HANDBOOK

OF PROJECTIVE

TECHNIQUES

ALSO BY BERNARD I. MURSTEIN

Theory and Research in Projective Techniques, "Emphasizing the TAT"

HANDBOOK OF PROJECTIVE TECHNIQUES

EDITED BY

BERNARD I. MURSTEIN

BASIC BOOKS, INC.

PUBLISHERS / NEW YORK & LONDON

Copyright © 1965 by Basic Books, Inc.
Library of Congress Catalog Card Number: 65-21190
Manufactured in the United States of America
DESIGNED BY VINCENT TORRE

TO DANIELLE AND COLETTE

from

Freddy Frog and Samuel Snake

Preface

More than half a century has passed since projective techniques formally became part of the clinical armamentarium. During this time, many articles and books have been written about these techniques. In teaching a course on projective techniques and in speaking to the needs of other behavioral scientists with interests in projective testing, it surely would be helpful if one could select, as readings, those articles that reflect the strengths, weaknesses, unsolved problems, and various approaches surrounding the administration and interpretation of the techniques. Why not conduct a poll to determine the key articles? The list could then be published in the *Journal of Projective Techniques* and serve as an aid to instructors trying to choose an appropriate selection of readings. Such, in short, was my thinking during the winter of 1963.

Ideally, I should have liked to poll the entire membership of the Society for Projective Techniques. Since the membership contained somewhat under one thousand members at that time, I decided, for financial reasons, on a more limited sample. All Fellows of the Society were polled, as well as some eighty psychologists who were not members but who seemed to me to have made outstanding contributions to the literature of projective techniques. In sum, about 320 packets were mailed. Each respondent was asked to list for each of seven areas at least three articles that had had an outstanding impact on thinking, practice, or methodology in projective techniques. The individual could, however, list as many articles as he wished in each area. Ten points were to be awarded to a first-place vote, nine to a second, and so forth.

The areas were, (1) general and theoretical, (2) Rorschach, (3) TAT, (4) Draw-a-Person, (5) Bender-Gestalt, (6) Sentence-Completion, and (7) other. The list was, of course, finite, whereas the kinds of test are infinite. Where were the CAT, the VAT, the PAT, Play Therapy, Howard Ink Blot Test, Lowenfield Mosaic Test, and so on? The list should not overly tax the patience of the respondents and had best restrict itself to the basic techniques.

Of the 320 letters sent, 49 individuals, constituting some 15 per cent of the sample polled, replied. Of these, 5 could not furnish data immediately, for one reason or another, 11 said that they were too busy, 17 said that they were not qualified, and 17 sent in their responses. Of those classified as "too busy," several sent reprints of their own articles; and a few suggested that the editor read sections in their books for helpful information. Among the 17 who stated that they were not qualified to respond at this time are recorded some of the best-known names in the area of projective techniques. Finally, of the 17 persons sending in their lists, only 5 had complete lists, the others contributing titles for one or more but not all of the areas. The lists did not overlap much and were, in any case, numerically insufficient to serve as a guide for the selection of articles. Moreover, the rapid increase in the projective-technique literature and the fact that many former experts had moved into other areas made it unlikely that any reasonable consensus of valuable articles might be obtained by polling. The project, in short, failed to achieve its purpose. I should, nonetheless, like to express publicly my appreciation to those individuals who took time from obviously busy schedules to participate in the poll.

Daunted by the small response to my poll, but not irretrievably so, I decided to select the articles myself. Gone was the dream of a representative vote from the *vox populi*. There were, nevertheless, certain advantages gained. First, a considerable number of the newer articles, despite their excellence, would not have received many votes because sufficient time would not have elapsed so that the majority of respondents would have been able to read them. Second, certain excellent articles have appeared in journals that are, relatively speaking, not widely circulated and, consequently, would not have received popular support on this account. Third, I had recently completed a book on projective techniques for which I had collected an annotated bibliography of approximately one thousand titles.

I proceeded to check each volume of *Psychological Abstracts* from 1927 to the time the manuscript was submitted to the publisher in 1964. Last, I surveyed all the recent issues of journals for articles that had not as yet been abstracted.

Despite the large size of this volume, some readers may note that some of their favorite articles are not reproduced. Obviously, no book could encompass even a small fraction of the total literature on projective techniques.

For a handbook, I prefer comprehensive articles, and, accordingly, I chose many articles that summarize or review considerable portions of the literature. I have tried to emphasize research that has had a broad scope, rather than that which tested a specific or limited question of scoring or interpretation. Further, the quantitative and hypothesis-testing articles have been chosen at the expense of the more descriptive, less quantitative approaches. I do recognize, however, that projective-technique interpretation is dependent on certain presently ill-defined artistic skills, as well as on knowledge about behavior in general and projective-technique behavior in particular. Nevertheless, it seems to me that useful information about projective techniques can be much more readily transmitted to the reader via the printed word than can artistic skills.

Certain omissions are a function of mechanical necessities, rather than of philosophy. In composing a handbook, there are inevitably more articles that "should be" included in it than is feasible for a single volume. Some otherwise-well-qualified papers were eliminated, therefore, because their considerable length would have necessitated the omission of several articles of average length. At other times, two equally excellent articles seemed to cover closely allied problems, and, hence, it was reluctantly decided to eliminate one of them.

This volume is intended as a basic text for courses in projective techniques and seeks to indicate how projective techniques are employed in research, the extent of their utility in various research problems, and their strengths and weaknesses in the assessment of personality. Each article is preceded by a brief critique by the editor. Where possible, I have tried to indicate problems raised by the findings and to offer comments on the techniques employed and conclusions drawn by the authors.

Because the book deals with a myriad of research problems in personality and examines the psychometric status of many of the projective techniques, I believe that it may serve as an auxiliary text for a course in personality and for a course in tests and measurements. Moreover, the volume should have considerable utility as a reference work for the researcher and practicing clinician because much of the important research in the field, since the inception of projective techniques, is included either as articles in full or as references within these articles.

I am deeply appreciative of the kindness of the authors, who graciously gave their permission to have their articles reproduced. Special thanks are due to my colleague Prof. Philip Goldberg, who wrote a review of the sentence-completion method at my request and also gave the entire manuscript the benefit of his criticism. I further wish to acknowledge the financial assistance of the Faculty Research Fund of Connecticut College and the contributions of those sleuths of script, our Psychology Department secretaries, Mrs. Ruth K. Booth and Mary Jane Waldo (Mrs. Peter Waldo). For bearing with the hardships attendant upon the family of a writer, I should like to close with a toast to my wife Prof. Nelly K. Murstein and to that delightful duo, our daughters Danielle and Colette.

BERNARD I. MURSTEIN

New London, Connecticut
July 1965

The Authors

GORDON W. ALLPORT   Professor of Psychology, Harvard University; past president, American Psychological Association, recipient of the American Psychological Association Distinguished Scientific Contribution Award.

JOHN W. ATKINSON   Professor of Psychology, University of Michigan.

MARCELLA V. BALDWIN   Psychologist at the Child Evaluation Center, Morristown Memorial Hospital, Morristown, New Jersey.

E. EARL BAUGHMAN   Professor of Psychology and Director of Clinical Training, University of North Carolina.

FRED Y. BILLINGSLEA   Chief Psychologist, V.A. hospital, New Orleans.

JOSEF BROŽEK   Research Professor of Psychology, Lehigh University.

EUGENE BYRD   Behavioral Science Consultant, National Institute of Child Health and Human Development.

RUTH D. CHURCHILL   College Examiner and Professor of Education and Psychology, Antioch College.

RUSSEL A. CLARK   Late Director of Morale and Motivation in the Research Division and Acting Director of the Statistical Division, United States Navy.

SIDNEY E. CLEVELAND   Chief Psychologist, VA Hospital, Houston; Associate Professor of Psychology, Baylor University College of Medicine.

LOREN V. COROTTO   Clinical Psychologist II, Napa State Hospital, California.

VAUGHN J. CRANDALL   Late Professor of Psychology, Antioch College; Senior Research Associate, Fels Research Institute.

RUE L. CROMWELL   Associate Professor of Clinical Psychology and Director of Research, Department of Psychiatry, Vanderbilt University Medical Center.

LEE J. CRONBACH   Past President, American Psychological Association; Professor of Education and Professor of Psychology, Stanford University.

xi

ROBERT H. CURNUTT Clinical Psychologist II, Napa State Hospital, California.

VIRGINIA W. EISEN School Psychologist, Pequannock Township Public School, New Jersey.

LEONARD D. ERON Professor of Psychology, State University of Iowa.

SEYMOUR FISHER Professor of Psychology, State University of New York Upstate Medical Center, Syracuse.

DONALD W. FISKE Professor of Psychology, University of Chicago.

LAWRENCE K. FRANK Former Lecturer, Department of Planning, MIT.

LEWIS R. GOLDBERG Associate Professor of Psychology, University of Oregon; Research Associate, Oregon Research Institute; Field Selection Officer, U.S. Peace Corps.

PHILIP A. GOLDBERG Assistant Professor of Psychology, Connecticut College.

ARMIN GRAMS Leader of the Human Development Program, Merrill-Palmer Institute.

ALBERT V. GRIFFITH Associate Professor of Psychology, East Carolina College.

HAROLD GUETZKOW Professor of Political Science and Professor of Psychology, Northwestern University.

EMMANUEL F. HAMMER Chief Psychologist, Lincoln Institute for Psychotherapy, New York.

WAYNE H. HOLTZMAN Professor of Psychology, and Dean of the College of Education, University of Texas; creator of the Holtzman Ink Blot Test.

ALICE JOSEPH Senior Assistant Psychiatrist, Lenox Hill Hospital, New York.

BERT KAPLAN Professor of Psychology, University of California, Santa Cruz.

IRWIN J. KNOPF Chairman and Professor of Psychology, Emory University.

ELIZABETH M. KOPPITZ School Psychologist, Board of Cooperative Educational Services, Bedford Hills, New York.

ANNELIESE F. KORNER Research Associate, Department of Psychiatry, Stanford University School of Medicine, Palo Alto; and Senior Psychologist, Department of Psychiatry, Mt. Zion Hospital, San Francisco.

RICHARD S. LAZARUS Professor of Psychology, University of California, Berkeley.

GERALD S. LESSER Professor of Education and Developmental Psychology and Director of the Laboratory of Human Development, Harvard University.

GARDNER LINDZEY Chairman and Professor of Psychology, University of Texas.

KENNETH B. LITTLE Chairman and Professor of Psychology, University of Denver.

RICHARD M. LUNDY Professor of Psychology, Pennsylvania State University.

JOSEPH M. MASLING Professor and Director of the Training Program in Clinical Psychology, Syracuse University.

JOHN F. McGOWAN Professor of Education and Assistant Director of the Testing and Counseling Service, University of Missouri.

PAUL E. MEEHL Past President of the American Psychological Association;

Professor of Psychology and Professor of Clinical Psychology, University of Minnesota Medical School.

JULIAN MELTZOFF   Chief Psychologist, VA Outpatient Clinic, Brooklyn, New York.

S. M. MILLER   Professor of Sociology and Senior Research Associate, Syracuse University Youth Development Center.

ROBERT B. MORTON   Director of the Atlanta Division of Harless & Kirkpatrick Associates, Inc.

HENRY A. MURRAY   Professor Emeritus of Psychology, Harvard University; creator of the Thematic Apperception Test.

BERNARD I. MURSTEIN   Professor of Psychology and NIMH Principal Investigator, Connecticut College.

ARTHUR NEWBURG   Formerly associated with Harvard University.

ROBERT C. NICHOLS   Director of Research, National Merit Scholarship Corporation, Evanston, Illinois.

HARVEY PESKIN   Associate Professor of Psychology, San Francisco State College.

DOUGLAS A. R. PEYMAN   Director of the Psychology Departments for the Alabama State Hospitals; Professor of Psychology, University of Alabama.

ZYGMUNT A. PIOTROWSKI   Professor of Psychology, Jefferson Medical College, Philadelphia.

KENNETH PURCELL   Director of the Behavior Science Division of the Children's Asthma Research Institute and Hospital; Assistant Clinical Professor of Psychology, University of Colorado Medical School, Denver.

JANET E. RAFFERTY   Assistant Professor of Psychology and Research Associate, Southern Illinois University.

MARIA A. RICKERS-OVSIANKINA   Professor of Psychology, University of Connecticut; Charter Member of the Society for Projective Techniques.

FRANK RIESSMAN   Member, Department of Psychiatry, Albert Einstein College of Medicine.

LAWRENCE RINDER   Clinical Psychologist, Black Hawk County Mental Health Center, Waterloo, Iowa.

JULIAN B. ROTTER   Professor of Psychology and Director of the Clinical Psychology Training Program, University of Connecticut; creator of the Rotter Incomplete Sentences Blank.

JOSEPH M. SACKS   Chief of the Clinical Psychology Section, VA Hospital, Fresno, California.

HENRY SAMUELS   In private practice as a Clinical Psychologist, Columbus, Ohio.

RICHARD SANDERS   Director of Psychological Services, Philadelphia State Hospital.

EVA SCHACHITZ   Formerly engaged in research at Ohio State University.

LYLE D. SCHMIDT   Associate Professor of Psychology, Ohio State University.

BERNARD A. STOTSKY   Psychologist, VA Hospital, Brockton, Massachusetts.

DEODANDUS J. M. STRÜMPFER   Professor of Psychology, University of Port Elizabeth, Port Elizabeth, Republic of South Africa.

CLIFFORD H. SWENSEN, JR.   Associate Professor of Psychology, Purdue University.

ARTHUR S. TAMKIN   Chief Clinical Psychologist, VA Regional Office, Providence, Rhode Island.

CHARLOTTE TEJESSY   Social worker formerly associated with Harvard University.

CHARLES VAN BUSKIRK   Clinical Psychologist, Duluth Mental Hygiene Clinic, Duluth, Minnesota.

JULIA R. VANE   Associate Professor of Psychology, Hofstra University.

HENRY WEINBERG   Professor of Psychology, Boston University.

Introduction

There was a group of psychologists in the 1930's that found the increasing quantification emloyed in psychological assessment most distressing. In the world of quantification, the individual was but one among others in a distribution of scores. Could the unique configuration of habits, traits, and genetic background that made up his personality really be understood by a score of "27" on a neurotic inventory? Those who answered this question in the negative eagerly seized on the newly arrived projective techniques as "saviors" of the "unique personality." These techniques would measure the whole man via a set of semiquantitative signs, as were employed in the Rorschach and the TAT.

The academicians — more knowledgeable in statistics and perhaps less interested in personal interaction — resisted this movement, called the projective techniques a series of quack instruments and their adherents worse, and tried to force the movement out of "serious psychology."

The basic differences between these groups were unfortunately projected onto projective techniques, which were thus endowed with virtues and sins not intrinsically native to them. The result was that its adherents made exaggerated claims for the techniques, whereas those more skeptical devised unrealistic tests of validity from which projective techniques had little chance of emerging unscathed.

The techniques, proclaimed its supporters, would provide an X ray to the covert world: "No one can fake these tests," said they. The reader will find in this volume that the subjects often could and did control and vitiate the meaning of their responses. The skeptics, on the other hand, tested the ability of the techniques to predict, for example, a criterion such as "success as a psychologist." My reasons for concluding that this was a patently unfair test of the utility of projective techniques are stated in the critique of Samuel's article (Chapter 13). We may simply note here that the task was immeasurably hindered because we really cannot define what constitutes "success as a psychologist."

The early exponents of projective techniques claimed, in general, that the stimulus was unimportant to the analysis of the response and, somewhat contradictorily, that the stimulus should, in at least some instances, be quite similar to the person taking the test. These claims are refuted specifically in Chapter 29, as well as in numerous other articles included herein.

The relative ambiguity of the stimulus, however, does directly contribute to the excessive variability of the responses from one occasion to the next since variability seems to be a strong correlate of ambiguity (Chapter 5). Additional findings that emerge from the studies reported within this book are as follows:

1. The original belief that the needs of the subject might be directly transcribed to the projective protocols has been rejected. It is clear that mediating variables relating to ego functions must be studied along with drive level. The article by Lesser (Chapter 34) clearly illustrates this point.

2. The earlier studies sought to demonstrate that validity either was or was not an inherent characteristic of projective techniques. Today we realize that validity has meaning only in a specific situation. Accordingly, the emphasis has switched to studying various problems, such as the need for affiliation or achievement, in which the projective technique is used as a *technique* to study the problem and not as the *object* of study itself. The result of the use of projective techniques as instruments rather than as objects of study has led, in the case of the thematic tests, to the construction of cards specifically designed to tap the need or trait in question (e.g., achievement) rather than the continued use of the TAT as a broad-band instrument.

3. It is now clear that the stimulus is a crucial factor in the analysis of the response. Until we accurately determine stimulus impact, we will continue to experience difficulty in separating the component of the response attributable to the stimulus properties of the card from the more interesting component tapping the subject's personality.

4. The void left by the demonstration that many of the basic tenets of projective techniques, derived by observation of clinical populations, could not be verified by research has led to attempts to derive newer, more verifiable data by creating more appropriate psychometric versions of the older techniques. A prime example of this is the Holtzman Ink Blot technique.

5. The fact that many subjects can control their responses has been demonstrated, in the main, for the analysis of *content*. Some success, even in dealing with relatively sophisticated subjects, has been demonstrated when *formal analysis,* or *how the subject tells the story* rather than *what he tells,* has been investigated.

6. The difficulties experienced in the validation of content measures with adults were often absent when children were studied. Apparently,

in the more undeveloped egos of children, the awareness and/or concern about the direct projection of needs onto the projective protocol is largely absent. Projective techniques have so far proved more successful with children than with adults.

7. Projective techniques have clearly failed to serve as useful aids in psychiatric diagnosis. While this finding seems clear, the causal factors are more uncertain. The lack of agreement from one psychiatrist to another on diagnosis is a prime contributing factor, for without adequate reliability one cannot hope to gain even moderate validity. But the difficulties go beyond unreliability of the criterion. A psychiatric diagnosis provides only a minute coverage of the total personality configuration of a patient. Within the classification of manic-depressive, for example, we find some angry and some unconcerned individuals; some aggressive, some passive. All these facets may be picked up by the projective techniques, but they may provide little help in the psychiatric classification. Small wonder, then, that projective techniques have shown better predictive utility with regard to criteria relating to behavioral dynamics than to psychiatric classification.

8. In our almost exclusive emphasis on the personality of the subject as the primary determinant of the projective response, we have been guilty of gross provincialism. Not only is the stimulus important, but also the ambiguity of the projective situation allows the examiner to confuse his own dynamics with those stemming from the subject. Further, we should give more weight to the purpose of the testing, as perceived by both the examiner and the testee, as well as its sociological meaning. Thus, for example, the offer of $1.25 for finishing at a certain percentile in a laboratory task may serve to trigger the *intrinsic* motive to succeed, in upper middle-class subjects, whereas for lower-class ones it is the *monetary funds themselves* that are important, not the desire to win. Hence, unless the significance of the reward is considered in the nature of the experimental design, it may serve to mute the differences in the conditions with which the experiment is primarily concerned.

Moreover, as Peskin shows (Chapter 10), a study favorable to the Rorschach in the San Francisco area would have more meaning than one supporting this technique in New York in that certain biases regarding projective techniques are geographically distributed.

9. Insufficient attention has been paid to the kind of population studied. In the study of the prediction of "success as a psychologist," for example (Chapter 13), the population consisted of hand-picked, top grade, graduate students in a VA clinical psychology program. How much success could there be in searching for psychological differences within such a selective population?

10. The Rorschach has been described as a perceptual test, yet Baughman has clearly shown (Chapter 17) that most subjects are not

aware of the perceptual determinants of their responses. Has the inability to validate the Rorschach in some studies been a function of the lack of correlation between the perceptual determinants of a response and the determinants verbalized by the subject? The more widespread employment of the Baughman version of the Rorschach (Chapter 17) should serve to provide an answer to this question.

11. The perhaps most unexpected finding involving projective techniques over the past twenty years has been the strong showing made by the sentence completion method in a variety of studies with adults, as demonstrated clearly by Goldberg's review (Chapter 49). Why should this modest technique, generally considered the most easily controllable and furthest from involving unconscious processes, have done so well as compared to such allegedly "deeper" techniques as the Rorschach and DAP, which are believed to tap unconscious aspects of personality? Perhaps it is because the validity criterion selected for most sentence completion studies involves either ratings by counselors, people going into psychotherapy, or discharges from mental hospitals. Why are individuals considered "disturbed" in the first place? Because they see crazy things on ink blots or make drawings of people with sharp fangs and transparent bodies? Hardly likely!

People are admitted into mental hospitals often because they "talk funny." A person goes to a counselor because he claims that he does not feel well emotionally, but this is precisely what the sentence completion method is best equipped to measure. Is it, after all, so strange that a student writing, "At school . . . I feel miserable," shortly afterward goes in to see his school counselor? If he can write it on the sentence completion that others see, he presumably can and wants to communicate his problems to the counselor in a yet more gratifying way. Why then, should not a strongly conscious test prove more valid than a less conscious one, such as the Rorschach, when rating a highly conscious criterion? In justice to the Rorschach, perhaps, we ought to seek more suitable criteria than conscious and publicly avowed feelings of emotional malaise. But we do not know enough about personality theory to know how to detect most problems before they reach us, more or less fully developed.

This statement leads us to the problem of accounting for the relatively poorer status of such "deeper" projective techniques as the Rorschach, DAP, and TAT. Should we allow the inchoate state of personality theory lead us to accept the empirical findings that, for example, the Rorschach is not a very valid test since it often shows little or no relationship to psychiatric classification or ratings gained from observational data? Perhaps instead, we ought to *validate the psychiatric ratings by employing the Rorschach as the criterion* against which to compare them. Being a pragmatist at heart, I have no objection to using highly conscious criteria, just so long as we note that in so doing, while waiting for the further development of personality theory, we are handicapping those techniques claiming to probe beyond the surface.

Another crucial question, which seems to have been investigated rarely (Meehl excepted; see Chapter 2) has been the question of whether the information we get from projective techniques is something we might obtain, sooner or later, by simpler means. In short, we might profitably take a page from the time-study merchants and compare our psychological cost with our gain. We should thus not ask whether projective techniques tell us something that is true, but whether the information thus gained is more true and less expensive than the same information gained by other means. These alternate modes of gathering information, following the law of parsimony, might include asking the patient what his problem is, or simply noting the base rate of a psychological diagnosis among all of our patients and employing this information in deriving conclusions about any incoming patient. If we have to aid the patient to his chair and place the pencil in his faltering fingers before he can draw figures with broken Gestalts which we then interpret as indicative of visual-motor disorganization, can we then claim that the Bender-Gestalt is significant because it enables us to pick 10 out of 10 brain-injured patients?

In closing, let it be noted that the lot of the projective technique enthusiast is not so sanguine as it was formerly. In fact, he finds himself in somewhat of a bind. As a consequence of the collapse of the X-ray theory and the findings that simple content is easy to control, he must now devise newer and more subtle formalistic methods (see Chapter 30) to bypass the censoring eye of the ego. In so doing, however, he becomes increasingly inferential and wanders in the opaque world of symbols and signs, touching areas in which personality theory, despite the important beginnings of Freud and Jung, has precious little to say.

Caught on the horns of this dilemma, some researchers have abandoned research in this area. Yet, though projective techniquies today appear not so glamorous nor so able to provide the panacea to the riddle of personality assessment hoped for twenty years ago, they seem in no immediate danger of expiring. The research shortcomings of such instruments make little impression on many clinical practitioners—so long as they feel they gain something from the testing—when they are not especially keen to tack a quantitative score onto a person whith whom they are interacting.

On the other hand, a number of researchers have discovered that projective techniques are quite useful in the measurement of motivation in situations in which the persons tested have been subjected to varying aroused conditions and then given projective measures. Apparently, these tests are a more sensitive barometer of changes in motivation than are more rigidly ingrained verbal response habits or writing patterns as represented by paper and pencil tests.

It may be, therefore, that the projective techniques await only a maturer theoretical understanding of personality before experiencing a renaissance in which their open-ended approach to the study of personality can be employed advantageously, compared with the more circumscribed paper and pencil tests.

The following fifty-six articles, it is hoped, reveal the soaring aspirations, the disappointments, reappraisals, and renewed but cautious vigor which has characterized projective technique research in the last twenty-five years.

Contents

PART IV : THE DRAW-A-PERSON TEST

PART V : BENDER-GESTALT

PART VI : THE SENTENCE COMPLETION TEST

PART 1

GENERAL AND THEORETICAL STUDIES

1

Projective Methods for the Study of Personality

L A W R E N C E   K .   F R A N K

An acknowledged classic in the field of projective techniques, Frank's article attacked the concern with group norms and group laws which, as George Kelley is alleged to have said, "left the individual no place to sit but on his continuum." Viewed from today's vantage point, the "numbers" men, or nomotheticists, seem not to have been as insensitive to the "individual" as portrayed. Frank's article, however, was written in a period when there were few clinical psychologists and the majority of academic psychologists simply ignored projective techniques as one step removed from crystal-ball gazing.

This article provided the leadership that projective technique adherents were to follow. Paper-and-pencil tests were contaminated by the factor of social desirability. Only projective techniques, it was believed, could tap the private world of the subject that he could not or would not otherwise reveal. The stimulus was held to be ambiguous and intended only as a trigger to elicit the private fantasies and perceptions of the subject. The usual concepts of validity and reliability developed for group processes were unsuited for this type of analysis. Temporal validity (validation over a period of time) and reliability as a function of congruency of interpretation among several projective techniques were to be the methods of assessing reliability and validity.

Time has proved many of these assumptions wrong. For many projective tests (the TAT in particular), the stimulus is the chief determinant of response content, and failure to measure its influence correctly has delayed progress in personality assessment. Further, the normal individual has proved unusually able to protect his "private world" from manifesting itself on projective techniques, so that new, more indirect methods have had to be devised instead of the simple analysis of content. Last,

1

projective techniques have proved amenable to treatment by standard statistical methods and are rapidly being converted to more psychometrically acceptable instruments.

Despite these changes, Frank's article is important historically as the signal for the emergence of "depth" testing. If the assumption that the private world of the individual could easily be tapped was in error, how much more naive to have believed that the intent of the personality inventories of that period could not be even more readily deciphered by subjects! At the time it was written, it represented a great step forward; and with increased refinement of scoring strategy, projective techniques may yet fulfill some, if not all, of the expectations for them so proudly put forth by Frank.

An initial difficulty in the study of personality is the lack of any clear-cut, adequate conception of what is to be studied. The recent volumes by Allport (1937) and by Stagner (1937) and the monograph by Burks and Jones (1936) may be cited as indicators of the confusion in this field, where, as they show, there are many conflicting ideas and concepts, each used to justify a wide variety of methods, none of which is wholly adequate.

A situation of this kind evokes different responses from each person, according to his professional predilections and allegiances. Obviously, pronouncements will be resisted, if not derided, while polemics and apologetics will only increase the confusion. The question may be raised whether any light on this situation can be obtained by examining the process of personality development for leads to more fruitful conceptions and more satisfactory methods and procedures.

Personality as the Result of Interaction, Socialization, and Individuation

Specifically, it is suggested that we reflect on the emergence of personality as an outcome of the interaction of cultural agents and the individual child. In the space here available, only a brief summary statement is permissible of the major aspects of this process in which we may distinguish an individual organism, with an organic inheritance, slowly growing, developing, and maturing under the tutelage of parents and teachers intent on patterning him to the culturally prescribed and socially sanctioned modes of action, speech, and belief.

As elsewhere stated (Frank, 1938; Frank, 1939), the child is not passive clay but a reacting organism with feelings, as are the parents, nurses, and

teachers who are rearing him. He receives, therefore, training in the prescribed cultural and social norms of action, speech, and belief, according to
their personal bias and feelings, and he accepts this training with varying
degrees of observance, always idiomatically and with feelings toward these
instructors. What we can observe, then, is the dual process of *socialization*, involving sufficient conformity in outer conduct to permit participation in the common social world, and *individuation*, involving the
progressive establishment of a private world of highly idiosyncratic
meaning, significances, and feelings that are more real and compelling
than the cultural and physical world.

The foregoing does not imply any subjective duality or other traditional
dichotomy; it is an attempt at a simple statement of the well-known and
generally accepted view that in all events we may observe both similarities
or uniformities and also individual deviations. We may concentrate on
the larger uniformities and ignore the individual components that are
participating, as we do in measuring the temperature, pressure, and other
properties of a gas, or we may look beyond the aggregate uniformities to
the individual, discrete molecules and atoms and electrons which, as we
are now realizing, are highly erratic, unpredictable, and far from that uniformity of behavior described statistically. Thus, we may observe a similar
antithesis between the group uniformities of economic, political, and
social affairs and the peculiar personal conduct of each of the citizens
who collectively exhibit those uniformities and conformities.

Culture provides the socially sanctioned patterns of action, speech, and
belief that make group life what we observe; but each individual in that
group is a personality who observes those social requirements and uses
those patterns idiomatically, with a peculiar personal inflection, accent,
emphasis, and intention (Benedict, 1934; Mead, 1935; Bateson, 1936).
Strictly speaking, there are only these individuals, deviating from and
distorting the culture; but with our traditional preoccupation with
uniformities, we have preferred to emphasize the uniformity of statistical
aggregates of all activities as the real and to treat the individual deviation
as a sort of unavoidable but embarrassing failure of nature to live up to
our expectations. These deviations must be recognized, but only as minor
blemishes on and impediments to the scientific truths we seek!

Those ideas flourished in all scientific work up to about 1900 or 1905
when X rays, quantum physics, relativity, and other new insights were
developed that made these earlier ideas obsolete, except in a number of
disciplines which still cling to the nineteenth century. Thus it is scientifically respectable, in some circles, to recognize that uniformity is a
statistical group concept that overlays an exceedingly disorderly, discon-
tinuous array of individual, discrete events that just won't obey the
scientists' laws! It is also respectable to speak of organization and
processes "within the atom," although it is recognized that no direct
measurements or even observations can be made within the atom—infer-

ences being drawn from activities and energy transformations that are
observable and frequently measurable.

For purposes of discussion, it is convenient to see individuals (1) as
organisms existing in the common public world of nature, (2) as
members of their group, carrying on their life careers, in the social world
of culturally prescribed patterns and practices, but living (3) as personalities in these *private worlds* which they have developed under the
impact of experience. It is important to recognize these three aspects of
human behavior and living because of their implications for scientific
study.

As organisms reacting to the environmental impacts, overtly and physiologically, human activity presents a problem of observation and measurement similar to that of all other organisms and events. The human body
moves or falls through geographical space, captures, stores, and releases
energy, and so on. As members of the group, individuals exhibit certain
patterns of action, speech, and belief that may be aggregated into larger
categories of uniformity or cultural and group norms; at least, we find
certain pronounced, often all-inclusive modes in their observed activities
in which they tend to conform to social and cultural prescriptions.

When we examine the personality process or private worlds of individuals, we face a somewhat peculiar problem, because we are seeking not
the cultural and social norms of the uniformities of organic activity, but
rather the revelation of just that peculiar, individual way of organizing
experience and of feeling which personality implies.

In this context, then, we may emphasize that personality is approachable as a process or operation of an individual who organizes experience
and reacts affectively to situations. This process is dynamic in the sense
that the individual personality imposes upon the common public world
of events (what we call nature) his meanings and significances, his organization and patterns, and he invests the situations thus structured with an
affective meaning to which he responds idiomatically. This dynamic
organizing process will of necessity express the cultural training he has
experienced so that, until he withdraws from social life, as in the
psychoses, he will utilize the group-sanctioned patterns of action, speech,
and belief, but as he individually has learned to use them and as he feels
toward the situations and people to whom he reacts.

If it were not liable to gross misunderstanding, the personality process
might be regarded as a sort of rubber stamp which the individual imposes
upon every situation by which he gives it the configuration that he, as an
individual, requires; in so doing, he necessarily ignores or subordinates
many aspects of the situation that for him are irrelevant and meaningless
and selectively reacts to those aspects that are personally significant. In
other words, the personality process may be viewed as a highly individualized practice of the general operation of all organisms that selectively
respond to a figure on a ground (Frank, 1926) by reacting to the config-

urations in an environmental context that are relevant to their life careers.

It is interesting to see how the students of personality have attempted to meet the problem of individuality with methods and procedures designed for study of uniformities and norms that ignore or subordinate individuality, treating it as a troublesome deviation which derogates from the real, the superior, and only important central tendency, mode, average, etc. This is not the occasion to review these methods, and the writer is not competent to assess them critically; but it is appropriate to point out some aspects of the present methodological difficulty we face in the accepted quantitative procedures.

Since individuals, as indicated earlier, learn to conform to the socially sanctioned patterns of action, speech, and belief (with individual bias and flavor of their own), it is possible to establish the social norms appropriate for *groups* of like chronological age, sex, and so on and to construct standardized tests and to calculate statistically their validity (i.e., do they measure or rate what they are expected to measure or rate for each group?) and their reliability (i.e., how well or reliably do they measure or rate the performance of the groups?) (Frank, 1939a).

While standardized tests are generally considered to be measurers of individual differences, it would be more appropriate to say that they are ratings of the degree of likeness to cultural norms exhibited by individuals who are expected, as members of this society, to conform to those group patterns. In other words, the standardized test does not tell very much about the individual, *as an individual*, but rather how nearly he approximates to a normal performance of culturally prescribed tasks for which a more or less arbitrary, but internally consistent, scheme of quantitative ratings is utilized (Kent, 1938). By the use of an over-all total figure for an individual, it becomes possible to assign numerical evaluations to individuals in various categories of achievement, skill, conformity, and so forth, such as accelerated, average, or retarded mentally; manual or verbal proficiency, etc. Having assigned him to a rank order in a group or class according to the standardized test, the individual is disposed of and adequately explained (Lewin, 1935[1]). The history of the use of standardized tests shows how they are used to place individuals in various classifications that are convenient for administration, for remedial work and therapy, or for segregation for purposes of social control, with little or no concern about understanding the individual so classified or placed or discovering his characteristics *as an individual*.

It would seem fair to say, therefore, that standardized tests offer procedures for rating individuals in terms of their socialization and how nearly they approximate to the acceptance and use of the culturally prescribed patterns of belief, action, and speech for which statistical norms can be

---

[1] See especially Chapter I on Aristotelian and Galilean modes of thought and the class theory of investigation.

calculated from actual observations of performance of *groups* of individuals, according to age, sex, etc.

In order to apply these and more recently developed quantitative methods to the study of personality, it has been necessary to adopt a conception of the personality as an aggregation of discrete measurable traits, factors, or other separable entities which are present in the individual in differing quantity and organized according to individual patterns. But since the personality is more than overt activity, some way of getting at the underlying personality is necessary. The need for quantitative data has led to the use of the culturally standardized, socially sanctioned norms of speech and belief and attitudes in and through which the individual has been asked to express his personality, as in questionnaires, inventories, rating scales, etc.

If time allowed, it would be desirable to examine more fully the implications of this procedure which attempts to reveal the individuality of the person by using the social stereotypes of language and motives that necessarily subordinate individuality to social conformity, emphasizing likeness and uniformity of group patterns. This point becomes more significant when we recall that almost identical actions and speech may be used in extraordinarily different senses by each individual using them; while, conversely, the widest diversity of action and speech may have almost identical sense and significance for different individuals exhibiting them. Moreover, the conventional traits and motives and objectives derived from traditional concepts of human nature and conduct carry meanings often alien to the investigator using them as data. Words are generalized symbols, usually obscuring of, when not actually misleading about, the individual idiomatic personality using them (Willoughby & Morse, 1936).

It should be further noted that many procedures for study of personality rely on the subject's self-diagnosis and revelation of his private world of personal meanings and feelings which the social situation compels the individual to conceal, even if, as is unusual, he had any clear understanding of himself. When we ask an individual to tell what he believes or feels or to indicate in which categories he belongs, this social pressure to conform to the group norms operates to bias what he will say and presses him to fit himself into the categories of the inventory or questionnaire offered for self-diagnosis (Vigotsky, 1939).

Moreover, as Henry A. Murray has observed, the most important things about an individual are what he cannot or will not say. The law has long recognized testimony as unreliable, to be accepted only after many checks and tests as formulated in the law of evidence.

At this point, there may be a feeling of dismay, if not resentment, because the discussion has led to a seeming impasse, with no road open to study the personality by the accepted methods and procedures of present-day quantitative psychology. Moreover, the insistence upon the unique, idiomatic character of the personality appears to remove it from the area of scientific study conceived as a search for generalizations, uniformities, invariant relationships, etc. It is proposed, therefore, to discuss a few recent developments in scientific concepts and methods and the new problems they have raised in order to indicate a way out of this apparent impasse.

The Field Concept

It is appropriate to recall that the uniformity and laws of nature are statistical findings of the probable events and relationships that occur among an aggregate of events, the individuals of which are highly disorderly and unpredictable. Theoretical physics has adjusted itself to the conception of a universe that has statistical regularity and order and individual disorder, in which the laws of aggregates are not observable in the activity of the individual making up these aggregates. Thus quantum physics and statistical mechanics and many other similar contrasts are accepted without anxiety about scientific respectability. The discrete individual event can be and is regarded as an individual to whom direct methods and measurements have only a limited applicability. We can, therefore, acknowledge an interest in the individual as a scientific problem and find some sanction for such an interest.

Another recent development is the concept of the field in physics and its use in biology. The field concept is significant here because it offers a way of conceiving this situation of an individual part and of the whole, which our older concepts have so confused and obscured (Burr & Northrop, 1935). Instead of a whole that dominates the parts, which have to be organized by some mysterious process into a whole, we begin to think of an aggregate of individuals which constitute, by their interaction, a field that operates to pattern these individuals. Parts are not separate, discrete, independent entities that get organized by the whole, nor is the whole a superior kind of entity with feudal power over its parts; e.g., a number of iron filings brought close to a magnet will arrange themselves in a pattern wherein each bit of iron is related to the other bits and the magnet and these relations constitute the whole; remove some bits, and the pattern shifts as it does if we add more filings or bits of another metal. Likewise, in a gas, the gas may be viewed as a field in which individual molecules, atoms, and electrons are patterned by the total interactions of all those parts into the group activity we call a gas. Ecology studies this interaction of various organizations in the circumscribed life zone or field which they constitute (Du Nouy, 1937[2]).

This field concept is highly important because it leads to the general notion that any "entity" we single out for observation is participating in a field; any observation we make must be ordered to the field in which it is made; or, as we say, every observation or measurement is relative to the frame of reference or field in which it occurs.

There are many other far-reaching shifts in concepts and methods that should be discussed here, but the foregoing will suffice to indicate that the study of an individual personality may be conceived as an approach to a somewhat disorderly and erratic activity, occurring in the field we call culture (i.e., the aggregate interaction of individuals whose behavior is patterned by participation in the aggregate). Moreover, the observations we make on the individual personality must be ordered to the field of that individual and his life space. We must also regard the individual himself as an aggregate of activities which pattern his parts and functions.

Here we must pause to point out that the older practice of creating entities out of data has created many problems that are unreal and irrelevant and so are insoluble. In bygone years, it was customary to treat data of temperature, light, magnetic activity, radiation, chemical activity, and so on as separate entities, independent of each other. But the more recent view is to see in these data evidences of energy transformations that are transmitted in different magnitudes, sequences, etc., and so appear as heat, light, magnetism, etc. This has relevance to the study of personality, since it warns us against the practice of observing an individual's actions and then reifying these data into entities called traits (or some other discrete term), which we must then find some way of organizing into the living total personality who appears in experience as a unified organism.

With this background of larger, more general shifts in scientific procedures, let us examine some more specific developments that are relevant to our topic.

Within recent years, new procedures have been developed for discovering not only the elements or parts composing the whole but also the way those parts are arranged and organized in the whole, without disintegrating or destroying the whole. The X rays are used, not merely for photographs or to show on a fluorescent screen what is otherwise invisible within an organism or any object, but also for diffraction analysis, in which the X rays are patterned by the internal organization of any substance to show its molecular and atomic structure. Spectrographic analysis reveals the chemical components qualitatively, and now quantitatively, and in what compounds, by the way light is distributed along a continuous band of coarse and fine spectral lines, each of which reveals a different element or isotope. The mass spectroscope offers another exceedingly delicate method for determining the composition of any substance that gives off radiations whereby the electrons or their rate of travel can be measured and the composition of the substance inferred.

---

² Other part-whole fields are a candle flame, a fountain jet, a stream of water, etc.

X rays, however, are only one of the newer methods whereby any complex may be made to reveal its components and its organization, often quantitatively, when approached by an appropriate procedure. Recently, it has been found that the chemical composition of various substances, especially proteins, can be ascertained by the reflection of a beam of light on a thin monomolecular film of the protein substance spread on a film of oil on water over a metallic surface. Again, it has been found that metallic ores and coal may be analyzed — i.e., be made to reveal their chemical composition and other properties—by the "angle of wetability," the angle of reflection, or the color of the light reflected from a liquid film that adheres to the surface of the unknown material.

Polarized light has also become an instrument for revealing the chemical composition of substances without resort to the usual methods of disintegration or chemical analysis. Electrical currents may also be passed through substances—gaseous, liquid, or solid—and used to discover what they contain and in what form. Indeed, it is not unwarranted to say that these indirect methods that permit discovery of the compostiion and organization of substances, complexes, and organisms seem likely to become the method of choice over the older destructive analytical procedures, because these methods do not destroy or disturb the substance or living organism being studied.

In this connection, reference should also be made to the development of biological assays, whereby a living organism, plant, or animal is used for assaying the composition of various substances and compounds and determining their potency, such as vitamins, hormones, virus, drugs, radiation, light, magnetism, and electrical currents (including electrophoresis for separating, without injury or change, the different subvarieities of any group of cells, chemical substances, etc.). In these procedures, the response of the living organism is utilized as an indicator, if not an actual measurement, of that about which data are sought, as well as the state, condition, maturation, etc. of the organism being tested. It is appropriate to note also that physicists are using such devices as the Wilson cloud chamber and the Geiger counter to obtain data on the *individual* electrical particle, which reveals its presence and energy by the path traced in water vapor or by activation of the counter, although never itself observable or directly measurable.

These methodological procedures are being refined and extended because they offer possibilities for ascertaining what is either unknowable by other means or undeterminable because the older analytic methods destroyed part or all of that which was to be studied. They are being accepted as valid and credible, primarily because they are more congruous with the search for undivided totalities and functioning organisms and are more productive of the data on organization on which present-day research problems are focused. They are also expressive of the recent concepts of whole and parts and their interrelations which no longer invoke the notion of parts as discrete entities upon which an organization is imposed by a superior whole but rather employ the concept of the field. Finally, they offer possibilities for studying the specific, differentiated individuality of organized structures and particulate events which are ignored or obscured by the older quantitative determinations of aggregates.

Since the threshold task in any scientific endeavor is to establish the meanings and significances of the data obtained by any method of observation and measurement, it should be noted that these indirect methods for revealing the composition and organization of substances and structures rely on experimental and genetic procedures to establish reliability and validity, not on statistical procedures. That is to say, these newer procedures establish the meaning of any datum by employing the procedure on a substance or structure of known composition, often made to order, so that it is possible to affirm that the resulting bending, patterning, arrangement of light, radiation, and so on, are reliable and valid indicators of the substance or structure when found in an unknown composition. These methods for establishing reliability and validity are therefore genetic in the sense of observing or tracing the origin and development of what is to be tested so that its presence or operation may be historically established: they are also dependent on the concurrent use of other procedures that will yield consistent data on the same composition which are therefore validated by such internal consistency and congruity of findings.

Psychology developed the statistical procedures for establishing reliability and validity because the only data available were the single observations or measurements taken at one time on each subject. Since no other data were available on the prior history and development of the subjects, reliability had to be determined by statistical manipulation of these test data themselves, also, since no other data were available on the subject's other functions and activities, only statistical validity could be established. It would appear that these tests of reliability and validity, devised to meet the difficulty presented by absence of other data, now act as barriers to the use of any other procedures for personality study in which reliability and validity for each subject is tested through these other nonstatistical methods.

Methods of *temporal validation* offer great promise because they permit testing of the validity of data for a *specific subject*[3] over a period of time, and the method of congruity among data obtained by different procedures from the same subject offers large possibilities for testing the reliability of any data for a *specific subject*. It is appropriate to recall here that the accepted methods for testing reliability and validity of tests, inventories, etc. offer indexes only for the *group*, not for any individual subject in that *group*.

We may, therefore, view the problem of personality in terms of these more recent ideas and conceptions and consider the application of these indirect procedures for revealing the composition and organization of substances and energy complexes.

As indicated earlier, the personality may be viewed as a dynamic process of organizing experience, of "structuralizing the life space" (Lewin) according to the unique individual's private world. This conception may be made precise and operational by seeing the individual and his changing environment as a series of fields that arise through the interaction of the individual personality (with his selective awareness, patterned responses, and idiomatic feelings) with the environmental situations of objects, events, and other persons. A field organization or configuration arises out of this interaction wherein, as suggested, the personality distorts the situation, so far as it is amenable, into the configurations of its private world, but has to adjust to the situation in so far as it resists such distortion and imposes its necessities upon the personality. What we have called personality and fumblingly have tried to formulate as the total responses of the whole individual and similar additive conceptions becomes more understandable and approachable for investigation when conceived as the living process in this field created by the individual and the environing situation.

The objective world of objects, organisms, and events likewise may be seen as fields of interacting object situations upon which cultural patterns operate in the conduct of human beings who, by very reason of behaving in these learned patterns, create the cultural fields of interacting human conduct. What is highly important to note is that every observation made must be ordered—given its quantitative and qualitative interpretation—to the field in which it occurs, so that the idea of pure objectivity becomes meaningless and sterile if it implies data not biased, influenced, relative to the field in which observed. Likewise, the conception of a stimulus that may be described and measured apart from the field and the organism in that field is untenable.[4] The "same" stimulus will differ in every field and for every field and for every organism which selectively creates its own stimuli in each situation. Indeed, this dynamic conception of the personality as a process implies that there are no stimuli to conduct (as distinct from physical and physiological impacts), except in so far as the individual personality selectively constitutes them and responds to

---

[3] See Bateson (1936), in which appears a discussion of diachronic and synchronic procedures.

[4] See Vigotsky (1939, p. 29): "The investigator who uses such methods may be compared to a man, who, in order to explain why water extinguishes fire, analyzes the water into oxygen and hydrogen and is surprised to find that oxygen helps the process of burning and hydrogen itself burns. This method of analyzing a whole into elements is not a true analysis which can be used to solve concrete problems."

them in its idiosyncratic patterns. In other words, the stimuli are functions of the field created by the individual interacting with the situation.

Thus, the movement in various areas of scientific work is toward recognition of the field concept and the devising of methods that will record not merely data but the fields in which those data have been observed and find their significance. Those who are appalled by the seeming anarchy thus threatening scientific work may be reminded that the present-day standards of scientific work and of methods are part of a development that will inevitably make today's ideas and procedures obsolete. It is well to recall how proud (justly so) chemistry was to achieve quantitative determinations of the composition of substances; and now, how crude those early quantitative methods and findings appear, when they are seeking today to find out not merely what and how much, but the spatial arrangement of the constituents, as in stereochemistry, where the same atoms in the same quantity produce different substances according to their spatial arrangement. It is likewise worth recalling that about 1900, young physicists could find no problems except the more precise measurement of the pressure, temperature, etc., of a gas and were content with such crude quantitative findings. Furthermore, biologists today are accepting as commonplace that the same nutritive components, amino-acids, carbohydrates, fats, minerals, and vitamins are selectively digested, assimilated, and metabolized in different ways by each species and by each individual. Moreover, it is conceded that the proteins of each species are different, as are those of each individual, with the possibility of an almost unlimited number of different protein molecules in which the same basic elements are organized into unique spatial-temporal configurations appropriate to the organic field of the individual organism.[5]

Projective Techniques

Coming directly to the topic of projective methods for personality study, we may say that the dynamic conception of personality as a process of organizing experience and structuralizing life space in a field leads to the problem of how we can reveal the way an individual personality organizes experience, in order to disclose or at least gain insight into that individual's private world of meanings, significances, patterns, and feelings.

Such a problem is similar to those discussed earlier, where indirect methods are used to elicit the pattern of internal organization and of

---

[5] The concepts of individuality and of individuation are being used by biologists because they find themselves confronted with individual organic activities and idiomatic processes (Blumenthal, 1939; Coghill, 1930; Coghill, 1936).

composition without disintegrating or distorting the subject, which is made to bend, deflect, distort, organize, or otherwise pattern part or all of the field in which it is placed—e.g., light and Xrays. In similar fashion, we may approach the personality and induce the individual to reveal his way of organizing experience by giving him a field (objects, materials, experiences) with relatively little structure and cultural patterning, so that the personality can project upon that plastic field his way of seeing life, his meanings, significances, patterns, and especially his feelings. Thus we elicit a projection of the individual personality's private world, because he has to organize the field, interpret the material, and react affectively to it. More specifically, a projection method for study of personality involves the presentation of a stimulus situation designed or chosen because it will mean to the subject, not what the experimenter has arbitrarily decided it should mean (as in most psychological experiments using standardized stimuli in order to be "objective"), but rather whatever it must mean to the personality who gives it, or imposes upon it, his private, idiosyncratic meaning and organization. The subject will then respond to *his* meaning of the presented stimulus situation by some form of action and feeling that is expressive of his personality. Such responses may be *constitutive*, as when the subject imposes a structure or form or configuration (Gestalt) upon an amorphous, plastic, unstructured substance such as clay, finger paints, or upon partially structured and semiorganized fields like the Rorschach cards; or they may be *interpretive*, as when the subject tells what a stimulus situation, like a picture, means to him; or they may be *cathartic*, as when the subject discharges affect or feeling upon the stimulus situation and finds an emotional release that is revealing of his affective reactions toward life situations represented by the stimulus situation, as when he plays with clay or toys. Other expressions may be *constructive* organizations, wherein the subject builds in accordance with the materials offered but reveals in the pattern of his building some of the organizing conceptions of his life at that period, as in block building.

The important and determining process is the subject's personality, which operates upon the stimulus situation as if it had a wholly private significance for him alone or an entirely plastic character which made it yield to the subject's control. This indicates that, as suggested earlier, a personality is the way an individual organizes and patterns life situations and effectively responds to them—"structuralizes his life space,"—so that by projective methods we are evoking the very process of personality as it has developed to that moment (Dunbar, 1938[6]). Since the way an individual organizes and patterns life situations imposes his private world of meanings and affectively reacts upon the environing world of situations and other persons and strives to maintain his personal version against the coercion or obstruction of others, it is evident that personality is a persistent way of living and feeling that, despite change of tools, implements, and organic growth and maturation, will appear continuously and true to pattern.

When we scrutinize the actual procedures that may be called projective methods, we find a wide variety of techniques and materials being employed for the same general purpose: to obtain from the subject "what he cannot or will not say," frequently because he does not know himself and is not aware what he is revealing about himself through his projections.

In the following statements, no attempt has been made to provide a complete review of all the projective methods now being used, since such a canvass would be beyond the present writer's competence and intention. Only a few illustrations of projective methods are offered, to show their variety and their scope in the hope of enlisting further interest in and creating a better understanding of their characteristics and advantages.[7]

The Rorschach ink blots, to which the subject responds by saying what he "sees" in each of a number of different blots, are perhaps the most widely known of these procedures. They have been utilized in Europe and in the United States, frequently in connection with psychiatric clinics and hospitals, for revealing the personality configurations and have been found of increasing value. In so far as life histories and psychiatric and psychoanalytic studies of the subjects who have had the Rorschach diagnosis are available, the ink-blot interpretations are being increasingly validated by these clinical findings. Such comparative findings are of the greatest importance because they mutually reinforce each other and reveal the consistency or any conflicts in the different interpretations and diagnosis of a personality.

A similar procedure is the cloud-picture method, developed by Wilhelm Stern to evoke projections from a subject on more amorphous grounds, with advantages, he believed, over the Rorschach blots. The more amorphous or unstructured the ground, the greater the sensitivity of the procedure, which, however, loses in precision, as in most instruments. Hence the Rorschach may be less sensitive than cloud pictures or clay but more precise and definite. Both the ink blots and the cloud pictures offer a ground upon which the subject must impose or project whatever configural patterns he "sees" therein, because he can see only what he personally looks for or "perceives" in that ground. The separate details of the responses, however, are significant only in the context of the total response to each blot and are meaningful only for each subject.

---

[6] An individual may express his feelings, otherwise blocked, in illness or physiological dysfunctions.

[7] Cf. Horowitz and Murphy (1938) for further discussion of different procedures and their use.

This does not imply an absence of recurrent forms and meanings from one subject to another but rather that the same letters of the conventionalized alphabet may recur in many different words and the same words may be utilized in a great variety of sentences to convey an extraordinary diversity of statements, which must be understood within the context in which they occur and with reference to the particular speaker who is using them on that occasion.[8]

Play techniques are being increasingly employed for clinical diagnosis and for investigation of the personality development of children. As materials, almost any kind of toy or plaything or plain wooden building blocks may be presented to the subject for free play or for performance of some designated action, such as building a house, sorting into groups, setting the stage for a play, or otherwise organizing the play materials into some configuration which expresses for the subject, an affectively significant pattern. In children, it must be remembered, there are fewer disguises and defenses available to hide behind, and there is less sophisticated awareness of how much is being revealed in play. The investigator does not set a task and rate the performance in terms of skill or other scale of achievement, since the intention is to elicit the subject's way of "organizing his life space" in whatever manner he finds appropriate. Hence, every performance is significant, apart from the excellence of the play construction or activity, and is to be interpreted, rather than rated, for its revelation of how the subject sees and feels his life situations that are portrayed in the play constructions and sequences. The question of how to decide whether a particular activity is or is not meaningful is to be decided, not by its frequency or so-called objective criteria, but by the total play configuration of that particular subject, who, it is assumed, performs that particular action or uses that specific construction as an expression of his way of seeing and feeling and reacting to life—i.e., of his personality. But the degree of relevance is to be found in the context, in what precedes and what follows, and in the intensity of feelings expressed. If these criteria appear tenuous and subjective and lacking in credibility, then objections may be made to the use of various methods for discovering the composition and structure of an unknown substance through which light, electric current, or radiations are passed, to give patterned arrangements or a spectrum photograph in which the position, number, intensity of lines, and the coarse and fine structure indicate what the unknown substance is composed of, how organized internally, and so on. Personality studies by projective methods have not, of course, been as extensively studied, nor have the patterns

---

[8] Since each personality must use socially prescribed cultural patterns for his conduct and communications, he will exhibit many recurrent uniformities; but these are significant only for revealing the patterns or organizations or configurations which the personality uses to structuralize his life space.

used by subjects been so well explored. The important point is that the way is open to the development of something similar to spectroscopic and diffraction methods for investigation of personality.

If the foregoing appears farfetched, it may be recalled that the lines on the spectroscopic plate were established, not by statistical procedures, but by experimental procedures through which a known chemically tested substance was spectroscopically tested so that its identifying line could be precisely located and thereafter confidently named. In much the same fashion, it is being established that a child who is known to be undergoing an affective experience will express that feeling in a play configuration that can be so recognized. Thus, children who have lost a beloved parent or nurse, or have been made anxious by toilet training, or are insecure and hostile because of sibling rivalry, etc., will exhibit those feelings in their play configurations. Experimentally produced personality disturbances can be established and their severity investigated by subsequent play forms and expressions. Moreover, the insights derived from play configurations yield interpretations that are not only therapeutically effective but often predictive of what a child will show in the near future.

Not only play toys and objects are utilized but also various plastic amorphous materials such as modeling clay, flour and water, mud and similar substances of a consistency that permits the subject to handle freely and manipulate into various objects. In these play situations, the subject often finds a catharsis, expressing affects that might otherwise be repressed or disguised or symbolically releasing resentments and hostility that have been long overlaid by conventionally good conduct. Dolls capable of being dismembered can be used to evoke repressed hostility and aggression against parents and siblings. Dramatic stage play with toy figures and settings have also provided occasions in which a subject not only revealed his personality difficulties but also worked out many of his emotional problems. Clay figures are modeled by child patients in which they express many of their acute anxieties and distortions. Reference should be made to eidetic imagery, which, as E. R. Jaensch, in his constitutional studies, has shown, indicates one aspect of the subject's way of expressing what enters into his personality make-up or way of organizing his life space.

Artistic media offer another series of rich opportunities for projective methods in studying personality. Finger-painting has given many insights into child personality make-up and perplexities. Painting has been found very fruitful for study of personality make-up and emotional disturbances. Other clinical uses of painting have been reported that indicate the way paintings and drawings supplement the clinician's interviews and evoke responses that are exceedingly revealing, often more so than the verbal responses. Puppet shows elicit responses from child patients that are both diagnostic and therapeutic because the intensity of the dramatic experience arouses the child to a vehement expression of his feelings toward authority and toward parents and of his repressed desires to hurt others. Roles have been assigned to individuals who are then asked to act out those roles impromptu, thereby revealing how tangled and repressed their feelings are and how release of pent-up emotion leads to insight into one's personality difficulties. Drama teachers are finding clues to personality in the way individuals portray the characters assigned them in a play. Music offers similar and often more potent possibilities for expression of affects that are revealing of the personality. It is interesting to note that as psychotherapy proceeds to free the patient, his art expressions, painting, modeling, music, and dramatic rendition become freer and more integrated.

As the foregoing indicates, the individual rarely has any understanding of himself or awareness of what his activities signify. In the thematic perception methods this unawareness offers an opportunity to elicit highly significant projections from subjects who are asked to write or tell stories about a series of pictures showing individuals with whom they can identify themselves and others of immediate personal concern. Likewise, the subjects project many aspects of their personality in the completion of stories and of sentences, in making up analogies, in sorting out and grouping objects, such as toys, and similar procedures in which the subject reveals "what he cannot or will not say."

Expressive movements, especially handwriting, offer another approach to the understanding of the personality who reveals so much of his characteristic way of viewing life in his habitual gestures and motor patterns, facial expressions, posture, and gait. These leads to the study of personality have been rejected by many psychologists because they do not meet psychometric requirements for validity and reliability, but they are being employed in association with clinical and other studies of personality, where they are finding increasing validation in the consistency of results for the same subject when independently assayed by each of these procedures. In this group of methods should be included observations on tics of all kinds and dancing as indications of tension, anxiety, or other partially repressed feelings.

If we will face the problem of personality, in its full complexity, as an active dynamic process to be studied as a process rather than as entity or aggregate of traits or factors or as a static organization, then these projective methods offer many advantages for obtaining data on the process of organizing experience that is peculiar to each personality and is useful in understanding him throughout his life. Moreover, the projective methods offer possibilities for utilizing the available insights into personality which the prevailing quantitative procedures seem deliberately to reject.

Here, again, it may be re-emphasized that the study of personality is not a task of measuring separate variables on a large group of individuals at one moment in their lives and then seeking, by statistical methods, to measure correlations, nor is it a problem of teasing out and establishing the quantitative value of several factors (Jersild & Fite, 1939[9]). Rather the task calls for the application of a multiplicity of methods and procedures which will reveal the many facets of the personality and show how the individual "structuralizes his life space" or organizes experience to meet his personal needs in various media. If it appears that the subject projects similar *patterns* or *configurations* upon widely different materials and reveals in his life history the sequence of experiences that make those projections psychologically meaningful for his personality, then the procedures may be judged sufficiently valid to warrant further experimentation and refinement. In undertaking such explorations, the experimenter and clinicians may find reassurance and support in the realization that they are utilizing concepts and methods that are receiving increasing recognition and approval in scientific work that is today proving most fruitful.

---

[9] Especially p. 102.

REFERENCES

ABEL, THEODORA M. Free designs of limited scope as a personality index. *Charac. & Pers.*, 1938, 7, 50–62.

ACKERMAN, N. W., with the technical assistance of VIRGINIA REHKOPF. Constructive and destructive tendencies in children. *Amer. J. Orthopsychiat.*, 1937, 7, 301–319.

ALLPORT, G. W. *Personality: A psychological interpretation.* New York: Holt, 1937.

ALLPORT, G. W., & VERNON, P. E. *Studies in expressive movement.* New York: Macmillan, 1933.

ANDERSON, H. H. Domination and integration in the social behavior of young children in an experimental play situation. *Genet. Psychol. Monogr.*, 1937, 19, 343–408.

BARKER, R. G. The effect of frustration upon cognitive ability. *Charact. & Pers.*, 1938, 7, 145–150.

BARKER, R. G., DEMBO, T., & LEWIN, K. Experiments in frustration and regression studies in topological and vector psychology. *Iowa Child Welf. Res. Sta. Monogr.*, 1939.

BATESON, G. Naven. Cambridge: Cambridge Univer. Press, 1936.

BECK, S. J. Autism in Rorschach scoring: A feeling comment. *Charact. & Pers.* (News and Notes), 1936, 5, 83–85.

BECK, S. J. Introduction to the Rorschach method. *Amer. Orthopsychiat. Ass. Monogr.*, No. 1, 1937. (a)

BECK, S. J. Psychological processes in Rorschach findings. *J. abnorm. & soc. Psychol.*, 1937, 31, 482–488. (b)

BECK, S. J. Personality structure in schizophrenia. *Nerv. ment. Dis. Monogr.*, 1938, No. 63.

BENDER, LAURETTA. Art and therapy in the mental disturbances of children. *J. nerv. ment. Dis.*, 1937, 86, 229–238. (a)

BENDER, LAURETTA. Group activities on a children's ward as methods of psychotherapy. *Amer. J. Psychiat.*, 1937, 93, 1151–1173. (b)

BENDER, LAURETTA. A visual motor Gestalt test and its clinical use. *Amer. Orthopsychiat. Ass. Monogr.*, 1938, No. 3.

BENDER, LAURETTA, KEISER, S., & SCHILDER, P. Studies in aggressiveness. *Genet. Psychol. Monogr.*, 1936, 18, 357–564.

BENDER, LAURETTA, & SCHILDER, P. Form as a principle in the play of children. *J. genet. Psychol.*, 1936, 49, 254–261.

BENDER, LAURETTA, & WOLTMANN, A. The use of plastic material as a psychotherapeutic method for behavior problems in children. *Amer. J. Orthopsychiat.*, 1936, 6, 341–354.

BENDER, LAURETTA, & WOLTMANN, A. Puppetry as a psychotherapeutic measure with problem children. *Mon. Bull. N.Y. State Ass. occup. Ther.*, 1937, 7, 1–7. (a)

BENDER, LAURETTA, & WOLTMANN, A. The use of plastic material as a psychiatric approach to emotional problems in children. *Amer. J. Orthopsychiat.*, 1937, 7, 283–300. (b)

BENEDICT, RUTH. *Patterns of culture.* Boston: Houghton Mifflin, 1934.

BLUMENTAL, H. T. Effects of organismal differentials on the distribution of leukocytes in the circulating blood. *Arch. Path.*, 1939, 27, 510–545.

BOOTH, G. C. Personality and chronic arthritis. *J. nerv. ment. Dis.*, 1937, 85, 637–662. (a)

BOOTH, G. C. The use of graphology in medicine. *J. nerv. ment. Dis.*, 1937, 86, 674–679. (b)

BOOTH, G. C. Objective techniques in personality testing. *Arch. Neurol. Psychiat.*, 1939.

BURKS, BARBARA S., & JONES, MARY C. Personality development in childhood: A survey of problems, methods and experimental findings. *Monogr. Soc. Res. Child Develpm.*, 1936, 1, 1–205.

BURR, H. S., & NORTHROP, F. S. C. An electro-dynamic theory of life. *Quart. Rev. Biol.*, 1935, 10, 322–333.

CAMERON, N. Functional immaturity in the symbolization of scientifically trained adults. *J. Psychol.*, 1938, 6, 161–175. (a)

CAMERON, N. Individual and social factors in the development of graphic symbolization. *J. Psychol.*, 1938, 5, 165–183. (b)

CAMERON, N. Reasoning, regression, and communication in schizophrenics. *Psychol. Monogr.*, 1938, 50, 1–34. (c)

CAMERON, N. Deterioration and regression in schizophrenic thinking. *J. abnorm. soc. Psychol.*, 1939, 34, 265–270.

COGHILL, G. E. Individuation versus integration in the development of behavior. *J. Gen. Psychol.*, 1930, 3, 431–435.

COGHILL, G. E. Integration and motivation of behavior as problems of growth. *J. Genet. Psychol.*, 1936, 48, 3–19.

CONN, J. H. A psychiatric study of car sickness in children. *Amer. J. Orthopsychiat.*, 1938, 8, 130–141.

CURRAN, F. F. The drama as a therapeutic measure in adolescents. *Amer J. Orthopsychiat.*, 1939, 9, 215–231.

DESPERT, J. LOWSE, & POTTER, H. W. The story, a form of directed phantasy. *Psychiat. Quart.*, 1936, 10, 619–638.

DUNBAR, H. F. *Emotions and bodily changes.* (2nd ed.) New York: Columbia Univer. Press, 1938.

DU NOUY, P. L. Biological time. New York: Macmillan, 1937.

ERIKSON, E. H. Configurations in play: Clinical notes. *Psychoanal. Quart.*, 1937, 6, 139–214.

FITE, MARY D. Aggressive behavior in young children and children's attitudes toward aggression. *Genet. Psychol. Monogr.*, 1939.

FRANK, L. K. The problem of learning. *Psychol. Rev.*, 1926, 33, 329–351.

FRANK, L. K. Fundamental needs of the child. *Ment. Hyg.*, N.Y., 1938, 22, 353–379.

FRANK, L. K. Comments on the proposed standardization of the Rorschach method. *Rorschach Res. Exch.*, 1939, 3. (a)

FRANK, L. K. Cultural coercion and individual distortion. *Psychiatry*, 1939, 2, 11–27. (b)

GERARD, MARGARET W. Case for discussion at the 1938 symposium. *Amer. J. Orthopsychiat.*, 1938, 8, 1–18.

GITELSON, M. Clinical experience with play therapy. *Amer. J. Orthopsychiat.*, 1938, 8, 466–478.

GITELSON, M. (Chairman), et al. Section on "play therapy," 1938. *Amer. J. Orthopsychiat.*, 1938, 8, 499–524.

GRIFFITHS, R. *Imagination in young children.* London: Kegan Paul, 1936.

HANFMANN, EUGENIA. Social structure of a group of kindergarten children. *Amer. J. Orthopsychiat.*, 1935, 5, 407–410.

HANFMANN, EUGENIA, & KASANIN, J. A method for the study of concept formation. *J. Psychol.*, 1937, 3, 521–540.

HANFMANN, EUGENIA, & KASANIN, J. Disturbances in concept formation in schizophrenia. *Arch. Neurol. Psychiat.*, 1938, 40, 1276–1282.

HANFMANN, EUGENIA. Analysis of the thinking disorder in a case of schizophrenia. *Arch. Neurol. Psychiat.*, 1939, 41, 568–579.

HERTZ, MARGUERITE R. The method of administration of the Rorschach ink blot test. *Child Develpm.*, 1936, 7, 237–254.

HERTZ, MARGUERITE R., & RUBENSTEIN, B. B. A comparison of three "blind" Rorschach analyses. *Amer. J. Orthopsychiat.*, 1939, 9, 295-314.

HOLMER,, P. The use of the play situation as an aid to diagnosis. *Amer. J. Orthopsychiat.*, 1937, 7, 523–531.

HOROWITZ, RUTH E. Racial aspects of self-identification in nursery school children. *J. Psychol.*, 1939, 7, 91–99.

HOROWITZ, RUTH E., & MURPHY, LOIS B. Projective methods in the psychological study of children. *J. exp. Educ.*, 1938, 7, 133–140.

HUNTER, MARY. The practical value of the Rorschach test in a psychological clinic. *Amer. J. Orthopsychiat.*, 1939, 9, 287–294.

JAENSCH, E. R. *Eidetic imagery and typological methods of investigation.* New York: Harcourt, Brace, 1930.

JERSILD, A. T., & FITE, MARY D. The influence of nursery school experience on children's social adjustments. *Child Develpm. Monogr.*, No. 25, 1939.

KASANIN, J., & HANFMANN, EUGENIA. An experimental study of concept formation in schizophrenia: I. Quantitative analysis of the results. *Amer. J. Psychiat.*, 1938, 95, 35–48.

KELLEY, D. M., & KLOPFER, B. Application of the Rorschach method to research in schizophrenia. *Rorschach Res. Exch.*, 1939, 3, 55–66.

KENT, GRACE H. Use and abuse of mental tests in clinical diagnosis. *Psychol. Rec.*, 1938, 2, 391–400.

KLOPFER, B. *Rorschach Res. Exchange.* September, 1936, to date.

KLUVER, H. The eidetic child. In Murcheson, C. (Ed.), *Handbook of child psychology.* Worcester: Clark Univer. Press, 1931. Pp. 643–668.

LEVY, D. M. Use of play technique as experimental procedure. *Amer. J. Orthopsychiat.*, 1933, 3, 266–277.

LEVY, D. M. Hostility patterns in sibling rivalry experiments. *Amer. J. Orthopsychiat.*, 1936, 6, 183–257.

LEVY, D. M. "Release therapy" in young children. Psychiatry, 1938, 1, 387–390.

LEVY, J. The use of art techniques in treatment of children's behavior problems. Proč. Amer. Ass. ment. Def., 1934, 58, 258–260.

LEVY, J. The active use of phantasy in treatment of children's behavior problems. Unpublished paper presented at Amer. Psychiat. Ass.

LEWIN, K. Environmental forces. In Murchison, C. (Ed.), Handbook of child psychology. Worcester: Clark Univer. Press, 1931. Pp. 94–127.

LEWIN, K. A dynamic theory of personality. New York: McGraw-Hill, 1935.

LEWIN, K. Principles of topological psychology. New York: McGraw-Hill, 1936.

LEWIN, K. Psychoanalysis and topological psychology. Bull. Menninger Clin., 1937, 1, 202–211.

LISS, E. Play techniques in child analysis. Amer. J. Orthopsychiat., 1936, 6, 17–22.

LISS, E. The graphic arts. Amer. J. Orthopsychiat., 1938, 8, 95–99.

LOWENFELD, V. The nature of creative activity. London: Kegan Paul, 1938.

MASSERMAN, J. H., & BALKEN, EVA R. The clinical application of phantasy studies. J. Psychol., 1938, 6, 81–88.

MEAD, MARGARET. Sex and temperament. New York: Morrow, 1935.

MORENO, J. L. Who shall survive? Nerv. ment. dis. Monogr., 1934, No. 58.

MORENO, J. L. Creativity and cultural conserves—with special reference to musical expression. Sociometry, 1939, 2, 1-36. (a)

MORENO, J. L. Psychodramatic shock therapy—A sociometric approach to the problem of mental disorders. Sociometry, 1939, 2, 1–30. (b)

MORENO, J. L., & JENNINGS, H. Spontaneity training, a method of personality development. Sociomet. Rev., 1936.

MORGAN, CHRISTINE D., & MURRAY, H. A. A method for investigating fantasies: The thematic apperception test. Arch. Neurol. Psychiat., 1935, 34, 289–306.

MURPHY, LOIS B. Social behavior and child personality. An exploratory study of some roots of sympathy. New York: Columbia Univer. Press, 1937.

MURRAY, H. A. The effect of fear upon estimates of the maliciousness of other personalities. J. soc. Psychol., 1933, 4, 310–329.

MURRAY, H. A. Facts which support the concept of need or drive. J. Psychol., 1937, 3, 27–42.

MURRAY, H. A. Techniques for a systematic investigation of fantasy. J. Psychol., 1937, 3, 115–143.

MURRAY, H. A., et al. Explorations in personality. New York: Oxford Univer. Press, 1938.

NEWMAN, S. Personal symbolism in language patterns. Psychiatry, 1939, 2, 177–184.

NEWMAN, S., & MATHER, VERA G. Analysis of spoken language of patients with affective disorders. Amer. J. Psychiat., 1938, 94, 913–942.

NEWMAN, S., & MATHER, VERA G. The M, FM, and m responses as indicators of changes in personality. Rorschach Res. Exch., 1937, 1, 148–156. (a)

PIOTROWSKI, Z. The methodological aspects of the Rorschach personality method. Kwart. Psychol., Poznan, 1937, 9, 29. (b)

PLANT, J. S. Personality and the culture pattern. J. soc. Philos., 1938, 3.

PORTER, E. L. H. Factors in the fluctuation of fifteen ambiguous phenomena. Psychol. Rec., 1937, 2, 231–253.

ROSENZWEIG, S., & SHAKOW, D. Play technique in schizophrenia and other psychoses: I. Rationale; II. An experimental study of schizophrenic constructions with play materials. Amer. J. Orthopsychiat., 1937, 7, 32–35, 36–47.

SAPIR, E. The emergence of the concept of personality in a study of culture. J. soc. Psychol., 1934, 5, 408–415.

SENDER, SADIE, & KLOPFER, B. Application of the Rorschach test to child behavior problems as facilitated by a refinement of the scoring method. *Rorschach Res. Exch.*, 1936, Issue No. 1, 1–17.

SHAW, R. F. *Finger painting.* Boston: Little, Brown, 1934.

STAGNER, R. *Psychology of personality.* New York: McGraw-Hill, 1937.

STEIN-LEWINSON, THEA. An introduction to the graphology of Ludwig Klages. *Charact. & Pers.*, 1938, 6, 163–177.

TROUP, EVELYN. A comparative study by means of the Rorschach method of personality development in twenty pairs of identical twins. *Genet. Psychol. Monogr.*, 1938, 20, 465–556.

VAUGHN, J., & KRUG, OTHILDA. The analytic character of the Rorschach ink blot test. *Amer. J. Orthopsychiat.*, 1938, 8, 220–229.

VIGOTSKY, L. S. Thought and speech. *Psychiatry*, 1939, 2, 29–54.

WERNER, H. William Stern's personalistics and psychology of personality. *Charact. & Pers.*, 1938, 7, 109–125.

WILLOUGHBY, R. P., & MORSE, MARY E. Spontaneous reactions to a personality inventory. *Amer. J. Orthopsychiat.*, 1936, 6, 562–575.

WOLFF, H. A., SMITH, C. E. & MURRAY, H. A. The psychology of humor. 1. A study of responses to race-disparagement jokes. *J. abnorm. soc. Psychol.*, 1934, 28, 341–365.

2

Theoretical Considerations Concerning the Scope and Limitations of Projective Techniques

ANNELIESE F. KORNER

> "The fault, dear Brutus, is not in our stars,
> But in ourselves, that we are underlings."

So speaks Cassius in Shakespeare's Julius Caesar, *Act I, Scene 2. Likewise, Korner holds that if we cannot predict overt behavior through the use of projective techniques, the responsibility rests not with the projective techniques but with our failure to advance the present inchoate state of personality theory.*

The verity of her conclusion is important, for, if we consider these techniques as merely opportunities to elicit samples of behavior, then much energy is wasted in creating ever new techniques that will always have to rely on the sparse knowledge concerning personality theory. On the other hand, if we hold projective techniques at fault, where does the fault lie? Does it reside in supposing that the perception of ink blots or the telling of stories in response to the presentation of pictures is a basically unsound way to study personality? Or, perhaps the onus should be put on our methods of analysis rather than the materials we work with? Korner's article is valuable in pointing out that we need to know much more about personality theory before we can pass ultimate judgment on the value of projective techniques.

23

With the increasing enthusiasm for projective methods and the construction of new and modified techniques, we tend to lose ourselves in our pragmatic efforts and to make only feeble or no attempts to relate our new discoveries to basic personality theory. The literature abounds with papers stressing the value of various projective techniques, and yet there is a real neglect of theoretical formulations regarding the workings and interrelationships among these techniques and fundamental psychodynamic theory. In this chapter, an attempt will be made to trace some of these interrelationships. An effort will be made to clarify some of the principles and rationale underlying projective techniques, to discuss some of the factors involved in prediction from these tests, and, through this very process, to demonstrate the scope and some of the limitations of these techniques.

Basic Rationale

The first assumption on which projective techniques draw heavily is the fact that all behavior manifestations, including the most and least significant, are expressive of an individual's personality (Rapaport, 1942). If this assumption is correct, it becomes clear that any behavior sample elicited by any technique is potentially capable of mirroring or reflecting personality at work and that the merit of the different techniques varies largely with the degree that these techniques have been explored and the familiarity of the examiner with the various behavior manifestations elicited by a given technique. This view is not generally shared, as demonstrated by the mushrooming of new techniques. Instead of realizing that all of these techniques operate on the same principles and instead of exploring a few techniques thoroughly aiming at an integration between the tests and the body of personality theory, we are busy devising new gadgets that in each instance require new standardization and new validation (MacKinnon, 1949).

The merit of a test varies not only with the degree to which its dimensions and potentialities were explored (and we see a good example of this in Rorschach, which is probably one of the most informative tests by virtue of having been most thoroughly investigated), but also with the skill and clinical insight of the interpreter. This realization is very disturbing to some who wish to see in tests totally objective and independent indicators of personality and who quiet their doubts in this respect by referring to an objectifying scoring system. Actually, though, scoring may be viewed merely as the psychologist's shorthand used for the purpose of reducing behavior to manageable proportions. It is important that we are aware that our tests merely record behavior and that we can arrive at clinical insights only through inference, which in turn requires a thorough familiarity with the principles of psychodynamics on the part of the interpreter. In viewing test results, we should at all times be aware that what dictates test performance is not some magic inherent in the test, but the basic personality characteristics of the person taking it. More concretely, when on Rorschach for example, an individual shows an affinity for small details, it is not because the ink blots contain a good many small details, but because such an individual would show similar compulsiveness on other tests and in whatever he undertook. Since so much is dependent on clinical inference from what is observed on tests, an examiner must know not only what the indications for schizophrenia, for obsessive-compulsiveness, for hysteria are on tests, but must know also how schizophrenics, compulsives, and hysterics behave, what some of their basic problems are, and what set of defenses they are most apt to use. It becomes clear then that for meaningful interpretation of any test's results it is as important for the examiner to be thoroughly familiar with psychodynamic theory as it is for him to be familiar with the tests he uses to observe behavior. Nowhere does the relation between the two disciplines become as clear as here. After all, what we observe on tests is nothing more than a reflection of those personality characteristics that are also at work in other situations.

The question might well be raised, why then do we need tests to make such observations. Could not interviews achieve much the same end? The reasons why they could not lie in the fact that interviews are more diffuse and less predefined situations, which have an infinite number of variables, in both subject and observer. The prime advantage of tests consists in their being standard sets of stimuli against which characteristic ways of thinking, speaking, and perceiving are easily detected and compared. Because of this standard screen, fine nuances of behavior, which in a free situation easily get lost, stand out very clearly. Also, in a quantitative sense, it is this standard situation which permits the establishment of statistics and norms which are essential for effective comparison among individuals.

The second assumption underlying projective tests is that the individual taking them gives material that he either will not or cannot give otherwise. Projective techniques usually involve the presentation of purposely ambiguous material that to the subject does not mean what the experimenter had arbitrarily decided it should mean, as in questionnaire-type tests, but rather whatever it must mean to the person who interprets it. When confronted with such ambiguous material, the subject chooses his own form of presentation and, in so doing, makes conceptualizations most implicit and characteristic of his case. The assumption for all these techniques is that when a subject gets absorbed in explaining what seems to be an objective bit of material, he loses sight of the fact that in his interpretations he discloses his preoccupations, his wishes, his fears, and his aspirations. Thus his resistance against disclosing personal and sometimes painful material may be substantially diminished.

Another assumption on which projective techniques draw heavily is that of psychic determinism, which precludes a story or a response from being a chance event. Each response is supposed to be brought about by a distinctive set of causal influences. The objection has frequently been raised that instead of producing personally meaningful material in his stories, a patient may merely recount the plot of a movie he has seen or introduce the content of a recent book. This objection disregards the fact, however, that from all the experiences a patient has, he selects certain ones to remember and to recount and that these selections in turn have personal meaning. There are some projective techniques that are based exclusively on the idea that selected and distorted recollections give clues to personality characteristics. Despert (1938), for example, asks children to retell popular fairy tales. She finds valuable clues in the children's deviations from the original, in their emphasis and their omissions. Duess (1944) uses a similar technique in checking therapeutic progress in the analysis of her child patients. She usually presents them with six incomplete fables, each symbolizing a fundamental conflict, and studies their resistances through the tenacity with which the children cling to the same completion pattern in spite of repeated interpretation.

Scope and Limitations

Returning to the assumptions underlying projective techniques, it is probably the first one listed which defines their scope and implies their limitations most clearly. By virtue of being standard sets of stimuli, projective techniques elicit behavior samples, verbatim and complete, that invite minute analysis and clinical comparison. This analysis should reveal characteristic ways in which an individual organizes ambiguous and unfamiliar material. By inference, this organizational process gives clues as to how the subject is apt to tackle new tasks and assimilate new experiences. Such an analysis also allows a dissection of the structural aspects of language and verbalization, which gives valuable diagnostic and personality-descriptive indications. Much can be learned in analyzing speech, whether it is circumstantial, evasive, fuzzy, qualifying, apologetic, disjointed, bizarre, or incoherent. Furthermore, these techniques permit observation of perceptual processes that are very sensitive in reflecting incipient and manifest structural changes concomitant with schizophrenia, intracranial pathology, and deterioration.

A case in point is that of a man, 52 years of age, who was referred for routine psychological examination with the diagnosis of paranoid schizophrenia. This diagnosis was largely made on the basis of the man's complaints. He stated that a whole clique of people were after him, bent on driving him out of business. His Rorschach did not reflect the typically bizarre thought processes commonly seen in schizophrenics, but instead revealed perceptual perseverations and distortions usually found only in organically deteriorated patients. Careful neurological examination confirmed intracranial pathology. His ideas of persecution, therefore, developed in response to a very real situation, namely his inability to cope with the complex responsibilities involved in his highly competitive occupation as an insurance salesman.

This is just one case demonstrating that it lies within the scope of Rorschach to function as a tool in differential diagnosis. On a larger scale, numerous studies (e.g., Benjamin & Ebaugh, 1938; Hertz, 1941; Hertz & Rubenstein, 1939) have shown the very high diagnostic validity of Rorschach. This is not surprising in view of the fact that clinical diagnosis can be made not only on the basis of a life history and content of conflict, but also through analysis of ideation, which reflects characteristics pathognomonic for the various clinical groups.

It is also within the scope of projective techniques, particularly the Thematic Apperception Test and related tests, to explore fantasies, attitudes, aspirations, identifications, and preoccupations. This, too, has been done successfully, as there is usually a very high correlation between the fantasies uncovered through testing and those brought out in a series of psychiatric interviews. I recall a little girl of twelve, for instance, who recounted a great many fantastic, fairy-tale-like stories when presented with the TAT cards. Almost all her stories had an inherent wish-fulfillment quality. She was an illegitimate, deprived, and undernourished child, brought up by her alcoholic father together with two defective younger siblings. She had incestuous relations with her father at about the age of ten. Her father married a much older woman when patient was eleven. It was noted that the themes or fantasies reflected in her TAT stories were the same as those she revealed in a series of play interviews and in a number of symptomatic acts. In her stories and play fantasies she tried to supplant the new mother figure through identification with her. She pictured herself as assuming all the household tasks, as being a mother and having babies, as traveling to faraway places with her husband, as living in beautiful houses, and as having all the food she wanted to eat. Many of her activities, symptomatic and otherwise, were based on similar fantasies. She assumed the role of an adult woman, sought to do as much of the household chores as her stepmother would permit her to do, baked pies, and sat with the neighbors' children in preference to going to the movies. She stole money from her stepmother, even though she had plenty saved up herself, hoarded trinkets, papers, and insisted on wearing her stepmother's costume jewelry, even though the latter had bought exactly the same for this patient. She showed a good deal of jealousy toward anyone who captured her father's attention, and she openly declared that she would never get married. In all her fantasies, she seemed to want to take her stepmother's place.

Psychiatrists often find TAT results very useful and sometimes more meaningful than Rorschach findings, because they furnish material and fantasies closely related to the kind elicited during psychiatric interviews. It is not surprising that such fantasies can be elicited relatively easily, if we consider that in responding to a given set of ambiguous stimuli a subject is unaware that he is speaking of himself. This process, and the fact that he is making personally meaningful selections from an infinite number of possible choices, act as a short cut to his fantasy life.

It has, then, been established that projective techniques potentially have very high diagnostic validity and also show themselves valid in exploring the content of fantasy life. The next question is, are projective techniques valid in predicting reality behavior? Psychologists all too often are either evasive, inarticulate, overoptimistic, or apologetic on this subject. The remainder of this paper will, therefore, be devoted to an attempt at clarification of some of the problems involved in prediction.

I have become acutely interested in this problem through a study which explored the relationship between hostile fantasies as revealed through a series of play situations and actual hostile behavior in a group of preschool children (Korner, 1949). These children were entirely consistent in their expression of hostility when observed through various play techniques. By contrast, no consistency was observed when their play was contrasted with their reality behavior. The results indicated that no inference could be drawn regarding the degree or the form of a child's hostile behavior in real life on the basis of observing his play. It was interesting that in the sample studied, half the children remained consistent in all the situations in which they were observed; that is, they were either strongly hostile or submissive throughout, while the other half reversed their position, being strongly hostile in the play situations and submissive in actual behavior, or vice versa. Clearly, since there was an even chance for consistency and inconsistency, prediction from one situation to the other was impossible.

On a much larger scale, this same lack of consistency between fantasy and reality behavior was observed by Sanford (Sanford et al., 1943). In examining the relationship between needs as they were expressed on TAT and in overt behavior, his average correlation was plus .11, from which he concluded that we cannot assume that a need which appears on TAT will be manifested behaviorally. There are not many other systematic studies that have explored this relationship, but clinical experience bears out the lack of correspondence between fantasy and reality behavior again and again. It has been my experience at the student health service of a midwestern university to find an alarming proportion of ambulatory schizophrenics as observed through Rorschach among students who clinically functioned quite well. Similar observations have been reported from other universities. Conversely, frank psychotics, as seen clinically, often produce Rorschachs that reflect less of a schizophrenic process than do records of preschizophrenics. In other words, Rorschach workers are constantly confronted with the discrepancy between extent of psychopathology and clinical behavior.

One may very well dismiss the whole issue by just stating that it is not the purpose of projective techniques to predict reality behavior. While this may be perfectly obvious to clinicians who constantly see patients who superficially make a fairly adequate adjustment, but who underneath show vast pathology, many psychologists find it difficult to accept that it is not the function of projective techniques to predict reality behavior. The very fact that so many psychologists attempt to determine the validity of projective techniques through correlation with reality behavior shows a nonacceptance of this fact. Antagonists to projective techniques take the tests' inability to predict reality behavior as proof positive that they are invalid, and workers in the field constantly furnish material for these objections by seeking validity of that kind. For example, Tomkins (1947), who wrote a comprehensive volume on the Thematic Apperception Test, states that the acid test of any technique is its usefulness in successful prediction. In a later article (Tomkins, 1949) he reports with apparent surprise that he has seen cases in whose TAT he could not detect the specific nature of behavior disorders nor the occurrence of antisocial acts. Much of the research on projective techniques reflects this desire to predict reality behavior. Currently, both homicidal and suicidal inclinations are being studied, not through direct examination of the clinical syndromes leading to such an intent, but through the study of their secondary configurational patterns as reflected by Rorschach. Projective techniques also have been used as predictive tools in job selection and for prognostication of future success in a given field. It has been tried, and usually unsuccessfully, to predict through projective techniques success in salesmanship, piloting, engineering; and various psychoanalytic institutes have attempted to use them in their selections of candidates. Quite often, particularly when the tests were used as a screening device in filling vacancies, employers made the presence or absence of pathology the basis of their decision, which, in terms of the psychic requirements needed to succeed in various fields, is entirely unwarranted. In clinical practice, predictions are constantly being made which, if not too specific, and if considered as a product of speculation, may be very useful and even correct. Such predictions are necessary and desirable in a clinical situation if taken primarily as working hypotheses and subjected to constant revision. However, all too often these predictions are too literal a transcription between needs expressed in fantasy and reality behavior. This suggests a lack of acceptance and awareness of the fact that it is not the purpose of projective techniques to predict reality behavior, which is confirmed by the widespread feeling that a psychologist's contribution is being sharply curtailed if his ability to make such predictions is being questioned. There are really no grounds for such feelings, if we examine the reasons and rationale why such prediction is precarious. Besides, the contribution which these tests do make in the area of diagnosis and fantasy exploration is sufficiently valuable in and of itself to justify their use.

Why, then, is it so difficult to make predictions of reality behavior from projective techniques? What are the reasons, theoretical and practical, why such predictions are incorrect as often as not? The rationale for this difficulty is again inherent in the first assumption underlying projective techniques; namely, that tests merely elicit behavior and that any conclusion derived from the test results is by way of inference. Psychological inference, strictly speaking, is not inherent in the projective tests themselves, but enters the realm of psychiatric and psychodynamic personality formulations. Inferences from test data, then, are not only bound by the extent of the interpreter's awareness and familiarity with psychodynamic principles, but also by the limits of our present-day knowledge of such principles. Daily, psychiatrists and psychologists are confronted with the puzzling lack of one-to-one relationships and with the unpredictability of cause and effect in the psychic organization of an individual. While in each case we attempt to establish causality between existing pathology and historical events, we all know that we have only incomplete awareness of all the factors involved. This is shown not only in the fact that practically any parental attitude or childhood situation is being blamed for, or can potentially produce, maladjustment, but also in the lack of correspondence between the psychic damage, the narcissistic wounds received, and the end product, the personality as it functions. Every so often we are amazed, in listening to our patients' histories and the tales of the traumata they have suffered, to find them to be relatively well-integrated personalities, just as we are puzzled when we uncover a lot of latent pathology through Rorschach in individuals who clinically appear to be fairly intact. We frequently ask ourselves, what holds these people together? Conversely, we frequently search in vain for sufficient historical causation to explain the profound disturbance of some childhood or adult schizophrenias. We are confronted daily with the evidence that a given symptom may arise from vastly differing disease processes, and conversely we see a given disease entity express itself in vastly differing symptoms. We have here, then, problems that clinical psychiatry has not solved, problems that are the crux of all ego psychology. Is it not, therefore, unrealistic on the part of a referring psychiatrist, and presumptuous or unenlightened on the part of a psychologist, to expect that inferences from projective techniques enable us to make predictions which clinical psychiatry cannot yet make? Is this not endowing these tools with magic in the vain hope that they may furnish us with the most important link missing in basic personality theory today?

For prediction, ego psychology has to solve two important problems—problems which are so complex that perhaps they will never be solved. The first one is the detection of all the innumerable variables that are at work in the process of an individual's reality adaptation to a need. It is probably not only the existence of these variables but also their interaction which determines what form his adaptation will take. The other problem is to find the secret of ego synthesis, which probably consists of an organismic process involving more than the sum of the variables at work and which possibly is at the root of all the clinical discrepancies mentioned before.

Unfortunately, much of our present-day research is not helping us solve these problems. Too much psychological research today consists of taking a certain experimental or clinical group and finding what common denominators it presents. While cautious mention is being made that the coincidence of two variables does not assume that they stand in a one-to-one or causal relationship, we are nevertheless left with just such an impression. Such research usually assumes that all variables, other than the ones studied, remain constant, which results in the total neglect of those variables that are most important for the purposes of prediction; namely, those that intervene in and condition a response. Even control groups which establish a significantly smaller occurrence of a given trait are not necessarily helpful for purposes of prediction, for usually that trait occurs even in the control group to a lesser degree.

Perhaps, as long as our knowledge of ego psychology is as incomplete as it is, our most fertile field of investigation lies in the individual case. If we gather a large sample of an individual's behavior over a long period of time, we can sense a certain internal consistency, and certain behavioral laws, which help us make pretty accurate predictions for this individual. This, of course, is the approach taken by the psychoanalytic investigator. Perhaps a large collection of individual cases, and careful scrutiny of their needs on the one hand and their defense mechanisms on the other hand, will yield certain clusters of interacting variables that may have predictive value not only for a given individual, but also for other individuals in whom these clusters operate.

Returning to projective techniques, if we are aware of the constantly intervening variables between the needs of an individual and the adaptation he makes to them in reality, we do not expect reality behavior necessarily to correspond with fantasy or with pathology. It would be a mistake to question the validity of observations of either reality behavior or the test data. Each has its own validity, as each is a valid sample of an individual's behavior. For this reason, I think we are making a mistake if we disregard Rorschach findings, for example, if they do not jibe with our clinical impression. In such cases, it would be tempting to say that the Rorschach did not yield an accurate picture. For instance, not infrequently we find very pathological Rorschachs in children who clinically are relatively undisturbed, but whose parents show gross psychiatric disorders. Usually these children's Rorschachs uncover pathology way out of proportion with the pathology noted through observation. This discrepancy between Rorschach and clinical behavior does not necessarily cast a reflection on the validity of these Rorschachs, but perhaps furnishes a clue to this curious phenomenon of these children, who through some inexplicable reason remained relatively undisturbed despite their very neurotic parents. Since adverse parental influence and attitudes must of necessity affect children in some ways, one may possibly construe that evidence gathered through Rorschach may constitute a valid indicator for latent pathology, which potentially, with developmental changes or altered parent–child relationships, may come to the fore. Perhaps it is in this way that we can explain why it happens so frequently that therapeutic progress in the parent may bring forth manifest difficulties in the child and vice versa, that the economy of interaction between parent and child is so changed with improvement of the child that parents whose major initial problem is their child's behavior disorder all of a sudden show all sorts of symptoms and neurotic difficulties themselves.

These considerations are of real importance in defining treatment objectives for patients as well as in the choice of treatment suitable for a given patient. If, instead of discarding Rorschach findings as being inaccurate or exaggerated, we consider the evidence as a potential within the patient, we may have a safer estimate of what might occur during treatment and may thereby reduce the number of therapeutic failures.

A case in point for such planning is a man in his late thirties who recently was referred for testing. His wife was also seen. They were both given Rorschachs to help determine what temperamental differences caused their incompatibility. The wife was largely the complainant. The husband had had previous psychiatric treatment, but discontinued therapy after a short time. Aside from revealing some of his personality difficulties, this patient's Rorschach definitely reflected organic brain pathology. This was seen in strong perseverative tendencies, in marked rigidity and a total inability to shift his thought patterns, and in a very obvious defect in abstract and categorical thinking. He was also color-blind. Clinically, there was no reason to suspect intracranial pathology. Careful probing on the part of the referring psychiatrist established that this man must have had a structural defect from birth, for he had always had difficulty in the area of concept formation and did not comprehend what he was reading; and while he excelled at solving practical and concrete problems, he was so defective in inductive and deductive reasoning that he could not make the abstraction of understanding what rules he had followed in solving a problem. He was aware of his defect but kept it to himself. He bluffed himself through three years of college, he covered up his deficiency in his business transactions, and he never mentioned his difficulty to his first psychiatrist. The reason this case is instructive is that clinically this patient presented a facade of purely neurotic difficulties that appeared amenable to psychoanalytic therapy. However, the uncovering of this structural defect with the concomitant nonneurotic rigidity, and the patient's inability to reason through analogies, casts a serious doubt on this patient's capacity to benefit by such therapy.

Similarly, serious errors in therapeutic planning may be made if Rorschach evidence of schizoid mentation is dismissed lightly and disregarded in the face of a clearly neurotic clinical picture. Such evidence also constitutes a potential, which may come to the fore once the effectiveness of a patient's defenses is diminished. Perhaps serious therapeutic hazards could be avoided if such a potential were taken into consideration.

It follows from this that test results probably do not err in constituting sins of commission. Latent pathology is never revealed if it does not exist. By contrast, test results, in their frequent incompleteness, can commit serious acts of omission. These omissions can be a grave source of error, particularly for prediction of reality behavior. If projective techniques were more sensitive in detecting a larger array of defense mechanisms, accurate prediction of reality behavior would be more easily accomplished.

Perhaps, in conclusion, I should add what function, in my opinion, projective techniques can fulfill in research of predictive problems. Since, in predicting behavior from projective techniques, we have to rely on psychological inference, it is the function of general psychological research, rather than that of endless pragmatic studies with projective techniques proper, to establish predictive criteria. In other words, if we wish to know what kind of a person would make a good engineer, a good pilot, or a good psychoanalyst, let us first establish clinically and theoretically what kinds of needs, what patterns of impulse control, are helpful and which are a hindrance in a given field. After these clinical criteria are validly established, projective techniques will be very helpful and will constitute a short cut in the selection of candidates.

Furthermore, projective techniques may be used as a very valuable tool in ego-psychology research. Instead of deploring the fact that fantasy and reality behavior do not necessarily correspond, as we currently seem to be doing, we can use projective techniques as a short cut to a person's fantasy and ideational life, which then can be compared and examined in the light of his present and past actual behavior patterns. After all, is it not in the adaptations, the compromises, and the balances achieved between needs or fantasies and the demands of reality that we find the key to personality at work?

REFERENCES

BENJAMIN, J. D., & EBAUGH, F. G. The diagnostic validity of the Rorschach test. *Amer. J. Psychiat.*, 1938, 94, 1163–1178.

DESPERT, J. LOUISE. *Emotional problems in children*. Utica, N.Y.: State Hospital Press, 1938, 128.

DUESS, T. Etude expérimentale des phénomènes de résistance en psychoanalyse infantile. *Z. Kinderpsychiat.*, 1944, 11, 1–11.

HERTZ, MARGUERITE R. Validity of the Rorschach method. *Amer. J. Orthopsychiat.*, 1941, 11, 512–520.

HERTZ, MARGUERITE R., & RUBENSTEIN, B. A comparison of three "blind" Rorschach analyses. *Amer. J. Orthopsychiat.*, 1939, 9, 295–315.

KORNER, ANNELIESE F. *Some aspects of hostility in young children*. New York: Grune & Stratton, 1949, p. 194.

MACKINNON, D. W. Clinical practice and personality theory: a symposium. II. Psychodiagnosis in clinical practice and personality theory. *J. abnorm. soc. Psychol.*, 1949, 44, 7–13.

RAPAPORT, D. Principles underlying projective techniques. *Charact. & Pers.*, 1942, 10, 213–219.

SANFORD, R. N., et al. Physique, personality and scholarship. *Monogr. soc. Res. Child Developm.*, 1943, No. 34, 705.

TOMKINS, S. S. *The thematic apperception test; the theory and technique of interpretation*. New York: Grune and Stratton, 1947.

TOMKINS, S. S. The present status of the thematic apperception test. *Amer. J. Orthopsychiat.*, 1949, 19, 358–362.

3

The Trend in Motivational Theory

GORDON W. ALLPORT

In this penetrating analysis, Allport throws down the gauntlet to those who believe that "depth" methods represent the only means to circumvent the defenses of the testee. He states that normal *subjects will ofttimes communicate more readily and with a great saving of time what would take hours to tease out with a battery of projective techniques. Second, in those cases where the subjects do not wish to reveal anything, they will omit reference to disturbing material without the examiner's being one whit the wiser. Projective methods, therefore, should be used only in conjunction with direct methods so that the two modes of response may be compared.*

The article—certainly one of the most thought-provoking in the field—leads to the formation of several questions which all of us may well ponder. Is there really a discontinuity between normal *and* neurotic *subjects, as Allport seems to imply? If most individuals manifest at least some neurotic tendencies, could these problem areas really be evaluated consciously by the individual in question? Do even normal subjects truly know in which areas they have difficulties so that they can communicate these to others? The issue is far from resolved, but there are many who do not believe that such self-knowledge is very rampant.[a]*

With regard to Allport's contention that projective techniques are unable to dent the defenses of the relatively normal subject, the literature largely supports him with regard to content measures.[b] The use of more subtle measures, however,[c] indicates that it is currently possible, if

---

[a] See L. J. Cronbach, Essentials of Psychological Testing (2nd ed.; New York: Harper, 1960).

[b] See B. I. Murstein, "Assumptions, Adaptation-Level, and Projection Techniques," *Perceptual and Motor Skills,* 12(1961), 107–125, or Chap. 4 of this volume.

[c] See S. Epstein, "The Measurement of Drive and Conflict in Humans:Theory

not yet clinically practical, to differentiate relatively normal individuals on the basis of their projective responses despite defensive "sets" regarding the self.

Motivational theory today seems to be turning a corner in the road of scientific progress. In attempting to characterize this change in direction, I wish to pay special attention to the problem of psychodiagnostic methods, for the successes and failures of these methods can teach us much about psychodynamic theory.

Let us start by asking why projective methods are so popular in both diagnostic practice and research. The answer, I think, is to be found in the history of motivational theory during the past century. All the major influences have pressed in a single direction. Schopenhauer, with his doctrine of the primacy of the blind will, had little respect for the rationalizations invented by the individual's intellect to account for his conduct. Motives, he was sure, could not be taken at their face value. Darwin followed with his similar anti-intellectual emphasis on primordial struggle. McDougall refined the Darwinian stress on instinct, retaining in his *horme* the flavor of Schopenhauer's will, Darwin's struggle for survival, Bergson's *élan*, and Freud's libido. All these writers were irrationalists—confident that underlying genotypes in motivation should be sought rather than the surface phenotypes. All of them were reacting against the naive intellectualism of their predecessors and against the rationalizations offered by self-justifying mortals when called on to account for their conduct. Among these irrationalists who have dominated western psychology for the past century, Freud, of course, has been the leading figure. He, like the others, correctly perceived that the mainsprings of conduct may be hidden from the searchlight of consciousness.

In addition to irrationalism, modern dynamic psychology has developed another earmark: geneticism. The original instincts laid down in our nature are regarded as decisive; or if not, then the experiences of early childhood are held to be crucial. At this point, the leading nondynamic school of thought, stimulus-response psychology, joins forces with geneticism. Stimulus-response theorists agree with instinct psychologists and psychoanalysts in viewing adult motives as conditioned, reinforced, subli-

---

and Experiment," in M. R. Jones, ed., *Neraska Symposium for Motivation* (Lincoln: University of Nebraska Press, 1962), pp. 127–206, and B. I. Murstein, "The Effect of Stimulus, Background, Personality, and Scoring System on the Assessment of Hostility through the TAT (unpublished manuscript, Connecticut College, 1964).

mated, or otherwise elaborated editions of instincts, drives, or of an id whose structure, Freud said, "never changes."

Not one of these dominating theories of motivation allows for an essential transformation of motives in the course of life. McDougall explicitly denied the possibility; for our motivational structure is laid down once and for all in our equipment of instincts. New objects may become attached to an instinct through learning, but the motive power is always the same. Freud's position was essentially identical. The concept of "sublimation" and of shifting object "cathexis" chiefly accounted for whatever apparent alterations occur. Stimulus-response psychology is likewise geared to the assumption of remote control operating out of the past. We respond only to objects that have been associated with primary drives in the past, and we do so only in proportion to the degree that our responses have been rewarded or gratified in the past. From the stimulus-response point of view, the individual can hardly be said to be *trying* to do anything at all. He is simply *responding* with a complex array of habits that somehow were rewarded year before last. The prevailing dictum that motivation is always a matter of "tension reduction" or of "seeking equilibrium" is consistent with this point of view, but scarcely consistent, I think, with all the known facts.

This prevailing atmosphere of theory has engendered a kind of contempt for the "psychic surface" of life. The individual's conscious report is rejected as untrustworthy, and the contemporary thrust of his motives is disregarded in favor of a backward tracing of his conduct to earlier formative stages. The individual loses his right to be believed. And while he is busy leading his life in the present with a forward thrust into the future, most psychologists have become busy tracing it backward into the past.

It is now easy to understand why the special methods invented by Jung, Rorschach, and Murray were seized upon with enthusiasm by psychodiagnosticians. At no point do these methods ask the subject what his interests are, what he wants to do, or what he is trying to do. Nor do the methods ask directly concerning the subject's relation to his parents or to authority figures. They infer this relationship entirely by assumed identifications. So popular is this indirect, undercover approach to motivation that many clinicians and many university centers spend far more time on this type of diagnostic method than on any other.

Occasionally, however, a client may cause the projective tester consternation by intruding his unwanted conscious report. The story is told of a patient who remarked that a Rorschach card made him think of sexual relations. The clinician, thinking to tap a buried complex, asked him why. "Oh, because," said the patient, "I think of sexual relations all the time anyway." The clinician scarcely needed a Rorschach card to find out this motivational fact.

Still, it is probably true that most psychologists prefer to assess a person's needs and conflicts by going the long way around. The argument, of course, is that everyone — even a neurotic — will accommodate himself fairly well to the demands placed on him by reality. Only in an unstructured projective situation will he reveal his anxieties and unmasked needs. "Projective tests," writes Stagner (1951), "are more useful than reality situations for diagnostic purposes." To my mind, this uncompromising statement seems to mark the culmination of a century-long era of irrationalism, and therefore of distrust. Has the subject no right to be believed?

Fortunately, the extensive use of projective methods at the present time is yielding results that enable us to place this technique in proper perspective and to correct the one-sided theory of motivation on which their popularity rests.

Let us consider first the wartime research conducted with 36 conscientious objectors who lived for six months on a semistarvation diet (Brožek, Guetzkow, Baldwin, & Cranston, 1951). Their diet was so rigorously meager that on the average they lost one quarter of their initial body weight in the course of the six months. The food need was agonizingly great; their incessant hunger most poignant. Unless occupied with laboratory or other tasks, they found themselves thinking of food almost constantly. Typical daydreaming is reported by one subject as follows: "Today we'll have Menu No. 1. Gee, that's the smallest menu, it seems. How shall I fix the potatoes? If I use my spoon to eat them I'll be able to add more water . . . If I eat a little faster the food would stay warm longer—and I like it warm. But then it's gone so quickly." Now the curious thing is that while these men were clearly obsessed by their food drive, and all their energy seemed directed toward its fulfillment, yet on projective tests the need failed to appear. The investigators report that among the tests used (free word association, first-letters test, analysis of dreams, Rorschach, and Rosenzweig's P-F Study) only one gave a limited evidence of the preoccupation with food; viz., the free association test.

Here is a finding of grave significance. *The most urgent, the most absorbing motive in life failed completely to reveal itself by indirect methods.* It was, however, entirely accessible to conscious report. Part of the explanation may be that the subjects turned in relief to laboratory tasks to forget for a while their obsessive motive. They responded to the projective tests with heaven knows what available, habitual associational material. The failure of night dreams to reveal a significant amount of wish fulfillment is somewhat more perplexing. It can scarcely be ascribed to a defensive mental set. But both types of result suggest a possible law: Unless a motive is repressed, it is unlikely to affect distinctively the perception of, and responses to, a projective test. It is too early to tell whether this is a valid generalization, but it is a hypothesis well worth testing.

Other studies on hunger seem to yield supporting evidence (Levine, Chein, & Murphy, 1942; Sanford, 1936). Their trend suggests that on projective tests the number of explicit food associations actually declines in longer periods of fasting, apparently because the motive itself gradually becomes completely conscious and is not repressed. It is true that instrumental associations (ways of obtaining food) continue to appear in the subject's word responses as the state of hunger grows. This finding, however, is quite consistent with the hypothesis, since while hunger is fully conscious, the subject in the experimental situation is prevented from seeking satisfaction and thus is still repressing his instrumental action tendencies.

Another revealing line of evidence comes from the research of J. W. Getzels (1951). This investigator utilized two forms of a sentence-completion test—one couched in the first person and one in the third. His pairs are of the following type:

When they asked Frank to be in charge he . . . .
When they asked me to be in charge I . . . .

When Joe meets a person for the first time he usually . . . .
When I meet a person for the first time I usually . . . .

In this experiment, of course, the items were randomized. In all, there were 20 diagnostic items of each type. The subjects were 65 veterans, 25 diagnosed as well adjusted; 40 were psychoneurotic cases discharged from service with disability involving personality disorder.

It turned out that to a highly significant degree the well-adjusted men gave *identical* responses to the first- and to the third-person completions. If we assume that the third-person sentence is a "projective method," then the results obtained by this method for well-adjusted subjects squared almost perfectly with the results obtained from the direct, first-person questioning. The psychoneurotics, on the other hand, to a highly significant degree varied their responses. They said one thing when queried directly (e.g., "When they asked me to be in charge I agreed") and another on the projective item (e.g., "When they asked John to be in charge he was afraid"). The first-person completion is so direct that in the psychoneurotic it invokes the mask of defense and elicits a merely conventionally correct response.

Thus the direct responses of the psychoneurotic cannot be taken at their face value. The defenses are high; the true motives are hidden and are betrayed only by a projective technique. The normal subjects, on the other hand, tell you by the direct method precisely what they tell you by the projective method. They are all of a piece. You may therefore take their motivational statements at their face value, for even if you probe you will not find anything substantially different.

This research adds weight to the tentative judgment we formed in the case of the starving subjects. It is not the well-integrated subject, aware of his motivations, who reveals himself in projective testing. It is rather the neurotic personality, whose facade belies the repressed fears and hostilities within. Such a subject is caught off guard by projective devices; but the well-adjusted subject gives no significantly different response.

There is, however, one difference between the two researches. The starving subjects actually *avoided* any betrayal of their dominant motive in the projective tests. The well-adjusted veterans, on the other hand, gave essentially the *same* type of response in both direct and projective testing. It may be that the dissimilar nature of the tests used in the two situations accounts for this difference in results. But this detailed difference need not detain us here. What seems to be important is the implication of these researches that *a psychodiagnostician should never employ projective methods in the study of motivation without at the same time employing direct methods.* If he does not do so, he will never be able to tell whether there are strong conscious streams of motivation that are entirely evading the projective situation (as in the case of the starving subjects).

The trend of evidence that I have presented seems to indicate that a normal, well-adjusted individual with strong goal-directedness may on projective tests do one of two things: (1) either give material identical with that of conscious report—in which case the projective method is not needed—or (2) give no evidence whatever of his dominant motives. It is only when emotionally laden material comes forth in projective responses that is contradictory to conscious report, or to other results of direct assessment, that we find special value in projective testing. And we shall never know whether or not a neurotic situation prevails unless we use both diagnostic approaches and compare the yield.

Consider for a moment the diagnosis of anxiety. Using various responses on the Rorschach and TAT cards, the clinician might infer a high level of anxiety. Now, this finding taken by itself tells us little. The subject may be the sort of person who is enormously effective in life because he harnesses his anxiety to performance. He may know perfectly well that he is a harried, worried, bedeviled overachiever. Anxiety is an asset in his life, and he has enough insight to know the fact. In this case, the yield by projective methods is matched by the yield from direct methods. The projective technique was not really needed, but it does not harm to use it. Or, as in our starvation cases, we might find that projective protocols reveal no anxiety, while in actuality we are dealing with a person who is as harried, worried, and bedeviled as our first subject but who effectively controls his jitters. In this case, we assume that his large measure of control enables him to tackle the projective tests with some mental set unrelated to his anxious nature. But we may also find—and here is where projective methods have their uses—that an apparently bland and calm individual, denying all anxiety, reveals profound disturbance and fear in projective performances. It is this type of disassociated nature that projective tests help to diagnose. Yet they cannot do so unless direct methods also are employed.

In speaking so frequently of "direct" methods, I have referred chiefly to "conscious report." To ask a man his motives, however, is not the only type of "direct" method that we may employ. It is, however, a good one—especially to start with.

When we set out to study a person's motives, we are seeking to find out what that person is trying to do in this life, including, of course, what he is trying to avoid and what he is trying to be. I see no reason why we should not start our investigation by asking him to tell us the answers as he sees them. If the questions in this form seem too abstract, they can be recast. Particularly revealing are people's answers to the question, "What do you want to be doing five years from now?" Similar direct questions can be framed to elicit anxieties, loyalties, and hostilities. Most people, I suspect, can tell what they are trying to do in this life with a high degree of validity, certainly not less on the average than the prevailing validity of projective instruments. Yet some clinicians disdain to ask direct questions.

But by "direct methods" I mean also to include standard pencil-and-paper measures, such as the Strong Interest Inventory and the recently revised Allport-Vernon-Lindzey Study of Values. Now, it often happens that the yield on such instruments is not what would come from the subject's conscious report. The subject may not have known, for example, that compared with most people his pattern of values is, say, markedly theoretical and aesthetic or far below average in economic and religious interest. Yet the final score on the Study of Values is itself merely a summation of a series of separate conscious choices that he has made in forty-five hypothetical situations. While his verbal report on the pattern as a whole may be faulty, yet this pattern not only squares with all his separate choices but is known on the average to have good external validity. People with certain patterns of interests as measured by the test do, in fact, make characteristic vocational choices and do in their daily behavior act in ways that are demonstrably consistent with the test results.

To sum up: direct methods include the kind of report that is elicited in careful interviewing, whether it be of the simple psychiatric variety, the sort employed in vocational or personal counseling, or in nondirective interviewing. Autobiographic methods, when employed at their face value, are likewise direct. So, too, are the results of any kind of testing where the final scores represent a sum or pattern of a series of conscious choices on the part of the subject.[1]

The currently fashionable term *psychodynamics* is often equated explicitly with psychoanalytic theory. Projective techniques are considered psychodynamic because they are thought to tap deepest layers of structure and functioning. We have already indicated reasons for doubting the sufficiency of this assumption. Many of the most dynamic of motives are more accurately tapped by direct methods. At the very least, the discoveries by projective techniques cannot be properly interpreted unless they are compared with discoveries yielded by direct methods.

Devotees of psychodynamics often say that no discoveries are of value unless the unconscious is explored. This dictum we find in the valuable book by Kardiner and Ovesey (1951), *The Mark of Oppression*, dealing with the seriously disordered and conflictful motivational systems of Negroes in a northern city. Unless I am greatly mistaken, however, the authors discover little or nothing about their cases through psychoanalytic probes that is not evident in the manifest situation. The conscious handicaps of a Negro in our society, the economic misery, the deteriorated family situations, the bitterness and despair, constitute a painful psychodynamic situation in individual lives that in most instances receives no further illumination when depth analysis is employed.

Most of the psychodynamic evidence given by Kardiner and Ovesey concerning their cases is, in fact, drawn from straightforward autobiographical report. Their use of this method is acceptable and their findings highly instructive. But their theory seems to me out of line with both the method actually used and the findings obtained. Psychodynamics is not necessarily a hidden dynamics.

This point is well made by the psychiatrist J. C. Whitehorn (1950), who correctly holds that psychodynamics is a general science of motivation. Into its broad principles one may fit the specific contributions and insights of psychoanalysis. But psychoanalysis itself is by no means the sum and substance of psychodynamics. Whitehorn insists that the proper approach to psychotic patients, especially to those suffering from schizophrenic or depressive disorder, is through such channels of their normal

---

[1] For the purposes of the present argument, this simplified disussion of "direct" and "indirect" techniques is adequate. Psychodiagnosis requires, however, a much more discriminating classification of the methods currently employed and of the "levels" of organization that each normally taps. An excellent beginning is Rosenzweig's proposal (1950) that three classes of methods be distinguished, each adapted in principle to tapping three levels of behavior. What he calls *subjective* methods require the subject to take himself as a direct object of observation (questionnaires, autobiographies). *Objective* methods require the observer to report on overt conduct. *Projective* methods require both subject and observer to "look the other way" and to base the diagnosis on the subject's reaction to apparently "ego-neutral" material. Broadly speaking, Rosenzweig's subjective and objective procedures correspond to what I here call "direct" methods, and projective procedures to "indirect" methods.

Especially noteworthy is the author's statement that the significance of projective methods (e.g., his own P-F Study) cannot be determined unless the subject's projective responses are examined in the light of his subjective and objective responses.

interest systems as remain open. It is not the region of their disorder that requires primary attention but those psychodynamic systems that still represent sturdy and healthy adaptations to reality. In White-horn's words, the therapist should seek "to activate and utilize the resources of the patient and to help thereby to work out a more satisfying way of life with a less circumscribed emphasis upon these special issues" (1950, p. 40.)

Sometimes we hear it said that psychoanalytic theory does not do justice to psychoanalytic practice. What is meant is that in the course of therapy an analyst will devote much of his time to a direct discussion with his patient of his manifest interests and values. The analyst will listen respectfully and accept, counsel, and advise concerning these important, and not buried, psychodynamic systems. In many instances, as in the cases presented by Kardiner and Ovesey, the motives and conflicts are taken at their face value. Thus the method of psychoanalysis as employed is not fully sustained by the theory that is affirmed.

Nothing that I have said denies the existence of infantile systems, troublesome repressions, or neurotic formations. Nor does it deny the possibility of self-deception, rationalization, and ego defense. My point is merely that methods and theories dealing with these aberrant conditions should be set in a broad conception of psychodynamics. The patient should be assumed insightful until he is proved otherwise. If you asked a hundred people who go to the icebox for a snack why they did so, probably all would answer, "Because I was hungry." In ninety-nine of these cases we may—no matter how deeply we explore—discover that this simple, conscious report is the whole truth. It can be taken at its face value. In the hundredth case, however, our probing shows that we are dealing with a compulsive overeater, with an obese seeker after infantile security who, unlike the majority of cases, does not know what he is trying to do. It is peace and comfort he is seeking—perhaps his mother's bosom—and not the leftover roast. In this case—and in a minority of all cases—I grant we cannot take the evidence of his overt behavior, nor his account of it, at their face value.

Freud was a specialist in precisely those motives that cannot be taken at their face value. To him, motivation resided in the id. The conscious, accessible region of personality that carries on direct transactions with the world—namely, the ego—he regarded as devoid of dynamic power.

It is a misfortune that Freud died before he had remedied this one-sidedness in his theory. Even his most faithful followers tell us now that he left his ego psychology incomplete. In recent years, many of them have labored to redress the balance. Without doubt, the principal current in psychoanalytic theory today is moving in the direction of a more dynamic ego. This trend in theory is apparent in the work of Anna Freud, Hartmann, French, Horney, Fromm, Kris, and many others. In a communication to the American Psychoanalytic Association, Kris points out that the attempt to restrict interpretations of motivation to the id aspect only "represents the older procedure." Modern concern with the ego does not confine itself to an analysis of defense mechanisms alone. Rather it gives more respect to what he calls the "psychic surface." Present psychoanalytic techniques, he tells us, tend to link "surface" with "depth" (Kris, 1951). In a similar vein, Rapaport (1951) has argued that a measure of true autonomy must now be ascribed to the ego.

To illustrate the point at issue, we might take any psychogenic interest of maturity; for example, the religious sentiment. Freud's handling of the matter is well known. To him, religion is essentially a neurosis in the individual, a formula for personal escape. The father image lies at the root of the matter. One cannot, therefore, take the religious sentiment, when it exists in a personality, at its face value. A more balanced view of the matter would seem to be this: *sometimes* one cannot take this sentiment at its face value, and *sometimes* one can. Only a careful study of the individual will tell. In a person in whom the religious factor serves an obviously egocentric purpose—talismanic, bigoted, self-justificatory—we can infer that it is a neurotic, or at least immature, formation in the personality. Its infantile and escapist character is not recognized by the subject. On the other hand, in a person who has gradually evolved a guiding philosophy of life where the religious sentiment exerts a generally normative force upon behavior and confers intelligibility to life as a whole, we infer not only that this particular ego formation is a dominant motive but that it must be accepted at its face value. It is a master motive and an ego ideal whose shape and substance are essentially what appear in consciousness (Allport, 1950a).

Let us consider a final example. It is well known that most boys around the age of four to seven identify with their fathers. They imitate them in many ways. Among other things, they may express vocational aspirations for daddy's job. Many boys when grown do in fact follow their fathers' footsteps.

Take politics. Father and son have been politicians in many families: the Tafts, Lodges, Kennedys, La Follettes, Roosevelts, to mention only a few. When the son is at a mature age, say fifty or sixty, what is his motivation? Is he working through his early father identification or is he not? Taken at its face value, the interest of the son in politics now seems to be absorbing, self-contained, a prominent factor in his own ego structure. In short, it seems to be a mature and normal motive. But the strict geneticist would say: "No, he is now a politician because of a father fixation." Does the geneticist mean that an early father identification started him in a political direction of interest? If so, the answer is yes, of course. All motives have their origin somewhere. Or does he mean, "This early fixation now, today, sustains the son's political conduct"? If so, the answer is normally no. The political interest is now a prominent part of the ego structure, and the ego is the healthy man's source of energy. To be sure, there may be cases where a person mature in years is still trying to curry father's favor, to step into his shoes, to displace him with the mother. A clinical study of a second-generation politician may conceivably show that his behavior is compulsively father-identified. In such a case, his daily conduct is in all probability so compulsive, so ungeared to realistic situational needs, so excessive, that the diagnosis can be suspected by any skilled clinical observer. But such instances are relatively rare.

To sum up: we need in our motivational theory to make a sharper distinction between infantilisms and motivation that is strictly contemporary and at age.

I am fully aware of my heterodoxy in suggesting that there is, in a restricted sense, a discontinuity between normal and abnormal motivation and that we need a theory that will recognize this fact. Discontinuities are distinctly unpopular in psychological science. One theory of abnormality tells us that we are merely pleased to regard the extremes on our linear continuum as abnormal. Further, some culture theorists insist that abnormality is a relative concept, shifting from culture to culture and from one historical period to another. Likewise, there are many borderline cases which even the most experienced clinician could not with confidence classify as normal or as abnormal. Finally, and most important, is the fact that in many normal people one can by scratching deeply enough find some infantilism in their motivation.

Granted all these familiar arguments, there is still a world of difference —if not between normal and abnormal people—then between the healthy and unhealthy mechanisms involved in the development of motivation. What we call integrative action of the nervous system is basically a wholesome mechanism that keeps motivation up to date. It tends to bring about both an internal consistency and a reality testing among the elements entering into motivational patterning. Effective suppression is another healthy mechanism, not only harmless to the individual, but making possible the arrangement of motives in an orderly hierarchy (Belmont & Birch, 1951; McGranahan, 1940). With the aid of effective suppression, the individual ceases to act out infantile dramas. Insight, a clear self-image, and the little-understood factor of homeostasis may be mentioned among the balancing mechanisms.

As Getzels' experiment shows, direct and projective performances in healthy people are all of a piece. A further test of normality— unfortunately one psychologists have not yet developed—may lie in the harmony of expressive behavior (facial expression, gestures, handwriting) with the individual's fundamental motivational structure. There is evidence that disco-ordination between conscious motives and expressive movement is an ominous sign (Allport & Vernon, 1933). This lead for research should be followed through.

In unhealthy motivation, unbalancing mechanisms have the upper hand. There is always some species of dissociation at work. The individual represses ineffectively; repressed motives erupt in autistic gestures, in tantrums, in nightmares, in compulsions, perhaps in paranoid thinking. Above all, self-knowledge is lacking in large regions of the life.

My point is that normally the balancing mechanisms have the upper hand. Sometimes, in certain badly disordered lives, the unbalancing mechanisms take over. Occasionally, too, we find them operating in a segmental way in lives that are otherwise healthy. When the clash in mechanisms is marked, diagnosis is then aided by the use of projective techniques. But when there is essential harmony within the personality system, projective methods will teach us little or nothing about the course of motivation.

From what has been said, it is clear that a satisfactory conception of psychodynamics will have the following characteristics. (1) It will never employ projective methods or depth analysis without allowing for a full diagnosis of motives by direct methods as well. (2) It will assume that in a healthy personality the great bulk of motivation can be taken at its face value. (3) It will assume that normal motivation of this order has a present and future significance for the individual that is by no means adequately represented by a study of his past life. In other words, it will allow that the present psychodynamics of a life may in large part be functionally autonomous, even though continuous with early motivational formations (Allport, 1950b, pp. 76–113). (4) It will, at the same time, retain the epochal insights of Freud and others to the effect that infantile fixations frequently occur and that we do well to check on conscious report and to supplement direct methods by indirect.

Before such an adequate conceptualization can be achieved, there is one current dogma in motivational theory that demands re-examination. I refer to the oft-encountered statement that all motives aim at "the reduction of tensions." This doctrine—found in instinctivism, psychoanalysis, and stimulus-response psychology—operates to keep us on a primitive level of theorizing.

We cannot, of course, deny that basic drives seem to seek "reduction of tension." Oxygen need, hunger, thirst, elimination, are examples. But these drives are not a trustworthy model for all normal adult motivation. Goldstein remarks that patients who seek only tension reduction are clearly pathological. They are preoccupied with segmental irritations from which they seek relief. There is nothing creative about their interests. They cannot take suffering, or delay, or frustration as a mere incident in their pursuit of values. Normal people, by contrast, are dominated by their "preferred patterns" of self-actualization. Their psychogenic interests are modes of sustaining and directing tension rather than escaping it (Goldstein, 1940).

We should, I think, agree with Goldstein that tension reduction is not an adequate statement of the functioning of mature psychogenic motives. At the time of his inauguration as president of Harvard, James Bryant Conant remarked that he was undertaking his duties "with a heavy heart but gladly." He knew he would reduce no tensions by committing himself to the new job. Tensions would mount and mount and at many times become almost unbearable. While he would in the course of his daily work dispatch many tasks and feel relief, still the over-all commitment—his total investment of energy—would never result in any equilibrium. Psychogenic interests are of this order: they lead us to complicate and strain our lives indefinitely. "Striving for equilibrium," "tension reduction," "death wish," seem trivial and erroneous representations of normal adult motivation.

Recent years, as I have said, have brought a wholesome turn in theorizing. Few authorities on war neuroses, for example, wrote in terms of tension reduction. They spoke rather of "firm ego structure" or "weak ego structure." Grinker and Spiegel say, "As the ego becomes stronger the therapist demands increasing independence and activity from the patient" (Grinker & Spiegel, 1945, p. 94).

After successful therapy, these and other writers sometimes remark, "The ego now seems in full control." In such expressions as these—and one encounters them with increasing frequency—we meet post-Freudian ego psychology again. True, the flavor of these theoretical statements varies. Sometimes they still seem close to the conception of the ego as rationalizer, rider, and steersman. But often, as in the statements just quoted, they go far beyond. They imply not only that the ego is normally able to avoid malignant repression, chronicity, and rigidity but that it is also differentiated dynamism—a fusion of healthy psychogenic motives that can be taken at their face value.

There is no need to take fright at the conception of an "active ego." As I see the matter, the term "ego" does not refer to a homunculus but is merely a shorthand expression for what Goldstein calls "preferred patterns." The term means that normally healthy personalities have various systems of psychogenic motives. They are not limitless in number. Indeed, in a well-integrated adult they may be adequately indicated on the fingers of two hands, perhaps one. What a person is trying to do persistently, recurrently, as a function of his own internal nature is often surprisingly well focused and well patterned. Whether these leading motives are called desires, interests, values, traits, or sentiments does not greatly matter. What is important is that motivational theory—in guiding diagnosis, therapy, and research—should take these structures fully into account.

REFERENCES

ALLPORT, G. W. *The individual and his religion.* New York: Macmillan, 1950. (a)
ALLPORT, G. W. *The nature of personality: Selected papers.* Cambridge: Addison-Wesley, 1950. (b)
ALLPORT, G. W., & VERNON, P. E. *Studies in expressive movement.* New York: Macmillan, 1933.
BELMONT, L., & BIRCH, H. G. Re-individualizing the repression hypothesis. *J. abnorm. soc. Psychol.,* 1951, 46, 226–235.
BROŽEK, J., GUETZKOW, H., BALDWIN, M. V., & CRANSTON, R. A quantitative study of perception and association in experimental semi-starvation. *J. Pers.,* 1951, 19, 245–264.
GETZELS, J. W. The assessment of personality and prejudice by the methods of paired direct and projective questionnaires. Unpublished thesis, Harvard Coll. Lib., Cambridge, 1951.
GOLDSTEIN, K. *Human nature in the light of psychopathology.* Cambridge: Harvard Univer. Press, 1940.
GRINKER, R. R., & SPIEGEL, J. P. *War neuroses.* Philadelphia: Blakiston, 1945.
KARDINER, A., & OVESEY, L. *The mark of oppression.* New York: Norton, 1951.
KRIS, E. Ego psychology and interpretation in psychoanalytic therapy. *Psychoanal. Quart.,* 1951, 20, 15–30.
LEVINE, R., CHEIN, I., & MURPHY, G. The relation of the intensity of a need to the amount of perceptual distortion: A preliminary report. *J. Psychol.,* 1942, 13, 283–293.
McGRANAHAN, D. V. A critical and experimental study of repression. *J. abnorm. soc. Psychol.,* 1940, 35, 212–225.
RAPAPORT, D. The autonomy of the ego. *Bull. Menninger Clin.,* 1951, 15, 113–123.
ROSENZWEIG, S. Levels of behavior in psychodiagnosis with special reference to the picture-frustration study. *Amer. J. Orthopsychiat.,* 1950, 20, 63–72.
SANFORD, R. N. The effect of abstinence from food upon imaginal processes. *J. Psychol.,* 1936, 2, 129–136.
STAGNER, R. Homeostasis as a unifying concept in personality theory. *Psychol. Rev.,* 1951, 58, 5–17.
WHITEHORN, J. C. Psychodynamic considerations in the treatment of psychotic patients. *Univer. west. Ontario med. J.,* 1950, 20, 27–41.

4

Assumptions, Adaptation Level, and Projective Techniques[1]

BERNARD I. MURSTEIN

In this article, several basic assumptions underlying projective techniques are discussed. Some of them, such as the assumption that the stimulus is of little importance since it is "ambiguous" and "standard," have been shown to be patently invalid. Other assumptions are not simply true or untrue but require greater specificity. Such an assumption is the belief that the more similar the stimulus is to the subject, the greater the degree of projection. Here, the research indicates that physical similarity per se is not of crucial significance. It is but one of several determinants. Other important stimulus determinants include the cultural status of the figure and his psychological significance to the subject.

The finding that many of these assumptions are inaccurate or insufficient to account for projective technique responses emphasizes the fact that the earnest efforts to win recognition for these techniques as reputable assessment tools of personality have led to a heavy emphasis on empirical validation studies. The theoretical underpinning of projective techniques has been built largely on the theorizing of a relatively small number of individuals. These theories have rarely been supported by empirical evidence. In recent years, therefore, as the evidence has filtered in, it appears that many of these assumptions need to be drastically revised. The newer theoretical approaches of Epstein and Atkinson,[a]

[1] This investigation was supported by a Public Health Service Grant (M-4698) from the National Institute of Mental Health.

[a] S. Epstein, "The measurement of Drive and Conflict in Humans: Theory and Experiment," in M. R. Jones, ed., *Nebraska Symposium on Motivation* (Lincoln: Univ. of Nebraska Press, 1962), pp. 127–206; J. W. Atkinson, "Thematic Apperceptive Measurement of Motives within the Context of a Theory of Motivation," Chapter 26, *infra*.

to name but two, have the advantage of being operationally oriented and have been supported to some degree by empirical results. It seems appropriate, nonetheless, to state that these studies are just beginning to scratch the surface, and we are still far from having a viable theory tying projective behavior to personality theory.

It has been almost forty years since the introduction of projective techniques on a formal basis. Ignored at first, attacked later as unscientific, these instruments have currently achieved wide empirical employment if not theoretical acceptance. Perhaps now that the first flush of youth has passed, it is time for some "middle-aged" self-reflection. It is the purpose of this paper to examine some ten more or less popularly held assumptions regarding these techniques, which are believed to be contrary to current research findings, logic, or both. The critique will be followed by a conceptual approach directed toward achieving a better understanding of projective responses in the behavior system of the individual being examined.

Assumptions

1. *The more ambiguous the stimulus properties of the projective technique, the more response reflects the personality of the perceiver.*

This assumption at first sight appears incontrovertible and has been seconded by clinicians (Abt, 1950; Shneidman, 1956) and nonclinicians (Bruner, 1948). It is held that if, to use an extreme example, a blank card (Card 16, TAT) is presented to S and he is asked to tell a story, he must of necessity project, since there are no stimulus properties to guide his themes. To adhere to this view, however, is to commit the grievous error of assuming that the stimulus presented to S is the stimulus to which he reacts. It is not meant by this statement to enmesh the reader in the morass of the old objective reality–phenomenological reality dichotomy. Rather it is our purpose to state that the cards of themselves are only part of the total stimulus situation. Also to be considered are the environmental variables and those relating to S himself. Hence, the blank card, though it is bare of stimulus imprint, may so structure the testing situation that the response repertoire of S shows less variation than would be the case were he to receive a more structured card. Thus, the *actual stimulus* impinging upon S may result in his perceiving himself as being called upon to *reveal something of himself through a story, since there is obviously no objective picture for him to talk about.*

In that case, we should be dealing with a *response set* of a fairly stereo-typed nature having as its purpose the censoring of any material which would cause S to appear in an unflattering light.

A still further problem is the multiple-connotative usage of the term *ambiguity*. Sometimes ambiguity has been used to describe the physical properties of the cards, as in the "hazy appearance" of some TAT cards (Weisskopf, 1950b). Bijou and Kenny (1951), however, give the term more of a psychological meaning in defining it as the number of possible interpretations that could be given to a card. The important distinction has not been made between physical structure and ambiguity. It is proposed that the Funk and Wagnall's dictionary provides a basis for distinguishing the two terms. *Structure* is defined as "the arrange-ment and organic union of parts in a body or object" (Funk & Wagnalls, *New Standard Dictionary of the English Language*, p. 2401). *Ambiguity* is defined by the same dictionary as "the quality of being ambiguous, obscure, or uncertain in meaning, especially where either of two inter-pretations is possible" (p. 86).

The correlation between lack of structure and ambiguity is not unity. Card 16, for example, as stated earlier, is quite unstructured. It does not possess a high degree of ambiguity, however, since the extreme absence of structure also limits the number of possible interpretations of the card (Eron, 1950; Ullmann, 1957). Accordingly, Ss often claim they can-not give a story and when pressed give a trifling banality. Despite the variation of meaning in ambiguity, the research literature is hardly con-ducive to the belief that ambiguity is linearly related to projection.

In the field of projective techniques, and specifically the TAT, Weiss-kopf (1950a) found that photographs of the test given in reduced expos-ure, thus making them more hazy, did not increase projection. Using time of presentation as a measure of ambiguity, she found that cards exposed for a sufficient length of time so that they were clearly perceived were superior for projective purposes to cards only fleetingly seen. Again (Weisskopf, 1950b), completely traced line drawings were found to be more effective in evoking fantasy than incompletely traced drawings.

Murray himself has described the TAT cards as "divided into two series of ten pictures each, the pictures of the second series (numbers 11 through 20), being purposely more unusual, dramatic and bizarre than those of the first" (1943, p. 2).

The question arises as to which of these series is the more ambiguous? By way of answer, Bijou and Kenny (1951) had groups of men and women (college students) rank 21 "male series" TAT cards on the dimension of "ambiguity" (estimated number of different interpretations that might be derived from each card). A *t* test between the means of both series indicated that the "fairy-tale" series was more ambiguous at the .05 level. Granted the fairy-tale series is more ambiguous, does it elicit more projection on the part of S? Weisskopf (1950a) found that her sample of college students projected with more fantasy to the "everyday" series.

Can we, then, assume that the least ambiguous pictures precipitate the greatest amount of projection? While the foregoing data might hint at such an interpretation, two studies specifically aimed at this question indicate that the relationship is curvilinear rather than linear. Kenny and Bijou (1953) divided 15 TAT cards into three piles of low, medium, and high ambiguity. The stories derived from these cards were rated for "personality-revealingness" with the result that cards of medium ambiguity were the most "revealing." Murstein (1958c), using Bijou and Kenny's ranking for ambiguity and frequency of theme appearance rankings obtained from Eron's study (1950), correlated the two variables using both product-moment and curvilinear methods. While the linear correlation was nonsignificant, the curvilinear one proved to be quite significant. The moderately ambiguous cards produced the most themes, while the high and low ambiguous cards were less productive.

In another study, Murstein (1958a) had female Ss rank a "female" series of cards for "pleasantness" and for "psychological ambiguity." He correlated these rankings with each other and with Eron's "emotional tone" scores obtained from the TAT stories of a similar female population (1953). "Ambiguity" was found to correlate significantly (rho) with "pleasantness," .40; and with "emotional tone," .56.

In sum, it appears that extremely ambiguous TAT cards do not stimulate S's private world so much as they elicit a "response set" resulting in a sparsely themed pleasant type of response. The study of ambiguity has received little attention apart from the TAT, and it is to be hoped that the Rorschach and other techniques will stimulate further studies of this type.

2. *The more similar the stimulus to S, the greater the degree of projection.*

This question has been discussed at some length elsewhere (Murstein, 1959). The experimental literature was reviewed with regard to the Negro TAT versus white TAT, modification of the central character to resemble S, who might be a student, nun, crippled, or obese person, and the use of animal versus human pictures with children. The results are in general negative to the belief that making the central character in the picture more similar to S increases projection and to the belief that children project more readily to pictures of animals than they do to humans. Such views do not adequately consider the importance of the "background" factors and Ss' "personalities."

Also overlooked is the fact that the stimulus is perceived in accordance with *cultural experience*, resulting in perceptions which cannot be understood solely on the basis of a description of the physical properties of the picture. Negroes, for example, perceive the TAT figures *not as whites*, *but as people in general* (Cook, 1953). Such is the adaptation of the

Negro to the "white" norms that being shown a Negro TAT card arouses suspicion because of the novelty of such a test. Accordingly, one is hardly surprised to find that such cards given to Negroes have often been reported as resulting in *less* projection than when the usual TAT cards were used.

In the case of animal versus human pictures, the evidence is largely in favor of the use of humans in preference to animals. CAT versus TAT comparisons offer only indirect evidence, since the quality of response is a function of the *kind of situation depicted* as well as the use of animals or humans. Happily, several studies have used humanized analogues of the CAT pictures and noted the superiority of the analogues.

In sum, projection is enhanced by the use of the same species as *S* (*homo sapiens*) but, within species, increased physical similarity to *S* in terms of physical affliction, occupation, or appearance does not produce more meaningful objective responses.

3. *Since the stimulus is more or less ambiguous, it is of little importance as compared to the value of the response elicited.*

The proponents of this view hold that the determinant of the response is hardly so much the immediate stimulus as the basic idiosyncratic perceptions which stem from *S*'s "private world" (Rosenzweig, 1951). Since the stimulus is standard for all *S*'s, differences in response are said to stem from *S*'s projections. Actually, there has been less variation in response than commonly believed. Eron (1950, 1953) demonstrated that his *S*'s, regardless of their psychiatric classification (schizophrenic, neurotic, normal), tended to tell stories to the TAT that were of sad emotional tone. Murstein (1958a) found the unpleasantness in the emotional tone of TAT stories scored by Eron's scale to be positively related to the lack of ambiguity of the cards. Several TAT-type cards have been scaled for aggression and sex by the Guttman technique (Auld, Eron, & Laffal, 1955; Lesser, 1958; Murstein, Coulter, Bowdish, David, Fisher, Furth, & Hansen, 1959). These results imply that the TAT is not nearly so ambiguous as has been thought.

4. *No response is accidental. Every response is meaningful for the analysis of personality.*

Taken literally, the first of these two statements is beyond dispute if one adheres to a concept of psychic determinism. The second statement, however, would seem to run contrary to what general test theory propounds; namely, that a certain portion of the variance accounting for a response may be profitably treated as "error variance." This "error variance" stems from two factors. First, the fluctuation caused by lack of consistency of response. Second, *S*s differ not only with regard to personality but in many other ways. One of these ways is in experience. An emphasis on anatomical details in a farmer has different implications from similar perception by a medical student. *S*s differ in their verbal fluency and habits (most projective tests may be nominally perceptual, but *it is the verbalizations, not the perceptions, which are scored*).

Intellect is still another factor making for differences in response. Lastly, Ss differ in the cognitive response habits or response sets which they bring to the testing situation. Where these response sets are themselves analyzed, there is no problem. Often, however, these habits are not discerned by the examiner. A habit, for example, which is very difficult to detect is the "saw-tooth phenomenon" which has been extensively described by Atkinson with reference to the TAT (1950). Using a Latin square design for order of presentation, he showed that there was a significant difference between mean achievement-motive scores for odd and even serial positions (adjusted to remove systematic differences attributable to the pictures). Further, he found a significant relationship (rho = .66) between Ss' mean achievement scores for the first four positions and the size of the decrease from these scores to the scores based on the last four positions with scores, again equated for systematic differences due to the pictures. A logical explanation of this phenomenon is that the expression of achievement in early stories leads to a relative satiation with regard to the occurrence of this motive in later stories.

The conclusions to be derived are that there is considerable variation in the meaningfulness of a response to a projective technique, depending on the effects of Ss' experience, intelligence, verbal ability, and the "response set."

5. *Projective techniques are complementary in tapping the various layers of personality* (Harrison, 1940; Henry, 1947; Stern & Horinson, 1949).

One of the popular views among clinical psychologists is that the Rorschach delves into the "basic personality," while the TAT is said to be more sensitive to situational influences. Thus, Shneidman (1956) depicts the Rorschach as probing the unconscious, while the TAT seems to tap the unconscious, preconscious, and conscious. There has been some research which seems to indicate that, rather than being complementary, two projective techniques may on occasion give contradictory findings.

Shatin (1953, 1955), using a sign approach in his analysis of the Rorschach, obtained a Rorschach Adjustment Inventory (RAI) for a psychiatric patient population. Adjustment on the Rorschach was found to correlate with the following TAT variables: "unpleasant feeling tone" ($p < .10$), "degree of inner conflict" ($p < .05$), and "verbal and emotional aggression" ($p < .04$).

In a study by Murstein and Wheeler (1959), 36 female breast cancer patients at a southwestern hospital received the Rorschach and a Thematic Stories Test (TST), consisting of five TAT cards and five cards from the Caldwell Picture Series[2] a thematic-type test depicting mainly

---

[2] An unpublished test by B. M. Caldwell, Washington University School of Medicine, 1953.

elderly persons. Holding word count on the TST and number of responses on the Rorschach constant, the correlation between the measurement of hostility on the Rorschach and on the TAT was —.41 which was significant at the .01 level for a one-tailed test of significance. A study by Murstein (1960) on parents of hospitalized children resulted in a correlation of .31 (p < .05) between the pleasantness of the "emotional tone of stories" as scored on the TAT and the anxiety score on the Taylor Manifest Anxiety Scale. Carr (1956) tested 50 neurotic male patients to whom he administered the TAT, Sentence Completion, and Rorschach tests. Many of the "signs" on one test were contrary to those of the others. Thus, *the perception of less than two females on the Rorschach was correlated with a lack of mother-hostility on the TAT and Sentence Completion.*

Two points should be made with regard to these studies. The first is that often the assumption that two quantitative signs taken from two different tests are "qualitatively" equivalent is not sufficently justified by research evidence. We may thus do serious insult to the data by engaging in "miniature psychoanalysis" utilizing these signs. Hence, one may ask with considerable justification whether the lack of perception of females on the Rorschach is related to hostility toward them for the majority of test takers. Until research supports this assumption with experimental evidence, we might be wiser to avoid the utilization of such "face validity."

Secondly, however, negative correlations have been reported in which the operations used in measuring a trait in different tests have pretty much the same meaning (e.g., the projection of hostility on the Rorschach and TAT). If one keeps in mind the fact that the techniques are structured to a different degree with regard to their stimulus properties, then a negative correlation may be more easily understood. Accordingly, a "well adjusted" individual might get a high hostility score on the TAT because many of the cards are so structured as to depict violence and aggression (Eron, 1950; Murstein, 1958b). Getting a high hostility score on the TAT would not then indicate a person possessing considerable hostility, but instead one who manifested a high degree of confidence in perceiving the stimulus properties objectively. Such a person, however, would be expected to manifest little hostility in the more ambiguous Rorschach because there is little need for the release of hostility and because the stimulus properties of the Rorschach are not necessarily structured in a hostile manner. While such a hypothetical "normal" S's behavior would not be *constant*, it would be *consistent*. Much more work is needed in which the stimulus properties of the cards, in addition to environmental and personality variables, are utilized in assessing the complementary or contradictory results obtained.

6. *A protocol is a sufficiently extensive sampling of S's personality*

to warrant formulating judgments about it (Macfarlane & Tuddenham, 1951, p. 34).

It is true that one can learn something from the omission of response to a technique such as the Rorschach or TAT. Webb and Hilden (1953) have shown, however, that there is a fairly high correlation between the amount of words used in stories to the TAT and S's intelligence (.40) and verbal fluency (.50). Thus, while absence of an adequate number of responses for interpretation conceivably may be a function of personality disturbance, it also might be a function of intelligence or verbal fluency. The evidence, therefore, seems to indicate that the absence of response is not nearly so meaningful for personality interpretation as the presence of an adequate number of responses. Consequently, one can expect to encounter protocols from time to time which reveal little of S except that his response set is not geared to excessive production. One must therefore conclude that individual protocols vary in the amount of knowledge that may be gained from their analysis.

7. *S is unaware of what he discloses about himself.*

The impetus for this assumption may be traced to L. K. Frank's important article in which he suggested that projective techniques were an excellent medium with which to tap the "private world of the individual comprising as it does, the feelings, urges, beliefs, attitudes, and desires of which he may be dimly aware and which he is often reluctant to admit even to himself much less to others" (1948, p. 66).

Murray, in similar vein, also has said that "whatever peculiar virtue the TAT may have, if any, it will be found to reside not as some have assumed, in its power to mirror overt behavior or to communicate what the patient knows and is willing to tell, but rather in its capacity to reveal things that the patient is unwilling to tell because he is unconscious of them" (1951, p. 577).

Disagreeing sharply is Allport, who has stated: "Normal subjects . . . tell you by the direct method precisely what they tell you by the projective method. They are all of a piece. You may therefore take their motivational statements at their face value, for even if you probe you will not find anything substantially different" (1953, p. 110).

The evidence seems to favor Allport not only in so far as normal Ss are concerned but also for those whose adjustment is considerably less than optimal. Scodel and Lipetz (1957) and Wirt (1956) found that neurotics projected more hostility on the TAT and Rorschach, respectively, than did equally hostile psychotics. Indeed, Rader (1957) posits that projection is closely related to strength of ego control as well as to general sociocultural background. "Thus, with poor control one may find a positive correlation between content (which was earlier hypothesized to be an index of underlying drive) and behavior, while with strong control one may find a negative correlation" (Rader, 1957, p. 304).

Clark's work (1952) also supported the relationship of projection to ego control. He found that male Ss expressed little sexual content on the TAT after seeing nude pictures. The use of alcoholic beverages to loosen ego control resulted in an increase in sexual fantasy to the cards.

Murstein (1956) gave the Rorschach to fraternity men designated hostile-insightful and hostile-noninsightful on the basis of pooled rankings. The hostile-insightful men projected significantly more hostility on the Rorschach than the hostile-noninsightful men. He concluded that projection on the Rorschach was in part a function of the willingness of the individual to disclose data from his "private world."

A curvilinear relationship between overt hostility and hostility measured via the content of the Rorschach was hypothesized and found by Smith and Coleman (1956). Persons with little overt hostility and those with a good deal of overt hostility projected little hostility as compared with those occupying the middle range. Comparing dreams with TAT protocols, Gordon (1953) concluded that the TAT protocols reflected the idealized self (subject to conscious control) compared to the more need-oriented self depicted in dreams. Lindzey and Tejessy (1956) found that aggressive indexes derived from the TAT correlated more highly with self-ratings than with other ratings, including those of clinical observers.

Finally, a study by Davids (1955) seems to bear on the issue very well. He employed the usual rationale in recruiting Ss from a college population in that they were told that they were contributing time to the furthering of science. Several measures of maladjustment were obtained, including the use of two projective techniques, and the intercorrelations were fairly high. When, however, a new group of students were led to believe that, from their protocols, an individual of considerable emotional stability and maturity would be selected for a high-paying job, the intercorrelations dropped considerably. It would hardly appear conceivable that these changes occurred independently of the Ss' volition.

The experimental evidence seems to indicate a good deal of awareness on the part of S as to what he "projects" on a projective technique. It has also been shown that a "response set" to an ambiguous picture often results in pleasant but superficial associations (Murstein, 1958a). Synthesizing these two findings, we may adumbrate a schema whereby many Ss quite consciously control their words in an ambiguous situation, issuing more or less pleasant banalities in order to appear in a pleasing light to the examiner. The key to this guarded behavior lies in the ego-involving aspect of being probed psychologically in order to find out whether one is "adjusted or maladjusted."

This interpretation of the projective test situation is consistent with the results of Singer and Young (1941) in an experiment which did not involve projective techniques. The authors presented students with a series of tones, tastes, odors, and odor-taste alternations and had them rate this more or less representative series on "pleasantness" and "unpleasantness." The students also participated in a heterogeneous array of thirty activities which was followed by their being presented with a series of words or phrases to which they associated activities and then evaluated these activities for their attractiveness. In addition, they rated their moods. The ratios of pleasant to unpleasant ratings were as follows: Mood, 4.48; Activity, 1.77; Words, 1.59; Odor, .54; Odor-taste, .53; Taste, .46; Tone, .38.

It is noteworthy that the more personal the category rated, the more pleasant was the rating. Thus, moods reflect the emotional life of the student and, accordingly, they rated their moods of the previous hour as quite pleasant. With regard to activities and word associations, there is no direct reference to emotion, and yet one must favorably impress the examiner that one is a "pleasant sort of chap." Odors, tastes, and tones have little ego involvement, and perhaps the tediousness of the tasks results in unpleasant ratings. The important finding is that in situations where they were personally involved, the students tended to give pleasant ratings, though this "response set" took on a negative cast when sensory discriminations were called for.

In sum, then, if one returns to a consideration of projective techniques, one is struck by their relative inefficacy in dealing with sophisticated Ss. The very ambiguity of projective techniques as well as lack of stimulus structure (Lazarus, 1953) alerts S to the possibility that what he says "may be held against him." Accordingly, the resulting protocol is often most consistent with the "public self," which "self" the clinicians are usually not very interested in examining.

8. *The strength of a need is a function of its manifestation directly or symbolically on the projective technique.*

The work of Pittluck (1950) has indicated that no simple relationship exists between a need and its manifestation on a projective technique. Assuming that the expression of a need is a function of the need and of the anxiety opposing its expression, she was able to show that Ss who relied heavily on defense mechanisms such as "rejection" or "denial of aggression," putting aggression in a socially approved context or displacing it to nonhuman characters, were not apt to act out their hostility despite protocols containing many expressions of hostility. Murstein (1956) found that merely taking account of a need without considering the stimulus, self-concept, and environment surrounding an administration of the test would be of little predictive value with regard to overt behavior. He was able to show that two equally hostile groups differed significantly in the projection of hostility on the Rorschach as a function of their self-concepts. That even prolonged semistarvation does not significantly increase the number of food responses on the Rorschach was reported by Brožek and co-workers (1951). Levine and associates (1942) found that the number of food responses given in response to an ambiguous picture was less after 9 hours than it had been after 3 to 6 hours. Rader (1957), studying prison inmates, found only certain kinds of hostile projection (mutilation) related to overt hostile behavior. In a study by Smith and Coleman (1956), persons with high and low overt hostility (not including prison inmates) were found to project little hostility on the Rorschach as compared to those possessing a moderate amount of hostility.

It appears that the strength of a need is only one of many variables determining the projection of hostility. An accurate prediction of the manifestation of a need in overt behavior must consider the total situation (stimulus properties of cards, examiner, S, environment, and their interactions). More will be said about this point shortly.

9. *There is a parallel between projective technique behavior and behavior in the social environment.*

This assumption has been recently supported (Piotrowski, 1957) but more often than not disavowed (Murray, 1943; Symonds, 1949). It has already been indicated that persons expressing overt hostility may project little hostility on the projective techniques. Does the converse occur, so that persons projecting a lot of hostility on the Rorschach manifest little hostility in the outside world? Smith and Coleman (1956) found that their high hostility projection on the Rorschach occupied a medium range in the manifestation of overt hostility. Murstein (1956), however, found that those persons projecting the most hostility on the Rorschach of the four groups which he used were both hostile and insightful with regard to their hostility as measured by pooled rankings. Rader (1957) has further emphasized the parallel when socioculture conditions sanction aggressive behavior as well as when ego control breaks down. Moving to the TAT, however, one might expect to find the expression of hostility via the protocols to show either no relationship or a negative one to the manifestation of overt hostility. This reversal from the behavior vis-à-vis the Rorschach should occur because, while the Rorschach is more or less ambiguous, the TAT is negatively structured (Eron, 1950; Eron, 1953; Murstein, 1958b). Thus, people who have the confidence to correctly perceive the objectively structured negative stimuli may be those persons who as a correlate of this confidence have little need to manifest anxiety in their behavior. By way of support of this thesis, Murstein (1960) found a positive correlation between pleasantness of emotional tone on TAT stories and anxiety on the Manifest Anxiety Scale for a population of parents of hospitalized children.

It seems clear that the various arguments supporting or refuting the parallel between overt and test behavior have not indicated sufficient awareness of differences in the stimulus and background values often encountered in the two situations. Unless the total interaction between person, test, and background is quite similar in stimulus value in both projective and overt situations, we have little reason to expect a correspondence in behavior.

10. *The Rorschach is idiopathic? qualitative? a game of misperception?*

Were it not for the serious effects upon graduate students, psychiatrists, and the lay public, the amount of anthropomorphizing and projections orbiting about the Rorschach might be amusing. Some believe it is the answer to the nomothetic monster tests which "swallow up the individual" (Rosenzweig, 1951). Others believe it is a "qualitative oasis" in a vast "quantitative desert" (Murstein, 1958c) or yet "a game of controlled misperception" (Gibson, 1956). One feels, therefore, as if he possessed a great deal of "gall" in stating that the Rorschach is a series of ten blots which has served as a *technique* for analysis of what people *verbalize* about their perceptions of these blots. Surely we have heretofore countenanced a serious error in not realizing that the technique has often been *confounded with the interest of the researcher.* Some authors have implied that the Rorschach could not be quantified. Perhaps they should have said that they could not or would not devise quantifiable variables from the Rorschach. During the 1930's and early 1940's when clinicians were almost the only psychologists interested in the Rorschach, the technique was viewed as essentially idiopathic. Currently, we are witnessing an increasing number of nomothetic studies as well as theoretical articles on the Rorschach. Shall we now call it an idiopathic-nomothetic-theoretical instrument, or simply an ambivalent one?

A Conceptual Model for Studying Projective Techniques

My remarks up to this point have been made for the purpose of illustrating that several cherished beliefs have been accepted by some clinicial psychologists without the support of sufficient research validation. Several current viewpoints, however, are helping to give us a clearer understanding of the projective technique situation. One view holds that the Rorschach, for example, should be analyzed through focus on the examiner–S interaction (Sarason, 1954; Schafer, 1954). On the other hand, Piotrowski (1957) has favored an avenue of approach centered on the analysis of the formal characteristics of the blots. Perhaps one of these schools of thought is not necessarily better than the other. Because of the undue emphasis on one aspect of the testing situation, neither of these approaches is sufficiently inclusive to account for the determination of response to projective techniques.

Some ten years ago, a theory was published which appears of considerable help in this problem. Helson's theory of adaptation level (1948) was initially formulated as a means of accounting for the perception of certain visual phenomena. The theory has been successfully extended to the fields of social psychology and personality (Helson, 1955; Rosenbaum & Blake, 1955). The theory briefly stated is:

Operationally, the adaptation-level (AL) is represented by the stimulus to which the organism responds either not at all or in an indifferent or neutral manner. In a large variety of situations the AL proves to be a weighted log mean of three classes of stimuli; the stimulus in the focus of attention; all stimuli in the field forming the context or background; and residuals from past experience. These three classes of stimuli pool or interact to determine the AL and hence the adjustment of the organism. As stimulation of behavior varies, the adaptation-level fluctuates accordingly. A simple formula expresses these facts more clearly and concisely, as follows:

$$\log A = p \log X + q \log B + r \log R$$

where p, q, and r are weighting factors showing the relative importance of X, the stimulus, B, the background, and R, the residual (Helson, 1955, pp. 91–92).

In adapting the theory for use with projective techniques, the projective technique may be regarded as the stimulus (e.g., TAT card); the effect of the examiner, his instructions, and the locale of the test serve as "background" factors; and S's needs, self-concept, and goals (e.g., "life space") serve as the residual or (perhaps more appropriately termed) organismic factor. A somewhat more detailed account of these variables may be found elsewhere (Murstein, 1959). Translating Helson's terms into those more meaningful for describing response to a projective technique,

$$PR = S^a B^b O^c,$$

where PR stands for the projective response, S for the stimulus, B for the background characteristics, and O for the organismic variable. a, b, c stand for the weights for each variable.

Both the "stimulus" and "background" may be objectively determined without reference to the individual. For example, a TAT card could be readily scaled for stimulus pull for hostility. The background factors also could be scaled for hostility without too much difficulty. It should be possible, for example, to draw up a continuum of environments varying in permissiveness of the perception of hostility and to place the particular projective test situation at some point on the continuum. The most difficult variable to quantify is O. If the individual experiences an elevation of a tension gradient in some trait (hostility), the likelihood of maximum contribution from the O component is a function of the individual's need and his expectancy of satisfaction of the need. Rotter (1954) states that

$$BP = (E \& RV),$$

where BP is the behavior potential, E is the expectancy, and RV, the reinforcement value.

Since the objective characteristics of S and B are considered in addition to O, Rotter's equation has been subsumed under the O component so that

$$O = (E, RV),$$

where E and RV have the same meaning as before.

To allow for interaction between E and RV, the components are treated in a multiplicative manner. It should be emphasized, however, that the O component refers to the totality of the individual's experience prior to his being confronted with the testing situation. This allows one to view the projective response as the resultant of the objective stimulus and background conditions and the individual's needs and expectancies which influence his reaction to these conditions.

The use of a term such as "expectancy" implies a strong volitional component on the part of S with regard to the determination of the response he makes. One must not suppose, however, that S's awareness necessarily results in the prevention of the appearance of highly personal material. Rather, this awareness has the effect of more carefully filtering the material to be manifested so that it is consistent with S's self-concept. Thus, if S needs to express his hostility visually via the Rorschach and finds such material not ego-threatening, he may perceive "angry men" or "fierce-looking tigers." If, however, the individual publicly or privately believes himself to be friendly, he will not permit such perceptions to be exhibited to the examiner. Instead, he will substitute contrived but more pleasant associations.

Implicit in the foregoing has been the belief that S is capable of differentiating between responses which are favorable and unfavorable to his self-concept. The validity of this belief will vary with the stimulus properties of the projective technique. Previous experience and research (Murstein, 1956; 1958a; 1958d) indicate, however that the more popular techniques, such as the Rorschach and the TAT, are the most susceptible to S's control. It is logical to presume that not all S's are completely capable of sensing the import of their responses. Nevertheless, the average intelligent college student, who makes up a good deal of man power employed in psychological research, can readily distinguish between the personality-revealing properties of an "azalea" and "an axe buried in the head of an old lady with blood oozing down the handle."

Under what circumstances do uncontrollable responses occur? They may occur when the stimulus is so clearly defined that the need cannot dent the reality context. Likewise, when a need becomes overwhelmingly strong, S may exhibit an inability to censor some particular perception he otherwise might not release. Admittedly, such occasions are rarely encountered when the techniques are administered to normal or only slightly disturbed populations whose ego control remains fairly strong.

Another approach would be to disguise the techniques so that we could be fairly confident that S was not aware of what an adequate response was as opposed to an inadequate one. This approach has been tried in a recent personality inventory by equating the choice of responses for social desirability (Edwards, 1954). Still another method would be to use a full range of stimuli from nonambiguous to highly ambiguous for any given personality dimension the researcher is interested in tapping. One might then study the strength of relationship between the degree of ambiguity and the response educed. By thus extending the range of stimuli past the current narrow continuum of a test like the TAT, we widen the appropriate range of response. In this way, a person who employs a rigid "set" to see "good" regardless of the stimulus properties of the cards is less likely to mask his perceptual shortcomings. If, for example, an ego-defensive S decides to see "good" on every picture, he will see highly ambiguous pictures as "good," as well as pictures which are highly structured in a negative sense. The latter responses, however, will be inadequate in terms of the stimulus properties of the cards.

Let us consider two examples of how previous work might be analyzed from the AL viewpoint. Brožek and co-workers (1951) did a study in which a group of volunteers (conscientious objectors) went on a semi-starvation diet for six months. Ss were given a series of tests before the diet started and after several intervals during the course of their regime, followed by testing during the subsequent rehabilitation period. The results were in general negative, in that despite the fact that Ss talked about food all day long and daydreamed of huge feasts, very little material relating to food was obtained on any of the projective tests measures. Centering on just one test, the Rorschach, let us examine possible reasons for the lack of projection of the need for food. Are there stimulus limitations to the perception of food on the Rorschach (Eriksen, 1954)? There is no direct experimental evidence on this question, but the possibility should not be overlooked.

McClelland and Atkinson (1948) found that the use of ink blots resulted in fewer perceptions of food objects than did blank cards. In view of the high intensity of the hunger need in Brožek's study, however, we must look further for a more complete explanation.

It may be a temptation to ascribe the lack of perception of food on the Rorschach to the fact that the conscientious objectors wanted to "prove" to the Navy officials (psychological examiners) that they were "as tough as the armed forces personnel." The fact that Ss talked freely about their hunger fantasies and even rated their increasing degree of hunger for these same examiners negates this possibility.

If a need (hunger) is manifest and the expectancy of satisfaction of the need is not immediate, fantasy may serve as a homeostatic mechanism. The adequacy of the fantasy is dependent on the anticipated reduction of the need. Hence, an exceedingly hungry person driving across country will be able to control his hunger more adequately if he believes that food may be obtained in the next town than if he thinks that he will not encounter a restaurant for several hundred miles. Further, the more the fantasy resembles a real life possibility, the more satisfying it is apt to be. Accordingly, for our driver at least, the thought of getting a club sandwich at a local restaurant will probably have more meaning than fantasies relating to eating *pâté de foie gras* at the Waldorf-Astoria.

This statement is in accordance with the conclusions arrived at by Knapp (1948), who stated that as a need increased in intensity there was a "Drang nach Realität." "That is, as a need gets more intense a person's phantasy and perception begins to concern itself more and more with realistic means of satisfying the need. For example, a relatively satiated person may dream of food, but a hungry person begins to dream of ways of getting food—of walking out of the room for example" (Knapp, 1948, p. 219).

In short, where a need is strongly present, the closer the fantasy comes to satisfying the need the more readily it will be employed. In a choice between two kinds of fantasy, the fantasy promising a more realistic solution of the need will be the one apt to be employed by the individual concerned. It follows that the free discussion of the satisfaction of hunger needs with an associate, or with the examiner, allows more fantasy gratification than the perception of food on the Rorschach. There are, after all, few limitations to the *verbalization of fantasy*, while the perception of fantasy on the Rorschach is limited due to the limitations attendant on the components of the examiner–S interaction and the stimulus properties of the cards. Consequently, one could hardly expect to find anyone perceiving a restaurant with himself as owner, on the Rorschach, although this image was verbalized fully by several Ss in their conversations with each other and with the examiner. In sum, *within the possibilities of tension reduction through the use of fantasy, certain outlets take priority. These are the ones which are most applicable for use in approximating a real life situation.* Thus, we would conclude that within the universe of fantasy gratification, the perception of food did not occur, because there was less expectancy of fantasy gratification via the Rorschach medium than by free verbalization. Had Ss been isolated or not permitted to discuss food, it would be predicted that Ss' perceptions would contain a great deal of food imagery.

From the adaptation-level viewpoint, the foregoing can be outlined as follows. The stimulus—the Rorschach—is not very structured toward the perception of food, and the background is not very influential in this study for the organism; (1) need is quite high and intense while (2) expectancy of satisfaction is low for two reasons. First, it was known that the experiment would continue for a period of six months. Second, other means of fantasizing were more satisfactory than that afforded by structural limitations of the blots. Referring to our equation, $PR = S^a B^b O^c$, the weighting of the stimulus and background are quite low. The weighting of O is also low, due to the fact that the mode of response (perception of food) provides less alteration of the need than that obtainable by free verbalization.

If one wished to study the effect of manipulation of the stimulus, background, and organismic variables on perception, the following factorial design might be employed. The stimulus would be thematic cards which would differ in stimulus pull for food, one group being high, the other low. The background might be represented by the examiner's inducing both high and low arousal states for the perception of food. The organismic variable might be the differing expectancy of receiving food by two groups of hungry Ss. Thus, one group would expect to receive food immediately after administration of the cards, while the other would be told several further tasks would need to be completed before they were free to leave the testing situation. This design should provide further insight into some of the determinants of the perception of food on a projective card when a need state is high.

It should be noted that the conceptual model sketched here places considerable emphasis on the importance of the stimulus as a determiner of perception. Heretofore, the stimulus properties of the projective techniques have been given short shrift. It was assumed that R-R theory emphasizing the correlation of responses to projective techniques with responses to other situations was the royal road to the understanding of personality (Rosenzweig, 1951). The stimuli of a given test for any particular group of Ss were assumed to be standard so that differences in response were presumed to be due to differences in personality. The exact degree of stimulus pull exerted by the cards was of little concern. There is no reason, however, why TAT and Rorschach cards could not be scaled for dimensions such as aggression and sex, as Auld and co-workers (1955), Lesser (1958), and Murstein and associates (1959) have done. The assignment of a quantitative objective value for each card for different personality dimensions should enable us to learn the significant personality correlates of perceptual adherence to stimulus properties of the cards as opposed to the neglect of these same properties. Under present circumstances, if a person has a high hostility score derived from his TAT stories, we do not know whether it reflects his respect for the obviously negatively structured pictures or is indicative of a projection of hostility to the relatively unstructured ones.

Considered in conjunction with the manipulation of the background and organismic variables, it should be possible to broaden our understanding of the relationship of projective technique behavior to overt behavior by noting the relative strength of each of the variables in both situations.

Further, we have often mouthed the glib phrase, "The response is a function of the total field." Perhaps it is time we converted this literary phrase to quantitative expression and proceeded to measure the components that comprise the "field."

Summary

Ten assumptions commonly held by users of projective techniques are evaluated in terms of relevant evidence, and a conceptual model for studying projective techniques is outlined. The need for measurement of the total field is emphasized.

REFERENCES

ABT, L. A theory of projective psychology. In L. E. Abt., & L. Bellak (Eds.), *Projective psychology*. New York: Knopf, 1950. Pp. 33–66.

ALLPORT, G. W. The trend in motivational theory. *Amer. J. Orthopsychiat.*, 1953, 23, 107–119.

ATKINSON, J .W. Studies in projective measurement of achievement motivation. Unpublished doctoral dissertation, Univer. of Michigan, 1950.

AULD, F., ERON, L. D., & LAFFAL, J. Application of Guttman's scaling method to the TAT. *Educ. psychol. Measmt.*, 1955, 15, 422–435.

BIJOU, S. W., & KENNY, D. T. The ambiguity of TAT cards. *J. consult. Psychol.*, 1951, 15, 203–209.

BROŽEK, K., GUETZKOW, H., & BALDWIN, MARCELLA V. A quantitative study of perception and association in experimental semi-starvation. *J. Pers.*, 1951, 19, 245–264.

BRUNER, J. S. Perceptual theory and the Rorschach test. *J. Pers.*, 1948, 17, 157–168.

CARR, A. C. The relation of certain Rorschach variables to expression of affect in the TAT and SCT. *J. proj. Tech.*, 1956, 20, 137–142.

CLARK, R. A. The projective measurement of experimentally induced levels of sexual motivation. *J. exp. Psychol.*, 1952, 44, 391–399.

COOK, R. A. Identification and ego defensiveness in thematic apperception. *J. proj. Tech.*, 1953, 17, 312–319.

DAVIDS, A. Comparison of three methods of personality assessment: direct, indirect, and projective. *J. Pers.*, 1955, 23, 423–440.

EDWARDS, A. L. *Edwards personal preference schedule, manual.* New York: Psychological Corp., 1954

ERIKSEN, C. W. Needs in perception and projective techniques. *J. proj. Tech.*, 1954, 18, 435–440.

ERON, L. D. A normative study of the Thematic Apperception Test. *Psychol. Monogr.*, 1950, 64, No. 9 (Whole No. 315).

ERON, L. D. Responses of women to the thematic apperception test. *J. consult. Psychol.*, 1953, 17, 269–282.

FRANK, L. K. *Projective methods.* Springfield, Ill.: Charles C. Thomas, 1948.

Funk & Wagnall's new standard dictionary of the English language. New York: Funk & Wagnalls, 1955.

GIBSON, J. J. The non-projective aspects of the Rorschach experiment: IV. The Rorschach blots considered as pictures. *J. soc. Psychol.*, 1956, 44, 203–206.

GORDON, H. L. A comparative study of dreams and responses to the TAT. A need-press analysis. *J. Pers.*, 1953, 22, 234–253.

HARRISON, R. Studies in the use and validity of the TAT with mentally disordered patients. II. A quantitative validity study. III. Validity by the method of "blind analysis." *Charact. & Pers.*, 1940, 9, 122–138.

HELSON, H. Adaptation-level as a basis for a quantitative theory of frames of reference. *Psychol. Rev.*, 1948, 55, 297–313.

HELSON, H. An experimental approach to personality. *Psychiat. res. Rep.*, 1955, 2, 89–99.

HELSON, H., BLAKE, R. R., MOUTON, J. S. & OLMSTEAD, J. A. Attitudes as adjustments to stimulus, background and residual factors. *J. abnorm. soc. Psychol.*, 1956, 52, 314–322.

HENRY, W. E. The TAT in the study of culture-personality relations. *Genet. Psychol. Monogr.*, 1947, 35, 3–135.

KENNY, D. T., & BIJOU, S. W. Ambiguity of pictures and extent of personality factors in fantasy responses. *J. consult. Psychol.*, 1953, 17, 238–288.

KNAPP, R. H. Experiments in serial reproduction and related aspects of the psychology of rumor. Unpublished doctoral thesis, Harvard Univer., 1948.

LAZARUS, R. S. Ambiguity and non-ambiguity in projective testing. *J. abnorm. soc. Psychol.*, 1953, 48, 443–445.

LESSER, G. S. Application of Guttman's scaling method to aggressive fantasy in children. *Educ., psychol. Measmt.*, 1958, 18, 543–550.

LEVINE, R., CHEIN, I., & MURPHY, G. The relation of the intensity of a need to amount of perceptual distortion: a preliminary report. *J. Psychol.*, 1942, 13, 283–293.

LINDZEY, G., & TEJESSY, CHARLOTTE. Thematic apperception test: indices of aggression in relation to measure of overt and covert behavior. *Amer. J. Orthopsychiat.*, 1956, 26, 567–576.

MACFARLANE, JEAN W., & TUDDENHAM, R. D. Problems in the validation of projective techniques. In H. H., & G. L. Anderson (Eds.), *An introduction to projective techniques.* New York: Prentice-Hall, 1951. Pp. 26–54.

McCLELLAND, D. C., & ATKINSON, J. W. The projective expression of needs. I. The effect of different intensities of the hunger drive on perception. *J. Psychol.*, 1948, 25, 205–222.

MURRAY, H. A. *Thematic apperception test manual.* Cambridge: Harvard Univer. Press, 1943.

MURRAY, H. A. Uses of the TAT. *Amer. J. Psychiat.*, 1951, 107, 577–581.

MURSTEIN, B. I. The projection of hostility on the Rorschach and as a result of ego threat. *J. proj. Tech.*, 1956, 20, 418–428.

MURSTEIN, B. I. Nonprojective determinants of perception on the TAT. *J. consult. Psychol.*, 1958, 22, 195–199. (a)

MURSTEIN, B. I. The relationship of stimulus ambiguity on the TAT to the productivity of themes. *J. consult. Psychol.*, 1958, 22, 348. (b)

MURSTEIN, B. I. Review of Klopfer, Bruno and others. *Developments in the Rorschach technique.* Vol. II. *Fields of application. J. proj. Tech.*, 1958, 22, 248–250. (c)

MURSTEIN, B. I. Some determinants of the perception of hostility. *J. consult. Psychol.*, 1958, 22, 65–69. (d)

MURSTEIN, B. I. A conceptual model of projective techniques applied to stimulus variations with thematic techniques. *J. consult. Psychol.*, 1959, 23, 3–14.

MURSTEIN, B. I. The effect of long-term illness of children on the emotional adjustment of parents. *Child Developm.*, 1960, 31, 157–171.

MURSTEIN, B. I., COULTER, W., BOWDISH, C., DAVID, C., FISHER, D., FURTH, H., & HANSEN, I. A study of scaling methods applied to the TAT for the dimension of hostility. Univer. of Portland, 1959 (mimeographed).

MURSTEIN, B. I., & WHEELER, J. I., JR. The projection of hostility on the Rorschach and thematic stories test. *J. clin. Psychol.*, 1959, 15, 316–319.

PIOTROWSKI, Z. A. *Perceptanalysis.* New York: Macmillan, 1957.

PITTLUCK, PATRICIA. The relation between aggressive fantasy and overt behavior. Unpublished doctoral dissertation, Yale Univer., 1950.

RADER, G. E. The prediction of overt aggressive verbal behavior from Rorschach content. *J. proj. Tech.*, 1957, 21, 294–306.

ROSENBAUM, M., & BLAKE, R. R. Volunteering as a function of field structure. *J. abnorm. soc. Psychol.*, 1955, 50, 193–196.

ROSENZWEIG, S. Idiodynamics in personality theory with special reference to projective methods. *Psychol. Rev.*, 1951, 58, 213–223.

ROTTER, J. *Social learning and clinical psychology.* New York: Prentice-Hall, 1954.

SARASON, S. B. *The clinical interaction.* New York: Harper, 1954.

SCHAFER, R. *Psychoanalytic interpretation in Rorschach testing.* New York: Grune & Stratton, 1954.

SCODEL, A., & LIPETZ, M. E. TAT hostility and psychopathology. *J. proj. Tech.*, 1957, 21, 161–165.

SHATIN, L. Rorschach adjustment and the TAT. *J. proj. Tech.*, 1953, 17, 92–101.

SHATIN, L. Relationships between the Rorschach and the TAT. *J. proj. Tech.*, 1955, 19, 317–331.

SHNEIDMAN, E. S. Some relationships between the Rorschach technique and other psychodiagnostic tests. In B. Klopfer (Ed.), *Developments in the Rorschach technique.* Vol. II. *Fields of application.* New York: World Book Co., 1956. Pp. 595–642.

SINGER, W. B., & YOUNG, P. T. Studies in affective reaction. I. A new affective rating—scale. *J. gen. Psychol.*, 1941, 24, 281–301.

SMITH, J. R., & COLEMAN, J. C. The relationship between manifestations of hostility in projective tests and overt behavior. *J. proj. Tech.*, 1956, 20, 326–334.

STERN, E., & HORINSON, S. Concordances et divergences du test de Rorschach et du Thematic Apperception de Murray. *Proc. Int. Orthoped. Cong., II.* Amsterdam, 1949. Pp. 448–455.

SYMONDS, P. M. *Adolescent fantasy: an investigation of the picture-story method of personality study.* New York: Columbia Univer. Press, 1949.

ULLMANN, L. P. Productivity and the clinical use of TAT cards. *J. proj. Tech.*, 1957, 21, 399–403.

WEBB, W. B., & HILDEN, A. H. Verbal and intellectual ability as factors in projective test results. *J. proj. Tech.*, 1953, 17, 102–103.

WEISSKOPF, EDITH A. An experimental study of the effect of brightness and ambiguity on projection in the TAT. *J. Psychol.*, 1950, 29, 407–416. (a)

WEISSKOPF, EDITH A. A transcendence index as a proposed measure in the TAT. *J. Psychol.*, 1950, 29, 379–390. (b)

WIRT, R. D. Ideational expression of hostile impulses. *J. consult. Psychol.*, 1956, 20, 185–189.

5

Variability of Responses and the Stability of Scores and Interpretations of Projective Protocols

DONALD W. FISKE

Focusing on a problem not nearly so researched as its importance warrants, Fiske reviews some of the research on the stability of response. He concludes that stability is proportionate to stimulus structure. The less structure, the more variability. Since many projective techniques have relatively unstructured stimuli, their responses are quite variable. But is it not possible that though the manifest content varies, the underlying dynamics remain steadfast? Work on the sentence completion shows a high correlation between manifest content change and change in psychological meaning. Further, in 25 per cent of the cases, the intersubject comparisons yielded more similar interpretations than intrasubject ones. What is needed, therefore, is, on the one hand, a broad conceptual approach which can account for perhaps complementary successive protocols for many subjects who eschew repetitive performances. On the other hand, those aspects of protocols which are stable must be searched out and differentiated from their less stable brethren.

The literature on projective tests contains very little information on the consistency of responses. Very little is known about the stability of responses to the same stimuli at different times, and almost nothing is known about the stability of interpretations of such different protocols.

69

This paper is concerned primarily with these problems. We shall see that responses to the same stimuli tend to be different on different occasions and that such instability of response seems to have serious effects on the stability of interpretations. On the other hand, some scores or ratings derived from successive protocols show fair stability.

From work on the variability of a person's behavior over time, I have come to the postulate that behavior in the absence of external stimulation is completely variable. The more structured the stimulation and the more intense the stimulation (up to a point), the more consistent the behavior. Stimuli exercise constraints on behavior (Fiske, 1957a).

This position is strongly supported by several kinds of evidence. First let us consider dreams as an example of "behavior" of a sort, behavior in the absence of stimulation.

In the systematic work of Kleitman, Dement, Wolpert, and Kamiya (Dement & Wolpert, 1958), all the dreams a person has during a night are recorded immediately after they occur. For a number of subjects, the dreams of several nights have been recorded. Inspection of these shows no exact repetitions. The content of each dream is essentially unique, although one can, of course, find instances of similar themes or the development of a theme, especially in contiguous dreams. Much of the repeating material is associated with the experimental situation.[1] Thus, one subject had several dreams, usually the first each night, about the situation, the electrodes, etc. Another had two dreams about people slanting or biasing the dream material they reported. It is worth noting that the general topic of these reported dreams is common across subjects and is largely determined by the general experimental situation.

Another systematic collection of protocols in the relative absence of stimulation is in the work of Rechtschaffen and Mednick (1955) on the autokinetic word technique, in which it is suggested that the fixed point of light will trace letters, words, or sentences. Here also, there is no exact repetition of content.[2] Reports from stimulus deprivation studies seem to be consistent with these data. In a study by Goldberger and Holt (1958), subjects' verbalizations during an eight-hour period of marked stimulus reduction were recorded. Inspection of these protocols and of postsession interview reports of experiences during the experimental period showed minimal repetition of content.[3] There were two types of exceptions: two subjects repeated the same tune twice; some subjects, especially those who were anxious to escape the situation, repeated content such as wondering what time it was and wondering how he looked as he lay there. The latter type of repeated material related to

---

[1] I am indebted to Drs. William Dement and Joe Kamiya for access to these dream protocols.

[2] I am indebted to Dr. Allan Rechtschaffen for access to these protocols.

[3] I am indebted to Drs. Robert R. Holt and L. Goldberger for access to these protocols.

the situation is strikingly consistent with the repeated dream material noted above.

When relatively unstructured stimuli are present, behavior is more consistent than in the absence of stimulation, but it is still highly variable. One implication of this viewpoint is that a person has a very wide distribution of potential responses, the width or range of the distribution being greater when the stimuli are less constraining. Since projective techniques are rather unstructured, the stimuli and instructions impose relatively little constraint on responses.

Thus Weiner, Brown, and Kaplan (1956) have found that on a second testing, normal people can give almost as many new responses to the Rorschach cards as they gave the first time. In a study by Willis (1958), subjects gave an average of four or five different plots (themes) to a TAT card in 10 minutes. I have found that subjects can give several responses to each sentence completion stem.

While this evidence is not definitive, I am sure most of you would agree with the notion that a projective stimulus at any point in time for a single person has several potential responses, with varying response strengths. Now what is the evidence on the variability of emitted responses over time?

For word association, Willis and I have some preliminary data indicating that almost one-third to one-half of the responses are changed when the same stimulus word is repeated in a single session or in a second session. (We asked subjects to give two associations to each stimulus. Fifty to 85 per cent of the second associations are changed.)

For sentence-completion responses, three studies show that 64 per cent to 80 per cent of the responses are changed from one trial to the next (Fiske, 1957b; Osterweil & Fiske, 1956; Raine & Hills, 1959). In one study, subjects averaged six or seven different responses over nine trials.

The TAT does not permit similar comparisons. However, I have examined some sets of protocols, each set consisting of three trials 1 to 30 months apart. Rather than estimate similarity, I counted the number of times that the three stories the person told to a card were quite different, one from the other, in manifest content. This occurred in about 20 per cent of the subject-card combinations. In the remaining 80 per cent, the similarity ranged from two stories having one detail in common, which did not appear in the third, to sets of three almost identical stories. Some of the repetition was obviously straight recall, as one subject made explicit who "saw" each time in the blank card a polar bear in a snowstorm!

Swift (1944) reports that about 50 per cent of Rorschach responses by four- and five-year-old children are repeated two to four weeks later. Siipola, Kuhns, and Taylor indicate that for presentations of parts of these blots, about half the responses were changed on retest. Of these changed responses, about half were similar on the two occasions.

On the Blacky Test, Granick and Scheflen (1958) have reported that judges considered that about 57 per cent of the thematic content of two repetitions was similar, but a comparison with a matched group yielded one-third similarity between responses from different children!

For the Picture Arrangement Test, Tomkins and Miner report that 33 per cent of the order responses were changed over a three-week interval and 45 per cent were changed over three years (1957, p. 37).

The figures we have given are overestimates of response stability because there is much evidence that subjects remember many of their projective responses over several weeks (cf. Swift, 1944).

The reader may be thinking that while the manifest content may be changed, the psychological meaning would be essentially the same. To check this, Van Buskirk estimated the changes in psychological meaning over the nine trials of the sentence completion data mentioned earlier. He found a high correlation (.80) between the extent of change in the psychological meaning of a person's responses and the extent of change in the manifest responses. But this was merely suggestive. So we compared the interpretations of different protocols from the same individual (Fiske & Van Buskirk, 1959).

We asked this specific question: are the differences between the interpretations of protcols from the same person less than the differences between interpretations of protocols of different persons? Thus interindividual variation—variation between individuals—provides a frame of reference for evaluating the extent of intraindividual variability—variation or inconsistency within a person—over time.

We found that in 25 per cent of the judge-protocol combinations, the interpretation was more similar to interpretations of protocols from different subjects than to interpretations of other protocols from the same subject. This 25 per cent misclassification was not due to the homogeneity of the subjects. The manifest content differentiated the subjects better than the judges' interpretations.

Once again, such a single study is not definitive. It should be repeated with other tests and with complete batteries. It does suggest, however, that the changes in manifest content on at least one projective test make the interpretations clearly unstable over time.

I hope that the material I have presented has indicated to some of you the existence of considerable variability over time in projective responses presents a serious difficulty for clinical diagnosis and for personality assessment as a whole. But the picture is not entirely negative: there is considerable evidence that some characteristics of responses are reasonably stable over time.

For example, for the Incomplete Sentence Blank, Arnold and Walter (1957) found the Rotter Adjustment Score to have a stability over a week of .82. Churchill and Crandall (1955) report coefficients of .70 to .38 for six-month to three-year intervals. Rohde (1957) found stability coefficients of .68 and .64 (over an eight-month period) for need variables rated on her Sentence Completion Test. The cathections of objects were even more stable: less than 4 per cent were changed. For the TAT, Tomkins (1947, p. 6) reports r's from .50 to .80 over two to ten months for ratings using a need-press schema. For a two-month interval, Lindzey and Herman (1955) report 17 r's ranging from .co to .94. For a similar period, Helen Koch[4] has obtained a comparable range of coefficients on the CAT. In the Granick and Scheflen study (1958) of the Blacky cited earlier, 75 per cent of the subjects were consistent in their liking or disliking of each Blacky card. For the Sargent Insight Test, Fassett (1948) reports several coefficients all below .46. Rorschach scores have stabilities from .98 to — .16 (Eichler, 1951; Holzberg & Wexler, 1950; Kerr, 1936; Swift, 1944). In some unpublished Draw-a-Person test data of Shanan[5] the correlation between total area used for two figures over a six-month interval is only .44. This is similar to the only correlations reported in Swensen's review of the literature on the test (1957). The evidence for the stability of characteristics of such drawings is not impressive, but Wagner and Schubert (1955), cited by Swensen (1957, p. 435), report a coefficient of .86 for the stability of ratings of over-all quality.

Many of these coefficients indicate that the scores involved are sufficiently stable over time to permit comparisons between groups. However, few are high enough for dependable use in differentiating individuals. There is a possibility that certain temperamental and expressive attributes have higher stability: for example, productivity as measured by word count. Rechtschaffen[6] has obtained an r of .72 for the autokinetic procedure and Koch[7] found an r of .78 for the CAT. But such characteristics are not unique to projective techniques and are certainly not the kind of variable which such techniques are designed to assess.

What does the total picture look like?

1. The actual content of responses to projective tests varies considerably from trial to trial, and there are large individual differences in the extent of this change in content.

2. The stability of some scores and ratings based on projective protocols is reasonably adequate.

3. There is reason to believe that changes of responses may have serious effects on the stability of interpretations of total protocols.

The problem is not that successive protocols are psychologically inconsistent but that they often complement each other; material in one may not be present in the next. The problem then becomes that of determining the significance of such material for the enduring personality.

---

[4] Personal communication.
[5] Personal communication.
[6] Personal communication.
[7] Personal communication.

One promising approach has been neglected, at least in research literature. This is Murray's suggestion (1938, p. 604-605) of a unity thema: a central theme, compounded from dominant needs and press, which can be seen to run through a person's life.

We need to investigate this notion. Does material from different sources —such as TAT and other thematic protocols—indicate the same central theme? And do protocols gathered at different times embody the same thema?

We can safely assume that the "personality" we wish to assess and measure is that part of the person's dispositions and response tendencies which is stable, at least over weeks if not years. Therefore it is essential that we develop methods to distinguish between stable and temporary dispositions, between pre-eminent and subordinate response tendencies. I have found few explicit discussions of this problem (Rohde, 1957, p. 109; Lindzey, 1952; Bolgar, 1956; Klopfer & Spiegelman, 1958) and no development of adequate methods. It is my conviction that the validity of projective scores and interpretations will continue to be unsatisfactory until such methods are available.

REFERENCES

ARNOLD, F. C., & WALTER, V. A. The relationship between a self- and other-reference completion test. *J. counsel. Psychol.*, 1957, 4, 65–70.

BOLGAR, HEDDA. A re-evaluation of projective theory. In B. Klopfer, Mary D. Ainsworth, W. G. Klopfer, R. R. Holt. *Developments in Rorschach technique.* Vol. II. Yonkers-on-Hudson: World Book Co., 1956.

CHURCHILL, RUTH, & CRANDALL, V. J. The reliability and validity of the Rotter incomplete sentences test. *J. consult. Psychol.*, 1955, 19, 345–350.

DEMENT, W., & WOLPERT, E. R. Relationships in the manifest content of dreams occurring on the same night. *J. nerv. ment. Dis.*, 1958, 126, 568–578.

EICHLER, R. M. A comparison of the Rorschach and Behn-Rorschach inkblot tests. *J. consult. Psychol.*, 1951 15, 185–189.

FASSETT, K. K. A preliminary investigation of the Sargent test. *J. clin. Psychol.*, 1948, 4, 45–55.

FISKE, D. W. The constraints on intraindividual variability in test responses. *Educ. psychol. Measmt.*, 1957, 17, 317–337. (a)

FISKE, D. W. An intensive study of variability scores. *Educ. psychol. Measmt.*, 1957, 17, 453–465. (b)

FISKE, D. W., & VAN BUSKIRK, C. The stability of interpretations of sentence completion tests. *J. consult. Psychol.*, 1959, 23, 177–180.

GOLDBERGER, L., & HOLT, R. A. Experimental interferences with reality contact (perceptual isolation): I. Method and group results. *J. nerv. ment. Dis.*, 1958, 127, 99–112.

GRANICK, S., & SCHEFLEN, NORMA A. Approaches to reliability of projective tests with special reference to the Blacky pictures test. *J. consult. Psychol.*, 1958, 22, 137–141.

Holzberg, J. D., & Wexler, M. The predictability of schizophrenic performance on the Rorschach test. *J. consult. Psychol.*, 1950, 14, 395–399.

Kerr, M. Temperamental difference in twins. *Brit. J. Psychol.*, 1936, 27, 51–59.

Klopfer, B., & Spiegelman, M. Methodological research problems. In B. Klopfer, Mary D. Ainsworth, W. G. Klopfer, and R. R. Holt. *Developments in Rorschach technique*, Vol. II. Yonkers-on-Hudson, World Book Co., 1956.

Lindzey, G. Thematic apperception test: interpretive assumptions and related empirical evidence. *Psychol. Bull.*, 1952, 49, 1–21.

Lindzey, G., & Herman, P. S. Thematic apperception test: A note on reliability and situational validity. *J. proj. Tech.*, 1955, 19, 36–42.

Murray, H. A. *Explorations in personality.* New York: Oxford Univer. Press, 1938.

Osterweil, J., & Fiske, D. W. Intraindividual variability in sentence completion responses. *J. abnorm. soc. Psychol.*, 1956, 52, 195–199.

Raine, W. J., & Hills, J. R. Measuring intraindividual variability within one testing. *J. abnorm. soc. Psychol.*, 1959, 58, 264–266.

Rechtschaffen, A., & Mednick, S. A. The autokinetic word technique. *J. abnorm. soc. Psychol.*, 1955, 51, 346.

Rohde, Amanda R. *The sentence completion method.* New York: Ronald, 1957.

Siipola, Elsa, Kuhns, Florence, & Taylor, Vivian. Measurement of the individual's reaction to color in ink blots. *J. Pers.*, 1950, 19, 153–171.

Swensen, C. H., Jr. Empirical evaluations of human figure drawings. *Psychol. Bull.*, 1957, 54, 431–466.

Swift, Joan W. Reliability of Rorschach scoring categories with preschool children. *Child Developm.*, 1944, 15, 207–216.

Tomkins, S. S. *The thematic apperception test: The theory and technique of interpretation.* New York: Grune & Stratton, 1947.

Tomkins, S. S., & Miner, J. B. *The picture arrangement test.* New York: Springer, 1957.

Wagner, M. E., & Schubert, H. J. P. *DAP quality scale for late adolescents and young adults.* Kenmore, New York: Delaware Letter Shop, 1955.

Weiner, L., Brown, E., & Kaplan, B. A comparison of the ability of normal and brain injured subjects to produce additional responses on a second administration of the Rorschach test. *J. clin. Psychol.*, 1956, 12, 89–91.

Willis, V., Jr. The relationship of conceptual flexibility to personal adjustment. Unpublished master's thesis, Univer. of Colorado, 1958.

6

Problems in the Validation of Projective Techniques

KENNETH B. LITTLE

In this concise, excellently written description of problems in valida-
tion, Dr. Little offers no "miracle" cure. He questions the assumption
that in one fashion or another the kernel of the "whole personality" is
manifested on a projective protocol. He is also skeptical of the attempt
to analyze multiple facets of personality on the basis of a few responses
for each dimension. Last, he prescribes an antidote which calls for more
than a modicum of hard work.

We are discussing today the general issue of the validation of projective
techniques. However, I will limit my remarks to the effective validity of
such instruments rather than attempt to cover all forms of validation.
"Effective validity" may be subsumed under predictive validity but is
restricted to the class of useful predictions rather than any and all predictions.

In the clinical situation, where most projective techniques are administered, validity has a most pragmatic air. The construct validity of the
instrument may be of theoretical interest to the psychologist and the
concurrent validity an issue of some curiosity, but as far as the case in
hand is concerned, one usually wishes to make meaningful and useful
predictive statements about a patient. When one administers a Rorschach
or a TAT to such a person, the implicit or explicit questions are of a
rather prosaic sort: "Will this patient attempt suicide?", "Does he have
some form of organic impairment?", "Would psychotherapy be an appro-

priate form of treatment?", and the like. The questions are those the psychologist, as a psychodiagnostician, was hired to answer.

Other information may be, and usually is, provided in the test report. And certainly there is little expectation that the answers to the questions will reach such a degree of specificity as, "This patient will jump out of the ward bathroom window at 5:54 a.m. on Thursday." The report should include, however, statements about the subject that raise the probability of making correct assumptions as to his future behavior. The predictions involved may be quite indirect and dependent on fairly complex chains of inferences; but if personality assessments are to be other than exercises in composition, some information with implications for behavior must be included. It is the accuracy of the significant predictions, the correctness of the answers to the perennial questions, that may be called effective validity.

After this preamble, it is somewhat embarrassing to have to say that the published evidence on projective techniques indicates that they have either zero or, at best, very low positive effective validity indexes. Even in those studies with the most positive of results, correlations are of an order of magnitude that make predictions for the individual largely a waste of time.

This distressing state of affairs has been with us unchanged for a rather long period of time. During the thirty-five or so years in which, for example, the Rorschach has been subject to systematic investigation, the only noticeable change has been in the sophistication of design and analysis. Negative or ambiguous results, however, are just as disheartening when determined by an F ratio as when determined by a critical ratio.

The situation as described has been pointed out by several people (e.g., Cronbach, 1956), so I will not spend time in citing evidence. Instead I would like to consider the questions of "Why?" and "What do we do now?" A definitive answer to either of these would still require far more time than is available in this paper, so I will perforce be quite arbitrary about what I present.

An answer to the question of why our projective techniques fail so miserably at practical predictions is obviously required before any rational solutions can be proposed. However, the determinants involved in the failure are numerous and quite difficult to eliminate. The fact that behavior is a function of both the organism and the situation means that any prediction based on evaluation of the former alone will always be a contingent one. Since the number of possible alternative stimulus situations is astronomical, the problem of raising the validity of our instruments seems an impossible one. Fortunately humans as well as rats are capable of, and facile at, generalization, so it is possible to reduce the number of stimulus situation categories sharply. We are able to say that one man's candy is another man's brandy and call both consummatory responses, or oral behavior, etc. This leads inevitably to a loss in precision in the prediction of specific behavior, so we find ourselves anticipating alcoholism when obesity in fact occurs. However, correlations of less than unity are a fact of life with which psychologists have already learned to live.

However, there are other issues having to do more directly with the assessment process and with the instruments used. In our limited time, I wish to talk about two of these, one quite speculative and the other rather concrete. The speculative issue has to do with the interpretation of the basic postulate of projective testing, that of psychic determinism. The term *interpretation* is used deliberately since few people now argue that personality factors have no effect whatsoever on responses to projective technique stimuli. The rub occurs when we assume that all or a majority of the responses are determined by dominant and enduring characteristics, equally operative in the everyday life of the individual, as in the testing situation. The experienced tester allows for set, defensive factors unique to the particular situation, and the like in his interpretations. Then at this point he often assumes that what remains represents the regnant motives, ego-protective mechanisms, behavior style, and so forth that characterize the individual in all situations. I wonder if this is necessarily the case. Perhaps all that is revealed is a micropersonality of limited extent.

This amounts to a questioning of the unity of the personality, its Gestalt quality. It does not deny psychic determinism but merely raises the query as to whether that aspect of the psyche involved in responding to semistructured ambiguous stimuli is of any practical significance in the rest of man's behavior. During great stress, when the individual is fighting for physiological or psychological survival, all forces are mobilized toward a common end and common response patterns may be apparent in all or most all situations. Under less extreme conditions, perhaps the individual is far more differentiated than we expect, with a wide selection of response roles. Even in physiologic functions, such an effect may be observed; systolic and diastolic blood pressure, for example, correlate .60 in subjects suffering from combat fatigue, but the relationship drops to .06 after recovery (Wenger, 1948). A similar phenomenon may occur among psychic functions.

The above, as stated earlier, is obviously speculative; there are, however, specific aspects of our assessment instruments toward which we can point with some assurance in the attempt to determine why they fail. These have been examined at some length by Anastasi (1954), Cronbach (1956), Macfarlane and Tuddenham (1951), and others, so I will discuss only the sampling problem.

In the Rorschach one has ten stimuli and from ten to sixty or so responses; in the TAT twenty pictures eliciting hopefully twenty stories; in other projective techniques a varying number of stimuli but of a similar order of magnitude. With these stimuli we secure a small sample of the behavior of the individual and assume it is representative of his total

population of imaginative responses. Then, to make life even more difficult, we attempt to "measure" 5 to 75 different variables with this one
sample. The wise tester soon learns to restrict his assessment endeavor,
but typically we find that we are still assigning values to the variables we
do use on the basis of one or two responses. Since these few responses
are simply a sample of a number of potential responses to the stimuli,
the reliability of the measurement is quite questionable. The projective
technique interpreter is in a position analagous to that he would be in
if one took a random sample of 50 items from the MMPI, permitted the
subject the option of answering them in any fashion he chose (including
not answering them at all), and then asked the psychologist to describe
the MMPI profile. Depending on the sample of items, the subject's
choice of answer categories, and the tester's knowledge of the MMPI
scales, there might be an occasional fairly correct reproduction of the
whole profile, a slightly more frequent fair approximation of one or two
scale scores and most probably, an over-all accuracy index that resembled
strongly the validity coefficients for projective techniques.

Since others on the symposium have discussed this point also, I would
like to turn to my second question, i.e., what do we do now. This
discussion I will limit to some suggestions regarding increasing the
precision of measurement of projective techniques.

There are several different ways in which this might be done—all relatively painful. The first, which continues the idiographic global approach,
would be simply to increase the length of the current instruments—a
Rorschach of 50 cards, a TAT of 100, for example. It is theoretically
possible in this fashion to secure enough replicated information about a
subject to determine the interrelations among personality characteristics
and to enable us to specify the links between personality structure and
behavior.

I do not have much hope for such a procedure; increasing the size of
our global instruments will increase proportionately the amount of irrelevant information to be handled, placing a still greater load on the
intellectual and experience level of the clinician. Unless we are to increase
training time indefinitely, it is almost mandatory that our instruments do
a certain amount of predigesting for us, sacrificing coverage for precision.
As Tomkins and Miner describe it (1957), we must be prepared to throw
away information in order to raise the probability of correctness of that
we do obtain.

If we adopt such an austerity program, there appear to be two modes
of approach which might be used. The first way might be considered
analogous to the item-analytic techniques used in objective-test construction. The literature on the existing techniques can be searched for stable
and hopefully useful determinants of responses to projective stimuli and
special scales constructed for their measurement. After construction of
the scale, there will be a long and tedious period of establishing the

empirical correlates of the scale. A good example of this method is Barron's (1955) M scale for measuring the human movement response to ink blots. If such single determinant scales are too molecular, then additional scales can be constructed for configural combinations; the essential point is that there be sufficient stimuli for reliable measurement.

The second approach is the construction of projective instruments designed to measure specific personality variables within certain theoretical frameworks. The Blacky Test (Blum 1950) incorporates this idea to some extent but still attempts to measure too many variables with too few items. For precision of measurement, a minimum of about five reasonably independent projective "items" seems essential. Some of the sentence completion tests (Forer, 1950; Rotter & Rafferty, 1950) might be considered illustrations of this approach. McClelland's use of the TAT pictures for assessing need achievement is also a method of measurement that can be considered of this type.

A final example of a thematic projective technique devised for measurement of a specific personality characteristic is one developed by C. L. Winder and myself. It is similar in its general construction to an instrument developed quite independently by Lesser (1958). This test, which has no formal title, is designed to tap two aspects of the fantasy life of boys—fantasy aggression and fantasy aggression anxiety. In constructing it we started with 100 pictures drawn by an artist to represent a variety of boy–boy, boy–girl, and boy–adult interactions and with varying degrees of pull for aggressive response. The subjects wrote stories to the pictures under general TAT-type instructions. Reliability of scoring is better than .92, and split-half reliabilities (alpha coefficients) range between .71 and .88, depending on the type of aggression fantasy—e.g., boy–boy, boy–adult —being assessed. Since this is but the first round of refinement, we hope to increase those reliability figures somewhat.

Such instruments as this last demonstrate very well the advantages and disadvantages of the projective inventory approach. A tremendous amount of information is sacrificed in the interest of precision, without, it should be added, any guarantee that the resulting scores will be any more useful for predicting behavior than the global assessment. But since the global methods do not appear to work, we must, of necessity, try something else. Such inventories, moreover, do not permit the integration of multiple factors into a unique personality description, at least when administered singly. However, since it is my belief that unique descriptions that do not generate accurate predictions are merely works of art and not clinically meaningful, I think the gamble is worth taking.

There are other experimental variations of projective techniques, such as the PAT (Tomkins & Miner, 1957), which time does not permit me to discuss. They represent, I think, a very healthy trend toward exploration of all possible methods for personality assessment. If projective techniques are to be other than examples of the ingenuity of psychologists and their interpretation other than a measure of the clinicians' verbal ability, then some modification of our present instruments is essential.

REFERENCES

ANASTASI, ANNE,. *Psychological testing.* New York: Macmillan, 1954.

BARRON, F. Threshold for the perception of human movement in inkblots. *J. consult. Psychol.*, 1955, 19, 33–38.

BLUM, G. S. *The Blacky pictures: A technique for the exploration of personality dynamics.* New York: Psychological Corp., 1950.

CRONBACH, L. J. Assessment of individual differences. In P. R. Farnsworth (Ed.), *Annual review of psychology.* Stanford, Calif.: Annual Reviews, 1956.

FORER, B. R. A structured sentence completion test. *J. proj. Tech.*, 1950, 14, 15–29.

LESSER, G. S. Conflict analysis of fantasy aggression. *J. Pers.*, 1958, 26, 29–41.

MACFARLANE, JEAN W., & TUDDENHAM, R. D. Problems in the validation of projective techniques. In H. H. & G. L. Anderson (Eds.), *An introduction to projective techniques.* New York: Prentice-Hall, 1951.

ROTTER, J. B. & RAFFERTY, JANET E. *Manual for the Rotter incomplete sentences blank, college form.* New York: Psychological Corp., 1950.

TOMKINS, S. S., & MINER, J. B. *The Tomkins-Horn picture arrangement test.* New York: Springer, 1957.

WENGER, M. A. Studies of autonomic balance in Army Air Forces personnel. *Comp. psychol. Monogr.*, 1948, 19, No. 4.

7

Structured and Projective Tests: Some Common Problems in Validation

PAUL E. MEEHL

With his typical forthrightness, Meehl skirts past the usual approach to the problem of validation to pose some hard-hitting but more realistic questions. He has little patience for the global approach which, whether successful or unsuccessful, fails to identify "the variables doing the work." He refuses to accept the excuses proffered by some that the tests were analyzed by nonexperts. A test which "plays beautiful music" only in the hands of "virtuosos" is of limited concern to the average "fiddler." Some potent questions that might be asked are, "How much information is intrinsically contained in the test behavior? How much valid information does the instrument yield that is not readily available from other sources? Further, even if the information is not already present, if it will be obtained elsewhere (say in psychotherapy) within a few sessions, is it worth while to take extra time to give the projective techniques?" These questions, for the most part, have been largely avoided, but they seem to be much more appropriate than many of the validation studies extant.

Some of us at Minnesota have been trying to rethink, as objectively as human frailty permits, the principles involved in the clinical use of that structured test with which we are identified.

In preparing for this symposium, I discovered that most of the considerations which arise in validating such devices as the MMPI apply with very little modification to those open-ended tasks which have come to be known as the projective techniques. Faced with a choice between rigorously developing a point or two and offering a more extensive list of suggestions in a brief and dogmatic form with only a sketch of justification underlying each, I have preferred the latter.

In terms of the recommendations of the APA committee on test standards, the great majority of validation problems posed by both structured and projective tests are problems of construct validity. Careful scrutiny of apparent cases of content or concurrent validity will usually reveal that these rubrics are only superficially appropriate. The most obvious example of this is in the use of tests as an aid in formal diagnosis, where there is no point in giving a test in order to predict the verbal behavior of the psychiatric staff. Think of the so-called "hits" and "misses" in a validation study employing routine psychiatric diagnosis as criterion. Almost the sole value of such investigations is their relevance in deciding whether the test can be used as a probabilistic indicator, along with psychiatric judgment or any other "criterion," of the presence of that inner state which is theoretically definitive of a particular taxonomic entity. An important minority of exceptions are those of truly predictive validity (e.g., prognosis), although even here I would agree with Loevinger's recent emphasis that if predictive validity is to be generalizable over different clinical populations, good construct validity is necessary (Loevinger, 1957).

It follows that there is very little point in carrying out validation studies unless the nontest indicators are superior, both qualitatively and quantitatively, to the kinds of judgment, rating, or classification which are routinely available. If we want the Rorschach or the Bender or the MMPI to play a role analogous to what the EKG or gold-colloid tests play in organic medicine, we may have to adopt a causal and statistical model more like that of organic medicine. We have nothing strictly analogous to the pathologist's report (a face-valid "criterion"); therefore validation studies must employ multiple assessments of the same construct, numerous internal checks (sufficiently patterned but preserved from contamination), and some procedure for further checks on whether an apparent test miss is actually a miss or only seems to be so. For example: We study the *subset* of cases in which the Rorschach strongly indicated a schizophrenic structure but which were, by the usual concurrent validity criterion, not so diagnosed; then we might determine whether Q sorts by the residents on each case tended to show a higher Q correlation with an idealized Q-sort description of "pseudoneurotic schizophrenia" than is observed in randomly chosen nonschizophrenic cases.

Another approach with which we are currently working in our Multiphasic studies utilizes "temporal convergence" to the psychometrics. That is, recognizing that neither the test nor the nontest indicators (I prefer the term *indicator* to the term *criterion* in such contexts) are infallible, one can at least study the extent to which the nontest indicators and judgments tend to converge to the characterization yielded by the test as more nontest information is accumulated. Remembering the attenuation formula, the demonstration that a set of relatively unreliable clinical indicators converge over time (as a function of repeated and qualitatively diverse exposure to the patient) toward the perception of the patient provided by the test is encouraging, even when the absolute magnitude of the asymptote of this convergence function is mediocre.

A perennial problem in the validation of projective devices (which they share with structured devices when the latter are multivariate) is the exact role that should be given in validation studies to the so-called "global" approach. While the method of correct matchings has been urged as the solution of this problem, and while I would readily agree that it has a definite place (especially in the early stages), I do not believe it can be defended as the method of choice. It does not present a very true-to-life validation context, since we are practically never concerned clinically to identify "who somebody is." The method does not reveal which variables are doing the work; a device which purports to tell us several different kinds of things may appear better or worse than it actually is on the basis of a small number of crude and clinically uninteresting dimensions to which matchers have learned to attend selectively. Our global thinking must not mislead us into forgetting that in the training of students we do teach them to pay attention to certain scores to which the test gives rise and to attach differential interpretive significance to each. That this is done contextually, i.e., with reference to the pattern of the remaining scores, does not suffice to justify the matching method, although it does demonstrate the inappropriateness of confining a statistical analysis to the calculation of Pearson correlations between single-test dimensions and single-criterion variables. My own opinion is that Q sort provides both quantifiability and globality and is therefore preferable both to the traditional single-variable correlation on the one hand and the method of correct matchings on the other. There are unsolved problems with Q technique, but our MMPI research has pretty well convinced us that for many clinical validation purposes it is the best method available. I think it unfortunate that the method detailed by Cronbach (1948) has not been more widely used, although the number of judges required has no doubt militated against its application.

It would be nice to have some statistical gimmick for measuring the similarity of two complex characterizations of one person's dynamics and structure. This is not achieved by the method of matching, by single-trait correlations, by Q correlations nor, so far as I'm aware, by any method yet proposed. If I describe a person by the usual mixture of genotypic and phenotypic statements, the dynamic point of view sees each facet of the phenotype as an indicator of the genotype; and it is in some sense a more serious mistake to utter the single proposition, "This patient has rigid reaction formations against his unusually strong unconscious hostile impulses" (if that statement is in fact false), than it is to include erroneously a frequently present indicator, e.g., "The patient will be docile in accepting interpretations [because he will perceive disagreement as an aggressive act]." If the characterization were presented in numerical form as estimates of the patient's co-ordinates in the variables of the indicator or surface trait space, and similar estimates in the underlying casual or factor space, one of the available distance measures might be appropriate (Cronbach & Gleser, 1953). Short of that idealized situation, however, one has the feeling that any numerical measure of the "closeness of fit" between two structural dynamic characterizations would be excessively arbitrary.

I cannot refrain from a critical comment here with regard to the globality problem. Some clinicians are still confused between the complex psychological processes of the test interpreter, in arriving at his final integrated characterization of the patient, and the statistical problem of validating that interpretation. After he has weighed the various possibilities and taken account of the higher-order interactions as best he can, the clinician *does* produce a set of utterances which are, taken singly, accurate in varying degrees. It is quite appropriate to determine the number or average amount of errors in the final description by considering the statements individually. Such a procedure, which studies the final result of the clinician's cerebrations, seems to me to be an unavoidable part of validation. This methodological point was made crystal clear by Kelly and Fiske (1951) in their exposition of the Michigan assessment program's design, but in spite of the lack of any rational reply to their arguments the principle has even yet not completely sunk in.

A tough practical problem in the validation of multivariate instruments is that of utilizing higher-order interaction effects among the test variables. The qualitative merits of the independent construct variable estimates should be excellent, as I've pointed out above; otherwise we are wasting our time. This usually means that the patients have been subjected to intense scrutiny by judges of a high level of clinical competence. On the other hand, the capitalization of random sampling errors increases horrendously as patterning effects are taken into consideration, so that the determination of a function and the assignment of optimal weights requires a large sample. In other branches of applied psychology, or even in clinical psychology where predictive validity is really the problem, it often suffices to know a very little bit about a large number of persons; for other purposes, as in carrying out individual psychotherapy, it suffices to know a very great deal at a deep level about a single person. In validating the configural indicators of a multivariate test, we find ourselves in the unhappy position of requiring to know a *great* deal about a *large* number of persons.

I come now to some considerations relating validation studies to clinical practice. Since the interpretation of multivariate devices involves the test-clinician combination (i.e., mechanical or cookbook procedures do not exist), at what level of clinical skill should the clinicians in validation studies be chosen? One can put several questions, each of which makes theoretical and practical sense. We cannot dismiss negative validation studies on the grounds that the Rorschachs used were not being read by Klopfer but by "ordinary" clinicians of only moderate skill. One empirical property of a clinical device is how much valid information is extracted from it by persons who have achieved that degree of proficiency typical of the population of users. Suppose that only 5 per cent of people who are ABEPP diplomates, have attended Rorschach workshops, and have administered 300 or more Rorschachs under supervision can arrive at clinically useful conclusions with the instrument; the taxpayer is being somewhat defrauded if the other 95 per cent draw part of their salary on this basis. A second question is, "How much valid and clinically useful information can be extracted by the most skillful interpreters of an instrument?" Finally, one may ask, "How much information is intrinsically contained in the test behavior?" We are beginning to collect some evidence with regard to the MMPI that nobody gets all the information out (Halbower, 1955; Meehl, 1959; Sines, 1957), and I would assume that to be equally true of less structured devices.

"Clinically useful information" is actually a rather complicated notion. The weakest claim that can be made for a test is that it tells us things about the patient which are true. It is a remarkable social phenomenon that, within an allegedly scientific profession, even this claim has not as yet been clearly supported with respect to the majority of the inferential uses to which our favorite devices are being put. Secondly, one may ask, "How much valid information does the instrument yield which is not readily available from other sources present in any clinical context, and who will routinely be making these judgments regardless of whether we use the test?" A third question is, "How much sooner in the time sequence does such incremental information become available to us through the use of the test?" If my test tells me something about the patient that I do not get from the initial diagnostic interview but which I will be able to assess with a relatively high degree of probability by the end of the fifth therapeutic hour, the use of the test is hard to justify.

Finally, the really important question: "What is the incremental efficiency in clinical handling (that is, both in gross administrative decision making and in the moment-to-moment decisions made in the course of psychotherapy) achieved through incremental information provided in advance by the test?" The difficulties of designing experiments to answer this fourth question are considerable, but it seems to me obvious that the ultimate justification for the clinical use of devices, projective or otherwise, must lie here. I am myself inclined to be somewhat skeptical in this regard, and it is a source of continual amazement to me the extent to which many clinicians take the answer for granted.

In concluding, I cannot miss the opportunity to attack an unfortunate tendency, springing no doubt from overidentification with our favorite devices (combined with a lurking fear that they may not be quite as valid as "everybody knows" they are), to reject any experimental or statistical design which is offered, on the ground that it is artificial or not in accord with actual clinical practice. True, some unimaginative designs have been employed to produce negative results when a more sophisticated approach would have elicited the validities actually present. But I think it is time for some blunt speaking within our profession about the disparity that exists between even the best available studies of validity and the amount of faith—and I use here a theological word deliberately—invested by a large number of practitioners in current methods. Studies such as that of Kostlan (1954), in which the incremental information provided by each of several instruments is estimated by showing the effect of *subtracting* that source from the total pattern of data available, are sufficiently close to "real life" clinical practice that no one is ethically and scientifically entitled to ignore the findings. There is far too great a tendency to invoke "clinical experience" as though it were a satisfactory answer to the validation question. Such a mistake could only be made by someone ignorant of the history of science (particularly of the medical sciences) or remarkably naive about those errors in observation, memory, and interpretation to which the human intellect is subject.

REFERENCES

CRONBACH, L. J. A validation design for qualitative studies of personality. *J. consult. Psychol.*, 1948, 12, 365–374.

CRONBACH, L. J., & GLESER, GOLDINE C. Assessing similarity between profiles. *Psychol. Bull.*, 1953, 50, 456–473.

HALBOWER, C. C. A comparison of actuarial versus clinical prediction to classes discriminated by MMPI. Unpublished doctoral thesis, Univer. of Minnesota, 1955.

KELLY, E. L., & FISKE, D. W. *The prediction of performance in clinical psychology.* Ann Arbor. Univer. of Michigan Press, 1951.

KOSTLAN, A. A method for the empirical study of psychodiagnosis. *J. consult. Psychol.*, 1954, 18, 83–88.

LOEVINGER, JANE. Objective tests as instruments of psychological theory. *Psychol. Rep.*, Monogr. Suppl. 9, 1957, 3, 635–694.

MEEHL, P. E. A comparison of clinicians with five statistical methods of identifying psychotic MMPI profiles. *J. counsel. Psychol.*, 1959, 6, 102–109.

SINES, L. K. An experimental investigation of the relative contribution to clinical diagnosis and personality description of various kinds of pertinent data. Unpublished doctoral thesis, Univer. of Minnesota, 1957.

8

Ambiguity and Nonambiguity in Projective Testing

RICHARD S. LAZARUS

This brief article by Lazarus nestled away in the Critiques and Notes section of the Journal of Abnormal and Social Psychology *is important because it represented a turn from the prior tendency to ignore the stimulus impact on the subject. Up to the time of Lazarus' article, the stimulus of most projective techniques was described as standard, ambiguous, and consequently unworthy of further study.*

Lazarus points out that a continuum of ambiguity should be used in projective techniques and that even unambiguous stimuli may have diagnostic value because of the defenses they elicit. A review of the role of the stimulus and ambiguity is in part reproduced in Chapter 29.

In recent years, many psychologists have been experimenting intensively with the ways in which personality variables shape the perception of various kinds of stimuli. Some of this research has greatly strengthened many of the assumptions underlying the use of projective techniques (Eriksen, 1951a; Lazarus, Eriksen, & Fonda, 1951; McClelland & Liberman, 1949). However, some of the implications of this work have not been made fully clear in the clinical literature. Nor has full practical advantage been taken of the ideas generated from this area of experimental work. It is the purpose of this note to point out one particular instance where the concepts of need and perception may be fruitfully used in psychodiagnosis.

The projective techniques have always depended on the use of highly

89

ambiguous stimuli. The use of ambiguous ink blots, ambiguous incomplete sentences, ambiguous pictures of people, etc. has largely dominated the testing procedures of psychodiagnosis. The concept of ambiguity, as has been pointed out in other articles (Eriksen & Lazarus, 1952; Lazarus, Yousem, & Arenberg, 1953), seems to depend on the number of reasonable interpretations that may be given to any stimulus by any particular sample of people. For example, if everyone interprets some pictorial stimulus as two people fighting, then such as stimulus has little or no ambiguity. There is no variation in interpretation. Little information about the needs and defense mechanisms of people can be gained from such stimuli unless there is at least some variability in response. On the other hand, if a number of interpretations are possible, the stimulus is called ambiguous, and it is useful in diagnosis because differences in interpretations may be related to personality dynamics.

The use of highly ambiguous stimuli in diagnosis presents one very serious problem. We are in no great difficulty when someone offers an interpretation that is obviously deviant. For example, on the TAT an individual may offer a very high frequency of aggressive interpretations of the pictures. He may present themes which revolve preponderantly about family hostilities, sibling rivalry, etc. Because such a performance is not typical, we are reasonably justified in suspecting that this person has a problem pertinent to aggressive needs.

However, a primary difficulty in making inferences about personality dynamics from projective performance arises when we find records in which there is no such deviation in performance from some interindividual or intraindividual norm. It is not so easy, then, to infer that the individual has no tension in this area. It is quite possible, for example, that if hostility does not appear in an individual's projective performance, it is being avoided as part of an ego-defense process. A recent study with the Rorschach test (Eriksen & Lazarus, 1952) supported the clinical assumption that failure to accept aggressive interpretations of the ink blots was related to emotional problems in this area. A similar finding has been reported for the TAT (Eriksen, 1951b). But because of the great ambiguity of the stimuli typically used in projective tests, it is difficult to tell whether lack of aggressive interpretations occurred because of lack of interest or because of ego defenses against aggressive impulses. In this event, we sometimes depend on qualitative information such as signs of emotion, blocking, etc. For example, when we observe emotional behavior on Card 6 of the Rorschach test, we often relate this to the sexual symbol which is so prominent on this card. But we are on shaky ground in such an interpretation because other aspects of the situation may have produced the emotional response. The ego threat of the stimulus is not clear and unequivocal.

The point that is being made here is that to depend on only the most ambiguous kinds of stimuli in projective procedures results in uncertainty as to when an interpretation is avoided because of repressive defenses and when it is ignored because of lack of tension. We want to know when certain needs are so strong and open that they result in ready verbalizations and fantasies. But we also want to know when certain needs are so unacceptable that they lead to avoidance and distortion. Ambiguous stimuli are not very well suited to this latter chore. What we need in our tests is stimuli which range from the most to the least ambiguous. It would be revealing to confront the individual with material which is emotionally charged and observe the ways in which he handles it. How far does the individual go in distorting perceptually what other people perceive? What is the form of the distortion? Is the defense process such as to raise the threshold of recognition and impair the recall of the dangerous material, or does it lead to very rapid recognition and facilitated recall?

That this is no brand-new idea is evidenced by Bellak's (1944) use of the term "adaptive" to characterize one aspect of projective behavior. But projective tests, with the exception of the word-association approaches, have never really been designed with this concept in mind. The need and perception literature abounds in references to "perpetual defense" (Eriksen, 1952; Eriksen & Lazarus, 1952; Eriksen, 1951a; Lazarus, Eriksen & Fonda, 1951; McGinnies, 1949). The experimental literature on selective forgetting makes use of this notion by ego-involving individuals in problem-solving tasks and testing for selective memory for successes and failures later on (Alper, 1946; Eriksen, 1952; Rosenzweig & Sarason, 1942). In spite of the fact that defense against threat has been discussed with many different frames of reference, few clinical psychologists have made direct use of nonambiguous threatening material in psychodiagnosis. Perhaps one reason for this is the fear of upsetting the patient or driving him away. In the therapeutic interview, this kind of threat is usually avoided, with considerable justification.

One illustration from the experimental literature should make clear what might be involved in a testing sense in the use of nonambiguous, threatening material. Recently an experiment was reported (Lazarus, Eriksen, & Fonda, 1951) in which auditory perceptual recognition of emotional and nonemotional sentences was studied. Among the diagnostic procedures used was a sentence completion test which was found to correlate with perceptual accuracy for the emotional and nonemotional sentences. Some of the items on the sentence completion test were very ambiguous in the sense that they suggested very little by way of an aggressive response (to take one content category). Others were relatively nonambiguous in this regard. An example of the former type was, "He has longed for . . .". An example of a nonambiguous item was, "He hated . . .". Most subjects responded to the latter item with an aggressive completion, such as, "He hated his sister," "He hated mean people," etc. This kind of answer was largely dependent on the phraseology of the item in the first place. However, some subjects responded with, "He hated to be caught out in the rain without his umbrella," or "He hated to get up in the morning." In many of these latter instances, subjects consistently went to great lengths to avoid an aggressive response. This kind of item is ideally suited to get at defenses related to hostility which involve denial or avoidance. It confronts the individual directly with the threat and offers some opportunity for him to either accept or reject the implication. The approach has something in common with the procedure of testing the limits on the Rorschach test or with using a picture on the TAT whose stimulus value is known. Such knowledge allows us to assess deviations from the typical response.

Both highly ambiguous and relatively unambiguous stimuli could easily be used in the projective method of psychodiagnosis. The very ambiguous material allows us to identify most readily instances where significant interpretations are given gratuitously without encouragement from the stimulus. Ruminations and strong phantasies about hostility are apt to show themselves in ready and frequent aggressive interpretations. Unacceptable aggressive impulses which are dealt with by repressive mechanisms are likely to result in infrequent aggressive interpretations even when they are suggested or demanded by the stimulus, or when most people typically give such interpretations. Lack of tension with respect to a particular need is likely to be reflected in nondeviant behavior; that is, in interpretations which are characterized neither by exaggerated frequency in special areas nor by excessive avoidance or distortion.

The projective stimuli may be presented for perceptual recognition or for learning and recall. What is important is that they range from a highly structured to a highly ambiguous nature and that extensive normative data be accumulated on many kinds of individuals. For any particular need variable like aggression, succorance, achievement, etc., the use of a well worked-out stimulus dimension of ambiguity could lead to the more accurate specification of the strength of a need and the nature of the ego-defense process.

REFERENCES

ALPER, THELMA G. Memory for completed and incompleted tasks as a function of personality. *J. abnorm. soc. Psychol.*, 1946, 41, 403–420.

BELLAK, L. The concept of projection: An experimental investigation and study of the concept. *Psychiatry*, 1944, 7, 353–370.

ERIKSEN, C. W. Defense against ego-threat in memory and perception. *J. abnorm. soc. Psychol.*, 1952, 47, 230–235.

ERIKSEN, C. W. Perceptual defense as a function of unacceptable needs. *J. abnorm. soc. Psychol.*, 1951, 46, 557–564. (a)

ERIKSEN, C. W. Some implications for TAT interpretation arising from need and perception experiments. *J. Pers.*, 1951, 19, 282–288. (b)

ERIKSEN, C. W., & LAZARUS, R. S. Perceptual defense and projective tests. *J. abnorm. soc. Psychol.*, 1952, 47, 302–309.

LAZARUS, R. S., ERIKSEN, C. W., & FONDA, C. P. Personality dynamics and auditory perceptual recognition. *J. Pers.*, 1951, 19, 471–482.

LAZARUS, R. S., YOUSEM, H. & ARENBERG, D. Hunger and perception. *J. Pers.*, 1953, 21, 312–328.

MCCLELLAND, D. C., & LIBERMAN, A. M. The effect of need for achievement on recognition of need-related words. *J. Pers.*, 1949, 18, 236–251.

MCGINNIES, E. Emotionality and perceptual defense. *Psychol. Rev.*, 1949, 56, 244–251.

ROSENZWEIG, S., & SARASON, S. An experimental study of the triadic hypothesis: reaction to frustration, ego-defense, and hypnotizability. I. Correlation approach. *Charact. & Pers.*, 1942, 11, 1–19.

9

Social Class and Projective Tests[1]

FRANK RIESSMAN AND
S. M. MILLER

Does a bias exist among projective techniques with regard to social class? Riessman and Miller think so. Some tests, such as the TAT, are too heavily weighted with middle-class figures for the lower class to be able to identify with the characters. Further, the tests are uninteresting to many working-class subjects, so that they do not involve themselves in the testing situation. On the Rorschach, this may lead to fewer responses and concomitantly fewer color responses, indicating a lower emotional reactivity on the part of this class. The interpersonal situation is also often tense for the lower-class subject, who reacts with a "stressful" performance.

The problem may be partially offset by using more figures with whom workers may more readily identify and also a special set of norms just for workers. Riessman and Miller thus believe that the signs of maladjustment found for the working class, as compared to the middle class, are not basic to their personality, whereas, countless other studies have interpreted these differences as indicative of real personality differences between the classes. Though they do not present conclusive evidence to support their views, they perform the valuable service of alerting the reader to an important factor in interpretation often overlooked—social class.

---

[1] Data presented in this article are based in part, on Frank Riessman, "Workers' Attitudes Toward Participation and Leadership," unpublished doctoral dissertation, Columbia University, 1955. Special thanks are due the Institute for Research in Human Relations for making portions of the data available.

95

Allison Davis (1948), Ernest Haggard (1954), and their associates have demonstrated that various test-relevant variables, such as motivation, practice, etc., can markedly affect intelligence test performance. In particular, Haggard has indicated that such factors as test-taking experience, rapport with the examiner, motivation, language used in the test items, reading ability, and speed required can decidedly limit the test performance of the lower-class child[2] and thus contaminate our picture of his intelligence.

It is possible that similar factors are operative with regard to many other kinds of measurement. In this article, we shall begin to examine possible effects of some of these variables on two very different types of projective tests: the Rorschach and the F (Fascism) scale. Residual attention will be given to the Thematic Apperception Test.

Auld (1952) has observed that most personality tests indicate that the lower class is more maladjusted or neurotic. He raises the possibility, however, that the observed class differences may be artifacts of the tests rather than valid differences. An example of the difficulties of tests is found in a personality test for high-school students which contains the question, "Are you often left out of things other kids do?" An affirmative reply is interpreted as indicating shyness, while a negative response signifies sociability. But it is quite possible, Auld states, that the answer is simply an accurate reflection of the situation, observed by Hollingshead (1949) as well as by a number of other writers, that the lower-class adolescent is in fact frequently left out of school affairs. An affirmative reply may mean, not that the lower-class adolescent is shy, but that he is accurately reporting the reality situation.

Another more striking example reported some years ago by Rosenberg (1949) concerns the Bernreuter Neurotic Inventory, on which working-class individuals score in the neurotic direction more often than do middle-class subjects. The following items on the Bernreuter are defined as normal and well adjusted by the tests:

1. Do you see more fun or humor in things when you are in a group than when you are alone? (The supposedly "normal" answer is "No.")

2. Can you usually understand a problem better by studying it alone than by discussing it with others? (The well-adjusted answer is "Yes.")

3. Do you usually face your troubles alone without seeking help? ("Yes" is the nonneurotic answer.)

4. Do you like to bear responsibilities alone? ("Yes" is the "normal" answer.)

The responses required for "normalcy" by this test are of a highly individualistic order. Responses of this type may not be congruent with co-operative group norms and traditions of the worker (Douvan, 1956).

---

[2] "Lower class" and "working class" are used interchangeably in this article because of the widespread practice in this regard.

The appreciable class differences found on the Bernreuter, particularly on the "self-sufficiency" subscale (Auld, 1952), *may reflect class differences in norms of individualism rather than neurotic tendencies!*

It is interesting to observe in this connection that a more recent article on the Bernreuter found that this test was sharply biased toward middle-class values; the authors concluded that the "working-class scores on the inventory are spuriously high (neurotic)" (Hoffman & Albizer-Miranda, 1955).

Another source of difficulty in interpreting scores of working-class individuals on these tests arises from the probability that middle-class subjects are probably much more adept at giving the conventional "adjusted" responses. Gough (1948) found on the Minnesota Multiphasic Personality Inventory that the middle-class students were much more evasive in their replies, tending to deny having problems of adjustment.

The Rorschach

In a recent study, Haase (1956) found that essentially identical Rorschach records were *interpreted* quite differently depending on the designated social-class origin of the patient.

The protocols of individuals reported as lower-class were diagnosed as more maladjusted with poorer prognosis than were their middle-class counterparts with essentially similar records who were used as controls. It is also interesting to note that the working-class records were more frequently categorized in terms of psychosis and character disorder, while the essentially identical middle-class records were diagnosed as neurotic and normal.

Haase does not object to a class differential analysis per se, but rather he notes that the analysis unwittingly, but consistently, concludes that the lower class is more maladjusted. Haase points out that considering the lack of opportunity and difficult life conditions of the worker, a lower-class record which is identical with that of a middle-class person might be presumed to indicate greater health and better prognosis.

While data are somewhat sparse on actual class differences in response to the Rorschach, a trend is suggested by a number of the studies. Auld (1952), in presenting class differences on the Rorschach based on a comparison of two previous studies, notes a number of significant differences, including a greater total number of responses for the middle-class group as well as proportionately more color and movement responses. (It should also be noted that the lower-class profile includes an equal number of animal and human movement responses, while the middle-class profile shows a greater proportion of human movement.)

Color responses on the Rorschach are interpreted as revealing the emotional life of the person: how responsive he is to other people and the environment. The lower-class boys tested would seem to be less responsive to their environment and lacking in the emotional warmth, since they have fewer color responses of all kinds (Auld, 1952).

A recent study by Stone and Fiedler (1956) also reports class differences in Rorschach responses of children, although not all the differences are in the same direction as in the two studies summarized by Auld. Consistent with the previous findings, Stone and Fiedler find that the lower-class group shows a higher proportion of *FM* (animal movement), a higher *A*% (animal responses), less *CF* (color-form), less *W*% (whole responses), and a lower *Dd*% (small details). However, they found the lower-class group exhibiting a higher *R* (number of responses) and more *FC* (form-color), contrary to previous findings. Stone and Fiedler also report a special breakdown made for them by Carlson for the eight-year-old children used in Carlson's study (1952). Here, the lower-class group had significantly less *FC* (form-color) and *CF* (color-form) responses and the middle-class group used far more color in general, consonant with the Auld report.

Auld (1952) recommends that psychologists using the Rorschach should be provided with lower-class norms in order to avoid making misleading (and negative) interpretations of lower-class protocols because of the inadequacy of the usual standards of Rorschach analysis and interpretation which are predominantly based on middle-class subjects. This suggestion may not be an adequate solution. To see if it is, we must study the factors, following the Davis-Haggard model, which may affect the performance of working-class individuals on this test.

Eichler (1951), in discussing the relationship of situational stress to Rorschach scores, points out that there is likely to be a decrease in color responses in stress situations. Klatskin (1952), in reviewing the literature on the effect of the *test situation* on Rorschach responses, notes that color responses, of all responses, are most affected by stress. Kimble (1945) found that subjects tested under standard (usual formal) conditions give significantly fewer *M* (movement) and *C* (color) responses than others tested in the more informal atmosphere of a cafeteria.

It is quite possible that the worker experiences much more stress in the Rorschach test situation than does the average middle-class individual.

An important factor probably contributing to a more stressful reaction to the situation on the part of the worker is his lack of familiarity with the Rorschach test, as well as his lack of skill in test taking in general. Moreover, he is likely to have poorer rapport with the middle-class examiner.

Haggard (1954) found with regard to intelligence test administration that rapport with the examiner and experience in test taking were important variables limiting the performance of lower-class children.

It is possible, then, that the test situation may produce situational stress for the worker. It is interesting to note that, as Eichler (1951) reports, experimentally induced stress produces Rorschach response patterns which resemble those of the worker with regard to color responses.

An alternative hypothesis which should be explored further is that lower-class responses to the Rorschach are more characterized by lack of interest and apathy than by stress or anxiety. This view is consistent with Davis' report (1948) that on intelligence tests lower-class children endeavor to finish as quickly as possible and typically are uninterested in the task.

Impressionistically, it appears that workers find the test material of the Rorschach particularly unstimulating. It is not the kind of task which is found to be immediately meaningful to them. The ambiguity of the Rorschach task may be in opposition to workers' *desire for structure* and definiteness (Riessman, 1955). In a sense, the "easiest" responses to give on the Rorschach are those determined by form and animal: that is, these responses can be given when the person is least involved or interested in the test as well as when one is situationally anxious. These are the more predominant responses of the lower-class subjects.

Undoubtedly, many clinicians would contend that these responses to the test are indicative of personality characteristics of the lower class and therefore can be utilized in interpretations. There are a number of important objections to this view. As pointed out above, the lower-class response may indicate a localized situational reaction, not an enduring, deep personality trend. Furthermore, the precise determinants of the lower class responses are uncertain, and cautious procedure would call into question the imputing of personality interpretations to these responses. The responses may be reactions to the nature of the test and test situation rather than to the content of the Rorschach. While the former may have importance for certain kinds of differential diagnosis, the Rorschach itself does not provide a mode of interpreting such extratest reactions except by considering the Rorschach session as an interview or by assuming that these responses are symmetrical with all other responses.

A challenging point is that Rorschach responses and interpretations of the worker are difficult to reconcile with conclusions about his personality as inferred from other kinds of evidence. For example, community studies of the worker furnish a very different picture of him than one would obtain from the Rorschach syndrome. While data are often coerced to fit an interpretation of the worker as impulsive and over-emotional, there is considerable evidence pointing to a personality pattern built around a co-operative, solidaristic, outgoing, emotionally responsive orientation, hardly reflected in the Rorschach pattern, especially the lack of color responses (Douvan, 1956; Useem, Tangent, & Useem, 1942).

For a variety of reasons, then, the Rorschach may, at the present time, be an inadequate test for working-class subjects. Providing lower-class norms for clinicians would not completely overcome these difficulties. Employing separate norms in analyzing a lower-class record may tell us how the individual compares with other lower-class subjects in response to situational test anxiety, skill in test taking, etc., but still does not give us an adequate picture of his basic, enduring personality tendencies. It is possible that the Rorschach may be one of the various tests that are not equally applicable to different cultural groups, because of the nature of the test material in relation to the background of the group.

The Thematic Apperception Test

The Thematic Apperception Test is another projective technique applied across class lines without awareness of the difficulties which may arise. Mason and Ammons (1956) report a number of class differences in response to the TAT, including language differences, differences related to the recording of the stories, differences in willingness to participate, and differences in stories elicited by the various cards. "For example, burglar stories were told to Card 14 by every class, but the burglar was clever and escaped in upper class stories, while he was caught in lower class stories" (Mason & Ammons, 1956).

Korchin (1950) found that middle-class subjects gave longer stories on the TAT than did lower-class subjects. Again we may hypothesize that rapport difficulties and concomitant situational stress may partially explain the shorter stories of the lower-class subjects.[3]

Nevertheless, in many respects this test may be more appealing than the Rorschach to working-class individuals. The task seems more stimulating to them, and what is required is perhaps clearer. However, two difficulties limit the usefulness of this instrument. In the first place, most of the pictures include people who appear to be middle-class; some are ambiguous, but very few suggest working-class individuals, symbols, or situations. In the second place, very few lower-class individuals have had much experience making up stories from pictures. This second

---

[3] Length of story may not be the best index of lower-class involvement, inasmuch as educational deficiencies would probably limit the length of the story, regardless of how deeply the worker identified with the individuals in the pictures.

objection is not quite as serious as the first, because working-class individuals have been exposed to movies and television stories and might be able to participate in this task if the pictures were more suggestive of working-class people, themes, and symbols. We do not mean to imply that such pictures should include labor struggles and strike scenes. More probably, everyday scenes which included workers' homes, manner of dress, and recreational activities would be more effective.

One adaptation of the TAT which makes an effort in this direction was developed in Mexico for rural children (Shore, 1954). Thus far no similar test has emerged for urban working-class subjects.

Some of the difficulties involved in instituting such tests is revealed by the several grounds on which Riess, Schwartz, and Cottingham (1950) criticize the Thompson TAT cards for Negro subjects. Perhaps the most troubling difficulty with the Thompson cards is that they explicitly and unambiguously portray Negro figures. This situation may constrain against full relaxation and involvement on the part of many Negro subjects, who find this experience strikingly different from most test situations which customarily do not involve Negroes. Providing Negroes with "familiar" material is unfamiliar (and perhaps disturbing) to them in this particular context. It is for this very reason that we have suggested that a "working-class TAT" not employ strike scenes and labor issues, but rather introduce in a more indirect manner situations and symbols reflecting lower-class life. We might also suggest that Negro TAT cards be constructed in which the race of the characters is ambiguous rather than explicitly white or Negro. These cards might evoke more response from many Negro subjects. Also, it might be possible to develop new cards reflecting themes and symbols emanating from Negro culture and not simply reproduce a standard TAT with the characters blackened to appear Negro, as in the Thompson TAT.

It is interesting that there are special cards for different age and sex groups within the regular TAT set but not for different class groups.

The F Scale or Fascism Scale

Another very important projective test on which significant class differences appear is the so-called Fascism scale or F scale, as it is usually called (Adorno et al., 1950). This test, unlike the Rorschach or the TAT, is highly structured in the sense that only certain definite, forced-choice responses may be given in answering the questions. (It is projective (Campbell, 1950) in the sense that the implication or meaning of the questions is disguised.) One of the most important attributes of this scale is its definite relationship with social attitudes such as leadership, prejudice, and political apathy.

A few of the items from an abbreviated form of the F scale

(Sanford, 1950), called the A-E scale (authoritarianism-equalitarianism), will clarify its meaning:

1. There are two kinds of people in the world: the weak and strong. (A positive answer is scored in an authoritarian direction.)

2. A few strong leaders could make this country better than all the laws and talk. (A positive answer is recorded in the authoritarian direction.)

Results from a number of studies indicate that the working class is more authoritarian on both the F and the A-E scales (Janowitz & Marvick, 1953).

Again the question arises: what does this mean? Adorno et al. (1950) indicate that the original F scale was developed on an almost entirely middle-class sample. Hyman and Sheatsley (1954) point out that differences in response may simply reflect differences in formal education rather than be symptomatic of deep personality trends.

In support of this position, Riessman (1955) found that education was a very decisive factor accounting for differences in response to the authoritarianism-equalitarianism scale. Of the grade-school educated workers, 62 per cent gave authoritarian responses while only 37 per cent of the high-school educated workers responded in an authoritarian direction. It is, therefore, possible that the scale items may have a very different meaning for the educated individual than they have for the less educated person.

If this is the case, we can expect the scale to be much more predictive of authoritarian relevant attitudes within the middle class, the group with more formal education.

Riessman (1955) found no relationship for the working-class group between authoritarianism, as measured by the A-E scale, and response to leaders as "people-oriented" (likes people, kind, understanding, etc.). That is, the workers who were classified as authoritarian in terms of the A-E scale showed just as many "people-oriented" responses to leadership as the equalitarian workers. In the middle-class group, on the other hand, the authoritarian individuals as measured by the A-E items were much less likely to select "people-oriented" humanitarian characteristics in indicating their response to leadership than were the middle-class equalitarians.

This lack of predictive value of the F scale for working-class groups is further corroborated by Farris (1956) in a study of the relationship of authoritarianism and political behavior (political activity, confidence, information, etc.). He concludes that "within groups of working-class respondents . . . authoritarianism does not usually correlate with observed variations in political behavior or attitudes."

There is, then, considerable reason to believe that the F scale and its derivatives are not applicable to the working-class subculture, while it may be appropriate for the middle class, on which the scales were originally developed.

One final point is relevant here: Christie (1954) points out that the middle-class person who feels that people are prying into his affairs (a standard F scale item) may suffer from paranoid tendencies, whereas an individual in the working class, where probing by various public functionaries is not uncommon, may *realistically* offer the same response. Also the statement "There are two kinds of people in the world: the weak and the strong" might have quite different implications for those whose class membership places them among the "strong," i.e., middle class, and the "weak," i.e., lower class. It is a reasonable hypothesis that those in a favorable hierarchial position are not as aware of the discrepancy in freedom of action or of their own privileges as those who are constantly faced with the reality of status differences.

Florence Goodenough (1950), in reappraising her own work on the Draw-a-Man test, has eloquently stated the issue: "The search for a culture-free test, whether of intelligence, artistic ability, personal-social characteristics, or any other measurable trait is illusory." While this view may be prematurely skeptical, it seems that, at least in their present form, authoritarian tests are limited in application by their middle-class orientation.

Conclusion

1. The typical response tendencies of lower-class individuals on the Rorschach may not be indicative of enduring personality tendencies. Rather they may simply reflect a response to a localized stress situation; namely, the stress involved in taking the test from a middle-class examiner in the context of workers' general lack of experience in test taking. There is evidence that situational stress is associated with fewer color responses, which appear to be one of the typical characteristics of workers' records. It also appears possible that situational stress will diminish those responses which require a more relaxed, interested involvement on the part of the testee, such as W, M, R, O.

We also suggest another hypothesis (not necessarily in contradiction to our major point): the workers' Rorschach response may be characterized by lack of interest and involvement. The worker shows a higher proportion of the responses which are "easiest" to give when least involved (A, F, etc.). It is possible that both lack of interest and test anxiety characterize workers' response at different times, but considerable research is needed before anything conclusive can be said.

The Rorschach may, at the present time, be a very limited test for determining personality patterns of lower-class individuals. The difficulties in using the instrument with these individuals cannot be surmounted by simply providing lower-class norms for the examiner.

2. There appears to be a need for a test like the Thematic Apperception Test in form but *including* working-class people, symbols, and situations. At the present time no such test is available for workers.[4]

In the absence of such a test, the need for caution on the part of psychiatrists and clinicians utilizing the standard personality tests is considerable. *Even if a new test equally appropriate in structure for both working-class and middle-class subjects were to become available, problems of rapport, experience in test taking, etc. would have to be overcome* before a full and accurate picture of the worker could be obtained from a battery of personality tests.

3. Although the lower-class individual scores in an authoritarian direction on the F scale and its derivatives, the items probably have a very different meaning or referent in his subculture; consequently we should be very cautious in inferring anything about his personality, authoritarian tendencies, etc. from these scales. It is most striking that the scales are not predictive of authoritarian relevant attitudes (such as people-oriented leadership and political apathy) in the lower class, while they are predictive in the middle class.

Many of the difficulties encountered in personality tests when they are applied across cultural and subcultural lines arise also on the *attitude* tests and polls employed by social psychologists and sociologists. While the authoritarianism scales were developed as projective personality tests, they are actually quite similar to numerous attitude scales. Katz's (1942) finding that white-collar interviewers received fewer pro-labor responses from workers than did working-class interviewers is highly relevant in this connection.

4. Considerable research is needed in order to determine exactly how the test-relevant variables, such as practice, motivation, etc., affect the performance of different groups on various projective tests. We need to know more about how the lower-class individual responds to different tests, which he likes better, and, more particularly, how he responds to test anxiety. Are there class differences in response to test (situational) anxiety, and if so, what are they? In regard to the Rorschach, specifically, we need to know whether workers' responses are characterized by lack of interest, anxiety, or both. This knowledge, of course, would have to be flexibly, not mechanically, applied. For example, it is not always true that a Negro psychologist will have better rapport with every Negro child, although the presence of a Negro psychologist in the clinic

---

[4] A number of projective picture tests similar to the TAT have been developed, but these are oriented toward determining social attitudes rather than personality patterns. See, for example, H. Lennard and F. Riessman, A proposed projective attitude test. *Psychiatry*, 1946, 9.

would probably provide a more favorable climate for relationship between Negro children and white examiners.

If new TAT pictures apparently more suited to the lower class are developed, research will be needed to ascertain whether in fact these pictures lead to a more full response on the part of the worker and whether they provide a more accurate portrayal of his personality.

5. Clinicians utilizing projective tests with members of different class groups should consider the possible effects of the test situation, language (and referents) used in the test, educational differences, motivation, timing of the test (speed factors), and cross-class rapport problems. In order to be able to do this effectively, clinicians need considerable training in sociology as well as fairly extensive knowledge concerning the culture of the subgroups with which they are likely to be working.

Many of the test-relevant variables we have been considering apply to any individual in any class, and clinicians have to attempt to appraise their role in making a diagnosis.

These variables probably function, however, in a more consistent and decisive fashion across class and cultural lines.

REFERENCES

ADORNO, T. W., FRENKEL-BRUNSWICK, ELSE, LEVENSON, D. J., & SANFORD, R. N. The authoritarian personality. New York: Harper, 1950.

AULD, F. The influence of social class on tests of personality. Drew Univer. Stud., No. 5, December, 1952, 1–16.

CAMPBELL, D. The indirect assessment of social attitudes. Psychol. Bull., 1950, 47, 15–38.

CARLSON, RAI. A normative study of Rorschach responses of eight year old children, J. proj. Tech., 1952, 16, 56–65.

CHRISTIE, R. Authoritarianism reexamined. In R. Christie & Marie Jahoda (Eds.), Studies in the scope and method of the authoritarian personality. Glencoe: The Free Press, 1954.

DAVIS, A. Social class influences upon learning. Cambridge: Harvard Univer. Press, 1948.

DOUVAN, ELIZABETH. Social status and success striving, J. abnorm. soc. Psychol., 1956, 52, 219–223.

EICHLER, R. M. Experimental stress and alleged Rorschach indices of anxiety. J. abnorm. soc. Psychol., 1951, 46, 344–355.

FARRIS, D. Authoritarianism as a political behavior variable. J. Polit., 1956, 18.

GOODENOUGH, FLORENCE, & HARRIS, D. B. Studies in the psychology of children's drawings: II. 1928–1949. Psychol. Bull., 1950, 47, 369–433.

GOUGH, H. G. A new dimension of status, II. Amer. sociol. Rev., 1948, 13, 401–409.

HAASE, W. Rorschach diagnosis, socioeconomic class, and examiner bias. Unpublished doctoral dissertation, New York Univer., 1956.

HAGGARD, E. Social status and intelligence: An experimental study of certain cultural determinants of measured intelligence. *Genet. Psychol. Monogr.*, 1954, 49, 145–185.

HOFFMAN, K., & ALBIZER-MIRANDA, C. Middle class bias in personality testing. *J. abnorm. soc. Psychol.*, 1955, 51, 150–152.

HOLLINGSHEAD, A. B. *Elmtown's youth.* New York: Wiley, 1949.

HYMAN, H., & SHEATSLEY, P. The authoritarian personality—a methodological critique. In R. Christie & Marie Jahoda (Eds.), *Studies in the scope and method of the authoritarian personality.* Glencoe: The Free Press, 1954.

JANOWITZ, M., & MARVICK, D. Authoritarianism and political behavior. *Publ. opin. Quart.*, 1953, 17, 185–201.

KATZ, D. Do interviewers bias poll results? *Publ. opin. Quart.*, 1942, 6, 248–268.

KIMBLE, G. A. Social influences on Rorschach records. *J. abnorm. soc. Psychol.*, 1945, 40, 89–93.

KLATSKIN, ETHELYN. An analysis of the effect of the test situation upon the Rorschach record. *J. proj. Tech.*, 1952, 16, 193–198.

KORCHIN, S. J., MITCHELL, H. E., & MELTZOFF, J. A critical evaluation of the Thompson TAT. *J. proj. Tech.*, 1950, 14, 445–452.

MASON, BETH, & AMMONS, R. B. Note on social class and the thematic apperception test. *Percept. mot. Skills*, 1956, 6, 88.

RIESS, B. F., SCHWARTZ, E. K., & COTTINGHAM, ALICE. An experimental critique of assumptions underlying the Negro version of the TAT. *J. abnorm. soc. Psychol.*, 1950, 45, 700–709.

RIESSMAN, F. Workers' attitudes towards participation and leadership. Unpublished doctoral dissertation, Columbia Univer., 1955.

ROSENBERG, M. The social roots of formalism. *J. soc. Issues*, 1949, 5, 14–23.

SANFORD, F. H. *Authoritarianism and leadership.* Philadelphia: The Institute of Research in Human Relations, 1950.

SHORE, A. *Autoritarismo y agresión en una aldea Mexicana.* Mexico, D.F.: 1954.

STONE, L. J., & FIEDLER, MIRIAM F. The Rorschachs of selected groups of children in comparison with published norms: II. The effect of socio-economic status on Rorschach performance. *J. proj. Tech.*, 1956, 20, 276–279.

USEEM, J., TANGENT, P., & USEEM, RUTH. Stratification in a prairie town. *Amer. J. Sociol.*, 1942, 7, 331–342.

10

Unity of Science Begins at Home: A Study of Regional Factionalism in Clinical Psychology

HARVEY PESKIN

This unusual article consists largely of a replication of an earlier study by Kostlan. In the present study, the relative validity of several sources of psychodiagnostic information (case history, Rorschach, MMPI, SCT) was tested using psychiatric outpatients, the basis of validation consisting of statements taken from psychological reports. The method was to pool all information obtained, with the exception of the particular source to be validated. Therapists' reports of the patient served as a criterion.

In Kostlan's study, the case history was the most potent source of accurate prediction. The MMPI, but neither the Rorschach nor SCT, improved prediction significantly when added to the case history. In Peskin's study, similar results were found, except that any two tests added to the case history improved prediction over the case history alone. The relative superiority of the MMPI over the projectives thus was not found in the secondy study. Why did this occur? Peskin used exclusively eastern psychologists, while Kostlan used western ones. The bias of the former in favor of the MMPI and against psychodiagnosis and the projectives is said to be counteracted by the opposite bias in the latter group. Training locale is thus a pertinent factor in the efficacy of tests for clinical evaluation. Another problem that needs to be considered was the relatively small reduction in errors when the tests were added to the case history as compared with the use of the case history alone.

The results serve to stimulate the following questions.

1. Should more time be spent in perfecting case histories than in validating projective techniques in view of the small reduction in errors occasioned by the use of these techniques?

2. How well would the Rorschach, SCT, or MMPI have done as sole sources of prediction for the psychotherapy statements?

3. Should we not emphasize the quality *of information contributed rather than the* quantity? *In other words, do the projectives contribute more important information than the case history? Do they perhaps contribute information that is not obtainable elsewhere?*

The studies of Kostlan and Peskin are extremely valuable, but they serve only to whet the researcher's appetite rather than satisfy it. Much more research of this type is needed before we may allow any conclusions to jell.

The bonanzas and hard times borne by the field of clinical psychology over the past three decades have spirited its members into the much-discussed unevenness of professional identity (Kahn & Santostefano, 1962) and led its own burgeoning social structure into a peculiar factionalism. Concerning the latter, the most persistent example is the strain that tends to prevail between members of university clinical faculties and those in clinical practice. Not the least of the complications that ensue is the danger that clinical opinion, theory, or research of each camp becomes excessively polarized, leading to a cultish disregard of and provincial indifference to the thinking of the other. This tendency toward intellectual isolationism was nicely demonstrated by Levy and Orr (1959), who successfully predicted with which of the two professional groups researchers were affiliated by whether their published *statistical* findings professed to validate or invalidate selected aspects of Rorschach theory and practice. The academic setting "sponsored" more research favorable to the construct validity of the Rorschach and more research unfavorable to its criterion validity, while studies from the clinic situation more often approved than disapproved of the Rorschach as a useful instrument in criterion-validity research oriented to practical service goals. Such internecine warfare suggests that the social structure of clinical psychology inherits and perpetuates the unresolved academic-clinic conflict endured by the predoctoral candidate as discussed by Kahn and Santostefano.

Factionalism in clinical psychology exists elsewhere. Those clinicians whose training or employment have taken them over wide stretches of the United States may have been impressed by the often salient *regional* differences in what clinical psychologists, in practice, teaching, and research, appear to value or ignore professionally. For others, this kind of factionalism goes unnoticed, compared to the academician-practitioner situation where the parties must coexist in the community and co-operate in the training of graduate students.

Such an impression stimulated the present investigation, which observes the patterning of psychodiagnostic skills in a group of clinical graduate students whose university and clinical training was in progress in the East, particularly in New York City, and in a graduate clinical group in the West, from the San Francisco Bay area.

The psychodiagnostic milieu in both the university and clinical setting appears qualitatively different between these regions. In terms of the traditional classes of diagnostic instruments in clinical psychology, projective techniques in New York City have a nearly exclusive hold on the imagination of the clinician in his role as psychodiagnostician. And among these, the Rorschach appears the most popular, judging especially from interns' reports. Moreover, it is interesting to note the explicit reference made to projective techniques in graduate course *titles* published in the bulletins of the New York schools. The 1961–1962 catalogues of graduate studies at New York University, Columbia Teachers College, and the City College offer courses where "projective techniques" appears in the course name or else list classes given over completely to one technique, e.g., "Rorschach method," "Interpretation of the TAT," or "Play techniques in child study." No such explicit mention is made in the bulletins of the Western schools.

In the San Francisco Bay area, the graduate centers of the University of California (Berkeley) and Stanford and the clinical agencies serving them present the contrasting picture of the predominant use of objective tests, particularly the MMPI. Formal teaching of the Rorschach has tended to be compressed into no more than the equivalent of a semester, along with other projective or semiprojective instruments, such as sentence completion methods. Graduate bulletins always refer to this course work by such inclusive titles as "Personality assessment" or "Diagnostic testing." Nevertheless, the Rorschach does not seem to have undergone the complete exclusion suffered by the MMPI in the East. Rather, the fate of the Rorschach hangs on such uncertainties as the particular supervisor to which an intern is assigned. Whether this test is permanently valued or ignored may depend on this assignment.

One notices not only differential diagnostic emphases, but a generally greater involvement in the East than the West in psychodiagnostic study. This speculation arises partly from the likelihood that variations in regard to bases of inference and historical heritage tend to be greater among projective tests than among objective tests. Objective testing has expanded intramurally with no substantial change in the guiding theory of scale construction. The MMPI is constantly extended by the addition of new scales, each markedly similar to the empirical principles of the original clinical scales. (Objective scales derived by factor analysis or by methods of face validity have had little impact to date upon the clinic setting.) That the East may infuse greater commitment to the diagnostic role carries no implication about over-all superiority in diagnostic skill, a talent that certainly transcends the size of the clinician's repertoire of familiar tests and even of psychodiagnostic training, per se. Rather, the argument implies that eastern psychologists are apt to garner knowledge from a larger number of test sources, although the sum total of knowledge need not be absolutely greater.

This suggested differential involvement in diagnostic practice may be viewed as reflecting the intrusion of the academic-clinic cleavage into regional differences. According to Levy (1962), clinical psychologists with their doctoral degrees from the New York City schools publish less than do those from institutions in the San Francisco Bay area. The median number of publications from Columbia Teachers College and New York University in a twelve-year period are 2.2 and 2.3, respectively; from the University of California and Stanford, 3.9 and 4.8, respectively. Since the academic orientation implies a decided commitment of energy to research pursuits (and perhaps greater skepticism concerning the power of tests as *clinical* instruments), it may be reasonable to assume that clinical psychologists in these western schools have less investment in psychodiagnostic services, per se. The same reasoning would hold, of course, for the selective encouragement of the practice of psychotherapy in the East. The issue of psychotherapy in clinical psychology is, however, far more complex. By sharing this function with other healing professions, the extent and fate of psychotherapeutic training is also contingent on the quality of the relations prevailing in the region among the disciplines of psychology, psychiatry, psychoanalysis, and social work, and the politics thereof, as well as on the community's definition of mental illness and treatment.

Procedure

The scientific study of psychodiagnosis is by no means compromised by studying the clinician in a context which resembles the actual conditions of his service function. Kostlan (1954) reasoned that a pertinent method would be a comparison of the relative validity of representative *batteries* of tests, and the present study is an exact replication of Kostlan's research. Since Stanford and University of California students—20 in all—composed his sample, his results will be used to reflect the performance of the western group. A group of 20 students representing the East attended Columbia Teachers College (11), New York University (5), Harvard (1), Buffalo (1), Boston

University (1), and Illinois (1). In terms of age and level of training, the members of the Western group were generally older, and while several staff psychologists were included in this sample, the majority were interns in the third and fourth years of graduate work. The eastern graduate students were most often in their second and third years of schooling.

Kostlan's method will be summarized here. Four sources of psychodiagnostic information were used: the Rorschach, MMPI, Stein Sentence Completion Test, and a standard social case history. Each clinician was randomly deprived of one of these four sources for each of four Veterans Administration outpatients and given only minimal or face-sheet data for a fifth patient. Thus, there were five experimental conditions presented to each clinician.

Accuracy of prediction was measured by marking a true-false questionnaire made up of statements previously validated from the patient's therapy progress notes. Only behavior that could be observed directly by the therapist or that was reported by the patient is considered in this comparative regional study. Examples of therapists' observations are: "he is in contact with reality"; "the patient concentrates on physical complaints"; "he would tend to ask advice of the therapist"; "the patient would assiduously keep his therapy appointments." Items determined by patients' reports include: "he says that he has always feared being self-assertive"; "he is in psychotherapy because he is convinced that he needs this kind of treatment"; "he sometimes openly doubts his ability to take the role of a husband and father." (A second set of statements garnered from psychodiagnostic reports and inferential in nature were validated by a group of expert psychologists. Since these experts were all trained in the West, this part of Kostlan's design is excluded because of the obvious circularity.)

TABLE 10–1   *Summary of Analysis of Variance of the Pooled Data for East and West Samples*

SOURCE	df	EAST MS	EAST F	WEST[a] MS	WEST[a] F
Conditions (test batteries)	4	74.67	4.81[c]	143.52	7.01[d]
Patients	4	95.79	6.17[d]	112.72	5.50[d]
Interns	19	32.84	2.11[b]	60.52	2.96[c]
Squares × Patients	12	17.95	1.16	30.10	1.47
Residual (error)	60	15.53		20.48	
Total	99				

[a] From Kostlan (1954).
[b] p = .05.
[c] p = .01.
[d] p = .001.

Every experimental condition for every patient could not be given to every clinician since the clinicians would remember characteristics of a given patient from one experimental condition to the next and thus be contaminated. It was necessary to restrict the patient-battery combinations so that each of five clinical interns had all five patients and all five experimental conditions, but neither a patient nor a condition was repeated for any intern. Such an arrangement fulfills the properties of a 5 × 5 Latin square. Four such squares were separately drawn, each with five different interns. For each region separately, the data were combined for the final statistical analysis. Finally, since it is the differential effectiveness of the various test batteries *within* regions that is the main focus of this report, errors were compared among the five experimental conditions by *t* tests for each group separately. This procedure has the added bonus of controlling for any possible differences in over-all ability as well as increasing the power of the comparison tests.

Results

As in Kostlan's study, the variance has been analyzed for the four replications combined. These data are summarized in Table 10–1. Variance contributed by patients, by conditions (test batteries), and by clinical interns in the East is significant and approximates Kostlan's results in the western sample. While it will only be the variance of the test conditions that receives further analysis, the significant *F* for interns suggests that no regional bias which this study may uncover can be so powerful as to stereotype clinical activity and eliminate individual differences in diagnostic skill.

The means for the five conditions are presented in Table 10–2. These means are based on the percentage of errors, since there were slight variations of possible correct answers for each patient, and then transformed into angles (equal to the arc sine of the square root of the percentage) to allow the assumption of homogeneity of variance to be made. These angles closely approximate percentage errors. Significance of the differences betweeen these means within each regional sample was tested by *t* tests, using the standard error of the mean differences to account for the correlational term. Kostlan's published results for the West and the present findings for the East are presented in Table 10–3.

Of the 10 possible comparisons between the five experimental conditions, 4 were significant beyond the .05 level for the West, 6 for the East.

Neither regional group could improve prediction over the minimal data condition without the case history being in a battery. That is, for both East and West, the number of errors made on the basis of the rather stereotyped information of age, marital status, occupation, education, and source of clinic referral did not exceed errors made from the battery of Rorschach, MMPI, and Sentence Completion.

Secondly, in the western sample, as Kostlan reported, only where the case history and MMPI appeared *together* could prediction exceed the

TABLE 10–2		*Mean Arc Sine Percentage Errors for the Experimental Conditions in East and West Samples*	
	CONDITIONS	EAST	WEST[a]
I	Battery minus the Rorschach	33.10	31.65
II	Battery minus the MMPI	33.50	34.40
III	Battery minus the Sentence Completion Test	33.65	31.65
IV	Battery minus the Social Case History	36.90	36.30
V	Minimal data only	36.95	37.35

a From Kostlan (1954).

minimal condition. This combination of the case history and MMPI arose in two batteries. In the eastern sample, however, the case history need

TABLE 10–3   *Summary of the t Tests for the Differences between Means of the Experimental Conditions for East and West Samples*

COMPARED CONDITIONS	EAST		WEST[a]	
	MEAN DIFFERENCES	t	MEAN DIFFERENCES	t
I–II	− .40	.27	−2.75	1.66
I–III	− .55	.36	0.00	0.00
I–IV	−3.80	3.22[c]	−4.65	3.69[c]
I–V	−3.85	2.16[b]	5.70	3.37[c]
II–III	− .15	.12	2.75	1.36
II–IV	−3.40	2.27[b]	−1.90	1.12
II–V	−3.45	2.76[b]	−2.95	1.86
III–IV	−3.25	2.48[b]	−4.65	2.77[b]
III–V	−3.30	2.52[b]	5.70	2.82[b]
IV–V	− .05	.03	−1.05	0.76

Note.—Experimental conditions are: I Battery minus Rorschach; II Battery minus MMPI; III Battery minus Sentence Completion; IV Battery minus Social Case History; V "Minimal" information only.

a From Kostlan (1954).

b $p = .05$.

c $p = .01$.

not have been accompanied by any specific test to exceed the minimal condition, for in the East all three batteries containing the case history exceeded the minimal condition.

The West could improve prediction, therefore, only if the MMPI were available, along with the case history. Given these two sources of information, it did not matter what third cue (Rorschach or Sentence Completion) was available. By contrast, the East could improve prediction with any paired combination of the three tests. But the eastern clinicians did no better with both projective tests than with one, plus the MMPI.

The remaining significant differences for East and West exactly repeat this analysis above, now using not the minimal condition but the battery lacking the case history as the comparative condition. For the West, only when the MMPI accompanies the case history and one other test (Rorschach or Sentence Completion) could prediction exceed the battery containing all three tests and lacking the case history; for the East, any paired combination of the three tests with the case history resulted in significantly fewer errors than the battery missing the case history.

Discussion

Both the unity and disunity of the psychodiagnostic function between regions are suggested by these data. Clinicians so reared apart reveal a common bond in what they require as a *necessary* condition for valid diagnosis: the availability of the historical and actuarial information that comprise the standard case history. For those who demand that skill in psychodiagnosis be gauged by the ability to do without such material—the "blind" diagnostic evaluation—this finding may not reflect an inspired contribution to the "unity of science." Others may evaluate this result as simply a realistic picture of competent clinical work everywhere and happily be reassured that regional bias leaves such competence, as revealed here, undisturbed: that the psychologist must capitalize on the actual sociocultural setting in order to return predictions of actual sociocultural *behavior* such as made up the present criterion in Kostlan's design.

The groups differ according to what constitutes the *sufficient* conditions of prediction in the present study, and in these divergences one may discern the effects of the regional factionalism discussed earlier. In the San Francisco Bay area, prediction exceeds the minimal condition and the all-test battery *only* when the MMPI accompanies case history material. In the East, no such contingency arises, and prediction succeeds with *all* paired combinations of the three tests (along with the case history).

Given Kostlan's results for the West alone, one might have concurred with a prevailing opinion or lore among users of objective tests that the MMPI is better suited to *behavioral* (as opposed to dynamic) predictions than projective techniques. (Kostlan did not draw such a conclusion.) Performance of the eastern sample suggests, however, that projective techniques (i.e., the battery containing the Rorschach and Sentence Completion) can do about as well in this regard when in the hands of those devoted to their study. It is tempting, therefore, to suspect the workings of the "self-fulfilling prophecy" in this rather western view of the exclusiveness of the MMPI, where the western group may have reaffirmed this special view of the MMPI by ignoring other available diagnostic instruments. By contrast, the eastern sample, by being as effective with all paired combinations of the three tests, seems to display more versatility, whether through a larger test repertoire or from more serious attention to and patience with the general psychodiagnostic enterprise.

The present research is offered not only for its specific results but as a vehicle for establishing an aspect of the structure of clinical psychology that complicates the teaching of scientific principles to which the profession is seriously committed. The "dissension" between the metropolitan areas of New York City and the San Francisco Bay area, which this discussion tries to make vocal rather than provoke, may be viewed as an instance of the operation of broad spheres of professional influence that divide the country along various axes. While the geographical boundary line may be unclear, a general East-West split has evolved under the impact of well-known historical forces which at once shape both the complexity and provincialism of clinical psychology.

The Rorschach and its attendant psychoanalytic spirit were migrants from Europe and naturally took stronger hold in the East. While the Rorschach tradition clearly diverged from the early American "objective" test movement whose chief representative was the Bernreuter, a definite projective-objective test polarization did not take hold until the early forties, with the construction of the basic clinical scales of the MMPI. The empirical and pragmatic approach of the MMPI (itself a revolt against the face validity of the Bernreuter) aptly reflected the functionalism of American psychology at one of the more western points of the widening professional frontier. Not only abstract social forces but the devoted, forceful, and original teaching of key psychologists have accounted for the currency of the Rorschach and MMPI. Yet it can be argued that these psychologists could have flourished only in a region whose intellectual bent invited and welcomed their style of thinking and creating.

The accessibility of the large research and theoretical literature of both test philosophies certainly has served to "desegregate" clinical thought.

Prevailing isolation must then be attributed to the trend for clinical psychologists, compared with those in other fields of psychology, neither to ask nor be asked to stray far from the sphere of influence under which they were trained. Such a conjecture may be examined by consulting the "ecology" of clinical psychology—the paths of migration from Ph.D. to professional employment. Such a method as Kostlan's may also be applied to other regions to help map the whereabouts of current insularity and applied over time to determine the degree to which professional polarization succumbs to or overtakes efforts toward the unity of clinical thought. There is, of course, no laudable achievement in a "unified" body of knowledge that is contrived and premature, for unity then gives way to mere uniformity of thought. If the questionable side of factionalism is the cleavage of thought, its brighter side is dedicated energy and productivity within regions. A sound unity of science in clinical psychology, as perhaps in other intellectual areas, may indeed be the heir of an unhurried factionalism.

Epilogue

The field of clinical psychology is volatile enough, and conclusions of the movement may rapidly date themselves. Five years have passed since the eastern data were collected, and five more years between Kostlan's original work and the present replication in the East. Without a more current replication, it is difficult to judge the timeliness of the present discussion. But, as a final conjecture, the author has no strong impression that these comparative findings have become obsolete or that the nature of clinical training between regions has significantly converged.

REFERENCES

KAHN, M. W., & SANTOSTEFANO, S. The case of clinical psychology: A search for identity. *Amer. Psychologist*, 1962, 17, 185–189.

KOSTLAN, A. A method for the empirical study of psychodiagnosis. *J. consult. Psychol.*, 1954, 18, 83–88.

LEVY, L. H. The skew in clinical psychology. *Amer. Psychologist*, 1962, 17, 244–249.

LEVY, L. H., & ORR, T. B. The social psychology of Rorschach validity research. *J. abnorm. soc. Psychol.*, 1959, 58, 79–83.

11

The Influence of Situational and Interpersonal Variables in Projective Testing

JOSEPH M. MASLING

The belief that projective techniques provided an X ray to the private world of the subject is said by Masling to be chiefly responsible for the failure to assess correctly the influence of situational and interpersonal factors on the projective response. Subsequent investigation has shown that the method of administration, the nature of the testing situation, the sex, status, and personality of the examiner, as well as the behavior of the subject, all influence the nature of the response and/or the interpretation given to it.

This importance of the interpersonal element need not be treated as "error variance" hindering the effectiveness of the test. Rather, it should be viewed as a bona-fide aspect of the testing situation, and its influence should be measured and assessed. In short, this article helps to point out the necessity of a "field" approach to personality assessment in which all elements affecting the subject's behavior must be taken into account.

Since the advent of projective techniques, psychologists have devoted considerable energy to the creation and utilization of various methods for assessing the "deeper layers" of personality. The impressive results often obtained with these instruments have led to a proliferation of projective methods, most of which are greeted with enthusiasm and validated by

117

endorsement. The early, uncritical acceptance of projective testing produced studies which were mainly concerned with the characteristics of such clinical populations as delinquents, psychotics, and organics. In general, the assumption was made that a projective test was as single-minded as the X ray (Frank, 1939), revealing information only about the patient without in any way being influenced by the person who administered the test, the method of administration, or the situation in which it was used. In the words of Cronbach (1956), "Test research has been dominated by the Galtonian view that the test is a sample of the subject's responses to a standardized nonpersonal stimulus" (p. 175).

However, with growing sophistication regarding the nature of psychological testing, a number of writers have explicitly commented on the influence in projective testing of factors other than the S's personality. One of the first to delineate the subjective factors in Rorschach testing was Schachtel (1945), who described four common elements in the Rorschach situation: the relationship of the E and S; the assignment of the task by the E to the S; the E's need to interpret the S's behavior; and the specific qualities of the task, such as the ambiguity or the lack of familiarity with the stimuli. Miller (1953), Sarason (1954), and Luchins (1947) have also indicated the subtle ways in which subjective forces may influence the course of a projective testing situation.

It is the purpose of this paper to review the considerable evidence regarding situational and interpersonal influences in projective testing. Experiments dealing with the effects of these factors on interviewing or intelligence testing and those studies concerning the effects of psychotherapy, psychosurgery, and individual versus group tests will not be reviewed, since these issues are considered to be part of essentially different problems. Four arbitrary, overlapping categories will be used to present these studies: method of administration, the testing situation, examiner influence, and subject influence.

The Influence of Method of Administration

INSTRUCTIONS TO MAKE A GOOD OR BAD IMPRESSION

The ability of projective tests to withstand attempts by Ss to disguise or alter their "real" responses has been investigated several times. The usual procedure in these studies is to test the same Ss several times under varying instructions; comparisons are then made between the test responses produced under standard instructions with those yielded by experimental instructions.

Fosberg (1938; 1941; 1943) has reported on the process of trying to produce a good or bad impression on the Rorschach. In one study (Fosberg, 1938), a husband and wife were each administered the Rorschach under four sets of instructions. Despite the instructions to create a given impression, it was concluded that the Ss were unable to avoid revealing basic aspects of their personality, the psychograms on the four examinations remaining essentially the same. In a later study (Fosberg, 1941), the Rorschach was given four times under different instructions to 25 male and 25 female Ss. A special experimental group of 16 Ss took the fourth examination under instructions to look for particular determinants. When Fosberg compared group means produced under the different instructions, he found few consistent differences. There was little change in the test as a whole, only the content of the responses showing marked changes. One reason for the failure of these instructions to produce differences in responses is that each S defined for himself the manner in which to deceive the E, so that six Ss increased their responses in order to make a good impression, while four increased their responses in order to make a poor impression. While there was no consistency among all Ss on how to create an artificial image for the E, most Ss felt that they could falsify their reactions by adopting a particular set. Of special importance to this review is the fact that in trying to make a bad impression several Ss seemed to concentrate on the E, rather than the test; three Ss annoyed the E, two acted stubborn and ornery, two proceeded very slowly, and four paid little attention (Fosberg, 1943).

Fosberg's studies were essentially repeated by Carp and Shavzin (1950), who also found that taking the Rorschach under instructions to make a good impression ("you are in a state hospital and the results on this test may help you get out") and under instructions to make a bad impression ("you are to be drafted for the Army and the results on this test may help keep you out") produce no significant group differences (except for the z score, significant at the .05 level). "This does not mean, however, that no changes were produced. The data clearly showed the differences. But the direction taken was so diverse, among the individual Ss, that they were balanced out in the analysis" (Carp & Shavzin, 1950, p. 232). The authors directly challenged Fosberg's conclusions that the Rorschach could not be manipulated by the Ss. "On the contrary, this study shows that there are some subjects who can manipulate their responses, who can vary their personality picture as reflected by the Rorschach, under instructions to make 'good' or 'bad' impressions" (p. 233).

Weisskopf and Dieppa (1951) administered three cards of the TAT to hospitalized psychoneurotic veterans, giving the standard instructions in one administration, asking the Ss to give the best possible impression on another administration and the worst possible impression on the third administration. Of the nine dimensions rated by judges, five showed significant differences as a function of the instructions. When the Ss tried to give their worst impression, they were rated as less well adjusted, more hostile, less willing to conform, and more spontaneous. Wallon and

Webb (1957) asked naval aviation cadets to take the Rosenzweig P-F test and a sentence completion test under several variations of instructions and test structure. One group took the P-F test in a multiple-choice form, another took it in standard form, while the third group was told in taking the test to try to make the best impression. It was concluded that as the test became less ambiguous, the results more closely resembled responses produced under instructions to fake.

INSTRUCTIONS EMPHASIZING PARTICULAR DETERMINANTS OR LOCATIONS

In the process of studying suggestibility, Coffin (1941) demonstrated how S's set may influence his responses to the Rorschach test. The Ss were first asked to read a fictitious article by a "Harvard professor" describing how professional men usually saw whole responses, while businessmen saw animals, skilled laborers saw inanimate objects, and WPA employees saw details. A second group of Ss read the article that now described professional men as seeing details, businessmen inanimate objects, etc. Following the reading of this article, each S was administered six Rorschach cards. The results clearly showed the influenec of the suggestion on the responses, each group tending to respond in the same direction as the socially acceptable norms. "Apparently the suggestion sets up a determining tendency operating upon the observer's perceptual and imaginal processes. This acted to direct the 'search' " (Coffin, 1941, p. 62).

In a better-controlled study, Abramson (1951) equated two groups of college students on the basis of W, D, and Dd responses to the first administration of the Rorschach. One group of Ss was then told that successful business and professional men saw whole responses, while the second group was instructed that these men saw detail responses. As a consequence of the difference in instructions, the two groups differed significantly on the second Rorschach test not only in the number of whole and detail responses but on several other determinants ($F\%$, FM, m, Hd, Ad) as well, although there were no significant differences between groups on the first test. Evidently establishing a set for area will also affect those determinants dependent on the area of the blot. The evidence of Keyes (1954) also supported the notion that the number of whole responses can be influenced by special instructions.

Hutt, Gibby, Milton, and Pottharst (1950) and Gibby (1951) investigated the effects of instructing Ss to pay particular attention to specific aspects of the Rorschach blots. In each study, various parts of the blots were emphasized to the Ss after the standard administration of the test but prior to the experimental administrations. A study of test-retest reliability of the Rorschach under these conditions showed certain determinants to be more stable and less resistant to change than others. "What appears to be crucial is how the individual perceives the total test situation. If we do not know this, we are likely to make serious errors in interpretation" (Gibby, 1951, p. 185).

After first administering the Rorschach under standard instructions, Fabrikant (1954), in his instructions to the experimental group, stressed movement, color, shading, and texture responses. In the experimental group, 15 Ss showed differences between first and second administrations in at least 3 of the 4 response categories, while in the control group only 3 Ss showed significant changes in at least 3 categories.

INSTRUCTIONS REGARDING THE PURPOSE OF THE TESTING

The most impressive evidence regarding the effects of telling the S the purpose of the testing comes from the study of Henry and Rotter (1956), who simply told their experimental group of female undergraduates what most college students have already presumably learned about the Rorschach test from television, the movies, and *Life* magazine: "This is a test to discover serious emotional disturbances." It was found that the experimental group gave fewer responses (at the .01 level), more good form responses (.05 level), more popular responses (.05 level), and more animal responses (.05 level) than a control group given a standard administration. It was evident that making explicit the purpose of the test produced more constriction and more attempts to be safe than leaving the purpose unstated.

A study by Calden and Cohen (1953) investigated the influence of both ego involvement and instructions regarding the nature of the Rorschach test. Half their senior high-school Ss were given ego-involving instructions and half were given neutral instructions; one-third of the Ss were told that the Rorschach tested intelligence, another third that it tested "nervousness," and the last group that it measured imagination. An analysis of variance computed for 27 selected variables showed 19 differences significant at the .05 level. In general, the resulting personality pattern that emerged from the intelligence test instructions resembled the same constricted, safe picture found by Henry and Rotter, form and animal responses increasing, movement responses decreasing. "Needless to say, predictions based on 'blind' interpretations of the Rorschach protocol, without knowledge of the testing situation or the S's reactions to the testing, are so much more fallible when viewed in the light of the results of this study" (Calden & Cohen, 1953, p. 308-309).

The TAT has also been used to study the effects of informing Ss of the purpose of the test (Summerwell, Campbell, & Sarason, 1958). Four different groups were used, each group receiving one of the following instructions regarding the purpose of the test: (1) the usual Murray instructions, (2) intelligence test instructions, (3) projective test instructions, (4) neutral instructions. It was found that the neutral instructions produced significantly different emotionally toned stories than any of the other three groups, with story outcomes significantly different from the standard Murray instructions and the projective test instructions.

THE MANIPULATION OF TIME OF RESPONSE

In giving the group Rorschach to 10 Ss under conditions of long time exposure (3 minutes) and short time exposure (10 seconds), Weisskopf (1942) noted that the same personality pattern emerged under both conditions of administration. Unfortunately, adequate experimental controls were not employed. A more rigorous procedure was utilized by Siipola and Taylor (1952), who gave the Rorschach test to experimental Ss seated in front of a noisy automatic timer which recorded reaction time of the first response. It was concluded that the pressure induced by the timer resulted in normal Ss behaving under stress much as disturbed patients do in a nonstress situation. "The moral of all this seems to be that the projective process, like any other psychological process, is not immune to the influences of the specific conditions under which it operates" (Siipola & Taylor, 1952, p. 46).

The Influence of the Testing Situation

The designs for the studies investigating the effects of varying testing conditions take several forms. The most rigorous of these utilizes a control group that has been given two administrations of the test to contrast with the experimental group which had experienced the special conditions between the first and second testing. If the projective test permits, some investigators prefer to counterbalance the order of presentation of the particular cards used, necessitating at least two experimental groups and two control groups. Another frequent design does not utilize a control group, the only comparison made being that of the first administration of the test with the second administration, with all differences between administrations assumed to be a function of the intervening conditions. A third procedure consists of administering a single test to groups known to differ on a particular dimension; all differences in test results are then attributed to the central, identifiable difference between the groups.

STRESS

The most careful, systematic effort to induce stress was that of Lindzey (1950a; 1950b), who frustrated his experimental Ss by subjecting them to 10 to 12 hours of food deprivation, inducing them to drink a large quantity of water and then preventing them from urinating for approximately three hours, taking a blood sample in a painful way with a spring lancet, and forcing them to fail in a group situation. As a consequence of these conditions, the Rosenzweig Picture-Frustration Test showed a significant increase in extrapunitive responses (Lindzey, 1950b). Of 12 predictions regarding changes in the TAT, 11 were in the expected direction, with 5 hypotheses confirmed at the .05 level of confidence or better (Lindzey & Herman, 1955). The effects of stress on the Rosenzweig P-F test were also studied by French (1950), who gave students in a social psychology class erroneous grades on an examination. Half the students who earned an A or B were given C or D, while half those earning a C or D were given an A or B. On the P-F test given immediately after the grades were returned, the good students given the poor grades (the stress group) did not differ from the good students who were assigned their correct grades. However, the poor students given the erroneously high grades showed fewer intropunitive ego-defensive responses than the poor students given their correct grade.

Eichler (1951) used an elaborate device resembling an electric chair to seat his Ss while taking the Rorschach. They were made to wear a helmet which looked as if it could conduct electricity and were told that while taking the test they would be given shock, "the longer the time interval that elapses without the receipt of shock the more intense the next shock will be." On the basis of an administration of the Behn-Rorschach test, the experimental group was matched on five variables with a control group that took the second Rorschach under standard conditions. Judges who made a blind global rating of the Rorschach protocols found a significant difference in anxiety between the two groups. On 15 anxiety indicators, however, they found that only 4 reflected a significant difference between groups, while 3 additional variables did not reach statistical significance but were in the predicted direction.

Less dramatic forms of frustration seem also to be effective in demonstrating how projective devices may reflect pretest conditions. Crandall's (1951) experimental Ss took tests of physical skills between administrations of the TAT and were informed that they had not met the "norm." A control group rested between test administrations. As a result of the failure situation, the experimental Ss' expectation for punishment as revealed in the TAT increased significantly.

Schwartz and Kates (1957) imposed stress by giving their Ss a fictitious "interpretation" of their Rorschach or Behn-Rorschach responses, showing them to be poorly adjusted. When the second test was administered, only 2 (FC and RT) of 16 preselected Rorschach variables showed significant differences as a function of the stress.

The best-adjusted and most poorly adjusted members of NYA camp were made to fail in performing with the Rotter Level of Aspiration Board. The pre- and postfrustration TAT records of the two groups differed in several ways, the poorly adjusted group showing a decrease in themes of superiority, aggression, and emotional states (Rodnick & Klebanoff, 1942).

Three studies did not impose stress experimentally but utilized Ss in "natural" stress conditions. Klatskin (1952) gave the Rorschach test to one group of patients the day before they were to receive gynecological surgery and to another group of patients the day before they were to be discharged from the obstetrical service. The hospital patients were matched on age and intelligence with a group of clerks. Of the 65 comparisons made between groups, 21 significant differences were found, generally indicating greater constriction and more self-preoccupation in the hospitalized Ss. In another study which utilized hospitalized Ss, Meyer, Brown, and Levine found that H-T-P drawings secured before surgery indicated far more regression than was apparent either clinically or in the postoperative drawings: "The contrast between the pre- and postoperative drawings were often so arresting as to cast doubt upon their being the product of the same individual" (1955, p. 431). Abel (1953), however, found conflicting patterns in human figure drawings in patients operated on for correction of facial disfigurement. Some patients made great changes in drawings as a result of corrective surgery, others made little change, while still a third group made dramatic changes in drawings even though no surgery had been performed.

Bellak (1944) made the stressful conditions part of the TAT test administration by criticizing ("These stories are about the worst I've ever heard," etc.) the S's efforts halfway through the testing session. He found that the stories following these remarks were characterized by an increase in aggressive words. Unfortunately, a control group was not used.

DRUGS

The effects of a wide variety of drugs have been studied by means of projective devices, particularly the Rorschach. While there is no record of a Rorschach being given under water, there are reports of Rorschachs given under the influence of mescaline, alcohol, sodium amytal, hyoscine, morphine, and oxygen deprivation. In general, these conditions produced limited effects on the test records. Sodium amytal seemed to make Ss more willing to co-operate in taking the Rorschach (Wilkins & Adams, 1947), and subsequent responses seemed less bizarre, permitting more detailed descriptions of personality (Kelley, Levine, Pemberton, & Katz, 1941). When Ss, given oxygen through a mask, reached a simulated altitude of 16,000 feet, their Rorschachs showed the same basic pattern as tests given under standard conditions, except for a decrease in movement responses and an increase in color responses (Hertzman & Seitz, 1942). Movement and color responses showed striking changes when the S was under the influence of mescaline (Guttman, 1936). Wertham and Bleuler (1932) have reported that the Rorschach test given under mescaline corresponded more closely to the personality as known in life than the standard Rorschach. They also reported the considerable difficulty in holding the experimental S to the task of attending to the Rorschach when he seemed to prefer to attend his own images. The administration of hyoscine to an S afflicted with encephalitis produced inconsistent changes in the Rorschach (Cofer, 1947).

While most Ss in these experiments were badgered, frustrated, and otherwise treated unpleasantly, in three studies Ss were served liquor in return for taking a projective test. In one investigation, between 9 and 15 ounces of 100-proof bourbon were served between administrations of the Rorschach. The conclusions of the experiment support the unsystematic observations of drinkers who have to buy their own: under the influence of alcohol, accuracy of perception, attention to details, self-critical attitudes, and self-controlling attitudes decrease (Rabin, Papania, & McMichael, 1954). Studies using the TAT (Tomkins, 1942) and the Rorschach (Kelley & Barrera, 1941) agree that projective responses given when the S is intoxicated may vary in minor details but do not differ in any consistent manner from responses given when sober.

Whether Brown's (1943) Ss were subjected to noxious or pleasant test conditions is a difficult distinction to make, since he administered morphine to 22 postaddict patients who had previously been abstinent from the drug for a minimum of six months. If the Ss did not experience the "right feeling" from the first experimental injection, the dose was increased until a euphoric state was reached. It was reported that intellectual control, originality, and organizational energy were not affected by morphine, but there was a shifting to greater imaginative living. There was no report on subsequent attitudes by the Ss toward the drug or this particular method of administering the Rorschach.

HYPNOSIS

The use of hypnosis with resistant test Ss was reported by Wilkins and Adams (1947), who found that this method produced co-operation and a useful test record. One S, studied intensively by having seven different moods induced while under hypnosis, was variously instructed that she was grief-stricken, euphoric, concerned about an undiagnosed illness, depressed, carrying on an extramarital affair, etc. While the content of the Rorschach test given immediately after the instructions changed from role to role, the similarity between records was great enough to show that the same underlying personality was being observed (Levine, Grassi, & Gerson, 1943; Levine, Grassi, & Gerson, 1944). A similar procedure was employed by Sarbin (1939), who told his S in one hypnotic session that she was Madame Curie and in another session that she was Mae West. A third Rorschach was given while the S was under hypnosis without any specific suggestion. It was found that the S tended to adopt the set imposed by the hypnotic instructions, so that half of her responses in the Madame Curie instructions concerned science while two-thirds of her responses in the Mae West set consisted of clothing and costume associations. The control Rorschach, given in the waking state, contained only two responses found in the hypnotic trance states. Hypnosis has also been used to study age regression (Bergmann, Graham, & Leavitt, 1947). The test responses of a 20-year-old S, given the Rorschach for the eight alternate years between 3 and 20, seemed to reflect the various stages in the development of his personality.

Two studies used the Rorschach with Ss who had been instructed under hypnosis to feel hostile toward the examiner (Counts & Mensh, 1950; Pattie, 1954). To illustrate the difficulties involved in using hypnosis for this purpose, the conclusions in one study were different from those in the other. Counts and Mensh (1950) found that the hostility to the E which appeared during the psychiatric interview was not reflected in the Rorschach, while Pattie (1954) could divide his 14 Ss into three groups, one of which (N=8) showed a twofold increase in hostile content in the posthypnotic Rorschach. The number of white space responses did not increase under the hostile instructions. A considerable degree of individual differences was also found by Arluck and Balinsky (1953), who used as the hypnotic suggestion "you are mature, warm and outgoing," etc. For some Ss the responses on both the Rorschach and a sentence completion test showed numerous differences with prehypnotic test records, but for others the two sessions produced highly similar results.

Qualitative and quantitative differences following the hypnotic induction of an elated mood and a despondent mood were found on a word association test (Fisher & Marrow, 1934). The reaction times were longest for unpleasantly toned words and were fastest for neutral words.

SPECIAL TRAINING AND EXPERIENCE

Several experiments have investigated the influence of perceptual training on Rorschach scores. Knopf (1954) provided pre-Rorschach perceptual training in finding animal or animal parts for one group of Ss, while the second group watched a film on the nature of color. He concluded that the over-all picture of the personality remained basically unchanged. Kurtz and Riggs (1954) similarly found no differences in group Rorschach scores in Ss who had first been exposed to a visual set to perceive animals. "So far as this study is concerned, Rorschach workers remain secure in the assumption that implicit peripheral sets will not influence test results to any appreciable extent" (p. 469). Nor did Norman, Leverant, and Redlo (1952) find that Rorschach scores were altered by having one group of Ss first look at colored food ads while another group looked at pictures of people in motion. Evidence that perceptual training can influence Rorschach performance has been reported by Keyes

(1954) and Leventhal (1956). Subjects trained on stimuli similar to the Street Gestalt pictures produced an increase in the number of whole responses on the group Rorschach (Keyes, 1954). Training on the Gottschaldt figures before an administration of the group Rorschach resulted in lower W and Z scores (Leventhal, 1956).

Giving children a "gratifying" experience prior to testing seemed to improve performance on the Draw-a-Person test (Reichenberg-Hackett, 1953). Coleman (1947) showed a neutrally toned film to children the evening before they took the second half of the TAT. Of the 370 stories told after the film, only one clearly reflected the content of the film. Kimble (1945) gave the Rorschach test twice, once in the standard office procedure and once in the college cafeterias with at least two other people present. The test results were quite similar in the two situations, the most important difference occurring in the experience balance, more color responses being given in the social situation. Gibby, Stotsky, and Miller (1954) concluded that the experience of taking a psychological test (Bender-Gestalt, TAT, Wechsler-Bellevue, or Goldstein-Scheerer) immediately before an administration of the Rorschach did not alter any of 11 selected Rorschach variables.

DEPRIVATION OR AROUSAL OF NEEDS

The effects of hunger on associations to ambiguous stimuli have received the attention of three investigators. School children showed more food associations on a word association test shortly before a regular meal than on the test given after the meal (Sanford, 1936). Undergraduates who had fasted for 24 hours before taking five projective tests gave more food responses than did Ss who had abstained from food for shorter periods of time. The increase was not a straight-line function of time, however, the most hungry Ss giving only slightly more food responses than the groups examined near the end of a normal eating cycle (Sanford, 1937). Atkinson and McClelland (1948) were able to derive a food score on TAT stories that could differentiate reliably among groups deprived of food for 1, 4, or 16 hours. While there was no increase in food imagery in these stories, there was a marked increase in food deprivation themes. While the TAT may be able to reflect a state of food deprivation, the report of Franklin and Brožek (1949) indicated that the Rosenzweig P-F test responses of a group of conscientious objectors did not change significantly from a period of semistarvation to a state of nutritional rehabilitation.

Two studies investigated the effects of motor inhibition on the production of movement responses in the Rorschach test. Korchin, Meltzoff, and Singer (1951) restricted normal motor behavior in their Ss by having them write a standard phrase as slowly as possible. Singer, Meltzoff, and Goldman (1952) reduced the motor behavior of Ss by requesting them to stand for five minutes without moving. In each experiment, the Ss denied motor activity gave more movement responses than a control group. However, Singer et al. (1952) also found that increasing motor behavior (by having Ss engage in five minutes of vigorous calisthenics) did not reduce the number of movement responses.

The relationship of experimentally aroused needs on projective test responses has also been investigated. When the need for achievement was induced by means of ego-involving instructions, stories of college men increased in achievement-imagery themes and themes of instrumental acts and attitudes related to achievement (McClelland, Clark, Roby, & Atkinson, 1949). The stories told by high school boys to pictures of male figures also showed an increased number of themes related to achievement as a result of special achievement-arousing conditions. These achievement-arousing conditions, however, were not effective in increasing achievement themes of either high school girls or college girls (Veroff, Wilcox, & Atkinson, 1953).

A sociometric test given prior to the administration of the TAT seemed to increase themes related to the affilation motive (Shipley & Veroff, 1952; Atkinson, Heyns, & Veroff, 1953). Freshmen who were rejected for membership in a fraternity gave more affiliation themes on the TAT than students who were accepted into fraternities (Shipley & Veroff, 1952).

Clark (1952) attempted to raise the level of sexual motivation by showing Ss slides of nude females before administering the TAT. A control group was shown slides of landscapes. Under these conditions, the group shown the slides of the nudes gave fewer manifest sexual responses and fewer themes of guilt than the control Ss. However, when the experiment was repeated after all the Ss had participated in a beer party, the experimental group gave more stories of manifest sex and guilt than those Ss who had been shown the landscape slides. Rabin, Nelson, and Clark (1954) had one group of undergraduate males waiting to take the Rorschach test remain in a room decorated with anatomical charts and surgical pictures; a second group, somewhat more fortunate in their assignment to experimental conditions, was seated in a room decorated with photographs of nude and seminude females; the control group waited in an undecorated room. While there was no difference between groups in the number of anatomy responses, there was a significant difference in the number of sexual responses.

The Influence of the Examiner

While the evidence regarding situational factors in projective testing has been compiled over the years, the studies dealing with interpersonal influences is of rather recent origin. Guilford and Lacey's study (1947) was the first in this area, and it was three years before the next experiments were reported. The relative neglect of this problem was not entirely due to lack of awareness of its importance, since Macfarlane wrote that "interpretation in the hands of the clinically inexperienced, the doctrinaire, or the methodologically uninformed easily degenerates into nothing more but one more predictive tool—to wit, one which discloses the organizing dynamics of the interpreter rather than the organizing dynamics of the research subject" (1942, p. 405), and Joel warned that "even if it were possible for the examiner always actually to feel the way he pretends he does, we should not forget that the subject reacts not only to the examiner's real attitude, but also to what he thinks the examiner's attitude is" (1949, p. 480). Probably the greatest deterrents to exploration of this question were the facts that the notion of E influence struck at the heart of the X-ray concept of projective tests, and the extreme complexity and subtlety of the interpersonal testing situation so aptly discussed by Schafer (1954), made experimentation difficult.

The first studies tested the hypothesis that Es would differ in the responses they elicited from Ss by analyzing test records secured from the files of a clinic. As interest turned to determining which characteristics of Es were related to differences in Ss' responses, such physical attributes of Es as skin color, size, and sex were investigated, as well as personality variables revealed in psychological tests, generally the Rorschach. The interaction of E and S has been studied on several occasions, either by controlling the warm-cold dimension or by contrasting tests taken with E present with those taken with E absent.

A completely different approach to this problem is through the use of hypnosis. While no study used hypnosis primarily to investigate the testing relationship, most of the experiments using hypnosis do report that S's test behavior varied with the hypnotic suggestion. Thus far only two studies (Gross, 1959; Wickes, 1956) have attempted to establish operant conditioning of S's verbal behavior, but this method seems so promising that undoubtedly it will become more widely used in investigating examiner influence.

THE EXAMINER'S PHYSICAL CHARACTERISTICS

The most immediately apparent characteristics of the E are his skin color, sex, and body build. Each of these attributes has been investigated for possible influence on the S's responses. Three studies related the sex of E to sexual responses on the Rorschach test. Alden and Benton (1951) selected 100 Rorschach records from the files of a VA hospital; all test Ss were males, 50 of them tested by a female E and 50 by a male. There were no significant differences in either overt or covert sexual responses that could be attributed to the sex of E. Exactly contradictory results were reported by Curtis and Wolf (1951). Again using the

Rorschach record of male veterans, comparisons were made of the overt and covert sexual responses given by 386 Ss to three female and seven male Es. Statistically significant differences were obtained. Rabin, Nelson, and Clark (1954) found that sometimes the sex of E makes a difference and sometimes it does not. The Ss who had waited for the Rorschach examination in a room decorated with anatomical charts did not differ in the number of anatomical responses given to the male and female Es, but those male Ss who had waited in a room decorated with pictures of nude women gave significantly more sexual responses to the male E than to the female. Clark (1952) found that male Ss gave more manifest sexual responses and more guilt responses on the TAT to a male E than to an attractive, rather seductive, female E.

The influence of the E's size and sex on Draw-a-Person productions were investigated by Holtzman (1952), who found that none of his 12 judges could guess better than chance either the sex or the identity of the Es by inspecting the drawings of 40 male and 40 female Ss. Two male Es, one of whom was nearly a foot taller and 60 pounds heavier than the other, and two female Es differing in "degree of feminine qualities," were used. Garfield, Blek, and Melker (1952) used two female and two male Es to administer the TAT to 54 male and 56 female Ss. Neither the sex of the E nor the interaction of the sex of E and S produced significant differences in the stories.

Riess, Schwartz, and Cottingham (1950) investigated the responses of Negro and white Ss to Negro and white stimulus figures on TAT cards administered by a Negro and white E and concluded that skin color of the E did not affect the length of stories. While most investigators look for the influence of the E in verbalized test responses, Rankin and Campbell (1955) used as their dependent variable the galvanic skin response of male Ss to a Negro and white E. In a word association situation, the E checked and adjusted on four occasions dummy equipment connected to S's left wrist. It was found that there was a higher differential galvanic skin response to the Negro E, but since he was nine years older, 2½ inches taller, and 27 pounds heavier than the white E, there was no conclusive proof that the difference was a function of skin color.

PRESENCE OR ABSENCE OF EXAMINER FROM THE TESTING ROOM

Bernstein (1956) found that TAT stories written in the absence of the E more frequently contained sad themes and outcomes and showed greater S involvement than stories written with the E present in the testing room. Certain aspects of H-T-P drawings secured from applicants for employment at a state school were found to be a function of the E's presence when the test was taken. Total size of the drawing, house size, house features, and person features all differed significantly between the group taking the test with E present and the group taking the test with the E absent (Cassel, Johnson, & Burns, 1958). VanKrevelen (1954b) tested 20 Ss with two cards of the MAPS series; one story was dictated to her, and the other was written in her absence. The only significant difference between the two groups was that the more ambiguous of the two cards produced more words in the written, E-absent situation. The absence of the e seemed to have more effect on Szondi test results (VanKrevelen, 1954a). The Ss were sometimes administered the Szondi by the E and at other times took the test themselves. When E was absent, Ss showed greater consistency, demonstrated more plus-minus reactions, and had a greater sum of open and plus-minus reactions than when E was present.

WARM-COLD EXAMINER BEHAVIOR

Luft (1953) varied the interaction between E and S by acting warm and friendly to some Ss and cold and blunt to others. The cold interaction consisted of asking the Ss their social security number and draft status and giving a short quiz on current events (e.g., "Which horse won the Kentucky Derby?") before administering 10 homemade ink blots. When the Ss were asked which ink blots they liked and which they disliked, the group treated in the warm fashion indicated that they liked a mean of 7.6 blots, while the cold Ss liked only a mean of 3.1 blots, a difference significant beyond the .001 level. Lord (1950) used three styles of administering the Rorschach—neutral, positive, and negative—and three male Es. In the positive interaction, E was instructed to look at S with a smile and to be warm and charming; the negative interaction called for E to assume the role of a harsh, demanding, authoritative figure, deliberately unconcerned about S. Each S took the Rorschach three times with the order of E and administration counterbalanced. As a result of the different methods of interaction, the protocols elicited from the warm administration produced more responses, more evidence of intellectual and creative imagination, less indication of stereotyped thinking, and increased evidence of greater ease in interpersonal relations. In the cold administration, responses indicating imaginative, creative thinking were reduced, there appeared to be a withdrawal from emotional stimuli, and there was a rise in self-questioning feelings.

OPERANT CONDITIONING OF SUBJECT'S VERBAL BEHAVIOR

Two studies investigated the extent to which S's associations to ink blots could be determined by the E's behavior. Wickes (1956) used 30 homemade ink blots, two Es, and 36 undergraduate Ss divided into two experimental groups and one control group. In one experimental group the first 15 cards were given in the standard manner; with Card 16 the E said, "fine," to the first movement response, "good," to the second movement response, and "all right" to the third movement response, making these comments in regular sequence to the end of the testing. In the second experimental group, the first 15 cards were given in standard fashion, but with Card 16 the E made various postural and gestural changes, nodding his head three times to the first movement response, and leaning forward in the chair after the third movement response, repeating this sequence to the end of the testing. When the responses on the first 15 and second 15 cards were compared for all groups, it was found that the experimental group given verbal reinforcement made a significant increase (.025 level) in movement responses on the second half of the test, the experimental group given postural reinforcement made a significant increase (.005 level) in movement responses in the second half of the test, while there was no difference in the number of movement responses in the control group. Gross (1959) verbally reinforced ("good") one group of Ss for each human response on the Rorschach, while for a second group he nodded his head once following each human response. Both the verbally reinforced group and the nonverbally reinforced group produced more human responses than a control group.

THE EFFECT OF THE EXAMINER AS A PERSON:
NO ASSESSMENT OF EXAMINER PERSONALITY

In a report not seen by the writer, but quoted by Lord (1950) and others, Guilford and Lacey (1947) concluded that some Es elicited more responses from their Ss in administering the Rorschach test than other Es. Baughman (1951) also noted that certain Es seemed to produce more responses in selected Rorschach categories than other Es. He selected 633 protocols secured by 15 Es from the files of a veteran's outpatient clinic and found 12 of 22 scoring categories differing significantly at the .001 level, with 4 additional differences significant at the .05 level. Unfortunately, the protocols were not scored by the investigator, so that the differences found may have resulted from the psychologists' procedures in scoring rather than from their influence on S. Both Wickes (1956) and Bernstein (1956) used two Es in their studies, and each concluded that the psychologists did not exert any significant influence on the Ss' responses.

To control for some of the sources of variation in responding to the Rorschach, Gibby (1952) had 9 Es use a standardized inquiry in testing 135 Ss. Despite this, significant differences in responses were found for 6 of the 11 determinants investigated. "The stimulus value of the examiner therefore must be considered a factor which influences the inquiry responses of the subject and therefore the final Rorschach psychogram. Standardization of the inquiry does not eliminate examiner differences" (Gibby, 1952, p. 452). An attempt was made by Gibby, Miller, and Walker (1953) to secure a homogeneous group of patients whose

Rorschach records could be analyzed for E influence. All Ss used were male veterans, white, 25 to 32 years old, had functional rather than organic ailments, and were the most recent patients tested by E. All 12 Es whose records were analyzed had a minimum of two years experience, used Beck's Rorschach method, and had tested at least 20 Ss who met the criteria for the study. All protocols were coded and scored blindly. Of the nine absolute scores which were investigated, three were significant at the .05 level or better, and of the eight percentage scores, three were significant at the .05 level or better. The investigators concluded that "there are significant over-all differences in the determinants obtained by various examiners from comparable groups of subjects. . . It is also probable that certain examiners tend to obtain successively dysphoric records while others with comparable patients will seldom elicit such reactions" (Gibby et al., p. 426).

Robinson and Cohen (1954) examined the case reports prepared by three psychological interns. The last 30 reports for each of the three interns were examined for the variables of dependence, independence, aggression, and abasement. When the incidence of these variables in the case reports was compared for each of the three psychologists, 6 of the 12 comparisions were significant at the .05 level. When components of these variables were considered, 12 of the 24 comparisons were significant at the .05 level of confidence. The investigators concluded that this study raises "a serious question about the objectivity of methods of evaluation and prediction if they must rely solely upon psychological reports for their basis" (Robinson & Cohen, 1954, p. 335).

THE EFFECT OF THE EXAMINER AS A PERSON; EXAMINER'S PERSONALITY ASSESSED

Hammer and Piotrowski (1953) asked three staff psychologists and three interns to rate 400 H-T-P drawings on a 3-point scale of aggression. The clinicians were themselves rated by one of the investigators on the degree of aggression and hostility they manifested in dealing with patients and staff members. In addition, the clinicians also took the Szondi test, which was scored by Susan Deri for degree of hostile and aggressive impulses. A rank-order correlation of .94 was found for the degree of hostility the clinicians saw in the H-T-P productions and the evaluation made of their interpersonal hostility. The rating of the clinicians' Szondi tests also yielded a rank order correlation of .94 with their evaluations of the hostility in the H-T-P. The authors concluded that "just as a subject's performance on a projective technique is a function of his personality, his needs, conflicts, desires and past experiences, so too, although to a lesser degree, is the interpretation of a projective protocol influenced by the personality pattern of the interpreter" (Hammer & Piotrowski, 1953, pp. 214-215). Filer (1952) analyzed 156 case reports submitted by 13 male clinicians for references to hostility, hostility turned inward, passive dependency, and feelings of inferiority. Evaluations were also obtained of the clinician's behavior in terms of ascendancy, depression, intropunitiveness, extrapunitiveness, and impunitiveness. The results indicated a complex relationship between the judgments of the clinician and the judgments made by the clinician. For example, Es who stressed hostility turned inward were rated depressed and intrapunitive. A separate study of references to defense mechanisms indicated that the three most frequently mentioned mechanisms were more characteristic of E than the test S.

Berger (1954) used the personal Rorschach results of eight VA trainees to compare with the Rorschach records these Es elicited from VA patients. Contrary to the findings of most other studies, Berger found no significant differences in E influence on 12 variables in the patients' Rorschachs. However, when both the E and his Ss were rank-ordered on the 12 variables, a rho correlation of .86 was found for the number of popular responses, a rho of .80 for white space responses, and a rho of — .54 for Y responses.

Lord (1950) did not attempt to make a formal assessment of the personalities of her three female Es, but she obtained descriptions of them at a subjective, intuitive level from two clinicians, relating these descriptions to the Rorschach responses secured from Ss. The first E, described by the judges as a cold, inflexible, masculine, castrating woman, produced Rorschachs from her Ss that made it appear that they had faced a threatening, frustrating situation. The second E, described as the most feminine of the group, the softest and most motherlike, elicited Rorschach records that suggested her Ss had been under controlled excitement without great anxiety or tension and had not been greatly stimulated intellectually. The third E was the oldest of the three and was described as the most flexible, exuberant, sympathetic, intermediate in feminine qualities. Her Ss' Rorschach records suggested that they had been challenged and made anxious, but there was also evidence of easy rapport and a relative absence of controlling devices.

The TAT and MMPI records of nine Es were evaluated and compared with the Rorschach responses the Es had elicited. An analysis of E variance showed 22 of 37 selected Rorschach variables significant at the .05 level or better (Miller, Sanders, & Cleveland, 1950). Sanders and Cleveland (1953) trained nine second-year graduate students to administer the Rorschach test after first obtaining a personal Rorschach from each. After a period of training, each E administered 20 Rorschachs to undergraduate Ss; at the end of each testing session S was asked to rate E on measures of overt anxiety and hostility. Indications of Es' covert anxiety and hostility were obtained by rating their personal Rorschach records. When the number of responses given by each S was held constant, it was found that of the 20 variables investigated, 9 differed significantly among Es. The Es rated high on overt anxiety by their Ss elicited more responses, more white space responses, and more color responses than those rated low in overt anxiety. No differences in Ss' scores could be accounted for by scores of the Es on covert anxiety. The Es rated high on hostility by their Ss elicited greater Y%, and A% in the Rorschachs they administered and secured less hostile and human content than those Es whose Ss rated them low in hostility. The Ss' reaction times seemed slower when E was perceived as hostile, a finding in agreement with the observation made of the test behavior of Ss with hypnotically induced hostility to E (Counts & Mensh, 1950; Pattie, 1954). When Es' personal Rorschachs were examined for hostility, it was found that the more hostile Es elicited less Y% less A%, more hostile content, and more human content than those Es with low covert hostility. The authors concluded, "The results of this study provide evidence that a subject's responses on the Rorschach test are not solely a product of his own emotional problems and personality structure" (Sanders & Cleveland, 1953, p. 48). While the investigators clearly indicated that E as a person can influence the test results, they estimated that the extent of this influence can account for only 3 to 7 per cent of the total variance in the Rorschach scores.

The Influence of the Subject

While there is wide theoretical agreement that each party in the testing situation exerts an influence on the other, the experimental evidence is limited almost entirely to the effect E has on S. Perhaps the chief reason for the failure to investigate the manner in which S can influence the psychologist is the lack of traditional experimental procedures that can afford control of the S's behavior while the E's behavior is allowed to vary. The one study in this area (Masling, 1957) controlled S's behavior by using attractive female accomplices who posed as test Ss, acting warm or cold to E. The dependent variable was the interpretation placed on sentence completion protocols by eight graduate-student Es. It was found that when S acted warm to E, her protocol was interpreted more favorably (i.e., she was seen in better mental health) than when she acted cold. In addition, the results indicated that when E saw two Ss, one of whom was cold and the other warm, the protocol of the warm S was interpreted more favorably than that of the cold S.

Discussion

The studies presented in this paper have been reviewed rather uncritically, with the emphasis on content rather than on adequacy of experimental design. Since faulty experimental procedures appear with regularity in the studies in this area, it might be worth while to examine more closely the more commonly found limitations in design.

1. No study reviewed here extensively sampled the E population. As Hammond (1954) has indicated, representative design demands that both E and S populations be adequately sampled if generalizations are to be made to larger groups of S and E. Most studies cited here, however, utilized only one E, with only Baughman (1951) using as many as 15 Es. The general results of the work on E differences makes clear how tenuous it is to assume that one E is drawn from the same population as any other E.

2. Not only has the E population been inadequately sampled, but the little attention given to Es has been directed for the most part to graduate students. While it is legitimate to work with a graduate-student population, it is inappropriate to generalize findings to a population of older, more experienced Es.

3. Those studies which investigated the influence of E differences by utilizing a random sample of cases found in the files of a clinic make the assumption, as Levy (1956) has indicated, that the cases were originally assigned on a random basis. This assumption may not always be valid, due to differences in E schedules, interests, and competence. As a result, differences in test records may be in part a function of uncontrolled bias in the selection of Ss. It is far better procedure for the investigator to control the assignment of cases than to assume existing cases had been randomly assigned.

4. A frequent method of assessing E personality has been to ask the E to take a psychological test. As the results of this review make quite clear, the orientation S has toward the test considerably influences his responses. Few graduate students in psychology are naive regarding the more common projective tests, even if they have never seen them before. The meaning of a Rorschach test taken by a graduate student, therefore, is unclear and cannot be easily related to differences in Ss' responses. A better way of evaluating E's personality might be to obtain judgments by his supervisors and colleagues. Another method that shows promise is that used by Sanders and Cleveland (1953), who asked the test Ss to make ratings of their impressions of E.

5. Most investigations of susceptibility of Ss' responses to situational influence have been conducted empirically, with no prior attempt made to predict where differences would be found. Research on the Rorschach has been particularly culpable in this regard. Since the Rorschach is still primarily an empirically, rather than theoretically, based instrument, most investigators have attempted to determine only if differences would occur between experimental and control groups, but, on finding differences, have been unable to interpret their meaning. As a result of this approach, almost every Rorschach score has at one time or another

been found to be a function of some experimental variable: Z, W, W%, Ds, D, Dd%, F—, F+%, F%, FM, m, M, CF, C, Y, Y%, A, A%, P, R, reaction time, and experience balance have all been reported to change as a result of experimental conditions.

6. Many of the Rorschach studies appearing before Cronbach's (1949) critique of Rorschach research did not control for the number of responses, but assumed that all differences in determinants could be attributed to the experimental variable. To a large extent, investigators now attempt to partial out differences in the number of responses, but an occasional study will still disregard this factor. While most of the other statistical errors Cronbach discussed occur far less frequently in later research, inflation of probability levels continues to be a major source of error.

Despite these flaws in design, the studies cited here presented strong evidence of situational and interpersonal influences in projective testing. It is important to note, however, that the projective response did not change with any and all conditions imposed by the E. The use of drugs produced only minimal changes in the protocol, and there was conflicting evidence regarding the importance of such physical differences among Es as skin color, sex, and size. What appeared to be the crucial element was the extent to which S's attitude toward the *total* testing situation was influenced by the experimental conditions. Where the experimental variable was peripheral to the examination, as in Coleman's (1947) showing of a film the night before administering the TAT, no appreciable effect was introduced in the protocol; when the condition was sufficiently unique and sufficiently contiguous to the testing session, as in the use of a waiting room decorated with pictures of nude women (Rabin, Nelson, & Clark, 1954), Ss evidently construed the experimental conditions to be a part of the total testing situation.

There is considerable evidence that Ss in an unstructured situation will utilize all available cues to complete their assigned task. The S in the projective test setting will not only use those cues furnished by the ink blot or picture but also those supplied by his feelings about the examiner, those furnished by his needs, attitudes, and fears, those implied in the instructions, the room, and previous knowledge of the test, and those cues supplied consciously or unconsciously by E. When E faces the ambiguous situation of supplying meaning to a series of isolated, discrete responses, he will rely not only on S's responses, but also on those cues furnished by his training and theoretical orientation, his own needs and expectations, his feelings about S, and the constructions he places on S's test behavior and attitudes. In short, these studies demonstrate that E and S behave as we should expect, considering our knowledge of behavior in ambiguous settings.

Thus, the procedure that many clinicians hoped would serve as an X ray proves, on close examination, to function also as a mirror, reflecting impartially S, E, the situation, and their interactions. This need not be a cause for despair, except for those who feel that E and situational influences contaminate a protocol. These influences are not sources of error, however, but indications of adaptation to the task. One reason for the poor record of blind analysis as a procedure for validating projective devices is that this method can utilize only a fraction of the material available in a protocol. Instead of trying to eliminate interpersonal and situational influence, E might better make a more thorough search of his own attitudes and of S's attitudes toward the test and the situation (Leventhal, Rosenblatt, Gluck, & Slepian, 1958). The interpersonal situation "is not an evil. It should not be striven against. As in psychoanalytic technique, this relationship must be regarded as inevitable, as a potentially significant influence on the patient's productions, and as a possible goldmine of material for interpretation" (Schafer, 1954, p. 6).

The important problems in this area remain unsolved. What effect does experience have on E's sensitivity to the attitudes of S? Of what importance is the psychological health of S in his response to the attitudes of E? Little is understood about the circumstances which prompt an S to rely heavily on interpersonal cues, nor do we know much of the forces acting on an E who is faced with a belligerent or overly co-operative or suspicious S. Most important of all, the great bulk of the studies cited here indicate only that situational and interpersonal variables influence the projective protocol, without in any way describing how these variables impinge on E and S. How S senses that E is hostile and how E realizes S is trying to control him can only be determined by studying the interaction process itself. It is interesting to note that no study reviewed here used verbatim recordings of the testing session, despite the growing popularity of verbatim transcripts in research on psychotherapy. Hopefully, future research on projective testing will investigate more fully the step-by-step transactions between E and S.

REFERENCES

ABEL, T. M. Figure drawings and facial disfigurement. *Amer. J. Orthopsychiat.*, 1913, 23, 253–264.

ABRAMSON, L. S. The influence of set for area on the Rorschach test results. *J. consult. Psychol.*, 1951, 15, 337–342.

ALDEN, PRISCILLA, & BENTON, A. L. Relationship of sex of examiner to incidence of Rorschach responses with sexual content. *J. proj. Tech.*, 1951, 15, 230–234.

ARLUCK, E. W., & BALINSKY, B. Possible shifts in functioning through hypnotic suggestion. *J. proj. Tech.*, 1953, 17, 447–454.

ATKINSON, J. W., HEYNS, R. W., & VEROFF, J. Effect of experimental arousal of the affiliation motive on thematic apperception. *Amer. Psychologist*, 1953, 8, 313–314. (Abstract)

ATKINSON, J. W., & McCLELLAND, D. C. The projective expression of needs: II. The effect of different intensities of the hunger drive on thematic apperception. *J. exp. Psychol.*, 1948, 38, 643–658.

BAUGHMAN, E. E. Rorschach scores as a function of examiner differences. *J. proj. Tech.*, 1951, 15, 243–249.

BELLAK, L. The concept of projection: An experimental investigation and study of the concept. *Psychiatry*, 1944, 7, 353–370.

BERGER, D. Examiner influence on the Rorschach. *J. clin. Psychol.*, 1954, 10, 245–248.

BERGMANN, M. S., GRAHAM, H., & LEAVITT, H. C. Rorschach exploration of consecutive hypnotic chronological age level regression. *Psychosom. Med.*, 1947, 9, 20–28.

BERNSTEIN, L. The examiner as inhibiting factor in clinical testing. *J. consult. Psychol.*, 1956, 20, 287–290.

BROWN, R. R. The effect of morphine upon the Rorschach pattern in post-addicts. *Amer. J. Orthopsychiat.*, 1943, 13, 339–343.

CALDEN, G., & COHEN, L. B. The relationship between ego-involvement and test definition to Rorschach test performance. *J. proj. Tech.*, 1953, 17, 300–311.

CARP, A. L., & SHAVZIN, A. R. The susceptibility to falsification of the Rorschach diagnostic technique. *J. consult. Psychol.*, 1950, 3, 230–233.

CASSEL, R. H., JOHNSON, ANNA, & BURNS, W. H. Examiner, ego-defense and the H-T-P test. *J. clin. Psychol.*, 1958, 14, 157–160.

CLARK, R. A. The projective measurement of experimentally induced levels of sexual motivation. *J. exp. Psychol.*, 1952, 44, 391–399.

COFER, C. N. Psychological test performance under hyoscine: A case of post-infectious encephalopathy. *J. gen. Psychol.*, 1947, 36, 221–228.

COFFIN, T. E. Some conditions of suggestion and suggestibility: A study of certain attitudinal and situational factors influencing the process of suggestion. *Psychol. Monogr.*, 1941, 53, No. 4 (Whole No. 241).

COLEMAN, W. The thematic apperception test: I. Effect of recent experiences. II. Some quantitative observations. *J. clin. Psychol.*, 1947, 3, 257–264.

COUNTS, R. M., & MENSH, I. N. Personality characteristics in hypnotically induced hostility. *J. clin. Psychol.*, 1950, 6, 325–330.

CRANDALL, V. S. Induced frustration and punishment reward expectancy in thematic apperception stories. *J. consult. Psychol.*, 1951, 15, 400–404.

CRONBACH, L. J. Statistical methods applied to Rorschach scores. *Psychol. Bull.*, 1949, 46, 393–429.

CRONBACH, L. J. Assessment of individual differences. In P. R. Fransworth (Ed.), *Annual review of psychology*. Stanford: Ann. Rev., 1956.

CURTIS, H. S., & WOLF, ELIZABETH. The influence of the sex of the examiner on the prediction of sex responses on the Rorschach. *Amer. Psychologist*, 1951, 6, 345–346. (Abstract)

EICHLER, R. M. Experimental stress and alleged Rorschach indices of anxiety. *J. abnorm. soc. Psychol.*, 1951, 46, 344–355.

FABRIKANT, B. Rigidity and flexibility on the Rorschach. *J. clin. Psychol.*, 1954, 10, 255–258.

FILER, R. M. The clinician's personality and his case reports. *Amer. Psychologist*, 1952, 7, 336. (Abstract)

FISHER, V., & MARROW, A. Experimental study of moods. *Charact. & Pers.*, 1934, 2, 201–208.

FOSBERG, I. A. Rorschach reactions under varied instructions. *Rorschach Res. Exch.*, 1938, 3, 12–30.

FOSBERG, I. A. An experimental study of the reliability of the Rorschach psychodiagnostic technique. *Rorschach Res. Exch.*, 1941, 5, 72–84.

FOSBERG, I. A. How do subjects fake results on the Rorschach test? *Rorschach Res. Exch.*, 1943, 7, 119–121.

FRANK, L. K. Projective methods for the study of personality. *J. Psychol.*, 1939, 8, 389–413.

FRANKLIN, J. C., & BROŽEK, J. The Rosenzweig P-F test as a measure of frustration response in semistarvation. *J. consult. Psychol.*, 1949, 13, 293–301.

FRENCH, R. L. Changes in performance on the Rosenzweig picture-frustration study following experimentally induced frustration. *J. consult. Psychol.*, 1950, 14, 111–115.

GARFIELD, S., BLEK, LIBBY, & MELKER, F. The influence of method of administration and sex differences on selected aspects of TAT stories. *J. consult. Psychol.*, 1952, 16, 140–145.

GIBBY, R. G. The stability of certain Rorschach variables under conditions of experimentally induced sets: I. The intellectual variable. *J. proj. Tech.*, 1951, 15, 3–26.

GIBBY, R. G. Examiner influence on the Rorschach inquiry. *J. consult. Psychol.*, 1952, 16, 449–455.

GIBBY, R. G., MILLER, D. R., & WALKER, E. L. The examiner's influence on the Rorschach protocol. *J. consult. Psychol.*, 1953, 17, 425–428.

GIBBY, R. G., STOTSKY, B. A., & MILLER, D. R. Influence of the preceding test on the Rorschach protocol. *J. consult. Psychol.*, 1954, 18, 463–464.

GROSS, L. Effects of verbal and nonverbal reinforcement in the Rorschach. *J. consult. Psychol.*, 1959, 23, 66–68.

GUILFORD, J. P., & LACEY, J. I. (Eds.) Printed classification tests. (*AAF Aviat. Psychol. Program Res. Rep. No. 5.*) Washington: U.S. Government Printing Office, 1947.

GUTTMAN, E. Artificial psychoses produced by mescaline. *J. ment. Sci.*, 1936, 52, 203–221.

HAMMER, E. F., & PIOTROWSKI, Z. A. Hostility as a factor in the clinician's personality as it affects his interpretation of projective drawings (H-T-P). *J. proj. Tech.*, 1953, 17, 210–216.

HAMMOND, K. R. Representative vs. systematic design in clinical psychology. *Psychol. Bull.*, 1954, 51, 150–159.

HENRY, EDITH, & ROTTER, J. B. Situational influence on Rorschach responses. *J. consult. Psychol.*, 1956, 6, 457–462.

HERTZMAN, M., & SEITZ, C. Rorschach reactions at high altitudes. *J. Psychol.*, 1942, 14,, 245–257.

HOLTZMAN, W. H. The examiner as a variable in the draw-a-person test. *J. consult. Psychol.*, 1952, 16, 145–148.

HUTT, M., GIBBY, R. G., MILTON, E. O., & POTTHARST, K. The effect of varied experimental "sets" upon Rorschach test performance. *J. proj. Tech.*, 1950, 14, 181–187.

JOEL, W. The interpersonal equation in projective methods. *Rorschach Res. Exch.*, 1949, 13, 479–482.

KELLEY, D., & BARRERA, S. Rorschach studies in acute experimental alcoholic intoxication. *Amer. J. Psychiat.*, 1941, 97, 1341–1364.

KELLEY, D., LEVINE, KATE, PEMBERTON, W., & KATZ, K. Intravenous sodium amytal medication as an aid to the Rorschach method. *Psychiat. Quart.*, 1941, 15, 68–73.

KEYES, E. J. An experimental investigation of some sources of variance in the whole response to the Rorschach ink blots. *J. clin. Psychol.*, 1954, 10, 155–160.

KIMBLE, G. A. Social influence on Rorschach records. *J. abnorm. soc. Psychol.*, 1945, 40, 89–93.

KLATSKIN, ETHELYN. An analysis of the test situation upon the Rorschach record: Formal scoring characteristics. *J. proj. Tech.*, 1952, 16, 193–199.

KNOPF, I. J. The effects of recent perceptual training and experience on Rorschach performance. *J. clin. Psychol.*, 1954, 10, 52–56.

KORCHIN, S., MELTZOFF, J., & SINGER, J. L. Motor inhibition and Rorschach movement responses. *Amer. Psychologist*, 1951, 6, 344–345. (Abstract)

KURTZ, JOSEPHINE, & RIGGS, MARGARET. An attempt to influence the Rorschach test by means of a peripheral set. *J. consult. Psychol.*, 1954, 18, 465–470.

LEVENTHAL, H. The influence of previous perceptual experience on the variance of the Rorschach W and Z scores. *J. consult. Psychol.*, 1956, 20, 93–98.

LEVENTHAL, T., ROSENBLATT, B., GLUCK, M., & SLEPIAN, H. The use of the psychologist-patient relationship in individual diagnostic testing. *Amer. Psychologist*, 1958, 13, 345. (Abstract)

LEVINE, KATE, GRASSI, J. R., & GERSON, M. J. Hypnotically induced mood changes in the verbal and graphic Rorschach: A case study. *Rorschach Res. Exch.*, 1943, 7, 130–144.

LEVINE, KATE, GRASSI, J. R., & GERSON, M. J. Hypnotically induced mood changes in the verbal and graphic Rorschach: Part II. The response records. *Rorschach Res. Exch.*, 1944, 8, 104–124.

LEVY, L. H. A note on research methodology used in testing for examiner influence in clinical test performance. *J. consult. Psychol.*, 1956, 20, 286.

LINDZEY, G. An experimental examination of the scapegoat theory of prejudice. *J. abnorm. soc. Psychol.*, 1950, 45, 296–309. (a)

LINDZEY, G. An experimental test of the validity of the Rosenzweig picture-frustration study. *J. Pers.*, 1950, 18, 315–320. (b)

LINDZEY, G., & HERMAN, P. S. Thematic apperception test: A note on reliability and situational validity. *J. proj. Tech.*, 1955, 19, 36–42.

LORD, EDITH. Experimentally induced variation in Rorschach performance. *Psychol. Monogr.*, 1950, 64, No. 10 (Whole No. 316).

LUCHINS, A. S. Situational and attitudinal influences on Rorschach responses. *Amer. J. Psychiat*, 1947, 103, 780–784.

LUFT, J. Interaction and projection. *J. proj. Tech.*, 1953, 17, 489–492.

MCCLELLAND, D. C., CLARK, R. A., ROBY, T. B., & ATKINSON, J. W. The projective expression of needs: IV. The effects of need for achievement on thematic apperception. *J. exp. Psychol.*, 1949, 39, 242–255.

MACFARLANE, JEAN W. Problems of validation inherent in projective methods. *Amer. J. Orthopsychiat.*, 1942, 12, 405–410.

MASLING, J. M. The effects of warm and cold interaction on the interpretation of a projective protocol. *J. proj. Tech.*, 1957, 21, 377–383.

MEYER, B. C., BROWN, F., & LEVINE, A. Observations on the House-Tree-Person drawing test before and after surgery. *Psychosom. Med.*, 1955, 17, 428–454.

MILLER, D. R., SANDERS, R., & CLEVELAND, S. E. The relationship between examiner personality and obtained Rorschach protocols: An application of interpersonal relations theory. *Amer. Psychologist*, 1950, 5, 322–323. (Abstract)

MILLER, D. R. Prediction of behavior by means of the Rorschach test. *J. abnorm. soc. Psychol.*, 1953, 48, 367–375.

NORMAN, R., LEVERANT, S., & REDLO, MIRIAM. The influence of a superficial immediately preceding "set" upon responses to the Rorschach. *J. consult. Psychol.*, 1952, 16, 261–264.

PATTIE, F. A. The effect of hypnotically induced hostility on Rorschach performance. *J. clin. Psychol.*, 1954, 10, 161–164.

RABIN, A., NELSON, W. & CLARK, MARGARET. Rorschach content as a function of perceptual experience and sex of the examiner. *J. clin. Psychol.*, 1954, 10, 188–190.

RABIN, A., PAPANIA, N., & MCMICHAEL, A. Some effects of alcohol on Rorschach performance. *J. clin. Psychol.*, 1954, 10, 232–255.

RANKIN, R. E., & CAMPBELL, D. T. Galvanic skin response to negro and white experimenters. *J. abnorm. soc. Psychol.*, 1955, 51, 30–33.

REICHENBERG-HACKETT, W. Changes in Goodenough drawings after a gratifying experience. *Amer. J. Orthopsychiat.*, 1953, 23, 501–516.

RIESS, B. F., SCHWARTZ, E. K., & COTTINGHAM, ALICE. An experimental critique of assumptions underlying the Negro version of the TAT. *J. abnorm. soc. Psychol.*, 1950, 45, 700–709.

ROBINSON, J., & COHEN, L. Individual bias in psychological reports. *J. clin. Psychol.*, 1954, 10, 333–336.

RODNICK, E. H., & KLEBANOFF, S. G. Projective reactions to induced frustration as a measure of social adjustment. *Psychol. Bull.*, 1942, 39, 489. (Abstract)

SANDERS, R., & CLEVELAND, S. E. The relationship between certain examiner personality variables and subjects' Rorschach scores. *J. proj. Tech.*, 1953, 17, 34–50.

SANFORD, R. N. The effects of abstinence from food upon imaginal processes: A preliminary experiment. *J. Psychol.*, 1936, 2, 129–136.

SANFORD, R. N. The effects of abstinence from food upon imaginal processes: A further experiment. *J. Psychol.*, 1937, 3, 145–149.

SARASON, S. B. *The clinical interaction.* New York: Harper, 1954.

SARBIN, T. R. Rorschach patterns under hypnosis. *Amer. J. Orthopsychiat.*, 1939, 9, 315–318.

SCHACHTEL, E. C. Subjective definitions of the Rorschach test situation and their effect on test performance. Contributions to an understanding of Rorschach's test, III. *Psychiatry*, 1945, 8, 419–448.

SCHAFER, R. *Psychoanalytic interpretation in Rorschach testing.* New York: Grune & Stratton, 1954.

SCHWARTZ, F., & KATES, S. L. Behn-Rorschach and Rorschach under standard and stress conditions. *J. consult. Psychol.*, 1957, 21, 335–338.

SHIPLEY, T. E., & VEROFF, J. A. A projective measure of need for affiliation. *J. exp. Psychol.*, 1952, 43, 349–356.

SIIPOLA, ELSA, & TAYLOR, VIVIAN. Reactions to ink blots under free and pressure conditions. *J. Pers.*, 1952, 21, 22–47.

SINGER, J. L., MELTZOFF, J., & GOLDMAN, G. D. Rorschach movement responses following motor inhibition and hyperactivity. *J. consult. Psychol.*, 1952, 16, 359–364.

SUMMERWELL, HARRIET, CAMPBELL, MARY, & SARASON, I. The effect of differential motivating instructions on the emotional tone and outcome of the TAT stories. *J. consult. Psychol.*, 1958, 22, 385–388.

TOMKINS, S. S. The limits of material obtainable in a single case study by daily administration of the TAT. *Psychol. Bull.*, 1942, 39, 490. (Abstract)

VANKREVELEN, ALICE. Some effects of subject-examiner interaction on projective test performance. *J. proj. Tech.*, 1954, 18, 107–109. (a)

VANKREVELEN, ALICE. A study of examiner influence on responses to MAPS test materials. *J. clin. Psychol.*, 1954, 10, 292–293. (b)

VEROFF, J., WILCOX, SUE, & ATKINSON, J. W. The achievement motive in high school and college age women. *J. abnorm. soc. Psychol.*, 1953, 48, 108–119.

WALLON, E. J., & WEBB, W. The effect of varying degrees of projection on test scores. *J. consult. Psychol.*, 1957, 21, 465–472.

WEISSKOPF, EDITH A. The influence of the time factor on Rorschach performance. *Rorschach Res. Exch.*, 1942, 6, 128–136.

WEISSKOPF, EDITH A., & DIEPPA, J. J. Experimentally induced faking of TAT responses. *J. consult. Psychol.*, 1951, 15, 469–474.

WERTHAM, F., & BLEULER, M. Inconstancy of the formal structure of the personality: Experimental study of the influence of mescaline on the Rorschach test. *Arch. Neurol. Psychiat.*, 1932, 28, 52–70.

WICKES, T. A. Examiner influence in a test situation. *J. consult. Psychol.*, 1956, 20, 23–26.

WILKINS, W. L., & ADAMS, A. J. The use of the Rorschach test under hypnosis and under sodium amytal in military psychiatry. *J. gen. Psychol.*, 1947, 36, 131–138.

12

A Quantitative Study of Perception and Association in Experimental Semistarvation

JOSEF BROŽEK,
HAROLD GUETZKOW,
AND MARCELLA V. BALDWIN

This is a study of the psychological test performance of a group of conscientious objectors to military service who for twenty-four weeks voluntarily underwent a semistarvation diet of 1,570 calories per day. That these men were intensely preoccupied with thoughts of food is amply documented by a host of indexes. Yet, by and large, the projective techniques employed (Free Word Association Test, Restricted Word Association Test, dreams, Rorschach, Rosenzweig's P-F Study) did not prove sensitive to the expression of the hunger need. Why? Possible factors which need to be considered are:

1. The meaning of hunger in relation to the self-perception of these individuals.

2. The effect of the use of such a selected group of unusual volunteers on the results. Would a more representative group of persons have responded differently?

3. Could hunger have been more readily detected through analysis of formal characteristics of the projective responses rather than a content-centered approach?

Werner (1949) indicated the focal point of a recent symposium on the interrelationships of perception and personality by referring to the projective nature of perception and citing Murphy's dictum that "the perceived world pattern mirrors the organized need pattern within" (1947, p. 351). Bruner and Postman described the steps to be taken in developing a "theory of behavior which treats the organism as an organized whole and which contains laws stating the manner in which perceiving is an instrument of adjustment activity" (1949, p. 16). The first step involves investigation of motivational variables (directive states of the organism) which bring about systematic changes in perceptual functioning. It is a plausible hypothesis that a reduction in food intake, resulting in a frustration of one of the basic drives and—if continued—in profound changes in the organism's physiology and biochemistry, may influence man's cognitive processes and color his mood.

Diaries of marooned explorers and reports from famine areas provide anecdotal material indicating the extent to which food may become the center of thought of the starving individual. Eating was reported to have been a frequent topic of dreams in a small group of severely starved and debilitated men, survivors of John Franklin's expedition to the shores of the Arctic Sea, while they were waiting for relief at Fort Enterprise (Franklin, 1823). Perhaps the best description of the effects of hunger on perception and imagination has been provided by Mikkelsen. He noted that hunger had given to him and to his companion, Iversen, "sort of a second sight, making it the easiest thing in the world to find anything in the shape of food (Mikkelsen, 1913, p. 238). After killing the last two dogs and eating their livers, Mikkelsen fell asleep. He dreamt of food—"enormous quantities of food, huge smoking joints, mountains of bread and butter, with great green piles of vegetables and salad. But it is all moving, moving continually; shifting just out of reach" (1913, p. 270). The hallucinations of "finding" sandwiches among the Greenland rocks are described in a particularly vivid manner (p. 303). Sorokin (1942) points out that under conditions of famine, food becomes the central topic of thought, of conversation, and of writing. It intrudes at all times into the consciousness of the starving man, disturbing the association of images and the flow of ideas.

The food need and its effect on association and perception were the subject of several recent experimental investigations. In a preliminary study, Sanford (1936) compared the total number of food responses before and after lunch. He obtained a ratio of 2.0 for word associations and 2.5 for picture interpretations. The subjects were 10 school children. In a subsequent investigation, Sanford (1937) used five different tasks (word association, picture interpretations, chain association, completion of drawings, and completion of words). The composite food-response scores for subgroups of subjects (college students) examined 1, 2, 3, 4, and 5 hours after a meal were 1.5, 1.7, 1.7, 2.4, and 2.4, respectively.

Twenty-seven subjects who were tested after a 24-hour fast obtained an average score of 2.7 as compared with 1.7, the mean of 37 control subjects. Levine, Chein, and Murphy (1942) attempted to measure the "autistic" aspects of perception by determining the number of food responses to meaningless and ambiguous pictures at different time intervals elapsed since eating. With five experimental subjects, the total average number of food response obtained 1, 3, 6, and 9 hours after eating was 9.0, 12.5, 14.3, and 10.8 for the 20 achromatic cards, 4.8, 8.5, 7.6, and 6.6 for the 20 chromatic cards.

McClelland and Atkinson (1948) tested candidates for a submarine training school. The subjects were given the impression that the purpose of the investigation was to test the ability to perceive faint visual cues. Actually, no objects were projected on the screen. Out of 14 possible answers, 2.1, 2.9, and 3.2 were related to food when the men were tested 1, 4, and 16 hours after a meal. The difference between the control and the 16-hour value was statistically significant. In the second experimental series of Atkinson and McClelland (1948), the subjects were to write brief stories in response to 7 pictures, drawn mostly from Murray's Thematic Apperception Test. After 4 and 16 hours of food deprivation, there was no over-all increase in references to food or eating. However, analysis of specific scoring categories revealed several significant trends. As the length of time without food increased, there was an increase in the frequency of stories in which deprivation of food was the central plot, someone in the story wanted food, and someone was engaged in activity aimed at removing the source of food deprivation. Interestingly enough, there was a decided decrease in the frequency of references to actual eating (from 74 to 62 to 36 per cent).

We shall not survey investigations on perceptual organization by G. Murphy and those by Bruner and Postman and their colleagues concerned with other motivational factors than hunger. These studies were reviewed in detail and critically analyzed by Pastore, who comes to the conclusion that "the experimental evidence cited in support of the view that need is a determinant of perception is inadequate" (1949).

In the Minnesota starvation-rehabilitation experiment, the clinical observations yielded material indicating the tendency of perceptional processes, thought, and memory to be directed toward food. It is the purpose of the present study to investigate whether and to what extent these changes in the perception and association can be objectively measured by a variety of psychological tests.

Subjects and Conditions

The subjects were 36 "normal" young men, conscientious objectors who volunteered to serve as subjects in the experiment. Their physical and psychological characteristics and the conditions of the experiment carried out in 1944–1945 were described in detail elsewhere (Keys, Brožek, Henschel, Mickelsen, & Taylor, 1950). Briefly, the experiment consisted of three main periods: control (12 weeks), semistarvation (24 weeks), and controlled rehabilitation (12 weeks). The average body weight at the end of the three periods was 69.4, 52.6, and 58.6 kg., respectively.

Physiologically, the reduction of caloric intake from about 3,500 Cal. during the control period to the average of 1,570 Cal. for 24 weeks of semistarvation resulted in profound alterations of the composition and the machinery of the body. Psychologically, depression, narrowing of interests, social introversion, preoccupation with thoughts of food, decrease in spontaneous activity, physical as well as mental, and marked diminution of libido were among the principal characteristics of the "semistarvation neurosis" (Franklin, Schiele, Brožek, & Keys, 1948; Schiele & Brožek, 1948). The average scores on the Depression scale of the Minnesota Multiphasic Personality Inventory (normal average = 50, 1 SD = 10) rose from 54.2 during the control period (C) to 73.9 after 24 weeks of starvation (S24) and declined to 65.7 after the first 12 weeks of rehabilitation (R12).

In animal experiments, clear evidence can be obtained that deprivation, partial or total, of food increases the food (hunger) drive. The concept of "drive" is a construct derived from behavior. In animal experiments, we postulate an intensification of the food drive when there is increase in the number of times a rat will cross a charged grid (Warner, 1928), or depress a lever releasing a food pellet (Heron & Skinner, 1937).

In man the conditions are much more complex, and the definition of a "drive" loses the beauty of exactness and simplicity the term has in the vocabulary of the animal psychologist. In adult man, operating within the conventional cultural framework, it is difficult to make meaningful direct observations on overt, nonverbal behavior, and it is even more difficult to put them into quantitative terms. The experimenter must supplement his observations by reports made by the subjects. In the Minnesota Experiment this was done in regularly scheduled interviews and through ratings. The intensity of the "food" drive, together with the activity and sex drives, was rated at monthly intervals, using a scale ranging from 0 (normal) to +5 (extremely large increase) and –5 (extremely large decrease).

In order to facilitate the ratings, some of the possible manifestations of the changes in the intensity of the drive were brought to the attention of the subjects in the form of questions. In reference to the food drive the following points were mentioned: To what extent do topics related to food enter your thinking, reading, and conversation? Is food and eating important to you? Do you think of the good old days when you could get as much food as you wanted? Do you often think of your old favorite dishes? To what extent are you conscious of your need for food?

The results indicating a rise of the food drive and a decrease in the sex and activity drive are indicated in Figure 12–1. In this context, we are concerned primarily with the altered food drive. The numerical values assigned to the ratings by the subjects appear to be under-estimates. It may be noted that at the end of the starvation period 59 per cent of the subjects reported that they felt hungry most of the time.

On a scale from 0 (normal) to 5 (extreme), the mean ratings for Appetite, defined as "the desire for food," rose to 2.7 after 12 weeks of semistarvation (S12) and to 3.1 after 24 weeks of semistarvation (S24), declining to 1.6 after 12 weeks of rehabilitation (R12). Whereas Appetite was defined as a craving for food not referred to any special region of the body, Hunger Pain referred to a gnawing sensation in the epigastric region. Although definitely present throughout the semi-starvation period, the Hunger Pain was rated as less prominent than the desire for food, with ratings of 1.7 at S12, 1.8 at S24, and 0.4 at R12.

In a few cases, striking increases in the food drive were observed.

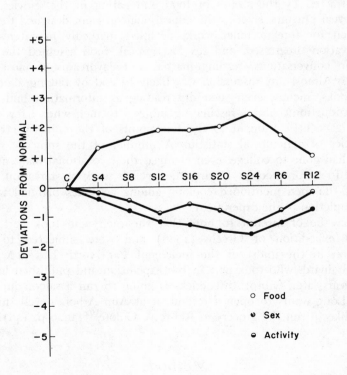

Figure 12–1. Average values of drive ratings during the control period (C), 24 weeks of semistarvation (S), and 12 weeks of nutritional rehabilitation (R). N = 32.

Four of the men, although they had committed themselves voluntarily to participate in the experiment the rigors of which were clearly indicated to them, were unable to stay on the semistarvation diet. Subject No. 234 broke the diet during the eighth week of the experiment. He ate several sundaes and malted milks. He stole some penny candies and later attempted to cover his dietary violations, made obvious by the lack of decrease in the body weight in spite of the absence of edema, by fabrication of weight records. Subject No. 235, while working as accountant in a co-operative grocery one evening, impulsively ate cookies, popcorn, and bananas. On returning to the laboratory, he "gave back the cookies." Subject No. 234 confessed minor offenses against the strict dietary rules by the tenth week of starvation. Later, he developed fascination for garbage, ate a sandwich found on the ground, and stole a student's lunch.

These instances were exaggerated expressions of the increase in the "food drive" present, in varying degrees, in all the subjects. During starvation the thoughts of food, in all its ramifications, came to dominate the men's minds. They talked and read about food. Their attention was attracted by the scenes of food and eating in the movies. While intellectual pursuits, such as the educational program designed to prepare the men for foreign relief work, declined markedly in interest value as starvation progressed, and sex lost appeal, food assumed the central place in conversations, reading matter, and daydreams of most of the subjects. Almost any discussion was likely to end by talking about food. Cookbooks, menus, even such dry reading as information bulletins on food production, became fascinating subjects to men who, a few months earlier, gave little thought to the fine points of the culinary art or the intricacies of agricultural statistics. A number of the subjects, most of whom had gone to college, even changed their vocational plans and now wanted to become cooks. During the twelfth week of starvation, 38 per cent of the men mentioned cooking among activities planned for after the completion of the experiment.

It may be of interest to note that the men who took part in the ill-fated expedition of Greely (1886) and were subjected to severe starvation in the midst of the inclement Far North had very similar ideas. Brainard, who took part in the expedition and published his diary many years later, wrote: "Fredericks is going to run a saloon in Minneapolis. Long wants to open a restaurant at Ann Arbor. Jewell thinks he would like to run the grocery in Ralston's Colony" (1929 p. 148).

Methods

In order to investigate the effect of the heightened food drive on perception and association, five sources of data were used: (1) free association, (2) restricted association, (3) dream content, (4) the Rorschach, and (5) Rosenzweig's Picture-Frustration Test. Only limited aspects of the Rorschach and Rosenzweig tests will be considered for present purposes.

FREE WORD ASSOCIATION TEST

The Worcester State Hospital (Special Military Project) Free Association Test, consisting of 100 stimulus words, was used. Fifty of the words had been selected from the Kent-Rosanoff Association Test (Kent & Rosanoff, 1910). Of the remaining 50 stimulus words, 40 had been chosen because of their potential significance in psychological dynamics. Ten were originally included in the test because of their value in the study of schizophrenia and were not analyzed in the starvation experiment. The method of giving the test was the time-honored one of presenting the stimulus words to the subject, one at a time, and asking him to respond with the first word that occurred to him.

The responses were timed and recorded. After the series of stimulus words had been presented, the subject was asked to recall as many as he could, together with responses he gave. All recalled words were recorded, but in the analysis only the first ten were used in order to minimize the individual differences in memory.

The 50 words from the Kent-Rosanoff list, selected on the basis of having the highest frequencies of "Most Common" answers, were scored according to the O'Connor (1933) norms. The responses were classified as *Most Common* (given most frequently by O'Connor's norm group of 1,000 men in industry), *Common* (responses occurring among O'Connor's subjects), *Individual* (words not present in the responses of the norm group but which represented synonyms, antonyms, or were in other logical ways related to the stimulus words), or *Unusual* (not falling in the first three categories). No satisfactory norms were available for the forty special words, so this large pool of material unfortunately could not be fully utilized. Multiple-word responses and delayed responses (beyond 3 seconds) were noted for all words.

Close scrutiny of the O'Connor scoring system reveals that, while the *Most Common* category is satisfactorily defined, the *Common* category is too broad. Since *all* responses given by his norm group are called "Common," this category includes responses of all frequencies: a reaction word given by 5 out of his 1,000 subjects, or even by a single person, is scored *Common* even though it is obviously the reverse.

A more finely discriminating analysis has been made possible by using O'Connor's tables listing those reaction words which occurred at least ten times either among Kent and Rosanoff's 1,000 subjects or his own group of 1,000. Reaction words not appearing in these lists are those which were given by less than 1 per cent of either of these large samples. Such words will be considered as "idiosyncratic" responses.

Thirty-one conscientious objectors, who participated in other projects carried out at the laboratory, acted as control group for the evaluation of the Free Word Association Test. For administrative reasons the free association test was given only once, toward the end of the starvation period.

RESTRICTED WORD ASSOCIATION TEST (FIRST LETTERS)

The restricted word association test was a part of the intellective battery administered throughout the three phases of the experiment (control, starvation, rehabilitation). It was restricted in the sense that the subjects were asked to write down words which begin with a specified letter. The test was referred to as *First Letters* (Thurstone & Thurstone, 1941) and was used as a measure of "verbal facility." The subjects were requested to include no proper names, to use no word more than once, and to avoid automatic series such as sixty-one, sixty-two, and so on (Guetzkow & Brožek, 1947). The group of 36 subjects was split at random into 6 subgroups, given B, C, F, P, S, and T as their "first letter." In successive sessions the same first letters were used but were assigned to different subgroups. For the purposes of the present study, the reproduced words were analyzed according to their content and the number of items related to food or eating was recorded.

Only three sets of records were analyzed. These were obtained during the control period, after one week, and after four weeks of semistarvation diet, respectively.

DREAMS

In order to obtain a random sampling of the content and frequency of the dreams, the subjects were asked at irregular intervals to describe briefly the dreams they had had during the preceding night. This was done during morning testing sessions. The times at which these surveys would be made were not announced in advance. There is good reason to believe that the sampling of the dreams was free of bias.

The content of the dreams was analyzed into "food dreams" and "other dreams." The data on dreams were obtained during the eighth, twelfth, and twentieth week of starvation and the seventh week of rehabilitation.

THE RORSCHACH

The Rorschach cards were projected on a screen in a small auditorium, following the directions given by Harrower-Erickson and Steiner (1945). The responses were recorded on the Group Rorschach Blanks. The individual booklets provide a separate page for an answer or answers to each of the ten ink blots and an additional space for further comments by the subject.

The responses were examined using the following criteria of "food responses": foods and foodstuffs (e.g., potato), references to cooking, kitchen utensils, eating places; and references to eating. The total number of food responses was used as a score. The test was administered during the control period, at the end of the semistarvation, and after 12 weeks of rehabilitation.

ROSENZWEIG'S P-F STUDY

The test (Rosenzweig, 1945) was administered at the end of 6 months of semistarvation and 12 weeks of rehabilitation. The responses were examined with reference to items related to food and eating.

Results

FREE WORD ASSOCIATION TEST

The data on the mean frequency with which the reactions of the experimental and the control groups were classified in the several O'Connor categories are presented in Table 12–1. One might have

TABLE 12–1	Free Word Association Test. Mean Frequencies, per Subject, of Reaction Words in Different Response Categories			
GROUP RESPONSE CATEGORY	EXPERIMENTAL (N=34)		CONTROL (N=31)	
	M	S.D.	M	S.D.
Most Common	16.8	8.3	19.7	6.2
Common	24.6	5.4	23.4	4.2
Individual	3.2	3.4	2.0	1.7
Unusual	4.8	4.4	4.9	4.3
Delayed*	2.7	4.2	3.7	3.9
Multiple Word	1.0	1.4	2.2	3.2
Delayed*	4.4	5.5	5.5	4.2
Multiple Word*	2.5	2.3	3.9	3.8

* The responses refer to the 50 Kent-Rosanoff stimulus words, except for the last two rows, which represent the responses to the 40 additional words.

expected that the experimental group would give a larger number of Unusual, Delayed, and Multiple Word responses. This was not the case. The mean number of Most Common responses was greater for the Controls but the difference was not statistically significant ($t = 1.49$; $t_{0.05} = 2.00$).

As seen from Table 12–2, the Experimental group had a higher mean percentage of idiosyncratic responses per word both on all 50 Kent-Rosanoff words and, more strikingly, on the food words; it was only in the case of the latter, however, that the difference was statistically significant ($t=2.71$; $t_{0.02}=2.62$).

It has generally been found that the content of reaction words only rarely gives information with regard to the individual's problems and attitudes. Nevertheless, in view of the intense preoccupation with food on the part of the semistarved group, one would expect that a greater

---

TABLE 12–2   *Free Word Association Test. Mean Percentage Frequencies of Idiosyncratic Responses per Word*

	EXPERIMENTAL (N=34)		CONTROL (N=31)	
	M	S.D.	M	S.D.
50 Kent-Rosanoff words	27.0	11.6	24.2	12.5
8 Kent-Rosanoff "Food" words*	27.2	9.5	15.7	5.9

* Eating, Bitter, Fruit, Sweet, Hungry, Sour, Thirsty, Cabbage.

---

number of the responses would relate to food and eating than in the well-fed group. The data do not substantiate such a hypothesis. In the semistarvation group, out of 3,069 responses, 181 (5.9 per cent) were related to food or eating. In the control group, out of 2,790 responses 162 (or 5.8 per cent) fell into this category.

The results presented so far were concerned only with the associated responses given originally to the stimulus words. Did the semistarvation group remember a greater number of food-related stimulus words? The

---

TABLE 12–3   *Free Word Association Test. Percentage Frequency of Recall by the Semistarvation (Experimental) and the Control Groups*

GROUP WORD	EXPERIMENTAL (N=34)	CONTROL (N=31)
Baby	41	39
Boy	41	45
Father	41	35
Mother	41	39
Girl	35	35
Brother	29	32
Hungry	26	0
Home	24	23
Ocean	24	0
Blue	24	26
Black	24	0

words included among the first 10 stimulus words recalled are tabulated, together with their frequency of occurence, in Table 12–3. The word "Hungry" was included among the first 10 words recalled by 26 per cent of the semistarved subjects but was in no case among the first 10 stimulus words recalled by the control group. It should be noted that none of the other stimulus words related to food and eating were prominent among those recalled by the semistarvation subjects.

THE FIRST LETTERS TEST

The results are presented in Table 12–4. There was a slight rise in The average number of food responses after one week of semi-starvation. The change did not reach the level of statistical significance ($F = 3.75$; $F_{0.05} = 4.16$). Three weeks later, at a time when the body

---

TABLE 12–4   *Restricted Word Association, First Letters Test, the Average Number of Food Responses (N = 32 Subjects)*

ITEM	CONTROL PERIOD	AFTER ONE WEEK OF SEMI-STARVATION	AFTER ONE MONTH OF SEMI-STARVATION
No. of food responses	1.6	2.3	1.9
Food responses as % of all responses	3.5	5.3	4.0

---

weight had decreased by about 5 kg., the mean value returned to that obtained during the control period ($F = 0.98$, not significant).

In view of these meager results, the data obtained in subsequent months were not analyzed with reference to the number of food responses.

DREAMS

The frequency and content of the dreams, sampled at intervals during the starvation-rehabilitation experiment, are indicated in Table 12–5.

TABLE 12–5   *Frequency of Dreams during Starvation and Rehabilitation*

	NO. OF SUBJECTS	FOOD DREAMS	OTHER DREAMS
Starvation, 8th week	36	0	10
Starvation, 12th week	35	3	13
Starvation, 20th week	34	1	13
Rehabilitation, 7th week	32	1	9

It is evident that food dreams of any kind were rare. No definite relationship between reduced food intake and dreams was observed.

THE RORSCHACH TEST

The data in Table 12–6 indicate a rise in the number of food responses after six months of starvation. On the percentage basis, the increase is negligible. Strangely enough, the trend continues at the same average rate during the rehabilitation period. The changes in the direction of an increase did not occur uniformly in all the subjects. Seven subjects had no food responses at any time. The distribution of the changes of the scores in the remaining 25 subjects is reproduced in Table 12–7.

TABLE 12–6   *Total Number of Food Responses in the Rorschach Test (N = 32 Subjects)*

ITEM	CONTROL PERIOD (c)	END OF 6 MOS. OF STARVATION (s24)	END OF 3 MOS. OF REHABILITATION (R12)
No. of food responses	15	36	45
Total no. of responses	931	1472	1442
Food responses as % of all responses	1.6%	2.4%	3.1%

TABLE 12–7   *Frequency of Subjects Showing a Change in the Number of Food Responses on the Rorschach Test (N = 25 Subjects Who Had One or More Food Responses)*

CHANGE Periods compared	−4	−3	−2	−1	0	+1	+2	+3	+4	+5	+6
S24-C		1	1	1	3	13	5		1		
R12-S24	1		2	6	5	5	2	3		1	

ROSENZWEIG'S PICTURE-FRUSTRATION STUDY

At the end of the starvation period, only one subject recorded a food response. In Picture No. 7 the subject answered to the waiter's accusation of being too fussy: "No sir, I'm paying to have *good* food served." The same subject answered to the neighbor bringing back a borrowed newspaper torn by the baby (Picture No. 24): "As long as he didn't eat it!" After three months of rehabilitation another subject commented on Picture No. 7: "Food is an important part of life, you know!" These answers do reflect the starvation mentality, but their occurrence was infrequent indeed.

Comment

Along with Atkinson and McClelland (1948), we feel that the expression of need in a projective fashion is anything but a straight forward matter and that there is an imperative need for studies of the responses in projective tests administered to subjects whose psychological condition is experimentally induced and is operationally clearly established. Unfortunately, the psychological setting in the Minnesota starvation-rehabilitation was not as simple and unequivocal as one would wish.

It is obvious that starvation as a total experience has a different psychological meaning for a man in the midst of a famine and for a person in a laboratory situation. Less obvious, but psychologically important, is the fact that food and eating have symbolic significances which vary from person to person and that the effects of an intensification of even such an apparently simple and straightforward viscerogenic drive as that of hunger may be tied up with the peculiar personality organization of the individual. While the peripheral manifestations of starvation are essentially identical from person to person (the extreme physiological changes, together with the concomitant reports of fatigue, depression, etc.), on a higher level of personality organization an experience which is truly frustrating to one individual, perhaps representing loss of love and the reactivation of infantile fears, may actually be satisfying to another individual. A person who feels the need of punishment and deprivation in order to expiate his guilt may find relief through physical suffering. The presence of the obvious, the peripheral, frustration in the Minnesota starvation experiment cannot be doubted. The extent to which its effects were counteracted or concealed by the subjects' personal *Einstellung* with regard to hunger and food is a difficult problem.

Klein and Schlesinger (1949) have emphasized that we are not justified in expecting a push-button relationship between "hunger" and the perceptual effects. One should not lose sight of the interaction of the biologically determined need stimuli and the ego structure. In spite of all the inconveniences and discomfort experienced by the subjects, the participation in the starvation experiment had its rewards. The assignment was "tough" and was more closely an equivalent of militaray service then planting trees in a work camp or serving as an orderly in a mental hospital. Symbolically, the men carried the ball for their fellow conscientious objectors and for starving humanity. The experiment received a considerable amount of publicity in the C.O. publications as well as in the general press. All these factors tended to mitigate the frustrating impact of the persisting hunger and the reduced physical fitness. Nevertheless, the paradox remains. On the one hand, the change in hunger-need structure was severe and prolonged and affected the observed and reported behavior. On the other hand, the quasi-objective and projective devices largely failed to reflect the change in perceptual and associative phenomena. The tests used seemed adequate for the purposes intended and in some cases had even been validated for short-term fasts by other experiments.

Let us consider the results of the individual tests used in this study.

FREE WORD ASSOCIATION TEST

The Free Word Association Test results indicate that the effects of semistarvation on the associative processes are fairly specific and chiefly influence reactions to those stimulus words whose content has to do with some aspect of eating. The alterations were not of a gross variety such as blocking, failure to follow directions, or peculiar ideation, which are characteristic of various types of mental illness, but consisted rather in a personalized kind of response. These personalized, idiosyncratic responses were not necessarily illogical or even farfetched but were statistically defined as reactions given by less than 1 per cent of either of two 1,000-subject samples. Thus it might be said that the "uncommonness" of these reactions was in keeping with the unusual personal circumstances of the subjects with regard to the eating complex.

The failure to find an increased number of food responses in the Experimental group, in spite of abundant clinical evidence of their preoccupation with food as well as the test indications that the food stimulus words were touching a psychologically sensitive area, is consistent with clinical experience that the content of the reaction words is only occasionally relevant.

FIRST LETTERS TEST

The number of food-related words given in the First Letters Test was small and showed no significant increase after one month of semistarvation. This fits in with the results of the Free Word Association Test, administered toward the end of the starvation period, which indicated no difference in the number of food responses given by the experimental and the control groups. Results obtained in subsequent administrations of the First Letters Test, which was a part of an intellective test battery, were not analyzed from this point of view.

It may be noted that after six months of starvation there was no significant change in the total number of words reproduced in the First Letters Test. This indicates that mental functions, as measured by this and other short mental tests, were not affected by marked changes in nutritional status.

DREAMS

Dreams are interpreted by psychoanalysts as one of the mechanisms for the release of driving forces which cannot find fulfillment in real life. Should not the starving man dream about food and eating? It is a reasonable hypothesis that the frequency of food dreams should increase under conditions of food deprivation.

References to food dreams can be found in reports of the victims of natural starvation. Sorokin (1942) states, without adequate evidence, that the dreams of the hungry persons are occupied predominantly with food. The validity of this and similar statements is doubtful or, at any rate, unknown, as detailed information on the total number of dreams and their topics is not indicated. It is very likely that the concern with food during the waking hours would act as a selective factor. The food dreams have a better chance to be remembered and talked about. Food dreams were reported, in poststarvation interviews, by 4 out of 12 men who lost about 10 per cent of their body weight (Benedict, Miles, Rothe, & Smith, 1919). It is of interest that a prominent place in the dreams was occupied by situations in which the men were about to break the dietary restrictions. However, recalling dreams which occurred over a period of months is not a very safe procedure.

In the Minnesota starvation-rehabilitation experiment, a determined effort was made to eliminate bias in sampling the dreams to be analyzed for their content. The subjects were asked to fill out the dream questionnaire during several of the relatively frequent morning testing sessions, without previous announcement. Under these conditions, semistarvation has not resulted in a definite increase in food dreams. At the same time, it should be noted that only the manifest, overt content of the dreams was used in making this analysis. Had the dreams been described in detail, a content analysis of the night dreams along the TAT lines could have been undertaken and might have proved more revealing.

The daydreams of the subjects were frequent and often passionately devoted to food-related topics. Although no systematic check was made of the frequency and duration of the daydreams, the interviews, and particularly the diaries of the subjects, brought out an increase in the amount of time devoted to daydreaming as well as the polarization of the dream content around food. In part, the increased time devoted to daydreaming was a consequence of the subject's lowered level of overt activity.

The following is an example of the nature of the daydreams, as reported in the diary of one of the subjects:

Today we'll have menu No. 1. Gee, that's the smallest menu, it seems. How shall I fix the potatoes? If I use my spoon to eat them I'll be able to add more water. Should I make different varieties of beverages tonight? Haven't had my toast yet today. Maybe I should save some for a midnight snack with my buddy. What kind of a sandwich could I make? Maybe I'd better write these ideas down, so I don't forget them. If I eat a little faster the food would stay warmer longer—and I like it warm. But then it's gone so quickly. . . .

The subjects reported that such musings sometimes would continue for hours unless their laboratory duties or other external stimuli interrupted these satisfying daydreams.

RORSCHACH

The results of the Rorschach test will be analyzed in detail in a separate publication (Kjenaas & Brožek, 1952). In starvation there was an increase in the total number of responses, interpreted as a retest phenomenon. The analysis of covariance, applied to Rorschach characteristics which showed an increase during starvation, indicated that in no case was the rise larger than could be expected from the increase in the total number of responses.

Even had the starvation increase in the number of food responses been statistically significant, its psychological significance would have remained uncertain. Obviously it could not be interpreted simply as an expression of the increased food drive, because the trend was still present after three months of rehabilitation, at a time when the need for food had definitely decreased.

ROSENZWEIG'S P-F STUDY

The P-F Study was not designed with any special reference to food or eating. However, when the need for food assumes such a dominant position in the person's life as it did in the Minnesota subjects after six months of semistarvation, it might be expected to color the answers to at least some of the test situations. Certainly item No. 7 in which the scene takes place in a restaurant might have elicited food-oriented responses. We have seen that the hypothesis was not substantiated by the facts.

The data obtained by the P-F Study have been analyzed in full elsewhere (Franklin & Brožek, 1949), using Rosenzweig's scoring categories. The starvation subjects had a larger number of extrapunitive and obstacle-dominant but a smaller number of impunitive and ego-defensive responses than "normal" subjects. The differences were statistically significant, but the absolute values of the differences were small and their psychological relevance appeared questionable. We have noted that on occasion Rosenzweig's (1945) two standardization samples differed from each other as much as the semistarvation subjects differed from either of the two normal groups. When the test was given after 12 weeks of nutritional rehabilitation, during which definite improvement took place in physiological functions and personal adjustment, no significant differences were obtained in the P-F scores.

Summary and Conclusions

1. A quantitative study was made of the processes of perception and association in experimental starvation and nutritional rehabilitation.

2. Thirty-six young men served as volunteer subjects, losing one-fourth of initial body weight within six months.

3. The tests considered in this paper included Free Word Association, the First Letters Test, analysis of the content of the dreams, the Rorschach, and Rosenzweig's P-F Study.

4. Only the Free Word Association Test provided limited evidence that semistarvation, resulting in an unquestionable increase in the "hunger drive," altered the associative processes.

REFERENCES

ATKINSON, J. W., & McCLELLAND, D. C. The projective expression of needs: II. The effect of different intensities of the hunger drive on thematic apperception. J. exp. Psychol., 1948, 38, 643–658.

BENEDICT, F. G., MILES, W. R., ROTHE, P., & SMITH, H. M. Human vitality and efficiency under prolonged restricted diet. Washington: Carnegie Institute, 1919, Publ. No. 280.

BRAINARD, D. L. The outpost of the lost. Indianapolis: Bobbs-Merrill, 1929.

BRUNER, J., & POSTMAN, L. Perception, cognition, and behavior. J. Pers., 1949, 18, 14–31.

FRANKLIN, J. Narrative of a journey to the shores of the polar sea. London: Murray, 1823.

FRANKLIN, J. C., & BROŽEK, J. The Rosenzweig P-F test as a measure of frustration response in semistarvation. J. consult. Psychol., 1949, 13, 293–301.

FRANKLIN, J. C., SCHIELE, B. C., BROŽEK, J., & KEYS, A. Observations on human behavior in experimental semi-starvation and rehabilitation. J. clin. Psychol., 1948, 4, 28–45.

GREELY, A. W. Three years of Arctic service. New York: Scribner, 1886.

GUETZKOW, H., & BROŽEK, J. Intellective tests for longitudinal experiments on adults. Amer. J. Psychol., 1947, 60, 350–366.

HARROWER-ERICKSON, MOLLY R., & STEINER, M. E. Large-scale Rorschach techniques. Springfield, Ill.: Charles C Thomas, 1945.

HERON, W. T., & SKINNER, B. F. Changes in hunger during starvation. Psychol. Rec., 1937, 1, 51–60.

KENT, G. H., & ROSANOFF, A. J. A study of association in insanity. Amer. J. Insanity, 1910, 67, 317–377.

KEYS, A., BROŽEK, J., HENSCHEL, A., MICKELSEN, O., & TAYLOR, H. L. The biology of human starvation. Minneapolis: Univer. of Minn. Press, 1950.

KJENAAS, NANCY K., & BROŽEK, J. Personality in experimental starvation. Psychosom. Med., 1952, 14, 115–128.

KLEIN, G. S., & SCHLESINGER, H. Where is the perceiver in perceptual theory? J. Pers., 1949, 18, 32–47.

LEVINE, R., CHEIN, I., & MURPHY, G. The relation of the intensity of a need to the amount of perceptual distortion. *J. Psychol.*, 1942, 13, 283–293.

McCLELLAND, D. C., & ATKINSON, J. W. The projective expression of needs: I. The effect of different intensities of the hunger drive on perception. *J. Psychol.*, 1948, 25, 205–222.

MIKKELSEN, E. *Lost in the Arctic.* London: Heinemann, 1913.

MURPHY, G. *Personality.* New York: Harper, 1947.

O'CONNOR, J. *Born that way.* Baltimore: Williams & Wilkins, 1933.

PASTORE, N. Need as a determinant of perception. *J. Psychol.*, 1949, 28, 457–475.

ROSENZWEIG, S. The picture-association method and its application in a study of reactions to frustration. *J. Pers.*, 1945, 14, 3–23.

SANFORD, R. N. The effect of abstinence from food upon imaginal processes: A preliminary experiment. *J. Psychol.*, 1936, 2, 129–136.

SANFORD, R. N. The effect of abstinence from food upon imaginal processes: A further experiment. *J. Psychol.*, 1937, 3, 145–159.

SCHIELE, B. C., & BROŽEK, J. "Experimental neurosis" resulting from semistarvation in man. *Psychosom. Med.*, 1948, 10, 31–50.

SOROKIN, P. A. *Man and society in calamity.* New York: Dutton, 1942.

THURSTONE, L. L., & THURSTONE, THELMA G. Factorial studies of intelligence. *Psychometr. Monogr.*, 1941, No. 2, 1–94, esp. p. 60.

WARNER, L. H. A study of hunger behavior in the white rat by means of the obstruction method. *J. compar. Psychol.*, 1928, 8, 273–299.

WERNER, H. Introductory remarks .*J. Pers.*, 1949, 18, 2–5.

13

The Validity of Personality-Trait Ratings Based on Projective Techniques[1]

HENRY SAMUELS

The attempt to predict selected graduate students' over-all suitability for clinical psychology was the challenging task which the Veterans Administration program took on in the summer of 1947. The study showed poor predictability in this regard, and projective techniques did more poorly than other indexes, such as actuarial data. Samuels, in this thorough, masterful study, clearly shows the limitations of projective techniques in this regard. The criterion was the final pooled personality ratings of a diagnostic council having all possible data available. Projective techniques showed a significant but very low correlation with the criterion. Moreover, certain tests, notably the Rorschach, yielded mainly descriptions of disturbance on the personality traits, while the TAT yielded interpretations seeing mainly the "good" in subjects. Last, there appeared to be more correlation between ratings made by different

[1] I wish to acknowledge my indebtedness to all the people who helped to make this study possible. I am especially grateful to Professor E. Lowell Kelly for his counsel, instruction, and labor, without stint. Such value as may be derived from the study must, for the most part, be attributed to him. I am indebted to Dr. Donald G. Marquis, Dr. George A. Satter, Dr. Max L. Hutt, and Dr. Wm. Clark Trow for their suggestions and criticisms and to Dr. Donald W. Fiske and Dr. Ernest C. Tupes for their willing help. My wife Helen was, as always, inspiring and stimulating and, in addition, labored long and arduously with the data. Caroline Weichlein and Phyllis E. Moore were most zealous with the secretarial chores.

The opinions expressed herein are the author's and do not necessarily reflect the views of the Veterans Administration.

raters with the same projective technique than between ratings of a single judge when he used different projective techniques.

In defense of projective techniques, there are many questions that might be raised.

1. Are we asking too much of a technique when we expect ratings of over-all suitability for clinical psychology to correlate highly with diagnostic council ratings? How do we know that these council ratings are in any way truly related to the degree of adequacy which the candidate will eventually manifest in his professional setting?

2. Is it reasonable to expect that differences between strongly selected above-average graduate students will relate to over-all suitability for psychology? The WAIS, for example, is not a good predictor of academic success for graduate students.

3. What are the criteria of over-all suitability? If there is no attempt to determine agreement on what it is, can one expect to predict it accurately?

4. Shouldn't the projective technique methodologies have been more adequately determined? We are told, for example, that ten TAT cards were given, but the particular cards employed are not stated. The assumption apparently is that one TAT card is as good as another, but this assumption is explicitly false.

In view of these comments, one must question whether any test could have done well under these circumstances; and, indeed, none did well. The situation was not suitable for a fair judgment regarding the efficacy of projective techniques in general or even in the particular assessment situation.

Considerable importance has been attached to projective techniques by clinical psychologists and professional personnel in allied fields. Such devices have been used in psychiatric diagnosis, academic and industrial selection, educational and vocational guidance, research studies of personality development, and psychotherapy. One of the outstanding problems with respect to such techniques in their validity in their various applications.

A review of the literature on projective techniques emphasizes the need for determining the extent to which projective techniques agree with independent criteria in the description of personality. We may have different kinds of validities, depending on the function projective techniques are asked to serve.

The purpose of the present investigation is to continue the study of the validity of projective techniques by considering the following questions:

1. How well are projective clinicians who use the same projective method able to *describe* personality? Are there differences among clinicians in this ability?

2. Are there differences in the extent to which personality is correctly described which are related to the kind of projective method used?

3. Are there differences among attributes of personality which make for differences in the degree to which they can be correctly described?

Procedures and Methods

The present investigation was done as part of the research project on the Selection of Clinical Psychologists sponsored by the Veterans Administration under a contract with the University of Michigan, under the direction of Professor E. Lowell Kelly (1947; Kelly & Fiske, 1950).

THE ASSESSMENT PROGRAM

During the summer of 1947, 140 students who had been selected by universities for first-year positions in the Veterans Administration clinical psychology training program came to Ann Arbor in "classes" of 24 per week to be assessed. During the assessment week, a student completed a battery of paper-and-pencil objective tests and had administered to him in group form the Thematic Apperception Test (10 cards) and the project's form of a sentence completion test. During the first day or two, the student was administered the Rorschach and the Bender-Gestalt individually and at separate sessions. Each student was interviewed twice (Soskin, 1949), filled out a 131-item Biographical Inventory, wrote an autobiography, was put through a variety of situations, and filled out a sociometric questionnaire.

The subjects, on whom the ratings investigated in this study were made, consisted of 128 male college graduates who had been accepted by various universities for graduate training in clinical psychology. The twelve women who were part of the total assessed group have been omitted from this study.

Because they are crucial to the present study, a detailed discussion is given to the rating scales, the projective ratings, and the criterion ratings.

THE RATING SCALES

The rating scales cover 42 variables divided into three sections which are given the letter designations A, B, and C.[2] Scale A, consisting of 22 variables, was designed to describe more overt or phenotypical dimen-

---

[2] Complete definitions of all 42 personality traits may be found in a doctoral dissertation by Samuels (1950, App. A).

sions of personality and was adapted from Cattell's (1946) factorial studies, with modifications made on the basis of experience with the scale in earlier pilot assessments. In the present study, 5 of the 22 Scale A variables are used. These 5 were selected on the basis of a factorial analysis by Fiske (1949). Each of these 5 selected Scale A variables has highest factor loadings for Fiske's five factors which are nearly orthogonal to each other. These 5 selected variables are:

No. 4. Depressed–Cheerful

No. 17. Conscientious–Not Conscientious

No. 18. Imaginative–Unimaginative

No. 21 Dependent Minded–Independent Minded

No. 22. Limited Overt Emotional Expression-Marked Overt Emotional Expression

The definitions of Scale A variables were designed to depict these variables as sharply as possible as surface behavior, i.e., how the individual would appear directly to the observer.

The 9 Scale B variables were designed to provide opportunity for judgment of the more covert, genotypical, dynamic, or interpretive aspects of personality. Despite the known intercorrelations between the Scale B variables (from –.57 to .79), all 9 have been used in this study, since it is in the description of these aspects of personality that projective techniques are commonly thought to be most useful. These 9 Scale B variables are:

No. 23. Social Adjustment

No. 24. Appropriateness of Emotional Expression

No. 25. Characteristic Intensity of Inner Emotional Tension

No. 26. Sexual Adjustment

No. 27. Motivation for Professional Status

No. 28. Motivation for Scientific Understanding of People

No. 29. Insight into Others

No. 30. Insight into Himself

No. 31. Quality of Intellectual Accomplishments

Scale C included 11 variables on which staff members were asked to make predictive judgment. Of these, only No. 42, "Over-all Suitability for Clinical Psychology," is used here, since this was the variable toward which the entire assessment program was oriented. Throughout the remainder of the discussion, Variable 42 is treated as though it were a Scale B variable for simplification in statistical summary. This assumes that the rating on "Over-all Suitability" represents an inference about a covert, although perhaps extremely complex, dimension of personality and is essentially similar to Scale B variables.

All ratings were made on an eight-point scale with a theoretical distribution of ratings of 3, 7, 15, 25, 25, 15, 7, and 3 per cent for points from 1 to 8 respectively. Raters were instructed to use a reference population of first-year clinical psychology graduate students in American universities.

THE PROJECTIVE RATINGS

As was stated above, during the early part of the week each student was examined with the Rorschach and the Bender-Gestalt *individually*. Each record was scored, interpreted, summarized, and the applicant rated on the scales described above by the test administrator, without other knowledge about the individual than could be gained from the particular projective technique and the personal contact involved during the testing period. The Thematic Apperception Test and the project form of a sentence completion test were administered as *group tests*. Each subject was then rated on each variable of Scale A and Scale B by four different staff members, each rater basing his ratings on a different projective technique. A single staff member was concerned with only one projective method per subject and was instructed to keep himself in ignorance of the findings of the other staff members for that subject. After each of the four projective techniques had been independently analyzed and subjects rated on the basis of each, the Rorschach analyst, serving in a new role of "projective integrator," made another set of ratings on each variable of Scale B based on *all* the projective data, with the exception of the actual ratings which had been independently made on the basis of each projective technique.

The number of students seen by a given clinician was not the same for a given technique, nor was the number of students seen by a given clinician the same, necessarily, for two or more techniques. The number of students per rater per technique is shown in Table 13–1.

TABLE 13–1   *Number of Students Rated by Each Rater on Four Projective Techniques*

TECHNIQUE	RATER								
	W	O	L	F	T	G	R	Q	M	P
	SCALE A								
Rorschach	11	11	12	10	5	9			
TAT	7	8	9	15	3*	14			
SC	4	8	14	4	13	2†			
BG							19	14	15	13
	SCALE B								
Rorschach	18	23	22	22	20	20			
TAT	22	22	14	28	4	25			
SC	16	13	37	4	26	6			
BG							32	29	33	33

* With an N of three, r is either indeterminate or fluctuates widely.

† With an N of two, r is .00 or 1.00.

A given rater may have analyzed more Rorschachs than another, fewer TATs than any or all the others, and some other number of SCs. The differences in N between the two Scales, A and B, are attributable to the fact that cases which were integrated by the "projective integrator" were not rated on Scale A by the "projective integrator" nor by the other projective technique raters. The projective raters used in this study are fewer in number than the total number of projectivists on the assessment staff. Only six are used, each of whom rated enough students via Rorschach, Thematic Apperception Test, and sentence completion to make comparisons among them possible. Four other projective raters were concerned only with the Bender-Gestalt. The latter four, coded by letters R, Q, M, and P, were graduate students at the University of Michigan at the third-year level of training in the VA training program for clinical psychologists and had been trained in the clinical use of the Bender-Gestalt by the same instructor. The other projectivists are coded W, O, L, F, T, and G. They were initially selected on the basis of professional competence, and the choice of another group of projective analysis raters similarly selected would probably not have resulted in any better interpretation of the projective tests. The sampling of techniques and the sampling of variables are both regarded as adequate. Raters were given full freedom with respect to scoring, interpretation, and report writing. The only formal imposition placed on them was the conversion of impressions, deductions, inferences, or conclusions into single numbers on each of the rated variables.

Although students were assigned randomly for projective examination, it was possible that the relatively small number of students seen by a given projectivist using one of the projective devices might have represented a different student population from that seen by another projective rater using the same projective instrument. That is, differences between projectivists' ratings might be found which might be attributable to differences in the students examined and not to differences in the projective techniques. As an additional check on the random assignment of students for projective testing, the following test was made. Distributions of the FinP ratings[3] on students on Variable 42, "Over-all Suitability," were made separately for each of the four projective techniques used in this study. For a given technique, these ratings for students were distributed for each of the projective raters.

In this way it was possible to compare the mean FinP ratings on Variable 42 with respect to the student population seen by each of the projectivists for each of the projective techniques. Epsilon square was computed, and no significant differences were found among the mean ratings for students assigned to different projective raters using

---

[3] Final Pooled Ratings. PI will be used as an abbreviation for the Projective Integrator and the Projective Integration.

the same technique. Since the students had been randomly assigned for projective testing and since no differences were found between students for Variable 42, there was no reason to believe that systematic differences would be found between students on other variables, and no other tests were made.

THE CRITERION RATINGS

In the seven-day period of each student's assessment, three staff members rated the student at frequent intervals. A given staff member would receive certain data on a student and rate, then receive other data and rate again, having filed away his previous ratings, and continue to make independent ratings based on various kinds of data. The first team conference (Preliminary Pooling Conference) produced a single set of ratings which represented a combination of the judgments of the staff team based on these materials: objective and projective tests, credentials, autobiography and Biographical Inventory, and the information obtained by way of the interview (Soskin, 1949). At the final pooling conference, all previous material and all previous ratings were made available to the staff team. Also available at this time were the student's self-ratings, ratings of each student by the other three members of the student team, the separate ratings based on projective methods, and the ratings made by a team of staff members who had observed the student in situation tests with no other knowledge about him. A separate final pooled rating was made on each variable of Scale A and of Scale B. These ratings are regarded as the best available measures of each of the 42 personality traits for each subject assessed and are the criterion measures of this study. They are designated FinP.

The FinP ratings are the most comprehensive and inclusive ratings to come out of the entire week's assessment. These ratings were made by different combinations of three staff members. The staff were initially selected on the basis of professional competence. They had had opportunity to study the student in a wide variety of ways and had had the benefit of judgments of many other skilled clinicians at various points. Although they are admittedly fallible, there can be little doubt that these FinP ratings are as valid criterion measures of these variables as are obtainable at the present time from skilled clinicians using present techniques in an assessment situation.

The FinP ratings are composite criteria consisting of the pooled judgments of three staff members who had available to them the results of the tests and procedures indicated above. A separate FinP rating was made for each variable of Scale A and Scale B. Since staff members were free to arrive at their final judgments as they chose, it would be difficult to say whether FinP ratings emphasized abilities, capacities, past achievement, or personality characteristics. Of interest in this connection is "the fact that assessment staff members tended to be uniformly of the opinion that the interview contributed most to their 'understanding of the case,' followed by either the projective tests or autobiography" (Kelly & Fiske, 1950, p. 404).

Two problems must be considered with respect to the relationship between the ratings based on projective techniques and the FinP ratings. First, how much influence did any or all the projective techniques have on the criterion measures? Second, are there differences in the criterion ratings when the Projective Integrator is and is not a member of the criterion team?

With respect to the first problem of the influence of projective techniques on criterion measures, a quantitative answer cannot be given. The projective technique protocols and the ratings based on them were available to the final pooling team. This constitutes a theoretical defect in the design of this study which was a sacrifice that had to be made in consideration of other aspects of the over-all project design. It would have been preferable, of course, if the ratings based on each projective technique could have been checked against a criterion based on all available data except that technique. This deficiency with respect to experimental independence would have the effect of spuriously raising the correlations between the ratings based on projective techniques and the criterion. The possible effect of dominance in criterion ratings by any one criterion team member tended to be canceled by the rotation of staff members from week to week in such a way that for each of the student classes the criterion teams were differently constituted. This does not eliminate the possibility of what might be called group bias with respect to projective methods. For example, many of the staff members, not themselves projectivists, spoke very respectfully of the value of the Rorschach and may have given careful attention to the Rorschach ratings in arriving at the criterion ratings. The possibility exists that another staff, or the same staff assessing at another time, might have another attitude toward projective methods and arrive at a different set of criterion ratings for the same subjects. Since there is small likelihood of another assessment designed to measure the reliability of criterion ratings by the test-retest technique, these obtained criterion measures must be regarded as the only ones available and therefore, in a practical sense, as universe (not sample) measures.

The problem of the effect of the Projective Integrator as a criterion team member on the criterion team ratings can be evaluated. The Projective Integrator was a member of the criterion team for half the number of poolings. Since the Projective Integrator was also the Rorschach analyst, it might be hypothesized that if he exerted a constant influence on the criterion ratings in the direction of his Rorschach ratings, then the correlations between ratings based on Rorschach and criterion ratings would be higher when the Projective Integrator was a member of the criterion team than they would when he was not. A comparison of correlations between Rorschach ratings and FinP ratings when the Projective Integrator was and was not a member of the criterion team found none of the differences between correlation coefficients under these conditions to be significant at the .05 level, nor was the direction of difference consistent.

Results

THE PROJECTIVE TECHNIQUES

Validities of Ratings Based on Projective Techniques

To determine the extent to which ratings based on projective techniques correlated with FinP ratings, the ratings made by the six raters (four in the case of the Bender-Gestalt) were entered into a single scatter plot for each technique and variable. It was found that something other than "chance" operated to generate statistically significant correlations, since, for Scale A variables, only 1 correlation in 20 was expected to be significant at the .05 level by chance, and we find 9 in 20 significant at this level. With respect to Scale B, where 40 correlations were computed, we would expect 2 to reach the .05 level, and we find 30 of the 40 correlations are significant at this level. In addition, it was noted that only 2 of the 60 coefficients were negative. These two findings, the relatively large number of statistically significant correlations, and the high proportion of positive correlations suggest that the ratings based on projective techniques have some validity. However, these results are, to some extent, spurious since, in addition to the fact that the criterion measures by the six raters were not completely independent, the intercorrelations among Scale B variables were more often positive than negative and fairly high.

The median correlation coefficients between ratings based on each of four projective techniques and FinP ratings are presented in Table 13–2. It was noted that correcting the technique-FinP r's for attenuation in the FinP ratings raised the median r only slightly, the greatest increase being from .31 to .35 in the case of the SC on Scale A. That is to say that even had the FinP ratings been perfectly reliable, the ratings based on projective techniques would have correlated only slightly higher with the FinP ratings.

Differences in the Validities of Ratings among the Projective Techniques

In order to test the hypothesis that there are no differences in the validities of ratings made on the basis of the four techniques used in this study, the following analysis was made. The validity coefficients for each of the techniques for each of the 15 variables were transformed into Fisher's z function and analysis of variance was done for each of the two sets of variables. There was no rater variance here, since raters had been combined for each technique. The results of the analysis of variance for the transformed validity coefficients for techniques for Scale A

TABLE 13–2   *Medians of Correlations between Ratings Based on Each of Four Projective Techniques and Final Pooled Ratings for Scale A and B Variables*

					TECHNIQUE			
SCALE	Ror.	n	TAT	n	SC	n	B-G	n
Scale A	.20	58	.32	56	.31	45	.21	61
Scale B	.29	125	.26	115	.28	102	.14	127
Both Scales	.27		.27		.28		.19	

---

showed no significant differences in validity at the .05 level for the techniques or for the variables. The analysis of variance of the Scale B variables showed no significant differences between variables but a difference between techniques significant at the .01 level. Further analysis showed that this difference was attributable to the ratings based on the Bender-Gestalt; this technique differed significantly from each of the other three techniques which did not differ significantly among themselves. Since the Bender-Gestalt raters were four different people from those whose ratings were based on the other three techniques, conclusions from these findings must be made with great care.

Comparison of Technique Validities on Scales A and B

When the median validity coefficients, which are given in Table 13–2, are examined, one is struck by the fact that with the exception of the Rorschach the coefficients are somewhat higher for Scale A, which is not a result that might have been readily hypothesized beforehand. It may also be noted that while many of the median values are statistically significant (.05 level), none of them may reasonably be regarded as predictively useful. Thus, for the techniques studied (with the exception of the Rorschach), we see that projective methods do not lead to more valid inferences about the more presumably covert aspects of personality, as is frequently argued, than they do of the more obvious aspects of personality. On the other hand, and particularly with reference to the TAT and the SC where the student was not seen by the rater (Ror and B-G were administered by the rater) and behaviorial manifestations of the student were inferred from the protocol only, we find that ratings are as valid, by and large, for overt variables as for covert variables.

The possibility that these findings may have been related to the unreliability of the criterion ratings has been shown to be dismissible. Another criticism of these findings may ask if it is fair to require clinicians (in this instance projective clinicians) to express their impressions and judgments in the form of ratings. The core of the argument is that clinicians are accustomed to describing their findings in the form of language (interpretive findings beyond the scores, ratios, percentages, etc. required by the various test instruments) and not in the form of ratings. While this problem must, perhaps necessarily, remain largely a matter for individual judgment, there is considerable merit in the argument that numbers may be more precise than words and are definitely far more useful in the verification of hypotheses. This position does not deny the possibility that ratings may not accurately represent the judgments about people which clinicians can make from personality test data, nor does it deny the possibility that such judgments may be more accurately communicated in some form other than ratings.

That there are not more differences in validities between the two scales for the projective techniques is a curious finding and difficult to understand. It is not unreasonable to believe that if one has understanding of the dynamics of the behavior one can infer one step more to the overt behavior of a given individual, but in making the additional inferential step there is additional opportunity for error. It would not have been surprising to find that ratings of overt personality characteristics had less relationship to the criterion ratings than ratings of the covert traits. That they do not—and since in both cases the relationships with the criterion ratings are low—suggests further study to determine, for example, how much correlation there is between the criterion measures and ratings based on observations of the subject in the projective testing situation and how much with ratings based on projective data without direct observation of the subject.

Correlations between Projective Technique Ratings

Up to this point, the four projective techniques have been considered as generically related. They have been called by a class name and regarded as methods of evaluating personality characteristics. We have found that ratings based on each of the four techniques show but low correlation with the criterion measures. We shall turn to the question, to what degree are personality ratings based on each of the separate techniques in agreement? This was investigated by intercorrelating the ratings, variable by variable, for each of the four techniques. The results are shown in Table 13-3. While there is a tendency toward positive relationships (101 out of 120) among the independent ratings (no two ratings of a single subject on a given trait were made by the same projective technique rater), there is very little basis for a feeling of confidence that these instruments serve similar functions, i.e., that these instrument-clinician

TABLE 13–3　　　　　*Correlations between Ratings Based on Each of the Projective Techniques**

SCALE A

VARIABLE	Ror/TAT	Ror/SC	Ror/B-G	TAT/SC	TAT/B-G	SC/B-G
4	.02	.08	.08	−.05	.11	.14
17	.11	−.01	.11	.09	.13	−.01
18	.11	.21	.10	.23	.06	.09
21	−.20	.22	.06	.05	.10	−.02
22	−.11	−.01	.27	.46	.03	.04

SCALE B

VARIABLE	Ror/TAT	Ror/SC	Ror/B-G	TAT/SC	TAT/B-G	SC/B-G
23	.12	.04	.11	−.07	.04	.04
24	.02	.09	−.04	.00	.06	−.02
25	−.14	.03	−.01	−.05	.02	−.14
26	.08	.00	.17	.14	.05	.19
27	.11	.08	−.09	.14	.05	.16
28	.15	.02	.07	.04	.13	.10
29	.01	.05	−.16	.13	.07	.01
30	.05	.08	−.09	.09	.09	.08
31	.03	.13	−.07	.06	.34	.15
42	.18	.22	.06	−.05	.10	.17

SCALE	MEDIAN CORRELATION FOR					
Scale A	.02	.08	.10	.09	.10	.04
Scale B	.06	.06	−.02	.05	.06	.09
Both Scales	.05	.05	.06	.06	.07	.08

* Correlation coefficients which are underlined are significant at the .05 level. For Scale A, N equals 61. For Scale B, N equals 128.

combinations are measuring the same thing. Although the proportion of positive correlations is large, only 9 correlations out of 120 are significant at the .05 level, where 6 correlations are expected to reach this level by chance.

THE PROJECTIVE RATERS

Relative Validities of Ratings for Individual Raters

Beyond the techniques per se, we are interested in the relative validities of the individual raters by technique and by variable. In Table 13–4 may be found the median validity coefficients for all traits in Scale A and Scale B respectively and for both Scales together. These are the median correlations for each of the six raters for ratings based on the Rorschach, TAT, and SC, respectively. Table 13–5 contains the same information for the Bender-Gestalt.

TABLE 13–4   *Medians of Correlations between Projective*
Technique e Ratings and Final Pooled Ratings
*for Each of Six Projective Raters**

Rorschach

MEDIAN CORRELATION FOR

SCALE	W	n	O	n	L	n	F	n	T	n	G	n	All
Scale A	.26	11	.10	11	.05	12	.16	10	.00	5	.43	9	.12
Scale B	.30	18	.21	23	.26	22	.44	22	.48	20	.20	20	.36
Both Scales	.30		.21		.22		.44		.48		.30		.19

TAT

MEDIAN CORRELATION FOR

SCALE	W	n	O	n	L	n	F	n	T	n	G	n	All
Scale A	.71	7	.33	8	.37	9	.30	15	—	3	.30	14	.33
Scale B	.26	22	.16	22	.22	14	.44	28	.46	4	.23	25	.28
Both Scales	.28		.21		.26		.40		—		.28		.30

SC

MEDIAN CORRELATION FOR

SCALE	W	n	O	n	L	n	F	n	T	n	G	n	All
Scale A	−.19	4	.54	8	.18	14	.82	4	.52	13	—	2	.52
Scale B	.04	16	.36	13	.32	37	.60	4	.45	26	.46	6	.36
Both Scales	.04		.47		.30		.74		.47		—		.37

* Correlation coefficients which are underlined are significant at the .05 level.

The results obtained (of which only the medians are presented here) suggest that two of the six Rorschach analysts were able to make ratings

TABLE 13–5   *Medians of Correlations between Bender-Gestalt*
Ratings and Final Pooled Ratings for Each
of Four Bender-Gestalt Raters

RATER

SCALE	R	n	Q	n	M	n	P	n	All
Scale A	.23	19	.00	14	.27	15	.30	13	.25
Scale B	.14	32	.10	29	.22	33	.12	33	.15
Both Scales	.14		.10		.26		.20		.16

which correlated with the criterion ratings beyond chance expectancy at the .05 level. For these two raters, F and T, the median coefficients for Scale B are, respectively, .44 and .48. These are the only median coefficients which are statistically significant for the six raters on both scales.

The number of statistically significant individual (not median) correlations is, considering both scales, greater than would be expected in chance occurrence for any rater, since at the .05 level only 1 in 20 coefficients is expected to reach this level by chance. The median value, however, is regarded as a better representation of the validity of a rater, in that it allows for the fact of intercorrelation between the traits within each Scale.

While the evaluation of a correlation coefficient in terms of what may be called its social significance is quite subjective, there is little reason for enthusiasm toward the efficiency with which these six Rorschach analysts were able to predict the criterion ratings. Although the validity coefficients for Rorschach raters may seem somewhat discouraging, it is emphasized that the ratings of Rorschach projectivists F and T appear to be reasonably valid. This finding is congruent with the situation which exists in the area of projective testing in which, to a very considerable extent, adeptness in the use of projective methods is acquired through instruction by masters. In the practical situation of assessment, however, four of the six Rorschach raters, initially selected on the basis of clinical competence, did not make as valid ratings as the other two. The high proportion of positive correlations suggests that, under assessment conditions, the Rorschach method provides a basis for some validity of rating.

These findings and observations also apply, in general, to the data obtained for raters using the TAT, SC, and BG.

RELATIVE CONTRIBUTIONS OF RATERS, TECHNIQUES, AND TRAITS TO VALIDITIES OF RATINGS

In order to determine the relative contributions of each of the three sources of variance investigated in this study to the validities of ratings, the following analysis was carried out. The validity coefficients were regarded as scores, and, after being transformed into their respective z functions, were treated by the method of analysis of variance. Analyses were done separately for Scales A and B, and additional analyses for the Bender-Gestalt.

For Scale A traits, the results indicated that significant differences in validity may be attributed both to techniques and to raters (.05 level) and that the interaction of techniques and raters makes for differences in validity (.01 level). That is to say that for Scale A traits, the traits themselves do not contribute significantly to differences in validity. However, the different techniques make for differences in the validity of ratings, and the different raters make for differences in validity of ratings. We find differences in validity dependent on who rates and on what technique is being used and differences in validity for the combinations of raters and techniques.

A similar analysis of Scale B traits showed significant differences in the validity of ratings for technique-rater combinations. Further analysis, however, showed this difference to be largely the contribution of rater differences in validity of rating. As with the Scale A traits, the traits themselves are not a source of differences in validity of ratings. While the techniques did contribute to differences in rating validity for Scale A traits, they are not sources of difference for the Scale B traits. For the presumably covert aspects of personality, it appears that differences in validity depend chiefly on the rater.

Separate analyses of variance for each of the two Scales for the Bender-Gestalt showed that neither variance due to raters nor variance due to traits was significantly greater than variance due to chance. Since only the one projective method was involved in these analyses, there was no technique variance.

It seemed reasonable to expect that some personality traits would be relatively more validly rated than others by one or all of the projective techniques or by one or all of the projective raters. The absence of statistically significant differences in validities of ratings attributable to differences among traits is necessarily qualified in that to the extent to which there is correlation among traits, it is more difficult to find existing differences. This is not a particularly cogent objection in the case of the Scale A variables for which the intercorrelations were low. The Scale B traits do have, in some instance, sizable correlation between them, resulting in an underestimation of the significance of the between-variable variance.

Other Factors Related to Validity

In this section are presented data with respect to factors, other than those originally considered in the scope of this study, which may have had an effect on the validity of ratings based on projective techniques. Consideration will be given to the possibility of bias in rating; to differences in dispersion (confidence) of ratings; to some additional factors concerning raters; and to the possible effects of unreliability in the predictor and criterion ratings.

BIAS IN RATING

One factor which may be related to the validity of ratings based on projective techniques is the frame of reference in which ratings were made. By "frame of reference" is meant an attitude of optimism represented by a tendency to make ratings in the direction of the "laudatory" or socially desirable end of the rating scale. It is possible that if ratings on a given technique tend, consistently, to be either more or less "laudatory" than the Final Pooled Ratings, this attitude might be related to the validity of such ratings. Similarly, it is possible that such differences in attitude might be related to differences between the relative validities of ratings among the techniques. In order to determine whether such "frame of reference" differences did obtain, the following was done. First, in order to compare the ratings by each of the techniques with the FinP ratings, the significance of the difference between the mean ratings was calculated. This was done by the usual method of obtaining the quotient of the difference between means divided by the standard error of the difference. In each instance, the FinP means were subtracted from the technique means and the arithmetic sign recorded in order that the direction of difference be known. This procedure was followed for the four techniques for the fifteen traits studied. A comparison of FinP means with those of the Projective Integrator was necessarily limited to the ten Scale B traits. Second, the mean ratings by each of the techniques on the fifteen traits were compared with the mean ratings by each of the other projective techniques, again by calculating the significance of each of the differences.

The results of the comparison of mean ratings for techniques and FinP ratings are presented in Table 13–6 in the form of an abbreviated table of signs. Either a plus or a minus sign is entered in the table where a statistically significant (.05 level) difference between means occurs. The plus sign is used to indicate that the technique mean was in the "laudatory"

TABLE 13–6   *Table of Signs Showing Statistically Significant Differences between Mean Technique Ratings and Mean Final Pooled Ratings**

VARIABLE	Ror–FinP	TAT–FinP	SC–FinP	B-G–FinP	PI–FinP
4					†
17	+		+		†
18					†
21					†
22		+			†
23					−
24	−				−
25				+	−
26			+		
27		−			
28					
29	−		−		−
30	−				
31		+	+		
42					−

* In this table, the "+" sign indicates that there is a statistically significant difference (.05 level) with the technique mean in the "laudatory" direction. The reverse is true for the "−" sign.
† The Projective Integrator did not rate Scale A variables.

direction, while the minus sign indicates that the FinP mean was in the "laudatory" direction. An examination of Table 13–6 reveals that the number of statistically significant differences found exceeds the number which might have been expected if only chance were involved, but these differences are not consistently in the same direction. In the case of the Projective Integrator, the obtained significant differences are always in the direction of being less "laudatory," and for the Rorschach one may note a trend in the same direction.[4] These data may be of interest in so far as they characterize the PI and the Rorschach as tending to look on the dark side of personality but probably have little, if any, relation to validity.

TABLE 13–7   *Table of Statistically Significant Differences between Mean Ratings Based on Each of the Projective Techniques**

VARIABLE	Ror–TAT	Ror–SC	Ror–B-G	TAT–SC	TAT–B-G	SC–B-G
4						
17						+
18						
21						
22	−	−				
23			−	+		−
24			−			
25						
26	−	−		−		+
27		+		+		−
28				+		
29	−			−		−
30	−		−			
31						
42						−

* In this table, the "+" sign indicates that there is a statistically significant difference (.05 level) with the first of the two techniques at the head of the column in the "laudatory" direction. The reverse is true for the "−" sign.

When the differences shown in Table 13–6 were compared with the validity coefficients which are statistically significant for the techniques and for the Projective Integrator, it was apparent that statistically significant validity coefficients were obtained at least as frequently when there was not a difference between means as when there was a mean difference. It may also be noted that statistically significant validity coefficients

[4] Soskin (1949) analyzed ratings based only on student behavior in a series of standard situations and found that Situationists "see the sample of subjects are being characterized predominately by the condemnatory pole . . ."

are not consistently associated with differences either toward or away from the "laudatory" end of the rating scale.

In Table 13–7 are presented the signs of statistically significant differences between the mean ratings among the techniques. In this table the minus sign indicates that the first of the two technique abbreviations at the head of the column has a mean rating in a less "laudatory" direction. Thus, the minus sign for Trait No. 22 in the first column signifies that

TABLE 13–8   *Table of Statistically Significant Differences between Standard Deviations of Technique Ratings and Final Pooled Ratings* *

VARIABLE	Ror–FinP	TAT–FinP	SC–FinP	B-G–FinP	PI–FinP
4					†
17					†
18	+				†
21					†
22					†
23				+	
24	+				
25	+	+	+	+	
26					
27				+	
28		−			
29		+			
30					
31				+	
42		−			

* In this table, the "+" sign indicates that there is a statistically significant difference (.05 level) with the technique ratings having the larger standard deviation. The reverse is true for the "−" sign.
† The Projective Integrator did not rate Scale A variables.

there is a significant difference between the mean ratings of the Rorschach and TAT on this trait and that the difference is in the direction of the Rorschach being less "laudatory." The apparent tendency for ratings based on the Bender-Gestalt to be more often in the "laudatory" direction than ratings based on the Rorschach or Sentence Completion may suggest a relationship to differences in validity, since both the Rorschach and Sentence Completion yielded more and higher statistically significant validity coefficients than the Bender-Gestalt. This argument is weakened, however, by the observation that the TAT, too, yielded more and higher statistically significant validity coefficients than the Bender-Gestalt without there being any differences between the means for these two techniques. Again, one might characterize the Rorschach raters as tending to view people darkly, while the Bender-Gestalt raters tend in the direction of rating personality in a relatively benign fashion.

DISPERSION (CONFIDENCE) OF RATINGS

Another factor which needs to be evaluated, since it might be related to validity of ratings, is the spread of scores or ratings. When there is more spread, the likelihood of obtaining higher correlation coefficients is increased. If one is willing to assume that where a rater lacks confidence in his rating he will tend to rate closer to the mean than he will when he does feel confident, then we can use a measure of spread as an index of confidence in evaluating confidence in rating as a factor in validity.

Table 13–8 is a table of signs showing where significant differences in spread (standard deviation) occur. A plus sign indicates that the spread

TABLE 13–9 *Table of Statistically Significant Differences between Standard Deviations of Ratings on Each of the Projective Techniques*[*]

VARIABLE	Ror–TAT	Ror–SC	Ror–B-G	TAT–SC	TAT–B-G	SC–B-G
4						
17						
18		+				
21						
22						
23					−	−
24		+				
25						
26						
27			−			
28					−	
29				−		−
30						
31		+		+	−	−
42	+	+	+			

[*] In this table, the "+" sign indicates that there is a statistically significant difference (.05 level with the first of the two techniques at the head of the column having the larger standard deviation. The reverse is true for the "−" sign.

for the technique ratings is significantly greater than that for the FinP ratings, and vice versa for the minus sign. These data suggest that dispersion of ratings has little or no relation to validity. The ratings based on the Bender-Gestalt, which are the least valid of the four sets of ratings, most often show significantly greater spread than the FinP ratings, whereas the Projective Integration ratings, which are more valid for more traits than the ratings based on the Bender-Gestalt, are in no instance significantly different in spread from the FinP ratings. It is interesting to note that ratings based on each of the four projective techniques (but not the Projective Integration) have significantly larger standard deviations in Trait No. 25, "Characteristic Intensity of Inner Emotional Tension," than the FinP. If this represents a feeling of confidence, it appears not to be justified consistently, since the TAT and BG ratings on this trait did not correlate significantly with the criterion ratings.

A comparison of the techniques with each other in terms of willingness to spread ratings was carried out. The results are presented in Table 13-9. The data suggest that ratings based on the Rorschach tend to be made with more spread than those based on the Sentence Completion and TAT. Similarly, the Bender-Gestalt tends to inspire dispersion of ratings at least equal to the Rorschach. This may be a function of the fact that both the Ror and BG were administered by the rater; i.e., face-to-face contact may be related to dispersion of ratings (confidence). This would be consistent with the staff's opinion that the interview contributed most to their understanding of the case.

ADDITIONAL FACTORS CONCERNING RATERS

It has been shown that different raters contribute significantly to differences in validities of ratings. One possible explanation of this finding, that "good" raters may have been assigned to one technique and "poor" raters to another, is not too tenable, since all the projective raters used the same techniques (except for the Bender-Gestalt) and, in addition, cases were randomly assigned to raters. On the other hand, the number of cases seen by each projective rater varied, and the obtained difference in validities for raters may have been related to difference in size of samples. As a way of evaluating whether there are differences in validity associated with the numbers of cases seen by "good" and "poor" raters, the rank-order positions of raters was used as an index of ability to rate. If we consider that those raters in the upper half of the ranking are "good" raters and those in the lower half are "poor" raters, then for Scale B, we find the following. For the Rorschach the "good" raters, W, F, and T, saw 65 of a total of 125 cases; for the TAT the "good" raters, W, F, and T, saw 54 of the 115 cases; for the SC the "good" raters, F, T, and G, saw 36 of 102 cases. Also, the size of the median validity coefficient for the SC compares favorably with those of the Rorschach and TAT. We may conclude that the size of sample for different raters is not significantly related to validity of rating.

Another possibility to be considered is the effect of a given projective technique on a rater. There may be something in the nature of a given technique which effects a change in the clinician who uses it. The data in Table 13-6 suggest that the Rorschach is more often associated with a tendency to see people in a less benign light than are the other techniques. When the Rorschach rater in his role of Projective Integrator makes a new set of ratings, incorporating the results of the other projective techniques with his own Rorschach results, this tendency to see people in a less benign light is increased.

FURTHER EVIDENCE ON INTERJUDGE AND INTERTECHNIQUE AGREEMENT

As was reported earlier in this chapter, this study found that unreliability of criterion ratings has very little effect on the validity of ratings based on projective techniques. There is no way of knowing, from the present data, to what extent the low validities found are a function of the unreliability of raters. The question may be asked in two ways: to what degree do judges agree when they use the same technique; to what degree does a judge agree with himself using different techniques? In order to answer these questions, another study was carried out, and some preliminary results were available at the time of writing. In this new study four projectivists made ratings based on each of four projective technique records from each of a total of 20 subjects. The number of subjects and raters was limited by practical considerations. On each of the 16 days of the experiment, a rater made ratings based on five projective technique records from five different subjects. For example, on the first day Rater A would have worked with the Rorschach records of Subjects 1 and 16, the TAT of Subject 10, the SC of Subject 12, and the B-G of Subject 4. This same "block" of records would be given to Rater B on the eighth day, to Rater C on the fifth day, and to Rater D on the sixteenth day. In this way each of the 16 blocks of five projective technique records would be worked with by each of the four raters, so that at the end of the 16 days each rater would have rated all the projective records on all 20 subjects. Tables of random numbers were used to assign the projective technique records to the 16 "blocks," after which the blocks were

TABLE 13–10   *Median Intercorrelation Coefficients for Each of Four Raters When Ratings Based on Four Techniques Are Intercorrelated**

VARIABLE	RATER			
	A	B	C	D
4	.32	.12	.19	.06
18	.08	.31	.23	.17
23	−.06	.20	−.03	.02
25	.04	−.15	.06	.18
31	.02	.32	.51	.20
42	.05	.26	.16	.14

* Correlation coefficients which are underlined are significant at the .05 level.

treated as units and distributed by random numbers to the raters. The ratings were then examined for consistency of rating for a rater over the four techniques and for the consistency of ratings on a given technique by the four raters, in both cases for 20 subjects.

In Table 13–10 are shown the results for the consistency of the individual raters, i.e., the intrarater consistency over all four techniques. The data are presented in the form of median values for the 6 intercorrelations of the four techniques. The single correlation which appears to be significant (Rater C, Trait No. 31) may be meaningless in that at the .05 level 1 correlation in 20 may be expected to reach this level of significance.

In Table 13–11 are shown the interrater (intratechnique) agreements. These again are median correlations for the 6 intercorrelations of the ratings of four raters for the same technique. It appears, from the data in

---

TABLE 13–11   *Median Intercorrelation Coefficients for Each of Four Techniques When Ratings by Each Rater on That Technique Are Intercorrelated**

VARIABLE	Ror	TECHNIQUE TAT	SC	B-G
4	.28	.49	.34	.18
18	.52	.22	.78	.44
23	.35	.20	.36	.20
25	.22	.40	.17	.20
31	.58	.16	.51	.34
42	.56	.34	.34	.48

* Correlation coefficients which are underlined are significant at the .05 level.

---

these two tables, that a projective technique tends to generate more coinsistency in rating behavior than the use of a single projective rater. Stated another way, it would appear that different raters will tend to rate a subject in the same way if they use the same projective technique. A given rater will tend to rate the same subject in a nonconsistent manner when he uses different techniques.

Summary and Conclusions

OBJECTIVES

The principal objectives of this study were:

1. To determine the relative validities of ratings based on four projective techniques when these were used to describe personality and to predict "over-all suitability" as a clinical psychologist;

2. To determine whether there were differences in the relative validities of ratings based on projective techniques which were ascribable to the rater;

3. To determine whether there were differences in the relative validities of ratings based on projective techniques which were ascribable to the technique;

4. To determine whether there were differences in the relative validities of ratings based on projective techniques which were attributable to the personality trait being rated.

Other related problems were also investigated.

METHODS AND PROCEDURES

During an intensive assessment program, a total of 128 male first-year graduate students in clinical psychology were rated by ten staff members on 15 personality variables after analysis of protocols from each of four projective techniques, and again after all the projective material (except the actual ratings) from the four techniques had been examined by a "projective integrator." These ratings were correlated with another set of ratings which were arrived at in a "pooling" conference of three staff members who had studied each subject intensively for a week. Since staff members had all the information it was possible to obtain about a subject during an assessment week, the ratings which the three staff members agreed upon in their final conference were taken as the best-rated descriptions of a subject's personality and used as criterion measures. These criterion measures were "contaminated" in that they included the protocols and ratings of the predictors, the effect of which would be spuriously to raise the correlations between ratings based on projective techniques and criterion measures. Under these conditions, the correlations between ratings based on projective techniques and the final staff ratings were regarded as validity indexes. By comparing the correlation coefficients which were obtained in this manner, the objectives of this study could be achieved.

SUMMARY OF FINDINGS

1. The projective techniques.

(a) Ratings based on the projective techniques correlated significantly with the criterion measures more frequently than was expected by chance. These correlations were preponderantly positive, but were, by usual standards, low.

(b) Correcting the criterion measures for attenuation raised the median correlations between ratings based on projective techniques and the criterion measures only slightly. The greatest increase was from .31 to .35.

(c) Ratings based on the Rorschach and the Bender-Gestalt (made by the raters who had administered these techniques) tended to be made with greater confidence, i.e., showed greater spread, than ratings based on the Thematic Apperception Test and the Sentence Completion (which were rated "blind").

(d) Ratings based on the Rorschach tended to be made away from the "laudatory" end of the ratings scale when compared with ratings based on the other projective techniques and with the criterion ratings.

(e) There appeared to be little or no relation between validity of ratings and bias of ratings toward either the "laudatory" or "derogatory" ends of the rating scale.

(f) There appeared to be little or no relation between validity of ratings and spread of ratings.

(g) Preliminary findings suggested that there was more correlation between ratings made by different raters using the same projective technique than between ratings made by a single rater using different projective techniques.

2. The projective raters.

(a) Differences in the validity of ratings based on projective techniques were found which could be attributed to the individuals making the ratings.

(b) Significant differences in the validity of ratings obtained not only between raters, but for the interaction between rater and technique, for both scales and for the Rorschach, the Thematic Apperception Test, and the Sentence Completion; interaction could not be tested for the Bender-Gestalt.

(c) Although some raters were "better" than others, in no instance did the median validity coefficients of statistical significance exceed $r = .48$.

3. The traits

No significant differences were found in the validity of ratings which were attributable to the differences in personality traits rated.

CONCLUSIONS

The conclusions which are drawn from the findings of this study are:

1. Projective techniques, used in the assessment of personality characteristics, measure very little in common.

2. There are significant individual differences in the ability to make valid ratings of personality traits from projective techniques, which appear to be independent of the technique used.

3. The dispersion of ratings made by clinicians on personality traits on the basis of projective techniques does not appear to be related to the validity of ratings.

4. The assessment of the degree to which a subject possesses socially desirable personality traits is, in part, a function of the projective technique which is used in making the assessment.

5. The value of projective techniques as instruments for the assessment of specified personality traits in a group of normal superior adults is apparently limited by low validities.

REFERENCES

CATTELL, R. B. *Description and measurement of personality.* Yonkers-on-Hudson: World Book Co., 1946.

FISKE, D. W. Consistency of factorial structures of personality ratings from different sources. *J. abnorm. soc. Psychol.*, 1949, 44, 329–344.

KELLY, E. L. Research on the selection of clinical psychologists. *J. clin. Psychol.*, 1947, 3, 39–42.

KELLY, E. L., & FISKE, D. W. The prediction of success in the VA training program in clinical psychology. *Amer. Psychologist*, 1950, 5, 395–406.

SAMUELS, H. An analysis of some factors affecting ratings of personality traits based on projective techniques. Doctoral thesis, Univer. of Michigan, 1950.

SOSKIN, W. F. A study of personality ratings based upon brief observations of behavior in standard situations. *Microfilm Abstr.*, 1949, 9, 170–171. (Doctoral thesis, Univer. Microfilms, Ann Arbor, Mich. Publ. No. 1208.)

TUPES, E. C. An evaluation of personality trait ratings obtained by unstructured assessment interviews. *Psychol. Monogr.*, 1950, 64, No. 11 (Whole No. 317).

14

Reliability

BERNARD I. MURSTEIN

The multiple problems of reliability measures for projective techniques are examined. It is shown that projective techniques have lower reliabilities than multiple-choice paper-and-pencil tests because, in addition to the usual sources of error, they add new ones. These include, to name just a few, scorer reliability, the influence of a response on succeeding responses, differences among subjects in the part of the stimulus focused on, and the ofttimes peculiar distributions of scores.

Further, the basic philosophy that "conventional" statistics are inapplicable to projective techniques is held to be untenable. Several solutions, including parametric and nonparametric methods of analysis, are used to illustrate this point.

In the following pages, reliability will be defined and its value in research discussed. Then consideration will be given to the attitudes toward reliability formerly held by many clinicians, followed by specific examples of what they considered the inappropriate use of statistics. A discussion of problems affecting reliability estimates for projective techniques follows, including problems of standardization, stimulus, scoring, examiner effects, length of protocol, length of test, nonnormal distributions, and heterogeneity of the population studied. At this point, several studies using differing measures of reliability will be reviewed, and, in closing, some proposed solutions to problems in reliability will be offered.

"Realiability is the degree of accuracy of a test in measuring whatever

189

it measures" (Jensen, 1959a, p. 4).[1] Statistically speaking, reliability refers to the ratio of true to total variance. Reliability essentially has two aspects, stability and equivalence, the most popular example of the former being test-retest reliability. Even where change from one test situation to another is expected, it is important to estimate the reliability of the change (Green, 1954). This brings into focus the need for equivalence scales. It is presumed that scales based on equivalent samples of items from the same universe of items should produce quite similar scores. Among the most popular equivalence measures of reliability are the split-half, odd-even, and alternate forms. In the split-half, through random procedures or by matching, the original pool of projective cards may be divided into two subsets. The correlation between subsets yields a co-efficient which is corrected by the Spearman-Brown formula, yielding a reliability estimate for the original scale. The odd-even method is similar, differing only in that odd cards in a test, e.g., Rorschach Cards 1, 3, 5, 7, 9, are compared with even Cards 2, 4, 6, 8, 10. In the alternate-forms approach two separate tests are correlated, the Spearman-Brown formula not being used since there is no artificial dichotomy of the cards into two halves.

It is also possible to obtain an estimate of reliability without using alternate forms or separating the test into two separate halves. Coefficients of equivalence from a single set of nondichotomized scores depend on the degree of homogeneity of the test, which is obtained by assessing the magnitude of the interrelationship of the items (projective cards). These measures of internal consistency are often estimated through the various Kuder-Richardson formulas (Gulliksen, 1950). If a high degree of homogeneity is attained, the test is said to measure a single variable and is thereby unidimensional. Operationally speaking, according to Green, unidimensionality and homogeneity have the same meaning and are defined in terms of the degree of covariation among the projective cards or items. Highly interdependent items are homogeneous, and the homogeneous test is also unidimensional. A homogeneous scale is in general a reliable one, but it is not necessary to have homogeneity to ensure reliability. In parallel tests, for example, if test A, intended as a measure of n Achievement, also taps n Affiliation and n Power, it may yet correlate highly with test B if this test contains similar stimulus pull for n Achievement, n Affiliation, and n Power.

Guttman's coefficient of reproducibility (Green, 1954) also gives a single-score estimate of reliability. This coefficient reflects the degree to which the individual's response pattern may be predicted solely by a knowledge of his total score. The items have a cumulative property, so that a person responding positively to the third item on a scale will usually

---

[1] The coverage of the topic of reliability has been made much easier by the publication of two excellent papers by Jensen (1959a; 1959b), to which the interested reader may want to refer for some detailed solutions not presented in this [paper].

also respond positively to the previous two items. If the three items were, respectively, "I am at least 4 feet tall," "5 feet tall," "6 feet tall," and the respondent, a lengthy 6 feet 3 inches, answers the third item affirmatively, we may be fairly confident that he will answer the first two items similarly. In like manner, one can scale a projective technique like the TAT. Consider three cards, differing in stimulus pull for the trait of hostility. If the first card has an average stimulus pull of 60 per cent (that is, 60 per cent of the judges perceive the cards as hostile), the second one 40 per cent, and the third 20 per cent, we expect that the individual who gives an affirmative answer to the card with the least stimulus pull (third card) also will perceive the first and second cards as hostile.

The coefficient of reproducibility gives a slightly inflated reliability estimate in that the test constructor chooses the order of the items so as to give the highest possible value and thereby capitalizes on error variance. A more serious problem is that the minimum possible reproducibility value is a function of the difficulty of the items. Accordingly, it is possible to obtain a value of .85 but have a minimum possible value of .80, indicating negligible improvement in scaling. Several alternatives to this problem are provided by White and Saltz (1957). Generally, a coefficient of at least .90 is considered necessary to establish a scale. A value below this figure leads to the suspicion that the items are multidimensional and that further refinement is necessary.

An alternative variation of the coefficient of reproducibility is the H technique of Stouffer, Borgatta, Hays, and Henry (1952). Space does not permit a detailed description of this method, but basically it consists of increasing the coefficient of reproducibility by pooling items into clusters called "contrived" items. To receive credit for a score, a "contrived" item consisting of three individual items must have two or more of these individual items answered affirmatively. H technique is thus analogous to those subtests on the Stanford-Binet where a subject must answer at least two out of three parts correctly to receive credit for the subtest.

The Reliability of a Reliability Coefficient

The formula for the standard error of a reliability coefficient sets confidence limits for the reliability coefficient. It is dependent on the size of the sample, as the following formula indicates:

$$Se_{r_{11}} = \frac{1 - r_{11}^2}{\sqrt{N-1}} \tag{1}$$

where r_{11} = the reliability of the test
N = the size of the sample

If we obtain an r of .90 for a sample of size 17, the odds are about 2 to 1 that the true population value lies between .85 and .95. This formula, however, does not hold for projective techniques where more than sampling error is involved. Since a projective test involves scoring errors, examiner effects, and variations in administration, the error is larger than for a true-false test, the degree of error increment varying for every specific occasion on which the test is administered. Since this error is indeterminate in so far as the usual reliability coefficient is concerned, another method must be utilized to tap these sources of error. In a following section, we shall outline the solution offered by Jensen (1959b).

Errors of Measurement, Substitution, and Prediction

The applicability of research data on projective techniques to the clinic will often depend on the extent of the errors of measurement, substitution, and prediction. These, in turn, are a function of the relationship of the standard deviation and the reliability of the test. Each of these errors will be briefly discussed and its applicability to projective techniques illustrated.

ERROR OF SUBSTITUTION

Suppose that in a clinic we have parallel forms of a projective test such as the Holtzman Ink Blots. We wish to know how comparable a score on one test is to a score on the parallel form. Our reason might be that the first form has been used earlier, but henceforth we propose to use the second form. We should like to know what error we incur in substituting the score from one form to that on another. The formula which gives us this information is

$$S_d = S \sqrt{2(1-r_{12})} \qquad (2)$$

where S = the standard deviation of test scores
$\quad r_{12}$ = the correlation of the two parallel halves

If, for example, a person gets a color score of 3 for the first form, the standard deviation for the population of subjects from which our individual was drawn is 2, and the correlation of color for the two parallel forms is .91, then $S_d = 2 \sqrt{2(-.91)} = .85$. In other words, an individual whose observed score was 3 on the first form might be expected to score between .81 and 5.19 on the second form 99 per cent of the time (i.e., $3 \pm 2.58 \, S_d = .81$ and 5.19).

ERROR IN ESTIMATING THE OBSERVED SCORE

If a regression equation is used to estimate the score on one test from that on the parallel form as above, the "error of estimate" gives the measure of minimal error. This measure also may be used when retest reliability is known and an estimate is desired for the probable limits within which a score obtained on one test will fall on the second test. The formula is

$$S_d = S \sqrt{(1-r_{12}^2)} \tag{2}$$

where S = the standard deviation
r_{12} = the correlation of two parallel halves, or repeat reliability

If, then, the standard deviation of a group of TAT stories scored for n Achievement is 2 and the test-retest reliability of n Achievement is known to be .91, the standard error of estimate $= 2\sqrt{1-(.91)^2} = .83$. A person whose n Achievement score was 3 therefore would score between .86 and 5.14 on a retest 99 per cent of the time.

ERROR OF MEASUREMENT

In measuring some aspect of personality through a projective technique, it is our fervent desire to assign each person a "true" score. Human fallibility being what it is, we must content ourselves with obtaining an observed score which is part truth, part error. The error made in substituting the observed score for the true score is called the "error of measurement." This measure may be used to tell us the probable limits within which the true score lies. Where we have only one opportunity to test a person, this measure will be more useful than the "error of estimate." In an earlier study (Murstein, 1961), peer-ranking scores on the trait of hostility were normalized and the standard error of measurement was used to determine cutting points for the possession of hostility. The error of measurement also can be used to select personality types from projective techniques, provided some measure of reliability is obtained. The formula is

$$S_e = S\sqrt{1-r_{11}} \tag{4}$$

where S = the standard deviation
r_{11} = the reliability of the test

Suppose that we want to select a group of persons who are high need achievers as determined by their high n Achievement scores on a thematic test. We realize that error is involved in that some persons may have achieved their high n Achievement scores as a function of random error. We determine, therefore, that our risk of falsely calling a nonachiever a high achiever will be 1 per cent. We would, therefore, use the following equation employing the error of measurement:

$$X_i + 2.58(S \sqrt{1-r_{11}}) > T_i > X_i - 2.58(S\sqrt{1-r_{11}}) \tag{5}$$

where X_i = the score of any individual i
$S \sqrt{1-r_{11}}$ = the standard error of measurement
T_i = the "true" score of any individual i

If an individual obtained a score of 3, the standard deviation of the score being 2, and the reliability of the test was .91, the standard error of measurement would be .60, and the individual's true score would lie between 1.45 and 4.55 exactly 99 per cent of the time. We might then confidently select individuals with scores above 4.55 as high achievers and those below 1.45 as low achievers.

ERROR IN ESTIMATING A TRUE SCORE

In the previous equation, we described the error in substituting the observed score for the true score. Assume that we have an equation to *predict* the true score from the observed score, as, for example,

$$\hat{t} = r_{xt} \ \frac{s_t}{s_x} \ \text{x} \qquad \text{(Gulliksen, 1950, p. 43)} \tag{6}$$

where $\hat{t}$ = the predicted true score
r_{xt} = the correlation between the true and the observed score (equals the square root of the reliability of the observed scores)
s_x = the obtained standard deviation
s_t = the true standard deviation (equals the observed standard deviation multiplied by the square root of the reliability)
x = the obtained score expressed in deviate form

Then it can be shown that the error in predicting the true score (that is, the difference between the prediction and the actual true score) is equal to

$$S_e = S\sqrt{r_{11}} \sqrt{1-r_{11}} \tag{7}$$

where S = the observed standard deviation
r_{11} = the reliability of the test

If, as in the previous cases described, the standard deviation of our achievement scores is 2 and the reliability is equal to .91, then $S_e = .57$. For a person who obtained a score of 3, therefore, we could say with 99 per cent accuracy that his true score lay between 1.53 and 4.47. In any given set of data $S_e < S_e < S_d < S_d$. In our examples the respective values were .85, .83, .60, and .57. These measures apply to projective as well as to "objective" data. They will indicate the discriminating ability of the scores employed in many of the projective techniques.

All the reliability estimates mentioned earlier have been employed in projective studies, as we shall shortly see. Errors of measurement have rarely been applied, though there is no reason why they should not also be utilized. Regardless of whether a reliability coefficient is obtained, every test has a reliability value somewhere between 0 and 1.00, although it may not always be possible to obtain a reliability estimate. A reliability value ≥ .90 is considered adequate for tests of individual prediction such as the Wechsler and Stanford-Binet. Most personality tests show much lower reliabilities, often inhabiting a range of .50 to .90 with the mode probably around .80. Although such a figure seems adequate, it should be noted that it accounts for only 64 per cent of the variance. High reliability does not assure high validity, or any validity, for that matter. Low reliability does, however, put an upper limit to validity, since validity cannot exceed the square root of the product of the reliabilities of the test and the criterion. It follows therefore, that, if test A has a reliability of .70 and criterion B one of .75, the validity cannot exceed .72. There are situations, however, where tests with low reliabilities, even in the .30 to .50 range, may still be of value. In multiple correlation, for example, a test with low reliability which does not correlate with another, but does correlate significantly with the criterion, may be preferable to a test which is very reliable but correlates highly with other tests in the battery, thus adding little to the battery's predictive ability. Nevertheless, without adequate reliability a single test used for individual prediction will rarely be useful. It is often possible, consequently, to spare oneself useless hours in undertaking a study if the reliability of the measure to be employed is not adequate.

In view of these considerations it is difficult to appreciate the pronouncements that reliability has no place in projective techniques. Consider the statements of Frank:

Psychology developed the statistical procedures for establishing reliability and validity because the only data available were the single observations or measurements taken at one time on each subject. Since no other data were available on the prior history and development of the subject, reliability had to be determined by *statistical manipulation* of these data themselves; also since no other data were available on the subject's other functions and activities, only statistical validity could be established. It would appear that these tests of reliability and validity devised to meet the difficulty presented by absence of other data now act as barriers to the use of any other procedures for personality study in which reliability and validity for each subject is tested through these other non-statistical methods [*italics mine*] (Frank, 1939, pp. 399–400).

The substitute measure of reliability offered by Frank is the method of congruity among data obtained by different procedures. This method, while popular, has not been used as a measure of reliability, else we might have the phenomenon of negative reliability coefficients (Murstein & Wheeler, 1959). In my opinion, the attitude which characterized the views of the front ranks of "clinical" psychologists in 1940 stemmed from a concern with the whole functioning person which the "experimental" psychologists did not share and an unfamiliarity with many basic statistical methods. It is, therefore, no accident that clinical psychologists such as Zubin, thoroughly versed in statistics, did not deride their contribution.

Objections to Reliability Estimates with Projective Techniques

There is a basic difference of opinion in the philosophy of the meaningfulness of thematic data. Murray speaks of separating the wheat from the chaff (1951), implying that some responses will not be meaningful in analyzing a protocol. Bellak (1950), on the other hand, believes that every response has value. We are thus faced with a dilemma. General test theory holds that a certain portion of the variance found in responses may be profitably treated as random "error variance," while the concept of "psychic determinism" holds that no response is accidental. The resolution of this problem lies in the knowledge that a projective technique has no invariable reliability but has a degree of reliability for a specific method of analysis and another degree of reliability for a different task. Murray is thus alluding to a specific use of the TAT when he speaks of chaff, and Bellak is stating that what is error variance for one approach may not be error variance in some other kind of analysis. The two men thus do not differ in their philosophy when the semantic confusion is lifted. With this orientation to "specific" reliability, let us consider some objections to the use of "conventional" reliability estimates with projective techniques.

One objection concerns the attention given to the reliability of a specific component of a profile score when it is the Gestalt that is important. So long as the configural score on the Rorschach, say $\Sigma M : \Sigma C$, is said to have meaning, however, the components which make up the score must be reliable or the total score cannot be reliable. In statistics if not perception, the reliability of the whole is definitely related to the reliability of the parts. If one speaks of the over-all reliability of a protocol obtained by reading it and jotting down a diagnostic impression, it is conceivable that one might have high reliability for diagnostic impressions and low reliability for a given component. But that is not the same problem as was mentioned above, where the configural score is the unit for interpretation.

The split-half method has been criticized by Watson (1949), Symonds

(1949), and Sargent (1945) as being inappropriate because both the Rorschach and the TAT differ radically in the stimulus properties of the cards, so that it is next to impossible to obtain comparable halves. Actually, one way to approach a solution of this problem is to obtain an average of reliabilities of all possible halves through the use of Gulliksen's formula 11 (Gulliksen, 1950, p. 224).

Another method of obtaining a split-half estimate despite the diverse stimulus pull of the cards is to use subjects rather than cards as the unit of analysis. Suppose that we have 20 students ranked for n Achievement on the first half of a thematic test. We can compare these students for ranking on the second half and correlate the ranks by Spearman's rho. There are two reasons why this method is unusually attractive. First, split-half reliability is often obtained by correlating the two halves of the test and estimating the reliability of a test twice the length of the half through the Spearman-Brown formula

$$r_t = \frac{2r_{AB}}{1 + r_{AB}} \tag{8}$$

where r_t = the reliability of the whole test and is obtained by correcting
        the split-half correlation to double length
and r_{AB} = the correlation between the test halves

The use of this formula assumes, however, that one deals with parallel halves. This fact may be demonstrated if (1) each half has equal errors of measurement and (2) each person's true score on one half is equal to his true score on the other half. For more practical purposes, these assumptions mean that the means and standard deviations of the scores must be equal for both halves. These conditions will probably be met only when using rank scores rather than raw scores.

Second, a unique "measurement error" is found in the TAT which is not found with the usual "objective" tests. This error has to do with the fact that, even though two halves may be truly parallel with regard to stimulus pull for a given need, say, n Achievement, the second half may reveal far less achievement imagery. This occurrence may be due to the "saw-tooth" effect (Atkinson, 1950) whereby the fact that an individual gives achievement imagery in one card may lead him to desist from repeating the same kind of story in future cards. Here again, however, so long as we assume that this effect is equal for each person, the rank order of the subjects should remain the same despite the drop in raw score. Raw scores rather than ranks, we shall shortly see, have been used in most split-half reliability studies, resulting in a violation of the assumptions in the use of the Spearman-Brown formula and an attendant overestimate of the true reliability.

The split-half approach, however, is not the only reliability approach deemed inappropriate by some clinicians. The test-retest reliability has been criticized because:

1. A retest is psychologically not the same experience as the initial test.

2. The subject may remember his initial responses and therefore retesting is only a measure of recall and not of reliability.

3. Projective techniques are so sensitive to the slightest changes in the subject, reflecting transient moods, etc., that a lack of correspondence between test and retest is said to be due to genuine changes in the subject (Jensen, 1959a, pp. 7–8).

In view of the above, the "antireliability" group must be suspected of "doublethink," for, unmindful of the ephemeral nature of the test results, the TAT has been used to determine the effect of psychotherapy by administering it before this treatment began and after it had been terminated. Moreover, despite the transient nature of the TAT responses, the test is supposed to give an X ray of the private world, presumably a fairly stable private world. In short, it is difficult to consider seriously objections to the application of reliability measures to the TAT which are based on ignorance of statistical measures and on the "flexible" logic which enables some psychologists to argue that the TAT reflects the immediate environment predominantly, while others maintain that it taps the deep underlying aspects of personality. One could, of course, argue that the content reflects situational changes but that the formal properties reflect basic personality. In this eventuality, however, there is no reason why repeat-reliability measures cannot be applied to either of these approaches. Let us therefore consider some more pressing problems in the measurement of reliability with projective techniques.

Reliability Problems Peculiar to Projective Techniques

THE PROBLEM OF STANDARDIZATION

Everyone who takes the MMPI gets 566 questions to answer, all administered in approximately the same manner. The scoring also is standardized, and even the interpretation may be considered somewhat invariate, in that certain profile scores are said to have fairly specific meanings. With projective techniques, the situation is often quite different. A wide variety of instructions may be used with the TAT, from Murray's instructions to the clinician's own "home-brewed" system. Different cards with different stimulus pulls are used at the discretion of the administrator, and he may record the stories verbatim or jot down only the important segments. Some clinicians attempt to inquire for missing parts of the story, while others do not press the subject at all. I shall not argue that these variations may not be of value in some instances, but it is difficult to compare two or more divergent reliability estimates when in essence we have different tests united only by the rubric "TAT cards."

THE STIMULUS

The construction of alternate forms for a true-false test is relatively easy with regard to motivating the subject, since he is set to respond to the same aspect of each item, namely, whether it is true or false. On a projective technique, however, the subject may respond to any part of the stimulus he wishes to. One might scale a given Rorschach or TAT card for a number of variables, but it is impossible to scale all conceivable parts of the card to which the subject might respond. Accordingly, it is always questionable as to just how similar a parallel set of blots or cards is to the primary set.

Another difficulty has to do with the random choice of both the Rorschach and TAT cards by their founders. In neither case was the selection random with regard to empirical utility, for both sets were chosen on the basis of clinical experience. Rather, "random" here refers to the underlying personality or need dimensions tapped by the cards. The TAT, for example, is heavily weighted to represent hostility and negative emotionality. Relatively few cards from the point of view of the stimulus tap the need for affiliation. In a situation where some needs are depicted on several cards and other equally important needs are rarely depicted, it is unwarranted to assume that the need content of stories reflects the importance of these needs in the personality (Macfarlane & Tuddenham, 1951).

DIFFERENCES IN SCORING ABILITY

Scorers may differ greatly in their ability to judge a protocol. What makes for these differences among scorers is a fascinating subject that has not been extensively studied, but it is obvious that adequate inter-scorer reliability necessitates two good scorers with the same "set" toward scoring. Another problem is the "halo" effect, that is, the tendency to judge any given response by the over-all impression of the protocol. The effect is most marked where there is ambiguity as to the scoring of an item. Suppose that we deal with a protocol replete with hostile expression. If, then, an ambiguous response is considered, there is a tendency to presume that it is simply a subtle expression of hostility. This effect is more pronounced in some scorers than others and is a deterrent to obtaining adequate reliability.

SCORING PHILOSOPHIES

Some clinicians believe that the projective protocol should be scored as a whole rather than by reference to specific atomistic components. The difficulty with this approach is that it is impossible to separate the value of the method from the acumen of the scorer. One atomistic principle has been to stay close to the data and make no inferences. The *descriptive content categories* are an example of this philosophy. Which aspects of content are to be scored, however? Once one begins to specify these aspects, the categories become limited and interpretation must be made as to whether to score a given sentence or two in a TAT story. Hence, increasing specificity may be offset by decreasing agreement (Macfarlane & Tuddenham, 1951). Another problem is the fact that, for the TAT at least, content is strongly influenced by the stimulus pull of the cards, and a simple content analysis may not yield adequate validity.

The use of *formalistic categories* is in keeping with the newer trend in clinical appraisal. Such methods usually offer high reliabilities, but it is difficult to decide which of the thousands of scoring possibilities are meaningful. At a yet more abstract level are the *interpretive categories*, which involve classification in terms of inferred meaning. Presumably, the interpretation of the meaning of a TAT story should yield better predictability about the personality patterns of an individual than any of the other categorizations. The difficulty is that interpretive scoring depends heavily on the subjective judgment of the scorer and his theoretical leaning. Moreover, it is always a question as to whether the judgments are more descriptive of the subject or of the interpreter.

None of the scoring approaches has proved clearly superior to the others. On the TAT, simple content analysis has proved to be of little value with highly structured pictures because of the stimulus pull of these pictures. The use of formalistic variables appears promising, but no extensive superiority has been demonstrated in the research. The use of interpretive categories is theoretically best, but scoring difficulties have made this approach largely an abandoned method.

EFFECT OF THE EXAMINER

The reader will recall that the discussion of the effect of examiner differences in the study of n Achievement indicated that faculty examiners tended to elicit significantly more n Achievement than graduate students.[1] Suppose, then, that two tests are given to the same group such that the pretest is followed by the experimental condition, followed by the posttest. Assume further that a faculty member serves as the administrator for the first session with a graduate assistant administering the follow-up test. The differences in examiners will not only affect the reliability of the test adversely but in this instance will also be confounded with the effect of the experimental treatment. The "examiner" effect on reliability is often overlooked in otherwise thorough studies.

---

[1] See Chapter 5 in Bernard I. Murstein (1963).

LENGTH OF TEST, LENGTH OF PROTOCOL, AND VERBAL FLUENCY

In most true-false tests, the longer the test is, the higher the reliability is likely to be. A test constructor, therefore, seeks to increase his test to maximum length, consistent with the time available and the tolerance of the test taker. The general formula for relating length of test and reliability is the Spearman-Brown formula

$$R_{LL} = \frac{K r_{11}}{1 + (K - 1) r_{11}} \tag{9}$$

where r_{11} = the reliability of the original test

K = the increase or decrease in comparison to the unit original test

R_{LL} = the reliability of the lengthened or decreased test

If the formula could be applied to the TAT and a reliability of .50 had been achieved for 10 TAT cards, what would the reliability be for 20 cards? According to the formula, it would be .67. Before anyone rushes to get 10 more cards, it should be noted that it is doubtful whether this increment in reliability would actually be achieved. The use of the Spearman-Brown formula assumes that the new items are parallel to the previous ones. Accordingly, merely doubling the number of cards does not meet the "parallel" requirements. In fact, adding cards beyond an optimum number may well decrease reliability, as Reitman and Atkinson (1958) report. After a given number of cards, the subject may seek to vary his themes so as to avoid telling the same story. The effect of this maneuver would be to lower split-half reliability.

Intelligent people are usually verbally fluent, and verbally fluent people tell longer stories than taciturn individuals. Any kind of scoring system on the TAT which involves counting words connoting a particular need will yield positive relationships between intelligence, verbal fluency, and the trait measured. If we measure hostility on the TAT by counting the number of aggressive words, we will probably find a substantial correlation between number of words and hostility score. Exactly the same situation exists for the Rorschach, where the number of responses is correlated with a large number of determinants (Fiske & Baughman, 1953). Clearly, it is necessary to correct for this factor, and solutions will be discussed in the section, "Some Remedies for Reliability Problems."

UNORTHODOX MEASUREMENTS AND DISTRIBUTIONS

Many of the raw data elicited from projective techniques do not seem amenable to analysis by the parametric statistics such as the Pearson coefficient of correlation and, to a lesser degree, the t test. The Pearson r presumes that we are dealing with interval data. Interval data are recognized by the fact that the distance from 1 to 2 is equal to the distance from 2 to 3. The Fahrenheit thermometer is an example of interval measurement. It is doubtful, however, that most "need" scores on the TAT fulfill this condition for definition as an interval scale.

Another factor limiting the use of parametric techniques is that the distributions of projective scores are often badly skewed, with a clustering of scores at the low end of the scale. Not infrequently J-shaped distributions occur, with most of the scores at zero and the remainder scattered throughout the rest of the scale. The solution is to transform the data where possible to interval scales which are also symmetrical and employ parametric statistics in the analysis. In some cases, no suitable adjustment of the data can be made (J-curve data), and the use of nonparametric tests is the only choice. These measures will be discussed shortly.

HETEROGENEITY OF THE POPULATION AND RELIABILITY

It is seldom appreciated that reliability is usually very much a function of the heterogeneity of the characteristics studied in the population. Tests reported in the literature often are standardized on a heterogeneous population. The impressed reader tries the test out on the relatively narrow range of personality types found in his hospital or clinic, often with disappointing results. The narrowing of range and the constricted standard deviation affect both reliability and validity, but we shall concentrate our attention on the former for the moment.

Assume that a simple, projective sentence completion test is employed at a military induction center and yields a reliability of .90 with a standard deviation of 15. What can the clinician expect the reliability to be if the test is used at an outpatient clinic specializing in neurotics, where the standard deviation for a given sample of clients is 8? The answer is provided by the formula listed by Gulliksen (1950, p. 124), with the terminology slightly modified for our purposes:

$$R_{11} = 1 - \frac{s^2}{S^2} (1 - r_{11}) \tag{10}$$

where R_{11} = the new reliability in the outpatient clinic
S^2 = the variance at the induction center
s^2 = the variance at the outpatient clinic
r_{11} = the reliability (.90) at the induction center

The new reliability turns out to be a disappointing .65. This value is only a rough approximation, since the motivation of the subject, if not the administration and scoring of the test, may be expected to vary from situation to situation, adding a further source of error. There is no "cure" for low reliabilities resulting from restricted range where the range cannot be altered. The wisest solution is to estimate the variability to be found in the clinic and to choose a test whose reliability has been obtained under just such circumstances, or whose reliability coefficient is sufficiently high to withstand a decrease due to curtailment of range.

Some Remedies for Reliability Problems

Earlier, several pressing problems concerning reliability were discussed briefly. For several of these difficulties little can be done.

STANDARDIZATION

Lack of standardization is not a statistical problem but a volitional one. While standardization obviously is of value, practical considerations prohibit standardization with regard to national samples for all possible traits. Even where standardization has been achieved for a finite trait population as Veroff, Atkinson, Feld, & Gurin (1960), have done, there is always the problem of needing special cards for a specific purpose. Suppose, for example, that the investigator wishes today to investigate the possibility of an oedipal situation in a young boy, tomorrow to examine sibling rivalry, and the next day to explore passive-aggressive feelings. The possible areas of conflict far outweigh the possibilities of depicting these scenes on cards. It is this sort of situation which leads to variations in cards used, instructions, and manner of inquiry. Consequently, it is impossible to standardize one set of TAT cards which will be equally useful for all personality problems. Where a specific area is of interest—for example, marital adjustment—something can be done, and we shall discuss some alternatives under the following heading, "The Stimulus."

THE STIMULUS

It has been stated earlier that the "shotgun" approach of randomly selecting thematic cards and the concomitant unequal stimulus representation of need areas yielded themas whose frequency or intensity of appearance did not correspond to the importance of these areas in the personality. It is possible, nonetheless, to construct a set of cards to tap a relatively specific area (Murstein, 1963, pp. 167–235). Here it will suffice to state that the principle involves a selection of cards representing the entire range of the trait and the use of judgments to remove cards which frequently elicit other motives than the one desired. Such tests often have very high internal consistency as reflected by the coefficient of reproducibility.

SCORER RELIABILITY

The literature reviewed indicates that several principles may be of value here. The first involves keeping the scoring system as simple as possible. We have seen how dichotomized scoring possibly may yield higher reliability indices than the use of many categories. This does not mean that there is anything intrinsically unsound about the latter procedure; as a matter of fact, all things being equal, if we compute a Pearson r with a scale having few interval units, the correlation will be lower than it ought to be, because of the effects of coarse grouping. In many cases, however, the difficulty in judging subtle differences in the manifestation of the trait studied lowers the reliability more than it strengthens the discriminating power of the test. It is best to score each card on a simple quantitative basis, but to use a sufficient number of cards to thereby gain a broad range of scores necessary for successful validation. The second and third principles have been discussed earlier and will simply be listed here. They involve the use of a training manual with practice protocols and the use of a standardized set of cards with whose scoring problems the scorers may readily become familiar.

Often persons who administer tests for research purposes also score them. There are two main objections to such a procedure. First, there is a confounding of scoring reliability and the effect of the examiner in testing. Second, the examiner often forms a clinical impression of the subject during testing. If he should also score the protocols, he is likely to score ambiguous responses in accordance with his clinical diagnosis. This "halo" effect even operates in a situation where the scorer is not the examiner but does score the whole protocol. In this case, an early "sick" response will influence the scoring of ambiguous responses encountered later in the protocol. This factor has been controlled by Pope and Jensen (1957) in scoring Rorschach responses for "pathological thinking" by having *each* individual response of the whole protocols of the subjects typed on separate cards and shuffled before delegating the responses to the scorers.

The use of ex post facto data derived from clinic files provides a wealth of information if the scoring of the protocols by the original scorers is highly correlated with the present scorers. Dana (1955) provides a method which indicates whether the data can be used as they are or whether they need to be rescored. The steps are:

1. Select a small random sample of protocols for each examiner represented in the clinic file.

2. Have these records scored independently by two or more new scorers.

3. Obtain a measure of correlation between the two new scorers.

4. Obtain a correlation between each of the new scorers and each of the original scorers.

If the correlation between the new scorers is not appreciably higher than that between any one of the new scorers and the old scorers, the data may be used intact. If any of the correlations between old and new scorers is appreciably lower than that between the two new scorers, the protocols of this particular old scorer must be scored anew by the current crew of scorers.

The usual practice in research is to accumulate as many subjects as feasible while paying scant attention to the number of scorers, with the result that often the minimum number of two is employed. The advantage of using three or more scorers with a modest number of subjects rather than two scorers with a large number of subjects may be readily demonstrated. When an analysis of variance is computed, scorer reliabiliability may be determined by a formula given by Jensen (1959b, p. 36).

$$r_{RR} = \frac{V_p - V_{pR}}{V_p} \tag{11}$$

where r_{RR} = the correlation between raters (scorers)
V_p = the variance between persons (subjects)
V_{pR} = the interaction between subjects and scorers which is used
as the error term

Dividing both numerator and denominator by the error term to obtain F ratios, we obtain

$$r_{RR} = \frac{F - 1}{F}$$

The degrees of freedom will be n_1 = (subjects −1) for subjects and n_2 = (subjects −1) (scorers −1) for scorers. Suppose that we ask what value the F ratio must reach to be significant at the .05 point if we have three scorers and 15 subjects. Consulting an F table, we observe that for 2 and 14 degrees of freedom an F value of 3.68 will be significant at the .05 point. How many subjects would be needed to match that value for significance if we have only two scorers? The F table reveals that even with an infinitely large population we would still need a value of 3.84 to reach significance at the .05 point. For research purposes, therefore, there is much to be gained by increasing the sample of scorers to three or more rather than adding unnecessary computation and administrative time costs by utilizing large numbers of subjects and only two scorers.

EXAMINER EFFECTS

The large number of sources of error in projective techniques makes the usual procedure of estimating reliability by correlation methods inadequate because these methods consider only random sources of error. Sources of error such as scoring differences, examiner effects, and their interaction, for example, are not revealed in split-half methods. Through analysis of variance methods, however, it is possible to obtain independent unbiased estimates of the population variance as well as reliability estimates of each of these sources of error. The analysis of variance model used to illustrate the study of examiner and scorer effects is a Type III design (Lindquist, 1953). This design is particularly suited to this problem if every examiner does not test every subject, but every scorer scores every subject. It will serve just as well if the examiner administers the test to each subject but the scorers score only a portion of the total number of protocols. What we are considering in short is a "mixed" design containing independent and "correlated" treatment effects.

Assume, then, that we deal with three examiners, two administrative conditions (neutral instructions, instructions designed to make the sub-ject appear at his best), and three scorers. The dependent variable will be *n* Achievement. It will be recalled that every examiner does not administer the test to each subject, as this would involve practice effects, but instead the examiners are randomly assigned five subjects for each of the two administrative conditions. The independent treatment effects are thus realized within a 3×2 factoral design, with the "correlated" effects (scorers score *all* the protocols) constituting the second part of the analysis. Table 14–1 illustrates the nature of the design.

TABLE 14–1   *An Analysis of Variance Design for the Study of Examiner, Instructional, and Scorer Effects on TAT Responses Scored for Achievement*

SOURCE OF VARIANCE FOR BETWEEN (INDEPENDENT) TREATMENTS	d.f.	SOURCE OF VARIANCE FOR WITHIN (CORRELATED) TREATMENTS	d.f.
Between:		Within:	
Subjects $abn - 1$	29	Subjects $abn(c - 1)$	60
Instructions $(a - 1)$	1	Scorers $(c - 1)$	2
Examiners $(b - 1)$	2	Scorers $\times$ instructions	
Instructions $\times$ examiners $(a - 1)(b - 1)$	2	$(c - 1)(a - 1)$	2
Error (between)		Scorers $\times$ examiners $(c - 1)(b - 1)$	4
$ab(n - 1)$	24	Scorers $\times$ instructions $\times$ examiners	
		$(c - 1)(a - 1)(b - 1)$	4
		Error (within) $ab(c - 1)(n - 1)$	48
		Total $abcn - 1$	89

From this one experiment we obtain estimates of differences between subjects, instructions, examiners, and scorers, as well as estimates of the significance of the important interaction effects. These provide information as to whether some examiners elicit more achievement with a particular set of instructions, scorers vary for different instructions, scorers differ according to which examiner's subjects they are scoring, and the scorer $\times$ instructions interaction differs across examiners. If we had wished, we could also have assessed the stimulus properties of the thematic cards used, the personality characteristics of the subjects, and the effect of administering the test on two or more occasions. The only limitation imposed would be the increasing difficulty of having at least five subjects for each experimental condition as the number of these conditions became very large. Jensen (1959b) presents another type of design and methods of obtaining reliability estimates for the various components influencing the projective response. In sum, the analysis of variance would seem to be an efficient yet relatively little-used method for the study of the determinants of the projective response.

LENGTH OF TEST AND LENGTH OF PROTOCOL

It is difficult to generalize as to the effect of lengthening a projective test on the reliability of the test. The usual Spearman-Brown formula for increased length does not apply, since the added cards are seldom parallel to the previous ones. On the TAT, for example, we have noted a "saw-tooth" effect whereby alternate cards are more highly correlated than succeeding ones. Fatigue and the avoidance of previously given themes are "measurement errors" which also void the use of the Spearman-Brown formula. Perhaps the only plausible recourse is to compare tests employing similar or identical cards. The use of standardized sets of cards, as in the McClelland series, also facilitates comparison.

I have previously alluded to the fact that many trait scores are as much a function of verbal fluency as of more underlying personality dimensions. It is clearly necessary to control this factor. One method is to partial out the effect of length of protocol by use of a regression equation. Thus, we correlate n Achievement and occupation, holding length of protocol constant. Unfortunately, we may also partial out some of the "treatment" effect to the extent that occupation and length of protocol are correlated. Another method is to divide the protocols collected into different categories as a function of length and analyze reliability separately for each group. Otherwise, if the reliability is determined on the basis of considerations of protocols of all lengths, the standard error of measurement will hardly be applicable for any given protocol. The Spearman-Brown formula cannot be used here because one would have to make the untenable assumption that the first half of a TAT story is parallel to the second half. Lastly, the variable of productivity can be sacrificed to the gain of obtaining an equal number of responses from everyone. Thus, the subject may be asked to give just three responses to a Rorschach record. The suitability of this procedure will depend on the purpose of the analysis.

The Use of Distribution-Free Statistics

In recent years there has been a big switch to the use of nonparametric statistics in analyzing projective technique data. The reason for this occurrence lies in the fact that these statistics usually avoid the assumptions of normality of distribution, homogeneity of variance, and equal interval data, sometimes made requisite for the use of parametric techniques like the t and F tests. The distribution-free methods, however, are hardly "cost-free." The price paid is that the use of these instruments by and large results in a loss of much information contained within the data. For example, the use of rank scores neglects the fact that the distance between a rank of 1 and a rank of 2 may be much larger in terms of the underlying dimension measured than the distance between a rank of 2 and a rank of 3. Consequently, these statistics are usually less powerful than tests which make assumptions in that they have a larger tendency to accept the null hypothesis when it is false than do parametric tests. The state of data, however, is often so precariously limited by errors of measurement that the use of "weak" tests is sometimes sufficient to opiate an otherwise clearly significant result. Some evidence (Boneau, 1960; Lindquist, 1953) exists that both the t and F tests are extremely robust and may be safely used with almost any kind of data. The chief exceptions, according to Norton (quoted in Lindquist, 1953), occur when sampling takes place from populations with *both* different shapes and heterogeneous variances. This statement, however, presumes equal sample sizes. The violation of the homogeneity of variance assumption may result in extensive distortion in utilizing t and F tables *if* the sample sizes differ radically from group to group.

Boneau's concluding remarks regarding his study of the t test are sufficiently important to quote in some detail. He states that in most situations the accuracy of the t test will be sufficiently high to warrant its use, even though the assumptions of homogeneity of variance and normality of the underlying distributions are untenable.

The large number of situations in which the t test is applicable have the following general characteristics:

(a) The two sample sizes are equal or nearly so; (b) the assumed underlying population distributions are of the same shape or nearly so. (If the distributions are skewed they should have nearly the same variance.) ... If the sample sizes are unequal, one is in no difficulty provided the variances are compensatingly equal. A combination of unequal sample sizes and unequal variances, however, automatically produces inaccurate probability statements which can be quite different from the nominal values. One must in this case resort to different testing procedures. . . . If the two underlying populations are not the same shape, there seems to be little difficulty if the distributions are both symmetrical. If they differ in skew, however, the distribution of obtained *t*'s has a tendency itself to be skewed, having a greater percentage of obtained *t*'s falling outside of one limit than the other. . . . Increasing the sample size has the effect of removing the skew, and, due to the Central Limit Theorem and others, the normal distribution is approached by this maneuver. By the time the sample sizes reach 25 or 30, the approach should be close enough that one can, in effect, ignore the effects of violations of assumptions except for extremes. Since this is so, the *t* test is seen to be functionally nonparametric or distribution-free (Boneau, 1960, pp. 62–63).

As an additional point, Boneau states that Bartlett's test for homogeneity of variance, which is extremely sensitive to nonnormality, is often used to determine whether data can be treated by analysis of variance. Quoting Box, he states that the use of this unrobust test to determine whether an analysis of variance can be used is "rather like putting out to sea in a rowing boat to find out whether conditions are sufficiently calm for an ocean liner to leave port" (Boneau, 1960, p. 62).

These remarks indicate that psychologists have largely overrated the effect of violations of the assumptions of parametric statistics. Yet, even in those relatively few instances where the data cannot be analyzed by an analysis of variance, other steps are possible. If one can assume that the population involved is normally distributed for the trait scored, then the data may be normalized. It is not necessary to assume that the raw scores are normally distributed, and this fact is a boon, since the crude measures employed with projective techniques make such an occurrence rare. Particularly in the case of Rorschach and TAT scores, a positive skewness is often observed with many zero scores and few extremely high ones. Among the more useful transformations excellently discussed by Jensen (1959b) are square root, cube root, reciprocal, powers, logarithms, and arcsin. Once transformed, the data may usually be analyzed by any of the parametric techniques.

Where the data are somewhat J-shaped, U-shaped, or bimodally distributed, it is possible that no transformation except a normalizing one will be of help. If, however, the trait represented by the score cannot be assumed to be normally distributed in the population from which the sample stemmed, nonparametric tests may be used as a final resort. If the data are very badly J-shaped and contain very many zero scores, as often occurs with projective data, normalizing may not be of help, and here too, recourse must be made to nonparametric statistics. We shall now consider some of these nonparametric methods likely to prove serviceable.

PHI COEFFICIENT

This coefficient assumes neither underlying linearity nor a normal distribution and on that account has been used in some factor analytic studies with the Rorschach (Murstein, 1960). It is useful when the distributions are truly dichotomous or are continuous but treated dichotomously for convenience. It also assumes that the cells in its fourfold table are independent of each other. Therefore, ratio scores which are not independent because of the presence of common denominators will yield spurious reliability estimates. Other crucial limitations are that the phi coefficient is not an estimate of a parameter, has no confidence limits, and does not always vary from $+1$ to -1. This latter limitation can be overcome by dividing the obtained phi by the marginal frequencies. In this way a picture of the intrinsic relationship of the variables will be produced, although this figure is not of utility in actual prediction. Confidence in phi values can be tested by conversion to chi square (Guilford, 1950, p. 341).

CHI SQUARE AND THE COEFFICIENT OF CONTINGENCY

Where more than two classes are scored by each judge, a coefficient of contingency is used. A hypothetical example of its use would involve two raters scoring a TAT for emotional tone, identification with hero, outcome, etc. One scorer is represented along the ordinate, his judgments for each variable described by each row, while the other scorer's judgments appear in the columns. The coefficient of contingency is limited in size as a function of the number of categories and is tested for significance via chi square (Guilford, 1950, p. 345).

RHO

This rank-order correlation is often useful when the underlying trait can be assumed to be normally distributed, in which case the ranks are converted to normalized scores by reference to Hull's table (Guilford, 1954, p. 182). Even when this assumption cannot be met, rho is useful in providing a measure of relationship where the scale qualities of data are unknown. It is thus especially valuable in judgments of the adequacy of the Draw-a-Person and Bender-Gestalt tests. It can also be used for a quick estimate of Pearson r. Used in this way, however, it inherits the assumptions of linearity and homoscedasticity of that statistic.

PERCENTAGES

In the face of uncertainty regarding the use of parametric measures, many projective technique researchers have turned to percentage agreement between scores as a measure of reliability. This approach is repugnant to Jensen, who would be happier "if this measure were abondoned entirely." His reasons are as follows:

In the first place, percentage agreement tells us none of the things we wish to know from a measure of reliability. It tells us nothing about the properties of variance in obtained scores that is attributable to variance in true scores. It tells us nothing about the standard error of measurement of the scores or of their potential discriminating power. Furthermore, the meaning of percentage agreement differs from one score to another, depending upon the amount of agreement that could be attributable to chance alone. Finally, percentage agreement should not even be regarded as a rough index of reliability, since its relation to reliability is hardly more than coincidental. The writer has never seen a case where a better measure could not be used in its place (Jensen, 1959b, p. 58).

To show how wasteful of information percentage agreement is, Jensen quotes the following example of judges making rank judgments. In two cases percentage of agreement is found to be equal while rho correlation differs radically.

| Judge A: | 1 | 2 | 3 | 4 | 5 | — 60% agreement |
| Judge B: | 4 | 2 | 3 | 1 | 5 | rho = .10 |

| Judge A: | 1 | 2 | 3 | 4 | 5 | — 60% agreement |
| Judge B: | 2 | 1 | 3 | 4 | 5 | rho = .90 |

The reason for this disparity resides in the fact that, in so far as percentage agreement is concerned, a big disparity in judgment is weighted equally with a small disparity. In rho correlation, on the other hand, the size of the disparity is reflected in the size of the correlation.

Even where percentage agreement might legitimately be used, as in obtaining a measure of agreement for categorized data, additional information is required for useful interpretation but is seldom provided. Consider the inspection of the Rorschach for schizophrenic signs within a guidance clinic. We may expect that these signs will occur but rarely, and accordingly agreement on the absence of the signs is highly probable. In fact, if the signs occurred in but 3 per cent of the cases, and one scorer adopted the uniform "set" of judging all protocols as nonschizophrenic while the other scorer made no errors of judgment, percentage agreement would still be 97. What is crucial, therefore, is the number of times the scorers agree on the presence of the schizophrenic signs. This effective percentage agreement is obtained by consideration of only those instances where one or more scorers have stated that schizophrenia is present. If 100 protocols are examined and Judge A says that he sees schizophrenic signs 5 times, while Judge B sees them only 2 times, and both of Judge B's positive judgments agree with those of Judge A, we have an effective percentage agreement of 2 out of 5, or 40. If we had considered percentage of agreement without reference to the ratio of the presence of schizophrenic signs to the absence of such signs, the percentage agreement would have been 97.

The feeling of uselessness of percentage agreement is not universal. Dana (1955), for example, prefers percentage of agreement because it makes no assumptions, as do parametric techniques. The use of correlation rather than percentage of agreement has been attacked by Brown, Lucero, and Foss (1962), particularly when the data are grouped in a five-point scale. They cite their own example of percentage agreement and correlation discrepancy with a group of hospital patients. In the convalescent ward, raters agreed 82 per cent in their five-point judgments, while their Pearson r was −.09. In the regressed ward, one scale yielded only 38 per cent agreement, but a substantial r of .72. The authors state that the meaningfulness of r is lost if the data are limited as to range or are coarsely grouped. To illustrate this point, they created a fictitious example, shown in Table 14–2, where all the judgments are either 1 or 2, and agreements are represented by $N_{11} + N_{22}$.

TABLE 14–2   *Hypothetical Ratings by Two Raters on a*
                           *Five-Point Scale**

		RATER Y					
RATER X		1	2	3	4	5	
	1	N_{11}	N_{21}	O	O	O	$N_{1.}$
	2	N_{12}	N_{22}	O	O	O	$N_{2.}$
	3	O	O	O	O	O	O
	4	O	O	O	O	O	O
	5	O	O	O	O	O	O
		$N_{.1}$	$N_{.2}$	O	O	O	N

* From Brown, Lucero, & Foss, 1962; reproduced by permission of the *Journal of Clinical Psychology.*

The Pearson r is in this case equal to

$$\frac{NN_{22}-N_{2.}N_{.2}}{\sqrt{N_{1.}N_{2.}N_{.1}N_{.2}}}$$

Inspection of the table indicates that, if N_{22} is equal to zero, the correlation will be negative even though percentage of agreement may be quite high.

To add to the confusion, suppose that we have two raters judging on a six-point scale. Judge A may confine his judgments to categories 1, 2, 3. Judge B may confine his judgments to categories 4, 5, 6. Yet it is theoretically possible to have zero percentage agreement and perfect correlation. To accomplish this unlikely fact, Judge B's and Judge A's scores would have to covary perfectly, with Judge B's rating always two points higher than the corresponding rating given by Judge A.

To emerge from this miasmatic morass, it should be said that neither of these tools can be favored over the other on purely theoretical grounds without reference to the specific situation. Where the crude data can be transformed into normalized form, where class intervals are preferably eight or more in number, where the range is not restricted, and where the amount of disagreement is important to note, the coefficient of correlation is the method of choice. Where the data are grossly nonnormal, where transformation is impossible, where judgments are on a five-point or less scale and consist of scores grouped at either extreme with accompanying restricted range, and where a slight discrepancy in judgment is as "good as a mile" in terms of psychological importance, then percentage agreement or "effective" percentage of agreement is likely to be the more useful tool. Cases in between will have to be judged on their psychological or practical merits rather than on statistical issues.

MATCHING

This method, quite popular some years ago, now seems to be on the wane. This decreasing popularity is not a function of lack of success. Palmer (1952), for example, had eight medical students match 100 stories of 20 outpatients on five cards. The over-all degree of success obtained via a coefficient of contingency was a respectable .79 ± .07. The difficulty lies in identifying the source of the success or failure in matching. While the globalness of matching may appeal to the "holist," it also makes the technique an examiner-test situation effect with no possibility of identifying the means of success or failure. The judge is at the mercy of the material given him to work with. The projective technique may be falsely blamed or praised for results which indeed are not characteristic of it. The information provided may emphasize, for example, minor aspects of the TAT which throw the matcher off stride, while the crucial material is never presented to him.

On the other hand, given a heterogeneous population, the matcher may identify protocols belonging to individuals on the basis of similarity and differences in vocabulary. This factor is not peculiar to the TAT and does not constitute a fair test of its efficacy. Lastly, some matchers may be highly skilled at picking up these clues whereas others are not, and it is unwarranted, therefore, to attribute resulting success or failure to the technique. If one is interested in determining the skill of particular clinicians with TAT stories, it is permissible to establish a reliability of interpretation by having each clinician sort the protocols into various diagnostic categories. What is being assessed, however is clinician-thematic responses used for classification. So long as no claims are made that this constitutes a test of the reliability of the TAT, no complaint can be raised.

Q SORT

An increasingly popular approach is the Q sort, which has been described earlier. If two judges sort the same statements obtained from a TAT protocol on a "most like" the subject to "least like" him continuum, we have, in effect, interjudge reliability. This technique could also be used for test-retest and parallel-form reliability as well as in validity studies. The Q sort is similar to matching in involving a measure of examiner-test interaction rather than an evaluation of the TAT or of the examiner alone. Because of its forced normal distribution, however, it is readily amenable to treatment via the Pearson r. Considerable question has been raised, nevertheless, as to the applicability of a forced-choice solution to the study of personality. By way of reiteration, let it be said that the justifiability of a forced sort depends on whether the statements sorted are representative of the particular individual's personality characteristics. In essence, this means that the applicability of the population of statements to the person should always be determined before testing. In the event of disparity between the two, there are serious limitations to the use of this method. In addition to the difficulties involved in trying to fit every head into the same hat, so to speak, we must contend with the irritation of the subject doing a self-sort in being forced to place items which he may feel are not like him at all into the "most like me" continuum. This irritation may result in a decrease in the care of sorting and a concomitant loss of reliability.

Furthermore, there are statistical problems involved when, for example, an analysis of variance is intended. Strictly speaking, the use of analysis of variance assumes that the sorting of one statement should be independent of the sorting of any other statement and that the probability of any alternative in choice of statements should remain the same for each statement (Gaito, 1962). This requirement is clearly not met in the forced sort except with regard to the placement of the first statement. Thereafter, the probability of the placement of any item in a given category increases until in a 100-item sort the last item is completely determined once the first 99 items have been accounted for. This may readily be seen by the following example. Let us assume that the subject has sorted 97 items and has one space left in columns 1, 2, and 3, respectively. When he picks up the ninety-eighth item, there is a probability of .33 that he will place it in column 1. Let us further assume that he puts it in column 2 instead. Now he has two statements left, and the probability of placing the ninety-ninth item in column 1 is .50. This time he places it in column 1, and the hundredth item can only go in the last remaining space, column 3. Because of the loss of information when all subjects are forced to have the same mean and variance as in the Q sort, Cronbach and Gleser (1953) advocate the use of a free sort, in which an individual is free to place any number of items in any of the columns. If the data assume the shape of a normal distribution, they may be treated by any of the conventional methods of analysis. Regardless of the distribution, however, the D measure advocated by Cronbach and Gleser may be used as an index of similarity between scores. The formula, as it might apply to a comparison of self-sorts for two persons, is

$$D = \sqrt{\sum_{j=1}^{K} (S_{j1} - S_{j2})^2} \qquad (12)$$

where D = the distance between the total number of items
  sorted by the two subjects
S_{j1} = one subject's self-sort for the jth item
S_{j2} = the second subject's self-sort for the jth item

This formula is readily recognizable as related to the formula for the distance between two points appearing in any textbook on analytic plane geometry.

In sum, the choice of free versus forced sort will depend on the specific conditions as just described.

A Potpourri of Reliability Problems

CAN TEST-RETEST RELIABILITY BE TESTED APART FROM THE MEMORY FACTOR?

As Jensen has indicated (1959b), if we wish to consider test-retest reliability, eliminating the memory factor, we note the effect that the time interval has on the internal consistency of the test. Suppose that on the Rorschach we have one group give two responses to each card and compute the internal consistency by any one of the Kuder-Richardson formulas cited earlier. A second group is given the cards and told to give but one response to a card. Two months later the latter group again takes the test, and the subjects are told that the one response per card which they are to give must not repeat a response previously given. The internal consistency measure is repeated for this second group and compared with that of the first group. If there is no noteworthy difference, than the time lapse has not significantly affected the reliability of the test.

If one wishes to maintain freedom of response, a somewhat different procedure is followed. One half of the test is given on one occasion and the second half on a subsequent occasion. By means of an analysis of variance procedure (Jensen, 1959b, p. 56) we compare the average correlation between cards within one session with the average correlation between cards administered in separate sessions.

THE WHOLE AND THE SUM OF THE PARTS IN RELIABILITY

The revolt against the "atomists" led many projective theorists to stress the value of configurational analysis. Just as a chain is no stronger than its weakest link, however, a profile score is no more reliable than its most reliable component and is often considerably less reliable. A formula for the reliability of the difference between two scores appears in Gulliksen, 1950, p. 353:

$$r_{x-y} \; \frac{\bar{r} - r_{xy}}{1 - r_{xy}} \qquad\qquad (13)$$

where r_{x-y} = the reliability of the difference between x and y

r_{xy} = the correlation of x with y

$\bar{r}$ = one half of the sum of the reliabilities of tests x and y

Assume that for a clinic population we wish to relate thematic expression of aggression with overt behavior as judged in the clinic. Being leery of taking it for granted that we have a simple straightforward relationship between thematic aggression and overt aggression, we want to know something about inhibitions to the expression of aggression. We therefore construct two separate scales, one for aggression and one for anxiety over expression of aggression. Our measure of thematic behavior which considers inhibition is the net score of expressed aggression minus anxiety over aggressive expression. The reliability for aggression is .80 and for anxiety is also .80. The correlation between the two scores in this somewhat inhibited population is .50. What is the reliability of our difference score? By means of the formula given above we find that, while each of the components has a reliability of .80, the profile score has a reliability of .60. Unlike the old Gestalt adage that the whole is greater than the sum of its parts, for the reliability difference scores, at least, the whole is equal to or less than the sum or difference of the parts.

Summary and Conclusions

The vast majority of studies show poor or mediocre reliability estimates. Unfortunately, this problem has been largely ignored by many practicing clinical psychologists. The questionable validity of many projective techniques is in part the inevitable consequence of the low reliability of these measures. There are many more sources of error variance in dealing with projective media than with true-false type tests. Whereas the latter type of test usually involves only random error, reliability estimates of projective techniques must take into consideration the varying stimulus properties within a test, scoring differences, examiner effects, and the motivation of the subject, to mention but four additional sources of error. One solution to this dilemma is to tighten the administrative procedure by measuring the stimulus properties, training scorers with a standardized manual, and developing a standard series of pictures and instructions. Another approach is to analyze the contribution of these variables to the projective response through analysis of variance procedures. This approach has been relatively little used in projective techniques research because of overconservative beliefs that it could not be justifiably applied to projective techniques and the lack of familiarity with complex statistical methods by many clinically oriented psychologists. Increased familiarity with statistics and a growing realization of the applicability of parametric methods to projective data should lead to an improvement in the reliability of these tests and an increasing tendency to approach them with both a qualitative and quantitative viewpoint.

REFERENCES

ATKINSON, J. W. Studies in projective measurement of achievement motivation. Unpublished doctoral dissertation, Univer. of Michigan, 1950.

BELLAK, L. Thematic apperception: failures and the defenses. Trans. N.Y. Acad. Sci., 1950, 12, 122–126.

BONEAU, C. A. The effects of violations of assumptions underlying the t test. Psychol. Bull., 1960, 57, 49–64.

BROWN, B. W., JR., LUCERO, R. J., & FOSS, A. B. A situation where the Pearson correlation coefficient leads to erroneous assessment of reliability. J. clin. Psychol., 1962, 18, 95–97.

CRONBACH, L. J., & GLESER, GOLDINE C. Assessing similarity between profiles. Psychol. Bull., 1953, 50, 456–473.

DANA, R. H. Rorschach scorer reliability. J. clin. Psychol., 1955, 11, 401–403.

FISKE, D., & BAUGHMAN, E. E. Relationships between Rorschach scoring categories and the total number of responses. J. abnorm. soc. Psychol., 1953, 48, 25–32.

FRANK, L. D. Projective methods for the study of personality. J. Psychol., 1939, 8, 389–413.

GAITO, J. Forced and free Q-Sorts. Psychol. Rep., 1962, 10, 251–254.

GREEN, B. F. Attitude measurement. In G. Lindzey (Ed.), Handbook of social psychology. Vol. 1. Cambridge: Addison-Wesley, 1954. Pp. 335–369.

GUILFORD, J. P. Fundamental statistics in psychology and education. (2nd ed.) New York: McGraw-Hill, 1950.

GUILFORD, J. P. Psychometric methods. (2nd ed.) New York: McGraw-Hill, 1954.

GULLIKSEN, H. Theory of mental tests. New York: Wiley, 1950.

JENSEN, A. R. The reliability of projective techniques: Review of the literature. Acta Psychologica, 1959, 16, 108–136. (a)

JENSEN, A. R. The reliability of projective techniques: Methodology. Amsterdam: North Holland Publishing Co., 1959. Pp. 32–67. (b)

LINDQUIST, E. F. Design and analysis of experiments in psychology and education. Boston: Houghton-Mifflin, 1953.

MACFARLANE, JEAN W., & TUDDENHAM, R. D. Problems in the validation of projective techniques. In H. H. & Gladys L. Anderson (Eds.), *An introduction to projective techniques*. Englewood Cliffs: Prentice-Hall, 1951. Pp. 26–54.

MURRAY, H. A. Uses of the thematic apperception test. *Amer. J. Psychiat.*, 1951, 107, 577–581.

MURSTEIN, B. I. Factor analyses of the Rorschach. *J. consult. Psychol.*, 1960, 24, 262–275.

MURSTEIN, B. I. The relationship of the possession of the trait of hostility to the accuracy of perception of hostility in others. *J. abnorm. soc. Psychol.*, 1961, 62, 216–220.

MURSTEIN, B. I. *Theory and research in projective techniques: emphasizing the TAT.* New York: Wiley, 1963.

MURSTEIN, B. I., & WHEELER, J. I. The projection of hostility on the Rorschach and thematic stories test. *J. clin. Psychol.*, 1959, 15, 316–319.

PALMER, J. O. A note on the intercard reliability of the TAT. *J. consult. Psychol.*, 1952, 16, 473–474.

POPE, B., & JENSEN, A. R. The Rorschach as an index of pathological thinking. *J. proj. Tech.*, 1957, 21, 59–62.

REITMAN, W. R., & ATKINSON, J. W. Some methodological problems in the use of thematic apperceptive measures of human motives. In J. W. Atkinson (Ed.), *Motives in fantasy, action, and society*. Princeton: Van Nostrand, 1958. Pp. 664–684.

SARGENT, HELEN. Projective methods, their origins, theory, and application to personality research. *Psychol. Bull.*, 1945, 42, 257–293.

STOUFFER, S. A., BORGATTA, E. F., HAYS, D. G., & HENRY, A. F. A technique for improving cumulative scales. *Publ. Opin. Quart.*, 1952, 16, 273–291.

SYMONDS, P. M. A review of literature on the thematic apperception test. In *Adolescent fantasy: an investigation of the picture-story method of personality study*. New York: Columbia Univer. Press, 1949. Pp. 10–51.

VEROFF, J., ATKINSON, J. W., FELD, SHEILA C., & GURIN, G. The use of thematic apperception to assess motivation in a nationwide interview study. *Psycholog. Monogr.*, 1960, 94, No. 12 (Whole No. 499).

WATSON, R. I. *The clinical method in psychology*. New York: Harper, 1949.

WHITE, B. W., & SALTZ, E. Measurement of reproducibility. *Psychol. Bull.*, 1957, 54, 81–99.

PART II

RORSCHACH

15

The Role of Stimulus in Rorschach Responses[1]

E. EARL BAUGHMAN

Reviewing many of the studies dealing with the stimulus properties of the Rorschach, Baughman lays several long-cherished assumptions to rest. Chief among these is the belief that color has powerful, pervasive effects on the responses of the subject. He shows that color affects the subjects more with regard to their feelings about the cards than it affects their formal scores. Moreover, the scores and time latencies said to occur with "color shock" are also found with achromatic counterparts of the Rorschach color cards, thus vitiating the significance of this concept.

Relatively few researchers have experimented with changing the stimulus properties of the Rorschach, but over all, their results indicate that the contour of the blots is the chief determinant of the response in so far as the response is represented by psychogram scores. The real question, however, is, do the scores obtained really reflect the subjects' perceptions, or are they verbalizations reflecting defensive sets, judgments about what the subject thought determined his responses, or perhaps responses by the subject that will satisfy the examiner and save him from a laborious inquiry? For a solution to this dilemma, the reader should examine another article by Baughman, Chapter 17 in this volume.

[1] This article was developed as part of a project supported by grant M-1027 from the United States Public Health Service.

221

The use of ink blots to analyze personality represents a creative effort of Hermann Rorschach, a man trained in medicine and a practicing psychiatrist. A similar statement can, of course, be made with regard to Freud and psychoanalytic theory. The subsequent histories of both these creative efforts, however, have emphasized their essentially psychological natures, and it is with general psychological principles that both must ultimately make their peace. Tremendous efforts with this objective in mind, have been made in recent years by both psychologists and psychoanalysts interested in psychoanalytic theory. Individuals working with the Rorschach technique have become aware recently of quite similar pressures and have begun to respond in constructive fashion to such demands. Although it is not our purpose to analyze these forces, it should be noted that many of the same criticisms are directed against the Rorschach technique which in the past have been leveled against psychoanalytic theory. Perhaps more than anything else these trends reflect an increasing concern with the need to construct a unified behavior theory that encompasses behavior wherever it is found, be it on the analytic couch, in the animal laboratory, or in response to a series of amorphous ink blots. Recognizing the need to bring Rorschach theory into a closer relationship with general psychological principles, this article presents a review and evaluation of studies which have been carried out in an attempt to clarify the perceptual basis of the Rorschach technique.

Perceptual Theory and Rorschach Theory

A large portion of general psychological theory has been built on the assumption that one must somehow relate observed behavior to the critical aspects of the stimulating situation in which the behavior is evoked. Put in other terms, certain stimuli lead to particular responses, and it is one of psychology's major tasks to discover these relationships at an empirical level and then integrate these findings so as to formulate general psychological principles or laws. A primary objective for psychology thus becomes the discovery of the stimulus for a given response, a principle elucidated by Dewey (1896) a half-century ago in his famous discussion of the reflex arc and underlined in recent discussions by Boring (1952) and Zubin, Eron, & Schumer (1965). Much of current-day behavior theory has been structured so as to be consistent with the spirit of this formulation, even though the details of the different theories vary considerably. At an empirical level, acceptance of this principle has resulted in a multitude of research studies in which various aspects of the stimulus situation have been varied in order to observe their effects on behavior. Each time that another such study appears in print, one can see at least an implicit acknowledgment of the Dewey-Boring assertion that "a stimulus is not something given in research but something to be discovered by research" (Boring, 1952, p. 141).

In view of the fact that Thurstone (1948) and others have criticized the Rorschach technique as being based on principles not within the bounds of psychological science, it is perhaps startling and somewhat paradoxical to find that the core of the technique formulated by Rorschach rests on a concern with a question quite identical with that which Dewey, Boring, and others acknowledge as being the primary task of psychology. To clarify this statement, one need only be reminded that the major responsibility of the examiner in a Rorschach testing situation is to discover what it is about the stimulus that evoked the response, i.e., discover the stimulus for the response. Early in his work, Rorschach recognized that individuals were differentially sensitive to the several dimensions (e.g., form, color, shading) of the stimulus, and it was his major hypothesis that this differential sensitivity was in turn related to particular personality characteristics of the respondents. Thus, if one could determine the attributes of the blots to which an individual had responded, he would then be in a position to infer the existence of certain personality traits. The inquiry was the means by which the examiner proceeded in his attempt to clarify the determinants of the responses. "What about the blot made you think of ———?" is a question that all experienced users of the technique have repeated almost ad infinitum.

In light of these facts, then, why is the Rorschach considered to be outside the bounds of psychological science by many psychologists? Obviously no single answer will suffice to a question such as this, but three considerations do stand out. The first involves the fact that many observers recognize a close affinity between psychoanalytic theory and the type of thought brought to bear on a Rorschach protocol, an affinity given clearest expression in the recent work of Schafer (1954). To some of these observers, psychoanalytic thinking has never settled very well in the digestive tract, and these attitudes find rather easy transfer to an evaluation of the Rorschach technique and preclude a reasonably objective appraisal. A second consideration revolves around the fact that many psychologists pride themselves on the quantitative nature of their science and eschew anything that smacks of subjectivity. The difficulties in dealing quantitatively with many aspects of Rorschach performance are too well known to bear repeating here. At the same time, however, it should be noted that increased sophistication in quantitative techniques is beginning to provide procedures to overcome some of the major problems in this regard (Cronbach, 1949).

The third consideration (and the one which is the focal point of this article) turns on the relationship between Rorschach theory and perceptual theory. Ultimately, of course, there cannot be one theory of perception which applies to the Rorschach and another theory which applies to extra-Rorschach situations. Rorschach thought of his technique as being fundamentally perceptual in nature, and it was with the formal properties of the response or how the response came about that he was most deeply concerned. Despite this early formulation of the theoretical basis for the technique, and despite the fact that this emphasis on the structural aspects of the response has continued until very recent years, it nevertheless remains true that Rorschach theory and orthodox psychological theories of perception have made little contribution to each other. As a matter of fact, one must search for communication, let alone contribution.

By looking more intensively at historical trends, it is possible to discern a basis for this failure to mutually enrich. Psychologists interested in the classical laboratory problems of perception typically went about their work by introducing variations into the stimulus input and correlating these variations with the behavioral output. The Ss in such experiments were merely means to an end, and it was usually the hope that they were somehow representative of people in general. Little or no attention was given to the needs, wishes, drives, and similar variables resident within the S. Over in the area of Rorschach work, quite a different situation existed, for here the focus was on the individual as an individual, with motivational variables being of central concern. Hundreds of investigations were reported in the literature in which Ss with different personal characteristics were studied in their response to the Rorschach blots, but it was not until 1948 that research was reported in which there had been carried out an experimental manipulation of one of the properties of the Rorschach blots (Lazarus, 1948). Since that time twenty-four additional studies of this type have appeared (six unpublished), but that they only begin to scratch the surface is indicated by Hutt's recent statement that "very little work has as yet been done on the theoretical import of the nature of the stimulus material itself" (1954, p. 199).[2] One thus finds that classical experimental work has been focused on stimulus material (to the neglect of the perceiver), while Rorschach workers have been riveted to the perceiver (to the neglect of the stimulus material). Only in comparatively recent years have perceptual theorists given adequate recognition to the need for including both stimulus and S variables in a comprehensive theory of perception (Blake & Ramsey, 1951).

An early recognition of the need to unite perceptual theory and Rorschach theory may be found in the paper by Brosin and Fromm (1942) in which they attempt to apply principles of Gestalt psychology

---

[2] The paucity of such research becomes evident when one finds that more than 2,500 research articles and books have been published on the Rorschach to date (Klopfer, 1956).

to the Rorschach experiment. Bruner (1948) presents a similar argument for union (without the Gestalt emphasis) in a more recent paper. The most detailed discussion of this problem may be found in the forthcoming volume by Zubin, Eron, & Schumer (1965), who rely heavily on the work of Gibson (1950) in their analysis. Wertheimer (1957) has also published an interesting discussion of perception and the Rorschach. The concern here, however, will not be primarily with these theoretical discussions but rather with the question of what the empirical research studies to date have to offer in terms of furthering our understanding of the role of the stimulus in Rorschach responses.

To prevent confusion, the reader should recognize that when reference is made to the stimulus or stimuli, the Rorschach blot(s) are intended. What effects do the various properties of these blots have on the S's behavior? Does color somehow make a difference? Are variations in shading or brightness immaterial as far as the S's responses are concerned? What about figure-ground contrast? Do small form areas within larger portions of the blot modify responsiveness in an appreciable manner? How do the blots compare with one another in terms of the problems they present to the S? Is the sequence of stimuli important in shaping behavior? These are the kinds of questions to which attention is directed. In so limiting the task, there is no intention to imply that the stimulus is just the blot; obviously it is more than that, as recent research has demonstrated (Sarason, 1954). Such variables as instructional set, examiner characteristics, and purpose of the testing are clearly part of the stimulus context for the S. It remains true, however, that the core of the stimulus for most Ss is the blot, and this core needs to be understood more completely.

Primary attention will be devoted to those studies which have attempted to clarify the role of the stimulus through experimental manipulation of its properties, since, as noted above, this procedure is in direct keeping with classical experimental procedure. Chronologically, however, such research is of recent date. Following discussion of these studies, briefer mention will be made of other investigations which somewhat more indirectly contribute to clarification of the general problem.

Studies Involving Experimental Manipulation of Stimulus Properties

Boring provides a succinct rationale for these experiments with his statement that "the effective stimulus is not an object but a property of the stimulus-object, some crucial property that cannot be altered without changing the response . . ." (1952, p. 144). Implied in this statement is the generally accepted notion that objects (including ink blots) are vested with a number of properties and that one property of the object may be more instrumental than another property in directing response to that object. To determine if and how this is so, the experimenter needs to vary the properties in question and note the resultant variations in behavioral response (if any) to the object.[3]

Table 15–1 presents a summary of the empirical studies which have been reported within the above methodological framework. The studies are listed in chronological order based on publication date, except for unpublished studies, which are listed according to date of completion.

Twenty of the 25 investigations listed in Table 15–1 are concerned with the effects of color; only the studies reported by Balloch, Barnett, Baughman, Belden and Baughman, and Grayson attempt to evaluate the effects of attributes other than color. This focus of research reflects the central role of color in Rorschach theory plus the relative ease with which suitable achromatic renditions of the standard blots may be constructed for research purposes. Shading also plays a central role in Rorschach theory, but the technical problem posed for the experimenter who desires to treat shading as an independent variable is much more formidable.

While there has been considerable agreement that color should be the first stimulus attribute to be studied intensively as an independent variable by such methods, there has been wide variation in the selection of Ss, research designs, and dependent variables. Color-shock signs, reaction time, productivity, 8-10/R%, and preference values have received major attention as dependent variables, but in some investigations most of the commonly utilized summary scores have been analyzed as related to the color variable. Subject populations have included normals, neurotics, organics, and psychotics, but the college psychology student continues to show up as an S more often than members of any other single class. Research designs have used both individual and group administration techniques; they have also used counterbalanced orders of administration as well as single administrations of the test to equated groups of Ss. When counterbalanced designs have been employed, the interval between readministrations has varied from two days to four months.

Before taking a closer look at the structure of the research designs summarized in Table 15–1, mention should be made of the modified stimulus materials used in these experiments, since the experimental blots are not uniform from one study to another in the same sense as are the standard blots. Beginning with Wallen (1943), achromatic reproductions of the standard colored blots were made by each investigator

---

[3] In retrospect, one might argue that this type of research should have been carried out in the early formative years of work with the Rorschach. Had this been done, much of the confusion and controversy related to such concepts as "color shock" and "gray-black shock" might have been avoided.

TABLE 15–1 *Studies Based on Experimental Manipulations of Rorschach Stimulus Properties*

AUTHOR	PRIMARY PURPOSE	SUBJECTS	METHOD	MAJOR FINDINGS AND CONCLUSIONS
Lazarus (1948; 1949)	To determine if color influences scoring categories other than those making direct use of color; to see if color shock is dependent on color.	100 high-school seniors (50 males). Ages: 16–21. $\overline{X}$ IQ (Otis): 103.	Group method. Standard and achromatic series in counterbalanced order six weeks apart to groups equated for age, sex, education, IQ.	1. Higher S and $F\%$ scores on achromatic series; special analysis indicates possibility of elevated P scores on achromatic. 2. Color-shock indexes do not depend on color. 3. Presence or absence of color had little effect on scoring categories.
Wallen (1948)	To determine if liking of Cards 2, 3, 8, 9, 10 is affected by color.	419 males in military service (71 neurotics). Ages: 17–37. Education: 0–15 years.	Individual administration. Ss shown each of 10 cards and asked to tell if they liked it. 283 Ss shown standard series, 136 Ss shown achromatic series. 45 Ss asked to compare chromatic-achromatic versions of Cards 2, 3, 8, 9, 10.	1. Normals prefer colored version of 8, 9, 10 achromatic version of 3; no difference for 2. 2. Neurotics prefer 8, 10 in color; tend to prefer 9 in color; no difference for 3; tend to prefer achromatic 2. 3. The neurotics' dislike of 2 is related to their association of it with blood. 4. Color may produce shock because it facilitates associations with a disturbing effect; in general, however, contour and organization of blot are the primary determiners of affective reactions

227

(Continued on next page)

TABLE 15–1 (*continued*)

AUTHOR	PRIMARY PURPOSE	SUBJECTS	METHOD	MAJOR FINDINGS AND CONCLUSIONS
Reece (1949)	To study influence of color on Rorschach protocol.	54 psychology students (44 males). Ages: 18–43.	Group administration. Standard and achromatic series administered to two groups (N =27) equated for age, sex, and major area of study. No retesting. Ss also asked to indicate if they liked each card.	1. D responses more frequent (.01 level) and W responses less frequent (.05 level) on Cards 2, 3, 8, 9, 10 of standard series. 2. Form responses more frequent (.01 level) on Cards 2, 3, 8, 9, 10 of achromatic series. 3. Color did not affect "liking" of cards.
Sappenfield & Buker (1949)	To determine if 8–10/$R\%$ is affected by color.	238 psychology students (153 males). $\overline{X}$ Age: 21. $\overline{X}$ Otis S–A: 60.	Group method. Standard and achromatic series administered in counterbalanced order one week apart to groups equated for age, sex, education, IQ.	1. Total R and 8–10/$R\%$ not affected by color.
Dubrovner, von Lackum, & Jost (1950)	To determine if productivity and reaction time are affected by color.	30 nurses. Ages 18–34.	Individual administration. Standard and achromatic series in counterbalanced order. Average of two weeks between administrations.	1. Color does not affect productivity, 8–10/$R\%$, or reaction time.
Siipola (1950)	To determine influence of color on reaction	132 college females.	Individual administration. Twenty colored areas cut	1. Color increases reaction time, frequency of both positive and nega-

TABLE 15-1 (continued)

AUTHOR	PRIMARY PURPOSE	SUBJECTS	METHOD	MAJOR FINDINGS AND CONCLUSIONS
	time, emotional attitudes, and conceptual content.		from Rorschach blots and achromatic copies made. One group ($N=72$) responded to chromatic areas; second group ($N=60$) responded to achromatic. Ss also indicated like or dislike of each blot.	tive emotional accompaniments of response, and number of rejections. 2. Whether content of response is affected depends on whether the color is appropriate to the content suggested by the form of the blot.
Siipola, Kuhns, & Taylor (1950)	To determine effects of color by administering chromatic and achromatic blots to same Ss.	98 college females.	Individual administration. Group C ($N=72$) responded to two series of blots (chromatic and achromatic). Group A ($N = 26$) responded to two series of achromatic blots. Twenty blots in each series similar to forms used by Siipola (see above). One month between administrations.	1. Decreases in reaction times on second administration are traced to memory factor, not color. 2. Color alters conceptual content.
Barnett (1950)	To study influence of color and shading.	40 psychology students (26 males). $\overline{X}$ Age: 21.	Individual administration. Two series of blots, standard and outline series. Two groups of Ss responded to both series one month apart; counterbalanced order.	1. Shock was as frequent on outline series as on standard. 2. P, A, and An responses were more frequent (.01 level) on standard series; FM and Bt were more frequent at .05 level. W responses

(Continued on next page)

229

TABLE 15-1 (continued)

AUTHOR	PRIMARY PURPOSE	SUBJECTS	METHOD	MAJOR FINDINGS AND CONCLUSIONS
			Groups equated for age, education, sex. (Outline blots conformed to the basic form of standard blots but were devoid of shading and color.)	were less frequent on standard series (.05 level). No difference in R, M, m, Ds, H, Hd, Ad, Ls. 3. Texture responses were more frequent on Card 4 of standard series but not on Card 6; vista responses were more frequent on outline series (Cards 4 and 6).
Sterling (1950)	To determine if color shock is due to color; to study other color effects.	20 neurotic males. Ages: 21–45.	Individual administration. Ss given 4 series, 2 days between each: achromatic, standard, series of colored parts taken from standard, and achromatic reproductions of the colored parts. All Ss took the 4 series in the order above.	1. Color has a major role in incitement of disturbance; it is a contributing element in the provocation of color shock. 2. Color affects the shock reaction by contributing to the reality of certain disturbing percepts; it is the incongruity rather than the incongruity which is the basis of disturbance.
Allen, Manne, & Stiff (1951)	To determine relationship between color and color-shock signs.	25 college students.	Individual administration. Standard and achromatic series in counterbalanced order six weeks apart.	1. Frequency of color-shock signs was as great on achromatic as on standard series; concludes that normal Ss do not show color-shock signs.

(Continued on next page)

TABLE 15-1 (*continued*)

AUTHOR	PRIMARY PURPOSE	SUBJECTS	METHOD	MAJOR FINDINGS AND CONCLUSIONS
Allen (1951)	To determine if reaction time is affected by color.	Same as for Allen et al. above.	Same as for Allen et al. above.	1. Reaction times are not significantly different for standard and achromatic series.
Buker & Williams (1951)	To determine effect of color on scoring categories other than direct color scores.	21 male schizophrenics. Ages: 20–40. $\overline{X}$ CVS IQ: 99. Education: 6–16 years.	Individual administration. Standard and achromatic series in counterbalanced order one month apart. (11 Ss took standard series first.)	1. Color increases reaction time to Cards 2, 3, 8, 9, 10; it may depress the $F+\%$ for 1, 4, 5, 6, 7, without affecting the $F+\%$ for 2, 3, 8, 9, 10. 2. Color, as a discrete variable, does not materially influence responsiveness (26 scores tested).
Canter (1951)	To study effect of color on performance.	76 psychology students (32 males). $\overline{X}$ Age: 21.	Individual administration. Standard and achromatic series administered to two groups ($N=38$) matched for age, sex, and "emotional constriction." No retesting.	1. R, $T/1R$, and $F+$ scores did not vary significantly as a function of color; no other dependent variables were tested.
Meyer (1951)	To determine if color shock is due to color.	60 psychology students (30 males).	Individual administration. One group ($N=30$) given standard series; second group (matched for sex, age) given achromatic series. No retesting.	1. About 80 per cent of both groups showed color shock; no sex differences. Color shock is not due to color.

231

(*Continued on next page*)

TABLE 15-1 (*continued*)

AUTHOR	PRIMARY PURPOSE	SUBJECTS	METHOD	MAJOR FINDINGS AND CONCLUSIONS
Perlman (1951)	To determine if 8–10/R% is affected by color.	36 university students (20 males). Median age: in 20's. 34 NP patients (17 males). Median age: 25. Median education: 12 years.	Individual administration. Standard and achromatic series in counterbalanced order one to eight weeks apart. Groups not matched.	1. Color does not affect 8–10/R%. 2. On retest the 8–10/R% tends to regress toward the mean.
York (1951)	To determine color effects.	32 neurotics. Ages: 20–40. Education: above sixth grade. $\overline{X}$ Verbal IQ (W-B): 112.	Individual administration. Standard and achromatic series to all Ss two weeks apart; counterbalanced order. Groups matched for age, education, IQ.	1. Color significantly impaired form perception ($F+\%$). 2. Reaction times ($T/1R$) were faster and popular (P) responses fewer due to color when achromatic series was given first. 3. Variables other than color make the chromatic cards more difficult to interpret than the achromatic cards.
Balloch (1952)	To determine effect of degree of shading contrast on responses.	75 college students (54 males). $\overline{X}$ Age: 20.	Individual administration. First seven cards of Rorschach, Behn-Rorschach, and Harrower were photographed at three different contrast	1. No changes in physiological responses. 2. Total number of times shading was used did not vary significantly with degree of contrast.

(Continued on next page)

232

TABLE 15-1 (*continued*)

AUTHOR	PRIMARY PURPOSE	SUBJECTS	METHOD	MAJOR FINDINGS AND CONCLUSIONS
			levels (N=63 blots). Each S in three matched groups was shown 21 cards, 7 at each contrast level. Latin-square design. Circulatory and respiratory changes recorded in addition to verbal responses.	3. As contrast increased, the number of C' responses increased; the number of FK responses also varied significantly with contrast (highest frequency at medium contrast).
Allen, Manne, & Stiff (1952)	To determine if color changes the consistency of responses on retest.	Same as for Allen et al. above.	Same as for Allen et al. above.	1. About 30 per cent of responses on retest are identical to those given originally; color does not influence consistency of response.
Allen, Stiff, & Rosenzweig (1953)	To determine if frequency of color-shock signs for neurotics and psychotics is affected by color.	18 male NP patients (10 neurotics, 8 psychotics).	Same as for Allen et al. above.	1. Shock signs are as frequent on achromatic as on standard series.
Brody (1953)	To determine color effects for both neurotics and normals.	100 males (50 neurotics). Ages: 18–35. Education: at least some college work. $\bar{X}$ W-B Vocabulary score: 32.	Individual administration. 25 neurotics and 25 controls took standard Rorschach followed a week later by achromatic series. Matched groups (age, sex, education) took achromatic series first fol-	1. Control Ss were not disturbed by the color, but neurotics were. Neurotics became disorganized and variable in their responses from one test or half of a test to the other.
				2. In terms of a number of scoring categories, the presence or absence

(Continued on next page)

TABLE 15–1 (continued)

AUTHOR	PRIMARY PURPOSE	SUBJECTS	METHOD	MAJOR FINDINGS AND CONCLUSIONS
			lowed a week later by standard series.	of color did not affect the responses of any of the groups.
Swartz (1953)	To test the validity of the color-shock hypothesis as a color phenomenon and to determine how hue affects the protocol.	50 neurotics and 30 normals (all males). Age: 20–47. Intelligence (Wonderlic): at least dull normal. Education: Grade 6 through post-college.	Individual administration. Each population divided into two subgroups. Standard and achromatic series presented in counterbalanced order with 2–4 month interval between tests. Subgroups equated for age, intelligence, and education.	1. Removal of color increases the number of form responses; no other clearly established color effects. The elimination of color did not affect the incidence of color shock.
Baughman (1954)	To determine how perceptual behavior changes when color, shading, figure-ground, and form characteristics of the blots are altered.	100 male neurotics. $\overline{X}$ Age: 31. $\overline{X}$ W-B IQ: 114. $\overline{X}$ Education: 11 years.	Individual administration. Four modified series of blots (achromatic, silhouette, simple outline, complex outline) plus standard series. Each of 5 series administered to equated groups of 20 Ss. No retesting. Ss also rank-ordered cards for preference.	1. The major dimensions of perceptual behavior remain constant, even though marked alterations are made in stimulus attributes. 2. The basic form of the blot is of overwhelming importance in determining perceptual behavior, compared to stimulus attributes such as color and shading. 3. The importance of figure-ground contrast is also emphasized.

(Continued on next page)

TABLE 15-1 (continued)

AUTHOR	PRIMARY PURPOSE	SUBJECTS	METHOD	MAJOR FINDINGS AND CONCLUSIONS
Belden & Baughman (1954)	To determine relationship between figure-ground contrast and perception.	140 male psychology students.	Individual administration. Seven variations of Card 2: a line drawing corresponding to outline of blot plus 6 solid grays (no light variations within blot) with different contrast values. Seven matched groups (age, IQ, sex, education) responded to one card only.	1. Responses to line drawings differ markedly from those with a bright-ness contrast. 2. There is a level of figure-ground contrast at which perception becomes most efficient. More responses are given in shorter time, with greater accuracy, and with greater variety in content when contrast is intermediate in value.
Crumpton (1956)	To determine if color is actually the stimulus for reactions commonly attributed to color.	60 male NP patients (20 psychotics, 20 neurotics, 20 organics). Ages: about 35. Education: about 11–12 years.	Individual administration. Standard series administered to 10 psychotics, 10 neurotics, 10 organics. Achromatic series administered to comparable group. No retesting. Ss also asked to choose most preferred and least preferred blot in addition to comparing chromatic and achromatic versions of same blot (for preference).	1. Color influences performance so that it can be detected by judges. 2. Color-shock signs as frequent on achromatic series as on standard. 3. Color changes the distribution of content categories: More *Hd* and *Ge* on standard series, less *Aobj*. 4. More attention to form on achromatic series. 5. Judges find more aggressive and submissive concepts on chromatic blots; also more expression of un-

(Continued on next page)

TABLE 15–1 (*continued*)

AUTHOR	PRIMARY PURPOSE	SUBJECTS	METHOD	MAJOR FINDINGS AND CONCLUSIONS
				pleasant affect. Ratings of anxiety and pleasant affect are not influenced. 6. High hue-form incongruity not associated with lengthened reaction times. 7. Ss in general preferred chromatic cards to their achromatic counterparts, especially on Cards 8, 9, 10.
Grayson (1956)	To determine effect of color and shading on productivity and card preference.	30 nurses in psychology course.	Group method. Standard series plus 9 experimental series; 3 achromatic (different degrees of blackness) and 6 monochromatic sets (blue, green, yellow, orange-tan, brick, red). Standard sequence of forms used, but each card was from a different one of the 10 series. Latin-square design with triple replication. Preference ratings obtained for each card.	1. Interaction between form and color was significant in influencing productivity, but not color or shading alone. 2. Color and shading significantly influence the "pleasantness" rating given to a card.

through his own photographic processes. Because of this fact, one cannot be certain of the identity of the stimuli used in the various researches; actually it is most probable that the stimuli prepared in this way differ from one another in terms of such attributes as brightness, contrast, and clarity of internal form areas. An improvement in this regard was introduced by Allen (1951), who had the achromatic versions of colored cards made by Verlag Hans Huber in Switzerland, using the same presses, the same black ink as in printing the noncolor cards, and the same pressure as in printing the standard color cards. Others have recently begun to follow Allen's lead in this regard and have made use of the Huber achromatic modifications. Although this refinement in construction of experimental materials is highly desirable from a technical standpoint, the effects of the earlier lack of uniformity in materials is probably not very great. Balloch (1952), for example, deliberately varied contrast levels but found that this did not significantly affect the number of times shading was used as a determinant.

A more important variation in the studies of color effects would seem to be that of S population, although evidence to be discussed later suggests that results are substantially the same despite marked differences in groups studied. Three groups of psychotics and one group of organics have been subjected to evaluation, but the total number of Ss in these classifications has been small ($N = 69$). Most investigators have chosen instead to work either with normals or neurotics, as an examination of Table 15–1 will indicate. Allen (1951) has argued strongly for the need of basal work with nonpsychiatric Ss, to be followed by comparative analyses of various maladjusted groups. York, in contrast, has chosen to do his initial work with neurotics and states emphatically, "The validity of color shock, a set of reactions assumed by all Rorschach workers to be mainly characteristic of neurotics, cannot be adequately tested with a normal group" (1951, p. 24). Primarily, of course, the question here is one of research strategy, since most investigators would probably agree that any complete understanding of color effects necessitates study of various groups. One advantage to be gained by working initially with neurotics, however, resides in the fact that theorists have consistently postulated more pronounced effects upon response due to color in this diagnostic group than in any other group. Failure to verify the reality of such effects through tight experimental procedures in a group where these effects are supposed to be maximized would lessen the urgency for similar testing of groups where the effects are supposed to be less pronounced.

The need to consider carefully the question of S population before interpreting the results of an experiment is illustrated by Lazarus' (1949) report. One of his major conclusions is that color does not affect the frequency of the color-shock indexes. His experiments, however, cannot be considered critical in this regard, for he worked with normals, who have been hypothesized to show fewer signs of shock than maladjusted groups. The results of this study contribute to the norms that Allen argues for, but they do not provide a firm basis for drawing conclusions about the relationship between color and color-shock signs. Later studies with maladjusted Ss, however, are in essential agreement with Lazarus' conclusion.

Only four studies (Grayson, 1956; Lazarus, 1949; Reece, 1949; Sappenfield & Buker, 1949) have made use of group testing procedures as part of the experimental design, and of these, three represent work carried out in 1949 or earlier. Subsequent research has utilized the individual method of administration almost exclusively. There are several reasons for this preference, among the most obvious of which is the fact that one is unable to measure the latency of responses in the group situation. Inasmuch as latency of response has always figured heavily in the formulation of color and shading shock, studies which purport to examine color and/or shading effects but which do not provide time scores thereby weaken the effectiveness of their arguments. Another obvious disadvantage of the group procedure is the fact that it does not usually provide inquiry data for scoring of responses in as adequate detail as does the individual method. If such scores are to be used as dependent variables (and they have been in most studies), clearly their measurement should be as precise and reliable as technique permits. Added to these obvious disadvantages is the fact that most Rorschach workers have been reluctant to accept the group procedure as equivalent to the individual method. To use the group procedure faces the researcher with an inevitable question: "But would an individual technique give comparable results?" For these reasons, it appears wise that most investigations have been built around individual technique, even though comparison of group and individual studies reveals no essential contradictions between the conclusions to be drawn from them.

The question of what type of research design is preferable for analyzing color and shading effects has elicited divided opinion. Ten studies have utilized a test-retest design in which Ss have responded to both the standard blots and an achromatic series, half of the Ss receiving the standard series first and the remaining half receiving the achromatic series first. As already noted, the length of time between successive administrations has varied from a few days to four months. The remaining studies have avoided retesting the same Ss; most of them have tried instead to use matched groups of Ss who responded to series of blots which differed in some specified way. Two studies have made use of a Latin-square design.

Perhaps the most cogent criticisms of the test-retest design for problems of this sort have been advanced by Canter (1951). In his analysis, Canter raises five objections, two of which penetrate most deeply and are interrelated. The first questions the validity of assuming (as one must in using such a design) that the influence of presenting A before B is equivalent to the influence of B before A. The second points up the error introduced by memory factors which affect the S's set and his responses on repeated administrations of the Rorschach; such factors are well-nigh impossible to evaluate.

Without pursuing this matter in detail, an example of a possible difficulty in evaluating behavior elicited in a test-retest design may assist in clarifying the general point. Subject A responds to the achromatic series; ten days later he looks at the standard series, and when he comes to Card 2 he evidences a startle reaction. Is this due to the sudden introduction of color, or is it because he suddenly realizes that he is not going to be looking at the same series of blots after all? Subject B gives a similar startle reaction to Card 2 when he initially responds to the standard series; on repeat administration with the achromatic series, he again appears ruffled on Card 2. Does this mean that color had nothing to do with his initial reaction? Or might color have been instrumental initially, with "change" being the effective stimulus in the repeat administration? It is clear in such designs that variables other than the intended independent variable are being introduced and that a design which is useful for much psychological research has limited utility for the question at hand. This would indicate an advantage for the matched-group approach, if the groups are carefully equated on pertinent variables. Again, however, there appears to be essential agreement in the results obtained by utilization of these two designs.

In order to examine more closely this question of the degree of agreement in results among the studies in which color[4] has been treated as an independent variable, Table 15-2 has been prepared. This table contains most of the dependent measures which have been reported by several different investigators. To construct the table, it has been necessary to take a few liberties in translating some scoring symbols into Beck's (1949) system. By examining each column, the reader may determine the extent of agreement on the question of whether or not the presence or absence of color affects a particular scoring category. For example, thirteen investigators all agree that color does not significantly affect the number of responses (R) given by Ss; the remaining investigators do not present data on this variable.

Inasmuch as most researchers analyze several dependent variables, occasional significant relationships are likely to be found which can in fact be attributed to chance considerations. Because of this, a positive finding should be confirmed by other research before it is given much weight. Holding this in mind, and examining Table 15-2, it is clear that color has little effect on Ss' behavior, at least to the extent that behavior is

---

[4] Two studies (Balloch, 1952; Belden & Baughman, 1954) listed in Table 15-1 treat only blot attributes other than color; one study (Barnett, 1950) alters color, shading, and figure-ground properties in a manner so that it is not possible to consider resultant variations in behavior as being related to a single blot dimension.

TABLE 15-2 Relationships between Color and Various Rorschach Measures

SENIOR AUTHOR	Preference	Content	Shock Signs	T/1R	R	8-10%	P	S	W	D	Dd	F+% or F+	M	m	FM	Y	V	F or F%	H	PH	An	A%
Lazarus (1948, 1949)	X	O	O			O		X	O	O	O	O	O	O	O	O	O	X	O	O	O	O
Wallen (1948)	O	O	O									O	O	O	O	O	O	X	O	O	O	O
Reece (1949)					O	O																
Sappenfield (1949)					O	O																
Dubrovner (1950)	X	X			O				X	X								X	X			
Siipola (1950)	X	X		O	O	O				X												
Siipola et al. (1950)	O[a]			X																		
Sterling[b] (1950)			X	O[a]																		
Allen et al. (1951)		O	O	O																		
Allen (1951)				X	O	O																O
Buker (1951)				O	O	O	O		O	O	O	O	O								O	O
Canter (1951)				O		O	O	O				O	O	O	O	O	O	X	O	O	O	O
Meyer (1951)			O	O	O	O		O				O										
Perlman (1951)			O		O	O																
York (1951)		O	O	O[c]	O	O	O[c]					X										
Allen (1952)		O	O	O	O	O																
Allen (1953)		O	O	O	O	O	O															
Brody[d] (1953)		O	O	O	O	O	O		O			O	O	O	O	O	O	O	O	O	O	
Swartz (1953)		O	O	O	O	O	O		O	O		O	O	O	O	O	O					
Baughman (1954)	X	X	O	O	O	O			O	O		O	O	O	O	O		X	O	O	O	O
Crumpton (1956)	X	X		O	O	O				O						O		X	O	X	O	O
Grayson (1956)	X			O	O	O												X				O

X Indicates author reports significant relationship between color and this score.

O Indicates author finds no significant relationship between color and this score. No entry indicates author did not report for this score.

[a] Authors attribute this to their experimental design and the memory factor; do not believe that Siipola's original findings are unsupported.

[b] Sterling reports the frequency of various shock signs related to measures in this table, but not individual tests of their significance.

[c] York reports significant relationship between color and these measures when S is administered achromatic series before standard.

[d] Brody...

240

accurately reflected in these scores. Total productivity, productivity on the last three cards, color-shock signs, popular responses, figure-ground reversals, location scores, form accuracy, projection of movement, shading responses, and the most common content categories are little affected by the presence or absence of color.[5]

The weight of the evidence also suggests that latency of response $(T/1R)$ is not significantly affected by color, although two reports are in disagreement with this conclusion. Siipola's (1950) work is cited most frequently in this regard. The problem situation confronting her Ss, however, differed from that facing Ss in the usual Rorschach test, and it is quite possible that this difference accounts for the discrepancy in results. Siipola's Ss were given single blot areas which they had to interpret even though the object suggested by the form might have a color incongruent with the color of the blot area. Ss with high need for form-color congruity might easily block in such a situation with resultant increase in response time; in the usual Rorschach test situation, however, Ss are not forced to respond to such incongruous areas but may select other areas which pose no such problems of congruity. Siipola has thus created a type of set and demand for her Ss which is not comparable to that faced by Ss in the Rorschach situation. Crumpton's (1956) findings, based on the full Rorschach, tend to confirm this interpretation of Siipola's results.

The other significant relationship between color and latency was reported by Buker and Williams (1951) in their study of schizophrenic Ss. Altogether they analyzed 26 dependent variables, reporting no other material influence on responsiveness attributable to color. It may be, then, that this one significant finding would not hold up on replication. The consistency of findings from other studies showing no significant relationship between color and latency suggests this as a possibility.

At this point, it is clear that the evidence is overwhelming in its refutation of the idea that color has broad, pervasive general effects on Ss' Rorschach behavior, as asserted by numerous theorists. In the final analysis, however, it may be the positive findings contained in Table 15-2 that prove to be the most significant. First of all, it is apparent that color does make a difference to Ss in their feeling or aesthetic response (listed as preference in Table 15-2) to the blots. Wallen (1948) was the first one to demonstrate this, and subsequent research has confirmed his early finding, even though a variety of procedures have

---

[5] Since the scores C, CF, and FC cannot be applied to responses on the achromatic series, significant decrements in these categories when compared with the standard series are inevitable; hence these scores are not listed in Table 15-2. In a similar way, one would anticipate an increase in F% (responses based on form only) when other attributes (such as color) are not available for the S to use. Four studies have shown significant increases in the number of form-determined responses on the achromatic series; other studies show a tendency in this direction, even though the difference is not sufficiently large to reach statistical significance.

been used to get at an *S*'s preference for particular blots.[6] Second, it is suggested that color may influence the conceptual content elicited, even though frequency of response in the major content categories is unaffected. The lack of agreement regarding this second point (which is evident in Table 15–2) arises in part from the fact that the studies have differed widely in their analyses of content data; some have treated it rather superficially, whereas others have carried out rather minute analyses. It is, perhaps, misleading to include conceptual content as a separate category, since there has been so little uniformity in its treatment. The thing to be remembered, however, is that content differences traceable to color can be demonstrated if one looks closely enough and if a sufficient number of *S*s are examined.

It is difficult, however, in this context to fully appreciate the significance of the positive findings regarding color as related to preference and content, engulfed as they are by numerous negative results pertaining to other variables. Perhaps the most that can be hoped for is that they suggest to the reader that color does somehow make a difference to most *S*s in the way they perceive and respond to ink blots. In a later paper, considerable attention will be devoted to a new method of inquiry which will make clear the fact that much of the difficulty encountered in demonstrating both color and shading effects is methodological in nature. By developing an entirely new inquiry procedure, it is possible to show color and shading effects which are to a great extent obscured in the studies under consideration. In this instance, as in many other scientific endeavors, a major bottleneck proves to be methodological in nature.

The results summarized in Table 15–2, however, make it clear that one cannot begin with variations in summary scores and use these as bases for inferring color effects. The same conclusion will probably prove to hold true for shading, although sufficient research on shading has yet to be completed. An individual's summary scores can be traced predominantly to the interaction of his personality characteristics with the form properties of the blots; color and shading effects are more subtle and do not affect behavior in a gross enough way to modify such scores appreciably. Another way of putting this is to state that summary scores are not sufficiently sensitive to reflect color and shading effects.

It is also true that on the basis of available data one cannot take particular content categories of responses and draw inferences about the effects of certain stimulus variables. For example, the response "fire" or "blood" suggests immediately that the *S* is responding to color, but when an examiner receives these responses to achromatic cards he realizes that

---

[6] The exception is Reece's study (1949). The reason for this one discrepancy is not clear, although it may be due to the fact that Reece used slides in a group situation and a relatively insensitive method for getting at preference behavior.

he is faced with a more complex problem. Several authors (Baughman, 1954; Canter, 1951; Reece, 1949) point out examples of such responses in the color area. Barnett (1950) raises a similar problem for shading when he reports vista responses given in response to outline blots in which no shading variations exist. In fact he reports a higher frequency of these responses for Cards 4 and 6 of the outline series than for the standard series. Baughman (1954) also obtained vista responses to outline figures, but the frequency was not as great as for Ss responding to the regular or achromatic series.

In summary, the following major points may be made with respect to studies attempting to clarify the role of the stimulus by manipulation of blot properties:

1. Almost all the work has focused on the effect of color; shading, figure-ground contrast, and other stimulus dimensions have been neglected.

2. Despite marked variations in research design and Ss studied, the results of the investigations are in substantial agreement.

3. Summary scores and color-shock signs do not vary significantly as a function of color.

4. Color does affect Ss, however, most noticeably in their "preference for" or "liking of" particular blots, but also to some extent in the content elicited by the blot.

5. The Rorschach, as currently used, elicits little in the way of behavior that can be taken as a basis for inferring color effects. The same statement is probably valid also for shading.

6. Rorschach behavior, as reflected in summary scores, is a product primarily of the S and the form properties of the blots.

Studies Dealing with Physiological Correlates

Rather than taking summary scores as dependent variables, a number of researchers have turned instead to investigations of physiological activity occurring during administration of the blots. Since color, shading, and other dimensions of the test situation are supposed to stimulate affective responses, these workers have reasoned that analysis of physiological activity (especially autonomic activity) should further our understanding of the Rorschach test. Skin conductance (the psychogalvanic response) has been studied most frequently (Frost & Rodnick, 1948; Goodman, 1950; Hughes, Epstein, & Jost, 1951; Levy, 1950; Milner & Moreault, 1945; Rockwell, Welch, Fisichelli, & Kubis, 1946; Rockwell, Welch, Kubis, & Fisichelli, 1948; Siple, 1948; Steinberg, 1949), but investigations making use of blood pressure (Hughes et al., 1951), heart rate (Hughes et al., 1951; Siple, 1948), respiration (Hughes et al., 1951), and the eye blink (Siple, 1948) have also been reported.

The research methodology used in these studies has been quite uniform; in most instances the investigator has simply made continuous records of the physiological activity in which he was interested while his Ss were responding to the standard Rorschach blots. Research populations have included pathological groups (Frost & Rodnick, 1948; Goodman, 1950; Rockwell et al., 1946) as well as normals (Frost & Rodnick, 1948; Goodman, 1950; Hughes et al., 1951; Jacques, 1946; Levy, 1950; Rockwell et al., 1946; Siple, 1948; Steinberg, 1949), and both individual (Frost & Rodnick, 1948; Goodman, 1950; Hughes et al., 1951; Jacques, 1946; Levy, 1950; Siple, 1948; Steinberg, 1949) and group administrations (Rockwell et al., 1946; Rockwell et al., 1948) have been utilized. It has been customary also to divide Ss into those showing color shock and those not showing shock (Rockwell et al., 1946; Rockwell et al., 1948; Siple, 1948; Steinberg, 1949) as determined by usual Rorschach criteria. The question has then been asked as to whether such groups differ in their physiological response to the blots.

A frequent finding in these studies is an adaptation effect, by which is meant that autonomic activity tends to be elevated at the beginning of the test series but levels off as the S presumably adjusts to the situation and becomes less anxious. The validity of this interpretation, however, is not firmly established, since only Levy (1950) and Steinberg (1949) report work in which the order of presenting the cards was varied. The possibility remains, therefore, that there are specific card effects related to those ordinarily coming early in the sequence which are independent of card position. The findings of Levy and Steinberg, however, argue against the likelihood of this possibility.

The experimental designs utilized in the physiological studies make it impossible to draw any definite conclusions about the relationships between autonomic activity and specific blot attributes. Although several authors contrast autonomic response to the colored blots of the standard series with similar responses to the noncolored blots of the standard series, it is evident that these two groups of blots differ from each other in terms of form, figure-ground contrast, symbolic associations, and other properties in addition to color differences. Even if one were to find significant differences in autonomic activity through such comparisons, one would not know what the critical dimensions were of the stimuli which were creating such differences. The most that can be learned through such designs is whether there are significant card differences in the provocation of autonomic activity; even this cannot be determined, however, unless order effects are also investigated.

Rockwell et al. (1948) report the only study available in which experimental manipulation of blot properties has been combined with autonomic measurements in order to get at the effect of a blot dimension (color) more directly. Twenty-three Ss were administered color slides of the standard Rorschach while a record was made of their palmar skin resistance; a repeat testing with achromatic cards was then carried out. The data were described as showing color-shock Ss differing from non-color Ss in that the former did *not* evidence differential effects in skin resistance btween the two situations, whereas the latter group did. This finding is only suggestive, however, because of both the small number of Ss and the failure to use a counterbalanced order of presentation. Nevertheless, the study is valuable in the sense of suggesting how measures of autonomic activity might be used as dependent variables along with experimental alteration of the stimulus material in order to clarify the effect of specific stimulus attributes; investigators need not be limited in their work to an analysis of verbal behavior.

Several workers in this area have been concerned primarily with the question of whether different groups of Ss differ in their autonomic response to the Rorschach blots (Frost & Rodnick, 1948; Goodman, 1950; Rockwell et al., 1946); correlates with blot properties have been of secondary interest to them. This appears to be one of the reasons why the experimental designs have such marked limitations in terms of the question that is central to our interest here. Keeping this in mind, the following tentative conclusions can be drawn from the studies under consideration:

1. There are marked inter-S differences in autonomic response to the Rorschach blots.

2. Individual cards have different affective values for different Ss, but cards cannot be termed emotional or nonemotional since they are not consistent in their effects on all or even a majority of Ss.

3. Physiological activity while an S is giving a color response does not appear to be significantly different from that occurring while he is giving a noncolor response.

4. The position of a card in the series is significant, there appearing to be adaptation effects.

Perhaps the most pertinent summary, however, with respect to the status of investigations utilizing this approach is to be found in the words of Siple as he reports on his study: "The treatment of data used in the present investigation does not permit a clear differentiation between effects of color and effects of other factors" (1948, p. 39). Perhaps additional investigations making use of the method employed by Rockwell et al. (1948) will assist in clarifying some of these questions regarding stimulus influences at a nonverbal level.

Symbolic Meanings of Rorschach Figures

From almost the beginning of Rorschach work, individuals have concerned themselves with the symbolic properties of the blots. Male or female blots, father or mother cards, are only a few of the concepts that have been advanced in this regard. Persons interested in the role of the stimulus in this sense seem to have been preoccupied primarily with the question of the total impact of the blot on the S rather than with any attempt to analyze the blot so as to determine the relative influence of the various stimulus dimensions. To oversimplify, perhaps, it has been a question of defining whether Card 7 is more feminine than Card 4 rather than attempting to define empirically the basis for this difference, if it is in fact found to exist.

Three studies illustrate the point just made. Meer and Singer (1950) asked fifty college males to select both a mother and a father card. Cards 4 and 2 were chosen most often as father cards, Cards 7 and 10 most often as mother cards. It is not clear, however, what it was about the cards that led to these differences. In a similar fashion, Shaw (1948) requested 50 college males to locate sexual areas on the cards. Only Card 6 produced more male than female responses, there being about twice as many female as male responses for all ten cards. Again, the bases in the stimuli are not identified; in fact, Shaw points out that one cannot even be certain whether the predominantly female gender of the percepts is a function of the structure of the blots or is due to the male composition of the group. Pascal, Reusch, Devine, and Suttell (1950) help clarify this latter question when they report that both male and female Ss give more female than male responses. Also, like Shaw, they found cards 1, 3, 2, and 6 to be the most sexually suggestive in the series. From studies of this type, it is possible to conclude that there are intercard differences in sexual properties and that femaleness predominates over maleness, i.e., there is what might be termed a sex bias in the stimuli. The studies do not, however, give a basis for understanding the emergence of these responses as a function of particular stimulus properties or combinations thereof.

Rosen extended the empirical investigation of symbolic meanings by asking 193 psychiatry students (118 males) to choose that card which suggested each of the following feelings or associations: (1) male sex organ, (2) masculine aggression, (3) authority, (4) father symbol, (5) mother symbol, and (6) family symbol. He also considered the states of emotional security and insecurity. Among the findings was that Card 4 was associated with the father symbol (confirming Meer and Singer), with masculine aggression, and with authority. Card 7 was related to the mother symbol (again confirming Meer and Singer). Card 6 was associated with the male sex organ; Card 10 was seen as the family card, also as suggesting emotional insecurity. Cards 2 and 7, in contrast, provoked associations of emotional security. Despite these significant findings, however, Rosen emphasizes that no card approaches identity in meaning for all Ss. He concludes, "The Rorschach would thus appear to consist of stimuli which have a partial, but not a total, symbolic communality for Ss" (Rosen, 1951, p. 244).

In another study, Guertin and Trembath (1953) attempted to determine the significance of Card 6 as a stimulator of behavior related to psychosexual disturbance, with generally negative results. Most discussions (e.g., Earl, 1941; Jacob, 1944; Lindner, 1946; Lindner, 1947; Lindner, 1950; Lindner, 1955; Phillips & Smith, 1953; Schafer, 1953) of content and symbol interpretation have remained, however, at primarily a theoretical level with insufficient empirical data. In fact, the few empirical studies referred to do little more than confirm what the experienced user of the Rorschach already knew. Carefully controlled work on symbols has been confronted with methodological obstacles since the beginning of interest in this problem, and resolution of these difficulties appears to remain a formidable challenge.

Other Studies Related to Stimulus Properties

COMPARISON OF RORSCHACH WITH PARALLEL SERIES

Responses to the Behn and Harrower series of ink blots have been compared to those elicited by the Rorschach blots in several studies (Buckle & Holt, 1951; Eichler, 1951; Mayman, 1947; Rosenwald, 1947; Singer, 1952). The major interest has been in the equivalence of the various series of blots. It is only indirectly that such research touches on the stimulus problem, although the research itself is based on the recognition that the stimulus factors are critical. Although Buckle and Holt (1951) address themselves to the differences between each pair of ink blots, most researchers have been interested instead in the question of whether the various series give identical or near-identical summary scores. Two studies (Rosenwald, 1947; Singer, 1952), for example, suggest that the Behn tends to elicit more color responses than the Rorschach. Since each blot in research of this type differs simultaneously from its counterpart in terms of not only color but form, shading, and other stimulus attributes, it is not possible to proceed very far toward identifying the relevant stimulus dimensions. One can say that two blots do or do not differ in terms of the behavior they stimulate, but not the basis for the result. This fact is pointed up by Buckle and Holt when they indicate that "We have no systematic theory of how responses can be influenced by changes in the ink blots" (1951, pp. 486–487).

INTERCARD COMPARISONS

Differentials in response to the ten Rorschach blots have always been recognized, in the formal as well as the content sense. Reaction time to Card 5 is fast, productivity is low, and the bat is a frequently perceived form, compared to the characteristics of responses to Card 10. Ranzoni,

Grant, and Ives (1950) were among the first to present extensive empirical data of this type in order to define what they called "card pull" for each of the cards. Other studies (Beck, Rabin, Thiesen, Molish, & Thetford, 1950; George, 1953; George, 1955; Hershenson, 1949; Matarazzo & Mensh, 1952; Meer, 1955; Mensh & Metarazzo, 1954; Mitchell, 1952) also provide data which may be used for analyses of this type.

As long as the responses alone to each card provide the total data for study, such research is faced with the same limitations as those pointed out for comparisons made with parallel series. That is, one can describe how two or more cards compare in productivity, reaction time, and similar variables, but the reasons for difference are often obscured. For practical work it is, of course, extremely important to understand card tendencies of this sort since it is against them that the individual response of a particular S must be compared, but the basic theoretical questions remain unanswered.

Some of the empirical studies referred to above, however, do attempt to go beyond this descriptive level (George, 1955; Hershenson, 1949; Mitchell, 1952). They do so by asking the S to indicate card preferences and then to give his reasons for his choices. Through this and related procedures, the following tentative conclusions are suggested:

(1) For some groups, preference for a card is inversely related to its sexual suggestiveness (George, 1953).

(2) More intelligent Ss tend to prefer more complex cards (George, 1955).

(3) Color tends to be a more important factor than content in determining preference for a card by normal Ss (Hershenson, 1949).

(4) Normals give color as the major reason for liking a card best, neurotics give ease or difficulty of the card, and psychotics give specific content as the primary factor (Mitchell, 1952).

The differential significance of various blot attributes for different S groups is suggested by these studies, but their results must be considered keeping in mind the limitations of introspective analysis.

CARD-ORDER EFFECTS

Stimulus effects are complicated by the fact that the S, after responding to Card 1, no longer responds to subsequent blots independently of his experience with previous blots. These order effects have not been studied extensively, despite an early report on the problem by Rabin and Sanderson (1947). Placement of a card in a series influences certain components of response, although the precise extent and nature of the influence is not known. Maradie (1953), however, has demonstrated through use of a Latin-square design that later-appearing cards produce more responses than earlier-appearing cards. Effects of order on other aspects of response appear to be in need of similar clarification.

MISCELLANEOUS

An early study utilizing a rather ingenious methodology is the often-quoted study by Brosin and Fromm (1940) making use of color-defective Ss. Several possibilities were advanced to explain why neurotic color-blind Ss showed color shock, but the authors neglected to consider that what was termed color-shock behavior might not be due to the color dimension of the stimuli. Subsequent research (see second section of this paper) indicates this to be the likely factor. A subsequent theoretical paper by the same authors (1942) gave explicit recognition to the need for clarifying the role of the stimulus and proceeded to analyze the Rorschach figures in terms of eleven basic principles coming from Gestalt psychology. In similar fashion, Klein and Arnheim (1953) argued that the perceptual characteristics of the blots as visual stimuli should be explored in their own right. They then proceeded to an intensive analysis of Card 1 in terms of Gestalt principles. Earlier, Arnheim (1951) had distinguished between two types of human movement responses, one based on a kinesthetic experience and the other on visual properties of the stimulus. Following Arnheim's lead, Eckhardt (1955) carried through an empirical study in which he was able to demonstrate that certain shape gradients (e.g., an ellipse) evoked more movement responses than did regular shapes (e.g., a circle).

Using a quite different technique (but one which might be used to advantage by those interested in the Gestalt characteristics of the blots), Blake (1948) photographed eye movements of Ss as they looked at the blots. The initial fixations tended to be embedded inside the blot, with later ones moving toward the periphery. Blake interprets his data as supporting the hypothesis that specific features of each card determine the fixations after the initial centering tendency has been completed. He then lists those areas of each card which seem to have the greatest demand value as judged by ocular behavior. The stability of these findings on achromatic versions of the standard chromatic cards would prove an interesting approach to color effects at a nonverbal level.

Stein undertook an exhaustive study of the perceiver's role in perception utilizing tachistoscopic exposure of the cards. Of interest here, however, is his suggestion that color and shading may reverse their order of importance as determinants, depending on exposure time. "At very brief exposures, the hierarchy of determinants based on the sensory aspects of the blots is form first, shading second, and color third. . . . The hierarchy which emerges at the longer exposures changes to form first, color second, and shading third" (Stein, 1949, p. 409). The writer has unpublished data, however, which are not consistent with Stein's findings; further research is needed to clarify this inconsistency.

Numerous studies have attempted to examine the question of

whether an *S*'s response to a particular stimulus quality (e.g., color, white space) is related in a consistent way to extra-Rorschach behavior. Ultimately, of course, this is a very important question, but it is somewhat tangential to the primary purpose of this paper. The reader is referred to reports by Bandura (1954), Sarason and Potter (1947), Matarazzo et al. (1952), Ruesch and Finesinger (1941), and Holzberg and Schleifer (1955) for illustrative examples of such research.

Conclusions

It is apparent, from the studies reviewed, that the definition of Rorschach stimulus effects is more a task for the future than an accomplishment of the past. In fact, empirical concern with this question appears to have been something of an afterthought with users of the technique. Variation in the stimulus, in order to define an independent variable, has been such a standard procedure in psychological research that it is surprising to find it being applied only during very recent years to an analysis of the Rorschach. Other methods, as indicated, have contributed to the clarification of this problem, but they have not, as yet, gone very deep.

Studies addressed to "card pull" substantiate what every experienced clinician knows; namely, that the individual blots vary widely in the classes of responses they evoke. Productivity, latency, content, and other response variables are not ordinarily independent of the stimulus to which the *S* is responding. Such studies are valuable, of course, even to the experienced tester, for they assist him in correcting for his own sampling biases. For the beginner, they are even more important. At the same time, it must be recognized that this approach does not go much beyond the descriptive definition of differences.

The 25 experiments attempting to go beyond this descriptive level by introducing variations into the stimulus conditions tempt one to conclude that the form or shape of the blot is the only relevant dimension. Certanly color does not appear to affect behavior very much, and if color is ineffective shading seems even less likely to be a significant variable. Other blot properties (such as figure-ground structure) have at best evoked the interest of an occasional researcher.

Perhaps this is the point at which to indicate a most important limitation in these studies. They do not really provide a basis for concluding that color, shading, and other blot dimensions do not affect an *S*'s behavior or the way he experiences and reacts to the blots. Actually, the only conclusion that appears to be justified by empirical research is that color has little or no effect on *S*'s behavior *to the extent that his behavior is represented by psychogram or similar scoring scales.* One may anticipate that a similar conclusion will prove to be justified for shading, but the necessary research is not yet in. About other dimensions, only guesses are possible.

Concern with behavior, in the overt sense, has led many to forget that one of the primary assets of techniques like the Rorschach is the providing of a basis for knowing about another person's subjective experience. Two individuals may be passive in their behavior, but one may experience the world as continuously threatening while the other does not. Similarly, two individuals may respond to the Rorschach with such identity as to receive equivalent psychogram scores, but can one be certain that there has been a similar equivalence in the way that they have experienced the blots? Does the absence of shading scores, for example, mean that two persons have been equally unresponsive to the shading properties?

Statements about another person's experience are always inferential, never directly observable. The starting point is observation; and the task for the person who desires to know another person's experience is to create a situation which will evoke behavior that can be used to draw the inference. In the Rorschach, this means that the examiner is limited primarily to the verbal statements made by the S during the free association and inquiry. Recognition of this fact immediately focuses attention on the question of whether the inquiry, as usually conducted, gives an adequate basis for drawing inferences about how the S has experienced color, shading, and other blot properties during the association period. Until alternate methods of inquiry are developed and compared, the question must remain unanswered. To anticipate, however, work completed by the author and planned for publication will show significant effects traceable to method of inquiry—effects which markedly alter the inferences drawn.

The research reviewed makes it clear that color does not have the pervasive effects on overt behavior that have been so often claimed. These studies should not, however, lead to an equally erroneous conclusion in the opposite direction. Simple requests for preferences have made it clear that Ss do experience the blots differentially related to various blot dimensions, even though their overt behavior as reflected in summary scores may give no basis for drawing such an inference. To evaluate the role of the stimulus correctly, new methods must be devised for drawing samples of behavior that will permit proper inferences to be made.

REFERENCES

Allen, R. M. The influence of color in the Rorschach test on reaction time in a normal population. J. proj. Tech., 1951, 15, 481–485.

ALLEN, R. M., MANNE, S. H. & STIFF, MARGARET P. The role of color in Rorschach's test: A preliminary normative report on a college student population. *J. proj. Tech.*, 1951, 15, 235–242.

ALLEN, R. M., MANNE, S. H., & STIFF, MARGARET P. The influence of color on the consistency of responses in the Rorschach test. *J. clin. Psychol.*, 1952, 8, 97–98.

ALLEN, R. M., STIFF, MARGARET P., & ROSENZWEIG, M. The role of color in Rorschach's test: a preliminary survey of neurotic and psychotic groups. *J. clin. Psychol.*, 1953, 9, 81–83.

ARNHEIM, R. Perceptual and aesthetic aspects of the movement response. *J. Pers.*, 1951, 19, 265–281.

BALLOCH, J. C. The effect of degree of shading contrast in ink blots on verbal response. *J. exp. Psychol.*, 1952, 43, 120–124.

BANDURA, A. The Rorschach white space responses and perceptual reversal. *J. exp. Psychol.*, 1954, 48, 113–118.

BARNETT, I. The influence of color and shading on the Rorschach test. Unpublished doctoral dissertation. Univer. of Pittsburgh, 1950.

BAUGHMAN, E. E. A comparative analysis of Rorschach forms with altered stimulus characteristics. *J. proj. Tech.*, 1954, 18, 151–164.

BECK, S. J. *Rorschach's test. I. Basic processes.* (2nd ed.) New York: Grune & Stratton, 1949,

BECK, S. J., RABIN, A. I., THIESEN, W. G., MOLISH, H., & THETFORD, W. N. The normal personality as projected in the Rorschach test. *J. Psychol.*, 1950, 30, 241–298.

BELDEN, A. W., & BAUGHMAN, E. E. The effects of figure-ground contrast upon perception as evaluated by a modified Rorschach technique. *J. consult. Psychol.*, 1954, 18, 29–34.

BENJAMIN, E. A psycho-biological approach to the nature of the color shock phenomenon on the Rorschach test. Unpublished master's thesis, Univer. of Chicago, 1948.

BLAKE, R. R. Ocular activity during the administration of the Rorschach test. *J. clin. Psychol.*, 1948, 4, 159–169.

BLAKE, R. R., & RAMSEY, G. V. (Eds.). *Perception: An approach to personality.* New York: Ronald, 1951.

BORING, E. G. Visual perception as invariance. *Psychol. Rev.*, 1952, 59, 141–148.

BRODY, G. G. A study of the effects of color on Rorschach responses. *Genet. Psychol. Monogr.*, 1953, 48, 261–311.

BROSIN, H. W., & FROMM, E. O. Rorschach and color blindness. *Rorschach Res. Exch.*, 1940, 4, 39–70.

BROSIN, H. W., & FROMM, E. O. Some principles of Gestalt psychology in the Rorschach experiment. *Rorschach Res. Exch.*, 1942, 6, 1–15.

BRUNER, J. S. Perceptual theory and the Rorschach test. *J. Pers.*, 1948, 17, 157–168.

BRUNER, J. S., & KRECH, D. (Eds.) *Perception and personality: A symposium.* Durham, N.C.: Duke Univer. Press, 1950.

BUCKLE, D. F., & HOLT, N. F. Comparison of Rorschach and Behn ink-blots. *J. proj. Tech.*, 1951, 15, 486–493.

BUKER, S. L., & WILLIAMS, M. Color as a determinant of responsiveness to Rorschach cards in schizophrenia. *J. consult. Psychol.*, 1951, 15, 196–202.

CANTER, A. An investigation of the psychological significance of reactions to color on the Rorschach and other tests. Unpublished doctoral dissertation, Univer. of Iowa, 1951.

CRONBACH, L. J. Statistical methods applied to Rorschach scores (a review). *Psychol. Bull.*, 1949, 46, 393–429.

CRUMPTON, EVELYN. The influence of color on the Rorschach test. *J. proj. Tech.*, 1956, 20, 150–158.

DEWEY, J. The reflex arc concept in psychology. *Psychol. Rev.*, 1896, 3, 357–370.

DUBROVNER, R. J., VON LACKUM, W. J., & JOST, H. A. A study of the effect of color on productivity and reaction time in the Rorschach test. *J. clin. Psychol.*, 1950, 6, 331–336.

EARL, C. J. A note on the validity of certain Rorschach symbols. *Rorschach Res. Exch.*, 1941, 5, 51–61.

ECKHARDT, W. An experimental and theoretical analysis of movement and vista responses. *J. proj. Tech.*, 1955, 19, 301–305.

EICHLER, R. M. A comparison of the Rorschach and Behn-Rorschach ink-blot tests. *J. consult. Psychol.*, 1951, 15, 185–189.

FROST, C. F., & RODNICK, E. H. The relationship between particular Rorschach determinants and the concomitant galvanic skin responses for schizophrenic and normal subjects. *Amer. Psychologist*, 1948, 3, 277. (Abstract)

GEORGE, C. E. Some unforeseen correlates between the studies of Shaw and Wallen. *J. abnorm. soc. Psychol.*, 1953, 48, 150.

GEORGE, C. E. Stimulus value of the Rorschach cards: a composite study. *J. proj. Tech.*, 1955, 19, 17–20.

GIBSON, J. J. *The perception of the visual world.* Boston: Houghton Mifflin, 1950.

GOODMAN, H. W. An experimental investigation of the affective value of color on the Rorschach test. *Amer. Psychologist*, 1950, 5, 321–322. (Abstract)

GRAYSON, H. M. Rorschach productivity and card preferences as influenced by experimental variation of color and shading. *J. proj. Tech.*, 1956, 20, 288–296.

GUERTIN, W. H., & TREMBATH, W. E. Card VI disturbance on the Rorschach of sex offenders. *J. gen. Psychol.*, 1953, 49, 221–227.

HERSHENSON, JEANNE R. Preference of adolescents for Rorschach figures. *Child Develpm.*, 1949, 20, 101–118.

HOLZBERG, J. D., & SCHLIEFER, M. J. An experimental test of the Rorschach assumption of the impact of color on the perceptual and associative processes. *J. proj. Tech.*, 1955, 19, 130–137.

HUGHES, H., EPSTEIN, L. J., & JOST, H. The relationship between certain measurable functions of autonomic nervous system activity and color responses on the Rorschach test. *J. clin. Psychol.*, 1951, 7, 244–249.

HUTT, M. L. Toward an understanding of projective testing. *J. proj. Tech.*, 1954, 18, 197–201.

JACOB, Z. Some suggestions on the use of content symbolism. *Rorschach Res. Exch.*, 1944, 8, 40–41.

JACQUES, MARY. A comparison of Rorschach and physiological indications of neurotic disturbance. *Amer. Psychologist*, 1946, 1, 264. (Abstract)

KEEHN, J. D. Rorschach validation. III: An examination of the role of color as a determinant in the Rorschach test. *J. ment. Sci.*, 1953, 99, 410–438.

KLEIN, A., & ARNHEIM, R. Perceptual analysis of a Rorschach card. *J. Pers.*, 1953, 22, 60–70.

KLEIN, G. S. The personal world through perception. In R. R. Blake & G. V. Ramsey (Eds.), *Perception: An approach to personality.* New York: Ronald, 1951. Pp. 328–355.

KLOPFER, B. (Ed.) *Developments in the Rorschach technique. II. Fields of application.* Yonkers-on-Hudson: World Book Co., 1956.

LACEY, J. I., BATEMAN, DOROTHY E., & VAN LEHN, RUTH. Autonomic response specificity and Rorschach color responses. *Psychosom. Med.*, 1952, 14, 256–260.

LAZARUS, R. S. An experimental analysis of the influence of color on the protocol of the Rorschach test. *J. Pers.*, 1948, 17, 182–185.

LAZARUS, R. S. The influence of color on the protocol of the Rorschach test. *J. abnorm. soc. Psychol.*, 1949, 44, 506–516.

LEVY, JEANNE R. Changes in the galvanic skin response accompanying the Rorschach test. *J. consult. Psychol.*, 1950, 14, 128–133.

LINDNER, R. M. Content analysis in Rorschach work. *Rorschach Res. Exch.*, 1946, 10, 121–129.

LINDNER, R. M. Analysis of the Rorschach test by content. *J. clin. Psychopath.*, 1947, 8, 707–719.

LINDNER, R. M. The content analysis of the Rorschach protocol. In L. E. Abt & L. Bellak (Eds.), *Projective psychology.* New York: Knopf, 1950. Pp. 75–90.

LINDNER, R. M. The clinical uses of content analysis in Rorschach testing. *Psychoanalysis*, 1955, 3, 12–17.

MARADIE, L. J. Productivity on the Rorschach as a function of order of presentation. *J. consult. Psychol.*, 1953, 17, 32–35.

MATARAZZO, J. D., & MENSH, I. N. Reaction time characteristics of the Rorschach test. *J. consult. Psychol.*, 1952, 16, 132–139.

MATARAZZO, R. G., WATSON, R., & ULETT, G. A. Relationship of the Rorschach scoring categories to modes of perception induced by intermittent photic stimulation—a methodological study of perception. *J. clin. Psychol.*, 1952, 8, 368–374.

MAYMAN, M. A comparative study of the Rorschach, Harrower, and Behn-Eschenburg inkblot tests. *Amer. Psychologist*, 1947, 2, 270–271. (Abstract)

MEER, B. The relative difficulty of the Rorschach cards. *J. proj. Tech.*, 1955, 19, 43–53.

MEER, B., & SINGER, J. L. A note on the "father" and "mother" cards in the Rorschach inkblots. *J. consult. Psychol.*, 1950, 14, 482–484.

MENSH, I. N., & MATARAZZO, J. D. Rorschach card rejection in psychodiagnosis. *J. consult. Psychol.*, 1954, 18, 271–275.

MEYER, B. T. An investigation of color shock in the Rorschach test. *J. clin. Psychol.*, 1951, 7, 367–370.

MILNER, B., & MOREAULT, L. Etude du test Rorschach en relation au réflexe psychogalvanique. *Bull. Canad. psychol. Ass.*, 1945, 5, 80. (Abstract)

MITCHELL, M. B. Preferences for Rorschach cards. *J. proj. Tech.*, 1952, 16, 203–211.

PASCAL, G. R., REUSCH, H. A., DEVINE, C. A., & SUTTELL, BARBARA J. A study of genital symbols on the Rorschach test: presentation of a method and results. *J. abnorm. soc. Psychol.*, 1950, 45, 286–295.

PERLMAN, JANET A. Color and the validity of the Rorschach 8-9-10 per cent. *J. consult. Psychol.*, 1951, 15, 122–126.

PHILLIPS, L., & SMITH, J. *Rorschach interpretation: advanced technique.* New York: Grune & Stratton, 1953.

RABIN, A. I., & SANDERSON, M. H. An experimental inquiry into some Rorschach procedures. *J. clin. Psychol.*, 1947, 2, 216–225.

RANZONI, JANE H., GRANT, MARGUERITE Q., & IVES, VIRGINIA. Rorschach "card-pull" in a normal adolescent population. *J. proj. Tech.*, 1950, 14, 107–133.

REECE, M. M. Color shock in the Rorschach test: the effect of achromatic reproductions. Unpublished master's thesis, Stanford Univer., 1949.

ROCKWELL, F. V., WELCH, L., FISICHELLI, V., & KUBIS, J. Changes in palmar skin resistance during the Rorschach experiment. *Amer. Psychologist*, 1946, 1, 287. (Abstract)

ROCKWELL, F. V., WELCH, L., KUBIS, J., & FISICHELLI, V. Changes in palmar skin resistance during the Rorschach test. II. The effect of repetition with color removed. *Mschr. Psychiat. Neurol.*, 1948, 116, 321–345.

ROSEN, E. Symbolic meanings in the Rorschach cards: a statistical study. *J. clin. Psychol.*, 1951, 7, 239–244.

ROSENWALD, A. K. A comparison of the Rorschach and Behn-Rorschach tests based on a study of chronic alcoholic subjects. *Amer. Psychologist*, 1947, 2, 270. (Abstract)

RUESCH, J., & FINESINGER, J. E. The relation of the Rorschach color response to the use of color in drawings. *Psychosom. Med.*, 1941, 3, 370–388.

SAPPENFIELD, B. R., & BUKER, S. L. Validity of the Rorschach 8-9-10 per cent as an indicator of responsiveness to color. *J. consult. Psychol.*, 1949, 13, 268–271.

SARASON, S. B. *The clinical interaction.* New York: Harper, 1954.

SARASON, S. B., & POTTER, E. H. Color in the Rorschach and Kohs block designs. *J. consult. Psychol.*, 1947, 11, 202–206.

SCHAFER, R. Content analysis in the Rorschach test. *J. proj. Tech.*, 1953, 17, 335–339.

SCHAFER, R. *Psychoanalytic interpretation in Rorschach testing: Theory and application.* New York: Grune & Stratton, 1954.

SHAW, B. Sex populars in the Rorschach test. *J. abnorm. soc. Psychol.*, 1948, 43, 466–470.

SIIPOLA, ELSA M. The influence of color on reactions to ink blots. *J. Pers.*, 1950, 18, 358–382.

SIIPOLA, ELSA M., KUHNS, FLORENCE, & TAYLOR, VIVIAN. Measurement of the individual's reactions to color in ink blots. *J. Pers.*, 1950, 19, 153–171.

SINGER, J. L. The Behn-Rorschach ink blots: a preliminary comparison with the original Rorschach series. *J. proj. Tech.*, 1952, 16, 238–245.

SIPLE, H. L. Physiological correlates of color shock in the Rorschach test. Unpublished doctoral dissertation, Northwestern Univer., 1948.

STEIN, M. Personality factors involved in the temporal development of Rorschach responses. *J. proj. Tech.*, 1949, 13, 355–414.

STEINBERG, A. An experimental investigation of the relation of galvanic skin response to Rorschach shock. Unpublished doctoral dissertation, Boston Univer., 1949.

STERLING, M. E. Color shock on the Rorschach test. Unpublished doctoral dissertation, Univer. of Kentucky, 1950.

SWARTZ, M. B. The role of color in influencing responses to the Rorschach test: An experimental investigation of the validity of the color shock hypothesis as a sign of neurotic distburance and as a phenomenon induced by the color stimulus. Unpublished dissertation, New York Univer., 1953.

THURSTONE, L. L. The Rorschach in psychological science. *J. abnorm. soc. Psychol.*, 1948, 43, 471–475.

WALLEN, R. The nature of color shock. *J. abnorm. soc. Psychol.*, 1948, 43, 346–356.

WERTHEIMER, M. Perception and the Rorschach. *J. proj. Tech.*, 1957, 21, 209–216.

YORK, R. H. The effect of color in the Rorschach test and in selected intellectual tasks. Unpublished doctoral dissertation, Boston Univer., 1951.

ZUBIN, J., ERON, L. D., & SCHUMER, FLORENCE. *An experimental approach to projective techniques.* New York: Wiley, 1965.

16

Relationships between Rorschach Scoring Categories and the Total Number of Responses[1]

DONALD W. FISKE
AND E. EARL BAUGHMAN

The influence of the number of responses (R) given to a Rorschach protocol on the elicitation of all other determinant scores is, on the average, considerable. The problem is that the high number of color, shading, or movement responses may be to some degree the result of a drive for productivity rather than of the factors usually attributed to these determinant scores. One could elect several methods of controlling the influence of R, including limiting the subject to perhaps three responses per card.

The method utilized by Fiske and Baughman, however, is to study the relationship of R and the various determinant scores by dividing their 633 outpatients into nine categories as a function of their number of R. For comparative purposes, they employed the 157 normal subject profiles of Beck. In addition to providing norms for each Rorschach score, they also plotted several of them graphically.

In general, there is little difference between the normal and outpatient groups, the most noteworthy differences being the tendency of patients to employ more shading at all levels of response, with the greatest divergence between the groups occurring at high response levels. Some of the

---

[1] We are indebted to Drs. Samuel Beck, George Calden, Lee Cronbach, David Grant, E. Lowell Kelly, E. H. Porter, Jr., and Morris Stein for their critical comments and to the Social Science Research Committee of the University of Chicago for a grant facilitating this study.

257

determinant and R *relationships appear to be linear, but many are curvilinear. These tables and figures should be very useful in providing norms for clinicians.*

The outstanding recognition accorded to the Rorschach technique has brought it to the attention of those research investigators who seek to further the scientific understanding of personality. Rorschach himself noted its research value (1942, p. 13). These experimenters, together with those interested in making the interpretation of Rorschach protocols more objective, have tried to convert the procedure into a standardized psychometric instrument. Investigators have looked for critical diagnostic signs, with dubious success. Such laborious statistical methods as factor analysis have been used in the effort to increase our understanding of the test (Hughes, 1950; Wittenborn, 1949; Wittenborn, 1950a; Wittenborn, 1950b). Cronbach (1949) has provided an excellent guide to the many difficulties involved in the quantitative investigation of Rorschach protocols.

The purpose of this paper is to examine one aspect of the adequacy of the Rorschach test as a psychometric instrument: to what extent are the frequencies of responses in the several scoring categories related to the total number of responses? It is hoped that the results of this study will be useful to investigators who might want to use the test for research purposes and also to clinicians using the test in clinical practice. Unless the Rorschach is to be used solely in a qualitative manner, it is essential that the properties of the various scores be studied empirically.

Lest there be any misunderstanding, let us state explicitly that in this paper we are not primarily concerned with the validity problem. A gradually accumulating body of evidence suggests that some Rorschach scores do measure consistent aspects of a person's response tendencies (Goldner, 1950; Orange, 1951; Williams, 1947). While definitive investigations are not available, there is strong reason to believe that many of Rorschach's insights point to dimensions of temperament and personality which when isolated and adequately measured will help to structure the complex phenomena studied in the embryonic science of personality.

Sources of Data

Outpatients. To investigate differences between Rorschach psychograms obtained by different examiners, Baughman (1951) collected 633 protocols from the files of the Chicago VA Mental Hygiene Clinic. These included all cases examined by each of 15 examiners. The number of records per examiner varied from 21 to 69, except for one examiner who had tested 126 cases. The median number of records was 30. The records, collected over a three-year period, were from male veterans whose psychiatric status ranged from mild neurosis to definite psychosis, with abnormal cortical functioning present in some cases. The majority were, however, neurotics.

These examiners followed the scoring system of Beck (1949) rather closely, but added certain variables from the approach of Klopfer and Kelley (1942). The scoring of the original examiner was used in all cases. Baughman's study found that for each of 22 scoring categories there was at least one examiner whose records had a distribution significantly different from that for all 15 examiners combined. Hence the examiners were divided into two groups: Group A included 9 examiners, each of whom had a distribution of R (total number of responses) which did not deviate significantly from that for the total group. Group B included 6 examiners with deviant distributions on R. The examiners in Group A had significantly deviant distributions on from 0 to 6 scoring categories out of 22, whereas those in Group B deviated on from 7 to 12 categories. The total number of records from each group was 259 and 374, respectively. Some analyses were made for each subgroup separately, as well as for the two groups together. For simplicity in exposition, however, the results for Group B by itself are not presented.

Normal group. Beck has reported his analysis of a group of 157 employees of a mail-order house (Beck, Rabin, Thiesen, Molish, & Thetford, 1950). He and his associates sought to obtain "a representative sample of the community." The group contained 71 males and 86 females. The age range was 17 to 69, with a mean of 30.5. Four vocational groups and a wide range of educational achievement were represented. Our analysis indicates that the two examiners who collected all the records had similar distributions of R, even when broken down into the four vocational groups. Each tested the same proportion of each of these four groups.[2]

Analysis

To facilitate tabulation, each case was placed into one of nine classes on the basis of R. For each class in each sample, the median frequency of

---

[2] The psychograms were made available to us through the courtesy of Dr. Beck and Dr. Thetford. We are deeply indebted to them for their cooperation.

TABLE 16-1   *Median Frequencies in Rorschach Scoring Categories*
for Protocols Grouped by Total Number
of Responses

SCORING CATEGORY	POPULATION	RANGE OF R FOR EACH GROUP								
		1	2	3	4	5	6	7	8	9
		0-9	10-14	15-19	20-24	25-29	30-34	35-39	40-49	50-175
Mdn R	Outpt. A	7.6	12.8	17.2	22.3	26.5	31.5	36.2	42.7	62.0
	All outpts.	7.8	12.7	16.8	22.0	27.1	31.8	37.1	43.3	66.0
	Normal	a	12.8a	18.0	22.3	27.4	31.6	36.3	42.0	61.2
W	Outpt. A	3.4	5.9	6.2	5.7	7.5	6.7	7.5	6.7	8.0
	All outpts.	3.4	5.7	6.1	5.3	6.1	6.4	7.7	6.9	7.6
	Normal		3.0	5.8	4.2	4.9	5.4	6.0	4.5	6.0
D	Outpt. A	3.0	5.2	9.9	14.9	16.5	22.5	24.5	27.3	39.7
	All outpts.	3.0	5.7	9.8	14.6	16.3	22.1	24.1	27.0	41.0
	Normal		7.2	11.3	16.2	20.0	23.2	26.2	31.8	45.2
Dd	Outpt. A	0.3	0.4	1.0	1.3	2.2	2.5	4.0	7.7	22.0
	All outpts.	0.2	0.3	0.7	1.3	2.8	2.5	4.1	7.2	16.5
	Normal		0.9	0.3	0.8	1.8	1.8	2.3	4.0	11.8
M	Outpt. A	0.3	0.4	0.7	0.8	2.1	1.5	2.3	2.7	4.0
	All outpts.	0.2	0.4	0.7	0.9	1.7	2.3	2.4	3.0	5.6
	Normal		0.7	0.7	2.1	2.7	3.0	2.8	5.0	9.0
C	Outpt. A	0.0	0.0	0.1	0.2	0.3	0.1	0.2	0.4	0.3
	All outpts.	0.0	0.1	0.1	0.2	0.2	0.1	0.3	0.4	0.4
	Normal		0.0	0.1	0.1	0.3	0.5	0.3	0.3	1.1
CF	Outpt. A	0.1	0.4	0.8	1.0	1.8	1.3	2.2	2.0	2.7
	All outpts.	0.2	0.6	1.0	1.2	1.8	1.4	2.4	2.4	3.3
	Normal		0.2	1.0	0.5	1.0	1.0	0.8	1.3	2.6
FC	Outpt. A	0.3	0.2	1.0	0.9	1.5	1.3	1.5	1.7	3.0
	All outpts.	0.2	0.2	0.5	0.5	0.9	1.0	1.3	1.7	2.7
	Normal		0.2	0.8	1.1	0.8	1.2	1.4	1.8	1.2
Sum C	Outpt. A	0.4	1.1	1.7	2.5	4.1	2.3	4.6	4.5	7.5
	All outpts.	0.2	1.2	2.0	2.8	3.8	2.9	4.7	4.8	7.5
	Normal		0.4	2.4	1.2	2.1	2.6	1.8	2.5	6.4
Y	Outpt. A	0.0	0.0	0.0	0.0	0.0	0.0	0.1	0.1	0.1
	All outpts.	0.0	0.0	0.0	0.0	0.0	0.0	0.1	0.1	0.1
	Normal		0.0	0.0	0.0	0.0	0.1	0.0	0.1	0.1
YF	Outpt. A	0.1	0.1	0.2	0.2	0.5	0.5	0.9	0.6	1.4
	All outpts.	0.1	0.1	0.2	0.3	0.4	0.5	0.5	0.6	1.5
	Normal		0.0	0.1	0.2	0.2	0.4	0.2	0.5	0.6
FY	Outpt. A	0.6	0.9	1.9	2.2	3.3	3.5	5.2	6.7	7.0
	All outpts.	0.6	0.7	1.5	1.9	2.4	3.0	3.9	5.8	6.8
	Normal		0.1	0.4	0.4	1.1	1.2	1.2	1.9	2.0
VF	Outpt. A	0.0	0.0	0.0	0.0	0.0	0.0	0.1	0.1	0.1
	All outpts.	0.0	0.0	0.0	0.0	0.0	0.0	0.0	0.1	0.1
	Normal		0.0	0.1	0.0	0.1	0.0	0.1	0.3	0.1
FV	Outpt. A	0.0	0.0	0.1	0.2	0.2	0.2	0.2	0.6	1.1
	All outpts.	0.0	0.0	0.1	0.2	0.3	0.2	0.3	0.7	0.8
	Normal		0.0	0.1	0.3	0.3	0.9	1.0	1.2	2.0
F+	Outpt. A	3.4	6.5	7.8	9.7	10.2	15.2	13.5	16.3	22.2
	All outpts.	4.0	6.0	7.6	9.6	11.1	14.8	15.3	17.3	23.5
	Normal		8.2	9.7	13.0	15.6	16.4	19.8	22.0	26.8
F-	Outpt. A	1.1	1.9	2.2	3.2	3.0	2.9	5.5	6.6	11.0
	All outpts.	0.8	2.0	2.1	3.2	3.4	3.8	5.9	6.8	10.8
	Normal		2.2	2.2	2.7	3.1	4.8	5.7	6.2	9.1

a One case in the normal group had 9 responses. It was added to the 6 cases in the 2nd R group.

TABLE 16–1 Continued
Median Frequencies in Rorschach Scoring Categories for Protocols Grouped by Total Number of Responses

SCORING CATEGORY	POPULATION	1 0–9	2 10–14	3 15–19	4 20–24	5 25–29	6 30–34	7 35–39	8 40–49	9 50–175
F%	Outpt. A	70	73	62	61	54	59	57	54	56
	All outpts.	72	70	61	60	60	60	56	56	56
	Normal		92	72	72	75	69	74	68	62
F+%	Outpt. A	85	75	77	75	78	82	71	71	62
	All outpts.	84	75	79	75	74	76	70	71	66
	Normal		75	82	82	84	78	78	76	74
P	Outpt. A	3.1	4.2	5.1	4.6	5.2	6.3	6.5	7.4	7.3
	All outpts.	2.8	4.0	5.2	5.0	5.5	6.5	6.7	7.1	7.7
	Normal		3.8	4.8	6.9	7.2	6.8	7.2	8.0	9.0
S	Outpt. A	0.4	0.5	1.1	2.1	2.1	1.2	2.7	3.3	4.7
	All outpts.	0.3	0.5	1.1	1.7	2.0	1.7	2.9	3.6	4.4
	Normal		0.4	0.7	1.0	1.4	1.1	2.5	1.5	2.9
H	Outpt. A	0.4	1.0	1.0	1.1	1.9	2.4	2.2	2.5	4.6
	All outpts.	0.3	0.9	1.2	1.2	2.1	2.5	2.2	3.2	6.2
	Normal		0.8	1.4	2.6	3.6	3.4	4.5	5.5	10.0
Hd	Outpt. A	0.2	0.4	0.5	0.8	1.2	2.2	1.8	5.2	6.8
	All outpts.	0.2	0.3	0.4	0.8	1.7	2.2	1.9	3.3	6.8
	Normal		0.7	0.4	1.0	2.0	1.2	2.2	2.5	4.4
A	Outpt. A	3.9	5.8	8.0	8.4	10.2	12.0	12.5	12.0	17.3
	All outpts.	3.5	5.8	7.7	9.0	9.7	11.4	12.6	12.4	17.3
	Normal		5.2	8.6	9.2	9.9	11.1	12.2	13.5	20.2
Ad	Outpt. A	0.2	0.4	1.3	1.8	1.8	3.5	3.2	3.3	6.1
	All outpts.	0.3	0.4	1.0	1.7	2.0	3.2	2.8	3.9	6.1
	Normal		1.0	0.8	2.5	1.9	2.8	2.5	4.0	5.2
An	Outpt. A	0.4	0.2	0.5	0.8	1.7	1.1	2.5	1.7	5.7
	All outpts.	0.2	0.4	0.5	0.8	1.5	1.2	1.7	1.5	2.5
	Normal		0.1	1.0	0.5	1.2	0.8	0.9	1.9	2.8
Sex	Outpt. A	0.0	0.0	0.0	0.0	0.0	0.2	0.2	0.1	0.4
	All outpts.	0.0	0.0	0.1	0.1	0.1	0.1	0.2	0.1	0.4
	Normal		0.0	0.0	0.0	0.0	0.0	0.0	0.1	0.0
A%	Outpt. A	57	54	53	50	46	52	40	40	37
	All outpts.	57	54	50	50	44	48	42	38	38
	Normal		57	53	54	44	45	43	43	41
F	Normal		0.0	0.0	0.1	0.0	0.0	0.2	0.2	1.0
Z	Normal		10.0	11.5	19.2	17.0	17.0	21.8	22.8	34.5
FM	Outpt. A	0.2	1.3	1.7	2.0	4.2	4.0	3.2	4.0	5.9
	All outpts.	0.2	1.1	1.3	1.9	3.3	3.7	3.6	3.7	6.8
m	Outpt. A	0.1	0.1	0.1	0.4	1.2	0.9	1.1	1.6	2.5
	All outpts.	0.1	0.1	0.2	0.3	1.1	0.5	1.2	1.8	2.2
8–10/R	Outpt. A[b]	31	29	33	33	39	36	35	37	36
	All outpts.[b]	22	29	33	35	36	35	39	34	35
Geog.	Outpt. A	0.1	0.1	0.2	0.2	0.3	0.5	0.4	1.0	2.0
	All outpts.	0.1	0.1	0.2	0.2	0.3	0.4	0.4	0.9	1.2
T/1R	Outpt.A[b]	19.5	30.0	21.8	22.7	15.3	17.0	14.3	12.5	11.7
	All outpts.[b]	27.0	29.5	23.2	24.0	21.0	17.2	17.0	14.5	12.5
N[c]	Outpt. A	19	40	43	51	24	24	20	17	21
	All outpts.	38	102	109	114	66	62	39	45	58
	Normal	(1)	7	17	30	23	31	16	18	15

b Data not available on many cases.
c Total N: Outpatient A group, 259; All outpatients, 633; Normal group, 157.

each Rorschach score was obtained. The median was selected as the measure of central tendency because most Rorschach scoring categories have marked skewness in their distributions. The medians are presented in Table 16–1.

While the frequency in some classes is unfortunately small, we felt that a more coarse grouping might obscure some trends. However, it must be recognized that the reliabilities of the medians vary from class to class because of differences in frequency.

To provide a single index for the degree of relationship between each scoring category and R, contingency coefficients (C) were computed. These are presented in Table 16–2. In the analysis of each scoring category for each sample, the median was obtained first. Then each R class was divided at this median for the sample, yielding a $2 \times n$ table of frequencies, where n is the number of R groups. The value of n was 9 for the outpatient population. (In these computations, the two outpatient groups were thrown together because the curves for the medians of the two groups were fairly congruent.) For the normal sample, it was necessary to combine adjacent classes to obtain acceptable theoretical frequencies. The three lowest R classes were combined. Contingency coefficients were computed from the resulting 2×7 tables and also from 2×5 tables obtained by combining the three highest R classes which had small frequencies. The two sets of coefficients were almost identical, those based on the 2×7 tables tending to be a few points higher. Since these larger tables seemed to represent the data better, the coefficients obtained from them are the ones presented in Table 16–2. Churchill (1951) indicates that the maximal value for a contingency coefficient derived from a $2 \times n$ table is .71.

On the basis of an examination of the contingency table for each score, a minus sign was attached to certain contingency coefficients to indicate instances where the relationship to R was generally negative. Inspection suggests that most of the obtained relationships between R and the several scoring categories are not simple linear relationships. The irregularities are in part a function of the number of cases. As a rule, the relationships are more regular for the total outpatient sample than for Group A alone or for the normal sample. These data indicate that in Rorschach studies, as in other psychometric research, the amount of random fluctuation found in small samples is so great that any trends in the data must be interpreted with extreme caution.

Most of the coefficients show significant positive relationships. However, in interpreting these relationships, one must recognize that all the coefficients are "spurious" because they are part-whole correlations: the total number of responses includes the frequency in each scoring category, and some categories (e. g., D) make major contributions to R. Nevertheless, this condition presumably has no general effect on the *form* of the relationship.

TABLE 16–2   *Relationship between Each Scoring Category and R*
(Coefficients of Contingency)

	POPULATIONS	
SCORING CATEGORY	ALL OUTPATIENTS ($N=633$)	NORMAL GROUP ($N=157$)
W	.22	(.13) †
D	.63	.63
Dd	.51	.46
M	.45	.41
C	.25	.34
CF	.30	.28
FC	.39	(.22) †
ΣC	.44	.33
YF	.30	.28
FY	.47	.38
FV	.33	.45
F+	.56	.57
F−	.43	.49
F%	−.16	−.26
F+%	−.19	−.34
P	.41	.39
S	.41	.36
H	.43	.49
Hd	.47	.40
A	.52	.53
Ad	.47	.40
An	.30	.37
Sex	.25	*
A%	−.29	−.31
Z	*	(.23) †
FM	.45	*
m	.41	*
8–10/R	.25	*
Geog.	.30	*
Median of above variables	.41	.38
T/1R	−.31	*
T/R	−.30	*

† With the exception of these three, all values of C are significant at the .05 level.
* Omitted values were not computed because scores were not available or because frequencies were too small.

As Figure 16–1 indicates, the various scoring categories show diverse types of relationship to R.[3] However, certain variables appear to show similar relationships with R. Thus the curves for D, F+, and A have comparable slopes, perhaps because each represents a general tendency to give commonly perceived responses. These three categories have the largest contingency coefficients for both populations. The same trend may be present in another cluster which also has approximately linear, but flatter, curves: FC, Sum C, FV, F—, and P. (The curve for P might resemble that for D if there were no limit to the number of possible P responses.) Still linear, but almost horizontal, slopes are found for C, Y, YF, and Sex, all of which occur very infrequently.

Most of the other variables appear to have curvilinear trends. Dd has a hyperbolic, rapidly accelerating curve. If it is true that a subject usually gives only one response to an area, it is not surprising that as total R increases, the number and also the proportion of responses to unusual details must increase even more rapidly.

The three percentage scores, F%, F+%, and A%, show relatively low negative relationships with R. As R increases, proportionally more responses tend to use uncommon determinants and content. It is interesting to note that with higher R, the latency of the first response (T/1R) also drops off.

The relationship patterns for most of the other variables seem to be complex: they usually have a leveling off or a dip in the curve. For example, the curves for the total outpatient group for M, H, Hd, and Ad (and possibly for FM, FV, and Geog) show a fairly even increase except for a flattening or a slight reversal in R classes 6 and 7 (30 to 39 responses). While the corresponding curves for the normal group are irregular, they are not congruent with those for the outpatient group or even with each other. (Parenthetically, we may observe here that for both the outpatient and the normal groups, the H and Hd curves resemble each other, whereas the A and Ad curves are not similar.)

A similar reversal of trend is found in the outpatient group's curves for m, CF, Sum C, and S: the median for Class 6 (30–34 responses) is definitely below those for the two adjoining classes. (The Dd curve also has a slight break at this point.) Again, the normal group does not repeat this effect.

How should we evaluate these irregularities? The magnitudes of the changes are not great, and the trends may be a consequence of the

[3] Graphical representations of all relationships referred to in this paper (similar to those presented in Fig. 16–1) have been filed with the American Documentation Institute. To secure a copy of these graphs, order Document 3701 from American Documentation Institute, 1719 N Street N.W., Washington 6, D.C., remitting $1.00 for microfilm (images 1 in. high on standard 35-mm. motion picture film) or $4.80 for photocopies (6×8 in.) readable without optical aid. A limited number of mimeographed sets of graphs are also available. To obtain these, write to E. E. Baughman, Department of Psychology, University of Wisconsin, Madison, Wisconsin.

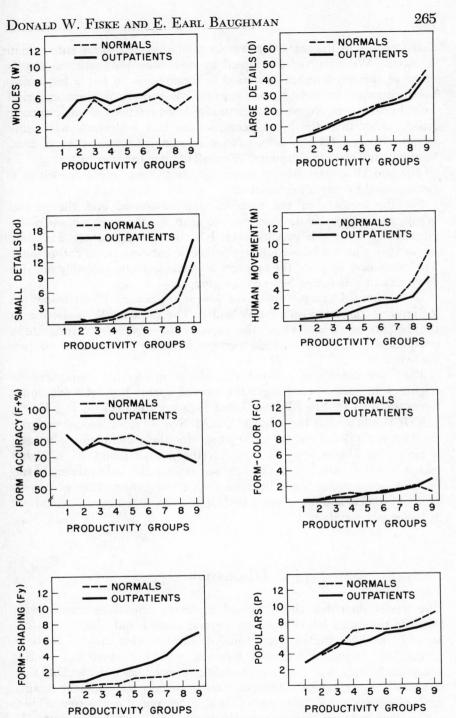

Figure 16–1. Graphic illustrations of relationships between productivity (R) and other Rorschach scores (W, D, Dd, M, FC, FY, P, F+%).

characteristics of the particular samples which happen to fall into certain R classes. We have not attempted to determine the statistical significance of these differences because it is meaningless to test a few exceptional discrepancies out of many possible comparisons in these empirical data. Furthermore, we see no meaningful interpretations of these specific trends, other than the broad generalization that individuals who differ in productivity (R) also differ in their thresholds for some determinants, locations, and content categories. We shall develop this point later.

The two W curves show a remarkable congruence in pattern which is not repeated for any other variable.

For the majority of the variables, the outpatient and the normal groups show fairly similar relationships with R: there are no sharp discrepancies. With the exception of FY, the general slopes are quite consistent. The median contingency coefficients are almost the same. The differences between the two sets of coefficients are probably not due to systematic differences between the groups.

In the normal group, two of the lowest coefficients (both below the .05 level of confidence) are for W and Z. The value for W is also low in the outpatient group. Thus, the capacity to organize or integrate a complex stimulus into a single percept is largely independent of productivity.

There are differences between the two groups in the proportions of responses in various categories: the normal group had relatively lower scores on W, CF, YF, FY, and S, but higher scores on F+, F% F+%, and H. While we did not tabulate the M: Sum C ratio, we can compare the two sets of medians for each group: for the patient group, Sum C is higher for almost every R class; for the normal group, M is higher except where R is below 20. We do not believe that safe inferences can be drawn concerning these differences since the groups differ in proportion of women and were not matched for age, intelligence, education, or socioeconomic status.

Discussion

The results presented above seemed to be in general agreement with the data published by Wittenborn (1950a; 1950b) and Hughes (1950). In each of those studies, factor analysis yielded what appears to be a productivity factor. We cannot, however, readily compare our contingency coefficients with the corresponding Pearson r's (Wittenborn) or tetrachoric r's (Hughes). Different scoring systems and different scoring categories were used. Moreover, C and r are not directly comparable.

Our data seem to differ from Wittenborn's in another respect. He found no evidence of nonlinear relationships with R (1950a, p. 263), whereas many of the relationships in our data appear to be nonlinear.

Scores based on the response frequency in a particular Rorschach scoring category are unsatisfactory psychological measures (Eichler, 1951). While it is clear that frequencies in most categories are related to the total number of responses, we cannot state, on the basis of the present data, which influences the other. We believe that a subject may take a set toward a certain productivity level and then seek to find the necessary responses to reach it . On the other hand, it is true that subjects with predispositions to perceiving H and Hd responses in Dd areas would tend to have comparatively high R's.

Most of the category scores cannot be improved by handling them as percentages of the total number of responses (cf. Beck et al., 1950, p. 253). While much of the relationship is removed by the process, there is still a relationship between the percentage measures and R. In the cases of W, P, and A, percentage scores would be comparable if computed by omitting the first three responses in that category; i.e., the formula $(A-3)/R$ yields a score unrelated to R. Since the great majority of subjects give at least three responses in each of these categories, individual variability related to R appears most clearly in the number of responses beyond that point. Furthermore, the use of percentage scores cannot remove all the effect of R: the variability of these scores may itself be related to R.

With respect to the relationship between P and R, Thompson (1950) reports that for group Rorschachs administered to college students, the curve for P flattens out after forty responses. This tendency was not marked in either of our groups.

For the clinical application of the Rorschach, it would be possible to prepare norm tables for each R class (cf. Fonda's table for S [1951, p. 374]). However, these would have to be based on sizable frequencies in each class to yield stable norms. Furthermore, separate norms should probably be prepared for various groups classified by intelligence, education, psychiatric status, etc. While such material would enable the clinician to be more objective in his evaluation of protocols, considerable labor would be involved in preparing the norms. Moreover, norms would be useless as long as examiner differences in scoring are present (cf. Baughman, 1951).

The numerous irregularities in the relationship curves are probably due in part to examiner differences and to examiner subject interactions (cf. Miller, Sanders, & Cleveland, 1950). A Rorschach response is determined by the subject's perception of the total situation, including the instructions, the card, his previous responses, the purpose of the testing situation, and the examiner, as well as by his usual modes of reaction. In research studies, it is imperative that no examiners be used whose response distributions differ appreciably from some standard and whose method of administration is not highly consistent from day to day. On the other hand, for clinical purposes the Rorschach can, of course, be used as a structured interview in any way the clinician sees fit.

One may question the value of using the Rorschach technique in research studies to measure particular variables. The fundamental insights of Hermann Rorschach can probably be incorporated into much more satisfactory instruments. For example, at the University of Chicago, L. L. Thurstone and Eckhard H. Hess are developing efficient tests for assessing color-form preferences. A series of such tests should yield a profile of response tendencies with more scientific value than the present Rorschach psychogram (cf. Zubin's suggestions [1950]). It may even be possible to create a technique for the simultaneous measurements of the principal dimensions of personality, thus preserving interactions between dimensions and making the total procedure less artificial.

Productivity or reactivity should be measured in a test or series of tests developed for that specific purpose. Such a test would require carefully worked out instructions. It is our tentative hypothesis that each subject perceives the Rorschach test situation as calling for some given degree of application to the task of finding percepts in the rather unstructured card. Energy output and rate of expenditure may be relevant concepts here: recall that the interval before the first response is negatively related to R. A smiliar relationship is found for time per response, T/R (which probably measures the interval between responses), for a portion of the outpatient group on whom this value was computed.

Given a set to expend a certain amount of energy on the task, certain perceptions are easier than others. Thus, subjects with a high energy-output set give proportionally fewer W and P responses because these rapidly become more difficult after the first few; on the other hand, Dd responses are comparatively easy for some subjects and may therefore becomes proportionately more frequent. Accuracy of perceptions $(F+\%)$ diminishes only slightly with increasing productivity, and $F-$ increases at a nearly constant rate. While M and Hd become proportionately more frequent, the other content and determinant categories make a fairly constant contribution to the total R.

Can the relationships between scoring categories and productivity be understood in terms of Maslow's concepts of the expressive and the coping components of behavior (Maslow, 1949)? Perhaps productivity is primarily coping or adaptive behavior. The subject meets the requirements of the test situation (as he perceives them) by giving a certain number of responses. On the other hand, many of the other scoring categories reflect the expressive component: the content and the determinants of a response may not contribute significantly to the subject's adjustment to the immediate test situation but may essentially be products of the state of the organism. We should not deny, of course, that a particular response may be adaptive in so far as it reduces tension or that the total number of responses may not be in part expressive of inner personality trends. We are suggesting that the major sources of variability may be usefully related to this dichotomy. We agree with the view of Klein and Schlesinger (1949) that we should recognize the adaptive properties of perceptual acts, but we would distinguish between the aspect of perception contributing primarily to adaptation to the external environment and that aspect contributed by internal processes which are relatively independent of the specific external situation.

What are the solutions to the problems raised by these data? We have suggested above that the Rorschach test be replaced by a series of tests measuring the same variables, possessing a more firm psychometric basis, and retaining some provision for recording interactions between them. Such a radical plan is of no present value—it will take years to develop such tests. In the meantime, it may be profitable to explore ways of controlling R. Werner (1945, p. 60) tried one method: since his groups had different mean R's, he used only the first three responses to each card in computing Dd%. Eichler (1951) has employed the analysis of covariance to adjust for differences in R. Another possibility is to alter the instructions by giving a specific set for, say, three responses per card; the same result might be better achieved by stopping the subject after the third response and encouraging unproductive subjects until they give three responses. Such modifications would sacrifice some information obtained by the standard instructions.

While the primary purpose of this paper has been to contribute to our understanding of the Rorschach test, we hope that the tables will be useful to the clinician. He can compare the psychogram of a given protocol with the median psychogram for members of our normal or outpatient group who gave a comparable number of responses.

Summary

For a group of 633 outpatients at a mental hygiene clinic and for the 157 cases in Beck's normal group, the median frequency in each Rorschach scoring category was obtained for classes based on total number of responses (R). Contingency coefficients between R and each category were computed. The findings were that:

1. The relationships between R and each scoring category often appear to be complex and nonlinear.

2. The form of the relationship with R seems to vary for the various categories, although some have similar patterns.

3. The forms of the relationships with R are fairly similar for the normal and the outpatient groups.

On the basis of these data, we agree with Cronbach (1949) that scores based on frequencies of responses in particular scoring categories are unsatisfactory psychological measures and that taking these scores as percentages of R is only a partially adequate solution to the problem. For research on the dimensions of personality, improved measures must be developed for promising Rorschach variables.

REFERENCES

BAUGHMAN, E. E. Rorschach scores as a function of examiner difference. *J. proj. Tech.*, 1951, 15, 243–249.

BECK, S. J. *Rorschach's test. I. Basic processes.* (2nd ed.) New York: Grune & Stratton, 1949.

BECK, S. J., RABIN, A. I., THIESEN, W. G., MOLISH, H., & THETFORD, W. N. The normal personality as projected in the Rorschach test. *J. Psychol.*, 1950, 30, 241–298.

CHURCHILL, E. Review of McNemar, *Psychological statistics.* In O. K. Buros (Ed.), *Statistical methodology reviews* 1941–1950. New York: Wiley, 1951. Pp. 270–271.

CRONBACH, L. J. Statistical methods applied to Rorschach scores: A review. *Psychol. Bull.*, 1949, 46, 393–429.

EICHLER, R. M. Some comments on the controlling of differences in responses on the Rorschach test. *Psychol. Bull.*, 1951, 48, 257–259.

FONDA, C. P. The nature and meaning of the Rorschach white space response. *J. abnorm. soc. Psychol.*, 1951, 46, 367–377.

GOLDNER, R. H. An investigation of the whole-part approach as a problem solving process. *Amer. Psychologist*, 1950, 5, 342. (Abstract)

HUGHES, R. M. A factor analysis of Rorschach diagnostic signs. *J. gen. Psychol.*, 1950, 43, 85–103.

KLEIN, G. S., & SCHLESINGER, H. J. Where is the perceiver in perceptual theory? *J. Pers.*, 1949, 18, 32–47.

KLOPFER, B., & KELLEY, D. M. *The Rorschach technique.* New York: World Book Co., 1942.

MASLOW, A. H. The expressive component of behavior. *Psychol. Rev.*, 1949, 56, 261–272.

MILLER, D. R., SANDERS, R., & CLEVELAND, S. E. The relationship between examiner personality and obtained Rorschach protocols; an application of interpersonal relations theory. *Amer. Psychologist*, 1950, 5, 322–323. (Abstract)

ORANGE, A. Consistency of manner of apperception under varying conditions of structure. Unpublished doctoral dissertation, Univer. of Chicago, 1951.

RORSCHACH, H. *Psychodiagnostics.* (Trans. by P. Lemkau & B. Kronenberg) (2nd ed.) New York: Grune & Stratton, 1942.

THOMPSON, G. M. Rorschach "populars" as a function of the length of record. *J. consult. Psychol.*, 1950, 14, 287–290.

WERNER, H. Perceptual behavior of brain-injured, mentally defective children: An experimental study by means of the Rorschach technique. *Genet. Psychol. Monogr.*, 1945, 31, 51–110.

WILLIAMS, M. An experimental study of intellectual control under stress and associated factors. *J. consult. Psychol.*, 1947, 11, 21–29.

WITTENBORN, J. R. A factor analysis of discrete responses to the Rorschach ink blots. *J. consult. Psychol.* 1949, 13, 335–340.

Wittenborn, J. R. A factor analysis of Rorschach scoring categories. *J. consult. Psychol.*, 1950, 14, 261–267. (a)

Wittenborn, J. R. Level of mental health as a factor in the implications of Rorschach scores. *J. consult. Psychol.*, 1950, 14, 469–472. (b)

Zubin, J. Test construction and methodology. In R. E. Harris, et al. (Eds.), *Recent advances in diagnostic psychological testing.* Springfield, Ill.: Charles C Thomas, 1950.

17

A Comparative Analysis of Rorschach Forms with Altered Stimulus Characteristics[1]

E. EARL BAUGHMAN

*The basis for much Rorschach scoring results from the verbal com-
munication between the subject and the examiner during the inquiry.
How much of the determinant score is a function of how the subject
actually saw the blot, and how much is the result of the manner of
carrying on the inquiry? Baughman's results contain the startling finding that most subjects do not know the determinants of their perceptions
and, accordingly, can hardly be expected to communicate them. Using
five varieties of the Rorschach called the Peripheral Form, Silhouette,
Internal Form, Achromatic, and Chromatic (usual) series, he found
that the "bat" response to Card 1 occurred only once on the two series
which did not have either a gray or black figure (Peripheral Form,
Internal Form). With the black or shaded forms, the bat was seen
very frequently, although few subjects verbalized anything other than
form or movement. Apparently, most persons did not realize the
importance of blackness in determining their percept.*

*Other findings indicated that color and shading were not nearly as
potent determiners of the response as form. Moreover, animal movement
(FM) and human movement (M), usually considered as closely related,
were differentially affected by the altered forms. The frequency of FM*

[1] Based on a dissertation submitted to the Department of Psychology of the University of Chicago in partial fulfillment of the Ph.D. degree requirements. The author
wishes to express his appreciation to Professors D. W. Fiske, H. Bolgar, L. L.
Thurstone, and R. Brener for their supervision of this research. The assistance of R.
McFarland is also gratefully acknowledged.

273

remained relatively invariant among the various sets, whereas M *was strongly affected by some sets in comparison to others.*

The main effect of Baughman's study is that it illustrates pointedly that the Rorschach test as usually scored is largely a verbal *test and not a perceptual one. Baughman's method indicates how the test can be made to reflect perceptual processes more adequately, and in another article in this section (Chap. 15), he spells out his method still further.*

The problem undertaken may be stated as follows: How is perceptual behavior altered when certain specified modifications are made in the color, shading, figure-ground, and form characteristics of the standard Rorschach blots? The specific modifications will be described in the following section, but the point now to be emphasized is that the study focuses on the attempt to clarify further the role of the stimulus in determining the Rorschach response. The need for such clarification of the stimulus has been clearly stated in an article by Zubin (1949) and in research reported by Allen, Manne, and Stiff (1951) and Siipola (1950).

Method

STIMULUS MATERIALS

Four experimental series of designs were constructed in addition to the standard series of Rorschach blots. The ten forms in each of the modified series maintained a peripheral form, however, which was identical with its counterpart in the standard series. (Peripheral form is defined as that form produced by tracing with a stylus in such a way that the stylus is always in contact with the white ground and a shaded or colored area of the card.) Within this limitation of constant peripheral form, each series differed from every other series in terms of one or more of the following attributes: color, shading, figure-ground contrast, and internal form characteristics. The five series may be described as follows.

Series P (Peripheral Form Series)

Series P was created by placing a sheet of transparent paper over each of the standard Rorschach figures and tracing in ink along each contour formed by the juxtaposition of white ground with shaded or colored areas. This simple line drawing was then photographed and the print was mounted on cardboard of a weight and size comparable to that of the standard Rorschach cards. It is to be noted that each card in Series P is a solid white except for the irregular thin line corresponding to the peripheral form of the standard Rorschach figures.

Series S (Silhouette Series)

Series S was constructed by taking a standard series of Rorschach cards and covering all the shaded and colored areas with a solid coat of black India ink. Photographing and mounting were then carried out as described under Series P. The result was a series of solid black designs without differential light values, maintaining the same form as Series P, but with a very marked figure-ground contrast.

Series I (Internal Form Series)

Series I may be described as a complication of Series P in the sense that lines or forms were added to the peripheral forms of Series P. These added forms are called internal forms since they always occur within the figure part of the original Rorschach blot. Only those lines were added, which are created by sharp differentials of light values on the standard series or by the juxtaposition of shaded and colored areas. Thus, the outline of the frequently seen human figure was added on Card 2.

Series A (Achromatic Series)

Series A was constructed by photographing the standard series in black and white on panchromatic film. Thus, color was eliminated but differential light values were maintained as closely as possible to those found in the standard series.

Series C (Chromatic Series)

This is the standard series of Rorschach blots.

An overview of the five series may be achieved by beginning with Series C, the most complex. It contains not only color and shading but also a complexity of form due to internal highlights and contrasts. Series A maintains the same complexity of form and shading but eliminates color. Series I maintains complexity of form but eliminates both color and shading. Series S eliminates complexity of form, differential shading, and color but gives the subject stimuli with accentuated figure-ground contrast with which to work. Series P eliminates all the above-mentioned characteristics and presents only a simple line figure. By varying these major characteristics of the stimuli, it was believed that it would be possible to evaluate the effects of color, shading, figure-ground contrast, and internal form characteristics on the perceptual behavior of a group of subjects. An example of the experimental modifications as applied to Card 2 may be seen in Figure 17–1.

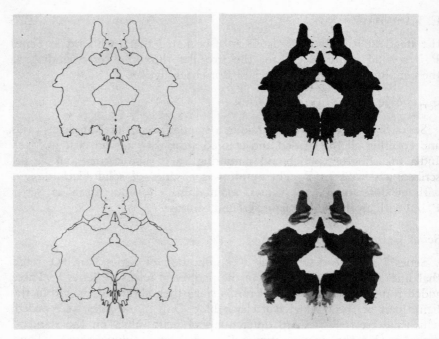

Fig. 17–1—Series P, I, S, and A modifications of Card 2, reading left to right, top to bottom. (Series A was actually a lighter and more differentiated gray than this miniature reproduction suggests.)

EXPERIMENTAL DESIGN, SUBJECTS, AND TESTING PROCEDURE

One hundred subjects participated in the experiment, 20 being randomly assigned to each of the 5 series. All subjects were hospitalized neurotic male veterans. Diagnosis was made independently of the present study by the psychiatric staff. Neurotics were chosen as the study population because Rorschach literature has consistently indicated that these are the individuals who are most strongly affected by color and shading. Identification of color and shading effects should be most apparent in such a group.[2]

Each subject was evaluated in terms of intellectual and educational level. Analysis of variance revealed no significant group differences in respect to these variables. A summary picture of the "typical" subject in this study would run somewhat as follows: a white male veteran, emotionally disturbed but not psychotic, of above-average intelligence

---

[2] Specific symptoms and psychiatric diagnoses were tabulated for each subject in each group. No systematic differences between groups were detected by this procedure, but the unreliability of such procedure is recognized. This is especially true since the total size of the sample necessitated participation by several psychiatrists with somewhat different theoretical orientations. Our method did ensure, however, a strict random assignment from within a clearly defined neurotic population and hence should minimize any possible bias due to selective assignment of specific diagnostic categories.

(mean IQ = 113.5), approaching his thirty-first birthday (mean age = 30.5 years), the possessor of 10.5 years of formal education, and coming from one of the lower socioeconomic levels.

All subjects were evaluated by the psychiatric staff prior to referral to the writer. Subjects were tested as part of their hospital study and did not know that they were also participating in a research project. All testing was done by the writer. Subjects who had taken the Rorschach test on any prior occasion were eliminated from the study.

After a brief initial interview with the subject (designed to obtain information regarding his educational background, age, occupation, socio-economic level, and related data), the VIBS (Kriegman & Hansen, 1947) was administered in order to assess his intellectual level. Administration of one of the Rorschach series followed, administrative procedure conforming to that suggested by Beck (1949), with the following exceptions: (1) identical instructions were given to each subject; (2) no encouragement was given after completion of Card 2; and (3) the word *designs* was substituted for the words *ink blots* in the instructions. In addition, the subject was asked to rank-order the ten cards in order of "liking" or preference after the inquiry had been completed. Upon completion of testing, subjects in Group C were examined for color blindness; no subject was found deficient in this respect.

SCORING OF PROCTOLS AND TREATMENT OF DATA

Beck's (1949) scoring procedure was utilized to evaluate and summarize each of the protocols, except for the addition of Klopfer's (Klopfer & Kelley, 1946) FM, m, and F% categories. All scoring was carried out by the writer, whose ability to score in a standardized manner had been demonstrated by a prior study (Baughman, 1951).

Analysis of the data was carried out in terms of two major dimensions: (1) group comparisons in regard to primary scoring categories and (2) comparative card analyses in terms of the differential response to each card in each of the five series. The group analysis involved the following steps.

1. Computation for each subject of a total score for each of the categories listed in Table 17–1.

2. Pooling of the total 100 scores for each category and determination of a cutting point for each category at or as close to the median value as possible.

3. Determining, for each group, the numbers of subjects falling above and below the cutting point for each category.

4. Comparing each group with every other group in terms of each of the scoring categories in order to determine significant differences. The test of significance utilized was the Fisher-Yates exact method (Finney, 1948).

Tests of significance were first run on the basis of raw scores. Then, where applicable, each raw score for each individual was converted into a percentage score based on his total number of responses. This was done in order to take into account effects of different productivity levels (Fiske & Baughman, 1953). Tests of significance were then run in a manner similar to that described for raw scores.

In addition, an analysis of time and response patterns was carried out. This was done by giving time and response data to three experienced Rorschach workers for each of the 100 subjects and asking them to judge independently which patterns were indicative of color and/or shading shock. The judges did not know, of course, to which groups the subject belonged.[3] For each subject, the judge received the following information: time per first response for each card, total time devoted to each card, number of responses given to each card, average time per response, average time per first response, average time per first response for Cards 1, 4, 5, 6, and 7, average time per first response for Cards 2, 3, 8, 9, and 10, and total time devoted to the test.

The analysis of card data may be divided conveniently into two parts: (1) comparison of each card with its counterpart in each of the other four series to determine significant differences in productivity (R), time per first response to card $(T/1R)$, total time devoted to card (Total Time), and preference rating (Preference) and (2) frequency analyses concerned with changes in location, determinants, and content through the five series for each card. The Fisher-Yates exact method was utilized to determine significance levels for the first type of analysis, according to the methodology described above for the group data analysis.

Results I: Group Data

Table 17–1 presents a summary of the significant differences between groups according to scoring categories. No group differed significantly (.05 level) from any other group in respect to 21 of the 39 scoring categories; consequently these categories are not listed in the body of Table 17–1. Entries in this table are based on percentage scores, except for categories R and $F +$, which are based on raw scores. Table 17–2 presents median raw scores for each group for each scoring category in order that trends in data may be noted where differences have not reached a significant level. Results will now be summarized following customary Rorschach groupings.

---

[3] The author wishes to thank Drs. M. E. Grier, R. W. Pugh, and D. Grauer for their assistance in this analysis.

TABLE 17–1   *Groups Differing Significantly*
                  According to Scoring Category

SCORING CATEGORY	LEVEL .01	.05	SCORING CATEGORY	LEVEL .01	.05
R		C-P	F +		I-P
D%		C-P, A-P	S %	P-C, P-A	I-C, I-A
		I-P, S-P		P-S, I-S	
		S-C, S-A	(H+Hd) %		S-C, S-A
M%		S-P, I-P			S-P, I-C
					I-A
C%		C-A, C-I	Aobj %		C-I
		C-S, C-P			
CF%	C-A, C-I		An %	C-I	
	C-S, C-P				
FC%	C-A, C-I		X-ray %	C-I, C-P	C-S, A-I
	C-S, C-P				A-P
YF%	C-I, C-P		(Ge+Ls) %		I-S, P-C
	A-I, A-P				P-A, P-I
					P-S
FY%	C-I, C-S		Ink %	C-P	C-I, A-P
	C-P, A-I				
	A-S, A-P				
	S-I				
FV%	A-I, A-S	A-C	F %	I-C, I-A	
	A-P			I-S, P-C	
				P-A, P-S	

Note:—Scoring categories for which none of the differences reached the .05 level are not listed in the table. These categories are W%, Dd%, FM%, m%, Y%, VF%, TF%, FT%, F+%, F−, P%, T/1R, T/R, T/1R for Cards 2, 3, 8, 9, and 10, T/1R for Cards 1, 4, 5, 6, and 7, Total Time (A+Ad)%, Sex%, Bt%, Total Number Content Categories, and VIII — X/R%. Scoring categories are more completely identified in text.

The first letter in each table entry indicates which of the two groups exceeded the other in respect to the particular scoring category. For example, Group C exceeded Group P in terms of R.

PRODUCTIVITY

Series P evoked the fewest number of responses (R), while Series C stimulated the greatest productivity. High productivity on Series C is the reverse of what might be anticipated on the basis of color-shock theory in relation to neurosis (Beck, 1946). Although Group P was least productive, an interesting fact is to be noted if the raw-score distributions are studied; namely, that as high productivity occurs on Series P as on the other series. Thus, the three top individuals in Group P scored 77, 59, and 41 compared to 81, 57, and 43 in Group C; 44, 42, and 42 in Group A; 78, 58, and 56 in Group I; and 60, 40, and 41 in Group S. The fact that the remaining subjects of Group P dropped off markedly in produc-

TABLE 17-2   *Median Raw Scores for Each Group*
                                for Each Scoring Category

SCORING CATEGORIES

GROUP

	R	W	D	Dd	FM	m	M	C
Chr.	24.5	6.8	18.0	0.4	3.8	0.5	1.1	0.2
Achr.	20.5	5.5	13.5	1.3	3.1	0.4	1.8	0.0
I-Form	22.5	4.8	14.5	1.5	2.9	0.4	2.8	0.0
Silh.	21.5	6.8	13.2	1.0	2.4	0.1	5.3	0.0
P-Form	14.5	6.0	6.8	0.4	2.0	0.1	0.8	0.0

	CF	FC	Y	YF	FY	VF	FV	*TF*
Chr.	0.5	1.1	0.1	0.3	1.5	0.0	0.1	0.0
Achr.	0.0	0.0	0.1	0.3	1.5	0.1	0.4	0.1
I-Form	0.0	0.0	0.0	0.0	0.0	0.0	0.0	0.0
Silh.	0.0	0.0	0.0	0.1	0.3	0.0	0.0	0.0
P-Form	0.0	0.0	0.0	0.0	0.1	0.0	0.0	0.0

	FT	F+	F+%	F-	P	S	T/1R	T/R
Chr.	0.0	14.5	76.5	3.1	6.8	1.4	23.7	48.1
Achr.	0.1	13.5	79.8	3.8	5.1	0.5	21.9	46.3
I-Form	0.0	15.5	80.0	4.2	5.8	4.0	32.6	57.5
Silh.	0.0	11.5	71.3	4.2	6.8	0.7	25.0	49.7
P-Form	0.0	8.2	66.5	4.5	2.5	4.2	35.4	64.0

	T/1R (Cards 2,3,8,9,10)	T/1R (Cards 1,4,5,6,7)	Total Time	F%	VIII-X/R%	(H+Hd)	(A+Ad)Aobj
Chr.	22.2	26.3	1092	68.5	34.2	2.5	11.0	0.9
Achr.	18.5	23.0	983	75.6	25.6	3.5	9.5	0.7
I-Form	36.6	30.7	1187	89.0	29.8	5.0	8.0	0.2
Silh.	23.5	25.3	1017	73.7	35.9	7.0	7.8	0.5
P-Form	39.6	27.3	981	93.3	29.2	1.5	5.2	0.6

	An	X ray	Sex	Bt	(Ge+Ls)	Ink	Total Content
Chr.	1.3	0.3	0.2	1.2	0.5	0.4	9.5
Achr.	0.3	0.2	0.1	0.8	1.5	0.2	9.5
I-Form	0.3	0.0	0.0	1.4	1.8	0.1	9.5
Silh.	0.7	0.1	0.0	0.9	0.5	0.1	7.9
P-Form	0.4	0.0	0.0	0.5	2.5	0.0	7.5

Note:—All time scores are given in seconds and tenths therof.

tivity, however, produced a change in the shape of the distribution compared to the other groups. Apparently those individuals who have a strong need to be productive will be so even though given comparatively little to work with. The distribution of scores for Group A suggests that the continued presentation of massive grays may dampen responsiveness for some subjects. Comparison of Group S in turn with Group P suggests that a definite figure-ground relationship enhances productivity even though the geometrical forms being worked with in the two series are identical. Consideration of Group I with Group P indicates that the productivity lost by the elimination of figure-ground contrast may be compensated for by the addition of discrete form areas.

MENTAL APPROACH

The stability of mental approach (W, D, Dd) in the face of pronounced assaults on the stimulus figures is emphasized by the data. As long as basic form is held constant, the stability of one's approach to interpretation is undeniable. Only on Series P is a significant distortion of the approach of subjects produced by the alteration of stimulus attributes considered in this study. Subjects in this group produced conspicuously fewer responses to major part areas (D responses) than did subjects in the other groups. It is surprising to note, however, that subjects did not experience a similar difficulty in "breaking up" the solid black forms (Series S). Despite the added unity given to these figures by making them one uniform "color," subjects were able to produce only the usual number of whole responses, and they maintained a comparable productivity level by breaking up the blots to produce major detail responses. Subjects in Group P, in contrast, produced a comparable number of whole responses but did not then proceed to break up the stimuli for major detail responses. It should also be noted that there was a tendency for subjects in Group I to produce fewer whole responses, although no significant decrement was obtained. The added prominence given to certain detail areas in this series probably made it difficult for some subjects to free themselves from the dominance of particular detail responses and go on to an integrated whole response.

DETERMINANTS

Movement (M, FM, m)
The most striking result involves the marked increase in the number of human movement responses (M) given to Series S. Seventeen of the 20 subjects in this group gave at least three M responses. The fact that this series was more "alive" than the standard Rorschach became apparent early in the testing. In contrast, Series P, which differed from Series S in figure-ground characteristics, was least productive of M responses.

Color (C, CF, FC)

Since color responses are possible only to Series C, one would anticipate that the remaining groups would differ significantly from Group C
but not among themselves, as shown by Table 17–1.

Shading (Y, YF, FY)

Nine of the eleven significant differences involve either Series P or
Series I, in which no differential light values are present. A rather
unexpected finding, however, is the fact that Groups A and C do not
differ significantly in frequency of shading responses, since Series A
seems to present considerably more opportunity for such responses to
develop than does Series C.

Vista (VF, FV)

The only three VF responses obtained occurred on Series A. Consistent with this trend is the fact that Group A differed significantly from
every other group with respect to FV responses. The factor of increased
opportunity referred to under *Shading* above may be apropos here as an
explanation of these differences. In comparing Groups C and A, however,
the problem arises as to why such differences are found in relation to
vista responses but not in regard to shading responses. The data indicate
that if the color impact affects the psychological processes underlying
vista responses, the effect is one of suppressing their manifestation or
shifting their manifestation to other forms. The data do not point to a
similar conclusion for shading responses. It is apparent that the present
study does not adequately resolve these problems.

Texture (TF, FT)

Such responses are too infrequent to be handled adequately in groups
composed of twenty subjects.

Form Accuracy (F+, F−, F+%).

The absolute number of $F+$ and $F-$ responses is probably less important than the relationship between the two, which is reflected in the
$F+\%$. When $F+\%$ is considered, it is found that the distributions are
almost identical for Groups C, A, and I, thus emphasizing the independence of form accuracy from color and shading effects. The drop in
form accuracy on Series S and P does not quite reach statistical significance except when Series I and P are compared. Series S and P are
the two series which present the subject with fewer discrete form areas
to interpret. The press for productivity provided by the structuring of

the test situation, however, is not lessened. One may infer, therefore, that productivity may be achieved through a lowering of the standards that the subject imposes on the accuracy of his response; rather than not produce, most subjects may settle for somewhat poorer responses. This inference can, of course, be rather easily checked by experimentally manipulating the press for productivity.

CONTENT

Humans (H + Hd)

Both Groups S and I produced an abundance of human percepts. In Group S, all but one of the subjects gave at least three responses with human content, whereas in Group C only three subjects gave three or more such responses. The modifications made in the stimulus cards were of such a nature as to give added demand value in Series S and I to areas which are commonly interpreted as human in content. The fact that Series P evoked no such increase should make one cautious in inferring a direct influence of color or shading in producing these data. This follows, since one would predict that if color and shading acted directly to set off affective reactions leading to a depression in the number of human responses, then a significant increment in such responses would be found when these two attributes are eliminated, as on Series P.

Animals (A+Ad)

The groups did not differ significantly in terms of animal content when productivity level was taken into account. If animal content is interpreted as a reflection of stereotypy of thought (Beck, 1946), then it is clear that the stimulus characteristics under question have no marked influence on such stereotypy.

Animal Objects (Aobj)

The usual animal objects (pelts, rugs, etc.) were less frequent only on Series I. The equal number of such responses given to Series S and P is most surprising since a shading determinant is frequently held to be essential. Series I and P differed in the production of these responses because of the addition of discrete forms to the center portions of Cards 4 and 6. The addition of these forms made it more difficult for subjects to integrate the total blot and produce a skin or rug percept.

Anatomy (An)

Anatomical responses occurred more frequently in response to Series C. Since many such responses involve a color determinant, this finding would appear to be predictable. An alternative hypothesis is possible, however; namely, that color stimulates an affective reaction of such a nature as to lead to greater bodily preoccupation.

X Ray

Groups C and A differed significantly from every other group in respect to X-ray responses. The necessity (in most cases) of having shading differentials present in order to form such percepts apparently accounts for these results. It is interesting to note, however, that each series provoked at least one X-ray response, despite the absence of shading differentials in Series I, S, and P.

Sex and Botany (Bt)

No significant group differences were obtained.

Geography and Landscape (Ge + Ls)

The high frequency of Ge and Ls percepts in Series P appeared to be related to the difficulty felt by many subjects in interpreting this series; yet rather than give no response they would oftentimes indicate a vague type of island or map percept. Thus, these responses were frequently a reflection of poverty in associational content: responses given when nothing more adequate could be produced.

Ink

It will be recalled that in the instructions no mention of ink or ink blots was made to the subjects. Yet in the free associations at least one such response was given by one or more subjects of each group. As expected, however, such content was more frequent on Series C and A.

Total Number of Content Categories

No significant differences between the groups occurred in terms of the number of content categories that the associations fell into. The trends parallel the findings for (A+Ad) noted above and support those findings regarding stereotypy of thought as related to stimulus attributes.

T/1R, T/1R (Cards 2, 3, 8, 9, 10), T/1R (Cards 1, 4, 5, 6, 7), Total Time, and T/R.

Although the groups do not differ significantly, the trend is for responses to be produced more slowly when figure-ground contrast is eliminated (Series I and P). No blocking effect due to color or shading is indicated.

Time and Response Patterns

As indicated in the section on *Method*, three experienced Rorschach interpreters were asked to consider the time and response patterns for each subject and to judge whether the patterns conformed to what is typically called "color shock" and/or "gray-black shock." The number of positive judgments made by each judge for each series was then tabulated, and the significance of differences between groups was determined by the exact method. Out of sixty possible comparisons (each judge for each group against every other group) only two significant differences were obtained: one judge found "color-shock" patterns more frequently on Series P than on Series C or A.

OTHER SCORES

Popular (P)

Although data regarding popular responses are presented in Tables 17–1 and 17–2, in actuality no satisfactory analysis of the psychological processes underlying P appears possible for the present study. To deal with numerical totals of P, when the responses to be called P have been determined empirically by reactions to Series C only, is misleading.

TABLE 17–3   *Significant Differences between Series According to Scores for Individual Cards*

SCORING CATEGORIES

Card Number	R .01	R .05	T/$_1$R .01	T/$_1$R .05	TOTAL TIME .01	TOTAL TIME .05	PREFERENCE .01	PREFERENCE .05
1	C-P, A-P, I-P, S-P		I-P		S-A		I-A, I-S, I-P	I-C
2	C-S		I-S, P-S					
3								
4		A-P, I-P						
5			I-C, P-C	P-A, P-S			I-C, S-C	A-C
6	C-P, A-P	I-P, S-P						
7	C-P, A-P			P-A	C-P			
8			I-C, P-C, P-A	I-A, P-S				C-A, C-I
9	C-P	A-P, S-P	P-C, P-S	P-A				
10		C-P, S-P						

Note:—The first letter in each entry indicates which of the two groups exceeded the other group in respect to the particular scoring category. For example, Group C exceeded Group P in productivity (R) on Card 1 at the .01 level of significance.

Thus the response "map" is more frequent on Series I and P for Card 1 than the response "bat," yet "bat" is P and "map" is not.

White Space (S)

Responses to areas called S on Series C were also scored S if they occurred on the other four series. As expected, such responses were most frequent in Groups P and I. With no brightness contrast existing between intended figure and ground, the restructuring of figure-ground relationships becomes much easier for the subject.

VIII – X/R%

No significant differences between the groups were found.

F%

Groups P and I give comparatively more form-determined responses than do the remaining groups. This is understandable, since they are given no opportunity to respond to shading or color attributes. Group S is comparable to Groups C and A because of its many M responses, as noted above.

Results II: Card Data

Table 17–3 presents a summary of differences in R, T/1R, Total Time, and Preference (according to each card) which were great enough to reach either the .05 or .01 level of significance. In addition, each card was analyzed in terms of alterations of response to discrete areas of the card in its five modifications. Most of the latter data is too detailed for presentation here; the interested reader is referred to the original dissertation. Some of the more interesting findings of this analysis for each card will now be listed, however.

1. The bat response to Card 1 occurred only once on the two series which did not have either a gray or black figure. Thus, the importance of a determinant other than form is indicated, even though few subjects verbalize anything other than form or movement. Witches were also seen on Card 1 only when the form was black or gray.

2. Response to the colored areas of Card 2 was slightly more frequent on Series C. Despite the prevalence of blood percepts on Series C, however, the preference level for the card did not drop significantly in that series.

3. The perceptual handling of Card 3 was remarkably constant throughout the modifications, and no systematic effects could be uncovered.

4. When Card 4 contained shading differentials (Series C and A), an animal form dominated the W responses; when shading was eliminated, however, human forms dominated the content. It was also found that skin percepts were given to each of the modified blots.

5. The bat was given less frequently on Card 5 when blackness or grayness was eliminated, thus supporting the findings relevant to Card 1. The differences were less pronounced, however, suggesting that the form itself is easier to reconcile with that of a bat proper than is the case with Card 1.

6. W skin or rug percepts on Card 6 were produced with equal frequencies on all series except I, thus emphasizing the dominance of form as a determinant. The decreased frequency on Series I is brought about by the accentuation of inner D areas, a fact which makes perception of a skin form for the whole a more difficult task. Card 6 was also rejected more frequently on Series I and P, i.e., when figure-ground contrast was eliminated.

7. Cloud percepts were given for Card 7 only on Series C and A. It is also of interest that figure-ground reversals did not occur more frequently on Series I and P, although such an increase was found for the central white area of Card 2.

8. Except for the increased preference for Card 8 when it is colored, the effect of color and shading on the perceptual handling of the card is quite minimal.

9. Negative effects due to color could not be demonstrated on Card 9. Among other findings, the number of rejections of the modified cards was of the same magnitude as for the colored stimulus.

10. The number of W interpretations of Card 10 is not significantly affected by color, shading, or figure-ground attributes. As was true for Card 9, negative effects due to color could not be demonstrated.

Discussion

The data are clear and impressive in their demonstration that the major dimensions of perceptual behavior in the Rorschach task remain remarkably constant even though marked alterations are made in the stimulus attributes. In 21 of the 39 scoring categories, no group differences occurred at or above the .05 level of significance. Moreover, all the differences in Table 17–1 which are significant at the .01 level can be explained on the basis of diminished availability of a particular stimulus attribute in one of the series being compared. Thus, all the significant differences involving scoring categories C, CF, and FC can be understood in terms of the fact that only one out of the five groups is given the opportunity to respond to color. In a similar fashion, one would expect Groups I and P to exceed the remaining groups in F%, since individuals in Groups I and P are given no opportunity to respond to shading. Comparable arguments can be made for the other differences at the .01 level of significance, as well as for many at the .05 level. Dimensions commonly referred to as productiveness, mental approach, accuracy of perception, reaction time, time of involvement in task, diversity of associational content, and productiveness during final portions of task are minimally affected by alterations in the stimulus attributes under consideration. The conclusion which appears to be justified by these findings is that the basic form of the blots is of overwhelming importance in determining perceptual behavior, to the extent that such behavior is determined by properties of the stimulus rather than processes within the perceiver functioning relatively independently of the stimulus situation.

The data are also clear in their implications regarding the effects of figure-ground organization on perceptual behavior. The effects of varying this stimulus attribute appeared to be considerably more far-reaching than did variation of color and shading. Of primary interest is the fact that accentuation of figure-ground contrast led to a very significant increase in human movement responses. This finding would seem to refute the suggestion made by Zubin (1950) that movement responses will be more frequent in response to chiaroscuro blots than to contour blots. A report of research now nearly complete will further clarify this problem of the relationship between perceived movement and figure-ground contrast.

It is worth noting here, however, that the findings in the present study were not identical for animal and human movement. The writer has often wondered whether or not the psychological process (or processes) underlying these two types of responses were not essentially the same, despite theoretical argument to the contrary. The fact that *FM* is independent of all the modifications made in the present study, whereas *M* is definitely not independent of them, suggests the lack of identity in the underlying processes.

The constancy of perception throughout these series stresses another fact that has been brought out by several pieces of recent research, namely, that the generalizing of dynamic effects of color on total perceptual behavior appears to be considerably less than Rorschach theory has postulated.[4] The present data also indicates that one is justified in drawing the same conclusion regarding the dynamic or generalizing effects of shading. In reference to color, support is thus offered for

---

[4] It must be clearly understood that the interpretation of "constancy of perception" as suggested here is dependent on the assumption that the groups did not differ in personality characteristics in such a way as to introduce systematic bias. That the random assignment of subjects successfully equated the groups with respect to such variables as intelligence, education, and age has been demonstrated quantitatively, but the equation in terms of other factors rests on a qualitative examination of symptoms and diagnoses as indicated in the section on method at the beginning of this article.

Lazarus' (1949) findings. Actually the present research is rather crucial in this respect, since it is fair to state that Lazarus was not justified in drawing his conclusions regarding color effects because of both the subjects and the method that he used. The use of normals and group administration (thus eliminating such measures as time scores) provided him with a critical test only if he secured positive results, which of course he did not. The present research, however, which has attempted to correct these two points of criticism, indicates the correctness of his conclusions, even though criticism of his method can be made. It then goes one step further in arguing for a comparable conclusion regarding shading effects.

The data resulting from the card analysis, however, suggests that part of the over-all constancy, as represented by psychogram scores, can be attributed to what might be called compensatory deviations within each series. By this is meant the fact that a deviation in one direction for a particular score on a particular card may be balanced by a deviation in the opposite direction for the same scoring category on a different card within the same series. For example, productivity was significantly decreased on Card 2 of Series S as compared to Series C, but there were sufficient increases in productivity on some of the remaining cards of Series S so that no over-all differences in productivity eventuated between Series S and C. This may reflect a "total productivity set," as suggested by Fiske and Baughman (1953) in a previous paper. Although the card data draw this fact to our attention, they do not negate our previous statement. One may, in fact, argue that the group data are a more reliable basis on which to draw conclusions regarding the effects of the stimulus attributes being considered, since dependence on a single form structure is eliminated.

Card data also support the group data in pointing to the fundamental importance of form and figure-ground contrast as being the two dimensions of the stimulus which most affect perception (40 of the 45 significant differences in Table 17–3 involve either Series I or P.) By contrast, the effects of color and shading appear to be quite minimal (only 1 significant difference in Table 17–3 when Series A and S are compared; two significant differences when Series C and A are compared). When effects of color and shading are noted, the effect is usually in terms of content (e.g., blood instead of heads on D2 of Card 2). The importance of figure-ground contrast had been suggested earlier by Sappenfield and Buker (1949) as one possible explanation of their findings in regard to the 8-9-10 per cent. Our results point in a similar direction and suggest the need for a more systematic investigation of the relationship between contrast and perception.

As the data were examined pertaining to each card in its variations, it became clear that certain stimulus attributes were necessary for the formation of particular percepts, even though the subject had not indicated awareness of such determinants (e.g., only one subject in Groups I and P gave a bat response to Card 1, whereas 22 subjects in Groups C, A, and S produced a bat percept). This, of course, is not a startling result since Rorschach workers have long been aware of the difficulties posed by the necessity of depending on the verbal report of the subject in order to carry out an inquiry. Experience gained in carrying out the present study suggests that a considerable part of this difficulty would be overcome by proper use of our experimental materials. Moreover, these materials provide a methodology whereby one should be able to differentiate those individuals who are aware of the external determinants of their perceptual behavior from those who are unaware of the correct determinants.

Changes in procedure of inquiry may be particularly desirable in research studies which place heavy emphasis on the interpretation of determinant scores. By proper selection of one or more of the experimental forms of each card to be presented to the subject during the inquiry (or following a regular inquiry), it should be possible to determine the primary and secondary determinants of each response with considerably more precision than one can do at the present time. If such a procedure were carried out following completion of a standard inquiry, one would then have data that would permit assessment of the extent to which the subject has been aware of the determinants of his behavior.

Many of the measures that we make of the perceptual behavior in the Rorschach test appear to be primarily dependent on processes inherent in the perceiver (to use Zubin's [1949] term) rather than on properties of the stimulus. Time patterns, productivity, and assocational breadth would be examples of such measures. The stimulus properties limit perceptual behavior, of course, but only in a very broad sense. These limitations, in turn, should be thought of primarily in terms of form and figure-ground characteristics.

The fact that perceptual behavior is so minimally affected by major changes in stimulus characteristics should make us feel more secure in our use of such techniques for personality evaluation. The fact that we affect behavior so little by such changes in external conditions points up the extent to which such behavior is determined by personal characteristics of the individual, a not unhappy finding. Our need now is to pursue more clearly the formulation of these internal or personal determinants.

Summary

This study was designed to analyze the role of stimulus attributes in determining the Rorschach response. In addition to the standard

Rorschach series, four experimental series of cards were constructed which are identical to the original series in regard to peripheral form but which varied in terms of color, shading, internal form, and figure-ground characteristics. Each of the five series was administered to a different group of twenty neurotic male veterans, the groups being equated for intelligence, educational background, and age. The groups were then compared as to scores on thirty-nine Rorschach categories and comparative analyses of each card were carried out. In addition, clinical judgments of time and response patterns were analyzed. On the basis of these data, the following conclusions were drawn:

1. Despite marked differences in stimulus attributes, similar perceptual behavior is elicited.

2. The dynamic or generalizing effects of color and shading on total perceptual behavior are not as extensive as Rorschach theory has postulated.

3. Constancy in psychogram scores for the five series is due in part to compensatory trends occurring within each series.

4. The importance of the geometrical form and the figure-ground dimensions of the stimuli in determining perceptual behavior is emphasized.

5. The importance of psychological processes inherent in the perceiver in determining perceptual behavior is pointed out.

6. The dependence of the formation of certain percepts on particular stimulus attributes is indicated, as well as the inability of many subjects to report the influence of the pertinent attribute.

Suggestions regarding a change in the method of conducting the Rorschach inquiry are also made.

REFERENCES

Allen, R. M., Manne, S. H., & Stiff, Margaret P. The role of color in Rorschach's test: A preliminary normative report on a college student population. *J. proj. Tech.*, 1951, 15, 235–242.

Baughman, E. E. Rorschach scores as a function of examiner differences. *J. proj. Tech.*, 1951, 15, 243–249.

Beck, S. J. *Rorschach's test: II. A variety of personality pictures.* New York: Grune & Stratton, 1946.

Beck, S. J. *Rorschach's test: I. Basic processes.* New York: Grune & Stratton, 1949.

Finney, D. J. The Fisher-Yates test of significance in 2 × 2 contingency tables. *Biometrika*, 1948, 35, 145–156.

Fiske, D. W., & Baughman, E. E. Relationships between Rorschach scoring categories and the total number of responses. *J. abnorm. soc. Psychol.*, 1953, 48, 25–32.

Klopfer, B., & Kelley, D. M. *The Rorschach technique.* New York: World Book Co., 1946.

KRIEGMAN, G., & HANSEN, F. W. VIBS: A short form of the Wechsler-Bellevue intelligence scale. *J. clin. Psychol.*, 1947, 3, 209–216.

LAZARUS, R. S. The influence of color on the protocol of the Rorschach test. *J. abnorm. soc. Psychol.*, 1949, 44, 506–516.

SAPPENFIELD, B. R., & BUKER, S. L. Validity of the Rorschach 8-9-10 per cent. *J. consult. Psychol.*, 1949, 13, 268–271.

SHIPOLA, ELSA M. The influence of color on reactions to ink blots. *J. Pers.*, 1950, 18, 358–382.

ZUBIN, J. Personality research and psychopathology as related to clinical practice. *J. abnorm. soc. Psychol.*, 1949, 44, 14–21.

ZUBIN, J. *Quantitative techniques and methods in abnormal psychology.* New York: Columbia Univer. Press, 1950.

18

An Attempt to Sort Rorschach Records from Four Cultures[1]

BERT KAPLAN,
MARIA A. RICKERS-OVSIANKINA,
AND ALICE JOSEPH

Are there basic similarities of personality common to a culture, so that individuals of one culture may be differentiated from those of another culture? To answer this question, the authors selected Rorschach records from the Zuni, Navaho, Mormon, and Spanish-American subcultures. An experienced Rorschacher who, however, was unfamiliar with the cultures in question, could not sort the records into their respective cultures. An experienced Rorschacher who was also familiar with the cultures to some degree could sort them at a better-than-chance ratio. The discriminant function did as well, based on three Rorschach scores, even when submitted to a cross-validation study using the signs derived from the first group.

Unfortunately, while rigorous from the point of view of analysis, the design suffers from a multitude of difficulties regarding the selection of subjects. Some subjects were selected randomly, while others were selected on the basis of acquaintanceship. The Spanish-American sub-

[1] This study was supported by a grant from the Laboratory of Social Relations, Harvard University. The writers wish to express their special appreciation to Dr. Clyde Kluckhohn for his stimulating suggestions and support. Dr. Frederick Mosteller and Goodhue Livingston gave invaluable help with the statistical problems and Drs. John Adair and Evon Z. Vogt, Jr., provided assistance in the field phase of the study without which the data could not have been collected.

[a] B. Kaplan. "A Study of Rorschach Responses in Four Cultures," *Peabody Museum of Harvard University, Papers,* 42 (1954), No. 2.

jects were largely obtained from a bar, the others not.[a] *Further, such
important factors as age, education, facility with the English language,
and experience with tests were not controlled, nor was the fact that the
Navaho and Spanish-American subjects were paid to participate, while
the others were not.*

*Consequently, the differences found between cultures may be wholly
or in part due to these uncontrolled variables. The study is interesting,
nonetheless, and points the way to a rigorous approach to the study of
the impact of culture on personality.*

In 1947, the senior author, while participating in a field study of Navaho
and Zuni war veterans,[2] had the opportunity to collect a series of 156
Rorschachs and other projective test data from individuals in four cultures situated in the same part of New Mexico. The cultures were the
Navaho, the Zuni, the Mormon, and the Spanish-American. Since these
materials lent themselves to cross-cultural comparisons, an analysis of the
differences among the four groups of tests was undertaken with the aim
of relating them to differences in the four cultural patterns. In addition,
it was hoped that a description of the four modal personality patterns
would emerge from tests. As the analysis of the material progressed,
an unexpected situation became apparent. The individual variability within
the cultures on every personality dimension studied was so great that it
was very difficult to find trends that would characterize any large portion
of the subjects within any of the groups. At the same time, differences
among the central tendencies of the groups, on the variables studied,
while present, seemed disappointingly small. This situation raised the
possibility that the data would not support the prevailing expectations
among workers in the field of culture and personality that the personality
characteristics of individuals in the same culture group tend to cluster
about some central or modal type and that such types differ widely
from group to group. Such expectations had good theoretical bases in
the work of writers like Kardiner, Linton, Mead, Kluckhohn, Benedict,
Hallowell, and others, but convincing empirical demonstrations to support them were more scarce.

The research aim was, therefore, reoriented from an attempt to discover what were the personality differences among the four groups to
the question of whether substantial differences did exist and whether
any of the groups was homogeneous enough with respect to some per-

---

[2] This study was carried on by the anthropologists John Adair (1948; Adair &
Vogt, 1949) and Evon Vogt, Jr. (Adair & Vogt, 1949; Vogt, 1951).

sonality variables to support the modal personality hypothesis. The latter questions seemed more appropriate to our present stage of knowledge, since they did not prejudge the issue, as did the former one.

Preliminary analysis of the Rorschach data was somewhat inconclusive.[3] Of 48 comparisons between pairs of cultures, 13 yielded differences significant at the 5 per cent level of confidence. Analysis of variance and chi-square tests showed that of 14 Rorschach variables, there was culture variability in five of them, FC, CF, T/R, FC, and m, which was significant at the 5 per cent level. At the same time, however, the individual variability within the cultures on all the variables was extremely high, so that despite the substantial number of significant differences, the overlap between the cultures was very great. In addition, the cultures were quite similar with respect to the content categories and popular responses. In drawing conclusions from these results, it seemed possible to emphasize the differences that were demonstrated and infer that the modal personality hypothesis was supported. On the other hand it seemed equally plausible to emphasize the similarities among the groups and the high degree of heterogeneity that existed in each of them and thus find support for the opposite conclusion.

It was in this somewhat indecisive situation that the sorting test was conceived as a method that would allow us to choose between the conflicting alternatives. Instead of asking whether the Rorschachs in the four cultures were different, we could now ask whether they were different *enough* so that they could be distinguished from each other. Instead of asking whether the Rorschachs from the same culture were similar to each other, we could now ask whether they were similar *enough* so that they could be matched as coming from the same group. The sorting and matching procedure should supply a criterion on the basis of which it might be possible to decide on the applicability of the modal personality hypothesis. The experiments on which this paper reports consist of three attempts at blind sorting of Rorschach tests into the four cultural groups. Two of the experiments are clinical in nature, in that experienced clinicians performed the sorting. The third attempt was made with the use of a statistical technique known as the "discriminant function" test. The circumstances in which the Rorschach tests were administered are described in Kaplan's monograph mentioned above (1954), and that description will not be repeated here. It should be said, however, that both the Navaho and the Zuni cultures are vigorous intact cultures which have retained to an unusual degree their separateness and integrity. For a description of these groups, the reader is referred to Kluckhohn and Leighton's work (1946) on the Navaho, Goldman's essay (1937) and Adair's monograph (1948) on the Zuni.

---

[3] These results are described elsewhere (Kaplan, 1954).

The Mormon group from which our sample was drawn consisted of the community of Ramah. This town of 200 individuals was founded in 1883 by settlers from Salt Lake City and later augmented by an influx of Mormons who had left their settlement in Mexico. The population is quite stable and very self-sufficient. The Spanish-American sample was drawn for the most part from the town of Grants, New Mexico. This town of 3,000 consists mostly of Spanish-Americans and is the center of a farming district. Only a small part of the Spanish-American population is indigenous, most of it having arrived in the past decade from small nearby villages. Only two individuals in our sample had been born in Grants, and fifteen had arrived there during the past ten years.

Procedure

For the first two experiments, 24 Rorschach records were selected, six from each of the four cultures. In the total sample from which the 24 tests were chosen, half of the individuals were veterans and half non-veterans. In order to rule out this difference as a source of confusion, only the Rorschachs of veterans were used. It probably would have been more correct to use the nonveteran Rorschachs, since these were presumably more representative of their cultures. The veterans were chosen, however, because the field workers were more familiar with them and thus might better understand the sorting. It was done on individuals who were well known to us. It was for this reason also that we departed from randomness in the selection of our sample. In three of the groups whose members were about equally well known to us, the six Rorschachs were chosen by random numbers from the veterans' Rorschachs. In the Zuni group, however, the Rorschachs of the six individuals best known to the experimenter were utilized. It is difficult to say whether this biased selection of the six Zuni records prejudices the results in any way. The main bias of these records is that they are probably somewhat more expressive than most Zuni Rorschachs. All identifications were removed from the records, including remarks in the record itself which might have given away the culture from which it came.

One of the writers,[4] who will be referred to as "A" in this paper, performed the first experiment. The conditions of this experiment were the most rigorous possible. The judge was not told anything about the Rorschachs beyond the fact that four cultural groups were represented. Her task consisted of two steps. First she was to separate the 24 records into four meaningful subgroups. In the second part of the experiment, the 24 Rorschach records were divided into two parts by the use of

---

[4] Maria A. Rickers-Ovsiankina.

random numbers. The first 12 were then grouped according to cultural membership, with three records in each of the four groups. These groups were not identified. The judge was asked to match each of the 12 remaining records to one of the four groups. Our idea was that if the Rorschachs within a culture were similar enough to each other, the already sorted records would provide cues which would facilitate the correct completion of the sorting.

The second experiment was performed after the first was completed and the results has been obtained and interpreted. It is by and large a duplication of the first with one important change. Another of the writers,[5] known here as "B," attempted the sorting in this experiment. In contrast to "A," she knew the names of the four cultures and had had some contact with the Navaho and with the Hopi, a culture similar in many ways to the Zuni. In addition, she had done some work with Rorschachs of Hopi children (Thompson & Joseph, 1945). This difference, however, had important consequences, since it changed the psychological task from one of finding what similarities existed within the subgroups of the 24 records to one of finding the records which best fitted a set of preconceived expectations.

The third sorting test performed was a statistical one in which the "discriminant function" technique was applied to see if Rorschachs from the four different cultures could be placed correctly in four separate hoppers. This technique (Johnson, 1949) enables the research worker to combine the discriminating power of several variables by a rather complicated procedure involving multiple correlations.

The test was performed on the 116 Rorschach records available, in all possible combinations of culture pairs. The records from each culture were divided into two groups, and those in the first group were used to derive the discriminant scores. For each pair of cultures the differences on eight variables, W%, A%, T/R, M, F%, FC, CF, and R, were examined and the three variables on which the t values were greatest were chosen. For the Navaho and Zuni they were M, CF, and F%; for the Navaho and Mormons, FC, CF, and T/R; for the Navaho and Spanish Americans, A%, F and T/R; for the Zuni and Mormons, R, FC, and T/R; for the Zuni and Spanish-Americans, T/R, M, and F%; and for the Mormons and Spanish-Americans, R, M, and T/R. These three variables were then combined into distributions of Z scores, and the point in the two distributions which would yield the fewest errors was chosen as a discriminating score. This score was then used in the sorting of the second half of the group of tests. A statistical test was performed to see whether the number of correct discriminations was larger than could have been expected by chance alone.

---

[5] Alice Joseph.

Results

The results of the first test, as given in tables 18–1 and 18–2 indicate that both "A's" sorting and matching attempts were unsuccessful. In her attempts to sort the 24 Rorschach records into homogeneous groups, "A" felt that the records seemed to separate most naturally into five groups, rather than four. However, seven of the 24 records could not be placed in any of the five groups nor were they similar to each other. "A" did feel that a number of the records could be grouped into pairs, and it will be noted that many of these pairs contain members of the same culture. In addition, "A," in looking at the records from different perspectives, formed four additional groups. In these groups there is somewhat greater success, but the successes appear to be limited to the grouping of Mormons. Of the five main groups, four contain records from at least three cultures. A fifth consists of three Zuni and one Mormon, and while this result could undoubtedly be explained in terms of the operations of chance, there is the real possibility that this is a partly successful grouping.

"A" had little confidence that her classification would correspond to the cultural groupings, although an examination of her notes indicates that her groupings were psychologically meaningful and consisted of records homogeneous with respect to some psychologically rather basic personality characteristics. These characteristics, however, happened to be represented in all four of the cultures. It is entirely possible that had the experiment continued with "A" seeking different bases for classification, she would eventually have found one that would coincide with the cultural variance. In the second part of the experiment, the matching problem, "A's" efforts were equally unsuccessful. As is shown in Table 18–2, only one of the 12 attempts at matching was successful. It is possible to say on the basis of this matching experiment that for "A" the records within each of the four cultures were not similar enough to each other so that they could be identified as belonging together.

Tables 18-3 and 18-4 indicate that "B," applying herself to the same task, achieved considerable success. In her initial grouping "B" sorted 13 out of 24 Rorschachs correctly. Six out of 24 would be the mean number of hits expected by chance, and the standard deviation of the distribution of random successes is 2.1. If we decide that we shall accept a result further than two standard deviations from the mean as sufficient to reject the hypothesis that this result could have occurred by chance, we find that "B's" sorting exceeds this criterion which requires 10.2 hits.

"B" was equally successful in the second task, with 8 out of 12 correct. In this problem, the mean number of correct matchings which would be obtained by purely random choice would be

TABLE 18-1   *"A's" Groupings of Twenty-four Unidentified Rorschachs*

FIVE MAIN GROUPS

1. Zuni	2. Navaho	3. Zuni	4. Navaho	5. Mormon
Mormon	Spanish-American	Zuni	Mormon	Navaho
Mormon	Mormon	Zuni	Spanish-American	Navaho
Navaho		Mormon		Zuni

SECONDARY COMPARISONS

S, S	M, Z
N, M, S, M, M	M, Z
M, M, M	M, N
N, Z	N, N
N, S	M, Z, S, M, N
S, M	Z, S
	M, M, Z, M
	M, M

TABLE 18-2   *"A's" Matching of Twelve Unidentified Rorschachs to Four Groups of Identified Rorschachs*

GROUP A	GROUP B	GROUP C	GROUP D
Spanish-American	Mormon	Navaho	Zuni
Navaho	Zuni	Spanish-American	Zuni
Zuni	Navaho	Spanish-American	Mormon
Mormon	Navaho	Mormon	Spanish-American

TABLE 18-3   *"B's" Groupings of Twenty-four Unidentified Rorschachs*

NAVAHO	ZUNI	MORMON	SPANISH-AMERICAN
Navaho	Zuni	Mormon	Spanish-American
Navaho	Zuni	Mormon	Spanish-American
Navaho	Mormon	Mormon	Spanish-American
Navaho	Mormon	Mormon	Mormon
Zuni	Spanish-American	Zuni	Zuni
Zuni	Spanish-American	Navaho	Navaho

TABLE 18-4   *"B's" Matchings of Twelve Unidentified Rorschachs to Four Groups of Identified Rorschachs*

NAVAHO	ZUNI	MORMON	SPANISH-AMERICAN
Navaho	Spanish-American	Mormon	Spanish-American
Navaho	Zuni	Mormon	Zuni
Navaho	Mormon	Zuni	Spanish-American

three, and the standard deviation of the distribution of such correct matchings would be 1.57.[6] If we place our level of confidence two standard deviations above the mean figure, we find that 6.14 correct hits are required before we can reject the hypothesis that random variation only was operating. Since "B" exceeded this figure, we must conclude that her eight correct hits constitute a successful matching of the records to their fellows from the same culture. These successes seem to us to be conclusive proof, established under extremely rigorous conditions, that the Rorschachs are to a degree similar within cultures and that they differ among cultures.

The results of the "discriminant function" test are given in Table 18-5. Since the discriminating scores were fitted in *ad hoc* fashion to the particular distribution of scores in the A group (those upon whom the computations were made), it is necessary for us to disregard the substantial success that was achieved in these first sortings. Group B, however, provides a severe test of our ability to make correct discriminations on the basis of independently derived discriminating scores. Even here, however, there are some impressive successes. In two pairs, the Navaho and Mormon and the Navaho and Spanish-American, the cultures are plainly distinguishable, with almost 85 per cent of the records being labeled correctly. In four other pairs, the excess of correct over incorrect placements may be accounted for by chance. The success of the discrimination between Navaho and Zuni, however, approaches the 5 per cent level of significance very closely.

TABLE 18-5   *Number of Correct and Incorrect Placements Made on Basis of the "Discriminant Function Test"*

	TRIAL SCORES* CORRECT	INCORRECT	TEST SCORES CORRECT	INCORRECT	CHI SQUARE
Navaho-Zuni	16	8	25	14	3.70
Navaho-Mormon	20	4	19	2	13.05
Navaho–Spanish-American	23	1	20	5	9.18
Zuni-Mormon	16	8	21	12	Not significant
Zuni–Spanish-American	18	6	19	15	Not significant
Mormon–Spanish-American	20	4	11	8	Not significant

A chi square of 3.84 is required for significance at the .05 level.
A chi square of 6.6 is required for significance at the .01 level.

---

* These scores show the number of correct and incorrect placements when a discriminating score was determined in *ad hoc* fashion so as to obtain the best results. The same discriminating score was applied to the test groups for a more rigorous test.

---

[6] The statistical problem involved in this computation has been worked by Frederick Mosteller (1948). This reference gives the formulas used to derive the mean number of correct matchings to be expected by chance as well as the variance.

It would be interesting to compare the efficiency of the statistical technique for sorting with that shown by the clinical method as exemplified by "B's" sorting. However, the tasks performed by the two methods were not quite comparable, since the "discriminant function" technique was used to distinguish between two groups while the clinicians were faced with the problem of dividing the records into four groups. The clinicians' task was much more difficult, and it is therefore not possible to say which approach was the more efficient. Both approaches achieved some important successes. On the other hand, both had failures. It is very possible that the two approaches were approximately equal in their successes in sorting. Although this cannot be proven in the present investigation, future studies can establish this point either by using the more elaborate "discriminant function" analysis in which more than two groups are differentiated or by simplifying the clinician's task by presenting him with material from only two groups. If there is substantial similarity in the successes of the two approaches, we might infer from this that the "failures" in discrimination were the result, not of inadequacies of the technique, but of the lack of differences between the groups.

The fact that "B" had considerable success in the clinical sorting and matching experiments and "A" did not requires some discussion. "B" had developed, as a result of her work with and interest in anthropological materials, a considerable amount of sophistication in analyzing such data. Knowing the names of the cultures and having at least a minimum acquaintance with them, she was able to view the 24 Rorschach records in terms which were relevant to the task of finding differences among these particular cultures. She was able to form in advance some conception, whether accurate or inaccurate, of what a Navaho, Zuni, Mormon, or Spanish-American record should be like and attempt to match the records to these conceptions. For example, she believed that the Indians more frequently than the other cultural groups would treat the blot percepts as concrete reality and that the Navaho would be more prone to do this than the Zuni. She also thought that the Mormons would show more intellectualized defenses and that there would be a lower W% in the Navahos. Not all her hypotheses were correct, and some led to wrong placements. On the basis of her results, we can say that her conceptions had some validity. For "A," the situation was very different. Not knowing which cultures were involved in the experiment, she could have no preconceptions to which the Rorschach records might be matched. Instead, she was forced to address herself to the somewhat different problem of whether the Rorschachs could be grouped in some psychologically meaningful way. Even if these groups were psychologically meaningful, and an examination of "A's" notes reveals that they were, there could be no assurance that they would coincide with the cultural classification. "A" could not know which was the correct classification without some knowledge of the cultures. All we can conclude from "A's" failure is that the classification which was most salient Rorschachwise did not correspond to cultural differences.

Discussion

These results suggest that Rorschachs from the four cultures are different enough to be sorted with considerable success. This differentiation is more possible with some cultures than with others. It is facilitated by a knowledge of the cultures. What is the significance of such findings? First in importance is the proof offered that the Rorschachs of the four cultures are different from each other in meaningful ways, and with this there is a strong presumption that certain personality characteristics of individuals in these cultures are also different. This, taken together with the fact that within each culture the test protocols were similar enough so that they could be matched with considerable success, might be viewed as a demonstration of the applicability of the "modal personality" concept. While no interference may be made about the ratio of the area of applicability to the total personality processes, the fraction is at least a discernible one. In other words, although we are unable to tell whether the so-called "modal personality" comprises a large or a small part of all personality processes, it is not so insignificant that it is totally obscured by "nonmodal personality" processes. Many workers in the field of culture-personality relationships may not be satisfied with such a limited claim. It has been generally assumed not only that modal personality characteristics exist but that they play dominant roles in the total personality configuration. It has been our purpose here to test the narrower assumption, and our results have indicated that it is correct. The more general assumption receives no support from these results. On the contrary the difficulty of the task and the occurrence of negative findings in both clinical and statistical analyses indicates that this latter assumption may be incorrect. More detailed study of the exact nature and magnitude of the differences among the cultures is required before definitive conclusions may be drawn.

One possible objection to the conclusions we have drawn from the results occurs to us. An important source of confusion in the field of culture and personality has been the confusion of cultural processes with personality processes. This has resulted from a lack of sharpness in the differentiation of the two concepts. For many, culture and personality are so highly interrelated that they are indistinguishable. These writers, as pointed out by Seeman (1946), have included processes which are clearly cultural, such as manners, or folkways, in their analysis of personality differences between cultures. Research that is oriented to this framework will inevitably discover differences in "personality" which are in fact differences in culture. The research project of which the present study is a part, has been keenly aware of this danger and has attempted to meet it by utilizing psychological tests of a projective nature such as the Rorschach, the Thematic Apperception Test, and the Sentence Completion Test. These tests are constructed so as to give the subject relative freedom to respond as he likes. The cultural structuring of his responses is thus minimized. However, the projective tests are a long way from being completely free from cultural influences. Implicitly, if not explicitly, the culture in no small degree defines the test situation and its requirements for the subject. The question that is important, even crucial, for the interpretation of our results is whether it is possible that the differences among the Rorschachs from the four cultures upon which the sortings were based are attributable to varying ways in which the cultures defined the test situation. Such differences might then be interpreted as reflecting, not personality differences, but cultural differences.

In addition to the varying definitions of the test situation, there exists the possibility that cultural influences may be imposed on the Rorschach performance through other channels. Certainly the modes of expression in the four cultures may vary, even if the same language is used. An obvious factor is the difference in experiential matrices from which the Rorschach responses emerge. Individuals in one culture— for instance, the Navahos—may lack the knowledge of and experience with a great many artifacts of our civilization and so are very unlikely to include perceptions of such objects or situations in their responses. The Mormons, on the other hand, might not have the intimate acquaintance with and interest in the world of nature which the Indian groups are thought to have. Perhaps more subtle is the influence of the time sense of the culture which may be reflected directly in the time scores of the Rorschach test.

With respect to the varying definitions of the test situation, the only systematic difference that is striking to us is the apparent lack of involvement and motivation for outstanding performance on the part of many of the Spanish-Americans. This we first thought was a result of the commercial aspect of the test situation in this group in which most of the subjects were paid a dollar for taking the test. However, some of the records of subjects who were not paid seemed similar to those of subjects who were paid.[7] Whatever the cause of their definition of the test, it seems clear that the Spanish-American subjects appeared not to be more than superficially involved and were not attempting to give more

---

[7] Spanish-American and Navaho subjects were, with a few exceptions, paid to take the test; Zuni and Mormon subjects were not paid.

than a minimum number of responses to the tests. These particular attitudes may very well reflect personality characteristics. On the other hand, they may represent stereotyped attitudes in the culture.

One would like to be able to say how the Rorschach situation is defined differentially in these four cultures. Unfortunately, this is very difficult to do at present. This may seem to be an inadequacy of our field work, but one has only to ask whether Rorschach workers in our own culture are able to describe the psychological meaning of the test situation for each subject to find that this is not a simple matter. Although some investigators, among whom Schachtel (1945) is a notable example, have given this problem their attention, by and large no satisfactory understanding has been reached.

Let us turn now to the varying experiential matrices as another type of cultural influence which may have contaminated our results. While there is considerable overlap in the kind of experience which members of various cultures have, the differences in such experiences are substantial and might lead one to expect differences in Rorschach content. Such differences might form the basis of "B's" sortings, even though they were not among the explicit factors mentioned by her. Fortunately, some data are available to help us evaluate this possibility. In the study by Kaplan (1954) previously mentioned, the four groups were compared with respect to certain content categories, of which animal responses and popular responses are the most pertinent. The finding, surprisingly enough, was that in neither of these categories were there substantial differences among the cultures. With a few exceptions, the animals frequently seen were the same in all four cultures, as were the popular responses. Although these results were derived from a larger number of Rorschachs than are studied in the present research, they provide us with some reason to doubt whether "B's" sortings were based on content differences.

While the extent of cultural contamination cannot be assessed satisfactorily, it is still possible to draw from our data some tentative conclusions, cautiously held and subject to revision if contrary evidence is forthcoming. Our procedures of analysis do reveal certain characteristic differences among the four cultures. It seems appropriate to formulate these differences in terms of the modal personality concept.

REFERENCES

ADAIR, J. A study of cultural resistance: The veterans of World War II at Zuni Pueblo. Unpublished doctoral dissertation, Univer. of New Mexico, 1948.
ADAIR, J., & VOGT, E. Z. Navaho and Pueblo veterans: A study of contrasting modes

BERT KAPLAN, MARIA A. RICKERS-OVSIANKINA, AND ALICE JOSEPH   305

of culture change. *Amer. Anthropologist,* 1949, 51, 547–561.

GOLDMAN, I. The Zuni Indians of New Mexico. In Margaret Mead (Ed.), *Cooperation and competition among primitive peoples.* New York & London: McGraw-Hill, 1937. Pp. 313–353.

JOHNSON, P. O. *Statistical methods in research.* Princeton: Prentice-Hall, 1949.

KAPLAN, B. The modal personality hypothesis tested in four cultures. Unpublished doctoral dissertation, Harvard Univer., 1949.

KAPLAN, B. A study of Rorschach responses in four cultures. *Peabody Museum of Harvard University, Papers,* 1954, 42, (2).

KLUCKHOHN, C., & LEIGHTON, DOROTHEA. *The Navaho.* Cambridge: Harvard Univer. Press, 1946.

MOSTELLER, F. Questions and answers: A matching problem. *Amer. Statistician,* 1948, 2 (1), 18–19.

ROBERTS, J. M. Three Navaho households: A comparative study in small group cultures. *Peabody Museum of Harvard University, Papers,* 1951, 40, (3).

SCHACHTEL, E. G. Subjective definitions of the Rorschach test situation and their effect on test performance. *Psychiatry,* 1945, 8, 419–448.

SEEMAN, M. An evaluation of current approaches to personality differences in folk and urban societies. *Soc. Forces,* 1946, 25, 160–165.

THOMPSON, L., & JOSEPH, ALICE. *The Hopi way.* Chicago, Univer. of Chicago Press, 1945.

VOGT, E. Z. Navaho veterans: A study of changing values. *Peabody Museum of Harvard University, Papers,* 1951, 41 (1).

19

Rorschach Summary Scores in Differential Diagnosis[1]

IRWIN J. KNOPF

The extent to which Rorschach summary scores can discriminate among psychiatric populations (131 psychoneurotics, 106 psychopaths, 100 schizophrenics) is the subject of this study. Chi-square tests were run for 34 summary scores, and 6 significant differences were reported (Dr%, A%, FM, P, Sex, and Anatomy). Since so many tests were run, thus capitalizing on chance factors, a subsample of 150 cases was drawn from the parent sample and the chi squares recomputed for this new sample. The result was that four of the six formerly significant values retained their significance (Dr%, P, Sex and Anatomy). This procedure does not appear justified because the sample drawn is not independent of the original sample and still capitalizes on chance factors.

The reason for the failure of these summary scores to differentiate the group is that they do not appear very frequently. Almost half of the scoring categories had medians of zero, and, accordingly, the small number of cases compared reduced the probability of significant chi-square values. Moreover, Contaminated and Position responses, often believed to be diagnostic of schizophrenia, were not found to differentiate the groups significantly.

Over all, there appears to be little confidence that Rorschach summary scores are practical aids in the differentiation of psychiatric syndromes. It is highly probable that intersubject differences in personality within a

[1] A portion of this paper was presented at the American Psychological Association meetings in New York, 1954.

given psychiatric syndrome are often of greater magnitude than the differences between psychiatric classifications.

The discrepancy between reports of clinical experience and research data has been a serious dilemma in Rorschach circles for a number of years. On the one hand, many clinicians have been impressed with the usefulness and the validity of the Rorschach method in a range of applications, while, on the other, research findings have not in the main supported this confidence. One such application has been the considerable use of the Rorschach as an aid in differentiating psychiatric disorders.

Formulated on the assumption that differences in psychiatric conditions would be reflected in Rorschach data, early investigations were primarily concerned with descriptive reports of the typical Rorschach performance of one or more psychiatric populations. As a result, statistical and/or experimental controls were not generally employed, but, instead, clinical description was accepted without more rigorous verification. Later, some workers attempted to isolate the qualitative differences purported between patient groups and yet preserve the "holistic" nature of the test findings by deriving patterns or signs which collectively seemed to discriminate among nosological groups. Thus, a variety of signs were reported; for example, signs which were found in brain-damaged individuals, in psychoneurotics, in schizophrenics, and which were useful as indexes of adjustment in the evaluation of psychotherapy (Piotrowski, 1936-37; Piotrowski, 1937; Miale & Harrower-Erickson, 1940; Harrower-Erickson, 1942; Thiesen, 1952; Muench, 1947). However, when many of these signs were employed in subsequent investigations, the significant discriminations reported earlier were not corroborated (Nadel, 1938; Cronbach, 1949; Rubin & Lonstein, 1953; Hamlin, Albee, & Leland, 1950; Knopf, 1956). The fact that signs derived in the original investigations provided better discrimination within the initial sample than within subsequent populations is not too surprising. In some of these studies, signs were obtained by selecting for prediction those few aspects of Rorschach performance which showed the highest relationships from among the available predictors which had a low correlation with the criterion. Such a procedure tends to capitalize on chance fluctuations within the sample and consequently may result in a spuriously high multiple-correlation coefficient. When signs which were derived in this manner are applied to subsequent populations, it can be expected that the coefficient will be of lower magnitude and of less predictive value than that obtained in the parent population.

Other investigators have studied the extent to which Rorschach single summary scores can discriminate among psychiatric groups. Wittenborn and Holzberg (1951) studied 39 summary scores with five patient groups and found that one score (CF) significantly discriminated the manic from the depressed patients. Friedman (1952) evaluated the discriminative effectiveness of Rorschach scores with two groups of normal adults and 30 schizophrenics. He found eight Rorschach variables which significantly differentiated the schizophrenics from both groups of normal subjects. Reiman (1953) evaluated 86 scores with replicated samples of ambulatory schizophrenics and neurotics. The results indicate that six scores were significant at the .10 level of confidence or better between the clinical groups for both samples. Kobler and Steil (1953) reported no statistical differences of any consequence between the Rorschach scores of the paranoid and depressive subgroups of involutional melancholic patients.

While the findings with respect to single summary scores are predominantly negative, unequivocal evaluation of these data is difficult. Most studies were able to obtain a few scores which discriminated among psychiatric groups. However, in some instances, the positive findings could be expected by chance because of the large number of tests of significance computed. It should also be noted that although a variety of Rorschach scores have been reported as differentiating diagnostic groups, there has not been a great deal of consistency for these scores to appear repeatedly as diagnostic from study to study. In addition, certain methodological limitations such as small samples, incomplete statistical or experimental controls, and vaguely defined diagnostic criteria have complicated the interpretation of the results.

In the light of the ambiguous nature of the research findings and the extensive application of the instrument, the need for a systematic evaluation of the Rorschach as a psychodiagnostic technique seems indicated. An investigative program of this sort is under way at the Iowa Psychopathic Hospital. The present study represents one minor phase of this research program and it specifically deals with the problem of determining the extent to which Rorschach summary scores can differentiate psychiatric groups.

Procedure

Our subjects were selected on the basis of the following criteria: (1) chronological age of 15 years or older; (2) unanimous agreement among psychiatrists as to diagnosis both on admission to and discharge from the hospital; (3) diagnosis was restricted to psychoneurosis (Pn), psychopathy (Pp), or schizophrenia (Sc); (4) diagnosis was independent of the Rorschach data;[2] and (5) the number of Rorschach responses (R) would not contribute to a significant difference in the mean number or the variance of responses for the three groups.

Initially, over 800 case records of patients who were 15 years or older, and who were given the Rorschach test during the six-year period from 1948 to 1953, were examined in order to check on the agreement and consistency of the psychiatric diagnosis. Each case folder contained an initial diagnostic impression usually made by a psychiatric resident or a staff psychiatrist, an admission and staff diagnosis, and a final discharge staff diagnosis, both of which were made by several residents and one or more staff psychiatrists. In this way 339 Rorschach records were obtained, and the number of responses per record was determined. Statistical tests showed no significant difference between the mean number of responses for the three groups, while the variances between the groups were significantly different. Inspection of the data indicated that two cases in the Pn group, each with 153 responses, were contributing greatly to the heterogeneity of variance. Consequently, they were withdrawn from the sample, and statistical tests of means and variances were recomputed. The groups showed no differences in either the total number of responses or variances, so that the effects of R on other Rorschach scores for the three groups were considered approximately equal.

A total of 337 Rorschach protocols meeting all the criteria and obtained from 131 Pn's, 106 Pp's, and 100 Sc's comprised the basic data for this study. In order to assure equal treatment of the data for all subjects, each protocol was rescored according to the scoring system described by Hertz (1938).[3] The incidence of clinical types which were included within each of the three major diagnostic groups is presented in Table 19-1. Additional subject characteristics of the three groups are given in Table 19-2. From this it will be noted that there was an unequal number of males and females in each group and that this was most discrepant in the Pp's. The small differences in age between the groups were not statistically reliable, although the differences in education and length of hospitalization were significant at the .01 level of confidence. The educational level of the Sc's was slightly higher than that of the Pn's and Pp's, while the length of hospitalization was slightly shorter for the Pp's than for the other two groups. Data were also available with regard to the subject's previous admission and illness. Thirty-seven per cent of the Pn group had been ill prior to this admission, whereas 24 per cent of the Pp's and 23 per cent of the Sc's had been ill previously. Generally these figures indicate that approximately 72 per

---

[2] It was not possible to obtain complete independence of diagnosis and Rorschach data. However, this criterion was met to the extent that the initial impression and the admission staff diagnosis were made prior to the Rorschach administration.

[3] The author wishes to express his appreciation to Donald Spangler for rescoring each Rorschach protocol.

TABLE 19–1   *Frequencies of Subclinical Types within Each Major Diagnostic Group*

PSYCHONEUROTICS		PSYCHOPATHS		SCHIZOPHRENICS	
Mixed	31	Psychopathetic pers.	38	Paranoid	46
Anxiety	30	Path. sexuality	18	Simple	13
Psychasthenia	28	Path. emotionality	14	Hebephrenic	8
Hysteria	22	Psychotic episodes	12	Mixed	7
Neurasthenia	5	Neurotic traits	8	Catatonic	4
Impulse neurosis	5	Inadequate type	7	Acute	3
Hypochondriasis	4	Asocial trends	3	Defect state	1
Psychosomatic	2	Alcoholism	2	Unclassified	18
Reactive depress.	2	Paranoid tendencies	2		
Unclassified	2	Exhibitionism	1		
		Malingering	1		
Total	131		106		100

cent of the total sample were first admissions at the time of the Rorschach administration, and that their condition was not, for the most part, considered chronic.

Medians, means, and standard deviations were computed for each clinical group on the following summary scores: R, W%, D%, Dr%, S, F%, F+% of 80, F+% of 60, M, FM, Fm, FC, CF, C, Fch, chF, ch, Fch', ch'F, ch', Fc, cF, c, A%, Ad, H%, Hd, Nature, Blood, Sex, Anatomy, Object, Fire, Position, Contamination, P, O%, and Rejection. Inspection of these figures indicated marked differences in the medians and the means for many of the scores, supporting previous observations that most Rorschach scores are not distributed normally (Berkowitz & Levine, 1953; Fiske & Baughman, 1953). In addition, almost half of the scoring categories had medians of zero and means of less than 1.0, which suggests not

TABLE 19–2   *Subject Characteristics for the Three Groups*
$(N = 337)$

	PSYCHONEUROTICS (56 M, 75 F)		PSYCHOPATHS (79 M, 27 F)		SCHIZOPHRENICS (57 M, 43 F)	
SEX	MEAN	SD	MEAN	SD	MEAN	SD
Age	27.3	8.6	26.9	9.8	27.7	9.6
Educ.	11.7	2.5	11.1	2.5	12.4	3.2
Length of hosp. (days)	58.1	43.7	40.5	37.5	55.8	45.3

only that these scores occurred very rarely but also that they have very limited utility in individual differential diagnosis. With the exception of the c, ch', Position, and Contamination scores which occurred very infre-

TABLE 19–3   *Medians, Means, and Sigmas for the Larger Clinical
Groups on the Significant Scores and the Probability
Values Obtained from Intergroup Comparisons*

	Pn (N=131)			Pp (N=106)			Sc (N=100)			INTERGROUP CHI-SQUARE VALUE PROBABILITIES*		
SCORE	MDN	MEAN	SD	MDN	MEAN	SD	MDN	MEAN	SD	Pn–Pp	Pp–Sc	Pn–Sc
Dr%	11.0	14.4	13.8	6.5	10.0	11.4	15.0	15.8	12.8		.01	
A%	50.0	48.0	17.4	51.0	50.2	18.0	44.0	43.4	17.0		.01	
FM	2.0	2.7	2.4	2.0	2.6	2.5	2.0	2.0	2.0			.02
P	5.0	5.1	2.2	5.0	5.2	2.5	4.0	4.1	2.0		.01	.02
Sex	0.0	0.5	1.2	0.0	0.2	1.0	0.0	0.9	2.8	.01	.01	
Anatomy	1.0	2.5	3.3	1.0	1.7	2.4	1.0	2.6	4.3	.01	.01	

* Only probability values at or beyond the .05 levels are reported.

quently, chi-square tests of independence were employed to evaluate
the significance of differences between the groups for the remaining 34
summary scores. The over-all median derived from the total sample
(337) for each score was used as the empirical cutoff point. Yates's correction for continuity was applied to the data wherever cell frequencies were
lower than ten (Lewis & Burke, 1949). The null hypothesis was retained
with those chi-square values which did not meet the minimum requirement of the .05 level of confidence.

Results

Although tests of significance were not computed, the incidence of
occurrence of contaminated and position responses will be presented
because some Rorschach workers have regarded these responses as diagnostically important in that they are almost always associated with
schizophrenia or psychosis (Beck, 1947; Beck, 1950; Klopfer & Kelley,
1946; Rorschach, 1951). Our data, however, indicate that these responses
can and do occur in other psychiatric conditions. For example, we found
contaminated responses in 9 Sc's, 2 Pn's, and 1 Pp and position responses
in 2 Sc's, 5 Pn's, and 1 Pp. Moreover, when we consider that only 12
patients out of the total sample of 337 produced contaminated responses
and only 8 patients produced position responses, it is apparent that
diagnostic classification cannot be effectively made solely on the basis of
the presence or absence of these responses.

The over-all chi-square tests applied to each Rorschach score for the
three clinical groups resulted in significant values for the following six

scores: Dr%, A%, FM, P, Sex, and Anatomy. Three additional chi-square values were computed for each of these significant scores to determine more specifically which group or groups the scores discriminated among. Table 19-3 lists the medians, means, and standard deviations for these scores, as well as the probability level obtained from the separate comparisons of the clinical groups. Most apparent from this table is the failure of any one score to discriminate among all three groups, although three scores were discriminative in two comparisons. It will also be noted that five scores significantly differentiated the Pp's from the Sc's, whereas only two scores differentiated the Pn's from the Pp's and the Pn's from the Sc's. Inspection of the data and reference to the medians and means listed in Table 19-3 indicates the direction of significance. There were more Pp's who were lower on Dr% and higher on FM than Sc's; more Pn's who were lower on Dr% and higher on A% than Sc's; more Pn's who were higher on FM than Sc's; more Pp's and Pn's who were higher on P than Sc's; and more Pn's and Sc's who were higher on Sex and Anatomy responses than Pp's.

The $F+\%$ score is often regarded as important in differentiating psychotic from nonpsychotic subjects. However, the over-all median value of 80 per cent which was obtained from the total sample did not discriminate among the clinical groups. Beck (1947) has suggested 60 per cent as a diagnostically useful cutoff point, and consequently this score was employed with the present data. The chi-square values indicated significant differences between the Sc's and the Pn's, and the Pp's and Pn's at the .001 and .05 levels of confidence, respectively, while no significant difference was obtained between the Pp's and the Sc's. Recognizing that there are differences in the Hertz and Beck scoring

TABLE 19-4   *Medians, Means, and Sigmas for the Clinical Groups of Fifty Cases on the Significant Scores and the Probability Values Obtained from Intergroup Comparisons*

SCORE	Pn (N=50) MDN	MEAN	SD	Pp (N=50) MDN	MEAN	SD	Sc (N=50) MDN	MEAN	SD	INTERGROUP CHI-SQUARE VALUE PROBABILITIES* Pn–Pp	Pp–Sc	Pn–Sc
Dr%	8.0	12.7	13.0	7.0	9.9	11.1	14.0	16.5	13.2	.01		.05
M	1.0	1.8	2.2	1.0	1.8	1.5	1.0	1.6	2.8		.01	
Fch'	1.0	1.1	1.5	0.0	0.5	1.3	0.0	0.5	1.0	.01		.05
P	5.0	4.9	2.2	5.0	5.2	2.4	4.0	4.0	2.0		.01	
Sex	0.0	0.6	1.6	0.0	0.1	0.4	0.0	1.0	2.5		.02	
Anatomy	1.0	2.6	3.2	1.0	1.5	1.9	2.0	2.8	2.9	.05	.01	

* Only probability values at or beyond the .05 levels are reported.

systems which include $F +$ tables and procedures for computing $F+\%$, these findings nevertheless suggest that Beck's empirical cutoff point of 60 per cent may also be discriminative with Hertz's scoring method.

In evaluating the results, it seemed important to consider the extent to which chance factors could account for the significance of differences between the groups for the seven Rorschach scores. Having computed 34 overall chi-square values, we can expect approximately two to be significant merely by chance at the .05 level of confidence. In the light of this possibility, a more rigorous examination of the stability of the present findings seemed essential. Therefore, 150 cases, 50 from each clinical group, were randomly selected from the total parent sample of 337. Statistical treatment and the analysis of the data for this sample was the same as that previously described for the parent population. Chi-square values were obtained separately for the 34 Rorschach scores, and only those scores which were significant on both samples were regarded as stable.

The analysis of the data for the new sample revealed that the $Dr\%$, M, Fch', P, Sex, and Anatomy scores significantly differentiated the groups at the .05 level of confidence or better. The medians, means, and standard deviations for each score together with the probability levels obtained from the separate comparisons of the groups are shown in Table 19-4. These results indicate the Pp's and the Sc's were significantly differentiated by five scores, whereas only two scores differentiated the Pn's from the Pp's and the Pn's from the Sc's. In comparing these findings with those obtained from the parent sample, we find that only the $Dr\%$, P, Sex, and Anatomy scores significantly discriminated the clinical groups on both samples and thus met the criterion of stability. While all four stable scores discriminated the Pp's from the Sc's, these scores were less sensitive in differentiating the Pn's from the Sc's and the Pn's from the Pp's in that only one score for each comparison was found to be significant with both samples ($Dr\%$ and Sex, respectively).

Summary and Conclusions

To determine the extent to which Rorschach summary scores could discriminate among psychiatric populations, a total of 337 carefully selected Rorschach records obtained from 131 Pn's, 106 Pp's, and 100 Sc's were analyzed. Chi-square tests of independence were computed on 34 Rorschach summary scores for the total sample and also for a second sample of 150 cases drawn randomly from the parent sample. Only scores which were discriminative on both samples were considered stable. The results showed that:

1. Most Rorschach summary scores are not normally distributed.

2. Almost half of the scoring categories had medians of zero and means of less than 1.0, not only indicating the rareness of these responses but also underscoring the limited utility of these scores for differential diagnosis.

3. Contaminated and position responses can and do occur, albeit infrequently, in all three groups and cannot be regarded as pathognomonic of psychosis or schizophrenia.

4. On an over-all basis, four scores: — Dr%, P, Sex, and Anatomy— significantly discriminated among the groups on both samples at or beyond the .05 level of confidence.

5. When specific tests of significance were made, no single summary score significantly differentiated all three clinical groups.

6. For practical purposes, Rorschach summary scores cannot be regarded as effective in differentiating psychiatric groups.

REFERENCES

Beck, S. J. Rorschach's test: I. Basic processes. (2nd ed.) New York: Grune & Stratton, 1949.

Beck, S. J. Rorschach's test: II. A variety of personality pictures. (2nd ed.) New York: Grune & Stratton, 1949.

Cronbach, L. J. Statistical methods applied to Rorschach scores: A review. Psychol. Bull., 1949, 46, 393–431.

Berkowitz, M., & Levine, J. Rorschach scoring categories as diagnostic "signs." J. consult. Psychol., 1953, 17, 110–112.

Fiske, D. W., & Baughman, E. E. Relationships between Rorschach scoring categories and the total number of responses. J. abnorm. soc. Psychol., 1953, 48, 25–32.

Freidman, H., A comparison of a group of hebephrenic and catatonic schizophrenics with 2 groups of normal adults by means of certain variables of the Rorschach test. J. proj. Tech., 1952, 16, 352–360.

Hamlin, R. M., Albee, G. W., & Leland, E. M. Objective Rorschach "signs" for groups of normal, maladjusted, and neuropsychiatric subjects. J. consult. Psychol., 1950, 14, 276–282.

Harrower-Erickson, Molly R. The values and limitations of the so-called "neurotic signs." Rorschach Res. Exch., 1942, 6, 109–114.

Hertz, Marguerite R. Scoring the Rorschach ink-blot test. J. genet. Psychol., 1938, 52, 15–64.

Klopfer, B., & Kelley, D. M. The Rorschach technique. Yonker-on-Hudson, N.Y.: World Book Co., 1946.

Knopf, I. J. The Rorschach test and psychotherapy. Amer. J. Orthopsychiat., 1956, 26, 801–806.

Kobler, F. J., & Steil, Agnes. The use of the Rorschach in involutional melancholia. J. consult. Psychol., 1953, 17, 365–370.

Lewis, D., & Burke, C. J. The use and misuse of the chi-square test. Psychol. Bull., 1949, 46, 433–489.

Miale, Florence, & Harrower-Erickson, Molly R. Personality structure in psychoneuroses. Rorschach Res. Exch., 1940, 4, 71–74.

MUENCH, G. A. An evaluation of nondirective psychotherapy by means of the Rorschach and other indices. *Appl. Psychol. Monogr.*, 1947, No. 13.

NADEL, A. B. A qualitative analysis of behavior following cerebral lesions. *Arch. Psychol.*, N.Y., 1938, 32, No. 224.

PIOTROWSKI, Z. A. On the Rorschach method and its application in organic disurbances of the central nervous system. *Rorschach Res. Exch.*, 1936–37, 1, 23–40.

PIOTROWSKI, Z. A. The Rorschach ink-blot method in organic disturbances of the central nervous system. *J. nerv. ment. Dis.*, 1937, 86, 525–537.

REIMAN, G. W. The effectiveness of Rorschach elements in the discrimination between neurotic and ambulatory schizophrenics. *J. consult. Psychol.*, 1953, 17, 25–31.

RORSCHACH, H. *Psychodiagnostics.* New York: Grune & Stratton, 1951.

RUBIN, H., & LONSTEIN, M. A cross validation of suggested Rorschach patterns associated with schizophrenia. *J. consult. Psychol.*, 1953, 17, 371–372.

THIESEN, J. W. A pattern analysis of structural characteristics of the Rorschach test in schizophrenia. *J. consult. Psychol.*, 1952, 16, 365–370.

WITTENBORN, J. R., & HOLZBERG, J. D. The Rorschach and descriptive diagnosis. *J. consult. Psychol.*, 1951, 15, 460–463.

20

The Projection of Hostility on the Rorschach and as a Result of Ego Threat[1]

BERNARD I. MURSTEIN

Can a subject disguise his responses on the Rorschach so as to prevent the expression of an ego-alien trait which is definitely characteristic of his behavior in the opinion of his peers? This study indicates that individuals judged extremely hostile by their peers, but who considered themselves extremely friendly, projected no more hostility on the Rorschach than friendly individuals, regardless of whether their self-concept was friendly or hostile. All three groups projected significantly less hostility than hostile individuals who acknowledged their hostility in their self-concept. Apparently, possession of the trait and acceptance of this possession were necessary before a considerable amount of hostility was projected.

These results seem to imply that the Rorschach does not, as has been alleged, enable the examiner to find out that which the subject cannot or will not tell. But this is only one study with one kind of population, with one kind of trait on one occasion. Moreover, the scoring system involved a content approach. Perhaps a formalistic scoring system would have yielded different findings. The over-all implication is, therefore, that the normal college student is far more capable of defending his private world than he has been given credit for, and consequently more

---

[1] The author wishes to express his thanks to Dr. Ira Iscoe, Dr. W. H. Holtzman, Dr. Philip Worchel, and Dr. Carson McGuire for giving the study the benefit of their valuable criticisms.

317

sophisticated approaches are required to breach the defenses of those whose egos are relatively intact.

The term *projection* is one of the most widely used in the field of clinical psychology and personality study. Unfortunately, the concept is one of the most difficult to define, chiefly because projection has been viewed conceptually in varying ways by workers in the field. All the definitions agree to the extent that projection is viewed as the ascribing of one's own motivations, feelings, and behavior to other persons. Nevertheless, these definitions differ sufficiently so that three different aspects may be described.

1. Naive projection: the tendency to project may steam from a limited field of experience and the projector's insensitivity to differences between his limited experience and a novel situation.

2. Rationalized projection: perception may be distorted by emotional biases or feelings. The projector often shows insight with regard to the expression of these feelings but distorts in trying to justify the biases on rational grounds. Thus, the person buying in the "black market" says, "Everybody else is doing it."

3. Classical projection: a situation in which the ego feels threatened is likely to result in the ego's refusing to acknowledge the trait and in the subsequent attribution of the trait to the outside world.

Certain questions of increasing concern to the clinical psychologist arise from an examination of this trichotomy. What kind of projection occurs on projective tests? How may it be measured? What is the relationship between overt behavior and the projection of fantasy material on projective techniques?

In an attempt to answer these questions, the trichotomy set forth in this paper was applied in interpreting previous research on the nature of projection (Bellak, 1944; Gluck, 1955; Holt, 1951; Murray, 1938; Murstein, 1955; Pattie, 1954; Sargent, 1945). Several experimenters (Bellak, 1944; Murray, 1938; Pattie, 1954), have shown that projection has occurred on the Rorschach and TAT when feeling tone was aroused but have not clearly demonstrated that projection occurs when the subjects are ego-defensive. It might be claimed, however, that "classical projection," being a dynamic construct, should not be expected to operate in a comparatively tension-free environment such as occurs in the usual administration of the Rorschach. If, however, an ego-threatening situation were to be created in which the subjects were severly criticized and told that they were hostile, this objection could not be raised.

Therefore, two hypotheses were formulated:

1. In a nonego-threatening situation, those persons who are hostile

but possess insight into this fact ("rationalized projectors") will project a significantly greater amount of hostility on the Rorschach than those persons who are equally hostile but lack self-insight.

2. In an ego-threatening situation, those persons who are hostile but lack insight into this fact ("classical projectors") will project more hostility as a result of ego threat than those persons who are hostile and insightful, friendly and insightful, and friendly and noninsightful.

In an attempt to measure adequately the mechanism of projection, the control of the following five variables was believed to be necessary: (1) The subject's possession of the trait to be examined must be objectively evaluated. (2) The subject's self-concept with regard to this trait must also be ascertained. (3) The trait must be amenable to examination by the instruments to be used in the study. (4) The conditions under which projection can and cannot be expected to operate must be fully investigated. (5) A projective score quantitatively sensitive enough to differentiate between various personality syndromes is necessary.

The attempt to control variables 1 and 2 was made through the use of the method of pooled ranks. The ranks were converted to normalized scores, using Hull's tables (Guilford, 1954, p. 182), and the mean score attributed to an individual by his peers was used as an objective estimate of his possession of a given trait. The individual's self-ranking provided a measure of his self-concept with regard to the trait.

Variable 3 was controlled by selecting the trait of "friendliness" for study. This trait did not arouse undue opposition from the subject because of reluctance to say anything unfavorable about the other members of his group;[2] it could be easily ranked by subjects who were not professional psychologists and was a trait with which the Rorschach dealt.

At first glance, the assumption that the least friendly persons were the most hostile might seem questionable. The manner in which the least friendly persons were defined, however—"By most friendly is meant that person who is the most co-operative, easiest to get along with, and least hostile in the fraternity"—left little doubt that the least friendly persons were the most hostile ones.

Variable 4 was controlled by proposing two conditions to be tested; viz., the projective test situation (Rorschach) and an ego-threatening situation.

An attempt to control variable 5 was made by using the Examiner Rating Sheet as an index of the projection of hostility under ego threat.

---

[2] In a previous "pilot study," the trait of "hostility" had been used. The use of this trait met, however, with considerable resistance on the part of the subjects, who were reluctant to term any of their fraternity brothers as hostile. Consequently, the trait deemed at the other end of the continuum, "friendliness," was employed, with the assumption that those subjects who were the least friendly were the most hostile. The use of this continuum stems from a list used by Cattell (1946).

This scale consisted of 19 statements taken from the larger Interview Rating Scale used by The University of Texas Testing and Guidance Bureau (1954). A typical statement taken from this sheet was, "The interviewer is a warm, sincere individual." The subject rated each statement on a five-point scale: 5 for "strongly agree," 4 for "agree somewhat," 3 for "undecided," 2 for "doubtful," and 1 for "strongly disagree." The highest possible score was 95; the lowest, 19.

Elizur's Rorschach Content Test (hereafter referred to as the RCT) had previously been used to measure hostility as derived from the content of the Rorschach (Elizur, 1949). This scale, however, measures projection by means of a two-point scale; and the possibility existed that this scale might therefore be insensitive to differences in hostile projection between the experimental groups investigated in this study. A new scale was therefore developed (see Appendix A), called the Rorschach Hostility Scale (hereafter referred to as RHS). This scale has point values running from zero, for no manifestation of hostility in the content of the Rorschach, to seven, for extreme manifestation of hostility. The scale is essentially two-dimensional. One dimension extends from impersonal expressions of hostility through actions expressed by variously more complex forms of phyla, culminating in direct expression of hostility by man. The higher the phyla, the higher the hostile score for a given action. The other dimension has to do with the overt-covertness of the action itself. Thus, "two bears vying for a piece of fish" receives a smaller hostility score than "two bears fighting." Using 40 randomly selected records, the average Pearson r between three psychologists was .96. This indicates that the RHS has satisfactory reliability for use as a clinical instrument.

Since the author measured the projection of hostility with the RCT as well as the RHS, it was necessary to ensure that his scoring had not been biased in favor of the latter scale. Hence, twenty different records were selected at random and scored by an experienced psychologist, an advanced graduate student, and the author, using the RCT. The average r was .70, with the factor of bias being eliminated, since the author's correlation with each of the other two scorers was higher than their correlation with each other.

Description of the Study

SELECTION OF SUBJECTS

On the basis of group- and self-judgments of hostility, 80 men divided among four experimental groups of 20 men each (hostile-insightful, hostile-noninsightful, friendly-insightful, friendly-noninsightful) were drawn from 536 students in 23 fraternities and two dormitories at the

University of Texas. To ensure that individuals chosen for the four experimental groups were either very hostile or very friendly, cutting scores based on consideration of the standard error of measurement of each of the group judgments were set up as criteria. The 20 most extreme cases exceeding the criteria scores for each of the four experimental groups were selected as subjects. Split-half reliability coefficients were obtained by dividing members of each fraternity and dormitory group randomly into two halves and computing the product–moment correlation by correlating the means of the ranking of each half for each person in the group. The Spearman-Brown formula was then used to estimate the full-length correlation. The scores for each fraternity and dormitory will henceforth be referred to as G scores.

The self-scores (hereafter referred to as S scores) were obtained in another manner. Ideally, the reliability of S might be obtained from a complete reranking. The length of time consumed through such a procedure, in view of the large number of subjects, would have been quite extensive. Therefore, another method was adopted. A previous study by Calvin and Holtzman (1953) suggested that the reliability of S in pooled rankings is at least .90. As a check on this finding, a group was selected at random and requested to make a second set of rankings a month later. The correlation between initial and second ranking for the 15 members was .89. In view of the high reliability despite the passage of time, it seems conservative to assume a reliability of .90 for self-rankings for the total population of subjects. To reduce the greater sampling fluctuation of the S score as compared to the G score, the standard deviation of self-rankings also was computed for the total population of subjects rather than for each individual group.

The chance of selecting an extreme subject incorrectly was to be no greater than .01. Hence, the criteria for selection of the hostile-insightful group was $G \geq 2.58$ (standard error of G) + mean of G, and $S \geq 2.58$ (standard error of S) + mean of S. (The standard error and mean will hereafter be referred to as SE and M, respectively).

For the friendly-insightful group a similar formula was used except that now the cutting scores were below the mean. The criteria were, therefore, $G \leq 2.58\ SE_g - M_g$, and $S \leq 2.58\ SE_s - M_s$.

The hostile-noninsightful and friendly-noninsightful groups were chosen in the following manner: for the first of these groups, G was $\geq 2.58\ SE_g + M_g$. To ensure noninsightfulness, the self-ranking had to be sufficiently below the G ranking so that the risk of error was to be .01 or less. Hence, the (G-S) discrepancy had to be $\geq 2.58\ \sqrt{SE_g^2 + SE_s^2} + M$ (g-s). For the friendly-noninsightful group, G was $\geq 2.58\ SE_g - M_g$. The amount by which an individual's S score had to exceed his G score for the individual to be noninsightful was $\geq 2.58\ \sqrt{SE_g^2 + SE_s^2} + M$ (g-s). The average reliability of the G scores for the 25 student groups was .86, the range being from .50 to .94. The standard deviation range of

G varied from .57 to 1.21, while the standard errors ranged from .24 to .64. The reliability of the S scores was estimated to be .90, and the standard deviation and standard error values computed for the total population were 1.79 and .56, respectively. These S values were used as constant S criteria for the selection of subjects from each of the 25 groups.

Procedure

The eighty experimental subjects were given a Rorschach individually and asked to give three responses for each card. There was no formal inquiry for determinants, and only the content, animation, and description of the perceptions was recorded. At the conclusion of the administration of the cards, the examiner, after carefully glancing over the subject's record, said, "Now I shall give you a brief interpretation of what you have seen."

Each experimental group of 20 subjects was divided and each half matched according to the means of the normalized group and self-rankings and their respective standard deviations. None of the halves of each group differed from the other half by more than .02 for the G mean, .03 for the S mean, .13 for the G standard deviation, and .22 for the S standard deviation. None of these differences was significant at the .05 level.

Within each experimental group, one half received the interpretation "friendly" while the other half received the interpretation "hostile." Initially, in selecting the subjects, the experimental group to which each subject belonged was, of course, known. The author detached the name from the group so that at the time of testing (five weeks later) the author did not know to which experimental group any of the subjects belonged.

The following points were stated in the "friendly" report: (1) You co-operated very nicely in taking this test. You saw things readily because you were interested and really "put yourself" into it. (2) Your perceptions are very rich in creativity and imagination. (3) Your perceptions reveal a lot of feeling for people and a lot of warmth; you are a friendly, co-operative person. (4) Your perceptions indicate a deep sensitivity for the needs of others. (5) You are, therefore, psychologically speaking, a mature and fairly well-adjusted person.

The following points were stressed in the "hostile" report: (1) You showed a lack of co-operation in taking this test. Your perceptions indicate that you were bored and uninterested, and didn't bother with the test. (2) Your perceptions are accordingly poor in imagination and indicate a lack of creativity. (3) You are pretty "cold" toward people and an unco-operative, hostile person. (4) Your perceptions indicate a lack of sensitivity to the needs of others. (5) You are, therefore, psychologically speaking, immature and not too well adjusted.

The examiner then presented the Examiner Rating Sheet to the subject, saying,

"Now I shall ask you to fill out anonymously a rating sheet whereby you evaluate me. This is a part of some research that the psychology department is currently running. Do not put your name on this sheet. When you have finished the rating, put the sheet in this envelope, seal it, and drop it in this box. I shall return in about five minutes."

When the examiner returned, he explained that the report which he had given the subject was used for experimental purposes and was not meaningful and that the "anonymous" ratings were coded for indentification purposes.

Results

The mean and standard deviation of scores for the four experimental groups scored by the RHS and the Elizur RCT are listed in Table 20–1. It may be observed from an examination of this table that the hostile-insightful group projected more hostility than the other groups as measured by both scales.

A t test was undertaken to test the significance of these differences. Since the hostile-insightful group variance was significantly greater than any of the other groups measured by the RHS ($p < .05$), the degrees of freedom were cut in half (d.f. = 19 instead of 38) (Edwards, 1950, p. 170). Even with this added restriction, an inspection of Table 20–2 indicates the hostile-insightful group's hostility content as measured by RHS, to be significantly greater than any of the other three groups ($p < .01$). None of the other groups differ significantly from each other. Examining Table 20–2 with reference to RCT scores, one notes that only the hostile-insightful and friendly-noninsightful groups show a difference in the predicated direction at the .05 level.

TABLE 20–1	Mean Score and Standard Deviation for Each Experimental Group When Scored for Rorschach Hostility Content by the RHS and RCT			
GROUP	RHS		RCT	
	MEAN	S.D.	MEAN	S.D.
Friendly-insightful	11.10	6.07	5.55	2.28
Friendly-noninsightful	12.05	6.93	4.95	3.35
Hostile-insightful	23.15	11.78	7.40	4.02
Hostile-noninsightful	12.40	7.97	5.15	3.85

TABLE 20–2   t *Values between Groups of Rorschach Hostility*
Content as Determined by the RHS
and the RCT (Indicated in
Parentheses)

GROUP	HOSTILE-INSIGHTFUL	HOSTILE-NONINSIGHTFUL	FRIENDLY-INSIGHTFUL
Hostile-noninsightful	3.29[b] (1.76)	—	—
Friendly-insightful	3.96[b] (1.74)	.56 (.39)	—
Friendly-noninsightful	3.54[b] (2.04[a])	.14 (.17)	.45 (.64)

[a] Significant at .05 level.
[b] Significant at .01 level.

Hypothesis 1, "In a nonego-threatening situation, those persons who are hostile but possess insight into this fact will project a significantly greater amount of hostility on the Rorschach than those persons who are equally hostile but lack self-insight," seems clearly demonstrated through the use of the RHS.

To test hypothesis 2, "Those individuals who are hostile but lack insight will project more hostility as a result of ego threat than those persons who are hostile and insightful, friendly and insightful, and friendly and noninsightful," an analysis of variance was undertaken with reference to the three variables, group ranking, self-ranking, and kind of interpretation received. The analysis was through a factorial design with three variables, each of which was varied independently of the other in two ways. Thus there were eight experimental conditions, with ten replications or subjects for each condition. Bartlett's test for homogeneity of variance yielded a chi square of 10.162, which was not significant at the .05 level.

TABLE 20–3   *Analysis of Variance of Projection Scores*
in Ego-Threat Situation

SOURCE OF VARIATION	D.F.	MEAN SQUARE	F
Between Group Rankings	1	45.00	.84
Between Self-Rankings	1	.80	.01
Between Interpretations	1	1805.00	33.85[a]
Interaction: Group × Self	1	72.20	1.35
Interaction: Group × Interpretation	1	.80	.01
Interaction: Self × Interpretation	1	273.80	5.13[b]
Interaction: Group × Self × Interpretation	1	.80	.01
Within Groups	72	53.32	—

[a] Significant at .01 level.
[b] Significant at .05 level.

TABLE 20–4   *Numerical Data Underlying Significant Interaction between Interpretation and Self-Ranking**

INTERPRETATION GIVEN SUBJECTS	SELF-RANKING FRIENDLY	HOSTILE
Friendly	(a) 1758	(b) 1688
Hostile	(c) 1494	(d) 1572

* Numbers shown are sums of projection scores as a result of ego threat. The lower the score, the higher the projection.

Hence, any differences found in the analysis might be attributed to the differences in the means and not the variances.

The complete analysis of variance for the eight experimental conditions is shown in Table 20–3. An examination of this table indicates that whether a person was hostile or friendly bore no significant relation of itself to the elicitation of projection under ego threat. Also, no significant differences were found between those persons whose self-concept was friendly and those whose self-concept was hostile. There is a significant difference well beyond the .01 level between those persons receiving a "friendly" interpretation of their Rorschach perceptions and those receiving a "hostile" one. This indicates that regardless of the group evaluation or self-concept, the majority of subjects tended to project under ego threat.

TABLE 20–5   *Standard Deviation, Mean, Projective Index, and t Values for Each Experimental Group**

GROUP	INTERPRE-TATION	S.D.	MEAN	PROJECTIVE INDEX (MEAN DIFFERENCE)	t (MEAN DIFFERENCE)
Friendly-insightful	Friendly	3.69	89.6	13.2	4.78[a]
	Hostile	7.41	76.4		
Hostile-insightful	Friendly	4.78	84.8	6.2	1.79
	Hostile	9.23	78.6		
Hostile-noninsightful	Friendly	7.57	86.2	13.2	3.38[a]
	Hostile	8.96	73.0		
Friendly-noninsightful	Friendly	7.45	84.0	5.4	1.53
	Hostile	7.55	78.6		

* The higher the score, the more favorably the examiner was rated on the Examiner Rating Sheet.
d.f. = 9 for Hostile-insightful and Friendly-insightful groups because of unequal variances.
d.f. = 18 for other groups.
a Significant beyond .01 level.

The only significant interaction at the .05 level was between the self and type of interpretation. This finding indicated that differences noted in projection under ego-threat scores for the different types of interpretation were a function of the self-ranking.

In order to examine the course of this significance more closely, a 2×2 table was constructed (Table 20–4) for the variables, self-ranking, and type of interpretation. An examination of this table indicates that the greatest amount of projection (lowest score) was manifested by those subjects who considered themselves friendly (friendly-insightful and hostile-noninsightful groups) but who received a hostile interpretation (group [c] in Table 20–4).

The projective index for each group, shown in Table 20–5, was obtained by subtracting the mean score attributed to the interpreter by that half of each group receiving a hostile report from the mean score given to him by the half receiving a friendly report. While all the groups tended to project, Table 20–5 reveals that the projection scores of only two of the groups, the friendly-insightful and hostile-noninsightful ones, reached significance beyond the .01 level. Hypothesis 2, therefore, was not confirmed.

Discussion

In view of the results indicating confirmation of hypothesis 1 and rejection of hypothesis 2, further clarification of the concept of projection would be helpful if it is to be fruitfully employed in the description of personality functions.

NAIVE PROJECTION

According to the concept of "naive projection," those persons perceiving themselves as hostile (friendly-noninsightful and hostile-insightful groups) should have projected more hostility than those persons perceiving themselves as friendly (friendly-insightful, hostile-noninsightful groups). This expectation was not fulfilled. The friendly-noninsightful group did not project a significantly greater amount of hostility on the Rorschach than the two groups in which the members perceived themselves as friendly. Likewise, in the ego-threatening situation, the subjects considering themselves hostile did not project more hostility than those considering themselves friendly. Therefore, the concept of "naive" projection is seen to be inadequate as a means of dealing with the experimental results.

RATIONALIZED PROJECTION

All subjects receiving a "hostile" interpretation should have reacted with feelings of anger and hostility. These feelings would then have been rationalized by saying that the anger was justified because of the incompetence of the examiner. Accordingly, the subjects would then have rated him quite low on the Examiner Rating Sheet. The results confirm this expectation in that all the groups show at least a tendency toward projection. Specifically, however, hostile-insightful subjects, being more tolerant of their hostility, should have projected to a greater degree than the hostile-noninsightful group. Actually, the opposite occurred, in that the hostile-noninsightful persons projected more hostility than the hostile-insightful ones. Moreover, the significant projection of the friendly-insightful group under ego threat seems antithetical to the concept of "rationalized" projection and indicates its inadequacy as an explanation of the occurrence of projection under ego threat.

CLASSICAL PROJECTION

Holt (1951) and Sargent (1945) imply that the defenses of ego-defensive persons are not sufficient to prevent the expression of repressed materials when the subject is given a projective technique such as the TAT and the Rorschach, albeit the material may be disguised. According to Freudian theory, the denial of the possession of a trait should make the individual more prone to use projection as a defense mechanism than would be the case of persons possessing self-insight into an unfavorable trait. This did not occur on the Rorschach, in that the hostile-noninsightful (ego-defensive) group did not project significantly more hostility than the other groups.

While it was possible to object to the employment of a projective test situation as a suitable test for the presence of "classical" projection, no such objection could be made for the employment of an ego-threatening situation. When told in the interpretation of their Rorschach responses that they were unfriendly and hostile, the hostile-noninsightful persons projected hostility to a greater degree than either the hostile-insightful or friendly-noninsightful groups. Freudian projection would seem a plausible explanation for this occurrence, were it not for the behavior of the friendly-insightful group. This group projected quite as much hostility as the hostile-noninsightful group.

The question might be raised as to whether the friendly-insightful group was actually projecting in response to a "hostile" report when they rated the examiner as incompetent. Were they not rightfully objecting to an inaccurate appraisal of themselves? This view does not appear justified, since the items of the Examiner Rating Sheet were based for the most part on the subjects' reaction to the manner in which the interpretation was presented rather than its content.

The results are unexplainable from the viewpoint of Freudian or "classical" projection. The friendly-insightful group cannot be said to have repressed. They were judged by their peers as being friendly. They considered themselves to be friendly. Still, they projected hostility.

The results are more amenable to analysis from a phenomenological frame of reference. Both the hostile-noninsightful and friendly-insightful groups had one characteristic in common. In both groups, the members considered themselves friendly. Objectively speaking, the members of the friendly-insightful group were correct; the members of the hostile-noninsightful group were in error. The objective circumstances were not crucial in this instance. What was important was the way in which each individual perceived himself. The experimental findings are consistent with the belief of Lecky that "any value . . . which is inconsistent with the individual's valuation of himself cannot be assimilated; it meets with resistance and is likely, unless a general reorganization occurs, to be rejected" (1951, p. 153).

The members of the friendly-insightful and hostile-noninsightful groups who received a hostile interpretation found this report contradictory to their self-concept, and they retaliated by perceiving the examiner as "the hostile one" (i.e., they perceived him as "cold, superficial, a clock watcher"). Apparently, the presence of an appropriate stimulus object— namely, the examiner who gave the interpretation—acted as a spur for the manifestation of the mechanism of projection. In sum, "classical" projection is incomplete as an explanation of the behavior elicited under ego threat as well as being inadequate as an explanation of the hostility content of the Rorschach protocols.

The concepts of "naive," "rationalized," and "classical" projection are therefore seen to be either incomplete or invalid, or, because of a lack of clarity and specificity, too crude for application to the two conditions examined within this study. Much of the contradictory evidence in experimental studies of projection may be laid to this lack of clarity and specificity. One may add that the difficulty in establishing a relationship between overt behavior and the material obtained through the use of projective techniques has arisen from lack of control of the aforementioned five important variables related to the manifestation of projection. The importance of these variables is indicated in the following conclusions which may be drawn from this study while noting the limitation that the sample consisted solely of college fraternity men.

1. Under a fairly nonego-threatening situation such as encountered on the Rorschach, projection of hostility is dependent on the *actual possession* and *self-acceptance* of the trait.

2. A revision of thinking as regards the supposedly negative relationship between insight and projection is warranted. The hostile-insightful group, possessing self-insight, projected more hostility on the Rorschach than any of the other three groups. Under an ego-threatening situation, however, the hostile-insightful group projected less hostility than the hostile-noninsightful group. The possession of insight, therefore, is seen to be of itself an inaccurate gauge of the amount of projection elicited in a given situation.

3. The situational quality of projection would seem to be clearly emphasized in that the hostile-noninsightful subjects did not project hostility on the Rorschach but did so as a result of strong ego threat.

4. The self-concept is of primary importance in determining the extent of projection under ego threat. In a projective test situation it must be studied in conjunction with the objective characteristics of the subject in order to make accurate predictions.

5. The sensitivity of the measure of projection may determine the conclusion as to whether projection has occurred. Measuring the same data, the RHS tapped significant instances of projection which the RCT failed to indicate, in spite of the fact that the two measures show a correlation of .84.

In view of the conclusions above, a redefinition of the concept of projection seems necessary. One may speak of projection under nonego-threatening and ego-threatening conditions. A twofold definition is thereby offered:

Projection, Nonego-Threatening Conditions. An individual tends to perceive the world in accordance with his personal characteristics or "life style," provided that the perceptual environment does not threaten the self to such an extent as to cause denial of the percept on either a conscious or unconscious level.

Projection, Ego-Threatening Conditions. As a consequence of an ego-threatening situation, most persons tend to project negative traits ascribed to them onto others. This projective process is more marked for those who deny possession of the traits which they are said to possess than it is for those who are willing to accept such an evaluation. This mechanism is more or less independent of insight but is dependent on the perceived threat to the self.

Summary

An attempt was made to test some of the different concepts of projection used by workers in the field. Four groups of subjects were selected on the basis of whether they were hostile or friendly persons and whether or not they possessed insight into this fact. They were tested for the projection of hostility on the Rorschach and as a result of ego threat. The important conclusions resulting were:

1. The projection of hostility on the Rorschach is dependent on the actual possession and self-acceptance of the trait.

2. The possession of self-insight is of itself an inaccurate gauge of the amount of projection elicited in a given situation.

3. The kind of projection elicited is a function of the situation in which projection is studied.

4. The self-concept is of primary importance in determining the extent of projection under ego threat.

5. The sensitivity of the measure of projection may determine the conclusion as to whether or not projection has occurred.

An attempt to explain these conclusions completely through use of the concepts of "naive," "rationalized," and "classical" projection failed. Therefore, a new definition of projection was offered for the kinds of projection operant within this study.

REFERENCES

BELLAK, L. The concept of projection. Psychiatry, 1944, 7, 353–370.
CALVIN, A. D., & HOLTZMAN, W. H. Adjustment and the discrepancy between self concept and the inferred self. J. consult. Psychol., 1953, 17, 39–44.
CATTELL, R. B. Description and measurement of personality. Cleveland: World Book Co., 1946.
EDWARDS, A. L. Experimental design in psychological research. New York: Rinehart, 1950.
ELIZUR, A. Content analysis of the Rorschach with regard to anxiety and hostility. J. proj. Tech., 1949, 13, 247–284.
GLUCK, M. R. The relationship between hostility in the TAT and behavioral hostility. J. proj. Tech., 1955, 19, 21–26.
GUILFORD, J. P. Psychometric methods. (2nd ed.) New York: McGraw-Hill, 1954.
HOLT, R. R. The thematic apperception test. In H. H. & G. L. Anderson (Eds.), An introduction to projective techniques. Englewood Cliffs, N. J.: Prentice-Hall, 1951. Pp. 181–229.
LECKY, P. Self-consistency. New York: Island Press, 1951.
MURRAY, H. A. Explorations in personality. New York: Oxford Univer. Press, 1938.
MURSTEIN, B. I. A study of the projection of hostility on the Rorschach, and in a stress situation. Unpublished doctoral dissertation, Univer. of Texas, 1955.
PATTIE, F. A. The effect of hypnotically induced hostility on Rorschach responses. J. clin. Psychol., 1954, 10, 161–164.
SARGENT, HELEN. Projective methods: Their origins, theory, and application in personality research. Psychol. Bull., 1945, 42, 257–293.
Univer. of Texas Interview Rating Scale (Form A), Testing and Guidance Bureau (mimeographed), 1954.

APPENDIX A

Hostility Scale for Content of Rorschach

(RHS)

General Considerations

A person's hostility score is the sum of the scores of all hostile perceptions on the Rorschach. It assumes strict comparability in number of responses between subjects. Generally speaking, as the perceptions move from abstract or vague expressions to more active, violent ones, the point score increases.

1 Point

(a) Predatory animal or part of a predatory animal seen with no accompanying description. Examples: lion, tiger, gorilla, hyena, manta ray. Not bear or eagle, as these are too popular.

(b) An implement of destruction or of war or part of such an instrument, seen in a dormant state. Examples: tank, gun sawed in half, jet bomber.

(c) Something that is not ordinarily considered a weapon which is capable of piercing, cutting, crushing, or hammering kind of action, perceived in a dormant state. Examples: wire cutter, pliers, vise, ice tongs, hammer, sharp icicles, stalactites.

(d) Parts of the anatomy perceived which are capable of wreaking havoc. Examples: teeth, claws, pincers, horns.

(e) People or animals eating food.

2 Points

(a) Something not ordinarily considered a weapon seen in a piercing, crushing, squeezing or hammering kind of action. Examples: a stake hammered into ground; something gripped in a vise; acid seeping through metal; poison seeping.

(b) A finger pointing.

(c) A human or animal described as fierce, aggressive, dangerous, evil. Examples: boar rushing aggressively forward; evil-looking spider; fierce-looking hawk.

(d) Bisected animal; cut spinal cord; animal laid open; animal pinned. The implication is that the action has occurred in past and is somewhat impersonal. If the animal is given a name and is said to have just been injured or there is implication of injury, score as a wounded animal.

(e) Human or animal figures leering. The presence of an eye or eyes peering or watching.

(f) Explosion or fire without excessive accompanying description. Examples: volcano erupting with fire and smoke; remnants of an explosion; house on fire; match burning.

(g) Stained blots; paint splattered; ink splattered; big puddle. If constructive action is used to save response, do not score. For example, "looks like the paint a painter uses to wipe his brush with to try out new colors" is not scored.

(h) Some perception of people or animals in derogatory positions or shapes. Examples: begging people, gossiping women, prehistoric men, Martian monsters, monster with pointed head, court jester with elfin head.

(i) Lair of predatory animal; spider web; evil cobweb.

3 Points

(a) Human symbol being injured. Example: statue of man with head broken off.

(b) An unfavorable human characteristic. Examples: piano-legged fat lady, angry people, frowning people, stupid-looking people, vicious, crazy, dumpy, etc. Old fat Germans. Fatness or skinniness or baldness are not scored unless implication is derogatory.

(c) Implements of war exploding, or explosions or fire with excessive detail. Examples: cannon firing; volcano erupting, with molten lava pouring down; fire tearing through woods, hungrily eating up the timber.

(d) Any injury to an insect, including death. If implication is that insect has been dead for long time and is decayed, do not score. Examples of scorable responses: squashed insect, mangled butterfly.

(e) Dog howling or barking. If barking at object with vicious intent, score three points. If barking at nothing in particular, score two.

4 Points

(a) Two animals or humans in some competitive struggle but not fighting in anger. Examples: two bears vying for a piece of fish; two guys wrestling, boxing.

(b) Two or more people or animals angry at each other; may be seen as quarreling, but not taking action leading to violence.

(c) Impersonal conflict. Example: "The red reminds me of war." "This symbolizes conflict." If people are involved, it becomes a fight and is scored five points.

(d) Blood. In any manner or description, this is scored at least four points. Examples: "Red reminds me of blood." "This looks like a bloody dissection." "This is blood dripping." (If the blood is connected with an animal or human injury, score five points.)

(e) Any animal which is committing some predatory action. Example: a lion stalking a deer.

(f) The following animals, which are considered symbols of predatory living: black-widow spider, praying mantis.

5 *Points*

(a) A wounded person or animal (not insect). May be seen as shot, blood flowing, gashed, mangled, etc. An animal or human perceived merely as dead is not scored.

(b) Two or more humans or animals fighting, but not to the death, with no mention of injury or gore.

(c) Violence depicted without showing a personal causal element. Examples: woman with head cut off; man severed in two. If the perception is of a person without a head but there is no mention of injury, do not score at all. Example: woman with no head.

6 *Points*

Two or more animals in a gory struggle, with blood or injuries and/or death occurring. Score 5 points for an animal seen as wounded without a description of a struggle.

7 *Points*

Two humans seen in hostile or destructive action toward each other with death occurring or blood flowing, etc.

Addenda

Critical remarks about the blots themselves are not scored. In the event that a response embodies two or more scorable aspects, only the highest is scored. Example: "A bloody dissection." Do not score 4 for blood and 2 for dissection. Score only highest value, which is blood (4).

In case of ambivalence or an attempt to vitiate the hostile implication of the perception, subtract 1 from what the hostile score would normally be. Exception: if the score would normally be one, the score remains one despite the vitiating remark. Examples: "This is either a rat or a wolf." (Score 1. Since this score is only one normally, nothing is subtracted despite the ambivalence.) "These people are killing each other, but it's only a movie we're seeing." (Score 7 − 1 = 6.) "Either they're angry or they're dead." (Score 3 − 1 = 2.)

21

The Relationship between Certain Examiner Personality Variables and Subjects' Rorschach Scores[1]

RICHARD SANDERS
AND SIDNEY E. CLEVELAND

The authors of this study believed that the Rorschach performance was too often viewed simply as a function of the subject's personality while ignoring the contribution of the examiner.

To correct this omission, they had nine graduate students take the Rorschach and then proceeded to train these students to be Rorschachers. The trainees were then assigned 30 college students at random, to whom they administered the Rorschach. The subjects, in turn, rated their examiners on a number of personality traits

Examination of 38 Rorschach scores for the 270 subjects (30 per examiner) showed significant differences on 20 of the scores. No exact probability tests are possible since the scores are nonindependent, but the high number of significant differences clearly suggests differences between the examiners. Relationships were found between ratings of the examiners on covert hostility and anxiety and their subjects' performances on these and other variables. The results, in short, point to a strong examiner influence on psychogram scores. It is, therefore, somewhat strange to note that the authors believed that the examiner influence

[1] From doctoral dissertations completed at the University of Michigan in 1950. The authors are indebted to Dr. Daniel R. Miller for his constant stimulation and efforts in seeing the study carried to completion.

*will usually not account for more than 3 to 7 per cent of the total vari-
ance in Rorschach scores. This conclusion is misleading because it fails
to take cognizance of the fact that the reliability of these scores is often
so low that the total* true *variance may range from 10 to 50 per cent.
Seven per cent, therefore, is hardly to be sneezed at. The authors also
err in correlating their hostility score with hostility per cent (hostility/
number of responses) to see if they have controlled for the presence of
R by employing this ratio. The correlation remains high simply as an
artifact of their procedure because both variables contain the common
component score "hostility." Despite these errors, the article serves to
emphasize that the examiner is an important figure in the testing situation.*

Recent developments in psychological theory and some research work
with the Rorschach test suggest the hypothesis that a Rorschach protocol
may vary significantly as a function of a number of factors not usually
considered: (1) the environmental setting, (2) the subject's mental set
toward the test, and (3) the nature of the interpersonal relationship
established between examiner and subject.

If these three factors are shown to be related significantly to Rorschach
scores, they must be considered in the interpretation of results. Aside
from such practical considerations, the Rorschach test, as a measure of
the subject's perception of relatively unstructured visual material, should
be particularly suited to reflecting the effects of the interplay between
two persons in an interpersonal situation. If a subject's performance on
the Rorschach test is in part a function of the personality of the examiner,
then differences in responses to examiners should provide a partial
measure of the relationship between examiner and subject. A subject's
perceptions of ink blots are determined not merely by the physical
characteristics of the blots themselves but also in large degree by his
"apperceptions" or organized strivings, which are largely influenced by
his needs, desires, and current emotional experiences. Schachtel refers
to the subject's organization of his needs as a "dynamic perception":
"A perception that is part and parcel of the entire interpersonal relation
between the perceiving and the perceived person" (1941).

The Rorschach test has traditionally been interpreted exclusively in
terms of the personality variables of the subject. The test protocol has
usually been regarded solely as a product of the subject; its interpretation
has been largely restricted to a description of his personality structure,
and there has been little recognition of the possible relationship between
the number, nature, and quality of the subject's responses and the
personality of the examiner. Among the few who recognize the role of

the examiner needs in data collection are Joel (1949), Murray (1938) and Schachtel. Schachtel has specifically emphasized the influences of interpersonal relationships and the subject's subjective definition of the test situation on the Rorschach test performance. He states:

By far the greater part of the literature on personality testing assumes that the way in which the subject experiences the test situation is irrelevant to the results of the test. Actually, each person will define the test situation according to his own needs, wishes and fears and his definition of the test situation will affect his performance. Also, it goes without saying that these experiences on the Rorschach and other tests are affected by the personality of the examiner. Although he is more of a blank mirror than the psychoanalyst can remain in his prolonged contact with the patient, it would be an illusion to think that he is an entirely neutral factor. He will benefit if he is aware of his own reactions in the Rorschach situation and of his effect on people in general and on the testee in particular (Schachtel, 1941).

The literature on general personality investigation offers ample evidence that environmental pressures, either from within the individual or as a part of his general surroundings, can distort or alter his perception and that these pressures are the more effective, the more unstructured the stimuli. In the specific area of Rorschach testing, there are only a few investigations which bear on examiner influence. Guilford (1947), who used the Rorschach experimentally as part of a vast testing battery in pilot selection with the Army Air Force during World War II, found that the total number of responses varies directly as a function of the examiner. When the mean numbers of responses for 9 examiners are compared for all possible combinations, 12 t's are obtained which are significant at the 1 per cent level, and 3 more are obtained at the 5 per cent level of significance. Guilford feels that this is "well above the expectation on the assumption of homogeneity of the examiners."

Traditionally, examiner variance has been attributed solely to lack of rapport. However, a poor relationship would not appear to be a complete explanation. As usually defined, the concept of rapport is relatively static in the assumption that individual differences among examiners are more or less equated if certain basic prerequisites are met in terms of friendliness and professional mien. The present authors agree with Joel, who writes:

It has been argued that the effect of the examiner should be reduced to a minimum by assuming a constant warm attitude which does not change under the impact of the subject's personality. There can be no argument about the desirability of a friendly attitude on the part of the examiner or about its beneficial effect on rapport. But we make a fundamental mistake if we believe that the assumed attitude of the examiner can really nullify the dynamics of the testing situation. Clinical psychologists are human, and the assumed attitude of warmth notwithstanding, they react to different subjects in different ways, partly because of irrational attitudes. So we must reckon with the effect of the examiner's actual continuously changing feelings underneath the assumed attitudes (Joel, 1949).

Experimental evidence on this point is provided by Lord (1950), whose different examiners gave the Rorschach first in the examiner's usual manner of administration, secondly in a standard situation with negative emotional loading, and lastly in a standard situation with positive emotional loading. She finds a greater number of differences among the examiners when they give the test in their normal manner than when they administer the test under different sets. She therefore concludes that the underlying personality of the examiner, his "true" attitudes as Joel calls them, influences the subject's Rorschach test to a greater extent than any assumed attitude or rapport.

The present experiment is concerned with the relationship between the examiner's personality and the records which he obtains from his subjects. Two general hypotheses were formulated. In the first, it was anticipated that various examiners would obtain significantly different Rorschach protocols from randomly assigned subjects. Secondly, it was predicted that significant relationships would be found between the kinds of records that examiners tend to get and independent measures of their own overt and covert anxiety and hostility. The variables, anxiety and hostility, were selected for study because they have been repeatedly reported as important and distinct components of personality.

Procedure

SELECTION OF SUBJECTS

Subject volunteers were selected from among second-year undergraduate students in elementary psychology. Of approximately 1,300 students enrolled, about 1,000 volunteered. In order to control the sex variable in the interpersonal situation, only white, male sophomores 18 to 24 years of age were selected.

A brief description of projective tests, and particularly the Rorschach test, was included as part of the curriculum of the elementary psychology class. This, in part, may have served to heighten the subject's motivation to take the test. In addition, the opportunity was offered them to discuss their Rorschach protocol with the authors at the conclusion of the experiment. Nearly all the subjects expressed an interest in this discussion, and over half actually requested interviews.

SELECTION OF EXAMINERS

The use of examiners who were well trained in administration and interpretation of the Rorschach test might have been expected to yield results more capable of generalization than those obtained with the present design. However, because such sophisticated examiners are acquainted with projective techniques, it would not be possible to obtain valid Rorschach records from them. Therefore, it was decided to train naive but highly motivated graduate psychology students in test administration.

The twelve graduate students who volunteered as potential examiners were asked if they would be interested in participating in a study of "Interpersonal Relations" in which they would be required to administer 30 Rorschach tests. At the same time, they were promised individual supervision in the administration, scoring, and interpretation. These potential examiners were recruited from among volunteer male, white, second-year graduate students in the projective techniques course at the University of Michigan. None had had any extensive contact with projective tests; some had taken the Thematic Apperception Tests as part of a research study; none had interpreted or used these tests in a clinical setting. In order to ensure that the examiners had an adequate theoretical and practical background for clinical testing, it was required that the volunteers have completed a course in advanced personality theory.

The twelve volunteers were informed that a good introduction to projective tests entailed the experience of taking them. They were asked, therefore, to arrange two periods of two hours each when they could take a battery of tests. The Rorschach was administered individually to all twelve by one of the authors, and, during this testing, the subject was seated with his back to the examiner because it was hoped that this would standardize the interpersonal situation between them. Following testing, the examiner discussed some of the administrative details as part of an introductory training session. Of the twelve volunteers, nine were finally chosen by the authors. The selection criteria were adequate motivation, dissimilar personalities, and absence of obvious physical deviations.

TRAINING OF EXAMINERS

Following this introduction to the Rorschach, the test procedure was further demonstrated in group sessions by both experimenters, who acted out the roles of subject and examiner. The examiner volunteers then followed this procedure and took turns as examiners and subjects. Finally, the student examiners administered the Rorschach test under supervision. This experience was offered in addition to the regular course instruction.

No attempt was made to make the examiners adequate in scoring or interpretation, but in order to prepare them for conducting the inquiry, the scoring categories and their meanings were discussed in detail, both by the authors and in the regular class sessions. Since differences in the method of conducting an inquiry may represent one possible source of variance among examiners, an attempt was made to standardize the inquiry by requiring that each examiner routinely ask only the following questions in order:

1. "Where (show me, etc.) in the blot is . . .?"
2. "What about this blot makes it look like . . .?"
3. "What else about this blot makes it look like . . .?"

If the examiner felt that these questions did not elicit adequate information, he was permitted to inquire further by saying: "Tell me more about it."

After this training period, the examiners were permitted to begin the testing of subjects assigned to them. The first two administrations of the Rorschach were observed by the authors through one-way screens, without the examiners' being aware of this. The purpose of this check was to see that all test procedures were correctly fulfilled. All examiners then came for individual conferences. At this time, any errors in technique observed by the authors were discussed with the examiners and their specific problems in testing were resolved. Each examiner was assigned 30 subjects to be tested during the 1949 fall semester. The only criterion for assignment was the matching of available free time of examiner and subject. Since all the subjects offered from three to seven free periods, it was assumed that there was a random assignment of subjects. Each examiner tested approximately 20 per cent of his subjects at night. Several testing rooms were used in an irregular manner so as to randomize any environmental effects. All these rooms were in university buildings and were specially designed for individual testing. Each subject was given a code number, and standard directions for orienting the subject to the Rorschach were read by the examiner. Following the test administration, the examiner gave the subject a questionnaire in which the subject was asked to respond concerning his feelings about the examiner. The questionnaire was filled in by the subject only after the examiner had left the room, and the completed questionnaire was then sealed in an envelope and placed in a box in the testing room.

SCORING OF RECORDS

All the Rorschach protocols were given to a secretary, who removed all identifying data; and from that time on, the protocols were identified only by code and order numbers. All records were scored blindly according to Beck's (1944) scoring system. In addition, Klopfer and Kelley's (1946) animal movement responses (FM), inanimate movement responses (m), and achromatic color (C') were also scored. Finally, the protocols were scored in accordance with Elizur's (1949) Rorschach Content Test procedure.

The records were assigned randomly to each author for scoring in order to control any constant scoring errors. Each author scored approximately an equal number of each examiner's records. In order to estimate variable scoring errors, the same twenty records obtained at the beginning of the experiment were scored independently by each author. Product–moment correlations which were computed for 15 of the scoring variables range from .81 to .99, only 4 falling below .90. In view of the high reliability of the scoring and the randomization of scoring errors, the degree of error contributed by the scoring is considered insignificant.

CRITERIA OF THE EXAMINER'S ANXIETY AND HOSTILITY

A Measure of the Examiner's Overt Anxiety and Hostility

At the conclusion of the Rorschach test, each subject completed a questionnaire which was designed to measure some of his feelings toward the examiner. One portion of the questionnaire consisted of a list of 15 adjectives and phrases. Five of these phrases were synonyms of anxiety: under some strain, uneasy, apprehensive, nervous, worried. Five were synonyms of hostility: critical, expecting too much, somewhat prying, irritating, disdainful. Five suggested the absence of anxiety or hostility: easy-going, unruffled, nonchalant, undisturbed, self-assured. Each subject was required to indicate whether or not each adjective or phrase applied to his examiner. The total number of adjectives selected as pertaining to an examiner was then used as a basis for ranking the nine examiners as to anxiety and hostility. Since this measure of examiner anxiety and hostility was established on the basis of the subjects' description of their examiners, it is inferred that this criterion provides an index of that aspect of the examiner's anxiety and hostility which is overt and apparent to the subject.

The odd-even reliability of the questionnaire anxiety and hostility items, corrected by the Spearman-Brown prophecy equation, was .83 and .72, respectively. The examiners were ranked (1) on the total number of phrases attributed to them by odd-numbered subjects and (2) on the total number of phrases attributed to them by even-numbered subjects. A rank-order correlation was computed. This was corrected to Pearsonian r and then entered in the Spearman-Brown equation. Although the use of rho in the Spearman-Brown formula is questionable, it is believed that this gives an indication of the potential reliability of the questionnaire.

The split-half reliability, similarly computed, was .92 for anxiety and .89 for hostility. The examiners were ranked (1) on the total number of phrases attributed to them by their first fifteen subjects and (2) on the total number of phrases attributed to them by their last fifteen subjects. As before, rank-order correlation was computed, converted to Pearsonian r, and entered in the Spearman-Brown equation.

Apparently the examiners tended to be perceived consistently as hostile or nonhostile, anxious or nonanxious throughout the experiment. Their first 15 subjects ascribed approximately the same number of hostile or anxiety phrases to them as their last fifteen subjects. The odd-numbered subjects considered their examiners approximately as hostile as the even-numbered subjects. Thus, if the examiners' attitudes to the testing situation were at all variable throughout the experiment, it was not reflected in the subjects' reported impressions.[2]

A Measure of the Examiner's Covert Anxiety and Hostility

In addition to the subjects' records, the Rorschach tests of the nine examiners were scored for anxiety and hostility according to Elizur's (1949) Rorschach Content Test. A ranking of the examiners according to this objective measure was used as a second criteron of examiner anxiety and hostility. It is assumed that this criterion measures the anxiety and hostility present in the examiner's perceptual and fantasy living and hence is covert rather than that acted out by the examiners. Elizur cites convincing evidence for the validity of his system for scoring the content of a Rorschach protocol for anxiety and hostility. In this study, the interscorer reliabilities on these measures of anxiety and hostility were .99 and .98, respectively. This compares favorably with Elizur's reported interscorer reliability of .89 and .93.

Results

EXAMINER DIFFERENCES IN OBTAINED RORSCHACH SCORES

The major problem of this study was to investigate whether different Rorschach examiners elicited characteristically different Rorschach records from their subjects. In order to study this problem, differences among examiners in the Rorschach protocols of their subjects were investigated by an analysis of variance technique. Thirty-eight F's were computed, one for each scoring symbol. The results of these thirty-eight analyses are reported in Table 21–1. Examination of this table reveals that nine of the scoring categories yield scores which differ among the examiners at the 1 per cent level of probability or beyond. Eleven more scores yield differences which are significant between the 2 to 5 per cent levels. In brief, 20 scores of the 38 tested yield significant differences.

Since all the scores are related in varying degrees to the total number of responses in a Rorschach record or may be highly interrelated with

---

[2] Rank-order intercorrelations were computed for the four criterion measures, overt and covert hostility and overt and covert anxiety. With $N = 9$, a correlation of .67 is significant at the 5 per cent level and .80 is needed at the 1 per cent level of confidence. Only the criterion measures of overt and covert hostility correlated significantly: $-.79$.

other scores, intercorrelations between scores (based on all cases, N = 270) were computed. Only those scores which differed significantly among the examiners were included in this analysis. The resulting matrix of correlations is reported in Table 21–2. As was anticipated from clinical experience, many of the raw scores proved to be moderately or highly correlated with R. However, ratios obtained by dividing the raw scores by R caused the relationship between the resulting ratio scores and R to become insignificant or only minimally significant. For example, in Table 21–2 it will be noted that the correlations between raw scores and R range from .44 to .93. However, the range of correlations between the ratio scores and R varies from .00 to .24. Interestingly, though, correlation of the raw scores and their ratio scores remains high. For example, Hostility and Hostility % correlate .80 and Y and Y% .78. This suggests that the same variable is being measured to a large degree even when R is partialed out.

Also, as was expected from clinical experience, a few of the other scores intercorrelated highly and must be regarded as closely related either to each other or to a third common variable, probably R. For example, M and H correlate .79, D and F+, .80, and D and Number of Content Categories, .80.

Since many of the Rorschach scores correlate highly with R and a few intercorrelate highly with each other, the twenty scores found significantly related to examiner differences should therefore also be evaluated in terms of their intercorrelations as well as their relationship with R. Since a correlation of .50 or less with R or other scores accounts for only 25 per cent of the variance in the individual scores, we may use this as a cutting point to select the Rorschach scores which are related to examiner differences but are also relatively independent of each other. Nine of the 20 scores found to be related to examiner differences correlate .50 or less with R and differ significantly among the examiners: the raw scores R and M and the ratios A, VIII-X, Hostility, Y, m, S, and Achromatic Color. An even more conservative estimate is derived if a correlation of .25 is considered as a prerequisite for independence. This intercorrelation accounts for only 6 per cent of the variance in any score. Using this standard, 8 of the 20 scores are relatively independent of each other and significantly related to examiner differences. Only 2 of the 38 scores would be expected to be significantly related to examiner differences by chance alone.

In addition, all the significant F's (5 per cent level and beyond) yield epsilons ranging from .16 to .27. The epsilons squared suggest that the variability among the examiners accounts for about 3 to 7 per cent of the total variance in the obtained scores. Thus, even a conservative estimate of the results indicates examiner differences beyond chance expectancy as well as a small but significant relationship between examiner differences and subjects' Rorschach scores.

TABLE 21-1   *Means, Standard Deviations, and Differences between Subjects' Rorschach Scores for the Nine Examiners*

SCORING CATEGORY	MEAN	STANDARD DEVIATION	F	EPSILON
R	43.3	20.0	2.3^b	.20
W	7.5	5.6	1.6	.13
W%	20.4	14.8	1.7	.14
D	27.3	12.5	2.4^b	.20
D%	63.6	11.1	1.0	.09
Dd	8.3	9.4	1.4	.10
Dd%	16.0	13.0	1.4	.11
S	4.1	4.1	2.7^c	.22
S%	8.5	6.3	3.1^c	.24
F+	18.1	9.7	1.8	.15
F+%	73.6	13.1	1.6	.13
F−	6.6	4.7	1.8	.15
F%	57.4	14.3	1.2	.08
M	5.5	4.0	2.4^b	.20
M%	13.4	8.9	1.1	.05
C	4.9	3.7	2.5^b	.21
C%	11.7	7.4	1.7	.14
Y	3.7	3.4	2.6^c	.21
Y%	8.3	6.0	3.2^c	.25
FM	4.8	3.6	1.7	.14
m	2.7	2.8	2.5^b	.21
m%	6.0	5.4	2.0^b	.17
Achromatic Color	2.3	2.7	3.3^c	.25
Achromatic Color %	5.4	5.4	3.6^c	.27
H	9.5	9.8	2.6^c	.21
H%	22.3	10.5	a	—
A	17.6	8.1	1.4	.11
A%	42.5	11.8	3.1^c	.24
No. of Content Categories%	33.7	8.8	2.1^b	.18
No. of Content Categories	13.6	4.7	2.1^b	.18
VIII-X%	37.5	7.4	2.0^b	.16
Hostility	6.9	6.1	2.4^b	.20
Hostility %	15.0	10.9	2.2^b	.18
Anxiety	10.7	6.9	2.6^c	.21
Anxiety %	25.3	12.9	1.2	.07
R/1T	16.4	9.8	1.7	.14
R/T	37.4	15.2	1.0	.00
P	6.4	2.2	1.1	.04

a Within group variance greater than between group variance.
b Significant at .02–.05 level.
c Significant at .01 level and beyond.

TABLE 21-2

Intercorrelations of Rorschach Scores

	A%	S%	Color%	m%	Cat%	X%	S	M	Host	Host%	Anx	C	Y	Y%	D	H	Cat	m	Color
			Achro	Cont VIII-													Cont		Anchro
R	-.25	.24	.00	.09	-.59	-.23	.66	.44	.67	.20	.64	.55	.58	.08	.93	.64	.83	.49	.46
A%		—	—	—	—	.15	-.22	-.31	-.26	-.17	-.12	-.32	-.23	-.13	-.17	-.32	-.21	-.27	-.10
VIII-X%							-.13	-.06	-.11	-.01	-.09	.02	-.12	.01	-.18	-.17	-.21	-.12	-.07
S								.30	.51	.22	.49	.43	.38	.05	.57	.41	.55	.40	.31
M									.53	.38	.37	.20	.21	-.01	.44	.79	.33	.23	.22
Host										.80	.52	.39	.35	.01	.61	.58	.55	.41	.35
Host%											.26	.14	.07	-.05	.18	.31	.19	.20	.09
Anx												.56	.51	.20	.60	.42	.50	.48	.46
C													.53	.26	.51	.19	.56	.40	.48
Y														.78	.54	.24	.51	.50	.57
Y%															.08	.08	.11	.26	.34
D																.59	.80	.44	.44
H																	.44	.19	.25
Cont Cat																		.11	.37
m																			.30

THE RELATIONSHIP BETWEEN EXAMINER ANXIETY AND HOSTILITY
AND SUBJECTS' RORSCHACH SCORES

In the preceding section, it was found that variances in subjects'
Rorschach scores attributable to examiner differences are beyond chance
expectancy. These results then suggested a need for investigation of the
possible relationships between the differences in subjects' Rorschach
scores and specific aspects of the examiners' personalities.

In order to study this second major problem, the examiners were
ranked in accordance with the four criterion measures of overt and
covert anxiety and hostility. Then only the three highest and the three
lowest of the nine examiners on a criterion measure were compared in
each of the analyses. The use of extremes was considered desirable
because (1) the group of examiners was relatively homogeneous with
regard to the personality variables under consideration, (2) differences
between extremes on the criterion measures should be more reliably
discriminated, and (3) the assumption of a linear relationship between
examiner personality variables and subjects' Rorschach scores might result
in the unwarranted rejection of possible relationships. The results of the
following analyses are presented in tables 21–3 to 21–6.

*Comparison between Overt Examiner Anxiety and Subjects' Rorschach
Scores*

The variances of only the twenty Rorschach variables which were
previously found to be significantly related to examiner differences were
analyzed. In Table 21–3, it will be noted that in the case of three scores,
differences between extreme examiners are significant at the 1 per cent
level or beyond; six differences are significant at the 1 per cent level
or beyond; six differences are significant at the 2 to 5 per cent levels.
However, the difference in mean R is also significant at the 1 per cent
level, and since it is likely that R is contributing to the variance in
the raw scores, only the following scores were considered significantly
related to overt examiner anxiety: (1) R, (2) $S\%$, and (3) C. Although
C correlates .55 with R, it is included since it seems unlikely that this
degree of communality with R accounts for all the variance.

These findings may be summarized in the following manner: examiners ranked high on overt anxiety elicit from their subjects more general responsiveness (R), more oppositional trends $(S\%)$ and more responsiveness to external and emotional stimuli (C).

*Comparison between Covert Examiner Anxiety and Subjects' Rorschach
Scores*

As before, analyses of examiner variances were made on only the
twenty Rorschach scores previously found to vary significantly among all

TABLE 21-3   *Differences between Subjects' Rorschach Scores Obtained by Examiner Extremes on Overt Anxiety*

RORSCHACH SYMBOL	MOST ANXIOUS EXAMINERS MEAN	LEAST ANXIOUS EXAMINERS MEAN	F
R	47.7	39.7	7.04[c]
A%	39.3	42.5	3.16
VIII–X%	37.3	36.4	[a]
S	4.9	3.5	4.94[b]
M	5.8	5.4	[a]
Hostility	8.4	6.3	5.20[b]
Hostility %	17.1	14.6	2.09
Anxiety	7.5	9.0	1.89
C	6.0	4.1	12.91[c]
Y	3.8	2.8	1.17
Y%	7.7	6.9	1.17
D	30.0	25.1	6.50[b]
H	10.4	9.3	1.45
No. of Content Categories	14.5	13.1	3.97[b]
M	2.9	2.5	[a]
Achromatic Color	2.6	1.8	2.26
S%	9.7	7.5	5.20[b]
Achromatic Color %	5.3	4.6	1.05
m%	5.7	5.9	[a]
No. of Content Categories %	32.4	35.9	4.24[b]

[a] Within group variance greater than the between group variance.
[b] Significant at .02—.05 level.
[c] Significant at .01 level and beyond.

the examiners. Again, in order to maximize examiner differences, only the three highest and lowest covert-anxiety ranked examiners were included. In Table 21-4 are found the results of this analysis. Inspection of this table reveals that examiners with high covert anxiety elicit significantly more human responses (H), more human movement (M), more Y, higher Hostility scores, and a smaller percentage of animal responses (A) than do low-ranked examiners. Since there is no significant difference in the total number of responses elicited by these two groups of examiners, it may be concluded that the differences in their scores were not generated by differences in R.

Comparison between Overt Examiner Hostility and Subjects' Rorschach Scores

Table 21-5 reveals that four of the twenty scores, H, A% Y%, and Hostility %, are related significantly to differences in overt examiner hostility. Since R does not differ significantly between the extremes of the hostility continuum and since these scores intercorrelate minimally, it may be concluded that these four are relatively independent scores. This number of significant findings exceeds those expected by chance. These results may be interpreted as follows: the more overt the hostility of the examiners, the more the Rorschach records of their subjects suggest passivity ($Y\%$) and stereotypy ($A\%$). Compared to examiners perceived as least hostile, those who are described by their subjects as overly hostile elicit Rorschach protocols with significantly less hostile content (Hostility $\%$) and fewer human responses (H).

Although the initial reaction times of the subjects were not found to be significantly different among all the examiners, Kamman (1944) suggests that this variable might be worthy of further investigation. Accordingly, the difference in initial reaction time between subjects of examiners perceived as low in hostility and subjects of overtly hostile examiners was tested and found significant at the .04 level of prob-

TABLE 21–4   *Differences between Subjects' Rorschach Scores Obtained by Examiner Extremes on Covert Anxiety*

RORSCHACH SYMBOL	MOST ANXIOUS EXAMINERS MEAN	LEAST ANXIOUS EXAMINERS MEAN	F
R	44.8	40.0	2.53
D	28.4	25.9	1.77
S	4.5	3.5	2.43
S%	8.9	7.5	2.20
C	5.3	4.6	1.57
Y	4.3	3.7	1.28
Y%	10.2	7.7	7.19
M	5.7	4.6	4.83[b]
m	2.6	2.4	[a]
m%	5.7	5.7	[a]
Achromatic Color	2.8	2.5	2.26
Achromatic Color %	6.0	6.0	[a]
A%	41.3	46.7	9.84[c]
H	9.9	8.0	6.45[c]
VIII–X%	38.1	37.3	2.14
No. of Content Categories	13.8	12.6	3.16
No. of Content Categories %	33.1	33.7	[a]
Anxiety	10.7	10.8	[a]
Hostility	7.6	5.0	9.55[c]
Hostility %	16.3	11.5	9.38[c]

[a] Within-group variance greater than the between-group variance.
[b] Significant at .02–.05 level.
[c] Significant at .01 level and beyond.

ability. The less hostile the examiners appear to their subjects, the faster the initial reaction times of the latter. Conversely, when subjects perceive their examiners as hostile, they block on their initial responses. Kamman offers the hypothesis that the subjects' unconscious hostility may prolong their reaction times. The question of whether or not subjects who perceive their examiners as hostile develop unconscious hostility against their examiners cannot be answered by the results of this study. However, the prolonged initial reaction times of such subjects are consistent with this hypothesis.

Comparison between Covert Examiner Hostility and Subjects' Rorschach Scores

In Table 21–6, 6 of the 20 F's are significant between the 1 and 5 per cent levels. The 6 scores significantly related to examiner differences

TABLE 21–5   *Means and Differences between Subjects' Rorschach Scores as Obtained by Examiner Extremes on Overt Hostility*

RORSCHACH SCORES	MOST HOSTILE EXAMINERS MEAN	LEAST HOSTILE EXAMINERS MEAN	F
R	41.1	45.3	1.83
D	26.7	28.5	a
S	3.8	4.8	2.28
S%	8.4	9.5	1.13
C	4.6	4.8	a
Y	3.9	3.2	2.07
Y%	9.2	6.7	8.48[c]
M	4.9	6.0	3.08
m	2.4	2.9	1.08
m%	5.5	6.3	1.01
Achromatic Color	1.8	2.3	2.66
Achromatic Color %	4.3	5.1	1.15
A%	44.3	39.7	6.48[b]
H	8.6	10.9	5.86[b]
VIII–X%	36.6	37.3	a
Content Cat	13.2	14.3	2.28
Content Cat/R	33.7	34.0	a
Anxiety	10.9	10.5	a
Hostility	6.1	7.8	3.77
Hostility %	13.2	16.6	4.56[b]
R/1T	17.5	14.5	4.23[b]

[a] Within group variance greater than the between group variance.
[b] Significant at .02—.05 level.
[c] Significant at .01 level and beyond.

TABLE 21–6   *Means and Differences between Subjects' Rorschach*
                 Scores as Obtained by Examiner Extremes
                 on Covert Hostility

RORSCHACH SCORES	MOST HOSTILE EXAMINERS MEAN	LEAST HOSTILE EXAMINERS MEAN	F
R	45.3	39.9	3.0
D	28.4	25.8	1.8
S	4.8	4.0	1.4
S%	9.5	8.1	2.0
C	4.8	5.2	a
Y	3.2	3.9	1.9
Y%	6.7	9.0	6.4[b]
M	6.0	5.4	1.2
m	2.5	2.4	a
m%	6.3	5.5	a
Achromatic Color	2.3	2.8	1.1
Achromatic Color %	5.1	6.5	3.1
A%	39.7	44.5	7.3[c]
H	10.9	8.2	9.4[c]
VIII–X%	37.3	37.0	a
Content Categories	14.3	12.7	5.0[b]
Content Categories/R	33.9	34.4	a
Anxiety	10.5	10.2	a
Hostility	7.8	5.8	4.8[b]
Hostility %	16.6	13.5	3.9[b]
R/₁T	14.5	15.9	1.2

a Within group variance greater than the between group variance.
b Significant at .02 —.05 level.
c Significant at .01 level and beyond.

in covert hostility are: Hostility, Hostility %, Y%, H, A% and Number of Content Categories. Hostility and Hostility % intercorrelate highly (.80) and are considered to be equivalent scores. However, the ratios of A, Y, and Hostility correlate minimally and may be considered as relatively independent scores. A correlation of –.45 between Content Categories and A% still leaves 80 per cent of the variance in these two scores unexplained, and accordingly these scores are considered separately in the present analysis.

This number of significant findings leads to a rejection of the null hypothesis that examiners who differ in the amount of hostility they reveal in their own projective records do not obtain significantly different Rorschach records from their subjects. The significant differences in subjects' Rorschach scores may be interpreted as follows: compared to examiners who rank low on covert hostility, the high examiners elicit less Y% (passivity), less A% (stereotypy), more Hostility and Hostility %, more Content Categories (diversified content), and more H (responses involving humans).

Analysis of Emotional Distance from Examiner

In addition to checking a series of adjectives and phrases describing the examiner, the subjects also had the opportunity on the questionnaire of indicating the degree of emotional closeness and liking which they felt toward their examiner. This they did by checking multiple-choice items to statements referring to their perception of the nature of the relationship between themselves and their examiner.[4] A chi-square test was then made of the subjects' responses to these items. This chi-square value of 28 (df—8) was significant beyond the 1 per cent level of confidence. That is, the examiners are liked differently by their subjects, and different degrees of emotional distance are described.

Inspection of the subjects' feelings as expressed on these items reveals that examiners rated low on overt anxiety or hostility are described as "close friends," while examiners described as most anxious or most hostile are liked "mildly" or "somewhat." The low anxiety or hostility-ranked examiners are liked "a great deal" or "pretty much," and according to their subjects these examiners would be "affectionate" or "rather warm" with children. In contrast, high anxiety or hostility examiners would be only "tolerant" or "pay some attention to it (child)."

A chi-square test was also made of the responses to questionnaire items referring to emotional distance between the three examiners ranked high and the three ranked low on anxiety according to Elizur's measure. This chi-square value failed to attain statistical significance. That is, subjects did not indicate any significant difference in their degree of liking or desire for emotional distance between examiners who are ranked high or low on covert anxiety. However, the more covertly hostile (Elizur's RCT) the examiners, the more the subjects like them and the "closer" the subjects want to be to these examiners.

Discussion

The findings of the present study indicate that the personality of the examiner is significantly related to the type of Rorschach protocol which

---

[4] Questionnaire statements referring to emotional distance and liking of the examiners:

    (a) If the examiner lived near me, I would like to (1) be close friends, (2) be neighborly, (3) be a casual acquaintance, (4) nod to him on the street.

    (b) If the examiner had a child, he would tend to (1) be affectionate, (2) be rather warm, (3) be tolerant, (4) pay some attention to it.

    (c) All in all, I tended to like the examiner (1) mildly, (2) somewhat, (3) pretty much, (4) a great deal.

he obtains when his technique has been standardized and his subjects have been selected at random from a pool of normal students.

Subjects indicate a greater liking for examiners whom they perceive in general as low in anxiety than they do for high-anxiety examiners. Compared to examiners ranked low on overt anxiety, those ranked high elicit from their subjects relatively more general responsiveness, more white space, and more color responses. Total responsiveness (R) in the present study is found related only to anxiety of the examiner as described by the subject. In the presence of examiners consciously recognized as anxious, the subjects produce more responses, possibly as a means of pleasing these threatening examiners or as a means of smoothing over any periods of uncomfortable silence. In addition to this increase in responsiveness, the subjects of examiners high on overt anxiety become more responsive to emotional and external stimuli (C) and they evidence more oppositional trends (S). One interpretation of these reactions may be to regard them as active, outwardly directed efforts on the part of the subjects. It is probable, also, that the desire for greater emotional distance is a means by which these subjects express the discomfort felt in the presence of the high-anxiety examiners. This may represent an effort on the part of the subject to cope with a disturbing and unpleasant situation.

Examiners ranked high or low on covert anxiety obtain a small but significant number of differences in the Rorschach scores of their subjects. The more anxious examiners do not elicit significantly more responses from their subjects than do the ones who are less covertly anxious. However, they do elicit more hostile content, more passive trends (Y%) and more fantasy and self-awareness (M and H). In this case, the subjects apparently are not aware of the source of the anxiety, even though certain of their perceptions on the Rorschach tests are influenced by the anxiety. At any rate, the subjects indicate no significant differences in their degree of liking for these high-and low-ranked examiners. The nature of their reaction, in general, in the presence of this kind of anxiety may be interpreted as a relatively less active one than in the presence of anxiety of which they are more consciously aware. It may be that the subjects tend to avoid acting out their disturbance. They indulge in increased fantasy, probably with a hostile content, and they become more passive. This is in contrast with the relatively more active and outwardly directed efforts in the presence of overt examiner anxiety.

A comparison of the Rorschach correlates of overt and covert examiner hostility reveals that four of the seven Rorschach scores significantly related to measures of examiner hostility are related significantly to both overt and covert hostility. These scores are Hostility %, A% (stereotypy), H (human responses), and Y% (passivity). The more overt the examiners' hostility, the more stereotypy and passivity and the less human and hostile content the subjects reveal in their Rorschach records. However, the more the examiners are covertly hostile, the less stereotypy and passivity and the more human and hostile content in the subjects' records. There is thus an inverse relationship between overt and covert hostility and these Rorschach scores.

As judged by initial reaction times and questionnaire scores, subjects of the more overtly hostile examiners tend to become constricted and inhibit any possible expressions of counter hostility. They become more passive, and it may be inferred that they react intrapunitively. The diminution of their expressiveness may represent a withdrawal from the threatening examiner. In addition, the more overt the examiners' hostility, the less their subjects prefer them as close friends. Sullivan (1947) refers to this as a "disjunctive" reaction.

On the other hand, examiners who have high Elizur RCT hostility scores elicit more hostile content from their subjects. Their subjects are less passive; their thinking is less stereotyped, and they are able to perceive the ink blots in more diversified contexts. Apparently where the hostility of the examiner is covert, the subjects are less threatened and can respond more freely. These examiners are even preferred as close friends.

A number of Rorschach scores were found to be relatively uninfluenced by examiner differences: the location ratios (W, D, Dd), amount of pure form F%), form quality (F+%), and popular responses (P). These scores represent intellectual rather than emotional factors in the personality. It may be that the former constitute more stable aspects of the personality and hence do not vary with examiner differences. In any event, for populations homogeneous with that of the present study, more reliance can be placed on these scores which are independent of examiner influence, and the interpretation need not take such influences into account.

Implications for Further Research

The results of this study provide evidence that a subject's responses on the Rorschach test are not solely a product of his own emotional problems and personality structure. In addition, subjects' Rorschach score differences among examiners have been found related in minimal degree to the examiner personality variables, anxiety and hostility.

A natural consequence of such findings is the question as to whether this study suggests the presence of a source of error so great as to render the Rorschach an unreliable instrument. Such an implication seems unwarranted. In the first place, examiner variance was found to account for only 3 to 7 per cent of the total variance in subjects' Rorschach scores. It seems questionable whether these differences in scores, significant at a statistical level, will also prove to be of importance at the level of test interpretation. Still to be tested is the hypothesis that different examiners will interpret a random sampling of Rorschach records in significantly different degrees.

Another problem suggested by the results of the present study is the extent to which examiners can control consciously their influences on subjects' perceptions. Lord's study demonstrates that the examiners' "true" attitudes influence the subjects' Rorschach protocols to a greater extent than certain assumed attitudes. On the other hand, it may be postulated that personal therapy will produce an awareness of previously unconscious needs and so enable the examiners to minimize these needs or their manifestations sufficiently to eliminate them as significant factors in the testing situation.

At still another level of investigation is the question as to whether examiners' personalities are related to the scores which they assign to Rorschach protocols. For example, do more anxious or hostile examiners project their anxiety or hostility by assigning higher anxiety and hostility scores to their subjects' records? This might be ascertained by testing the significance of the differences in scores assigned to a set of Rorschach records by two groups of examiners known to differ in degree of anxiety or hostility.

Lastly, to what extent can the results of the present study be generalized? This study was based on a college population of relatively normal males. If this sample is representative, the findings can be replicated with other populations of normals. However, populations with greater personality pathology might yield markedly different results. It might be expected that the more severely disturbed the subjects are, the less their Rorschach scores will be influenced by examiner differences. Psychotics, whose perceptions tend to be dominated primarily by inner needs, may be expected to show fewer interpersonal effects than normals. Communication with these subjects is difficult because their capacity to co-ordinate behavior with the requirements of reality is so limited. The interpersonal bonds between examiners and psychotic patients may therefore be expected to be very idiosyncratic and tenuous.

Most neurotics, on the other hand, because of their concern with the reactions of others, may be expected to show greater examiner influence on the variability of their Rorschach scores than most psychotics. This should be particularly true for the hysterics, because of their suggestibility. Their sensitivity to the feelings of others might conceivably lead them to be more reactive to examiner personality variables than even the normals.

Summary and Conclusions

This study was concerned with two major problems: (1) whether different examiners elicit from their subjects significantly different Rorschach scores and (2) whether these differences in the subjects' scores are related to examiner anxiety or hostility.

Nine male graduate psychology students, unsophisticated as to projective tests, were trained in the administration of the Rorschach test. Each examiner then administered 30 Rorschach tests to randomly assigned male college sophomores.

Two experienced clinical psychologists scored the records blindly and independently. The relationship between examiner differences and obtained Rorschach scores was tested by the analysis of variance technique. Of 38 Rorschach scores, 20 differ significantly among the 9 examiners. However, the total number of responses (R), which is one of the statistically significant variables, correlates highly with many of the raw scores. Elimination of those scores which correlate .25 or more with R or with each other still leaves 8 scores which differ significantly among the examiners. This number of significant differences is beyond chance expectancy and suggests that different examiners elicit significantly different Rorschach scores from their subjects.

The nine examiners were ranked on continua of anxiety and hostility on the basis of (1) the content of their own Rorschach tests and (2) the subjects' perceptions of the examiners. By analyses of variances, certain patterns of the subjects' Rorschach scores were found related to examiner extremes on overt and covert anxiety and hostility.

REFERENCES

BECK, S. J. Rorschach's test: I. Basic processes. New York: Grune & Stratton, 1944.
ELIZUR, A. Content analysis of the Rorschach with regard to anxiety and hostility. Rorschach Res. Exch. & J. Proj. Tech., 1949, 13, 247–284.
GUILFORD, J. P. Printed classification tests, Report No. 5, AAF Aviation Psychology Research Reports. Washington: U.S. Government Printing Office, 1947.
JOEL, W. The interpersonal equation in projective methods. Rorschach Res. Exch. & J. Proj. Tech., 1949, 13, 479–482.
KAMMAN, G. R. The Rorschach method as a therapeutic agent, Amer. J. Orthopsychiat., 1944, 14, 21–27.
KLOPFER, B., & KELLEY, D. McG. The Rorschach technique. New York: World Book Co., 1946.
LORD, EDITH. Experimentally induced variation in Rorschach performance. Psychol. Monogr., 1950, 64, No. 10.
MURRAY, H. A., JR. Explorations in personality. New York: Oxford Univer. Press, 1938.
SCHACHTEL, E. The dynamic perception and the symbolism of form. Psychiatry, 1941, 22, 79–96.
SULLIVAN, H. S. Conceptions of modern psychiatry. Washington: W. A. White Psychiatric Foundations, 1947.

22

Statistical Methods Applied to Rorschach Scores: A Review[1]

LEE J. CRONBACH

This article has had a considerable influence on the caliber of Rorschach research, which rose several notches after its publication. Among the numerous errors and problems Cronbach calls attention to are the use of inflated N's; the use of the sign approach without prior hypotheses, thus capitalizing on favorable chance factors; difficulties in applying ratio scores; unequal psychological units in most Rorschach scores; and the problems accruing from the nonindependence of many scores from each other and from the number of responses given.

Among his suggestions are the use of counting procedures (e.g., chi square) over additive ones (t test) in view of the likelihood of unequal psychological units. For the same reason, the median rather than the mean is the choice for the measure of central tendency.

Cronbach's suggestions may be viewed, however, as more palliative than curative. The psychometric weaknesses of Hermann Rorschach's scoring approach, until recently relatively closely adhered to, has led to several innovations which are described in other articles in this section (Baughman, Chap. 17; Holtzman, Chap. 24).

While the Rorschach test grew out of clinical investigations and is still primarily a method of individual diagnosis, there is increasing

---

[1] The writer wishes to express appreciation to Frederick Mosteller and to N. L. Gage, who read this manuscript and contributed many suggestions for its improvement.

355

emphasis on statistical studies of groups of cases. On the whole, the statistical methods employed have been conventional, even though the Rorschach test departs in many ways from usual test methodology. The present review proposes to examine the methods which have been employed to deal with Rorschach data and to evaluate the adequacy of those often used. It attempts to provide a guide to future investigations by indicating statistically correct studies which can serve as models. There is no intent here to review the generalizations about the test arising from these studies or to call into question general research procedures, sampling, and other aspects of the studies.

This report may be considered an extension of a review by Munroe (1945a). In 1945, she considered the objectivity of previous Rorschach research. She distinguished between the goals attainable by clinical intuitive interpretation and the goals to be reached by more quantitative procedures. She traced the trend in Rorschach literature, noting the gradual decrease in studies based solely on impressionistic treatment of data or on mere counting of scores and the introduction of significance tests, standard deviations, and other signs of adequate effort to test generalizations statistically. She also pointed out some errors in statistical thinking that lead to faulty conclusions about the Rorschach test. Munroe takes the position—and the writer fully concurs—that statistical research on the Rorschach test is not only justifiable but indispensable. The flexibility of clinical thinking creates excellent hypotheses, but these hypotheses can only be established as true by controlled studies. Among the propositions suggested by clinical work, some are certainly untrue, due to faulty observation, inadequate sampling, and errors of thinking. Statistical controls are essential to verify theories of test interpretation and to validate proposed applications of the test. Even though the clinician studying one person makes no use of statistics, he employs generalizations about the test which must rest on scientifically gathered evidence. Munroe demonstrated that the Rorschach test lends itself to objective studies; the writer reviews the same material more technically to evaluate the soundness of the statistical procedures on which the conclusions are based.

Clinical Treatments of Data

While this paper deals principally with statistical methods applied to raw Rorschach data, we shall consider briefly the statistical procedures used when clinically interpreted case records are used in a study. The Rorschach record is usually interpreted qualitatively and in a highly complex manner when the test is given in the clinic, and many studies have been based on these interpreted records. In only a few studies of this type do statistical problems arise.

DICHOTOMIZED RORSCHACH RATINGS

In one type of study, the interpreter of the records makes a final summary judgment, dividing the records into such groups as "adjusted-maladjusted" or "promising-unpromising," etc. This method is most used for validation studies, where the Rorschach judgment is compared with a criterion of performance or with a judgment from some other test. Simple statistical tests suffice to test the degree of relationship. If the criterion is expressed in two categories (as when the criterion indicates success or failure for each case), chi square is simple and appropriate. This is exemplified in a study of success of Canadian Army officers (Ross, Ferguson & Chalke, 1945), where a prediction from the Rorschach is compared with a later rating, of success and failure. If the criterion is a set of scores on a continuous scale, biserial r is usually an adequate procedure. In biserial r, one assumes that the dichotomy represents a continuous trait which is normally distributed. This assumption is generally acceptable for personality traits and for ratings of success.

RORSCHACH RATINGS ON CONTINUOUS SCALE

In some studies, the Rorschach interpretation is reported in the form of a rating along a scale, rather than as a dichotomy. When the criterion is dichotomous, biserial r is appropriate (e.g., a prediction of probable pilot success is so correlated with elimination-graduation from training [Guilford, 1947, p. 632]). For a continuous criterion, like grade-average, product-moment r is conventionally used.

These methods are not entirely satisfactory, because of a limitation of rating scales. If units on the rating scale are not psychologically equal, the correlation may not indicate the full size of the relationship. If ratings are careful, one can assume that men rated "Good" are superior to men rated "Fair" and that men rated "Excellent" are superior to both of these. But it may be unwise to assume that the jump from "Good" to "Excellent" is equal to the jump from "Fair" to "Good," as one automatically does in correlating. One solution to this difficulty is to assume that the trait rated is normally distributed in the men studied. Then we can condense the five-point scale into a dichotomy, which is the case discussed in the preceding paragraph. Alternatively, one may convert the ratings into scaled values which will yield a normal distribution (Leverett, 1947). Biserial r is then appropriate, if the criterion is dichotomous. Similar reasoning applies to the correlation of a rating with a continuous criterion; one will obtain the most meaningful results by dichotomizing the rating and using biserial r or by normalizing

TABLE 22–1   *Preferred Methods for Comparing Rorschach*
                           Interpretations with Criteria
                                  of Various Types

JUDGMENT MADE FROM RORSCHACH

| | | CONTINUOUS SCALE, |
CRITERION	DICHOTOMY	UNEQUAL UNITS
Dichotomy	x^2	x^2 after dichotomizing rating; r_{bis} after normalizing rating[a]
Continuous scale, unequal units	x^2 after dichotomizing criterion; r_{bis} after normalizing criterion[a]	x^2 after dichotomizing both variables; r_{bis} after normalizing one, dichotomizing the other; product-moment r after normalizing both
Continuous scale, equal units	r_{bis}[a]	r_{bis} after dichotomizing rating; product-moment r after normalizing rating

[a] Point biserial must be used if the two parts of the dichotomy cannot reasonably be considered subdivisions of a continuous scale.

before using product-moment r. These suggestions are summarized in Table 22–1.

Munroe (1945b), comparing a Rorschach adjustment rating with success in academic work, where both variables were reported on a four-category scale, used a coefficient of contingency. Where the correlation surface is nearly normal, this coefficient with proper corrections should give approximately the same result as the product-moment r for normalized data, corrected for broad categories. Yates (1948) has offered an alternative method of adapting the contingency method to take advantage of trends in the relationship between variables expressed as ordered categories.

MATCHING METHODS

Another favorite technique for evaluating Rorschach results is blind matching, which permits a study of each case "as a whole." When a set of Rorschach records (interpreted or not) and another set of data regarding the same individuals are available, one may request judges to match the two sets in pairs. The success of matching is evaluated by a formula developed by Vernon (1936). An example of its use is a study by Troup (1938), in which judges tried to match two Rorschach records for each person. One hundred fourteen matches were correct out of a possible 120, judges considering five pairs at a time. By the Vernon formula, this corresponds to a contingency coefficient of .88. A coefficient of .40 was obtained when judges attempted to match the record of each case with that of his identical twin. Another excellent illustration of the method is provided by J. I. Krugman (1942), who used it to establish that different evaluations of the same Rorschach protocol could be matched and that the interpretations could be matched to the raw records and to criteria based on a case study.

The limitations of this method are not statistical; they lie more in the human limitations of judges. A portrait based on the Rorschach may be nearly right, yet be mismatched because of minor false elements. Matching, on the other hand, might be excellent, even perfect; the study would still not guarantee that each element in each portrait was correct, especially if the subjects were quite different from each other. In fact, the portrait might be seriously wrong in some respects, without preventing matching.

A complex modification of the blind-matching method has been proposed and tried by Cronbach (1948). Judges are asked to decide whether each statement on a list fits or does not fit a case described in a criterion sketch. Since only about one-third of the statements in the list were actually made about the given case, one can test by chi square whether the matching is better than chance. The method yields many interesting types of information: (1) an allover estimate of the validity of predictions with relation to the criterion, (2) a separate estimate of the validity of the description for each case or for subgroups, and (3) an estimate of the validity of statements dealing with any one aspect of personality (e.g., social relations).

Errors in Statistical Studies

The majority of statistical studies with the Rorschach test have treated Rorschach scores directly, with clinical judgment eliminated. This is an important type of investigation which presents numerous problems. Before considering general questions of procedure, however, it is necessary to deal with several errors and unsound practices found in the literature reviewed. These miscellaneous errors must be pointed out lest they be copied by later investigators and to suggest that the studies in which the errors occurred need to be re-evaluated.

SIGNIFICANCE TESTS FOR SMALL SAMPLES

The critical ratio is not entirely satisfactory when applied to small samples. When there are fewer than 30 cases per group, the t test is preferable. This would apply, for example, in Goldfarb's (1943) comparison of obsessionals with supposedly normal adolescents. His significance ratios are a bit too high, since he used the formula σ_{diff}. with groups of 20 cases. (It may be noted also that Goldfarb's study does not permit sound generalizations about obsessionals as compared to other adolescents. The obsessionals had a mean IQ of 120 compared to 97 for the normals, so that differences between the groups may be due to intelligence rather than obsessional trends.)

Chi square is generally useful for small samples, but it is important to apply corrections when the number of cases is below 50. This is especially important when the expected frequency in any cell of a 2×2 table is five or lower, under the null hypothesis. Many Rorschach studies fail to recognize the need for corrections, Kaback's (1946, pp. 24, 38–39) being a striking example. She compares the distribution of such a score as M in each of two groups. To do so, she makes the distribution in a great number of intervals, with only a few cases per interval, and tests the similarity of the distributions by chi square. In such a case, with many small cell frequencies, no significant result could be expected. Nor is it useful to inquire, as her procedure does, whether the precise distribution of M scores is the same for the two groups (in her case, pharmacists and accountants.) Her major question was whether one group used M more than the other, and this could be answered by dichotomizing the distribution and then applying chi square, with proper correction. In applying chi square to the 2×2 tables, one should as a standard practice apply Yates's correction (1948, p. 169). The importance of this correction will be demonstrated in Table 22–4. Where groups are dichotomized, it is best to make cuts toward the center, so that marginal totals will remain reasonably large. Special problems in the application of chi square to successive tests of the same hypothesis, and to problems of goodness of fit, are discussed by Cochran (1942).

TESTS FOR SIGNIFICANCE OF DIFFERENCE IN PROPORTIONS

Throughout the Rorschach literature, the formula for the significance of differences between proportions is misused. The resulting inaccuracy is slight in most problems, fortunately. This error is common in other work, and even some statistics books appear to endorse the faulty procedure. The usual formula,

$$\sigma_{p_1 - p_2} = \sqrt{\frac{pq}{N_1} + \frac{pq}{N_2}}$$

may not be entered with p_1 and p_2, the proportions obtained in the two samples. Instead, one should substitute p_0 for p, where

$$p_0 = \frac{N_1 p_1 + N_2 p_2}{N_1 + N_2}.$$

A significance test inquires whether p_1 and p_2 might arise by chance in sampling from a homogeneous population in which the true proportion is p_0 (see Lindquist, 1942, pp. 126-129). Employing p_1 and p_2, instead of entering p_0 in both terms, almost always increases the critical ratio over what it should be. Because no correct model is found in the Rorschach literature, the following example is given, using Hertz's data (1942).

Five boys out of 41, and 0 girls out of 35, gave zero color responses.

$$p_0 = \frac{5 + 0}{76} = .066$$

$$s.d._{diff.} = \sqrt{\frac{.066 \times .934}{51} + \frac{.066 \times .934}{35}} = .057$$

$$p_1 = .122; \quad p_2 = .00; \quad \frac{diff.}{s.d._{diff.}} = \frac{.122}{.057} = 2.14 \ (P = .032)$$

This compares to the critical ratio of 2.41 $(P=.016)$ computed by the formula Hertz and other workers have inadvisedly used.

The computation above is equivalent to the determination of significance by chi square and yields an identical result. But in this instance the expected frequencies are so low that the correction for continuity becomes important. Applying Yates's correction, we find that P becomes .10, and the reported difference is not significant.

Several studies use the formula for proportions in independent samples when the formula for paired samples should be used. Thus Hertz (1942), to compare the 12-year-old and 15-year-old records of the same cases, should use a formula for correlated samples as given by Peatman (1947, p. 407) or by McNemar (1947; see also Edwards, 1948; Swineford, 1948). The correct formula would have yielded significant differences where Hertz found none. Other studies employing matched samples, where the significance of differences was underestimated by a formula for independent groups, are those of Hertzman and Margulies (1943), Meltzer (1944), M. Krugman (1946), Richardson (1944), and Goldfarb (1943). In studies where the subjects were children varying widely in age, the proper formula would probably have yielded quite different results.

A study by Brown (1943) committed this error and one even more serious. He compared records of 22 subjects without morphine and then with morphine. He found that 14 increased in R and 7 decreased. He then treated these as independent proportions of the 22 subjects, computing the critical ratio for the difference 64 per cent minus 32 per cent. These are not proportions in independent samples, and

Brown's statistical tests are meaningless. No manipulation of the increase-decrease frequencies is as satisfactory for this problem as the formula given by McNemar. Brown could properly have set a cutting score (e.g., 2oR) and compared the percentage exceeding this level with and without morphine.

Siegel's procedure (1948), in which the "percentage incidence" of a factor in one group is divided by the incidence in the second group, will be likely to produce misleading results.

An alternative formula for the significance of differences in matched groups is used by Gann (1945). In applying the formula, however, a serious error was made. The formula given by Engelhart, which Gann adopted, is

$$\sigma_{diff.}^2 = (\sigma_{M_1}^2 - \sigma_{M_2}^2)\,(1 - r_{if}^2)$$

where r_{if} is the correlation of the matching variables with the variable in which a difference is being tested. This formula may be extended to differences in proportions, although the estimated population value (p_0) for the proportion should be substituted for M_1 and M_2, as explained above. Gann's major error was to use a value of .9741 for r in all her calculations. From the context, this seems to be a multiple correlation of all matching variables with *all* dependent variables. The proper procedure, for any single significance test such as the proportion of cases emphasizing W, would be to correlate the matching variables with W tendency alone. This correlation would almost certainly be close to zero. By the procedure Gann used, the critical ratios are very much larger than they should be. In one comparison where Gann reported a CR of 6.o2, the writer has established that the true CR cannot be greater than 2.23 and is almost certainly less.

COMPARISONS OF TOTAL NUMBER OF RESPONSES

It is thoroughly unsound to compare the total number of responses of a given type in two samples. Swift (1945) tested 37 boys and 45 girls. The boys gave a total of 248 F responses; all girls combined gave 246. Swift used chi square, demonstrating that these 494 responses were divided in a way which departs significantly from the theoretical ratio 37:45. But this assumes 494 independent events in her sample, whereas she really had 82. The F responses are not independent, since some were made by the same person. She might properly have used the *t* test, applied to the means of the groups. The only correct way to use chi square on her problem is to compare the number of cases exceeding a certain F score (cases, not responses, being the basis of sampling). A similar error has been made by Hertzman (1942), Rickers-Ovsiankina (1938, p. 231), and Werner (1945).

Richardson (1944) followed a different erroneous procedure. In her Table 9, she determined what proportion of all responses in each of her groups were W responses and tested the difference in proportions for significance, using the number of subjects in the denominator of the significance formula. The "proportion" she was studying is actually the ratio $Mean\ W/Mean\ R$, and the standard deviation of this is not correctly given by the formula $\sqrt{pq/N}$. If she must test the W/R ratio, in spite of the difficulties to be considered later, it is necessary to determine the ratio for each person separately and test differences between the groups in one of the conventional ways (e.g., chi square, t test, etc.).

INFLATION OF PROBABILITIES

Rorschach studies are peculiarly prone to an error which can arise in any statistical work. If a particular critical ratio or chi square or t test corresponds to a P of .05, we conventionally interpret that as statistically significant because "such a value would arise by chance only once in twenty times." While this usually refers to once-in-twenty-samples, it may also be thought of as "once in twenty significance tests," if the several tests are independent. In some Rorschach studies, a vast number of significance tests are computed. Thus, Hertz in one study reported the astonishing total of 800 significance tests (1942). Many of these comparisons reach the 1 per cent level or the 5 per cent level, but even these are not all statistically significant. Quite a few of these differences did arise by chance, and unfortunately we cannot estimate how many because the tests were not experimentally independent. The proper procedure, in such a case, is to recognize that an inflation of P values has taken place. The analogy to monetary inflation is a fair one: The increase in the number of significance tests in circulation causes each P to have less worth than it would normally. We may accordingly raise our "price" arbitrarily and insist that P reach a higher level than .05 before we label it "significant" and a higher level than .01 before we label it "very significant." Of the differences reported in the Rorschach literature as "significant at the 5 per cent level," probably the majority are due to chance.

There are several ways in which significance levels may be inflated so that they become falsely encouraging. One is the common procedure of testing differences on a great many Rorschach scores. This is, of course, sound practice, but one must then take the total number of significance tests into account in evaluating P. The inflation is more subtle when the investigator rejects a large number of hypotheses by inspection without computing significance tests and reports only a few significance tests. Thus Piotrowski, Candee, Balinsky, Holtzberg, and von Arnold (1944) compared superior and inferior mechanical workers on "all the components used in conventional scoring as well as many others." They finally invented four composite scoring signs on which differences between the two samples were large enough to encourage a significance test. Suppose, for simplicity, that those four tests had yielded *P*'s of .02. The significance of those *P*'s must be minimized in view of the fact that four such differences were found in several hundred implied comparisons which were not actually computed, and two per hundred is chance expectation.

A comparable inflation arises when an investigator slices a distribution in order to take advantage of chance fluctuations and find some "hole" where a test will yield a low *P*. Hertz applied the formula for significance of the difference in proportions, to compare two groups on *M*% (Table 22–2). She introduced a spurious element by slicing the *M*% distribution in so many places, and making so many significance tests. If a distribution is dichotomized in many ways, the chances of a "significant" difference rise greatly. Here only one test yielded a *P* of .05, out of nine attempted. The interpretation "It may be said with certainty, that more girls than boys at 15 years give over 11% *M*" (1942, p. 180) is unjustified. In another sample, this fluctuation would not occur. It is not necessary to test explicitly all possible dichotomies for this type of error to arise. If the investigator examines his distribution and makes his cut at the place where the difference is greatest, he has by implication examined and discarded all other possible hypotheses. One of the several studies where this occurs is that of Margulies, discussed later.

Multiple-correlation procedures give rise to a similar error. Suppose ten scores are tried as predictors. These scores might be combined in a prediction formula in an infinite number of ways. When an investigator computes correlations and works out the best possible predictive combination for his particular data, he implicitly discards all the other combi-

TABLE 22–2   *Significance Data Reported by Hertz (1942)*
                    for Differences in M% *between 15-Year-Old*
                    Boys and Girls

DIFFERENCE TESTED	CRITICAL RATIO	P
Difference in means	1.47	.15
Difference in medians	2.32	.05
Difference in proportions		
in interval 0–1	.81	—
in interval 0–3	.81	—
in interval 0–5	1.83	.10
in interval 0–7	1.68	.10
in interval 0–9	.90	—
in interval 0–11	2.34	.05
in interval 0–13	1.24	—
in interval 0–15	1.81	.10
in interval 0–17	1.23	—

nations. Even though his combination gives a substantial multiple R for the original sample, it is certain to give a lower correlation in a new sample where the formula can no longer take advantage of chance fluctuations. The common practice of comparing two groups on a large number of signs and developing a check-list score in which the person is allowed one point for every sign on which the two groups differ is open to the same objection. In a new sample, many of these signs will no longer discriminate.[2] When a significance test is applied to a difference in check-list scores or to a multiple correlation in the sample on which the combining formula was derived, the significance test has only negative meaning. If, even after taking advantage of chance differences, one's formula cannot discriminate, it is indeed worthless. But if the result gives a P better than .05, the formula may still be of no value. Rorschach studies which have reported "significant" differences based on an empirical formula without confirming them on fresh samples are those of Montalto (1946), Harris and Christiansen (1946), Hertzman, Orlansky, and Seitz (1944), and Ross and Ross (1944). Thompson (1948) reports spurious r's but does not claim significance for them. Buhler, Buhler and Lefever (1948, Tables X, XX) mix new cases with the sample used in deriving scoring weights and therefore fail to provide an adequate test of significance. Significance tests on fresh samples have been properly made by Guilford (1947), Gustav (1946), Margulies (1942), Ross (1941), and Kurtz (1948). The latter gives a particularly clear discussion of the issue involved. In most studies, correlations nearly vanish when a Rorschach prediction formula is tried on a new sample.

Still another method of inflating probabilities is to recombine groups of subjects in a way to maximize differences. If one has several types of patients, all of whom earn different mean M scores, these groups may be recombined in many ways, and in one of the possible regroupings a pseudosignificant difference may be found. Rapaport and his co-workers (1946) have carried inflation to bizarre levels. Not only did they consider scores in great profusion and in numerous combinations. They recombined their subjects so that the number of implicit significance tests in their volume is incalculable. They began with subjects in 22 subgroups. Significance tests were then made, on any score, between any pair of subgroups or combinations of them which seemed promising *after* inspection of the data. There were 231 possible pairs of subgroups and an endless variety of combinations. Thus at times Unclassified Schizophrenics Acute were lumped with one, two, or more of the following: Paranoid Schiz. Acute, Simple Schiz., Uncl. Schiz. Chronic,

---

[2] Harris (1948) claims that in his experience the Rorschach behaves differently from other tests and that signs found to differentiate in one sample are usually confirmed in other samples. This appears improbable on logical grounds, and no evidence in the literature supports such a statement.

Par. Schiz. Chr., Uncl. Schiz. Deteriorated; or with all the schizophrenics and preschizophrenics; or with Paranoid Condition, Coarctated
Preschiz., Overideational Preschiz., and Obsessive-Compulsive Neurosis.
Such willingness to test any hypothesis whatever leaves these workers
open to the charge of having regrouped their cases to augment differences.
They have undoubtedly reported differences which were created by
artificial combinations of chance variations between groups. Every time
cases are recombined for a significance test, one must recognize that a
large number of implied significance tests were also made, since many
other recombinations were rejected without actual computation.

Rorschach studies, because of the great number of scores and the
large number of subgroups of subjects involved, are more prone to
inflation than other research. The suggestions to be made for sound
practice are these:

1. Compare the number of significant differences to the total number
of comparisons in the study, both those computed and those rejected by
implication.

2. Raise the P value required for significance as the number of comparisons increases.

3. Never accept an empirical composite score or regression formula until
its discriminating power has been verified on a new sample.

4. In general, do not trust significance tests unless the hypothesis
tested was set up independent of the fluctuations of a particular sample.

These suggestions require that the investigator have clearly in mind
the number of comparisons considered. Comparisons are of three types:
those rejected as improbable before the data are looked at, i.e., before
the study is begun; those not computed because a cursory inspection
showed no apparent difference; and those computed. Sometimes the
investigator begins with, say five groups of subjects and ten scores and
frankly wants to unearth all possible differences between types of subjects.
Then there are ten ways the groups may be paired against each other,
and since each pair may be compared on each score, there are a total of
one hundred comparisons in the study. If, on the other hand, the investigator sets out to check only certain relationships—"Schizophrenics differ
from neurotics in $F+\%$," "Manics differ from all other groups combined in $FC:CF+C$"—those limited hypotheses may be laid down in
advance of the study, and only those comparisons are counted as implied
significance tests. To avoid confusion, it is also well for the investigator
to specify his cutting point, if a variable is to be dichotomized, before
examining the differences between groups. This may be set by an arbitrary
rule—for instance, that each distribution is to be divided as near to its
median as possible—or by an a priori decision to divide at some point
such as $2M$. In essence, the investigator must ask himself before he gathers
his data, "How many comparisons do I intend to look at and charge
myself for?" A P of .01 may be called significant if it is one of three

comparisons charged for, but not if the investigator has looked at three hundred comparisons in order to salvage this one impressive value.

Methods of Comparing Groups on Rorschach Scores

NECESSITY FOR CHOOSING BETWEEN STATISTICAL PROCEDURES

Because Rorschach scores are numbers which can be added, averaged, distributed, etc., most investigators have used conventional mental test statistics without question. The most common need for statistics is to compare the test scores of groups and determine the significance of differences. The prominent methods encountered in Rorschach literature are as follows: significance of difference between means (critical ratio or t test); analysis of variance; biserial r; significance of difference in proportions exceeding a particular score, or chi square; and significance of difference between medians.

Apart from such errors as those listed in the preceding section, there is no reason for considering any of the procedures under discussion as mathematically incorrect. If a significant difference is revealed by any proper significance test, the null hypothesis must be rejected. Nevertheless, the investigator may not choose one of the techniques at random. *Different methods of analyzing the data will lead to different conclusions.* In particular, some procedures lead to a finding of no significant difference, even though a true difference could be identified by another attack.

Let us illustrate first with some of Kaback's data (1946). She administered the group Rorschach to men in certain occupations, and, *inter alia*, compared her groups on the number of popular responses. The mean for accountants is 7.0; for accounting students, 7.3. By the t test, the difference between means is not significant (P ca. .40). (Point biserial r applied to the same data gives the same significance level. Point biserial r and t are interchangeable procedures, and there is no merit in testing the hypothesis in both ways.) But if she had chosen the chi square test, quite proper for her data, Kaback would have found a significant difference between the groups. Chi square would be applied to compare the proportion of cases in each group having five or more popular responses. From her Table IV, this proportion is 60/75, accountants; 72/75, accounting students. The difference between accountants and accounting students is significant (P<.01). In this and other instances, Kaback disregarded a difference when the null hypothesis could be confidently rejected.

Further illustrative data are taken from Hertz's comparison of Rorschach scores of boys and girls. She tested each possible difference by several statistical devices, yielding results such as those for M% reproduced in Table 22–2. By any of nine methods, she is informed that the two sex groups differ no more than might two chance samples. By the other computations, she is informed that the difference is significant at the 5 per cent level. If different significance tests disagree, what one concludes depends nearly as much on what procedure one adopts as on the data themselves.

Hertz compared her boys and girls in 46 instances. Each time, she tested the significance of differences between means and between medians. Four times the means differed significantly; five times, the medians differed significantly. But in only one out of 46 comparisons was the difference significant by both methods. It is greatly to Hertz's credit that she saw the applicability of more than one significance test. But conclusions of research will be hopelessly confused and contradictory, unless we can find a basis for choosing between the procedures when one says " 'Tis significant" and the others say " 'Tain't."

The choice between comparison of means and medians or between the *t* test and chi square cannot be left to the inclination of the experimenter; the whole point of statistical method is to make an analysis freed from subjective judgment. The reason different methods yield different results is that they make different assumptions or try to disclose different aspects of the data. It is therefore important to recognize the ways in which the techniques differ. Differences that are of little concern in connection with most studies have peculiar importance in Rorschach work. The difficulties which make choice of procedures an important problem arise from three causes: the skewness of Rorschach scores, the complications introduced by ratio scores, and the dependence of Rorschach scores on the total number of responses.

CHOICE OF TECHNIQUES IN VIEW OF THE INEQUALITY OF UNITS IN RORSCHACH SCALES

Many of the significant Rorschach scores give sharply skewed distributions for most populations. This fact is reported repeatedly (Beck, 1938; Hertz, 1942; Rapaport, 1946). Skewness is usually found where many subjects earn 0, 1, or 2 points (i.e., M, FM, m, the shading scores, CF, and C), and in the location scores W, D, Dd, and S. Skewness itself is no bar to conventional significance tests. But in skew distributions the mean and median are not the same. Two distributions may have a significant difference in medians and not in means (or vice versa) if either is skewed.[3] Furthermore, it is doubtful if a satisfactory estimate of $s.d._{mdn}$ can be obtained for a skewed distribution.

---

[3] This argument is presented by Richardson (1944). In attempting to study differences in medians, Richardson unfortunately uses an incorrect method of determining $s.d._{mdn}$.

Disadvantages of the Mean and Related Procedures

In any statistical computation based on addition of scores (mean, s.d., t, analysis of variance), numerical distances between scores at different parts of the scale are treated as equal. Thus, since the average of 3W and 7W is the same as that of 1W and 9W, these computations assume that a shift 3W to 1W is equivalent to, or counterbalances, a shift 7W to 9W. There is no way of demonstrating equality of units unless one has some knowledge of the true distribution of the trait in question or a definition of equality in terms of the characteristics of the property being measured. This problem is present in virtually all psychological tools, but other tests yield normal distributions which are assumed to represent the true spread of ability. On the other hand, *Rorschach interpretation based on clinical experience constantly denies the equality of units for Rorschach scores.* The average W score is near 6, and scores from 1 to 10 are usually considered to be within the normal range. No matter how extremely a person is lacking in W tendency, his score cannot go below zero. For one who overemphasizes W, the score may go up to 20, 30, or more. A W score only six points below the mean may be considered clinically to be as extreme in that direction as a score fifteen points from the mean in the other direction. Munroe (1945b) has prepared a check list which shows how units of certain Rorschach scores would have to be grouped in order to represent a regularly progressing scale of maladjustment. Her groupings, based on clinical experience, are of approximately this nature:

W (or W%): 0 (or 1 poor) W response; 1–14%; 15–60%; 61–100%.
Dd%:   0–9%; 10–24%; 25–49%; 50–100%.
m: 0–1; 2–3; 4–5; 6 or more.

If these units represent increasing degrees of maladjustment, the raw Rorschach scores do not form a scale of psychologically equal units. It is advisable to accept the clinical judgment on this point, especially in the absence of evidence for the assumption of equal units.

Use of Median and Chi Square

Unlike procedures involving the addition of scores, procedures based on counting of frequencies make no assumption about scale units. In fact, they give the same results, no matter how the scale units are stretched or regrouped. The median, or the number of cases falling beyond some critical point (e.g., 10 W), depends only on the order of scores. This appears to justify the recommendation that counting procedures, such as the median, be given preference over additive procedures, such as the mean, in dealing with skew Rorschach distributions. To test the significance of a difference between two groups, the best procedure is to make a cut at some suitable score and compare the number of cases in each group falling beyond the cut, using chi square. This procedure is used by Rapaport (1946) and Abel (1945). The test of significance of differences between proportions yields the same result (see above). One virtue of cutting scores is that we may test for differences between groups both in the "high" and "low" directions. This is important, since either very high $F\%$ or very low $F\%$, for example, may have diagnostic significance. In the usual analysis based on means, deviations of the two types cancel.

In contrast to the chi-square method, many tests of significance involve computation of the standard deviation. These include the critical ratio of a difference between means or medians, analysis of variance, and the t test. In these procedures, great weight is placed on extreme deviations from the mean. If mean W is 6, a case having 25 W increases Σd^2 (which enters the computation of the *s.d.*) by about 361 points; a case having 15 W increases Σd^2 by about 81 points; and 0 W, by only 36 points. In skewed Rorschach distributions, the few cases with many responses in a category have preponderant weight in determining σ and the significance of the difference. Whether weighting extreme cases heavily is acceptable depends on whether one considers the difference between 15 W and 25 W to be psychologically large and deserving of more emphasis than, say, the difference from 0 W to 5 W. Chi-square weights equally all scores below (or above) the cutting point.

Normalizing Distributions

One method used to obtain more equal units is to assume that the trait underlying the score is distributed normally in the population. Raw scores are converted to T scores which are normally distributed (Lindquist, 1942; Walker, 1943). (This procedure must be distinguished from another conversion, also called a T score, used by Schmidt [1945]. Scores of the type Schmidt used are not normally distributed.) The effect of normalizing is to stretch the scale of scores as if it were made of rubber. Extreme scores below the median are weighted symmetrically to extreme scores above the median. Thus, in the conversion table prepared by Rieger and used by the writer (Cronbach, 1949), the median ($6\frac{1}{2}$ W) is placed at 100, and a score of 0 W is converted to 66, while 28 W becomes 134. This in effect compresses the high end of the W scale and expands the low end. This conversion does not alter any conclusion or significance test obtained by dichotomizing raw scores and applying chi square. But the conversion alters markedly any conclusion based on variance or on comparison of means.

There is obviously much merit in using a procedure which leads to a single invariant result, independent of the assumption of the investigator about the equivalence of scores. Even if scores are normalized, it is advised that the median be used to indicate central tendency and chi square to test significance. If, for some experimental design, the data must be treated by analysis of variance, the writer believes normalized scores will give results nearer to psychological reality than raw scores, but this judgment is entirely subjective.

Comparison of Mean Rank

Attention should be drawn to a new technique invented by Festinger (1946), which is peculiarly suitable to the problem under discussion. This method assumes nothing about equality of units or normality of distributions, being based solely on the rank order of individuals. To test whether two groups differ significantly in a score, one pools the two samples and determines the rank of each man in the combined group. The mean rank for each group is computed, and the significance of the difference is evaluated by Festinger's tables. The method has not yet been employed in Rorschach research.

The Festinger method and chi square are not interchangeable. Which should be used depends on the logic of a particular study. Chi square answers such a question as "Does Group A contain more *deviates* than Group B in the score being studied?" The Festinger method gives weight to differences all along the scale and therefore asks whether the two groups differ, all scores being considered. In one study, absence of M is quite important, but differences in the middle of the range have no practical importance. In another study, differences all along the scale are worth equal attention.

The Festinger method appears to have the advantage of greater stability for small samples. Chi square is much easier to use in samples of 30 or more per group. The Festinger method is not useful when there are numerous ties in score. Further experience with the new method may disclose other important distinctions.

SIGNIFICANCE TESTS COMPARED WITH ESTIMATES OF RELATIONSHIP

Some investigators have perhaps not conveyed the full meaning of their findings to the reader because of a failure to distinguish between tests of the null hypothesis and estimates of the probable degree of relationship between two variables. The former type of result is a function of the number of cases, whereas the latter is not, save that it becomes more trustworthy as more cases are included. When an investigator applies chi square, the t test, or the like, he determines whether his observations force him to conclude that there is a relationship between the variables compared. But if the degree of relationship is moderately low and the number of cases small, the null hypothesis is customarily accepted even though a true relationship exists. It is proper scientific procedure to be cautious, to reject the hypothesis of relationship when the null hypothesis is adequate to account for the data. But in Rorschach studies, where sample size has often been extremely restricted, nonsignificant findings may have been reported in a way which discouraged investigators from pursuing the matter with more cases.

The study of McCandless (1949) is a case in point. McCandless compared Rorschach scores with achievement in officer candidate school. In each instance save one, the *t* test showed *P* greater than .05 that the difference would arise in chance sampling. But the samples compared contained only thirteen men per group. Under these circumstances, it would take a sharply discriminating score to yield a significant difference. If the sample size were raised to about 50 per group and the differences between groups remained the same, twelve more of McCandless' thirty significance tests would be significant at the 5 per cent, or even the 1 per cent, level. When more cases are added, the differences will certainly change, and most of them will be reduced in size. In fact, the writer believes, on the basis of other experience with statistical comparisons of the Rorschach with grades, that McCandless' negative findings are probably close to the results which would be found with a larger sample. But the point is that McCandless, and other investigators using small *N*'s, have submitted the Rorschach to an extremely, perhaps unfairly, rigorous test. One way to compensate for the necessary rigor of proper significance tests is to report also the degree of relationship. A chi square test may be supplemented by a contingency coefficient or a tetrachoric *r*. A *t* test may be supplemented by a biserial *r* or point biserial (not to determine significance, as Kaback used it, but to express the magnitude of the relationship). Sometimes reporting the means of the groups and their standard deviations, to indicate the degree of overlapping, is an adequate way to demonstrate whether the relationship looks promising enough to warrant further investigation.

To restate the problem: the investigator always implies two things in a comparison of groups: (1) that he considers the null hypothesis is definitely disproven by his data, or else that the null hypothesis is one way to account for the data, and (2) in case the null hypothesis still remains tenable, that he does or does not judge further investigation of the question to be warranted. He can never prove that there is no relationship. So, if his data report a nonsignificant difference, he must judge whether the difference is "promising" enough to warrant further studies. This judgment is not reducible to rules in the way the significance test is. Whether to recommend further work depends on the difficulty of the study, on the probable usefulness of the results if a low order of relationship were definitely established by further work, and on the investigator's general confidence that the postulated relationship is likely to be found.

METHODS OF PARTIALING OUT DIFFERENCES IN R

The usual approach when comparing groups is to test the differences in one score after another and then to generalize that the groups differ in the traits to which the scores allegedly correspond. The various scores, however, are not experimentally independent — a man's total record is obtained at once, and his productivity influences all his scores. If two groups differ in R, they may also differ in the same direction in W (whole responses), D (usual details), and Dd (unusual details). Thus, consider the Air Force data in Table 22–3.

TABLE 22–3   *Rorschach Scores Compared to Success in Pilot Training**

RORSCHACH SCORE	MEAN OF SUCCESSFUL CADETS	MEAN OF UNSUCCESSFUL CADETS	BISERIAL r
R	18.5	15.8	.14
W	9.2	7.3	.24
D	7.1	6.7	.03
W%	60.2	55.8	.08
D%	31.7	37.6	−.15

* Guilford, 1947, p. 632.

The first group has more responses than the second. From the means in W and D, it would appear that the first group has more W tendency than the second, but is equal in D. But when responsiveness is controlled by converting scores to percentages, the difference in W becomes small and the second group is shown to be stronger than the first in emphasis on D.

The most striking illustration of this difficulty is Goldfarb's comparison of obsessionals and normals. The obsessional group averages 55 R; the normals, 14. Under the circumstances, it is not at all informative to proceed to test W, D, and Dd; all differ significantly in the same direction. One learns nothing about differences between groups in mental approach, which is the purpose of considering these three scores. Most of Goldfarb's other comparisons also merely duplicate the information given by the test in R, that is, that the obsessionals are more productive. Although the discrepancy between the groups in R is unusually striking in Goldfarb's group, it is present to a lesser but significant degree in a great number of other studies, including those of Buhler et al. (1948), Hertzman (1942), Kaback (1946), Margulies (1942), and Schmidt (1945).

A similar problem complicated Beck's comparison of schizophrenics and normals on D. The means were 19.0 and 19.9, respectively; the σ's were 13.5 and 9.9. Beck comments as follows:

The small difference is accentuated in the very small Diff./S.D. diff: 0.34. There is, however, probably a spurious factor in this small difference. The ogives give us a hint: up to the eighty-second percentile, the curves run parallel, with that for controls where we should expect it, higher. Above this point, the schizophrenics' curve crosses over, and continues higher, and more scattering, as we should expect from the S.D. The spurious element lies undoubtedly in the fact that the schizophrenics' higher response total would necessarily increase the absolute quantity of D, since these form the largest proportion of responses in practically all records. Absolute quantity of details is then no indicator of the kind of personality we are dealing with. . . . The medians for D are 14.46, 17.2 (1938, pp. 31–32).

When one makes several significance tests in which the difference in R reappears in various guises, one becomes involved in a maze of seemingly contradictory findings. And interpretation tempts one to violate the rule of parsimony, that an observed difference shall be interpreted by the fewest and simplest adequate hypotheses. To answer the question, how do obsessionals and normals differ? it is simpler to speak of the former as more productive than to discuss three hypotheses, one for each approach factor. And one may certainly criticize Hertzman and Margulies (1943) for interpreting differences in D and Dd between older and younger children as showing the former's greater "cognizance of the ordinary aspects of reality" and greater concern with facts. The older group gives twice as many R's as the former, which is sufficient to account for the remaining differences.

One might argue that R is resultant rather than cause and that the differences in W, D, Dd, etc. are basic. But the Air Force demonstration that R varies significantly from examiner to examiner (Guilford, 1947) suggests strongly that responsiveness is a partly superficial factor which should be controlled.

Only two studies examine their data explicitly to determine if differences in other categories could be explained in terms of responsiveness alone. Werner (1945) found a significant difference in dd% between brain-injured and endogenous defectives. But the latter gave significantly more R's. He therefore counted only the first three responses in each card and arrived at new totals. With R thus held about constant, he found the dd difference still marked and could validly interpret his result as showing a difference in approach.

Freeman, Rodnick, Shakow, and LeBeaux (1944) found that groups who differed in glucose tolerance also differed significantly in R. After testing differences in M and sum C on the total sample, they discarded cases until the two subsamples were equated in R. Since differences between the groups in M and C were in the same direction even when

R was held constant, they were able to conclude with greater confidence that glucose tolerance is related to M and C.

After differences in R are tested for significance, it is appropriate to ask what other hypotheses are required to account for differences in the groups. But these other hypotheses should be independent of R; otherwise one merely repeats the former significance test and obscures the issue. The usual control method is to divide scores by R, testing differences in $W\%$, $D\%$, $M\%$, $A\%$, $P\%$, etc. Such ratios present serious statistical difficulties, discussed in the next section. Moreover, these formulas fail to satisfy the demand for independence from R. There may be correlation between R and $W\%$, etc. (For a sample of 268 superior adults from a study by Audrey Rieger, the writer calculates these r's: $W\% \times R$, $-.45$; $M\% \times R$, $.03$; $F\% \times R$, $.06$. In the latter two cases, there is no functional relation of the percentage with R, but the distributions are heteroscedastic. $\sigma_{W\%} = 3.30$ when R 5–19 [74 cases] but 2.09 when R 40–109 [82 cases]. The corresponding sigmas for $M\%$ are 3.85 and 3.35; for $F\%$, 3.23 and 2.29. Only $M\%$ is really independent of R.)

One may control differences in R by other methods, provided many are available. One procedure is to divide the samples into subgroups within which R is nearly uniform (e.g., R 20–29) and make significance tests for each such set. A method which requires somehat fewer cases is to plot the variable against R for the total sample or a standard sample and draw a line fitting the medians of the columns. This may be done freehand with no serious error. Then the proportion of the cases in each group falling above the line of medians may be compared by chi square.

DIFFICULTIES IN TREATING RATIOS AND DIFFERENCES

More than any previous test in widespread use, the Rorschach test has employed "scores" which are arithmetic combinations of directly counted scores. One type is the ratio score, or the percentage in which the divisor is a variable score. Examples are $W:M$, $M:sum\ C$, W/R ($W\%$), and F/R ($F\%$). The other type of composite is the difference score, such as $FC-(CF+C)$. In clinical practice, scores of this type are used to draw attention to significant combinations of the original scores; the experienced interpreter thinks of several scores such as FC, CF, and C at once, placing little weight on the computed ratio or difference. When these scores are used statistically, however, there is no room for the flexible operation of intelligence; the ratios are treated as precise quantities.

It may be noted in passing that a few workers (e.g., Tulchin & Levy, 1945) appear to assume that Mean a/Mean b is the same as Mean $\frac{a}{b}$. This is, of course, not true; the mean of the ratios and the ratio of the means may be quite unequal. One cannot, as Kaback did (1946, pp. 33, 53, 55), assume that if the ratio of the means is greater for one group than another, the groups differ in the ratio scores themselves. The reader may convince himself by computing the mean ratio for each of the following sets of data in which Mean a/Mean b is constant:

$$\frac{0}{2}, \frac{2}{4}, \frac{4}{6}, \frac{6}{8}, \frac{8}{10}; \quad \frac{0}{6}, \frac{2}{8}, \frac{4}{2}, \frac{6}{10}, \frac{8}{4}; \quad \frac{0}{10}, \frac{2}{8}, \frac{4}{6}, \frac{6}{4}, \frac{8}{2}.$$

One difficulty with ratio scores is their unreliability. Consider a case with 5 W, 1 M. The ratio W; M is 5. But M is a fallible score. On a parallel test, it might shift to 0 or 2. If so, the ratio could drop to 2½ or zoom to infinity; such a score is too unstable to deserve precise treatment. The unreliability of another ratio is illustrated in Thornton and Guilford's data (1936). The reliabilities were, in one sample, .92 for M, .94 for C, but .81 for M/C. In a second sample, the values were .77, .65, and .31. If unreliable ratios are added, squared, and so on, one commits no logical error, but psychologically significant differences become overshadowed by errors of measurement.

Ratios based on small denominators are in general unreliable (Cronbach, 1941). $W\%$ is unreliable for a subject whose R is 12 but relatively reliable for a case whose R is 30. In the former case, addition of one W response raises $W\%$ by 8 per cent; in the latter, by 3 per cent. Errors of measurement always reduce the significance of differences by increasing the within-groups variance. A significant difference in $W\%$ might be found for cases where $R > 25$. A difference of the same size might not be significant for cases where $R < 25$ because of the unreliability of the ratio. If the significance test were based on all cases combined, the difference might be obscured by the unreliability of the ratios in the latter group. One possible procedure is to drop from the computations all cases where the denominator is low. (If there is a significant difference even including the unreliable scores, this need not be done.)

The issue of skewness must again be raised. In the M:sum C ratio, all cases with excess C fall between zero and 1. Those with excess M range from 1 to ∞. The latter cases swing the mean and sigma. Following the argument of a preceding section, it is injudicious to employ statistics based on the mean and standard deviation, as McCandless (1949) did. By such procedures, different conclusions would often be reached if both M: sum C and sum C: M were tested. Procedures leading to a chi-square test are to be recommended, as illustrated in several studies (Rapaport, 1946, pp. 251; Rickers-Ovsiankina, 1938; etc.) Another solution, less generally suitable, is to convert ratio scores to logarithmic form to obtain a symmetrical distribution (Thornton & Guilford, 1936).

A hidden assumption in ratios and differences is that patterns of scores yielding equal ratios (or differences) are psychologically equal. Thus, in

W% the same ratio is yielded by 2 W out of 10 R, 8 W out of 40 R, and 20 W in 100 R. One can always define and manipulate any arbitrary pattern of scores without justifying it psychologically, but better conclusions are reached if the assumption of equivalence is defensible. The regression of W and R is definitely curved. A person with 2 W out of 10 R is low in W tendency, since it is very easy to find two wholes in the cards. Only people with strong tendency and ability to perceive wholes can find 20 W in the ten cards, regardless of R. As R rises above 40, W seems to rise very little; the additional responses come principally from D and Dd. The resulting decline in W% reflects a drive to quantity, rather than a decreased interest in W (cf. Rapaport, 1946, p. 156). Put another way: a strong drive to W can easily lead to 90 or 100 per cent W when R<15; but such a ratio in a very productive person is unheard of. If the regression of a on b is linear and a close approximation to (a/b)=some constant ratios may be used as a score with little hesitancy. Otherwise, the ratio is a function of the denominator.

This factor is recognized by Munroe, who indicates repeatedly in her check list that the significance of a particular ratio depends on R. Thus 30–40 per cent M is rated + if R=10, but 16–29 per cent is rated + if R=50. Numerically equal Rorschach ratios, then, are not psychologically equal. Rapaport reflects the same point in testing differences between groups in W/D. Instead of applying chi square to the proportions having the ratio 1:2 or lower, he adjusted his standard.

"In records where R is too low or too high, we took cognizance of the fact that it is difficult not to get a few W's and difficult to get too many. Thus, in low R records the 1:2 norm shifted to a 'nearly 1:1' while in high R records, the 1:2 norm shifted to a 1:3 ratio" (Rapaport, 1946, p. 134).

This adjustment was evidently done on a somewhat subjective basis and is therefore not the best procedure. It is unfortunate that most other workers have unquestionably assumed that a given score in W%, M%, or FC–(CF+C) has the same meaning regardless of R.

At best, ratio and difference scores introduce difficulties due to unreliability and to assumptions of equivalence. There is a fairly adequate alternative which avoids statistical manipulation of ratios entirely. One need only list all significant patterns and determine the frequency of cases having a given pattern. Thus M: sum C can be treated in these categories: coarctated (M and C 2 or below); ambiequal, M orC<2, M and C differ by 2 or less; introversive, M exceeds C by 3 or more; extratensive, C exceeds M by 3 or more. Any other psychologically reasonable division of cases may be made, and significance of differences tested by chi square, provided that the hypothesis is not chosen to take advantage of fluctuations in a particular sample. Even this method, however, does not escape the criticism that a given pattern of two scores, such as 3 M, 3 C, has different significance in records where R differs greatly.

To cope with this limitation, the pattern-tabulation procedure is suggested later.

A detailed consideration of certain work by Margulies is now appropriate, since it affords an illustration of many problems presented above. Her study of the W:M ratio employed a procedure almost like that just recommended, but with departures which are unsound. Margulies compared Rorschach records of adolescents having good and poor school records (1942). Only her 21 successful boys and her 32 unsuccessful boys need be considered here. She was interested in comparing them on the W:M pattern, in view of Klopfer's belief that this ratio indicates efficient or inefficient use of capacity. She not only tested her data in several ways but reported the data so that other calculations can be made. Table 11-4 reproduces a part of her data and shows the results of seven different procedures for determining the significance of the difference.

It should be noted first that Yates's correction is essential for tables with 1 d.f. and low frequencies; in each case where it is applicable, the correction lowers the significance value importantly. Second, attention may be turned to the use of chi square to test differences between two distributions. Even if more cases were available, it would be unwise to apply chi square to the distribution cell by cell (procedures 2, 3), since this procedure ignores the regular trend from class interval to class interval. Instead, the distribution should be dichotomized. Therefore, procedure 5 is preferable to 2, and 6 is preferable to 3. It will be noted that these recommended procedures indicate higher significance than the tests in which the distributions are compared cell by cell.

Margulies is one of the few writers to note the unsoundness of assuming that equal ratios are equal. She pointed out that 20 W: 10 M is not psychologically similar to 2 W: 1 M, and she demonstrated that the regression of M on W is significantly curvilinear. She therefore was properly critical of procedures such as 3 and 6. She next turned to the scatter diagram of M and W and found successful boys predominating in some regions and unsuccessful boys in others. After grouping scores into regions as shown in Distribution III, she divided the surface into two areas, one area including cases where W is 0 to 5 and M is 2 or over, plus cases where W is 6 to 10 and M is 3 or over, plus cases where W is over 10 and M is 2 or over. In other words, instead of testing whether the groups are differentiated by a cut along the straight line M = 2 (Procedure 5), she made her cutting line an irregular one. This hypothesis, tested in Procedure 7, gave apparently quite significant results. The results are of little value, however, since the hypothesis was "cooked up" to fit the irregularities of these specific data. In the cells where W is 6 to 10 and M is 2, there happens to be a concentration of unsuccessful boys. But to draw the cutting line irregularly to sweep in all areas where the unsuccessful predominate is a type of gerrymandering which vitiates a

TABLE 22–4   *Results Obtained When a Set of Data Is Treated by a Variety of Procedures**

	DISTRIBUTION I		DISTRIBUTION III			DISTRIBUTION II		
NUMBER OF M	SUC-CESSFUL BOYS	UNSUC-CESSFUL BOYS	W/M RATIO	SUC-CESSFUL BOYS	UNSUC-CESSFUL BOYS	PATTERN OF W AND M	SUC-CESSFUL BOYS	UNSUC-CESSFUL BOYS
3 or more	5	5	<1	1	1	$W<6$, M 0–1	0	10
2	9	8	1.00	0	2	$W<6$, $M>1$	8	2
1	3	11	1.1–2.9	8	5	$W>5$, M 0–1	7	9
0	4	8	3.0–4.9	5	7	W 6–10, M 2	3	7
			>4.9	3	9	W 6–10, $M>2$	1	4
			∞ ($W/0$)	4	8	$W>10$, $M>1$	2	0

significance test. Hundreds of such irregular lines might be drawn. Therefore, it would be expected that in any sample some line could be found yielding a difference "significant" at the 1 per cent level. At best, the irregular line sets up a hypothesis which, if found to yield a significant difference in a new and independent sample, could be taken as possibly true.

The law of parsimony enters this problem. Wherever a set of data may be explained equally well by two hypotheses, it is sound practice to accept the simpler hypothesis. Irregular cutting lines and explanation in terms of patterns of scores are sometimes justified and necessary. But in this case the difference between the groups is explained as well by the hypothesis that the successful boys give more M's as by any non-spurious test of the $W:M$ relationship. Therefore, procedure 5 is the soundest expression of the significance of the Margulies data. With more cases, this difference might be found to be truly significant.

In the analysis above, we find again that different procedures, more than one of which is mathematically sound, give different conclusions. The results from chi square are less compatible with the null hypothesis than is the critical ratio. Chi square applied to a dichotomy gives evidence of a possible relationship, whereas chi square applied to the frequency distribution does not. Attention is again drawn to the necessity of re-garding with great suspicion any significance test based on a complex hypothesis set up to take advantage of the fluctuations of frequencies in a particular sample. Finally, it is noted that explanations in terms of

TABLE 22–4 *(continued)*

TYPE OF ANALYSIS	PROCEDURE	RESULT	P	RESULTS WITH YATES'S CORRECTION χ^2	P
Central tendency	1. Significance of difference in mean M	CR = .70[a]	.48	—	—
Cell-by-cell comparison	2. Chi square applied to Distribution I (3 d.f.)	$\chi^2 = 3.78$[c]	ca. .30	—	—
	3. Chi square applied to Distribution II (5 d.f.)	$\chi^2 = 5.30$[a]	ca. .40	—	—
	4. Chi square applied to Distribution III (5 d.f.)	$\chi^2 = 17.73$[a]	$<$.01	—	—
Dichotomy	5. Chi square applied to number of cases with $M>1$ (Dist. I)	$\chi^2 = 3.46$[b]	.06	2.54[b]	.11
	6. Chi square applied to number of cases with $W/M>3$ (Dist. II))	$\chi^2 = 1.86$[b]	.18	1.13[b]	.30
Frequency of selected patterns	7. Chi square applied to frequency having $M>1$ if $W>6$ or >10; having $M>2$ if $6<W<10$ (Dist. III)	$\chi^2 = 6.58$[b]	.01	5.13[b]	.03

* Data from Margulies, 1942, pp. 23, 26, 44.
[a] Computed by Margulies.
[b] Computed by the writer.
[c] Computed by the writer. Margulies reports 3.64.

ratios and patterns should not be sought unless they can account for observed differences more completely than can hypotheses in terms of single scores.

Treating Patterns of Scores

Rorschach workers continually stress the importance of considering any score in relation to the unique pattern of scores for the individual. While this is done in clinical practice, there is no practical statistical procedure for studying the infinite complex interrelations of scores and indications on which the clinician relies. Instead of considering the individual patterns, the statistician can at best study certain specific patterns likely to occur in many records. A pattern can be exceedingly complex; there is no statistical reason to prevent one from studying whether (for example) more men than women show "high S on colored cards accompanied by emphasis on M and excess of CF over C." The only limitation the statistical approach imposes is that the same pattern of scores must be studied in all cases.

Patterns of scores may be considered by means of composite scores, by definition of significant "signs," and by the pattern-tabulation method. The composite score is simply an attempt to express, in a formula, some psychologically important relationship. Examples include M: sum C ratio and the more complex composites developed by Hertz or Rapaport. These scores may be treated statistically like any score on a single category, although most of them are ratios or differences and suffer from the limitations already discussed.

COMPARING INCIDENCE OF "SIGNS"

The "signs" approach has been widely used. It is simple and well adapted to the Rorschach test. Normally, an investigator identifies some characteristic of a special group, such as neurotics, from clinical observation. Then this characteristic is defined in a sign, i.e., a rule for separating those having the characteristic. One such sign, for example, is FM>M. After the investigator hypothesizes that some sign is discriminative, the necessity arises for making a test of significance to see if the sign is found more often in the type of person in question. One may soundly compare a new sample of the diagnosed group with a control sample by noting the frequency of the sign in each group and applying chi square. This procedure is illustrated in studies by Hertzman and Margulies (1943) and Ross (1941).

The investigator may invent his own signs, if he follows due precautions to avoid misleading inflation of probabilities. Often it is easier and equally wise to use a predetermined set of signs. The most useful set of signs available at present is the Munroe check list. She has identified numerous ratios and patterns of scores which she considers significant of disturbance in her subjects (adolescent girls). She has stated that she does not think of her method as a set of signs (1945a), but the difference between her list and others appears to be (1) that it provides an inclusive survey of all deviations in a record and (2) that the list is designed as a whole to minimize duplication from sign to sign. There is no reason why two groups may not be compared by applying the check list to every record and then comparing the groups on the frequency with which they receive each of the possible checks. Chi square is the proper significance test, as used in one of Munroe's studies (1946). The Munroe signs sometimes are simply defined (e.g. *P*–is 0 or 1 popular response), but some involve patterns of several scores (thus the sign *FM*+ is defined in terms of *FM*, *M*, and *R*).

PATTERN TABULATION

Pattern tabulation is a method devised by Cronbach for the study of relations between two or three scores (1949). It has the advantage of permitting one to study the distribution of patterns in a group. To deal with any set of three scores, e.g. *W*, *D*, *Dd*, one normalizes the three scores for each person and considers the resulting profile. The profile is expressed numerically in terms of the deviation of the converted scores from their average for each person. These three scores can be plotted on a plane surface, and the resulting scattergram shows the distribution of patterns in a group. If two groups are compared, any type of pattern found more commonly in one group than another can be identified and the difference in frequency tested by chi square. The significance level for rejecting the null hypothesis must be set conservatively, as this method involves many implied significance tests. An analysis of variance solution is also possible but not recommended in view of the fact that distribution of patterns are often nonnormal.

This method cannot consider hypotheses involving more than three scores at once. It functions best when the three scores are equally reliable and equally intercorrelated. It encounters difficulty due to the fact that some Rorschach scores are unreliable, since any serious error of measurement in one score throws an error into the profile. The method does, however, appear flexible and especially useful for such meaningful patterns as *W-D-Dd* and *M-sum C-F*.

Another group of procedures leading to composite formulas for discriminating groups is treated in the next section.

Discrimination by Composite Scores

In many problems, it is desired to use the Rorschach to discriminate between two groups. Thus, one might seek a scoring formula to predict pilot success or a "neurotic index" to screen neurotics from a general population. The methods used to arrive at composite scores are the check list, the multiple-regression equation, and the discriminant function.

CHECK-LIST SCORES

The check list consists of a set of signs. Each person is scored on the check list, and the total number of signs or checks is taken as a composite score. This method has had considerable success, notably in

Munroe's study (1945b) and in the formula of Harrower-Erickson and Miale for identifying insecure persons. There are no serious statistical problems in the use of check lists. The total score can be correlated (though eta may be preferable to r). Differences between groups may be tested for significance, preferably by chi square. Chi square is advised because a difference in the nondeviate range is rarely psychologically significant; the investigator is usually concerned with the proportion of any group in the deviate range. Buhler et al. justifiably apply analysis of variance to their check-list score, to study its ability to differentiate clinical groups (1948).

Problems do arise, however, in developing check-list scores. A common method is to compare two groups on one raw score after another, noting where their means differ. Each score where a difference arises is then listed as a sign and counted positively or negatively in obtaining the check-list score for each case. This method takes advantage of whatever differences between samples arise just from accidents of sampling. If sample A exceeds B in mean M, allowing one point in the total score for high M will help discriminate A's and B's. In this sample, the A's will tend to earn higher check-list scores. But often in a new sample such a difference will not be confirmed, and the M entry in the composite will not discriminate.

One study employing the sign approach should be pointed out to Rorschach workers. Davidson (1945) sought to determine the relationship between economic background and Rorschach performance in a group of highly intelligent children. Her treatment of data is noteworthy because of the flexibility of her procedures; statistics are applied with great intelligence, new procedures being adopted for each new type of comparison. While the reviewer disagrees with some of the judgments she made in selecting procedures, her treatment is free from overt errors and well worthy of study by other Rorschach investigators.

Davidson divided her 102 cases among seven economic levels. She studied the Rorschach performance in various ways. First, she made a clinical analysis of each child and placed him in one of nine categories (introvert adjusted, childish, constricted, disturbed, etc.). The distribution which resulted is a 7×9 table. Recognizing that the expected frequency in each cell is quite small, she combined groups to form a 3×3 table before applying the chi square test for significance. This same type of condensation would have been advisable in some other comparisons she made, such as that between personality pattern and IQ. Davidson next applied a list of signs and obtained for each case the total number of signs of maladjustment. The number of signs was correlated with economic level, and the correlation was shown not to differ significantly from zero. She tested the significance of the difference in mean number of signs by the critical ratio. These procedures appear well suited to her data. A third attack on the data treats one Rorschach score at a time. Here Davidson placed her cases in seven categories, ranging from highest to lowest economic level. By analysis of variance, she demonstrated that differences among the seven groups were significant only for a few of the scores. The application of analysis of variance to continuous data appears to have been an unwise decision. Analysis of variance, like chi square or eta applied to a variable divided in several categories, ignores the order of the categories. Consider the following set of means in the score $M - sum$ C:

Economic level:	1	2	3	4	5	6	7	TOTAL
Mean Score:	1.17	1.86	1.29	0.96	−0.75	−.13	−0.71	0.63

The downward trend from Group 1 to Group 7 gives great support to the hypothesis that this score is related to economic level. Analysis of variance estimates significance witout considering this trend; the same significance estimate would be arrived at if Group 2 had had the mean of −0.13 and Group 6 the mean of 1.86. Davidson might have computed the correlation between each score and the economic level, but the skewness of some Rorschach scores weighs against this suggestion. The simplest procedure for testing this trend is to split the group into a 2×2 table by combining adjoining categories in the economic scale and dichotomizing the Rorschach score at a convenient point. Chi square would then give the significance estimate. Such a procedure might have yielded significant differences in several instances where Davidson found none.

In justice to Davidson, it should be repeated that her data have been singled out for critical comment because of their exactness and completeness rather than because they were improperly handled. The foregoing suggestions point to ways in which she might have arrived at additional important findings.

THE MULTIPLE-REGRESSION FORMULA

A limitation of check lists is that they are simple additive combinations of signs which individually discriminate. But in such a composite a given trait may enter several times if it is reflected in several signs and thus have greater proportionate weight then it deserves. The check-list method does not allow for the possibility that certain signs may reinforce each other to indicate more severe maladjustment than is indicated by a combination of two other nonreinforcing signs or for the possibility that two signs which are individually unfavorable may operate to neutralize each other. Multiple regression and the discriminant function are more powerful procedures than the usual check-list score because they consider the intercorrelations of scores and weight them accordingly.

By multiple correlation, one arrives at a regression equation which assigns weights to those variables which are correlated with a criterion and relatively uncorrelated with each other. This formula may be used to predict or to discriminate between groups. One such formula is that of the Air Force, used in its attempt to predict pilot success (Guilford, 1947):

$$2(Dd+S\%)+6FM+8W-1.5D\%+R-(VIII-X\%).$$

Multiple correlation does not seem especially promising for Rorschach studies. Even such an elaborate formula as that above turns out to have little or no predictive value when applied to a fresh sample. Even if it were stable, any formula of this type must assume that strength in one component compensates linearly for weakness in another. In this formula, emphasis on Dd would cancel weakness in FM in estimating a man's pilot aptitude. It is most unlikely that the factors cancel each other in the personality itself. The simple linear-regression formula provides an efficient weighting if the assumption of linear compensation is valid, but interrelations between aspects of personality are probably far too complex to be adequately represented in this way. The most that can be said for a regression formula is that, when derived on large samples (and this may require 5,000 cases), it is a more precise prediction formula than the simple check-list score can be. It cannot hope to yield very accurate predictions if interrelations within personality are as complex as Rorschach interpreters claim.

The discriminant function is a relatively new technique giving a formula which will separate two categories of men as thoroughly as possible from a mixed sample. It would be used to develop an effective index for separating good from poor pilots (not for predicting which man will be best, as the regression formula does) or for distinguishing organics and feeble-minded. A practical procedure for dealing with multiple scores has just been published by Penrose (1947), and has not been employed in Rorschach research. It appears likely to have real value in studies comparing different types of subjects.

Like the regression formula, however, the discriminant function provides a set formula. In this formula, it is assumed that one factor compensates for or reinforces weakness in another factor. The interactions within personality are probably too complex to be fully expressed by linear or quadratic discriminant functions.

Correlation and Reliability

CORRELATIONS OF SCORES

For one purpose or another, several studies have tried to show the relationship between the several Rorschach scores or between Rorschach scores and external variables. The conventional procedure for showing that two characteristics are associated is to compute a product-moment correlation between the variables. This has been done by Kaback (1946), Vaughn and Krug (1938), and others.

This method is unable to show the full relationship between variables when the regression of one on the other is curvilinear. Such a regression often occurs when one variable or both have a sharply skewed distribution. In fact, Vaughn and Krug note that one of their plots is curvilinear. The extent to which association may be underestimated is suggested by the following data. The data used are taken from tests administered individually by Audrey Rieger to several hundred applicants for employment, usually for managerial or technical positions. The tests were carefully scored by the Beck method. Generalization from the data must be limited because the group is not a sample of any clearly defined population. For 268 men, the product-moment correlation between D and Dd is .735. The curvilinear correlations are η_{DdD}, .785; η_{DDd}, .823. There is significant curvilinearity. If D and Dd are normalized, the $= 0$; for the converted scores, $r = .767$.

Brower employs rank-difference correlations in comparing certain Rorschach scores to physiological measures (Brower, 1947). This is a useful method for small samples and is equally sound for linear and nonlinear regressions. Thus, a rank correlation of W/M with another score is the same except for sign as the correlation for the inverted ratio M/W, but the product-moment correlations are far different.

The rank method does have the disadvantage of weighting heavily the small and unreliable differences in the shorter end of skew distributions, where many cases have the same rank. This might lower the correlations for a score like Fc but is not a difficulty with scores distributed more symmetrically over a wide range, such as F or $VIII-X\%$. Normalizing has the same disadvantage. This is a reflection of the inability of the test to discriminate finely among cases in the modal end of a severely skewed distribution.

RELIABILITY COEFFICIENTS

Test reliability is ordinarily estimated by the retest or the split-half method. These methods are not very appropriate for the Rorschach test, the former because of memory from trial to trial, the latter because the test cannot be split into similar halves. Nevertheless, both methods have been used in the absence of better procedures.

The split-half method introduces a statistical problem which not all investigators have noted; namely, that the Spearman-Brown formula must not be applied to ratios with variable denominators such as $W\%$ and $M/sum\ C$. Methods for estimating the reliability of ratio scores have been treated elsewhere (Cronbach, 1941; Cronbach, 1943), but these procedures are not useful when the denominator is relatively unreliable (as in $M/sum\ C$).

It is desirable to estimate reliability of scores separately for records of varying length. Vernon (1933) found that Rorschach scores were much more reliable for cases where $R>30$ than when $R<30$. This implies that it is unsatisfactory to estimate just one reliability coefficient for a group with varied R. Instead, the standard error of measurement of W, or W%, should be determined separately for cases where $R = 10$–15 $R = 15$–25, $R = 25$–35, or some such grouping.

The reliability of patterns of scores is a difficult problem. If both M and W were perfectly reliable, any pattern or combination based on the two scores would also be perfectly reliable. But these scores are unstable; subjects vary from trial to trial in M or W or both. Nevertheless, Rorschach users insist that the "pattern" of scores is stable. If there is any substance to this claim, it means that certain definable configurations of the scores are stable even though the separate scores are not. The configurations may be as simple as the W/M ratio or may be complex structures of several scores. One may establish the reliability of any composite score by obtaining two separate estimates from independent trials of the test.

The method of determining reliability by independent estimates has rarely been used. A study by Kelley, Margulies, and Barrera (1941) is of interest, even though based on only twelve cases. The Rorschach was given twice, and between the trials a single electroshock was given, reportedly sufficient to wipe out memory of the first trial without altering the personality. In the records so obtained, R shifted as much as 50 per cent from trial to trial, and absolute values of some other scores shifted also. In several cases where scores shifted, it can be argued that the *relationship* between the scores did not shift and that the two records would lead to similar diagnoses. The authors made no attempt at statistical treatment. Probably this ingenious procedure will rarely be repeated. Useful studies could certainly be made, however, by comparing performance on two sets of ink blots without shock (cf. Swift, 1944). Even if the two sets are not strictly equivalent, the data would indicate more about the stability of performance than any methods so far employed.

At first glance, it appears logical to set up composite scores, obtain two separate estimates, and correlate them. Even this is unsuitable for Rorschach problems, however. As pointed out before, a given ratio such as 20 per cent W or W/M 2.0 has different meaning in different records, depending on the absolute value of W. The pattern might conceivably be defined by a curvilinear equation, but this becomes unmanageable, especially as several variables enter a single pattern. The problem is one of defining when two patterns are psychologically similar and of defining the magnitude of the difference when they are not equivalent. No one would contend that the W/M balance is unchanged if a subject shifts from 12 W: 2M to 60 W: 10 M. The problem is to define and measure the balance in a numerical way. The approach pattern W-D-Dd has three dimensions. If we wish to estimate reliability by comparing two sets of these three scores, we have a six-dimensional array, for which no present methods are adequate. So far, even the pattern-tabulation method reduces such data only to four dimensions, which leaves the problem still unmanageable. All that can be recommended is that additional attention be given to this challenging problem. We can now obtain adequate evidence on the stability of Rorschach patterns only by such a method as Troup's (1938), discussed in the first section of this paper. It will be recalled that she had two sets of records interpreted clinically and employed blind matching to show that the inferences from the Rorschach remained stable.

Two unique but entirely unsound studies by Fosberg (1938; 1941) employed a novel procedure to estimate the reliability of the total pattern. He gave the test four times under varied directions. He then compared the four records for each person. In one study he used chi square to show that the psychograms for each person corresponded. But this statistical test merely showed that the D score in record 1 is nearer to D in record 2 than it is to W, C, or other scores. That is, he showed that the scores were not paired at random. But, since each score has a relatively limited range for all people—i.e., D tends to be large, m tends to be small, etc.—he would have also obtained a significantly large chi square if he applied the same procedure to four records from *different* persons. One may also point out that finding a P of .90 does not prove that two records do come from the same person but only that the null hypothesis is tenable, or possibly true. Fosberg's second study, using correlation technique, is no sounder than the first. Here the two sets of scores for one person were correlated. That is, pairs of values such as $W_1—W_2$, $D_1—D_2$, etc. were entered in the same correlation chart. As before, the generally greater magnitude of D causes the two sets to correlate, but high correlations would have been obtained if the scores correlated came from two different subjects.

Objection must also be made to several procedures and inferences of Buhler et al. (1948) in their attempts to demonstrate the dependability of their proposed Basic Rorschach Score. (1) They used the split-half method on the total score by placing half the signs in one list, the other half in a second list, and scoring each person on both lists (p. 112). They then correlated the two halves to indicate reliability. Because the correlation was computed on cases used to determine the scoring weights for the items, the resulting correlation is spuriously high. Even if new cases were obtained, the split-half method would be incorrect because the check-list items are not experimentally independent. A single type of performance enters into a great number of separately scored signs (in their checklist, M affects items 1, 2, 5, 6, 7, 8, 10, 11, 12, 51, 52, 53, 86, 93, 94, 95, 96, 99, 100, 101 and 102). A "chance" variation in

M would alter the score on all these categories and would spuriously raise the correlation unless these linked categories were concentrated in the same half of the test. (2) They derived separate sets of weights from the comparison of Normals versus Schizophrenics, Nurses versus Schizophrenics, and other groups. The correlation between the scoring weights is high, which they take as evidence for reliability (pp. 112 ff.). At least one serious objection is that the weights were derived in part from the same cases. If, by sampling alone, FK happened to be rare among the Schizophrenic group, this would cause the sign FK to have a weight in both the Normal-Schizophrenic key and the Nurse-Schizophrenic key. The evidence is not adequate to show that the weights would be the same if the two keys were independently derived. This objection does not apply to another comparison of the same general type, where the four samples involved had no overlap. (3) Certain papers were scored repeatedly, using sets of weights derived in comparable but slightly different ways (p. 116). The correlations of the resulting sets of scores are advanced as evidence of reliability. Any correlation of separate scorings of the same set of responses is in part spurious. If responses of individual subjects were determined solely by chance, there would still be a correlation when keys having any similarity to each other were applied to the papers. The reliability of the performance of the subject—and that is what reliability coefficients are supposed to report—cannot be revealed by rescorings of the same performance.

Conclusions

The foregoing analysis and the appended bibliography are convincing evidence that Rorschach workers have sought statistical confirmation for their hypotheses. But the analysis also shows that the studies have been open to errors of two types: (1) erroneous procedures have led to claims of significance and interpretations which were unwarranted; and (2) failure to apply the most incisive statistical tests has led workers to reject significant relationships. So widespread are errors and unhappy choices of statistical procedures that few of the conclusions from statistical studies of the Rorschach tests can be trusted. A few workers have been consistently sound in their statistical approach. But some of the most extensive studies and some of the most widely cited are riddled with fallacy. If these studies are to form part of the base for psychological science, the data must be reinterpreted. Perhaps 90 per cent of the conclusions so far published as a result of statistical Rorschach studies are unsubstantiated — not necessarily false, but based on unsound analysis.

Few of the errors were obvious violations of statistical rules. The Rorschach test is unlike conventional instruments and introduces problems not ordinarily encountered. Moreover, statistical methods for such tests have not been fully developed (Cronbach, 1950). It is most important that research workers using the Rorschach secure the best possible statistical guidance and that editors and readers scrutinize studies of the test with great care. But statisticians have a responsibility, too, to examine the logic of Rorschach research and the peculiar character of clinical tests in order to sense the limitations of conventional and mathematically sound procedures.

Present statistical tools are imperfect. And no procedure is equally advisable for all studies. Within these limitations, this review has suggested the following guides to future practice.

1. Matching procedures in which a clinical synthesis of each Rorschach record is compared with a criterion are especially appropriate.

2. If ratings are to be treated statistically, it is often advisable to dichotomize the rating and apply chi square or biserial r.

3. Common errors which must be avoided in significance tests are:

    (a) Use of critical ratio and uncorrected chi square for unsuitably small samples.

    (b) Use of sample values in the formula for differences between proportions.

    (c) Use of formulas for independent samples when matched samples are compared.

    (d) Interpretation of P values without regard for the inflation of probabilities when hundreds of significant tests are made or implicitly discarded.

    (e) Acceptance of conclusions when a significant difference is formed with a hypothesis based on fluctuations in a particular sample.

4. Counting procedures are in general preferable to additive methods for Rorschach data. The most widely useful procedures are chi square and analysis of differences in mean rank. These yield results which are invariant when scores are transformed.

5. Normalizing scores is frequently desirable before making significance tests involving variance.

6. Where groups differ in total number of responses, this factor must be held constant before other differences can be soundly interpreted. Three devices for doing this are: rescoring a fixed number of responses on all papers, constructing subgroups equated on the number of responses, and analyzing profiles of normalized scores (pattern tabulation).

7. Ratio and difference scores should rarely be used as a basis for statistical analysis. Instead, patterns should be defined and statistical comparisons made of the frequency of a certain pattern in each group. Use of chi square with frequencies of Rorschach "signs" is recommended.

8. Multiple-regression and linear-discriminant functions are unlikely to

reveal the relationships of Rorschach scores with other variables, since the assumption of linear compensation is contrary to the test theory.

9. Rank correlation, curvilinear correlation, or correlation of normalized scores are often more suitable than product-moment correlation.

10. No entirely suitable method for estimating Rorschach reliability now exists. Studies in this area are much needed.

There are in the Rorschach literature numerous encouraging bits of evidence. The question whether the test has any merit seems adequately answered in the affirmative by studies like those of Troup, Judith Krugman, Williams (1947), and Munroe. Supplemented as these are by the testimony of intelligent clinical users of the test, there is every reason to treat the test with respect. One cannot attack the test merely because most Rorschach hypotheses are still in a preresearch stage. Some of the studies which failed to find relationships might have supported Rorschach theory if the analysis had been more perfect. How accurate the test is, how particular combinations of scores are to be interpreted, and how to use Rorschach data in making predictions about groups are problems worth considerable effort. With improvements in projective tests, in personality theory, and in the statistical procedures for verifying that theory, we can look forward to impressive dividends.

REFERENCES

ABEL, T. M. Group Rorschach testing in a vocational high school. Rorschach Res. Exch., 1945, 9, 178–188.

BECK, S. J. Personality structure in schizophrenia. Nerv. ment. Dis. Monogr., 1938, No. 63.

BROWER, D. The relation between certain Rorschach factors and cardiovascular activity before and after visuo-motor conflict. J. gen. Psychol., 1947, 37, 93–95.

BROWN, R. R. The effect of morphine upon the Rorschach pattern in post-addicts. Amer. J. Orthopsychiat., 1943, 13, 339–342.

BUHLER, CHARLOTTE, BUHLER, K., & LEFEVER, D. W. Rorschach standardization studies. Number I. Development of the basic Rorschach score. Los Angeles: C. Buhler, 1948.

COCHRAN, W. G. The chi-square correction for continuity. Iowa St. Col. J. Sci., 1942, 16, 421–436.

CRONBACH, L. J. The reliability of ratio scores. Educ. psychol. Measmt, 1941, 1, 269–278.

CRONBACH, L. J. Note on the reliability of ratio scores. Educ. psychol. Measmt, 1943, 3, 67–70.

CRONBACH, L. J. A validation design for personality study. J. consult. Psychol., 1948, 12, 365–374.

CRONBACH, L. J. Pattern tabulation: a statistical method for treatment of limited patterns of scores, with particular reference to the Rorschach test. Educ. psychol. Measmt, 1949, 9, 149–171.

CRONBACH, L. J. Statistical methods for multi-score tests. J. clin. Psychol., 1950, 6, 21–25.

DAVIDSON, HELEN H. *Personality and economic background.* New York: King's Crown Press, 1945.

EDWARDS, A. L. Note on the "correction for continuity" in testing the significance of the difference between correlated proportions. *Psychometrika,* 1948, 13, 185–187.

FESTINGER, L. The significance of difference between means without reference to the frequency distribution function. *Psychometrika,* 1946, 11, 97–105.

FOSBERG, I. A. Rorschach reactions under varied instructions. *Rorschach Res. Exch.,* 1938, 3, 12–31.

FOSBERG, I. A. An experimental study of the reliability of the Rorschach technique. *Rorschach Res. Exch.,* 1941, 5, 72–84.

FREEMAN, H., RODNICK, E. H., SHAKOW, D., & LEBEAUX, T. The carbohydrate tolerance of mentally disturbed soldiers. *Psychosom. Med.,* 1944, 6, 311–317.

GANN, EDITH J. *Reading difficulty and personality organization.* New York: King's Crown Press, 1945.

GOLDFARB, W. A. A definition and validation of obsessional trends in the Rorschach examination of adolescents. *Rorschach Res. Exch.,* 1943, 7, 81–108.

GOLDFARB, W. A. Effects of early institutional care on adolescent personality. *Amer. J. Orthopsychiat.,* 1944, 14, 441–447.

GUILFORD, J. P. (Ed.) *Printed classification tests.* AAF Aviation Psychology Program Research Reports, No. 3. Washington: U.S. Government Printing Office, 1947.

GUSTAV, ALICE. Estimation of Rorschach scoring categories by means of an objective inventory. *J. Psychol.,* 1946, 22, 253–260.

HARRIS, R. E., & CHRISTIANSEN, C. Prediction of response to brief psychotherapy. *J. Psychol.,* 1946, 21, 269–284.

HARRIS, T. M. The use of projective techniques in industrial selection. In *Exploring individual differences,* American Council on Education Studies, Series 1, No. 32, 1948. Pp. 43–51.

HERTZ, MARGUERITE R. Personality patterns in adolescence as portrayed by the Rorschach ink-blot method: I. The movement factors. *J. gen. Psychol.,* 1942, 27, 119–188.

HERTZMAN, M. A comparison of the individual and group Rorschach tests. *Rorschach Res. Exch.,* 1942, 6, 89–108.

HERTZMAN, M., & MARGULIES, HELEN. Developmental changes as reflected in Rorschach test responses. *J. genet. Psychol.,* 1943, 62, 189–215.

HERTZMAN, M., ORLANSKY, J., & SEITZ, C. P. Personality organization and anoxia tolerance. *Psychosom. Med.,* 1944, 6, 317–331.

KABACK, GOLDIE R. *Vocational personalities: an application of the Rorschach group method.* New York: Bureau of Publications, Teachers College, Columbia Univer., 1946.

KELLEY, D. M., MARGULIES, HELEN, & BARRERA, S. E. The stability of the Rorschach method as demonstrated in electric convulsive therapy cases. *Rorschach Res. Exch.,* 5, 1941, 35–43.

KRUGMAN, J. I. A clinical validation of the Rorschach with problem children. *Rorschach Res. Exch.,* 1942, 6, 61–70.

KRUGMAN, M. Psychosomatic study of fifty stuttering children. *Amer. J. Orthopsychiat.,* 1946, 16, 127–133.

KURTZ, A. K. A research test of the Rorschach test. *Personnel Psychol.,* 1948, 1, 41–51.

LEVERETT, H. M. Table of mean deviates for various portions of the unit normal distribution. *Psychometrika,* 1947, 12, 141–152.

LINDQUIST, E. F. *A first course in statistics.* (Rev. ed.) Boston: Houghton Mifflin, 1942.

McCANDLESS, B. R. The Rorschach as a predictor of academic success. *J. appl. Psychol.,* 1949, 33, 43–50.

McNemar, Q. Note on the sampling error of the difference between correlated proportions or percentages. *Psychometrika*, 1947, 12, 153–157.

Margulies, Helen. Rorschach responses of successful and unsuccessful students. *Arch. Psychol.*, N.Y., 1942, No. 271.

Meltzer, H. Personality differences between stuttering and non-stuttering children. *J. Psychol.*, 1944, 17, 39–59.

Montalto, F. D. An application of the group Rorschach technique to the problem of achievement in college. *J. clin. Psychol.*, 1946, 2, 254–260.

Munroe, Ruth L. Objective methods and the Rorschach blots. *Rorschach Res. Exch.*, 1945, 9, 59–73. (a)

Munroe, Ruth L. Prediction of the adjustment and academic performance of college students by a modification of the Rorschach method. *Appl. Psychol. Monogr.*, 1945, No. 7. (b)

Munroe, Ruth L. Rorschach findings on college students showing different constellations of subscores on the A.C.E. *J. consult. Psychol.*, 1946, 10, 301–316.

Peatman, J. G. *Descriptive and sampling statistics.* New York: Harper, 1947.

Penrose, L. S. Some notes on discrimination. *Ann. Eugenics*, 1947, 13, 228–237.

Piotrowski, Z., Candee, B., Balinsky, B., Holtzberg, S., & Von Arnold, B. Rorschach signs in the selection of outstanding young male mechanical workers. *J. Psychol.*, 1944, 18, 131–150.

Rapaport, D. *Diagnostic psychological testing*, Vol. II. Chicago: Year Book Publishers, 1946.

Richardson, La Varge H. The personality of stutterers. *Psychol. Monogr.*, 1944, 56, No. 7.

Rickers-Ovsiankina, Maria. The Rorschach test as applied to normal and schizophrenic subjects. *Brit. J. med. Psychol.*, 1938, 17, 227–257.

Ross, W. D. The contribution of the Rorschach method to clinical diagnosis. *J. ment. Sci.*, 1941, 87, 331–348.

Ross, W. D., Ferguson, G. A., & Chalke, F. C. R. The group Rorschach test in officer selection. *Bull. Canad. Psychol. Ass.*, 1945, 84–86.

Ross, W. D., & Ross, S. Some Rorschach ratings of clinical value. *Rorschach Res. Exch.*, 1944, 8, 1–9.

Sarbin, T. R., & Madow, L. W. Predicting the depth of hypnosis by means of the Rorschach test. *Amer. J. Orthopsychiat.*, 1942, 12, 268–271.

Schmidt, H. O. Test profiles as a diagnostic aid: the Rorschach. *J. clin. Psychol.*, 1945, 1, 222–227.

Siegel, M. G. The diagnostic and prognostic validity of the Rorschach test in a child guidance clinic. *Amer. J. Orthopsychiat.*, 1948, 18, 119–133.

Snedecor, G. W. *Statistical methods.* Ames: Iowa State College Press, 1940.

Swift, Joan W. Reliability of Rorschach scoring categories with preschool children. *Child Develpm.*, 1944, 15, 207–216.

Swift, Joan W. Rorschach responses of 82 pre-school children. *Rorschach Res. Exch.*, 1945, 9, 74–84.

Swineford, F. A table for estimating the significance of the difference between correlated percentages. *Psychometrika*, 1948, 13, 23–25.

Thompson, G. M. College grades and the group Rorschach. *J. appl. Psychol.*, 1948, 32, 398–407.

Thornton, G. R., & Guilford, J. P. The reliability and meaning of Erlebnistypus scores on the Rorschach test. *J. abnorm. soc. Psychol.*, 1936, 31, 324–330.

Troup, Evelyn. A comparative study by means of the Rorschach method of personality development in twenty pairs of identical twins. *Genet. Psychol. Monogr.*, 1938, 20, 461–556.

Tulchin, S., & Levy, D. Rorschach test differences in a group of Spanish and English refugee children. *Amer. J. Orthopsychiat.*, 1945, 15, 361–368.

VAUGHN, J., & KRUG, OTHILDA. The analytic character of the Rorschach inkblot test. *Amer. J. Orthopsychiat.*, 1938, 8, 220–229.

VERNON, P. E. The matching method applied to investigations of personality. *Psychol. Bull.*, 1936, 33, 149–177.

WALKER, HELEN M. *Elementary statistical methods.* New York: Holt, 1943.

WERNER, H. Perceptual behavior of brain-injured, mentally defective children. *Genet. Psychol. Monogr.*, 1945, 31, 51–110.

WILLIAMS, M. An experimental study of intellectual control under stress and associated Rorschach factors. *J. consult. Psychol.*, 1947, 11, 21–29.

YATES, F. The analysis of contingency tables with groupings based on quantitative characters. *Biometrika*, 1948, 35, 176–181.

23

Factor Analyses of the Rorschach Test[1]

BERNARD I. MURSTEIN

Factor analysis is here used to test certain Rorschach hypotheses and to ferret out new information regarding the factorial composition of Rorschach determinants.

One finding is that CF and FC do not load on the same factor. While it is true that no one has ever formally claimed that CF and FC are factorially distinct, the use of both scores additively in the ΣC score implies such an assumption—an assumption which would appear, however, to be unjustified.

Many scores whose psychological meanings are usually treated as being independent of each other are nevertheless found to load highly on the same factor. Factor analyses have revealed, for example, that D, d, Dd, and F are all largely functions of productivity. This should temper the weight given independently to these scores, since to a considerable degree they all measure the same thing.

A key finding of these studies is that factors elicited from psychiatrically abnormal populations are not essentially different from normal patterns. What this seems to imply is that if the Rorschach is capable of psychiatric differentiation, this ability is relatively independent of the formal properties of the major scores that are currently analyzed.

Another implication of this review is that the Rorschach presents so many difficulties in attempting analysis from a psychometric point of view that a more refined psychometric instrument might be more useful. In this respect, both the Baughman and the Holtzman revisions (Chaps. 15 and 24 in this volume) seem promising.

[1] The author would like to thank William A. Botzum and Walter G. Klopfer for generously giving of their time in reading the manuscript and offering their criticisms.

395

Despite the plethora of studies utilizing the Rorschach (currently well past the 2,000 mark), the amount of knowledge obtained has been disappointing. The reasons for this unfortunate circumstance have been the refractoriness of the technique to crucial experimentation. While tens of iconoclastic researchers have hammered away at the folklore of the Rorschach (e.g., the number of responses to Cards 8, 9, 10 reflect emotional reactivity), the "defenders" have retorted that current statistical methods are insensitive to the important configurational and test-interpretive aspects of the instrument.

The increasing importance of factor analysis in psychology made it inevitable that it would be utilized in research involving the Rorschach. It is the purpose of this paper to assess the contribution that factor analysis has made with regard to this technique.

The problems inherent in the use of factor analysis will be dealt with first. Next, the difficulties peculiar to the use of the Rorschach as a psychometric instrument will be discussed, followed by a section on the various Rorschach hypotheses tested by means of factor-analytic methodology. Then, a section listing the major new contributions to the Rorschach will be presented, followed finally by a discussion of the newer Rorschach innovations which have attempted to create an instrument more amenable to psychometric treatment. A summary of each factor analysis involving the Rorschach only is presented in Table 23–1. Studies in which the Rorschach was investigated in addition to other variables are summarized in Table 23–2. These tables indicate the population sampled, the number and kinds of variables studied, the types of correlations used, and the factors obtained.

PROBLEMS INHERENT IN FACTOR ANALYSIS

In a study of Yale undergraduates, Wittenborn (1950a) used the factor-analytic method to test hypotheses. Thus, he stated four hypotheses and attempted to substantiate them via his rotated factors. Whether this is a valid test is debatable, since solutions with or without rotation are not mathematically unique. There are many possible rotations, and one may rotate the axes infinitely until one gets them into the position that best substantiates the hypothesis.

It would seem that an "objective" means for evaluating his hypotheses would have been through "blind rotations" (i.e., rotation according to some criterion such as "simple structure," but without knowledge of the nature of the variables involved). It is not apparent from the report that Wittenborn followed this procedure.

TABLE 23–1   *Summary of Factor Analytic Studies with the Rorschach*

INVESTIGATOR	SUBJECTS	NO. OF VARIABLES ANALYZED	TYPE OF CORRELATION	FACTORS EXTRACTED AND SOLUTION
[a]Hsü (1947)	76 emotionally disturbed children, ages 5–15	15	Tetrachoric	*Orthogonal* Facility in use of words; Facility in use of nouns; "Face" factor; Facility for verbs and adjectives; "Human" factor
[b]Wittenborn (1949)	247 Yale undergraduates	18	Tetrachoric	*Orthogonal* Six factors; *Oblique* Seven factors; interpretation of factors is largely avoided
Wittenborn (1950a)	92 Yale undergraduates	21	Pearson	*Orthogonal* Productivity; Low perceptual control; Empathy; One unnamed factor
Wittenborn (1950b)	160 in- and outpatients from psychiatric clinic	21	Pearson	*Orthogonal* Bizarre originality; Low perceptual control; Productivity; Empathy?
Adcock (1951)	88 Cook Island children; 30 New Zealand children	15	Tetrachoric	*Cook Island Ss: Oblique* Fluency; Introversion; Intelligence; Construction; *New Zealanders: Orthogonal* Fluency; Introversion; Intelligence
Coan (1956)	Wittenborn (1950a) 92 Yale undergraduate data	12	Pearson	*Orthogonal* Productivity; Low perceptual control (anxiety); Low perceptual control (passive submission to emotional impulses); Intratensivity; Inner control and empathy; Outer control
Stotsky (1957) Location	148 Schizophrenics	3	Tetrachoric	*Orthogonal (location scores)* Whole; Common and rare details
Determinants	148 Schizophrenics	5		*Orthogonal (determinant scores)* Form; Color and shading

[a] Only Card 1 administered.
[b] Group administration (Harrower-Erickson check list).

TABLE 23–2   *Rorschach Included among Other Tests*

INVESTI- GATOR	SUBJECTS	NO. OF VARI- ABLES ANA- LYZED	TYPE OF CORRELA- TION	VARIABLES	FACTORS EXTRACTED AND SOLUTION
Sen (1950)	100 Indian college students in England	38	Tetrachoric	Verbal Intelligence, Nonverbal Intelligence and 36 Rorschach variables	*Orthogonal* Fluency Cognitive (synthetic vs. analytic) Emotional (neurotic vs. nonneurotic) Group factors Fluency (basic factor) General intelligence General emotionality Reproductive association
Hughes (1950)	100 psychiatric hospitalized patients	22	Tetrachoric	22 signs of organicity from Rorschach	*Orthogonal* Organic factor; factors 2 through 8 not labeled
Cox (1951)	120 (60 normal school boys, 60 child guidance clinic boys)	27	Tetrachoric	School vs. clinic category, IQ, 25 Rorschach variables	*Orthogonal* Productivity Normal vs maladjustment Intelligence vs. lack of intelligence Initiative—Passivity Accurate-inaccurate perception
Sandler & Ackner (1951)	50 psychiatric patients	50	?	50 psychiatric patients (Modified Q analysis)	*Orthogonal* High vs. low productivity Perception of internal, anatomical objects vs. perception of external objects Animate percepts vs. inanimate percepts Defensive percepts vs. well-defined human parts
Lotsof (1953)	30 college students	11	Pearson	Intelligence test, total words, adjectives, verbs, 7 Rorschach determinants	*Orthogonal* Verbal intelligence Productivity Elaboration Individuality
Williams & Lawrence (1953)	100 psychiatric patients	22	Tetrachoric	Verbal IQ, Performance IQ, 20 Rorschach determinants	*Orthogonal* Productivity Lack of perceptual control, Intelligence Movement, Shading
Williams & Lawrence (1954)	100 psychiatric patients	32	Pearson & Tetrachoric	21 Rorschach 11 MMPI	*Orthogonal and Oblique* Rorschach productivity Ego strength Expressive-Repressive MMPI maladjustment
Foster (1955)	1. 54 Policemen	11	Tetrachoric	Vocabulary, Verbal IQ, Anxiety ratings, 8 Rorschach variables	Factors identified from two matrices on the basis of similar loadings on common items (proportional profiles)

(Continued on next page)

TABLE 23–2 *(continued)*

INVESTIGATOR	SUBJECTS	NO. OF VARIABLES ANALYZED	TYPE OF CORRELATION	VARIABLES	FACTORS EXTRACTED AND SOLUTION
	2. 28 college students	19	Tetrachoric	Allport-Vernon Scale of values 6, MMPI 6, Wechsler 3, Rorschach variables 4	*Orthogonal* Inhibition of spontaneity Verbal intelligence Emotional drive Anxiety Manic-depressive
Borgatta & Eschenbach (1955)	125 Air Force personnel	40	Pearson	Rorschach variables 15, Interpersonal performance scores 11, rating scales 7, PMA 3, Actuarial 4	*Orthogonal* Rorschach productivity Formal properties Rorschach Abstract intelligence Social intelligence Emotional assertiveness Task leadership Social acceptability Maturity-adjustment
Singer, Wilensky & McCraven (1957)	100 male veteran schizophrenics	23	Phi coefficient	Rorschach variables 7, Wechsler - Bellevue IQ, Barron's Movement Threshold Ink Blots, TAT Transcendence Index, Planning Self-Ratings, Porteus Mazes, Wechsler's Number Square Test 3, Time Estimation, Block Authority Reaction, Motor Inabilities Test, Digit Frustration, Behavior Ratings 4	*Oblique* Motor inhibition and planfulness Ambitiousness Emotional surgency Introspectiveness
Consalvi & Center (1957)	45 adults (6th grade education to professional college)	14	Pearson	Raven progressive matrices, Vocabulary, 12 Rorschach Variables	*Orthogonal* Intelligence Low form Productivity Movement
Lotsof, Comrey, Borgartz & Arsfield (1958)	72 underachieving school children	33	Pearson	Actuarial Variables 3, Verbal IQ, Performance IQ, Wechsler subtests 12, Rorschach variables 16	*Orthogonal* Verbal Intelligence Productivity Perceptual nonhuman movement Age Performance IQ Seven unnamed factors
Vernier, Stafford & Krugman (1958)	150 physically disabled male war veterans	35	Tetrachoric	Otis S. A. test of mental ability, Bender-Gestalt 4, Rorschach 12, Draw-a-Person 6, Sentence Completion 7, Physical pathology 5	*Oblique* Withdrawal Tension Need for social approval, Anxiety Dependence-Passivity Affective Liability Pseudointellectual Defensiveness

Among the assumptions made in the use of factor analysis, two are especially cogent with reference to the Rorschach. These are: (1) the variables must be linearly additive, and (2) the variables must be formally independent. A violation of the latter assumption occurs in the work of Adcock (1951). He treats as independent scores the ratios $W : M$ and $M : C$. The common element in both (M) assures that if the former ratio is low due to the presence of many Ms, the latter ratio must be high because M is now in the numerator of the second ratio as compared to its being in the denominator of the first ratio. Another example of linear dependency is the use of percentage scores. Hence, a high negative loading for $W\%$ virtually assures a negligible or high positive loading for $D\%$ or $Dr\%$.

The variation in methods of rotation also has doubtlessly contributed to the emergence of different factors. While the centroid solution with either orthogonal or oblique rotation has been favored, other variations have been used. The British analyses have included Burt's simple summation and group methods. Other variations have included the Kaiser varimax method and various principal components solutions. The use of different methods contributes somewhat to the differences in solution.

Another problem is the fact that there is currently no method of obtaining a standard error of a factor loading. Hence, the stability of the position of each factorial loading can be only indirectly assessed via such criteria as the number of subjects (Ss) used and the type of correlation employed. There are ways of reducing the risk of error by the employment of techniques such as repetition of previously found factors, rotation to known "psychological conditions," and the use of "marker" variables whose factorial make-up is known. These aids, however, are often not present in the first factorial investigation of a test.

Problems Specific to the Rorschach

NONSTATISTICAL PROBLEMS

While the Rorschach is ostensibly a perceptual test, operationally speaking it must be considered a verbal task only indirectly getting at the perception via the verbalization. This fact may not cause any consternation until one reflects fully on the fact that the testee must manifest an extreme sensitivity to the determinants of his perception. He must communicate the importance of form, and in the case of using shading, whether the concept is two- or three-dimensional, whether it involves the perception of "texture" or perhaps "vista"—to mention just a few possibilities. But even if a person possesses a keen awareness of the determinants of his perception, does he possess the vocabulary with which to communicate them to the examiner? It is apparent that to convey verbally the nuances of his perception a person needs a precise and extensive vocabulary. One may well wonder whether the dearth of determinants found in low socioeconomic class protocols reflects a "simple" perceptual world or a small and limited vocabulary.

The fact that a few "incidental" words may change the scoring of a determinant is yet another difficulty. If two men are seen on Card 3, the determinant might be an F. But if on inquiry the two men are "sitting down," the response is scored not F but M. The examiner's task is to determine whether the original percept involved movement but was not verbalized or whether the movement really was not a kinesthetic perception but a verbal embellishment.

The fact that a single perception may be subject to many different scorings, depending on the verbalization of the S, is another weakness in the test as Levin (1953), Baughman (1954; 1958; 1959), and Murstein (1958) have pointed out. This point is amply demonstrated in a study by Stotsky (1957), where the determinants D and F loaded .93 and .96, respectively, on the same factor. If almost every percept scored D for location is also form-determined (F), then they can hardly be conceived of as independent variables.

The same situation holds for the treatment of certain determinants and content scores as independent items. Can there be human movement (M) by other than a human being (H)? In a small number of cases the answer is yes, e.g., animals perceived as "dancing a polka." In most instances, however, the number of M correlates .90 or above with the number of $H + Hd$. Such a correlation then involves little psychologically meaningful covariation but is in essence an artifact. Its presence is the factor matrix may lead to erroneous interpretation.

Another problem is that if a perception involves several determinants, a specific order of scoring may be used which allows only the determinant highest in the hiearchy to appear to be present more often than the less-favored determinant. Accordingly, M takes predominance over C, which takes predominance over Fc, etc. For maximal interpretative value, however, the number of responses should be independent of the frequency of occurrence of the determinants.

Clinicians through the years have grumbled over the necessity of learning at least two systems of scoring (the Beck and the Klopfer systems), not to mention the somewhat less popular Hertz and Buhler variations. The minor difficulty of understanding the various Rorschach dialects is simple in comparison to the man-sized task facing the reader of the Rorschach factor analyses. It is common knowledge that factors are not invariant when the population or tests used in the factorial matrix are varied extensively. A brief listing of procedural variations should suffice to indicate that no two Rorschach matrices reviewed herein have been identical.

1. Different tests have been used. The Harrower-Erikson check list, for example (Wittenborn, 1950a), is not comparable to the usual Rorschach.

2. Different scoring systems have been used, such as the Beck and Klopfer ones, in addition to mixtures in varying strengths of the two.

3. Some analyses include the form level of a given determinant; others do not.

4. Sometimes the whole test has been analyzed, at other times only a part of the test.

5. Sometimes the instructions have been the "usual"[2] ones, while at other times the Ss have been told to produce a fixed number of responses.

6. The researchers have differed in their choice of variables to analyze. No two matrices analyzed by different investigators have contained the identical variables.

7. The telescoping of scores has been freely undertaken. Thus, one investigator used three separate color variables, *FC*, *CF*, and *C*; another used only *C*. Some have analyzed shading and texture as separate scores, while another has combined shading and texture into one score.

8. Some researchers have correlated the raw scores; others normalized scores; still others used percentages and ratios.

STATISTICAL PROBLEMS

Choice of Correlation

The Pearson product-moment correlation is the most frequent statistic used when a measure of linear regression is involved, and several studies have utilized it. It is, however, justifiably applied, only when (1) the regression is linear and (2) the variables possess the property of homoscedasticity. It is apparent from common clinical experience, as well as such articles as the one by Fiske and Baughman (1953), that the relationship between most of the Rorschach variables is not linear, due to the stimulus limitations of the cards which favor the differential occurrence of the determinants.

Some investigators have realized the inapplicability of the Pearson *r* and substituted instead the tetrachoric correlation. This statistic, however, also assumes normality of distribution and linear regression. In addition, the tetrachoric *r* has a greater standard error than the Pearson *r* and tends to overestimate the true correlation. To avoid the dubiousness of using the Pearson *r* as well as the tetrachoric *r*, the phi coefficient has been used because it does not assume underlying linearity or a normal

---

[2] Their "usual" instructions are "usual" only in a gross sense since, as has been brought to this author's attention in a personal communication by Walter G. Klopfer, the Beck system by its instructions implies a much stronger set to produce responses than does the Klopfer system.

distribution. Its limitations, however, are formidable. It is not an estimate of a parameter, does not always vary from $+1$ to -1, and has no confidence limits. Another approach is to normalize the raw scores and then correlate the normalized scores, using the Pearson r. This approach, however, seems to violate the logic involved in normalizing data. The assumption is usually made in normalizing data that the trait or ability would be distributed normally in the population if we had sensitive enough measurements. It is the nature of the Rorschach itself, and not only the crudeness of the quantitative scores, which does not justify a normalizing procedure. With the small number of ten cards and the various stimulus limitations inherent in these cards, it is unlikely that the perception of the various determinants can in any way be assumed to be basically normally distributed. In any event, it could hardly be claimed that the small select populations used in the factor-analytic studies were themselves normally distributed, thus justifying the use of such scores with them.

Yet another problem involved in the use of normalized scores is that they have the further disadvantage of transformations in general, in that they render the original data meaningless; or, as Wittenborn has succinctly put it, it "analyses the Rorschach as it isn't." The resulting conclusion is that the use of correlational indexes are, strictly speaking, unjustified. The crucial question, then, is how much does one distort the findings in using a given statistic? This question is extremely difficult, if at all possible, to answer. Until some statistician solves the dilemma, one may only conclude that most of the correlational matrices used have had an indeterminate amount of error variance and gave at best only approximate factorial solutions.

Another problem is the nonmutually exclusive character of Rorschach scores. These scores, by their nature, determine that the correlations between the components must on the average be negative. This is easily seen with the location determinants, W, D, and Dd. If, in a given protocol, the total number of responses is 30, and 8 responses are scored W, the limitation is that the remaining responses must total 22. In a series of protocols, then, there must be a perfect negative relationship between W and D + Dd, if R is a constant. That R is not constant from person to person in most studies simply means that this relationship will be attenuated somewhat but still present.

The use of percentages instead of raw scores may often lead to unwarranted conclusions, as illustrated in a study by Sen (1950). By means of judges' ratings and Burt's Rorschach content method, a significant correlation was reported between the score "imagination" and the "productivity" factor. Sen noted that M, often assumed to tap "inner creativity," had no loading on this factor. This finding is attenuated because M% was used instead of number of M. Consequently, it may well have been that imaginative individuals manifested a high R along with a high number of M. If, however, the slope of $\triangle M / \triangle R$ is one of negative acceleration as R increases, as seems indicated by the data of Fiske and Baughman (1953), the $M\%$ will not remain constant with the increase in number of responses, but rather decrease somewhat. Thus, the failure of $M\%$ to load on the factor of productivity may reflect not lack of imagination but the stimulus limitation for the perception of M on the cards.

Unfortunately, the Rorschach Psychodiagnostic was not conceived by a man familiar with the problems of quantitative measurement. Indeed, Rorschach scores like M, F, CF, etc. are not scores at all but a shorthand for clinical impressions. By way of comparison, a Wechsler Vocabulary Scale score of 18 indicates that the S is extremely conversant with words and probably of extremely high intelligence level (r of .85 with Full Scale IQ). That a S has seven Ms in his protocol tells us very little. One wishes to know what the form level is, whether the Ms are manifested spontaneously or elicited via inquiry, whether the Ms were given on Card 3 or 4, and whether they refer to a large or small section of the blot. All these questions are important to the clinician, but usually none are reflected in factor analyses of the Rorschach. It is little wonder, then, that successive analyses with these "scores" are seldom comparable.

Another problem, often ignored, is the extremely low reliability of many Rorschach scores, including the various color and shading measures. One cannot expect very meaningful factors unless the components which compose these factors, i.e., the correlations, possess adequate reliability.

The problem of R—the number of responses as a variable contributing spurious variance to the factorial structure—has been excellently dealt with in a study by Coan. He states:

> The correlation of R with any location or determinant score is actually a part-whole correlation, since the sum of either the primary determinant scores or of the location scores will equal R. Similarly, P and O are functions of protocol length, since their size is limited by the total number of responses and longer protocols present more opportunity for popular and original responses to occur. On a similar basis, certain specific location and determinant scores may be expected to correlate especially highly with R, so that even percentage scores will show certain systematic correlation effects (Coan 1956, p. 282).

As an antidote to this problem, Coan proceeded to analyze his data omitting R. The omission of R, however, does not necessarily remove the spurious component of correlation from any two determinant scores whose correlation is due to their mutual dependence on R. In short, Coan's analysis is only partially free of spuriousness and accordingly does not reflect the "intrinsic" relationship between the determinants. On the other hand, since it has some of the spurious variance removed, it does not reflect the "external" relationship either.

Along the same line, Glickstein (1959) recomputed two of Wittenborn's matrices (Wittenborn, 1950a; Wittenborn, 1950b) with R partialed out. The results showed that the mean of the matrices with R partialed out approximated zero, while Wittenborn's original matrices appear to have a mean of about .30. The reply of Wittenborn (1959) indicates that their differences may be due to different assumptions. Wittenborn holds that R is the resultant of the number of responses in the various scoring categories and not the generator of these responses, as Glickstein seems to imply. There is no direct evidence on this point. Webb and Hilden (1953), however, have shown that productivity on the TAT is related to verbal fluency. If it could be demonstrated that Rorschach productivity is related to productivity in other areas (i.e., verbal fluency), the argument that R generates the determinants, rather than vice versa, would be greatly strengthened. The origin of R is important since if R is due to a "set," the benefit of partialing it out may be the resulting gain in knowledge about the interrelationship of the determinants. If R is not due to a "set," Wittenborn is correct in stating that we do violence to the data in partialing it out. Until further research is forthcoming, the issue remains in doubt.

Wittenborn (1959) is on firmer ground when he points out that the use of partialing techniques ignores the actual responses given to the Rorschach which are the most meaningful from an interpretative point of view, "At present one has the unhappy choice of studying the Rorschach 'as it is,' of studying it 'as it isn't,' or of ignoring it altogether" (1959, p. 77).

Evaluation of Rorschach Hypotheses

Many factor analysts have been interested in submitting much of the Rorschach folklore handed down from clinician to clinician to a factorial test. In the following pages, some of their findings will be briefly discussed.

M : Σ 3 (Erlebnistyp)

Wittenborn (1950a), in a study of 92 Yale undergraduates, found M to be factorially distinct from C and CF, though not from FC, which partially substantiated his hypothesis that M and the color responses would be factorially distinct. Such evidence seems to be detrimental to the continued use of the M : Σ C ratio. Ainsworth (1954), in a rebuttal, makes much of the fact that the Rorschach categories are not based on a factorial rationale. Most Rorschachers do not treat color undimensionally. FC is held to be qualitatively as well as quantitatively distinct from CF and C. Further, the relationship of M and FC is not unexpected in the normal adjusted personality. Even from a formal point of view, it should be readily apparent that M and FC might have a good deal more in common than FC and CF. The scoring of M invariably implies the presence of form, for it is impossible to conceive of formless humans. It is possible that the movement response also might have included the perception of color, although this might not be scored, since M takes precedence over C in some scoring schemes. One may conclude therefore, that the appearance of M and FC on the same factor probably indicates their mutual emphasis of form as well as their socially adjustive implications. While FC and CF have color in common, they differ in the importance of form for the perception, and apparently this latter difference is the more important one since it results in their loading on separate factors. These statements put the Rorschacher in the position of having his cake and eating it, too. It should not be possible to defend the act of distinguishing between FC and CF in one breath and in the next breath proceed to treat both as similar in compiling a $M : \Sigma\, C$ ratio.

Adcock (1951) investigated the hypothesis that *Erlebnistyp* ("Experience Balance") is indicated by several indices: (1) $M : \Sigma\, C$, (2) $FM + M : Fc + c + C'$, and (3) number of responses to Cards 8, 9, 10. The validation of the hypothesis was held to be dependent on their high loading on a common factor. This did not occur, and Adcock concluded that all three indexes did not measure *Erlebnistyp*. To some Rorschachers, this conclusion would not be valid. They could argue that $FM + M : Fc + c + C'$ represented a potential ratio of intraversive to extratensive tendencies which were not currently realized. There is no reason, however, why one's potential extratensive tendencies should be a simple function of one's "realized" degree of extratensiveness. The exact opposite might be argued, in that if one is realizing much of his reservoir of extratensivity, there should be little left in reserve. While this argument weakens Adcock's finding, it does not inspire confidence in the testability of the Rorschach hypotheses.

INTELLIGENCE

Many Rorschachers have held that intelligence can be estimated from several Rorschach determinants as well as nonformal scores, such as variety of content and originality of percept. Among the formal scores, intelligence is asserted to be present when W, M, R, and F are present, to name just a few scores. The factorial studies have in general supported these hypotheses. M has been highly loaded on the intelligence factors found by Sen (1950), Lotsof (1953), Williams and Lawrence (1953), and

Consalvi and Center (1957). W has been highly loaded in three of these studies, with F and R each represented in one study. Only Lotsof, Comrey, Borgartz, and Arsfield (1958) failed to find any of these determinants on their "intelligence" factor. Their study, however, utilized children as Ss, and the "intelligence" hypothesis has not been generally extended to apply to children.

NEUROTICISM

The number of "neurotic signs" referred to in the Rorschach literature is legion. It is difficult to assess whether factor analysis aids in validating these signs when we cannot state an operational Rorschach definition of neuroticism. Despite the variation in choice of "neurotic" determinants, however, one category seems to be present on almost all lists. This is the color category, with particular reference to CF and C. These determinant scores have been used in studies where Rorschach "neurotic" factors were obtained. Sen's "neurotic" factor (1950) does contain high loadings for C and C + F, which is somewhat expected in view of the common component, C. These signs are given substantial support by virtue of their correlating highly with several other "internal" and "external" criteria. The factor was found to correlate approximately .7 with Burt's Rorschach Content Method Neurotic Rating and with peer-judges' ratings for neurotic tendencies. Both CF and C also had a significant negative loading on an "adjustment" factor reported by Cox (1951).

Lotsof (1953) reported putatively contrary findings. Since Σ C and Y (shading) had loadings of .70 and .40, respectively, on the same factor, Lotsof concluded that his study had serious negative implications for Rorschach theory since "anxiety [Y] and affect [C] should not appear correlated for a 'normal' population to the extent that they do in this study, . . ." (1953, p. 24). By way of retort, one may state that without knowledge of what is meant by "anxiety" and "affect" it is hardly possible to say whether or not they are correlated in a "normal" population. Besides, the equating of Σ C to "affect" and Y to "anxiety" without any further investigation into the form level and configural aspects of both of these categories is without justification.

The picture is clouded, however, by the results of Williams and Lawrence (1954). Their "ego strength" factor contains moderately high positive loadings for C and CF, whereas the expectation should be for negative loadings.

In sum, the over-all picture is unclear as to the determination of any kind of neurotic sign or validation of Erlebnistyp. The evidence seems favorable for the use of Rorschach determinants for intelligence. One vital flaw which would be emphasized by many clinicians is that most of the studies have no reference to the form level of the determinants. This appears to be a valid criticism, and it is strange that no experimenter has taken cognizance of this important point. Accordingly, without reference to form level, the use of the determinants cannot constitute an adequate test of Rorschach hypotheses which do emphasize the value of form level in reference to *Erlebnistyp*, intelligence, and neuroticism.

Other Rorschach Findings

The use of factor analysis has importance for increasing knowledge concerning the Rorschach, apart from testing the commonly used hypotheses. The following section lists some of the newer findings.

PRODUCTIVITY FACTOR

Most of the Rorschach studies have reported a "productivity" factor which reflects the degree to which the manifestation of the various determinants is a function of the total number of responses in the protocol. The importance of this factor for clinicians is that it enables them to test hitherto untested hypotheses as well as suggesting new ones. For example, the presence of a large number of D has usually been interpreted as indicating a preference for the larger details of a task rather than the organizational aspect. Factor analysis, however, has indicated that D, d, Dd, F, and R are highly loaded on the "productivity factor." Since the major portion of common variance of each of these determinants is accounted for by this factor, it is possible to examine the usual psychological meaning applied to each of these determinants and see whether the simultaneous existence of all these psychological hypotheses is clinically meaningful. In the aforementioned factor, this would mean that the tendency to attend to the larger details of a situation (D) is also accompanied by the tendency to attend to small but articulate details (d) and to the tiny aspects (Dd). In short, we could economize by saying that the tendency to attend to details is general, no matter what the size of the detail. But, the productivity factor also indicates that contour-determined perceptions (F) and general productivity (R) should be related to the tendency to perceive details. It is apparent, then, that in so far as meaning exists in determinants codified so as to be amenable to factor analysis, the factors extracted are helpful in testing the validity of psychological hypotheses as to the meaning of these determinants.

PSYCHIATRIC DIAGNOSIS

Several researchers have addressed themselves to the question of whether the factorial structure of psychiatric patients could be differentiated from that of normals. The evidence would appear to be negative.

Wittenborn undertook factor analyses of both kinds of populations. The Ss were unmatched, the normal population consisting of 92 Yale undergraduates (1950a), while the psychiatric one was composed of 160 in- and outpatients from a psychiatric clinic (1950b). Four factors were obtained for each group, of which three appear highly similar (Productivity, Low Perceptual Form, and Empathy). The chief difference between the two populations was a splitting of a factor found in the normal population which had high loadings of M, m, Fc, C', FC and original responses O (presumably reflecting a healthy controlled degree of empathy and originality) into two separate factors, one reflecting the movement and form-controlled determinants, the other possessing high loadings on O and S, which now reflected a bizarre kind of originality.

The similarity of the factorial make-up for the two populations is surprising. It may well be that the formal determinants investigated in an atomistic way without regard to configural pattern or form level may not be differentiated by mental disease. This might be due to the stimulus properties of the cards, the Ss' test-taking attitudes, or a myriad of other reasons.

Moreover, the meaningfulness of the factors is difficult to assess because of the lack of external criteria. Ainsworth (1954) correctly points out, for example, that rather than reflecting disturbance, the splitting of the factor referred to in the student population into two factors in the psychiatric one may reflect the fact that some of the patients possess ego strength in seeing things differently (O, S) than other less-adjusted patients. In the absence of known personality correlates of the patients' protocols, identification of the factors from a clinically meaningful point of view is difficult.

Hughes (1950) investigated the protocols of 100 psychiatric patients (32 organics, 39 psychoneurotics, 29 schizophrenics). Tetrachoric intercorrelations of 22 different signs representing the above-mentioned syndromes were factored and yielded 8 orthogonal factors. The results were disappointing in that only the "organic" factor was clearly defined.

The factoring of persons (Q technique) on the basis of Rorschach scores was undertaken by Bendig and Hamlin (1955). Sixteen patients from four psychiatric categories were intercorrelated on 42 Rorschach element scores. The inverted factor-analytic method (Q technique) did not separate the psychiatric categories, although clinicians were able to do so via blind analyses. Apparently there is a great deal of meaningful information in the Rorschach protocol which is not represented in the scores obtained from it.

FACTORIAL RELATIONSHIP OF RORSCHACH AND MMPI

The relationship between the Rorschach and MMPI was investigated by Williams and Lawrence (1954) in a study which also included the

Wechsler Scale of Adult Intelligence. The usual Rorschach "productivity" factor manifested no substantial MMPI subscale loadings. The second factor, labeled "ego strength," was represented by all the tests: Rorschach variables W (.82), k (.60), K (.59), C (.55), CF (.72); Wechsler Verbal IQ (.54); and MMPI variables K (.51), F (-.47), Sc (-.45), and Ego Strength (.71). A "repression" factor was not clearly defined but had highest loadings on the MMPI for the R (repression) scale (.55), D (.40), Hy (.54), and on the Rorschach by D (-.48), FM (-.49), FC (-.48), and R (-.44). The last factor was termed a "maladjustment" one and was heavily loaded with most of the MMPI subscales. Surprisingly, no Rorschach variable was represented to any degree on this factor. The authors concluded that a considerable amount of variance in each test was not accounted for by covariation between them.

RORSCHACH AS A MEASURE OF BASIC PERSONALITY

A study by Borgatta and Eschenbach (1955) utilized a wide range of Rorschach variables, aptitude scores, actuarial background data, and personality ratings obtained from 125 normal male Air Force personnel. Three of the eight factors obtained loaded highly with Rorschach variables. These included a "productivity" factor, a "formal properties" factor—loaded highly on C, texture and shading, S, and W, which would be perhaps more accurately labeled as "low perceptual form,"—and an "intelligence" factor. Of chief interest to the authors was the fact that the Rorschach did not contribute significantly to factors which they labeled as "social intelligence," "emotional assertiveness," "task leadership," "social acceptability," and "maturity adjustment." In view of these findings, the authors believed that the use of the Rorschach as a tool for tapping the basic personality seemed questionable.

ONE OR TWO KINDS OF M

A dimension of personality associating fantasy tendencies with the control of motility and impulsive behavior was hypothesized by Singer, Wilensky, and McCraven (1956). The population consisted of 100 male veteran patients bearing the diagnosis of schizophrenia. These Ss received the Rorschach, TAT, and a battery of motor tests. Behavior-rating scales were obtained from ward personnel. The M determinant was believed to represent both a tendency to inhibit motor activity and a considerable imagination or use of fantasy. While M loaded highly on two of the factors obtained—"motor inhibition" and "introspection,"—the fact that this hypothesized unitary factor emerged as two separate factors precluded a simple conclusion as to the meaning of M. The authors implied that the category M may be too gross in linking introversive individuals with those possessing considerable ability for restraining impulsive behavior. A key problem that remained unanswered was whether the factors might be a function of the population employed, with little generality for more representative groups.

THE PROBLEM OF "EXTERNAL" VALIDATION

The difficulty of interpreting factors in clinical studies when no behavorial correlates are used is illustrated in a study by Vernier, Stafford, and Krugman (1958), who investigated the relationships among several projective tests (Rorschach, Sentence Completion, Bender-Gestalt, and Draw-a-Person). Another purpose was to determine the relationships between four kinds of physical pathology (orthopedic, respiratory, cardiac, and neurological) and the projective scores. The Ss, 150 VA patients (105 inpatients, 45 outpatients), received the Otis Self-Administered Test of Mental Ability in addition to the aforementioned projective techniques.

Tetrachoric correlations of 53 variables obtained from the tests were reduced to a 35 × 35 matrix by eliminating intercorrelations approaching zero as well as those over .75. The analysis yielded seven oblique factors which are extremely unclear in meaning. The lack of clarity is a function of the lack of experimental evidence as to the import of many of the "signs" obtained from projective techniques. For example, the "withdrawal" factor had substantial loadings on "hands omitted" from the Draw-a-Person test (.63) and on the "need affiliation" score from the Sentence Completion test (−.49). What this has to do with a third highly loaded variable—"not rejecting cards on the Rorschach" (.64)—is unknown. Do people who withdraw from interpersonal contact tend not to reject Rorschach cards? Similarly, the six other factors obtained are difficult to interpret. The weakness of this study lies in the fact that the interpretive implications of clusters of signs from projective techniques are themselves meaningless unless we know the personality correlates of these responses. The crucial task, then, for researchers employing factor analysis is to indicate the common variance between projective responses and behavior in important personal-social situations rather than the common variance between responses from different projective techniques.

A study which deals with this problem is that of Sandler and Ackner (1951). Here the "external" validation was obtained by correlating 200-odd psychiatric ratings with the Rorschach factors treated as scores, using the formula given by Sandler (1949). Space does not permit a full discussion of these interesting data. Suffice it to mention that Factor 2, for example (the perception of internal, anatomical objects as opposed to the perception of external objects), correlated beyond the .01 level with such current symptoms of the patient as "overt aggressive behavior" (.53), "complaints of feelings of aggression" (.41), "confabulations" (.41), as well as with previous personality traits of "appearing self-distrustful" (.42) and "feeling tense" (.36). This interesting study shows the possibilities of obtaining new information when sufficiently broad external behavior scores are compared with factors treated as scores.

Present Innovations in the Rorschach

In the foregoing pages, an attempt has been made to discuss the problems attendant on the use of the Rorschach as a psychometric instrument and at the same time to present some of the important findings resulting from factorial studies. In a way, the two tasks are contradictory. If the Rorschach is so ill-fitted for psychometric treatment, why bother to review studies at all? The reason for reviewing the content of many of these studies is that they present an admixture of "true" and "error" variance which is difficult to separate so long as we retain the Rorschach in its present form. In an effort to retain the baby, we have saved the dirty bath water, too. Though the Rorschach may be a means of probing the depths of personality in the hands of some practicing clinicians, from the point of research it must be considered a psychometric sow's ear. The small number of cards, quasi-quantitative scoring system with resulting low reliability, variable number of R, use of multiple scores from single responses, attests to its ancestry. Yet another difficulty lies in the fact that scoring is completely dependent on the self-knowledge, verbal fluency, and vocabulary strength of the testee, not to mention the skill of the examiner in asking the right questions. The Rorschach is operationally, then, hardly a *perceptual test* but rather an *interpretation of an interpretation.* Several researchers have attempted to remedy this situation. Cronbach (1949) has offered several statistical approaches to the Rorschach. He favors counting procedures over additive methods. Where correlation is desired, the scores should be normalized. Ratio and difference scores should be replaced by patterns. His suggestions have had some influence on Rorschach research. They are, however, of a "let's make the best of a bad situation" kind and are intended as stopgap measures pending the arrival of a more statistically sophisticated ink-blot technique.

Rust (1947), McReynolds (1951), and O'Reilly (1956) have constructed interesting subsystems designed for specialized use either in determining the presence of a given determinant or for psychiatric diagnosis. In the interest of space, however, only those systems dealing with a new total scoring system will be considered. The Howard Ink Blot Test (Howard, 1953) does contain 12 new blots, but the system of scoring employed is identical to the Beck system, and there is therefore little point in reviewing the technique.

Zubin (Zubin & Eron, 1953), the first to apply more adequate quantitative methodology, constructed 60 scales measuring location, objective stimulus attributes, determinants, interpretation, content, organization, and other attributes somewhat difficult to categorize. The scores obtained are rated on a five-point scale. Zubin's system has not been generally accepted for two reasons. One, a very basic reason, is that the system has not until very recently been published in book form. Secondly, the excessive number of characteristics is a bit too detailed for the current state of knowledge about the stimulus correlates of the Rorschach.

A more recent variation is that of Holtzman (1959), who employs his own set of ink blots. He has borrowed Zubin's rating scheme, trimming the number of scoring categories utilized, however, to six. These are Location, Form Appropriateness, Form Definiteness, Color, Shading, and Movement Energy Level, which are rated on from three- to seven-point scales. In addition, several new innovations are introduced for the purpose of making the scores more amenable to treatment as normal continuous data. Two sets of parallel cards are employed, each set containing 45 cards. With this large set of cards, it was possible to ensure that not only would each card be used, but the same number of responses would be given to each card. Accordingly, the S is instructed to give only one response to each card.

The system is a major advance in obtaining higher reliabilities in the scoring of the categories. Interscorer reliability is in the .90's, while estimates of reliability based on internal consistency using Gulliksen's matched random subtest method yielded correlations ranging from .80 to .91.

In view of these important advances, it seems unfortunate that in one respect the system has remained stagnant. This is in the manner of recording the response. Here Holtzman has relied more or less on the highly unsatisfactory standard inquiry method. The disadvantage of this method, which relies on the S's ability to verbalize the determinants of his perception, is apparent in the data presented by Baughman (1954). It is known that most people who see a bat on Card 1 give form as the chief determinant. Very few mention the black color and shading as influencing their percept. When, however, Baughman presented a modified version of Card 1 which had only the color removed, very few people saw the bat. Further evidence in this regard is reported in a recent study comparing two methods of inquiry (Baughman, 1959). One method was the standard Beck approach. The other was the paired-comparison inquiry. This method, briefly stated, presents the orthodox card and one of several various modifications during the inquiry period. The modifications currently employed are as follows.

Achromatic (A): Color is eliminated; remaining blot properties are retained as in the standard series. Complex Silhouette (CS): Shading variations are removed; differentiation between major detail areas is retained, however, by giving each major detail area a different contrast value. Silhouette (S): All shading variations and differentiations between major detail areas are eliminated, making a uniform gray. White (W): A white figure is placed on a uniformly gray background. Complex Form (CF): Figure-ground contrast due to brightness difference is removed; forms of major detail areas are retained. The form is like that of CS. Form (F): A form comparable to S and W is created, but figure-ground contrast due to brightness difference is eliminated (Baughman, 1958, p. 382).

The examiner chooses the modification to suit his question. If, for example, S sees "bat" on Card 2 and E wishes to determine the role of shading in the perception, the silhouette Card 2 might be compared to the standard chromatic one and S asked if he still sees the bat.

The Beck-Baughman inquiry comparison indicated that much more shading was actually utilized by most Ss on the Rorschach than was verbalized under the Beck inquiry.

The Baughman method, which retains the original 10 cards, will probably not supply quite as reliable data as the more refined statistical procedures seem to give the Holtzman modification. On the other hand, Baughman's studies have the advantage of being more readily related to the vast Rorschach literature and should prove of greater interest to most practicing clinicians. Both have the disadvantage of requiring an excessive number of cards, 45 in each of the two Holtzman series and 65 in Baughman's group. It is too early to state which of these procedures will prove to be the more fruitful for personality study, but both represent a considerable improvement over the current Rorschach procedure.

The importance of these new revisions for factor analysis is considerable. To the extent that the current Rorschach is inadequate as a quantitative test, the use of factor analysis will yield questionable results. If factor analysis is to be utilized more fully in the future, the Rorschach will have to be superseded by a more appropriate test. The newer variations, with increasing reliance on quantification and reliability, should more readily justify the use of factor analyses and increase our confidence in the results obtained from such studies.

REFERENCES

ADCOCK, C. J. A factorial approach to Rorschach interpretation. *J. gen. Psychol.*, 1951, 44, 261–272.

AINSWORTH, MARY D. Problems of validation. In B. Klopfer et al., *Developments in the Rorschach technique*. New York: World Book Co., 1954. Pp. 405–500.

BAUGHMAN, E. E. A comparative analysis of Rorschach forms with altered stimulus characteristics. *J. proj. Tech.*, 1954, 18, 151–164.

BAUGHMAN, E. E. A new method of Rorschach inquiry. *J. proj. Tech.*, 1958, 23, 381–389.

BAUGHMAN, E. E. The effect of inquiry method on Rorschach color and shading scores. *J. proj. Tech.*, 1959, 23, 3–7.

BENDIG, A. W., & HAMLIN, R. M. The psychiatric validity of an inverted factor analysis of Rorschach scoring categories. *J. consult. Psychol.*, 1955, 19, 183–188.

BORGATTA, E. F., & ESCHENBACH, A. E. Factor analysis of Rorschach variables and behavioral observation. *Psychol. Rep.*, 1955, 1, 129–136.

COAN, R. A factor analysis of Rorschach determinants. *J. proj. Tech.*, 1956, 20, 280–287.

CONSALVI, C., & CENTER, A. Rorschach scores as a function of four factors. *J. consult. Psychol.*, 1957, 21, 47–51.

COX, S. M. A factorial study of the Rorschach responses of normal and maladjusted boys. *J. genet. Psychol.*, 1951, 79, 95–115.

CRONBACH, L. J. "Pattern Tabulation": A statistical method for analysis of limited patterns of scores, with particular reference to the Rorschach test. *Educ., Psychol. Measmt*, 1949, 9, 149–171.

FISKE, D. W., & BAUGHMAN, E. E. Relationships between Rorschach scoring categories and the total number of responses. *J. abnorm. soc. Psychol.*, 1953, 48, 25–32.

FOSTER, A. The factorial structure of the Rorschach test. *Tex. Rep. Biol. Med.*, 1955, 13, 34–61.

GLICKSTEIN, M. A note on Wittenborn's factor analysis of Rorschach scoring categories. *J. consult. Psychol.*, 1959, 23, 69–75.

HOLTZMAN, W. H. Objective scoring of projective tests. In B. M. Bass & I. A. Berg (Eds.), *Objective approaches to personality assessment*. New York: Van Nostrand, 1959. Pp. 119–145.

HOWARD, J. W. The Howard ink blot test: A descriptive manual. *J. clin. Psychol.*, 1953, 9, 209–254.

HSÜ, E. H. The Rorschach responses and factor analysis. *J. gen. Psychol.*, 1947, 37, 129–138.

HUGHES, R. M. A factor analysis of Rorschach diagnostic signs. *J. gen. Psychol.*, 1950, 43, 85–103.

LEVIN, M. The two tests in the Rorschach. *J. proj. Tech.*, 1953, 17, 471–473.

LOTSOF, E. J. Intelligence, verbal fluency, and the Rorschach test. *J. consult. Psychol.*, 1953, 17, 21–24.

LOTSOF, E. J., COMREY, A., BORGARTZ, W., & ARSFIELD, P. A factor analysis of the WISC and Rorschach. *J. proj. Tech.*, 1958, 22, 297–301.

McREYNOLDS, P. Perception of Rorschach concepts as related to personality deviations. *J. abnorm. soc. Psychol.*, 1951, 46, 131–141.

MURSTEIN, B. I. Review of B. Klopfer et al. *Developments in the Rorschach techniques. Vol. II. Fields of application. J. proj. Tech.*, 1958, 22, 246–248.

O'REILLY, B. O. The objective Rorschach: A suggested modification of Rorschach techniques. *J. clin. Psychol.*, 1956, 12, 27–31.

RUST, R. M. Some correlates of the movement response. *J. Pers.*, 1947, 16, 369–401.

SANDLER, J. The reciprocity principle as an aid to factor analysis. *Brit. J. Psychol., statist. Sect.*, 1949, 2, 180–187.

SANDLER, J., & ACKNER, B. Rorschach content analysis: an experimental investigation. *Brit. J. med. Psychol.*, 1951, 23, 180–201.

SEN, A. A study of the Rorschach test. *Brit. J. Psychol., statist. Sect.*, 1950, 3, 21–39.

SINGER, J. L., WILENSKY, H., & McCRAVEN, V. G. Delaying capacity, fantasy, and planning ability: A factorial study of some basic ego functions. *J. consult. Psychol.*, 1956, 20, 375–383.

STOTSKY, B. A. Factor analysis of Rorschach scores of schizophrenics. *J. clin. Psychol.*, 1957, 13, 275–278.

VERNIER, CLAIRE M., STAFFORD, J. W., & KRUGMAN, A. D. A factor analysis of indices from four projective techniques associated with four different types of physical pathology. *J. consult. Psychol.*, 1958, 22, 433–439.

WEBB, W., & HILDEN, A. H. Verbal and intellectual ability as factors in projective test results. *J. proj. Tech.*, 1953, 17, 102–103.

WILLIAMS, H. L., & LAWRENCE, J. F. Further investigation of Rorschach determinants subjected to factor analysis. *J. consult. Psychol.*, 1953, 17, 261–264.

WILLIAMS, H. L., & LAWRENCE, J. F. Comparison of the Rorschach and MMPI by means of factor analysis. *J. consult. Psychol.*, 1954, 18, 193–197.

WITTENBORN, J. R. A factor analysis of discrete responses to the Rorschach ink blots. *J. consult. Psychol.*, 1949, 13, 335–340.

WITTENBORN, J. R. A factor analysis of Rorschach scoring categories. *J. consult. Psychol.*, 1950, 14, 261–267. (a)

WITTENBORN, J. R. Level of mental health as a factor in the implications of Rorschach scores. *J. consult. Psychol.*, 1950, 14, 469–472. (b)

WITTENBORN, J. R. Some comments on confounded correlations among Rorschach scores. *J. consult. Psychol.*, 1959, 23, 75–77.

ZUBIN, J., & ERON, L. Experimental abnormal psychology (prelim. ed.). New York: New York State Psychiatric Institute, 1953.

24

A Brief Description of the Holtzman Ink Blot Test[1]

WAYNE H. HOLTZMAN

Dissatisfied with the problems attendant on the use of the Rorschach technique as a psychometric instrument, Holtzman has formulated a new instrument: the Holtzman Inkblot Test. This test overcomes certain difficulties of the Rorschach due to the low reliability of scores by defining a broader range of scores, e.g., three levels of form appropriateness in place of the single F+ or F— scores of Beck. Reliability is also increased by the use of 45 cards instead of 10. Last, the obtaining of but one response per card assures that the frequency of occurrence of the various determinant scores will not be related to the number of responses given, a problem in the interpretation of most Rorschach protocols.

These improvements are not accompanied, however, by the badly needed reform for the method of inquiry. As Baughman has shown (reproduced in this book, Chap. 17), most subjects do not know the determinants of their perceptions. The best method of finding the determinants of response would, therefore, appear to be perceptual discrimination rather than verbal report. In this sense, the use of the traditional method of inquiry with an otherwise greatly improved test is analogous to attempting to get by with old, low-octane gas for a new, high-horsepower vehicle.

[1] Initial impetus for this research was given the writer by a Faculty Research Fellowship from the Social Science Research Council, Inc., of New York. More recently the research program has been supported by a grant-in-aid from the Hogg Foundation for Mental Health, the University of Texas.

417

The fundamental question of how to develop psychometrically sound scoring procedures for responses to ink blots while also preserving the rich qualitative projective material of the Rorschach has been approached from a new point of view at the University of Texas.[1] The major modifications undertaken consist of greatly increasing the number of ink blots, while limiting the number of responses per card to one, and extending the variety of stimulus colors, pattern, and shadings used in the original Rorschach materials. From an exploratory study, it was concluded that a test containing 45 ink blots, to each of which only one response is given, would be feasible to construct and would probably tap essentially the same variables as the classical Rorschach method. Special efforts might have to be made, however, to develop materials which have high "pulling power" for responses using small details, space, and color and shading attributes to compensate for the tendency to give form-determined wholes as the first response to an ink blot.

Such a test would have several advantages over the standard Rorschach: (1) The number of responses per individual would be relatively constant. (2) Each response would be given to an independent stimulus, avoiding the weaknesses inherent in the Rorschach, where all responses are lumped together regardless of whether they are given to the same or different ink blots. (3) Making a fresh start in the production of stimulus materials, especially in view of recent experimental studies of color, movement, shading, and other factors in ink-blot perception, would yield a richer variety of stimuli capable of eliciting much more information than the original 10 Rorschach plates. And finally, (4) a parallel form of the test could easily be constructed from item-analysis data in the experimental phases of test development, and adequate estimates of reliability could be obtained independently for each major variable.

The research to date has borne out all original expectations. Two matched alternate forms, A and B, of the Holtzman Inkblot Test have been developed, each containing 45 ink blots. Two additional blots are common to both forms of the test and appear as practice blots before the others. Instructions to the subject are similar to those used in the standard Rorschach, with the exceptions that the subject is asked to give just the primary response to each card, and a brief, simple inquiry is made after each response where necessary to clarify the location or determinants. Administration of the test is easier than the Rorschach, and the subject generally finds that giving only one response per card is a fairly simple task.

Six major variables are scored for each response, while a number of minor variables or qualitative signs are scored when deemed appropriate.

The major variables were selected and defined according to the following criteria: (1) The variable had to be one which could be scored for any legitimate response. Variables which occurred only rarely were set aside for the moment. (2) The variable had to be sufficiently objective to permit high scoring agreement among trained individuals. (3) The variable had to show some a priori promise of being pertinent to the study of personality through perception. And (4) each variable must be logically independent of the others. Location, Form Appropriateness, Form Definiteness, Color, Shading, and Movement Energy Level were selected for intensive study and provided the basis for item analyses in the final selection and matching of ink blots for Forms A and B.

Location as a variable was defined strictly in terms of the amount of blot used and the extent to which the natural Gestalt of the blot was broken up by the response. A three-point weighting system was adopted, with o for wholes, 1 for large details, and 2 for small areas, making possible a theoretical range of scores from o to 90.

The scoring of color was based entirely on the apparent primacy or importance of color, including black, gray, and white, as a response determinant. When the subject named the color in his response, scoring was relatively simple. On rare occasions, when it was apparent that the response would have been highly improbable without the presence of color, credit for color was given even though never mentioned by the subject. A four-point system similar to the Rorschach was adopted, with o for completely ignoring color and 3 for use of color as the sole determinant. Total scores for Color have a theoretical range from o to 135.

While subtle distinctions in the different uses of shading as a determinant are usually made in the Rorschach, no such differentiations are made in the Holtzman Inkblot Test. As with Color, the scoring of Shading was based solely on the apparent primacy of shading as a determinant. Because pure shading responses are so rare, only a three-point scoring system was used, yielding a theoretical range from o to 90.

The scoring of movement is linked closely to content in most contemporary scoring systems for the Rorschach. Too frequently such practices lead to highly arbitrary convention as to whether or not movement is scored or how it is scored. In the Klopfer system (Klopfer & Kelley, 1942), for example, "airplane" and "bat" present difficult problems. Can you be sure the airplane is flying? Even when an airplane does fly, there is no movement of its parts and no movement relative to any frame of reference unless landscape is added. Is "bat" to be scored *FM* for animal movement, while "airplane" is scored *Fm* for inanimate movement, when both concepts are really precision alternatives rather than uniquely different responses? The resulting picture is often highly confusing from a psychometric point of view. The essential character of the movement response is the energy level or dynamic quality of it rather than the particular content. Leaning heavily on Zubin (Zubin & Eron, 1953), Sells (Sells, Frese, & Lancaster, 1952), and Wilson (1952), a five-point scale was adopted, varying from o for no movement or potential for movement through static, casual, and dynamic movement to a weight of 4 for violent movement such as whirling or exploding. Movement Energy Level ranges theoretically from o to 180.

Different authorities vary in the extent to which concept elaborations and specifications are confounded with the goodness of fit of the concept to the form of the ink blot. In the Holtzman Inkblot Test, Form Definiteness was defined independently of form level in the usual sense; it refers solely to the definiteness or specificity of the form of the concept represented in the response, disregarding completely the characteristics of the ink blot. Working independently with a large number of concepts culled from ink-blot responses, five psychologists placed them in rank order with the most form-definite concept at the top. The independent sets of ranked concepts were then merged to yield an overall rank order for the entire list. Cutting points were chosen so that five levels of form definiteness could be distinguished. The resulting set of examples served as a scoring manual, with a weight of o for the most indefinite concepts, such as anatomy drawing, squashed bug, or fire, and a weight of 4 for the most definite concepts, such as Indian chief, violin, or knight with a shield. Form Definiteness has a theoretical range from o to 180.

Form Appropriateness, the last of the six major variables, is by its very nature a subjective variable, requiring extensive preliminary work to make scoring reasonably objective. And yet it is this very subjectivity which gives the variable great theoretical importance. Beck (1944) recognized the likelihood that goodness of fit of the concept to the form of the ink blot would be closely related to degree of contact with reality and undertook a major study of form level that has proved to be one of the most valuable contributions to the Rorschach. Considerable effort was spent in arriving at acceptable standards for scoring Form Appropriateness. Different responses to each ink blot were listed separately for each location and rated independently by at least three judges. A seven-point scale was used, with o representing extremely poor fit. Although there was good agreement of judges in most cases, a final judgment for each response was reached only after full discussion in conference. The resulting manual provides a guide to the scoring of Form Appropriateness on a three-point system, with o for unusually poor form and 2 for unusually good form. Form Appropriateness can range theoretically from o to 90.

The agreement among independent but well-trained scorers for a sample of 46 records proved in general to be very high: product-moment correlations of .99 for Location, Form Definiteness, and Movement Energy Level, .97 for Shading, .95 for Color, and .91 for Form Appropriateness. Good estimates of reliability based on internal consistency were obtained by using Gulliksen's (1950) matched random subtest method. Correlations ranged from .80 for Form Appropriateness to .91 for Shading. All six variables proved to be reasonably normal and continuous in distribution. Studies are now under way to determine the correlations between Forms A and B with several time intervals and populations of subjects.

Once the standardization of the Holtzman Inkblot Test is complete, it should be possible to develop specialized multiple-choice versions of tests for measuring variables of particular interest. Seymour Fisher and Sidney Cleveland (1958), have already had some success in developing a series of multiple-choice items, to be used with 40 of Holtzman's ink blots, which yields a measure of their Barrier Score. The particular ink blots used were selected on the basis of earlier item-analysis data so that each blot would be accompanied by three fairly acceptable choices, one representing a barrier response (such as "a knight in armor"), one representing a penetration response (such as "X ray"), and one which was neutral (such as "flower"). The subject was asked to check the one he liked most and place a different mark on the one he liked least, leaving the third choice blank. Both the Group Rorschach and the new multiple-choice test were given to 60 college students by Fisher and Cleveland. The correlation between the two sets of Barrier Scores was .64[2]. This fairly high correlation, coupled with the fact that the distribution of scores on the multiple-choice test was much greater than on the Rorschach and was more normally shaped, suggests that the multiple-choice Barrier Score would be superior to the measure reported earlier by Fisher and Cleveland (1958).

---

[2] Personal communication from Dr. Sidney E. Cleveland.

REFERENCES

BECK, S. J. Rorschach's test: I. Basic processes. New York: Grune & Stratton, 1944.

FISHER, S., & CLEVELAND, S. E. Body image and personality. Princeton: Van Nostrand, 1958.

GULLIKSEN, H. Theory of mental tests. New York: Wiley, 1950.

KLOPFER, B., & KELLEY, D. M. The Rorschach technique. Yonkers-on-Hudson, N.Y.: World Book Co., 1942.

SELLS, S. B., FRESE, F. J., JR., & LANCASTER, W. H. Research on the psychiatric selection of flying personnel. II. Progress on development of SAM group ink-blot test. Project No. 21–37–002, No. 2, Randolph Field, Texas: USAF School of Aviation Medicine, April, 1952.

WILSON, G. P. Intellectual indicators in the Rorschach test. Unpublished doctoral dissertation, Univer. of Texas, 1952.

ZUBIN, J., & ERON, L. Experimental abnormal psychology. (Prelim. ed.) New York: New York State Psychiatric Institute, 1953.

PART III

THEMATIC TESTS

25

Uses of the Thematic Apperception Test[1]

HENRY A. MURRAY

Murray here takes the opportunity, on the basis of extensive experience with the TAT, to state his beliefs as to what it can and cannot do. He points out that the stories are potent predictors, not of overt behavior, but rather of that which the subject cannot or will not reveal about himself. Note the contrasting position to that of Allport (Chap. 3), who believes that projective tests display this power only with neurotic individuals, whereas normal individuals tell you quite openly whatever might be derived from their projective protocols. In the opinion of the editor (Chap. 4), the research so far favors Allport's view in so far as content analysis is concerned. Whether formal analysis will prove able to pierce successfully the defenses of relatively emotionally intact persons remains to be demonstrated.

The reader should note also the rather modest assumptions put forth by Murray compared to other adherents of the TAT. Bellak, for example, disagreeing with Murray, does not believe that the TAT may contain much chaff. According to him (Bellak, 1950), it is all wheat or nearly so if interpreted correctly. The argument is more semantic than real. What is "wheat" or "chaff" depends on what one is looking for. Possibly another thousand studies may reveal all kinds of subtleties of response that are not apparent now. The real question is, what is the quality of wheat (information) obtained by analysis of the response as compared to the cost of manufacture (analysis)? With this criterion, one must agree that much of the TAT harvest in the past has contained a goodly portion of chaff.

---

[1] Read at the 106th annual meeting of The American Psychiatric Association, Detroit, Michigan, May 1–5, 1950.

The choice of "projective techniques" as topic for the theoretical section
at the 1950 meeting of The American Psychiatric Association is another
heartening sign — an authoritative sign — of multiplying articulations
of interest and purpose between practitioners of psychiatry and practitioners of psychology. It seems that the older and more venerable of
the two professions is today both secure enough and magnanimous
enough to give the bumptious younger one an opportunity to speak up
and be heard.

The choice of this topic also indicates, it seems to me, a mounting
enthusiasm among psychiatrists for investigations of a strictly psychological sort in addition to the ever-important researches of a physiological
sort.

I would be not a little embarrassed to devote, as I will now, all
the allotted time to a test with which my name is sometimes linked,
if this test were not a product of more brains than mine. The germinal
suggestion for the TAT came from a brilliant student in abnormal
psychology at Radcliffe, Mrs. Cecilia Roberts,[2] and, during the first
phases of its development, much of the picture selection and picture
drawing, the administration and interpretation, was done by Mrs.
Christiana D. Morgan. Since then, a host of ladies and gentlemen—Drs.
White, Sanford, Tomkins, Bellak, Henry, Rapaport, Stein, Rosenzweig,
and others—have succeeded more than I have in shaping its character.

This afternoon, with your tolerance, I shall assume the role of
protagonist and, to sharpen the argument, put forth the preposterous
proposition that the psychiatrist *himself*—particularly the psychoana-
lytically trained psychiatrist—should learn the simple art of administering and interpreting the TAT.

My first reason for suggesting this is tinged with selfish prejudice.
Having a certain sentimental regard for the TAT, I am anxious that
the young lady be given every opportunity for refinement and for the
exhibition eventually of all her potential charms and talents. Without
the aid of the psychoanalyst, this goal is scarcely attainable, because
not only is the analyst in the best relational position to kindle the
patient's whole capacity for projective story telling, but with the
knowledge he acquires from free associations and dream analyses, he,
more than anyone, is capable of discriminating grain from chaff in the
TAT stories, and thus of laying hold on the facts required for the
construction of dependable principles of interpretation.

---

[2] Now Mrs. Crane Brinton.

Whatever peculiar virtue the TAT may have, if any, it will be found to reside, not, as some have assumed, in its power to mirror overt behavior or to communicate what the patient knows and is willing to tell, but rather in its capacity to reveal things that the patient is unwilling to tell or is unable to tell because he is unconscious of them. Since it is only the depth therapist who, in the regular course of his work, exposes components of the personality that have been unconscious to the patient, it is only the depth psychotherapist who is in a position to validate the most significant inferences drawn from the TAT stories. Thus, further straight-line progress in the development of this technique depends to a considerable extent on whether or not a few competent psychiatrists will decide that the TAT is a strategic instrument for explorations of subterranean mental processes.

More specifically and more cogently, I would recommend the use of this device at the start, in the middle, and at the end of courses of therapy: first of all as an aid in identifying suppressed and repressed dispositions and conflicts and in defining, as Bellak (1950) has suggested, the nature of the patient's resistances to these dispositions; second, as a therapeutic agent, since the stories, like dreams, provide admirable starting points for free associations; third, as a means of estimating the effects of therapy; and fourth, as an instrument of research, especially in the psychosomatic disorders.

Administration

Although the TAT is rarely administered as I believe it should be, the technique is very simple, if you happen to be the kind of person who is disposed to hearten people in their creative efforts. All you have to do is to recite a short paragraph of plain instructions and with an encouraging expression—I won't say a grin—hand the patient Picture No. 1.

In order to prevent the much too common occurrence of more or less irrelevant reactions—such as mere descriptions of parts of the picture—we at the Harvard Clinic have adopted the practice of requesting the patient to examine the picture carefully for about 20 seconds and then put it aside.

Also, in order to facilitate the establishment in the patient of a single individual point of orientation through identification with a preferred figure, we ask him or her to choose a proper name for the chief character before proceeding with the story.

It is often necessary, after the completion of the first story, to repeat some of the directions, explaining unambiguously to the patient that every story he tells must have a plot with a definite ending. But after this—except for an occasional guiding comment and some judicious praise—the administrator should not say anything until ten stories have been told and the hour is over.

If properly "warmed up," most subjects (instructed to devote about 5 minutes to each response) will tell stories that are 200 words or more in length (as recorded, say, on a dictaphone). Although there are certainly some psychotics and an occasional neurotic who cannot be induced under ordinary circumstances—say, without the administration of a drug—to tell stories of this length, or even to speak at all, we consider that to come out with stories averaging less than 200 words apiece usually indicated that the rapport between administrator and the patient and/or the "warming up" process were defective.

At the moment, we are testing the effectiveness of other directions given to the testee. Instead of asking for one long story, we request the subject to respond to each picture by presenting the outline of as many plots as possible. Although something is lost by this method, something is gained: we obtain about seventy themes instead of twenty. It is too early to say whether, on the average, the gains outweigh the losses.

Test Material

Physically speaking, as some of you may know, the TAT is no more nor less than a set of nineteen pictures and one blank card arranged in a definite order.

The advantages of keeping the stimulus conditions of a test uniform—of presenting, say, an unchanging set of pictures in an unchanging sequence—are generally known and appreciated. No argument for this principle seems necessary today, despite the fact that the majority of TAT workers, as far as I can determine, have not seen fit to abide by it.

Unless we accept *this* amount of standardization, it will not be possible to do what we so often want to do: compare the responses of one subject, or of one class of subjects, or of one social group, with the responses of other subjects, classes, social groups. Every TAT worker knows that the kinds of responses—in this case, stories—that he gets are largely determined by the characteristics of the pictures. In order to raise the proportion, say, of homicidal and suicidal themes, one has only to introduce one new element in one picture—a gun leaning against a wall.

In view of these weighty considerations, we TAT workers might be disposed to stick to the standard set of pictures, were it not that so many of us believe that some of these pictures are not as significantly provocative as they might be. We can hardly doubt, for example, that Thompson and Bachrach (1949) are correct in stating that color increases the stimulating power of the pictures. The introduction of two or three abstract or symbolic pictures—less definite, less structured—might also improve the series.

It is not unlikely that the deeper layers of fantasy would be more successfully invited by pictures that were less closely related to settings and personages of everyday American life. A foreign landscape, a fairy-tale scene, or an animal picture might arouse fewer defenses than do some of the pictures now in use. Furthermore, as Shakow[3] and others have pointed out, certain often-critical conditions—such as sibling rivalry, separation from a supporting person, and so forth—are not suggested by any of the pictures in the present collection. Finally, in order to avoid antagonizing subjects who have æsthetic sensibilities, it is evident that several of the Harvard pictures must be redrawn, and all of them should be more satisfyingly reproduced.

Thus, we have two conflicting aims: one, to establish and agree to use a standard set of pictures, and two, to improve the present set. These aims, as I see them, can be reconciled only by delegating to an elected committee the responsibility of judging whether or not each new picture submitted for membership in the series is more effective than the least effective picture in current use.

In terms of what criteria should these judgments be made? In my opinion, the most readily obtainable criteria—length, vividness, and dramatic intensity of the stories—criteria proposed by Symonds (1949), Thompson and Bachrach (1949), and others—are not at all dependable. What we really need to know is how much each picture commonly contributes to an understanding of the patient's latent, repressed, and unconscious dispositions. Since the TAT is not designed to exhibit the overt action patterns of people, the possession by any picture of this kind of virtuosity is almost wholly irrelevant. If the TAT selection committee agrees with this opinion, the data they will require in appraising the effectiveness of any picture can be obtained only through an extensive study of the covert personalities of a large number of subjects who have taken the test.

Besides an improved set of 20 to 30 pictures for general use, I would strongly recommend several special sets, of 4 or 5 pictures each, for testing the presence of specific dispositions or complexes.

Constituents of TAT Stories

The efficacy of the TAT, like that of most projection tests, depends on the degree to which the following assumptions are valid.

---

[3] Personal communication.

1. In characterizing the hero of a story and in portraying his actions and reactions, the storyteller will commonly utilize some of the components, conscious or unconscious, of his own past or present personality—for example, an assumption, an expectation, an idea, a feeling, an evaluation, a need, a plan, or a fantasy that he has experienced or entertained.

2. In characterizing the other major figures of a dramatic narrative and in portraying their actions and reactions, the storyteller will commonly utilize some of the personality components (as he has apperceived them) of persons—such as parents, siblings, rivals, loved objects—with whom he has had, or is having significant interactions.

Not infrequently, some of the depicted qualities and reactions of the other major characters will be derived from once-fantasied figures—inventions of the child's imagination—rather than from apperceptions of actual people; or they may be derived from aspects of the storyteller's own personality (as in the first assumption). That is to say, the interactions in a story may involve two different parts—two subsystems—of the subject's total self.

3. In constructing the plot, describing the endeavors of the hero, his transactions with the other major figures, and the outcome and final consequences of these efforts and interactions, the storyteller will commonly utilize memory traces, conscious or unconscious, of some of the actual or fantasied events that have exerted a significant influence on his development.

Note that these are not only very modest assumptions—assumptions that have been made by generations of literary critics—but that they have been repeatedly demonstrated.

According to the three stated propositions, only a fraction—as a rule a relatively small fraction—of the aggregate of words, phrases, and sentences that make up a set of stories represent important constituents (as defined above) of the patient's past or present personality. As a rule, most of the obtained material consists of statements that are not representative of anything that needs to be included in a formulation of his personality. In short, the larger fraction of the protocol is chaff; the smaller fraction, grain. The crucial question—how does one thresh out the grain from these stalks of stories—will be discussed shortly.

The assumption that a set of TAT stories will contain a fair amount of grain—sometimes a large amount of rich grain—cannot be verified by observing the subject's behavior in everyday life. The patterns of the imagination and the patterns of public conduct are more apt to be related by contrast than by conformity. But the psychiatrist can prove to himself and others how much real grain is concealed in TAT stories by waiting a few months until he has acquired a great deal of information and feels thoroughly at home in his patient's stream of consciousness.

If then, at this later date, he examines the set of stories, with mind alert to every symbolic possibility, he will almost surely discover that a good deal of what he has learned during the course of the analysis is there, varyingly disguised, in the stories.

Of course, some important things, as Tomkins (1949) and Bellak (1950) have pointed out, will not be found there. Two hours of story-telling is not enough to reveal all the important potentialities of a person; and besides this, the ego has its defenses that operate even when self-consciousness is half-lost in the process of composing dramatic plots.

If, say, in the middle of an analysis, the psychiatrist uses the critical elements and incidents in the stories as points of departure for free associations, and by tactful questioning discovers the known sources of as many items as possible, and then adds this information to the knowledge he has already acquired, he will usually find that the grain—that is, the significant personal references in the stories—can be assigned to one or more of the following periods of the life history.

1. *Testing period.* The TAT protocol is likely to include some indica-tion of the patient's apperception, appraisal, and reaction to the total testing situation and/or, more specifically, the administrator of the test.

2. *Current period.* Many of the TAT grains are straight or distorted representations of constituents of what historians call the "specious present." That is, they portray the patient's evaluations, emotional reac-tions, and expectations in relation to the ongoing course of events—the events that in the last days, weeks, or months have most frequently or intensely affected him.

3. *Past periods.* Of these, the period of childhood is perhaps most important from a therapeutic standpoint.

According to our experience, almost all TAT protocols contain grains that can be interpreted as symbolic representations of childhood occurrences. I would be surprised if there were any traumatic event or complex known to child psychology that has not been found in some disguised form in TAT protocols.

So much for the constituents of TAT stories and the periods of the life history from which they are commonly derived.

Let us now turn to the as-yet-unsolved, or only partly solved, problem of how to pick the significant elements and forms out of a web of irrelevancies, when one's knowledge of the patient's past history and character is nil.

Here I must be brief. Time is running out. The most dependable criteria, I submit, for distinguishing the relevant elements and forms in a set of stories are the following.

1. *Symbolic significance:* i.e., an element or thematic structure that resembles in some familiar way an element or theme that is known to

be very commonly important in childhood. Here I am referring to plausible inferences based on our knowledge of the principles of dream interpretation.

2. *Repetition*: i.e., an element or theme that recurs three or more times in the series of stories.

3. *Uniqueness*: by referring to the set of norms recently published by Rosenzweig (1949), the inexperienced interpreter can, for the first time, make use of this criterion.

4. *Interrelatedness*: i.e., an element or theme that is known to be mutually related with an element or theme that has already been judged to be significant (according to one of the three above-listed criteria).

5. *Subject's self-involvement*: i.e., indications that the subject's emotions—interests or defenses—were excited when mentioning a certain element or during the entire composition or part of it.

So much for the huge subject of diagnosis.

This brings me to the end of my allotted time and the end of the most condensed summary I could contrive of the Thematic Apperception Test and its uses.

REFERENCES

BELLAK, L. Thematic apperception: Failures and the defenses. *Trans. N.Y. Acad. Sci.*, 1950, 12, 122–126.

ROSENZWEIG, S. Apperceptive norms for the thematic apperception test. *J. Pers. Psych.* 1949, 17, 475–482.

SYMONDS, P. *Adolescent fantasy.* New York: Columbia Univer. Press, 1949.

THOMPSON, C. E., & BACHRACH, A. J. The use of color in the thematic apperception test. Paper presented at the Annual Meeting of the American Association for the Advancement of Science, New York, 1949.

TOMKINS, S. S. The present status of the thematic apperception test. *Am. J. Orthopsychiat.*, 1949, 19, 358–362.

26

Thematic Apperceptive Measurement of Motives within the Context of a Theory of Motivation

JOHN W. ATKINSON

In this well-written paper, Atkinson describes his theoretical approach to the measurement of motives within the context of a theory of motivation. Briefly stated, his approach involves holding incentive constant and assuming that a person's thematic response is then a multiplicative function of the motives aroused in him and his expectancies of goal attainment. In measuring achievement, it is expected that some pictures are more relevant to some individuals than others, but that, given a sample of pictures, these individual differences should cancel out. Atkinson thus states that a blue-collar worker might project more need achievement to a picture of a blue-collar worker than to that of a white-collar worker, whereas the converse might be true of a white-collar worker. In actuality, however, as Veroff (1961) and Murstein (1963) have subsequently shown, it is the cultural status of the character depicted, more than physical similarity, which determines the nature of the projection.

A more serious difficulty with his assumption is that it does not account for the relevancy of the picture to the particular motive structure of a given individual. In a study by Lesser, Krawitz, and Packard (1963), it was shown that some high-school girls project more achievement to pictures of women, while others project more to male pictures. The difference reflected the fact that overachieving women identified with women figures, while the lower achievers more traditionally identified with male figures. It is apparent, therefore, that optimum stimuli for measuring a particular motive in a given individual can be most appro-

priately known only by prior knowledge of the subject. While this fact limits the prediction of individual behavior without extensive preknowledge of the individual, such would appear to be the "projective" facts of life. What is suggested, therefore, is that the use of the TAT as a narrow-band instrument is favored only when earlier background information helps to pinpoint the interpretation to be assigned to the thematic stories.

Can we turn now to the measuring instrument and see it in the context of ideas about motivation and behavior suggested by the empirical findings of studies which have used it to assess the strength of motivation? Thematic apperception is, after all, a particular kind of behavior. One test of the adequacy of some of the ideas which have been advanced is to see whether or not they can be used to provide at least the outline of a theory of the measuring instrument, one which will help to define the path for further research aimed at increasing the validity of inferences about motivation drawn from imaginative behavior.

One potential value of an analysis of the measuring instrument is coming face to face with the fact that the problems of assessing individual differences in motivation and the problems faced in the search for general laws relating motivation and behavior are completely intertwined. Lewin has made the oft-neglected point as clearly as anyone:

> A law is expressed in an equation which relates certain variables. Individual differences have to be conceived as various specific values which these variables have in a specific case. In other words, general laws and individual differences are merely two aspects of one problem; they are mutually dependent on each other and the study of one cannot proceed without the study of the other (1951, p. 243).

Three important questions are to be considered: What is a need or motive?[1] How is the strength of a particular motive related to overt adaptive behavior? And how is the fact of a changing level of motivational content in thematic apperceptive stories, both as a function of systematic changes in the situation at the time of testing and of the pictures used to elicit stories, to be reconciled with the conception of a motive, or need, as a relatively stable and enduring attribute of personality? (A fourth question, the historical issue of how motives

---

[1] These two terms have been used interchangeably throughout the book. The term *motive* is, however, preferred because it does not imply that activation and direction of behavior are necessarily linked to conditions of deprivation. Of all the possibilities available, the term *motive* seems the most general in its connotation.

are acquired, has been dealt with more fully elsewhere by McClelland, Atkinson, Clark, & Lowell, 1953, Chaps. II and IX).

The only feasible way to deal with all three questions is to take them one at a time and to try to keep the others from intruding until it is their turn for discussion. The plan is to review ideas which have been presented in earlier portions of Atkinson (1958) and to present rather dogmatically what is admittedly an incomplete conceptual scheme. In the process, we shall point to the empirical findings that seem, at the moment, to demand such a scheme. Along the way, we shall try to uncover the problems for future research which the scheme suggests.

What Is a Need or Motive?

The conception of a need, or a motive, as a relatively enduring disposition of personality was developed by Murray et al. (1953) in an attempt to formulate a comprehensive system for description of personality. The core of personality, as viewed by Murray, is a configuration or hierarchy of basic needs. McClelland (1951) has extended and elaborated the general argument for this theoretical position, particularly in his analysis of the origins of motivational dispositions in the primary learning experiences of childhood.

A motive, or need, is a disposition to strive for a particular kind of goal state or aim, e.g., achievement, affiliation, power. The aim of a particular motive is a particular kind of effect to be brought about through some kind of action. The aim of a motive defines the kind of satisfaction that is sought, e.g., pride in accomplishment, a positive affective relationship with another person, a sense of being in control of the means of influencing the behavior of other persons. The attainment of a goal state is accompanied by feelings of satisfaction; disruption of goal-directed activity, or nonattainment of a desired goal state, is accompanied by feelings of dissatisfaction. The aim of a motive is not identified with performance of particular kinds of acts, such as approval seeking or attempts at influence, or with particular qualities of instrumental action, such as persistence or rigidity. A particular kind or quality of instrumental action may, however, come to be associated with attainment of the aim of a particular motive and hence provide a fairly reliable clue to the presence of that motive. The question of how many basic motives it may be useful to consider and the problem of what criteria are relevant for deciding on a limited set of basic motives are matters beyond the scope of the present discussion. These issues have been dealt with at length by both Murray et al. (1938) and McClelland (1951). It is doubtful whether anything new can be added to their discussion of this problem before empirical studies directly pertinent to it are undertaken to provide something concrete to talk about.

The linkage between affective reactions and the attainment or non-attainment of goals has made it possible to clarify the definition of the aims, or goal states, of particular motives by experiment. When a particular kind of motivation is experimentally aroused, thematic apperceptive stories produced by the motivated person contain elaborate imaginative descriptions of the kinds of circumstances which will produce feelings of satisfaction and dissatisfaction in him. The definitions of the goal states of three motives presented in Atkinson (1958, pp.-179-233) are hence to be viewed as *empirically derived* generalizations from analysis of hundreds of thematic apperceptive stories produced by persons in whom these motives had been experimentally aroused. In some cases, the initial task of clarifying the definitions of the aim of a motive has taken one to two years of repeated trial-and-check analysis of the material. The write-ups of experiments often fail to communicate the trial-and-check nature of the procedure.

McClelland (1951, Chap. 12) has produced a number of cogent arguments rooted in accepted principles of learning to support the view, advanced chiefly in psychoanalytic writings, that motives are developed early in childhood and become relatively stable attributes of personality which are highly resistant to change. Implicit in the studies reported by Atkinson (1958) is an assumption that the motives of an individual are relatively stable dispositions which he carries about with him from situation to situation. This conception of a motive poses two problems: (1) How are motives related to overt adaptive behavior? (2) If the strength of a motive is a relatively stable thing, how can it be measured through thematic apperception when the motivational content of thematic apperception is extremely sensitive to situational influences?

How Is the Strength of a Particular Need or Motive Related to Overt Adaptive (*i.e., Instrumental*) Behavior?

Let us, for the moment, assume that the index of the strength of a particular motive as obtained from thematic apperception in a "neutral" situation *is* a valid measure of the strength of a relatively stable disposition, acquired early in life, to strive for a particular goal state. We shall make a thorough analysis of the measuring rod, itself, in the next section and examine this assumption critically. But for now, let us accept it in order to turn to the question of the relation of motives to behavior.

Do we always expect the individual's motives to be clearly manifested in his overt behavior? Do we expect the person who is highly motivated to achieve always to show concentration in the task at hand, a heightened desire to perform well, a willingness to persist in the face of obstacles? Do we expect the person who is strong in the need for affiliation constantly to display approval-seeking tendencies in his actions? Do we expect the person who is high in the power motive invariably to attempt to influence the behavior and opinions of others?

The intuitive answer to these questions, when put in so bald a form, is obviously no; and experimental findings (Atkinson 1958) confirm our intuition that the answer should be no. We find that the situation at the time of performance somehow defines the relevance or functional significance of alternative paths of action for the individual. Our theoretical task, then, is to conceptualize the effect of the situation in a way that will clarify the problem for further experimental analysis. This, hopefully, may lead to a technique for independent and more precise assessment of the salient features of situations which have a profound influence on behavior. Here we come face to face with the stubborn problem of the interaction of personality and situation as it arises in studies of the effects of human motives on behavior. And to solve the problem, we have adapted several ideas developed over the years chiefly by Tolman (1951, 1955). Our analysis of the situation pursues a course that is similar in many respects to that also developed in the recent writings of Rotter (1954, 1955).[2]

Our experiments have suggested that a particular motive (e.g., n Achievement) is aroused or engaged in performance of an act when the cues of the situation can be interpreted to mean that performance of the act will be instrumental in attaining some satisfaction (an incentive) of that particular motive. In other words, when the situation seems to arouse in the person a *cognitive expectancy* (now to use Tolman's concept) that performance of the act will produce an effect he is generally interested in bringing about, his motive is aroused and manifested in overt performance of the act. The influence of the situation seems to be reducible to the kinds and relative strengths of the cognitive expectancies it arouses in a person (given his recent life history) concerning the possible rewarding or punishing consequences (given his motives) of this versus that path of action. Rotter (1955) has directed attention to the central role of the situation in defining the *expectancies* and *reinforcement values* (incentives) which determine behavior. The present conception tends to highlight the role of individual differences in the strength of motives.

To simplify the present analysis of the interaction between personality (motive) and situation (expectancy of goal attainment), we will assume that incentive, i.e., the amount of satisfaction of a motive offered in a situation, is held constant. Obviously the amount of satisfaction of

---

[2] See also the clarifications of expectancy theory presented by MacCorquodale and Meehl (1953; 1954).

a motive can vary from situation to situation, just as the degree to which any satisfaction expected from that motive can vary from situation to situation. But the present "limited" conception will ignore possible variations in the value of the incentive. (Elsewhere [Atkinson, 1958, Chaps. 20 and 22], we have attempted to deal with the specific effects of variations in the incentive to achieve, the special case where incentive value is dependent on the strength of expectancy.)

Where does our conception of the role of the situation in the determination of behavior lead us? It can be assumed that every individual has acquired a number of different kinds of motives. And any particular situation in which he may find himself—e.g., a college classroom, a business office, a walk in the park with a friend, a luncheon with strangers—is likely to arouse a number of different cognitive expectancies concerning possible consequences of performing this or that act. It may be expected, for example, that a pleasant comment about the weather will provoke a positive reaction in a stranger at lunch but have little, if any, rewarding consequence if produced while one is working alone late at night in one's business office. On the other hand, it may be expected that silent concentration on the task at hand will move one closer to that sense of pride in accomplishment sought on the job, but the same degree of silent concentration on the task of eating one's lunch may be expected to heighten interpersonal tension rather than to contribute to the affiliative satisfaction of a friendly luncheon conversation.

Some situations arouse expectancies of satisfying different motives through performance of different acts: the college student torn between continued study in his room and going to the movie with his friends. In such cases, the individual experiences a conflict between the two tendencies to act which have been aroused in him: one instrumental to achievement, the other to affiliation. When, on the other hand, the cues of a situation arouse expectancies of simultaneously satisfying several different motives through performance of the same act, these several different motives should be engaged in performance of the same act. The resultant behavior should then reflect the combined strengths of the several motives which have been engaged. The total strength of motivation to perform the act will be greater than the strength contributed by any one of the particular motives which has been engaged. The behavior, in other words, is *overdetermined*.

This discussion of how the motives of an individual are engaged by expectancies aroused in a situation may seem to imply that the person is completely conscious of his decision-making processes. Such an implication is certainly not intended. Both the motives of the individual and the expectancies aroused in him are inferences to be made from relevant and independent observations of his past behavior i.e., from a survey of his developmental history or from behavior as recorded on some instrument specially designed for assessment of motives or expectancies. What a person consciously experiences when a motive is aroused is an interesting empirical question for future study. Our hunch is that the motivated person will report only the feeling of wanting to perform some act and certain images pertaining to the consequences of the act when asked to describe his inner experience.

We see here the need for a distinction in terminology. The term *motive* (or *need*) has been used to refer to dispositions to strive for rather general goal states, kinds of satisfaction, or effects. These dispositions, it is assumed, have their origins in childhood experience and are relatively stable and enduring after childhood. They are carried about from situation to situation by the adult and constitute the core of what is called personality. Our discussion has suggested that these dispositions be thought of as latent, with respect to overt adaptive behavior, until the cues of a situation arouse the appropriate expectancy of goal attainment through performance of some act. The cognitive expectancies cued off in particular situations are also acquired. But we assume that specific expectancies of attaining this or that goal through performance of this or that act in a particular situation are normally acquired later than motives, that expectancies can be acquired through verbal training, as well as through actual experience, and that the more situationally defined expectancies are more amenable to change than the more general motive dispositions. Expectancies, in other words, are the stuff of which beliefs, social norms, and social roles are made.

But to return to the need for a distinction in terminology: if the term *motive* refers to the more general and relatively stable disposition, what shall we call a person's *temporarily aroused state* produced when the cues of a situation elicit an expectancy of goal attainment which engages the motive? I should like to use the term which immediately comes to mind to designate the aroused state: *motivation*. The term *motivation* refers to the arousal of a tendency to act to produce one or more effects. The term *motivation* points to the final strength of the action tendency which is experienced by the person as an "I want to ———." The particular aim of the momentary state of motivation is situationally defined. It is specific and concrete; it is the aim of the moment, e.g., to get a high score on this test, to be warmly received by that person. The aims of the one or more motives which may be contributing to the momentary strength of motivation, on the other hand, are more general and refer to the kinds of experience of satisfaction that may be sought on the particular occasion. For example, one may experience strong *motivation* to eat a hamburger or a piece of lemon pie; the general aim of the *motive* is the satisfaction that accompanies eating something.

One may be strongly motivated to complete a task; the general aim of the motive may be a sense of personal accomplishment. The term *motivation* points to the over-all strength of the tendency to strive which has been aroused on this particular occasion. The term motive is used to define the functional significance of the striving in relation to the more general and relatively enduring dispositions of the individual. The term motive points to the one or more "meanings" of the act for the individual, *of which meanings he may be completely unaware.*

The distinction intended between motive as disposition and motivation as aroused state is presented schematically in Figure 26–1.[3]

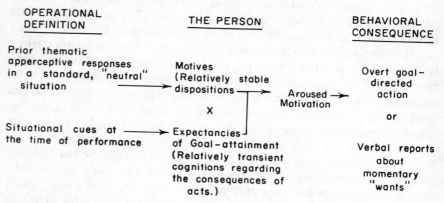

FIGURE 26–1. The interaction of the motives of an individual with the situation in the determination of the momentary strength of motivation to perform some act.

This conception of motivation to perform an act as a joint function of the motives of the individual and the expectancies of motive-satisfying consequences elicited by situational cues is supported by a number of experimental facts (Atkinson, 1958, pp. 270–349) which can be summarized briefly.

1. Performance is positively related to the thematic apperceptive index of the strength of a particular motive when the situation cues have aroused the expectancy of attaining the goal state of that motive through performance of the act and few or no other expectancies of goal attainment have been aroused. In this case, the strength of motivation to perform the act, as measured by response output or some equivalent index, should largely be a function of the strength of the one motive which has been systematically engaged.

2. Performance is unrelated to the strength of a particular motive

---

[3] As mentioned earlier, the effect of *incentive*, i.e., the amount of satisfaction of the motive offered in the situation, is not included in the present formulation. But the reader may note that many of the points that are made concerning the influence of expectancies on strength of motivation can be repeated concerning the effects of variations in incentive value.

when the cues of the situation have been deliberately rigged to mini-mize the probability that anyone would expect to satisfy *that* motive through performance of the act. In this case, motivation to perform the act must be attributed to various other unmeasured motives which are unsystematically engaged in performance of the act.

3. When the cues of a situation are deliberately controlled to arouse the expectancy of attaining the goal of a particular motive, but expectancies of satisfying other motives through performance of the same act are also systematically aroused, the relationship between performance and thematic apperceptive indices of the strength of the particular motive of interest is greatly reduced or washed out completely. In this case, the person who is weak in the particular motive which has been measured may be strong in some other motive which has also been systematically aroused. To the extent that several different motives are now contributing to the total motivation to perform the same act, a simple relationship between the strength of any one of them and performance is confounded.

Can we now point to other empirical findings that also fit the scheme?

One of the important results of Groesbeck's (1956) analysis of the personality correlates of thematic apperceptive indices of *n* Achievement and *n* Affiliation in the data accumulated by Kelly and Fiske (1951) in their assessment of clinical psychology trainees illustrates another implication of this conception. In the course of the assessment program, a group of prospective clinical trainees were brought together for a week-long period of testing and observation. During this period, they lived together and spent most of their leisure time in each other's company. Toward the end of the week, each individual was rated by his peers on a number of personality traits. Each individual was also rated on these same traits by a group of staff psychologists who had observed the trainees in a number of test situations and in interviews throughout the week.

Staff ratings were made chiefly in terms of behavior observed in achievement-oriented contexts, while trainees presumably had their best opportunity to size each other up in the interpersonal contexts of their leisure hours. When Groesbeck examined the personality correlates of these motives taken singly, he found that the staff ratings of the trainees were related almost exclusively to differences in *n* Achievement. Ratings by peers, on the other hand, were related almost as exclusively to differences in *n* Affiliation (1956, pp. 26 and 28). The result can reason-ably be attributed to the different kinds of expectancies of goal attainment normally aroused in the situations in which the most reliable observations by the two groups were likely to be made. The staff observed behavior aroused in the various test situations and so motivated to a great extent by *n* Achievement; the peers, on the other hand, were presumably basing their ratings on behavior motivated chiefly by *n*

Affiliation and other interpersonal motives engaged in the off-duty hours when they were more free to observe their associates. One may wonder, in the light of these suggestive findings, how general a description of personality in terms of behavioral ratings is ever likely to be when the behavior observed occurs in fairly circumscribed situations capable of arousing expectancies that make a limited appeal to the motivational structure of the individual.

One of the findings in a project dealing with conformity, reported by Walker and Heyns (1956), is also consistent with the present scheme. They report that subjects were put into a conflict in which continued hard work at a task, instrumental to personal accomplishment, was pitted against slowing up to satisfy the appeal of a friend and partner who was being put in a position of invidious comparison by the subject's high level of performance. A group of subjects who were classified high in n Affiliation but low in n Achievement showed the greatest tendency to be influenced by the appeal of the friend to slow down. In this case, expectancies of satisfying two different motives through performance of incompatible acts were aroused. A willingness to slow down should be expected in a group who are strong in n Affiliation but relatively weak in n Achievement. Along the same line, French (1956) has found that persons highly motivated to achieve but low in n Affiliation prefer a successful stranger to an unsuccessful friend as a work partner, while just the reverse is true of persons high in n Affiliation but low in n Achievement.

In the light of the present conception of the relationship between particular motives and overt behavior, it is not at all surprising that the correlations that have been reported between thematic apperceptive measures of particular motives and complex performance criteria like academic grade average are, at best, low to moderate (Morgan, 1953; Ricciuti & Sadacca, 1955) and vary from school to school. A high grade-point average in school or college is an *accomplishment* requiring performances which undoubtedly are overdetermined in the sense of involving more than one of the individual's motives. The strength of motivation to get good grades in school, for example, is in part a function of the strength of the achievement motive, but few will quarrel with the idea that performance in school is also perceived by many students as instrumental to gaining the approval of parents (affiliation) or as the path to an influential vocation (power), to list but two other possible "meanings" that working hard in school may have for particular individuals.

A more promising approach to investigation of factors which contribute to academic accomplishment, in light of the present analysis, would be to assess the expectations of particular individuals regarding the consequences of their working to get good grades. Such an assessment of expectations, together with thematic apperceptive measurement of the various motives which, as a result, may be engaged in academic work, should bring us much closer to the accurate prediction of academic success from motivational variables that we have been seeking for so long in a relatively blind empirical way. The same idea may be applied to many other instances in which an overdetermined performance criterion is to be predicted.

A Theoretical Conception of the Thematic Apperceptive Index of Motive Strength

Let us turn now to the question which we put aside earlier: How is the conception of motives as relatively enduring and stable dispositions to be reconciled with the fact that the level of motive-related imagery in thematic apperception, which provides the index of the strength of a motive, is not constant but varies as a function of systematic changes in the situation prior to administration of the test and of the pictures used to elicit stories? How, in other words, can the strength of a stable disposition be inferred from the frequency of particular kinds of imaginative responses when the frequency of such responses is known to vary?

These questions can be satisfactorily answered if the distinctions between *motive*, *expectancy*, and *aroused motivation* which we are forced to make in an analysis of instrumental action are now applied to the imaginative response of the subject to a particular picture. The fact that changes in average level of motivational imagery in stories occur as a result of certain experimental procedures and the idea of a relatively stable strength of motive can be reconciled if imaginative content is thought of as an expression of the *momentary state* of *aroused motivation* in the person.

According to our theoretical formulation, the momentary state of motivation is a changing thing. It is a joint function of a stable element—the motive—and a transient or changing element—the momentary expectancy of attaining some degree of satisfaction of the motive—which has been aroused by situational cues. When we refer to the total score for a particular kind of motivation (e.g., n-Achievement score) as obtained from a series of thematic apperceptive stories, we are referring to a summation of the amounts of that kind of motivation which has been expressed in a series of stories *in a particular situation, e.g., under certain experimental conditions*. The strength of motivation aroused by expectancies cued off by the situation is assumed to remain fairly constant throughout the 20- to 30-minute test period. When, on the other hand, we view the changing level of motive-related imaginative response from picture to picture *within* the test period, we are observing an additional effect on the level of motivation of particular expectancies aroused by the cues of different pictures. Our theoretical task, then, is to define the conditions, both situationwise and picturewise, under which the inferring of individual differences in strength of *motive* from observed differences in an index of strength of *motivation* is reasonably valid and to discover the conditions under which inferences about the strength of motive from this motivation score might be very erroneous.

Let us start with a generalization of the findings of experiments dealing with the effects of experimental arousal of motives on thematic apperception (Atkinson, 1958, Part I): when reasonable and generally acceptable procedures are used to arouse experimentally a particular kind of motivation by controlling the motivating cues prior to the test, the imaginative thought sequence is increasingly saturated with imagery that is expressive of that kind of motivation. The arousal of a particular kind of motivation is, in other words, accompanied by an increase in a particular *kind* of imaginative content.

According to the present theoretical formulation, the experimental procedures employed in these studies can be described as manipulating the cues which arouse particular kinds of expectancies, e.g., of having performance evaluated in terms of standards of excellence (achievement), of being liked or disliked by others (affiliation), etc. If we consider the over-all frequency of a particular kind of motivational content in a series of stories to be a measure of the strength of that kind of motivation in the person at the time of writing the stories, the index obtained in the so-called "neutral" or standard situation for assessing individual differences must represent the strength of that kind of motivation which has been aroused in that situation. In experiments dealing with the relationship of individual differences in strength of particular motives to behavior, the thematic apperceptive measure has normally been administered in a college classroom or some similar situation, and stories are written without any attempt by the experimenter either to arouse a particular motive prior to the test or deliberately to relax the subjects. Nevertheless, this so-called "neutral" situation is obviously not neutral with respect to the motives of the individual. The cues of a college classroom should arouse particular kinds of expectancies by virtue of the relatively limited range of kinds of satisfactions that have been experienced by individuals in such a situation.

We have been willing to proceed on the assumption that the kinds of expectancies cued off in the so-called neutral situation are very similar, i.e., relatively constant, among the individuals tested. It is not too bad an assumption in most cases. There are few situations which can make a greater claim of being illustrative of what is meant by a common or shared learning experience in our society than the average classroom situation. It is the geographic locus of activity of all members of the society for six hours a day, five days a week, from age five to sixteen or beyond. To the extent that the assumption is warranted, the state of motivation at the time of writing thematic apperceptive stories, following our theoretical scheme, should be largely a function of the relative strengths of various motives in the individuals. Let us check this assumption, tentatively, as one to be scrutinized carefully a little later on and proceed, for the moment, to a discussion of the instrument itself. The reader who finds it difficult to grant the assumption—even tentatively—may simply imagine an "ideal" standard situation for assessment of motives in a number of individuals. This is one in which the expectancies aroused by the situation cues are the same for all individuals, so that differences in the aroused state of a particular kind of motivation can be unambiguously attributed to differences in the strength of motive.

In the neutral situation, or for that matter in any situation, the average score of a group of individuals for a particular kind of motivation varies significantly from picture to picture. Pictures of men working in a shop or of a young man seated at his desk in school, for example, elicit more achievement-related responses than relatively unstructured or obviously nonachievement-related pictures. Similarly, pictures of a group of persons sitting in a clubroom or of two young people apparently conversing are the kinds of pictures which provoke the greatest affiliative response. The picture which produce the greatest amount of imagery symptomatic of a particular motive are, in other words, pictures of situations which normally arouse expectancies of satisfying that particular motive through some kind of action (Figure 26–2).

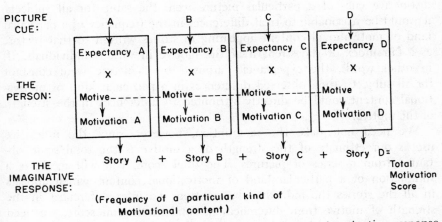

FIGURE 26–2. A conception of the determinants of the imaginative response in which the strength of motive is constant throughout a series of stories, and the expectancies aroused by the cues of the real-life situation (not included in diagram) are constant throughout the test period, but the expectancies of goal attainment aroused by the cues of particular pictures vary. As a consequence, the momentary strength of motivation expressed in particular stories varies.

If the situation portrayed in a picture arouses the expectancy that evaluation of performance in terms of standards of excellence is the normal consequence of behavior in that setting, we should expect the achievement motive to be engaged and the motivational content of the imaginative story to contain a variety of associations related to the achievement-directed sequence of behavior. The characters of the story should be trying to achieve something. They should experience feelings of satisfaction when they have performed well and unpleasant feelings when their efforts to accomplish are thwarted in some way. Similarly, if the picture portrays a situation which normally elicits expectancies having to do with the attainment of power, the stories written in response to such a picture should be saturated with associations related to the power-directed sequence of behavior. The motivational content of the story should, in other words, reveal the kinds of motives normally aroused in real-life situations similar to those contained in the picture.

The imaginative story, however, tells us more about the state of motivation than does simple observation of the vigor of acts in a real-life situation; the imaginative story contains specific statements of aim and imagery related to the subtleties of feeling that are never directly observed in action. *The imaginative story defines the motive by describing the kinds of circumstances which produce affective reactions in the characters of the stories.*

If it were plausible to assume that the expectancies aroused by the distinctive cues of a particular picture were the same for all subjects, it would be reasonable to treat differences in the frequency of a particular kind of motivational content appearing in stories written to that picture as a fair index of the strength of the motive in various individuals. If, in other words, the expectancies aroused by a picture were constant for all subjects, then observed differences in a particular kind of motivational content could be directly attributed to differences in the strength of the motive.

We need not make this assumption, however, since the index we use as our estimate of the strength of a motive is the total score obtained from a series of pictures. The total score, you will recall, is a summation of a particular kind of motivational content which appears in all the stories the individual has written. To infer differences in the strength of motive from differences in total motivation score, we need only assume that the *average strength* of a particular expectancy (e.g., the expectancy of achievement or of power, etc.) aroused by all the pictures in the series is approximately equal for all subjects. When such an assumption is warranted, every subject has had a fair opportunity to reveal his motive in the test as a whole.

The point may be clarified by an example. Let us take two hypothetical young men known to have had the kinds of early childhood experiences which would account for their having developed equally strong motives to achieve. But let us suppose that the later cultural experience of one of these men had emphasized apprenticeship training for a job as a skilled machinist. He has quit school very early and has had expectations of achieving strengthened in the blue-collar work situation. The other young man, however, has had a different kind of later indoctrination and experience. His father is in business, and the son has had a number of influences play on him at home and in summer jobs as a clerk in an office which point toward the long-term goal of an executive role in business.

How do we expect these two young men to respond in thematic apperception when confronted with pictures of a "man working in a shop" and a "business-office scene"? For the first young man, achievement-related expectancies should be relatively strong in response to the blue-collar picture and relatively weak in response to the white-collar picture. Just the reverse should be true of the second young man. Given equally strong motives to achieve, the frequency of achievement-related imaginative responses should be greater in response to the blue-collar picture for the first young man and greater in response to the white-collar picture for the second young man. But their total scores from the two stories should be very comparable. Both should have higher total scores, for example, than young men who have had similar *later* cultural learning experiences which define cognitive expectations in these particular situations but who have not had the significant *early* affective experiences of childhood which contribute to the development of a strong motive to achieve at something.

In summary, our conception of the determinants of the imaginative response is directly analogous to our conception of the joint role played by motives and situationally aroused expectancies in the determination of adaptive, instrumental acts. The cues preceding the test period and of the test situation itself are thought to arouse certain expectancies in each individual. This accounts for a base level of motivation before the first picture is even presented. (In the "ideal" test situation, the expectancies aroused would be the same in all the persons tested.) The pictures used to elicit stories are conceived as arousing particular kinds of expectancies of goal attainment which engage particular motives of the individual. These are expressed in the motivational content of the imaginative story. The story reveals the kinds of associations that situations similar to the one portrayed in the picture would elicit in the person in real life. Inferring individual differences in strength of a motive from the total motivation score is justified only when it can be assumed that all individuals tested have had an equal opportunity to express that motive in the test as a whole. This condition is likely to be *approximated* when the situations portrayed in the pictures are representative of a wide variety of life situations in which people can satisfy the particular motive. But the "ideal" instrument—and this point is worth repeating—is one in which the average strength of the expectancies of attaining the goal of a particular motive aroused by all the pictures is equal for all individuals tested. And the "ideal" test situation is one which arouses the same goal expectancies in everyone.

We can organize most of the known facts about the index of motivation derived from thematic apperception in terms of this scheme. In the first place, the assumption that the thematic content related to a particular aim, e.g., achievement imagery or affiliation imagery, corresponds to the state of motivation, rather than directly to the strength of the motive, enables us to account for the fact that we are able to develop valid scoring procedures by defining the particular kinds of content which increase in frequency in imaginative stories when a particular kind of motivation is experimentally aroused. The motive, conceived as a relatively stable disposition, cannot change when motivating cues are introduced; but the state of motivation can change. Secondly, the assumption that picture cues also arouse expectancies of goal attainment which engage particular motives and heighten the momentary strength of that kind of motivation enables us to account for a number of facts concerning the average response to particular pictures. For example:

1. In college students, the average n-Achievement score is greater in response to pictures of culturally defined achievement situations than to pictures of unstructured or unrelated situations (McClelland et al., 1953). The same is generally true of n-Affiliation and n-Power scores, although systematic studies have not been performed except for achievement.

2. Rosenstein (1952) has shown that a group of physical education majors and a group of chemistry majors obtain nearly equal high average n-Achievement scores in response to pictures of athletic competition situations, a fairly universal achievement-training experience for all males in this society; but the chemistry majors had a significantly higher n-Achievement score than physical education majors in response to pictures portraying laboratory situations. It seems reasonable to attribute this difference to the rather specialized kinds of learning experiences a group of young men who decide to major in chemistry have had, experiences which would account for their having stronger achievement-related expectancies in laboratory situations.

3. The average n-Achievement scores of American male and female students in high school and college are significantly greater in response to pictures of men in culturally defined achievement settings than in response to pictures of women in very comparable settings (Veroff, Wilcox, & Atkinson, 1953). Mead (1949) has argued that ideas of achievement are defined out of the female role in our society at about

the time of adolescence. The girl begins to realize that trying to achieve puts her in competition with men and elicits a negative reaction from these potential marriage partners. As a result, we should expect that expectations of achievement are stronger, even in women, in response to pictures of men rather than women in work situations.

A Conception of Conflict Which Inhibits the Expression of Motive in Thematic Apperception

We have been lucky in our choice of the achievement motive for most of these early experimental excursions. Had we started our research with sex or aggression, the motives which interest clinicians most in societies which have made them special problems, we should not have been led so easily to as simple a scheme as that outlined in the preceding paragraphs. Our society does not generally punish the expression of a motive to achieve. Quite the contrary. So we have been able to avoid, to this point, discussing a question that frequently arises concerning the ultimate utility of thematic apperception for measuring the strength of motives about which the individual is seriously conflicted.

Let us see what happens when we impose the motive-expectancy distinction on the classic motivations, sex and aggression. Our scheme would lead us to look to early childhood for experiences which contribute to the development of these two motives, conceived as dispositions to attain certain kinds of gratifying effects or aims. The sense of having injured another person might serve, tentatively, as a definition of the aim of the aggressive motive, and sensuous pleasure will serve as a definitition of the general aim of the sex motive. The question of type of act is, as in the cases of the other motives, left out of the definition of the aim.

Now, we might ask, when are these two motives expressed in overt action? Our theoretical answer is that these motives, like all others, are engaged when the cues of the situation, as a result of prior learning, arouse the expectancy of satisfying the motive through performance of some instrumental act. These two motives, like all others, are aroused by expectancies of satisfaction.

But—and this is an important but—there is a tremendous accumulation of evidence which indicates that overt expression of these motives is often inhibited. And, as Clark (1952) has shown, even direct expression in thematic apperception is inhibited or distorted. We cannot expect, so the argument runs, to infer the strength of these motives simply by counting the frequency of manifest, motive-related responses, as is the case for achievement, affiliation, and hunger.

The expression of sexual or aggressive motivation is inhibited when some other motive has also been engaged and the resultant motivations are incompatible. The conception of approach-avoidance conflict introduced by Lewin (1931), extended and refined by Miller (1951) within the framework of S-R reinforcement theory, and employed by Clark (1952) has become the conventional model for discussion of inhibition produced by conflict. We can employ this general model. But instead of accounting for the relative strengths of the competing tendencies in terms of the concepts of drive and habit, as in the Miller (1951) scheme, we shall appeal to a multiplicative relationship between motive and expectancy (and incentive) as outlined in earlier paragraphs.

What are the motives for avoidance? Fear or anxiety over painful consequences is the by now well-documented general answer to this question. Is there any reason that we cannot conceive of pain avoidance as the general aim of a family of avoidance dispositions? McClelland (1951) has stated affirmatively the argument for a two-factor theory of motivation. And the distinction between appetites and aversions, pleasure seeking and pain avoidance, hopes and fears, has been advanced in the writings of Tolman (1951), Mowrer (1950), Murray et al. (1938), and others. One can look to early childhood for the antecedents of pain-avoidance motives, e.g., a rejection-avoidance motive, a failure-avoidance motive, etc., just as easily as one can look there for antecedents of approach dispositions like achievement, affiliation, and aggression. It may be less cumbersome in discussion to call these avoidance dispositions fears, as McClelland (1951) has suggested, and to define them in terms of the particular kinds of punishing consequences that are to be avoided, e.g., fear of punishment, fear of rejection, fear of failure, etc.

Conflict will occur when an approach motive and an avoidance motive are simultaneously engaged by different expectancies cued off in a situation. For example, the same cues which arouse the expectancy of satisfying the aggressive impulse may serve also to arouse the expectancy of punishment. If so, two mutually incompatible *motivations* are aroused—to hit and not to hit. The person is in a state of conflict. Under such circumstances, the expression of the approach tendency is likely to be weakened or inhibited completely, as many experiments have shown. What will be expressed in its place? The answer to this question requires a theory of how particular conflicts are resolved by the person. It is at this particular point that the simple conception of motivation and behavior offered here must make contact with ideas about conflict and its resolution.

Does this mean that we cannot hope to measure a motive through the manifest content of thematic apperception if it happens to be one about which the individual often experiences conflict? The theoretical answer is: *not necessarily*. What is now clearly required, however, is specification of the conditions—in theoretical terms—under which the approach motive can be expressed without disguise and the conditions under which conflict with its attendant distortion of the approach tendency is to be expected. It is at least theoretically possible to imagine a situation that will arouse the expectancy of satisfying the approach motive without simultaneously arousing the expectancy of punishing consequences which would engage the avoidance disposition and hence inhibit expression of the approach tendency. The concept of displacement points to such conditions. And work of Sears (1951a) and others with doll play in children suggests the possibility of kinds of situations which allow fairly free reign to an otherwise inhibited approach tendency. The task for those who would like to extend the thematic apperception method to the point of fairly accurate assessment of sexual and aggressive motives is to construct a test situation and choose a set of pictures which meet the requirement of arousing the expectancy of satisfying the approach tendency without also arousing the expectancy of punishment for its expression. The experimental problem may be difficult, but it need not be decided in advance that it is impossible to solve.

The experiment by Clark (1952) on expression of sexual motivation in thematic apperception has shown that arousal of fear of punishment, or guilt, which inhibits free expression of sexual motivation, is reduced by alcohol. And Mussen and Scodel (1955, Chap. 8) have shown that the strength of the expectancy of punishment, and hence strength of the inhibiting motivation, can be increased and decreased by subtle changes in situational variables, viz., a stern versus a permissive experimenter.

Another hopeful possibility is that as our understanding of how conflicts are resolved advances (e.g., see McClelland & Apicella, 1945, and the recent work of Miller & Swanson, 1956), it may be possible to assess the relative strengths of the competing tendencies directly from the distorted expression which represents a particular mode of resolving the conflict. The studies of Clark and Sensibar (1955) and Beardslee and Fogelson (1958), for example, point the way to reading the strength of a motive from the frequency and extent of symbolic expression of it. There is every reason to believe that continued experimental analysis of this problem will lead to the development of valid and reliable techniques for *latent* content analysis.

In any case, the ultimate solution of this problem will require independent assessment of the expectancies aroused by both situation and picture cues. For unless there is some way of knowing in advance what the situation "means" to the individual, any attempt to infer motives from expressed motivations will continue to involve two unknown quantities—the motive and the expectancy aroused by momentary cues.

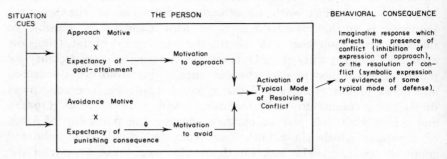

FIGURE 26–3. A conception of approach-avoidance conflict as it affects the attempt to assess the strength of an approach motive from manifest motive — related imagery in thematic apperception. (Suggested by the earlier conception and experimental evidence of Clark [1952] and the current conception of conflict and defense by Miller and Swanson [1956].)

Figure 26–3 summarizes the conception that is advanced for thinking about conflict in terms of simultaneously aroused approach and avoidance motives. Better than anything else, it defines the need for independent assessment of expectancies aroused by situation cues as a first step toward teasing out the effect of motives on thematic material and on instrumental activity.

Independent Assessment of Expectancies Aroused by Situational and Picture Cues

Rotter's (1954) social-learning theory gives a central role to the concept of expectancies aroused by situational cues. His own analysis of the directive role of situation cues has begun to produce a series of theoretically relevant attempts to assess expectations (1955). Our own attempts along the same line have focused chiefly on the problem of defining the cue characteristics of the pictures used in thematic apperceptive measurement of motives. And while the empirical research to date has dealt only with picture cues, the methodological implications would seem to hold as well for attempts to assess the cognitive meaning, in expectancy terms, of the cues of any real-life situation in which the behavior of a person might be observed.

The few excursions we have taken in trying to assess the cognitive meaning of the situation for a person suggest the possibility of constructing fairly standard conditions for the measurement of any human motive.

In our use to date of the thematic apperception method, we have felt compelled to hold the *physical* stimulation of situation cues and pictures as constant as possible for purposes of comparing individuals or groups presumed to differ in strength of a particular motive. If it is actually possible to obtain an independent measure of the particular cognitive expectancies aroused by both situation and picture cues, the experimenter will be in a position to loosen his control of the physical stimuli and substitute instead his readings taken on the cognitive meanings of these stimuli for particular subjects or particular groups of subjects. *The ideal test of strength of a particular motive may ultimately consist of different pictures for different individuals—pictures more alike in the expectancies they arouse than in their physical properties.* When and if we reach this stage of precision, we shall be controlling the psychological environment rather than having to assume some kind of rough equivalence produced by constant physical cues.

Final Comment

If nothing else, this theoretical analysis supports Rotter's (1955) emphasis of the need for an adequate technique for assessing the cue characteristics of the stimulus situation to which the individual responds. In adapting Tolman's (1955) concept of expectancy to deal with the "casual texture of the environment," I have deliberately sought a concept which captures the central idea of the Lewinian life space, or psychological environment, as distinct from geographic or physical environment.

Embedding the problem of assessing human motives in an expectancy theory of motivation and action tends, furthermore, to bring us a step nearer to the probability-utility model for decision making, which has had a durable history in economics and is currently engaging the interest of model builders with an empirical slant (Edwards, 1954). The possible fruits of a union between a method for assessing the strength of basic motives in an individual and a mathematical model for decision making seems worth the effort of a try.

The decision to employ the concept of expectancy to carry the burden of the meaning of the situation for the person is the result of another consideration. It is an appreciation of the extent to which an appeal to cognitive expectations is the core of what social scientists in other fields have in mind when they speak of the *norms* of a society and the definitions of *roles* within a society. Working in his own bailiwick, the psychologist has become sensitive to the need—argued forcefully by Sears (1951b)—for a conception of personality which makes contact with a theory of action, so that the individual will be described in terms of potentialities for action for which there are known principles. The psychologist may also be susceptible to another kind of argument.

It should influence his choice of concept when there are admittedly many different alternatives open to him. The ultimate point of contact between psychological and sociological conceptions lies in the analysis of the behavior of persons in particular concrete situations. The choice of concept and the development of methods for treating the effect of the situation on the individual can enhance or hinder the possibility of integrating the conception of personality and the conception of social structure in concrete research. The idea of measuring cognitive expectancies aroused in particular real-life situations seems to be a promising mediating link.

REFERENCES

ATKINSON, J. W. (Ed.), *Motives in fantasy, action, and society.* Princeton, N.J.: Van Nostrand, 1958.

BEARDSLEE, D., & FOGELSON, R. Sex differences in sexual imagery aroused by musical stimulation. In J. W. Atkinson (Ed.), *Motives in fantasy, action, and society.* Princeton: Van Nostrand, 1958. Pp. 132–142.

CLARK, R. A. The projective measurement of experimentally induced levels of sexual motivation. *J. exp. Psychol.,* 1952, 44, 391–399.

CLARK, R. A., & SENSIBAR, MINDA R. The relationships between symbolic and manifest projections of sexuality with some incidental correlates. *J. abnorm. soc. Psychol.,* 1955, 50, 327–334.

EDWARDS, W. The theory of decision making. *Psychol. Bull.,* 1954, 51, 380–417.

FRENCH, ELIZABETH G. Motivation as a variable in work-partner selection. *J. abnorm. soc. Psychol.,* 1956, 53, 96–99.

GROESBECK, B. L. Personality correlates of the achievement and affiliation motives in clinical psychology trainees. Unpublished doctoral dissertation, Univer. of Michigan, 1956.

KELLY, E. L., & FISKE, D. W. *The prediction of performance in clinical psychology.* Ann Arbor: Univer. of Michigan Press, 1951.

LEWIN, K. Environmental forces in child-behavior and development. In C. Murchison (Ed.), *A handbook of child psychology.* Worcester, Mass.: Clark Univer. Press, 1931. Pp. 94–127.

LEWIN, K. *Field theory in social science: selected theoretical papers.* D. Cartwright (Ed.), New York: Harper, 1951.

LESSER, G. S., KRAWITZ, RHODA N., & PACKARD, RITA. Experimental arousal of achievement motivation in adolescent girls. *J. abnorm. soc. Psychol.,* 1963, 66, 59–66.

MacCORQUODALE, K., & MEEHL, P. E. Preliminary suggestions as to a formalization of expectancy theory. *Psychol. Rev.,* 1953, 60, 55–63.

MacCORQUODALE, K., & MEEHL, P. E. Edward C. Tolman. In W. K. Estes et al., *Modern learning theory.* New York: Appleton-Century-Crofts, 1954. Pp. 177–266.

McCLELLAND, D. C. *Personality.* New York: Sloane, 1951.

McCLELLAND, D. C., & APICELLA, F. S. A functional classification of verbal reactions to experimentally induced failure. *J. abnorm. soc. Psychol.,* 1945, 40, 376–390.

McCLELLAND, D. C., ATKINSON, J. W., CLARK, R. A., & LOWELL, E. L. *The achievement motive.* New York: Appleton-Century-Crofts, 1953.

Mead, Margaret. *Male and female.* New York: Morrow, 1949.

Miller, D. R., & Swanson, G. E. The study of conflict. In M. R. Jones (Ed.), *Nebraska symposium on motivation.* Lincoln: Univer. Nebraska Press, 1956. Pp. 137–174.

Miller, N. E. Comments on theoretical models illustrated by the development of a theory of conflict behavior. *J. Pers.,* 1951, 20, 82–100.

Morgan, H. H. Measuring achievement motivation with "picture interpretation." *J. consult. Psychol.,* 1953, 17, 289–292.

Mowrer, O. H. *Learning theory and personality dynamics.* New York: Ronald, 1950.

Murray, H. A., et al. *Explorations in personality.* New York: Oxford Univer. Press, 1938.

Murstein, B. I. *Theory and research in projective techniques: Emphasizing the TAT.* New York: Wiley, 1963.

Mussen, P. H., & Scodel, A. The effects of sexual stimulation under varying conditions on TAT sexual responsiveness. *J. consult. Psychol.,* 1955, 19, 90.

Ricciuti, H. N., & Sadacca, R. *The prediction of academic grades with a projective test of achievement motivation. II. Cross validation at the high school level.* Princeton: Educational Testing Service, 1955.

Rosenstein, A. J. The specificity of the achievement motive and the motivating effects of picture cues. Unpublished honors thesis, Univer. of Michigan, 1952.

Rotter, J. B. *Social learning and clinical psychology.* Englewood Cliffs, N. J.: Prentice-Hall, 1954.

Rotter, J. B. The role of the psychological situation in determining the direction of human behavior. In M. R. Jones (Ed.), *Nebraska symposium on motivation.* 1955, Pp. 245–268.

Sears, R. R. Social behavior and personality development. In T. Parsons & E. A. Shils (Eds.), *Toward a general theory of action.* Cambridge: Harvard Univer. Press, 1951. (a)

Sears, R. R. A theoretical framework for personality and social behavior. *Amer. Psychologist,* 1951, 6, 476–483. (b)

Tolman, E. C. *Collected papers in psychology.* Berkeley: Univer. of California Press, 1951.

Tolman, E. C. Principles of performance. *Psychol. Rev.,* 1955, 62, 315–326.

Veroff, J. Thematic apperception in a nationwide sample survey. In J. Kagan & G. Lesser (Eds.), *Contemporary issues in thematic apperceptive methods.* Springfield, Ill.: Charles C Thomas, 1961. Pp. 83–110.

Veroff, J., Wilcox, Sue, & Atkinson, J. W. The achievement motive in high school and college age women. *J. abnorm. soc. Psychol.,* 1953, 48, 108–119.

Walker, E. L., & Heyns, R. W. Studies in conformity. Unpublished manuscript, Univer. of Michigan, 1956.

27

Levels of Prediction from the Thematic Apperception Test

SEYMOUR FISHER
AND ROBERT B. MORTON

This study is concerned with the classification of the behavior of tuberculosis patients into three categories on a continuum of ease of camouflaging scores to these classifications. Least subject to camouflage are the nonverbal behaviors, such as "rate of recovery from tuberculosis" and "remaining for the full length of treatment or leaving before this point." At an intermediate level were ratings by the patients of their present and past life on such relatively innocuous factors as socio-economic level of parents and kinds of organization to which the patient belonged. Most ego-involving were patient attitudes toward the hospital situation and family attitudes toward the hospitalization. The authors hypothesized that those measures least subject to camouflage would correlate best with two TAT measures, "definiteness of parental behavior" and "achievement orientation." The results supported their hypothesis.

The interesting findings are weakened somewhat by the failure of the authors to provide reliability values for the various measures. Since the nonverbal behaviors, by their objective nature, may be presumed to have very high reliability and ego-involving measures often have low reliability, the latter's failure to correlate significantly with the TAT measures may have stemmed from a lack of reliability rather than a lack of intrinsic validity. With such a small sample of TAT variables, it is dangerous to generalize to all thematic or other projective tests.

It should be noted also that the finding here is contrary to that

*reported by Lindzey and Tejessy (see Chap. 32 in this volume), in that
the latter report a correspondence between TAT hostility content and
self-appraisal of hostility, whereas Fisher and Morton report no association between their thematic measures and their patients' verbalized
behavior. The difference, however, may well lie in the fact that Lindzey
and Tejessy's thematic variables are not disguised, whereas Fisher's
would be difficult for a subject to control. It may be, therefore, that
there is a relationship between thematic content and verbal expression
when the thematic content is subject to control, but not when more
disguised variables, such as parental definiteness and achievement, are
employed. Further work in this area should lead to clearer insight into
the strength of subject control of responses.*

The literature is replete with studies and speculations concerning the
kinds of phenomena which can be predicted from projective test
responses. Summaries of this material are available elsewhere (Kagan
& Mussen, 1956; Mussen & Naylor, 1954; Tomkins, 1949). It is somewhat
confusing to examine the evidence concerning the validity of projective
tests, because it is so contradictory. One investigator reports great success
in predicting various behaviors from the Rorschach or TAT, and another
investigator reports completely negative results. These divergences are
in many instances due to obvious differences in subject populations
used and to variations in procedure. Thus, it is clearly easier to predict
in a heterogeneous group than in one that is highly selected. Likewise,
it is clear that some projective test indices are more cleverly devised
than others and therefore give more valid results. However, aside from
such obvious factors, there are important differences in results which
seem to be a function of the area of behavior one attempts to predict.

Kagan and Mussen (1956) have pointed out that past studies have
found less significant relationships between fantasy and behavior that
is prohibited or punished in the individual's social milieu than between
fantasy and behavior that is culturally sanctioned. This point is
illustrated by the fact that various researchers (Bach, 1945; Korner,
1949; Sanford, Adkins, Miller, et al., 1943) have not found significant
relationships between amount of aggressive TAT or doll-play fantasy
and degree of overt aggression among subjects from a middle-class milieu.
But Mussen and Naylor (1954) demonstrated a significant link between
TAT aggressive fantasy and overt aggressive behavior in a group of lower-
class boys for whom this sort of behavior is more likely to be approved.
Apparently, if the individual is set to conceal certain aspects of his
behavior, this decreases the correlation of such behavior with logically
related areas of fantasy.

In an analogous vein, might one not anticipate differences in fantasy versus behavior relationships as a function of other behavioral dimensions? Is verbal behavior easier to predict from fantasy than nonverbal behavior? Is behavior over which the individual has no conscious control easier to predict than behavior which he can consciously influence? Are certain kinds of verbal behavior less difficult to predict than others? Are behaviors that are usually conceptualized in purely physiological terms more or less predictable than behaviors occurring at the level of verbalization and striate muscular response? The present study represents an attempt to answer some of these questions. More specifically, the intent was to determine the relationships of two different TAT scores to a whole range of behaviors which had been measured in a population of individuals who were hospitalized for tuberculosis.

Methods

BEHAVIORAL MEASURES

The opportunity for examining such issues was provided in terms of a body of data which was collected by Moran, Fairweather, Morton, and others (Fairweather, Moran, & Morton, 1956; Moran, Fairweather, Fisher, & Morton, 1956). As part of a large-scale study of the adjustment of patients with tuberculosis, they obtained a wide variety of measures on a group of 140 male veterans who were receiving treatment for tuberculosis in a Veterans Administration hospital. The methods used in selecting this population and the behavioral measures obtained have already been described in detail elsewhere (Fairweather et al., 1956). Therefore, they will only be briefly listed and summarized. These measures were of the following order:

1. Verbal responses from each patient concerning his immediate attitudes toward the hospital situation. There were various items which touched on his feelings about ward regulations, ward personnel, and other patients. The items were expressed in terms of statements with which the patient could agree or disagree. Scoring of responses was based on an a priori judgment as to whether agreement or disagreement with a particular item represented an adaptive or maladaptive attitude toward the hospital situation. By and large, adaptive attitudes were equated with wanting to conform to regulations and expressing positive reactions toward personnel and other patients.

2. Verbal responses to a series of questions concerning prehospital adjustment. These questions concerned such a range of things as school attendance, number of close friends, and social achievement. Answers to questions were scored in terms of a priori judgments concerning which of the reported behaviors are adaptive versus maladaptive. Thus,

getting into fights, having few friends, and belonging to few organizations are examples of behaviors which would be scored in the maladaptive direction.

3. Verbal responses to a series of questions concerning the characteristics of the patient's original family orientation. The questions diversely concerned such topics as parents' economic status, parents' educational status, and parents' mode of disciplining children. Answers were scored relative to a priori standards of what is adaptive and maladaptive. Illustratively, adaptive scores were given for reports of high parental economic status and high parental occupational attainment.

4. Verbal responses to a series of questions concerning the status of the patient's current adjustments outside the hospital situation. Patients were questioned concerning such issues as their anticipated employabiliy when they recovered from their illness and attitudes of their dependents toward their hospitalization. Responses were considered to be adaptive if, for example, they indicated that the immediate family was well taken care of economically or that the family had a positive accepting attitude toward the patient's hospitalization.

5. Ratings of the actual ward behavior of each patient. Two aides and two nurses who had usually attended the patient for several months prior to rating independently evaluated him on a 64-item scale. The items in the scale related to conformance to regulations (e.g., staying in bed, covering coughs), relations with ward personnel (e.g., how demanding or convivial), and relations with other patients (e.g., hazing and disturbing others). Each rating item offered two alternatives, one of which was judged on an a priori basis to be adaptive. The score for a specific item was the number of times the adaptive alternative was checked by all four raters. Once again, adaptive response was considered to be in the direction of obeying regulations and getting along with others.

6. The ability of the patient to remain in the hospital for the full period required to complete treatment. Some patients find it difficult to tolerate the demands made on them as the result of living in a tuberculosis treatment ward. Such patients will leave the hospital despite the fact that they are still sick and will seriously endanger the health of members of their family if they return home prematurely. It is obviously a maladaptive response to leave the hospital in this fashion, and it provides a clear-cut index of poor adjustment to the hospital situation.

7. Rate of recovery from the tubercular infection. This rate of recovery variable was defined in terms of the length of time required for the patient to convert from positive to negative bacteriology. Each patient's sputum and gastric contents are routinely checked at intervals to determine their bacteriological status. A negative report means the absence of tubercle bacilli in the laboratory specimen. Within the context

of this study, the patient was considered to be "converted" from positive to negative bacteriologically after five successive negative laboratory reports. Only 46 patients were involved in this phase of the study. They were subjects who had been carefully selected to participate in a national research on the effectiveness of chemotherapy. Patients who converted bacteriologically within five to eight months were designated a fast recovery group and patients who did not convert within this time period were designated as a slow recovery group.

The various measures listed above provided samples of many different kinds of behavior of a group of men who were of lower to lower-middle socioeconomic status, who could be considered part of the normal population in that they did not exhibit an unusual frequency of personality disorders, and who at the time evaluated were living in a similar standardized environment.

For the purposes of the present study, a number of individual measures were derived from the total available array. These individual measures were selected so as to conform to a particular conceptual scheme. It was postulated that any behavior to be predicted may be categorized on a continuum having to do wth how easily the individual is consciously able to camouflage that behavior so as to make it appear socially acceptable or how motivated he is to do so. In illustration, there might be cited at one extreme the rate of bacteriological conversion or the long-term ward behavior of a tubercular patient who is intensively observed by nurses and aides. A patient cannot consciously influence his rate of bacteriological conversion. It is doubtful also that a patient could for long dissimulate sufficiently to prevent nurses and aides who observed him intimately from detecting his basic modes of reaction to the ward situation. At the other extreme are behaviors which simply involve the patient's own verbal descriptions of things. The patient is then free to shape and distort his descriptions within a wide range of possibilities that fit his needs. However, within this area of verbal report, there may be distinguished those descriptions which have important ego-involving significance to the patient and which might therefore be twisted by him in a self-enhancing manner. At quite a different level are verbal reports regarding matters that have relatively limited emotional significance and which the patient has only minor need to distort in terms of his own self-protective attitudes. Thus, a patient might self-protectively warp his answers concerning how much he likes the hospital or his ward physician but be without temptation to do so in reply to simple factual questions concerning how much he participates in sports or the kind of recreation he enjoys. In line with his conceptual scheme, the following behaviors were selected for study.

1. Those behaviors which are relatively difficult for the patient to influence or to camouflage in a self-protective, socially approved direction. Three measures are included in this category.

(a) Rate of bacteriological conversion.

(b) Evaluations made by nurses and aides of the patient's actual overt adaptation to the ward situation.

(c) The differentiation between patients who leave the hospital prematurely before treatment is complete and those who remain for an optimum treatment period. This differentiation involved 26 of 140 patients who left prematurely and a comparison group of 45 patients randomly selected who remained for full treatment.

2. Verbal reports concerning issues which have relatively low ego involvement for the patient and which are likely not to be camouflaged. Two measures are included here.

(a) A group of thirteen items concerning the patient's relationships with peers from childhood to the period just preceding his hospitalization. The items mainly refer to such factors as the number and kinds of social organizations in which membership was held; preferred forms of recreation with friends; number of friends; number of friendships formed in the army; and degree to which army friendships have carried over into civilian life. The scoring of the answers is intended to evaluate how actively and fully the individual has interacted with his peers. Two-thirds of the items refer to childhood and adolescent behavior rather than to adult behavior. It was considered that these questions would be relatively nonthreatening because their apparent intent was vague and because most of them were phrased in a bland innocuous fashion.

(b) A group of three items concerning the occupational level of the patient's parents. These were questions that simply requested information concerning the type of work done by the parents and how steadily they were employed.

3. Verbal reports concerning issues that have relatively high ego-involving significance and are likely to result in camouflage and distortion. Four measures are embraced by this category.

(a) Forty-five questions concerning how the patient feels about various aspects of his immediate situation in the hospital. These questions required the patient to express to the interviewer his opinions about his physician, the nurses, the aides, the quality of food served, and so forth. It was considered that such questions tapped opinions which the average patient would be embarrassed to voice openly. For example, if he disapproved of his physician or thought the nurses were inefficient, he might be anxious that an open expression of such feeling would get him into trouble. Thus, his tendency would be to play down the negative aspects of his attitudes.

(b) A cluster of three questions relating to how the patient currently perceives the attitudes of significant figures outside the hospital toward his hospitalization. The questions requested information as to how alarmed his dependents were by his illness, whether his dependents favored or did not favor his initial hospitalization, and whether any person significant to him was pressuring him to hurry up and leave the hospital. It seemed likely that such questions would probe into areas of high tension (e.g., guilt about the plight of dependents) and elicit defensive disguised verbal replies.

(c) A cluster of nine questions that refer to how well the patient's parents supplied him with a stable environment with consistent rules and limits. These questions concerned how much time the parents spent at home, the kind of discipline they administered, and whether they were given to unusual drinking or drug addiction. It was assumed that such questions would elicit defensive responses from patients because they touched on a deeply personal aspect of one's relationship to his parents (viz., discipline and punishment) and because they required reports about socially highly disapproved aspects of behavior (viz., drinking and drug behavior) of the parents.

(d) A group of ten questions regarding the patient's ability to get along with authority figures from the time of grade school to the present. These questions variously inquired concerning such issues as past arrests, failures in school, and failures in the army. Obviously, there would be marked temptation to distort answers to questions that had the intent of extracting so much negative information concerning one's past.

FANTASY MEASURES

Ten cards on the TAT were administered to each patient: 1, 2, 4, 12M, 8BM, 6BM, 17BM, 18BM, 6GF, 7BM. In choosing TAT measures which would be most likely to predict a wide range of behavior of tubercular patients, special consideration was given to the hospital situation in which this behavior occurs. The average patient who comes to be treated for tuberculosis in the VA hospital setting in which the present study was carried out is required to adjust to a very new way of life. He enters into a situation in which he has to change radically many of his previous ways of doing things. He has to endure a variety of procedures which are restraining and frustrating. He has to give up many of his immediate life goals with the hope that in so doing he will better his long-term prospects. In this setting, his physician becomes a central figure whose decisions take on magnified importance. These decisions determine how much freedom he has in the hospital and of course are always fraught with implications concerning how well the treatment is progressing. The patient comes to attach exaggerated importance to the words and gestures of his physician; and his mood tone may fluctuate up and down as he ascribes first one and then another significance to such words and gestures.

These special features of the hospital treatment situation suggested that two kinds of fantasy variables might be particularly pertinent as predictors of the behaviors of the tuberculosis patient:

1. The hospital situation is one which clearly requires an unusual degree of immediate passivity from the patient. Yet it also requires a long-term active or aspiring attitude in the sense of being willing to put up with immediate frustrations in anticipation of attaining basic future goals. It therefore seemed logical that a fantasy measure concerned with achievement and aspiration should be related to aspects of the tubercular patient's behavior. So many of the tubercular patient's problems seem to cluster about issues of activity versus passivity that one would expect his fantasies in this area to be meaningfully linked to his patterns of response. The TAT index which was selected to get at this dimension of fantasy is a measure developed for a previous study (Fisher & Cleveland, 1956). It is an Achievement score based on the number of instances in which story characters are described as having high aspirations, engaging in unusually hard work, attaining financial success, doing an excellent job, being obligated to great effort, or adopting a laudable aim. The score is simply a count of all instances in which such characteristics are depicted. An interscorer rank-order reliability of .62 was obtained on ten independently scored TAT records.

2. The fact that the tubercular patient finds himself in a situation where certain authority figures (viz., physician and nurse) take on great prominence in his life suggested that his fantasies about father figures and mother figures would have particular relevance. Since so many decisions about his treatment and his activities are in the hands of his physician and nurse, one would assume that his fantasies about the male authority figure and the female authority figure would have a significant bearing on many of his responses in the hospital situation. The TAT measure used to get at this dimension was also devised for an earlier study (Fisher & Cleveland, 1956). It is based on an analysis of the stories given to Cards 2, 6BM, and 7BM, which are cards that seem frequently to evoke the maximum number of themes concerning mother and father figures. The measure is concerned with the definiteness or clarity of the parental images that are projected into these TAT pictures. In a previous study (Fisher & Cleveland, 1956) it was shown that the definiteness of such images is significantly related to certain basic personality characteristics. The theory underlying the measure is that parents who stand for something definite (whether it is positive or negative) provide their children with well-defined values; whereas parents who are weak or fluctuating in their position on various issues leave their children without clear-cut standards of judgment. A parental figure in any TAT story was scored as definite if the story described the parent in a clearly domineering or unfriendly

role or in a clearly favorable or friendly role. A parental figure was scored as vague or weak if he was described as inadequate or if the story data were too fragmentary or unclear to permit classification in the "definite" category. An interjudge reliability of .81 on the dichotomous scores was obtained on twenty independently scored protocols. A special adaptation of this basic scoring procedure was utilized. It was assumed that the patient would usually project images of both the father and mother figures in his reactions to Card 2. Each image that was definite was given a score of $+1$. If either image was unclear or weak, it was given a score of -1. Thus, a maximum definiteness score of $+2$ and a minimum definiteness score of -2 could be earned for Card 7BM. The subject could, therefore, obtain a total score ranging from $+4$ to -4.

No predictions were made concerning the direction of differences

---

TABLE 27–1   *Chi-Square Tests of Differences in Various Behaviors between Those High and Those Low in TAT Parental Definiteness and Those High and Low in TAT Achievement*

| | PARENTAL DEFINITENESS | | | HIGH ACHIEVEMENT | | |
BEHAVIORS	GROUP W/ HIGHER SCORE	χ^2	LEVEL OF SIGNIFICANCE	GROUP W/ HIGHER SCORE	χ^2	LEVEL OF SIGNIFICANCE
Verbal Behavior:						
Attitude toward hospital situation	—		—			
Family attitude toward hospitalization	—		—			
Goodness of parental behavior	—		—			
Difficulties with authority	—		—			
Parent occupational status	H	3.7	.06	—		
Response to peers	H	4.3	.05–.06	H	7.9	.01
Nonverbal Behavior:						
Rated ward behavior	—		—		4.0	.05–.02
AMA vs. MHB[a]	MHB	5.5	.02–.01	MHB	3.8	.05
Rate of bacteriological conversion	L	4.0	.05–.02	—		

[a]AMA = Group leaving hospital against medical advice.
MHB = Group remaining in hospital for maximum hospital benefit.

that might be obtained from the Aspiration score and the Parental Definiteness score. It was simply hypothesized that both scores would tap fantasy areas that significantly influence behavior in the unique tuberculosis treatment situation. But more specifically, it was hypothesized that the fantasy scores should be most significantly linked with behaviors that the subject cannot consciously camouflage or that he would have little motivation to camouflage.

Results

The results shown in Table 27–1 tend to corroborate the expectations underlying this study. The Parental Definiteness score significantly differentiates subjects who are above the median and below the median in four behavior areas. Individuals who have the most definite parental images are slower in their rate of bacteriological conversion, less likely to leave the hospital before fully treated, more likely to describe themselves as having full, satisfying relationships with peers, and more likely to describe their parents as being of high occupational status. What is more important about these significant differentiations is that they all involve behaviors which are considered to be difficult to camouflage or of a sort that one would have little motivation to "dress up." None of the behaviors which have ego-involving import and which are subject to conscious manipulation could be predicted from the Parental Definiteness score.

The results shown in Table 27–1 concerning the Achievement score are in the same direction. Of three significant differences obtained, none falls outside of those behaviors which are considered least likely to be dissimulated. Those subjects with the higher Achievement scores are more likely to remain in the hospital for their full treatment; they have a greater probability of being rated by nurses and aides as adjusting well on the ward; and they are more likely to describe themselves as having satisfying involvement with their peers.

There is some temptation to try to account for the specific direction of the significant differences obtained. But this would be a long, involved task and is not pertinent to the main objective of this paper, which was to demonstrate that certain modes of behavior are more directly linked with fantasy (whether positively or negatively) than are other modes. The pattern of results suggests that fantasy and behavior are not two different realms, but rather that they are intimately connected. It would appear that the appropriate question is not whether fantasy influences behavior, but rather whether behavior conceptualized in certain ways can be predicted from measures derived from specific defined conceptualizations of fantasy data.

Summary

The purpose of the study was to relate two measures of fantasy derived from the TAT to a variety of behavioral measures obtained from a group of persons hospitalized for treatment of tuberculosis. It was hypothesized that the fantasy measures would predict best those behaviors least subject to camouflage by the subjects. The pattern of results was significantly in the predicted direction.

REFERENCES

BACH, G. R. Young children's play fantasies. *Psychol. Monogr.*, 1945, 59, No. 2 (Whole No. 272).

FAIRWEATHER, G. W., MORAN, L. J., & MORTON, R. B. Efficiency of attitudes, fantasies, and life history data in predicting observed behavior. *J. consult. Psychol.*, 1956, 20, 58.

FISHER, S., & CLEVELAND, S. E. Body image boundaries and style of life. *J. abnorm. soc. Psychol.*, 1956, 52, 373–379.

KAGAN, J., & MUSSEN, P. H. Dependency themes on the TAT and group conformity. *J. consult. Psychol.*, 1956, 20, 29–32.

KORNER, ANNELIESE F. *Some aspects of hostility in young children.* New York: Grune & Stratton, 1949.

MORAN, L. J., FAIRWEATHER, G. W., FISHER, S., & MORTON, R. B. Psychological concomitants to rate of recovery from tuberculosis. *J. consult. Psychol.*, 1956, 20, 199–203.

MUSSEN, P. H., & NAYLOR, H. K. The relationships between overt and fantasy aggression. *J. abnorm. soc. Psychol.*, 1954, 49, 235–240.

SANFORD, R. N., ADKINS, M. M., MILLER, R. B., et al. Physique, personality and scholarship: A cooperative study of school children. *Monogr. Soc. Res. Child Developm.*, 1943, 8, No. 1.

TOMKINS, S. S. The present status of the Thematic Apperception Test. *Amer. J. Orthopsychiat.*, 1949, 19, 358–362.

28

A Normative Study of the Thematic Apperception Test[1]

LEONARD D. ERON

This article serves as a landmark separating the period of unbridled and surely unwarranted enthusiasm for the use of projective techniques during and after World War II and the increasingly sober, critical, somewhat pessimistic air regarding these techniques commencing with the early fifties and rising to a crescendo during the late fifties and early sixties. Was this article the prophet of doom, or did it rather signal a retrenchment, a change in thinking, and a tendency to replace faith with empirical fact? If it disappointed some clinicians, it encouraged those engaged in personality research. What were its contributions?

To begin with, it provided one of the first reliable methods for scoring thematic stories and a brief description of how others could score the stories with the system. Second, it indicated that the search for the alchemist's stone to turn TAT leaden stories into psychiatric classifications of "pure gold" would be doomed to failure. There were smaller differences between the stories of normal college students and various psychiatric in- and outpatient groups and between the various psychiatric groups themselves than between those hospitalized and those not hospitalized, regardless of classification. Third, the crucial role of the stimulus in determining the content of TAT stories was clearly demonstrated, with most stories being moderately sad with little difference between the diagnostic groups. Henceforth, it would not be possible to ignore the importance of this crucial determinant of response under the

---

[1] The data included in this monograph were collected in part in connection with a Ph.D. dissertation, "An investigation of the fantasy productions of college students and neuropsychiatric patients," University of Wisconsin, 1949.

469

*belief that the TAT provided an X ray to the private world of the sub-
ject. Last, much of the folklore which had been written in the textbooks
of that period regarding signs of schizophrenia and homosexuality
faded quickly from the scene when exposed to the harsh daylight of
empirical research. The air was now cleared for finding out what the
TAT really could do, a process that is still going on. Perhaps then, this
article may signify not the beginning of the end for projective techniques,
but the end of an inappropriate beginning.*

A number of studies have indicated that the Thematic Apperception
Test, is a valid instrument for measuring the usual product of fantasy
central to an individual (Harrison, 1940; Morgan & Murray, 1935;
Murray et al., 1938; Sarason, 1944), and thus many investigators have
assumed that this technique can be used as a basis for diagnostic
differentiation among clinical groups. Preliminary investigations by this
writer, however, have indicated that no broad group differences could
be elicited, at least in respect to content (Eron, 1948) and emotional
tone (Garfield & Eron, 1948), and that hositalization itself might
be an important influence in determining the nature of the productions
(Garfield & Eron, 1948). It was also disclosed in these studies that
many of the diagnostic interpretations placed on certain characteristics
of TAT stories did not apply to the groups of subjects they included
and that there was thus a definite need for normative data comparable
with the Rorschach tables of Beck (1944) and Hertz (1946). Were
such data available to all who use the TAT, many false impressions
about certain records would be corrected and there would be less
danger than there has been of the examiner's projecting his own biases
into personality interpretations constructed on the basis of the TAT.
Furthermore, the dangerous practice of "cue analysis,[2] often based
on faulty analogical reasoning (Eron & Hake, 1948) and susceptible
to misuse by the inexperienced, might be considerably curtailed if the
examiner had recourse to adequate normative data.

   It is the purpose of the present research to clarify three fundamental
questions which were raised by these preliminary investigations:

   1. Do the fantasy productions of persons suffering from behavior
disorder resemble those of persons not diagnosed ill?

   2. Does the restricted environment of a psychiatric hospital affect
systematically the fantasy productions of patients?

---

   [2] The use of specific characteristics of form and content of the subject's productions as pathognomonic indicators for a given clinical syndrome or dynamic factor.

3. How can the material obtained from the TAT be standardized to furnish adequate norms for use in a clinical situation?

Procedure

SUBJECTS

The subjects of the present study consisted of 150 male veterans of World War II, divided into six groups of 25 each, which included: Groups C1 and C2, nonhospitalized college students; Group NHPN, nonhospitalized psychoneurotics; Group HPN, hospitalized psychoneurotics;[3] Group HS, hospitalized schizophrenics; Group GNPH, general neuropsychiatric hospital population. The clinical groups contained the following subclassifications (all final diagnoses rendered by a board of at least three psychiatrists):

1. Group NHPN, Nonhospitalized Psychoneurotics:

anxiety	19
mixed	3
anxiety, conversion reaction	1
anxiety with depression	1
obsessive with anxiety	1

2. Group HPN, Hospitalized Psychoneurotics:

anxiety	14
mixed	7
anxiety, conversion reaction	1
anxiety with depression	1
anxiety, sex deviate	1
anxiety, emotional instability	1

3. Group HS, Hospitalized Schizophrenics:

unclassified	14
simple	3
catatonic	3
paranoid	3
hebephrenic	2

4. Group GPNH, General Neuropsychiatric Hospital Population:

schizophrenic, paranoid	5
schizophrenic, catatonic	2
schizophrenic, unclassified	1
schizophrenic, simple	1

---

[3] Outpatients seen at Madison VA Mental Hygiene clinic; inpatients seen at Mendota VA Hospital. The writer wishes to thank Dr. R. W. Trent and Dr. A. Bomar for their co-operation in permitting him to see patients at these facilities.

incipient schizophrenia 2
manic depressive psychosis 2
psychosis, unclassified 1
psychoneurosis, anxiety 2
psychoneurosis, conversion reaction 1
reactive depression with alcoholism 1
transvestism 1
inadequate personality 1
psychopathic personality 1
drug addiction 1
encephalopathy 1
postepileptic 1
observation 1

The reasons for the breakdown into six groups of 25 each were to both simplify the statistical procedures (i.e., permit the use of frequency data in comparisons without converting to percentages) and to provide experimental control over any group characteristics which might emerge. If significant differences occurred, we could see: (1) whether they were more extensive than those between two unsystematically selected normal groups; (2) whether hospitalization itself accounted for some differences; (3) whether certain group characteristics could emerge even from a heterogeneous population (such as that constituted by Group GNPH). One of the shortcomings of the studies in the use of various tests in clinical diagnosis has been that not only do the diagnostic patterns derived from the examination of test protocols select individuals of the specific clinical group desired, but they also pick out individuals of every other clinical category. In this study, we have a check on whether the mere grouping of individuals into clusters of 25 does or does not in itself make for significant group characteristics.

The groups were distributed according to age, education, IQ and marital status, as shown in Table 28–1. They are comparable with respect to these variables, although Group GNPH is least homogeneous and has more extreme individuals than the other groups.

MATERIAL AND ADMINISTRATION

All 20 cards recommended for adult males (Harvard University Press, 3rd Edition) were used. Administration of the test was individual, and the only ones present in the testing room were the subject and examiner. The examiner took verbatim notes, as far as possible, of everything that the subject said. Although the authors of the test suggest an interval of one week between the administration of the first and second 10 cards (Murray, 1943), hospital and clinic routine did not permit such a procedure in this study. It was therefore necessary to administer the whole series at one session with a ten-minute break between halves. This method has been recommended by certain investigators (Rotter, 1946). Directions to all the subjects were identical and as follows: "This is a test of imagination. Here are some pictures about which I would like you to make up some stories. You are to tell what happened before, what is happening in the picture, and how it's going to turn out, what the characters are thinking and feeling. Take about four or five minutes for each one but be sure to include all these things. All that we want is a plot for each picture. No elaborate literary masterpiece is necessary. This is the first one, see what you can do with it."

Each subject was prompted when any of the elements of the story as given in the directions was omitted. However, during any single story no subject was prompted more than once for any particular element. After the first ten cards were administered, the subjects were told that the test was half over and that there would be a ten-minute break during which they could go to the lavatory, have a drink of water, etc. After approximately ten minutes the test was resumed with the following instructions:

TABLE 28–1   *Age, Education, IQ, Marital Status of Subjects*

GROUP[a]	N	AGE		EDUCATION		I Q		MARITAL STATUS	
								MAR-RIED	DI-VORCED
		RANGE	MEAN	RANGE	MEAN	RANGE	MEAN		
C1	25	20–36	25.9	13–17	14.4			7	
C2	25	20–35	25.8	13–18	14.5			7	
NHPN	25	20–34	25.4	12–16	13.5	103–128	114.2	7	2
HPN	25	19–35	26.1	12–15	13.0	100–126	111.3	15	
HS	25	20–30	24.2	12–17	13.3	100–133	112.9	6	
GNPH	25	20–49	30.6	9–17	12.1	90–128	109.7	9	2

[a]The following notation will be used throughout the tables to identify the various groups:

C1— First group of college students
C2— Second group of college students
NHPN— Group of nonhospitalized psychoneurotics
HPN— Group of hospitalized psychoneurotics
HS— Group of hospitalized schizophrenics
GNPH— Group of general neuropsychiatric hospital patients.

No IQ scores are available for the college students, but it is assumed they are at least of normal intelligence. It has been reported in the literature (Rotter, 1946) that, after a normal level of intelligence has been reached, there is no correlation between quantity or quality of response on the TAT and added increments of intelligence. Indeed, one investigator states that stories with satisfactory content for analysis have been obtained with subjects with IQ's as low as 80 and consistently satisfactory stories were obtained from subjects with IQ of 90 and above (Jacques, 1945). Since the IQ of no subject in the clinical groups is below normal, it is felt that this factor has been adequately controlled.

"The stories which you told in the first half were all very good—just the kind of story I wanted. But the pictures I'm going to show you now are even more difficult to make up stories about. They are more vague and ambiguous, not as clearly defined, and you're going to have to use your imagination to make up some meaningful stories. So give free rein to your imagination now and make up some good stories about these pictures."

For the sixteenth card, which is blank, there were the special directions as follows:

"Now look at this blank card. Imagine that you see some kind of picture there. Tell me what it is." After the subject described the picture he was then told, "Now make up a story about it."

TECHNIQUE OF ANALYZING STORIES

After the stories were all collected, they were analyzed for the following variables: themes, identification of characters, perceptual distortions, unusual details, level of interpretation, emotional tone of the body of the story and outcome, as follows:

1. *The thematic analysis* followed a check list of themes empirically derived in the following manner. After 50 protocols had been collected, they were perused at least twice. The first time, each story was read through and the action taking place was summarized in a few words. After this was done for all the stories, the author, with the help of another psychologist,[4] examined the summaries, and a check list of 98 themes was organized under the two general headings of disequilibrium and equilibrium, indicating the state of tension or adjustment displayed in the story. These two general groups were subdivided into interpersonal, intrapersonal, and impersonal classifications, depending on the sphere to which the situation was referred. The interpersonal classification was further broken down into sections dealing with parent,[5] partner, peer, and sibling. Each theme appearing in the classification was named and defined and examples of each given so that the same list could be used in further research. On the basis of additional experience, the list was revised and expanded to include 125 themes. The final check list used in this study, with definitions of each theme, appears in Eron, 1950, Appendix B. During the examination of the stories, each theme was tallied as it appeared, so that most stories have more than one theme and rarely are there stories with no themes which appear on the check list and which are thus impossible to classify. Only the manifest content was considered—the actual behavior of the characters

---

[4] Dr. Ann Magaret.

[5] Parent substitutes, such as older authority figures, are included under the heading of "parent." Authority figures of age range similar to hero are classified with "peer" or "partner," whichever is appropriate.

in the stories as narrated by the subject, regardless of its covert significance. The thematic analysis was done by the experimenter, since it is
actually merely a counting procedure with a minimal judgmental
function—a theme is either present or not, and the sole criterion is
the verbal statement of the subject.

2. *Identification of characters* included the sex and age of each of
the individuals depicted on the cards, the relationship when there were
two or more characters, and specific identifying features, including in
some cases nationality, occupation, physical characteristics, etc. In
determining perceptual distortions, the standard taken was the description of each picture offered by the authors of the test (Murray, 1943).
Any deviations from this standard were noted. Notice was also taken of
attention to unusual details such as pregnancy of the woman on Card 2,
lack of tie on man on Card 4, etc. Only one judge, the experimenter,
was used for identifications of characters, as this, too, is merely a counting
procedure.

3. *The level of interpretation* refers to whether the responses were
narratives, mere descriptions, symbolic, abstract, etc. and also to unusual
formal characteristics of the stories such as inclusion of the examiner
in the story, no connection between picture and story told, etc. A list
of these characteristics and their definitions appears in the latter part of
Eron (1950, Appendix B). Since the judgmental function is minimal here
also, only one judge was used.

4. To rate the *emotional tone of the stories and outcomes*, it was
decided to improve on the three-point scale used in a previous study
(Garfield & Eron, 1948). Consequently, a five-point scale was developed
by the author and two collaborators (Eron, Hake & Callahan, n.d.).
The scales (Eron, 1950, Appendix A) were derived in the following
manner: 500 TAT stories were read independently by three judges, who
indicated the rating of each story on a 10-cm. line representing a
continuum from happy to sad. On completion of the ratings, the lines
were divided into ten 1-cm. intervals and an average Pearson product-
moment correlation coefficient of .76 was obtained among the raters.
The 10-cm. lines were then divided into five 2-cm. intervals, and each
interval was assigned a weight as follows, ranging from sad to happy:
-2, -1, 0, $+1$, $+2$. Each interval was described on the basis of those
stories for which there was complete agreement among the three judges,
i.e., all three ratings fell in that particular interval.

Individual scales were constructed for each story for Emotional Tone
and Outcome, and general scales for the two variables were also devised.
The individual scales and the general scale for Outcome were so similar
that only the general scale was used in rating the outcome, although
the individual scales were used for emotional tone.[6] The interinter-

---

[6] Individual scales for emotional tone of stories and the general scale for outcome
appear in Eron (1950, Appendix A).

preter reliability of this scale, based on ratings of three judges for 200 additional stories (10 complete protocols), was rather high. The average Pearson r for emotional tone was .86; and for outcome, .75 (Eron et al., n.d.). It was felt that, since the rating of tone and outcome was a judgmental process, someone other than the investigator should rate the stories, as the latter might be biased by a knowledge of the diagnostic classification of the subjects. Therefore, independent ratings of the emotional tone and outcome were made by an individual who had no clue as to which were the normal stories and which belonged to members of the various clinical groups.[7]

STATISTICAL METHOD

All the data collected in this study (e.g., judgments of emotional tone, themes, perceptual distortions, etc.) were of the frequency type, and our comparisons, therefore, employ the chi-square technique. The formula was one with correction for continuity suggested for use when $p = q = 0.5$ (Child, 1946).

$$\text{Chi square} = \frac{([m - s] - 1)^2}{m + s}$$

In general, each variable was treated in two ways:

(1) First the data were analyzed on the basis of total responses; i.e., each group was compared with every other group on the basis of total number of times a given characteristic was present in those groups for all 20 stories. This means that each individual contributes more or fewer responses to the analysis.

2. Next, the data were analyzed on the basis of individuals, that is, the number of persons in each group contributing a given number or more of responses of each type. This provides information concerning whether the factor causing group differences was a greater mean number of responses per individual in the group or just a few extreme individuals. Also, if there are no significant differences between groups, the reason might be, not that all individuals in both groups contribute approximately the same number of responses, but that in the one, occasional subjects are responsible for the majority of responses, while in the other all are contributing just a few. In other words, we would have some indication of the homogeneity of variance within the groups. Presumably, also, if one group contributed significantly more of certain responses than another, and also contained significantly more individuals who made such responses, we could be more certain that these differences in responses represent real group characteristics. One of the inadequacies of past research on diagnostic testing is that it has been based on responses and not on individuals. This means that any generalization

---

[7] Mrs. Dorothy T. Hake rated all the stories for emotional tone and outcome.

of the conclusions from the groups on whom the work was done to other groups is unjustified, since intragroup variability has not been considered.

Chi-square tests of homogeneity (Garrett, 1949; Lindquist, 1940) were also performed in the analysis of individual themes and ratings of tone and outcome. The .05 level of confidence (Yule & Kendall, 1937) was adopted as the criterion of significance, and all differences significant at this level were noted, both in the individual chi square tests and in the tests of homogeneity.

Results and Discussion

EMOTIONAL TONE OF STORIES

It is obvious from Table 28–2 that the preponderance of stories told by all subjects in response to the TAT are sad, although there is a little significant intergroup variation with respect to the proportion of stories in each category of the scale (chi square of homogeneity, 94.9900, with 20 degrees of freedom, significant beyond the .001 level). A comparison of each group of subjects with every other group indicates that the six groups arrange themselves into two distinct populations depending on whether or not they are hospitalized. The hospitalized groups appear to be emotionally duller than the nonhospitalized ones, since those in the hospital tell more of the neutral stories and less of the extremely emotional ones than those not in the hospital.

These differences might be a function of the seriousness of the illness, since undoubtedly those in the hospital are more seriously ill than the outpatient group. However, the relationship is not always a progressive one, with the nonhospitalized psychoneurotics more like the hospital groups than are the normal subjects and the psychoneurotics more like the normals than the schizophrenics. There are some instances in which the nonhospitalized psychoneurotics differ significantly from the hospitalized ones and not from the schizophrenics (e.g., total number of sad stories). If degree of illness caused the increasingly neutral stories, it would be expected that the schizophrenics would have more neutral stories than the psychoneurotics and that the hospitalized psychoneurotics would be more like the nonhospitalized ones than the schizophrenics. This is not the case, and thus it seems that the differences obtained are a function of the hospitalization and not the degree of illness.[8]

---

[8] Of course, it is understood that the rough diagnostic categories here used are not the best indicators of severity of illness and that to study definitively the effect of hospitalization, duration of stay in the hospital would have to be strictly controlled and systematically varied. However, within the limits of this study it is highly suggestive that our obtained differences are the result of hospitalization and not severity of illness.

An analysis of the data according to the number of individuals contributing a given number or more of stories of each category of emotional tone produces the same result. *The hospitalized subjects, regardless of classification, give more stories which are neutral or flat in the amount of feeling invested in them.*

This is the same type of phenomenon that has been noted in individuals exposed to other kinds of restricted, routinized, and deprived environment, such as concentration camps, prisons, and orphanages (All-

TABLE 28–2   *Frequency of Stories of Different Emotional Tone, by Group*

TONE	C_1	C_2	NHPN	HPN	HS	GNPH	TOTAL	COMPARISON	CHI SQUARE	P
+2	18	15	15	13	13	6	80			
+1	74	60	64	52	55	54	359	−1, 0	186.5721	.001
0	85	97	77	142	159	171	731	0, −2	79.8755	.001
−1	249	254	246	201	205	201	1356	−2, +1	4.9220	.03
−2	74	73	85	79	60	55	426			
Total happy[a]	18.4	15	15.8	13	13.6	12	14.6			
	92	75	79	65	68	60	439	happy, sad	812.0000	.001
Total sad[a]	64.6	65.4	66.2	56	53	51.2	59.4			
	323	327	221	280	265	256	1782			

a Upper figures are percentages. Lower figures are frequencies.

port, Bruner, & Jandorf, 1942; Bettelheim, 1943; Bondy, 1943; Gesell & Amatruda, 1947; Goldfarb, 1945; Greenson, 1949; Nirembersky, 1956; Sarason, 1950). Reports of observations on such populations all stress the dulling of social adaptation, the apathy, indifference, and aimlessness which such controlled environments engender among their inhabitants. Greenson (1949) discusses the cases of men who had been exposed during the war to adverse conditions, often free of actual danger, but with poor food, in bad climate, or with severe boredom and great loneliness. The apathy which develops in such individuals, he believes is specifically caused by deprivation, which for Greenson refers to "lack or withdrawal of the necessary supplies of love (affection, deference) or food or both, which the individual requires from his environment." Apathy is the defense against painful perceptions and serves the purpose of avoiding "overwhelming feelings of annihilation."[9]

One possible explanation, thus, of the relatively flattened affect of the stories told by our hospitalized patients is that it is a reflection of the insulation they have built around themselves as a defense against the lack of affective bonds which they experience in this circumscribed

[9] It is interesting that the prewar histories in his group of patients showed that men from broken homes and orphan asylums formed a relatively high percentage of those who developed apathy.

environment. It is not an effect limited to just one kind of patient, e.g., schizophrenic, but one which applies to all our hospitalized subjects.

OUTCOME OF STORIES

As can be seen from Table 28-3, the outcomes are more variable for all groups of subjects than the emotional tone of the stories, which seems to be determined largely by the stimulus properties of the pictures themselves. The outcomes appear to be more clearly a function of the individual's creativity.

The most frequent outcome is that described as moderately happy, although the frequency in this category is not significantly greater than that in the neutral category. The fact that story outcomes tend to be happy does not agree with Rautman and Brower's findings with children (1945), although it does with Coleman's investigations with children (1947) and with a former study done with adults (Garfield & Eron, 1948). Rautman and Brower, however, worked with only ten cards, three of which are not in this series, and administered the test in

---

TABLE 28-3   *Frequency of Stories of Different Outcomes, by Groups*

OUT-COME	GROUP							COM-PARISON	CHI SQUARE	P
	C1	C2	NHPN	HPN	HS	GNPH	TOTAL			
+2	45	27	33	16	17	18	156			
+1	174	158	143	148	143	155	921	o, ?	180.5954	.001
0	120	147	108	135	172	162	844	+2, −2	59.2552	.001
−1	81	71	58	35	49	37	331			
−2	56	67	76	48	40	39	326			
?	24	29	69	105	71	76	374			
Total happy[a]	42.4	37.7	35.2	32.8	32.0	35.5	35.9			
	219	185	176	164	160	173	1077			
Total sad[a]	27.4	27.6	26.8	16.6	17.8	15.2	21.9	happy, sad	101.2462	100·
	137	138	134	83	89	76	657			

[a] Upper figures are percentages, lower figures are frequencies.

---

group fashion. Thus their results are not strictly comparable to those of the present study. However, they do mention the fact that happy endings were more common among teachers who took the test than with the children but give no indication of the extent of the difference. There might thus be a difference between children and adults on this variable.

There is also much more intergroup variability in relation to outcome than was found in a consideration of emotional tone (chi square of homogeneity = 184.61 with 25 degrees of freedom, significant far beyond the .001 level of confidence). The differences between the hospitalized and nonhospitalized groups are not so clearly defined as they were in the previous analysis, although the hospitalized groups give more neutral and less extreme outcomes than do the nonhospitalized groups. In addition, each nonhospitalized group gives significantly more sad outcomes than each hospital group. When the data are analyzed by the number of individuals in each group contributing a certain number or more of a given outcome, the pattern is the same: fewer individuals in the hospitalized groups give sad outcomes and fewer also give extreme outcomes. Significantly more nonhospitalized psychoneurotics give a large number of moderately sad outcomes than do hospitalized psychoneurotics, and, as in the analysis of emotional tone, it would thus seem that hospitalization itself is a factor in making the outcomes more bland.[10]

Both normal groups give significantly less questionable outcomes than each of the clinical groups. Of all the clinical groups, the hospitalized psychoneurotics give the most such conclusions, significantly more than both the nonhospitalized psychoneurotics and the schizophrenics. Essentially the same picture is obtained when the data are analyzed by individuals. No normal subject gives more than four such outcomes, whereas in the clinical groups there are individuals contributing as many as twelve. This excess of questionable outcomes among all the clinical groups is perhaps a reflection of the indecisiveness and uncertainty of these patients who are not as forthright and sure of themselves as are normal individuals. This is carried to an extreme by the hospitalized psychoneurotics.

SHIFT IN TONE FROM BODY OF STORY TO OUTCOME

The fact that many individuals turn unhappy stories into happy conclusions has been noted before (Coleman, 1947; Garfield & Eron, 1948), and the frequency of this phenomenon for all our groups of subjects appears in Table 28–4.

It has been stated that the shift to happier conclusions is characteristic of schizophrenic individuals (Harrison, 1943). Our data would demonstrate it to be more representative of normal persons than it is of schizophrenics. Other writers have characterized it as a "refusal to accept consequences which (in children) may lay the foundations for later neurotic behavior" (Rautman & Brower, 1945, p. 200). Actually, our normal subjects also manifest this characteristic more frequently than do the psychoneurotics; significantly so in the case of the outpatient group. That individuals often tack illogically happy endings onto very sad stories is not surprising since, by the mere instructions to make up a story, we are inviting the subject to indulge in fantasy. And one of the characteristics of fantasy is that it disregards logic and reason (Murray, 1957). Furthermore, the individual is following a cultural pattern illustrated by our movies which, producers seem to feel, must

---

[10] See notes to Table 28–8.

DIRECTION AND AMOUNT OF SHIFT	TOTAL	GROUP						SIGNIFICANT COMPARISONS	DIFFERENCES (CHI SQUARE)	P
		C1	C2	NHPN	HPN	HS	GNPH			
+4	9	3	2	1	3			C1-HS	4.3802	.04
+3	127	31	23	22	17	17	17	NHPN-C2	7.2000	.01
+2	588	111	103	100	98	81	95	NHPN-GNPH	7.2000	.01
+1	409	69	78	47	60	77	78	NHPN-HS	6.7280	.015
All stories shifting positively[a]	37.1 / 1133	42.8 / 214	41.2 / 206	34 / 170	35.6 / 178	35 / 175	38 / 190	C1-NHPN	4.8150	.03
Shifting 2 or more places positively[a]	24.1 / 724	29 / 145	25.6 / 128	24.6 / 123	23.6 / 118	19.6 / 98	22.4 / 112	C1-GNPH	3.9874	.05
								C1-HS	8.7078	.005
Shifting 3 or more places positively[a]	4.5 / 136	6.8 / 34	5 / 25	4.6 / 23	4 / 20	3.4 / 17	3.4 / 17	C1-HS	5.0196	.025
								C1-GNPH	5.0196	.025
								C1-HS	4.9543	.03
0	1578	237	245	269	270	288	269			
-1	198	39	38	35	35	26	25			
-2	29	7	8	5	3	3	3			
-3	14	3	2	8	1					
All stories shifting negatively[a]	8.0 / 241	9.8 / 49	9.6 / 48	9.6 / 48	7.8 / 39	5.8 / 29	5.6 / 28	NHPN-HS	4.0000	.05
								C1-GNPH	5.1948	.025
								C2-GNPH	4.7500	.03
								NHPN-GNPH	4.7500	.03
								C1-HS	4.6282	.035
								C2-HS	4.2078	.04
								NHPN-HS	4.1078	.04
								hosp. vs. non hosp.	9.5210	.005
All stories shifting 2 or more places negatively[a]	1.4 / 43	2.0 / 10	2.0 / 10	2.6 / 13	.1 / 4	.1 / 3	.1 / 3	NHPN-HS	5.0625	.025
								NHPN-GNPH	5.0635	.025

[a] Figures appearing in top row are percentages. Figures in bottom row represent frequencies.

481

always have happy endings in order to be successful financially and which thus reflect the demand of the movie-goers.

PERCEPTUAL DISTORTIONS

Misidentification of Sex

Instances in which the subject misidentifies the sex of characters in the pictures are frequent and there is no significant difference among the clinical and normal groups in the total number of such misidentifications (Table 28–5). Nor is there a significant difference in the number of individuals in each group making them. There are certain pictures in which sexual misidentification is frequent; others where it is completely absent. Some errors in sex identification are made by individuals in each group; others, only by individuals in the clinical groups; and one, only by a normal individual.

Many clinicians interpret the fact that a subject misidentifies the sex of a character in the picture as an indication of his own sex confusion. Numerous writers (Bellak, 1947; Harrison, 1943; Rapaport, Gill, & Schafer, 1946; Rotter, 1946; Stein, 1948) have specifically indicated that sexual misidentification of the character on Card 3BM is an indication of a high feminine component in the personality of the male subject. However, more than half the subjects are confused over the sex of this character, and this corroborates an earlier investigation (Eron, 1948). It is difficult to see how this can legitimately be called a projection of

TABLE 28–5   *Frequency of Instances of Sex Confusion**

CARD	GROUP						
	C_1	C_2	NHPN	HPN	HS	GNPH	TOTAL
3BM	15	12	19	12	12	15	85
5		1					1
6BM					1		1
8BM	1	1	1	1	1	2	7
10	1			4	1	2	8
12BM	3	2	4	3	2	6	26
14					1	1	2
15	1		2		1	2	6
20	6	4	4	3	5	5	27
Total	27	20	30	23	24	33	157
Percentage	5.4	4	6	4.6	4.8	6.6	5.0

* This includes outright misidentification and instances in which subject is unsure whether character is male or female. For exact nature of these confusions and all perceptual distortions, refer to Eron (1950, Appendix C).

the subject's feminine identification when fewer individuals identify it correctly than err in identification. This, too, would seem to be more a function of the stimulus properties of the card. There may be some justification in such a statement about the other pictures, where misidentification is rare and where it can be assumed there is actual distortion on the part of the subject when he misidentifies a character. It should be noted, however, that among our subjects are seven homosexuals, ranging from one diagnosed as latent homosexual to one who has been a transvestite for a number of years, and in no one of these cases is there a single instance of sexual misidentification.

Other Perceptual Distortions

Although the most frequent perceptual distortions are the sexual misidentifications, Table 28-6 shows that other distortions are also not infrequent and occur in each group. By "other perceptual distortions" are meant any departures from the standard description of the picture as described in the test manual (Murray, 1943). These include such things as identifying the violin in Card 1 as a typewriter, the gun in Card 3 as a pipe, the woman in Card 4 as a Negress.[11] Again, there are some cards for which distortions are frequent in all groups and other cards in which perceptual distortions are made only by members of the clinical groups. The general hospital group produces significantly more distortions than all other groups. But there are no significant differences among any of the groups as to number of individuals producing these distortions. From 70 per cent (Psychoneurotic inpatients) to 100 per cent (General hospital group) of the individuals in each group produce at least one distortion, and the schizophrenics produce significantly no more than do the normals or psychoneurotics.

A common characteristic ascribed to TAT productions of schizophrenic patients has been frequent distortion of objective characteristics of the pictures (Balken, 1943; Rapaport et al., 1946; Rotter, 1946). However, these data show that perceptual distortions are no more representative of our group of schizophrenics than they are of any of our other subjects, normal or ill. This is evidence of Cameron's "principle of continuity" (1947). Distortions of reality are common among normal individuals as well as among persons with behavior disorders. The only difference, important as it may be, is that normal people are better able to check up on their faulty perceptions through appropriate and practiced techniques of social validation. The critical point in the development of delusions, e.g., is, in addition to the need and the "reaction sensitivity," the failure of correction.

It is difficult to see, on the basis of our data, how perceptual

---

[11] For instances of specific distortions, see Appendix C in Eron (1950).

TABLE 28–6   *Frequency of Other Perceptual Distortions*

CARD	GROUPS							SIGNIFICANT INTERGROUP DIFFERENCES		
	C1	C2	NHPN	HPN	HS	GNPH	TOTAL	COMPARISONS	CHI SQUARE	P
1			1	3	1	1	6			
3BM	7	13	5	5	1	14	45			
4	3	6	2	1	6	3	21			
6BM					3	2	5			
7BM			1		1		2			
8BM	12	8	9	9	12	18	68			
9BM	3	6	2	5	4	3	23			
12BM	3	1	5	4	4	6	23			
13MF	1			3	5	6	15			
14			2		2	5	9			
15	3				1	5	9			
17BM	1				2	3	6			
18BM	6		3	2	5	5	21			
20					1	1	2			
Total	39	34	31	31	48	72	255	C1GNPH	7.2900	.01
Percentage	7.8	6.8	6.2	6.2	9.8	14.4	8.5	C2-GNPH	10.0104	.05
								HPN-CNPH	10.7895	.05
								NHPN-GNPH	10.0104	.005
								HS-GNPH	4.8090	.03[a]

[a] No significant differences when analyzed by individuals.

inaccuracies can be used as a diagnostic "cue" for schizophrenia. Of course, the schizophrenics in our sample are all young, just recently diagnosed, and with comparatively little deterioration. However, these are the cases which are the diagnostic problems. The TAT is not necessary in order to ascertain that a deteriorated schizophrenic has bizzare ideas or distorts reality. But when the TAT is used as a diagnostic instrument with suspected cases of schizophrenia, it is unjustifiable to employ presence or absence of perceptual distortions as a "sign."

THEMES

In the approximately 3,000 stories which were analyzed in this study, there were 6,210 discernible themes which could be classified according to our check list. These were contributed by the various groups as indicated in Table 28–7. All the groups except GNPH are about equally productive, with no significant difference in the number of themes produced. The last group contributes significantly less than each of the other groups except HPN and the difference, even in this comparison (chi square = 3.7809), approaches significance at our criterion. It is

TABLE 28–7   *Number of Themes Contributed by Subjects*
in Each Group

Group	No. of Themes	Average No. per Individual
C1	1,073	43
C2	1,088	44
NHPN	1,067	43
HPN	1,017	41
HS	1,034	41
GNPH	961	38

obvious that lack of productivity is not a characteristic of any of our more homogeneous groups (indeed, in average number of responses per individual there is little difference among any of the groups). Schizophrenics as a class do not show an unusual[12] amount of blocking, as has been reported (Balken, 1940; Bennett, 1941-1942).

As for the themes themselves, the 60 most popular ones, including all those appearing at least 30 times (or in approximately 1 per cent of the stories), are listed in Table 28–8. The inspection of this table makes it apparent that themes of violence, hostility, death, restriction, guilt, and frustration are common to subjects of all types in response to the TAT and are not peculiar to any particular clinical group, as has been reported in the literature (Balken & Masserman, 1940; Bennett, 1941–1942; Harrison, 1940; Klebanoff, 1947; Kutash, 1943; Leitch & Schafer, 1947; Masserman & Balken, 1938; Rapaport et al., 1946; Rotter, 1940; Sarason, 1943–1944). Themes for which these subjects do not comprise a homogeneous population appear in Table 28–9. There are 11 such individual themes in our classification scheme of 125 themes, which is more than could be expected by chance at the .05 confidence level. However, when individual comparisons between groups are considered, only 72 significant differences, listed in Table 28–10, occur out of a total of 1,875 comparisons (125 themes × 15 comparisons per theme). This is less than would be expected by chance 5 per cent of the time. It should be noted that significance could not be calculated by the chi-square procedure in 321 comparisons because there are 45 themes for which one or more groups have a zero frequency. But even on the basis of the remaining 1,554 comparisons, there are fewer significant differences than could be expected by chance. Thus it would seem that, at least on the basis here proposed, content analysis cannot differentiate diagnostic classifications.

In order to say that any given feature characterizes a certain clinical

---

[12] By "unusual" is meant a difference in frequency that is statistically significant at the .05 level of confidence.

TABLE 28–8 *Most Frequent Themes Contributed by 150 Subjects in 3,000 TAT Stories*

		THEME†				GROUP			
NO.		NAME	CI	C2	NHPN	HPN	HS	GNPH	TOTAL
1	IA1a	Pressure from parents	51	65	50	31	58	34	289
2	IC5	Aggression from impersonal source	43	49	47	39	45	44	267
3	IB1	Aspiration	46	54	45	46	41	32	264
4	IB3	Curiosity	34	41	32	20	38	42	207
5	IA1b	Succorance from parents	27	29	32	33	30	35	186
6	IB4	Behavior disorder	33	31	33	26	28	17	168
7	IB19	Vacillation	27	31	26	25	28	29	166
8	IA2j	Death or illness of partner	18	23	29	39	33	20	162
9	IB11	Occupational dissatisfaction	41	19	27	22	28	20	157
10	IB12	Physical illness or death of central character	20	22	23	31	24	31	151
11	IC1	Economic pressure	29	26	21	27	27	17	147
12	IC6	War	29	31	28	24	12	22	146
13	IIB6	Occupational satisfaction	16	20	27	24	32	27	146
14	IB7	Guilt—remorse	28	24	18	34	18	21	143
15	IA3b	Succorance from peer	24	19	22	14	23	32	134
16	IB8	Drunkenness	21	26	22	27	19	17	132
17	IA2a	Pressure from partner	23	20	25	19	17	22	126
18	IB16	Religion	15	16	18	25	30	22	126
19	IC4	Aggression toward environment	16	22	22	23	22	18	123
20	IB2	Inadequacy	17	23	17	23	15	13	108
21	IA2h	Illicit sex	25	29	14	15	14	7	104
22	IA1i	Death or illness of parent	22	9	22	15	14	13	95
23	IIA2c	Contentment of partner	16	12	13	17	19	15	92
24	IA3j	Belongingness	22	23	16	11	9	7	88
25	IC2	Legal restriction	6	11	10	29	18	14	88
26	IA1f	Departure from parent	16	12	20	7	18	11	84
27	IA3e	Aggression to peer	11	14	15	15	20	8	83
28	IC7	Escape from perilous environment	14	11	12	16	12	10	75
29	IB13	Retribution	10	9	11	16	15	10	71
30	IB5	Suicide	4	11	13	15	18	9	70
31	IB17	Loneliness	15	9	9	14	8	12	67
32	IB9	Fear	13	14	11	7	13	8	66
33	IIB2	Intrapersonal tranquility	15	13	13	7	6	9	63
34	IA3m	Hypnotism	14	7	9	12	6	13	61
35	IA1j	Death or illness of child	18	13	9	3	10	7	60
36	IA3d	Aggression from peer	6	9	17	9	12	6	59
37	IB21	Exhaustion	7	6	9	8	11	17	58
38	IA31	Death or illness of peer	11	8	10	8	10	10	57
39	IB10	Rumination	15	18	6	5	6	7	57
40	IA2f	Departure from partner	8	15	8	7	8	9	55
41	IIA1f	Contentment with parent	10	8	8	1	9	11	53
42	IA3a	Pressure from peer	11	12	6	9	5	9	52
43	IC3	Generalized restriction	17	14	7	5	4	4	51
44	IIB3	Reminiscence, happy	10	7	10	12	4	8	51
45	IA2B	Succorance from partner	6	7	6	11	8	7	45
46	IA2e	Aggression toward partner	4	8	9	12	8	2	43
47	IIB1	Self-esteem	9	10	8	6	3	7	43
48	IIB7	Ordinary activity intrapersonal	5	7	4	5	7	14	42
49	IA1m	Filial obligation	8	8	8	3	6	8	41
50	IA2n	Partner competition	3	4	8	7	7	9	38
51	IIC1	Favorable environment	9	8	5	8	7	1	38
52	IIA3e	Exhibition	8	7	6	3	4	8	36
53	IA1p	News of marriage to parent	5	11	2	6	5	6	35
54	IB14	Reminiscence, sad	6	6	6	3	8	5	34
55	IA1g	Parental concern	5	3	5	7	7	6	33
56	IA2c	Nurturance to partner	7	6	8	4	3	5	33
57	IA31	Competition with peers	10	6	4	2	5	6	33
58	IB6	Moral struggle	2	6	9	4	4	5	30
59	IA2m	Jealousy of partner	5	10	3	6	3	3	30
60	IA1k	Disappointment to parent	7	5	2	7	4	5	30

* Included are all themes appearing in 1 per cent (30) or more of the 3,000 stories. Themes are listed in order of decreasing frequency.
† For definition of specific themes, see Appendix B in Eron (1950).

TABLE 28–9   *Themes for Which All Groups of Subjects Do Not Mean Bender-Gestalt Z Scores and Standard at .05 Confidence Level*

No.	THEME NAME	CHI SQUARE OF HOMOGENEITY	P (5 DEGREES OF FREEDOM)
IA1a	Pressure from parent	19.2290	.01
IA1j	Death or illness of child	13.2000	.05
IA1c	Nurturance to parent	16.2500	.01
	Total themes, parental disequilibrium	14.9178	.02
IA2h	Illicit sex	21.5294	.001
IA2j	Death or illness of partner	12.2221	.05
	Total themes, partner disequilibrium	11.4887	.05
IA3j	Belongingness	15.3335	.01
	Total themes, interpersonal disequilibrium	17.0565	.01
IB10	Rumination	27.1578	.001
IB11	Occupational dissatisfaction	12.7306	.05
IC2	Legal restriction	21.8668	.001
	Total themes of disequilibrium	21.5186	.001
IC3	Generalized restriction of environment	20.3293	.01
IIA1d	Reunion with parents	12.0549	.05
	Total No. of themes	16.3409	.01

group, this feature must distinguish that group both from normal individuals and from other clinical groups. Not one of our classes of subjects differs significantly from *all* other classes in any given theme. Furthermore, no class differs from *both* normal groups in more than five themes, and there are no themes for which the nonhospitalized psychoneurotics differ from both normal groups. In fact, there are fewer significant differences between one normal group (C_1) and one clinical group (NHPN) than there are between the two normal groups (C_1) and (C_2). By chance there should be more than six such differences in 125 comparisons. There are only five pairs of groups that have more than six significant differences between them and thus differ more than could be expected by chance in regard to themes. These are C_1 and HPN with 10 significant differences, C_1 and GNPH with seven significant differences, C_1 and HS with eight significant differences, C_2 and HPN with seven significant differences, and C_2 and GNPH with eight significant differences.

As was mentioned above, there are 45 themes in which the frequency for at least one group is zero, and therefore 321 comparisons could not be made. The maximum number of such instances for any particular comparison, however, is 28, and when the total number of comparisons between any two groups is reduced by the number of times that the chi square could not be calculated, the number of differences more frequent than could be obtained by chance between any two classes is not greatly affected. The comparison between another pair of groups, HPN and GNPH, can now be added to the list above. It would seem, therefore, that we could say definitely no more than that hospitalized psychoneurotics tell certain kinds of themes that are distinctive, since this is the only group that differs from both normal groups and from a miscellaneous neuropsychiatric group more frequently than could be expected by chance.

When the data are analyzed by individuals, the latter statement must be even more circumscribed, because on this basis significant differences are still less frequent. Now, there are significant differences merely between each of the normal groups and each of the clinical groups; but the number of these differences ranges from only one to three—less than could be expected by chance. Thus it can justifiably be said only that this particular group of hospitalized psychoneurotics differs significantly more frequently than could be expected by chance from these particular normal groups and this particular general neuropsychiatric hospital group.

It is possible to rearrange the subjects so that there are larger classes, and thus the comparisons can be based on more individuals, as in Table 28–11. When all psychoneurotics, Groups NHPN and HPN, are compared with all normals, Groups C1 and C2, more significant differences appear. There are now eleven such differences, almost twice what could be expected by chance. And when, as in Table 28–12, all hospitalized groups, HPN, HS, and GNPH, are compared with all non-hospitalized groups, C1, C2, and NHPN, slightly more differences emerge. It may be that our original six classes are not large enough to permit significant group differences to emerge.

Some of the differences that are obtained when the subjects are regrouped into these larger classifications are interesting. The normal subjects give significantly more themes of parental disequilibrium than do the psychoneurotics, and within this category, more of both pressure from parents and nurturance to parents. These normals apparently project their parental difficulties into their fantasy more frequently than do these psychoneurotics. However, theirs is perhaps a more mature level of fantasy, because a greater number of themes of nurturance to the parent may be an expression of independence, even while more themes of parental pressure reflect a chafing at parental restrictions.

That the normal subjects contribute more themes concerning illicit sex may be due to fewer inhibitions in giving verbal expression to these thoughts—or, if one accepts the concept of need projection, perhaps they have a greater impulse to express them verbally since they are finding less expression actually. The fact that they do not contribute as many themes of death of partner possibly indicates less hostility towards the opposite sex, which might very well be a function of the

TABLE 28–10   *Differences in Themes and Interpretation Levels Significant at or Beyond .05 Confidence Level*

NO.	THEME NAME	GROUP	FREQUENCY	GROUP	FREQUENCY	CHI SQUARE	P
IA1a	Pressure from parent	C2	65	HPN	31	11.3437	.001[b]
		C2	65	GNPH	34	9.0909	.005
		HS	58	HPN	31	7.5955	.01
		HS	58	GNPH	34	5.7500	.02
		C1	51	HPN	31	4.4024	.035
		NHPN	50	HPN	31	4.0000	.05
IA1c	Nurturance to parent	C1	9[a]	HPN	1	4.9000	.03
		C1	9[a]	HS	1	4.9000	.03
		C2	8[a]	HPN	1	4.0000	.05
		C2	8[a]	HS	1	4.0000	.05
IA1f	Departure from parent	NHPN	20	HPN	7	5.3333	.025
IA1i	Death or illness of parent	C1	22	C2	9	4.6451	.035
		NHPN	22	C2	9	4.6451	.035
IA1j	Death or illness of child	C1	18	HPN	3	9.3333	.005[b]
		C2	13	HPN	3	5.0625	.025
		C1	18	GNPH	7	4.0000	.05
IA1p	Marriage of child	C2	11[a]	NHPN	2	4.9231	.03
IA2e	Aggression to partner	HPN	12	GNPH	2	5.7857	.02
IA2h	Illicit sex	C2	29	GNPH	7	12.2500	.001[b]
		C1	25	GNPH	7	9.0312	.005[b]
		C2	29	NHPN	14	4.5581	.035[b]
		C2	29	HS	14	4.5581	.035
		C2	29	HPN	15	3.8409	.05
IA2j	Death or illness of partner	HPN	39	C1	18	7.0175	.01[b]
		HPN	39	GNPH	20	5.4916	.02
		HS	33	C1	18	3.8431	.05[b]
IA3b	Succorance from peer	GNPH	32	HPN	14	6.2826	.015
IA3e	Aggression to peer	HS	20	GNPH	8	4.3213	.04
IA3d	Aggression from peer	NHPN	17[a]	C1	6	4.3478	.04
		NHPN	17[a]	GNPH	6	4.3478	.04
IA3j	Belongingness	C2	23	GNPH	7	7.5000	.01
		C1	22	GNPH	7	6.7586	.005
		C2	23	HS	9	5.2812	.025
		C1	22	HS	9	4.6451	.035[b]
IA3l	Competition	C1	10[a]	HPN	2	4.0833	.045
IB1	Aspiration	C2	54	GNPH	32	5.1279	.025[b]
IB3	Curiosity	GNPH	42	HPN	20	7.1129	.01
		C2	41	HPN	20	6.5574	.015
		HS	38	HPN	20	4.9828	.03

[a] No individual contributes more than one such response.
[b] Also a difference in number of individuals in each group.

(Continued on next page)

TABLE 28–10 *(continued)*

THEME		GROUP FREQUENCY		GROUP FREQUENCY		CHI SQUARE	P
NO.	NAME						
IB_4	Behavior disorder	C_1	33	GNPH	17	4.5000	.035
		NHPN	33	GNPH	17	4.5000	.035
IB_5	Suicide	HS	18	C_1	4	7.6818	.01
		HPN	15	C_1	4	5.2632	.025[b]
IB_7	Guilt—remorse	HPN	34	NHPN	18	4.3269	.04
		HPN	34	HS	18	4.3269	.04
IB_{10}	Rumination	C_2	18	HPN	5	6.2609	.015
		C_2	18	NHPN	6	5.0417	.025
		C_2	18	HS	6	5.0417	.025
		C_1	15	HPN	5	4.0500	.045
		C_2	18	GNPH	7	4.0000	.05
IB_{11}	Occupational dissatisfaction	C_1	41	C_2	19	7.3500	.01
		C_1	41	GNPH	20	6.5574	.015
		C_1	41	HPN	22	5.1428	.025
IB_{21}	Exhaustion	GNPH	17[a]	C_2	6	4.3478	.04
IC_2	Legal restriction	HPN	29	C_1	6	13.8286	.001[b]
		HPN	29	NHPN	10	8.3077	.005
		HPN	29	C_2	11	7.2250	.01
		HPN	29	GNPH	14	5.9394	.015
		HS	18	C_1	6	5.0416	.025
IC_3	Generalized restriction	C_1	17	GNPH	4	6.8570	.01
		C_1	17	HS	4	6.8570	.01[b]
		C_1	17	HPN	5	5.5000	.02
		C_2	14	GNPH	4	4.5000	.035
		C_2	14	HS	4	4.5000	.035
IC_6	War	C_2	31	HS	12	7.5348	.01
		C_1	29	HS	12	6.2439	.015
		NHPN	28	HS	12	5.6250	.02
IIB_4	Retirement	HS	32	C_1	16	4.6875	.035
IIB_7	Ordinary activity	GNPH	14	NHPN	4	4.5000	.035
IIC_1	Favorable environment	C_1	9	GNPH	1	4.9000	.03
		C_2	8	GNPH	1	4.0000	.05
		HPN	8	GNPH	1	4.0000	.05
Level of Interpretation							
III A	Symbolic	C_1	22	NHPN	6	8.0357	.005
		C_2	22	NHPN	6	8.0357	.005
		C_1	22	HPN	8	5.6333	.02
		C_2	22	HPN	8	5.6333	.02
		HS	18	NHPN	6	5.0417	.025
III C	Description	GNPH	21	C_2	3	12.0417	.001
		GNPH	21	C_1	4	10.2400	.005
		GNPH	21	NHPN	5	8.6538	.005
		HPN	15	C_2	3	6.7222	.01[b]
		HS	14	C_2	3	5.8823	.02
		HPN	15	C_1	4	5.2631	.025[b]

(Continued on next page)

TABLE 28-10 *(continued)*

NO.	NAME	THEME GROUP FREQUENCY		GROUP FREQUENCY		CHI SQUARE	P
		HS	14	C_1	4	4.5000	.03
		HPN	15	NHPN	5	5.0500	.025
III D	Unreal	C_1	19	GNPH	6	5.7000	.02
III G	Autobiographical	HPN	25	C_1	12	3.8919	.05
III I	Alternate themes	HPN	45	C_1	11	19.4464	.001[b]
		NHPN	35	C_1	11	11.5000	.001[b]
		GNPH	31	C_1	11	8.5952	.005
		HS	30	C_1	11	5.5609	.02[b]
		HPN	45	C_2	23	6.4853	.015
III J	Comments	GNPH	20	NHPN	4	9.3750	.005
		GNPH	20	C_2	6	6.5000	.015
		HS	16	NHPN	4	6.0500	.015
		GNPH	20	HPN	8	4.3214	.04
III L	Rejection	HS	12	C_2	1	7.6923	.01[b]
		GNPH	9	C_2	1	4.9000	.03
		HS	12	NHPN	2	5.7857	.02
		HPN	22	C_2	1	17.3913	.001[b]
		HPN	22	NHPN	2	15.0417	.001
III M	Peculiar verbalizations	HS	13	HPN[c]	1	8.6429	.005
III N	Confused	HS	18	C_1	1	13.4737	.001
		HS	18	NHPN	1	13.4737	.001[d]
		GNPH	11	C_1	1	6.7500	.01
		GNPH	11	NHPN	1	6.7500	.01[b]

[c] All other groups except GNPH have zero frequency. GNPH has frequency 4 which is not significantly different from 13.
[d] Groups C_2 and HPN have zero frequency.

fewer inhibitions just noted. The normal subjects offer more themes of belongingness, perhaps because, as college students, they are more concerned with problems of acceptance and fellowship; and the traditional preoccupation of college students with world problems and man's insignificance may be reflected in the preponderance of themes of rumination. Bennett (1941–1942) also found sexual topics and "disillusionment" (similar to our "rumination") more popular with normals.

Some of these same differences appear when hospitalized and nonhospitalized subjects are compared, and new ones of interest are also revealed. Those in the hospital give significantly fewer themes of interpersonal disequilibrium, including fewer themes of disturbance in the parental situation and fewer themes of illicit sex and belongingness. In general, they give fewer themes of disequilibrium, perhaps as a result of their simplified, protected environment which removes them from many everyday struggles. This is further illustrated by the fact that they have fewer themes of generalized restriction of the environment, yet more of legal restriction, the latter probably a reflection of their own

TABLE 28–11   *Differences in Themes Significant at or Beyond
.05 Confidence Level between All Normal
and All Psychoneurotic Subjects*

NO.	THEME NAME	NOR-MAL	PSYCHO-NEUROTIC	CHI SQUARE	P
IA1a	Parental pressure	116	81	5.8680	.02
IA1c	Nurturance to parent	17	4	6.8751	.01
IA1j	Death or illness of child	31	12	7.5344	.01
	Total parental disequilibrium	356	290	6.5402	.02
IA2h	Illicit sex	54	29	7.5300	.01
IA2j	Death or illness of partner	41	68	6.2018	.02
IA3j	Belongingness	45	27	4.0139	.05
IB10	Rumination	33	11	10.0227	.01
IB11	Occupational dissatisfaction	60	39	4.0404	.05
IC2	Legal restriction	17	39	7.8751	.01
IC3	Generalized restriction of environment	31	12	7.5349	.01
IIA1d	Reunion with parents	2	10	4.0833	.05
	Level				
III A	Symbolic	44	14	14.5000	.001
III C	Descriptive	7	20	5.3333	.05
III E	Fairy tale	8	1	4.0000	.05
III I	Alternate themes	34	80	17.7631	.001
III L	Rejection	1	24	19.3600	.001

position in the hospital. They also seem to be less concerned with war than the other veterans. The hospitalized subjects offer significantly more themes of inadequacy, perhaps because of their own inferiority feelings which are intensified by the hospital experience. More religious themes might be expected of more seriously ill neuropsychiatric patients, while fewer themes of rumination might indicate a lessened concern with other philosophical problems.

Although there is no indication of the significance, because chi-square tests could not be performed, it is important to note those instances where frequency of theme in one group was zero. This might indicate certain characteristics that are exclusively clinical or exclusively normal, at least for this sample. We find that no subject in any of the non-hospitalized groups offers a theme of homosexuality, while at least one such response is forthcoming from each of the hospitalized groups and five from the schizophrenic classification. However, in the latter group there are only two individuals who contribute such themes, since one contributes four of the five themes. Nor does a single theme of incest with siblings appear among the normal subjects, although there are two such schizophrenic responses and one in the nonhospitalized psychoneurotic group. However, one theme of incest with parents is contributed by a normal, and one by a hospitalized psychoneurotic, but

TABLE 28–12   *Differences in Themes Significant at or Beyond .05*
Confidence Level between Hospitalized
and Nonhospitalized Subjects

NO.	NAME	NON HOS-PITAL-IZED	HOS-PITAL-IZED	CHI SQUARE	P
Ia1a	Parental pressure	166	123	6.1038	.02
IA1c	Nurturance to parent	20	5	7.8400	.01
IA1f	Departure from parent	48	26	5.9595	.02
IA1j	Death or illness of child	40	20	6.0167	.02
	Total parental disequilibrium	521	423	9.9671	.01
IA2h	Illicit sex	68	36	9.2404	.01
IA3j	Belongingness	61	28	11.5102	.001
	Total peer disequilibrium	348	289	5.2810	.05
	Total interpersonal disequilibrium	1,290	1,127	10.9913	.001
IB2	Inadequacy	57	88	6.2069	.02
IB10	Rumination	39	18	7.0175	.01
IB16	Religion	49	77	5.7857	.02
IC2	Legal restriction	27	61	12.3750	.001
IC3	Generalized restriction of environment	38	13	11.2941	.001
IC6	War	88	58	5.7603	.02
	Total disequilibrium	2,864	2,609	11.8810	.001
IIB2	Tranquility	41	22	5.1428	.05
	Total themes	3,228	2,982	9.7449	.01
	Level				
III A	Symbolic	50	28	4.7619	.05
III C	Descriptive	12	50	12.2208	.001
III G	Autobiographical	41	68	6.2018	.02
III I	Alternate themes	69	106	6.6057	.02
III J	Comments	20	44	8.2656	.02
III L	Rejections	3	43	33.0652	.001

none by a schizophrenic or any other clinical subject. It cannot be said, then, that tabooed sexual themes (incest, rape, homosexuality, etc.) are exclusively schizophrenic, as has been stated in the literature (Rapaport et al., 1946).

It is interesting that although each group has at least one response of disregard for peer, there is no such response in the schizophrenic group. The same is true of the theme, self-pity. In general, there is only an occasional theme which is found exclusively in schizophrenic or exclusively in psychoneurotic or exclusively in normal groups. For in almost every classification to which one group contributes, some members of at least one other group also appear.

Although we have hypothesized about the significance of some of the intergroup differences, *the outstanding finding of this study seems* to be the similarity in fantasy content among our various groups of subjects. This is not at variance with what has been reported by some investigators using other projective techniques. More than 25 years ago Gardner Murphy (1921) reported that he could not establish any clear-cut differences among the responses of dementia praecox, manic-depressive, and paretic patients to the Kent-Rosanoff word list on the basis of preponderance of one type of association. A further study (Murphy, 1923) of dementia praecox and manic-depressive patients and normal subjects, classifying their responses according to the logical rela-tionship between S and R, also failed to differentiate among these groups. McDowell (1928) also found no difference between stuttering and nonstuttering children on the basis of the word-association test.

Anastasi and Foley (1944) found extensive overlapping in the type of subject matter portrayed by abnormal and normal groups in an investigation of their spontaneous drawings. Their findings are very similar to ours. They say:

Most of the subject matter categories do not differentiate significantly between normal and abnormal drawings. Although certain types of drawings appear to be more clearly diagnostic of abnormality, such drawings are made by a small minority of institutionalized patients. The majority of abnormal patients, although showing clearly psychotic behavior in other respects, produced drawings which were indistinguishable from the normal in subject matter (Anastasi & Foley, 1944, p. 174).

Recent studies have been carried out on populations similar to ours, using the Draw-a-Man technique. Royal (1949) found no statistically significant differences between neurotic and normal veterans on a check list of 28 drawing characteristics, although there was a tendency toward significance in eight of them. Albee and Hamlin (1949) found that 15 clinical psychologists could not distinguish the drawings of psycho-neurotic and schizophrenic outpatient veterans from each other.

Using the verbal summator technique, Grings (1942) found no discrimination in projective content among 24 schizophrenics, 15 manic-depressive, depressed patients, and 18 psychoneurotics.

The fact that there are no differences in the thematic content of individuals of the various nosological groups has implications for the theory of behavior pathology. It is further evidence for the hypothesis of continuity between normal and abnormal. According to J. F. Brown, "Abnormal psychological phenomena are simply exaggerations (i.e., overdevelopments or underdevelopments) or disguised (i.e., perverted) developments of normal psychological phenomena" (1940, p. 7). White (1948) has pointed out how maladjustments arise out of each stage or process of normal growth, and Cameron (1947) contends that normals, neurotics, and psychotics differ from one another only in degree and that any behavior found in psychiatric patients is somehow related to normal behavior. If we accept the notion that "fantasy is driven by need" (Murray, 1937, p. 118), it can be predicted from any of these points of view that there would be no difference in the content of fantasy productions of individuals of different diagnostic categories, since all individuals have the same needs, whether they are psychotic, neurotic, or normal. And these are, indeed, our findings.

If any one thing differentiates our subjects, it seems to be the factor of hospitalization, which has been discussed above in the consideration of emotional tone and outcome. The effect of the external environment on the content of fantasy productions has been pointed out by some investigators.

Bumke and Kant (1942), for example, report that patients in continuous hydrotherapy hallucinate lobsters and fish. Potter (1948) found that environmental factors, in this case a hospital stress situation, affected the fantasy of women awaiting gynecological surgery and obstetrics so that their Rorschach protocols were more similar to each other than to a matched group of clerical workers not in a hospital situation. This "leveling" effect, which also makes our hospitalized patients, regardless of clinical classification, more similar to each other than nonhospitalized subjects, is further evidence of the influence of situational factors, e.g., limitation of environment, on fantasy productions. Bondy (1943), in a discussion of the effect of internment camps on personality organization, attributes to the social isolation the eventual similarities in personality which emerge. "In consequence of this isolation in the internment camps, all social veneer and superficial personality traits soon disappear. With startling rapidity the internees reach a common denominator and lose their individuality" (Bondy, 1943, p. 462). Bettelheim found significant differences when comparing old and new prisoners, and the differences "seemed to originate in personality changes brought about by the impact of camp experiences on the prisoners" (1943, p. 437). The unnatural, restricted, and routinized environment to which our hospitalized patients are exposed may easily have a similar kind of effect on their fantasy productions.

LEVEL OF INTERPRETATION

Since the analysis of the TAT by content has failed to discriminate between diagnostic classifications and since it has been suggested by some (Leitch & Schafer, 1947; Wyatt, 1942) that analysis of the formal aspects of the productions would be more fruitful, the writer, in the course of analyzing the stories for themes, noted also when there were deviations from the instructions to make up a narrative. Of 16 different kinds of deviation from the instructions,[13] these groups

---

[13] See Appendix B of Eron (1950) for a description of these deviations.

TABLE 28–13   *Levels of Interpretation for Which All Groups*
                     of Subjects Do Not Make Up a
                     Homogeneous Population

		LEVEL	CHI SQUARE OF HOMOGENEITY	P*
III	A	Symbolic	20.1539	.01
III	C	Description	27.2000	.001
III	I	Alternate themes	22.6152	.001
III	J	Comments	19.3000	.01
III	L	Rejection	21.3750	.001

* Five degrees of freedom.

do not make up a homogeneous population in 5 (Table 28–13). The specific intergroup differences significant at or beyond the .05 level of confidence are noted in the latter part of Table 28–10; and there are 29 such differences, which is more than could be expected by chance. The hospitalized psychoneurotics reject more cards than do all other subjects, although each of the hospitalized groups rejects significantly more than each of the nonhospitalized groups. There are only two rejections among the nonhospitalized psychoneurotics, one in one normal group, and none in the other. Each of the hospitalized groups also gives significantly more descriptions than each nonhospitalized group. The nonhospitalized subjects seem to be more willing or able to co-operate than the hospitalized ones, since they comply more closely with the directions. All the clinical groups give significantly more alternate themes than one normal group. (The other normal group also has less of these than any clinical group, but the difference is significant only when comparison is made with the hospitalized psychoneurotic group.) The excess of alternate themes in these groups is no doubt a function of indecision and uncertainty of the subjects in them, just as the greater number of questionable outcomes is. Analysis by individuals does not change the picture very much, except that now fewer significant differences appear, but all are in the same direction.

In light of what has been stated in the TAT literature about the formal characteristics of stories of various clinical groups, it is appropriate to see how our data corroborate or are at variance with what has been reported. The fact that both groups of normal subjects give more symbolic stories[14] than each of the clinical groups, significantly more

---

[14] An example of a symbolic story contributed by a normal subject is as follows: It looks like Dante's inferno. Some sort of monstrosity—a primeval picture—symbolic of evil. This creature here is exploring the unknown—symbolic of man. Might even say it's all a picture of life—dark, cloudy, devastation. The way it's going to turn out is that this small creature is going to defeat this evil up here. More or less a symbolic approach. (Card 11.)

than the psychoneurotics, contradicts reports that this is a characteristic of the stories of schizophrenics (Rapaport et al., 1946) and
psychotic children (Leitch & Schafer, 1947). The normals also give
more abstract stories,[15] although this difference is not significant at the
.05 level. It has been said that ambitendency in story trend is also
a schizophrenic characteristic (Rotter, 1946); yet, as noted above, this
seems to be more characteristic of psychoneurotics. As compared with
normals, the schizophrenics do give more such themes, but they seem
to be representative of all clinical groups and not distinctive of schizophrenics. Story continuation from one picture to the next has been
listed as diagnostic of schizophrenics (Rapaport et al., 1946), but again
our data show this to be more characteristic of normal stories (Table
28–11). Statements that the depicted situations are unreal are also
more frequent among normals; and the difference is significant between
one such group and the hospitalized general neuropsychiatric group.
The schizophrenics and the general neuropsychiatric patients make
significantly more comments about the picture than do both of the
psychoneurotic groups and one of the normal groups. This, too, has
been called a psychoneurotic characteristic (Rotter, 1946).

Other unusual kinds of interpretation are also more common among
normals and often to not even appear among some of the clinical
groups, as shown in the latter part of Table 28–11. For example,
having the central character outside the picture is an interpretation
given by six normal subjects and two schizophrenics; and three normals
included the examiner in the story,[16] whereas only one each among the
hospitalized psychoneurotics and the general hospital group did likewise.
This latter has been called an exclusively psychotic characteristic
(Leitch & Schafer, 1947). As would be expected, peculiar verbalizations,
confused stories, and stories with no conceivable connection to the
picture are significantly more characteristic of schizophrenics than other
subjects, although the actual number of schizophrenics who produce
stories with such characteristics are very few.

The finding that there is more differentiation among groups on the
basis of the formal characteristics of the stories than on the basis of
content is comparable to the results of Anastasi and Foley (1944).
However, just as they report, none of the items occurs with a sufficiently
high frequency in any of the groups to be regarded as a regular feature
of its stories. Each of the deviations in the check list was observed
in only a small minority of each population, and very few of the items
were absent from any group.

---

[15] An example of an abstract story contributed by a normal subject is as follows: It
looks like Salvador Dali. Well, this is an emotional picture. It shows happiness and
contentment of this couple despite storms and adversities. They are secure in each
other's love. Happiness is expressed here—the ultimate in marital bliss—peace and
contentment. (Card 19.)

[16] One of the characters in each of these stories was a "Dr. Eron."

TABLE 28–14   *Rank Order of Pictures on Basis of Number*
                        of Themes Which Each Elicits

STIMULATORY VALUE	PICTURE	NO. OF THEMES
1	13MF	456
2	20	421
3	18BM	413
4	6BM	395
5	3BM	373
6	4	361
7	12M	352
8	15	340
9	7BM	316
10.5	10	301
10.5	17BM	301
12	8BM	287
13	9BM	273
14	14	264
15	5	255
16	2	239
17	1	237
18	19	225
19	11	202
20	16	199

Normative Data for the TAT

Certain pictures have been said to be more stimulating than others
(Kutash, 1943; Rotter, 1946). An analysis of the number of themes
elicited by each card corroborates this claim. Table 28–14 lists the
pictures in the order of their stimulatory value for these 150 subjects.
There was only one significant intergroup difference in the number
of themes aroused by each picture. This was for Card 16, in which
Group C2 has significantly more themes than Group GNPH (chi square
6.1538, significant at .05 level of confidence).

Since the test is usually administered in two parts with one half
of the cards presented in each session, it is desirable to know if
there is any difference in the kind of story told for either half. All
significant differences in themes and levels of interpretation for the
first and second 10 pictures appear in Table 28–15, and there are
significant differences for 48 themes and 8 levels, both many more than
could be expected by chance. Themes and levels for which there is
no occurrence in one or the other parts of the test are listed in Table

23–16. It is obvious from these two tables that each half of the test has a differential effect on the kind of stories it elicits. A study by Kannenberg (1948) indicates that this is not a function of order of presentation or special instructions to make the stories as imaginative as possible, as had previously been assumed (Eron, 1948).

Summary and Conclusions

1. Approximately 3,000 Thematic Apperception Test (TAT) stories contributed by 150 male veterans, including 50 college students, 25 nonhospitalized psychoneurotics, 25 hospitalized psychoneurotics, 25 hospitalized schizophrenics, and 25 miscellaneous neuropsychiatric patients, were analyzed for themes, level of interpretation, emotional tone, outcome, identification of characters, perceptual distortions, and attention to details. The data were arranged (1) according to total number of responses for all 20 cards presented and also (2) according to number of individual subjects contributing a certain number or more of a given response. Significant differences between groups were calculated on both of these bases by the chi-square method, and all differences significant at or beyond the .05 level of confidence were noted. In all, 400 significant intergroup differences were noted, as shown in Table 28–17. As seen in this table, the two most similar groups are C_1 and C_2, the two normal ones, since there were only 6 significant differences found between them, which is much less than would normally be expected by chance. Next in order of similarity are the normal group, C_1 and the nonhospitalized psychoneurotics, NHPN, and groups C_2 and NHPN, with 10 and 11 significant differences, respectively. Thus the three nonhospitalized groups are the most similar. Next in order of similarity are HPN and HS, the hospitalized psychoneurotics and schizophrenics; HS and GNPH, the hospitalized schizophrenics and the general neuropsychiatric hospitalized group; and HPN and GNPH, each with 12, 16, and 17 significant differences, respectively. The groups with the number of significant differences between them closest to this are NHPN and HS, with 24 such differences; all other "cross comparisons" (i.e., comparisons between hospitalized and nonhospitalized groups) yield a larger number of significant differences—up to 46 for group C_1 versus GNPH. It would seem, then, that our six groups of subjects arrange themselves in two clusters according to whether or not they are hospitalized, since the three nonhospitalized groups are most similar, followed by the three hospital groups, and finally by comparisons between groups of the two different classes.

2. When each of the six groups was compared with every other group on each of the six variables specified below, not many more significant

TABLE 28–15   *Differences in Number of Themes in Pictures 1–10 and 11–20 Significant at or Beyond .05 Confidence Level*

THEME

NO.	NAME	1–10	11–20	CHI SQUARE	P
IA1a	Pressure from parents	260	29	183.0450	.001
IA1b	Succorance from parents	172	14	132.5215	.001
IA1c	Nurturance to parents	20	5	7.8400	.005
IA1k	Disappointments to parents	25	5	12.0333	.001
IA1f	Departure from parents	73	11	44.2976	.001
IA1g	Concern of parents	30	3	20.4848	.001
IA1i	Death or illness of parents	79	16	41.7789	.001
IA1m	Filial obligation	38	3	28.1951	.001
IA1p	Marriage of child	34	1	29.2571	.001
	Total parent disequilibrium	809	135	479.7976	.001
IA2a	Pressure from partner	102	24	47.0555	.001
IA2b	Succorance from partner	38	7	20.5000	.001
IA2c	Nurturance to partner	25	8	7.7575	.01
IA2e	Aggression toward partner	8	35	15.7209	.001
IA2f	Departure from partner	48	7	29.0909	.001
IA2i	Illicit sex with violence	1	16	11.5294	.001
IA2j	Death or illness of partner	18	44	10.0806	.005
IA2n	Competition by partners for hero	34	4	22.1316	.001
IA2s	Unrequited love	5	19	7.0417	.01
IA2r	Seduction by partner	17	3	8.4500	.005
	Total sibling disequilibrium	29	12	6.2439	.015
IA3a	Pressure from peer	8	44	23.5577	.001
IA3b	Succorance from peer	14	120	82.2761	.001
IA3e	Aggression toward peer	23	60	15.6144	.001
IA3d	Aggression from peer	10	49	24.4746	.001
IA3i	Death or illness of peer	16	41	10.1052	.005
IA3j	Belongingness	59	29	9.5568	.005
IA3k	Unappreciated by peers	1	8	4.0000	.045
IA3l	Competition from peers	3	30	20.4848	.001
	Total peer disequilibrium	154	482	168.1273	.001
	Total interpersonal disequilibrium	1,396	1,021	57.8718	.001
IB1	Aspiration	196	48	83.8073	.001
IB4	Behavior disorder	56	112	18.0059	.001
IB6	Moral struggle	25	5	12.0333	.001
IB7	Guilt — remorse	44	99	20.2500	.001
IB8	Drunkenness	26	106	47.2803	.001
IB11	Occupational dissatisfaction	129	28	63.6943	.001
IB13	Retribution	23	48	8.1127	.005
IB16	Religion	14	112	74.6746	.001
IB17	Loneliness	16	51	17.2537	.001
IB20	Vacillation	34	132	56.6807	.001
	Total intrapersonal disequilibrium	972	1,186	21.0236	.001
IC2	Legal restriction	27	61	12.4842	.001
IC5	Aggression from environment	49	218	107.2283	.001
IC6	Escape from perilous environment	6	69	52.0324	.001
	Total impersonal disequilibrium	335	562	132.8426	.001
IIA1f	Contentment with parents	10	43	19.3207	.001
IIA2c	Contentment with partner	75	17	35.3152	.001
IIA2d	Reunion with partner	22	2	15.0417	.001
	Total partner equilibrium	111	29	46.8642	.001
IIA3d	Peer approbation	1	17	14.2223	.001
	Total peer equilibrium	13	80	46.8387	.001
IIB1	Self-esteem	2	41	33.5814	.001
IIB3	Reminiscence, happy	14	37	9.4902	.005

(Continued on next page)

500

TABLE 28–15 *(continued)*

THEME

NO.	NAME	1–10	11–20	CHI SQUARE	P
	LEVEL				
IIB4	Retirement	110	36	23.9427	.001
IIC1	Favorable environment	4	34	22.1316	.001
	Total impersonal equilibrium	4	36	24.0250	.001
	Total Equilibrium	334	404	6.4512	.015
III A	Symbolic	16	72	39.5852	.001
III B	Abstract	2	19	14.0870	.001
III D	Unreal	8	68	53.4405	.001
III G	Autobiographical	31	78	42.3500	.001
III H	Continuations	3	14	5.8823	.02
III I	Alternate themes	52	123	66.6475	.001
III J	Comments	22	42	5.6406	.02
III L	Rejection	13	33	7.8478	.005

differences emerged than would be expected by chance. The findings can be summarized briefly as follows:

Emotional tone. The most frequent stories of our entire group are moderately sad, regardless of the clinical classification of the subjects contributing them. The hospitalized subjects more frequently tell stories which are neutral in emotional tone than do the nonhospitalized subjects. This appears to be more a function of hospitalization than of seriousness of illness, because there is no steady progression in the number of such stories from normals through psychoneurotics to psychotics.

Outcome. The conclusions offered by the subjects seem to be more a projection of their own creativity than is the emotional tone, since there is considerably more interindividual and intergroup variability for this dimension. However, the most frequent outcome is *happy* for all except the schizophrenic group, which contributes more neutral outcomes. As in emotional tone, the hospitalized subjects give less extreme outcomes, either very happy or very sad, than do the nonhospitalized subjects; and again the hospitalization is considered the chief factor in accounting for this greater blandness.

Shift. Slightly less than half of the subjects terminate their stories with conclusions which are happier than the general tone of the body of the story. A shift to happier conclusions is less characteristic of our schizophrenic subjects than it is of the normal ones.

Perceptual Distortions. Misidentification of the sex of characters in the pictures and other perceptual distortions are frequent and no more characteristic of any of our specific nosological groups than of our normal subjects. It was demonstrated that to use misidentification of the sex of the figure in Card 3BM as an index of a high feminine component in the male personality is fallacious.

Themes. When the individual groups are compared on the basis of our 125-theme check list, only a few more differences appear than could be expected by chance. Themes of aggression, hostility, frustration, restriction, death, violence, and guilt are common to all groups. For no given theme does any one group of subjects differ from all others, and no group differs from both normal groups in more than five themes. The subjects were rearranged into larger groups, and comparisons were made between all normal and all psychoneurotic subjects, and between all hospitalized and all nonhospitalized subjects. On this basis, more significant differences emerged than could be explained by chance. The nature of these differences, as well as of those among the individual groups, was discussed both in the light of the present literature on the TAT and possible personality dynamics.

Level of interpretation. In an attempt to see if more intergroup differentiations could be made on the basis of a formal rather than a content analysis, the stories were classified according to deviations from the instructions to make up narratives, and many more significant differences were obtained than could be expected by chance. Again,

---

TABLE 28–16   *Themes and Interpretation Levels for Which There Is No Frequency in One Half of the Test*

THEME

NO.	NAME	1–10	11–20
IA1h	Incest		2
IA1n	Confession to parent	18	
IA1o	Bad news to parent	18	
IA1q	Collusion with parent	5	
IA4b	Succorance from sibling	1	
IA4e	Aggression to sibling	4	
IA3n	Envy of peer		4
IA3m	Hypnotism		61
IB18	Compensation		14
IB23	Inconsequential sadness	3	
IB24	Hurt feelings	18	
IB25	Jealousy (unspecified)	3	
IB28	Homesickness		4
IIA1b	Resignation of parent	1	
IIA1e	Fulfillment to parent	4	
IIA2a	Admiration of partner	3	
IIA3c	Reunion with friends		2
IIA3e	Exhibition		36
IIB6	Resignation to lot	3	
IIB7	Ordinary activity		42
IIC2	Rescue		2
	LEVEL OF INTERPRETATION		
III E	Fairy tale		10
III F	Central character out		8

our results were compared with those reported in the literature; and many of the differences which have been reported, when put to the statistical test, were found not only to be nonsignificant but often reversed.

TABLE 28–17   *Number of Significant Differences between Groups*

GROUPS	THEMES	LEVELS	TONE	OUT-COME	SHIFT	DIS-TORTIONS	TOTAL	GRAND TOTAL	RANK SIMILAR-ITY
A. Total responses									
C1-C2	2	1		1			4		
C1-NHPN	1	2		2	1		6		
C1-HPN	16	5	3	5			29		
C1-HS	12	4	3	6	5		30		
C1-GNPH	14	5	5	6	3	1	34		
C2-NHPN	4	2		3	1		10		
C2-HPN	10	7	2	3			22		
C2-HS	9	4	3	3	2		21		
C2-GNPH	21	7	3	4	1	1	37		
NHPN-HPN	8	3	3	5	1		20		
NHPN-HS	4	6	2	2	4		18		
NHPN-GNPH	10	4	3	5	3	1	26		
HPN-HS	5	2		2	1		10		
HPN-GNPH	14	1				1	16		
HS-GNPH	11	1			1	1	14		
Total							297		
B. Individuals									
C1-C2									
C1-NHPN		1					1		
C1-HPN	3	2	1	2			8		
C1-HS	3	1		1			5		
C1-GNPH	2		2	4		1	9		
C2-NHPN	1						1		
C2-HPN	1	2		2			5		
C2-HS	1	1	1				3		
C2-GNPH	2					1	3		
NHPN-HPN		1		1			2		
NHPN-HS		1					1		
NHPN-GNPH		1	3	1		1	6		
HPN-HS									
HPN-GNPH						1	1		
HS-GNPH									
Total							45		
C. Card by card					Details				
C1-C2				1		1	2	6	1
C1-NHPN	1			1		1	3	10	2
C1-HPN	4			3			7	44	13.5
C1-HS	4			1			5	40	11.5
C-1-GNPH	1			1	1		3	46	15
C2-NHPN								11	3
C2-HPN	3	1		2		1	7	34	10
C2-HS	2			2		1	5	29	9
C2-GNPH	3			1			4	44	13.5
NHPN-HPN	1		2	2			5	27	8
NHPN-HS	1		1	2	1		5	24	7
NHPN-GNPH	2		1	3	1	1	8	40	11.5
HPN-HS	2						2	12	4
HPN-GNPH								17	6
HS-GNPH	1					1	2	16	5
Total							58		
Grand Total								400	

3. We interpret these findings to mean the following:

(a) Fantasy productions of various clinical groups do not differ significantly from each other or from the productions of a normal population.

(b) Fantasy productions are affected by the external "objective" environment of the individual: in this case a limiting, routinized, hospital environment.

(c) The TAT, as a fantasy technique, should not be used as a diagnostic instrument in the sense of yielding "signs" or "patterns" characteristic of specific nosological entities.

4. In making a valid interpretation of a given protocol, due consideration must be given to the stimulus properties of the cards themselves, which appear to be as important a factor in determining an individual's response as the actual clinical group in which he may have been classified. As an aid to the proper utilization of this technique, a table has been prepared and is appended (Eron, 1950, Appendix C) that gives for each of the twenty cards in the adult, male series of the Third Edition of the TAT the most popular responses contributed by 150 subjects in terms of emotional tone, outcome, perceptual distortions, identification, attention to details, and thematic content.

5. Although the findings negate much of what has been reported in the TAT literature, they are not to be construed as an argument against the validity of the instrument. The TAT was introduced to investigate the fantasy of normal individuals. It was assumed that from this fantasy there could be inferred important strivings and needs in the narrator. Nothing here reported contradicts this assumption. What is demonstrated is the lack of justification for using the method as a diagnostic device for the differentiation of nosological groups. Schizophrenics, psychoneurotics, and normal persons all have the same needs and strivings, preoccupations, attitudes, delusions, and misconceptions. There may be a difference in emphasis and degree from individual to individual, but not from group to group. Normal persons check up on their ideas and correct their delusional thinking through techniques of social participation, role taking, and the sharing of perspective more readily than individuals with behavior disorders, in whom these skills are not as well practiced. But the fact remains, according to the evidence of the present study, that we all fantasy much the same things. Therefore, a technique such as the TAT cannot be used as a diagnostic instrument in the sense of pigeonholing people into different Kraepelinian categories. If we mean by diagnosis the determination of the dynamics and content of an individual personality and the understanding of his preoccupations and conceptions, the TAT may well be of great value. It is a diagnostic instrument in the sense that it gives an understanding of the individual in his own life setting. The results of this study

indicate that it does not yield differential patterns for classification into Kraepelinian nosological entities.

REFERENCES

ALBEE, G. W., & HAMLIN, R. H. A preliminary rating scale of adjustment inferred from drawings. *J. clin. Psychol.*, 1949, 5, 389–392.

ALLPORT, G. W., BRUNER, J. S., & JANDORF, E. N. Personality under social catastrophe: Ninety life histories of the Nazi revolution. *Charact. & Pers.*, 1942, 10, 1–22.

ANASTASI, ANNE, & FOLEY, J. P., JR. An experimental study of the drawing behavior of adult psychotics in comparison with that of a normal control group. *J. exp. Psychol.*, 1944, 34, 169–194.

BALKEN, EVA R. A delineation of schizophrenic language and thought in a test of imagination. *J. Psychol.*, 1943, 16, 239–271.

BALKEN, EVA R., & MASSERMAN, J. H. The language of phantasy: III. The language of the phantasies of patients with conversion hysteria, anxiety state, and obsessive compulsive neuroses. *J. Psychol.*, 1940, 10, 75–86.

BECK, S. J. *Rorschach's test. I: Basic processes.* New York: Grune & Stratton, 1944. Pp. 155–195.

BELLAK, L. *A guide to the interpretation of the thematic apperception test.* New York: Psychological Corp., 1947.

BENNETT, G. Structural factors related to the substitute value of activities in normal and schizophrenic persons: I. A technique for the investigation of central areas of the personality. II. An experimental investigation of central areas of the personality. *Charact. & Pers.*, 1941, 10, 42–50; 1942, 10, 227–245.

BETTELHEIM, B. Individual and mass behavior in extreme situations. *J. abnorm. soc. Psychol.*, 1943, 38, 417–452.

BONDY, C. Problems of internment camps. *J. abnorm. soc. Psychol.*, 1943, 38, 453–475.

BROWN, J. F. *The psychodynamics of abnormal behavior.* New York: McGraw-Hill, 1940, pp. 3–14.

BUMKE, O., & KANT, F. Cited in E. W. Jellinek (Ed.), *Alcohol addiction and chronic alcoholism.* New Haven: Yale Univ. Press, 1942. Pp. 98–99.

CAMERON, N. *The psychology of the behavior disorders.* New York: Houghton Mifflin, 1947, pp. 1–186.

CHILD, I. Note on Grant's new statistical criteria. *Psychol. Bull.*, 1946, 43, 558–561.

COLEMAN, W. The thematic apperception test: I. Effects of recent experience. II. Some quantitative observations. *J. clin. Psychol.*, 1947, 3, 257–264.

ERON, L. D. Frequencies of themes and identifications in the stories of schizophrenic patients and non-hospitalized college students. *J. consult. Psychol.*, 1948, 12, 387–395.

ERON, L. D. A normative study of the thematic apperception test. *Psychol Monogr.*, 1950, 64 (9).

ERON, L. D., & HAKE, DOROTHY T. Psychometric approach to the evaluation of the thematic apperception test. In J. Zubin & K. M. Young, *Manual of projective techniques.* Madison: College Typing Co., 1948. Chap. 15-A.

ERON, L. D., HAKE, DOROTHY T., & CALLAHAN, R. The use of rating scales with the TAT. Unpublished manuscript.

GARFIELD, S. L., & ERON, L. D. Interpreting mood and activity in thematic apperception test stories. *J. abnorm. soc. Psychol.*, 1948, 43, 338–345.

GARRETT, H. E. *Statistics in psychology and education.* New York: Longmans, Green, 1949, pp. 377–387.

GESELL, A., & AMATRUDA, C. S. *Developmental diagnosis.* New York: Paul B. Hoeber, 1947.

GOLDFARB, W. Psychological privation in infancy and subsequent adjustment. *Amer. J. Orthopsychiat.*, 1945, 15, 247–255.

GREENSON, R. R. Psychology of apathy. *Psychoanal. Quart.*, 1949, 18, 290–302.

GRINGS, W. W. The verbal summator technique and abnormal mental states. *J. abnorm. soc. Psychol.*, 1942, 37, 529–545.

HARRISON, R. Studies in the use and validity of the thematic apperception test with mentally disordered patients: II. A quanitative validity study. III. Validation by the method of "blind analysis." *Charact. & Pers.*, 1940, 9, 122–138.

HARRISON, R. The thematic apperception and Rorschach methods of personality investigation in clinical practice. *J. Psychol.*, 1943, 15, 49–74.

HERTZ, MARGUERITE R. *Frequency tables to be used in scoring responses to the Rorschach ink-blot test.* Cleveland: Western Reserve Univer., 1946, pp. 7–160.

JACQUES, E. The clinical use of the thematic apperception test with soldiers. *J. abnorm. soc. Psychol.*, 1945, 40, 363–375.

KANNENBERG, K. N. A comparison of results obtained from the thematic apperception test under two conditions of administration. *Amer. Psychologist*, 1948, 3, 363. (Abstract)

KLEBANOFF, S. G. Personality factors in alcoholism as indicated by the thematic apperception test. *J. consult. Psychol.*, 1947, 11, 49–54.

KUTASH, S. B. Performance of psychopathic defective criminals on the thematic apperception test. *J. crim. Psychopath.*, 1943, 5, 319–340.

LEITCH, MARY, & SCHAFER, SARAH. A study of the thematic apperception tests of psychotic children. *Amer. J. Orthopsychiat.*, 1947, 17, 337–342.

LINDQUIST, E. F. *Statistical analysis in educational research.* New York: Houghton Mifflin, 1940, pp. 41–46.

McDOWELL, E. D. *Educational and emotional adjustment of stuttering children.* New York: Columbia Univer. Press, 1928.

MASSERMAN, J. H., & BALKEN, EVA R. The clinical application of phantasy studies. *J. Psychol.*, 1938, 6, 81–88.

MORGAN, CHRISTINE D., & MURRAY, H. A. A method for investigating phantasies: The thematic apperception test. *Arch. neurol. Psychiat.*, 1935, 34, 289–306.

MURPHY, G. A comparison of manic-depressive and dementia praecox cases by the free association method. *Amer. J. Insanity*, 1921, 77, 545–558.

MURPHY, G. Types of word association in dementia praecox, manic-depressives, and normal persons. *Amer. J. Psychiat.*, 1923, 79, 539–571.

MURRAY, H. A. *Manual for the thematic apperception test.* Cambridge: Harvard Univer. Press, 1943.

MURRAY, H. A., et al. *Explorations in personality.* New York: Oxford Univer. Press, 1938, pp. 530–545.

NIREMBERSKY, M. Psychological investigation of a group of internees at Belsen Camp. *J. ment. Sci.*, 1946, 92, 60–74.

POTTER, E. H. An analysis of the effect of temporary situational factors upon Rorschach test results. Unpublished doctoral dissertation, Yale Univer., 1948.

RAPAPORT, D., GILL, M. M., & SCHAFER, R. *Diagnostic psychological testing.* Chicago: Year Book Publishers, 1946. Vol. II, pp. 395–459.

RAUTMAN, A. L., & BROWER, E. War themes in children's stories. *J. Psychol.*, 1945, 19, 191–202.

ROTTER, J. B. Studies in the use and validity of the thematic apperception test with mentally disordered persons: I. Methods of analysis and clinical problems. *Charact. & Pers.*, 1940, 9, 18–34.

ROTTER, J. B. Thematic apperception test: suggestions for administration and interpretation. *J. Pers.*, 1946, 15, 70–92.

ROYAL, R. E. Drawing characteristics of neurotic patients using a drawing-of-a-man-and-woman technique. *J. clin. Psychol.*, 1949, 5, 392–396.

SARASON, S. B. The use of the thematic apperception test with mentally deficient children: I. Study of high grade girls. *Amer. J. ment. Def.*, 1943, 47, 417–421. II. Study of high grade boys. *Amer. J. ment. Def.*, 1944, 48, 169–173.

SARASON, S. B. Dreams and thematic apperception test stories. *J. abnorm. soc. Psychol.*, 1944, 39, 486–492.

SARASON, S. B. *Psychological problems in mental deficiency.* New York: Harper, 1950.

STEIN, M. I. *The thematic apperception test: an introductory manual.* Cambridge: Addison-Wesley, 1948.

WHITE, R. W. *The abnormal personality.* New York: Ronald, 1948, pp. 102–174.

WYATT, F. Formal aspects of the thematic apperception test. *Psychol. Bull.*, 1942, 39, 491. (Abstract)

YULE, G. U., & KENDALL, G. M. *An introduction to the theory of statistics.* (11th ed.) London: Charles Griffin & Co., 1937, pp. 534–535.

29

The Stimulus

BERNARD I. MURSTEIN

In a study in 1907, Brittain,[a] finding that boys told more unified stories to a set of pictures than girls, attributed this fact to heredity. The fact that his pictures of moose, Indians, and broncos may have been more meaningful for masculine interests went unnoticed. Indeed, it is only in the last decade or so that the importance of the stimulus in determining the projective response has begun to be appreciated.

The following review traces the efforts to fathom the importance of the stimulus by varying it in a number of different ways, including lighting, exposure time, structure, pictureless TAT, and color. The central figure has been varied by making it a nun, a Negro, crippled, obese, similar to the subject, of different socioeconomic status, and animallike. Last, the attempts to measure the varying stimulus pull of needs from card to card are described.

It is difficult to summarize the findings in a few words. Suffice it to state, therefore, that the studies in general indicate that physical similarity per se is not nearly so important as is the cultural and personal meaning the stimulus holds in society and for the individual taking the test. Further, since so much of the response is influenced by the stimulus, it would seem mandatory that the cards be scaled for a wide variety of needs so that the reality-percept component of the thematic response may be readily separated from more personal projection.

---

[a] H. W. Brittain, "A Study in Imagination," *Pedagogical Seminars*, 14 (1907), 137–207.

509

The Stimulus and the TAT

The stimulus is by far the most important determinant of the content of a TAT response, as is indicated in the work of Eron (1950), Lowe (1951), Mason (1952), Starr (1960), and Murstein (1965a). The last-named study will illustrate this point. Though the study investigated the effect of socially evaluated behavior, self-concept, different instructions, and sex differences, as well as the various interactions, the stimulus properties of the nine TAT cards accounted for over half of the total variance.

If we consider the over-all impact of all the TAT cards, the general conclusion is that they are predominantly sad, as indicated in the rankings of Dollin (1960) and by the emotional tone of the stories as scored by Eron's system. This finding is corroborated by Lebo (1955), who found that his college students judged most of the cards to be sad. Newbigging (1955), however, found that most of the stories elicited from his London college population were rated happy. It is not known whether the differences in the studies are due to the greater structuring in Eron's scoring system, to cultural differences in the population studied, or to the fact that different TAT cards were utilized (Newbigging's cards were selected by virtue of their being spaced evenly along a happiness–sadness continuum). The median response time and median number of words per story correlated negatively with the happiness of the pictures. This finding unfortunately is confounded, as recognized by Newbigging, because the pictures had been given in the order "most happy" to "least happy." Ideally, each subject should have received the pictures either randomized or in Latin-square sequence.

"EVERYDAY" SERIES VERSUS "FAIRY-TALE" SERIES

H. A. Murray, in the manual for the TAT, describes the male series TAT as "divided into two series of ten pictures each, the pictures of the second series (Nos. 11 through 20) being purposely more unusual, dramatic, and bizarre than those of the first" (H. A. Murray, 1943, p. 2).

Eron (1948) gave the male series to a group of college males and neuropsychiatric patients. The patients were matched and their stories evaluated by his emotional tone and emotional outcome ratings. He found that the "everyday" series, which in the main contains human beings in common social situations, elicited the greater part of the themes of aggression, hostility, conflict, and occasional aspiration, while the "fairy-tale" series, which contains few instances of social situation, provoked stories of a descriptive, impersonal, and symbolic nature.

Weisskopf (1950b) found that college students, when asked to describe both sets, projected significantly more fantasy material to the everyday series than to the fairy-tale one. A heterosexual group of college students was asked by Kenny and Bijou (1951) to rank 21 male series TAT cards according to their ambiguity (estimated number of interpretations that might be derived from each card). The authors computed a *t* test between the mean ambiguity level for the first Murray series and that of the second one. The second, fairy-tale series proved to be more ambiguous, at the .05 level of confidence, although the authors did not reject the null hypothesis in postadopting an .01 level. They also compared the "personality revealingness" value of the first series as compared to the second by analyzing the themes of the TAT stories (Kenny & Bijou, 1953). The mean personality revealingness value of the everyday series proved to be somewhat higher than that of the fairy-tale series, but the *t* test of .92 was not statistically significant.

Dividing 15 cards, selected from the 21, into three groups of 5 cards each, according to high, medium, or low ambiguity, the authors found that 8 cards belonged to the everyday series, while 7 came from the fairy-tale series. No significant difference in transcendence (mean number of responses going beyond pure description) was found between the two groups of cards.

The studies reviewed here suggest that the TAT, like most projective techniques, yields predominantly "unhealthy" and sad protocols. Whereas the reason the DAP or Rorschach yields more negative than positive signs of emotional health may reside in the interpretive systems employed (Murstein, 1961a), the negative emotional tone of the TAT may be attributed in large part to the stimulus properties of the cards.

The claim that the fairy-tale series probes more deeply into the psyche than the everyday series has not been substantiated. The evidence, while not substantive, hints that the social facilitation of scenes compatible with the lives of the subjects results in greater identification and more meaningful projection to the everyday series.

Thematic Modifications

In the effort to ferret out the importance of different aspects of the stimulus, investigators have turned to TAT-type cards, modifying them to suit the particular question under investigation. In this section, we shall consider variations in lighting, exposure time, structure of the card, and color, as well as substituting verbal description of the cards for visual presentation.

VARIATIONS IN LIGHTING

Weisskopf (1950b) had college students write descriptions of several TAT cards which were presented either in an unaltered form or as pictures taken under reduced exposure, giving the pictures a hazy effect. No significant differences in transcendence were obtained. Bradley and Lysaker (1957), using a lifelike TAT-type picture, varied the illumination from normal to ·three successively darker stages, as well as three lighter ones. The subjects were several hundred housewives (range 122 to 171 for each stage), with each subject seeing the picture in only one stage. As in Weisskopf's (1950b) finding, no difference in productivity of response was noted. In analyzing the content of associations with regard to the picture, however, a clear positive linear relationship was found between increasing degree of darkness and pleasantness of association. When the picture was used with a varying degree of increasing light, the picture slightly lighter than the control elicited the most favorable association, followed by the next lighter picture, the lightest picture, and the control picture. The effect of light was apparently not a linear function, with a moderate amount of supranormal illumination considered most pleasant and either more or less illumination considered less pleasant.

It seems clear that with the absence of light the stimulus properties of the picture become increasingly vague, thus resulting in an increasingly "internal" perception on the part of the subject. In the relative absence of sensory stimulation, a person finds it easier to introspect and to relate personal material with considerably less inhibition than under normal circumstances. The soothing yet fantasy-enriching effect of darkness is what makes a motion picture more enjoyable in a movie house than in the semilighted atmosphere of a television room. Moreover, many psychotherapists have their seating arranged so as to be out of the patients' direct gaze, on the assumption that there is then less interference with the patients' private thoughts. Here, too, the darkened room is often more likely to induce free association than is the normally lighted one.

The supraillumination effects are more difficult to interpret. Possibly a limited amount of extra light obscures the picture and permits pleasant fantasies to be evoked. An increasing amount of light may be irritating to the nervous system and accordingly elicit less pleasant associations. The relative lack of "pleasantness" occurring under normal illumination may have stemmed from the stimulus properties being most clear at this stage, and hence the subject having been more likely to respect the neutral emotional tone of the pictures (woman baking a cake).

The question may arise as to why an association elicited under less than optimal sensory conditions should be pleasant rather than unpleasant. Two factors may be suspected of playing a part here. In the first place, fantasy often occurs as a temporary vicarious means of satisfying needs and tensions which are as yet unsatisfied in the outer world. The teen-age girl dreams of a Prince Charming; the young executive imagines himself as a junior vice-president. Many of our fantasies are thus related to a need to succeed in a variety of activities, the attainment of which would be associated with pleasant feelings. It is, of course, true that unpleasant, even hostile, tensions may also be present. The young girl may be annoyed because a rival seems to have currently won her Prince Charming; the young executive may chafe under the imposition of being a yes man to the boss. Nevertheless, militating against the appearance of hostility on the TAT would be the fact that the subject would probably deem the testing situation as inappropriate for the expression of hostility. The inhibitory effect of the "background" might be due to a weak generalization gradient from hostility to the expression of hostility because the subject felt that he was being judged and he wanted to make a good impression. Since it is socially acceptable to perceive pleasant things and not as acceptable to perceive hostility in others, more than likely, when the stimulus properties of the object being perceived are weak enough, the subject will be apt to fantasize publicly over only a narrow band of ideation, namely, those topics which do not conflict with what he perceives to be the ego demands of the social situation in which he is involved.

VARIATIONS IN TIME EXPOSURE

Weisskopf (1950b) presented college subjects with two sets of TAT pictures exposed for 0.2 second and for 5 seconds. The latter exposure resulted in a higher number of fantasy scores (transcendence). Kenny (1954) exposed the TAT pictures to college subjects for 5 seconds and 2 minutes, respectively. The correlation between personality revealingness of the themes elicited and trancendence was .62 and .64 for the 5-second and the 2-minute conditions of exposure, respectively.

Apparently, the individual's stories reflect greater personal involvement as well as greater productivity when he has enough time to appraise the stimulus qualities of the card. After a sufficient time has elapsed (optimally, perhaps, a few seconds), added length of exposure has little effect.

VARIATIONS IN STRUCTURE

Completely traced line drawings proved to be more effective in eliciting a greater Transcendence Index than incompletely traced ones in studies by Weisskopf (1950a) and Weisskopf-Joelson and Lynn (1953). Laskowitz (1959) also demonstrated greater transcendence with an increase from fuzzy to clear photographs and from incomplete line drawings to complete ones.

Bradley and Lysaker (1957) reported that varying the background of a picture, when the figure (woman baking a cake) remained constant, had no effect in altering the productivity of responses to the pictures.

These studies seem to indicate that ambiguity of the figure affects fantasy production, but alteration of the background has little effect, provided the activity of the figure remains clear.

PICTURELESS TAT

The novel idea of simply reading the descriptions of the TAT cards (as provided by H. A. Murray, 1943) to the subjects instead of presenting the cards themselves was hit upon by Lebo and Harrigan (1957). Their justification in so doing was the possibility that verbal descriptions might be easier to translate than redrawing a TAT picture to conform to another cultural milieu; also, it might be easier to administer the cards in this form to a group and might be valuable as a projective test for the blind. A counterbalanced order of presentation of TAT cards and their spoken descriptions was utilized, the subjects being college women. Over-all analysis of word count, idea count, story mood, outcome mood, level of response, and dynamic content indicated little difference between the presentations. Comparison was made between the normative data of Eron (1950), Eron, Terry, and Callahan (1950), and Terry (1952) and the responses to the pictures, as well as to the spoken description. The correlations on the aforementioned variables were only negligibly lower for spoken descriptions versus the norm than for the TAT picures versus the norm. In another study, Lebo and Sherry (1959) compared the spoken descriptions with the written descriptions (that is, H. A. Murray's descriptions were typed out, one description per page, and presented to the subjects, who also were college women). Comparison of the two versions yielded no significant differences for the variables number of words, number of ideas, emotional tone of story, emotional tone of outcome, response level, dynamic content, and perceptual range, with the written description being either equally good or superior for each variable. Both measures correlated significantly with the normative data for the variables story mood and common themes. The correlation did not quite reach significance for level of responses and outcome mood.

The results are a bit trying for the TAT. Apparently, many of the TAT pictures are so unambiguous that it matters little whether a visual or verbal description of the card is presented. It would be interesting to see whether these results would hold if a series of the more highly ambiguous TAT cards was utilized. The Lebo studies, rather than necessarily stressing the utility of nonpicture forms of the TAT, may well have indicated why the highly unambiguous TAT has repeatedly failed to differentiate varying psychiatric groups. Perhaps what is needed for accurate personality diagnosis is a new set of highly structured yet highly ambiguous cards. Another factor is that the results may have been specific to a college population, with the efficacy of the verbal descriptions varying inversely with age and maturity of the subjects.

VARIATIONS IN COLOR

It is known that color has a pronounced effect on the perception of Rorschach cards. Does the addition of color influence thematic responses? To test this hypothesis, Brackbill (1951) had an artist apply lifelike oil tints to 12 TAT cards. He administered 6 oil-tint cards and their achromatic counterparts to psychiatric and normal populations, balancing the order of presentation. The colored cards resulted in a greater number of depressive stories among neurotic subjects than did the uncolored ones. The control subjects, on the other hand, showed somewhat more positive themes to the colored cards. Reaction time to the colored cards was slower than to the achromatic ones for the neurotic group, but no difference existed for the controls. When Brackbill analyzed the categories "depressive," "intellectual," "destructive," and "other," he noted that the experimental group could not be distinguished from the controls on the basis of stories told to black and white cards but could be clearly distinguished on all the categories when the stories obtained from the color cards were analyzed.

Thompson and Bachrach (1951) formulated the hypothesis that individuals deal with color impressions in a manner consistent with their affective life. In testing their theory, they employed the group versions of the Thompson TAT (a reproduction of the standard TAT cards employing Negro figures rather than whites) and the standard TAT cards. Lifelike color was added to both series, and the Negro chromatic and achromatic versions administered to two Negro groups in ABBA form. Whites similarly received the standard TAT in chromatic and achromatic forms. In all groups, an interval of seven days separated the administration of the two forms. Using word count as an index of emotional impact, the authors found that both Negroes and whites projected significantly more words to the chromatic versions. Observation of their classification of various categories of mood and outcome seemed to indicate that the achromatic Thompson TAT elicited more unpleasant themes than the chromatic Thompson TAT. The standard TAT did not seem to show any great difference between the achromatic and chromatic sets. The results are confounded, however, by the fact that the Negro and white sets were not administered to the same groups.

Lubin (1955), in a similar study, found that mentally retarded subjects manifested a significantly greater number of words and themes to the colored TAT than they did to the standard version. In another study, Lubin and Wilson (1956) used the Bachrach and Thompson pictures of handicapped persons in both chromatic and achromatic forms with a handicapped and a control population. They found that the handicapped produced significantly more words to the colored cards than to the achromatic ones, while the normal control group produced significantly less to the colored set as compared to the achromatic one. Their conclusion is that color makes the picture more lifelike, thus furthering identification in the handicapped (increased verbal productivity) and decreasing identification in the normal group (less verbal productivity to colored cards than to achromatic ones).

The only study to show no effect of color was that of Weisskopf-Joelson and Foster (1962), who used a group of six-year-old children. The children received two CAT cards, one in color and one achromatic, and two CAT-like cards substituting human beings for the animals, one in color and one achromatic. No differences in transcendence were found for the chromacity-achromacity division.

The relationship of color and form apart from the TAT has been investigated by Berg and Polyot (1956) and Wright and Gardner (1960). The former authors found no superiority of varying hues over achromatic versions of semistructured pictures with regard to accuracy of perception. The latter group used the semantic differential in eliciting responses to the color squares red, yellow, and blue, which were presented alone and as a background to pictures of a family around a new car, two hands holding a strip of adding-machine tape, a plan of an adding-machine keyboard, and a large question mark. Judged by themselves, red was found to be a "strong-exciting" color but an "unsafe" one, and blue a "good-safe" one. When the red color was introduced into a picture context, however, the pictures were judged still "strong-exciting" but also "good-safe." The addition of blue, however, did not move the meaning of a picture into the "good-safe" range. The explanation of the role of red is that the conceptual organization of the picture modifies the otherwise threatening color stimulus so that it becomes "safe," while the impact of the color is to increase the liveliness of the conceptual organization of the picture, which then becomes more "exciting." The authors concluded that "the black and white pictures represent too much control, while the square of red represents too much impulse, and that their combination produced a color-form balance less provocative of anxiety, yet more emotionally satisfying than either alone" (Wright & Gardner, 1960, p. 304).

Some of the studies on color suffer from certain methodological weaknesses, such as absence of reliability measures (Thompson & Bachrach, 1951) and such conceptual deficiencies as the use of word count as a measure of emotional impact. Nevertheless, the studies, considered as a whole, support the assumption that the addition of color facilitates differentiation between the thematic responses of psychiatric and normal, and normal and handicapped, groups. Apparently, the dyspeptic effect of achromacity reinforces the already strong stimulus impetus of the TAT cards toward sadness. The effect of the introduction of color is to add a dimension of complexity and thus mitigate the potent impact of the stimulus structure on the responses elicited. Whether the gain is worth the greater cost of adding color, or of developing a new research literature, remains to be seen. Future research ought to stress more meaningful personality indices than word count and instead measure the gain in description of personality through the use of color. The experimental results surely seem to warrant serious consideration to the employment of color in future thematic tests.

Variations in Central Figure

H. A. Murray (1943) suggested that a least one card should be chosen showing a figure of approximately the same age and sex as the subject. Tomkins (1947), on the other hand, has proposed that the TAT may be interpreted most meaningfully by taking into account the psychological distance of the stimulus from the subject. Moreover, the meaningfulness of the responses elicited by the TAT should be a function of the "remoteness" of the thematic material presented, up to a certain point. Piotrowski concurs with Tomkins, stating,

The verbalization of an unpleasant tension-creating desire, pressing for outward manifestation, can be accomplished with less anxiety if the desire is projected into a person of an age or sex different from that of the testee; especially if that person is by virtue of his age, or social position, a more suitable person to entertain such a desire (Piotrowski, 1950, p. 108).

In the following sections, we shall attempt to compare the evidence on the two competing viewpoints with regard to racial characteristics, physical similarity, socioeconomic factors, similarity of need states, and the use of animals instead of human beings for thematic cards.

NEGRO TAT

Thompson (1949), adhering to Murray's suggestion, believes that the closer the stimulus resembles the actual subject, the more the subject will identify with the figure and accordingly be likely to produce more meaningful material. To test this hypothesis, he constructed a set of TAT cards similar to the original TAT, except that Negro characters were substituted for white ones. With 26 Negro college students from a Negro school as subjects, the Thompson TAT was group-administered by a Negro examiner, who flashed the cards on a screen by means of a projector. The subjects were instructed to write stories to the projected pictures. In order to compare the H. A. Murray and Thompson versions, the subjects were divided into two groups of 13 each, with half receiving the Thompson series first and the H. A. Murray series second, while the other half received both series with the order of presentation reversed. Thompson found a significant increase ($p<.01$) in a story length to the Thompson TAT for each of the ten cards used.

Later studies, however, have been highly critical of the value of the Thompson modification. Riess, Schwartz, and Cottingham (1950) used 30 Negro and 30 white females from Hunter College, in New York City. The usual ABBA order for the two TAT tests was followed, using a Negro examiner for half of both the Negro and white group and a white examiner for the other half. The results were:

Negroes and whites in the North produce stories that differ insignificantly in length regardless of whether the stimulus material is Negro or not, and regardless of the color of the examiner, with the exception of a tendency for northern whites to increase story length on Negro stimulus material with a Negro examiner (Riess et al., 1950, p. 708).

In another article, using the same data (Schwartz, Reiss, & Cottingham, 1951), the authors reported the number of ideas appearing in the stories rather than merely the length of stories. Their data showed that (1) Negroes expressed the most ideas when given the cards by a white examiner, the set of cards used being of little consequence; (2) whites gave more ideas when the Thompson set was used (this result was not a function of whether the examiner was white or Negro); and (3) the production of ideas was quite low when the stimulus, examiner, and subjects were of the same race.

Korchin, Mitchell, and Meltzoff (1950) used two groups of 80 Negro and 80 white male subjects from Philadelphia, half of each group being "middle class" while the other half was of "low" socioeconomic status. The examiner was white. An analysis of variance showed no significant effects due to race or any significant interaction between race and status for story length. Only the "class" differences were significant ($p < .01$), with the middle class telling the longer stories.

In still another experiment, Light (1955) divided 26 white students into two groups of 13 each, one half receiving the Murray TAT, the other the Thompson version. No significant differences in story length were evident, although Light found certain themes to be more frequent with the Thompson set. These themes were crime, poverty, occupational inferiority, witchcraft, and prostitution.

Cook (1953) used 60 male college students (30 Negro, 30 white), divided into four groups of 15 each. One half of the Negro and white groups each received the Thompson TAT, while the remaining two groups received the Murray TAT. The latter groups were composed of the remaining Negro and white subjects, respectively. The examiner here also was white, and most of the subjects had spent at least 15 years in the South. Cook wished to examine the relationship between the subjects and stimuli for such measures of ego defensiveness as word count, compliance with instructions given, vagueness of stories, number of words indicating uncertainty, number of alternatives offered, number of references to the pictures (i.e., excessive use of description), and number of different themes offered. No significant differences solely attributable to the two sets of pictures were found. Both the Negroes and whites were interviewed with regard to their perception of the test. It was found that the great majority of the Negroes perceived both the Murray and the Thompson TAT as dealing with "people in general." On the other hand, the whites perceived the Thompson TAT as dealing with Negroes rather than people in general. Hence, it would be expected that the chief differences between the Negro and white subjects would be found with regard to the Thompson TAT. This was precisely what happened. The Murray TAT yielded only two significant findings at the .05 level: Negroes used more words indicating uncertainty and made more references to the pictures. All measures were significant beyond the .01 level. Cook believed his findings indicated that the more remote the relationship between the stimulus and the subject, the less the ego defensiveness.

The foregoing studies lead to a consideration of the following.

1. Are Negroes to be treated as a homogeneous class? The data hardly suggest that such a treatment is warranted. Apparently, it would be more justifiable, if anything, to use a "socioeconomic" class approach to interpretation.

2. The degree of similarity between stimulus and subject is of itself insufficient as an explanation of the type of response elicited because it does not take cognizance of the background characteristics. Thus, in Schwartz et al.'s (1951) work, Negro subjects who were administered Negro cards by a Negro examiner manifested a smaller number of ideas in their stories than any other grouping. Negro subjects receiving the same cards from a white examiner expressed the greatest number of ideas. For the white subjects, however, the Negro cards seemed to educe the greatest number of ideas, regardless of the race of the examiner.

3. In view of the fact that the stimulus $\times$ background $\times$ person interaction seems to be of considerable importance in determining the nature of the response, the t test favored by previous investigation would appear to be a relatively insensitive statistic. The analysis of variance would seem to be more valuable in this regard.

4. The question arises as to whether story length or number of ideas expressed is an adequate measure of the subject's involvement in the TAT. Is it not conceivable that sophisticated subjects (college students) might display an excessive superficial verboseness to mask the projection of manifest or covert needs? What is needed is a quantitative scale measuring the personality meaningfulness of the stories rather than indirect and unproved correlates such as word count and number of ideas.

5. The influence of the stimulus is not a simple function of its similarity to the subject. The culture plays a crucial role in the interpretation of perception. Negroes tended to perceive the Murray TAT characters not as whites but as people in general. Whites, however, perceived

the Thompson cards as dealing with Negroes. Thus, majority populations are far more prone to perceive minorities as "different" than vice versa. They are also less likely to have had contact with them. Minority groups such as Negroes, however, must constantly live in a "white" world. Although certainly aware of the special privileges whites possess which they do not have, they must adapt perceptually to the majority white culture if they are to be maximally adjusted to their environment. Thus, the finding that Negro girls preferred white dolls to Negro ones (Goodman, 1952) should come as no surprise. When, however, Negroes are confronted with the Thompson figures, particularly in the presence of a white examiner, it is apparent to them that something unusual and different is involved, and they tend to be cautious and vague.

PHYSICAL SIMILARITY

McIntyre (1954) used short film strips as projective instruments and congruity of answers to MMPI items between the self and predictions for the character depicted in the film as an index of projection. His results indicated that the chief determinant of projection was the scene *depicted*. No evidence was found that subjects projected more onto figures of the same sex as their own. In fact, it is noteworthy that, although all the subjects were young college men and women, the most effective scenes for producing projection had as their chief protagonists an old man and an old woman, respectively. A subsequent study by Silverstein (1959) employed parallel sets of male and female pictures of approximately the same age and sex as his students. The Edwards Personal Preference Schedule (EPPS) also was administered. Correlations between nine needs as assessed by Murray's TAT system and the EPPS were quite low and did not differentiate same-sex identification via projection from opposite-sex projection, the findings thus agreeing with those of McIntyre.

There is, however, some evidence hinting at greater facilitation for opposite-sex projection in women. DeCharms, Morrison, Reitman, and McClelland (1955) report a study in which they found, in testing college women who held office, that n-Achievement scores derived from stories written to pictures of career women would *not predict* performance in an achievement situation. In order to manifest performance, the picture cues had to be of men or of women in nonachievement situations.

Even more explicit evidence is forthcoming from Veroff, Wilcox, and Atkinson (1953). Under both "relaxed" and "achievement-oriented" conditions, women students produced significantly more achievement themes to pictures of males than females. Both sexes were comparable in the situations depicted in the cards, differing essentially only in the sex of the figure. The authors suspected that background cues, the classroom situation, the male examiner, etc., may have influenced the women to strive harder. Consequently, a second experiment stressing low motivation to achieve was undertaken in which the presence of males was omitted. The results were identical to those of the first experiment.

Lubetsky (1960) had college men and women rate themselves and a series of photographs of men and women of varying ages on 27 personality traits. He hypothesized that projection (ascribing traits seen as belonging to the self to the photos) would be greater when judging photographed individuals who were similar to the self in terms of age and sex than when judging relatively dissimilar photographs. His results indicated that men did as predicted for photographs of both men and women. Women, however, saw themselves as more similar to the photographs of men than of women, making no age distinction with regard to degree of projection to photographs of men. When judging photographs of women, they followed the predicted age gradient, seeing themselves as more similar to young women than to either younger or older females.

Weisskopf and Dunlevy (1952) used three groups of 10 each of normal, crippled, and obese male undergraduates. Each subject received three sets of TAT cards, one of which was unmodified, the other sets being amended so that the central figure was obese in one set and crippled in the other. The subjects were asked to describe the cards rather than to tell a story. The results indicated that the mean Transcendence Index was significantly less for the obese figures than for the normal and crippled ones. This trend was consistent among all three groups.

In a related study, Greenbaum, Qualtere, Carruth, and Cruickshank (1953) administered several TAT pictures and modified versions which were generally similar except that the figures were depicted as physically handicapped. The method of assessment was a rating for depth of projection. The authors concluded that the original TAT series encouraged a greater level of productivity than the modified series (p < .04). They state:

> In pictures where the child is forced to perceive a handicap, his main preoccupation is with this barrier and he only cursorily treats the nature of the goal region from which the handicap is barring him. On the other hand, pictures which do not force a response to a handicap seem to encourage the production of fantasy material in which the child tells about the nature of his wishes in regard to interpersonal goals (Greenbaum et al., 1953, p. 43).

In another study, Weisskopf-Joelson and Money (1953) modified the TAT with sketches of the original drawings. In the first series, the head of the central character was a more or less neutral face. In the second series, the same cards had actual photos of the subjects' heads instead of the original neutral heads. A control group was used to account for the effect of repetition. No significant increase in projection was found for the "photo" set over the neutral set as measured by the Transcendence Index and word content. In addition, the diagnostic value of the photo set, when judged by two judges, was not found to be any higher than that of the other set.

In a study by Edgar and Shneidman (1958), a group composed of psychotics, psychoneurotics, and persons suffering from personality disorders was used. Material from "patient government" discussions was compared with that obtained from the MAPS technique and a variation of this technique, in which full-length cutout photos of every person in residence on the ward at the time, as well as all staff members, were used. Using the Bales Interaction Process Method to analyze the data, the authors found as much reluctance to show antagonism to photos of peer figures as to peers in face-to-face contact, such as occasioned by the group meetings. They suggest that one use of the photo technique may be to measure the feelings of need for evaluation from others and the feelings or need for direction. Nevertheless, the authors conclude that "photos, in general, seem to elicit more positive feeling than fantasy figures did, the latter calling forth more overt aggression" (Edgar & Shneidman, 1958, p. 11).

These studies indicate that similarity of the central character to the subject is not only noneffectual in furthering projection but actually may be detrimental. Since obesity is the butt of jokes in our society, it is unlikely that fat persons derive any satisfying tension reduction in identifying with obese characters. Crippled individuals also would prefer to forget their handicap.

It would seem that women as a class behave similarly to Negroes in following certain prescribed cultural rules. To women, the prototype of achievement in our society, the male, is much more important in stimulating themes of fantasy achievement than is the presence of a figure of the same sex as the perceiver. It appears likely that "culture" exceeds "narcissism" as a motivating agent for the other needs also, but here the experimental evidence is largely lacking.

Before concluding, however, that similarity per se inhibits projection, it may be of value to recall that the background characteristics (purpose of the experiment) are much more readily apparent to the subject under these conditions. Thus, while the subject is taking the TAT under the usual nomothetic experimental procedure, he may not suspect that his responses as an individual will be noteworthy. The subject who, as in Weisskopf-Joelson and Money's study (1953), sees a photo of his head planted somewhat out of context on a rough sketch, may not suffer this delusion. It may be that under nonsocial conditions similarity might well stimulate projection. Indeed, the mirror probably does richly stimulate fantasies in teen-agers, as they carefully preen themselves before going out on a heavy date. Some support for this statement comes from the data of Beier, Izard, Smock, and Tougas (1957), who gave young adults sets of photos of younger, peer, and older persons, having them signify the ones liked and disliked. Male subjects most frequently liked peer males, while female subjects preferred peer females.

In sum, however, as far as the usual testing procedure is concerned, it seems clear that similarity to the point of idiosyncratic identification promotes ego defensivness and a reduction of the degree of projection.

SOCIOECONOMIC FACTORS

Do subjects project more readily to characters engaged in similar occupational or vocational pursuits than to persons in differing vocations? Lasaga y Travieso and Martinez-Arango (1946), in working with nuns, found no improvement in the diagnostic value of the TAT stories when they substituted nuns for the usual TAT central figures. Rosenstein (mentioned in Atkinson, 1958, p. 611), however, separated chemistry majors from physical education majors by the use of pictures portraying laboratory scenes, to which the chemistry students projected more n-Achievement. Scenes depicting athletic competition did not separate the groups. The reason for this failure presumably is that athletic prowess is a fairly universal motive for college men. With the navy, Briggs (1954) employed a modification of the TAT depicting sailors, but no supporting research favoring this approach was presented. Likewise, Chowdhury (1960) has used an Indian TAT and Henry (1951) an American Indian version, but no direct test of the superiority of their modifications has been presented.

Veroff (1961) used pictures depicting various socioeconomic levels in his nationwide survey of motivation. Of particular interest here is his comparison of the responses of blue-collar workers (young skilled laborers) and white-collar workers (young professional and managerial men) to pictures of both these classes. He reported that n-Achievement scores from blue-collar pictures were better than scores from white-collar cards in predicting job dissatisfaction for *both* these groups. White-collar pictures, nevertheless, proved superior in predicting achievement gratification for both groups. Veroff believes these results may be due to suppression of associations toward situations very similar to the occupation in which one is engaged. An alternative explanation — and one more consistent with the findings reported in this chapter — is that the status value of the occupation depicted in thematic cards plays a greater role in the determination of the content of the thematic response than does the degree of similarity between the occupation of the subject and the occupation portrayed in the cards.

Women in his study were categorized by three educational levels: grade school, high school, and college-educated housewives. Their responses to three pictures, two of household action and one of a career work setting, indicated a weak negative relationship for all educational categories between dissatisfaction with housework as measured in an interview and n-Achievement for pictures of household action. There is some indication, therefore, that a strong achievement motive enables one to derive more satisfaction out of housework than a weak achievement motive. The career picture shows no over-all relationship to n-Achievement. When the educational levels are analyzed separately, the only noteworthy finding is the fact that for the college-educated housewives the career pictures elicited a slight positive relationship between n-Achievement and dissatisfaction with housework, and the household pictures yielded a negative relationship between dissatisfaction and n-Achievement. Again, the highest correlation, −.17, though it does not quite reach significance for the sample of 72 college-educated women, is found for a situation presumably more removed from the nucleus of this group's interest than is true of the less-educated groups.

The data warrant the conclusion that similarity of occupation itself is not the crucial factor eliciting projection; rather it is the "status" of the occupation. The prestige of a white-collar position is thus most sensitive to the expression of job satisfaction, while blue-collar pictures, which depict lower social status, most readily elicit themes of job dissatisfaction.

INFLUENCE OF PRESSING-NEED STATES

Does the portrayal of a need which the subject is experiencing lower the threshold for thematic expression of that need? Kagan (1956) found that cards highly structured for hostility (but not actually depicting hostile interaction) best differentiated boys rated as overtly hostile by their teachers as compared to nonhostile ones. Proshansky (1943) showed a "labor" TAT to college students of strong pro- and antilabor bent. Their responses, scored for attitude toward labor, were correlated with a Newcomb attitude scale toward labor, yielding high coefficients of .67 and .87 for both groups, respectively. These studies thus support the "sensitization" effect thesis of structured cards. Most of the studies, however, emphasize the opposite point of view and/or stress the importance of the experimental conditions. Clark (1952), for example, found that showing fraternity men slides of nude females inhibited direct sexual expression as compared to the responses of a control group which did not see the slides. In another experiment, the slides were again shown, but the TAT stories were written under the influence of alcohol in a beer-party setting. Here the aroused group showed more manifest sexual imagery than the controls. Similarly, Leiman and Epstein (1961) found that cards highly structured for sex yielded considerable sexual imagery only for men without sexual guilt. For guilt-ridden subjects, the sexual cards decreased the manifestation of sexual imagery, as compared to their performance on low-stimulus-relevant cards. Fenz and

Epstein (1962) found that parachutists, on the day of a jump, expressed fear not to pictures depicting parachutists but to neutral pictures. With regard to sleep, E. J. Murray (1959) found that subjects deprived of sleep for 96 hours projected significantly *less* sleep imagery to cards depicting sleep scenes than did a control group. Last, Walker, Atkinson, Veroff, Birney, Dember, and Moulton (1958) found that fearful soldiers (soldiers close to the site of an exploding atomic bomb) were able to express this fear more readily to a picture of women and children than to pictures of soldiers.

These experiments point out that presenting pictures which mirror the need experienced by a subject only facilitates expression of the need when such expression is consistent with the self-concept of the subject. Otherwise, the strongly structured card may inhibit expression of the need. This holds only, perhaps, for manifest imagery, for Clark (1952) found that aroused subjects who had had nothing to drink projected more sexual symbolism in their stories than did a control group, even though their manifest imagery was less.

SIMILARITY OF "SET"

Relatively little is known in this area. Solkoff (1959) used two sets of pictures selected from magazines, one set representing the dimension of hostility, the other the dimension of sexuality. The subjects were Iowa undergraduate college students. Half of them were told to give their stories in the first person, the other half in the third person. The cards consisted of six pictures from each stimulus dimension. Analysis of the stories indicated a significant interaction between instructions and stimulus dimension. Thus, initial reaction time was significantly increased from third- to first-person instructions only for the hostility pictures. Inhibition ratings were increased under first-person instructions only for the sexual pictures. Verbal productivity was greatest for the hostile cards and least for the sexual series. The only consistent finding was that inhibition ratings were highest for the cards within each dimension which were highest on the dimension characteristic. The author concluded that "verbal output as a response measure does not in fact operate in a consistent fashion in various 'socially' inhibiting situations" (Solkoff, 1959, p. 81).

ANIMALS VERSUS HUMAN BEINGS

Bellak and Bellak (1949), believing that children identify more readily with pictures containing animal figures than with human ones, created the Children's Apperception Test (CAT). Bills (1950) compared a series of pictures of rabbits with several TAT cards, using as subjects children (both male and female) aged 5 through 10. Significantly longer stories were obtained with the rabbit pictures. It should be noted, however, that the pictures of the rabbits were in color, whereas the TAT was achromatic. This provides a confounding of color and type of central figure. In view of the results with color discussed earlier, there is some cause for considering the possibility that color, more than the rabbits, may have been responsible for the longer stories. In another study (Bills, Leiman, & Thomas, 1950), a new group of third-grade subjects had six play-therapy sessions and then took the rabbit test and TAT. Both tests correlated only slightly with the material obtained from play therapy, using H. A. Murray's rating approach for manifest needs. Their correlations with each other also were rather low, ranging from —.09 to .58.

Biersdorf and Marcuse (1953) used a broad approach to the problem, employing CAT cards and specially constructed cards which were almost identical to the CAT cards except that persons were substituted for the animals while keeping the same emotional expressions. The subjects were 30 first-graders, the group containing both sexes. Not only were no significant differences found between numbers of words used in both tests, but also further analysis revealed no difference in length of time before response, length of response time, number of words used, number of ideas used, number of characters mentioned in the pictures, and number mentioned who were not in the pictures. Mainord and Marcuse (1954), using the same set of cards, tested emotionally disturbed boys and girls (mean age, 7 years) and found similar nonsignificant differences for the aforementioned quantitative measures. They, however, also asked five clinicians to rate the protocols as to "clinical usefulness," the judges being ignorant of the hypotheses of the authors and the stimulus properties of the cards eliciting the protocols. The human figure cards were considered to be more clinically useful at better than an .001 level of confidence.

In yet another study comparing the CAT with its "humanized" analogue, Furuya (1957) studied the protocols of 72 children ranging in age from 6 to 12. He was interested in answers to the following two questions:

1. With different criteria and age groups from those of Biersdorf and Marcuse (1953) and Mainord and Marcuse (1954), what kind of difference will be found between the productivity to animal pictures and to human pictures, equivalent in scenes and situations?

2. Is there any tendency toward relative decrease of productivity to animal pictures compared with human pictures as children grow older (Furuya, 1957, p. 248)?

The results are confounded with methods of presentation in that the youngest children received the cards individually, while the older ones received the cards as a group. Nevertheless, the results are consistent with earlier studies in indicating the superiority of the human pictures.

Of the 20 t tests, 4 proved to be significant at the .05 level or better. These indicated that the percentage of stories containing expressions of feeling and significant conflict, and having a definite outcome, was significantly higher for the human pictures than for the animal ones.

No tendency was found for any increase or decrease in the relative productivity of the animal or human pictures from the youngest to the oldest age range. Last, the author implies that the results might have been even more extensive but for the fact that "most of the animal pictures that have been used were 'personified or human-like' animal pictures" (Furuya, 1957, p. 252).

Light (1954), working with 9- and 10-year olds, found significant differences between the CAT and TAT. The TAT was found to elicit more feelings, different kinds of feelings, conflicts, number and kinds of outcomes, number and kinds of themes, and number of figures. Only the number of words was not significantly different from test to test. Light believed that this result may have been due to the imposed time limit of 7 minutes to write the stories after the pictures had been flashed on a screen.

Armstrong (1954), working with intellectually superior first-, second-, and third-graders, also found no difference in number of words used between the CAT and a set of pictures corresponding in style and composition but depicting human beings instead of animals. The Weisskopf Transcendence Index, however, indicated that the children gave significantly more nondescriptive statements to the human series.

The effect of variation in both stories and pictures was examined by Boyd and Mandler (1955) in a study of 8-year-olds. All subjects were first told a story containing either animals or human beings as the central characters, followed by a similar set of pictures. A $2 \times 2 \times 2$ factorial design was employed, based on the variables (1) type of stimulus story (animal or human), (2) content of stimulus story ("good" or socially approved behavior versus "bad" or socially disapproved behavior), and (3) type of stimulus picture (animal or human). The majority of the subjects preferred the animal stories but tended to be more involved in the human ones. Contrary to the studies previously mentioned, the animal pictures tended to elicit more emotional material.

Simson (1959) compared the human analogue with the CAT on a population of German children aged 8 to 9, the tests being administered in ABBA order. The results showed no effect of order of presentation but a clear superiority of the human series in terms of longer stories, more rapid verbalization, quicker reaction time, and more themes.

Budoff (1960) thought that the failures to substantiate the Bellaks' hypothesis might be due to the fact that the children tested in other studies ranged in age from 6 to 10, and that at this age level children might be already making their primary identification with human figures. He therefore compared the human analogue he had drawn with the

CAT, using children of age 4. His findings included the conclusion that at this age the stories are not too meaningful because of the immaturity of the children, despite the fact that every child's IQ was over 120. Comparisons of word count, story level, and Transcendence Index did show a trend (p .05>p .10) favoring the human set, when these variables were lumped together.

The work of Amen (1941) also serves to emphasize the extremely young age at which a concern with human relationships is emphasized in thematic stories. She showed her children a picture of a little boy and a little girl standing in a living room with a dog between them and asked them, "What is the picture about?" At age 2, 40 per cent of the group told stories centering solely around the dog, while only 20 per cent told stories involving the children. By age 3, however, the percentages respectively were 25 and 64, and at age 4, only 3 per cent of the stories dealt exclusively with the dog, while 95 per cent included the boy or girl in their stories.

Last, Weisskopf-Joelson and Foster (1962), in their study of kindergarten children, found no significant differences in transcendence scores between CAT pictures (one in color, one achromatic) and their humanized analogues.

CONCLUSIONS

These experiments clearly stress the superiority of the TAT to the CAT for the conditions described. The assumption that children who can tell stories will more readily identify with and project onto animal figures than to human ones gained no support at all. Yet, though it may seem that the potentiality of the CAT has been tested and found wanting, this is not the case.

First, let it be noted that only one study used "disturbed" children. It is possible that severely inhibited children may more readily identify with animal pictures than human ones. We need more research before this possibility can be ruled out. Second, the drawings of the CAT are designed to test *specific* problems, such as sibling rivalry and oral fixation. While granting the superiority of the TAT as a broad-band instrument, it is conceivable that the CAT may be superior with reference to the kind of problems the drawings are intended to tap. Future research, therefore, ought to avoid broad indices such as word count and reaction time and focus on the value of the test for the kinds of problems it was designed to measure.

As for the theoretical issue of the supremacy of animals or human beings, this issue can be tested only by employing a broader sampling of behavioral situations depicting animals than the relatively small number of 10 used in the CAT. Perhaps the kind of situation in which the animals are depicted also should be varied instead of using the "humanized" environment appearing on the CAT. In sum, there is a need for considerably more research on a much broader base than heretofore with regard to the CAT.

Scaling of Thematic Cards

One of the first researchers to report measurement of the stimulus properties of cards was Symonds (1939). He had judges rate a series of cards and stories told to the cards on a five-point scale in which adolescents were the central characters. The dimensions rated included goodness of story, genuiness of story, emotion expressed in picture, and lack of detail in picture. The 10 variables were intercorrelated, and the results indicated that the best pictures for meeting the afore-mentioned criteria were those which had a minimum of detail, were vague in theme, were incomplete in content, and yet suggested characters who were readily identified with by the adolescents.

Jacobs (1958) used average intercorrelation of judges' rankings for various personality dimensions. For 14 needs or goals described to the judges, the correlations ranged from .20 to .60 over 12 pictures. The pictures with high correlations may be conceived of as the most unambiguous, the ones with the lower correlations considered as the most ambiguous.

The rank method has been employed also by Birney (1958) on a series of achievement pictures. The ranks were found to correlate with percentage of achievement imagery in the stories ($r = .41$), despite the fact that most of the pictures were high in achievement pull. Starr (1960) employed 10 cards distributed throughout the range of hostility and found a correlation of .96 between judged rank and number of hostile stories told.

A possible difficulty with the rank method resides in the heterogeneity of the pictures. Where the pictures tend to be fairly similar, the rankings are bound to contain a good deal of error variance and the intercorrelations will be spuriously low. The result might be that the pictures would be erroneously described as more ambiguous than they actually are. This objection is overcome through the use of more absolute measures such as the Thurstone scales. More will be said about these scales in the next section.

A multicriterion method of selecting pictures having high stimulus pull for achievement was employed by Haber and Alpert (1958). Their three criteria were: (1) in pretests at least 75 per cent of the subjects had to write stories containing achievement imagery; (2) a paired-comparison method was employed to obtain values on achievement for each of the cards; (3) each picture was rated for several concerns. To be selected, the first three concerns ranked by every subject for a picture must have been achievement-related. Of a total of 120 pictures initially selected, 40 met all these criteria. For these pictures, the correlation between cue rank and achievement imagery was .71.

SCALING METHODS

The first actual scaling of thematic cards resulted from a study by Auld, Eron, and Laffal (1955). They felt that a scaling technique might supply the answer to two pressing problems:

(1) When should one consider two responses as indicative of a single underlying trait (habit or motive of the subject)? (2) Conceding that two or more responses both reveal the strength of the habit or motive, how can one combine the ratings obtained from the two responses into a single rating of the habit or motive (Auld et al., 1955, p. 423)?

The authors believed that the solution to both problems lay in a method which would order the subjects unequivocally, regardless of the weights assigned. An approximation to such a scale might be achieved with the Guttman technique, providing that the coefficient of reproducibility was greater than .90.

The subjects were 100 sailors at a submarine school; the test was the Navy Group TAT, an amalgam of specially drawn pictures and selected TAT cards. The task was to scale the cards for the dimensions of aggression and sex. The rationale underlying the construction of scales was that the pictures differed in stimulus pull for any given dimension (sex, for example). Subjects also differ in their need to tell stories with sexual themes. Moreover, the greater the need, the less strong the stimulus pull required to elicit a sexual theme. Subjects with little need to express sexual themes should react only, if at all, to blatantly sexual pictures. It should then be possible to order each person's "sexual story expression," once the stimulus properties of the cards are known. One measure of the stimulus pull is the percentage of subjects giving "sex stories" to each of the cards. Of the initial 10 cards, only three evoked stories indicating aggression from any appreciable number of subjects. The small number of cards, as well as the fact that they were not evenly spaced (78, 22, 21 per cent), led to an abandonment of the construction of an aggression scale. Four cards were extracted for the sex scale, however, the coefficient of reproducibility being .93.

The ordering of subjects by the test-retest method yielded a product-moment correlation of .13. This finding, however, is highly equivocal, since the subjects on the first occasion were applying for participation in an experiment and on the second occasion were just emerging from a submarine after having been submerged for 30 days. The authors do, however, give some important advice with regard to scale construction. First, they advise that the probability of achieving a scale is enhanced by having a large number of cards to start with. Further, cards should be selected which are specifically designed to elicit the motive in question. Moreover, the picture should, if possible, tap *no other motive*. One possible weakness of the Guttman scale is the fact that it fails to take into account the inhibitory forces acting on the subject. It has already been demonstrated in the work of Pittluck (1950), Kagan (1956), and Lesser (1958b) that consideration of these inhibitory factors greatly enhances predictive ability with regard to overt behavior.

Using 72 boys aged 10 to 13, Lesser (1958a) also attempted to construct a Guttman scale of aggression. A special set of pictures was drawn, each of which contained two boys, and an attempt was made to minimize motives other than aggression. The scale achieved contained seven pictures and had a coefficient of reproducibility of .91. Lesser suggests that scaling procedures which take account of inhibitory factors would improve prediction. If fantasy aggression and anxiety over fantasy aggression could both be scaled simultaneously, we might possess a very powerful predictor of overt behavior. To date, such a double scaling has not been attempted.

In a later study, Murstein, David, Fisher, and Furth (1961) had slides of the 31 TAT cards scaled for hostility by the Thurstone Equal Appearing Interval, Thurstone Successive Categories, Likert, Edwards Scale Discrimination, Guttman, and H-technique methods. The subjects were 100 students (50 men and 50 women) obtained from a beginning psychology course at the University of Portland. The results of the two Thurstone methods indicated that most of the cards fell below the midpoint of hostility. Whether this result was due to haziness over the meaning of "average," or represented the type of student body (middle-class Catholic) can only be checked by future studies with a more representative population.

The Likert results, however, indicated that the mean rating fell somewhat toward the hostile end of the continuum. Since the same students participated in the construction of both scales, it is possible that the discrepancy was accounted for by practice and/or position effects (the Likert followed the Thurstone procedure). On the other hand, the discrepancy might have been due to genuine differences in orientation because of the different judgments required in each scale. The Thurstone procedure consisted of sorting the cards in nine categories, with the fifth category described as the midpoint of hostility. The Likert procedure called for the following choice of judgments per card: very hostile, somewhat hostile, undecided, probably not hostile, definitely not hostile. Possibly the inclusion of the "undecided" category accounted for the disparity. It might be omitted from future scaling since, as Edwards (1957) points out, neutral categories contain a good deal more error variance than positive or negative categories.

The successive category judgments between men and women revealed no significant differences except for 17GF, which was seen as significantly more hostile by women than by men. By and large, however, the judgments of the two sexes are very close, as attested by the correlation of .93 between the successive category judgments of both sexes.

The size of the Q values of most of the cards is comparable to values found when scaling attitudes. This would tend to confirm the suspicion that the cards are highly structured. Along the same vein of thinking, it is possible to conceive of Q, the interquartile deviation, as an index of projection. The rationale for this belief would be that one of the signs of a good projective card is the fact that a great disparity of opinion exists as to whether the card is hostile or nonhostile. The occurrence of such a disparity might well be due to the fact that the objective stimulus offers little clue as to what is happening, resulting in a wide range of sorting judgments which reflect projection on the part of the judges.

There is, however, a fly in the ointment. *For the above to be true, it must follow that each card can be judged by the vast majority of the judges for the given dimension.* It is possible that a card cannot be meaningfully located on a dimension. Accordingly, individuals considered as a group might tend to randomly sort such a card, thus ensuring a high Q value. This possibility might be forestalled in the future by having the cards evaluated for relevance to the dimension under consideration and nonrelevance to the dimensions not under consideration.

The Likert item analyses consisted of taking the 25 persons whose ratings were the highest of the total group and comparing them, card for card, with the 25 persons whose scores were lowest in hostility for the total judgments. The computation of 31 t tests (one-tailed tests) for the entire series of cards yielded 3 nonsignificant t's, 10 significant beyond the .05 point, and 18 significant beyond the .01 point. The Equal Appearing, Q, Likert mean, t, and p values are shown in Table 29–1.

The least differentiating card was 16, the blank card. This result confirms the earlier finding of Murstein (1958a; 1958b; 1959; 1961b) concerning the ineffectuality of this card because of its lack of ambiguity. Although this card is unstructured, *it is not very ambiguous.* There is simply nothing to see, and the vast majority of judges perceive it as nonhostile. The second most undifferentiating card, 18GF, was highest in hostility according to the Equal Appearing Interval method. This card is described by H. A. Murray as follows: "A woman has her hands squeezed around the throat of another woman whom she appears to be pushing backwards across the banister of a stairway" (1943, p. 20). This card can hardly be called structureless. It is highly structured and relatively unambiguous, though it is sometimes seen as one person helping another.

In general, the least and most hostile ends of the continuum contain the greatest number of nondifferentiating cards. This is only a trend, however, for there are several exceptions. Thus, Card 10, whose Equal Appearing Interval Scale value was 1.27 and would thus be con-

TABLE 29–1   *Equal Appearing Interval, Q, Likert Mean, t, and* p
*Values for Each TAT Card**

CARD	EQUAL APPEARING INTERVAL SCALE VALUE	EQUAL APPEARING INTERVAL Q VALUE	LIKERT MEAN VALUE	t VALUES FOR HIGHEST QUARTILE VS. LOWEST QUARTILE LIKERT JUDGMENT	p
12BG	1.13	.31	1.11	2.00	.05
16	1.19	1.07	1.20	.55	ns
10	1.27	1.14	1.32	4.67	.01
8GF	1.41	.69	1.91	1.94	.05
9BM	1.67	1.00	1.18	2.45	.01
13G	2.31	1.35	1.94	2.89	.05
14	2.80	2.47	2.24	2.38	.05
17BM	2.89	1.69	2.08	3.17	.01
2	3.00	1.40	2.06	3.55	.01
13B	3.11	1.39	2.13	5.45	.01
1	3.60	1.61	3.28	2.23	.05
7GF	3.78	1.66	2.65	2.54	.01
5	4.43	1.49	2.25	1.86	.05
7BM	4.56	1.47	3.97	2.00	.05
19	4.62	2.09	3.09	2.77	.01
6GF	4.76	1.52	3.95	4.53	.01
17GF	4.77	2.52	3.50	2.75	.01
12F	5.23	1.85	3.78	3.74	.01
6BM	5.50	1.53	3.64	4.13	.01
20	5.56	1.81	3.59	2.36	.05
4	5.88	1.66	4.24	2.25	.05
8BM	5.90	2.49	3.37	3.78	.01
9GF	5.98	.69	3.86	2.71	.01
12M	6.11	1.89	3.96	2.11	.05
3BM	6.70	1.61	4.03	3.51	.01
11	6.79	2.38	3.29	1.53	ns
3GF	7.03	1.39	4.50	4.91	.01
18BM	7.82	1.06	4.75	2.90	.01
15	8.12	1.13	4.75	1.81	.05
13MF	8.15	1.17	4.77	3.75	.01
18GF	8.32	1.23	4.50	1.85	.05

* Murstein et al., 1961; reproduced by permission of the American Psychological Association.

sidered very low on the hostility continuum, had a t value of 4.67. This card is described as "A young woman's head against a man's shoulder" (H. A. Murray, 1943, p. 19). Clinical experience has shown that many persons see the figures as elderly people who are embracing. The explanations for this embrace are varied. Some see them as happily married for many years; others see them as joyfully reuniting after a long separation; still others perceive them as trying to comfort each other after the death of a child. It is apparent then that the *action engaged in by the figures is quite structured*, although the lack of structure of the faces makes the ages of the figures somewhat ambiguous. In any event, thre is no clue as to the cause of their embracing, and hence the *interpretation of the picture also is ambiguous*.

Card 13MF is almost as hostile as 18GF (Equal Appearing Interval value 8.15 as compared to 8.32). Nevertheless, the *t* value for this card is 3.75 (p<.01), as compared to the *t* value of 1.85 (p<.05) for 18GF. It will be recalled that 13MF is described by Murray as follows: "A young man is standing with downcast head buried in his arm. Behind him is the figure of a woman lying in bed" (Murray, 1943, p. 20). This picture is quite highly structured but also very ambiguous, as has been mentioned earlier.

The results of the Likert procedure help to emphasize the earlier confounding of the concepts of *structure* and *ambiguity*. It appears that the most differentiating cards with regard to this study were those highly structured and yet highly ambiguous. Cards low in structure, as well as those high in structure, have drawbacks for use in differentiating individuals on a perceptual basis. The former probably tend to induce "sets" to be on guard since little can be distinguished from the card itself. The subject is most likely, therefore, to be aware that his response is a function of his perceptual world rather than of the stimulus properties of the card. Under these circumstances, the depth of the response may well be a function of the motivation of the subject toward exhibiting his "private world" to the examiner. In the case of the highly structured, highly unambiguous card 18GF, the stimulus pull is so strong and the choice of explanations so narrow that to oppose this pull is to deny objective reality itself. This is not to deny that some individuals do perceive this card as nonhostile. The card would thus be of value in detecting persons with a strong need to avoid the objective properties of the card. For most people, however, the stimulus nature of such a card precludes the possibility of injecting personal values into the judgment.

In constructing the Guttman scale, the advice of Edwards (1957) was followed in utilizing an item analysis before testing the scale for unidimensionality. First, the cards had to be more or less evenly spaced throughout the hostility continuum. Second, they had to possess low Q values. Third, they had to differentiate very significantly with regard to *t* values as determined by the Likert method. The result of this analysis was the selection of nine cards. These cards, in order of least to most hostility, are 10, 13G, 13B, 7GF, 6GF, 9GF, 3GF, 18BM, and 13MF.

TABLE 29–2   *Equal Appearing Interval Scales Values, Q Values,*
and t Values for Nine Cards Selected
for Test of Unidimensionality

CARD	SCALE VALUE	Q	t
10	1.27	1.14	4.67
13G	2.31	1.35	2.89
13B	3.11	1.39	5.45
7GF	3.78	1.66	2.54
6GF	4.76	1.52	4.53
9GF	5.98	.69	2.71
3GF	7.03	1.39	4.91
18BM	7.82	1.06	2.90
13MF	8.15	1.17	3.75

* Murstein et al., 1961; reproduced by permission of the American Psychological Association.

They are shown in Table 29–2, together with their Equal Appearing
Interval Scale, Q, and t values. The method used to obtain the coefficient of reproducibility was the one proposed by Goodenough (1944).
The one recommended by Guttman is spuriously high because of the
fact that the experimenter takes advantage of sampling bias in selecting
the cutting point of the statement or card. Goodenough's method gives
an unbiased representation of the degree of accuracy with which the
responses to the cards can be reproduced from a knowledge of the total
scores alone. The obtained coefficient was .88, which is sufficiently
high to meet one of Guttman's standards for a "perfect scale." Guttman's
criterion is actually .90, but this figure is inflated because of the aforementioned spurious factor. The coefficient of marginal reproducibility
tells us what our accuracy of reproduction would have been had we just
used our marginal totals as a basis for cutting points. It was found to
be .74, indicating that we were able to improve our predictions considerably from knowledge of the total scores.

Last, eight of the nine cards were combined into three "contrived
cards," following the H-technique procedure (Edwards, 1957). By this
means, the coefficient of reproducibility was elevated to .965.

In another study, Murstein (1965b) obtained Likert scale values for
amount of achievement from a college male population, using the full
set of 31 TAT cards and several additional ones from Atkinson's list
(1958). Table 21–3 lists the scale values and the t values for differences
between persons whose judgment scores were in the upper quartile and
those in the lowest quartile. The nine cards most representative of the
scale and also differentiating between the low and the high groups are
indicated by the superscript b. These cards may be categorized as including three cards each for low, medium, and high n-Achievement

stimulus pull. They have been used in another experiment (Murstein, 1963b) testing Atkinson's theory of motivation. In this study, persons predicted by the theory as having maximal motivation (probability of success in a task = .50) could be differentiated from persons with lesser achievement motivation on the basis of their manifestation of n-Achievement to the medium set. The high and low stimulus pull sets did not differentiate between the groups.

Using a paired-comparison technique as well a a ranking procedure, Brayer, Craig, and Teichner (1961) scaled ten TAT cards for difficulty, which they defined as "the difficulty people would have in deciding what the picture is really about" (Brayer et al., 1961, p. 273). They found almost no difference between the positions of the cards for each scale, and both methods proved to be internally consistent when Mosteller's chi-square test of internal consistency was applied. Eight of the cards employed were the same as those used by Bijou and Kenny (1951) in their study of ambiguity. These authors had defined "ambiguity" as that which is open to a number of possible interpretations. Rank-order correlations between the ambiguity and the difficulty values for these cards were −.02 for the paired-comparison method for scaling these variables and −.18 for the rank-order method, both values being nonsignificant. The results suggest that the two dimensions are independent of each other. The small number of cards and the fact that different subjects were employed in each study, however, indicate that these results need replication before any confidence can be placed in them, a point noted by the authors.

In reviewing the data on scaling, several conclusions seem pertinent. Generally speaking, adequate success has been attained in scaling the cards by conventional scaling procedures. This fact would seem to confirm the suspicion, if it is still just a suspicion, that the TAT is as a whole quite structured. It is hardly conceivable that an instrument which professes to "tap the private worlds" of individuals would sound such a concordant note with regard to the dimensions of sex, aggression, and hostility as to result in coefficients of reproducibility exceeding .90 in each case. It would seem that a change is required both in the selection of cards for future thematic series and in the procedure utilized in measurement. As Lazarus has well pointed out, "to depend upon only the most ambiguous kinds of stimuli in projective procedures results in uncertainty as to when an interpretation is avoided because of repressive defenses and when it is ignored because of lack of tension" (Lazarus, 1953, p. 444). The solution, then, should be a series of graded stimuli for a given dimension, ranging from highly ambiguous to highly unambiguous. To distinguish between what is ambiguous and what is unambiguous, it is helpful to employ scaling methods. Once we have a card scaled for a dimension, we can proceed to investigate the meaning of conformity or deviancy from the stimulus value. There is extremely

TABLE 29-3   *Mean Likert Values and t Scores for Judged Amount of Achievement for Upper and Lower Quartiles (N=46) of Population of College Men*[*]

CARD	MEAN LIKERT VALUE	t
Scientist holding up test tube	2.54	.24
Track man at the starting block	2.30	.96
8BM	2.23	1.12
Pioneering chopping down tree[a]	2.22	3.04[c]
2[a]	2.22	2.48[c]
Office worker at desk	2.17	1.67
Two men working at a press	2.13	1.08
17BM[a]	1.91	3.22[c]
10	1.54	2.18[b]
12M	1.54	.45
7BM	1.52	1.58
17GF	1.48	3.71[c]
1	1.48	1.30
Student taking examination[a]	1.46	4.36[c]
13MF	1.39	4.93[c]
8GF[a]	1.33	4.18[c]
6GF	1.30	2.26[b]
14[a]	1.24	5.25[c]
4	1.24	3.25[c]
18GF	1.20	3.14[c]
15	1.13	2.53[c]
9GF	1.09	2.26[b]
13G	1.04	0.00
7GF	.98	2.18[b]
6BM	.96	.96
3GF	.96	3.04[c]
19	.96	1.62
5	.96	4.14[c]
11	.91	1.06
13B[a]	.91	4.19[c]
12F	.89	2.10[b]
18BM	.78	1.25
9BM	.74	3.48[c]
20[a]	.65	3.71[c]
12BG	.59	1.78[b]
3BM[a]	.48	4.33[c]

[*] o = little or no achievement in picture; 1 = somewhat low in achievement; 2 = somewhat high in achievement; 3 = very high in achievement.
[a] Nine cards selected as representative of entire range and most differentiating.
[b] Significant at .05 point.
[c] Significant at .01 point.

little information on this matter, since heretofore scaling methodology has been used for demonstrative purposes rather than in the investigation of perception and personality.

It is no secret that our so-called perceptual tests are really verbal tests, as the results of Webb and Hilden (1953) imply. Thematic cards, however, can be used as nonverbal perceptual judgment tasks by having the subject sort the cards into a number of categories for a given personality dimension. The sort can then be compared with the scaled values obtained from a population similar to the subject in age, socio-economic background, and other important variables. The sum of the discrepancies over all the pictures might represent the subject's perceptual deviancy scores. The same could be done, if desired, for the subject's stories. These deviancy scores could then be compared with other behavior to see whether they contribute anything to the measurement of personality.

There are still other possibilities, as Jacobs (1958) has indicated. If the experimenter wishes to determine whether certain perceptual responses are independent of the stimulus properties of the pictures, cards very high on the ambiguity continuum may be selected. An ambiguous group of pictures also would be suitable for investigating "background" variables. Subjects might be given varying instructions or exposed to different kinds of "arousal" stimuli. The responses to the pictures before and after the introduction of the experimental background factor could then be compared. The use of ambiguous pictures would ensure a minimum of response determination due to the stimulus and a maximum due to the background factor, organismic factor, and their interaction.

Nonambiguous pictures are useful for detecting "sets" on the part of the subject. One may speculate, for example, that adequately adjusted persons from a personality standpoint are apt to respect the stimulus properties of thematic pictures more than are maladjusted persons. If, then, a series of fairly nonambiguous "hostile" pictures is presented to a mixed group of "normal" and "ego-defensive" subjects, we might expect the normal group to perceive the cards as hostile, while the ego-defensive group might be less prone to acknowledge the stimulus properties of the cards in an effort to maintain a good impression before the examiner.

Rules in the Construction of Thematic Tests

In view of the impact of the stimulus on thematic responses, it is surprising to note that few psychologists have suggested rules to utilize in the construction of thematic tests.

In his important book on the TAT, Henry (1956) suggests several criteria for selecting or constructing thematic pictures.

1. The picture must have a potent *latent stimulus meaning*. In Card 1 for example, the picture of a boy with a violin "is a convenient symbolization of a person in an ambivalent emotional situation" (Henry, 1956, p. 48). It is the perceived struggle with frustration and authority that is of interest rather than attitudes toward the violin per se.

2. A number of pictures should depict *basic interpersonal relations*, such as various family dyads like mother-child, father-child, sibling; also heterosexual scenes, a person alone, two persons of the same age and sex, and persons in varying social roles.

3. The pictures should describe different aspects of reality. These include:

(a) *Clear-cut reality* (the basic content is portrayed in direct unambiguous fashion).

(b) *Illogical reality arrangement*. Here the components of the situation are realistic, but their relationship is somewhat illogical. Card 18BM, for example, shows a man being helped to his feet by *three* hands. To whom does the extra hand belong? The picture thus challenges the subject to explain the presence of three hands without attached bodies. The shading is dark so that it is possible to rationalize that the hands are affixed to someone who is in the shadows. There is, however, sufficient challenge to test the subject's reality integration.

(c) *Bizarre or unreal stimuli*. "Some of the pictures . . . should portray events in a bizarre, startling, or unexpected manner" (Henry, 1956, p. 49). These pictures further test integrative abilities in addition to often eliciting irregular or pathological thought content.

(d) *Ambiguous reality*. "Some of the pictures chosen should be unstructured and ambiguous" (Henry, 1956, p. 49).

4. The pictures should be sufficiently *intense in quality* to intrigue the subject and motivate him to propose a solution via his story.

5. The pictures may be *ambiguous for the reality of objects and persons portrayed and for the emotions, action, and outcome*. The latter are most important, since some excellent pictures show readily identifiable persons yet possess considerable emotion and outcome ambiguity.

6. "The pictures selected and the *situation portrayed should be appropriate to the culture* of the group being studied. The pictures should be so drawn or selected as to employ persons, dress, objects, and background that are not thought inappropriate by the persons being studied" (Henry, 1956, p. 51; italics mine).

Sherwood (1957) presents 13 criteria for the designing of pictures which he utilized in a study of the Swazi people. Those additional to Henry's suggestions are:

7. "The images of which each picture is composed must be *defined*

*neither with a sharpness sufficient to simulate reality nor with a vague-
ness sufficient to render the identification of the content uncertain"*
(Sherwood, 1957, p. 168).

8. "Each picture . . . while it tends to evoke associations bearing upon
a particular topic or theme, its content and the situation it suggests
will be *incomplete* to a degree such that the subject . . . will be obliged
to exercise his imaginative and creative faculties and thus to reveal
something of his inner self" (Sherwood, 1957, p. 173).

9. "Stimuli must be *compressed* into each picture to elicit associations to a wide range of relationships . . . and important themes auxiliary
to the specific area at which the picture is 'aimed' " (Sherwood, 1957,
p. 174).

10. "*The series . . . must comprise a range from pictures presenting
only one or two figures and objects to pictures presenting an appreciably larger number of items.* The order of presentation . . . is roughly
from pictures containing few objects toward pictures containing a relatively large number of objects" (Sherwood, 1957, p. 176).

Other suggestions by H. A. Murray (1943) and Crandall (1951)
include the following:

11. The pictures should contain at least one example where the central
figure is of the same sex and of relatively the same age as the subject
(H. A. Murray, 1943).

12. "There should be a maximum number of pictures to ensure reliability consistent with a minimum number to maintain high motivation in the subject" (Crandall, 1951, p. 401).

13. "The pictures should contain situations relevant to important needs
and strivings of the subject" (Crandall, 1951, p. 401).

14. "Pictures representing situations eliciting a given need should call
forth stories eliciting that need in a clear majority of the subjects"
(Crandall, 1951, p. 401).

15. "Two roughly equivalent sets of pictures should be developed"
(Crandall, 1951, p. 401).

The research literature on these rules is sparse; yet some evidence is
available. This chapter has presented evidence indicating that the "everyday" series has proved superior to the "fairy-tale" series. This finding,
however, does not preclude the use of the fairy-tale series to provide
information where the everyday series is lacking. Rule 3, therefore, is
not disproved by the emipirical data. The work of Murstein (1962a)
indicates that emotional-tone ambiguity is more important in gaining a
meaningful picture of the individual than is character-identification ambiguity, thus supporting Henry's point (Rule 5).

The support of medium-ambiguous pictures by the research literature
is in accordance with Rule 7. The work of Proud (1956) in pointing
out the superiority of incomplete backgrounds to more detailed ones is
in agreement with Rule 8. The one rule for which nonsupporting evi-

dence is available is Rule 11, in which the assertion that persons project more to figures of the same sex and age was promulgated. It has been shown that women project more to pictures of men under certain conditions than they do to pictures of their own sex. The other rules either are common-sense reliability measures which are scarcely debatable or have not yet been tested.

Summary and Conclusions

We have seen the stimulus emerge from a secondary role to one of prime importance in consideration of thematic responses. Moreover, the role of physical similarity between stimulus and subject has been over-valued, while the sociological value of the characters depicted has been underestimated. Other stimulus dimensions, such as color, clarity, and contour, also need to be investigated more thoroughly. The hypothesis that children tend to project more readily in response to animal figures than to human figures can be rejected if one is interested in a broad-band thematic test. The investigation of the utility of the CAT for testing specific psychoanalytic hypotheses has not been undertaken.

In constructing a new thematic test or improving the usefulness of the TAT, the following additional suggestions may be of value.

1. The pictures should be scaled for all personality dimensions by the use of various scaling devices.

2. The analysis of the stories shoud be considered in relation to the stimulus value of the picture.

3. The entire range of a stimulus dimension ought to be used.

4. It may be necessary, however, to employ different scoring systems for cards of differing stimulus value. Cards of low stimulus relevance appear to be fairly sensitive to direct content representation. Pictures of high relevance, however, especially if the drive is socially unacceptable, may have to be measured by the analysis of avoidance mechanisms.

5. A good way to learn more about the relationship of the response to the stimulus is to obtain several perceptual-type groups according to their response to a TAT and then measure their behavior on other variables. The person who follows the stimulus closely in his stories, the one who deviates, the one who follows the high stimulus-pull cards but not the low, and the one who responds to low stimulus pull but not highly structured cards — all these types and many more may be observed and measured in other behavioral situations to throw light on the meaning of their TAT behavior. Almost nothing of this sort has been done, with the exception of the work of Nelson and Epstein (1962), but such studies are probably destined for a more important role in the near future.

REFERENCES

AMEN, E. W. Individual differences in apperceptive reaction: a study of the response of preschool children to pictures. *Genet. Psychol. Monogr.*, 1941, 23, 319–385.

ARMSTRONG, MARY A. S. Children's responses to animal and human figures in thematic pictures. *J. consult. Psychol.*, 1954, 18, 67–70.

ATKINSON, J. W. Thematic apperceptive measurement of motives within the context of a theory of motivation. In J. W. Atkinson (Ed.), *Motives in fantasy, action, and society.* Princeton: Van Nostrand, 1958. Pp. 596–616.

AULD, F., ERON, L. D., & LAFFAL, J. Application of Guttman's scaling method to the TAT. *Educ. psychol. Measmt*, 1955, 15, 422–435.

BEIER, E. G., IZARD, C. E., SMOCK, C. D., & TOUGAS, R. R. Response to the human face as a standard stimulus: A re-examination. *J. consult. Psychol.*, 1957, 21, 165–170.

BELLAK, L., & BELLAK, SONYA S. *Manual of instruction for the children's apperception test.* New York: C.P.S. Co., 1949.

BERG, J., & POLYOT, C. J. The influence of color on reactions to incomplete figures. *J. consult. Psychol*, 1956, 20, 9–15.

BIERSDORF, KATHRYN R., & MARCUSE, F. L. Response of children to human and to animal pictures. *J. proj. Tech.*, 1953, 17, 455–459.

BIJOU, S. W., & KENNY, D. T. The ambiguity of TAT cards. *J. consult. Psychol.*, 1951, 15, 203–209.

BILLS, R. E. Animal pictures for obtaining children's projections. *J. clin. Psychol.*, 1950, 6, 291–293.

BILLS, R. E., LEIMAN, C. J., & THOMAS, R. W. A study of the validity of the TAT and a set of animal pictures. *J. clin. Psychol.*, 1950, 6, 293–295.

BIRNEY, R. C. Thematic content and the cue characteristics of pictures. In J. W. Atkinson (Ed.), *Motives in fantasy, action, and society.* Princeton: Van Nostrand, 1958. Pp. 630–643.

BOYD, NANCY A., & MANDLER, G. Children's responses to human and animal stories and pictures. *J. consult. Psychol.*, 1955, 19, 367–371.

BRACKBILL, G. A. Some effects of color on thematic fantasy. *J. consult. Psychol.*, 1951, 15, 412–418.

BRADLEY, J. E., & LYSAKER, R. L. Ambiguity as a variable in the use of projective technique. Minneapolis: Pillsbury Mills, Inc., 1957 (mimeographed).

BRAYER, R., CRAIG, GRACE, & TEICHNER, W. Scaling difficulty values of TAT cards. *J. proj. Tech.*, 1961, 25, 272–276.

BRIGGS, D. A. A modification of the thematic apperception test for Naval enlisted personnel. *J. Psychol.*, 1954, 37, 233–241.

BUDOFF, M. The relative utility of animal and human figures in a picture-story test for young children. *J. proj. Tech.*, 1960, 24, 347–352.

CHOWDHURY, U. An Indian modification of the thematic apperception test. *J. soc. Psychol.*, 1960, 51, 245–263.

CLARK, R. A. The projective measurement of experimentally induced levels of sexual motivation. *J. exp. Psychol.*, 1952, 44, 391–399.

COOK, R. A. Identification and ego defensiveness in thematic apperception. *J. proj. Tech.*, 1953, 17, 312–319.

CRANDALL, V. J. Induced frustration and punishment-reward expectancy in thematic apperception stories. *J. consult. Psychol.*, 1951, 15, 400–404.

DECHARMS, R., MORRISON, H. W., REITMAN, W. R., & McCLELLAND, D. C. Behavioral correlates of directly and indirectly measured achievement motivation. In D. C. McClelland (Ed.), *Studies in motivation.* New York: Appleton-Century-Crofts, 1955. Pp. 414–423.

DOLLIN, ADELAIDE P. The effect of order of presentation on perception of TAT pictures. Unpublished doctoral dissertation, Univer. of Connecticut, 1960.

EDGAR, CLARA L., & SHNEIDMAN, E. S. Some relationships among thematic projective tests of various degrees of structuredness and behavior in a group situation. *J. proj. Tech.*, 1958, 22, 3–12.

EDWARDS, A. L. *Techniques of attitude scale construction.* New York: Appleton-Century-Crofts, 1957.

ERON, L. D. Frequencies of themes and identification in stories of patients and nonhospitalized college students. *J. consult. Psychol.*, 1948, 12, 387–395.

ERON, L. D. A normative study of the thematic apperception test. *Psychol. Monogr.*, 1950, 64, No. 9 (Whole No. 315).

ERON, L. D., TERRY, DOROTHY, & CALLAHAN, R. The use of rating scales for emotional tone of TAT stories. *J. consult. Psychol.*, 1950, 14, 473–478.

FENZ, W. D., & EPSTEIN, S. Measurement of approach-avoidance conflict by a stimulus dimension in a test of thematic apperception. *J. Pers.*, 1962, 30, 613–632.

FURUYA, K. Responses of school children to human and animal pictures. *J. proj. Tech.*, 1957, 21, 248–252.

GOODENOUGH, W. H. A technique for scale analysis. *Educ. psychol. Measmt*, 1944, 4, 179–190.

GOODMAN, MARY E. *Race awareness in young children.* Cambridge: Addison-Wesley, 1952.

GREENBAUM, M., QUALTERE, T., CARRUTH, B., & CRUICKSHANK, W. Evaluation of a modification of the thematic apperception test for use with physically handicapped children. *J. clin. Psychol.*, 1953, 9, 40–44.

HABER, R. N., & ALPERT, R. The role of situation and picture cues in projective measurement of the achievement motive. In J. W. Atkinson (Ed.), *Motives in fantasy, action, and society.* Princeton: Van Nostrand, 1958. Pp. 644–663.

HENRY, W. E. The thematic apperception technique in the study of group and cultural problems. In H. H. & Gladys L. Anderson (Eds.), *An introduction to projective techniques.* Englewood Cliffs, N.J.: Prentice-Hall, 1951. Pp. 230–278.

HENRY, W. E. *The analysis of fantasy, the thematic apperception techniques in the study of personality.* New York: Wiley, 1956.

JACOBS, B. A method for investigating the cue characteristics of pictures. In J. W. Atkinson (Ed.), *Motives in fantasy, action, and society.* Princeton: Van Nostrand, 1958. Pp. 617–629.

KAGAN, J. The measurement of overt aggression from fantasy. *J. abnorm. soc. Psychol.*, 1956, 52, 390–393.

KENNY, D. T. Transcendence indices, extent of personality factors in fantasy responses, and the ambiguity of TAT cards. *J. consult. Psychol.*, 1954, 17, 283–288.

KENNY, D. T., & BIJOU, S. W. Ambiguity of pictures and extent of personality factors in fantasy responses. *J. consult. Psychol.*, 1953, 17, 283–288.

KORCHIN, S. J., MITCHELL, H. E., & MELTZOFF, J. A critical evaluation of the Thompson thematic apperception test. *J. proj. Tech.*, 1950, 14, 445–452.

LASAGA Y TRAVIESO, J. E., & MARTINEZ-ARANGO, C. Some suggestions concerning the administration and interpretation of the TAT. *J. Psychol.*, 1946, 22, 117–163.

LASKOWITZ, D. The effect of varied degrees of pictorial ambiguity on fantasy evocation. Doctoral dissertation, New York Univer., 1959.

LAZARUS, R. S. Ambiguity and non-ambiguity in projective testing. *J. abnorm. soc. Psychol.*, 1953, 48, 443–445.

LEBO, D., & HARRIGAN, MARGARET. Visual and verbal presentation of TAT stimuli. *J. consult. Psychol.*, 1957, 21, 339–342.

LEBO, D., & SHERRY, P. J. Visual and vocal presentation of TAT descriptions. *J. proj. Tech.*, 1959, 23, 59–63.

LEIMAN, A. H., & EPSTEIN, S. Thematic sexual responses as related to sexual drive and guilt. *J. abnorm. soc. Psychol.*, 1961, 63, 169–175.

LESSER, G. S. Application of Guttman's scaling method to aggressive fantasy in children. *Educ. psychol. Measmt*, 1958, 18, 543–550. (a)

LESSER, G. S. Conflict analysis of fantasy aggression. *J. Pers.*, 1958, 26, 29–41. (b)

LIGHT, B. H. Comparative study of a series of TAT and CAT cards. *J. clin. Psychol.*, 1954, 10, 179–181.

LIGHT, B. H. A further test of the Thompson TAT rationale. *J. abnorm. soc. Psychol.*, 1955, 51, 148–150.

LOWE, W. F. Effect of controlling the immediate environment on responses to the thematic apperception test. Unpublished master's thesis, Univer. of Louisville, 1951.

LUBETSKY, J. Assimilative projection as measured by trait attribution. Unpublished doctoral dissertation, Northwestern Univer., 1960.

LUBIN, N. M. The effect of color in the TAT on productions of mentally retarded subjects. *Amer. J. ment. Def.*, 1955, 60, 366–370.

LUBIN, N. M., & WILSON, M. O. Picture test identification as a function of "reality" (color) and similarity of picture to subject. *J. gen. Psychol.*, 1956, 54, 31–38.

McINTYRE, C. J. Sex, age, and iconicity as factors in projective film tests. *J. consult. Psychol.*, 1954, 18, 475–477.

MAINORD, FLORENCE R., & MARCUSE, F. L. Responses of disturbed children to human and to animal pictures. *J. proj. Tech.*, 1954, 18, 475–477.

MASON, BETH B. Cards, sequences of cards, and repetitions as factors in thematic apperception test behavior. Unpublished master's thesis, Univer. of Louisville, 1952.

MURRAY, E. J. Conflict and repression during sleep deprivation. *J. abnorm. soc. Psychol.*, 1959, 59, 95–101.

MURRAY, H. A. *Thematic apperception test manual.* Cambridge: Harvard Univer. Press, 1943.

MURSTEIN, B. I. Nonprojective determinants of perception on the TAT. *J. consult. Psychol.*, 1958, 22, 195–198. (a)

MURSTEIN, B. I. The relationship of stimulus ambiguity on the TAT to productivity of themes. *J. consult. Psychol.*, 1958, 22, 348. (b)

MURSTEIN, B. I. A conceptual model of projective techniques applied to stimulus variations with thematic techniques. *J. consult. Psychol.*, 1959, 23, 3–14.

MURSTEIN, B. I. A caution regarding the "levels" hypothesis and the use of psychological tests. Unpublished manuscript, Interfaith Counseling Center, Portland, Oregon, 1961. (a)

MURSTEIN, B. I. The role of the stimulus in the manifestation of fantasy. In J. Kagan & G. Lesser (Eds.), *Contemporary issues in thematic apperceptive methods.* Springfield, Ill.: Charles C Thomas, 1961. Pp. 229–273. (b)

MURSTEIN, B. I. The relationship of expectancy of reward to performance on an arithmetic and thematic test. *J. consult. Psychol.*, 1963, 27, 394–399.

MURSTEIN, B. I. A normative study of TAT ambiguity. *J. proj. Tech. pers. Assess.*, 1964, 28, 210–218.

MURSTEIN, B. I. The scaling of the TAT for n Achievement. *J. consult. Psychol.*, 1965, in press. (a)

MURSTEIN, B. I. The projection of hostility on the TAT as a function of stimulus, background and personality variables. *J. consult. Psychol.*, 1965, 29, 43–48. (b)

MURSTEIN, B. I., DAVID, CHARLOTTE, FISHER, D., & FURTH, H. The scaling of the TAT for hostility by a variety of scaling methods. *J. consult. Psychol.*, 1961, 25, 497–504.

NELSON, J. T., & EPSTEIN, S. Relationships among three measures of conflict over hostility. *J. consult. Psychol.*, 1962, 26, 345–350.

NEWBIGGING, P. L. Influence of a stimulus variable on stories told to certain TAT pictures. *Canad. J. Psychol.*, 1955, 9, 195–206.

PIOTROWSKI, Z. A. A new evaluation of the thematic apperception test. *Psychoanal. Rev.*, 1950, 37, 101–127.

PITTLUCK, PATRICIA. The relationship between aggressive fantasy and overt behavior. Unpublished doctoral dissertation, Yale Univer., 1950.

PROSHANSKY, H. M. A projective method for the study of attitudes. *J. abnorm. soc. Psychol.*, 1943, 38, 393–395.

PROUD, ANN P. Response to picture-thematic stimulus material as a function of stimulus structure. Unpublished doctoral dissertation, Univer. of California at Los Angeles, 1956.

RIESS, B. F., SCHWARTZ, E. K., & COTTINGHAM, ALICE. An experimental critique of assumptions underlying the Negro version of the TAT. *J. abnorm. soc. Psychol.*, 1950, 45, 700–709.

SCHWARTZ, E. K., RIESS, B. F., & COTTINGHAM, ALICE. Further critical evaluation of the Negro version of the TAT. *J. proj. Tech.*, 1951, 15, 394–400.

SHERWOOD, E. T. On the designing of TAT pictures with special reference to a set for an African people assimilating western culture. *J. soc. Psychol.*, 1957, 45, 161–190.

SILVERSTEIN, A. B. Identification with same-sex and opposite-sex figures in thematic apperception. *J. proj. Tech.*, 1959, 23, 73–75.

SIMSON, E. Vergleich von CAT und einer inhaltsanslogen Mensch-Bilderserie. *Sonderdruck aus Diagnostica*, 1959, 5, 54–62.

SOLKOFF, N. Effects of a variation in instructions and pictorial stimuli on responses to TAT-like cards. *J. proj. Tech.*, 1959, 23, 76–82.

STARR, S. The relationship between hostility-ambiguity of the TAT cards, hostile fantasy, and hostile behavior. Unpublished doctoral dissertation, Washington State Univer., 1960.

SYMONDS, P. M. Criteria for the selection of pictures for the investigation of adolescent phantasies. *J. abnorm. soc. Psychol.*, 1939, 34, 271–274.

TERRY, DOROTHY. The use of a rating scale of level of response in TAT stories. *J. abnorm. soc. Psychol.*, 1952, 74, 507–511.

THOMPSON, C. E. The Thompson modifications of the thematic apperception test. *Rorschach Res. Exch.*, 1949, 13, 469–478.

THOMPSON, C. E., & BACHRACH, J. The use of color in the thematic apperception test. *J. proj. Tech.*, 1951, 15, 173–184.

TOMKINS, S. S. *The thematic apperception test.* New York: Grune & Stratton, 1947.

VEROFF, J. Thematic apperception in a nationwide sample survey. In J. Kagan & G. Lesser (Eds.), *Contemporary issues in thematic apperceptive methods.* Springfield, Ill.: Charles C Thomas, 1961. Pp. 83–110.

VEROFF, J., WILCOX, SUE, & ATKINSON, J. W. The achievement motive in high school and college-age women. *J. abnorm. soc. Psychol.*, 1953, 84, 108–119.

WALKER,, E. L., ATKINSON, J. W., VEROFF, J., BIRNEY, R., DEMBER, W., & MOULTON, R. The expression of fear-related motivation in thematic apperception as a function of proximity to an atomic explosion. In J. W. Atkinson (Ed.), *Motives in fantasy, action, and society.* Princeton: Van Nostrand, 1958. Pp. 143–159.

WEBB, W. B., & HILDEN, A. H. Verbal and intellectual ability as factors in projective test results. *J. proj. Tech.*, 1953, 17, 102–103.

WEISSKOPF, EDITH A. An experimental study of the effect of brightness and ambiguity on projection in the TAT. *J. Psychol.*, 1950, 29, 407–416. (a)

WEISSKOPF, EDITH A. A transcendence index as a proposed measure in the TAT. *J. Psychol.*, 1950, 29, 379–390. (b)

WEISSKOPF, EDITH A., & DUNLEVY, G. P. Bodily similarity between subject and central figure in the TAT as an influence on projection. *J. abnorm. soc. Psychol.*, 1952, 47, 441–445.

WEISSKOPF-JOELSON, EDITH A., & FOSTER, HELEN C. An experimental study of stimulus variation upon projection. *J. proj. Tech.*, 1962, 26, 366–370.

WEISSKOPF-JOELSON, EDITH A., & LYNN, D. B. The effect of variations in ambiguity on projection in the children's apperception test. *J. consult. Psychol.*, 1953, 17, 67–70.

WEISSKOPF-JOELSON, EDITH A., & MONEY, L. Facial similarity between subject and central figure in the TAT as an influence on projection. *J. abnorm. soc. Psychol.*, 1953, 48, 341–344.

WRIGHT, B., & GARDNER, B. Effect of color on black and white pictures. *Percept. mot. Skills*, 1960, 11, 301–304.

30

The Thematic Apperception Test and Antisocial Behavior[1]

KENNETH PURCELL

This article is imposing in several ways. First, it received an accolade in 1957 as the projective technique research article of the year. Second, it is truly a tour de force of the possibilities of analysis. It shows clearly that, given a wide sample of personality types with respect to the trait of aggression and the use of various ratio and inhibition scores, one can very nicely predict antisocial behavior. The prediction of such behavior from simple TAT aggressive content proved to be not nearly as efficacious.

Purcell's findings further indicate that when approach and avoidance measures are both considered, there is a straightforward relationship between behavioral aggression and thematic aggression. Previously, others had suggested a compensatory relationship such that many individuals who projected thematic aggression were compensating for an inability to do so in real life. The present study indicates, however, that such individuals might be readily detected by the amount of internal punishment expressed in their studies. Antisocial persons seem to shun such defensive measures as internal punishment and remoteness in time, place, object, and level of behavior in favor of more direct thematic expression of aggression. Further research is badly needed for needs other than aggression, using an amalgam of approach and avoidance measures.

---

[1] The author wishes to express his appreciation to Richard Besnia, Carl Eisdorfer, Marvin Greenstein, Maurice Kouguell, and Dr. Phillip Kubzansky, who collected the data for this study and assisted in its statistical evaluation.

547

Antisocial behavior may be viewed in terms of disequilibrium between an impulse system and a control system, the latter involving assessments of reality consequences as well as internalized standards serving as restrictions on behavior. The present study is designed to examine certain disturbances of the impulse-control balance as they are manifested in TAT productions. Lindzey has referred to the "determination of the conditions under which inferences based on the projective material directly relate to overt behavior and the conditions for the reverse" (Lindzey, 1952, p. 18) as one of the major interpretive problems for the TAT. Studies examining the relationship between fantasy and overt behavior have yielded varied results (Murray, 1943; Sanford, Adkins, Miller, Cobb, & others, 1943). Neither Murray (1943) nor Sanford et al. (1943) found any substantial direct relationship between the intensity of fantasy expression and its overt expression. However, in explaining their respective results, each hypothesizes a factor of cultural prohibition serving to prevent the overt gratification of antisocial needs. In order to circumvent the complicating factor of middle-class inhibitions regarding aggressive behavior, Mussen and Naylor (1954) studied a group of lower-class boys whose culture presumably encourages rather than inhibits overt aggression. They found strong support for a positive relationship between fantasy aggressive needs and overt aggressive behavior. Moreover, they found suggestive evidence that the amount of punishment anticipated relative to aggressive needs was an important determinant of overt aggression. With the exception of Mussen and Naylor's work, previous investigations attempting to correlate covert needs and overt behavior have tended to neglect the role of inhibiting or defensive forces in modifying the behavioral resultant of covert needs. Mussen and Naylor, however, made no effort to distinguish between external and internal controlling forces.

Hypotheses

The major hypotheses of the present study may be stated with reference to different facets of the impulse-control balance:

IMPULSE SYSTEM

1. There is a direct relationship between degree of aggressive, antisocial behavior and the number of aggressive thoughts manifested in TAT stories.

2. The form as well as the number of TAT aggressions is related to the extent of overt aggressive behavior. More aggressive individuals are likely to express TAT aggressions crudely and directly, relatively un-hampered by repressive processes.

EXTERNAL CONTROL SYSTEM

3. Overt antisocial behavior varies inversely with the anticipated amount of fantasy punishment from an external source.

4. Among antisocial individuals, themes of external punishment are more likely to serve as justifications for aggression than among non-antisocial individuals. This hypothesis is derived from Redl and Wineman's (1951) detailed account of the "delinquent ego." By this is meant the ego whose every effort is bent toward obtaining guilt-free and anxiety-free enjoyment of delinquent impulsivity.

INTERNAL CONTROL SYSTEM

5. Overt antisocial behavior varies inversely with the anticipated amount of fantasy punishment from an internal source.

6. Of the two types of punishment, internal and external, anticipated internal punishment is the more significant inhibitor of antisocial behavior.

Method

Fifty-seven male Army trainees between the ages of 17 and 26 with a mean age of 20 were used as subjects (Ss) for this experiment. All were psychiatric referrals to the Mental Hygiene Clinic for whom psychological testing was requested. The only patients excluded were those suffering from organic brain damage or those diagnosed as psychotic.

Each S was seen individually by one of three clinical psychology specialists, who administered Cards 1, 3BM, 4, 6BM, 7BM, 8BM, 12M, 13MF, 14, and 18BM of the TAT. A fourth clinical psychology specialist and the author, neither of whom had administered any of the TATs, independently scored the TAT protocols for measures of aggressive impulses with respect to both quantity and quality, anticipated punishment from external agencies, and anticipated punishment from within.

The criteria used for identifying fantasy aggressions and punishments were based on those described by Mussen and Naylor (1954), with certain modifications. A fantasy aggression score was derived for each S by counting the frequency of instances of all aggression such as the following: fighting, criminal assault, getting angry, criticizing, running away, resisting coercion, being negativistic, lying, cheating, stealing, dominating or restraining someone, rejecting someone. The occurrence of death, illness, or accident to parents or other loved objects in a story was also regarded as fantasy aggression. Since the present study is concerned only with extrapunitive aggression, such items as suicide, self-injury, and self-depreciation were not scored as fantasy aggression. The Pearson r, used as the reliability measure in every case, showed the correlation between independent scorings to be .91.

An external punishment score was obtained by summing the frequency of such themes as the following when they were directed toward the hero: assault; injury; threat; quarreling; deprivation of some privilege, object, or comfort; domination; physical handicap such as blindness, etc; rejection. Scoring reliability was .81.

Internally based punishment included suicide, self-depreciation, and feelings of guilt, shame, or remorse. Since a broad definition of punishment encompasses "injury to a loved object," instances of death, illness, or accident to parents or other loved objects were recorded in this category of internal punishment. In instances in which the hero of the story was the direct agent of aggression, e.g., husband striking his wife, internal punishment was not scored except where there was a clear expression of remorse or shame. By contrast, accidental injury, death, or illness of a loved one always received a scoring of internal punishment unless the hero specifically denied anything resembling guilt feelings. Scoring reliability was .89.

Remoteness of fantasy aggression from overt behavior was rated on a seven-point scale with one representing the most direct form of fantasy expression. For each instance of fantasy aggression counted in the TAT story, a remoteness rating was made. The following considerations were kept in mind when evaluating remoteness: (1) object of aggression (person, society, animal, inanimate object), (2) time (present, past, future), (3) place (customary habitat, other countries, other planets), (4) level (behavior wish, memory, daydream, nightdream, special state of consciousness such as intoxication, dissociation, drug addiction, insanity), (5) social context and instigator (hero instigates aggression, merely tags along with crowd, or even has nothing directly to do with aggression, e.g., death of someone due to disease or accident). The reliability for the number of one and two remoteness ratings scored per S was .96.

Measurement of aggressive antisocial behavior was based on the social history data routinely obtained by the psychiatric social work specialists. Such information included a record of S's military delinquencies, e.g., AWOL, refusal to obey orders, assault, etc., as well as S's report of any delinquent civilian behavior, e.g., truancies, gang fighting, stealing, peddling of drugs, etc. The military information was, of course, easily verifiable, but the data pertaining to premilitary activities were not, except in certain instances in which records were requested from reformatories or other institutions mentioned by S. Several factors, however, indirectly testified to the substantial accuracy of Ss' accounts of their civilian behavior. First, the civilian and military behavior data were almost invariably consistent with respect to delinquent characteristics. Nevertheless, it was important to use the premilitary history to get a long-term picture of S's characteristic aggressive pattern, particularly for those individuals whose time in the military was relatively brief. Second, a subsequent check of psychiatric diagnosis revealed no case in which there was gross discrepancy between the clinical impression of the psychiatrist and S's report of his aggressive behavior pattern. Third, on every occasion in which independent confirmation of civilian behavior was available (15 cases), S's own account was corroborated.

Data pertinent to the variable of aggressive behavior were extracted from each S's social history by the three clinical psychology specialists who had been responsible for testing. The author and one of these specialists rated the behavior extracts for aggressivity on a seven-point scale, with "one" representing the least degree of aggressive behavior. The possibility of knowledge of test scores influencing behavior ratings or vice versa was negligible for two reasons. First, the specialist who served as a judge to check the reliability of the behavior ratings had administered only 25 per cent of the total number of TATs; and second, the behavior ratings were accomplished two months prior to the TAT scoring. Sample extracts of the extremes of the scale are presented below.

Rating of 1: Steady school attendance record through fifth term high school. After leaving school, worked his way up to level of assistant pressman in print shop at $110 per week. He was drafted from a firm which had employed him since 1948. Married and living with wife and child for three years. No military or civilian delinquencies reported.

Rating of 7: Long history of truancies, delinquency, and classroom misbehavior. In reform school four years. Prior to induction was confined two years eight months for armed robbery. While AWOL came in possession of drugs and jailed one month. Assaulted several people. Enlisted in Army on advice of parole officer to get reduction of sentence. History of eight AWOLs and four court-martials. Now facing a general court-martial, five years in prison, and a dishonorable discharge because he wrecked stockade dispensary.

The reliability of these behavior ratings was .91. In order to assure large enough groups for comparison, the seven-point scale was then consolidated into a three-point scale, combining ratings of one and two; three, four and five; and six and seven. Hereafter, Group I of 24 Ss refers to the least antisocial group, Group II of 19 Ss to the intermediate, and Group III of 14 Ss to the most antisocial group.

TABLE 30–1   *Product-Moment Intercorrelation of TAT Variables*

	REMOTENESS	INT. PUN.	EXT. PUN.
	FA	FA	FA	FA
Remoteness FA	.53[a]			
Int. Pun. FA	−.72	−.58		
Ext. Pun. FA	−.45	−.13	.38	
Int. Pun. Ext. Pun.	−.65	−.13	.89	.01

[a] An r of .36 is required for significance at the 1 per cent level.

Results

Since the interpretation of results depends in some degree on the relative independence of the five TAT variables, their intercorrelations are presented in Table 30–1. Most of the relationships are statistically significant, as seems logically required by the fact that complementary aspects of the impulse-control factor of personality are represented. However, in nearly all instances the amount of variance in one variable that can be accounted for by the variance in another (as measured by r^2) is very low to moderate. Therefore, each of the variables may be said to contribute some unique information beyond their common meaning.

As shown in Table 30–2, the analysis of variance indicates over-all significant differences between the means of the three groups. This does not tell us, however, how well the three groups are separated. Therefore, before describing these results in detail, more precise information on the differnces between the groups is presented in Table 30–3. Two-tailed tests of significance were used. It is apparent that in nearly all instances each group is significantly different from the other two.

The difference between the means of the three groups in number of fantasy aggression themes, as shown in Block A of Table 30–2, is highly significant beyond the value of $p = .001$. Since several authors have suggested the importance of social-class sanction as a factor governing the overt expression of covert aggressive needs, this variable was explored within the limits of the data. The bulk of the antisocial

TABLE 30–2		*Analysis of Variance for Three Groups Differing in Degree of Antisocial Behavior*				

TAT VARIABLES	MEAN			VARIANCES[a]	F	p
A. Fantasy Aggression						
Group I	6.08	Between Groups		136.69	23.98	.001
Group II	8.05	Within Groups		5.70		
Group III	11.64					
B. No. of 1 and 2 Remoteness Ratings						
Fantasy Aggression						
Group I	.10	Between Groups		.71	35.50	.001
Group II	.17	Within Groups		.02		
Group III	.49					
C. External Punishment						
Fantasy Aggression						
Group I	.87	Between Groups		.33	3.66	.05
Group II	.70	Within Groups		.09		
Group III	.62					
D. Internal Punishment						
Fantasy Aggression						
Group I	.79	Between Groups		2.88	20.57	.001
Group II	.32	Within Groups		.14		
Group III	.08					
E. Internal Punishment						
External Punishment						
Group I	1.03	Between Groups		3.63	12.96	.001
Group II	.52	Within Groups		.28		
Group III	.15					

[a] Between groups $df = 2$. Within groups $df = 54$.

group was of lower-class background, whereas the nonantisocial group was predominantly middle-class (χ^2 significant at 5 per cent level).

To press the examination further, the Ss in Groups I and III (least and most antisocial) were then separated according to social class. Using the u statistic described by Lord (1947), the significance of the difference in number of aggressions for middle-class Ss only was calculated. The same was then done for lower-class members of Groups I and III. Group III Ss produced significantly more aggressive themes than Group I Ss, regardless of social class. Although the number of Ss on whom these comparisons are based are relatively few (15 middle-class Ss in Group I and 5 in Group III, 6 lower-class Ss in Group I and 9 in Group III), the p values were .02 and .01. These several findings confirm the validity of hypothesis 1 which concerns the relationship between aggression in fantasy and behavior.

To evaluate hypothesis 2, the ratio of one and two remoteness ratings to total fantasy aggression score was compared for the three groups. The results, shown in Block B of Table 30–3, reveal the difference between the means to be significant well beyond $p = .001$. Not only does the antisocial individual respond with more aggressive themes, but the quality of his fantasy aggression is far more direct and undisguised than is true for the nonantisocial individual.

Block C of Table 30–3 compares the ratio of external punishment to fantasy aggression for the three groups. The significance of the difference between the means attains a value of $p=.05$. Thus, an important force inhibiting the nonantisocial group appears to involve some sort of anticipated punitive action from without, giving support to hypothesis 3.

Hypothesis 4 calls for a closer look at the fantasied external punishments. These were separated into three categories according to the following principles: (1) external punishment occurring subsequent t o fantasy aggression and as a direct consequence of such aggression, e.g., "he was sent to jail for stealing"; (2) external punishment occurring prior to fantasy aggression and used as a justification for such aggression, e.g., "she was mean to him so he hit her"; (3) external punishment having neither of the above relationships to fantasy aggression, e.g., "she held him back because she was afraid he might get hurt." The total number of external punishments is larger for Group III than Group I, with $p=.05$. It is clear, however, that TAT themes of external punishment are far more frequently utilized as excuses for aggression by antisocial members of Group III ($p=.001$), thus confirming Hypothesis 4. The mean number of themes classified in this manner was 3.64 for Group III, 1.25 for Group I. External punishment themes as a direct consequence of aggression are also more common among Group III Ss, although the t value of 1.89 falls just short of significance. Since the number of postaggression punishment themes is obviously dependent on the number of fantasy aggressions, an attempt was made to compare retaliatory punishment themes on a proportional basis. The data showed that the mean ratio of retaliatory punishment themes to fantasy aggression is identical for Groups I and III, so that it was not even necessary to calculate a significance statistic. Interestingly enough, the number of external punishment themes unrelated to fantasy aggression is larger among the nonantisocial members of Group I ($p=.01$).

Block D of Table 30–3 indicates that the differences between the group means, with respect to the quantity of guilt and shame themes proportional to aggression, is significant at the value $p=.001$. Since the

GROUPS COMPARED	FANTASY AGGRESSION	NUMBER OF 1 & 2 REMOTENESS RATINGS / FANTASY AGGRESSION	EXTERNAL PUNISHMENT / FANTASY AGGRESSION	INTERNAL PUNISHMENT / FANTASY AGGRESSION	INTERNAL PUNISHMENT / EXTERNAL PUNISHMENT
TABLE 30–3			*t Ratios of Group Differences**		
Group I vs. Group II	3.18	1.75	1.77	3.36	2.83
Group II vs. Group III	4.17	5.33	1.09	6.00	4.07
Group I vs. Group III	6.04	7.84	2.27	4.44	4.40

* Minimum *t* ratios required for significance: $1.69 = <.10$, $2.04 = <.05$, $2.75 = <.01$, $3.64 = <.001$.

antisocial Ss produced significantly more aggressive themes than the nonantisocial Ss, one may wonder whether this alone is not the crucial determinant in creating differential values of the ratio of internal punishment to fantasy aggression. If one were able to find individuals in Groups I and III with aggressive impulses of similar strength, then the effect of internal punishment expectations could be independently evaluated. Overlapping in the number of fantasy aggressions between Ss of Groups I and III permitted comparison of six members from each group. They were the six highest and lowest in Groups I and III, respectively, in

TABLE 30–4   *Discriminative Power of Indicators Obtained*
                              *from the TAT**

VARIABLES	GROUPS I & II	GROUPS II & III	GROUPS I & III
Fantasy Aggression	68	67	76
Number of 1 & 2 Remoteness Scores / Fantasy Aggression	58	82	90
External Punishment / Fantasy Aggression	63	58	66
Internal Punishment / Fantasy Aggression	77	88	97
Internal Punishment / External Punishment	70	82	92

* Numbers in table refer to percentage of cases correctly classified.

number of fantasy aggression themes. The u statistic shows no significant difference between the two groups with respect to fantasy aggression. However, the proportion of internal punishment to fantasy aggression is much larger for the nonantisocial group (p=.001). The mean ratio was .11 for the six Group III members and .54 for the six Group I members.

The relationship between socioeconomic class and antisocial rating raises a similar question regarding internal inhibition as was posed for fantasy aggression. Does the difference in number of internal punishment themes for antisocial and nonantisocial groups hold true irrespective of social-class membership? The u statistic shows clearly that Group I Ss produce significantly more internal punishment themes than Group III Ss, regardless of social class. The difference between the middle-class members of Groups I and III is significant beyond the .001 level, and among lower-class members of the two groups the difference achieves significance at the .01 level.

As shown in Block E of Table 30–3, the ratio of internal to external punishment themes differs significantly for the three groups (p=.001). The much higher ratio for Group I Ss suggests that internal punishment anticipations are a more potent deterrent to antisocial behavior than are external punishment anticipations, supporting hypothesis 6.

Discriminative Power

Since a widely used diagnostic instrument was employed in this study, it was deemed desirable to obtain some measure of diagnostic power or forecasting efficiency as distinguished from statistical significance. In order to evaluate discriminative power accurately, it is necessary to make three comparisons of overlapping scores: Group I with Group II, Group II with Group III, and Group I with Group III. In each instance, the median of the overlapping scores of the two populations being compared was selected as the cutoff point. Thus, there were three different cutoff points for three separate comparisons. The percentage of correct classifications is calculated from the number of cases in each two-group comparison falling on the predicted side of the overlap median score. The data in Table 30–4 suggest that the most discriminating variables are the two internal punishment ratios. In clinical practice, however, it would seem appropriate to approach this classification problem by judging the interrelationship among the factors. For example, one of the members of Group I had a high fantasy aggression score but fell well within the nonantisocial group in all other scoring categories.

Discussion

Since the finding of a positive relationship between fantasy and aggressive behavior held true for Ss of the middle as well as the lower class, some attempt at explanation seems warranted in view of the contrary results of Sanford et al. (1943) and Murray (1943). The range in severity of aggressive behavior among Ss in the present study seems far greater than was true for either of the previous studies, and this, of course, made for an easier discrimination. Furthermore, it is the author's impression, also suggested by Redl and Wineman (1951) and Feshbach (1955), that certain individuals who characteristically behave in impulsive, antisocial fashion not only find fantasy an unsatisfactory substitute for direct action but may actually be stimulated and provoked to act out by a succession of onrushing hostile images.

The association between lower-class membership and antisocial behavior is perhaps partially reflective of the freer rein given aggressive impulses in this group, as suggested by previous authors. It is important to note, however, that when antisocial behavior does occur, whether it be among middle- or lower-class Ss, these individuals manifest stronger aggressive impulses and/or a weaker internal control system than nonantisocial individuals. Thus, the distinguishing feature is the individual impulse-control balance, although specific cultural groups may tend to foster varying types of impulse-control balance with respect to aggression.

The analysis of remoteness of aggression is related to the problem of symbolic representation of impulses and conflicts in projective data. This investigation demonstrated that antisocial Ss were more direct in their expression of aggression than nonantisocial Ss. It appears, then, that defensive inhibitions alter not only the sheer quantity of aggressive themes but also the way in which they are formulated. This is a common enough clinicial observation but one which does not seem to have been given sufficient weight in experiments concerned with the problem of inferring behavioral tendencies from projective material.

Anticipation of punishment as a consequence of aggressive behavior was no more prominent among nonantisocial Ss than antisocial Ss. This is not to say that such expectation may not serve to deter antisocial action in many instances. However, the results do suggest that it is not one of the critical distinctions between the two groups. On the other hand, a significantly larger number of punishment themes unrelated to aggression either as retaliation or justification was characteristic of Group I Ss. The content of themes classified in this manner suggests a greater awareness and acceptance of external direction and restraint. This finding may relate to the demonstration by Pastore (1952) of the importance of perceived arbitrariness of the frustrating situation as a determinant of aggressive reaction.

As noted earlier in this paper, there is a marked tendency for antisocial Ss to justify their aggressive reactions by pointing to the harsh treatment imposed on them by others. If antisocial individuals can prove that the world is against them, then there is no need to recognize any obligations to others. The very fact that they so frequently find it necessary to resort to this projection technique argues that the delinquent ego is busily engaged in disposing of still existing remnants of guilt. One of the implications of this state of affairs is that any general policy of retaliation only reinforces this defensive maneuver and makes it easier for the delinquent to pursue his antisocial course on a guilt-free basis. The basic importance of internal controls in the inhibition of antisocial behavior is amply demonstrated by the data. Certainly the evasion of guilt, shame, or remorse is a far more vital mark of the delinquent than any lack of awareness concerning potential external punishment consequent to antisocial behavior.

Another pertinent topic involves the hypothesis that fantasy behavior has a compensatory function. Tomkins (1947) assumes this hypothesis in stating that TAT aggressive fantasies are found more commonly among neurotics and normals than antisocial characters. The results of the present study suggest that the opposite is the empirical fact, given Ss differing widely in antisocial behavior. However, this finding is not necessarily contradictory to the fantasy substitution hypothesis. One possibility is that the more potent and numerous aggressive impulses of the antisocial Ss obscure any relative increment in fantasy aggression in the nonantisocial Ss. An alternative suggestion mentioned earlier is that fantasy is not universally employed as a defensive or adaptive measure. Clinical experience tells us that individuals differ widely in the use of fantasy, and it may simply be that many directly hostile individuals have not learned to resort to fantasy for substitute gratification.

Summary

This study has relevance to two problems. Its first interest was to examine certain personality variables, particularly in terms of the impulse-control balance, in order to establish their relationship to overt aggressive tendencies. The TAT was the instrument through which information was gathered about the nature of and interrelationships between aggressive impulses, anticipated internal punishment, and anticipated external punishment. The second major issue concerns the relationship between fantasy and reality behavior and the task of formulating from projective data alone the various cues which might permit differential predictions about behavior tendencies in so far as overt expression is concerned.

Fifty-seven young adult soldiers, the large majority of them basic trainees and all of them psychiatric referrals to the Mental Hygiene Clinic, served as Ss. On the basis of social history data covering aggressive and antisocial behavioral manifestations in both civilian and military life, each S was rated as to overt antisocial tendencies. It was found that antisocial Ss differ from nonantisocial Ss in quantity and quality of fantasy aggressions, the former producing not only a larger number of fantasy aggressions but also finding it less necessary to obscure or minimize the hostile impulse. The superego variable as measured by anticipated internal punishments was found to be of far greater significance in inhibiting antisocial behavior than fear of retaliatory punishment, which did not even differentiate between groups. An intersting finding dealt with the tendency of antisocial Ss to utilize themes of external punishment as a justification for their fantasy aggressions. Some of the implications of these results were discussed. An effort was made to deal with the problem of socioeconomic class factors as they might relate to the data. Finally, emphasis was placed on the fact that, for behavioral prediction from projective material, the same attention must be given to repressive, inhibitory forces manifested in the data as is given to the impulse or drive system.

REFERENCES

FESHBACH, S. The drive-reducing functions of fantasy behavior. *J. abnorm. soc. Psychol.*, 1955, 50, 3–11.

LINDZEY, G. Thematic apperception test; interpretive assumptions and related empirical evidence. *Psychol. Bull.*, 1952, 49, 1–25.

LORD, EDITH. The use of range in place of standard deviation in the *t*-test. *Biometrika*, 1947, 34, 41–67.

MCNEMAR, Q. *Psychological statistics.* New York: Wiley, 1949.

MURRAY, H. A. *Thematic apperception test manual.* Cambridge: Harvard Univer. Press, 1943.

MUSSEN, P. H., & NAYLOR, H. K. Relationships between overt and fantasy aggression. *J. abnorm. soc. Psychol.*, 1954, 49, 235–240.

PASTORE, M. The role of arbitrariness in the frustration-aggression hypothesis. *J. abnorm. soc. Psychol.*, 1952, 47, 728–731.

REDL, F., & WINEMAN, D. *Children who hate.* Glencoe, Ill.: The Free Press, 1951.

SANFORD, R. N., ADKINS, M. M., MILLER, R. B., COBB, E. A., et al. Physique, personality, and scholarship: A cooperative study of school children. *Monogr. Soc. Res. Child Develpm.*, 1943, 8, No. 1.

TOMKINS, S. S. *The thematic apperception test.* New York: Grune & Stratton, 1947.

31

Projective Measurement of Experimentally Induced Levels of Sexual Motivation[1]

RUSSELL A. CLARK

The importance of situational factors in mediating the relationship between an aroused need and the manifestation of that need through thematic stories is the key finding of this study. Under the conditions of receiving the TAT from an attractive, somewhat provocative woman or viewing nude pictures prior to taking the TAT, the aroused sexual drive was more than compensated for by aroused guilt. The result was that the aroused groups indicated less projection of sex in their stories than control groups who had neither of these arousal stimuli. As a result of the influence of alcohol, however, a new experimental group viewing the nude pictures did project more sexual imagery than a control group who had also imbibed at a beer party.

The results demonstrate the utility of a dialectical approach to measuring needs. Every arousal situation probably elicits some defense against the change of behavior the subject would have to undergo to satisfy the need. This opposition of drive and defense against expression (in this case sex drive and guilt over expression) results in a synthesis which is the algebraic summation of these two competing forces. Depending on which of the two is stronger, the subject will either manifest sexual imagery or not. The effect of alcoholic consumption is apparently to lower the guilt gradient, thereby assuring the projection of sexual imagery.

[1] The present paper is a somewhat different form of a dissertation presented to the faculty of the Graduate School of Yale University in partial fulfillment of the requirements for the Degree of Doctor of Philosophy. The author is grateful to Drs. C. I. Hovland, I. L. Child, I. L. Janis, and D. C. McClelland for assistance in the planning and execution of this project.

This experiment thus negates the belief that the content of thematic stories is not subject to conscious control and further indicates the importance of the knowledge of mediating influences in predicting the manifestation of a need in a thematic response.

The primary purpose of the present research has been to investigate the measurement of sexual motivation by means of the TAT. The impetus for this study came from some findings by McClelland, Atkinson, Clark, and Lowell (1953). All the TAT scoring categories employed by Mc-Clelland and his associates for measuring the need for achievement (n-Achievement) varied as a direct function of increase in motivation. That is to say, with an increase in experimentally induced strength-of-achievement motivation there was a corresponding increase in the frequency of appearance of the various achievement-related categories. This seems to indicate that for n-Achievement there is no such thing as repression, suppression, or any sort of inhibition operating. This finding seems fairly plausible in view of the fact that in the American culture individuals are widely encouraged to work hard, get good grades in school, advance themselves in the business world, etc. There are few taboos attached to the attainment of achievement goals. However, these findings involved mean differences in frequencies based on groups of Ss. A further study by McClelland et al. (1953), involving case histories and psychiatric interviews indicated that there were a few individuals who were highly motivated to achieve but so anxious about achievement that they inhibited the expression of manifest achievement imaginery in their TAT stories. This tentative finding ran contrary to the common assumption that projective measures circumvent the usual defenses of the individual.

For investigating the degree to which inhibition occurs in the TAT, it seemed desirable to select some motive which was apt to differ from n-Achievement with regard to amount of anxiety that was apt to be involved. The sex motive, in our society at least, seems to have the necessary qualifications. There are all sorts of parental, social, and religious prohibitions against sexual activity. Because of this basic difference, and because it seemed possible to manipulate sex motivation experimentally, this motive was chosen as suitable for investigation.

Procedure

Three separate experiments (A, B, and C) were conducted in the course of the present investigation. Each experiment involved two groups of male college Ss, one of which (experimental) took a group TAT after having been exposed to some type of sexually arousing stimulus. The other group (control) consisted of comparable Ss who took the group TAT without prior sexual stimulation.

The TAT pictures employed were from the Murray 1942 series with one exception. They were presented in the following order: 7BM, 12BG, 14, 20, 10, 6F, picture of a man working late at night in an office, and 6BM. Not all of the groups saw all eight pictures. The first five were shown for Experiment A, the first six for Experiment B, and all eight for Experiment C. The instructions which were employed for the administration of the group TAT are the standard instructions used by McClelland et al. (1953), and McClelland, Clark, Roby, and Atkinson (1949).

EXPERIMENT A

The experimental group was first exposed to a series of photographic slides of attractive nude females and immediately thereafter given the TAT. The control group took the TAT immediately after having been exposed to a series of slides of landscape scenes, architecture, fashionably decorated rooms, etc. All slides used in this experiment were black and white.

The Ss were in two sections of an elementary psychology class. They were tested before there had been any formal discussion of projective techniques. Two Es (graduate students) met the control class; one to conduct an "investigation on factors affecting aesthetic judgment," which was the rationale for the control slides, and the other to conduct "a standardization of a test of creative imagination." The Ss were asked to rate each slide with respect to degree of attractiveness, stating what it was about the picture that makes it attractive or unattractive. They used mimeographed line rating scales with spaces for comment. All slides were presented briefly in order to enable Ss to get an over-all impression, and then on the second presentation the slides were shown for a longer period, thus enabling Ss to make the ratings and pertinent comments. The TAT was given by the second E immediately thereafter. Every effort was made to convince Ss that the rating of the slides and the TAT were separate experiments.

The experimental group was tested on the next day by the author and one of the previous Es. After again doing a variety of things to give Ss the impression that the presentation of the slides and the TAT were two different experiments, the author gave the rationale for the presentation of the nude slides, which was an attempt to make the presentation of the nude slides seem very plausible to the Ss. This rationale referenced the work of Sheldon (1949) on the correlation between body type and certain physical and mental disorders, explained why the pictures of nude females were drawn from art photography (because of social pressure against standardized body-typing photographs), and requested Ss to use a mimeographed line rating scale with space for comments in evaluating the eight pictures to be shown. The E indicated that comments such as "breasts just the right size and shape" and "legs long and shapely" were adequate. In order to further set Ss for sexual stimulation by the slides, E then said:

"I think that you will find that most of these pictures are of at least fairly attractive girls. We have purposefully included mostly those body types that we feel should be fairly appealing. So when you use the rating scale, don't be concerned if many of the ratings fall toward the attractive end of the scale, but try to make fine discriminations among the more attractive girls. Now, remember your job is to judge the sexual attractiveness of these girls. I don't think you will find this an especially unpleasant task."

The nudes were projected life-size on a large screen. After Ss had finished their ratings and pertinent comments about these slides, E collected the papers, packed up the slides, and left. The other E then came forward and administered the TAT with the same remarks and instructions that were given the control group.

EXPERIMENT B

Basically this experiment consisted simply of employing a very attractive female as administrator of the TAT for the experimental condition and a male administrator for the control group. No nude or neutral slides were involved. It was designed to determine whether the presence of an attractive, clothed female would elicit a type of sexual phantasy less apt to be guilt-ridden than that obtained in Experiment A.

The Ss were members of the freshman class who, for one reason or another, had missed taking the TAT as a part of a battery of personality and aptitude tests. The Ss for the experimental and control groups were assigned at random and received notices from the Dean's office to report for the test. These Ss were run in small groups of 4, 5, or 6 over a four-day period, with the male E (control) testing on the first two days, and the female E (experimental) testing on the last two days. All testing was at night and in an office, in order to assist in making the female's presence less formal and more intimate. The girl was dressed attractively and wore an allegedly stimulating brand of perfume. She had trouble with the projector in the first TAT picture in order to enable her to request the males to come to her assistance. They gathered around and did so. The privacy of Ss while writing was ensured by E, after having projected the TAT slide for 20 seconds, retiring to a remote easy chair during the 5 minutes allowed for writing about each TAT slide. Also, each S deposited his protocol in an envelope on completion of the test.

EXPERIMENT C

It is a very common assumption that alcohol reduces guilt, fear, or anxiety. In fact, recent work by Conger (1951) with white rats seems to demonstrate that this is the case. Experiment C employed alcohol in an attempt to reduce sex-involved guilt or anxiety. The experimental group took the TAT in a fraternity beer-party setting after having been exposed to nude slides as compared with a control group also in a beer-party setting but without exposure to any kind of slides.[2]

Two presumably comparable fraternity groups were used as the experimental and control groups. The test was rationalized on the ground that it was desirable to determine the effects of informal environment and alcohol on the test of "creative imagination." The test was given approximately 1¼ hours after the start of the beer parties, and Ss were permitted to continue drinking during the test. The nude pictures were exposed on slides to the experimental group through clandestine arrangements designed to dissociate these pictures from the later TAT. The TAT was given shortly after the last of eight nude pictures was shown.

SCORING

The scoring was done by the author and one other person. The author rescored the stories several times. The other scorer practiced on 150 stories under the author's tutelage before beginning the reliability check. In the case of discrepancies, the final scoring was decided on after a joint conference of the two scorers.

The first analysis of the TAT protocols was to reveal manifest sex imagery. Sexual relationships were categorized as (1) primary — explicit or implicit evidence for sexual intercourse, (2) secondary—evidence for the occurrence of such secondary sex activity as kissing, dancing, fondling, etc., (3) tertiary—characters in the stories perceived as sweethearts, on a date, courting, in love, etc., but not engaged in either primary or secondary sexual activity. Sexual activity was scored only once for each story, and that which was biologically most sexual received priority.

In addition to sex imagery, the protocols were also scored for guilt. A decision was made to score for guilt only in connection with sexual activity. It could be argued that sexual guilt might easily appear in a disguised form by being displaced to other types of activity. The author made an initial attempt to score for guilt regardless of the activity

---

[2] Neutral slides were omitted from this control group because a few stories in Experiment A seemed to be determined by a set for evaluation of the aesthetic qualities of the TAT slides which presumably was established by having rated the aesthetic qualities of the "control" slides.

involved and obtained no group differences whatsoever. Three general categories are scored as being indicative of the presence of guilt: (1) someone is ashamed, guilty, sorry, anxiety-ridden, morally concerned, embarrassed, etc. over sexual activity; (2) someone is punished, criticized, ostracized for sexual activity; and (3) someone punishes himself in some concrete fashion as a result of a sexual activity. Guilt is also scored only once for each story.[3]

The per cent agreements between the two scorers were 91 per cent for sexual imagery and 90 per cent for guilt over sex. These percentages were obtained by considering agreements to be those categories which both scorers had marked as being present. Those categories which one scorer had marked as being present but the other scorer had marked as absent were counted as disagreements. Those categories which both scorers had indicated as being absent were not considered in the calculations above. Thus, agreements of the present-present variety are considered but not agreements of the absent-absent variety.

Results

The chi squares in this study were calculated in the following manner. The frequency of appearance of any particular category was calculated for each S. The two groups under comparison were combined, and the dividing point for setting up the contingency tables was determined by selecting that frequency which most nearly enabled the placing of 50 per cent of all Ss above and below that dividing point. Yates's correction for discontinuity was used in every case, regardless of the magnitude of the cell entries.[4]

Table 31–1 demonstrates that the experimental groups for Experiments A and B exhibited significantly less manifest sex imagery than the controls. The experimental group for Experiment C, however, showed reliably more sex imagery than the control group.

Table 31–2 presents the comparisons of Experiment A and Experiment C. The reader is reminded that theoretically these two experiments differed only with respect to the fact that one of the conditions involved

---

[3] The stories were also scored for affect over sexual activity. A three-way breakdown was made involving: (1) passion, lust, etc.; (2) love, tenderness, etc.; and (3) no affect present. The results of this analysis are the same as those that obtain for the sexual activity and are not reported because they add little to the interpretation.

[4] There were 5 TAT pictures used in Experiment A, 6 pictures in Experiment B, and 8 pictures in Experiment C. In each case, calculations are based on the maximum number of pictures common to the groups being compared. Also, in examining the tables that follow, the reader should be warned that the percentage of Ss above the dividing point for a given group may vary from one comparison to another because a different dividing point is often involved.

a beer-party atmosphere. In practice, however, there were certain minor differences other than this. The Ss for Experiment A were mainly sophomores, with a few juniors and seniors. The Ss for Experiment C represented, of course, a cross-section of the four classes. Also, the nude slides were achromatic for Experiment A but chromatic for Experiment C. Finally, the control group for Experiment A was exposed to neutral slides, while the control group for Experiment C was not exposed to neutral slides. Interexperiment comparisons involving Experiment B are not presented mainly because the sexual-arousal stimulus differed markedly from that employed for the other two experiments, and only freshmen were employed as Ss in Experiment B.

TABLE 31–1   *Per Cent of Ss above the Dividing Point in Respect to the Frequency of All Sex Imagery*

CONDITION	Ss	% Ss ABOVE DIVIDING POINT	χ^2
Exp. A			
Exp.	40	27.5	10.12[b]
Control	38	65.8	
Exp. B			
Exp.	30	30.0	7.34[b]
Control	29	69.0	
Exp. C			
Exp.	35	60.0	5.85[a]
Control	27	25.9	

[a] Significant at 5 per cent level.
[b] Significant at 1 per cent level.

Table 31–2 indicates that in general the groups of Experiment C (alcohol) show more sexual imagery than the groups of Experiment A (nonalcohol). Comparison of groups was made also with respect to the three types of sexual imagery — primary, secondary, and tertiary. The general finding was that primary sexual imagery was the main contributor to the differences in over-all sex imagery contained in Tables 31–1 and 31–2. Also, Table 31–2 shows that there is no significant difference in over-all sex imagery between the control groups of Experiment A and Experiment C. However, the control group of Experiment C does have a significantly greater amount of primary sexual imagery than the control group of Experiment A.

Tables 31–3 and 31–4 reveal that those groups which show more sex imagery (see Tables 31–1 and 31–2) also exhibit more guilt over sexual activity.

Table 31–5 presents the comparisons of the amount of guilt involved in the different types of sexual imagery. It is clear that more guilt is evoked by primary sex than by secondary or tertiary sex. One also might expect that stories involving secondary sex would contain more guilt than those involving tertiary sex. This, however, is not the case. A number of explanations could be offered for this inconsistency. For example, one

---

TABLE 31–2   *Per Cent of Ss above the Dividing Point in Respect*
to the Frequency of All Sex Imagery

EXPERIMENT A			EXPERIMENT C			
		% Ss ABOVE DIVIDING			% Ss ABOVE DIVIDING	
CONDITION	Ss	POINT	CONDITION	Ss	POINT	
Exp.	40	27.5	Exp.	35	77.1	16.60[b]
Control	38	15.8	Exp.	35	45.7	6.51[a]
Exp.	40	27.5	Control	27	63.0	6.89[b]
Control	38	65.8	Control	27	63.0	

[a] Significant at the 5 per cent level.
[b] Significant at the 1 per cent level.

TABLE 31–3   *Per Cent of Ss above the Dividing Point in Respect*
to the Frequency of Sex-Involved Guilt

CONDITION	Ss	% Ss ABOVE THE DIVIDING POINT	χ^2
Exp. A			
Exp.	40	20.0	5.31[a]
Control	38	47.4	
Exp. B			
Exp.	30	16.7	8.01[a]
Control	29	55.2	
Exp. C			
Exp.	35	51.4	5.69[a]
Control	27	18.5	

[a] Significant at the 5 per cent level.

of the TAT pictures employed is usually perceived as a man and woman in an embrace. This picture elicited a large number of stories concerning a husband and wife in an embrace or kissing. This type of story would, of course, be scored as secondary sex. In our society, for husband and wife there are no moral sanctions against this type of activity. Also, some of these same stories involved embracing (secondary sex) but this was in a context of consolation for the loss of a son in the war, etc. These stories were scored in order to be consistent with the criteria, but in future work it would be well to eliminate this type of story either by special provisions in the scoring system or by avoiding the use of this type of picture (TAT 10).

Discussion

The two main factors considered in the present study are sex and sex-involved guilt. One logical way of interpreting these results involves an

TABLE 31–4   *Per Cent of Ss above the Dividing Point in Respect to the Frequency of Sex-Involved Guilt*

		EXPERIMENT A			EXPERIMENT C	
		% Ss ABOVE DIVIDING			% Ss ABOVE DIVIDING	
CONDITION	Ss	POINT	CONDITION	Ss	POINT	χ^2
Exp.	40	20.0	Exp.	35	82.9	26.89[a]
Control	38	47.4	Exp.	35	82.9	8.62[a]
Exp.	40	20.0	Control	27	59.3	9.07[a]
Control	38	47.4	Control	27	59.3	

[a] Significant at the 1 per cent level.

TABLE 31–5   *Per Cent of Guilt Involved in Each of the Three Types of Sex Imagery for All of the Groups Combined*

	PRIMARY SEX IMAGERY	SECONDARY SEX IMAGERY	TERTIARY SEX IMAGERY
Per cent of stories containing guilt	70.4	22.1	30.4
Standard error of per cent	3.0	5.0	4.1
	Primary Sex vs. Secondary Sex CR = 8.3 $p<.01$	Primary Sex vs. Tertiary Sex CR = 7.9 $p<.01$	Tertiary Sex vs. Secondary Sex CR = 1.2

approach-avoidance conflict-type analysis such as that proposed by Lewin (1931) and Miller (1948). However, before considering the results in the light of such an analysis, it is necessary to make a clear-cut distinction between two different aspects of both sex and guilt that are presumably involved in this study. First, there is the degree of sex arousal and accompanying guilt that is evoked by the experimental procedures involving the presence of an attractive female and the presentation of nude slides. These motives can be referred to as stimulus-produced sex and guilt motives. The second aspect concerns the sexual arousal and accompanying guilt that might result from the writing of stories of a sexual nature. These motives can be referred to as response-produced sex and guilt motives.

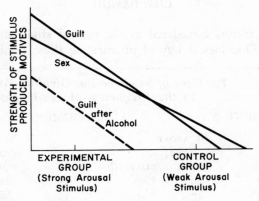

FIGURE 31–1. Hypothetical curves showing the strength of sex and guilt motives evoked by the arousal conditions for the experimental and control groups.

Figure 31–1 depicts the relative strengths of the stimulus-produced motives for the experimental and control groups. In this figure, the guilt gradient is shown as being reduced by the consumption of alcohol. The control groups are assumed to be located toward the weak end of the stimulus continuum. The experimental groups are located at a point in the strong end of the stimulus continuum. This figure also assumes that the guilt or avoidance gradient is steeper than the sex or approach gradient. In other situations, it has been found that avoidance gradients are steeper than approach gradients, and Miller (1948) has discussed possible reasons for this. In the discussion that follows, the conclusions drawn depend, of course, on the shapes of the gradients and the location of the experimental and control groups with respect to these gradients. For the purpose of simplicity, the gradients are assumed to be linear in nature. The exact location of the two groups with respect to these gradients is, of course, not known. If the positions depicted in Figure 31–1 were changed at all markedly, some of the conclusions to be drawn would no longer hold. Figure 31–2 presents the strengths of the response-produced sex and guilt that are evoked by writing stories containing the various kinds of sex imagery. The considerations that apply to the gradients in Figure 31–1 also apply here.

The question that arises next concerns the relationship between the stimulus-produced sex and guilt and the writing of stories containing sex imagery. The first assumption made is (1) that the expression of sex in the TAT stories is a direct function of the algebraic summation of the stimulus-produced sex and guilt gradients. That is, the higher the sex gradient above the guilt gradient, the greater will be the tendency to express sex. The second assumption is (2) that the guilt appearing in the TAT stories is a function of expressing sex in the stories and not a function of the guilt that is evoked by the arousal stimuli. There is some evidence to indicate that the second assumption is correct. If this assumption were true, there should be no difference in percentages of guilt over a given kind of sex imagery expressed in the TAT protocols between the experimental and control groups. That is to say, both groups should experience the same degree of guilt for writing a given kind of sex story. If the level of guilt evoked by the arousal conditions also has a tendency to be expressed in the stories, this should lead to a higher percentage of expressed guilt for the experimental group because of the greater strength of guilt due to the arousal conditions for this group. There is, however, no evidence for this. The percentage of guilt over primary sex obtained by combining the three experimental groups is 73.6 per cent and that for the combined control groups is 67.3 per cent. The critical ratio for this difference is 1.01, with a probability value of .31.

In the light of these assumptions and considerations, the findings will now be analyzed. The first major result to be explained is the finding that for Experiments A and B the control groups express more sex and guilt in the TAT stories than their respective experimental groups. By consulting Figure 31–1, it can be seen that for these experimental groups

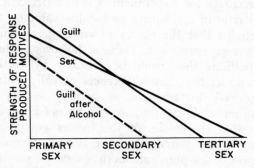

FIGURE 31–2. Hypothetical curves showing the strength of sex and guilt motives evoked by the writing of stories containing the various kinds of sex imagery.

the stimulus-produced guilt is at a higher level than the stimulus-produced sex. Just the reverse is true for these two control groups. Thus, one would predict that the control groups would have a greater tendency to express sex. Having expressed a greater amount of sex and especially a greater amount of primary sex, it follows that the control group should express more guilt. This can be understood by examining Figure 31–2 and recalling the assumption that expressed guilt is primarily a function of writing stories containing sexual imagery.

The second major finding is that for Experiment C the experimental group expressed more sex and guilt than did the control group. Again by examining Figure 31–1, the explanation for this can be sought. With a sufficient lowering of the guilt gradient due to alcohol, it can be seen that there is a greater difference between the sex and guilt gradients for the control group. The line of reasoning for this difference in expression of sex and guilt is the same as that applied to the previous finding.

The last major finding to be considered concerns the interexperiment comparisons involving Experiments A and C. In general, the alcohol groups of Experiment C express more sex and guilt than do the non-alcohol groups of Experiment A. By checking Figure 31–1, the reader can satisfy himself that for any of these particular comparisons the alcohol group in question should express more sex than the nonalcohol group in question. However, when one examines Figure 31–2, it can be seen that the alcohol groups should have less guilt over expressing sex because of the lowered guilt gradient in this situation. This, of course, does not conform with the empirical findings. On the other hand, one might expect a higher total frequency of guilt for the alcohol groups because of the higher total frequency of both over-all sex and primary sex. Nevertheless, according to Figure 31–2, one would expect a lower percentage of guilt over a given kind of sex imagery. However, this is not the case. The percentage of guilt over primary sex obtained by combining the experimental and control groups of Experiment C is 68.6 percent. The comparable percentage for Experiment A is 65.0 per cent. This difference yields a critical ratio of .43, with a probability value of .67. From this it might be concluded that the theory is wrong in assuming that alcohol reduces guilt over expressing sex. There is, however, at least one possible alternative hypothesis that could be checked by further work. This involves the consideration that differences actually exist in the stories that are categorized, for example, as primary sex. It is the author's impression from rereading the primary sex stories for the alcohol and non-alcohol groups that the stories of the former groups are more sexual in nature. That is, the statements "She became pregnant" and "They had an impassioned sex orgy" are both scored as primary sex, but the latter type of imagery seems, to say the least, a more powerful statement. A more refined scoring system, or the present system modified such that sex imagery could be scored more than once per story, might demonstrate this impression to be true. If the subjects in the alcohol groups are expressing a more primary type of sex, the increased guilt that this would involve might compensate for the decrease in guilt due to alcohol. This would account for the finding that there is no difference in the percentages of guilt involved in primary sex for the two conditions.

Summary

This study involved the projective measurement of experimentally induced levels of sex motivation. Sexual motivation was aroused by the presentation of slides of nude females in two instances and in another instance by the presence of an attractive female. The TAT protocols were analyzed for manifest sex imagery and sex-involved guilt.

The results showed that under normal conditions the experimental groups expressed significantly less sex and guilt in the TAT stories than did the control groups. Under conditions of alcohol, these results were just the reverse. That is, the experimental group showed significantly more sex and guilt than did the control group.

These results are interpreted by assuming that under normal conditions the guilt evoked by sexual arousal is sufficient to inhibit the expression of sex with a consequent lowering of guilt. Under alcohol, however, the guilt over sexual arousal is reduced enough to permit the expression of sex with a resulting increase in expressed guilt.

REFERENCES

CONGER, J. J. The effects of alcohol on conflict behavior in the albino rat. Quart. J. Stud. Alcohol, 1951, 12, 1–29.

LEWIN, K. Environmental forces in child-behaviour and development. In C. Murchison (Ed.), A handbook of child psychology. Worcester: Clark Univer. Press, 1931.

McCLELLAND, D. C., ATKINSON, J. W., CLARK, R. A., & LOWELL, E. L. The achievement motive. New York: Appleton-Century-Crofts, 1953.

McCLELLAND, D. C., CLARK, R. A., ROBY, T., & ATKINSON, J. W. The projective expression of needs. IV. The effect of the need for achievement on thematic apperception. J. exp. Psychol., 1949, 39, 242–255.

MILLER, N. E. Theory and experiment relating psychoanalytic displacement to stimulus-response generalization. J. abnorm. soc. Psychol., 1948, 43, 155–178.

SHELDON, W. H. Varieties of delinquent youth: An introduction to constitutional psychiatry. New York: Harper, 1949.

32

Thematic Apperception Test: Indexes of Aggression in Relation to Measures of Overt and Covert Behavior[1]

GARDNER LINDZEY
AND CHARLOTTE TEJESSY

*The thematic protocols of 20 volunteer Harvard men were scored for
10 TAT signs of aggression reputed to measure the covert aspects of
this variable and then correlated with various criteria. These criteria
included diagnostic council ratings (all tests of the subject including
autobiographies and interview data were used in the assessment),
observer ratings, Rosenzweig Extrapunitive and Intrapunitive Scores,
and the self-ratings of the subjects.*

*Contrary to prediction, the self-ratings showed the highest correla-
tion with TAT aggression, the diagnostic council ratings the poorest.
These findings indicate that the subject was able to control the hostile
content of his responses to the TAT so that they were in accord with
his self-concept. The implications are that earlier clinicians have erred
in assuming that the kinds of aggressive signs measured on the TAT*

[1] From the Harvard Psychological Clinic. This study is part of a program of
research conducted under the direction of Henry A. Murray and supported by grants
from the Rockefeller Foundation and the Laboratory of Social Relations, Harvard
University.

[a] B. I. Murstein. "The Effect of Stimulus Background, Personality and Scoring
System on the Assessment of Hostility through the TAT" (Unpublished paper,
Connecticut College, 1964).

were immune to the censoring eye of the subject. Rather, much more subtle means are necessary to gain access to his private world. In the opinion of the editor, there are three basic ways to achieve this step. First, measure the stimulus properties of the cards so that we may know what aspect of a subject's story represents projection and what part indicates his respect for the properties of the stimulus. Second, more subtle forms of analysis than the scoring of simple content are needed.[a] Third, more should be known by the tester about the subject coming for testing than is usually the case. When this information is lacking, the examiner might profitably employ an interview before administering the projective test to help him assess the context in which the projective productions are to be judged.

Perhaps most perplexing of all the many problems facing the user of projective techniques is the difficulty of assigning his inferences about the respondent to some "level" of behavior. Will this attribute be expressed freely in public settings? Is the subject aware of but unwilling to reveal this motive except under rarely encountered circumstances? Does it determine his behavior without awareness on his part? Is it displayed only in fantasy? Or is the attribute expressed under some still more complex set of conditions? The confusion introduced by these bewildering empirical possibilities is not at all lessened by existing formulations and findings dealing with the problem. In general, clinician and investigator alike have failed to provide an adequate conceptual statement to incorporate and systematize problems in this area, and further, there are all too few empirical findings that promise to be of appreciable importance in contributing to eventual clarification of this question.

The present study serves to underline the complexity of these problems and in addition provides evidence that bears directly on the validity of existing generalizations concerning aspects of Thematic Apperception Test response that reflect variations in aggression.

From a survey of empirical generalizations dealing with the TAT (Lindzey, Tejessy, Davids, & Heinemann, 1953), we selected ten "signs" of aggression that had been proposed by various individuals familiar with the instrument. The complete TAT protocols of a small number of intensively studied subjects were then analyzed in terms of these ten dimensions and related to independent measures designed to assess the variable of aggression under different conditions or at different levels. The measures used were: a clinical rating assigned by a diagnostic council, an observer rating based on a fact-finding interview and the subject's autobiography, the Picture-Frustration Study, and self-ratings by the subject.

While it is generally agreed that the TAT reflects or measures various levels of behavior (Lindzey, 1952), most psychologists would agree with Murray's statement: "Whatever peculiar virtue the TAT may have, if any, it will be found to reside, not, as some have assumed, in its power to mirror overt behavior or to communicate what the patient knows and is willing to tell, but rather in its capacity to reveal things that the patient is unwilling to tell or is unable to tell because he is unconscious of them" (Murray, 1951, p. 577).

Consistent with this assumption, we predicted that the measures of aggression derived from the TAT would be most sensitive to (correlate most highly with) aggression as measured by the clinical ratings and least sensitive to aggression as measured by the subjects' self-ratings. We expected that the measures based on the P-F Study and the observer ratings would be intermediate in the magnitude of their relationship to the TAT measures.

Procedure

The subjects were 20 Harvard College undergraduates, most of whom were sophomores at the time of data collection. While enrolled in an introductory psychology course, they had volunteered to participate in an intensive psychological study that would extend over several years. They were paid for their time at the customary student rate. Within the limitations imposed by the restricted range of the population from which they were drawn, the subjects were heterogeneous in socioeconomic status, religion, academic standing, and extracurricular activities.

INDEPENDENT MEASURES

Clinical Ratings

The diagnostic council judgments were arrived at for each subject after detailed discussion of a large amount of case material by a group of from 8 to 12 council members. The rating of aggression was made in terms of a six-point scale and was based on knowledge of a wide variety of test results, fantasy productions, interview material, autobiography, special ratings, etc. Although the ratings were made with a knowledge of the subject's autobiography and limited aspects of overt behavior, the clinicians gave a very heavy weighting to covert or fantasy material; e.g., in cases where an individual revealed no overt evidence of a given disposition but showed strong covert signs, he would secure a high rating. Our clinical measure, then, is somewhat contaminated by a knowledge of overt response but is heavily weighted in the direction of the kinds of material and inference processes that are conventionally employed to get at covert tendencies.

There is another and more serious source of contamination present in these ratings. Included in the mass of material available to the council were the raw TAT protocols. It is true that the TAT represented only a small proportion of the data available for each subject and further that the council did not have the specific scores or ratings that are of interest in this study, but it is, of course, possible that in a more intuitive way the council might lean heavily on just those aspects of the TAT protocols that our scored variables are designed to assess and thus produce a spurious correlation between the council ratings and the TAT measures. Thus, positive correlations between the diagnostic council ratings and the TAT "signs" must be evaluated in the light of this contamination of the measures.

Observer Ratings

A highly experienced clinician rated each subject on overt aggression, basing his ratings on a brief fact-finding interview and on a detailed autobiography. Again the ratings were made on a six-point scale.

Picture-Frustration Study

The P-F Study was administered in a group setting and scored by an individual who knew only the age and sex of the respondents. Only the variables of extrapunitiveness and intrapunitiveness will be dealt with in this study.

Self-Ratings

Each subject rated himself on a number of variables, among which was the variable of physical (overt observable) aggression. For each variable rated, the subject was provided with a number of specific components that were part of the general variable. He was asked first to check the elements, or components, that applied to him and then to make an over-all judgment, on a one-to-six scale, of the strength of this variable in his behavior.

THEMATIC APPERCEPTION TEST

The TAT was administered under standard conditions, with the two halves of the test given on separate days. The examiner took notes continuously throughout the test, and in addition, without knowledge of the subjects, the sessions were electrically transcribed. The combination of the examiner's notes and the recording permitted an almost verbatim record of each subject's stories.

The story protocols were analyzed in terms of ten variables that were selected from a relatively exhaustive summary of generalizations concerning the TAT (Lindzey et al., 1953). Each variable was defined as precisely as possible, and objective rules for rating the variable were established. In describing these variables, we shall in each case present first a brief quotation indicating the published source of the variable.

Avoidance of gun. "The gun is an aggressive object and the fact that patient avoids it suggests the possibility that he may have difficulty in handling aggression" (Stein, 1948, p. 57). "The revolver in Picture No. 3 and the rifle in Picture No. 8 may be omitted by patients with strong aggressive tendencies" (Stein, 1948, p. 42). ". . . A subject who has to repress his latent aggressiveness may completely deny the presence of the gun (No. 3 BM) by simply omitting reference to it, seeing it as a hole in the floor, as a cigarette case, or not at all" (Bellak, 1950, pp. 207–208).

Stories told to the appropriate cards were rated on a three-point scale in terms of whether avoidance of the gun was clearly present, was questionably present (e.g., several interpretations of what the gun might be are offered, one or more of which deny that it is a gun), or was absent.

Aggressive turns. "In a setting of otherwise orderly stories, sudden and not too elaborate aggressive turns which are not required by the card indicate strong suppressed aggression" (Rapaport, Gill, & Schafer, 1946, p. 445).

Individual stories were rated from o to 4, depending on the intensity and unexpectedness of the aggressive incident. Any aggressive act that is the result of careful preparation on the part of the hero is scored o.

Death as a result of external forces. "A frequent technique used by most patients who cannot express their aggression directly against the people to whom they feel hostile is to have them die in the stories because of natural causes or as a result of an accident" (Stein, 1948, p. 75).

This variable is scored as present or absent for each story. In order for the variable to be present, there must be reference to the death of a nonhero figure due to some cause other than an act of the hero.

Violence. "Aggression may be shown by stories of violence . . ." (Rotter, 1946, p. 89).

Each story is rated from o to 4 in terms of the amount of extreme destruction, aggression, or hostility.

Death or failure in nonheroes. "Aggression may be shown by stories . . . in which death, jail, failure, etc., occur in characters with whom the patient is not identified" (Rotter, 1946, p. 89).

Each story is scored as displaying this variable or not. Only obvious and explicitly stated incidents in the life of a nonhero lead to the score of present.

Misrecognition. "Where the patient is unable to accept physical violence or aggression because of a need to suppress his own aggression, misinterpretation of both objects in the picture and the facial expression of the characters is common in order to avoid aggressive stories" (Rotter, 1946, p. 81). "Repressed aggression may be indicated by the subject's failure to recognize or accept pictures where the action or expression of the character is usually interpreted as aggressive" (Rotter, 1946, p. 89).

Individual stories were rated from o to 4, depending on the existence of misperception or faulty reporting and the degree to which the error was clearly tied to aggression.

Strong aggressive fantasies. "The boys who are inhibited in expressing their aggression in behavior have strong aggressive fantasies" (Symonds, 1949, p. 99).

Again, each individual story was rated from o to 4, depending on the frequency and strength of the aggressive themes present in the story. This variable overlaps considerably with *violence* but is somewhat more inclusive as it covers less extreme forms of aggression as well as aggressive thoughts or wishes which would not be included under the earlier variable.

Forceful language. "Decision as to this factor (aggression versus passivity) is made from the content and general tone aspects of the stories. Useful in estimating this" is "the language used implying either forceful aggressive action or its opposite" (Henry, 1947, p. 45).

Each story was rated from o to 4, depending on how straightforward and unqualified the language was, e.g., use of the words definitely, surely, clearly, etc., and avoidance of such words as perhaps, maybe, possibly, etc.; and how ruthless, assertive, and domineering the behavior it described.

Constructive outcome. "The kinds of outcome and solutions given to various situations, the constructive forward-looking nature of these, versus their succorant and nurturant nature" (Henry, 1947, p. 45).

Each story was rated from o to 4, depending on the relative success in the outcome of incidents and stories.

TABLE 32–1	*Interrater Reliability of TAT Variables*
TAT VARIABLE	r $(n = 20)$
1. Avoidance of gun	.93
2. Aggressive turns	.81
3. Death as a result of external forces	.81
4. Violence	.78
5. Death and failure in nonheroes	.90
6. Misrecognition	.68
7. Strong aggressive fantasies	.86
8. Forceful language	.48
9. Constructive outcome	.67
10. Constructive character	.57

Constructive character. "The constructive and self-reliant versus the suppliant and retiring characteristic of central characters" (Henry, 1947, p. 45).

Individual stories were rated from 0 to 4, depending on the strength, purposiveness and forcefulness of central figures in the story.

Half of the stories for each subject were scored for each variable by a reliability rater who had no knowledge of the subjects or of the experimental rater's scores. The two sets of scores were compared by means of product-moment correlations. The resulting coefficients are summarized in Table 32–1. With the exception of the last three variables, which were difficult to define satisfactorily and furthermore seemed to have the least rational link to the variable under study, these reliability figures seemed relatively satisfactory.

Results and Discussion

The relations between the TAT variables and the various independent measures are summarized in Table 32–2. Contrary to our expectations, there was no consistent relationship between the *clinical ratings* and the TAT indexes. Only half of the correlations were positive, and the two highest correlations were negative. As these findings represented our best approximation of the kind of information the TAT is conventionally presumed to provide, these results came as a distinct surprise. They do serve to allay all qualms concerning the contamination of our diagnostic council ratings by inclusion of the TAT protocols. It is scarcely reasonable to be concerned over contamination when there is no evidence for any positive relationship between the measures at question.

The relationship between *observer ratings* and the TAT measures was somewhat more consistent, but still there does not seem to be much evidence for an intimate relationship between the two sets of scores. Nine of the ten correlations were positive, including the single correlation that was significant at the 5 per cent level (avoidance of gun). If we assume that the TAT measures are most sensitive to covert and unconscious aspects of aggression, these relatively low positive findings would not be surprising, as we are dealing here with an *overt* measure of aggression—judgments of an external observer making no attempt to infer latent aggression. However, the findings we have already reported make clear that things are not as they should be. While the indexes measure overt aggression imperfectly, as expected, they appear not to measure covert aggression at all.

Scores on the Rosenzweig Picture-Frustration Study showed a much stronger relationship to the TAT dimensions than either of the two independent measures thus far considered. All the TAT variables were positively related to extrapunitive scores and negatively related to intrapunitive scores. Further, three of the variables (aggressive turns, violence, forceful language) were significantly related to both of the P-F Study dimensions. It is somewhat difficult to interpret the significance of these findings because of the absence of clear-cut evidence as to just what level of behavior the P-F Study reflects. Rosenzweig (1950) considers the test most appropriate to measure what he terms Level II or the "objective level," which is behavior as seen by the trained, objective observer. Several studies by Lindzey and Goldwyn (1954) have provided only slight evidence supporting the contention that the P-F Study is sensitive to the "objective level" of behavior but have been relatively convincing in their demonstration that the test is not sensitive to the covert or "projective" level of behavior. Other studies (Fisher & Hinds,

---

TABLE 32–2   *Correlation between TAT "Signs" and Independent Measures of Aggression (N=20)*

TAT VARIABLES	DIAGNOSTIC COUNCIL RATINGS	OBSERVER RATINGS	P-F STUDY EXTRA-PUNITIVE	P-F STUDY INTRA-PUNITIVE	SELF-RATINGS
1. Avoidance of gun	−.11	.43[a]	.01	−.05	.51[a]
2. Aggressive turns	.18	.30	.49[a]	−.46[a]	.60[a]
3. Death as a result of external forces	−.05	.10	.20	−.08	.36[a]
4. Violence	.29	.25	.40[a]	−.39[a]	.50[a]
5. Death and failure in nonheroes	.05	.27	.30	−.19	.73[a]
6. Misrecognitions	.22	.17	.14	−.03	.36[a]
7. Strong aggressive fantasies	.35	.22	.33	−.26	.63[a]
8. Forceful language	−.20	−.07	.38[a]	−.41[a]	.02
9. Constructive outcome	−.61	.10	.18	−.27	.15
10. Constructive character	−.60	.16	.20	−.32	.09

[a] = Significant at 5 per cent level with one-tailed test.

1951; Holzberg & Posner, 1951; Lindzey, 1950; Rosenzweig, 1945) that have related TAT scores to the P-F Study show no consistent pattern of findings. Thus, this evidence of association with a paper-and-pencil projective measure cannot be considered convincing proof that the TAT indexes are sensitive to covert aspects of behavior.

Finally, we turn to the relation between the TAT dimensions and the subjects' *self-ratings*. We had predicted that these correlations would be the lowest of the four sets of relationships examined. Quite the contrary of our prediction, we find that for all ten TAT dimensions there is a positive correlation with the self-ratings, and seven of these correlations reach conventional significance levels. The seven variables that proved to be significantly related to the self-ratings are: avoidance of gun, aggressive turns, death as a result of external forces, violence, death and failure of nonheroes, misrecognitions, and forceful language. These findings suggest rather strongly that the scores we had derived painstakingly from the TAT protocols represent rather accurately the information we could have secured from the subjects themselves by simply asking them to appraise their own behavior. It is interesting to note that this finding, for a group of normal college students, fits well with the predictions made by Allport in his recent critique of projective testing. He suggests: "normal subjects . . . tell you by the direct method precisely what they tell you by the projective method. They are all of a piece. You may therefore take their motivational statements at their face value, for even if you probe you will not find anything substantially different (Allport, 1953, p. 110).

In summary, the empirical generalizations (signs) concerning the TAT and aggression seem to be ineffective. While there is some variability among the "signs," they appear to be much better indicators of conscious aspects of aggression than of covert or repressed aspects, in spite of the fact that most of the originators of the statements have suggested the reverse. At first glance, then, these findings present a rather bleak picture of the utility of the Thematic Apperception Test.

These discouraging conclusions are weakened by a single finding not yet reported. As part of this study, each clinician who administered the individual TAT's (four clinicians in all) rated each of his subjects on a number of variables, including aggression, without knowing anything about the subjects other than their performance on the TAT. These ratings were relatively intuitive judgments, as the psychologists arrived at their one to six ratings in any manner they chose without being asked to specify the grounds for their decisions. This set of ratings showed a .35 correlation with the diagnostic council ratings of aggression, just failing to achieve significance at the 5 per cent level and exceeding the positive relationship between all but one of the objectively scored TAT dimensions and the diagnostic council ratings. It is important to note that the single objective-dimension correlation of .35 represents the highest of ten correlations, all of which had the same prior status. Thus, interest in this particular relation is considerably lessened because of the very great likelihood that it is a product of chance factors. In general, then, our findings provide some evidence for believing that clinical or intuitive judgments are more likely to predict covert aspects of behavior than carefully specified, objective ratings.

This last finding suggests that our earlier results serve as an indictment or serious question of the value of the particular scoring methods we used *but* may have little to say about the general sensitivity of the instrument. While this is a truism in one sense, still we can evaluate an instrument only as we have specific scores or interpretations to use in the evaluation. Consequently, we must ordinarily accept negative findings for a particular scoring scheme as negative for the instrument until a counter example is given with more positive findings from another source. The result we have just reported for the intuitive ratings serves as such a counterexample.

We began this paper by pointing to the importance and difficulty of dealing adequately with the question of the level of behavior to which test inferences may validly be linked. Our findings have shown that for the particular indexes we have focused on, the appropriate level does not appear to correspond to that conventionally attributed to the test. Further, we have some slight evidence that using a different means of analyzing the test leads to results that are more consistent with our prior expectation. This implies that discussion of levels of behavior in connection with the TAT must specify, in addition to the instrument, the particular analysis technique used. Presumably, there are still other factors that will ultimately prove crucial in this specification, e.g., personal characteristics of the subject, the psychological variable under study, and the circumstances under which the test is administered.

Our results make clear that the TAT reflects different levels of behavior and thus suggest the importance of attempts to specify conditions or factors within the story protocols that may differentiate motives or dispositions that are reflected at different levels. A significant warning that may be derived from this study is that *the clinician or investigator who uses projective techniques must not assume that his results necessarily refer to unconscious or covert aspects of behavior*. The actual situation is much more complex than this.

The discrepancy between findings secured with the objectively scored dimensions and those secured with the more intuitive ratings implies that although the clinical use of the TAT may ordinarily result in sensitivity to covert dimensions of personality, attempts at specifying the objective basis of this clinical use have led to empirical control over conscious aspects of behavior rather than covert aspects. Thus, although most of our variables have been suggested by clinical practitioners, it seems that their efforts to become operational have diminished their control over covert components of personality. This lack of initial success should not lead to an abandonment of the goal of objectivity, for even though the early efforts to secure adequate specification and operational legitimacy may reduce the sensitivity of the clinician, it is only through resolute steps in this direction that we may hope to make the clinical sensitivity of the very few an attribute that can be acquired by many.

Summary

This study attempted to test the validity of 10 "signs" of aggression proposed by various users of the Thematic Apperception Test by exploring the relation between the TAT and measures representing various "levels" of behavior. The complete TAT protocols of 20 intensively studied subjects were analyzed in terms of the 10 variables and the resultant scores related to measures of aggression derived from: a diagnostic council rating, an observer rating, the Picture-Frustration Study, and self-ratings. We expected that the TAT would show the highest correlation with the diagnostic council ratings and the lowest correlation with the self-ratings.

Our results gave no evidence of any positive relation between the diagnostic council ratings and the TAT measures, little evidence of any association between the observer ratings and the TAT dimensions, convincing evidence of a relation between P-F Study scores and the TAT scores, and the strongest evidence of an association between the self-ratings and the TAT measures. Thus, the results neatly reversed our expectations. A clinical (intuitive) rating, which was made with no attempt to specify the basis for the judgment, showed a positive correlation, just short of significance, with the diagnostic council rating.

The major conclusions of the study are:

1. Although there was some variability among the "signs," they were in general ineffective in assessing covert aspects of aggression, in spite of the fact that most of their propounders had suggested them as indexes of covert or repressed aggression.

2. Depending on the particular method of analysis used, the TAT may or may not be sensitive to covert aspects of behavior. Consequently, the user of projective techniques must not assume that he is necessarily dealing with covert or latent aspects of behavior.

3. An adequate specification of "level of behavior" must include reference not only to the instrument being used but also to the particular method of analysis employed (and probably also to the exact circumstances surrounding administration of the test, personal characteristics of the subject, etc.). Related to this is the pressing need for research that inquires into the conditions within projective technique protocols that may differentiate motives that are operant at different levels of behavior. Undoubtedly these within-story conditions are at present reflected differentially within different scoring schemes.

4. The fact that initial attempts to objectify clinical judgment have proven relatively fruitless should not lead to discouragement. It is to be expected that first attempts at increasing intersubjectivity will result in a decrease in sensitivity. However, the goal of increasing precision and adequacy of specification remains a crucial one.

REFERENCES

Allport, G. W. The trend in motivational theory. *Amer. J. Orthopsychiat.*, 1953, 23, 107–119.

Bellak, L. The thematic apperception test in clinical use. In L. E. Abt & L. Bellak (Eds.), *Projective psychology*. New York: Knopf, 1950. Pp. 185–229.

Fisher, S., & Hinds, Edith. The organization of hostility controls in various personality structures. *Genet. psychol. Monogr.*, 1951, 44, 3–68.

Henry, W. E. The thematic apperception technique in the study of culture-personality relations. *Genet. psychol. Monogr.*, 1947, 35, 3–135.

Holzberg, J. D., & Posner, Rita. The relationship of extrapunitiveness on the Rosenzweig picture-frustration study to aggression in overt behavior and fantasy. *Amer. J. Orthopsychiat.*, 1951, 21, 767–779.

Lindzey, G. An experimental test of the validity of the Rosenzweig picture-frustration study. *J. Pers.*, 1950, 18, 315–320.

Lindzey, G. Thematic apperception test: Interpretive assumptions and related empirical evidence. *Psychol. Bull.*, 1952, 49, 1–25.

Lindzey, G., & Goldwyn, R. M. Validity of the Rosenzweig picture-frustration study. *J. Pers.*, 1954, 22, 519–547.

Lindzey, G., Tejessy, Charlotte, David, A., & Heinemann, Shirley H. Thematic apperception test: A survey of empirical generalizations. Unpublished manuscript, Harvard University, 1953.

Murray, H. A. Uses of the thematic apperception test. *Amer. J. Psychiat.*, 1951, 107, 577–581.

Rapaport, D., Gill, M., & Schafer, R. *Diagnostic psychological testing*. Chicago: Year Book Publishers, 1946.

Rosenzweig, S. The picture-association method and its application in a study of reactions to frustration. *J. Pers.*, 1945, 14, 3–23.

Rosenzweig, S. Levels of behavior in psychodiagnosis with special reference to the picture-frustration study. *Amer. J. Orthopsychiat.*, 1950, 20, 63–72.

Rotter, J. B. Thematic apperception test: Suggestions for administration and interpretation. *J. Pers.*, 1946, 15, 70–92.

Stein, M. I. *The thematic apperception test*. Cambridge: Addison-Wesley, 1948.

Symonds, P. M. *Adolescent fantasy*. New York: Columbia Univer. Press, 1949.

33

Thematic Apperception Test: A Tentative Appraisal of Some "Signs" of Anxiety[1]

GARDNER LINDZEY
AND ARTHUR S. NEWBURG

Using the "sign" approach, Lindzey and Newburg tested 18 TAT anxiety indexes against the criterion of anxiety rating of the 20 volunteer Harvard subjects by the diagnostic council. Three of the 18 signs correlated significantly with the council ratings at the .05 level. By selecting certain signs only, a correlation of .63 was achieved. This post hoc *approach, however, capitalizes on chance factors and is not likely to remain stable in a cross-validational study.*

The results over all suggest some validity for the sign approach, but of a rather low level, thus negating any serious possibility of applying this approach to the individual case. The reliability of the criterion group, which would help in determining the limits of possible validity, is not given. Another factor which undoubtedly limited the possibility of attaining a high validity figure was the use of such a select group as volunteer Harvard students. Validity would presumably be considerably higher with a more representative group.

In sum, the study indicates several good leads for anxiety indicators of a formal as opposed to content nature. It also indicates that several signs alleged by some experts to tap anxiety did not in fact do so. Much

[1] This study is part of a program of research conducted at the Harvard Psychological Clinic under the direction of Professor Henry A. Murray. The research is supported by grants from the Rockefeller Foundation and the Laboratory of Social Relations, Harvard University. We are grateful to Shirley Shapiro for her assistance in the statistical analysis.

more work is needed in determining just how anxiety is manifested on the TAT. The success of the formal anxiety signs further suggests that anxiety may be sufficiently general in nature to be measurable, despite the fact that its origins are quite diverse.

Generalizations concerning the relation between aspects of test performance and those attributes of the empirical world that the test intends to predict or diagnose stem from many sources. Perhaps the most fertile of these is careful observation by sensitive and experienced clinicians. By contrast, the role of controlled, empirical study in creating such generalizations is relatively slight. When it comes to evaluating or instituting a system of checks, however, the contribution of controlled investigation is very great. The free-ranging sensitivity of the clinical observer, which makes him an ideal generator of new ideas, also promises that individual bias and autistic factors will play some role in determining his statements. Thus, only when the clinician's generalizations have been submitted to test under circumstances designed to eliminate observer bias can we place much enduring confidence in them.

In the present study, we selected a small number of generalizations concerning the Thematic Apperception Test and its sensitivity to anxiety and attempted to test these under some degree of empirical control. As a result of an earlier survey of the literature (Lindzey, Tejessy, Davids, & Heinemann, 1953), we had available over 500 statements relating aspects of TAT response to characteristics of the storyteller. From this list we selected 18 generalizations concerning anxiety and attempted to translate each of these into an objective scoring system that would permit us to score TAT protocols reliably. In addition, we sought to secure a reasonable, independent measure of anxiety that could be correlated with our TAT "signs."

Procedure

SUBJECTS

The subjects of this study were 20 undergraduate males who had volunteered from an introductory course in psychology at Harvard College to participate in a program of personality study. They were paid for their time on an hourly basis at customary student rates. The subjects were selected so as to be heterogeneous in regard to such factors as socioeconomic and ethnic background, academic performance, and extracurricular activities.

THEMATIC APPERCEPTION TEST

Administration

The TAT was administered under standard conditions with the two sessions separated by 24 hours or more. In all cases the stories were electrically recorded without the subjects' knowledge and later transcribed verbatim.

Scoring

Our scoring procedures were based on statements culled from the literature. In describing these, we will first present the pertinent quotation, and following this we will summarize the variable or variables that were designed to correspond to those mentioned in the statement. The reader will notice that we have not attempted to exhaust the meaning of these quotations but have simply selected, somewhat arbitrarily, certain variables that seemed especially pertinent or easy to objectify. In all, there were 18 signs or variables, presumably sensitive to anxiety, that we attempted to measure.

While scoring, the examiner knew only that the subjects were male and college students. Every variable was scored individually for each story, and all stories told to a given card were scored before proceeding to the next set of stories. With the exception of the second variable, all scores were dichotomous, as the scorer simply indicated for each story that the variable was present or not present (high or low). In some cases, this required setting relatively arbitrary cutting points. Thus, for all but the second variable, the subject's score was made up of the sum of 20 yes-and-no scores and consequently could range from 0 to 20.

"[Anxiety is indicated by the] . . . presence of disruptions in the consistency of form characteristics, especially in organizational elements, in vacillation from concept to picture-dominated responses, and in rejections and refusals, content characteristics . . . of overt aggression, depression, mental conflicts or other outstanding emotional states . . ." (Henry, 1950, p. 48).

1. *Intrapicture vacillation from concept- to picture-dominated responses.* A concept-dominated response is one whose main theme deals with an idea the picture suggests rather than the picture itself. It may be abstract, symbolic, or allegorical and often relates the events of the story to the general case. A picture-dominated response is one whose main theme deals directly with the events of the picture itself. Often past and future action is omitted, and in general the story action takes place in the here and now of the picture. At its most restricted level, the response may be only a description of the picture

with little or no plot. If during a single story there was one or more shifts from one type of response to the other, the story was scored "vacillation."

2. *Interpicture vacillation from concept- to picture-dominated responses.* Each story was scored as concept, picture, or vacillation, as defined for the preceding variable. Then the number of changes from concept to picture domination and vice versa in the twenty stories was counted.

3. *Rejections and refusals.* The subject makes a negative comment about the picture or his ability to create a story from the picture. He contradicts or denies or reverses part of his story. He refuses to tell or finish a story.

4. *Outstanding emotional states.* The characters show strong and persistent overt aggression, depression, mental conflict, fear, extreme happiness, love, worry, etc.

Phantasies with marked anxiety were "characterized by moving, dramatic situations and intense, comparatively clearcut conflicts" [p. 75].... A high incidence of verbs denotes a kinetic release in the phantasy of anxious tensions in the narrator [p. 77].... Total number of verbs/total number of adjectives. High values connote restless, forceful, dramatic action in the phantasies, expressing libidinal tensions and anxiety in the subject [p. 79].... the phantasies in an *anxiety* state are brief; the action is most dramatic (highest verb-adjective quotient) and often compulsive; alternatives of conation are most frequently sought; special expressions connoting vagueness, hesitation, and trepidation are freely used; and direct identification of the narrator with characters in his phantasy frequently occur ... phantasied situations are left as unresolved as the underlying emotional conflicts of the subject [pp. 80–81] (Balken & Masserman, 1940).

5. *Intense conflicts.* The conflict may be intra- or interpersonal. It should involve violent emotional states, and if it is intrapersonal the individual should be seen as "torn" by the two sides of the conflict.

6. *Vagueness and hesitation.* The subject makes *two or more* statements showing either vagueness or hesitation or both, e.g., "I'm not sure," "I don't know," "I can't tell."

7. *Self-identification.* The narrator openly admits that one of the characters resembles or acts like himself. He indicates that part or all of the story is taken from his own life.

8. *Unresolved conflicts.* The story has no outcome. Conflicts, situations, plots are left unfinished. Statements like "I don't know how this comes out," "I don't know what comes after this," are common. Or conflict situations are seen as remaining so, e.g., "And he never forgives her for that," "And this couple continues to quarrel."

9. *Interjections.* The subject makes *two or more* statements not directly related to the story he is telling. These may be in the form of comments about the picture: "My God, what's that?" "I'll never be able to get anything out of that." Or he may break into his story

to ask the experimenter a question: "Is this the kind of story you want?" "Haven't I seen this picture before somewhere?" Or he may break the continuity of his story by suddenly commenting on his style, delivery, plot, etc.: "This is quite an allegory, isn't it?"

10. *Verb/adjective quotient.* First the total number of verb forms was counted. The whole predicate was counted as one verb. Then the total of verbs was divided by the total number of adjectives, and a ratio of 3.5 or better was considered high and all other ratios low. With this variable and the following variable, we used a random-number table to select three stories from each set of protocols and used these stories as unbiased estimates of the actual quotient for the entire 20 stories.

11. *Number of adjectives per 100 words.* The number of adjectives was computed in the same manner as in the previous variable. This figure was divided by the total number of words and a ratio of .12 or greater scored high and all ratios less than this scored low. Again the sampling technique described above was used.

12. *Briefness.* The total number of words in the story was counted. Any story with less than 175 words was classed as brief, and all others were considered long.

If the testing situation itself significantly raises the level of anxiety, a not uncommon sequel is invariance of stories on the level of object description: "The violin looks like a Stradivarius" [pp. 57–58]. Wishes may also be reactivated by memory. Individuals who suffer grief, shame or anxiety may tell such stories. . . . In our experience the sequence of memory-wish has usually signified serious disturbance in the inner life [p. 64]. Only when a protocol is invariant with respect to the level on which the stories proceed may we assume that this level is a literal representation of the predominant level on which the individual functions. An example of such invariance is the individual whose anxiety is reflected in his stories by exclusive reference to the level of feeling and expectations [p. 103] (Tomkins, 1947).

13. *Invariance on the level of object description.* With the exception of opening and concluding sentences such as "'Lemme' see," "Well, I guess that's about it," every scorable sentence must be restricted to the simple, physical description of the objects or people in the picture. Neither the feelings nor thoughts of any of the people in the story may be present in any sentence.

14. *Invariance on the level of feeling and expectation.* With the exception of the beginning and ending phrases noted in the previous variable, every sentence must contain affect. It is not necessary that the kind or quality of emotion expressed be the same. The narrator must attribute emotion or expectation throughout the story. "I feel that . . . ," "He is worried (afraid, in love, fears, hates, longs for, etc.)." A single sentence in which this was absent scored the story as negative.

15. *The sequence of memory followed by a wish.* Either the narrator or one of the characters recalls material from the past, and this stimulates

him to express a desire for something now. A sentence, clause, or phrase containing a verb of remembering is followed by a passage containing a verb of wishing or desiring, e.g., "The old man recalls his wife fondly; he wishes she were still alive."

"No suggestive diagnostic features other than sporadic blocking, flurries of anxiety in the course of telling the stories, and frequent themes of apprehensiveness are to be expected; even these do not occur frequently" (Schafer, 1948, p. 46).

16. *Blocking*. The subject's response to the picture is blocked; he is incapable of responding quickly and freely to the stimulus. A long pause before he responds, or two or more pauses during the story, indicates this. Any statement he makes which has a content indicating that he feels unable to produce a story, or that producing one would be difficult, was scored. Statements such as "I can't get any further" or "I seem to be stuck" are examples.

17. *Apprehensiveness*. The presence of themes in which there is anticipation of future evil or misfortune. The narrator or one of the characters in the story has feelings of dread or foreboding about the future. He has an expectation that unpleasantness lies ahead. "Things don't look too bright for the future." "I'm afraid the situation gets worse for these people."

"Anxiety neurotics had many plots emphasizing sudden physical accidents and mental traumas such as loss of wife, mother, sweetheart or jobs, house burning down, stock market crash, etc., thus reflecting their own fears and the instability of their world (Rotter 1940 p. 30).

18. *Trauma*. The content of the story deals with a theme in which: (1) one of the characters has a sudden physical accident, e.g., "and then he fell and broke his leg," " . . . when suddenly a rock dropped on her"; (2) someone undergoes a severe mental trauma, characterized by its lasting effects.

Reliability

In estimating the reliability of the TAT scoring, we selected at random 100 stories, and a reliability rater scored these for each of the variables. These ratings agreed with the experimental ratings in 82 per cent of the cases, indicating a relatively high degree of association between the two sets of ratings.

CRITERION MEASURE

The primary independent measure was a "diagnostic council" rating based on a very wide variety of information derived from observation, self-report, situational tests, and a large number of indirect measures. After preliminary analyses, this information was presented individually for each subject and discussed in a council of clinical psychologists.

During this session, the group assigned a tentative rating to each subject to indicate the importance of anxiety as a determinant of his behavior. Later all the subjects were considered jointly and ranked in terms of the degree or importance of anxiety. In addition to the diagnostic council ratings, scores were available for the Psychosomatic Inventory which presumably should bear some relation to anxiety. We obtained a rank-order correlation of .69 between the total score of the inventory and the clinical ranking.

STATISTICAL ANALYSIS

In most of our analyses, we relied on rank-order correlation as a statistic suited to the relative crudeness of our data. In attempting to relate our "signs" to the subscores of the Psychosomatic Inventory, we used a technique described by Mosteller (1946) for estimating correlation coefficients. This short-cut method was used as these relations were of relatively slight interest, and indicating the direction of the relation and the existence of strong relationships seemed sufficient. A perfect correlation would be signified by a score of 96 using this technique.

Results and Discussion

Our major results are summarized in Table 33–1, where we find that, of the 18 TAT signs, 13 show some trend toward positive association with the clinical rating of anxiety. Three of the positive correlations (vagueness and hesitation, self-identification, object description) are significant at the 5 per cent level, and there is one negative correlation (interpicture vacillation from concept- to picture-dominated response) of approximately the same magnitude. These findings are not encouraging so far as the utility of the particular TAT measures employed here are concerned. Although there is some evidence of a tendency toward association between the TAT variables and our criterion measure, as witnessed by the preponderance of positive correlations, this seems a very tentative link, and the existence of relatively high negative correlations suggest dramatically how far we are from an adequate formulation of how to measure anxiety with this instrument.

The correlations between the TAT signs and the Psychosomatic Inventory are also summarized in Table 33–1. In general, they conform to the tendencies revealed in the clinical rating correlations. Especially for the total score and the psychosomatic subscore, the direction of the correlations is quite similar to those we have already discussed, although the magnitude is generally less. In view of the presumed lesser sensitivity of this paper-and-pencil instrument, these findings are to be expected.

TABLE 33–1   *Relation of TAT "Signs" of Anxiety to Criterion Measures*

TAT VARIABLE	CLINICAL RATINGS	PSYCHOSOMATIC INVENTORY					
		TOTAL SCORE	PSYCHO-SOMATIC	GASTRO-INTESTINAL	NERVOUS TENSION	WORRY	FEAR
1. Intrapicture vacillation	.05[b]	−.32[b]	−38[c]	−49[c]	−21[c]	−28.5[c]	−1[c]
2. Interpicture vacillation	−.38	−.04	−14	−19.5	−8.5	+5.5	−4.5
3. Rejection and refusal	.30	.40[a]	+33.5	+13.5	+26.5	+27.5	+3
4. Outstanding emotional states	−.06	−.02	+10	−1.5	−1	−37.5	−7
5. Intense conflicts	.03	.06	+8.5	+3.5	+9.5	−30	−10.5
6. Vagueness	.40[a]	.15	+7.5	−7.5	−10	+29.5	+18.5
7. Direct identification	.39[a]	.09	−1.5	−5	+7	−1.5	0
8. Conflict unresolved	.22	−.02	−5.5	−28	−1	−29	−1.5
9. Interjections	.06	.21	+17.5	+9	+25.5	+9.5	+11
10. Verb/adjective quotient	−.09	−.13	−9	−31.5	−23	+2	−8
11. Adjectives per 100 words	.13	.09	+7.5	+33	+11.5	−5	−1
12. Briefness	.15	.31	+36	+51	+10	+26	+9
13. Object description	.38[a]	.53[a]	+43	+2	+37.5	+32.5	+35
14. Feeling and expectation description	.22	.02	+19.5	+3	−1.5	−9	−22.5
15. Sequence: memory to wish	−.16	−.09	−11	−22.5	−21.5	−29.5	−18.5
16. Blocking	.33	.20	+20.5	+11	+5.5	+2.5	+1.5
17. Apprehensiveness	.05	−.04	−8	−1	−2	−33	−11.5
18. Trauma	−.19	.10	+7.5	+22	+23	+1.5	−4

a Significant at 5 per cent level with one-tailed test.
b Rank-order correlation.
c Mosteller's correlation approximation.

In Table 33–2, we present the intercorrelations between the TAT signs. If we exclude the first two variables, which appear to have been reversed in their scoring, the general tendency is for low positive correlations. In general this table of intercorrelations does not suggest a set of indexes for the same or very similar variables. If some of these signs are in fact highly indicative of anxiety, then it seems evident that others are *not* very sensitive to this variable. Nevertheless, several interesting clusters appear. In one we find the following variables: strong emotional states, intense conflicts, apprehensiveness, and trauma; while in the other we find rejections, hesitations and vagueness, interjections, and blocking. The question of how much these represent related psychological variables and how much the association is artificially produced by scoring the same story attributes under multiple headings is not clearly answered by our data. Certainly an examination of the definitions of these eight variables suggests that some of these intercorrelations are the results of multiple scoring of the same aspects of the stories.

Speculation concerning the relatively strong negative correlation between our measure of interpicture vacillation and our criterion measure of anxiety suggested that a variable of rigidity or inflexibility might be mediating this relationship. A low picture-vacillation score implies that the subject adopts an initial set toward the story-construction process and maintains this without variation throughout the series of pictures. The widely observed "freezing" effect of anxiety makes it

---

TABLE 33–2   *Rho Intercorrelation of TAT "Signs" of Anxiety*

TAT VARIABLE	Intrapicture vacillation	Interpicture vacillation	Rejections and refusals	Emotional states	Intense conflicts	Vagueness and hesitation	Self-identification	Unresolved conflicts	Interjections	Verb/adjective quotient	Number of adjectives	Briefness	Object description	Feeling and expectation	Memory followed by wish	Blocking	Apprehensiveness
Intrapicture vacillation																	
Interpicture vacillation	−27[a]																
Rejections and refusals	−.28	−.10															
Emotional states	.25	−.03	−.18														
Intense conflicts	.25	−.25	−.13	.85													
Vagueness and hesitation	.14	−.52	.53	−.41	−.25												
Self-identification	.25	−.20	.52	−.19	.00	.33											
Unresolved conflicts	.60	−.20	−.03	.41	.53	−.04	.38										
Interjections	−.04	−.20	.75	.03	.21	.56	.19	−.01									
Verb/adjective quotient	−.18	.21	−.40	.36	.25	−.30	−.36	−.05	−.27								
Number of adjectives	.25	−.11	.37	−.36	−.33	.21	.42	−.04	.16	−.89							
Briefness	−.71	.26	.35	−.37	−.50	.02	−.12	−.33	−.02	−.02	.10						
Object description	−.10	.26	.54	−.32	−.37	.18	.47	.02	.11	−.30	.32	.30					
Feeling and expectation	−.26	.06	.21	−.11	−.15	.08	.12	.15	.03	−.24	.12	.41	.14				
Memory followed by wish	−.03	−.06	.03	.39	.34	−.03	−.17	.16	.37	.08	−.28	−.09	−.09	.25			
Blocking	.07	−.48	.75	−.29	.09	.78	.32	.16	.59	−.27	.18	.18	.20	.10	−.10		
Apprehensiveness	.19	−.05	−.18	.96	.83	−.31	−.22	.38	.13	.31	−.30	−.37	−.43	−.12	.36	−.07	
Trauma	−.02	.23	−.12	.63	.45	−.39	−.28	.00	.17	.12	.05	−.11	−.12	−.39	.17	−.17	.69

[a] A rho of .44 is required for significance at the 5 per cent level.

understandable that the individual high in anxiety might be relatively invariant in his approach to storytelling. Given this initial hypothesis, we looked for other variables that could be seen as related in some way to rigidity, lack of spontaneity, perseverative tendencies, or inflexibility. We then set up new ranks based on the pooled scores from these variables. First we combined scores from the interpicture vacillation and intrapicture vacillation variables, as these measures seemed obviously to be getting at related material in spite of their low intercorrelation. For these two variables, we reversed the direction of our original scoring because of the observed negative correlation and our *post hoc* rationale. The resulting correlation (.47) was somewhat better than the .38 correlation that our single measure had given us. Next, we included scores for the tendency to simply describe objects or aspects of the stimulus picture. This combined rank showed a correlation of .56 with our criterion. Following this, we developed a rank order based on these three variables plus scores for the tendency of the storyteller to specifically identify part of the story as coming from his own life or one of the characters as resembling himself. This last variable suggests a concreteness and lack of spontaneity that go with the other variables we have already mentioned. The rank order based on these variables correlated with our criterion measure .58. Finally, we introduced scores for vagueness or hesitation of the storyteller, reasoning that this indecisiveness was related to the lack of spontaneity we have already commented on. This ranking showed a .63 correlation with the criterion measure.

The fact that through the use of three variables we were able to secure a correlation of .56 with our criterion and that with the addition of two more variables we could raise this to .63 suggests that potentially the TAT may be a relatively sensitive indicator of anxiety. On the other hand, in evaluating these findings it is important to consider the small size of our sample and its composition. Our subjects all met some criteria of normality, although at least four of them presented rather serious adjustment problems. Even these four, when compared to severely disturbed patients, probably could be characterized as only moderately anxious. Thus our results are based on a restricted range of the variable of interest.

The relative success of our formal measures in predicting anxiety when compared to the content measures suggests that analysts of the TAT might well devote more of their time to this type of variable. It is, of course, possible that this finding may be rather specifically linked to the nature of the variable under study.

In summary, our results are somewhat discouraging for the utility of common generalizations concerning anxiety and the TAT. Nevertheless, the fact that we were able to find relatively substantial correlations between our criterion measure of anxiety and small clusters of

TAT variables that bore some rational relation to each other suggests the potential utility of the instrument in this area. If we take seriously the highly tentative evidence of this study, it seems that the TAT of the anxious person is characterized by an excessive sameness of rigidity in the approach of the storyteller, a preference for limiting himself to simple object description, a readiness to relate parts of characters in the stories explicity to himself, a tendency to be vague or hesitant in presenting his stories, and also a readiness to reject his productions and refuse to tell or complete his stories.

REFERENCES

BALKEN, EVA R., & MASSERMAN, J. H. The language of phantasy: III. The language of the phantasies of patients with conversion hysteria, anxiety state, and obsessive-compulsive neuroses. *J. Psychol.*, 1940, 10, 75–86.

HENRY, W. E. The analysis of fantasy: the thematic apperception technique in the study of behavior. Unpublished manuscript, Univer. of Chicago, 1950.

LINDZEY, G., TEJESSY, CHARLOTTE, DAVIDS, A., & HEINEMANN, SHIRLEY H. Thematic apperception test: a summary of empirical generalizations. Unpublished manuscript, Harvard Univer., 1953.

MOSTELLER, F. On some useful "inefficient" statistics. *Ann. math. Statist.*, 1946, 17, 377–408.

ROTTER, J. B. Studies in the use and validity of the thematic apperception test with mentally disordered patients. I. Method of analysis and clinical problems. *Charact. & Pers.*, 1940, 9, 18–34.

SCHAFER, R. *The clinical application of psychological tests: diagnostic summaries and case studies.* New York: International Univer. Press, 1948.

TOMKINS, S. S. *The thematic apperception test.* New York: Grune & Stratton, 1947.

34

The Relationship between Overt and Fantasy Aggression as a Function of Maternal Response to Aggression

GERALD S. LESSER

The problem of determining the relationship between thematic expression and overt behavior has remained a thorny one since the very onset of the TAT. It has become apparent that there are certain ego-mediating factors that intervene between the drive and the response and determine whether, for example, an aggressive person talks of tigers or tiger lilies. But what are these factors? In this study, Lesser shows that the attitude of the mother toward her child's expression of aggression determines whether there is a positive or negative correlation between his thematic expression of aggression and his overt behavior.

This study indicates that the thematic responses can be used for the prediction of overt behavior, providing some knowledge of the mediating responses are known. At the same time, it cautions us that projective techniques used without prior information about the important background influences are not apt to provide very much information regarding overt actions. In fact, in this study, as in many others, if one disregards the background information, the correlation between thema and physical behavior approaches zero.

In recent years, a voluminous literature has developed around the problem of establishing relationships between fantasy behavior and overt behavior. Different researchers have used different drive areas, different

599

populations, different theoretical bases, and different methods of measurement. The most conspicuous conclusion is that the empirical findings are not in agreement.

The importance of this area of investigation for both clinical practice and personality theory has been elaborated by Lindzey (1952). He concludes that one of the most important and difficult problems is the "determination of the conditions under which inferences based upon projective material directly relate to overt behavior and the conditions for the reverse" (Lindzey, 1956, p. 18). The present study concerns the differential conditions under which aggressive behavior is learned that may allow prediction of how aggressive expressions in fantasy are related to those in overt behavior.

Various studies (Kagan & Mussen, 1956; Murray, 1943; Sanford, Adkins, Miller, Cobb, et al., 1943; Symonds, 1949; Tomkins, 1947) have demonstrated that the degree of correspondence between fantasy behavior and the associated overt behavior is greater for certain drives than for others. Significant positive correlations have been reported between TAT fantasy and overt behavior for variables such as abasement, achievement, creation, dependence, exposition, nurturance, etc. Significant negative correlations have been reported for sex, and inconclusive results have been obtained for a wide variety of other variables. For the variable of aggression, results include significant positive correlations between fantasy and overt expressions (Kagan, 1956; Mussen & Naylor, 1954), significant negative correlations (Feshbach, 1955; Sanford et al., 1943), and inconclusive findings (Bach, 1945; Bialick, 1951; Child, Frank, & Storm, 1956; Davids, Henry, McArthur, & McNamara, 1955; Gluck, 1955; Korner, 1949; Murray, 1943; Pittluck, 1950; Sanford et al., 1943; Symonds, 1949).

To resolve these inconsistent results, it has been suggested (Murray, 1943; Mussen & Naylor, 1954; Sanford et al., 1943; Tomkins, 1947) that motives that are culturally encouraged are "likely to be as strong in their overt as in their covert manifestations" (Murray, 1943, p. 16), while motives that are culturally discouraged are apt to show little or no relationship between the strength of fantasy and overt expressions.

Mussen and Naylor have attempted to test the first segment of this formulation. They contended that lower-class culture encourages aggression, and predicted that "in a lower-class group, individuals who give evidence of a great deal of fantasy aggression will also manifest more overt aggression than those who show little aggression in their fantasies" (Mussen & Naylor, 1954, p. 235). A mixed group of white and Negro boys, "almost all of whom had been referred to the Bureau of Juvenile Research for behaviors which brought them into conflict with school and court authorities" (p. 236), were used as subjects. The authors report a statistically significant but not especially strong positive relationship between ratings of overt aggression and number of aggressive TAT themes. Further investigation of Mussen and Naylor's hypothesis would profit from more precise measurement of parental response to aggression, control comparisons, and a more representative sample.

The present study seeks to examine the comparative consequences of both encouragement and discouragement of aggression through the hypothesis that under conditions of maternal encouragement of aggression, a greater degree of correspondence exists between fantasy and overt aggression of children than under conditions of maternal discouragement of aggression.

Method

SUBJECTS

The subjects (Ss) were 44 white boys (ages 10–0 to 13–2) and their mothers. The boys were drawn from one fifth grade and two sixth grades in two public schools. All the boys and their mothers in these three classes participated except one mother who refused to be interviewed. The Kuhlmann-Anderson intelligence quotients of the boys ranged from 82 to 119, with a mean of 102. The two schools are in adjacent districts, and the families constitute a relatively homogeneous upper lower-class group.

MATERNAL ATTITUDES AND PRACTICES

Only one aspect of the environmental conditions of learning of aggressive behavior was measured, i.e., the maternal attitudes and practices supporting or prohibiting aggression. A structured questionnaire-interview schedule was orally administered to the mothers in their homes by a male interviewer. Questions regarding the support or prohibition of aggression constituted only one segment of the total interview; the entire interview schedule is described in detail elsewhere (Lesser, 1952). Pertinent to the present study were eight items concerning the mother's attitudes toward aggression in children and thirteen items about the mother's practices in dealing with the aggressive behavior of her child. An illustrative item measuring maternal attitudes toward aggression is: "A child should be taught to stand up and fight for his rights in his contacts with other children." The four response alternatives of agree, mildly agree, mildly disagree, and disagree were allowed for this item. An example of an item measuring maternal practices concerning aggression is: "If your son comes to tell you that he is being picked on by a bully at the playground who is his own age and size, there would be a number of different things you might tell him. Would you tell him to ignore him and turn the other cheek?" Response alternatives for this item were yes and no. Items that did not involve judgments on a four-point scale were transformed to have approximately the same range of scores as the items that involved four alternatives.

A single score was obtained for each mother by combining all items, assigning plus scores to the responses indicating support of aggression and minus scores to responses indicating discouragement of aggression. The range of scores was from $+9$ to -7, with a median score of $+2$. The corrected odd-even reliability coefficient was .80.

The distribution of scores for maternal response to aggression was dichotomized to form one group of mothers (with scores above or at the median) whose attitudes and practices were more supportive of aggressive behavior than those of the other group (with scores below the median). The hypothesis demands that the correlation between fantasy and overt aggression for the children of the mothers in the former group be significantly more positive than the corresponding correlation for the children of the mothers in the latter group.

FANTASY AGGRESSION

Fantasy agression in the children was measured through an adaptation of the TAT procedure (Murray, 1943, pp. 3–5). A set of ten pictures was designed. In each picture two boys are interacting. The pictures differed from one another in the degree to which the instigation to aggression was apparent.

To ensure complete and accurate transcription of the stories, tape recordings were taken. An introductory period preceding the fantasy task served both to establish rapport between the child and the male examiner and to familiarize the child with the recording device. Instructions were:

"I'm going to show you some pictures. These are pictures of two boys doing different things. What I'd like you to do is make up a story to each of these pictures. You can make up any story you wish; there are no right or wrong stories. Say what the boys are thinking and feeling and how the story will turn out."

The ten pictures, in the order of presentation, were:

1. One boy is holding a basketball, and the other boy is approaching him with arms outstretched.

2. One boy is stamping on an ambiguous object, and the other boy is reaching for the object.

3. One boy is sitting behind the other boy in a classroom and is leaning toward him.

4. One boy is walking down the street, and the other boy, with fists clenched, is glaring at him.

5. One boy, with fists clenched, is staring at the other boy who is sitting, head bowed, on a box.

6. One boy is sawing a piece of wood, and the other boy is leaning on a fence between them, talking to him.

7. The two boys, surrounded by a group of other boys, are approaching each other with arms upraised and fists clenched.

8. The two boys are making a fire. One boy is kneeling to arrange the wood, and the other boy is approaching, ladened with wood for the fire.

9. One boy, who is looking back, is running down a street, and the other boy is running behind him.

10. Two boys are standing in a field. One boy, with his hand on the other boy's shoulder, is pointing off in the distance.

A fantasy aggression score was obtained for each S by counting the number of times the following acts appeared in his stories: fighting, injuring, killing, attacking, assaulting, torturing, bullying, getting angry, hating, breaking, smashing, burning, destroying, scorning, expressing disdain, cursing, swearing, threatening, insulting, belittling, repudiating, ridiculing.

Fantasy aggression scores ranged from 1 to 15, with a mean of 5.3. The corrected matched-half reliability coefficient was .86; the interjudge scoring reliability coefficient was .92.

OVERT AGGRESSION

To measure overt aggression in the child, a modified sociometric device, the "Guess who" technique (Hartshorne & May, 1929), was adopted. The Ss were presented with a booklet containing a series of written descriptions of children and asked to identify each of these descriptive characterizations by naming one or more classmates. Fifteen overt aggression items were used, such as "Here is someone who is always looking for a fight." A diversity of aggressive behaviors were included; items depicted verbal, unprovoked physical, provoked physical, outburst, and indirect forms of aggressive behavior.

An overt aggression score was obtained for each subject by counting the number of times he was named by his classmates. There were substantial differences among the three classes in the distributions of the overt aggression scores; in order to combine into one distribution the scores of children in different classes, overt aggression raw scores were transformed into standard scores.

The biserial correlation coefficient between the overt aggression measure derived from the children and teacher entries for the same "Guess who" aggression items was .76 ($p < .01$).

Results

Two Pearson product-moment correlation coefficients were obtained. For boys ($N = 23$) whose mothers are relatively encouraging or supportive of aggression, the correlation between fantasy aggression and overt aggression is $+.43$ ($p < .05$, two-tailed test). For boys ($N = 21$) whose mothers are relatively discouraging of aggression, the corresponding correlation is $-.41$ ($p < .10$, two-tailed test). These coefficients are statistically different ($p = .006$, two-tailed test).

When the total sample is not separated into two groups on the basis of scores for maternal response to aggression, the over-all Pearson product-moment correlation coefficient is $+.07$. This coefficient is not significantly different from zero.

Discussion

Confirmation is found for the hypothesis that under conditions of relative maternal encouragement of aggression, a greater degree of correspondence exists between the fantasy and overt aggression of children than under conditions of relative maternal discouragement of aggression. Thus, the direction and extent of the relationship between fantasy and overt aggression in the child is apparently influenced by the maternal attitudes and practices surrounding the learning of aggressive behavior.

It has been predicted (Murray, 1943; Sanford et al., 1943) that those tendencies which are negatively sanctioned or prohibited will be high in fantasy expression and low in overt expression. This association is premised on a compensatory or substitutive role of fantasy where overt expression is not allowed. A scatter plot of the fantasy and overt aggression scores for the children whose mothers discourage aggression (from which the $-.41$ coefficient is derived) reveals a considerable number of such high fantasy aggression, low overt aggression scores. However, children with low fantasy aggression and high overt aggression scores are as well represented in this scatter plot as those with high fantasy aggression, low overt aggression scores. Although mothers of children in this group were classified (relative to the others) as discouraging aggression, perhaps certain of them do so ineffectively and thus allow the child sufficient release of aggressive feelings in overt behavior so that he may not need to express aggression in fantasy. An alternative speculation regarding the concurrence of low fantasy aggression and high overt aggression in the group exposed to maternal discouragement of aggression suggests that a child with strong aggressive needs whose mother prohibits aggression may assign this prohibitory attitude to the adult experimenter and suppress fantasy aggression expressions in the testing situation; yet this child may find avenues for overt expression of aggression among his peers.

In the present study, only one condition related to the learning of aggressive responses and controls was assessed, maternal attitudes and practices. Other possibly critical determinants that remain to be explored include fathers' behavior and teachers' attitudes and practices. This study has sampled a limited range of maternal attitudes and practices concerning aggression. Although there is no direct manner of determining the absolute degree of punitiveness of the most prohibitive mother in this sample, it appears unlikely that extremely severe and continuous maternal punitiveness is represented. Such severe condemnation of aggression might so limit or restrict both the fantasy aggression and overt aggression expressions of the child that no correlational analysis within such a group would be possible. Both the extremes of unimpeded permissiveness and severe condemnation warrant further investigation.

Summary

The relationship between fantasy and overt expressions of aggression was studied as a function of the maternal attitudes and practices toward aggression. Subjects were 44 boys and their mothers. The boys' fantasy aggression was assessed through a modified TAT approach, their overt aggression was measured through a modified sociometric technique, and maternal attitudes and practices toward aggression were measured by use of a questionnaire-interview device.

Support was found for the hypothesis that under conditions of maternal encouragement of aggression, a greater degree of correspondence exists between fantasy and overt aggression of children than under conditions of maternal discouragement of aggression.

REFERENCES

BACH, G. R. Young children's play fantasies. *Psychol. Monogr.*, 1945 59, No. 2 (Whole No. 272).

BIALICK, I. The relationship between reactions to authority figures on the TAT and overt behavior in an authority situation by hospital patients. Unpublished doctoral dissertation, Univer. of Pittsburgh, 1951.

CHILD, I. L., FRANK, KITTY F., & STORM, T. Self-ratings and TAT: Their relations to each other and to childhood background. *J. Pers.*, 1956, 25, 98–114.

DAVIDS, A., HENRY, A. F., McARTHUR, C. C., & McNAMARA, L. F. Projection, self-evaluation, and clinical evaluation of aggression. *J. consult. Psychol.*, 1955, 19, 437–440.

FESHBACH, S. The drive-reducing function of fantasy behavior. *J. abnorm. soc. Psychol.*, 1955, 50, 3–11.

GLUCK, M. R. The relationship between hostility in the TAT and behavioral hostility. *J. proj. Tech.*, 1955, 19, 21–26.

HARTSHORNE, H., & MAY, M. A. *Studies in the nature of character. II. Studies in service and self-control.* New York: Macmillan, 1929.

KAGAN, J. The measurement of overt aggression from fantasy. *J. abnorm. soc. Psychol.,* 1956, 52, 390–393.

KAGAN, J., & MUSSEN, P. H. Dependency themes on the TAT and group conformity. *J. consult. Psychol.,* 1956, 20, 29–33.

KORNER, ANNELIESE F. *Some aspects of hostility in young children.* New York: Grune & Stratton, 1949.

LESSER, G. S. Maternal attitudes and practices and the aggressive behavior of children. Unpublished doctoral dissertation, Yale Univer., 1952.

LINDZEY, G. Thematic apperception test: Interpretive assumptions and related empirical evidence. *Psychol. Bull.,* 1952, 49, 1–25.

MURRAY, H. A. *Thematic apperception test manual.* Cambridge: Harvard Univer. Press, 1943.

MUSSEN, P. H., & NAYLOR, H. K. The relationships between overt and fantasy aggression. *J. abnorm. soc. Psychol.,* 1954, 49, 235–240.

PITTLUCK, PATRICIA. The relation between aggressive fantasy and overt behavior. Unpublished doctoral dissertation, Yale Univer., 1950.

SANFORD, R. N., ADKINS, MARGARET M., MILLER, R. B., COBB, E. A., et al. Physique, personality, and scholarship. A cooperative study of school children. *Monogr. Soc. Res. Child Developm.,* 1943, 8, No. 1.

SEARS, R. R. Relation of fantasy aggression to interpersonal aggression. *Child Developm.,* 1950, 21, 5–6.

SYMONDS, P. M. *Adolescent fantasy: An investigation of the picture story method of personality study.* New York: Columbia Univer. Press, 1949.

TOMKINS, S. S. *The thematic apperception test.* New York: Grune & Stratton, 1947.

PART IV

THE
DRAW-A-PERSON
TEST

35

Empirical Evaluations of Human Figure Drawings[1]

CLIFFORD H. SWENSEN, JR.

Many of Machover's hypotheses regarding the psychological importance of various body parts are subjected to empirical evidence in this exhaustive review. The results almost totally fail to support the assumptions, the one sole body area for which support was found being "the neck." The huge number of tests, however, with attendant capitalization on chance factors, precludes the conclusion that this one "part" may be said to have psychological significance. Moreover, the evidence for this area is not presented in the review, but it hardly seems possible that the neck is of psychological significance when assumptions regarding the head, ears, nose, legs and feet, fingers, and so forth have not been supported. The safest conclusion would appear to be that the basic premise that the drawing of any part of a human figure involves the projection of important psychological characteristics has not been empirically demonstrated.

It is true that there is some support for the notion that over-all adequacy of the figure bears some relationship to personality adjustment. The relationship, however, appears to be so slight that the DAP at this stage hardly seems an efficient means for measuring personality adequacy. It might be interesting to speculate why such a poorly validated instrument has become so popular as to rank only behind the Rorschach and TAT in frequency of usage, but such speculation is beyond the pale of this critique.

[1] The author is indebted to Drs. Ernest Furchtgott and E. E. Cureton for many helpful suggestions in the preparation of this paper. He also wishes to express his thanks to Miss Rebecca Mallory, Mrs. Marjorie Truan, and Mrs. Ann Black.

Since the publication, in 1949, of Karen Machover's *Personality Projection in the Drawing of the Human Figure* (Machover, 1949), the Draw-a-Person Test (DAP) has become an instrument used routinely by many clinical psychologists. In the eight years that have elapsed since the publication of Machover's monograph, many research studies on the DAP have been published. It seems desirable at the present time to examine the hypotheses Machover presented in her monograph in the light of the empirical evidence that has accumulated.

It is the purpose of this paper to attempt to analyze all the research on the DAP reported in the literature from January, 1949, to December, 1956. Machover's hypotheses will be examined in the light of the evidence produced by these studies.

Reliability

Machover states that "structural and formal aspects of drawing, such as size, line, and placement, are less subject to variability than content, such as body details, clothing, and accessories" (1949, p. 6). Machover goes on to state that Ss render consistently such features as the following: size of the figure, placement of the figure on the page, kinds of lines (long, continuous lines versus short, jagged ones), stance of the figure, proportions of the body, observance of symmetry compulsions, tendency to incompletions, presence of erasures, and presence of shading.

Both Bradshaw (1952) and Lehner and Gunderson (1952) have attempted to determine the reliability of both the structural aspects of figure drawings and the content of figure drawings. Since the aspects of figure drawing that they investigated overlap considerably, these two studies will be considered together.

Bradshaw (1952) gave the DAP as a group test to 100 psychology students, both male and female, ranging in age from 19 to 55, with a mean age of 27.57. He used the test-retest method, with one week between the two administrations of the test. Bradshaw considered 25 different body areas or parts in his study. He scored for 17 possible different kinds of drawing treatment, and each body area or part was scored for as many of these kinds of drawing treatment as were applicable to it. For example, the hands were scored for whether they were present or not, whether they were clothed or not, presence of erasing, presence of shading, degree of detailing, proportional size, line quality, and shape. Bradshaw determined reliability by percentage of consistency from the first administration of the test to the second administration of the test. If, for example, of ten drawings, four had shading on the hands of both drawings and five had no shading on the hands of either drawing, and one had shading on one drawing and no shading in the other drawing, there would be 90 per cent consistency for shading in the treatment of the hands. However, he did use, in addition, the product-moment correlation coefficient in determining the consistency of quantifiable dimensions such as distance from the side of the paper, distance from the top of the paper, and vertical height. These are measured in centimeters.

Lehner and Gunderson (1952) gave the DAP to 91 psychology students, ranging in age from 18 to 26, with four months between the two administrations of the test. They also determined reliability by the test-retest method and in addition investigated intrajudge reliabilities and interjudge reliabilities. They scored the drawings on 21 "dimensions," using rating scales for the scoring. The authors report that most of the rating scales had 10 points, but some of the rating scales had as few as 2 points. They do not present the scales used to rate the dimensions. The authors state that "all results are per cent of agreement between the sets of ratings, i.e., per cent of cases in which the matched ratings are identical" (Lehner and Gunderson, 1952).

Table 35–1 summarizes the reliabilities reported by Bradshaw and Lehner and Gunderson on the content as indicated earlier. Bradshaw scored each body part on several different scales. For example, the hands might be scored for presence versus absence, presence of erasures, presence of shading, etc., so that for each body part several different percentages of agreement were reported. The range of these percentages of agreement is presented in the table, and to the immediate right of the range the mean of the ratings for that particular part is presented. It will be noted that Bradshaw found the lowest percentage of agreement (65 per cent) on the lips and the hips and the buttocks. He found the highest percentage of agreement (84 per cent in rating the whole drawing. Lehner and Gunderson found the lowest percentage of agreement (42 per cent) on the breasts and the highest percentage of agreement (70 per cent) on the hair.

Table 35–2 summarizes the reliabilities reported by the two studies on the structural and formal aspects of the DAP based on the analysis of the same drawings as reported in Table 35–1. Bradshaw reports three reliabilities (distance from top of paper, distance from left side of paper, and vertical height) in product-moment rs. All other figures are percentage of agreement. In this table, also, Bradshaw had several ratings for each of the aspects of the drawings. For example, presence of shading was rated in regard to several different body parts such

TABLE 35–1   *Reliabilities of DAP Content Reported*
                              by Two Studies

DAP PART	BRADSHAW RANGE[a], [b] PER CENT	MEAN PER CENT	LEHNER & GUNDER-SON
Whole drawing	(100–66)	84	—
Whole head	(100–59)	78	—
Whole trunk	(100–59)	83	—
Legs and feet as whole	(100–62)	75	—
Arms	(99–44)	72	—
Mouth	(94–50)	68	44
Lips	(74–54)	65	—
Chin	(91–57)	74	—
Eyes	(96–55)	76	61
Eyebrows	(90–68)	78	—
Ears	(78–62)	70	—
Hair	(84–35)	68	70
Nose	(97–55)	74	52
Face	(79–73)	76	—
Neck	(95–55)	68	—
Arms	(99–65)	77	—
Hands	(97–55)	76	67
Fingers	(87–54)	70	—
Legs	(98–60)	74	—
Feet	(97–54)	75	56
Shoulders	(96–59)	73	—
Hips, buttocks	(83–45)	65	—
Waistline	(78–60)	66	—
Breasts	(100–50)	71	42
Crotch	(78–44)	68	—

a All figures represent percentage of agreement.
b All parts were rated for many different characteristics, such as line quality, proportion, shape, etc.

as the arms, hands, face, etc. In this table, the range of percentage of agreement obtained by Bradshaw is reported, and to the immediate right of it the mean of the percentages of agreement is presented.

Bradshaw reports the lowest percentage of agreement (60 per cent) on the shape of the figure and the highest percentage of agreement (90 per cent) on the presence or absence of the various parts of the body. The three rs Bradshaw reports are all significant at the .01 level of confidence.

Lehner and Gunderson report the lowest percentage of agreement (45 per cent) on the position of the figure on the page and the highest percentage of agreement (93 per cent) on body type.

It will be recalled that Machover suggested that the structural and formal aspects of the DAP tend to be more reliable than the content. In order to give a comparison of the percentages of agreement obtained by Bradshaw and Lehner and Gunderson, Table 35–3 was prepared. In Table 35–3, the number of parts falling at each level of percentage of agreement for the body parts and the structural and formal aspects of the DAP for each study are presented. It will be noted that there is no great difference between the percentages of agreement on the content and the percentages of agreement on the structural aspects of the DAP.

Serious criticism must be leveled against the use of the percentage of agreement as a measure of reliability. The significance of the percentage of agreement on the DAP is entirely dependent on the base rate of

TABLE 35–2   *Reliabilities of Structural and Formal Aspects of DAP as Reported by Two Studies*

DAP ASPECT	RANGE[a, b] PER CENT	BRADSHAW MEAN PER CENT	LEHNER & GUNDERSON
Presence of parts	(100–72)	90	—
Presence of clothing	(98–65)	86	—
Presence of erasing	(98–54)	69	56
Presence of shading	(93–62)	76	59
Presence of accessories	—	75	—
Profile vs. full-face	(72–85)	80	65
Direction of profile	(70–89)	83	—
Sex first figure	—	68	—
Distance from left of paper	—	$r = .46^d$	45[c]
Distance from top of paper	—	$r = .54^d$	45[c]
Vertical height	—	$r = .61^d$	—
Degree of detailing	(65–90)	76	79
Proportional size	(52–100)	64	—
Line quality	(50–84)	72	71
Shape	(35–75)	60	—
Stance	(44–96)	72	78
Reinforcement	—	—	64
Body type	—	—	93
Transparency	—	—	77
Position of hands	—	—	46
Extraneous drawing	—	—	75
Symmetry	—	—	60

a All figures percentage of agreement unless otherwise noted.
b Several aspects were rated for presence on several different parts of DAP.
c Reported as "position on page," such as head, legs, breasts, etc.
d Significant at the .01 level.

the particular body part or structural aspect of the drawing that is being investigated. The "base rate" refers to the frequency with which a particular sign is ordinarily present in the population of Ss that is being studied. Meehl and Rosen (1955) have pointed out the importance of including the base rate in the validation of a clinical instrument. The more frequently a particular sign is found in a particular part of the DAP, the higher the percentage of agreement must be in order to be significant. If a particular sign is drawn by 90 per cent of the population on the DAP, then a consistency of 82 per cent would not be significant. This is illustrated in Table 35–4. Table 35–4 is a purely fictional table designed to illustrate this point. It will be noted in Table 35–4, on the first administration of the DAP, that of 1,000 subjects 900, or 90 per cent, drew hands and 100, or 10 per cent, omitted the hands. On the second administration of the DAP to this same group, 90 per cent drew hands and 10 per cent omitted the hands. So, it may be stated that the base rate for the drawing of hands on the DAP for this particular sample is 90 per cent. Of those who drew hands on the DAP at the first administration 810, or 81 per cent of the total sample, also drew hands on the DAP at the second administration. Of those who omitted the hands on the first administration 10, or 1 per cent of the total sample, also omitted the hands on the second administration of the DAP. Adding the 81 per cent who drew hands on both administrations to the 1 per cent who omitted the hands on both administrations, we arrive at a figure of 82 per cent consistency on the presence or absence of hands. However, if we calculate the significance of this relationship by either

---

TABLE 35–3   *Percentage Agreement of DAP Content Compared with Percentage Agreement of Structural and Formal Aspects of DAP*

NO. OF ITEMS REACHING PERCENTAGE OF AGREEMENT LEVELS

PERCENTAGE OF AGREEMENT LEVEL	BRADSHAW		LEHNER AND GUNDERSON	
	CONTENT	STRUCTURAL ASPECTS	CONTENT	STRUCTURAL ASPECTS
90–100	0	1	0	1
80–89	2	3	0	0
70–79	16	5	0	5
60–69	7	4	3	3
50–59	0	0	2	2
40–49	0	0	2	3

TABLE 35-4   *Hypothetical Frequencies Demonstrating How Percentage of Agreement Can Be High and Reliability Low*

DAP SECOND ADMINISTRATION	DAP FIRST ADMINISTRATION		
	HANDS PRESENT	HANDS OMITTED	TOTALS
Hands present	810	90	900
Hands absent	90	10	100
Totals	900	100	1,000

$x^2 = .00$
ϕ/ϕ maximum $= .00$
% agreement $= 82\%$

chi square or ϕ/ϕ maximum,[2] we find that in both cases we obtain a result of .00. In other words, we have obtained 82 per cent consistency, but it is not a statistically significant relationship, and the correct conclusion should be that the presence or absence of hands on the DAP has zero reliability.

Since neither Bradshaw nor Lehner and Gunderson report the base rates of the various parts and aspects of the DAP, it is impossible to tell the actual significance of the percentages of agreement that they report. Therefore, with the exception of the product-moment r's reported by Bradshaw, the author would suggest that these studies do not provide valid estimates of the reliability of the DAP.

Wagner and Schubert (1955) developed a scale for rating the "quality" of the DAP. They constructed this scale by having judges grade the drawings of 75 college girls into seven categories ranging from the poorest to best quality. The closer a drawing came to resembling a "real lifelike person" the higher it was to be rated in the quality categories. With this scale they obtained interjudge reliabilities of approximately .90 for experienced judges and .85 for inexperienced judges. The reliability of the quality of the same-sex figure for 176 coeds in a school of education was .86, apparently using the test-retest method and employing experienced judges for assessing reliability. The authors did not report the amount of time between the two administrations of the DAP.

Wagner and Schubert's study suggests that the "quality" of the DAP, when judged as a whole, is reliable. Bradshaw's data (1952) suggest that the placement of the figures on the page and the size of the figures also appear to be reliable, but less reliable than judgments of the quality of the total figure. No other data are available to determine the reliability

[2] This point was suggested by Dr. E. E. Cureton.

of the other parts or aspects of the DAP or to evaluate the validity of Machover's hypothesis that the structural and formal aspects of the DAP are more reliable than the content of the DAP.

Research Applying to the "Body-Image" Hypothesis

The basic hypothesis underlying figure-drawing interpretation is that when a person responds to the request to draw a picture of a person he draws a picture of himself. This is sometimes called the "body-image" hypothesis. Machover states that "the human figure drawn by an individual who is directed to 'draw a person' relates intimately to the impulses, anxieties, conflicts, and compensations characteristic of that individual. In some sense, the figure drawn *is* the person, and the paper corresponds to the environment. This may be a crude formulation, but serves well as a working hypothesis" (1949, p. 35).

Unfortunately, there have been few studies that would appear to bear at all upon the question of whether or not human figure drawings do, in fact, represent the drawer's perception of himself.

Berman and Laffal (1953) come the closest to testing the hypothesis. They were interested in determining if Ss, when instructed to draw a picture of a person, tend to draw a figure that represents themselves, or draw an idealized figure, or draw a figure that shows no discernible relationship to themselves. They used as their basic data the human figures drawn by 39 male patients in a VA hospital. Using an inspection technique, they rated the body type of the patient. They used Sheldon's types as the categories into which they placed the Ss. They then rated the body type of the figures drawn by these patients and correlated the ratings of the patient with the ratings of the drawings. The authors do not describe how they converted their ratings into numerical scores from which a Pearson r could be computed. They obtained a Pearson r of .35, which is significant at the .05 level of confidence. These results suggested to the authors that when an S is asked to draw a figure he tends to draw the type he is most familiar with, i.e., his own. However, inspection of Berman and Laffal's data shows that only 18 of their 39 Ss drew figures that were judged to be of the same body type as the S's body. This suggests the possibility that for some Ss the figure drawn represents the S's own body, but that for the majority of Ss the figure drawn represents something else.

In connection with a series of studies of obese women, Kotkov and Goodman (1953) made a careful investigation of the differences between the human figures drawn by obese women and the figures drawn by ideal-weight women. They used as Ss 25 obese and 20 ideal-weight women who were matched as groups for age, educational level, IQ, marital status, and the "career versus housewife" dichotomy. They compared both the male and female figures drawn by the Ss on 43 items of measurement. They ran 129 chi-square tests of significance and found that 32 of them were significant at the .20 level or better. Of the 32 chi squares that were significant at the .20 level, seven were found to be significant at the .05 level of confidence. In view of the fact that 129 chi squares were computed, this suggests the possibility that the significant statistics were due to chance alone. But examination of the report shows that most of the significant differences were due to the greater area on the page covered by the obese female. Kotkov and Goodman suggest that the female figures drawn by their subjects did represent a projection of the body image.

But the authors feel that certain inconsistencies in their results "lead us to look for the operation of dynamic personality principles in the determination of differences between the groups." In other words, they feel the body-image hypothesis accounts for only part of the differences they obtained.

Lehner and Silver (1948) and Giedt and Lehner (1951) were interested in determining the ages assigned to the figures drawn by Ss. These studies do not provide data showing a relationship between the physical dimensions of the patient's body and the dimensions of the figure he draws, but they do suggest a relationship between a characteristic of the S and the characteristics he assigns to the figures he draws. In the first study (Lehner & Silver, 1948), the DAP was given to 229 men (ages 17 to 45) and 192 women (ages 18 to 54). It was found that as the S's chronological age increased, he tended to ascribe a higher age to the figure he had drawn. This tendency continued until age 25, when the age of the figure drawn ceased to increase as rapidly as the S's age. This change in rate seems to be more pronounced for female Ss than for men subjects. Both sexes tended to assign older ages to the male drawing than to the female drawing. The authors also noted that the men tended to draw male and female figures that were similar to each other, and that this same tendency was noted in the women Ss. The second study (Giedt & Lehner, 1951) used as Ss 188 male neuropsychiatric patients in a VA hospital and 229 male students in a psychology class. The authors found that the age assigned to the figure drawn tends to increase with an increase in the S's age, but that younger Ss (students under 25 and patients under 35) tend to assign ages to the figures that are older than the subject's own age, and the older Ss (students over 30 years old and patients over 40 years old) tend to assign ages to the figures that are younger than the S's age.

Prater (1950) compared the human figure drawings of hemiplegic patients with the drawings of a matched group of normals. He was interested in determining whether or not there was any relationship between hemiplegia and the drawing of heads and limbs. He used as an experimental group of Ss 49 hemiplegics and a control group of 43 normals.

He obtained the ratio of the area covered by the head to the area covered by the trunk of the figure drawing and also measured the length of the limbs of the drawings of both groups. He found no significant differences between the drawings of the normals and hemiplegics on relative head size. He found that the drawings of the hemiplegics showed no tendency to emphasize the head or the limbs by excessive shading or by any other means. He found no differences between the limbs either on the part of the limbs that were on the same side of the body as the hemiplegics' paralyzed limbs, or those that were on the same side of the body as the hemoplegics' normal limbs. These results suggest that, for hemiplegics at least, abnormalities of the body are not reflected in the drawings.

These few studies suggest that there is slight basis for believing that the figure drawn usually represents the S's own body. The results suggest that for many, or perhaps most Ss, the figure drawn does not represent the S's own body. Goldworth (1950), on the basis of a review of the literature that had been published prior to 1948, has suggested that the body-image hypothesis may only be valid for Ss whose perceptions are determined primarily by senses other than the visual. He also points out that for adult Ss the drawings reflect the S's ability to evaluate his own drawing and thus reflect his capacity for self-criticism. He feels that research into factors affecting an S's ability for self-criticism would also throw some light on the meaning of human figure drawings.

It is apparent from the few studies reviewed above that the most outstanding conclusion that can be drawn is that definitive research on the basic meaning or signficance of human figure drawings is lacking.

Content and Structural and Formal Aspects of Drawings

Machover (1949, p. 21) stresses that, in interpreting the DAP, the patterns of the traits in the drawings must be considered when they are being interpreted. But she suggests that particular kinds of treatments of particular parts of the body tend to have a particular significance. Therefore, in the section that follows, the hypotheses of Machover which apply to particular parts of the drawings, or which deal with the meaning of a particular kind of treatment of a particular body part (e.g., shading the breasts), will be discussed.

In the following discussion, the various parts of the body will be discussed, first presenting Machover's hypothesis concerning the meaning of various kinds of rendering of the part of the body under consideration, followed by the results of the applicable studies. Discussion of those parts of the body for which no research is reported in the literature has been omitted.

In the following discussion, any statistic that is referred to as being "significant" is significant at the .05 level or higher. The specific level of significance will not be mentioned unless it is below the .05 level or unless the level of significance is of particular interest. This is done to eliminate much awkward repetition.

HEAD

Machover (1949, p. 36) feels that "the head is essentially the center for intellectual power, social balance, and the control of body impulses." A disproportionately large or small head suggests that the S is having difficulty in one of these areas of psychic functioning. For the most part, none of the studies get at any of these factors directly. Perhaps the investigator to come the closest was Cook (1951), who found that, in a group of 21 male college students, those who drew the female head larger than the male head attributed the "social function" to the female to a significantly greater degree than to the male. Cook determined "social function" by a 15-item attitude scale.

Goodman and Kotkow (1953) found no significant relationship between the size of the head on the DAP and repression or inhibition.

Machover also suggests that disproportionate heads will often be drawn by individuals who are suffering from organic brain damage or preoccupied with headaches or other special head sensitivity and that this will be because of the weakened intellectual power and control which fixates consciousness on the head as the primary organ in the hierarchy of body values. In addition, she hypothesizes that "a youngster whose emotional or social adjustments have been dislocated because of a severe reading or other subject disability will frequently draw a large head on his figure" and that "the mentally defective will . . . often give a large head" (1949, p. 37). She also feels that the paranoid, narcissistic, intellectually righteous, and vain individual may draw a large head as an expression of his inflated ego and that the inadequate male will draw the female figure with a much larger head than the male figure. Several studies bear directly on these points. Fisher and Fisher (1950) obtained DAP's from 32 paranoid schizophrenics. They rated these drawings on six signs Machover considers indicative of paranoid schizophrenia (eye emphasis, large grandiose figure, speared fingers, large head, rigid stance, and large ears). They found that only 13 of the 32 drawings had as many as 3 of the signs present. They concluded that their results cast doubt on the validity of these signs, including the large head, as being indicative of paranoid schizophrenia. Holzberg and Wexler (1950) compared 38 schizophrenic female patients with 78 student nurses on 174 scoring items of the DAP, including head size. Eighteen paranoid schizophrenics were included in their group of patients. They found no significant differences between the normals and paranoids in head size. Prater (1950) compared the DAP's of 49 male hemiplegics with a matched group of 43 normal males. He found no significant difference between the two groups in head size. Royal (1949) found no significant difference between the shape of the head on DAP's rendered by 80 VA mental hygiene clinic patients diagnosed as anxiety neurosis and the DAP's rendered by 100 VA dental patients. De Martino (1954) found no significant difference between the head size of the DAP's of mentally retarded homosexuals and mentally retarded normals.

On the other hand, Goldworth (1950) found significant differences between the heads drawn by normals, neurotics, psychotics, and brain-damaged patients. He compared the drawings of 50 normals, 50 neurotics, 50 psychotics, and 50 brain-damaged patients on 51 scoring items of the DAP. He scored each of the items with a rating scale. He tested the significance of the differences between the diagnostic groups of Ss with the chi-square technique. In addition to testing for the significance of the differences between the diagnostic groups, he also tested for the significance of the differences between the male and female Ss, using the chi square. He found differences significant at the .05 level or higher on 38 of the 51 scoring items. He found that normal Ss tend to draw heads that are more accurate, better proportioned, and better differentiated than heads drawn by neurotic, psychotic, or brain-damaged subjects. He particularly noted that the brain-damaged subjects either tended to draw heads that were grossly disproportionate or omitted significant details. Rarely, according to Goldworth, does a brain-damaged S draw a head that is reasonably correctly proportioned, with the correct shape, and containing the essential details that are included in a normal head. His research suggests that the normal tends to draw a "normal head"; neurotics tend to draw heads that are generally fairly accurate, well proportioned, well differentiated, and containing the essential details of a human head, but not quite as good as heads drawn by normals; that schizophrenics tend to draw relatively more frequently distorted heads, inaccurate heads, misproportioned heads, or heads with significant details missing; and brain-damaged generally draw the least well-proportioned heads. His research also suggests that there is a considerable amount of overlap between these groups. Kotkov and Goodman (1953) found that obese females tended to draw heads that were significantly larger than females of normal weight. However, since obese females draw figures that cover a larger area of the page than normal females do, it might be considered that the larger head area is a function of the general tendency of the obese female to draw a larger figure.

FACE

According to Machover, "the face is the most expressive part of the body" (1949, p. 40). Machover feels that the face is the center of communication and that it is the easiest part of the body to draw. She states that Ss who draw the head as the last feature usually show disturbance in interpersonal relationships. Subjects who deliberately omit facial features in their drawings are evasive about the frictional character of their interpersonal relationships. She feels that omitting facial features is a graphic expression of the avoidance of social problems. She states that superficiality, caution, and hostility may characterize the social contacts of an individual who omits drawing the facial features. However, she does feel that occasionally normal Ss will omit them.

Holzberg and Wexler (1950) found no significant differences between normal Ss and schizophrenic Ss in the presence or absence of facial features. On the other hand, Margolis (1948), in reporting the case of a schizophrenic girl treated by outpatient psychotherapy, noted that at the end of nine months of therapy this girl drew facial features last in sequence on the DAP. Margolis suggests that this indicates the difficulty the girl had in facing the world. However, this girl is reported as having improved her interpersonal relationships while in therapy.

Facial Expression

According to Machover, facial expression is one of the characteristics of drawings which may be judged directly with considerable confidence. Machover feels that regardless of the S's skill, he unconsciously sets the tone for the drawing by giving the figures expressions of fear, hate, aggression, meekness, etc. She mentions, for example, that schizoid individuals will frequently draw a facial expression reflecting autistic and narcissistic preoccupation, with "large size and aborted or blocked movement trends to reinforce the fantasy quality of the subject's ego concentration" (Machover, 1949, p. 42).

Fisher and Fisher (1950) found that there was low agreement among seven judges judging facial expression on drawings taken from 32 paranoid schizophrenics. The authors mentioned the fact that they repeatedly ran across wide disagreement between one rater and another in the judgment concerning the facial expression. In this study, Fisher and Fisher used two psychiatrists, three psychologists, and two stenographers as judges. Only the psychologists had experience in figure-drawing analysis. However, the highest agreement among judges on the facial expression was between the two stenographers, who agreed in regard to 13 of the 32 DAP's. On the other hand, Goldworth (1950) found significant differences between normals, neurotics, psychotics, and brain-damaged patients on facial expression. He noted that neurotics' drawings show fewer instances of "happy" expressions and more of "unhappy" expressions than the normal Ss. Schizophrenics show by far the largest incidence of "peculiar" and "doll-like" facial expression. The brain-damaged group resembles the schizophrenic group in the sense that they do not often draw "happy" expressions. The brain-damaged group shows many instances of an "unhappy" expression. "Empty" expression on a figure is drawn almost exclusively by brain-damaged subjects.

Mouth

According to Machover, "Oral emphasis is marked in the drawings of young children, primitive, regressed, alcoholic, and depressed individuals. Since the mouth is often the source of sensual and erotic satisfaction, it features conspicuously in the drawings of individuals with sexual difficulties. Overemphasis of the mouth is frequently tied up with food faddism and gastric symptoms, profane language, and temper tantrums" (1949, p. 43). According to Machover, mouth detailing with the teeth showing is considered an index of infantile, oral aggression often seen in simple schizophrenics or hysterical types. The concave or orally receptive mouth is, according to Machover, generally seen in the drawings of infantile, dependent individuals. The mouth that is defined by a heavy line slash is generally an indication of aggression and is found in verbally aggressive, overcritical, and sometimes sadistic subjects. The mouth that is "heavy but brief," that is, one in which an individual starts to draw a heavy line slash but then suddenly withdraws from the page during the drawing, is generally found in individuals who are aggressive but who anticipate rebuff for their aggression and so withdraw cautiously. A single line for a mouth is generally considered by Machover to be an indication that the individual is shutting the mouth against something. This kind of mouth is sometimes seen in individuals who have had active homosexual experience. The wide, grinning mouth, giving the effect of a grinning clown, is interpreted as forced congeniality, an effort to win approval, or even inappropriate affect, depending on other aspects of the drawing. Machover also states that asthmatics sometimes omit the mouth.

Holzberg and Wexler (1950) found that normal women more frequently drew female figures in which the corners of the mouth were turned up and in which the mouth was shaded than schizophrenic women did. They found there were no significant differences between schizophrenic and normal women in the frequency of having the corners of the mouth turned down and having the mouth represented by a single line. They found that normal women more frequently had the mouth turned up than hebephrenic women, but that there was no significant difference between normal women and hebephrenic women in having the corners of the mouth turned down, having an object in the mouth, having the mouth open, or having the mouth represented by a single line. They found that normal women significantly more frequently had shading in the mouth than paranoid women, but there was no significant difference between normal and paranoid schizophrenic women in having the mouth open, having an object in the mouth, having the corners of the mouth turned down, or the corners of the mouth turned up, or in having the mouth represented by a single line. There were no significant differences between normal women and any classification of schizophrenic women in the presence or absence of teeth.

Cramer-Azima (1956) found that a man recovering from the effects of exposure to beryllium dust showed changes in his treatment of the mouth that were concomitant with the changes in his behavior. He was originally meek, depressed, and uncooperative. At this time, nothing unusual was noted about his mouth by the author. As treatment progressed, he became moderately anxious, restless, and angry about certain conditions existing in his home. At this time he showed "aggressive treatment" of the mouth. After three weeks of treatment, he was expansive, somewhat grandiose, and anxious. At this time, the teeth were featured in the mouth as well as other "aggressive" indicators. After discontinuation of treatment, when he was feeling physically better and showing no overt signs of anxiety or hostility, it was noted that the drawing of his mouth showed fewer "aggressive" features.

Margolis (1948), in noting the changes of the DAP of a 16-year-old schizoid girl during nine months of psychotherapy, noted that at the beginning of treatment the girl was fearful, childish, with no social activities, no friends, and seeking to enter a convent. At this time, she drew a mouth which was a "forced, grinning one." After nine months of treatment, when the patient was more outgoing and sociable, and more efficient in intellectual functioning, she drew a mouth that was fuller but narrower. However, the author notes that at the termination of therapy the mouth was drawn with a more dissatisfied expression than in the drawings produced earlier in therapy.

Gutman (1952) in comparing patients who improved in therapy to patients who did not improve in therapy, found no significant differences between the two groups in representing the mouth with a single line or in drawing the mouth open.

Lips

Lips are difficult to separate from the mouth in treatment, as is indicated in some of the discussion which preceded in the case of the mouth. However, Machover states that full lips in a male figure generally indicate effeminacy and appear with other features reflecting "foppish and narcissistic interests" (1949, p. 45). She states that individuals who draw lips that resemble a phallus have had homosexual experience. Girls drawing elaborate cupid-bow lips in combination with other heavily cosmetized features are generally sexually precocious. Objects drawn in the mouth, such as a straw or toothpick or, on a more sophisticated level, cigarette or pipe, generally indicate oral erotic trends.

Holzberg and Wexler (1950) found that normal women significantly more frequently show line emphasis in the outline of the lips than schizophrenic women do. They found no significant difference between normals and schizophrenic women in shading the lips or drawing an object in the mouth. They found no significant differences between normal women and hebephrenic schizophrenic women in drawing objects in the mouth, shading, or line emphasis in the lips. De Martino (1954) found no significant differences between homosexual and nonhomosexual mentally retarded males in their drawing of the lips or in placing an object in the mouth.

Eyes

According to Machover, the eye can be regarded as the "window of the soul," revealing the inner life of the individual, and "is a basic organ for contact with the outside world" (1949, p. 47). Therefore, she feels that the eye is the chief point of concentration for the feeling of "self" and the vulnerability of "self." Since the eye is the window through which the self is revealed and also the means by which the individual maintains contact with the outside world, it follows that the individual who is most concerned with keeping contact with the outside world— namely, the suspicious individual looking for hostility from the outside world—is most apt to emphasize the eye. The paranoid, of course, is the psychopathological category most nearly fitting this description, and therefore we would expect to find that the paranoid most frequently draws overemphasized eyes. People concerned with social functions are more apt to detail the eye, elaborating such things as eyelashes. Since females are more sociable than males, according to Machover, women would be expected to have a greater tendency to elaborate the drawing of the eyes. Also effeminate men, such as homosexuals, would be expected to elaborate the eyes and perhaps draw eyelashes on the figure. Machover mentions that homosexuals will sometimes draw eyelashes and in addition draw a figure with a "well-specified pupil." On the other hand, she states that people with a tendency to shut out the world will tend to draw figures with the eyes closed or perhaps draw a circle for an eye and omit the pupil. She states that this is most apt to be seen in a patient who is emotionally immature and egocentric.

De Martino (1954) noted that his homosexual mentally retarded males drew eyelashes on their figures significantly more often than the nonhomosexuals.

Gutman (1952) found that patients who did not improve in therapy had a tendency to draw either piercing eyes or blank eyes. The piercing eyes would be characteristic of a paranoid schizophrenic and the blank eyes characteristic of the simple schizophrenic or schizoid individual, both types having a poor prognosis for psychotherapy.

On the other hand, De Martino (1954) found no significant differences between homosexual mentally retarded males and nonhomosexual males in the way they drew the parts of the eyes other than the eyelashes. Fisher and Fisher (1950) were unable to differentiate between normal Ss and paranoid schizophrenic Ss using six DAP signs. One of the six DAP signs they used was eye emphasis.

Holzberg and Wexler (1950) found that there was no significant difference between normals and paranoid schizophrenic women in any aspect of the eyes. However, they did find that hebephrenic women had a significantly greater tendency to draw eyes represented by circles, dots, or dashes and curves than normal women. Taking the schizophrenic group as a whole, however, they found that there was no significant difference between normal women and schizophrenic women in dealing with the eyes.

Eyebrow

Machover (1949, p. 49) suggests that the eyebrow is probably related to other hair indicators. The trim eyebrow reflects the refined and well-groomed individual, while the bushy brow suggests the primitive, rough, and uninhibited individual. The raised eyebrow suggests disdain, haughtiness, or query.

Holzberg and Wexler (1950) found that normals tend to be significantly more careful in detailing the eyebrows than schizophrenics, and normals tend significantly more often to have carefully detailed eyebrows than their paranoid schizophrenic subgroup. They found no significant difference between normals and schizophrenics in the presence or absence of eyebrows. De Martino (1954) found no significant difference between homosexual and nonhomosexual mentally retarded males in the presence of eyebrows.

Ear

The ears, according to Machover (1949, p. 50), are probably of less significance than some of the other parts of the body. However, if the ears are emphasized in a drawing, this suggests that the ears have been particularly sensitized for the individual who is doing the drawing. Particularly the paranoid individual, with his guardedness and suspiciousness, will likely give emphasis to the ears.

Holzberg and Wexler (1950) found that schizophrenics draw either no ears, or ears where none should be, significantly more often than normals. However, when Holzberg and Wexler compared the normals with the paranoid and hebephrenic schizophrenics divided into subgroups, neither subgroup alone differed significantly from the normals in the drawing of the ears.

Gutman (1952) found that the presence or absence of ears did not differentiate significantly between patients who improved and patients who did not improve in psychotherapy. Fisher and Fisher (1950) used large ears as one of the six signs by which paranoids might be distinguished from normals. In their study, these signs did not differentiate the two groups.

Hair

Machover notes (1949, p. 51) that hair emphasis, regardless of where it occurs, is generally considered an indication of striving for virility. This emphasis may be manifested by drawing a large amount of hair, with an elaborate coiffure, or with shading the hair. Machover feels that messy hair suggests immorality. A drawing of a hairy woman suggests the woman is viewed as being sexually passionate. She suggests that emphasis on wavy, glamorous, and cascading hair, when combined with other outstanding cosmetic details, is usually seen in the drawings of adolescent girls who are either sexually delinquent or entertain aspirations of an amorous sort.

Holzberg and Wexler (1950) found that normals drew the hair inadequately significantly more frequently than their total group of schizophrenics. However, when the paranoid schizophrenic subgroup and the hebephrenic subgroup were independently compared with the control group of normals, no significant differences were found in the treatment of the hair. When Cramer-Azima's (1956) beryllium-dust-poisoned man had received ACTH treatment for 21 days he began acting euphoric and exhibited considerable interest in a female patient. At this time, he drew a female figure with glamorous and wavy hair.

Royal (1949) was unable to find any significant difference between normals and anxiety neurotics in the shading of the hair. Gutman (1952) was unable to find any significant difference between patients who improved and patients who did not improve in psychotherapy on the amount of hair drawn on the figure or on excessive detailing of the hair. De Martino (1954) found no significant differences between homosexual and nonhomosexual mentally retarded males in hair treatment.

Nose

The nose is considered by Machover (1949, p. 54) to be a sexual symbol. She suggests that patients having sexual difficulties or feeling sexual immaturity, inferiority, impotence, or other sexual insufficiency are inclined to emphasize the nose by either reinforcing it, making it larger, erasing, or shading, or other emphasized treatment of this sort. She suggests that impotence in the older male, for example, is often symbolically indicated in the drawing by an excessively long nose. On the other hand, it is suggested that the shaded or cut-off nose is primarily related to castration fears, particularly castration fears stemming from autoerotic indulgence. She suggests that if nostrils are indicated with any degree of emphasis, they are regarded as a specific accent on aggression.

Holzberg and Wexler (1950) found no significant differences between normals and schizophrenics of any type in any aspect of the nose including size, shading, and shape. De Martino (1954) found no significant difference between homosexual and nonhomosexual mentally retarded males in the treatment of the nose. Goldworth (1950) found no significant differences between normals, neurotics, schizophrenics, and brain-damaged patients in drawing the nose. However, he did find that schizophrenic and normal men apparently tend to draw conflict indicators on the male nose more often than schizophrenic or normal women.

CONTACT FEATURES

Contact features are the legs and feet and the arms and hands. Machover feels (1949, pp. 59–60) that children and young adults will show more movement in their drawings than will older people because they are physically more active. As individuals grow older, Machover feels that the representation of movement in the drawings tends to decrease, just as the physical activity of people tends to decrease with age. In people in whom effective contact with the outside world has been weakened, such as in neurotic or psychotic patients, the contact features will be weakened. The figures may have stiff arms and legs or weak, poorly developed arms and legs in which the arms are held stiffly at the sides rather than extending out toward the environment.

Arms and Hands

The arms and hands are felt to be "weighted with psychological meanings referring primarily to ego development and social adaptation" (1949, p. 60). It is with the arms and hands that the individual feeds and dresses himself, either caresses or hurts other people, and maintains contact with the environment. Arms extending out to the environment in a warm, accepting fashion indicate good relationships with the environment. Machover feels that the direction of the arm placement is important in determining the contact of the individual with the environment. She feels that "in general, the direction and fluency of the arm lines relate to the degree and spontaneity of extension into the environment." She feels that omission of the arms should never be considered an oversight. Schizophrenics or extremely depressed subjects may omit the arms as an indication of withdrawal from the environment. She notes that sometimes the arms of the female may be omitted by males, in which case it suggests that the male has been rejected by his mother and has felt unaccepted by contemporary females. She notes that the hand is the most frequently omitted feature in the drawing, and the implication of missing hands or hands that are vague or dimmed out suggests the lack of confidence in social contacts or in productivity or both.

Holzberg and Wexler (1950) found that normal women significantly more often have the hands and arms present in the drawing than schizophrenic women, more frequently had the arms placed behind the back, more frequently had line emphasis on the outline of the arms, more frequently had the arms bent at the elbows, and more frequently shaded the arms. This, of course, suggests more conflict indicators were present in normal women than in schizophrenic women. However, the authors point out that their normal group was made up of girls who probably still had not completely resolved their adolescent conflicts related to contact with other people. Probably this difference is more a reflection of the fact that schizophrenics' drawings tend to be empty and lacking in detail, whereas the drawings of normals contain more detail and therefore would probably contain more conflict indicators.

Goldworth (1950) found statistically significant differences between normals, neurotics, psychotics, and brain-damaged Ss in the drawing of the arms and hands. He found that normal Ss predominantly drew arms on their figures that were scored "accurate." The normals drew arms that were correctly proportioned. Normals usually drew their arms in motion or in a natural pose. Normal men tended to redraw the arms of the female figure, making changes in the size of the arms. Normal women tended to do much erasing on the arms of the female figure. Normal Ss rarely omitted the arms from the female figure or drew reinforced lines in the arms of the female figure. Normals also rarely omitted the arms on the male figure, but they drew more reinforced lines and did more erasing on the arms of the male figure than did any other group.

Goldworth found that the neurotics also tended to draw arms that were scored "accurate" but not quite as frequently as did the normals. Neurotics rarely drew arms that were disproportionate. Neurotics drew arms that were rigid, or dangling, more frequently than did normals and drew fewer arms that were in motion or in a natural pose than the normal Ss did. Neurotics rarely omitted or reinforced the arms and shaded or erased the arms *less* frequently than any of the other groups.

Schizophrenics drew arms that were scored as "accurate" less frequently than the normals and neurotics. One-fifth of the schizophrenics drew arms scored "distorted." They drew disproportionate arms more frequently than the normals and neurotics. They drew arms that were rigid and lacking in muscle tone more frequently than any of the other groups. Schizophrenics omitted the arms and reinforced the lines in the arms more frequently than any of the other groups.

Brain-damaged Ss rarely drew arms that were scored "accurate." They drew well-proportioned arms less frequently than any other group. Their arms were drawn dangling more frequently than those of any other group.

They tended to draw many size changes on the female arms and tended to draw somewhat fewer reinforced lines, erasures, and shading on the arms of the female figure than did the other groups.

Normal Ss rarely drew distorted hands, but one-third of them attempted to hide the hands. Normals drew well-proportioned hands more frequently than any of the other groups. The normals had more shading and erasures in the hands than any of the other groups.

The neurotic Ss drew more distorted hands than the normals and did not hide the hands as frequently as the normals. They tended to draw well-proportioned hands, but not as frequently as did the normals. The neurotics did less shading and erasing than did the normals, but they made more changes in the size of the hands than the normals did.

Schizophrenics drew hands scored as "accurate" about as frequently as the neurotics and omitted the hands no more frequently than the neurotics did. They drew fewer well-proportioned hands than the normals. The schizophrenics erased less and drew less shading in the hands than the normals, but they redrew the hands, changing the size, more often than the normals.

Brain-damaged Ss rarely drew hands that had good accuracy, and they rarely evaded drawing the hands. They drew fewer well-proportioned hands than any of the other groups. The brain-damaged tended to change the size of the hands more frequently than did the normals.

Woods and Cook (1954) noted that there was an r of .43 (significant at the .01 level) between drawing proficiency and the tendency of eighth-grade students to draw the hands behind the back. Woods and Cook interpret this as indicating that as a student gets more proficient at drawing, he becomes aware that drawing the hands is difficult and thus has a tendency to avoid drawing them. This suggests that a tendency to hide hands goes with normality and increased maturity. This seems to agree with the findings of Goldworth which are mentioned above.

On the negative side, Holzberg and Wexler (1950) found no significant difference between normals and schizophrenics in poor proportion of arms (which does not agree with Goldworth), the drawing of very short arms, the drawing of very long arms, arms held at a distance from the body, arms held over the head, arms held in front of the body, arms perpendicular to the body, and arms misplaced in relation to the shoulders. They also found no significant difference in the drawings of muscular arms or in the hiding of hands or in the drawing of distorted hands or line emphasis or shading in the hands. De Martino (1954) found no significant differences between homosexual and nonhomosexual mentally retarded males in the drawing of the arms or the hands. Gutman (1952) found no significant differences between patients who improved and patients who did not improve in therapy in the drawing of arms or hands. Royal (1949) found no significant difference between normals and neurotics in drawing figures with missing or hidden hands or in the relation of the man's arms to the body or of the woman's arms to the body. As noted earlier, Prater (1950) found no significant differences between hemiplegics and normals in the drawing of the arms.

Fingers

According to Machover (1949, p. 63), the fingers are extremely important in the experiential pattern of the person, since they are the real contact points between the individual and the environment. Also they are important as the parts of the body that involve manipulation. Therefore she feels that grapelike fingers, though common in children, are generally indicative of either poor manual skill or infantility when found in adults. And she feels that shaded fingers or reinforced fingers are generally indicative of guilt. Speared or talonlike fingers indicate aggression and are considered to be paranoid features. She feels that the clutched fist, when held away from the body, indicates aggressive behavior which is fairly close to being acted out. When the clutched fist is held close to the body, it indicates inner repressed rebellion that is probably expressed in symptoms rather than in overt behavior. The mitten type of hand is also associated with repressed aggression but is more evasive and noncommittal, generally being manifested by occasional outbursts of aggression rather than by symptoms. Abnormally long fingers in a drawing that is generally regressed suggest people who have "shallow, flat, and simple types of personality development." Hands that are drawn with more than five fingers on them suggest that the drawer is an aggressive, ambitious individual. Fingers that have the joints and nails carefully indicated suggest obsessive control of aggression. This is also true of drawings in which the fingers are formed like a claw or a mechanical tool.

There are few data relative to these hypotheses. Holzberg and Wexler (1950) found that hebephrenic schizophrenic women had significantly fewer poorly proportioned fingers than normal women. Gutman (1952) found that there were no significant differences between the patients who improved in therapy and patients who did not improve in therapy in the drawings of useless or confused fingers. Fisher and Fisher (1950) found that speared fingers were not present in a majority of paranoid patients' drawings. De Martino (1954) found no significant difference between homosexual and nonhomosexual mentally retarded males in the drawing of the fingers.

Legs and Feet

The legs and feet are not only contact features but also bear the responsibility of supporting and balancing the body and of moving the body about. Therefore, Machover feels (1949, p. 65) that drawings showing nonexistent or weak legs and feet indicate an individual either unable to get about or having an uncertain footing or foundation. The legs of the female figure have sexual significance. If they receive conflict treatment in the form of reinforcement, erasures, or changes it suggests conflict in the sexual area. The foot may be a phallic symbol. An individual who draws a foot that looks like a phallus may be sexually inadequate and/or sexually preoccupied. Conflict treatment of the foot, such as erasures, lengthening, shortening, changing the line, or shading, suggests conflict in the sexual area. The foot may have aggressive implications, since it is an organ for propelling the body forward as well as an instrument for attack.

Goldworth (1950) found that there were significant differences among his groups in the accuracy with which they drew the legs. Four-fifths of the drawings of legs by normals were well proportioned. Normals were more accurate, particularly in the drawing of the female leg. There were a few distorted legs among the figures drawn by neurotics. Schizophrenics' drawings, he found, were much like those of the neurotics both in the accuracy of the legs and the proportion of the legs, but he did note that schizophrenics somewhat more frequently drew distorted legs than neurotics did. The brain-damaged group drew the greatest number of distorted legs and rarely drew accurate legs. He found that there was a slight tendency for normal men to be less accurate than women in drawing the feet. Therefore, he made comparisons only between the drawings of men. He found that there were significant differences (.09 level of confidence) among the four groups in the drawings of the male feet and a significant difference (.02 level of confidence) in the drawings of the female feet. He noted that normals omit the feet as they do the hands more frequently than any of the other groups. Neurotics' drawings of the female figure are very similar to those of normals, but neurotic men do not omit the feet on the male figure as often as normal men do. This is because neurotic men tend to draw smaller male figures and thus have enough room at the bottom of the sheet of paper for drawing the feet, whereas the normal men often draw a large male figure and do not have enough room at the bottom of the sheet of paper to get the feet on. Schizophrenics did not differ noticeably from neurotics. The brain-damaged drew the highest proportion of distorted feet. He found no significant differences among the four groups in the proportionate size of the feet. He found that there were significant sex differences in the female figure; he noted that schizophrenic women rarely drew conflict indicators on the feet, while schizophrenic men did a great deal of shading, erasing, and reinforcing compared to the women. Schizophrenic men more frequently reinforced, erased, or shaded the feet of the female figure than men in other groups. There were no significant differences between the groups in shading, reinforcing, or redrawing the feet on the male figure.

Holzberg and Wexler (1950) found that normal women significantly more often drew both legs and feet on their drawings than schizophrenic women, which is contrary to Goldworth's findings. Their normal women significantly more often drew very small, pointed feet on the drawings than schizophrenic women. The normals significantly more often than the hebephrenic schizophrenics drew the legs, drew a knee joint, and drew very small pointed feet. However, when the normal women were compared with the paranoid schizophrenics, it was found that the only significant difference was that the normals significantly more often used line emphasis on the outline of the legs. There were no significant differences between the groups in legs drawn off the bottom of the page, locked or closed legs, poorly shaped and disproportionate legs, stick legs, excessively short legs, or excessively long legs, shading the legs, naked feet, delineation of toenails, poorly formed feet, excessively large feet, penislike feet, single-dimensioned feet, shading the legs and feet, or line emphasis in the outline of the feet or shoes.

Toes

According to Machover, when toes are indicated in a figure that is not intended to be a nude they are regarded as an accent on aggressiveness that "is almost pathological in nature" (1949, p. 67). Holzberg and Wexler (1950) found no significant differences between normals and schizophrenics in drawing naked feet with the toes indicated or in drawing feet with the toenails delineated.

MISCELLANEOUS BODY FEATURES

Trunk

Machover states (1949, p. 68) that the trunk is often limited to a simple oblong, a square box, or a circular unit. She suggests that round figures are drawn by individuals who are passive and have feminine characteristics, whereas square trunks are drawn by masculine persons. The bottom of the trunk is left open in some drawings. Machover suggests that this indicates sexual preoccupation. Drawing an especially thin trunk on the figure of the same sex as the S is suggested as indicating that the subject is discontented with his body type. In the case of a thin individual, the thin trunk is a direct representation of body weakness, and in a heavy individual the thin trunk suggests "compensation for unwelcome rotundity."

Goldworth (1950) found that normal men drew the trunk with greater accuracy significantly more often than normal women. He also found that there were significant differences between normal men, neurotic men, psychotic men, and brain-damaged men. He observed that practically all normals drew trunks that scored at the "excellent" or "adequate" accuracy level. No normals scored at the "primitive" or "distorted" level. Neurotics drew few extremely good trunks, and several drew distorted trunks, but no neurotics drew primitive trunks. Schizoprehnics drew trunks that resembled those drawn by neurotics, but the schizophrenics drew primitive and distorted trunks more frequently than neurotics. The brain-damaged drew "primitive" trunks more frequently than the other three groups. Goldworth found that there were no significant differences between his four groups in the proportions of the male trunks they drew. There were significant differences between the four groups in proportions of the female trunks they drew. Normals drew female trunks that were correctly proportioned. Most of the grossly disproportioned female trunks were drawn by schizophrenics and brain-damaged patients.

Holzberg and Wexler (1950) found the only difference between normal women and schizophrenic women was that the normal women significantly more often drew shading in the chest and waist areas of their figures. There were no significant differences between normals and hebephrenic schizophrenic women in any of the body characteristics, but normal women significantly more often shaded the chest than the paranoid schizophrenic women.

Royal (1949) found in comparing his neurotics with normals that the neurotics tended to draw the head and trunk in a rectangular or circular shape significantly more frequently than normals. There was no significant difference between the two groups on the shading of the body.

Breasts

According to Machover, the most consistent emphasis on breasts is noted in the drawings of the emotionally and psychosexually immature male. This sort of emphasis is generally found to consist of erasures, shading, or the addition of lines. Machover feels that it is important whether the breasts on the figure are the low, pendant sort of breasts typical of a mother figure or the high, firm breasts of the youthful female figure. She notes that the female who draws large breasts and a well-developed pelvis on her female figure is strongly "identified with a productive and dominant mother-image" (Machover, 1949, p .69).

Holzberg and Wexler (1950) found that normal women significantly more often than schizophrenic women delineated the breasts and shaded the chest. When the subgroups were compared, no significant differences between normal women and hebephrenic schizophrenic women were found, but the normal women significantly more often delineated the breasts than the paranoid schizophrenic women. There were no significant differences between the normals and the schizophrenics in drawing a very narrow chest, drawing a nude breast or breasts, in the line emphasis on the outline of the chest, or delineating the nipples on the breast.

Goldworth (1950) found that breast emphasis was found primarily in the drawings of neurotic subjects.

Shoulders

According to Machover (1949, p. 71), the width and massiveness of the shoulders are the most common graphic expression of physical power and perfection of physique. In drawings by males, massive shoulders emphasized at the expense of other parts of the figure are generally drawn by adolescents and sexually ambivalent individuals as an overcompensation for feelings of body inadequacy. A female S who draws massive shoulders on the female figure may be suspected of having some degree of masculine protest. Massive shoulders on the figure of the same sex as the S indicate that the S feels physically inadequate.

Holzberg and Wexler (1950) found that normal women significantly more often had shoulders present on their drawings than did schizophrenics. When the schizophrenic group was split into paranoid and hebephrenic subgroups and compared with the normal group, it was found that normals significantly more often drew broad shoulders, had shoulders present in the drawings, and emphasized the lines of the outlines of the shoulders than did hebephrenic schizophrenics. Normals significantly more often drew broad shoulders than did the paranoid schizophrenics. Kotkov and Goodman (1953) found that obese females drew square shoulders more often than normal-weight females. Goldworth (1950) found that there were no significant differences among his groups and showed far fewer instances of omission, shading, or changing the size of the shoulders. He found that neurotics occupied a score position intermediate between the normals on one hand and the schizophrenic and brain-damaged on the other hand. The schizophrenic and brain-damaged women tended to have few erasures but had many omissions and much shading or size changes on the shoulders of the female figure.

These studies provide no clear-cut test of Machover's hypotheses, but they suggest that the shoulders may have more significance for female Ss than for male Ss.

Hips and Buttocks

According to Machover, emphasis on the hips and buttocks is characteristic of homosexually inclined or homosexually conflicted males. This may be indicated by confusion, a break or change in the line, a particular widening or other conspicuous treatment of the buttocks. In female figures drawn by females, exaggerated hips indicate that the woman is aware of the power that relates to the "functional potentialities of ample pelvic development" (Machover, 1949, p. 72).

Goldworth (1950) found no significant differences between males and females in treatment of the buttocks; however, he did find significant differences between normals, neurotics, psychotics, and brain-adamaged people. He found that normal individuals had the fewest conflict indicators in the drawings of male hips, while the brain-damaged showed the greatest number of conflict indicators on both the male and female hips. The neurotic drawings tended to fall midway between the drawings of normals and the drawings of the brain-damaged in the number of conflict indicators found in the hips.

No studies report a comparison of the drawings of hips by homosexual males with drawings of hips by nonhomosexual males. This seems rather strange, since this hypothesis would seem to be a fairly clear-cut and easy one to test.

Waistline

The waistline serves to separate the "above" part of the body from the "below" part of the body (1949, p. 72). In the man, the "above" part is the chest area which embraces the primary body features of physical strength. The "below" part refers to the area of sexual functioning. In the female, the "above" part refers primarily to the breasts and nutritional factors, whereas the "below" part in the female refers to the sexual and reproductive functions. The legs of the female also are related to the sexual allure of the girl; therefore, adolescent girls, "being at the threshold of adult sexuality," show the greatest amount of leg conflct. Machover feels that conflict in the waistline may be expressed by a delay in drawing the waistline, by a reinforced waistline, by a broken line at the waistline, by an elaborate belt drawn at the waistline, or by an excessively tightened waistline.

Holzberg and Wexler (1950) found that normal women significantly more often than schizophrenic women shaded the waist area. When comparing the schizophrenic subgroups with normal women, they found no significant differences between normal women and hebephrenic schizophrenic women but found that normal women did shade the waist area significantly more often than paranoid schizophrenic women; also normal women had an "absence of straight vertical lines for the waist" significantly more often than paranoid schizophrenic women. However, there were no significant differences between normal women and schizophrenic women in line emphasis on the outline of the waist.

De Martino (1954) found no significant difference between homosexual mentally retarded males and nonhomosexual mentally retarded males on shading of the waist.

Anatomy Indications

According to Machover (1949, p. 74), internal organs are not drawn in the DAP except by schizophrenics or actively manic patients. However,

Holzberg and Wexler (1950) found no significant difference between normal and schizophrenic women in the representation of internal organs. Few Ss in either group drew internal organs on their figures.

Machover feels that the inclusion of sexual organs in a drawing is not generally found except in the drawings of professional artists, people who are under psychoanalysis, and schizophrenics. But in this regard, too, Holzberg and Wexler (1950) found no significant difference between normal women and schizophrenic women in any representation of the genitals or in line emphasis or shading in the genitals.

Joints

Machover states that the drawing (1949, p. 75) of joints suggests a faulty and uncertain sense of body integrity. She feels that this sign is found chiefly in schizoid and schizophrenic individuals.

Holzberg and Wexler (1950) found that normal women showed the knee joints significantly more often than hebephrenic schizophrenic women. There were no significant differences between the normal and schizophrenic women in the representation of knuckles. These results are a direct contradiction of Machover's hypothesis.

CLOTHING

Machover feels that "it is generally accepted that clothes always have some libidinal significance" (1949, p. 75). She feels that clothing is essentially a compromise between modesty and body display and that most subjects tend to draw a vague indication of clothing. She feels that a person who asks whether or not he should draw a figure with clothes on it may be assumed to be troubled by a strong body self-consciousness. Often the identity of the drawn figure can be inferred from the clothes. For example, a male drawing a figure with clothes appropriate for the 1920's suggests that the S identified with his father. She also states that a small proportion of Ss tend to underclothe or overclothe their drawings. The overclothed figure is drawn by a "clothes-narcissist." The clothes-narcissist is a superficially quite sociable and extroverted individual, but this sociability is motivated primarily by a desire for social approval and dominance rather than by an interest in people. Those who underclothe the figure are called by Machover "body-narcissists." Body narcissists tend to display muscle power and tend to be schizoid and introverted.

Holzberg and Wexler (1950) noted that normal women had a significantly greater tendency to draw clothing on their figures than did schizophrenic women. When the schizophrenics were broken down into subgroups, they noted that normal women significantly more often than both the hebephrenic and paranoid schizophrenic women drew figures in which there were clothes. Paradoxically, Holzberg and Wexler also report that normal women drew figures which were nude significantly more often than the paranoid women. There were no significant differences between the normal women and the schizophrenic women in the drawing of minimal clothing, in having inadequate clothing represented, or in having a special emphasis on more or less unusual clothing items such as jewelry. Normal women significantly more often than schizophrenic women drew a figure with a wide skirt. There were no significant differences between the two groups in the drawing of the shoelaces, high heels, gloves, or overcoats.

STRUCTURAL AND FORMAL ASPECTS

Action or Movement

Machover states that action is more commonly found in the drawings of males than in the drawings of females (1949, p. 85). Drawings obtained from psychiatric hospital patients tend to be static. A figure which conveys an impulse to movement that is blocked is most often drawn by schizophrenics who have strivings toward actions that are blocked.

Holzberg and Wexler (1950) found no significant differences between normals and schizophrenics in action portrayed in drawings. There were no significant differences between the groups on figures running, sitting, kneeling, or bending. Royal (1949) found no significant differences between normals and neurotics in movement portrayed by the figure.

Goldworth (1950) found that normals drew the arms in motion more frequently than his other groups. Neurotics drew substantially fewer figures with the arms in a natural motion than did the normals. Schizophrenics had drawings that were similar to those of the neurotics, with the exception that the schizophrenics more frequently drew "floating figures." (This refers to figures who do not "have their feet on the ground.")

Succession

Most normal people draw a figure with some sort of systematic succession. It is suggested (Machover, 1949, p. 86) that people suffering from an impulse disorder, such as manic excitement or schizophrenic thinking, work in confusion, scattering all over the drawing without any particular plan. On the other hand, the compulsive individual will tend to develop each area quite carefully and in detail bilaterally. Holzberg and Wexler (1950) found no significant differences between normals and schizophrenics in a tendency to begin a drawing on one part of the page and then start someplace else on another part of the page, turning the page over, etc.

Mid-line

Mid-line emphasis may be indicated either by a line down the middle of the body or by an elaborate treatment of the Adam's apple, tie, buttons, buckle, or the fly on the trousers. Machover feels (1949, p. 89) that such emphasis indicates somatic preoccupation, feelings of body inferiority, emotional immaturity, and mother dependence.

Holzberg and Wexler (1950) found that their normal women significantly more frequently than schizophrenic women emphasized the mid-lines of their drawings. When the normals were compared with the hebephrenic schizophrenic subgroup, it was found that the normal women significantly more often than the hebephrenic women emphasized the mid-lines. However, no significant difference was found between the normal women and the paranoid schizophrenic subgroup.

Size and Placement

It is felt that a figure that is placed on the right side of the page indicates a subject who is environment-oriented, while a figure placed on the left side of the page suggests a subject who is self-oriented. A figure placed high on a page suggests optimism, while a figure placed low on a page suggests pessimism. Large figures suggest high self-esteem and high energy level, whereas small figures suggest low self-esteem and a low energy level; or, as Machover states in the case of regressed schizophrenics, a small figure is an expression of "a low energy level and a shrunken ego" (Machover, 1949, p. 89). Grandiose paranoid individuals tend to draw large figures which suggest high self-esteem. Individuals suffering paranoid conditions associated with alcoholism or senility, in which the self-esteem is low, may draw a figure which is small in size but high up on the page, the position of the figure on the page suggesting the optimism characteristic of these individuals. Large figures may also be drawn by the aggressive psychopath. However, Machover feels that the psychopath will draw his large figure on the left side of the page, which not only indicates that he has high self-esteem but also suggests the inadequacy he feels.

Cramer-Azima (1956), in her study of the drawings of a man under ACTH treatment for beryllium-dust poisoning, noted that when the patient was meek and depressed, at the beginning of treatment, he drew a figure that was about 3¼ inches high. After twenty-one days of treatment, the patient was showing signs of euphoria and later became grandiose. At this time, his figure was 8½ inches tall. After the discontinuation of treatment, when the patient's behavior became less euphoric and expansive, he drew a figure 6½ inches tall. In this case, the size of the figure seemed to increase as the subject became more euphoric, and the figure became smaller as he became less euphoric. Gutman (1952) noted that patients who improved in therapy tended to draw figures that were more than four inches tall. Patients who did not improve in psychotherapy tended to draw figures that were less than four inches tall. Lehner and Gunderson (1953) found that men tend to draw larger figures the older they get, until they get to 30 years of age. Beyond 30 years of age, men tend to draw figures smaller and smaller. Women tend to draw larger figures, the older they get, until they reach age 40. Beyond age 40, women tend to draw gradually smaller figures. This could be interpreted as a reflection of the self-evaluation of the individuals; that is, as a man grows older and more capable, he tends to draw larger figures, but as he passes the "prime of life" and begins getting older and less able, his figures become smaller. Kotkov and Goodman (1953) found that obese women tended to draw figures that covered more horizontal area on the page than did normal-weight women.

On the other hand, Goodman and Kotkov (1953), in their study of obese women, did not find any significant relationship between insecurity and a tendency to place the figure on the upper left-hand side of the page. Fisher and Fisher (1950), in their study of signs on the DAP which differentiate between paranoids and normals, used as one of the signs of paranoid schizophrenia the size of the drawing. In their study, they were unable to differentiate significantly between normals and paranoid schizophrenics using this sign. Gutman (1952) found no significant difference between patients who improved in psychotherapy and those who did not improve in psychotherapy in the tendency to draw their figures on the left side of the page. Holzberg and Wexler (1950) found that normal women tended to draw figures that were small or constricted in size significantly more often than schizophrenic women. They found that normal women tended to draw small figures significantly more often than the hebephrenic subgroup but that they did not draw small figures significantly more frequently than the paranoid schizophrenic subgroup. There were no significant differences between the normals and schizophrenics in a tendency to draw very large figures or in the placement of the figures on the page. The evidence presented here is conflicting. A carefully controlled definitive study of these hypotheses should clear up some of the conflict.

Stance

The stance in drawings is regarded as meaning the same thing as the stance of a real person. A figure in which the legs float off into space may be drawn by an individual with precarious stability. This kind of figure is supposed to be drawn, for example, by older chronic alcoholics. A stance in which the legs are closely pressed together suggests a tense, self-conscious, and repressed individual. In a female figure, this is suggested as "a fear (or repressed wish?) of sexual attack" (Machover,

1949, p. 92). It is suggested that when this is seen in the female figure drawn by a male subject, he anticipates resistance to sexual advances.

Goldworth (1950) found significant differences between his groups in the stance of their figures. He found that normals usually drew figures which had a "normal" stance. No normal subjects drew figures that lacked equilibrium or were floating. The neurotics tended to draw fewer figures in a natural motion or pose than did normal Ss. Several of the figures drawn by neurotics lacked equilibrium. However, floating figures were rarely drawn by the neurotics. Schizophrenics' drawings tended to be quite similar to the drawings of neurotics, with one major exception: there were a substantial number of floating figures drawn by schizophrenics. The brain-damaged subjects drew the least number of figures which had a definite equilibrium and the largest number of figures which were floating or lacked equilibrium. Over one-third of the drawings by the brain-damaged group were either floating or lacked equilibrium.

Gutman (1952) found no significant difference between the DAP's of those who improved in therapy and those who did not improve in therapy when compared for stance. However, when stance was combined with a tendency to draw the same sex larger, it was found that those patients who improved in therapy tended to draw figures with a firm, assertive stance and drew the same-sex figure larger than the opposite-sex figure significantly more often than did the group of patients who did not improve in therapy. When stance was combined with the position of the legs as a sign, it was found that patients who improved in therapy tended to draw figures with a firm, assertive stance and with the legs side by side, in parallel, significantly more frequently than patients who did not improve in therapy. However, an assertive stance, when combined with pressure of the lines of the drawings did not differentiate significantly between patients who improved and patients who did not improve.

Fisher and Fisher (1950) were unable to differentiate significantly between normal women and paranoid schizophrenic women using rigid stance as a sign of paranoid schizophrenia. Royal (1949) found no significant difference between normals and neurotics in the inclination of the figures from the vertical axis.

Perspective

It is felt (Machover, 1949, p. 93) that drawing the figure in profile indicates evasiveness. But drawing a figure from the front view does not necessarily indicate accessibility or frankness. Machover states that boys and men draw a figure in profile more frequently than girls or women do. This suggests that females are more sociable and more accessible to clinical contact than are men.

Cramer-Azima (1956) noted that when her subject, being treated with ACTH for beryllium-dust poisoning, was behaving in a rather expansive and euphoric manner, he drew his figures facing forward. In the other drawings, when he was inclined to be more depressed, tense, and anxious, he tended to draw the figures facing sideways. Royal (1949) found no significant difference between anxiety neurotics and normals in the direction they drew the men's or women's heads facing. Holzberg and Wexler (1950) found no significant difference between normal women and schizophrenic women in having one part of the body in profile and the other part of the body in front view.

Type of Line

The line delineating the contour of the body is felt to be the wall between the body and the environment (Machover, 1949, p. 95). Machover feels that chronic schizoid alcoholics and others suffering from fears of depersonalization or from acute conflict over withdrawal trends may draw a heavy, thick line as a barrier between themselves and the environment. She feels that "the body wall is built as a substantial structure as though to ward off an attack of the environment and to guard securely the contents of the body." She feels that the apprehensive neurotic individual may also draw heavy lines for the same reason. In such a drawing, conflicts which are aroused by drawing special areas in the figure will be expressed by a sudden change in the line or a gap in the line. Dim lines are most frequently drawn by timid, self-effacing, and uncertain individuals. The dim line may be sketched or fragmented. Also, a body drawn with such a line may have uncertain contours, and individual parts of the body may be blurred. Drawings in which the contour of the head is heavy and reinforced while the facial features are dimly sketched suggest that the drawer is an individual with a strong desire for social participation but shy and timid and self-conscious in actual social expression. Lines which fade in and out with spotty reinforcement are suggested as being drawn by people given to hysterical reactions. In these cases, the head and facial features may be well delineated, while the body is blurred and the arms and legs fade away into random lines. The very faint "ectoplasmic" line does not appear very often, and when it does it is generally drawn by withdrawn schizophrenics. Acutely excited schizophrenics generally draw very heavy lines. Broken or tremulous lines are generally drawn by the schizoid alcoholic, who is distinguished from the paranoid alcoholic who tends to draw the figure with a heavy line.

Gutman (1952) found that patients who did not improve in psychotherapy tended to draw continuous and reinforced lines. Patients who did improve in psychotherapy tended to draw their figures with light or sketchy lines. Royal (1949) found no significant difference between normals and anxiety neurotics on pencil pressure, continuity of lines, regularity of lines, or single-line and multiple-line drawings. Holzberg and Wexler (1950) found no significant difference beteeen normal females and various kinds of schizophrenic females in the use of very light lines throughout the whole drawing, in the use of light lines in parts of the drawing, in the use of fragmented or broken lines in all of the drawing, or in the use of broken lines in just parts of the drawing.

CONFLICT INDICATORS

Erasures

Erasures are a form of conflict treatment and are most apt to be noticed in the hands and feet, the shoulders, the arms, the nose, the ears, the crotch, and the hipline. Interpretation depends on the part of the body in which the erasure is found. This form of conflict treatment is felt by Machover (1949, p. 98) to be seen primarily in neurotics, obsessive-compulsive characters, and psychopaths with neurotic conflicts. Erasures are considered an expression of anxiety but differ from line reinforcement and shading in that they show overt dissatisfaction. She states that pubertal girls erase profusely.

Royal (1949) found no significant difference between his normal men and his anxiety-neurotic men in erasures. Holzberg and Wexler (1950) found that normal women tended to erase significantly more often than paranoid schizophrenic women but that there was no significant difference between normal women and hebephrenic schizophrenic women in this regard. Goldworth (1950) found that, in general, normals drew more conflict indicators, both erasures and shading, than did other groups. He notes that, in the case of the hands, arms, ears, and hips, neurotics tended to show the least number of conflict indicators. In the case of the shoulders, the neurotics tended to show fewer erasures than the normals but more erasures than the schizophrenic or brain-damaged patients. In the case of the nose, the neurotics showed fewer erasures than either normal men or schizophrenic men.

These results appear to contradict Machover.

Shading

Shading as an indicator of conflict has already been partially considered in connection with the discussion of the particular parts of the body, but some of this discussion will be repeated here. According to Machover (1949, p. 98), shading is an indication of anxiety. The particular area shaded suggests the source of the anxiety. Vigorous, aggressive scribling to cover up something is considered to be a discharge of aggression and an expression of concealment. The most frequent kind of shading is done by using light, dim, and uncertain lines which accent particular parts of the figure. The most frequently shaded parts of the figure are the chest of the male figure, which Machover feels indicates sensitivity to physical inferiority, and the breasts of the female figure done by the male S, which suggest conflict concerning mother dependence.

Female subjects may put a few subtle lines in the skirt in the area of the genitals, suggesting "furtive and inhibited sexual concern."

Goldworth (1950) summarized his findings on this topic by stating that the normals' drawings contained the least number of conflict indicators, including shading, of any group on only three scales: the male and female ears and the male hips. On all the other parts of the body, he found that the normals showed proportionately the same amount of conflict indicators as other groups. He found the brain-damaged group consistently drew the largest number of conflict indicators.

Holzberg and Wexler's (1950) findings regarding shading of particular parts of the body have already been presented in relationship to other parts of the body. Briefly these results will be repeated here. Normal women significantly more frequently than schizophrenic women tended to shade the following parts: mouth, arms, chest, and waist. Normal women did not shade any parts significantly more often than the hebephrenic schizophrenic subgroup. However, normal women did shade the following parts more frequently than the paranoid schizophrenic subgroup: mouth, hands, chest, and waist.

Royal (1949) found no significant differences between normal men and anxiety-neurotic men in the shading of the hair or of the body and clothing. Gutman (1952) found no significant difference between patients who improved in therapy and patients who did not improve in therapy in the amount of shading on the figure. De Martino (1954) found no significant differences between male homosexual mental defectives and male nonhomosexual mental defectives in the shading of the waist, arms, legs, or other body parts. The results seem to indicate that normals show at least as much shading, on most body parts, as any group of abnormal Ss.

Differential Treatment of Male and Female Figures

Machover hypothesizes that the individual who is identified with his own sex will draw the self-sex figure first. She states that "some degree of sexual inversion was contained in records of all individuals who drew the opposite sex first . . . " (1949, p. 101). She also feels that Ss who scramble the sexual characteristics of the two figures they draw are suffering from sexual maladjustment. A pair of figures in which one figure is drawn disproportionately larger than the other suggests that the larger figure is viewed as the stronger, while the smaller figure would suggest that the figure drawn smaller is the weaker sex.

Barker, Mathis, and Powers (1953) compared a group of 50 homosexual soldiers with a control group of 35 normal soldiers on the sex of the first-drawn figure. They found no significant difference between the two groups. Hammer (1954) found no significant difference between homosexual offenders in Sing Sing Prison and two groups of nonhomosexual offenders in the sex of the first-drawn figure. Granick and Smith (1953) found no relationship between the sex of the first-drawn figure and scores on the masculinity-femininity subscale of the MMPI. De Koningh (personal communication) found no significant relationship between sex of the first-drawn person and sexual differentiation as measured by Swensen's (1955) scale, which is described below.

Swensen (1955) developed a scale for rating sexual differentiation between the male and female figures on the DAP. Using this scale to measure sexual differentiation, he found that normals drew figures in which the differentiation between the male and female figures is significantly better than that of either neurotics or psychotics. Sipprelle and Swensen (1956) used this scale and three other sexual indicators on the DAP in an effort to determine the relationship between the DAP and the S's sexual adjustment. They found no significant relationship. Cutter (1956) used Swensen's scale to compare the sexual differentiation of normals, neurotics, and psychiatric patients suffering from severe personality disorganization (psychotics, alcoholics, etc.). He used as Ss 108 sexual psychopaths under observation at a state hospital, 59 sexual psychopaths committed to the hospital who were receiving psychotherapy, 22 psychiatric technician trainees who served as a control group, a group of 19 neurotics, and a group of 17 suffering from "personality disorganization." The "personality disorganization" group was composed of "alcoholics, psychotics in remission, etc." He found that there were no significant differences between the different groups of sexual offenders and that the sexual offenders did not differentiate between the sexes of the figures on the DAP any worse than the normals. However, he did find that the group of overt sexual offenders differentiated between the sexes on the DAP significantly better than the group of neurotics or the group suffering "personality disorganization."

Fisher and Fisher (1952) related the femininity of the female figure drawn by 76 female psychiatric patients to the sexual adjustment of these patients. The femininity of the female figure was rated on a four-point scale. They rated the Ss on the following indexes: general femininity, subjective satisfaction from sexual relations, range of past heterosexual experience, somatic sexual dysfunction, and bizarre sexual manifestations accompanying the onset of mental illness. Of 54 computed statistics, only 8 were significant at the .05 level. They reported that women who drew figures of low femininity tended to have had fewer heterosexual experiences than the other Ss, had more dysfunctions of the sexual organs, and had led constricted sex lives. Those who drew the most feminine figures tended to have had more promiscuous but unsatisfying sexual experiences. The Ss drawing figures of intermediate femininity reported more satisfaction from their sexual experiences.

Singer (1952) attempted to test Machover's hypotheses relative to the projection of sexual conflict on the DAP. Singer hypothesized that in our culture, pubescents should suffer more sexual conflict than pre-pubescents. He used a group of 18 pubescents matched with a group of 18 prepubescents for age, IQ, school grade, and socioeconomic status. He obtained DAP's from both groups and analyzed them by an "analytic" method, using signs obtained from Machover, and also analyzed them by a "holistic" method in which he judged the drawings as a whole rather than by paying attention to specific parts of the drawings. His techniques did not significantly differentiate between the drawings of the pubescents and the drawings of the prepubescents.

None of the studies cited above provides evidence to support Machover's hypothesis concerning the significance of the sex of the first-drawn person on the DAP. Only one of the studies cited suggests that particular sexual characteristics of drawings are related to the sexual adjustment of the Ss, and that one study (Fisher & Fisher, 1952) reports only 8 of 54 computed statistics significant at the .05 level. In view of the results reported by the other studies, it seems reasonable to suggest that the results reported by Fisher and Fisher (1952) were due to chance.

SUMMARY TABLE OF FINDINGS

For the purposes of illustration and discussion, the author prepared Table 35–5 to illustrate in a very rough way the conclusions the studies cited suggest concerning Machover's hypotheses about the significance of the content and structural and formal aspects of the DAP. It is not claimed that the table is entirely objective. If the reader prepared a table of his own, it would probably come out slightly different from that presented here. But it does suggest that no considerable empirical support for Machover's hypotheses exists at the present time. Perhaps the most charitable thing that can be said for the hypotheses concerning the content and the structural and formal aspects of the DAP is that few of Machover's hypotheses have been explicitly tested by definitive studies. But those which have, such as her hypothesis concerning the sex of the first-drawn figure, have not been supported by the experimental evidence.

Discussion and Conclusions

EVALUATION OF THE DAP AS A CLINICAL TOOL

The evidence presented in this paper does not support Machover's hypotheses about the meaning of human figure drawings. More of the evidence directly contradicts her hypotheses than supports them. And, even in the studies where some support for her hypotheses can be found, many of the cases did not render the human figure drawings in the way that would be expected according to Machover. For example, Berman and Laffal's (1953) study found a significant relationship between the body type of the S and the body type of the figure drawn by the S, but a majority of the Ss did not draw figures that were of the same body type as the S. Since in clinical work the reliable diagnosis of the individual case is of paramount importance, this lack of consistent

TABLE 35–5   *Results of Comparison of Experimental Results with Machover's Hypotheses Concerning Body Parts and Structural and Formal Aspects of the DAP*

SUPPORTED	CONFLICTING EVIDENCE	NOT SUPPORTED	NOT TESTED[a]
Neck	Facial Expression	Head	Chin
	Mouth	Ears	Eyebrow
	Lips	Nose	Trunk
	Eye	Legs and feet	Shoulders
	Hair	Fingers	Hips and buttocks
	Hands and arms	Toes	Clothing
	Waist	Anatomy	Pockets
	Buttons	Breasts	Tie
	Action	Joints	Shoes and hat
	Size	Succession	Theme
	Stance	Mid-line	Symmetry
	Perspective	Placement	
	Type of lines	Erasure	
		Shading	
		Sexual treatment	

a Items were included in this column if the reported research did not appear to test Machover's hypotheses or if no research concerning them was reported in literature. Those for which no research is reported have been omitted from the previous discussion.

evidence supporting Machover, on both the group level and the individual level, suggests that the DAP is of doubtful value in clinical work.

On the other hand, many clinicians routinely use the DAP and feel that it is a valuable tool. Machover wrote her monograph on the basis of extensive clinical use of the DAP which convinced her that it was a valuable instrument. This "clinical evidence" needs to be considered.

The discrepancy between the results of research studies and the testimony of people with extensive clinical experience may stem from the fact that the two figure drawings obtained in the DAP, as it is usually administered, do not provide enough data for making a reliable assessment of personality dynamics in most cases. This conclusion is suggested by Caligor's study (1952), in which he found that paranoid trends could be detected in only 25 per cent of a group of paranoid schizophrenics when only one drawing was used but could be detected in 85 per cent of the cases when a series of eight drawings was used. Although two drawings are not sufficient basis for the reliable diagnosis of most individuals, they can provide data that may be sufficient for the accurate diagnosis of some cases. Once in a while the clinician meets a client who draws figures that clearly illustrate his problem: for example, the Caspar Milquetoast–type client who draws a small, weak-looking male figure and a towering, overbearing, scowling female figure who bears a remarkable resemblance to the patient's wife. The clinician will probably remember this case long after he has forgotten twenty Caspar Milquetoasts who did not draw a weak-looking male figure and a powerful female figure. Since cases which do illustrate pretty clearly the dynamics of an individual case are more likely to stick in the memory of the clinician than cases which do not, this possibly explains why clinicians feel that the DAP is of value in clinical work and also explains the sources of Machover's hypotheses.

But even though there is much evidence which does not support the use of the DAP in clinical work, there still may be a place for it. If, as has been suggested above, the nonsignificant results obtained in using human figure drawings are primarily because two drawings do not provide enough data for reliable diagnosis, figure drawings may still be of some value as one part of a diagnostic battery composed of several different kinds of tests and behavioral data. And when it is used as a part of a diagnostic battery, it should be kept in mind by the clinician that the DAP, by itself, does not provide sufficient evidence for a diagnosis, but that the DAP must be considered in conjunction with other instruments. The DAP is easily and quickly administered, which is one advantage in using it as one type of data to be considered along with all the other data obtained from the psychological test battery.

Another use for the DAP might be as a rough screening device or as an indicator of "level of adjustment." That is, although it may not provide enough data for diagnosing the various factors or aspects of personality dynamics in the individual case, it may be useful as a device for screening large groups of people or as a rough gauge of how well the individual patient is functioning. Several studies that have been previously cited (Cutter, 1956; Goldworth, 1950; Holzberg & Wexler, 1950; Swensen & Sipprelle, 1956; Wexler & Holzberg, 1952) have reported significant differences between groups of normal Ss, neurotic Ss, psychotic Ss, and brain-damaged Ss on many different aspects of the DAP. Margolis (1948) and Cramer-Azima (1956) have reported changes in the DAP which were concomitant with changes in the adjustment of the individual Ss. Also, Modell (1951) studied the changes in the DAP's of 28 hospitalized regressed psychotics as they improved in adjustment. He gave the DAP to these patients serially during their course of treatment at the hospital. The DAP's of these patients were rated, using a scale devised by him, for "body image maturation" and "sexual maturation." On the "body image maturation" scale, the immature body is represented by an oval. The mature body is a trunk or pelvis that resembles in shape that of a normal human being, with clothing and other pertinent details present. On the "sexual maturation" scale, the drawing with immature sexual characteristics has few or no details which differentiate between the male and female figures. The drawing with mature sexual characteristics has male and female figures which can be clearly identified as male and female. In his study he found that as a patient recovered from regressed states, the "sexual maturation" and the "body image maturation" of their DAP's improved significantly. Albee and Hamlin (1949; 1950) obtained DAP's from 10 patients representing a wide range of emotional adjustment, and had 15 clinical psychologists rate the drawings, using the paired-comparisons technique. The judges judged which of the pair of DAP's was from the better-adjusted S. By comparing each DAP with every other DAP, they obtained a mean preference score for each DAP. The Ss were rated for emotional adjustment, the ratings being based on the patients' case histories. The rank-order correlation between the rating of the drawings and the rating of the case histories was .62, which is significant at the .05 level. Albee and Hamlin (1950) then used the drawings mentioned in the previous study as a scale with which they rated the drawings produced by 21 outpatients diagnosed as schizophrenics, 21 outpatient anxiety cases, and 30 dental patients. These cases were controlled for age, sex, education, and veteran status. It was found that the scale differentiated reliably between the normals (dental patients) and each of the outpatient groups but did not differentiate between the schizophrenics and the neurotics.

But even though the evidence cited above suggests that the DAP might be used as a gross indicator of "level of adjustment," it still needs more precise evaluation for this purpose than any study has so far provided. As Meehl (1956) has pointed out, it is possible for a test to significantly differentiate between two groups and still be useless or worse than useless in making predictions in the individual case.

SUGGESTED APPROACHES TO FUTURE RESEARCH

Research designed to systematically test the validity of a particular theoretical system is probably more likely to yield useful results than research randomly testing unrelated hypotheses. Since Machover's system of interpretation is probably going to continue to be used in figure-drawing analysis until a more valid system is proposed, future research is more apt to be fruitful if it is designed to test specific hypotheses of Machover's. It must have been evident to the reader, in the presentation of the studies reviewed in this paper, that few of the studies reported were designed to test specific hypotheses of Machover's.

Studies which attempt to evaluate the significance of patterns of signs on the DAP appear to be more promising than attempts to evaluate the significance of individual DAP signs. This is suggested by the results obtained by Goldworth (1950) and Gutman (1952). This, of course, has been pointed out by Machover (1949, p. 21).

Studies are needed in which DAP's are taken serially from Ss while the Ss are undergoing treatment. Such studies, if they included adequate control groups, should throw some light on those aspects of the DAP which vary concomitantly with variations in the Ss' behavior.

Caligor's Eight-Card-Redrawing Technique (1951; 1952; 1953) appears to be quite promising for research purposes. He developed this technique in an effort to get at factors that were buried too deeply in the unconscious to be revealed by the standard DAP method. In the Eight-Card-Redrawing Technique (usually shortened to 8 CRT), the S is given a pad with eight sheets of onionskin paper in it. He is asked to draw a full-length picture of a person. After he has completed his first drawing, the next sheet of onionskin is folded over the sheet on which he has made his first drawing, and he is told to draw another picture of a person making any changes he wishes to make. In this way he may see his first drawing through the transparent onionskin while he is drawing the second figure. When the second figure is completed, a sheet of cardboard is put between the first drawing and the second drawing. A third sheet of onionskin is folded over the second sheet, and he is again asked to draw a new figure, making any changes he wishes to make from the second figure. This is repeated until the S has drawn eight figures. While he is drawing each figure, except the first, he is able to see the drawing he has just finished. If, as Caligor suggests, this technique taps more reliably various personality factors, it would appear to be worth while to use it to explore the significance of various gross and fine details of the DAP.

A series of carefully planned, statistically sophisticated studies of the reliability of the various parts of the DAP are especially needed. Not only should the reliability of the individual parts and aspects be determined, but the reliability of patterns should also be studied. It would probably prove quite fruitful to factor-analyze the DAP in an effort to determine its basic dimensions.

Summary

1. Machover's hypotheses concerning the DAP have seldom been supported by the research reported in the literature in the past eight years.

2. It is suggested that the opinion of clinicians that the DAP is of value as a clinical instrument, despite the lack of experimental evidence to support this judgment, is due to the fact that the DAP, in a few cases which impress the individual clinician, does provide an indication of the nature of the individual client's problems.

3. Some evidence supports the use of the DAP as a rough screening device and as a gross indicator of "level of adjustment."

4. Approaches to future research are suggested.

REFERENCES

ALBEE, G. W., & HAMLIN, R. M. An investigation of the reliability and validity of judgments inferred from drawings. *J. clin. Psychol.*, 1949, 5, 389–392.

ALBEE, G. W., & HAMLIN, R. M. Judgment of adjustment from drawings; the applicability of rating scale methods. *J. clin. Psychol.*, 1950, 6, 363–365.

ANASTASI, ANNE, & FOLEY, J. P. A survey of the literature on artistic behavior in the abnormal: I. Historical and theoretical background. *J. gen. Psychol.*, 1941, 23, 111–142. (a)

ANASTASI, ANNE, & FOLEY, J. P. A survey of the literature on artistic behavior in the abnormal: II. Approaches and interrelationships. *Ann. N.Y. Acad. Sci.*, 1941, 42, 106. (b)

ANASTASI, ANNE, & FOLEY, J. P. A survey of the literature on artistic behavior in the abnormal: IV. Experimental investigations. *J. gen. Psychol.*, 1941, 25, 187–237. (c)

ANASTASI, ANNE, & FOLEY, J. P. A survey of the literature on artistic behavior in the abnormal: III. Spontaneous productions. *Psychol. Monogr.*, 1942, 52, No. 6.

ANASTASI, ANNE, & FOLEY, J. P. Psychiatric selection of flying personnel. V. The human figure drawing test as an objective psychiatric screening aid for pilots. *USAF, Sch. Aviat. Med. Proj. Rep.*, 1952, No. 21–37–002 (Rep. No. 5).

BARKER, A. J., MATHIS, J. K., & POWERS, CLAIR. Drawing characteristics of male homosexuals. *J. clin. Psychol.*, 1953, 9, 185–188.

BERMAN, A. B., KLEIN, A. A., & LIPPMAN, A. Human figure drawings as a projective technique. *J. gen. Psychol.*, 1951, 45, 57–70.

BERMAN, S., & LAFFAL, J. Body type and figure drawing. *J. clin. Psychol.*, 1953, 9, 368–370.

BLUM, R. H. The validity of the Machover DAP technique. *J. clin. Psychol.*, 1954, 10, 120–125.

BOUSSION-LEROY, A. Transparent drawings and level of development. *Psychol. Abstr.*, 1952, 26, 178. (Abstract)

BRADSHAW, D. H. A study of group consistencies on the draw-a-person test in relation to personality projection. Unpublished master's thesis, Catholic Univer., 1952.

BRILL, M. The reliability of the Goodenough draw-a-man test and the validity and reliability of an abbreviated scoring method. *J. educ. Psychol.*, 1935, 26, 701–708.

BROWN, F. House-tree-person and human figure drawings. In D. Brower & L. E. Abt (Eds.), *Progress in clinical psychology.* New York: Grune & Stratton, 1952. Pp. 173–184.

BUHRER, LYDIA, DE NAVARO, R. S., & VALASCO, EMMA. A classification experiment of Goodenough's draw-a-man test. *Psychol. Abstr.*, 1952, 26, 5603. (Abstract)

CALIGOR, L. The determination of the individual's unconscious conception of his masculinity-femininity identification. *J. proj. Tech.*, 1951, 15, 494–509.

CALIGOR, L. The detection of paranoid trends by the eight card redrawing test (8 CRT). *J. clin. Psychol.*, 1952, 8, 397–401.

CALIGOR, L. Quantification on the eight card redrawing test (8 CRT). *J. clin. Psychol.*, 1953, 9, 356–361.

COHN, R. Role of the "body image concept" in pattern of ipsilateral clinical extinction. *A.M.A. Arch. Neurol. Psychiat.*, 1953, 70, 503–509.

COOK, M. A preliminary study of the relationship of differential treatment of the male and female head size figure drawing to the degree of attribution of the social functions of the female. *Psychol. Newsltr*, 1951, 34, 1–5.

CRAMER-AZIMA, FERN J. Personality changes and figure drawings: A case treated with ACTH. *J. clin. Psychol.*, 1956, 20, 143–149.

CUTTER, F. Sexual differentiation in figure drawings and overt deviation. *J. clin. Psychol.*, 1956, 12, 369–372.

DE MARTINO, M. F. Human figure drawings by mentally retarded males. *J. clin. Psychol.*, 1954, 10, 241–244.

FEATHER, D. B. An exploratory study in the use of figure drawings in a group situation. *J. soc. Psychol.*, 1953, 37, 163–170.

FISHER, LILLIAN. An investigation of the effectiveness of the human figure drawing as a clinical instrument for evaluating personality. Unpublished doctoral thesis, New York Univer., 1952; Microfilm abstract, Ann Arbor, Mich.

FISHER, S., & FISHER, RHODA. Test of certain assumptions regarding figure drawing analysis. *J. abnorm. soc. Psychol.*, 1950, 45, 727–732.

FISHER, S., & FISHER, RHODA. Style of sexual adjustment in disturbed women and its expression in figure drawings. *J. Psychol.*, 1952, 34, 169–179.

GIEDT, F. H., & LEHNER, G. F. J. Assignment of ages on the draw-a-person test by male psychoneurotic patients. *J. Pers.*, 1951, 19, 440–448.

GLUECK, B., GRANUS, J. D., & PANES, R. The use of serial testing in regressive shock treatment. In P. Hoch & J. Zubin (Eds.), *Relation of psychological tests to psychiatry.* New York: Grune & Stratton, 1952. Pp. 244–257.

GOLDWORTH, S. A comparative study of the drawings of a man and a woman done by normal, neurotic, schizophrenic and brain-damaged individuals. Unpublished doctoral thesis, Univer. of Pittsburgh, 1950.

GOODENOUGH, FLORENCE. *The measurement of intelligence by drawings.* Yonkers-on-Hudson, N.Y.: World Book Co., 1926.

GOODENOUGH, FLORENCE, & HARRIS, D. B. Studies in the psychology of children's drawings: II. 1928–1949. *Psychol. Bull.*, 1950, 47, 369–433.

GOODMAN, M., & KOTKOV, B. Predictions of trait ranks from draw-a-person measurements of obese and non-obese women. *J. clin. Psychol.*, 1953, 9, 365–367.

GRAHAM, S. R. Relation between histamine tolerance, visual autokinesis, Rorschach human movement, and figure drawing. *J. clin. Psychol.*, 1955, 11, 370–373.

GRANICK, S., & SMITH, L. J. Sex sequence in the draw-a-person test and its relation to the MMPI masculinity-femininity scale. *J. consult. Psychol.*, 1953, 17, 71–73.

GUNDERSON, E. K., & LEHNER, G. F. J. Reliability in a projective test (the draw-a-person). *Amer. Psychologist*, 1949, 4, 387.

GUNDERSON, E. K., & LEHNER, G. F. J. Height of figure as a diagnostic variable in the draw-a-person test. *Amer. Psychologist*, 1950, 5, 472. (Abstract)

GUTMAN, BRIGETTE. An investigation of the applicability of the human figure drawing in predicting improvement in therapy. Unpublished doctoral thesis, New York Univer., 1952.

HAMMER, E. F. Relationship between diagnosis of psychosexual pathology and the sex of the first drawn person. *J. clin. Psychol.*, 1954, 10, 168–170.

HINRICHS, W. E. The Goodenough drawing in relation to delinquency and problem behavior. *Arch. Psychol.*, 1935, No. 175.

HOLTZMAN, W. H. The examiner as a variable in the draw-a-person test. *J. consult. Psychol.*, 1952, 16, 145–148.

HOLZBERG, J. D., & WEXLER, M. The validity of human form drawings as a measure of personality deviation. *J. proj. Tech.*, 1950, 14, 343–361.

JOLLES, I. A study of the validity of some hypotheses for the qualitative interpretation of the H-T-P for children of elementary school age: I. Sexual identification. *J. clin. Psychol.*, 1952, 8, 113–118.

KING, J. W. The use of drawings of the human figure as adjunct in psychotherapy. *J. clin. Psychol.*, 1954, 10, 65–69.

KOTKOV, B., & GOODMAN, M. The draw-a-person tests of obese women. *J. clin. Psychol.*, 1953, 9, 362–364.

LEHNER, G. F. J., & SILVER, H. Age relationships on the draw-a-person test. *J. Pers.*, 1948, 17, 199–209.

LEHNER, G. F. J., & GUNDERSON, E. K. Reliability of graphic indices in a projective test (draw-a-person). *J. clin. Psychol.*, 1952, 8, 125–128.

LEHNER, G. F. J., & GUNDERSON, E. K. Height relationships on the draw-a-person test. *J. Pers.*, 1953, 21, 392–399.

LEVY, S. Figure drawing as a projective technique. In L. E. Abt & L. Bellak (Eds.), *Projective psychology*. New York: Knopf, 1950. Pp. 257–297.

McCARTHY, D. A study of the reliability of the Goodenough drawing test of intelligence. *J. Psychol.*, 1944, 18, 201–216.

McCURDY, H. G. Group and individual variability on the Goodenough draw-a-person test. *J. educ. Psychol.*, 1947, 38, 428–436.

McHUGH, G. Changes in Goodenough I.Q. at the public school kindergarten level. *J. educ. Psychol.*, 1945, 36, 17–30.

MACHOVER, KAREN. *Personality projection in the drawing of the human figure*. Springfield, Ill.: Charles C Thomas, 1949.

MACHOVER, KAREN. Human figure drawings of children. *J. proj. Tech.*, 1953, 17, 85–91.

MAINORD, FLORENCE. A note on the use of figure drawings in the diagnosis of sexual inversion. *J. clin. Psychol.*, 1953, 9, 188–189.

MARGOLIS, MURIEL. A comparative study of figure drawings at three points in therapy. *Rorschach Res. Exch.*, 1948, 12, 94–105.

MEEHL, P. E. *Clinical versus statistical prediction*. Minneapolis: Univer. of Minnesota Press, 1954.

MEEHL, P. E. Wanted—a good cookbook. *Amer. Psychologist*, 1956, 11, 263–272.

MEEHL, P. E., & ROSEN, A. Antecedent probability and the efficiency of psychometric signs, patterns, or cutting scores. *Psychol. Bull.*, 1955, 52, 194–216.

MODELL, A. H. Changes in human figure drawings by patients who recover from regressed states. *Amer. J. Orthopsychiat.*, 1951, 21, 584–596.

MORRIS, W. W. Methodological and normative considerations in the use of drawings of human figures as a projective method. *Amer. Psychologist*, 1949, **4**, 267. (Abstract)

MORRIS, W. W. Ontogenetic changes in adolescence reflected by the drawing-human-figures techniques. *Amer. J. Orthopsychiat.*, 1955, **25**, 720–729.

NOLLER, P. A. & WEIDER, A. A normative study of human figure drawing for children. *Amer. Psychologist*, 1950, **5**, 319–320. (Abstract)

PRATER, G. F. A comparison of the head and body size in the drawing of the human figure by hemiplegic and nonhemiplegic persons. Unpublished master's thesis, Univer. of Kentucky, 1950.

ROYAL, R. E. Drawing characteristics of neurotic patients using a drawing-of-a-man-and-woman technique. *J. clin. Psychol.*, 1949, **5**, 392–395.

SCHILDER, P. *The image and appearance of the human body.* New York: International Univer. Press, 1950.

SINGER, H. Validity of the projection of sexuality in the drawing of the human figure. Unpublished master's thesis, Western Reserve Univer., 1952.

SIPPRELLE, C. N., & SWENSEN, C. H. Relationship of sexual adjustment to certain sexual characteristics of human figure drawings. *J. consult. Psychol.*, 1956, **20**, 197–198.

SLOAN, W. A critical review of H-T-P validation studies. *J. clin. Psychol.*, 1954, **10**, 143–148.

SMITH, F. O. What the Goodenough intelligence test measures. *Psychol. Bull.*, 1937, **34**, 760–761. (Abstract)

STEINMAN, K. The validity of a projective technique in the determination of relative intensity in psychosis. Unpublished doctoral dissertation, New York Univer., 1952.

STONE, P. M. A study of objectively scored drawings of human figures in relation to the emotional adjustment of sixth grade pupils. Unpublished doctoral thesis, Yeshiva Univer., 1952.

STONESIFER, F. A. A Goodenough scale evaluation of human figures drawn by schizophrenic and non-psychotic adults. *J. clin. Psychol.*, 1949, **5**, 396–398.

SWENSEN, C. H. Sexual differentiation on the draw-a-person test. *J. clin. Psychol.*, 1955, **11**, 37–40.

SWENSEN, C. H., & NEWTON, K. R. Development of sexual differentiation on the draw-a-person test. *J. clin. Psychol.*, 1955, **11**, 417–419.

SWENSEN, C. H., & SIPPRELLE, C. N. Some relationships among sexual characteristics of human figure drawings. *J. proj. Tech.*, 1956, **30**, 224–226.

WAGNER, M. E., & SCHUBERT, H. J. P. *D.A.P. quality scale for late adolescents and young adults.* Kenmore, N.Y.: Delaware Letter Shop, 1955.

WAXENBERG, S. E. Psychosomatic patients and other physically ill persons: a comparative study. *J. consult. Psychol.*, 1955, **19**, 163–169.

WEIDER, A., & NOLLER, P. A. Objective studies of children's drawings of human figures. I. Sex awareness and socioeconomic level. *J. clin. Psychol.*, 1950, **6**, 319–325.

WEIDER, A., & NOLLER, P. A. Objective studies of children's drawings of human figures. II. Sex, age, intelligence. *J. clin. Psychol.*, 1953, **9**, 20–23.

WEXLER, M., & HOLZBERG, J. D. A further study of the validity of human form drawings in personality evaluation. *J. proj. Tech.*, 1952, **16**, 249–251.

WHITMYRE, J. W. The significance of artistic excellence in the judgment of adjustment inferred from human figure drawings. *J. consult. Psychol.*, 1953, **17**, 421–422.

WOODS, W. A., & COOK, W. E. Proficiency in drawing and placement of hands in drawings of the human figure. *J. consult. Psychol.*, 1954, **18**, 119–121.

YEPSIN, T. N. The reliability of the Goodenough drawing test with feeble-minded subjects. *J. educ. Psychol.*, 1929, **20**, 448–451.

ZIMMER, H. Predictions by means of two projective tests of personality evaluations made by peers. *J. clin. Psychol.*, 1955, **11**, 352–356.

36

Critique of Swensen's "Empirical Evaluations of Human Figure Drawings"

EMANUEL F. HAMMER

The author courageously attempts to counter the review of Swensen which concluded that the DAP is of doubtful value in clinical practice. He points out that many deviant signs, while valid, occur so infrequently that comparisons between normals and, for example, schizophrenics will appear insignificant because the majority of each group will not show the sign. His point is well taken, but the rarity of appearance of these signs only leads to the question of whether they can be of much clinical use.

He further states that Swensen has regarded self-projection too narrowly. An individual projects not only his present self, but his idealized self, or his feared self, or the threat perceived in others. Hammer's more sophisticated approach, however, does not strengthen confidence in the DAP because he provides no means of detecting which of the selves is present. In sum, in pointing out that the overly simple studies have not done justice to the DAP rationale, he changes the status of the DAP from a moderately complex, unsubstantiated instrument to a more complex, unsubstantiated instrument. If the former approach yielded little support, will the latter improve on the situation?

In a recent review (Swensen, 1957) of research in the field of figure drawings, several fallacies are expressed which invite correction before

655

other research workers fall into the use of the same misconceptions. In the face of so comprehensive and integrated a review of the literature, criticism of Swensen's article is perhaps supererogatory, but three points of clarification must be made.

Swensen (1957) reports that Holzberg and Wexler (1950) found no significant difference between normals and schizophrenics in drawing naked feet with the toes delineated, in drawing feet with the toenails indicated, or in a tendency to begin a drawing on one part of the page and then start someplace else on the page, turning the page over, or showing other signs of disorganized sequence. Also, no significant differences were found between normals and schizophrenics in the frequency of drawing internal organs which showed through a transparent body wall. Swensen interprets these findings as contraindicating Machover's hypotheses concerning these signs' suggestion of schizophrenic processes in the subject.

The occurrence of naked feet with toenails delineated, the occurrence of disorganized and bizarre sequence in the order of the various parts of the human figure drawn, and the representation of internal organs almost invariably, in my experience, are associated with schizophrenia. In view of this experience, I cannot help suspecting that the responsibility for the lack of statistical support for these clinical findings lies on the shoulders of the experimental approach rather than on those of the hypotheses: All these three "schizophrenic signs" are relatively infrequent in projective drawings of the human figure, but where they do occur, they occur in the drawings of schizophrenics. Thus, to test these hypotheses adequately, only instances where the sign does occur should be included. For example, to wait to accumulate twenty such drawings and then compare the incidence of schizophrenia in the subjects who submitted these drawings would be the only way to assess fairly the validity of the sign. If one had to wait until two hundred drawings were accumulated in order to obtain twenty in which these signs occurred, and then one found that in eighteen of the twenty the subject was actually schizophrenic, this would then constitute an investigation of the meaning of such a sign. However, to investigate a relatively infrequent occurrence by comparing fifty "normals" with fifty schizophrenics and deducing from the respective instance of zero and two frequencies of such signs that there is "no statistically significant difference" between the two groups does violence to the actual clinical use of such signs and to the statistically sophisticated investigation of their meaning.

The second point this writer wishes to make concerns those studies investigating hypotheses which are formulated on a not-too-careful reading of Machover's contribution. Swensen states that Machover reports that the drawing of knee joints suggests a faulty and uncertain sense of body integrity and occurs chiefly in schizoid and schizophrenic individuals. Swensen then interprets Holzberg and Wexler's (1950) finding, that normal women show the knee joint significantly more often than hebephrenic schizophrenic women, as a direct contraindication of Machover's hypothesis.

Actually, a reading of the section of Machover's book in which the meaning of "joints" is discussed (and it is only one paragraph) will find the following sentences: "The schizoid, the frankly schizophrenic individual, and the body narcissist in decline, will lean on joint *emphasis* [italics mine, E.F.H.] in order to stave off feelings of body disorganization" and "Most drawings that involve joint *emphasis* [again my italics] . . . " (Machover, 1949). Thus, the flavor of the hypothesis concerns overemphasis on detailing of joints in the drawings. The mere inclusion of knee joints in the drawings, without overemphasis, is consistent with the better reality contact and assessment of the normal women as compared with the hebephrenic schizophrenic women and is not research data opposing the hypothesis as clinically employed.

Elsewhere Swensen points out that "erasures are considered an expression of anxiety" but that Goldworth (1950) found that, in general, normals employed more erasures than other groups. Swensen concludes, "These results appear to contradict Machover."

This type of research reasoning embodies a popular fallacy in which groups of subjects are compared with other groups of subjects and extremes in each group tend to cancel each other out, thus yielding a more benign mean for the group. But clinicians find that neurotic and psychotic groups tend to deviate from the norm in either direction. Thus, sick individuals will draw a figure much too large (at the grandoise side of the continuum) or much too small (reflecting direct feelings of inferiority and inadequacy); they will either draw with too light a line (reflecting anxiety, hesitancy, and uncertainty) or too heavy a line (reflecting aggression and inner tension); similarly they will erase too much or not erase at all. As with all areas of behavior, it is the deviation in either direction from the mean which is clinically noteworthy. Group comparisons, then, on any variable tend to obscure the extreme emphasis, in both directions, of that group and to cancel out the noteworthy occurrences.

In regard to the specific hypothesis about erasures, some erasure, with subsequent improvement, is a sign of adaptiveness and flexibility. Overemphasis on earasure, particularly in the absence of subsequent improvement in the drawing, is the correlate of excessive self-doubt, self-disapproval, and conflicts which result from perfectionistic demands on one's self. A total absence of erasures, on the other hand, may denote a lack of adaptive flexibility.

In cases such as this, a comparison of means has no valid meaning. The only research design that is applicable would involve employing a three-point (or five-point) rating scale: (1) overemphasis, (2) "normal" emphasis, and (3) underemphasis and absence. Then the comparison between groups which is appropriate would be in regard to percentages falling in the extreme categories, not with the obscured picture of the means.

The last point that requires clarification in Swensen's review concerns the basic premise of projective drawings as a reflection of the self. Swensen reports Berman and Laffal's (1953) comparison of figure drawings with the body type of the subjects offering the drawings. A Pearson r of .35 significant at the .05 level of confidence, was yielded on the basis of Sheldon's body types. In inspecting Berman and Laffal's data, Swensen points out that "only" eighteen of their 39 subjects drew figures that were judged to be of the same body types as the subject's body type and concludes that for some subjects, the figure drawn represents the subject's own body, but for the majority of subjects, the figure drawn represents something else. Swensen deduces, "Since in clinical work the reliable diagnosis of the clinical case is of paramount importance, this lack of consistent evidence supporting Machover . . . suggests that the DAP is of doubtful value in clinical work."

Here, Swensen is entangled in a relatively unsophisticated notion of the concept of the self. Some subjects tend to project themselves as they experience themselves to be, while other subjects tend to project themselves as they wish to be. The idealized version of the self is an integral component of the self-concept and is necessary in describing personality. It is not the chaff, to the real self as wheat. In actual clinical context, most drawings are neither one nor the other but actually represent a fusion of both the realistic perceptions of one's self and the ego ideal. In addition, the picture is further complicated by the fact that the perceptions of one's self *as one fears one might be* also color the total picture. Since the *self* actually includes what we are, what we wish to be, and what we fear we might sink to, we must expect all three to flood projective drawings and not regard any deviation from perfect correlation on any one of these variables between the drawing and the subject as a contraindication of the basic hypothesis.

The trouble with Swensen's interpretation of the results of Berman and Laffal's study is that he too narrowly defines the self as both experienced by the subject and as projected in his drawing. As the present writer points out elsewhere (Hammer, 1958), a still additional facet that must be reckoned with in the understanding and investigation of projective drawings involves a perception of significant figures in one's early developmental years. Thus, the projective-drawing interpreter and/or research worker must grapple with the problem of disentangling the influences of four different projections on the drawing page.

For example, a subject who suffers from "castration anxiety" will reveal in his drawing *the fear of what he may become*. A subject who feels himself to be obese may draw a fat person (*what he feels himself to be*); another subject who suffers from obesity but who has not yet lost the capacity to yearn and strive for an ideal figure will draw a very shapely person (*what he wishes to be*). A child who experiences his father as threatening may, as one subject recently did, draw a male with teeth bared, a dagger in one hand and scissors in the other, with a generally menacing facial tone and violent look in the eyes (*his perception of others*).

In the face of a complex world, the research worker is obligated to recognize the complexity of the variables he attempts to come to grips with in his investigations and steer vigorously away from the dangers of atomistic studies naively conceived and dogmatically interpreted.

REFERENCES

BERMAN, S., & LAFFAL, J. Body type and figure drawing. *J. clin. Psychol.*, 1953, 9, 368–370.

GOLDWORTH, S. A comparative study of drawings of men and women done by normal, neurotic, schizophrenic and brain-damaged individuals. Unpublished doctoral thesis, Univer. of Pittsburgh, 1950.

HAMMER, E. F. *The clinical application of projective drawings.* Springfield, Ill.: Charles C Thomas, 1958.

HOLZBERG, J. D., & WEXLER, M. The validity of human form drawings as a measure of personality deviation. *J. proj. Tech.*, 1950, 14, 343–361.

MACHOVER, KAREN. *Personality projection in the drawing of a human figure.* Springfield, Ill.; Charles C Thomas, 1949.

SWENSEN, C., JR. Empirical evalutions of human figure drawings. *Psychol. Bull.*, 1957, 54, 431–466.

37

A Factor Analysis of Draw-a-Person Test Scores

ROBERT C. NICHOLS AND
DEODANDUS J. W. STRÜMPFER

From a sample of VA psychiatric and nonpsychiatric patients, Nichols and Strümpfer factor-analyzed a series of DAP signs allegedly tapping maladjustment. Included was the marker variable "gross behavioral adjustment," which indicated whether a person was classified as normal, neurotic, or psychotic. The major factor resulting was "Quality of Drawing," which reflected the adequacy of the drawn figure in terms of completeness, accuracy, and artistic quality. This factor proved to be independent of behavioral adjustment. Only the last factor showed a moderate loading for behavioral adjustment, but this factor evidenced no strong loading for any other variable. In fact, the behavioral adjustment variable showed only 23 per cent of its variance accounted for by the factorial loadings, with 77 per cent being attributed to unique and error variance. It appears, in sum, that the alleged signs of maladjustment as derived from the DAP had best be considered signs of technical adequacy in the drawing of human figures that have no apparent relationship to behavioral abnormality.

In the interpretation of human figure drawings, clinicians have attributed different personality significance to a large number of drawing characteristics, and several scales have been developed for quantifying global evaluations of drawings along various dimensions. Research on the validity of the personality interpretation of various aspects of drawings

661

as reviewed by Swensen (1957) and a study of a number of global scales by Strümpfer (1959) indicates that the usual interpretations of figure drawings are of doubtful validity. Whitmyre (1953), among others, has shown that when psychologists think they are judging adjustment from drawings, they are really judging artistic quality. Thus, there is considerable evidence that clinicians cannot identify and correctly interpret the salient aspects of drawings. Nevertheless, a recent survey by Sundberg (1961) indicates that figure drawing, used as a projective test, is second only to the Rorschach in frequency of use in hospitals and clinics in the United States. Thus, further study of this technique is badly needed.

An alternative approach to the usual use of clinical intuition as a source of hypotheses about drawings is to determine empirically what dimensions are present in a number of drawing scores and to search systematically for personality correlates of these dimensions. It is the purpose of the present study to factor-analyze a variety of drawing scores in order to find what aspects of drawings might legitimately be considered independently and what aspects should be combined into a single score.

Method

SUBJECTS

Human figure drawings were available from two groups of subjects: a group of 107 male college students and a group of 90 male VA patients. The tests were presented to the college students as part of a research project during a regular class meeting of introductory psychology and were group-administered.

The 90 VA patients were carefully selected to include 30 "normal" patients hospitalized in a general hospital for nonpsychiatric disorders and with no psychiatric history, 30 patients with predominantly neurotic symptoms from the psychiatric ward of a general hospital and a VA outpatient clinic, and 30 patients with predominantly schizophrenic symptoms from the psychiatric ward of a general hospital. These groups were matched for mean age and education. All the VA patients were individually tested, with the test being presented as a regular part of the diagnostic procedure. Tests for the two psychiatric groups were taken from the files. Further details of the samples and testing procedures are given by Strümpfer (1959).

THE DRAWING VARIABLES

In a factor analytic study, it is necessary to sample adequately the domain to be factored so that all factors affecting measures in the domain will be represented. In the human figure drawing domain, there are an infinite number of drawing characteristics that could be considered. There are, however, a limited number of characteristics that have been noted by clinicians to reflect the personality of the subject making the drawing, and it is with these aspects that the present study is concerned. In the clinical interpretation of figure drawings, two main approaches have been used. (1) Global judgments are made of the degree to which the drawing taken as a whole reflects some characteristic such as adjustment, aggression, artistic quality, etc. (2) Specific details of the drawing are considered separately, and often several details felt to reflect a single personality trait are summed in a point scale to obtain a score for this trait.

A number of scales have been published for quantifying global judgments of drawings by comparing the drawing to be scored with a standard set of drawings selected to represent the points on the scale. All the scales of this sort that could be found in the literature were included in this study. These were scales for (1) "Adjustment" developed by Albee and Hamlin (1949), (2) "Sexual Differentiation" developed by Swensen (1955), (3) "Maturity" developed by Dunn and Lorge (1954), (4) "Aggression" developed by Strümpfer (1959), and (5) "Artistic Quality" developed by Wagner and Schubert (1955).

In addition to the global judgment scales, the point scales available in the literature were also included. These were the "Body Image" scale discussed by Fisher (1959), and the "Weighted Flaw" score, the "Weighted Good" score, the "Net Weighted" score, and the "Percent Raw G" score developed by Buck (1948).

A discussion of the method of scale construction and scoring for each of these scales can be found in Strümpfer (1959). For purposes of this study, the scoring direction of the Adjustment, Artistic Quality, Body Image, and Weighted Flaw scales was reversed so that high scores are indicative of good adjustment, good artistic quality, lack of body image distortion, and high intelligence, respectively. The other scales which were not reversed are scored so that high scores indicate a large amount of the quality indicated by the title. With scales scored in this way, the better-executed drawings obtain higher scores on most scales.

In addition to the scores for the scales listed above, the height of each figure was measured in millimeters, and these height measures were combined in two ways: (1) the sum of the heights of the male and female figures and (2) the ratio of the male and female figures. Also the 14 details that enter into the Body Image scale were scored separately as a sample of the specific drawing details that are commonly interpreted clinically. The 14 details, which are described in greater detail by Fisher (1959), are: Erasures, Transparency, Lack of any Body Part, Nose indicated by Two Dots, Mouth indicated by Single Line, Hands behind Back, Crude Clothing, Lack of Breasts in the Female

Figure, Shading of the Body, Lack of Delimiting Lines, Figure off Balance, Figure very Small, Shading of Crotch Area, and Opposite Sex Drawn First. Each of these details was scored as present if it occurred in either the male or the female figure and as absent if it occurred in neither figure.

The interrater reliabilities for scoring drawings on the various scales were determined by Strümpfer (1959). These reliabilities corrected by the Spearman-Brown formula to the reliability of the average of two raters as used in this study, were generally satisfactory and ranged from .59 for the Aggression scale to .95 for the Artistic Quality scale. The reliabilities of the drawing details were estimated by scoring the male and female drawings separately for each detail and calculating phi coefficients as an index of reliability over the two drawings. These coefficients, which were not corrected by the Spearman-Brown formula since the score used in the analysis was not a sum, are shown in Table 37–1.

TABLE 37–1   *Reliabilities of the Drawing Details for the Combined College and VA Samples*
(N = 197)

DRAWING DETAIL	RELIABILITY[a]
Erasures	.46
Transparency	.26
Lack of body part	.51
Nose as two dots	.35
Mouth as single line	.27
Hands behind back	.27
Crude clothing	.51
Shading	.31
Lack of lines	.45
Figure off balance	.38
Figure very small	.51

[a] Reliability is a phi coefficient showing consistency of the detail in the male and the female drawing.

Results

STATISTICAL ANALYSIS

The scores for the scales and drawing details described above plus the age of the subject and a dichotomous score indicating whether he was a member of the college or VA sample amounted to 32 scores for each of 107 college and 90 VA subjects. The intercorrelations of these 32 scores, based on all 197 subjects, were calculated using product-

TABLE 37–2	Rotated Orthogonal Factors from VA and College Samples Combined				
SCORE	I	II	III	IV	h²
Adjustment scale	.84	−.21	.00	−.16	.78
Sex differentiation	.84	−.30	.10	−.03	.81
Maturity (male figure)	.91	−.08	.07	.01	.84
Maturity (female figure)	.86	−.30	.05	−.03	.83
Total maturity	.92	−.20	.07	−.01	.89
Aggression (male figure)	−.12	−.04	.13	.79	.66
Aggression (female figure)	−.01	.09	−.02	.74	.56
Total aggression	−.08	.03	.07	.94	.90
Body image	.79	.17	.26	−.06	.72
Artistic quality	.90	−.14	.02	.01	.83
Weighted flaw	.85	−.08	.13	−.04	.75
Weighted good	.87	−.19	.09	.00	.80
Net weighted	.89	−.15	.08	.00	.82
% raw G	.89	−.14	.12	.02	.83
Height M/F	.02	−.27	−.03	−.07	.08
Height M + F	.22	−.06	.80	.08	.70
Erasures	−.06	−.20	−.04	.10	.06
Transparency	−.17	−.03	.06	−.09	.04
Lack of body part	−.58	−.16	.03	.02	.36
Nose as two dots	−.04	.19	.08	−.03	.05
Mouth as a single line	−.13	−.11	.02	−.03	.03
Hands behind back	.13	−.10	.13	−.14	.06
Crude clothing	−.67	−.03	.06	.08	.46
Lack of breasts on female	−.43	.26	−.15	.05	.28
Shading of body	.16	−.04	−.17	.25	.12
Lack of delineating lines	−.43	.01	−.01	−.04	.19
Figure off balance	−.33	.16	−.02	−.08	.14
Figure very small	−.17	−.12	−.80	.05	.69
Shading of crotch area	−.02	−.07	−.01	.08	.12
Opposite sex drawn first	.01	.04	−.05	.19	.04
Age	−.39	.81	−.04	.03	.81
Membership in VA sample	−.38	.89	−.06	.09	.95

moment coefficients for the correlation of two continuous variables, point-biserials for a continuous and a dichotomous variable, and phi coefficients for two dichotomous variables.[1] The resulting matrix was factored by the principal components method, with communalities

[1] The correlation matrices from the combined sample and the VA sample and the orthogonal factor matrix from the VA sample have been deposited with the American Documentation Institute. Order Document No. 7047 from ADI Auxiliary Publications Project, Photoduplication Service, Library of Congress, Washington 25, D.C., remitting in advance $1.25 for microfilm or $1.25 for photocopies. Make checks payable to: Chief, Photoduplication Service, Library of Congress.

[2] These calculations were performed on Purdue University's Datatron 205 computer.

estimated as the highest correlation in each row. On the basis of the size of the highest loadings and the size of the latent roots, it was decided to retain five factors, which were rotated analytically to the varimax criterion of orthogonal simple structure.[2] After rotation, the fifth factor had no appreciable loadings and was dropped from further consideration. The rotated loadings were presented in Table 37–2.

After the above-mentioned analysis was done, it was decided to make a further study of the factor structure of some of the variables in the sample of VA patients alone. This was considered desirable for three reasons: (1) An external criterion of adjustment in the form of the division of the sample into normal, neurotic, and psychotic groups was available for inclusion in the matrix. (2) The VA drawings were collected in the usual individual testing situation and are thus more typical of drawings used clinically than are the college drawings which were collected in a group. (3) If the patterns of correlations in the college and VA groups differ appreciably, factors present in only one of the samples may be obscured.

Fifteen of the variables were selected for further study from the 32 included in the first analysis by dropping part scores and variables with low communalities. A gross behavioral adjustment score was added by assigning the 30 psychotic patients a score of 1, the neurotic patients a score of 2, and the normals a score of 3. These variables were intercorrelated, using the 90 VA patients as subjects. The resulting

TABLE 37–3   *Oblique Factor Loadings from VA Sample*

	FACTORS				
SCORE	A	B	C	D	h^2a
Gross behavioral adjustment	−.02	.05	.06	.48	.23
Age	−.15	.02	−.16	−.12	.09
Adjustment score	.85	−.07	−.09	.02	.81
Sex differentiation	.76	.11	−.09	.31	.84
Total maturity	.83	.04	.02	.13	.92
Body image	.75	.25	−.08	.02	.86
Artistic quality	.82	−.02	.06	−.15	.90
Net weighted score	.64	.16	.05	.08	.65
Height M + F	.16	.46	.13	−.17	.38
Total aggression	−.04	−.06	−.01	−.02	.01
Lack of body part	−.78	.17	.49	−.02	.66
Hands behind back	−.02	.11	.29	.06	.11
Crude clothing	−.81	.11	.18	.15	.72
Lack of breasts on female	−.18	−.52	.06	−.38	.54
Lack of delineating lines	−.37	−.10	−.15	.01	.28
Figure off balance	−.23	.05	−.36	.11	.30

a Communalities obtained from orthogonal factor matrix.

matrix was factored by the principal components method, with communalities estimated as the squared multiple correlation of each variable with all other variables. On the basis of the size of the highest loadings and of the latent roots, it was decided to retain four factors, which were rotated analytically to the varimax criterion of orthogonal simple structure.

From an inspection of the orthogonal factors, it was felt that simple structure could be improved by oblique rotation of two of the factors. The factors were plotted graphically two at a time and rotated obliquely until inspection of the plots indicated that further rotation would not

TABLE 37–4 *C-Matrix Correlations between Oblique Factors from the VA Sample*

FACTOR	A	B	C
B	−.29		
C	−.37	.11	
D	.00	.00	.00

improve the simple structure. The loadings of the retained variables on the oblique factors are shown in Table 37–3, and the correlations between the reference vectors are shown in Table 37–4.

THE FACTORS

The rotated factor matrix of orthogonal factors from the first analysis done on the total group of subjects is shown in Table 37–2. These factors are labeled with Roman numerals to distinguish them from the oblique factors from the VA sample, which are designated by letters.

Factor I is a very large factor that accounts for most of the common variance among the drawing scores. All the scales, with the exception of the Aggression scale, have high loadings on this factor. The variables having considerable negative loadings seem to indicate poor or incomplete drawings. These are: Lack of Body Part, Crude Clothing, Lack of Breasts on Female Figure, Lack of Delimiting Lines, and Figure off Balance. When one asks himself what the variables which load on this factor have in common that is not present in those variables which do not load on the factor, one is faced with two possibilities: (1) The factor may represent some broad dimension of psychological adjustment, since most of the high loading variables have been felt to be related to some aspect of adjustment. (2) The factor may represent the dimension of drawing ability. Certainly the high-scoring drawings on all the scales loading on the factor appear to be better drawings, in the sense of looking more like a person, than the low-scoring drawings, and the Artistic Quality scale has a loading of .90.

A possible compromise interpretation is that drawing ability and adjustment are themselves highly correlated and are both reflected in the factor. The Artistic Quality scale and the Adjustment scale were correlated .86 with each other, and both load highly on the factor. The analysis of the VA data to be discussed below may aid in deciding between these possible interpretations.

Factor II is identified by the high loadings of age and membership in the VA sample. This factor is due to the fact that two groups differing greatly in age were included in the sample. Had the score indicating group membership not been included in the matrix, this factor would not have appeared, and age would have had a small communality. The group membership score was included because it was expected that many aspects of the drawings would vary from college to VA samples. However, this is clearly not the case. The only way in which VA and college drawings differ is in over-all quality or adjustment of the drawing, as is shown by the loading of group membership on Factor I and the low loadings of the drawing scores on Factor II.

Factor III is clearly a size factor, with Height and Figure very Small being the only variables with appreciable loadings. The small loading of the Body Image scale is probably due to the fact that size of figure is part of the Body Image score. The size of the drawing seems to have a low positive relationship with over-all quality of drawing, as is shown by the loading of the two size variables on Factor I. Other than this, however, size has little relationship with other aspects of the drawings, as is shown by the low loadings of the drawing scores on Factor III.

Factor IV is defined by the three Aggression scores and has no other high loadings.

The oblique factors from the VA sample are shown in Table 37–3.

Factor A is clearly the same large "Quality of Drawing" factor found in the total group. It is now possible to answer the question raised in the total sample of whether or not this factor could represent some broad dimension of psychological adjustment. If this were the case, gross behavioral adjustment, as represented by the division of the sample into normal, neurotic, and psychotic groups, would be expected to load highly on the factor. Instead, the loading of gross behavioral adjustment is –.02. The fact that this negative loading is not due to some artifact of the rotation is attested to by the correlation of –.03 between gross behavioral adjustment and the figure-drawing Adjustment score. Thus the most plausible interpretation of the factor is one of over-all quality of the drawing, perhaps due to individual differences in drawing ability which are independent of psychological adjustment.

Factor B evidently represents a tendency to draw big bosomy figures and is negatively correlated with Factor A.

Factor C is characterized by loading of Missing Parts and Hands behind Back and the negative loading of Figure off Balance. This might very tentatively be interpreted as defensiveness and constriction in drawing. It is negatively correlated with Factor A.

Factor D is the only factor on which gross Adjustment is loaded, and it is thus of great interest to see what drawing variables are also loaded on this factor. No drawing variable has its major loading on this factor, but the positive loading of Sexual Differentiation and the negative loading of Absence of Breasts in the Female Figure may be considered minimally significant.

Discussion

For the heterogeneous group of subjects represented by the combined college and VA subjects, a single factor, interpreted as over-all quality of drawing, accounts for most of the common variance among a wide variety of drawing scores. The additional factors found can be interpreted as artifacts of the method of scoring the variables. Although other interpretable factors were found in the VA sample, again most of the common variance was accounted for by a single factor.

In their early thinking about these results, the writers began referring to this large first factor as artistic quality, mainly because of the high loadings of the Artistic Quality scale. In a preliminary attempt to construct a scale of sample drawings to illustrate this factor, they began sorting drawings from a new sample according to artistic quality as defined by their experience with the scales loading highly on the first factor. They obtained very good interrater reliability among psychologists in this endeavor, but when an artist from a university art department was asked to rate the drawings on artistic quality, they found a near-zero correlation between the ratings of psychologists and the ratings of the artist. The explanation for the low correlation was found in differing conceptions of artistic quality. The psychologists, as do the scales loading highly on the first factor, gave high scores to drawings that looked like a person or in some cases that looked like the cartoon character or caricature that the subject seemed to be trying to portray. The artist, on the other hand, was primarily concerned with balance, symmetry, freedom of expression, and esthetic appeal. Thus, the first factor, called over-all quality of drawing, seems mainly to reflect the technical skill of the subject in executing a drawing and has little to do with esthetic appeal. Picasso would score very low on the first factor.

Investigators who have set out to develop measures of such aspects of drawings as adjustment, maturity, intelligence, sex differentiation, body image disturbance, and artistic quality have ended up with measures whose major differences are in their titles. Apparently, over-all quality is such a pervasive aspect of the drawing and has such a large variance compared with other factors affecting drawings that most measures have most of their reliable variance accounted for by this factor. Even a number of very specific aspects of drawings such as Lack of Body Part, Crude Clothing, Lack of Margins and Lines, and Figure off Balance correlate with this factor of over-all quality almost to the limit of their reliability.

It is surprising that over-all quality of drawing is not related to gross adjustment in the VA group, since the Adjustment scale has its major loading on this factor. Yet gross adjustment has very little communality (.23) with the drawing scores at all. Although Lack of Breasts on the Female Figure and perhaps other aspects of sex differentiation have a low relationship with gross adjustment, they cannot be used as measures of this variable because "lack of breasts" and the Sex Differentiation scale have their major loadings on other factors unrelated to gross adjustment.

The present analysis indicates that over-all quality of drawing accounts for most of the variance in aspects of figure drawings considered clinically significant. It also seems probable that the over-all quality of a person's drawings has little relationship to his psychological adjustment. If there are, indeed, aspects of figure drawings which are related to the personality of the person making the drawing, such a relationship is likely to be obscured in any group comparison by the large individual differences in over-all quality. Thus, further research might profitably be directed to study of the correlates of certain drawing scores when over-all quality of drawing is experimentally controlled.

Summary

A factor analysis of a number of aspects of human figure drawings, including global evaluations of the whole drawing and scores of particular aspects of the drawing, yielded a single factor which accounts for most of the common variance among the drawing scores in a heterogeneous group of subjects. Another factor analysis of a smaller number of drawing scores, using 90 VA patients as subjects, yielded the same large factor as the first analysis and three smaller, yet interpretable, factors. The major factor, interpreted as over-all quality of drawing, was unrelated to gross adjustment of the VA patients. Gross Adjustment defined a factor of its own on which the Sex Differentiation scale and Absence of Breasts in the Female Figure had low loadings.

REFERENCES

ALBEE, G. W., & HAMLIN, R. An investigation of the reliability and validity of judgments inferred from drawings. *J. clin. Psychol.*, 1949, 5, 389–392.

Buck, J. N. The H-T-P technique; a qualitative and quantitative scoring manual. *J. clin. Psychol.*, 1948, 4, 317–396.

Dunn, M., & Lorge, I. A Gestalt scale for the appraisal of human figure drawings. *Amer. Psychologist*, 1954, 9, 357. (Abstract)

Fisher, S. Body activity gradients and figure drawing variables. *J. consult. Psychol.*, 1959, 23, 54–59.

Strümpfer, D. J. W. A study of some communicable measures for the evaluation of human figure drawings. Unpublished doctoral dissertation, Purdue Univer., 1959.

Sundberg, N. D. The practice of psychological testing in clinical services in the United States. *Amer. Psychologist*, 1961, 16, 79–83.

Swensen, C. H. Sexual differentiation on the draw-a-person test. *J. clin. Psychol.*, 1955, 11, 37–40.

Swensen, C. H. Empirical evaluations of human figure drawings. *Psychol. Bull.*, 1957, 54, 431–466.

Wagner, Mazie E., & Schubert, H. J. P. *DAP quality scale for late adolescents and young adults.* Buffalo: Authors, 1955.

Whitmyre, J. W. The significance of artistic excellence in the judgment of adjustment inferred from human figure drawings. *J. consult. Psychol.*, 1953, 71, 421–424.

38

The Differentiation of Human Figure Drawings

LYLE D. SCHMIDT AND
JOHN F. McGOWAN

This study purports to demonstrate that physically handicapped persons can be differentiated from physically normal ones by their drawings. Unfortunately, the physically normal group was younger than the handicapped group (as determined by age range). Intelligence, socioeconomic class, influence of the handicap on physical ability to draw also were not strictly controlled. Consequently, the reader has no assurance that the differences reported were a function of differences in body image rather than of more extraneous variables. The fact that psychologists did no better than nonpsychologists in distinguishing the two groups is consistent with findings on the Bender-Gestalt (see Chap. 44 in this volume).

Human figure drawings as diagnostic tools are finding increased use and acceptance among psychologists. The purpose of this study was to determine whether or not human figure drawings by physically disabled persons could be differentiated from human figure drawings by physically normal persons and to investigate some of the factors involved in the differentiation.

The need for the investigation arose from the observation that previous studies yielded contradictory results. Abel (1953), Tolor (1955), and Tolor and Tolor (1955) indicated that figure drawings were valid projections of the drawer, while studies by Simms (1951) and Silverstein

673

and Robinson (1956) did not support this finding. Studies by Albee and Hamlin (1949; 1950) showed that judges could reliably judge figure drawings, although Tolor and Tolor (1955) and Silverstein and Robinson (1956) concluded they could not. In most of these studies, however, certain conditions existed in the design that would suggest that important variables which could have influenced the results may not have been adequately controlled.

Among these sources of variability was the wide variation in methods used by the investigators. Blanchard (1952) and Tolor (1955) tried global judgments, Lehner and Gunderson (1952) used signs and check lists, Abel (1953) employed categorization, while Simms (1951) and Silverstein and Robinson (1956) applied more than one of these methods.

Another source of variation was suspected to lie in the frequent use of children as subjects, since in studies by Goodenough and Harris (1950) and Machover (1953b) possible developmental factors, both in motor and personal adjustment areas, were frequently found in children's drawings. In addition, Tolor (1955), Simms (1951) and Silverstein and Robinson (1956) used children in their studies, and their results were mostly negative.

Still a third source, and one that this study attempts to evaluate, might have been in the usual practice of selecting judges for the studies solely on the basis of some academic and/or experience factor. Simms concluded that psychologically experienced judges who knew techniques of figure-drawing analysis did no better in judging the drawings than naive and unsophisticated judges. Albee and Hamlin (1950) concluded that nonpsychologists not experienced in projective techniques could make judgments of the figure drawings as reliably as the clinical psychologists used in the study. This would seem to indicate that some other factors were operating that might be only indirectly related to experience and knowledge of drawing analysis.

Two studies in the counseling area serve as examples of such a phenomenon. Dipboye (1952) discovered a tendency for "counselor style" to divide into "affective" and "cognitive" areas and for counselors to respond differently to each area. McGowan (1955) found further that counselors could be grouped according to whether their interview responses primarily concerned the "content" or "affect" of the client–counselor relationship and that counselor "style" is not so much attributable to professional training as to the counselor's own personality and his readiness to use or not use any specific counseling technique.

As related to the use of figure drawings, these studies would suggest that judges might evaluate figure drawings more in the light of their professional orientation or leanings than in the light of their formal training and experience. This would imply a potential variability in successfulness, particularly, if one orientation is more conducive to effective or reliable drawing analysis. In the present framework, one orientation might be considered "affective" and involve an impressionistic or "feeling" approach to the drawings, and the other orientation might be regarded as actuarial or "cognitive," with a tendency to evaluate the drawings more in terms of specific signs or factors.

When these possible sources of variation in the studies on figure drawings are considered, the contradictions found seem more understandable, and the present study represents an attempt to control for them in the following manner. First, the design of the study makes use of the short-inspection type of drawing analysis commonly used in their everyday application. Second, the subjects for the study were adults. Third, a preliminary attempt was made to select and separate judges not only on the basis of experience and familiarity with figure drawings but also on their professional or psychological orientation.

The hypotheses of the study are: (1) human figure drawings by physically disabled persons can be differentiated from human figure drawings by physically normal persons; (2) experienced psychologists with a similar knowledge of drawing analysis differ in their ability to judge the drawings; (3) judges with psychological training and knowledge of drawing analysis can differentiate the drawings with greater success than untrained judges naive in drawing analysis.

Subjects and Procedure

DRAWINGS

Human figure drawings were obtained from each of the 60 subjects (Ss) in the study in the manner suggested by Machover (1949), with a drawing of each sex comprising a pair. All identifying data, except the sex and age of the drawer, were removed, and the pairs were randomly intermixed and numbered from 1 to 60. The top drawing in each pair was the one made first.

These randomly ordered pairs were presented to each judge, and he was told to separate them into two groups—the drawings by the disabled in one and those by the physically normal in the other. The order of his placements was tabulated, and each was scored as "right" if placed in the group to which its drawer actually belonged or "wrong" if not so placed. His rights or wrongs could vary from 0 to 60, since his choices were not forced into equal piles. Individual and group results were analyzed by chi square, using a one-tailed test of significance and .05 as the accepted level of confidence.

SUBJECTS

The disabled group consisted of 20 males and 10 females ranging in age from 20 to 70. The criteria for their selection included their being at least 20 years of age and the presence in each of some visible physical disability such as an amputation. An S was not included if he also had some diagnosed psychological disability, such as neurosis or mental deficiency. There may have been some incidence of these, but none was discovered in the psychological examinations of this group. The group was essentially of average intelligence and from the lower-middle or lower socioeconomic backgrounds. The Ss were part of The Greater Kansas City Survey and Demonstration Project for the Handicapped, conducted by Community Studies, Incorporated, of Kansas City, Missouri.

The normal group was made up of 10 males and 20 females, aged 21 to 59. The selection criteria consisted of being at least 20 years of age, functioning adequately in an occupation, and with no visible physical disabilities. Factors of intelligence and psychological adjustment were held constant by randomly selecting people functioning adequately in an unselected group of occupations. An assumption was made that the incidence of atypical factors would be no greater than in any population of normal people. Occupations represented include: secretary, recreation worker, receptionist, clerical worker, and building maintenance (not custodian). The Ss were not objectively evaluated, but incomes, occupations, and social characteristics would tend to place them at a lower-middle or upper-lower socioeconomic level.

JUDGES

The judges for the study were selected with the aid of a short information form, developed to identify each judge's feelings toward professional questions concerning the use of tests, attitudes toward figure drawings, counseling style, etc. Responses to each item were evaluated by three doctoral candidates in counseling psychology as either tending toward a cognitive or toward an affective point of view, using criteria suggested by the investigator. An inspection of the results of the evaluations of all items for each judge roughly indicated the general direction of his professional orientation.

The three groups of judges were made up as follows. (1) Group I was composed of three persons with doctor's degrees in counseling or clinical psychology and professional experience beyond the degree. Each had a basic knowledge of figure-drawing analysis and some experience in its use. Their general professional orientation was determined to be "affective." (2) Group II consisted of three persons with doctor's degrees in counseling or clinical psychology and professional experience beyond the degree. Each had a basic knowledge of figure-drawing analysis and some experience in its use. Their general professional orientation was determined to be "cognitive." (3) Group III was made up of three persons with doctor's degrees in education and professional experience beyond the degree. No one in this group had any knowledge of figure-drawing analysis. Their professional orientation was unknown.

Results

In order to evaluate possible effects on the judge's decisions of the uneven distribution of males and females in the two groups of Ss, the judgments were first analyzed by sex; that is, contingency tables were developed to see if any relationship existed between the sex of the Ss and how the judges sorted their drawings. In other words, is there a relationship between the proportions of drawings, called disabled and called normal, and sex of the people drawing them? For the disabled Ss, the chi square was .74, for the nondisabled Ss .007, and for all the Ss together 3.60. For two degrees of freedom, chi squares as great as or greater than these could occur by chance at least 70, 98, and 20 per cent of the time, respectively. This indicates no significant relationship existing between the placements of the drawings and the sex of the drawer and permits one to infer that any significant

TABLE 38–1		Chi-Square Values and Significance Levels of Judgments		
GROUP	JUDGE	x^2	df	$P<$
Group I	1	1.35	1	.15
	2	.02	1	.45
	3	8.82	1	.005
Total I		5.34	1	.025
Group II	4	.42	1	.35
	5	.42	1	.35
	6	.00	1	—
Total II		.68	1	.25
Group III	7	.15	1	.40
	8	7.35	1	.005
	9	4.82	1	.025
Total III		10.28	1	.005
Total		14.34	1	.01
Between groups				
I, II, III		2.98	3	.50
I, II		.92	2	.70
I, III		.30	2	.90
II, III		2.56	2	.30

results in succeeding analyses are due to judgments on cues related to disability, not sex.

Contingency tables between all three groups of judges and between every combination of two resulted in probabilities that were in no case less than .30 (see Table 38–1). This signifies that null hypotheses of no difference in judging ability between groups could not be rejected (hypotheses 2 and 3). That is, it is not clear from this study whether cognitive, affective, or naive judges, as a group, are superior in judging figure drawings.

The judgments of each group were tested by chi square against a chance expectancy of .5, since judgments were between just two categories. The results found in Table 38–1 indicate Groups I and III were significantly better than chance in judging the drawings. These results, and the p of .01 for the total judgments, permit a rejection of the null hypothesis of no differentiability between the two groups of drawings (hypothesis 1). Drawings by physically disabled persons can be differentiated from those by physically normal persons under the conditions of this study.

Discussion and Conclusions

The results of the study indicate there is no significant difference between the groups of judges involved, in their ability to differentiate human figure drawings. This may point to a worth-while area for investigation, for although the number of judges per group in this study is small and the results on this point not decisive, the intimation is that the untrained judges did as well as the experienced judges in differentiating the drawings.

Another outstanding point in the results is the wide variability between individual judges. Probabilities that the scores obtained were due to chance ranged from as low as .005 to as high as .45. One conclusion that might be drawn from this is that facility with figure-drawing analysis is in the main dependent on some factor within the individual using the drawings and not on his particular knowledge of the theory of drawing analysis.

In conclusion, the study suggests that figure drawings really are projections of the drawer, but not merely simple projections of the self-image. As Machover says: "It is clear from the study of drawings of handicapped persons that the relation between body handicap and projection in the drawings is not a simple one. In the attitude toward a handicap there is the mediation of the whole personality. Drawings, as sensitive instruments recording realistic or shining self-evaluations, must be analyzed in the light of the whole personality" (1953a, p. 262).

It also implies that figure-drawing techniques have possible value in clinical and counseling situations, but the wide variability among the judges indicates that the effectiveness and applicability of the techniques may be a function of the individual using them. The usefulness of the drawings will probably be complemented by other evaluation procedures and methods and by background knowledge and understanding of the individual drawing the figures.

Finally, although the naive judges were quite accurate in their judgments, this should not be interpreted as a license for untrained persons to use figure drawings. Instead, many clinicians point out that since the drawings may contain considerable information about the drawer, they must be handled professionally by competent persons until their clinical meanings can be more conclusively ascertained.

Summary

Human figure drawings were obtained from 30 persons with visible physical disabilities and 30 persons without visible physical disabilities. They were randomized and presented to each of the members of three selected groups of judges, who were requested to sort the drawings into "disabled" and "normal" piles. Group I judges were experienced in drawing analysis and were determined to have generally an "affective" professional orientation. Group II judges were experienced in drawing analysis but had a general "cognitive" professional orientation. Group III judges had no experience in figure-drawing analysis.

From a chi-square analysis it was found that:

1. Figure drawings by physically disabled persons could be distinguished from figure drawings by physically normal persons under the conditions of this study.

2. There was no demonstrable superiority of any one group in the study in regard to drawing judgment, indicating that the group with no training in drawing analysis was able to sort the drawings with as great success as either of the experienced groups.

3. A wide variation existed between individual judges in the success of their drawing judgments. Probabilities that the discriminations were due to chance varied from as low as .005 for some judges to .45 or more for others.

REFERENCES

ABEL, THEODORA M. Figure drawings and facial disfigurement. Amer. J. Orthopsychiat., 1953, 23, 253–261.
ALBEE, G. W., & HAMLIN, R. M. An investigation of the reliability and validity of

judgments inferred from drawings. *J. clin. Psychol.*, 1949, 5, 389–392.

ALBEE, G. W., & HAMLIN, R. M. Judgment of adjustment from drawings: the applicability of rating scale methods. *J. clin. Psychol.*, 1950, 6, 363–365.

BLANCHARD, HELEN M. A preliminary study of the drawing of the human figure by brain injured children. Unpublished master's thesis, Univer. of Denver, 1952.

DIPBOYE, W. J. An analysis of an aspect of counselor style by topical discussion units. Unpublished doctoral dissertation, Univer. of Missouri, 1952.

GOODENOUGH, FLORENCE L., & HARRIS, D. B. Studies in the psychology of children's drawings: II. 1928–1949. *Psychol. Bull.*, 1950, 47, 369–433.

LEHNER, G. F., & GUNDERSON, E. K. Reliability of graphic indices in a projective test (the draw-a-person). *J. clin. Psychol.*, 1952, 8, 125–128.

McGOWAN, J. F. Client anticipations and expectancies as related to initial interview performance and perceptions. Unpublished doctoral dissertation, Univer. of Missouri, 1955.

MACHOVER, KAREN. *Personality projection in the drawing of the human figure.* Springfield, Ill.: Charles C Thomas, 1949.

MACHOVER, KAREN. Discussion of Theodora M. Abel: Figure drawings and facial disfigurement. *Amer. J. Orthopsychiat.*, 1953, 23, 262–264. (a)

MACHOVER, KAREN. Human figure drawings of children. *J. proj. Tech.*, 1953, 17, No. 1, 85–91. (b)

SILVERSTEIN, A. B., & ROBINSON, H. A. The representation of orthopedic disability in children's figure drawings. *J. consult. Psychol.*, 1956, 20, 333–341.

SIMMS, NANCY. An analysis of the human figure drawings of orthopedic and non-orthopedic children. Unpublished master's thesis, Univer. of Nebraska, 1951.

TOLOR, A. Teacher's judgments of the popularity of children from their human figure drawings. *J. clin. Psychol.*, 1955, 11, 158–162.

TOLOR, A., & TOLOR, B. Judgments of children's popularity from their human figure drawings. *J. proj. Tech.*, 1955, 19, 170–176.

39

Eye-Ear Emphasis in the Draw-a-Person Test as Indicating Ideas of Reference[1]

ALBERT V. GRIFFITH
AND DOUGLAS A. R. PEYMAN

The authors in this study found support for the hypothesis that eye-ear emphasis on the DAP is associated with ideas of reference. They were able to do this by referring to behavioral criteria as obtained from the case histories. Had they relied on psychiatric classification as a criterion, i.e., selecting paranoids on the assumption that they would have ideas of reference, their hypothesis would not have been substantiated. The study is important in emphasizing the superiority of actual overt behavior to psychiatric classification in the attempted validation of projective techniques.

The purpose of this study was to relate eye-ear emphasis in the DAP with the trait "ideas of reference." The Ss were drawn from 745 male patients who had consecutively entered Bryce Hospital. The DAP drawings of this population were jointly scanned by two staff psychologists. Eighteen Ss were selected as emphasizing eyes and/or ears. Only those Ss were selected when both judges were in agreement as to the presence of the sign. A conservative position was taken; i.e., only those Ss were chosen where eye and/or ear emphasis was obvious. An 8 per cent

[1] The authors wish to thank Clem C. Nesmith and Waters C. Paul, staff psychologists at Bryce Hospital, for serving as judges in the present study.

681

sample ($N = 58$), which was to serve as the control group, was then randomly selected from the remaining population.

The 76 hospital records (eye-ear emphasis $N = 18$; control $N = 58$) were randomly presented to two other staff psychologists. Judgments were jointly made by the latter as to the presence of ideas of reference for each S. These judgments were not based on any psychometric data. As the two judges worked together, no estimate of reliability was made. Both judges felt that it was much easier to judge the presence of ideas of reference than to decide in what diagnostic category each S should be placed.

Eleven of the 18 Ss in the eye-ear emphasis group were judged as having ideas of reference, while 13 of the 58 Ss in the control group were so judged. A statistical analysis of the data indicated that a significant difference existed between the two groups $\chi^2 = 7.754$ for one df; $P < .01$). It is concluded that the hypothesis is confirmed.

Swensen's judgment (1957, p. 461) that the DAP is of use in clinical work only as a rough screening device was based on studies that had certain defects of design. Most of these studies used psychiatric diagnoses as the criteria. The reliability of psychiatric diagnoses, however, has been questioned for years. If psychiatric diagnosis (paranoid involvement) had been the criterion in the present study, nonsignificant results would have been obtained. Only 5 of the 18 Ss in the eye-ear emphasis group were diagnosed as having paranoid involvement, while 8 Ss in the control group were so diagnosed.

What was being tested in most of the studies reviewed by Swensen was the efficiency of DAP signs in predicting various psychiatric labels. The most important thing for the clinician, however, is the validity of the sign; i.e., *when the sign is present*, does it signify beyond chance expectancy a given condition or trait? The present study was designed to investigate this type of problem. The result was that eye-ear emphasis in the DAP was demonstrated to be predictive of ideas of reference.

Our data indicate that eye-ear emphasis in the DAP, while valid, is inefficient in predicting ideas of reference. This should not surprise us, as it is generally recognized that tests are inefficient in predicting personality variables.

REFERENCE

SWENSEN, C. H., JR. Empirical evaluations of human figure drawings. *Psychol. Bull.*, 1957, 54, 431–466.

40

Signs of Homosexuality in Human Figure Drawings

ARMIN GRAMS AND LAWRENCE RINDER

Can homosexuality be determined from DAP drawings? Twenty-five delinquent boys who had committed homosexual acts were compared with 25 matched nonhomosexual delinquent boys. Fifteen Machover signs of homosexuality, as well as two other signs, were tested. None proved successful in differentiating the groups.

The conclusion is weakened by the failure of the authors to demonstrate that the boys committing homosexual acts were in fact homosexuals. It is known that occasionally homosexuals marry, but this does not truly make them heterosexuals. It makes no more sense to consider a young adolescent a homosexual because he has engaged in one homosexual act in which he was caught. Particularly does this classification seem hazardous if the boys committed the homosexual act while in the institution in which they were confined. Indeed, the ability to engage in social–sexual relationships yielding mutual satisfaction when no females were available might well have been counted as a sign of adjustment.

This study investigates the validity of the 15 signs in human figure drawing which Machover (1949) lists as predictive of homosexuality. Fifty adolescent inmates of a state training school were divided on the basis of homosexual experience into two groups matched for age, schooling, IQ, and race. Each subject was asked first to draw a person

683

and then to draw a person of the sex opposite that of the first-drawn figure. Three psychologists rated the drawings for the presence of signs purported to be indicative of homosexuality. To facilitate rating, Machover's signs were stated objectively as follows:

1. Ear large or heavily lined or much detail.
2. Detectable delineation of hips or buttocks.
3. Failure to complete drawing below waist.
4. Heavy line of demarcation at waist.
5. Failure to draw "V" of crotch.
6. Presence of shading on lips.
7. Pants transparent (legs showing through).
8. Naked presence of sexual organs (genitals only).
9. Trousers only clothing shaded.
10. Female figure transparent below waist.
11. Male nose large, erased, and redrawn.
12. Phallic foot (length at least three times width and/or shaded tip).
13. Belt shaded and speared to right of figure.
14. Presence of eyelashes.
15. Drawing of female figure first.

The extent to which all judges rated a sign present or absent in a drawing became the index of rating reliability. Agreement on the drawings of homosexuals was 76.5 per cent, on the drawings of controls, 83.1 per cent.

Three of the signs (1, 2, 4) resulted in chi squares whose P values were between .10 and .20, one (5) resulted in a chi square with a P value between .20 and .30, and three (12, 14, 15) resulted in chi squares whose P values were between .50 and .70. The eight remaining signs resulted in chi squares whose P values exceeded .70. Thus, none of the signs proved to have individual validity. To determine the predictive significance of the 15 signs taken as a group, the total number of signs present in a drawing was correlated with homosexuality and nonhomosexual experience. A point-biserial r of .15, not significant at the .05 level of confidence, was obtained. Thus, neither individually nor collectively did the signs studied validly predict the criterion.

REFERENCE

MACHOVER, KAREN. *Personality projection in the drawing of the human figure.* Springfield, Ill.: Charles C Thomas, 1949.

41

The Goodenough Draw-a-Man Test and Signs of Maladjustment in Kindergarten Children

JULIA R. VANE AND
VIRGINIA W. EISEN

This is one of the few articles to report a favorable outcome in the attempted validation of the DAP. The results are in keeping with the belief of the editor that projective techniques should prove most useful in the assessment of young children. It is further noteworthy that whereas the five-year-olds who were maladjusted could be differentiated by the use of four "signs," these signs lost much of their efficacy for the six-year-olds. A study by Stoltz and Coltharp[a] shows, in fact, that fourth-graders' DAP performances did not correlate with behavioral criteria of maladjustment. The reason for the loss of validity with advancing age is that the signs at the younger ages consist largely of omissions of parts of the body, but any omission is rare for a child of ten. The search for graphic correlates of behavior for older children and adults so far has not been very successful.

Problem

This study attempts to determine the sensitivity of the Goodenough Draw-a-Man Test to the school adjustment of kindergarten children as

---

a R. E. Stoltz and Frances C. Coltharp. "Clinical Judgment and the Draw-a-Person Test," *Journal of Consulting Psychology*, 25 (1961), 43–45.

rated by their teachers. Among the figure-drawing characteristics found to be related to maladjustment in children by Koppitz, Sullivan, Blythe, and Shelton (1959), Machover (1950), and Eisen (1951) were: excessive use of shading, figure placed in one corner of page, figure two inches or less in height, unfinished figure, slanting figure, three or more figures drawn spontaneously, figure with no eyes or with vacant eyes, figure showing separation between parts of the body, figure with no body, figure with no mouth or with no arms, grotesque figure. Only the last four signs showed promise for differentiating the well-adjusted from the poorly adjusted kindergarten children.

Subjects

A total of 662 kindergarten children were tested in two separate samples in March, 1960, and May, 1961. No overage children or repeaters were included. The 1960 sample included 307 children from five New York schools and one New Jersey school. The New York schools represented all socioeconomic levels except farmers and included Negroes and whites. The New Jersey school represented white middle and upper socioeconomic levels. The school populations ranged in mean IQ from 103 to 115. The mean age at time of testing was 5–9, with a range from 5–3 to 6–5.

The 1961 sample included 355 children from six New York schools. Five of these schools were the same as those used in obtaining the 1960 sample. The sixth school had a mean IQ of 100 and represented mostly lower socioeconomic levels. The mean age at time of testing was 5–11, range 5–5 to 6–5.

Procedure

The Goodenough Draw-a-Man Test was administered to groups of 10 to 12 children by the school psychologist. The directions were: "Draw a picture of a man, the best man you know how. Draw a whole man." All children were urged, "Finish the man. Don't leave anything out." This was repeated once to children who claimed they had finished, if they had omitted an important part.

During the week the Goodenough Test was administered, the kindergarten teachers, six in 1960 and eight in 1961, were asked to rate each child on a nine-item behavior-rating scale. The children were divided into "Good," "Fair," and "Poor" adjustment groups on the basis of scores on the behavior-rating scale.

Results

Table 41-1 shows that drawings made by children who were rated as showing poor adjustment contained significantly more of the four signs "grotesque," "no body," "no mouth," and "no arms" than did the drawings by children who were rated as showing good or fair adjustment.

TABLE 41-1   *Percentage of Drawings Containing Signs Associated with Maladjustment in the Three Rated Groups*

	1960 SAMPLE (N = 307) ADJUSTMENT RATINGS			1961 SAMPLE (N = 355) ADJUSTMENT RATINGS		
	GOOD	FAIR	POOR	GOOD	FAIR	POOR
SIGNS	N = 83	N = 179	N = 45	N = 104	N = 209	N = 42
Grotesque[a]	0	2	13[c]	0	1	7
No body	4	8	27[c]	13	11	45[d]
No mouth	1	7	15[b]	5	7	19[b]
No arms	6	15	13	6	12	31[c]
One or more signs	11	22	47[d]	20	26	71[d]

[a] A grotesque drawing shows gross distortions. It is scored rigidly. Samples of figures that would be scored as grotesque may be found in Goodenough's (1950) Specimen Drawings, Figures 1, 2, 3, 4, 17, 63, 72, and 77. None of the other Specimen Drawings would be scored as grotesque by our criteria.

[b] differs from good group at the .01 level
[c] differs from fair and good groups at the .01 level
[d] differs from fair and good groups at the .001 level

In order to give consideration to developmental changes taking place even within this relatively narrow age range, a comparison was made of the percentage of signs occurring in the drawings of the younger and older children. The 1960 and 1961 samples were combined for this analysis. Table 41-2 indicates that whereas it was possible to select 76 per cent of the poorly adjusted children, using one or more of the four signs, at age 5-6 to 5-11, only 45 per cent could be selected at age 6-0 to 6-5. This same trend was shown when the two samples were treated separately. The possibility that the older children were better adjusted was negated by the fact that the percentage of children rated by their teachers as showing good, fair, and poor adjustment was practically the same in both age groups. Reference to Goodenough's norms (1950) clarifies the finding. The norms indicate that by the time children reach the age of six, 85 to 90 per cent include mouth, body, and arms in their drawings. Failure to include these items in drawing a man at age six and above may be very significant in individual cases, but the absence of these items is so infrequent at this age level and above that it minimizes their practical value as indicators of maladjustment.

In view of the fact that the Goodenough Draw-a-Man Test was designed to measure intelligence, the question arose whether the four signs merely differentiated bright from less bright children. To test this possibility, it was necessary to hold the intelligence level constant. To do this, children in the poor adjustment group were matched with those in the good adjustment group on the basis of IQ's obtained from a vocabulary test[1] given at the time the Draw-a-Man Test was administered. A second matching was made on the basis of the Goodenough IQ's. Matching was rigid, reducing the number of pairs obtainable, but permitting more accurate comparisons. Each child was matched with another from his own school. The difference in IQ was no more than seven points. Of the 37 pairs obtained, 12 had identical IQ's and 16 varied by only one to three points.

TABLE 41–2   *Percentage of Signs of Maladjustment Occurring in Drawings of Younger (Age 5–6 to 5–11) and Older (Age 6–0 to 6–5) Children*

| | | | ADJUSTMENT RATINGS | | |
SIGNS	AGE GROUP	N	GOOD	FAIR	POOR
Grotesque	Younger	337	0	2	14
	Older	272	0	0	5
No body	Younger	337	11	10	45
	Older	272	5	6	26
No mouth	Younger	337	3	6	29
	Older	272	4	5	8
No arms	Younger	337	8	21	26
	Older	272	4	6	18
One or more signs	Younger	337	18	27	76
	Older	272	13	16	45

The results showed that of the 21 pairs of children matched on the basis of the vocabulary IQ, the good adjustment group had a mean IQ of 102.7 and the poor adjustment group a mean IQ of 103. None of the children in the good adjustment group had drawings which showed any of the four signs of maladjustment, whereas the drawings of 45 per cent of the children in the poor adjustment group showed one or more signs. Of the 16 pairs matched on the basis of the Goodenough IQ, the good adjustment group had a mean IQ of 108.0

---

[1] Vocabulary test standardized by Vane on over 1,000 children aged four through nine years. Correlation with Stanford-Binet Scale .77 for 100 kindergarten children. To be published.

and the poor adjustment group a mean IQ of 108.5. Again, none of the children in the good adjustment group had drawings which showed any of the four signs, whereas 31 per cent of the poor adjustment group showed one or more signs. In both instances, the difference between the groups was significant at the .01 level.

The fact that, when intelligence was held constant, the percentage of the poorly adjusted children identified by the signs decreased was felt to be related to the difficulty of finding matches among the good adjustment group for children in the poor adjustment group whose IQ's were below 85. Children who have IQ's this low almost always show signs of poor adjustment in school even at the kindergarten level. This is not surprising, in view of the fact that to be successful in school usually requires average intelligence. Children with less endowment are limited in their ability to adapt readily to the demands of the school situation and begin to show evidence of this early in their school careers.

Repeated studies have shown that more boys than girls evidence behavior problems, school failure, and poor school adjustment. Our data indicate that this trend exists in our kindergarten samples. More boys (17 per cent) than girls (8 per cent) were rated by their teachers as showing poor adjustment, and the drawings of more boys (28 per cent) than girls (16 per cent) showed one or more of the four signs indicative of maladjustment.

To investigate whether the signs indicative of maladjustment in the kindergarten might also be related to adjustment a year later, the first-grade teachers of 150 of the children who had comprised the 1960 sample were asked to rate the children on the same behavior-rating scale. The teachers rated the children in June, 1961 (15 months after they had completed the kindergarten Draw-a-Man Test), and had no knowledge of the ratings the children had received in kindergarten or the outcome of the Draw-a-Man Test.

TABLE 41–3 *Teachers' Ratings in Kindergarten and First Grade and the Percentage of Signs of Maladjustment in the Drawings of the Children Rated*

N	KINDERGARTEN RATINGS	FIRST-GRADE RATINGS	PERCENTAGE OF KINDERGARTEN DRAWINGS SHOWING SIGNS
14	Poor	Poor	50
16	Good, Fair	Poor	44
12	Poor	Fair, Good	33
12	Good	Fair	25
33	Fair	Fair	21
41	Fair	Good	10
22	Good	Good	9

Table 41-3 shows that the highest percentage of the signs of maladjustment in the drawings occurred in the group rated poor in both instances. The next highest percentage appeared in the group rated as good or fair by the kindergarten teacher but rated poor by their first-grade teachers. It would seem that kindergarten children whose drawings show any of the four signs of maladjustment, despite the fact that their adjustment is rated as good or fair by their teachers, should be considered as having possible problems. As might be expected, the children rated as good in both instances showed the smallest percentage of signs. Although the numbers in the subcategories of this part of the study are small, the results seem to lend validity to the predictive quality of the signs of maladjustment shown in the kindergarten drawings.

Summary

The Goodenough Draw-a-Man Test was evaluated as a tool for predicting the school adjustment of kindergarten children. Drawings were obtained from 662 kindergarten children ranging in age from 5-3 to 6-5. The same children were rated by their kindergarten teachers on a nine-item behavior-rating scale. The results indicated that there are at least four signs which identify a fairly high percentage of children who show poor adjustment in kindergarten. Many drawing signs considered by other investigators to be related to poor adjustment in children were not found predictive at this age level.

REFERENCES

Eisen, Virginia W. Comparison of human figure drawings by behavior problem and normal control boys. Unpublished doctoral dissertation, Fordham Univer., 1951.

Goodenough, Florence L. *Measurement of intelligence by drawings.* Yonkers-on-Hudson: World Book Co., 1926.

Goodenough, Florence L., & Harris, D. B. Studies in the psychology of children's drawings. *Psychol. Bull.*, 1950, 47, 369–433.

Koppitz, Elizabeth M., Sullivan, J., Blythe, D. D., & Shelton, J. Prediction of first grade school achievement with the Bender Gestalt test and human figure drawings. *J. clin. Psychol.*, 1959, 15, 164–168.

Machover, Karen. Sex differences in the developmental pattern of children as seen in human figure drawings. In A. I. Rabin, & Mary R. Haworth (Eds.), *Projective techniques with children.* New York: Grune & Stratton, 1950. Pp. 238–257.

42

Hostility as a Factor in the Clinician's Personality as it Affects His Interpretation of Projective Drawings (H-T-P)[1]

EMANUEL F. HAMMER AND
ZYGMUNT A. PIOTROWSKI

In this study, a strong relationship is found between hostility attributed to subjects by clinical trainees from their House-Tree-Person (H-T-P) drawings and hostility attributed to the trainees by their supervisors. The interpretation of the H-T-P by the trainees, therefore, represented a joint projective effort on the part of clinician and subject.

A question not discussed by the authors is whether this phenomenon is peculiar to the H-T-P or whether it is typical of projective tests in general. Little evidence is available from other tests, because few researchers have specifically measured the projection of the examiner in the scoring. One hypothesis which may be entertained is that those tests whose validity has been mediocre or worse may provide the most fertile ground for examiner projection. Regrettably, there is no evidence on this question, and it is to be hoped that future research will determine not only whether clinicians project aspects of their own personality onto the protocols but also under what conditions projection is increased or decreased.

[1] Grateful acknowledgment is made to Mrs. Susan Deri for her interpretation and ranking of the Szondi profiles and to John N. Buck for his fruitful suggestions and criticisms.

691

Previous studies in projective techniques have been aimed at obtaining insight into the manner in which personality dynamics, needs, conflicts, and phantasies of a subject are revealed by his responses to a projective device. The study of the role of the clinician and the significance of his personality factors in the interpretation of projective techniques have awaited study until the establishment of working tenets in regard to the interaction of the personality of the subject with the projective material. If psychodiagnostic tools are to be sharpened and made more valid, investigation must now be made of the correlation between the interpreter's own needs, conflicts, and phantasies and the interpretations he makes from a patient's projective protocols.

A study by Bruner and Goodman (1947) highlighting the connection between needs and perception deserves mention in this regard. It was found that poor subjects overestimated the size of coins more than did rich subjects. This was considered to be a reflection of the greater financial need of the poor children and was taken to substantiate the hypothesis that needs affect perception and judgment.

The present study was set up to investigate the question of whether or not clinicians' needs, as with the needs of the subjects in the study by Bruner and Goodman above, influence and distort their apperception or "reading" of a set of projective protocols, namely, a series of drawings of House, Tree, and Person (H-T-P).

There has already been some experimentation done on the effect of the clinicians' personality on his rating of the overt behavior of subjects by Frenkel-Brunswik. She states that "drive ratings may be influenced by . . . the intensity of the drive in question in the personality of the rater" (1951, p. 390). She found that raters showed a stronger tendency to project when rating children of their sex than when rating children of the opposite sex. Hence, she concludes that "we must acknowledge that there are various subjective factors that seem to influence the perception of others even in clinically trained observers" (p. 393).

Does the same hold true for clinically trained projective testers? This question is the aim of the present study. The particular trait (the expression of which represents a need) chosen for study in this experiment was that which is roughly referred to as "hostility" or "aggression." The decision to focus on this personality area grew out of the writers' experiences which have led them to feel that the two areas in which clinicians tend to differ most in their interpretations are those of hostility and sexuality. The former was investigated in the present study; and the latter is to be investigated in a subsequent study.

Procedure

The freehand drawings of House, Tree, and Person had been used in a previous study (Hammer, 1953) as a device to tap the personality of 400 children of elementary-school age ranging from grades 1 to 8. Of these 400, 148 were Negro children (Hammer n.d.,c) and 252 white children in gratifyingly representative (from a socioeconomic viewpoint) semiurban, semirural schools.

The H-T-P was employed because it is a quick and easy-to-administer projective technique which seems to be penalized less by group administration than most other projective devices. It was employed also because four of the six clinicians[2] who served as interpreters had received special training in the H-T-P technique directly under John N. Buck (1948a; 1948b; 1950), its innovator, and the remaining two had received their H-T-P training at Lynchburg State Colony, the institution at which this technique had been developed.

In the present study, these 400 H-T-P's were given to the clinician-judges to be rated independently on a scale of aggression from zero to 2. A rating of 0 represented no apparent aggression or hostility, a rating of 1 represented mild aggression or hostility, while a rating of 2 represented severe aggression and hostility. In regard to giving a rating of 1 or 2, the clinicians were instructed to give the former rating if in a psychological report on the subject's H-T-P they would ordinarily mention that there was mild aggression or hostility present and a rating of 2 if they would ordinarily cite severe aggression or hostility as present.

Three clinicians served as judges for the drawings of all eight grades of children, while three additional clinicians served as judges for the third, fifth, and seventh grades in order to afford the opportunities for a spot check.

Correlations of the judgments of the three principal judges were then computed. All six judges, principal and secondary, were put in rank order according to the degree of hostility they apperceived in the H-T-P's (of the students in the third, fifth, and seventh grades) they had rated. This rank order was then compared with the rank order in which the judges were rated for hostility by one of the writers, then supervisor of intern training at the institution at which the study was conducted. The supervisor rated the clinicians on the basis of the degree of overt aggression and hostility manifested by them in their interaction with patients and staff members. The clinicians were placed in rank order of hostility before they judged the drawings, and they did not know of

---

[2] Three of the six were experienced staff psychologists, while the other three were on an intern level.

the dual end to which their ratings would be put until after their data were handed in and their consent obtained.

The drawings were rated by the six clinicians on the basis of the following qualitative signs for aggression and hostility from the *Guide for Qualitative Research with the H-T-P*: (1954a.)

The drawing of attic windows which are open implies hostile phantasy which causes the person guilt. It has been observed that subjects who are extremely prone to phantasy in hostile fashion frequently provide themselves with what might be called "safety valves" by drawing open windows in the area symbolizing phantasy thinking, the roof.

Windows drawn without panes, curtains or shutters (hence, like the "keyhole" tree below, another depiction of unrelieved, enclosed, white space) may imply hostility.

A tree which consists of a looping line representing the tree's branch structure (unclosed at its junction with the trunk) and two vertical lines closed or unclosed at the trunk's base (thus resembling a key-hole) is taken to indicate strong hostile impulses.

Two-dimensional branches that are drawn resembling clubs or sharply pointed branches or leaves, especially with little organization, imply strong hostility.

A mutilated Person, or a degraded Tree or House, it goes without saying, serves to underscore the patient's hostility. The use of degrading details which serve to symbolize feelings of aggressive hostility may include such depiction as an outhouse drawn beside a House that is otherwise a mansion, a large conspicuous garbage can drawn on the front porch, or a dog drawn as urinating against the trunk of the Tree.

Sharply pointed fingers and toes, as well as other similarly treated details are a reflection of aggressive tendencies, as are teeth prominently presented in the drawing of the face.

Sharply squared shoulders in the drawing of the Person connote over-defensive, hostile attitudes.

Well-outlined, but unshaded hair, in the drawing of the Person suggests hostile phantasy concerning sexual matters.

Arms that are drawn folded across the chest suggest attitudes of suspicion and hostility.

The Person carrying weapons such as guns, blackjacks, etc., clearly indicates aggressive and hostile tendencies.

The Person presented in a threatening attitude (example, fist upraised, etc.) bespeaks aggressive hostility.

Drawings made conspicuously too large for the page, without adequate form page space framing them (particularly when they touch or almost touch the page's side margins), tend to indicate a feeling of great frustration produced by a restraining environment, with concomitant feelings of hostility and a desire to react aggressively (either against the environment or the self, or both) (Hammer, 1954b).

The qualitative points listed above were employed as broad guide-posts in an effort to increase, in some measure, the objectivity of the qualitative approach employed in the present study. The greater the number or intensity of signs of hostility and aggression in a set of drawings, the more inclined the clinicians were to go up the continuum from mild to severe in their ratings. Since the dynamic interrelationship of a sign with all other signs available is of prime importance, however, the drawings were viewed as a Gestalt. An attempt was made to take the total constellation into account at all times.

The six clinicians then submitted to six administrations of the Szondi Test each. The Szondi was chosen as a projective technique to tap the degree of hostility and aggression in each of the clinicians because it represented the clinical tool with which these particular clinicians had, as yet, had no experience and little orientation. In regard to the Szondi technique, the clinicians were, for the most part unsophisticated and uninformed. The Szondi profiles of the six clinicians were submitted to Mrs. Susan Deri for her to place the clinicians in rank order in regard to the degree to which, in her opinion, each clinician possessed hostile and aggressive impulses. This rank order was then correlated with the rank order of the clinicians in regard to the degree of aggression and hostility they interpreted in the 400 H-T-P's.

Results

Rank-difference correlations among the ranks of the three judges were .74, .78, and .84, with standard errors of .031, .030, and .014 respectively.

All six clinicians — the three main and the three secondary judges— were placed in rank order in regard to the degree of hostility they manifested in interpersonal relationships as judged by the supervisor. A comparison of this rank order with the rank order of the degree of hostility they saw in the H-T-P drawings is presented in Table 42–1.

A rank-order correlation of .94 with a standard error of .48 is obtained.

The correlation between the rank order of the clinicians in regard to the degree to which they apperceived aggression and hostility in the H-T-P drawings and the degree to which they revealed aggression and hostility on the Szondi, as a personality component, is also .94 with a standard error of .48. Table 42–2 indicates that a reversal in rank order is found in regard to clinicians C and D.

A similar correlation of .94 with the same standard error of .48 is obtained between the rank order of the clinicians' aggression as judged by the supervisor and as judged by Mrs. Deri's analysis of their Szondi profiles.

As high a correlation was found, then, between the degree of hostility the clinicians "saw" in the H-T-P's and the degree of their own hostility as judged by both their supervisor and Mrs. Deri as exists between the judgments of the supervisor and Mrs. Deri.

TABLE 42–1   *Comparison of Rank Order of the Average Hostility Index* Given the 400 Drawings by Each of Six Clinicians and the Rank Order of the Degree of Hostility in Each Clinican as Judged by His Supervisor*

CLINICIAN-JUDGE	AVERAGE HOSTILITY INDEX AWARDED THE DRAWINGS	RANK ORDER[a] OF HOSTILITY INDEX AWARDED THE DRAWINGS	RANK ORDER[a] OF SUPERVISOR'S RATING	DIFFERENCE IN RANK ORDER
A	0.49	1	1	0
B	0.51	2	3	1
C	0.57	3	2	1
D	0.63	4	4	0
E	0.90	5	5	0
F	1.12	6	6	0

* A rating of zero represents no apparent aggression and hostility, 1 represents mild and 2 represents severe aggression and hostility.
a In order of increasing hostility.

Discussion

To turn to the question of the correlation of the judgments made by the three main judges, correlations ranging between .74 and .84 suggest a reasonably high degree of reliability among clinicians rating qualitative factors such as hostility and/or aggression on the basis of the H-T-P In spite of these reassuringly high correlations, however, it appears that much subjectivity enters into and distorts the interpretation of these factors on projective drawings.

The supervisor's judgment[3] of the degree of the clinicians' hostility and aggression as manifested in their interrelationship with patients and staff members was found to correlate to a marked degree with the proneness of the clinicians to see hostility in the drawings of other subjects.

This finding may be partially explained by the differences in *sensitivity*[4] on the part of the various clinicians to the particular personality factor, aggression. In addition, the differences among the clinicians' interpretations of the projective technique is probably further due to the

[3] The validity of the supervisor's judgments was supported by the correlation with the clinicians' Szondi protocols.
[4] This term is used as a concept denoting *sensitivity* to the perception of existing situations or stimuli (in accord with the concept of Bellak and Abt that a stimulus that is congruent with a pre-existing configuration is more readily perceived than one that is not).

fact that when interpreting a projective technique, clinicians tend to project[5] as well as interpret. This conclusion appears to be supported by (1) the relatively high correlation between the supervisor's ratings of hostility in the clinicians and the degree to which they saw hostility in the 400 H-T-P's they interpreted, (2) the relatively high correlation between the degree of aggression and hostility in each clinician as suggested by his Szondi profile and the degree to which he apperceived aggression and hostility in the projective drawings he interpreted and (3) (Brink 1944) the fact that clinician F, for instance, awarded the drawings an average hostility index which approaches the point of being twice the mean hostility index awarded by the other five judges (so marked a deviation, on the part of one trained clinician, from the other five suggests the operation of *projected* hostility, beyond *sensitivity* on his part).

TABLE 42–2   *Comparison of Rank Order of the Average Hostility Index* Given the 400 Drawings by Each of Six Clinicians and the Rank Order of the Degree of Hostility in Each Clinician as Judged by His Szondi Profile*

CLINICIAN-JUDGE	AVERAGE HOSTILITY INDEX AWARDED THE DRAWINGS	RANK ORDER[a] OF HOSTILITY INDEX AWARDED THE DRAWINGS	RANK ORDER[a] OF HOSTILITY ON THE BASIS OF SZONDI	DIFFERENCE IN RANK ORDER
A	0.49	1	1	0
B	0.51	2	2	0
C	0.57	3	4	1
D	0.63	4	3	1
E	0.90	5	5	0
F	1.12	6	6	0

* A rating of zero represents no apparent aggression and hostility, 1 represents mild and 2 represents severe aggression and hostility.
a In order of increasing hostility.

Since all visual perception involves the process of selection to greater or less degree, it is to be expected that there would be individual differences between clinicians in the extent to which they interpret various personality factors from projective drawings of their subjects. Anyone who has had experience as a supervisor of psychology interns or has worked in a setting with many psychologist colleagues has been impressed with the shortcomings of the role objective factors play in the

---

[5] *Projection* is used to denote the process of attributing one's own feelings, conflicts, etc. to outside stimuli, people, or situations. This concept, when applied to projective tests, is broadened to include not only unacceptable and repressed but also acceptable and conscious tendencies.

interpretation of projective techniques and the degree to which sub-jective factors color such interpretations. Just as a subject's performance on a projective technique is a function of his personality, his needs, conflicts, desires, and past experiences, so, too, although to a lesser degree is the interpretation of a projective protocol influenced by the personality pattern of the interpreter.

Projective interpreting deals with material which is emotional, often-times subjective, and usually partly unconscious—material which the interpreter finds difficulty in viewing in a wholly objective manner. Projective drawings produce latent as well as manifest, symbolic as well as concrete, material, some of which cannot be directly assessed but must first be perceived and interpreted through the eyes of the interpreter. It is at this point that his own needs may infiltrate and influence his interpretive formulations.

Conclusions

As the results of the study were obtained from one group of clinicians only, and that group a small one consisting of but six members, the reliability of the results should be tested on other and larger groups. The following tentative conclusions, however (the further reliability and validity of which can be established only by future and more extensive studies), seem justified.

1. There is a relatively high degree of reliability among clinicians in the present investigation in their ability to judge the degree of aggression and hostility as manifested in a subject's freehand drawing of a House-Tree-Person.

2. In spite of this high degree of reliability, the clinicians' interpretations appear to have been, in part, determined by their own projections and areas of sensitivity.

3. Content or qualitative analysis of projective technique protocols, notably projective drawings, should therefore be employed with caution until more objective research is available and the subjective aspect of interpretation is controlled or minimized.

4. More extensive studies of the role played by the personality of the clinician in interpreting projective techniques should be undertaken with larger groups of clinicians and in investigation of other projective techniques such as the Rorschach and TAT.

REFERENCES

BENDER, LAURETTA. Art and therapy in the mental disturbances of children. *J. nerv. ment. Dis.*, 1937, 86, 249–263.

BRINK, MARIA. The mental hygiene value of children's art work. *Amer. J. Ortho-psychiat.*, 1944, 14, 136–146.

BRUNER, J., & GOODMAN, C. Value and need as organizing factors in perception. *J. abnorm. soc. Psychol.*, 1947, 42, 33–44.

BUCK, J. N. The H-T-P. *J. clin. Psychol.*, 1948, 4, 151–159. (a)

BUCK, J. N. The H-T-P technique, a qualitative and quantitative scoring manual. *Monogr. supp., J. clin. Psychol.*, 1948, 4, 1–120. (b)

BUCK, J. N. Administration and interpretation of the H-T-P test. Richmond, Va.: VA Hospital, 1950. Pp. 1–87 (mimeographed).

FLEMING, JOAN. Observations on the use of finger-painting in the treatment of adult patients with personality disorders. *Charact. & Pers.*, 1940, 8, 301–310.

FRENKEL-BRUNSWIK, ELSE. Personality theory and perception. In R. R. Blake & G. V. Ramsey (Eds.), *Perception, an approach to personality.* New York: Ronald, 1951. Pp. 356–419.

HAMMER, E. F. Frustration-aggression hypothesis extended to socio-racial areas: comparison of Negro and white children's H-T-P's. *Psychiat. Quart.*, 1953, 27, 597–607.

HAMMER, E. F. Guide for qualitative research with the H-T-P. *J. gen. Psychol.*, 1954, 51, 41–60. (a)

HAMMER, E. F. Comparison of intellectual functioning level of Negro children and adolescents on two intelligence tests, one an emergency scale. *J. genet. Psychol.*, 1954, 84, 85–93. (b)

LEVY, J. The use of art techniques in treatment of children's behavior problems. *J. Psychoaesthetics*, 1934, 39, 258–260.

NAUMBURG, MARGARET. Studies of the free art expression of behavior problem children and adolescents as a means of diagnosis and therapy. *Nerv. ment. dis. Monogr.*, 1947, 71, 225.

PIOTROWSKI, Z. A. A Rorschach compendium—revised and enlarged. In J. A. Brussel et al., *A Rorschach training manual.* Utica: State Hospital Press, 1950. Pp. 33–86.

PRECKER, J. A. Painting and drawing in personality assessment. *J. proj. Tech.*, 1950, 14, 262–286.

SCHMIDL-WAEHNER, T. Formal criteria for the analysis of children's drawings. *Amer. J. Orthopsychiat.*, 1942, 12, 95–104.

WAEHNER, T. S. Interpretations of spontaneous drawings and paintings. *Genet. psychol. Monogr.*, 1946, 33, 70.

WOLFF, W. The personality of the pre-school child. New York: Grune & Stratton, 1946.

PART V

BENDER-GESTALT

43

The Bender-Gestalt: A Review and a Perspective

FRED Y. BILLINGSLEA

It is rather surprising to note that such a brief test as the Bender-Gestalt (B-G), which involves copying nine geometric designs composed of dots, lines, angles, and curves, can be applied to such a broad spectrum of purposes. The B-G has been used, however, for personality description, as a measure of intelligence, and to diagnose brain damage. Stranger still is the fact that, despite this broad usage, surprisingly few generalizations can be made about the test. Various scoring systems have been employed, with great variability of results from one study to the next. Further, there is no hard core of accepted signs that have proved valid for any of the three tasks mentioned above. Usually a researcher replicating a study that resulted in one set of signs will reject the majority of these signs and find only a few still valid. He is also apt to discover new signs that, however, will not be validated by his successor, who will find new signs, etc., ad absurdum, ad nauseam.

The review of Billingslea indicates few hard conclusions one can draw from this test. Even in those studies where, for example, the B-G shows some diagnostic validity for detecting organicity, one may ask if it was necessary to diagnose this state through the use of the B-G or if simple observation could have yielded the same conclusion. More cost-oriented research is needed to determine just how helpful the B-G really is for the diagnosis of subtle behavior disorders.

The Bender-Gestalt Test (B-G) was built on the premise that accurate visual-motor behavior is a skilled act. Its nine geometrical designs are

composed of dots, lines, angles, and curves combined in a variety of
relationships. Individuals see and reproduce these geometrical designs
differently. It is believed by those utilizing this tool that there is a
"normalcy range" in the manner of reproducing the designs that is
highly correlated with the hypothetical average person. They further
assume that deviations from the normal range reflect deviations from
the average individual in intellectual capacity and functioning, emotional
stability, perceptual relevancy, attitudinal logicality, need-gratification patterns, adequacy of defense mechanisms, and soundness of brain tissues
and chemistry.

The reader may recall that even before 1932 Bender began utilizing
Wertheimer's designs as a means of tapping such processes as intelligence in children and the mentally defective, schizophrenic reactions,
and the organic brain disturbances correlated with trauma or toxic
agents. Since then, she has published two manuals that have served as
standards (Bender, 1938; Bender, 1946). Bell (1948), Billingslea (1948),[1]
Buros (1949; 1953), Pascal and Suttell (1951), Peek and Quast (1951),
and Woltmann (1950) published manuals describing their own scoring
and interpretation system or giving textbook accounts of the method.
In them will be found an adequate bibliography of the field through
1950. Hutt (1953)[2] republished his 1945 restricted Army manual with
some modifications but still omitted supporting research data. Gobetz
(1953) was the last to publish a manual-type monograph. In 1952 the
attitudes toward this tool were so uncrystallized that Burton, writing in
Buros (1953), reported:

Watching an expert, trained at one of the military installations interpreting
a Bender was to witness the crudest sort of crystal gazing. It was particularly
dismaying to have to come to terms with the fact that this kind of operation
was taking place in many university clinical facilities, those presumed citadels
of the new dynamo-scientfic clinical psychology. Reaction on the part of
competent[3] clinical psychologists was swift and also somewhat overgeneralized.
The scorn, which was justifiably poured on the crystal gazing, extended to
the instrument itself (p. 287).

Many studies have been published yearly on specialized aspects of this
test. It seems, therefore, that an up-to-date survey of the literature should
permit a re-evaluation of this clinicial procedure and its original assumptions and thus help set the foundations for its use today. Though this
report attempts to be inclusive, it cannot be complete. Some literature

---

[1] In my monograph, a Mason General Hospital Bender-Gestalt guide is listed as
having an "anonymous" author. By personal communication, Edith E. Lord reported
having authored it.

[2] Authors recently entering the field frequently use the Army reference for Hutt.
It was "restricted" material, but his 1953 publication is readily available.

[3] Burton seems to be implying, even then, acceptance of the "standardized" clinician
concept advocated later by Hunt (1959) and Meehl (1954; 1956; 1957).

was not readily available, some was hidden under unrevealing titles, and some may have been overlooked unintentionally.

Figures

No outstanding changes in the original designs have been made that have been accepted. Barkley (1949) developed a set of raised plastic plates of the designs, which he had prophesied would assist in discrimination of intracranial organic pathology. No one else has published results from using his plates. In 1948 I urged acceptance of one standard set of figures; yet Popplestone (1956) was forced to lament the many variations apparent in the seven published versions of the B-G figures he surveyed. Subjective methods of evaluation (Bender, 1938; Hutt, 1953) and even the relatively objective scoring systems (Koppitz, 1958a; Pascal & Suttell, 1951) utilize the stimulus design as the standard referent against which to judge the experimental subject's or the patient's reproduction protocol. Willingness to disregard such variations in stimulus designs assumes, at best, that as long as the essential Gestalt of the individual designs is maintained from set to set, the requirements of all significant perceptual principles have been met. I continue to believe such an assumption is untenable. If that opinion is sound, it follows that psychologists, functioning as clinicians, warrant some of the embarrassing criticism received from experimental colleagues. It seems feasible to establish procedures permitting the adoption of a standard set of stimuli with minimal difficulty.

Scoring Systems: Children and Early Adolescents

Bender (1938; 1946) incorporated a table of responses for each year of age from ages 3 through 11 to "adults." The examiner compares his subjects' protocols with these responses and thus obtains a suggested mental age (MA) level. Applying her approach to 100 hospitalized youths aged 3 to 20, two Frenchmen, Hewyer and Angoulvent (1949), found their obtained B-G MA's equal to or better than those obtained from Binet-Simon or Stanford-Terman batteries. Then Wolfsohn (1951–52), faced with a flood of children immigrating into Israel, combined the B–G with Patterson Form Boards and Goodenough scoring of Draw-a-Man Test. With children 6 to 11 years he found a correlation of .73 with the Goodenough MA's and he expressed the belief that the B-G Test was apparently culture-free.

Modifications in Bender's procedure were first reported by Keller (1955), who employed "a priori judgment" methods to develop a scoring system involving maturation levels for use with mentally handicapped children. Though no full account of the system seems to have been published, an observer of the procedure reported it to be "simple and fast." Apparently 114 signs selected by Keller are employed on all nine figures, and then the sum of the "passes" on these signs is taken as a "total score." The signs related to each figure were roughly assembled in order of increasing difficulty. He reports a twelve-month retest reliability of .89 on 36 boys. Correlations with the Binet and the Grace Arthur ranged from .63 to .77 on 37 boys, age range 7 to 11. On a 13-year-old group of boys with a higher average IQ, similar correlations ranged from .43 to .67. It is interesting that Keller found the correlations between his B-G total scores and the Reading and Arithmetic achievement test scores to be higher than the correlations between the Grace Arthur and these tests, but lower than the correlations between the Binet and these same tests. The Pascal and Suttell (P&S) scoring system was applied by Baroff (1957) to the protocols of 84 mentally deficient twins. He felt his results discriminated successfully seven different MA levels and also validated certain signs suggestive of organic brain damage. He believed that norms in the form of scores plus qualitative signs could be established for his seven MA ranges, which would discriminate the endogenous mentally deficient individual. Only 4 of 15 signs selected by Byrd (1956) to score the B-G protocols of 200 maladjusted youths 8 to 16 years old and those of a group of "normals" tended to discriminate the two groups. The signs were: orderly sequence, change in curvature, closure difficulties, and rotation. The abstract of Wewetzer's (1956) paper reports that the partial scores of his scoring method for children's B-G protocols will "satisfactorily differentiate" brain-damaged children from normals. Koppitz (1958a; 1960a) in 1958 hypothesized that if the B-G Test discriminated a group of children with low achievements in reading, writing, and spelling from a similar group with above-average achievements in those skills, the test would be discovering learning disturbances primarily due to problems in visual-motor perception. She modified P&S's scoring system to seven main factors, which were related to distortions in Figures A, 3, 5, and 7. The sum of the indexes for the seven factors gave a total score. She applied her procedure to an initial group of 41 above-average and 36 below-average achievers from the first to fourth grades, with an age range of 6 to 10 years. Then Koppitz (1958b) cross-validated her results on a group of 31 above-average and 20 below-average children of comparable age and education. This second group had the additional characteristic of being maladjusted. She reported a significant discrimination between the two groups. In 1960, Koppitz published the results of a normative study on her scoring system which she applied to the protocols of 1,055 kindergarten through fourth grade children having a range of 5–0—10–5 years. In this article, she presented the normative scores in a table containing 11 six-month groups throughout this age range. Likewise, Koppitz gave a table of mean scores for the five grade-school levels. She reports the system continues to discriminate significantly between her groups.

The stability of the scoring systems used on this 3 to 12-year age range for establishing MA's and giving clues to the presence of brain damage continues to show promise of rewards from further explorations. Most of the studies above, of course, only report significant group differences. The finding that the Binet was more efficient in predicting individual cases than was the B-G score points up the caution that is necessary when one interprets the individual subject's B-G protocol. Perhaps research results will be forthcoming which will more clearly define the limits of the test when the individual child's protocol is interpreted.

Scoring Systems: Late Adolescents and Adults

INSPECTION SYSTEMS

This approach was introduced by Bender (1938; 1946). The protocols, her minute observations of them, and the interpretive manner in which she combines the observations to fit diagnostic categories are still stimulating after many rereadings. Sullivan and Welch (1948) used her system to score the protocols of 101 experimental subjects and of a matched control group. The experimental group had a 6 to 17 year age range, including both sexes, and all had a history of poliomyleitis. The matched control group had not had "polio." The authors divided the two groups into two subgroups. One pair of the subgroups, experimental and control, received the Stanford-Binet, the California Test of Personality, the Hunt-Minnesota, and the B-G. The other pair did not receive the B-G or Hunt-Minnesota. The authors reported a significant discrimination by the B-G of the experimental group from the control group. A frequently mentioned Military Clinical Psychology Technical Manual (Department of the Army, 1951) simply paraphrases Bender's procedure and then recommends that it be used and interpreted by an experienced clinician.

Hutt (1953) modified Bender's inspection procedure distinctly. He defines 27 "scoring" factors descriptively. For the first three factors and the fifth, he gives his range for normals but does not list similar suggestions for the rest of the factors. One must suppose, therefore, that his normals accurately reproduced the stimulus figure. One or more psychodynamic or diagnostic grouping characteristics are attributed to each factor. Hutt frequently refers to "our data" and "our findings" but these are not disclosed in his publication, and they do not seem to have been published elsewhere. Though he rejects the term "syndrome," Hutt continues to list the groupings of his factors which he feels discriminate between selected psychiatric classifications. These groupings he calls "patterns." The system was used by Harriman and Harriman (1950) on the records of 30 five-year-old nursery-school children who had not commmenced to read and on 30 second-grade seven-year-old children who were judged to be making satisfactory progress in reading. They used 11 of Hutt's factors and tabulated the percentage of each group whose protocols appeared to contain positive aspects of the 11 factors. No statistical procedures were employed, but the authors judged that 4 of the 11 factors showed "sign differences" in favor of the second-grade group. The authors interpreted their results as showing that sensory-perceptual-motor activities of seven-year-old children more closely resemble those of adults than do those of nursery-school children. They feel this characteristic is a necessary correlate of reading readiness. Their study was repeated by Baldwin (1950) on two Negro adolescent sisters. One sister's B-G protocol supported Harriman's findings. The similar protocol of the other gave findings that were just opposite to Harriman's results. Hanvik (1951) employed Hutt's inspection procedure on regular and recall B-G protocols obtained from two groups of adult male veterans, one composed of patients in a Veterans Administration neuropsychiatric (NP) hospital for treatment of functional complaints. Using 19 of the factors, he gained a total score by tallying counts where any factor appeared in a protocol. Secondly, he had experienced judges sort the protocols on the basis of experimental or nonexperimental group membership. Finally, he scored the recall protocols for the number of total designs remembered. None of the three methods discriminated the two groups significantly. The rapid inspection system was also used by Matchabely and Bertrand (1953) on the B-G protocols of 82 hospitalized NP patients in a French hospital. The authors reported definite B-G factor patterns for schizophrenia, paranoia, alcoholism, melancholia, neurosis, epilepsy, oligophrenia, dementia, paralytica, hysteria, and psychopathic personality.

The "creatively interpretive" clinician feels fettered by the demands of experimental procedural controls. He prefers to inspect the results of his clinical examinations, searching for hunches and apparent trends in these data. Many well-designed but sterile pieces of research bear mute testimony to this point. An increasing number of statistical methods that objectify the data without destroying clinically apparent trends are available. Their use should help to allieviate much of the reticence now apparent and improve the quality of the publications.

OBJECTIVE SCORING SYSTEMS

Billingslea's (1948) monograph was the first published attempt at an objective scoring system. Following Bender's and Hutt's lead, he selected and defined 38 factors, using 137 indexes to score them. Measurements were made in an objective fashion. He used this system on the protocols of 100 neurotic adult male patients in an Army hospital and 50 adult male soldiers judged to fall within the normal range of emotional behavior. He was unable for the most part to demonstrate interfigure reliability for the test factors. Likewise, Hutt's pattern for the psychoneurotic record was not found to be valid. Though the monograph seemed to stimulate much research activity following its publication, the scoring method has proven too cumbersome for clinical and reasearch use. A scoring system employing graph paper to determine objectively the size factor of the B-G figures was reported by Kitay (1950). He used this method to obtain data for 25 indexes which in turn led to a D score. He expected D to designate an over-all expansion or contraction of size and reported it did so when he applied it to the protocols of 60 normal college undergraduates.

A compromise was adopted by Pascal and Suttell (1951). They settled on 105 factors and provided actual B-G records to assist the scorer in determining whether the factor is present in a particular protocol. Each factor is given a numerical value. The sum of the numerical values of the factors judged to be present in a protocol represents a "total raw score." A helpful scoring blank is provided. The authors used their scoring system on 271 protocols from adults with a high-school background and 203 protocols from adults with college background. The raw scores of each of those distributions translated into standard scores permitted the establishment of Z or weighted scores. Applying their scoring system to the protocols of a group of psychotic patients and a group of neurotic patients, they found significant differences between the groups with psychopathology as well as between these groups and the non-patient normals. They indicated the results were not adequate, however, for interpreting an individual protocol. The ability of this system to discriminate groups of patients displaying different types of psychopathology from nonpatient groups has been supported by the findings of Addington (1952), Swensen and Pascal (1953), Curnutt (1953), Robinson (1953), and Lonstein (1954).

Another series of studies, on the other hand, are less favorable. Curnutt and Lewis (1954) obtained B-G protocols and Rorschachs from 25 hospitalized NP patients. They hypothesized that the B-G Z score and the $F+$ percentage of the Rorschach were theoretically similar indexes and therefore should show a relatively close relationship. Their data disclosed no correlation between the two distributions. Likewise, Blum and Nims (1953) found that the P&S system failed to differentiate significantly the B-G protocols of a group of NP patients from a control group which was instructed to simulate neuropsychiatric illness. The authors also applied a clinical matching procedure to the same protocols, which significantly did differentiate the experimental from the control group. Incidentally, the authors found no significant difference between results gained from administering the B-G by group procedures or by individual testing.

Negative results were reported by Tamkin (1957), in an attempt to discriminate psychotic and nonpsychotic male veteran NP patients, and by Tucker and Spielberg (1958), who sought to separate "depressed" patients from those with other NP disturbances. Rosenthal and Imber (1955) described a somewhat different method of evaluating the P&S scoring system. The subjects were 13 NP outpatient cases variously diagnosed as some type of neurosis to some type of schizophrenia in a significant degree of remission. These subjects were tested in a before, during, and after type of experimental design. The design covered five periods of two weeks each. Psychiatrists saw the subjects once each period and rated their observations on a check list. The psychologist administered the B-G Test once each period. Between these periods, Mephenesion or a placebo was given in a prescribed dosage to the subjects by the psychiatrist in a random, blind manner. Statistical interpretation of the data revealed that the check list did not disclose any clinical improvement in the patients. Likewise, there was no correlation between P&S scores on the B-G protocols and times when Mephenesion was administered versus times when placebos were administered. Of added importance in this study was the impression of these authors that some changes they noted in the B-G protocol could be attributed to practice effects on the test.

Keehn (1957) examined the question of repeated testing by comparing series of B-G protocols obtained from four chronic schizophrenic patients. He tested his subjects from 13 to 15 times on the B-G with four-day intervals between testing. The author found no systematic trends in the P&S scores for all the patients. This was true of the total scores as well as the scores on the individual figures. Two of the subjects' protocols showed "improvement" on all figures during the testing period, whereas two others tended to regress somewhat. The scores for all subjects fluctuated markedly from individual testing to individual testing. The author also administered the Koh block designs from the Wechsler-Bellevue Intelligence Scale, Form II (W-B II) battery, to these four subjects at each administration of the B-G Test. Although variations also appeared in the subjects' scores on that measure, the final results displayed definite improvement through improved accuracy. It seems obvious that though this scoring system has many limitations, its assets probably outweigh the limitations. Further support for this conclusion is found in the fact that the literature reveals it to be the most widely used scoring system on the B-G Test today.

Peek and Quast (1951) published an objective scoring system which was not available to this reviewer, nor could a description of it be found elsewhere in the literature. Peek (1953) does report a study of the relationship between one B-G Test factor and personality character-istics. It is not clear whether this factor was included in the author's original scoring system. The factor relates to Figure 5 and depends on whether the subject, in drawing the dotted directional line of that figure, starts from the rim of the cup of the figure or starts from the outer edge of the line and approaches the cup accordingly. Seemingly, the "combination" of personality characteristics of 75 hospitalized male NP patients who started the diagonal at its upper edge is significantly different from the personality characteristics of a similar group whose directionality of line pattern was unknown. Goodstein, Spielberger, Williams, and Dahlstrom (1955) were concerned whether the method of "free recall" incorporated in the Peek and Quast scoring system might be affected unduly by the serial position of the figures and their varying levels of difficulty of recall. Using college students and an adequate experimental design, they concluded that B-G Figures A, 1, and 2 are the easiest to recall, while Designs 3, 4, and 7 are most difficult. They also found that recall adequacy is a function of the serial position of the designs as well as their difficulty level. Stewart (1957), noting their findings on Figures 3 and 4, wondered if, since these figures were located essentially in the middle of the sequence, the findings might also be a function of the learning principle that "ordinarily items toward the beginning and end of a series are easier to learn than those in the center." His preliminary results appeared to support that learning principle, though they do not, necessarily negate the previous study's results.

Japanese psychotic adults have been discriminated by Okino's (1956) 121-index scoring system, but Uffelmann (1958) failed to differentiate Canadian schizophrenic adults from hospital employees with a system he developed.

Comparisons of the effectiveness of the inspection system versus the P&S scoring method have been made. Bowland and Deabler (1956) found both approaches successfully separated the B-G protocols from four similar adult male groups judged to be nonneuropsychiatric patients, neurotic patients, schizophrenic patients, and patients with organic brain damage. Mehlman and Vatovec (1956) submitted 25 protocols of carefully matched patients to three nationally known B-G "experts," who employed their particular evaluatory approaches. One patient of the pair was judged to have a "functional" psychosis, while the other had an "organic" psychosis. Only two of the judges approached better than chance separation of the groups. The authors report difficulties in obtaining the participation of five other experts. I have no comment. Later Nadler, Fink, Shontz, and Brink (1959) described a well-designed study aimed at experimentally comparing the efficiency of P&S's scoring system on B-G protocols with that of clinical inspections. They set the task of discriminating the protocols of 27 patients with known organic brain damage from those of 26 patients judged to be without such damage. Both methods were reported to be equally successful. They then removed the 28 cases from the extremes of their distributions on organicity and found that neither method could discriminate the two groups significantly. The judges, by the way, were two psychologists familiar with the P&S system, two psychologists who were not familiar with that system, and two occupational therapists not trained in psychology. The reliability between the judgments of members of pairs of judges was high, and the reliability between judges generally was almost as high.

McPherson and Pepin (1955) asked whether the scores obtained on the same subject from his B-G protocols from two different motor methods of reproducing the figures would be the same. They argued that the scores from the two methods must be essentially the same if they were to be interpreted diagnostically. Their two methods involved (1) the usual administration procedure of the B-G and (2) having the subject construct the figures by placing pieces of felt on a felt board. They used 32 male and female senior college students as subjects. The results were rated on the degree of similarity between the stimulus figure and the reproduced figure. They found an acceptable agreement between the two methods of reproduction 77 per cent of the time, with a "total or extreme disagreement occurring only 6 per cent of the time." They concluded that B-G figure reproductions were more influenced by the perceptual factors than by motor factors.

The preceding survey seems to force the conclusion that both Bender's inspection system and P&S's objective scoring system have stood the test of time, when the problem is to separate grossly the B-G protocols reflecting major disturbances from those reflecting normal behavior. Neither approach adequately handles diagnostic evaluation of the individual case. The quality of the "standardization" of the clinician appears to be the important variable under these conditions. The "categorizing" approach was losing popularity in 1947 and now seems to be dying normally. Its place is being taken by a return to discriminatory evaluations of mental processes such as perception, problem solving or thinking, attitudes, need gratification, etc.

Specialized Interpretative Approaches to the Bender-Gestalt

Guertin (1952; 1954a; 1954b; 1955) set himself the problem of seeking "some systematic order which could be developed out of the relationships among the scoring factors for the B-G by the application of factor analysis." Initially, he obtained the B-G protocols from 100 hospitalized NP patients, psychiatrically classified as either psychotic or with organic brain pathology. His scoring procedure essentially followed Billingslea's definitions and included indexes for 41 variables. A factor analysis of the intercorrelation matrix on these variables yielded five factors which he labeled (1) propensity for curvilinear movement, (2) pure spatial contiguity, (3) constriction, (4) careless execution, and (5) poor reality contact. Next Guertin interested himself in the characteristics of the factor "propensity for curvilinear movement" discovered in his first study. He noted that it was most heavily loaded in catatonic and mixed schizophrenic subjects. From that, he hypothesized that poor emotional control might be basic to "certain types of distortion" of the designs and, in turn, might be an important variable in schizophrenia. Again he obtained the B-G protocols from 100 hospitalized NP patients, 26 of whom were females. Diagnostically the group included 13 nonschizophrenics, 15 catatonic schizophrenics, 14 hebephrenic schizophrenics, and 35 mixed schizophrenics. Five factors were revealed by an analysis of 42 signs: (1) unstable closure, (2) curvilinear distortion, (3) propensity for curvilinear movement Factor II, (4) fragmentation, and (5) irregular propensity for curvilinear movement. Factor 1 seemed related to an underlying general instability. Factor 2 appeared related to impulsiveness with a possible emotional basis. Factor 3 was related to emotional disorganization and display of affect. Factor 4 seemed related to either misperception or attempts to avoid unpleasant feelings through use of associations. Factor 5 was related to emotional conflicts and neurotic-type defenses against unpleasant feelings.

Still seeking for a B-G diagnostic formulation of schizophrenia in general, he next performed a transposed factor analysis on the B-G protocols of 32 hospitalized male, chronic, long-term schizophrenic patients with a variety of subtype diagnoses. No large group factor corresponding to schizophrenia emerged. On the other hand, the study did tend to group his subjects into four subtypes that he labeled chronic undifferentiated schizophrenia, disorganized schizophrenia, conforming and nondefensive schizophrenia, and actively defensive schizophrenia. Lastly Guertin (1955) did a transposed factor analysis of the B-G protocols of 30 male hospitalized NP subjects with recent onsets of a paranoid-type schizophrenic reaction. This study also disclosed four subtypes for this diagnostic grouping which he labeled chronic and deteriorated, hostile reactive, poorly integrated, and inadequate and withdrawn. The writer does not know the degree of impact Guertin's studies have had on the general use of the B-G. His work has been given an extended review here because it reflects a statistically synthesized organization of the many B-G indexes and factors used to discriminate the protocols of patients with schizophrenic reactions.

A truly amazing number and variety of symbolic interpretations have been produced by clinical psychologists for B-G protocols and made available to some of their colleagues on a private basis. Only three studies[4] have been concerned with this problem, however. Suczek and Klopfer (1952) sought to introduce a degree of realism in this activity by obtaining the free associations to each of the nine B-G figures of 48 beginning psychology college students who were viewing the projected designs in a group setting. Their free associations to each of the figures could be grouped under five headings: a list of objects frequently associated with each, the particular part of the figure on which average interest focused, the affective pull which the figure had on the average viewer, the average symbolic meaning of the figure for the standard group, and the experimenters' tentative interpretation of the figure as a symbol. Although the reader may not agree with those tentative interpretations, he at least has objective data to support the other four groupings.

Tolor (1957), following Suczek's and Klopfer's lead, had 50 Air Force NP patients give their associations to the nine B-G designs. He found the individual designs differed decidedly in their stimulus value for the subjects. There were many rejections, many vague associations, and many simple descriptions. The intellectual and educational backgrounds of the subjects were not described, however. He urged caution when interpreting a B-G protocol symbolically.

The child subjects of Greenbaum (1955) were asked to state what each B-G design reminded him of after he had reproduced all figures. Some of the nouns from each subject's statements were then selected and mixed in a commonly used word-association list. This modified list was administered to the subject on two different follow-up occasions. The subject's associations to the two word lists were subjectively interpreted and so cannot be evaluated by this reviewer.

It is probable that symbolic interpretations of the B-G protocol will continue to be popular. Little support for their a priori validation is given by the preceding research, however. Empirical hunches in this area should be put to scientific tests, or their dissemination should be prevented.

The clinician dealing with patients with varied cultural backgrounds must be alert for test stimuli that are influenced in a minimum manner by differing cultural milieus. Peixotto (1954) was faced with this problem in a Hawaiian clinic and wondered if the B-G would prove to be a culture-free instrument. She selected 35 NP patients active in the out-patient clinic who represented seven different ethnic groups on the islands. Age range was 14 to 31, and their IQ range was 82 to 135. The B-G protocols were scored according to the P&S method, and

---

[4] Three additional studies (Guertin & Davis, 1962 personal communication; Hammer, 1954; Tolor, 1960) have been done. Hammer's small but positive results were contaminated by questionable testing procedure, and the other two studies produced negative findings.

an analysis of variance of the raw scores was made, with the expectation of finding no important differences between ethnic groups. Variation between ethnic groups was significant at the 5 per cent level, however. Peixotto concluded that the instrument reflected characteristics common to any specific ethnic group but varied between groups and thus was not culture-free. One wishes for a cross validation on a much larger sample, for the N in each ethnic group was small in this study. Wolfsohn (1951–1952), as reported previously in this review, believed the B-G Test to be adequately culture-free when it was applied as an intelligence test to Jewish immigrant children.

Bender-Gestalt Discernment of Organic Brain Pathology

Rotation of the B-G designs seems to be widely accepted by clinicians as a discriminating factor in organic brain pathology. Yet it occurs in the protocols obtained from subjects carrying other diagnostic labels who are considered clinically to be free of any brain pathology. One must keep in mind that in the literature reviewed in this article, the brain pathology generally ascribed to the experimental subjects was of the lesion and/or blood circulatory types, rather than the toxic. The possibility of the presence of a metabolic toxic brain disturbance in functional psychosis certainly has not been disproven at this time. Thus, it is possible that Bender figure rotations reflect brain chemical pathology, too. Many studies already mentioned have included rotation as one of several factors investigated. There are several studies that seek to evaluate this one factor alone, however. Hanvik and Anderson (1950) compared a group of 44 brain-damaged hospitalized patients with a control group. They found 59 per cent of the experimental group produced one or more rotations of 30 degrees or more in the nine designs, while only 19 per cent of the control group did so. Later, Hanvik (1953) examined the EEG reports of 20 of his child patients whose B-G protocols contained 30 per cent or greater rotations. Eighty per cent of their EEG's were abnormal. Chorost, Spivack, and Levine (1959) attempted to validate Hanvik's (1953) findings. Their subjects were 68 "children" below the age of 18. Of the 68 protocols, 51 had one or more design rotations. The EEG's of 69 per cent of the 51 subjects were abnormal. However, 47 per cent of the EEG's of the remaining 17 subjects who did not rotate any B-G designs were also abnormal. The authors concluded that in their sample the "success of the B-G rotation test was not much better than chance probability."

The B-G protocols of 1,003 male NP veteran hospital patients were used by Griffith and Taylor (1960). They defined rotation as a movement of the design of 45 degrees or more with the figure still recognizable. Fifty-six per cent of the mentally deficient patients in their group gave protocols with such rotations. Forty per cent of the chronic brain syndrome cases in their group gave protocols with rotations. These percentages were significantly higher than those found in the schizophrenic reaction group, neurotic group, and the character disorder groups. The diagnostic significance of rotations of B-G designs is obviously not settled. Other pattern-evoking stimuli are being studied for this characteristic. Perhaps these efforts should be consolidated by administering the B-G to the subjects being studied with other rotation-evoking material and comparing results. We can hope also for more valid criteria of organic brain pathology than EEG's alone.

A recall protocol has not been routine procedure in B-G administration, to my knowledge. Apparently, Peek and Quast (1951) included it on the basis that it might "afford a measure of the learning taking place during the copying phase of the test, and (that it) fits the paradigm of one-trial serial learning under free recall conditions, with the important exception that the S is not instructed to learn" (Goodstein et al., 1955). Since Peek and Quast published their manual while at the University of Minnesota, it is possible that they were influenced by Sullivan and Welch's (1948) work.

The reader should have in mind the previously reviewed studies on the effects on the recall score of the serial position of the designs and their difficulty level when he considers the following reports. Hanvik and Anderson (1950), following Welch's lead, in addition to a rotation score, obtained a recall score by counting the number of designs correctly recalled following the usual reproduction procedure. The mean recall score did not discriminate significantly their brain-damaged group of patients from their normal group. Three recall scores were obtained by Niebuhr and Cohen (1956) for each of their subjects during one test period. Prior to the regular test, they used a ten-second exposure of the design card followed by immediate recall of each design. After the regular procedure was completed, a recognition memory score was obtained by asking the subject to select the correct design from a choice of six alternates constructed for each of the nine figures. Finally, after completing this procedure, they asked the subject to match one of the six alternates with the standard design. This permitted a second recognition score. They used 10 subjects in each of the four groups classified as normal nurses, acute schizophrenics, chronic schizophrenics, and neurological cases. They found a progressively increasing degree of perceptual memory inefficiency in the order of diagnostic groups listed. There was no doubt that the memory scores fully discriminated the neurological group, but they did not separate adequately the acute from the chronic schizophrenic reaction group.

Tolor (1956) determined the number of designs correctly recalled after the usual reproduction procedure and a score for digit span on

91 organics, 35 convulsives, and 49 psychogenic patients. The subjects ranged in age from 12 to 72 years and in IQ from 57 to 136 on the Wechsler-Bellevue Intelliegence Scale, Form I (W-B I). The recall scores discriminated the organic group more adequately from the psychogenic group than did the digit span. He cautioned against using this finding in interpreting individual cases. Later Tolor (1958) cross-validated this study and controlled the age variable better by group-matching his character-disorder, schizophrenic, and organic subjects. This time the organic group made significantly poorer recall scores on both the B-G Test and the Digit Span test, except for digits backwards. His other two groups were not discriminated by the immediate memory tests.

Reznikoff and Olin (1957) sought to validate Tolor's first study. They selected their "organics" from Tolor's original population. Their recall score was the number of whole designs accurately recalled. They found the score discriminated their organic subjects from their schizophrenic subjects at the .05 level of confidence. These authors (Olin & Reznikoff, 1958) then developed a somewhat different recall score by modifying P&S's scoring system. This score significantly discriminated their organic brain damage adult patient group and their schizophrenic adult patient group without brain damage from "normal" nurses. The score did not, however, discriminate the two patient groups.

Stewart and Cunningham (1958) published a study of incidental interest here. They obtained a modified P&S recall score on 18 psychotic patients, 17 nonpsychotic but NP patients, and 20 nurse subjects. All subjects were females and ranged in age from 15 to 59. The group means discriminated their groups significantly. Obviously, the results are not definite but do direct attention to the greater efficiency of certain types of recall scores over others.

Niebuhr and Cohen's (1956) procedure needs cross validating. Likewise, more realistic controls of intelligence and other variables need to be introduced into future investigations of Welch's recall method. These further research efforts are urged with the expectation of strengthening the instrument's overall-validity in the detection of the presence of organic brain pathology.

Several studies have dealt with the question of discerning the presence of organic brain pathology through the medium of the B-G protocol by employing individualized approaches. Guertin (1954b) was concerned over the tendency of psychologists and psychiatrists to ascribe certain test signs and symptoms to organic patients without regard to the "varied etiology and foci of pathology" in the brain. He obtained B-G protocols from 27 male adult schizophrenic subjects with readily recognizable organic brain pathology. A transposed factor analysis of the correlation matrix did not discriminate adequately factors that separated the patients' "organicity" from their psychosis, and so he urged extreme caution in utilizing organic test signs without reference to etiology. For example, can the B-G Test be used to detect the psychiatric disturbances aroused in normal subjects by LSD–25? Abramson, Waxenberg, Levine, Kaufman, and Kornetsky's (1955) results on 25 subjects tended to indicate they were psychiatrically disturbed but did not distinguish the etiology of the disturbance. On the other hand, Hirschenfang (1960) obtained B-G protocols from 25 right and 25 left hemiplegic hospitalized patients. The age range for the right group was 22 to 78 years. The age range for the left group was 46 to 83 years. Sex and intelligence were not controlled. He scored the protocols by the P&S system and found resulting group scores significantly discriminated the left group as being "worse."

The efficacy of the B-G Test versus flicker-fusion as devices for demonstrating brain pathology was studied by McGuire (1960). He tested two groups of 21 Navy men, matched for age, of whom the experimental subjects had known organic brain damage. He sent their B-G protocols to five judges, three of which had had long experience with the B-G Test. His flicker-fusion score correctly labeled 30 of the 42 subjects. Three of the judges correctly labeled 29 of the 42 subjects.

Bender-Gestalt as a Measure of Intelligence

Bender's Mental Age Scale for children and recent studies of it have already been discussed. Koppitz' (1958a, 1960a) scoring system for children's protocols has been reviewed earlier. She administered the WISC to 90 children for whom she had B-G protocols (Koppitz, 1958b). All children were clinic patients with school maladjustment due to learning or behavior difficulties. Their age range was from 6–7 to 11–7, and the WISC range in IQ was from 73 to 126. All the WISC scores correlated significantly with her B-G scores except those from the Coding, Information, Comprehension, and Similarities subtests. Likewise, Koppitz, Sullivan, Blyth, and Shelton (1959) found that the Koppitz B-G scores from the protocols of 143 first-grade students correlated significantly with their Metropolitan Achievement Test scores.

Some findings are available on "adult" subjects. For instance, Tolor (1956) correlated the usual B-G recall scores on 175 NP patients with an age range of 12 to 72 years with their W-B I Total IQ's; the $r = .50$. Also, Peek and Olsen (1955) obtained a B-G recall score, number of correct whole and one-half figures, on 193 hospitalized male and female patients, aged 14 to 72 years. They reported an r of .34 ($p=.001$) between that score and the patient's Shipley-Hartford CQ score. Since there was an essentially .00 correlation between the recall and Shipley-Hartford raw scores, they concluded the B-G was evaluating intellectual efficiency but not intellectual capacity.

A similar .co correlation between Shipley-Hartford "intelligence" and a 1.5 recall score was reported earlier by Aaronson, Nelson, and Holt (1953). Aaronson (1957) obtained B-G protocols on 42 male and 46 female epileptics who had also been given the Porteus Mazes. The recall score was obtained by the 1.5 procedure. The initial correlation of .46 between the patient's recall score and Porteus quotient reduced to .21 when age was partialed out. Lastly, Peek and Storms (1958) asked three trained judges to estimate the intellectual level of B-G protocols obtained from 100 NP patients without known organic brain damage. The subjects were of both sexes and ranged in age from 16 to 59 years. The correlation between the judges ranking and Shipley-Hartford T scores was not significant. The preceeding studies seem to substantiate further the earlier findings that the B-G Test is useful in estimating the intelligence of children ranging from 4–0 to 11–11 years but is inadequate for this purpose with younger and older individuals.

Determining Personality Psychodynamics with the Bender-Gestalt

The reader is referred to earlier material on Hutt's scoring system and the studies concerned with free associations to the B-G designs. No direction in the research results is apparent in this area, so the next studies are presented simply in order of publication. Wohl (1957) sought for the degree of generalization of "constriction" in an individual's B-G designs, Rorschach responses, Thematic Apperception Test (TAT) stories, an interest test, and a semantic differential device. Constriction was not revealed to be generalized throughout these tests by an inter-correlation procedure. Zolik (1958) obtained P&S's Z scores on the B-G protocols of 43 delinquents and 43 nondelinquents, aged 14 to 17. The groups were matched on age, IQ, and lack of "motor defect." A cutoff score of $Z = 60$ correctly grouped 69 per cent of the delinquents and excluded 95 per cent of the controls.

Koppitz (1960b) took matched groups of 16 first-grade students each and obtained B-G and Draw-a-Person protocols from each subject. One group studied under a relaxed, nontension-producing teacher, the other under a nervous, tension-producing teacher. The B-G protocols scored for tension did not discriminate between the two groups, whereas the

[5] Clawson's (1959) report is a survey of her Ph.D. dissertation completed in 1958. In 1962, she released the data in the form of a manual, available at Western Psychological Service in Los Angeles.

Draw-a-Person scores did.[5] Like Wohl's earlier study, Prado, Peyman, and Lacey (1960) tested if the B-G designs could be used to predict "flattened affect" psychiatrically judged to be present or not present in 120 NP patients and normals. They carefully and objectively scored the designs in a manner similar to Billingslea's method. The results did not discriminate between the groups.

Gavales and Millon (1960) obtained the usual recall scores and a size score on the protocols of 80 college students who had also taken the Taylor Manifest Anxiety scale (MA scale). They divided their subjects into two groups of 40 each, a high MA scale-score and a low MA scale-score group. Twenty subjects from each of the two groups took the B-G under artificial social stress. Both groups of "stressed" subjects tended to produce smaller figures, regardless of their MA scale scores. The same size relationship was found in their recall scores also. Further, all group recall scores showed reduction in size from the reproduction design scores. On the other hand, Lachmann, Bailey, and Berrick (1961) found that clinical psychologists' judgments for the presence of anxiety in B-G and Draw-a-Person protocols were not consistent, and their judgments did not agree with the MA scale score. It is evident that attempts to substantiate, experimentally, this use of the B-G continues to be unrewarding. Most of the difficulty stems from the fact that the characteristic under consideration fails to appear consistently throughout the whole protocol. The factor "size" remains the one possible exception to this generalization. It would appear that the individual designs are reacted to by subjects as if each is a symbolically discrete design. If this conclusion is correct, then each design must be studied individually for what it has to offer psychodynamically, and the sequential influence of one design on the others must be taken into account. Finally, the perceptual importance of other expressive behavior patterns that occur during the drawing period but seldom have been included in the published research need careful investigation.

Bender-Gestalt as a Standard for Judging the Effects of Treatment Procedures

When employing a test as a standard in a study just once, the experimenter is forced to use norms obtained from other subjects. When the instrument is used two or more times in a design, the resulting data can furnish their own controls or "norms." Byrd (1956) was interested in selecting children in need of psychotherapy by means of the B-G Test. Using 200 maladjusted subjects 8 to 16 years old and a normal control group, he found that only orderly sequence, change in curvature, closure difficulty, and rotation of his 15 factor indexes tended to discriminate the groups.

Ligthart, Johnston, and Sussman (1956) administered the B-G and W-B I to a group of adult NP patients before and after they were given an electroshock therapy (EST) with Coramine treatment series. They assumed P&S's Z scores would be indicative of the amount of psychopathology present. In an interesting variation, Crasilneck and Michael (1957) desired to know the absolute and relative age levels of behavior that would occur when they introduced various conditions, one of which was hyponotic age regression. They assumed the B-G protocols would disclose the MA levels on which a subject was functioning at a given time without his knowing how to depict this on the test. The subjects, 10 white nurses aged 19 to 22, were given the W-B I and the B-G first while awake. Next, still awake, they were asked to reproduce the designs as they thought they would if they were four years old. Next, while hypnotized to the somnambulistic state they again reproduced the figures as they thought they would if they were four years old. Finally, they regressed to the four-year-age level hyponotically and were asked to reproduce the designs. The mean MA's for the four groups of protocols were 11.2, 9.9, 7.8, and 7.3 years, respectively.

Lothrop (1958) wondered if the B-G with P&S scoring would discriminate between a group of nine male veterans who responded successfully to medical treatment for their duodenal ulcer from a similar group which did not. The IQ's for the successful group ranged from 71 to 126, while the failure group's ranged from 66 to 110. The correlation of age with IQ was significant. The group B-G means did not even overlap.

Schon and Waxenberg (1958) obtained pre- and posthospital B-G protocols from hypophysectomized subjects and developed P&S scores for them. The scores worsened significantly after surgery, when they resembled those of psychiatric patients. Pre- and post-W-B I scores were not significantly different. Finally, Higbee, Clark, and Henderson (1960) found P&S-scored B-G protocols did not differentiate the lengths of hospital stays of 72 male veterans.

If this survey accomplishes little else, it should demonstrate that the B-G as yet has not reached a stage of development where it can be employed to evaluate the effects of other variables.

Perspective

Although there are surprisingly few generalizations that can be made about the B-G test as a result of reviewing the published experiences with it over the past decade, the following seem justified in the light of the preceding discussion:

1. The test continues to be popular with clinicians and deserves to remain as an additional tool in his repertoire.

2. It is in great need of a universally accepted standard set of designs.

3. The P&S scoring system has proven useful on adult protocols, as has Koppitz' modification of it on children's protocols.

4. Reasonably valid MA's can be obtained with it for children 4 to 12 years and adults with equivalent MA's, but not adolescents and adults with higher MA's.

5. It can be employed as an additional tool in a battery of tests administered to an individual when clues for the possible presence of organic brain pathology are sought.

6. Whether evaluated with objective scores or with some systematic inspection procedure, the results tend to discriminate the psychotic from the nonpsychotic and nonpsychiatric subject, provided the MA is 13 or above. It does not detect effectively nonpsychotic emotionally disturbed children, however.

7. When the protocols are interpreted symbolically, the clinician must rely almost completely on the validity of his own subjective professional knowledge.

8. The test has not been standardized sufficiently to permit its use as a norm against which to judge other variables.

9. More research is needed on the perceptual contributions of each design and the effects on such perceptions of their sequential appearance in the protocol.

REFERENCES

AARONSON, B. S. The Porteus Mazes and Bender-Gestalt recall. *J. clin. Psychol.*, 1957, 13, 186–187.

AARONSON, B. S., NELSON, S. E., & HOLT, SHIRLEY. On a relation between Bender-Gestalt recall and Shipley-Hartford scores. *J. clin. Psychol.*, 1953, 9, 88.

ABRAMSON, H. A., WAXENBERG, S. E., LEVINE, A., KAUFMAN, M. R., & KORNETSKY, C. Lysergic acid diethylamide (LSD-25): XIII. Effect on Bender-Gestalt test performance. *J. Psychol.*, 1955, 40, 341–349

ADDINGTON, M. C. A note on the Pascal and Suttell scoring system of the Bender-Gestalt test. *J. clin. Psychol.*, 1952, 8, 312–313.

BALDWIN, MARCELLA V. A note regarding the suggested use of the Bender visual motor Gestalt test as a measure of school readiness. *J. clin. Psychol.*, 1950, 6, 412–415.

BARKLEY, B. J. A note on the development of the Western Reserve Hapto-Kinesthetic Gestalt test. *J. clin. Psychol.*, 1949, 5, 179–180.

BAROFF, G. S. Bender-Gestalt visuo-motor function in mental deficiency. *Amer. J. ment. Def.*, 1957, 61, 753–760.

BELL, J. E. *Projective techniques.* New York: Longmans, Green, 1948.

BENDER, LAURETTA. A visual-motor test and its clinical use. *Amer. J. Orthopsychiat. Monogr.*, 1938, No. 3.

BENDER, LAURETTA. *Instruction for the use of the visual motor Gestalt test.* New York: Amer. Orthopsychiat. Ass., 1946.

Billingslea, F. Y. The Bender-Gestalt: An objective scoring method and validating data. *J. clin. Psychol. Monogr.*, 1948, No. 1.

Blum, R. H., & Nims, J. Two clinical uses of Bender visual-motor Gestalt test. *USAF med. J.*, 1953, 4, 1592–1599.

Bowland, J. A., & Deabler, H. L. A Bender-Gestalt diagnostic validity study. *J. clin. Psychol.*, 1956, 12, 82–84.

Buros, O. K. *The third mental measurements yearbook.* Highland Park, N.J.: Gryphon, 1949.

Buros, O. K. *The fourth mental measurements yearbook.* Highland Park, N.J.: Gryphon, 1953.

Byrd, E. The clinical validity of the Bender-Gestalt test with children: A developmental comparison of children in need of psychotherapy and children judged well-adjusted. *J. proj. Tech.*, 1956, 20, 127–136.

Chorost, S. B., Spivack, G., & Levine, M. Bender-Gestalt rotations and EEG abnormalities in children. *J. consult. Psychol.*, 1959, 23, 559.

Clawson, A. The Bender visual motor Gestalt test as an index of emotional disturbances in children. *J. proj. Tech.*, 1959, 23, 198–206.

Crasilneck, H. B., & Michael, Carmen M. Performance on the Bender under hypnotic age regression. *J. abnorm. soc. Psychol.*, 1957, 54, 318–322.

Curnutt, R. H. The use of the Bender-Gestalt with an alcoholic and non-alcoholic population. *J. clin. Psychol.*, 1953, 9, 287–290.

Curnutt, R. H., & Lewis, W. B. The relationship between Z scores on Bender-Gestalt and F+% on the Rorschach. *J. clin. Psychol.*, 1954, 10, 96–97.

Department of the Army. *Military clinical psychology.* (Technical Manual No. 8–242) Washington: U.S. Government Printing Office, 1951.

Gavales, D., & Millon, T. Comparison of reproduction and recall size deviations in the Bender-Gestalt as measures of anxiety. *J. clin. Psychol.*, 1960, 16, 278–280.

Gobetz, W. A quantification, standardization, and validation of the Bender-Gestalt test on normal and neurotic adults. *Psychol. Monogr.*, 1953, 67, No. 6 (Whole No. 356).

Goodstein, L. D., Spielberger, C. D., Williams, J. E., & Dahlstrom, W. G. The effects of serial position and design difficulty of the Bender-Gestalt test designs. *J. consult. Psychol.*, 1955, 19, 230–234.

Greenbaum, R. S. A note on the use of the word association test as an aid to interpreting the Bender-Gestalt. *J. proj. Tech.*, 1955, 19, 27–29.

Griffith, R. M., & Taylor, Vivian H. Incidence of Bender-Gestalt figure rotations. *J. consult. Psychol.*, 1960, 24, 189–190.

Guertin, W. H. A factor analysis of the Bender-Gestalt tests of mental patients. *J. clin. Psychol.*, 1952, 8, 362–367.

Guertin, W. H. A factor analysis of curvilinear distortions on the Bender-Gestalt. *J. clin. Psychol.*, 1954, 10, 12–17. (a)

Guertin, W. H. A transposed analysis of the Bender-Gestalts of brain disease cases. *J. clin. Psychol.*, 1954, 10, 366–369. (b)

Guertin, W. H. A transposed factor analysis of schizophrenic performance on the Bender-Gestalt. *J. clin. Psychol.*, 1954, 10, 225–228. (c)

Guertin, W. H. A transposed analysis of the Bender-Gestalts of paranoid schizophrenics. *J. clin. Psychol.*, 1955, 11, 73–76.

Hammer, E. F. An experimental study of symbolism on the Bender-Gestalt. *J. proj. Tech.*, 1954, 18, 335–345.

Hanvik, L. J. A note on the limitations of the use of the Bender-Gestalt test as a diagnostic aid in patients with a functional complaint. *J. clin. Psychol.*, 1951, 7, 194.

Hanvik, L. J. A note on rotations in the Bender-Gestalt test as predictors of EEG abnormalities in children. *J. clin. Psychol.*, 1953, 9, 399.

HANVIK, L. J., & ANDERSON, A. L. The effect of focal brain lesions on recall and the production of rotations in the Bender-Gestalt test. *J. consult. Psychol.*, 1950, 14, 197–198.

HARRIMAN, MILDRED, & HARRIMAN, P. L. The Bender-visual-motor-Gestalt-test as a measure of school readiness. *J. clin. Psychol.*, 1950, 6, 175–177.

HEWYER, G., & ANGOULVENT, N. Le test de Lauretta Bender. *Enfance*, 1949, 2, 89–305.

HIGBEE, D. S., CLARK, J. R., & HENDERSON, W. E. The Bender-Gestalt test as a predictor of length of hospitalization with mental patients. *J. clin. Psychol.*, 1960, 16, 265–266.

HIRSCHENFANG, S. A comparison of Bender Gestalt reproductions of right and left hemiplegic patients. *J. clin. Psychol.*, 1960, 16, 439.

HUNT, W. A. An actuarial approach to clinical judgment. In B. M. Bass & I. A. Berg (Eds.), *Objective approaches to personality assessment.* Princeton: Van Nostrand, 1959. Pp. 169–191.

HUTT, M. L. Revised Bender visual motor Gestalt test. In A. Weider (Ed.), *Contributions toward medical psychology.* Vol. 2. New York: Ronald, 1953. Pp. 660–687.

KEEHN, J. D. Repeated testing of four chronic schizophrenics on the Bender-Gestalt and Wechsler block design tests. *J. clin. Psychol.*, 1957, 13, 179–182.

KELLER, J. E. The use of a Bender-Gestalt maturation level scoring system with mentally handicapped children. *Amer. J. Orthopsychiat.*, 1955, 25, 563–573.

KITAY, J. I. The Bender-Gestalt test as a projective technique. *J. clin. Psychol.*, 1950, 6, 170–174.

KOPPITZ, ELIZABETH M. The Bender-Gestalt test as a projective technique. *J. clin. Psychol.*, 1958, 14, 292–295. (a)

KOPPITZ, ELIZABETH M. Relationships between the Bender-Gestalt test and the Wechsler intelligence test for children. *J. clin. Psychol.*, 1958, 14, 413–416. (b)

KOPPITZ, ELIZABETH M. The Bender-Gestalt test for children: A normative study. *J. clin. Psychol.*, 1960, 16, 432–435. (a)

KOPPITZ, ELIZABETH M. Teacher's attitude and children's performance on the Bender-Gestalt test and human figure drawings. *J. clin. Psychol.*, 1960, 16, 204–208. (b)

KOPPITZ, ELIZABETH M., SULLIVAN, J., BLYTH, D. D., & SHELTON, J. Prediction of first grade school achievement with the Bender-Gestalt test and human figure drawings. *J. clin. Psychol.*, 1959, 15, 164–168.

LACHMANN, F. M., BAILEY, M. A., & BERRICK, M. E. The relationship between manifest anxiety and clinicians' evaluation of projective test responses. *J. clin. Psychol.*, 1961, 17, 11–13.

LIGTHART, P. W. K., JOHNSTON, R. P., & SUSSMAN, E. Evaluation of combined coramine-electroshock therapy in the treatment of schizophrenia. *Amer. J. Psychiat.*, 1956, 17, 619–623.

LONSTEIN, M. A. A validation of a Bender-Gestalt scoring system. *J. consult. Psychol.*, 1954, 18, 377–379.

LOTHROP, W. W. Relationship between Bender-Gestalt test scores and medical success with duodenal ulcer patients. *Psychosom. Med.*, 1958, 20, 30–32.

McGUIRE, F. L. A comparison of the Bender-Gestalt and flicker-fusion as indicators of central nervous system involvement. *J. clin. Psychol.*, 1960, 16, 276–278.

McPHERSON, MARION W., & PEPIN, LORETTA A. Consistency of reproductions of Bender-Gestalt designs. *J. clin. Psychol.*, 1955, 11, 163–166.

MATCHABELY, K., & BERTRAND, R. Quelques considerations pratiques sur l'application du test moteur de structuration visuelle de Bender en clinique psychiatrique. *Rev. Psychol. appl.*, 1953, 3, 326–332.

MEEHL, P. F. *Clinical vs. statistical prediction: A theoretical analysis and a review of the evidence.* Minneapolis: Univer. of Minnesota Press, 1954.

Meehl, P. E. Wanted: A good cookbook. *Amer. Psychologist*, 1956, 11, 263–272.

Meehl, P. E. When shall we use our heads instead of the formula? *J. counsel. Psychol.*, 1957, 4, 268–273.

Mehlman, B., & Vatovec, E. A validation study of the Bender-Gestalt. *J. consult. Psychol.*, 1956, 20, 71–74.

Nadler, E. B., Fink, S. L., Shontz, F. C., & Brink, R. W. Objective scoring vs. clinical evalution of the Bender-Gestalt. *J. clin. Psychol.*, 1959, 15, 39–41.

Niebuhr, H., & Cohen, D. The effect of psychopathology on visual discrimination. *J. abnorm. soc. Psychol.*, 1956, 53, 173–177.

Okino, H. Studies on the Bender-Gestalt test. *Folia psychiat. neurol. Jap.*, 1956, 9, 314–328.

Olin, T. D., & Reznikoff, M. A comparison of copied and recalled reproductions of the Bender-Gestalt designs. *J. proj. Tech.*, 1958, 22, 320–327.

Pascal, G. R., & Suttell, Barbara J. *The Bender-Gestalt test.* New York: Grune & Stratton, 1951.

Peek, R. M. Directionality of lines in the Bender-Gestalt test. *J. consult. Psychol.*, 1953, 17, 213–216.

Peek, R. M., & Olsen, G. W. The Bender-Gestalt recall as an index of intellectual functioning. *J. clin. Psychol.*, 1955, 11, 185–188.

Peek, R. M., & Quast, W. *A scoring system for the Bender-Gestalt test.* Minneapolis: Author, 1951.

Peek, R. M., & Storms, L. H. Judging intellectual status from the Bender-Gestalt test. *J. clin. psychol.*, 1958, 14, 296–299.

Peixotto, Helen E. The Bender-Gestalt visual-motor test as a culture free test of personality. *J. clin. Psychol.*, 1954, 10, 369–372.

Popplestone, J. A. Variability of the Bender-Gestalt designs. *Percept. mot. Skills*, 1956, 6, 269–281.

Prado, W. M., Peyman, D. A. R., & Lacey, O. L. A validation study of measures of flattened affect on the Bender-Gestalt test. *J. clin. Psychol.*, 1960, 16, 435–438.

Reznikoff, M., & Olin, T. D. Recall of the Bender-Gestalt designs by organic and schizophrenic patients: A comparative study. *J. clin. Psychol.*, 1957, 13, 183–186.

Robinson, Nancy M. Bender-Gestalt performances of schizophrenics and paretics. *J. clin. Psychol.*, 1953, 9, 291–293.

Rosenthal, D., & Imber, S. D. The effects of Mephensen and practice on the Bender-Gesalt performance of psychiatric outpatients. *J. clin. Psychol.*, 1955, 11, 90–92.

Schon, Martha, & Waxenberg, S. E. Effect of hypophysectomy on Bender-Gestalt test performance. *J. clin. Psychol.*, 1958, 14, 299–302.

Stewart, H. F. A note on recall patterns using the Bender-Gestalt with psychiatric and nonpsychiatric patients. *J. clin. Psychol.*, 1957, 13, 95–97.

Stewart, H., & Cunningham, S. A note on scoring recalled figures of the Bender-Gestalt test using psychiatrics, nonpsychiatrics, and controls. *J. clin. Psychol.*, 1958, 14, 207–208.

Suczek, R. F., & Klopfer, W. G. Interpretation of the Bender-Gestalt test: The associative value of the figures. *Amer. J. Orthopsychiat.*, 1952, 22, 62–75.

Sullivan, J. J., & Welch, G. S. Results with the Bender visual motor Gestalt test. *Monogr. Soc. Res. Child Develpm.*, 1948, 12, No. 2 (Ser. No. 45).

Swensen, C. H., & Pascal, G. R. A note on the Bender-Gestalt test as a prognostic indicator in mental illness. *J. clin. Psychol.*, 1953, 9, 398.

Tamkin, A. S. The effectiveness of the Bender-Gesalt in differential diagnosis. *J. consult. Psychol.*, 1957, 21, 355–357.

Tolor, A. A comparison of the Bender-Gestalt test and digit-span test as measures of recall. *J. consult. Psychol.*, 1956, 20, 305–309.

Tolor, A. Structural properties of Bender-Gestalt test associations. *J. clin. Psychol.*,

1957, 13, 176–178.

TOLOR, A. Further studies on the Bender-Gestalt test and the digit-span test as measures of recall. *J. clin. Psychol.*, 1958, 14, 14–18.

TOLOR, A. The meaning of the Bender Gestalt test designs: A study in the use of the semantic differential. *J. proj. Tech.*, 1960, 24, 433–438.

TUCKER, J. E., & SPIELBERG, MIMI J. Bender-Gestalt test correlates of emotional depression. *J. consult. Psychol.*, 1958, 22, 56.

UFFELMANN, RUTH. The Bender-Gestalt test: Manner of approach. *Canad. J. Psychol.*, 1958, 12, 184–186.

WEWETZER, K.-H. Bender-Gestalt-Test bei Kindren: Auswertungsmethode und differentialdiagnostiche Moglickheiten. [The Bender-Gestalt test in children: A method of evaluation and differential diagnostic possibilities.] *Z. diagnost. Psychol.*, 1956, 4, 174–186. (*Psychol. Abstr.*, 31:6147)

WOHL, J. A note on the generality of constriction. *J. proj. Tech.*, 1957, 21, 410–413.

WOLFSOHN, T. Liv'ayat hashimush b'm'ivhanim bilti miluliyim. [Using nonverbal tests in measuring intelligence of elementary school pupils.] *M'gamot*, 1951–52, 3, 48–157.

WOLTMANN, A. G. The Bender visual-motor Gestalt test. In L. E. Abt & L. Bellak (Eds.), *Projective psychology*. New York: Knopf, 1950. Pp. 322–356.

ZOLIK, E. S. A comparison of the Bender-Gestalt reproductions of delinquents and non-delinquents. *J. clin. Psychol.*, 1958, 14, 24–26.

44

The Effectiveness of Clinicians' Judgments: The Diagnosis of Organic Brain Damage from the Bender-Gestalt Test[1]

LEWIS R. GOLDBERG

This experiment is noteworthy because it asks many of the questions which ought to be asked in the attempt to validate the Bender-Gestalt (B-G). Can the test differentiate organics from nonorganics? Are experienced clinicians better at this task than trainees? Are trainees, in turn, better than nonpsychologists?

The results indicated that correct selections could be made from a pool of an equal number of organic and nonorganic protocols at a somewhat better-than-chance ratio for each of the three groups. None of the groups, however, differed from each other essentially in accuracy of production, their composite amounting to an average of 68 per cent. Clinical training and experience apparently added nothing to predictive ability. A "superexpert" called in did achieve a "hit" score of 83 per cent. In most situations where the B-G is given, however, the base rate of non-organics would probably be just as high or higher. Consequently, the prediction that every patient is not an organic might be more efficacious than testing each one.

Certain questions can be raised. Are many schizophrenics suffering

[1] The author wishes to express his gratitude to the personnel of the Ann Arbor VA Hospital for their help in making this study possible. Special thanks are due Philip A. Smith, of the hospital, and E. Lowell Kelley and Max Hutt, of the University of Michigan, for their encouragement and criticisms of this paper.

from a functional rather than an organic disorder? Is not the difficulty in diagnosis just as much a function of the inaccuracy of the psychiatric classification system as that of the test? Moreover, cannot the B-G be used in conjunction with other tests of organicity so that although any one of these tests may not have very high validity, their composite may give an accurate diagnostic picture?

No matter what position one takes on these questions, it is evident that the B-G, with the present theoretical and methodological framework used in assessing patients, is not a very powerful tool in diagnosing organicity.

One of the most penetrating criticisms of previous attempts at assessing clinical judgments has been that the experimental predictions asked of the clinician differed in class or in kind from those made in his day-to-day practice. More specifically, the clinician often felt that the prediction of success at flight school (Holtzman & Sells, 1954), competency in clinical psychology (Kelley & Fiske, 1951), or even outcome of psychotherapy (Barron, 1953) called for a range of inferences beyond those usually demanded of him. Some clinicians deny making predictions and, instead, characterize their usual work in terms of "personality description," "diagnosis," "dynamic formulations," or "understanding the patient." Seen in this light, a good many of the published studies of the clinician's effectiveness can be dismissed as irrelevant by practicing clinicians who see themselves primarily as diagnosticians or therapists.

To eliminate these objections and thereby place clinicians in their best light, clinical assessment must: (1) involve problems typically encountered by the practicing clinician (for example, diagnostic judgments of neuropsychiatric referrals), (2) allow the clinician to use his favorite techniques (be they tests, interviews, case history material, reports from other services, etc.) in his favorite manner of utilizing them, and then (3) independently validate his conclusions against evidence acceptable to science as a whole; moreover, this entire procedure should be compared with similar judgments made by nonpsychologists (for example, clerical help).

Once one has established the kinds of judgments which clinicians tend to make more validly than less-trained personnel, then the assessment process can be analyzed segmentally to see where and how this increased accuracy comes about. This would involve the same considerations mentioned above, with one important difference: now the clinician would be restricted to one specific instrument or one assessment technique. At this stage, one finds many studies aimed at validating a specific technique, yet very rarely do they attempt to approximate the criteria already considered. For this reason, the question of what each diagnostic technique contributes to over-all diagnostic competence lies still unanswered.[2]

The present paper does not concern itself with the value implications of what the clinician does. Only in the sense that his work is compared with less-trained personnel is any judgment made of the worth of his labors. Whether diagnostic work-ups utilize the clinician's time to best advantage, whether he should be able to predict overt behavior, whether he should concentrate on research and/or therapy—all such questions are omitted here. The assumption has been made that clinicians spend a good deal of their time in diagnostic testing, and the question asked here is, "How good a job are they doing?"

The experimental answer to this last question hinges on two ancillary ones: who is to be called a clinician, and what is the nature of the independent evidence to test his judgments. The frequent criticism heard when groups of clinicians "fail" in some experimental study is that they were not "expert" enough or that they were essentially "academicians." Moreover, the criteria typically utilized in studies of this kind are all too often dubious in nature. Even the broad classifications "psychotic," "neurotic," "character disorder," and "normal"—much less the more homogeneous nosological categories such as "paranoid schizophrenia," "obsessive-compulsive neurosis," etc.—have no commonly accepted operational definitions. For this reason, it is typical to accept as a criterion either the consensus of many (the majority of whom could be in error) or the judgment of an established few (typically psychiatrists, who are usually responsible for the diagnostic referral to the clinical psychologist in the first place).

In this paper, which reports the first of a proposed series of assessments of clinical practice, the major concern is with diagnosis rather than prediction to later behavior. The nosological category chosen for this study was "organic brain damage, cortical," because of its inherent criterion for ultimate operational definition; namely, the independent diagnosis of a competent neurological team.[3] The clinicians assessed

---

[2] These comments circumvent two related problems: (1) the "clinical-actuarial" controversy and (2) the "molar-molecular" controversy. Both issues lend themselves to parallel research within the framework mentioned above. For example, diagnoses arrived at actuarially could be compared with those of the clinician and the non-psychologist. And diagnoses made, using all the clinician's techniques, could be compared with ones made using a portion of these techniques or just one "favorite" technique.

[3] This statement is not meant to imply that present neurological techniques are as yet able to assess the many gradations along the continuum from complete absence of cortex to perfect cortical health, at least short of opening the skull and examining the brain microscopically. Nor is there any implication that localization, chronicity, and amount of cortical destruction will not influence performance on psychological tests. However, if a neurological team can separate cases on both extremes of the continuum, then these cases might serve as logical criteria for the evaluation of psychological techniques.

included those who were currently practicing as diagnosticians (either staff or trainees) at a large VA hospital, and their diagnostic performance was compared with that of nonpsychologists (hospital secretaries). This study was aimed at the second stage of a total assessment project, an appraisal of the validity of a specific diagnostic instrument in the hands of practicing clinicians. Since the Bender Visual-Motor Gestalt Test is the most widely used test for organic brain damage at the installation under consideration (and perhaps at many other installations), this instrument was chosen as the technique in question.

Procedure

Protocols of Bender-Gestalt tests were randomly selected from the files of a VA general medical and surgical hospital. Of these protocols, those from the first 15 patients who had been diagnosed by independent neurological examination as showing clear-cut evidence of cortical impairment were selected to represent patients manifesting organic brain damage (hereafter termed organics). As the nonorganic control group (hereafter termed nonorganics), the protocols of the first 15 patients from psychiatric wards were selected where (1) psychiatric diagnoses were clearly agreed upon, (2) no symptoms usually associated with organic brain damage were reported, (3) no record of cerebral trauma was noted, and (4) any routine examination by the neurological staff was negative to cortical impairment. These latter psychiatric patients were all fairly recent admissions to the hospital at the time they were tested and in general could be characterized as displaying acute rather than chronic symptomatology. Table 44-1 summarizes certain descriptive variables for these 30 patients.

The 30 Bender protocols were divided into three groups of 10 each, such that in Group I there were 2 organics and 8 nonorganics, in Group

TABLE 44-1   *Description of Patient Populations*

	ORGANICS ($N = 15$; MEAN AGE = 38; AGE RANGE = 24–61)			NONORGANICS ($N = 15$; MEAN AGE = 32; AGE RANGE = 23–54)	
ETIOLOGY (WHERE AVAILABLE) N	LOCALIZATION (WHERE AVAILABLE) N		SYMPTOMATOLOGY (WHERE AVAILABLE) N	FINAL PSYCHIATRIC DIAGNOSES	N
Trauma	7	Rt. cerebral		Convulsions	4	Paranoid schizophrenia	4
Tumor	3	hemisphere	1	Death	3	Catatonic schizophrenia	1
Multiple sclerosis	2	Lt. temporal lobe	1	Chronic brain		Manic-depressive	
Thrombosis	1	Rt. parietal lobe	1	syndrome	1	psychosis	1
Alvheimer's disease	1	Rt. front parietal		Hemiparesis	1	Character disorder	4
		lobe	1	Hemiplegia,		Conversion reaction	2
		Rt. carotid artery	1	spastic	1	Anxiety neurosis	2
				Headaches	1	Obsessive-compulsive	1
						neurosis	

II there were 5 of each, and in Group III there were 8 organics and 2 nonorganics. This was done so as to be able to investigate the relationship between frequency of occurrence of a diagnostic entity (base rate) and accuracy of its diagnosis; also, this allowed the work for each clinician to be broken down into more convenient sections. All protocols were assigned a code number which was printed on cardboard and stapled over the patient's name, thus removing this identifying datum. On the other hand, all descriptions of how the patient actually drew the Bender designs (i.e., arrows, circles, short notes, etc.) were left on the protocols.

Only the actual reproductions of the Bender designs were used in this study, since uniform elaborations and free associations were not available for all the patients.

Table 44–2 gives a breakdown of some variables concerning the judges who participated in this project. All the psychologists were actively engaged in diagnostic evaluations at the time the study was conducted, although they varied both in their general diagnostic testing experience and in their particular experience with the Bender. Many used the test almost routinely as part of their psychological examinations of referred patients, while a few used it only rarely. Without exception, the non-professional judges had had no contact with the technique.

Each judge was given the three packets of 10 protocols, one packet at a time in random order. Directions were essentially as follows for all participants:

You will be given 30 Bender protocols for your diagnostic impressions. For your convenience they have been divided into 3 groups of 10 each. Please judge each Bender individually, using any system you normally apply to such a task. Take all the time you want, and feel free to utilize any instruments (i.e., compass, protractor, ruler, etc.) which you feel will increase your diagnostic accuracy. Please do the very best job you possibly can.[4] Record your judgments on the face sheet attached to each packet.

This face sheet was a mimeographed form listing the patients' code numbers in a column down the left-hand side of the sheet. Along the top of the sheet were column headings Organic and Nonorganic, as well as a confidence rating scale labeled Positively; Fairly certain; Think so; Maybe; and Blind guess. Instructions on the form were to check the most appropriate diagnostic description for each patient and also to indicate one's degree of confidence in each of these judgments. Thus, each participant made one dichotomous diagnostic judgment and then qualified it on a five-point scale of confidence.

---

[4] To increase the judges' involvement in this diagnostic task, a bottle of Scotch was offered to the judge who performed most accurately. It was generally felt that all the judges "tried their best." Although the judges spent only 15 to 30 minutes diagnosing all 30 patients, in general they expressed their impressions that they had been as careful in these diagnoses as they would be typically in their regular professional evaluations.

TABLE 44–2   *Description of Participating Judges*

GROUP	N	MEAN AGE	LEVEL OF TRAINING IN PSYCHOLOGY	APPROXIMATE EXPERIENCE WITH THE BENDER	
				MEAN	RANGE
Psychology staff	4	35	Ph.D.plus 4–10 yrs. experience	6 yrs.	4–9 yrs.
Psychology trainees	10	27	M.A. plus 1–4 yrs. experience	3 yrs.	1–4 yrs.
Nonpsychologists	8	25	None	0	None

For the nonprofessional participants, the directions were amplified slightly. Since they had no basis at all for their judgments, they were administered the Bender as a patient would have received it. Then, they were given the following directions:

"Now you have an idea of the test itself. Psychologists use this test to help them diagnose patients with brain damage, on the assumption that brain-damaged persons draw the designs differently than persons without such damage. If you wish, you may use your drawings as a guide to the way a nonbrain-damaged person responds on the test."

Then followed the same directions given the psychologists.

After the 22 judges had completed the diagnostic task, the Bender reproductions were scored by the Pascal-Suttell Objective Index (Pascal & Suttell, 1951), for comparison purposes with the clinical judgments.[5]

Results

INTERJUDGE ANALYSIS

The most striking finding of this study is the complete overlap between groups of judges on diagnostic accuracy (see Table 44–3). Staff psychologists, psychology trainees, and nonprofessional persons did not differ from one another in their ability to differentiate organic from nonorganic patients by means of their Bender protocols. The judges' degree of successful diagnoses ranged from 57 to 77 per cent, with six judges differing at the .01 level and six more at the .05 level from statistical chance (50 per cent). The remaining ten judges did not differ in their diagnostic accuracy from that attributable to chance alone.

---

[5] The author wishes to thank Ronald Ribler, of Michigan State University, for his help in scoring the Bender protocols.

While the Pascal-Suttell Objective Index (1951) was developed to help differentiate psychotic from neurotic populations, it has been used for the diagnosis of organics (Bowland & Deabler, 1956). Cutting scores for this use of the index vary, and extensive normative data is as yet unavailable. If a Z score of 100 is used to separate the groups, the index accurately diagnoses 63 per cent of the patients in this study (Fisher's Exact: $p = .04$). When the cutting score is lowered to 90, the percentage of successful diagnoses increases to 67 per cent ($p = .01$). The optimum cutting score for this population seems to be around 80, at which point the index diagnoses with 80 per cent accuracy ($p < .005$). As the cutting point is lowered below this, accuracy slowly falls away (77, 73, and 70 per cent for Z cutting points of 70, 60, and 50, respectively); at a cutting score of 40 or below, only chance results occur.

TABLE 44–3   *Diagnostic Accuracy by Groups of Judges*

GROUP	N	MEAN PER CENT CORRECT	RANGE	NUMBER OF JUDGES DIFFERING SIGNIFICANTLY FROM CHANCE (50%) AT THE .05 LEVEL
Psychology staff	4	65%[a]	60–70%	1 (25%)
Psychology trainees	10	70%[a]	60–77%	6 (60%)
Nonpsychologists	8	67%[a]	57–73%	5 (62.5%)
All groups	22	68%	57–77%	12 (54.5%)

[a] All mean differences between groups are nonsignificant.

To check on group differences in interjudge agreement, the percentage of agreement for each group of judges was computed for each patient. The average percentage of agreement over all 30 patients, for each group of judges, ranged from 78 to 85 per cent (chance would predict 50 per cent), with no statistically significant intergroup differences.

Although the groups appeared quite similar with respect to diagnostic accuracy and interjudge agreement, there were large differences between the groups in the amount of confidence they placed in their judgments (Kruskal-Wallis H test: $p < .01$). The nonprofessional judges—with no training or experience in Bender interpretation (and therefore no apparent reason for developing confidence in the technique)—were, as a group, much more confident in their judgments than were either the staff or the trainees. And the trainees displayed more confidence in their diagnoses than the staff. The results present the surprising paradox of an inverse relationship between the amount of experience with the Bender and the degree of confidence placed in diagnoses made from it. Moreover, there was no relationship between individual diagnostic accuracy and degree of confidence!

To test whether the reduced confidence exhibited by the more sophisticated judges was the result of their finer discrimination between the easier and the more difficult judgments (with the more difficult ones being rated with less confidence), the average degree of confidence for each judge was computed for those cases he diagnosed correctly and again for those cases when he misdiagnosed the patient. The difference between these two averages (hereafter termed the index of discrimination), when computed for each group of judges, was found to show no significant intergroup differences. In general, judges were about as confident on cases they misdiagnosed as they were on those they diagnosed correctly. When the index of discrimination was used as the basis for ranking the judges, there was found to be no relationship between this measure and either total degree of confidence or total diagnostic accuracy.

A further measure was developed as an index of clinical judgment,[6] under the assumption that a misdiagnosis which had been given with little confidence should not count as heavily against the clinician as one which was given with great confidence. An index was constructed in the following manner: for each correct diagnosis qualified by more than his median degree of confidence, each judge was given two points; for each correct diagnosis given with less than his median degree of confidence, one point; for each misdiagnosis with greater than median confidence, minus two points; for each misdiagnosis qualified by less than median confidence, minus one point. When total scores were computed for each judge, analysis showed no differences between the psychologists, trainees, and the nonprofessional judges on this measure of clinical judgment.

An analysis was made of the judges' tendencies to overcall or undercall organicity in the population they were diagnosing. The trainees as a group made the most "organic" diagnoses, 13.5 per judge, and they were the nearest to judging the actual number of organics in the sample. The nonprofessionals made the least such diagnoses, only 8.5 per judge. These differences almost approach statistical significance (Kruskal-Wallis H: $p < .10$), but there was no relationship between the number of patients called organic and diagnostic accuracy. A measure of the discrepancy between the number of organics called and the actual number in the sample was computed for each group; neither this measure nor the gross number of organics called was related to any of the previously reported indexes. Table 44-4 summarizes the findings on these various measures.

Since the original material presented to the judges consisted of three packets, each containing different percentages of organic patients, the

---

[6] Suggested by Philip A. Smith, of the Ann Arbor VA Hospital.

TABLE 44–4   *Performances of the Three Groups of Judges*
on Some Selected Indexes

GROUP	INTERJUDGE AGREEMENT AVERAGE PER CENT	DEGREE OF CONFI- DENCE[a, b]	INDEX OF DISCRIMI- NATION[c]	NUMBER CALLED ORGANIC[d]	INDEX OF CLINICAL JUDGMENT[e]
Psychology staff	78%	2.1	1.3	12.1	16.2
Psychology trainees	85%	2.5	1.1	13.5	20.6
Nonpsychologists	85%	3.1	1.1	8.5	18.8
Totals	84%	2.6	1.1	11.1	19.1

a Intergroup differences in degree of confidence significant at the .01 level (Kruskal-Wallis H test); all other differences nonsignificant.
b Scored o for "blind guess"; 1 for "maybe"; 2 for "think so"; 3 for "fairly certain"; and 4 for "positive."
c Scored by subtracting the confidence score on misdiagnoses from that on correct diagnoses.
d The actual number of organics was 15.
e For method of scoring, see text.

data could be reanalyzed to investigate base rate differences on the variables already considered. In this respect, each packet can be thought of as a separate study, each comparable to one conducted at a different type of installation (for example, a GMS hospital, an NP hospital, a home for mentally deficients, etc.). All the previously reported indexes

TABLE 44–5   *Group Performance as a Function of Differing*
*Organic Base Rates**

GROUP	DIAGNOSTIC ACCURACY	INTERJUDGE AGREEMENT	CONFI- DENCE	DISCRIMI- NATION	NUMBER CALLED ORGANIC	INDEX OF CLINICAL JUDGMENT
Group I (2 organic; 8 nonorganic)						
Psychology staff	72%	78%	2.2	.2	3.0	7.0
Psychology trainees	62%	84%	2.3	.6	3.7[b]	4.9
Nonpsychologists	78%[a]	88%	3.1	.1	2.0[c]	9.5
Total	70%	84%	2.6[d]	.3	2.6	7.0
Group II (5 of each)						
Psychology staff	57%	78%	2.1	.5	3.8	3.2
Psychology trainees	73%	81%	2.5	−.2	4.3[b]	7.2
Nonpsychologists	68%[a]	80%	3.1	.2	3.0[c]	5.9
Total	68%	80%	2.6[d]	.1	3.7	6.0
Group III (8 organic; 2 nonorganic)						
Psychology staff	65%	80%	2.c	.7	5.5	6.0
Psychology trainees	75%	89%	2.6	.1	5.5[b]	8.5
Nonpsychologists	56%[a]	89%	3.1	.2	3.5[c]	3.4
Total	66%	87%	2.7[d]	.2	4.8	6.2

* For explanation of indexes, see Table 44–4 or text.
a Differences among nonpsychologists at the three base rates significant at the .05 level (Friedman two-way analysis of variance).
b Differences significant at the .01 level (Friedman).
c Differences significant at the .05 level (Friedman).
d Differences between groups significant at the .05 level for each base rate (Kruskal-Wallis one-way analysis of variance). Note.—All other differences nonsignificant.

(accuracy, interjudge agreement, degree of confidence, discrimination, clinical judgment, and number of patients called organic) were computed for each group of judges for each of the three different organic base rates. Table 44–5 summarizes these results.

The Friedman two-way analysis of variance (nonparametric) was run to test differences attributable to the differing base rates. The only statistically significant differences uncovered were on the "diagnostic accuracy" and "number called organic" indexes. The nonprofessionals were significantly more accurate in their diagnoses as the number of organics in the sample decreased (probably because of their consistent tendency to be the most sparing in their use of the diagnosis "organic"). All groups called more patients organic as the actual base rates of organics in the sample increased (although in the case of the staff judges, the small size of their group prevented statistical significance).

The Kruskal-Wallis one-way analysis of variance (nonparametric) was carried out to test if any of the differences between mean group scores, at each base rate, were statistically significant. Just as in the case of the over-all analysis, the three groups of judges were found to differ significantly only in their degree of confidence.

INTERPATIENT ANALYSIS

Sometimes the "majority opinion" of a group is more accurate than any of the opinions of its individual members. To check on this, a "group" diagnosis, generated by combining the diagnoses made by all 22 judges, was examined for each patient. The amount of agreement between judges ranged from complete agreement on one patient (a manic-depressive psychotic, correctly diagnosed by everyone as nonorganic) to a complete 11–11 split in opinion on two patients (both organics). There was less than 75 per cent agreement on 8 of the 30 patients.

For those 28 patients on whom there were "majority" diagnoses, the group as a whole misdiagnosed two nonorganics (both paranoid schizophrenics) and five organics (of whom three had symptoms which included grand mal convulsions, one was a case of posttraumatic encephalopathy, and one had a deadly glioblastoma multiforme). Thus, if one counts the evenly divided cases as errors (since no group diagnosis was generated), the group as a whole correctly diagnosed 70 per cent of the patients, a figure not significantly different from the mean of the individual diagnoses (68 per cent).

Interestingly, the degree of agreement among the judges did not correlate significantly with the accuracy of their combined diagnoses. Moreover, majority accuracy did not turn out to be related to such variables as the chronological age of the patient or to his nosological category. On the other hand, since most of the judges tended to underestimate the actual number of organics in the sample, they tended to be most in agreement on patients whom they diagnosed nonorganic (Fisher's Exact: $p = .013$).

Certain patients must have seemed easier to diagnose than others, since there was a strong relationship between the amount of agreement on a patient's diagnosis and the total pooled confidence ratings given for this diagnosis (Fisher's Exact: $p < .001$). Surprisingly, however, the judges were just as confident in rating their incorrect as their correct diagnoses; nor were they any less confident in diagnosing organic than nonorganic patients.

A SUBSEQUENT EXPLORATION

In the course of examining the relationship between diagnostic accuracy and experience with the Bender, it was noted that the judge who performed most accurately was a trainee who had spent considerable time (as part of his research for a doctoral dissertation) in administering, scoring, and interpreting tests for organic brain damage with a large group of brain-damaged patients. Although a staff judge also had considerable Bender experience and only performed at the median level on this task, one might still wonder whether specific intensive experience with the instrument might not increase diagnostic accuracy. In effect, this hypothesis would imply that although the practicing diagnosticians were not more accurate than nontrained persons on this task, real "experts" with the Bender could surpass them all.

To test this hypothesis, one of the country's foremost authorities on the Bender test was solicited to take part in this study.[7] This judge, taking some 20 hours to complete the diagnostic process, did perform more accurately than anyone in the original study—diagnosing 83 per cent of the patients correctly. His scores fell in the middle of the over-all distribution on degree of confidence and discrimination, but he was one of the most accurate in judging the actual number of organics in the sample. He also was at the top on the index of clinical judgment.

Since his performance lends support to the "expert" theory on Bender diagnosis, it seemed legitimate to combine the scores of the top two diagnostic judges in this study into a subgroup of Bender "specialists" and then to reanalyze the data comparing their performance on all the indexes with that of the three other groups. This analysis revealed no significant differences on measures other than those of accuracy and clinical judgment (Fisher's Exact: $p < .004$), on which variables the "specialists" were, in effect, selected.

[7] Special acknowledgment is due Max Hutt, of the University of Michigan, for the time and thought he invested in this phase of the study.

Discussion

In general, the results indicate that diagnostic accuracy (when using the Bender to diagnose organic brain damage) does not depend on experience or training in psychology (unless, perhaps, that training includes years of intensive work with the instrument in question). If he is not a real expert in the use of the Bender, a clinician will find that his secretary can probably do this particular job of differential diagnosis as well as himself. Moreover, she will most likely have considerably more confidence in her judgments than he would have in his. This makes it all the more unfortunate that one's degree of confidence bears no relationship to his diagnostic accuracy on this task!

Now these results, in themselves, may be embarrassing. And, when one considers the base rates of organics usually encountered in clinical practice, one might even become alarmed. For in most settings the actual base rate is closer to Group I (20 per cent organics) than to any of the other groups in this study. And it is in this Group I where the nonprofessionals—by virtue of their tendency to label most patients nonorganic — appear most likely to overshadow their professional employers in diagnostic accuracy (see Table 44–5). However, neither the nonprofessionals nor the group as a whole did as well as could have been done by merely calling all patients in this group "nonorganic" and thereby diagnosing with 80 per cent accuracy.

Before judging the Bender too harshly, however, the following factors should be considered: (1) the group as a whole did perform significantly above chance (50 per cent) on this task, thus supporting the premise that groups of organics do respond differently to the Bender test than do groups of nonorganics (but when discriminable differences do appear, they are typically so obvious that almost everyone can detect them); (2) this study provided no basis for comparing the Bender with other tests for organic brain damage in order to see whether the widespread faith in this technique is indeed comparatively justified; (3) it is, of course, possible that other tests taken in combination with the Bender may permit judges to diagnose more accurately; and (4) one cannot immediately discount the utility of the cues furnished by a face-to-face encounter with the patient—cues which were totally absent in this study.

On the other hand, these results might have been anticipated on the basis of previous work in this area (Bowland & Deabler, 1956). For example, Pascal and Suttell (1951), while formulating their Objective Index to differentiate psychotics from neurotics, have this to say about the differential diagnosis of organics:

The Bender-Gestalt test cannot, in the absence of other data, answer that question (is there cortical damage?) except occasionally in extreme cases which are also clinically apparent (p. 40).

Performance on the Bender-Gestalt test can indicate damage to the cortex only when the damage shows its effect by pronounced disturbance of the ability to execute the test. We know that nine-year-old children can produce the designs without marked deviation from the stimuli. When, therefore, an individual is functioning at a maturational level of nine years with respect to his ability to reproduce the designs, so to speak, we cannot distinguish between his deviation and those of individuals suffering from psychogenic disorders. This fact suggests that damage to the cortex has to be rather severe in its effect on the functioning efficiency of an adult of normal I.Q. before it can be detected by means of performance on the Bender-Gestalt test. This fact also suggests that actual lesions may exist which cannot, on the basis of the deviations noted by us, be detected in performance on this test (pp. 62–66).

Nevertheless, since the evidence suggests the possibility that real experts in the technique may perform with increased diagnostic accuracy on this task, it is conceivable that they might be able to communicate whatever interpretive refinements they possess. In effect, this has been tried with the Pascal-Suttell Objective Index, which, at its optimum cutting point, performed about as well as did the best of the individual judges. Significant in this connection, however, is the considerably greater length of time taken by the top expert in making his diagnoses, as compared to the amount taken by any of the others, and correspondingly the greater length of time needed to score records by the Pascal-Suttell method. Assuming that real experts—after considerable time and careful scrutiny—can slightly outperform hospital secretaries, the value of this potential increment in accuracy must be carefully evaluated.

Summary

Staff psychologists, psychology trainees, and nonprofessional (secretarial) judges made diagnostic judgments from the Bender protocols of 15 organic and 15 nonorganic patients and then indicated their degree of confidence for each of their diagnoses. The three groups of judges did not differ in their ability to diagnose organic brain damage from the Bender, although the nonprofessionals displayed considerably more confidence in their judgments than did either of the other groups. The Pascal-Suttell Objective Index approximately equaled the clinical judgments in diagnostic accuracy, but a renowned Bender expert was able to better the diagnoses of the practicing clinicians. The group as a whole diagnosed above a chance level, but when the base rate of organic patients typically encountered in clinical practice is considered, the results suggest that chances for misdiagnosis could be increased by utilizing the Bender-Gestalt Test.

REFERENCES

BARRON, F. Some test correlates of response to psychotherapy. *J. consult. Psychol.,* 1953, 17, 235–241.

BOWLAND, J. A., & DEABLER, H. L. A Bender-Gestalt diagnostic validity study. *J. clin. Psychol.,* 1956, 12, 82–84.

HOLTZMAN, W. H., & SELLS, S. B. Prediction of flying success by clinical analysis of test protocols. *J. abnorm. soc. Psychol.,* 1954, 49, 485–490.

KELLEY, E. L., & FISKE, D. W. *The prediction of performance in clinical psychology.* Ann Arbor: Univer. of Michigan Press, 1951.

PASCAL, G. R., & SUTTELL, BARBARA J. *The Bender-Gestalt test.* New York: Grune & Stratton, 1951.

45

The Effectiveness of the Bender-Gestalt Test in Differential Diagnosis[1]

ARTHUR S. TAMKIN

In this carefully controlled study, the author was unable to differentiate a group of psychotics from a group of neurotics and personality disorders, using the Pascal and Suttell Z score. Despite the fact that Pascal and Suttell had reported no relationship between the Z score and age, the author went ahead and controlled for this variable anyhow. It was well that he did so, because he reported a significant relationship between age and Z score. Since several studies reporting Z scores as successfully differentiating psychiatric groups failed to control for age, presumably on the basis of Pascal and Suttell's earlier study, the results of these studies are suspect. The fact that one study has failed to find such a relationship should not be taken as carte blanche to avoid the labor of controlling for this variable. Such are the peculiarities and complexities of behavior that any number of circumstances may yield a positive relationship in one situation and a negative relationship or none at all in still others. Until the factors causing this fluctuation are known and controlled, it may be wiser to seek justification for omitting a control from several consistent studies rather than relying on a solitary report.

[1] From the Veterans Administration, Northhampton, Massachusetts. The author wishes to thank the following members of the Clinical Psychology Service for their constructive review of the manuscript: Drs. Isidor Scherer, Arnold Trehub, Cesareo D. Peña, and C. James Klett.

741

PART V : *Bender-Gestalt*

Since the introduction of the Visual-Motor Gestalt test by Lauretta Bender (1938), there has arisen considerable interest in its use as a differentially diagnostic instrument for psychiatric disorders. While its efficacy in identifying cases of organic brain disease, in which there is a disintegration of visual-motor functions, has been considered to rest on firm ground, the question of its applicability to the functional mental disorders has not been settled. Bender found deviations of visual-motor Gestalt patterns in her studies of schizophrenic children and adults; but because the personality disturbances of psychoneurotics seldom invade their visual-motor sphere, she did not find that their records showed deviations. Hutt (1945), however, was able to delineate characteristic distortions in the Bender drawings of schizophrenics and psychoneurotics which distinguished these clinical groups from each other and from patients with organic brain damage. Billingslea (1948) found no support for Hutt's proposed psychoneurotic signs, nor was Hanvick (1951) able to differentiate between psychoneurotics with functional backache and control patients with proven organic disease of the back.

With the introduction of an objective scoring method by Pascal and Suttell (1951), successful separation between clinical groups with functional diagnoses has been reported. In addition to Pascal and Suttell, Lonstein (1954) and Bowland and Deabler (1956), all using the same scoring method, reported discrimination between hospitalized psychotics and nonpsychotic psychiatric patients at high levels of statistical significance. Because of Pascal and Suttell's findings that age did not materially affect scoring levels within the age range of 15 to 50 years, controls for age were ignored in these studies. Furthermore, the factors of education and chronicity were not uniformly controlled by these experimenters. The present study was an attempt to cross-validate the findings that the Pascal and Suttell scoring method of the Bender-Gestalt differentiates significantly between functionally psychotic patients and those with nonpsychotic, functional mental disorders.

Procedure

The subjects (Ss) used in this study consisted of a group of 27 psychotics and a group of 27 neurotics and personality disorders matched on the basis of age. They were all male patients at the Veterans Administration Hospital, Northampton, Massachusetts, who had taken the Bender-Gestalt in conjunction with other psychological tests for routine psychodiagnostic evaluations. Except for a few, they had been tested shortly after their arrival as new admissions or readmissions, and their diagnoses, representing functional psychiatric disorders, were established later by neuropsychiatric staff conferences. All Ss had sufficient education to permit the computation of Pascal and Suttell's Z score; that is, at least one year of high school. The psychotic group ranged in age from 20 to 42 years, with a mean age of 30.85, and the nonpsychotic group ranged in age from 21 to 43 years, with a mean age of 31.63. Thus, the Ss were representative of the high-school and college-educated hospitalized patients with functional mental disorders of recent exacerbation who might require differential diagnoses.

Each S's Bender-Gestalt protocol was scored by the Pascal and Suttell method without the scorer's knowledge of the diagnosis, and the corresponding Z score for the S's educational level was determined. For 37 Ss of these samples, scores on the F and Critical Item scales of the MMPI were obtained. These two scales have been shown to be related to degree of psychopathology when applied to similar patients (Tamkin, 1957), and they were used as indexes of psychopathology.

Results

The correlation coefficient between age and z score was found to be + .29, which is significant at the .05 level. The mean Z score of the group of psychotics was 59.19, and of the group of neurotics and personality disorders it was 61.59. A t test of the difference between the means yielded a value of 0.58, indicating no significant difference. Since the weights of the reproductive errors derived by Pascal and Suttell may not have been applicable to the samples used in this study, the numbers of raw errors produced by each group were compared. The mean number of raw errors of the psychotic group was 7.44, and for the group of neurotics and personality disorders it was 9.44. A t of 1.74, however, was not significant at the .05 level. Since MMPI profiles of 37 Ss were available, an attempt was made to determine if Z scores were correlated with test measures of psychopathology, if not with psychiatric diagnosis. Scores of both F and Critical Item scales seemed to be suitable criteria of degree of psychopathology since they each differentiated the two clinical groups at the .05 level, based on one-tailed hypotheses. Accordingly, correlation coefficients were computed for z and F and for z and the Critical Item scale. The obtained values of + .29 and + .17 were not significant.

Discussion

The failure to find significant differences between the Bender-Gestalt scores of these two clinical groups, when the important extraneous variables of age, education, and chronicity were controlled, contrasts sharply with the positive findings reported by other investigators using the Pascal and Suttell scoring method. In comparing the scoring levels of this psychotic group, one finds lower raw scores and Z scores than those reported by the other investigators, while for the nonpsychotic group the scores are more nearly similar (Addington, 1952; Bowland & Deabler, 1956; Lonstein, 1954; Pascal & Suttell, 1951). It may be of some significance in explaining the divergent findings of this study that none except Addington controlled for the age variable, nor did they uniformly control for education or chronicity. Addington, who selected subjects with at least two years of hospitalization, obtained the highest raw score in his schizophrenic group.

In conclusion, it appears that the Bender-Gestalt, scored by the Pascal and Suttell method, is of dubious effectiveness in differentiating between functional psychiatric disorders. In this study, it failed to separate hospitalized psychiatric patients with functional psychoses from hospitalized neurotics and personality disorders, nor did it correlate significantly with MMPI-derived indexes of psychopathology.

Summary

The effectiveness of the Bender-Gestalt, scored by the Pascal and Suttell method, in differentiating the functional mental disorders, was investigated. The Z scores were computed from the Bender-Gestalt protocols of a group of 27 functional psychotics and a group of 27 neurotics and personality disorders matched on the basis of age. All Ss were selected from newly admitted or readmitted hospital patients who had at least ninth-grade education. The findings showed no significant differences between the two clinical groups and no significant correlations between Z scores and two MMPI-derived indexes of psychopathology. A significant correlation between age and Z score was obtained, contrary to the findings of Pascal and Suttell. It was concluded that the Bender-Gestalt, scored by the Pascal and Suttell method, has dubious effectiveness as a differentially diagnostic instrument for the functional mental disorders.

REFERENCES

ADDINGTON, M. C. A note in the Pascal and Suttell scoring system of the Bender-Gestalt test. *J. clin. Psychol.*, 1952, 8, 312–313.

BENDER, LAURETTA. A visual motor Gestalt test and its clinical use. *Amer. Orthopsychiat. Assoc., Res. Monogr.* No. 3, 1938.

BILLINGSLEA, F. Y. The Bender-Gestalt: an objective scoring method and validating data. *Clin. Psychol. Monogr.* No. 1, 1948.

BOWLAND, J. A., & DEABLER, H. L. A Bender-Gestalt diagnostic validity study. *J. clin. Psychol.*, 1956, 12, 82–84.

Hanvick, L. J. A note on the limitations of the use of the Bender-Gestalt test as a diagnostic aid in patients with a functional complaint. *J. clin. Psychol.*, 1951, 7, 194.

Hutt, M. L. A tentative guide for the administration and interpretation of the Bender-Gestalt test. U.S. Army, Adjutant General's School, 1945 (Restricted).

Lonstein, M. A validation of a Bender-Gestalt scoring system. *J. consult. Psychol.*, 1954, 18, 377–379.

Pascal, G. R., & Suttell, Barbara J. *The Bender-Gestalt test.* New York: Grune & Stratton, 1951.

Tamkin, A. S. An evaluation of the construct validity of Barron's ego-strength scale. *J. clin. Psychol.*, 1957, 13, 156–158.

46

The Use of Bender-Gestalt Cutoff Scores in Indentifying Juvenile Delinquents

ROBERT H. CURNUTT AND LOREN V. COROTTO

The futility of attempting to diagnose fuzzily defined, too-inclusive diagnostic groups is emphasized in this brief study. The problem was to validate a Z score of 60 from the Pascal-Suttell scoring system as a good cutoff for the diagnosis of juvenile delinquency. Neither this cutoff score (suggested by Zolik) nor the score of 70 suggested by Pascal and Suttell proved to be effective. Apparently, the next step is to try the cutoff score with more specifically defined behavior problems than "juvenile delinquent."

Some studies indicate that the Bender-Gestalt (B-G) (Bender, 1938) Test can be used to differentiate various behavioral groups by the use of cutoff scores. This was first done by Pascal and Suttell (1951), who believe that statistical statements can be made regarding the probability of certain scores' being attained by a patient or nonpatient. This has led other authors to attempt to determine more effective cutoff scores. A study by Zolik (1958) indicated that by utilizing a cutoff score of 60, which represents one standard deviation above the mean, delinquents could be differentiated from nondelinquents. This study attempts to validate independently the various cutoff scores suggested by Zolik and

747

Pascal and Suttell and to evaluate whether these suggested cutoff scores do actually differentiate an independent sample of delinquents.

Method

All the adolescents referred to a children's psychiatric service for observation by the juvenile courts during a two-year period were examined. Any adolescent with a diagnosis or known history of psychosis, organic brain damage, or mental deficiency was excluded to eliminate gross psychopathology as a variable in the B-G protocols. In addition, any subject failing to meet the statistical criteria specified by Pascal and Suttell for their scoring system was eliminated. The final sample consisted of 120 adolescent delinquents, 63 males and 57 females. The protocols of these subjects were coded and subsequently scored by one of the authors who had no knowledge of any of the individual cases. A delinquent was operationally defined as an adolescent having had one or more contacts with a juvenile court, as well as a court placement in a children's psychiatric service for observation. The ages of the delinquent sample ranged from 15 to 19 years.

Results

The results in general question the efficiency of cutoff scores as a method of distinguishing juvenile delinquents. Simple inspection of Table 46–1 reveals marked variability which makes the use of cutoff scores a highly questionable procedure.

TABLE 46–1	*Mean Bender-Gestalt Z Scores and Standard Deviations*		
	MALES	FEMALES	TOTAL
Mean	62.70	55.75	59.40
S.D.	15.91	13.67	15.29
N	63	57	120

Thirty-six cases, or 30 per cent, of the juvenile delinquents in the present study obtained Z scores of 49 or lower, while 32 cases, or 26.7 per cent obtained Z scores in the 50 to 60 range, i.e., Zolik's questionable range. Fifty-two cases, or 43.3 per cent, yielded scores of 61 or higher, which are above Zolik's suggested cutoff score of 60. A chi-square test indicated a significant divergence (.01 level) of the observed results from those expected on the basis of Zolik's sample. There are significantly more cases below a Z score of 50, while, conversely, at the other end of the continuum there are signficantly less cases above a Z score of 60 than would be expected from Zolik's data. The present sample of delinquents yielded a distribution much closer to a normal distribution of Z scores than did Zolik's sample.

Pascal and Suttell's suggested cutoff score of 72 segregated 36 cases, or 30 per cent, of the delinquents. Forty per cent, or 48 cases, fell in Pascal and Suttell's questionable range i.e., 50 to 72, while the remaining 36 cases, or 30 per cent, had Z scores of 49 or less. This distribution of scores tends to fall between Pascal and Suttell's standardizing samples of normals and psychoneurotics.

A t test of the means of the male delinquents and the female delinquents yielded a difference that is significant at the .02 level. This diference is probably due to differences in choice of delinquent behavior rather than a true sex difference, as a previous study by Corotto and Curnutt (1960) demonstrated.

Discussion

The results indicate poor prediction in terms of differentiating delinquent behavior from nondelinquent behavior whether one utilizes the higher cutoff score suggested by Pascal and Suttell or the lower cutoff score suggested by Zolik. The wide variability of scores in the present sample may reflect the wide range of behavior that is encompassed in the term *delinquent*. It may be possible to utilize cutoff scores with some delinquent samples, provided the behavioral criteria have been systematically restricted to well-defined and consistent behavioral traits.

Summary

To determine the effectiveness of B-G cutoff scores as a screening device for juvenile delinquents, a sample of 120 B-G protocols of adolescent delinquents was coded and scored without knowledge of the individual case. The distribution was analyzed in terms of cutoff scores reported in the literature. The results indicate that extreme caution must be used in applying cutoff scores mechanically in any but the grossest type of differentiation.

REFERENCES

Bender, L. *A visual motor Gestalt test and its clinical use.* New York: Amer. Orthopsychiat. Ass., 1938.

Corotto, L. V., & Curnutt, R. H. The effectiveness of the Bender-Gestalt in differentiating a flight group from an aggressive group of adolescents. *J. consult. Psychol.*, 1960, 24, 368–369.

Curnutt, R. H. The use of the Bender-Gestalt with an alcoholic and non-alcoholic population. *J. clin. Psychol.*, 1953, 9, 287–290.

Pascal, G., & Suttell, Barbara J. *The Bender-Gestalt test.* New York: Grune & Stratton, 1951.

Zolik, E. S. A comparison of the Bender-Gestalt reproductions of delinquents and nondelinquents. *J. clin. Psychol.*, 1958, 14, 24–26.

47

The Clinical Validity of the Bender-Gestalt Test with Children: A Developmental Comparison of Children in Need of Psychotherapy and Children Judged Well Adjusted

EUGENE BYRD

In this well-executed study, several signs of maladjustment on the B-G proposed by Hutt were tested with groups of well-adjusted and poorly adjusted children of varying age levels. In general, though less than half the statistical tests proved significant, the differences were in accordance with the hypotheses. The fact that the majority of signs showed no significant differences is attributable to their low frequency of occurrence. Several differences found at earlier ages disappeared when the older children were tested. It is apparent, therefore, that at least some of these signs are influenced by maturation.

The one obvious flaw in the study is the failure to control the groups for intelligence. Byrd contends, by citing earlier research, that intelligence does not affect B-G performance when scores are in the normal range or above. Only one of the studies he quotes, however, dealt with children, and as Tamkin has shown (Chap. 45 in this volume), one study is not sufficient to avoid the responsibility of controlling such a crucial variable.

Problem

The Bender-Gestalt Test was originally conceived as a visual-motor performance test to explore gestalt functions of perception, but it has become widely used throughout the country in clinics and hospitals as a part of test batteries for personality evaluation of both children and adults. Since the publication of Bender's monograph (1938), research studies have been primarily concerned with the development of objective scoring systems and problems of interpretation and validation. For the most part, these studies have been concerned with adult performance. While there is general agreement on the ability of the Bender-Gestalt to identify organic, mental defective, and psychotic processes, there is a lack of agreement on its validity in differentiating neurotic from normal subjects. Pascal and Suttell (1951) and Hutt (1945; 1950) support this latter validity, while the conclusions of Billingslea (1948) and Gobetz (1953) are essentially negative.

Investigation of children's performance on the Bender has been relatively limited. Maturational aspects have been reported by Bender (1938) and Harriman and Harriman (1950). Fabian (1945) found that children who show reading reversals also tend to rotate horizontally oriented Bender designs to the vertical. Fabian considered this "verticalization persistence" to be a sign of an infantile pattern of behavior. A somewhat similar conclusion was drawn by Hanvik (1953), who noted that 16 out of 20 children who showed one or more rotations on the Bender had abnormal EEG records. Hanvik believed this behavior was a compensation for underlying deficiencies. Greenbaum (1955) has suggested the use of a word-association test as an aid to interpreting children's associations to the test design.

Two studies have been reported that include secondary data which are relevant to the present investigation. Sullivan and Welsh (1947), as part of their comparison of children who had poliomyelitis with normals, were unable to differentiate these groups on the basis of their Bender-Gestalt records. Pascal and Suttell (1951), in their volume on the validity and quantification for adults, report a significant difference in Bender-Gestalt scores between a group of 12 child patients in a residential treatment home and 12 nonpatient children. They also found a decrease in scores with an increase in age for a normal group of children between ages six and nine corroborating the findings of Bender (1938). No other studies are known to the writer that support or refute the validity of the Bender-Gestalt as an instrument to evaluate personality adjustment in children.

The individual most singularly influential in the development of the Bender as a tool for evaluation of personality dynamics has been Max

L. Hutt. During World War II, Hutt trained some 300 Army psychologists who later passed their indoctrination in the clinical use of the test on to others. At this time, he released the first detailed outline of the clinical interpretation of the test determinants (1945). This outline was later revised and expanded, and definitions were more explicitly formulated for publication in a widely circulated clinical reference text (1950). Hutt's interpretive criteria were developed on the performance of adult subjects and are based on a theoretical framework that is primarily psychoanalytic. There have been no reported standards nor validated interpretative hypotheses concerning personality dynamics developed for children on the Bender. It may be assumed, therefore, that, insofar as this test is being used as a diagnostic instrument with children, its interpretation is based primarily on formulated hypotheses from adult performance. There remains a need for validation of interpretive criteria of psychopathology in children's reproductions on the Bender-Gestalt Test.

This study is limited to an attempt to establish those factors of test performance which differentiate children needing psychotherapy from well-adjusted children. It is a study of empirical validity and attempts to define the test's uses and limitations in practical terms rather than identify psychological processes. With valid factors established, further exploration through clinical observation and experimentation will be necessary to determine the psychodynamic meaning of these signs.

The major assumption of this study is that personality adjustment and integration constitutes a continuum. A second assumption is that the ability of an instrument to differentiate groups of individuals along this continuum is a measure of validity of that instrument. It is further assumed that children in need of psychotherapy possess a markedly different personality structure and function from children who are judged well adjusted. The general hypothesis set up as a guide for this study is that children in need of psychotherapy, as a group, will differ significantly in the frequencies of occurrence for each test factor from a group of children judged well adjusted.

Method

Fifteen of Hutt's factors relating to test interpretation were used in this study because of their general acceptance, reported validity, and ease of definition and scoring. Unless otherwise stated, definitions and criteria of significance for scoring followed Hutt (1950). In those cases where this was not possible, due to lack of clarity and omission on the part of Hutt or obvious lack of applicability to children's records, criteria for scoring were determined empirically by the investigator on the basis of the performance of well-adjusted 14- and 15-year-old children. The test signs investigated and the objective critical scoring limits were established as follows.

1. *Placement of the first figure* was investigated in two areas on the paper. The upper middle area consisted of a rectangle, 3¼ by 5½ inches, horizontally located in the center of the paper 1 inch from the top. This area was slightly increased from that suggested by Hutt (1950) after preliminary scoring of the records revealed too few cases in any of the groups for a meaningful comparison. Hutt reports that two-thirds of "unselected" adult subjects place their first figure in this area. The second area was a 2¼-inch square in the extreme upper left-hand corner. The size of this area was arbitrarily established to determine extreme placement which is reported to be a sign of timidity and fear (1950) and would be expected to be found more in emotionally disturbed children. Only figures whose entire dimensions were in either of these areas were scored.

2. *Sequence* refers to the successive positions of the drawings as they appear on the record. The four types of sequence investigated were *orderly, irregular, overly methodical,* and *chaotic.* An orderly sequence was defined as one in which the child followed a regular succession in the placement of the figures, with the exception that one inversion or change in direction was allowed. An irregular sequence was one in which more than one change in direction was permitted, but it was still possible to determine by inspection that the change was logical, such as occurs in the need for greater space. An overly methodical sequence was defined as one with forced rigidity in which all figures followed an undeviating horizontal or vertical progression. A chaotic sequence consisted of a clear lack of any plan, with the figures scattered about the page.

3. *Use of space.* Excessive variability in the size of children's reproductions made the comparison of amounts of space between drawings inadequate as an indicator of use of space. Only *compressed* use of space was scored when all drawings were placed in an area of less than one complete half of the paper.

4. *Use of margin* refers to the use of the margin of the paper as a guide for placing the designs. Use of the margin was considered significant if six or more of the figures were within one-quarter-inch of any of the margins of the paper. Hutt (1950) suggests the use of seven figures as a criterion.

5. *Over-all change in size* was scored if five or more figures showed an increase or decrease of either the vertical or horizontal axis by more than one-quarter of the axis of the stimulus designs.

6. *Change in angulation* refers to a change in the degree of the angle of a figure or the angle of intersection between parts of a figure from that of the stimulus design. Only changes greater than 15 degrees were considered. This factor was scored when there was either an increase or

decrease in angulation in four or more of the eight figures with angles or when angulation was not reproduced or maintained in both Figures 2 and 6.

7. *Change in curvature* refers to the tendency to either accentuate or reduce curvature in curvilinear figures. It was determined by obtaining a ratio of perpendicular radii in Figure A and base–altitude ratios in Figures 4, 5, and 6. Deviations were scored as increase when the following ratios were exceeded; Figure A, elliptical with radial axis less than 8:10; Figure 4, 1:1; Figure 5, 1:1; Figure 6, 2:1 on the horizontal curve and 1.5:1 on the vertical. Significant decrease in curvature was scored when ratios were greater than: Figure 4, 3:1; Figure 5, 9:5; Figure 6, 5:1 on the horizontal curve or 6:1 on the vertical. A change in the majority of curves on either the horizontal or the vertical was necessary to score Figure 6. Change in curvature in two or more figures was considered significant.

8. *Closure difficulty* refers to the difficulty in bringing the joining parts of a figure together and is manifest in a drawing by failure to connect, or by overlapping, lines at points of connection. The presence of closure difficulty in two or more figures was considered significant.

9. *Overlapping difficulty* refers to failure to draw, or excessive distortion or erasure of, figures in which one line crosses another. This sign was scored if it occurred in either Figure 6 or 7.

10. *Rotation* is the reproduction of a figure with a rotation of the major axis of the drawing without a change in the position of the stimulus card or paper. The rotation of any figure more than 15 degrees was considered significant.

11. *Retrogression* is defined as the substitution of the stimulus by a more primitive Gestalt form. The presence of loops, lines, or dashes for dots anywhere in the record was considered significant.

12. *Fragmentation* is the reproduction of only a part of the stimulus figure and was scored if present anywhere in the records.

13. *Elaboration* is the adding of lines not present in the stimulus and was scored when present anywhere in the record.

14. *Collision* refers to the actual overlapping or running together of two or more adjacent figures and was scored if present anywhere in the record.

15. *Perseveration* is the persistence of drawing behavior which was appropriate for the previous figure but inappropriate for the present one. Perseveration was scored when dots replaced circles in Figure 2, loops replaced dots in Figure 3, or lines replaced dots in Figure 5.

Scoring limits for placement of first figure, use of space, use of margin, and changes in size, angulation, and curvature were indicated on clear plastic and placed directly over the records for scoring. All other factors were easily determined by inspection. The occurrence of all factors, with the exceptions of upper-middle placement of the first figure and orderly sequence, are considered by Hutt (1945) to be signs of psychopathology.

SUBJECTS

Bender-Gestalt records of 200 children, between ages 8 and 16, who had been diagnosed as in need of psychotherapy were obtained from child guidance clinics throughout the State of Florida. There was mutual agreement between clinic staffs and adults responsible for the children as to need for treatment. The control group consisted of 200 children who were independently judged "well adjusted" by at least two adults. These adults consisted of teachers, principals, or youth-center leaders who were responsible for the supervision of the subjects many hours each week. Selection and judgment were made on the basis of a check list containing the following criteria: (1) He (or she) is able to play well with other children. (2) He has reasonable control over his emotions. (3) He is able to think for himself. (4) He is achieving somewhere near his capacity. (5) He can be depended on. (6) He is relatively free from fears, tensions, and anxiety. (7) He is able to learn from experience. (8) He is kind and helpful to teachers and classmates. (9) He is liked and respected by his peers. (10) He is able to show satisfaction in his own ability without being dependent on adult approval. (11) He is able to share. Each child was judged to meet a least nine of the criteria and have no gross deviation from any criterion which he failed to meet. Selection was made by the teacher or youth-center leader, who was asked to limit the number selected to not more than 10 per cent of the child population from which he could choose. To reduce effect of halo and preconceptions, the phrase "well adjusted" was avoided by the investigator in the selection process. The children were not aware of the basis for their selection. It was assumed that personality adjustment of children constitutes a continuum and that an attempt to obtain a group of well-adjusted children for comparison would enable a better initial test of the discriminating ability of the Bender. It was felt that this was one step better than the frequently reported "clinic-nonclinic" or "neurotic-normal" comparisons.

No child with known brain damage, an obvious motor or uncorrected visual impairment, or IQ below 86 was included in either group. Gobetz (1953) and Pascal and Suttell (1951) found that IQ's within the normal range or above and sex of the subject did not affect Bender-Gestalt scores. However, because of the high ratio of approximately six boys to one girl in the group of children needing therapy, groups were matched for sex distribution at each age level.

TEST ADMINISTRATION

The test was individually administered in both groups according to the following directions by the examiner: "I am going to show you some cards, one at a time. Each card contains some figures. I want you to copy these figures on the paper as well as you can." Drawings were limited to one side of an 8½ by 11 inch paper. All nine cards were presented in regular order. There was no time limit, and a child was free to erase or change any design. In the case of the clinic group, the test generally constituted one of a battery of diagnostic tests.

TREATMENT OF THE DATA

In order to determine age levels at which the various test factors may discriminate, each group was divided into four subgroups of ages 8 and 9, 10 and 11, 12 and 13, and 14 and 15. Total frequencies for each subgroup and statistical significance of differences were determined between the clinic and the well-adjusted subgroups at each of the four age levels by means of chi square, corrected for continuity (Edwards, 1950, p. 86). Probabilities were computed by the direct method (Edwards, 1950, p. 84) when frequencies of less than five were involved. A probability level

TABLE 47–1   *A Comparison of Frequencies of Bender-Gestalt Test Factors of Fifty Children in Need of Psychotherapy and Fifty Well-Adjusted Children at Years Eight and Nine*

TEST FACTOR	CHILDREN IN NEED OF PSYCHOTHERAPY	WELL-ADJUSTED CHILDREN	P
Placement of first figure			
Extreme upper left	7	11	—
Upper middle	5	22	.01
Sequence			.01
Orderly	13	31	.01
Irregular	27	19	—
Overly methodical	1	0	—
Chaotic	9	0	.01
Compressed use of space	2	4	—
Use of margin	0	1	—
Over-all change in size	40	41	—
Change in angulation	31	35	—
Change in curvature	35	14	.01
Closure difficulty	47	33	.01
Rotation	18	7	.03
Overlapping difficulty	15	6	.05
Retrogression	26	18	—
Fragmentation	1	1	—
Elaboration	1	0	—
Perseveration	1	6	—
Collision	11	7	—

of .05 or less was considered significant, although some probabilities slightly above .05 are reported to provide developmental continuity.

Results

The data obtained are summarized in Tables 47–1 to 47–4. Test factors which showed significant differences between children needing psychotherapy and well-adjusted children are presented in Figure 47–1, with frequencies expressed as percent of occurrence.

Four test factors were found to differentiate children needing therapy from well-adjusted children at all ages from 8 through 15. These were: orderly sequence, change in curvature, closure difficulty, and rotations. Two additional factors, over-all change in size and angulation, occurred with significant differences at all ages above 10. Significantly more well-adjusted children up through age 11 placed their first figure in the upper

| TABLE 47–2 | *A Comparison of Frequencies of Bender-Gestalt Test Factors of Fifty Children in Need of Psychotherapy and Fifty Well-Adjusted Children at Years Ten and Eleven* |

TEST FACTOR	CHILDREN IN NEED OF PSYCHOTHERAPY	WELL-ADJUSTED CHILDREN	P
Placement of first figure			
Extreme upper left	11	8	—
Upper middle	5	19	.05
Sequence			
Orderly	14	29	.02
Irregular	24	21	—
Overly methodical	1	0	—
Chaotic	9	0	.01
Compressed use of space	4	1	—
Use of margin	0	0	—
Over-all change in size	39	25	.01
Change in angulation	32	11	.01
Change in curvature	23	12	.04
Closure difficulty	43	26	.01
Rotation	21	4	.01
Overlapping difficulty	11	3	.05
Retrogression	19	16	—
Fragmentation	2	0	—
Elaboration	1	0	—
Perseveration	3	0	—
Collision	11	5	—

TABLE 47–3   *A Comparison of Frequencies of Bender-Gestalt Test Factors of Fifty Children in Need of Psychotherapy and Fifty Well-Adjusted Children at Ages Twelve and Thirteen*

TEST FACTOR	CHILDREN IN NEED OF PSYCHOTHERAPY	WELL-ADJUSTED CHILDREN	P
Placement of first figure			
Extreme upper left	6	7	—
Upper middle	10	15	—
Sequence			
Orderly	15	26	.04
Irregular	30	24	—
Overly methodical	0	0	—
Chaotic	5	0	.06
Compressed use of space	6	4	—
Use of margin	0	0	—
Over-all change in size	36	19	.01
Change in angulation	23	11	.03
Change in curvature	17	4	.01
Closure difficulty	35	20	.01
Rotation	19	4	.01
Overlapping difficulty	0	4	—
Retrogression	22	15	—
Fragmentation	1	1	—
Elaboration	0	0	—
Perseveration	1	0	—
Collision	5	6	—

center of the page, but no significant differences were found for this factor at older ages. Overlapping difficulty was discriminating up through age 11, but thereafter the frequency of occurrence approached zero in both groups at age 15.

Use of margin, compressed use of space, fragmentation, elaboration, perservation, and collision occurred infrequently in both groups at all age levels and were not discriminating. The factor of collision, however, did discriminate between groups at ages 14 and 15. Use of margin occurred only once in all 400 subjects.

Of those factors which occurred with moderate or high frequencies, only two failed to differentiate, at all age levels, children needing therapy from well-adjusted children. These were extreme upper-left placement of the first figure and retrogression. However, retrogression was present more often in the clinic group at all ages. All factors which discriminated between the groups did so in the direction predicted by Hutt's interpretive hypotheses (1950); i.e., test factors considered signs of poor adjustment were more frequent among children needing therapy, and positive

TABLE 47–4   *A Comparison of Frequencies of Bender-Gestalt Test Factors of Fifty Children in Need of Psychotherapy and Fifty Well-Adjusted Children at Ages Fourteen and Fifteen*

TEST FACTOR	CHILDREN IN NEED OF PSYCHOTHERAPY	WELL-ADJUSTED CHILDREN	P
Placement of first figure			
Extreme upper left	15	19	—
Upper middle	3	4	—
Sequence			
Orderly	23	36	.02
Irregular	20	16	—
Overly methodical	0	2	—
Chaotic	7	0	.02
Compressed use of space	4	2	—
Use of margin	0	0	—
Over-all change in size	36	19	.01
Change in angulation	21	11	.05
Change in curvature	10	3	.07
Closure difficulty	38	24	.01
Rotation	20	1	.01
Overlapping difficulty	1	0	—
Retrogression	20	14	—
Fragmentation	0	2	—
Elaboration	1	0	—
Perseveration	3	1	—
Collision	7	0	.02

signs were more frequent in the well-adjusted groups. Only chaotic sequence and elaboration occurred exclusively in the clinic group.

Of 60 independent statistical comparisons made in this study, 26 were significant at a probability level of .05 or less. The chance probability of obtaining this number of significant statistics is less than .001 (Sakoda, Cohen, & Beall, 1954).

The effect of maturation on the occurrence of Bender-Gestalt Test factors is indicated by the slopes of the curves in Figure 47–1. Inspection of these curves shows this effect to be more marked in groups of well-adjusted children.

Discussion

The results of this study support the validity that the majority of test factors selected from Hutt (1950) are signs of personality adjustment.

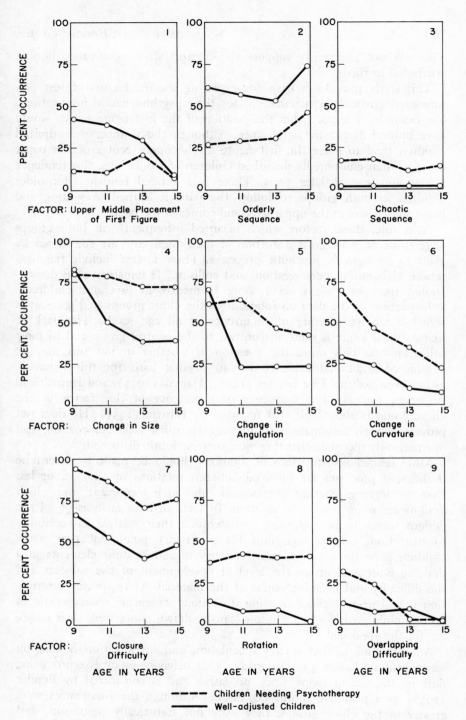

FIGURE 47-1. Factors discriminating children needing psychotherapy from well-adjusted children.

They do not necessarily support the interpretative significance he has attributed to them.

This study provides a basis for exploring specific factors of test performance, particularly in children, for their psychodynamic implications. For example, it appears that the position of the first figure drawn would have limited diagnostic significance. Although the younger well-adjusted children tend to place the first figure in the upper center of the paper more so than emotionally disturbed children of similar age, this tendency is not apparent at later years. There is a general tendency for older children in both groups to follow the pattern learned in writing and begin somewhere in the upper left-hand corner of the paper.

As a rule, those factors which occurred infrequently in both groups were those of more gross distortion of the designs and are considered by Hutt to be signs of psychotic processes. These factors include fragmentation, elaboration, perseveration, and collision. It remains to be demonstrated that these signs occur more frequently in psychotic children.

Inspection of the data on rotation for the clinic groups in Figure 47–1 shows a relative stability of occurrence at all age levels. This lack of maturational effect is quite in contrast to the control group and to most other factors. This raises the question of whether or not this may be considered additional evidence for an organic basis for this behavior, as has been indicated by Bender (1938), Hanvik (1953), and Hanvik and Anderson (1950). The frequency of occurrence of this factor in the clinic group is about half that reported by Hanvik (1953). He does not provide enough information on his subjects for a valid comparison, and one may only speculate that they were more seriously disturbed.

More refined investigations of rotations should be made to determine if different processes are involved between rotations of 180, 90, or less than 90 degrees; whether direction of rotation is significant; and which designs are more subject to rotation. In fact, an item analysis of all the designs seems to be indicated to determine their relative susceptibility to distortion. Goodenough and Harris (1950) point out that when children draw from models, the tendency to add or omit elements in a drawing is dependent on the level of development of the subjects and the difficulty and meaningfulness of the material. More specific information is still needed about drawing distortions which are characteristic of normal children before conclusions can be drawn concerning their meaning for the abnormal.

Another finding that invites speculation and investigation is that on retrogression (Tables 47–1 to 47–4). This behavior involves reproducing dots by the use of loops, lines, or dashes and is considered by Bender (1938) as a primitive motor expression. Although the frequencies were greater in the clinic groups, they were not statistically significant, and approximately one-third of the well-adjusted children demonstrated this behavior.

The maturational effect found in this study essentially agrees with the findings of Bender (1938) and others (Harriman & Harriman, 1950; Pascal & Suttell, 1951). Bender (1938) was primarily concerned with the "goodness" or completeness of children's designs and found that mastery of the Gestalt principles of the figures was usually complete around the eleventh year. Study of the finer aspects of reproducing the designs can extend this evaluation of maturation at least up to the sixteenth year.

The purpose of this study was to establish significant test variables in children's Bender-Gestalt records. A further word of caution is due regarding any direct clinical application of the findings in this study. It should be remembered that many of the signs appeared in both groups, although not always in the same context. Of particular note is closure difficulty. At age 15, 40 per cent of well-adjusted children show this behavior on two or more figures. Evaluation of a record involves far more than a listing of signs. The total test performance must be considered, which involves the temporal-special patterning of all the figures, the unique meaning the designs or test may have for the subject, the clinical setting, and other information and behavior known about the subject. Finally, psychodynamic interpretations of the test signs presented by Hutt and others (Guertin, 1954; Hammer, 1954) must still be considered hypotheses to be tested, particularly in children.

This study provides a broader base for knowing what may be expected from emotionally disturbed as well as from emotionally healthy children on the Bender-Gestalt Test. It also provides additional objective data on a test well known for its subjectivity and speculative interpretation. The Bender-Gestalt appears to be useful for evaluating, in children as young as eight years, more than the simple ability to perceive and reproduce designs.

Summary

This study was designed to establish valid scoring factors for the Bender-Gestalt as it is used to evaluate personality adjustment in children. Bender-Gestalt records of 200 children, ages 8 to 16 and diagnosed as needing psychotherapy, were compared to a similar age group of 200 children judged well adjusted. Fifteen independent test factors, originally suggested by Hutt and widely used in the evaluation of adults, were objectively defined and their frequencies of occurrence determined in subgroups of 50 children at age levels 8 and 9, 10 and 11, 12 and 13, and 14 and 15. Significance of difference between clinic and well-adjusted subgroups was determined by chi square.

At all age levels, well-adjusted children show significantly more use of orderly sequence and less change in curvature, closure difficulty, and rotations than children needing psychotherapy. After age 10, the clinic groups show more over-all change in size and change in angulation. Frequency of upper-middle placement of the first figure drawn is significantly greater in well-adjusted children only up to year 13. Chaotic sequence is absent in this group. Emotionally disturbed children have more difficulty with overlapping figures up to age 13, thereafter, this behavior is nearly absent in both groups.

Use of margin, compressed use of space, fragmentation, elaboration, perservation, and collision occurred infrequently in both groups and are not discriminating. Retrogression and extreme upper-left placement of first figure occur with moderate frequencies but fail to discriminate.

Maturational effects on reproduction of designs are noted up to age 16. Investigation of specific psychodynamic interpretation of test factors remains to be done. Other areas for research are suggested.

REFERENCES

BENDER, LAURETTA. A visual motor Gestalt test and its clinical use. *Amer. Ortho-psychiat. Ass., Res. Monogr.,* 1938, No. 3.

BILLINGSLEA, F. Y. The Bender-Gestalt: An objective scoring method and validating data. *J. clin. Psychol.,* 1948, 4, 1–27.

EDWARDS, A. L. *Experimental design in psychological research.* New York: Rinehart, 1950.

FABIAN, A. A. Vertical rotation in visual-motor performance: Its relationship to reading reversals. *J. educ. Psychol.,* 1945, 36, 129–154.

GOBETZ, W. A quantification, standardization, and validation of the Bender-Gestalt test on normal and neurotic adults. *Psychol. Monogr,* 1953, 67, No. 6 (Whole No. 356).

GOODENOUGH, FLORENCE L., & HARRIS, D. B. Studies in the psychology of children's drawings: II 1928–1949. *Psychol. Bull.,* 1950, 47, 369–433.

GREENBAUM, R. S. A note on the use of the word association test as an aid to interpretating the Bender Gestalt. *J. proj. Tech.,* 1955, 19, 27–29.

GUERTIN, W. H. A factor analysis of curvilinear distortions on the Bender Gestalt. *J. clin. Psychol.,* 1954, 10, 12–17.

HAMMER, E. F. An experimental study of symbolism on the Bender Gestalt. *J. proj. Tech.,* 1954, 18, 335–345.

HANVIK, L. J. A note on rotations in the Bender-Gestalt test as predictors of EEG abnormalities in children. *J. clin. Psychol.,* 1953, 9, 399.

HANVIK, L. J., & ANDERSON, A. L. The effect of focal brain lesions on recall and on the production of rotations in the Bender Gestalt test. *J. consult. Psychol.,* 1950, 14, 197–198.

HARRIMAN, MILDRED, & HARRIMAN, P. L. The Bender motor Gestalt test as a measure of school readiness. *J. clin. Psychol.,* 1950, 6, 175–177.

HUTT, M. L. *A tentative guide for the administration and interpretation of the Bender-Gestalt test.* U.S. Army Adjutant General's School, June, 1945 (restricted).

HUTT, M. L. Revised Bender visual-motor Gestalt test. In A. Weider (Ed.), *Contributions toward medical psychology*. New York: Ronald, 1950.

PASCAL, G. R., & SUTTELL, BARBARA J. *The Bender-Gestalt test*. New York: Grune & Stratton, 1951.

SAKODA, J. M., COHEN, B. H., & BEALL, G. Test of significance for a series of statistical tests. *Psychol. Bull.*, 1954, 51, 172–175.

SULLIVAN, J. J., & WELSH, G. S. Results from the Bender visual motor Gestalt test. In E. L. Philips et al. (Eds.), Intelligence and personality in poliomyelitis. *Monogr. Soc. Res. Child Develpm.*, 1947, 12, No. 2.

48

The Bender-Gestalt Test and Learning
Disturbances in Young Children

ELIZABETH M. KOPPITZ[1]

This study indicates that a modified version of the Pascal and Suttell z score does differentiate between children with learning problems and those with none. It would appear, however, that IQ is able to predict learning disturbances equally well. Are they measuring the same thing? This study does not permit any definite answer to this question, but by computing a multiple R it should be possible to determine whether the B-G contributes any unique variance to that predicted by the IQ.

This study, using young school children, was designed to explore the usefulness of the Bender-Gestalt Test (Bender, 1938) in discovering learning disturbances that are primarily due to problems in visual-motor perception. An attempt was made to find out how well the Bender-Gestalt Test can differentiate between children whose achievement in reading, writing, and spelling is above average, and those below average.

Method

SUBJECTS

Two groups of children served as Ss in this study. Group I was used to test and refine a scoring system for the Bender-Gestalt Test that was

[1] The writer wishes to express her appreciation to Mrs. Jenny Raduege, Miss Judy Ward, and David D. Blyth for their valuable assistance.

767

sensitive to school achievement. Group II was used to cross-validate the findings from Group I.

All Ss were of at least dull normal intelligence. Their age range was from 6–4 to 10–8. The mean age for both groups was 8–5. All Ss were elementary-school students in the first four grades. Group I included 77 Ss, 41 of whom were selected by their teachers on the basis of above-average adjustment and achievement; 36 had below-average achievement. Group II included 51 clinic patients. Twenty of these were referred to the Children's Mental Health Center primarily because of poor school progress and learning disturbances; the remaining 31 Ss were referred primarily because of emotional problems; their school achievement was satisfactory. All Ss in Group I came from upper middle-class residential sections of Columbus, Ohio. Group II included urban and rural children, and their social status ranged from lower to upper middle-class.

PROCEDURE

The Bender-Gestalt Test was administered to each S individually. The classroom teachers gave the test to the Ss in Group I after receiving careful instructions and a manual on procedure. In Group II, each S was given the Bender-Gestalt Test by the writer along with a battery of other tests at the time of psychological evaluation at the Children's Mental Health Center.

After testing numerous scoring items on random Bender protocols of school children, 20 categories were selected for use in this study. Most of these were adapted from Pascal and Suttell's (1951) scoring scheme. Each scoring category was operationally defined and examples were given. Each category was scored as either present or absent. In case of doubt, an item was not scored. The 20 scoring categories were as follows:

A. Distortion of Shape (all Figures)
B. Rotation (all Figures)
C. Workover or Second Attempt (all Figures)
D. Part Missing (all Figures)
E. Confused Order (total protocol)
F. Overlapping of Figures (all Figures)
G. Compression of Figures (total protocol)
H. Substitution of Circles or Dashes for Dots (Figures 1, 3, and 5)
I. Perseveration (Figures 1, 2, and 6)
J. Wavy Line (Figures 1 and 2)
K. Shape of Circle (Figure 2)
L. Deviation in Slant (Figure 2)
M. Dashes or Dots for Circles (Figure 2)
N. Blunting (Figure 3)
O. Number of Dots Incorrect (Figure 3)
P. Parts of Figure Not Joined (Figures 1 and 4)
Q. Three or More Angles in Curve (Figure 6)
R. Angles, Missing or Extra (Figures 7 and 8)
S. Guidelines (Figures 2, 3, and 5)
T. Enclosure of Figure (all Figures)

A reliability check with another psychologist yielded 93 per cent agreement on the independent scoring of 14 Bender protocols. The writer then scored all protocols "blindly." Thereafter, they were grouped according to grade placement and school achievement of the Ss. The presence or absence of deviations on the Bender protocols was next analyzed and compared by means of chi-square tests. Each scoring category was tested separately to see whether it differentiated significantly between the above average and below average students. This was done for the first two grades, for the third and fourth grades, and for all four grades combined. Only those scoring categories were considered as differentiating markedly between the good and poor students in which at least two of the three P values obtained were significant at the 5 per cent level or better. Seven of the 20 categories met this requirement. These were: Distortion of Shape; Rotation; Substitution of Circles or Dashes for Dots; Perseveration; Parts of Figure not joined; three or more Angles in Curve; Angles, Missing or Extra.

When each Bender figure was analyzed separately in the category Distortion of Shape, it was found that distortions (as defined in this category) occurred rarely in Figures 1, 2, 4, 6, and 8. When they did appear, it was equally often among good and poor students. On the other hand, distortions in Figures A, 3, 5, and 7 differentiated well between the two groups of students. Thus, only distortions in Figures A, 3, 5, and 7 were included in the final scoring system.

A comparison of those children using only one sheet of paper for the Bender with those using two or three pieces revealed no significant difference in regard to school achievement or Bender Test performance.

Final Scoring System

The original 20 scoring categories were reduced to a final scoring system which only included the seven significant categories. A Composite Score was then computed for each S by adding all his scoring points. The highest Composite Score a S could get was 31. The final scoring system was once more tested on Group I. After computing the Mean Composite Scores for the first two grades, the third and fourth grades, and all four grades, chi squares were used to compare the good and poor students whose Bender Composite Scores were above and below the Group's Mean Composite Score. Table 48-1 shows significant results indicating that good students tend to have a low Composite Score, that is, few deviations on the Bender, whereas poor students will tend to show a high Composite Score, or many deviations.

CROSS VALIDATION

A cross validation of the final scoring system was carried out on Group II. The test protocols were analyzed, and Composite Scores

TABLE 48–1   *A Comparison of Bender Composite Scores for*
                     Above- and Below-Average Students of
                     Groups I and II with χ² and P Values

	MEAN COMPOSITE SCORE	GOOD STUDENTS MEAN		POOR STUDENTS MEAN			
GRADES		ABOVE	BELOW	ABOVE	BELOW	χ²	P
Group I							
1 & 2	5.6	5	17	15	6	10.2	<.001
3 & 4	4.1	4	15	9	6	5.4	<.02
all	4.9	11	30	26	10	15.9	<.001
Group II							
1 & 2	8.7	1	10	12	2	14.5	<.001
3 & 4	5.7	0	9	12	5	11.8	<.001
all	7.2	2	18	21	10	16.4	<.001

were computed for each S in Group II. As would be expected, the
Mean Composite Scores for Group II were somewhat higher than for
Group I. It was felt that these higher scores are probably closer to
Mean Composite Scores for elementary-school children generally. Thereafter chi squares were computed to determine the validity of the scoring
system. The results in Table 48–1 indicate with a high degree of confidence that the Bender-Gestalt Test can differentiate between groups
of children with learning problems and with satisfactory school
achievement.

Bender-Gestalt Test and IQ

It is well known that bright children tend to have higher school
achievement than dull children. The Bender-Gestalt Test, a test of
visual-motor perception, was found to be related to school achievement
also. An attempt was made to explore the relationship of school achievement to IQ and the Bender Test.

All Ss in Group II had been given the WISC or the Stanford-Binet
Scale at the same time the Bender was administered. The distribution of
above-average and below-average IQ and high or low achievement was
compared by means of a chi square. Table 48–2 shows that a significant
relationship exists between IQ and school achievement. But a comparison of Tables 48–1 and 48–2 shows that the Bender is even more
closely related to achievement than is the IQ.

For the first two grades visual-motor perception and IQ are both
significantly related to school achievement and may overlap to a considerable degree. With one exception, all the good students had good

TABLE 48–2   *A Comparison of IQ's for Above- and Below-Average*
Students of Group II with χ^2 and P Values

| | GOOD STUDENTS | | | | | |
GRADES	IQ 99 BELOW	IQ 100 ABOVE	IQ 99 BELOW	IQ 100 ABOVE	χ^2	P
1 & 2	2	9	11	3	9.0	<.01 <.001
3 & 4	3	6	13	4	4.6	<.01 <.02
all	5	15	24	7	13.6	<.001

Benders, with few deviations (the one exception was a Bender of average quality), and all had an IQ of above 100, with the exception of two Ss whose IQ's were in the high 90's. All the poor students had poor Benders and low IQ's, with the exception of two very immature, slow-moving, nonverbal children. Two bright Ss with severe visual-motor difficulties were also among the poor students.

On the third- and fourth-grade level, there was found to be a somewhat greater discrepancy between school achievement and IQ than among the younger Ss. All good students were found to have good Benders—even the three Ss whose IQ's were below 100. Among the poor students with below-average IQ, 10 had poor Benders, while three had fairly adequate Benders but revealed severe emotional problems in addition to difficulties in auditory perception. Speech problems, poor auditory perception, and extremely low frustration tolerance were present in the four children who did poorly in school despite above-average IQ's. Two of these had quite adequate Benders.

Discussion

Very few children under the age of nine years can reproduce the Bender figures perfectly. However, not all deviations on the test are related to learning disturbances, nor is it felt that they all indicate serious problems in visual-motor perception. Of the 20 deviations tested in this study, only 7 proved to be related to school achievement. The other deviations appeared to be primarily related to age or to emotional factors.

Pascal and Suttell's (1951) table, comparing Bender deviations of psychotic patients, young children, and normal adults, was used to determine which deviations could be considered to be primarily of psychogenic origin and which were chiefly indications of immaturity.

Among young school children, there was found to be little relationship between school achievement and the ability to arrange the figures neatly on a sheet of paper, to draw a straight line, the omission of parts of a figure, and the blunting of the arrowhead and the addition of dots on

Figure 3. These phenomena were found equally often among good and poor students six years of age; they decreased as the Ss grew older.

There are other kinds of distortion on the Bender that are not related to school achievement, including the tendency to overlap figures, to draw careless and distorted circles, and the failure to maintain the slant on Figure 2. Both immaturity and emotional upset may produce these deviations. They were found among the very young and among psychotics.

Several deviations on the Bender seem to be primarily related to tension and anxiety, since they were found frequently among Pascal and Suttell's psychotic patients but not among the very young. These deviations include the tendency to rework figures, to make several attempts before completing a design, to constrict all nine figures into less than half the sheet of paper or to string them along the edge of the paper, and finally to substitute tense little lines or dots for circles in Figure 2. It seems significant that the good students in this study, who had been considered well adjusted by their teachers, showed more of these tension indicators than the poor students. The difference was, however, not statistically significant.

In contrast to the deviations discussed so far, there were two groups of deviations that were definitely related to learning disturbances. The first of these can be described by the inability to control lines both in directionality and in shape. The following deviations are included in this group: difficulty in drawing angles in Figures A, 7, and 8; the tendency to rotate figures; and the inability to draw sinusoidal curves on Figure 6. Since all these deviations are found among young children as well as among psychotic patients, according to Pascal and Suttell, it is hypothesized that we are dealing here with phenomena of either immaturity and/or a loss of control due to confusion or regression.

The second group of deviations related to learning problems can be described by the inability to integrate parts into wholes and the inability to control and terminate visual-motor activity. The following deviations are included in this group: distortions on Figures A, 3, 5, and 7; the substitution of dashes or circles for dots on Figures 1, 3, and 5; perseveration on Figures 1, 2, and 6; and the failure to integrate parts on Figures A, 4, and 7 into meaningful wholes. All these deviations occurred only among Pascal and Suttell's very young children but not to any great extent among their psychotic patients. It is, therefore, hypothesized that these phenomena indicate immaturity in younger children, while they suggest retardation and possible brain damage in older children.

Summary

A scoring system for the Bender-Gestalt Test sensitive to learning problems in young school children was developed on 77 first- to fourth-graders. Items from Pascal and Suttell's scheme were adapted for this study. Of the 20 scoring categories tested, only 7 were found to differentiate significantly between good and poor students, including: Distortion of Shape; Rotation; Substitution of Circles or Dashes for Dots; Perseveration; Parts of Figure Not Joined; Three or More Angles in Curve; Angles, Missing or Extra. For each S, a Composite Score was computed by adding the number of significant deviations in his protocol. The scoring system was cross-validated on a group of 51 school children. The results indicate that the Bender-Gestalt Test can differentiate significantly between above-average and below-average students in the first four grades of school.

REFERENCES

BENDER, LAURETTA. A visual motor Gestalt test and its clinical use. *Amer. Ortho-psychiat. Ass., Res. Monogr.* No. 3, 1938.

BENDER, LAURETTA. *Psychopathology of children with organic brain disorder.* Springfield, Ill.: Charles C Thomas, 1956.

ORTON, S. T. *Reading, writing and speech problems in children.* New York: Norton, 1937.

PASCAL, C. R., & SUTTELL, BARBARA J. *The Bender Gestalt test.* New York: Grune & Stratton, 1951.

STRAUSS, A. A., & LEHTINEN, L. E. *Psychopathology and education of the brain injured child.* New York: Grune & Stratton, 1947.

STRAUSS, A. A., & KEPHART, N. C. *Brain injured child.* Vol. 2. New York: Grune & Stratton, 1956.

PART VI

THE SENTENCE
COMPLETION TEST

49

A Review of Sentence Completion Methods in Personality Assessment[1]

PHILIP A · GOLDBERG

This is the most comprehensive and, in my opinion, the best review ever written on the Sentence Completion Method. Further, the thoroughness of the article reveals a very unanticipated fact (at least to the editor). The Sentence Completion Method is a valid test, generally speaking, and probably the most valid of all the projective techniques reported in the literature. If the reader doubts this, he may survey Goldberg's graphical summary (Figure 49-1), in which he reports the validity figures for all the SCT studies he could gather. Unfortunately, to the best of my knowledge, no such comparable figure exists for any of the other projective techniques. Yet, perusal of countless articles would seem to indicate no comparable validity attainment for any other technique. The reader may ask (1) Why should the SCT be more valid than other projective tests? (2) If it is so valid, why is it used less frequently than many other individually administered projective techniques?

It is more valid because of two factors. First, the test has by and large not been used with a broad variety of criteria or with all age groups. Its forte seems to be psychiatric evaluation, personality evaluation, and general adjustment of adults. Adjustment and personality evaluation are generally based on overt behavior or behavior that is readily verbalized. We know an individual is neurotic, for example, because he acts listless

---

[1] The author is indebted to his colleague, Dr. Bernard I. Murstein, for his aid and encouragement throughout the development of this paper and to Dr. Bertram R. Forer for his generous bibliographic assistance.

and uninterested in a work situation and he tells us he feels unhappy.

There are other criteria which are not related to self-evaluation, as, for example, achievement. Individuals who verbalize a strong need for achievement often do not manifest achievement in their behavior. Hardly strange, therefore, is the finding that the SCT is a poor index of achievement behavior.

Our answer to question 1, therefore, is that the superior validity of the SCT stems from the fact that more often than any other test it has tried to predict to criteria consistent with the nature of the test in emphasizing verbality and consciously controllable behavior.

As to question 2, I believe the test has been used less than other techniques, first, because it is not a broad-band instrument giving information on all facets of behavior, as do, for example, the Rorschach and TAT, including many different kinds of needs at many levels of behavior. Second, it is not as glamorous as the Rorschach and TAT and has little of the mystical about it to inspire a cult. Third, the many diverse forms it has taken have made it difficult to draw conclusions about it as a single test, as Goldberg has convincingly demonstrated. Last, until Dr. Goldberg pulled all the diverse literature on the SCT together, many of us did not know how well the test could function in certain circumscribed situations. Now that we have noted the test's efficacy, I should not be surprised to see it used more frequently in the future.

The sentence completion method has its origins in the work of Ebbinghaus (1897), Kelley (1917), and Traube (1916), who used the method to measure intellectual variables. Though there have been more recent attempts to use the test to investigate intellectual capacity (Copple, 1956; Piltz, 1957; West, 1958), it has been used primarily in recent years as a device for personality assessment. Payne (1928) and Tendler (1930) are generally credited with being the first to use sentence completions for personality assessment.

Since that time, sentence completion methods have become increasingly more popular and the sentence completion has become a regular part of standard clinical test batteries (cf. Carr, 1958; Peskin, 1963). The essence of the method is to present the subject with a sentence fragment or stem, which he is asked to complete. The instructions, content, and structure of the stem vary from form to form, as does the manner of categorizing the responses, but the method has generally attractive features. The content of the stems may be adapted to meet specific clinical and research purposes, and the method lends itself to group administration.

These two features of flexibility and economy seem to have been of paramount importance in gaining the sentence completion the wide popularity it currently enjoys. Sundberg (1961) found that of all the psychological tests and instruments used in clinical services, the sentence completion ranked thirteenth in frequency of use, and among the group personality instruments the sentence completion was second only to the MMPI.

The flexibility and popularity of the method have led to a proliferation of sentence completion forms, the origins of which are often obscure (cf. Rohde, 1948; Stein, 1949). The sentence completion method has been used to assess a variety of attitudes: attitudes toward Negroes (Brown, 1950), old people (Golde & Kogan, 1959), school life (Costin & Eiserer, 1949), peers and parents (Harris & Tseng, 1957), career choice (Getzels & Jackson, 1960), mental hospitals (Souelem, 1955), and attitudinal change (Lindgren, 1954).

The sentence completion method has often been used to predict achievement for specialized groups. Murray and MacKinnon (1946) used a sentence completion form to evaluate candidates in the classic OSS studies. The sentence completion has been used to predict the success of graduate students in clinical psychology (Kelly & Fiske, 1950; Kelly & Fiske, 1951; Samuels, 1952) and to predict the success of flight cadets (Holtzman & Sells, 1954).

The sentence completion has been used to assess differences between a wide variety of contrasted groups. Touchstone (1957) used a sentence completion test to investigate Negro–white differences. Smith (1952) compared stutterers to nonstutterers, MacBrayer (1960) investigated sex differences in sex perception, and Farber (1951) used a sentence completion to assess differences in national character.

The sentence completion has proved to be useful in virtually all areas of clinical psychological research. The method has been used to examine schizophrenic language (Cameron, 1938a; Cameron, 1938b; Ellsworth, 1951) and to examine the adjustment of patients to hospital routines (Luft, Wisham, & Moody, 1953). The sentence completion method has been used to evaluate counselor training (Kirk, 1956), and it has also been used in a case study of a mass murderer (Kahn, 1960).

In the bulk of these studies, the sentence completion methods used were "custom" tests, devised specifically for the particular research project. The ease of constructing sets of stems, the content of which bears a prima facie relationship to the variables under investigation, has encouraged a wide variety of research. Consequently, the development of a systematic and parametric body of information relevant to any one sentence completion method has been retarded. Additionally, in light of the number of sentence completion forms extant, general statements made about the method must be viewed with caution. The interchangeability of these various forms across populations and for different purposes is unknown.

There have, however, been several attempts to construct and present "standard" forms (Holsopple & Miale, 1954; Sacks & Levy, 1950; Rohde, 1946; Rohde, 1957; Stein, 1947; Forer, 1950; Forer, 1957; Forer, 1960a). Special standard sentence completion forms for use in the armed services were developed by Bijou (1947), Flanagan (1947), Trites, Holtzman, Templeton, and Sells (1953), and Willingham (1958). The attempt at standardizing a sentence completion form, which has probably been most rigorous, had most impact, and provided most stimulation for further research has been that of Rotter and his associates (Rotter, 1946; Rotter, Rafferty, & Schachtitz, 1949; Rotter & Rafferty, 1950; Rotter & Rafferty, 1953; Rotter, 1951; Rotter, Rafferty & Lotsof, 1954).

The Rotter Incomplete Sentences Blank (ISB) was developed out of earlier work done by Rotter and Willerman (1947), Shor (1946), Hutt (1945), and Holzberg, Teicher, and Taylor (1947). Though stemming from work done in the Army, Rotter has extended the ISB for use with college and high-school populations as well as the general adult population. The ISB consists of forty stems ranging in structure from "I . . ." to "My greatest worry is . . ." The general aims of the ISB are to provide an economical instrument for group use in assessing general psychological adjustment. A discussion of the theoretical rationale underlying the ISB, its structure, its scoring methods, and its weaknesses and strengths will be presented after a consideration of more general issues.

What Is the Sentence Completion?

The sentence completion is a method. Its status as a test or as a projective technique varies with the psychometric criteria used and with the specific sentence completion method. For Cronbach, "A test is a systematic procedure for comparing the behavior of two or more persons" (1960, p. 21). None of the available sentence completion methods would have any difficulty in meeting this criterion. If, however, the criteria are made somewhat more demanding, as in Anastasi's definition that "a psychological test is essentially an objective and standardized measure of a sample of behavior" (1954, p. 22), then the words *objective, standardized,* and *measure* in combination are sufficient to eliminate most sentence completion methods from further consideration as tests.

The decision as to whether the sentence completion method is or is not a test may perhaps be evaded safely as a matter of little pragmatic concern. The question as to the status of the sentence completion as a projective device is a matter of an entirely different magnitude that goes beyond taxonomic nicety. The data yielded by sentence completion methods can have no intelligibility unless there is a clear understanding of the psychological processes involved in the production of the data.

Are sentence completion responses to be treated as signs or samples? Is the response controlled by the subject and shaped by consciously maintained attitudes and beliefs devoid of deeper psychic meaning? Or does the sentence completion response tap deeper psychic levels, involving urges and desires of which the subject is, at best, but dimly aware? Is the sentence completion a projective test, and will the projection hypothesis[2] serve as an adequate theoretical rationale for the use of the method? What a test can or cannot do involves notions of validity and implies a relatively advanced stage in the development of a psychometric instrument. A prior stage is the determination of what a test, in principle, ought to be able to do. These questions concerning the nature of the sentence completion method need answering if this prior stage is to be successfully negotiated.

Few tests have so resisted consensual typological classification as has the sentence completion. There are those who are decisive in their appraisal of the sentence completion as a projective device. Rohde states, "In unconstrained response to sentence beginnings, the subject inadvertently reveals his true self, since there is no way in which he can anticipate the significance of his answers for personality study" (1946, p. 170). Holsopple and Miale (1954) and Sacks and Levy (1950) are all in substantial agreement with Rohde that the sentence completion is a projective technique and that the projection hypothesis serves as the theoretical rationale for its use.

Others have expressed reservations, though still regarding the sentence completion as a projective technique. Campbell (1957), in an attempt at test classification, believes the sentence completion to be a projective test but one that differs from the Rorschach and TAT in that "rarely is the respondent unaware that he has been revealing his own attitudes" (1957, p. 208). Lindzey (1959) similarly regards the sentence completion as a projective test but one that is most like the Rosenzweig P-F. Forer regards the sentence completion as a "controlled projective test" (1950, p. 3).

Still others are apparently not at all sure of what to make of the test. Hanfmann and Getzels regard it as "half way between a projective technique and a questionnaire" (1953, p. 294). Rotter and Rafferty are similarly perplexed ("The sentence completion method of studying personality is a semistructured projective technique. . . As in other projective devices, it is assumed that the subject reflects his own wishes, desires, fears and attitudes in the sentences he makes" (1950, p. 3). Such a statement is entirely consistent with the view that the sentence com-

---

[2] The projection hypothesis, which generally serves as the theoretical rationale underlying the use of projective tests, was made most explicit by Frank (1939; 1948). Presented simply, the projection hypothesis states: when an individual is forced to impose meaning or order on an ambiguous stimulus complex, his response is a "projection" of his "feelings, urges, beliefs, attitudes, and desires . . ." (Frank, 1948, p. 66). The general relevance and validity of the projection hypothesis have been critically examined and questioned by several authors (Bellak, 1950; Cattell, 1951; Murstein, 1963).

pletion is a bona-fide projective test. The following statement made by
the same authors is not: "The responses tend to provide information
that the subject is willing to give rather than that which he cannot help
giving" (Rotter & Rafferty, 1950, p. 3). The juxtaposition of these two
statements helps to highlight the difficulties involved in attempting to
assess the sentence completion, its limits, and its potential.

One of the major theoretical controversies in the field of projective
testing which has special relevance for the sentence completion revolves
around the "levels hypothesis." Stated most simply, this approach con-
ceptualizes personality as arranged at various and different levels of psychic
functioning and organization. Different tests tap different levels, and "the
expression of a motive in one context or at one level of psychological
organization is not highly correlated with its manifestations at another
psychological level or in another stimulus context" (Forer, 1957, p. 359).
Carr (1954; 1956; 1958) advances the levels hypothesis to explain the
lack of congruity among data derived from different projective techniques.

Accepting the level hypothesis forces us to raise the same question
in a slightly different context: Where do we position the sentence completion? What level of personality does it tap? Sacks and Levy help us
very little when they say, "The SSCT (Sacks Sentence Completion Test)
may reflect conscious, preconscious, or unconscious thinking and feeling"
(1950, p. 375). Carr (1954; 1956) and Hanfmann (1947) agree that the
material elicited by the sentence completion comes from a personality
level closer to awareness than material elicited by either the Rorschach
or the TAT. Hanfmann and Getzels are but a bit more precise: "The
[sentence completion] test elicits material from a range of levels but
with the bulk of it being fairly close to awareness" (1953, p. 290).
Fitzgerald (1958), in accepting this position, also points out that a less
"deep" test is not therefore a less valuable one. Where inferences about
overt behavior are to be made, he believes that a highly structured,
behaviorally oriented projective test such as the ISB may be more appropriate than the TAT, which he believes is better than the ISB as a
"source of inferences about conflict in a given need" (Fitzgerald, 1958,
p. 202).

Considering the significance of the levels hypothesis, there is unfortunately relatively little hard supporting empirical evidence. Murstein
says in this regard, "Although the 'levels' approach appears intuitively
tenable, no conclusive demonstration of the existence of discriminable
levels has been made through experimental research" (1963, p. 67).

Stone and Dellis (1960) have conducted what is probably the most
specific empirical test of the levels hypothesis. Stone and Dellis hypothesized an inverse relationship between level of personality tapped by
psychological tests and the degree of stimulus structure inherent in each
of the tests. The authors gave the WAIS, The Forer Sentence Completion
Test, TAT, Rorschach and Draw-a-Person to a group of twenty patients

hospitalized for psychiatric conditions. The tests, in the order named, were evaluated by the authors as possessing decreasing amounts of stimulus structure and were thus hypothesized to reach increasingly less conscious levels of personality organization.

Stone and Dellis submitted the protocols to judges for "blind" ratings of amount of psychopathology. The results of the study were in striking agreement with the hypotheses. The test protocols were rated for psychopathology in the precise order predicted by Stone and Dellis. The authors conclude, "If supported by future observation and research, the Levels Hypothesis could conceivably affect the entire concept of validity in regard to projective techniques" (Stone & Dellis, 1960, p. 339).

Stone and Dellis' work has, however, been criticized by Murstein (1963) for not having a necessary control. Murstein points out in reviewing Stone and Dellis' results, "The results might be explained on the grounds that most projective scoring systems emphasize unhealthy traits, and that projective responses are more likely to reflect frustrations than positive thought. Accordingly, the more a test permits projection in the responses made to it, the more likely it is to be scored as 'unhealthy' " (1963, p. 67). We believe Murstein's point to be well taken. Tests may vary in the degree to which they permit projection to occur without such demonstrated differences in tests' potential being related to structural differences in personality organization.

However, we believe Murstein's suggested control to be less well considered. He suggests that Stone and Dellis should have obtained protocols from a group of normal subjects as well. It is to be expected that a group of normals would have produced protocols with less rated psychopathology. The relationship among the five tests, however, should be the same as obtained with the psychiatric population. This would be the expectation whether one accepts Stone and Dellis' Levels Hypothesis or Murstein's suggestion that tests differ in the degree of projection allowed.

A reconciliation of these views, at least for purposes of positioning the sentence completion, is entirely possible. A position vis-à-vis the levels hypothesis is not really necessary in order to understand the potential limits of the sentence completion. Although, as already discussed, there exists some disagreement as to the nature of the material elicited by sentence completion methods, it does seem to be the general view that the sentence completion is truly a projective test. Beyond that, most theorists apparently agree that the material elicited by the sentence completion is typically less dynamic than the material elicited by such tests as the Rorschach, TAT, and projective drawings. All this may be so, whether personality is viewed as layered in different levels of psychic functioning or whether tests are arranged in a hierarchy according to degree of permitted possible projection.

Often implicit in the levels hypothesis is the notion that tests which tap deeper layers of personality organization are better or more valid than tests which tap less deep layers. This position has, however, failed to receive empirical support. Deep levels are not necessarily better predictions of various validity criteria than less deep levels. In fact, the sentence completion is probably better substantiated than the TAT, Rorschach, and DAP. Both reliability and validity tend to vary inversely with depth of level.

One further and final observation concerning the levels hypothesis; the levels hypothesis is too easily—and has been too often—abused. Accepting such a theoretical orientation in no way alters the standards for scientific rules of evidence. Though the levels approach may explain inconsistency in projective test findings, it is clearly not an alternative to an empirical test of validity. It continues to be the researcher's task to provide a behavioral referent to substantiate his claim of test validity, irrespective of the level at which he presumes to be operating.

The Effects of Instruction and Set

The instructional set given the subject varies from one sentence completion form to another. The instructions used with the ISB are as follows: "Complete these sentences to express your *real feelings*. Try to do every one. Be sure to make a complete sentence" (Rotter & Rafferty, 1950, p. 5). The emphasis of these instructions is on truthful rather than immediate responding. The instructions to the Miale-Holsopple test are even less demanding; they neither ask for quick responses nor for truthful responses. The subject is told to "complete each sentence in whatever way you wish." Rotter and Willerman (1947) and Rotter and Rafferty (1950) claim that the instructions that emphasize speed tend to produce short responses similar to responses typically obtained by word association methods. However, Sacks and Levy (1950), Stein (1947), Forer (1950), and Murray, MacKinnon, Miller, Fiske, & Hanfmann (1948) all stress speed of responding.

There is no clear evidence that instructional emphasis on quick responding produces more immediate responding than instructions lacking such emphasis. Carter (1947) found that neurotics produce longer latencies than normals. A study by Cromwell and Lundy (1954), comparing the effects of instructions stressing speed to instructions emphasizing real feelings, found no significant differences in speed attributable to the differences in the instructions.

However much instructions may differ, it is safe to say that all these authors wish to achieve essentially the same goal; namely, honest, noncensored responding, thereby eliciting material which will be differentially and predictively useful. If instructions vary, it is only because each author believes his instructions to be most efficient. The paucity of research findings relevant to the effects of different types of instructions on sentence completions encourages the continuation of this often gratuitous variation. Benton, Windle, and Erdice (1957), in reviewing the procedural differences among sentence completion forms, conclude, "The cumulative effect of these many procedural variations is a presumptive lack of comparability among studies" (1957, p. 6).

It might be expected that the sensitivity of sentence completion responses to variations in the preparatory instructions would vary with the purposes of the respondents taking the test. Certainly, where the test is used in an industrial research project to measure employee attitudes (Miller & Gekoski, 1959; Friesen, 1952), the respondents' orientation might be expected to be quite different from the orientation of the patient voluntarily seeking psychotherapeutic help at an adult outpatient clinic (Hiler, 1959). It is not unreasonable to speculate that such presumed differences in test-taking attitudes would either obliterate or intensify or, in any event, interact with differences attributable to variations in instructions. Whatever the test constructor might think of his test instructions, the crucial question is, What does the subject taking the test think of them?

A study by Meltzoff (1951) emphasizes the importance of mental set in response to sentence completion tests. Meltzoff hypothesized that the subject's set, as determined by (1) test instructions and (2) stimulus tone, directly affects the tone of the sentence completion response. To test these hypotheses, Meltzoff randomly assigned an equal number of a population of 120 college students to one of four treatment categories. All subjects were required to take a sentence completion test designed specifically for this study by the author. The test consisted of 30 of each of three types of stems: positive (e.g., He loves . . .), negative (e.g., He hates . . .) and neutral (e.g., He is usually . . .). The test was the same for all subjects, but the instructions given to the subjects varied with the treatment condition. One group of subjects worked anonymously and were asked to produce an impression of good emotional adjustment; a second group were required to sign their names to the tests and were told that the results would be discussed with the university authorities; a third group took the test anonymously and were told that it was the test that was being investigated; the fourth group also worked anonymously and were asked to try to produce emotionally disturbed protocols.

The test responses were rated by experienced judges for adjustment, and the results supported both the main hypotheses. The degree of threat inherent in the instructional set correlated with the frequency of positively toned responses and correlated inversely with negatively toned responses. Further, Meltzoff found that negatively toned stems produced more negatively toned responses and that there were several significant interactions between mental set and stimulus tone on the quality of the responses. "The mental sets imposed by variations of instructions had most differential effect with neutral stimuli, and least with negative stimuli. Negative stimuli tended to evoke negative responses regardless of the test condition, and in general exhibited the strongest effect among the three types of stimuli" (Meltzoff, 1951, p. 184).

From these findings, Meltzoff concludes that subjects can censor their responses to the sentence completion to a considerable degree. His incidental finding that subjects who experienced more threat took more time to complete the test supports the view that subjects are able to manipulate consciously their responses to the test in a manner consistent with the image of themselves that they wish to present. Meltzoff's conclusions are consistent with Rotter and Rafferty's (1950) speculation that the test provides information which the subject is "willing" to give. Rohde (1946), however, on purely theoretical grounds, denies that the subject is able to control his responses to the sentence completion method. Further, she believes that it is "immaterial" whether the subject is telling the truth or not; he reveals himself in either event.

The importance of Meltzoff's findings is considerable. It directly challenges the tenability of the projection hypothesis as applied to the sentence completion and raises questions about its validity with other projective devices. Meltzoff's findings would seem to require of the sentence completion user that he understand the subject's approach to the test if he is to understand the subject's responses.

One note of modification is, perhaps, in order. There is, of course, a very real question as to the generalizability of these findings from a normal group of college students to the clinical populations for which the sentence completion is most generally intended. Additional research is needed.

The Effects of Variation of the Sentence Stem

The flexibility of the sentence completion method, as noted previously has led to a proliferation of sentence completion tests, many of which were designed for a single and limited research purpose. The research purposes have determined the stem content and form, which typically have reflected sophistication at the level of face validity. Many researchers have assumed that structuring the stem with regard to content or need would elicit responses pertaining to the same content and or need. There is, therefore, a considerable literature involving the use of widely different stems.

There are, unfortunately, no definite experimental studies which have systematically investigated the effects of variation in stem structure or form. What work there has been investigating the effects of stem variation has tended to fall into one of two categories; (1) investigations dealing with stem structure or ambiguity and (2) investigations dealing with the person of reference in the stem, i.e., self or other reference.

STEM STRUCTURE

The structure of a sentence stem is defined by the determining power of the stem's content. Nunnally's definition, "If there is an agreed-on public meaning for a stimulus, it is referred to as a *structured stimulus*" (1959, p. 339), would probably be acceptable to most people working with the sentence completion method. Structure is high if the content of the stem tends to establish narrow response classes.

The content of sentence stems varies in kind and degree from one sentence completion test to another. Forer (1950) believes his test to be "fairly highly structured," whereas Rotter and Rafferty (1950) characterize their own test as "unstructured." On inspection, the two tests do seem to differ, and Rotter's ISB does seem to be less highly structured than Forer's test. The first stem on Forer's test is "When he was completely on his own, he . . ."; the first stem on the ISB is "I like . . .". There does, however, appear to be at least some overlap between the two tests. "Men . . ." is a stem from the Forer test, and "My greatest worry is . . ." is a stem from the ISB.

The use of structured items generally reflects the test constructor's desire to direct the responses of the subject to areas predetermined by him to be of special psychological significance. Such an approach has been exemplified by Forer (1950; 1960). Forer reasons that if we wish to use projective test stimuli to predict behavior, we must establish a stimulus equivalent between the test stimuli and the social stimuli in which we are predictively interested. Consequently, the stems in Forer's test were designed to correspond with limited areas of life in which the clinician is likely to be most interested.

The areas sampled by Forer's sentence stems are (1) various important interpersonal figures, (2) dominant needs, (3) environmental pressures, (4) characteristic reactions, (5) moods, (6) aggressive tendencies, and (7) affective level. Forer (1950) specifies which stems were designed to elicit material from each area, and he provides the user of his test with a check sheet which permits him to note the responses as well as the areas to which the responses relate. Forer says of such a procedure: "Systematic interpretation and critical diagnostic inferences are thereby encouraged and the phases of the diagnostic process can more easily be examined and systematized. In addition, quantitative norms become a distinct possibility" (1950, p. 29).

Other sentence completion test constructors have endorsed the use of structured, content-determining items. Stein (1947), in his development and extension of the OSS test, similarly used a priori content categories, and the sentence stems selected for use in the final form of the test had to meet criteria of category relevance and low response stereotypy. Stein's categories are (1) family, (2) past, (3) drives, (4) inner states, (5) goals, (6) cathexes, (7) energy, (8) time perspective, and (9) reactions to other.

All the stems in Sacks's test (SSCT) are similarly clustered in specific clinically significant content categories. The four categories chosen by Sacks are (1) family, (2) sex, (3) interpersonal relationships, and (4) self-concept. These four areas are further subdivided into fifteen sub-categories, each of which is represented by four sentence stems.

Shaping the content of stems to elicit material in specific areas of clinical interest is not, however, a universal approach. Rotter and Rafferty (1950) and Holsopple and Miale (1954) do not position their stems within specified categories. Holsopple and Miale say of their selection procedure, "For many items, the only criterion of selection which can now be identified is that they seemed to be a good idea at the time, and we suspect that some of them remained in the series because we liked them" (1954, p. 5).[3]

Though Holsopple and Miale's candor has a certain amount of charm, Nash's (1958) discussion of this problem of content selection is, perhaps, more cogent:

> Variations in response to a sentence fragment should be concentrated along a limited number of dimensions, preferably along a single dimension. Simultaneous variation along a variety of dimensions dissipates the information in the responses, leaving little information available in any given dimension which is of interest to E. There is, then, an optimum heterogeneity in S's responses: this optimum is characterized by maximum heterogeneity along a limited number of dimensions, and by maximum homogeneity along all other dimensions (1958, p. 570).

Nash suggests that in order to achieve this optimum and to increase the predictive efficiency of a sentence completion test, stems should be arranged in a "tight cluster." A tight cluster of stems is one in which the constituent stems are intimately interrelated in content and structure. Nash suggests that when stems have a specified and common content, the responses to these stems are less ambiguous and more easily interpretable.

Forer (1950, 1960b) and Nash are thus in substantial agreement. Forer similarly believes that unstructured stems produce responses which are more difficult to interpret. "The interpreter lacks sufficient information regarding the stimulus situations to determine what the response means. The less the interpreter knows of the stimulus situation the less able he is to determine the role of the response in the total personality and the less able to predict behavior" (Forer, 1950, p. 17). Additionally,

---

[3] Talland (1959), in his review of Holsopple and Miale's monograph, has some biting comments to make about such selection procedures.

Forer believes that unstructured stems make it easier for the subject to avoid getting involved. Structured items, however, force the subject to respond without evasion to areas the items were designed to tap.

The construction of sentence stems with content specifically designed to elicit "significant material" seems intuitively to be a reasonable approach. Unfortunately, support for this approach has remained largely at the level of intuition, and, as Rotter and others have shown, intuitions differ. There is no clear evidence to demonstrate that creating stems to conform to specific content areas increases the likelihood of eliciting responses which are significant as well as relevant to these areas. It is conceivable, in fact, that such content structuring may threaten the subject. Holsopple and Miale believe that highly structured stems do, indeed, constitute an obvious threat, which, in turn, leads the subject to evade by giving responses that merely reflect conscious attitudes. Clear experimental support for this position is similarly not available.

It must be understood that the issue is not between stems with content and stems without content. There is nothing contentless about the stems in the ISB. The difference between the Forer, Stein, and Sacks tests is that the authors of the more structured tests have explicitly prescribed the content areas for which they wish to elicit information. As for the unstructured tests, their stems are likely to have less obvious content structure, but to assume that there is no structure would require that every stem would have an equal probability of eliciting material in any given area. There is no experimental evidence demonstrating the existence of such stems, and it is unlikely that such stems could be constructed.

In the absence of evidence that structure facilitates assessment, the decision as to which approach to use will probably be answered by preference and purpose. As the aims of Rotter's test and Forer's test are quite different, it is possible that each has adopted the approach most valid for his purpose. The ISB was designed to be a group screening device that would provide a summary score of general psychological adjustment. Forer was more concerned with devising an aid to clinical personality analysis and description.

Dole and Fletcher (1955) present the most specific principles as to the effects of stem structure on sentence completion responses reported in the literature. The principles presented by Dole and Fletcher are based on an analysis of 500 protocols of the *Dole Vocational Sentence Completion Blank* (DVSCB) (Dole, 1958). Though the authors' specificity is impressive, the principles presented are largely grammatical ones; e.g., "When the stem is a coordinate clause, the completion is usually a subordinate clause" (Dole & Fletcher, 1955, p. 107). Similar precision involving principles of a somewhat more dynamic nature are to be hoped for.

Trites (1955; 1956) found that structured unambiguous stems tend to elicit responses that are unambiguous. Peck and McGuire (1959) similarly found that well-defined sentence stems yield less ambiguous data then relatively unstructured stems. King (1958) used a sentence completion form developed for his study to investigate sexual identificiation in a group of college males. He found that the responses that indicated "sexual confusion" were normatively tied to specific stems, and he concluded that the responses were, at least in part, a function of the stimulus properties of the specific stems. Rozynko (1959) correlated the rated social desirability of sentence completion responses obtained from fifty psychiatric patients. He found that "the social desirability of the sentence stem performs the function of establishing the direction of the response. A socially desirable stem tends to evoke a socially desirable response and vice versa" (Rozynko, 1959, p. 280).

Based on the available evidence, there seems little doubt that the *content* of a response can be controlled to a considerable degree by the structure of the stem. "My mother . . ." leads obviously to more predictable response content than the stem "My . . ." The question is, What is the effect on the *significance* of the content as the structure of the stem increases? It is possible that increasing stem structure provides the tester with greater control over less significant material. Advocates of structured stems have tended to stress the advantages of content control Advocates of unstructured stems have tended to stress the advantages of honest responding, which is presumed to be facilitated by relatively unstructured stems. Research is needed which will investigate the relationship of content control and response significance to varying degrees of stem structure.

PERSON REFERENCE

Two of the sentence stem properties that have generated most interest have been the person of the pronouns used and the effects related to variations in the personal reference of the stem. Logically consistent with the projection hypothesis is the assumption that a subject is more likely to reveal himself when talking about another person and more likely to manifest defensive behavior when talking about himself. Many workers have accepted this assumption and have cast their stems in the third person. Here too, however, agreement is far from complete.

Rotter and Rafferty (1950) and Sacks and Levy (1950) use stems that are neutral or cast in the first person. Forer (1950) and Stein (1947) use stems cast in both the first and third person. Stein, interestingly, refers to first-person stems as "personal" and third-person stems as "projective." Forer believes that third-person stems supplement first-person stems in eliciting material that would be too threatening in response to the more charged first-person construction. Holsopple and Miale (1954) use two first-person stems; the rest of their list of 73 stems in either in the third person or neutral.

Trites et al. (1953) employed a variation not so easily categorized. Their sentence completion form was intended for use as a screening device with Air Force flying personnel. The cadets taking the test were shown a large sketch of an aviation cadet and instructed to complete the sentences "by writing what the cadet in the picture is saying" (Trites et al., 1953, p. 7). Once again, though the purposes and aims of the test constructors are essentially the same, the procedures used to achieve the goal vary in almost all possible ways. Given the fact that this variability is occurring not among grossly different techniques, but rather within the limits of a single method, the variability is remarkable. It is hard to imagine a sound scientific model that would legitimatize all these approaches.

Fortunately, there has been a fair amount of work investigating the effects of person reference. The first and most important study dealing with this problem is one by Sacks (1949). Sacks developed two forms of a 60-stem sentence completion which were identical except that one form had stems that were all cast in the first person whereas in the other form the stems were in the third person. Both forms were given to 100 neuropsychiatric patients. Three psychologists rated the subjects for disturbance on the basis of the sentence completions, and the psychiatrists treating the patients rated them for disturbance on the basis of clinical impressions.

The results of the study clearly indicated that the first-person form manifested greater agreement with the psychiatric ratings than did the third-person form. An additional finding was that six of the seven psychologists who took part in the study preferred the first-person form for clinical use.

Sacks' study is an interesting and important one. Nonetheless, questions might be raised about the criterion used to evaluate the two sentence completion forms. It might be suggested that the psychiatrists in their ratings were responding to the more peripheral aspects of personality; that they were in fact responding mainly and merely to what the patients chose to tell them. If this were so, and if it is further assumed that first-person stems lend themselves to greater conscious control, Sacks's findings would assume a quite different significance. The congruence of the ratings based on the first-person form with the psychiatric ratings would demonstrate only an equal lack of profundity. The lack of agreement between ratings based on the third-person form with the psychiatric ratings would be consistent with the assumption that such a form taps the projective core of personality.

There is no wish to defend this highly speculative argument but merely to present it. There is no direct empirical support for such a position, but a study by Morton (1955) is interesting and suggestive.

Morton found that the ISB correlated .40 with the Mooney Problem Check List. This check list (Mooney & Gordon, 1950) consists of a number of statements, each of which refers to a specific problem. The subject is asked to check the problems which concern him. As is obvious, the information generated by the check list is limited by the subject's willingness to reveal the information. The significant correlation of the ISB (a first-person form) with such an instrument raises questions about the degree of conscious control the subject has and uses in responses to the ISB and other tests of this kind. It would be of some interest to know the correlation of a third-person form of the ISB with the Mooney.

Arnold and Walter (1957) corroborate Sack's finding that the person reference of the sentence stem is an important determinant of the response. They used the ISB as a self-reference form and a variation of the ISB as an other-reference form. They gave these forms to 120 female college students and found that the two forms correlated $r=$ .55. The authors concluded that first-and third-person forms are not interchangeable.

Cromwell and Lundy (1954) do, however, support Sacks's contention that first-person stems are superior to third-person stems. Thirty-nine clinical psychologists made personality inferences about 60 VA neuropsychiatric patients on the basis of data obtained from a sentence completion form designed for the study. The authors had the clinicians make specific hypotheses about the subjects and additionally asked the clinicians to indicate the specific sentences which had contributed to their evaluations. By this method, the authors were able to assess the differential productivity of the stems, and they found that first-person stems were clinically more productive than third-person stems. No attempt, it should be noted, was made to validate the clinical inferences.

In a study by Forer and Tolman (1952), it was found that clinicians asked to make judgments about the potential clinical value of each stem in the Forer Structure Sentence Completion Test showed no preference for either first- or third-person constructions. Though these results are not consistent with the findings of Cromwell and Lundy, it should be noted that the clinicians made their judgments using a blank form. It is entirely possible that had the clinicians seen what the stems could "do," they would have shown—as in the study by Cromwell and Lundy— a similar preference for first-person stems.

A study by Hanfmann and Getzels (1953) offers some support for the use of third-person stems. Using third-person stems, the authors tested a group of white and Negro high-school girls with a specially constructed sentence completion form. A special procedure was used, termed by the authors the *Self-Reference Technique*. This technique consisted of reviewing each of the responses with the subject and asking her whether or not the responses to the test were true of herself. Hanfmann and Getzels found that the subjects identified 70 per cent of the responses as personally relevant. On the basis of these data, the authors suggest that third-person stems elicit self-revelatory responses, the bulk of which tap a levey of personality organization fairly close to consciousness. This study did not provide a direct comparison of the efficacy of first-person versus third-person stems. Consequently, these findings are, at best, suggestive.

In summary, there is considerable variability in the treatment of the stem relative to the person of reference. This variability seems to be related to theoretical assumptions that are largely untested, unstated, or both. What empirical evidence there is, does seem to favor the first-person construction of sentence stems. The evidence is, however, far from being definitive.

Treatment of the Response

There are a variety of ways of treating sentence completion responses reported in the literature, and several authors use more than one method of analysis. Basically, however, responses are subjected to either (1) formal anaylsis or (2) content analysis, and content-analysis methods may be further classified as semiobjective or impressionistic.

Formal analysis refers to the assessment of the nonmeaningful properties of the sentence completion response. Benton et al. (1957) classify some of the formal analyses that have been reported:

(1) Length of completion (Carter, 1947; Wilson, 1949). (2) Use of personal pronouns (White, 1949).

(3) Time for reaction and for completion (Carter, 1947; Meltzoff, 1951; White, 1949). (4) Absolute and relative frequencies of parts of speech, such as verb/adjective ratio (Ellsworth, 1951; Mann, 1941). (5) Range of words used in relation to number of words used (Mann, 1941). (6) Grammatical errors, nonsensical responses, or neologisms (Cameron & Magaret, 1949; White, 1949). (7) First word used (Benton, Windle, & Erdice, 1952).

Guertin (1959), in a factor-analytic study of errors (e.g., misspelling) made on the ISB, found four factors that related to other clinically significant material. Wilson (1949), however, found that analyses of sentence completion data for misspellings, use of sentence fragments, response length, and other formal characteristics did not discriminate groups of well-adjusted and groups of maladjusted school children, and she suggests that a content-analysis approach would be more discriminating. This recommendation, whatever its merits, does seem to be consonant with general practice. The treatment of sentence completion responses most typically involves the analysis of content.

Content analysis is however, anything but a monolithic procedure. Approaches to the content analysis of sentence completion responses have been many and varied, but they have tended to polarize on a dimension of objectivity. Many authors have used highly subjective impressionistic methods. These methods have had historical priority in the development of the sentence completion, and they continue to be widely endorsed.

In contrast, there have been a number of attempts to develop objective scoring procedures for the analysis of content. It should be understood, however, that even the most objective methods of scoring sentence completion responses involve a high degree of subjectivity. Free-response tests defy clerical scoring, and though there have been variants of the sentence completion method that lent themselves to greater objectivity, these have typically involved the imposition of response limits (Grigg & Kelley, 1960, Izard, Rosenberg, Bair, & Maag, 1953; Shay, 1950). It is doubtful, as Benton et al. (1957) point out, that these variants are comparable with the traditional free-response forms.

IMPRESSIONISTIC METHODS

Of all the sentence completion test constructors, Holsopple and Miale (1954) are probably the ones most committed to a clinically impressionistic method of coping with sentence completion responses. They maintain:

> This desire to achieve a scoring system which would provide for a more "objective" handling of the data sounds like a reasonable desire, but we believe that an effort in this direction at the present time would be premature. . . . For the time being, however, we believe that more and better material can be acquired by a process of interpretation sentence by sentence until an acceptable global description is achieved (Holsopple & Miale, 1954, p. 6).

In order that the reader might gain a truer understanding of the clinical interpretation of the sentence completion, Holsopple and Miale present their clinical interpretation of a sample protocol, taken response by response. Toward this same end, the interpretation of the response "they are right" given to stem 1 (Children are usually certain that . . .) is presented in full:

> It did not occur to the subject to say that children are usually certain that they are loved or that they can have their own way. On the basis of our observation that adults here often ascribe certainty to children in areas of their own more important uncertainties, the question raised at the outset is "How right am I?" The implication is that being right is important, and the subject has some doubts about his judgment (Holsopple & Miale, 1954, p. 45).

Stein (1947) similarly regards the sentence completion as a method of generating useful data to which the clinician may respond interpretively. The validity of the clinician's interpretations are presumably correlated with his experience, sensitivity, and general clinical expertise. Sacks and Levy (1950) also believe that a nonquantitative or clinical approach is called for. Such an approach has greater flexibility, which they believe is required, considering our primitive understanding of human personality. Forer (1960) rejects the quantitative scoring systems of Rotter et al. (1949) and Rohde (1957) as having limited clinical utility. Elsewhere, in discussing objective quantitative scoring systems for the sentence completion, Forer says:

While such neatness facilitates validation, the evidence in the research literature is that the sheer occurrence of magnitudes of drives or traits has little predictive utility. Particularly does this appear to be the case because such labeling or quantification of needs provides no evidence of the likelihood or conditions or forms of expression of these needs. Rather a growing focus in description of the personality deals with the enduring organizing aspects, often conceptualized as the ego or the self (1960b, p. 215).

There is meager empirical support for the impressionistic approach to content analysis. Dean (1957) used the ISB in combination with other tests to assess the adjustment of blind subjects. Rotter's quantitative scoring system was unable to discriminate well-adjusted subjects from poorly adjusted subjects. Dean concluded that a qualitative approach would be more useful. Unfortunately, he did not put his faith in a qualitative approach to an empirical test. Stein (1947), Holsopple and Miale (1954), and Forer (1960) all offer clinical, nonquantitative data to support impressionistic analysis. Beyond this, there is little firm experimental evidence to support the impressionistic approach to content analysis.

Further, even Sacks, Stein, and Forer are apparently not entirely willing to submit their tests to completely free impressionistic analysis. These authors arrange their stems, as previously noted, in specified content categories, and they direct users of their tests to organize their clinical efforts within these categories. And though it is certainly true that these authors permit clinicians considerable lattitude in the interpretation of the responses, they do offer relatively pointed interpretive guides.

Sacks, in fact, uses a rating procedure similar to the one devised by Rotter and Willerman (1947). He clusters his sentence stems within each of his categories and rates the subject on a four-point scale for degree of disturbance in each of the fifteen clinical areas. These ratings are achieved through clinical acumen and no attempt is made to treat the ratings statistically. Sacks's method seems to be but a step—albeit a good-size step—away from being an objective, quantitative method of content analysis. There is also an attempt, reported in the literature, to apply Rotter and Willerman's rating procedures to Forer's stems. Karen (1961) reports reliability coefficients ranging from .90 to .96 for this method. Unfortunately, this work was based on only eight items, and no attempt was made to validate the procedure.

Stein eschews the use of ratings, but he does cluster his stems, and he presents seven principles to sensitize clinicians to critical responses. Forer, too, clusters his stems and presents the potential user of his test with a number of interpretive tips. These attempts to make the bases for clinical impression more public and consensual, coming as they do from people committed and sympathetic to the clinical approach, seem to emphasize the ultimate desirability of the clinical cookbook (Meehl, 1956). The issue is, however, as it has always been, the feasibility and not the desirability of a cookbook approach. Is an actuarial approach theoretically possible? And if it is theoretically possible, are we, at our present level of sophistication, ready for it?

These questions will not be answered here, but ready or not there is considerable evidence in the general clinical literature and in the sentence completion literature specifically that clinical impressionistic methods involve a too full measure of risk and uncertainty.

In a study by Masling (1957), eight clinical psychology graduate students were required to give and interpret ISB's obtained from female undergraduates. Unknown to the graduate students, the testees were accomplices who had been instructed to assume either a "warm" or "cold" role toward the examiner according to a predetermined schedule. Masling defines the roles as follows:

"In the warm role the accomplice was told to act friendly and interested in both the testing situation and the examiner, the goal being to make him feel comfortable and accepted. In her cold role she was to act in a formal, disinterested way and her object was to make him feel awkward and incompetent" (1957, p. 378).

Each examiner saw one "cold" and one "warm" testee. The protocols, though different in content, had been prepared so that they were equal in rated adjustment. The examiner-subjects were asked to write clinical interpretive reports for the two protocols. After all references to the examiner-testee relationships had been deleted, the reports were analyzed for number of positive and negative statements made about the testee. The ratings were done blind, and the results were as predicted, in that "warm" subjects were perceived more positively than "cold" subjects.

In evaluating the significance of these findings, it must be remembered that the examiners were relatively inexperienced graduate students. Nonetheless, the study is intriguing and the results provocative. The sentence completion method may be even more of a projective device than its adherents had ever intended. It is, moreover, unfortunate that Masling did not also have the examiner rate the ISB's using Rotter and Rafferty's procedure, which is alleged to involve a high degree of objectivity. It would have been of considerable interest to know if "objective" scoring procedures are similarly sensitive to the effects of "warm" and "cold" interactions.

A study by Horowitz (1962) attempted to assess the accuracy of clinical judgments based on projective test data. The clinicians were asked to predict to Q-sort descriptions made by patients' psychotherapists. *Michigan Sentence Completion Test* protocols were part of the projective data available to the clinicians. The major finding was that the clinical judgments were no more accurate than base-rate predictions.

In a study by Luft (1950), experienced clinicians and physical scientists were asked to identify patients' true responses to the OSS sentence completion test from among lists of five alternatives. The judges were presented with tape recordings of the patients' diagnostic interviews as a basis for their identifications. The clinicians and nonclinicians were equally unable to predict the sentence completion responses.

There have been a number of studies that have questioned the efficacy of the impressionistic approach.[4] Certain studies by Fiske and his associates, however, suggest that the problem may not be with the clinical method per se but rather with the instability of the data. Fiske and Van Buskirk (1959) had clinicians do a Q sort of thirty need variables, using sentence completion protocols. Three protocols obtained at different points in time were obtained from each of eight subjects. This procedure permitted Fiske and Van Buskirk to answer the question: "Are the differences between the interpretations of protocols from the same person less than the differences between interpretations of protocols of different persons?" (1959, p. 177). The authors found that "in 25 per cent of the comparisons, the agreement was higher with protocols for different subjects than with the other protocols from the same subject" (Fiske & Van Buskirk, 1959, p. 180).

This study developed from a more general interest in the problem of intraindividual response variability, reviewed by Fiske and Rice (1955). In other studies (Osterweil & Fiske, 1956; Fiske, 1957), it was found that sentence completion responses showed great variability on repeat testing. Of special significance was the finding by Osterweil and Fiske that those responses that were most individuating and useful to the clinician were the ones that were least stable over time.

Stephens (1960) reported that "the stems with lowest retest reliability were those which were rated by judges as being most likely to be sensitive to change in adjustment" (1960, p. 333). Such a finding tends to support the results obtained by Osterweil and Fiske, but in at least one important sense it alters the interpretation of Osterweil and Fiske's data. If Stephens' data are valid, then the instability of the sentence stems is a function of *true* personality change rather than random variability. Further, these results question the legitimacy of traditional notions of test-retest reliability as applied to a personality test like the sentence

---

[4] For a broader discussion of this issue, the reader is advised to consult Meehl (1954), Holt (1958), and Schafer (1949).

completion. This old and thorny problem has been discussed at length by Macfarlane and Tuddenham (1951) and others. The general conclusion seems to be that the projective test user must find other non-temporal methods of coping with the problem of reliability.

Nonetheless, however achieved, there does appear to be considerable intraindividual response variability—a fact which presents the actuary and the clinician alike with a problem of considerable magnitude.

SEMIOBJECTIVE METHODS

The validity and power of a sentence completion test analyzed impressionistically can be no greater than the skill of the clinician using the instrument. In general practice, the validity of the test and the astuteness of the tester are nonindependent. As methods of analysis become more objective, the analytic role of the clinician decreases. Whether this relationship is viewed with alarm or delight, the relationship as such is incontestable.

The most rigorous and objective system of scoring the content of sentence completion responses has been presented by Rotter and Rafferty (1950). Each completion is scored on a 7-point scale from 0 to 6 for degree of conflict (C). There are three classes of C responses, three classes of positive (P) responses, and a class of neutral (N) responses. The scoring of the responses is guided by examples supplied in the test manual, with separate scoring manuals provided for males and females. The ISB user compares the response to the examples found in the appropriate manual and assigns the rating given to the example which is most similar to the one he has obtained. The list of examples in the manual is not intended to be exhaustive, and the authors furnish general scoring principles to be used in combination with the specific examples.

As an illustration, item 10, "People . . .", is presented with the examples of scoring weights given in the male manual:

(6) C_3 disturb me; worry me; never understand me; frighten me; have it in for me; are hateful

(5) C_2 annoy me (strong criticism of people in general — e.g., destroy what they build; have a deplorable sense of value); (indication of unfavorable attitude toward subject — e.g., think that I am a snob)

(4) C_1 can be got along with if you try; do not co-operate enough; run around in circles most of the time

(3) N are sometimes good, sometimes bad; who are truthful will be rewarded; work to achieve something; inherit the world; are interesting to study (stereotypes — e.g., are funny; are crazy)

(2) P_1 are interesting; are fascinating; are nice

(1) P_2 are good; are basically good; I like

(0) P_3 are fun; I like them all; are wonderful; are the salt of the earth; touch wet paint in spite of wet paint signs (Rotter & Rafferty, 1950, p. 58).

After the responses are rated individually, the weights are totaled to produce an over-all "adjustment" score. The higher the score, the greater the degree of maladjustment.

In a validation study by Rotter et al. (1949), it was found that a cutting score of 135 correctly identified 68 per cent of maladjusted female college students, 69 per cent of maladjusted male students, 80 per cent of well-adjusted females, and 89 per cent of well-adjusted males. In light of the simplicity of the scoring system and the relative homogeneity of the population, these results are impressive. A cross-validation study by Churchill and Crandall (1955) yielded results in essential agreement with the original findings, and the authors suggest that the ISB norms may be applicable in a variety of college settings. Arnold and Walter (1957), however, found that for another college population the cutting score of 135 seemed to be pegged too low.

If the "objectivity" of an objective test is simply defined in terms of its ability to be scored with perfect agreement by a number of judges, then based on a number of empirical studies, it is clear that the ISB approaches being an objective test. Rotter et al. (1949) report interscorer reliabilities of .91 and .96 for male and female protocols, respectively. Using the high-school form of the ISB, Rotter, Rafferty, and Lotsof (1954) report interscorer reliabilities of .96 and .97 for the boys' and girls' manuals. Studies by independent researchers report interscorer reliabilities for the ISB that are comparably high. Jessor and Hess (1958) report an interscorer reliability of .97; Churchill and Crandall (1955) for a sample of female subjects report interscorer reliabilities ranging from .94 to .98; Bieri, Blacharsky, and Reid (1955) found interscorer reliability to be .95; Arnold and Walter (1957) found interscorer reliability to be .97; Chance (1958) obtained an interscorer reliability of .89; and Cass (1952b) reports an interscorer reliability of .90.

The success achieved by Rotter and his associates in developing reliable scoring methods has encouraged other attempts at objectifying the content analysis of sentence stems through the use of manuals of scoring examples. Sechrest and Hemphill (1954) devised a manual of scoring examples to be used specifically with Air Force personnel which proved to be sensitive to motivational variables involved in the assumption of combat responsibility.

Trites et al. (1953) report the development of a scoring manual based on the protocols of 1,038 flight cadets. The manual contained principles and examples that permitted the assignation of a response to one of thirteen categories. Each category had two properties: (1) it referred to a particular attitude and (2) it had either a positive or a negative tone. An example of one of Trites et al.'s categories (Category L, Sexuality Attitudes), as defined in their manual, is, "Expresses positive, mature, heterosexual attitude toward dating, courtships, love, marriage, sexual and marital relations" (1953, p. 21). Using a scoring manual to assign responses to such categories, judges achieved interscorer reliabilities ranging from .80 to .94. These reliabilities are quite respectable and are comparable to the reliabilities reported by Rotter and Rafferty (1950).

Rychlak, Mussen, and Bennett (1957) believe that objective methods of scoring sentence completion responses are more appropriate for research purposes than more impressionistic methods. Accordingly, in a study using a sentence completion test to measure social adjustment in native Japanese students enrolled at an American university, the authors attempted to construct a scoring manual that would facilitate the objective scoring of the sentence completions.

They made hypotheses about ten personality variables presumed to be related to social adjustment. Their scoring manual defined each of these variables, gave examples of responses that related to them, predicted the relationship of each variable to social adjustment, and presented the theoretical rationale underlying each prediction. Each response was scored on all appropriate variables, and the score for each variable was the number of responses which had been relevant to the particular variable. The percentage of interscorer agreement for this scoring procedure was .80.

In their study, Rychlak et al. correlated the sentence completion adjustment scores on each of the ten personality variables with social adjustment ratings based on interview data. Six of the ten correlations were significant at $p < .05$ or better. The authors concluded that the sentence completion test scored by their procedures proved to be a remarkably efficient predictor of the quality of the individual's social relationships" (Rychlak et al., 1957, p. 28).

Perhaps the most elaborate and ambitious scoring system is reported by Rohde (1946; 1957). Responses to each one of her 65 sentence stems are analyzed in terms of Murray's theory of needs and presses. She employs 38 categories of needs, inner integrates, inner states, and general traits, each of these variables being scored for strength. The criteria for assessing the strength of a variable are frequency and intensity. "Frequency is obtained by counting the number of occurrences of the variable. Intensity is estimated on a 1 to 3 scale: (1) low, (2) medium, (3) high. The determinant is the vividness and potency with which the variable is expressed. For example, a suggestion of annoyance is rated 1, and outright expression of dislike is rated 2, while intense hatred is rated 3 in reference to n Rejection" (Rohde, 1957, p. 63).

Rohde (1946) conducted a validation study of her test, using the scoring procedures described above. One hundred high-school students, 50 boys and 50 girls, were given the Rohde-Hildreth Sentence Completion Technique, and each of 33 variables abstracted from the test was rated on a ten-point scale. On the basis of interviews with teachers and school supervisors, another set of ratings for the subjects was obtained to serve as the criterion measure for the validation of the test. The correlations between these two sets of ratings were impressively high, .79 for the girls and .82 for the boys. However, as both Rotter (1951) and Zimmer (1956) note, the experimenter was involved in the rating of the criterion measure as well as the scoring of the test responses. The possibility of bias confounding the data is clear and unfortunate.

In studies by Jenkins and Blodgett (1960) and Jenkins (1961), attempts were made to quantify the changes in sentence completion responses on repeat testing. Using the Miale-Holsopple test, the authors paired responses given to the same stems at two different times. Judges were asked to compare the second response to the first and rate the response for improvement (+) or worsening (−). The pluses and minuses were summed to give an over-all improvement score. These scores were used to predict or postdict improvement for a group of juvenile delinquents (Jenkins & Blodgett, 1960) and for a group of schizophrenics (Jenkins, 1961). These scoring methods did have some success in predicting improvement and are considered by the authors to have considerable promise.

The scoring procedures used by Jenkins and Blodgett and by Rotter are characterized not only by features of objectivity and quantification but by emphasis on a single score, whether it be "improvement" (Jenkins & Blodgett) or "adjustment" (Rotter). This approach is quite different in procedure and purpose from other semiobjective methods, such as the one used by Trites et al. and Rychlak et al., who attempted to assess a number of variables.

Scoring all responses from a given sentence completion test for a single variable rather than for a number of variables has the obvious effect of increasing the test's length and reliability. The increasing monotonic relationship between test length and reliability is well known and accepted (Guilford, 1954). In a study by Mishler (1958), there is empirical support, specific to the sentence completion test, for the value of increasing the number of sentence stems in order to decrease instability.

Zimmer (1956) shares this view: "The attempt to derive only a single variable, rather than several from a test record may increase the likelihood that an adequate number of responses relevant to all aspects of the variable can be obtained, and may thereby contribute to the stability and accuracy of prediction" (1956, p. 67). In his review of sentence completion validation studies, he concludes that an objective scoring system is a more promising method than a global impressionistic evaluation. Most promising of all, he believes, are approaches that combine objective scoring systems with single-variable analysis.

Such an approach would seem to be the most generally useful method of treating sentence completion responses for research purposes. A single variable orientation is likely to maximize data relevance, and objectification facilitates replication, which, is, after all, the corrective that distinguishes the scientific enterprise. Is the single variable–objective scoring system treatment of responses an equally valuable method for general clinical purposes?

Merely raising the question tends to furnish the answer. Clinical purposes are typically different from research purposes. Data relevance and procedural replicability are, of course, important to the clinician. His purpose in using projective techniques for personality assessment, however, reside in the power of these tests to generate hypotheses that will help him to describe and understand the particular patient with whom he is confronted. A single summary score of psychological adjustment, however sophisticated psychometrically, is likely to be regarded by the clinician as limited at best.

Problems in the Assessment of Validity

In Table 49–1, some 50 studies bearing on the validity of the sentence completion method are summarized. Even a cursory inspection of the table suggests that there can be no unequivocal claim for the validity of the sentence completion method. Many tests, scored in many ways, using a variety of criteria, applied to a variety of populations, have yielded a variety of data.

STANDARD AND CUSTOM TESTS

Research with 26 different sentence completion forms is reported in Table 49–1. Of these 26 forms, 11 have been presented by their authors in standard forms; the others, referred to as *custom* tests, were by and large designed for the study of specific variables. Of the 50 studies summarized, the ISB has 15 citations, with the next most cited test having 4. No claim is made that this table is a perfect reflection within any of its categories of the nature and amount of work done with the sentence completion method. Nonetheless, whatever the true proportions, it is clear that the ISB has received more research attention than any other standard sentence completion form.

It is entirely possible, however, that sentence completion forms designed for more general clinical purposes like the Forer, SSCT, Miale-Holsopple, and Rohde are in wider clinical use than the research literature suggests. It is not entirely unlikely, though it would be unfortunate, that clinical instruments with least research support are most "used" and that instruments such as the ISB are most researched because they lend themselves to research purposes irrespective of pragmatic virtue.

One further note about the various completion forms. Many of the standard sentence completion tests available have their roots in work done during World War II (cf. Holzberg, Teicher, & Taylor, 1947; Hutt,

TABLE 49-1 A Summary of Fifty Representative Sentence Completion Validity Studies

TEST	E	N	METHOD OF ANALYSIS	Ss	CRITERION	RESULTS
Forer	Meyer & Tolman (1955)	20	Rated for attitudes toward parental figures	Therapy patients	TAT & interview data	r = N.S. (value of r not reported)
Forer	Carr (1956)	50	Rated for 4 affect categories	Male patients in a mental hygiene clinic	Rorschach variables	χ^2: 13 significant relationships at p<.10 or better
Forer	Stone & Dellis (1960)	20	Rated on Menninger Health–Sickness Rating Scale for amount of psychopathology	Schizophrenics	WAIS, TAT, Rorschach, DAP	Difference in amount of pathology between SCT & Rorschach; SCT & DAP p<.01
ISB[1]	Rotter & Willerman (1947)	200	Ratings on a 7-point scale of conflict using a scoring manual of examples	AAF convalescent hospital patients	Evaluation of severity of disturbance based on tests, case history, & interview data	Triserial r = .61
		148	Global clinical evaluation of disturbance		Presence or absence of psychiatric complaints	bis. r = .41 & .39
ISB	Rotter et al. (1949)	82f[3] 124m	Rotter & Willerman's procedures	College students	Adjustment ratings	bis. r = .64, p<.01 bis. r = .77, p<.01
ISB	Barry (1950)	38	Rotter & Willerman's procedures	College students in counseling	Adjustment ratings	bis. r = .67, p<.01
ISB	Rotter & Rafferty (1950)	299	Rotter & Willerman's procedures	College freshmen	Ohio State Psychological Examination	r = .11
ISB[2]	Rotter et al. (1954)	48f 45m 70f 68m	Rotter & Willerman's procedures	High-school students	Adjustment ratings Adjustment ratings Sociometric choice Sociometric choice	r = .37, p<.05 r = .20, N.S. r = .32, p<.05 r = .20, N.S.
ISB	Sechrest & Hemphill (1954)	340	Rated on 16 scales relevant to air-crew adjustment	Air-crew members	Assumption of combat responsibility	t test: 4 of 16 scales sig. at p<.05 or better
ISB	Bieri et al. (1955)	40	Rotter & Willerman's procedures	College students	Taylor MAS Accuracy of prediction of other S's MAS	r = .46, p<.01 r = .19, N.S.
ISB	Churchill & Crandall (1955)	188f	Rotter & Willerman's procedures	College students	Application for psychol. couns.	bis. r = .42, p<.01

(Continued on next page)

TABLE 49-1 (continued)

TEST	E	N	Ss	METHOD OF ANALYSIS	CRITERION	RESULTS
ISB	Morton (1955)	156m	College students	Rotter & Willerman's procedures	Application for psychol. couns.	bis. $r = .37$, $p < .01$
		44	Mothers		Adjustment ratings	$r = .49$, $p < .01$
		28	College students		Adjustment ratings	$r = .53$
					Mooney Problem Check List	$r = .40$
					Adjustment, therapy — non-therapy	bis. $r = .50$
ISB	Berger & Sutker (1956)	199m 154f	College students	Rotter & Willerman's procedures	Academic achievement	$r = .01$, N.S.
					Academic achievement	$r = .01$, N.S.
ISB	Dean (1957)	54	Blind Ss	Rotter & Willerman's procedures	Adjustment ratings	$t = -.16$, N.S.
ISB	Chance (1958)	52	College students	Rotter & Willerman's procedures	Prediction of other S's EPPS	$r = -.26$, $p < .10$
ISB	Fitzgerald (1958)	60	College students	Rated for n dependency using a scoring manual of examples	Sociometric ratings of dependency	$r = .25$, $p < .05$
					Interview ratings of dependency	$r = .28$, $p < .05$
ISB	Jessor & Hess (1958)	41	College students	Rotter & Willerman's procedures	Rotter Level of Aspiration Board	White's test $p < .10$
ISB	Denenberg (1960)	40 21	College students	Rotter & Willerman's procedures	Kinesthetic maze	$r = .39$ tris. $r = .46$
Miale-Hol-sopple	Jenkins & Blodgett (1960)	92	Delinquent boys	Rated retest improvement	Recidivism	χ^2 for 3 judges: $p < .005$, $p < .01$, $p < .025$
Miale-Hol-sopple	Jenkins (1961)	30	Schizophrenics	Schizophrenics	Improvement as measured by Lorr Multidimensional Scale	t test $= p < .05$
Michigan	Kelly & Fiske (1950)	78	Clinical psychol. grad. students in VA training	"Blind" prediction of criteria based on global ratings	Success in clinical psychology evaluated by clinical staff members	4 of 8 r's: $p < .05$ or better
Michigan	Hiler (1959)	70	VA psycho-therapy patients	Intensity ratings on 25 personality variables	Continuation in psychotherapy vs. termination	71% agreement with criterion
		95		Clinical impression to predict criterion		68% agreement with criterion

(Continued on next page)

TABLE 49-1 (continued)

TEST	E	METHOD OF ANALYSIS	N	Ss	CRITERION	RESULTS
OSS	Hardy (1948)	Scored for dominance, submission	25	Grad. students in course in nondirective counsel.	Nondirectiveness of counseling statements	Rho = −.26, N.S.
OSS	Hadley & Kennedy (1949)	Modified Rotter & Willerman procedures (3-point scale)	157	College students	High- vs. low-grade point	Critical ratio $p < .04$; of 12 $\bar{X}$ ratings 6 $p < .05$ or better
Peck	Peck & McGuire (1959)	Retest changes rated positive/negative	69	College students	Lefkowitz Rigidity Scale Worchel Self-Activities Index McGuire Q Check	$r = .11$, N.S. $r = -.02$, N.S. $.67\ p < .01$ $r = .00, .06, .19, .03$ (all N.S.)
Rohde	Rohde (1946)	Ratings based on Murray's need system	50m 5of	High-school students	Combined ratings of teacher judgments & interview data relative to Murray's need system	$r = 82,\ p < .01$ $r = .79,\ p < .01$
SAM	Trites et al. (1953)	Scoring manual used to rate 13 personality variables	100 413 539 639	Flight cadets	Success vs. failure in flight cadet training	bis. $r = .32,\ p < .005$ bis. $r = .21,\ p < .001$ bis. $r = .13,\ p < .001$ bis. $r = .18,\ p < .001$
SSCT	Sacks (1949)	Inpressionistic ratings on 3-point scale for disturbance	100	VA neuro-psychiatric outpatients	Psychiatric adjustment ratings	Agree. on 8/15 variables, $p < .001$ (1st-person form); agree. on 3/15 variables, $p < .001$ (3rd-pers. form)
SSCT	Sacks & Levy (1950)	Ratings for disturbance Interpretative summaries	100 50	VA neuro-psychiatric outpatients	Psychiatric ratings of disturbance Agreement with clinical findings	$r = .48$ to $.57$ 77% agreement

(Continued on next page)

TABLE 49–1 *(continued)*

Test	Author (year)	Measure	N	Comparison	Subjects	Results
SSCT	McGreevey (1962)	Pooled rankings on 4 personality traits using TAT & SSCT	40	Ego-threatened versus nonego-threatened	Student nurses	r's for nonego-threat. group N.S.; % r's for ego-threat. group $p < .05$ or better 6/12 t tests $p < .05$
Stein	Locke (1957)	3-point scale of disturbance	100	Imprisonment versus nonimprisonment	Naval Personnel	
Stein	Howard (1962)	Rank ordering of 10 of Murray's needs	10	Rorschach & TAT	VA psychiatric	$\bar{X}$ interjudge agreement between tests, $r = .05$, N.S.
Stotsky & Weinberg	Stotsky & Weinberg (1956)	Rated for positive or negative tone relative to 9 ego-strength dimensions	80	Work performance ratings	Psychiatric patients	χ^2 $p < .05$ or better on 8/9 vars.
			80	Work progress ratings		χ^2 $p < .05$ or better on 8/9 vars.
Stotsky & Weinberg	Stotsky (1957)	Rated on 9 ego-strength dimensions	32	Subject characteristics	Normals I	I & II differed ($p < .05$) on 2/9 vars; I & III differed ($p < .05$) on 8/9 vars. (χ^2)
		Positive treatment outcome	39		Schizophrenics II	t test: on 6/8 variables $p < .10$ or better
		Negative treatment outcome	39		Schizophrenics III	
Stotsky & Weinberg	Wolkon & Haefner (1961)	Stotsky & Weinberg procedures	48	Behaviorally improved group versus unimproved group	Psychiatric patients	
Custom	Wilson (1949)	Rated for grammar, spelling, and other formal aspects	22	Maladjusted children versus well-adjusted children	High-school students	No significant relationships observed $r = -.08$ to $.14$ (all N.S.)
Custom	Cameron & Magaret (1950)	Frequency of response "scatter"	45	Card-sorting test	College students	
Custom	Rosenberg (1950)	Rated for attitudes toward parents	72	Guilford Inventory	Psychoneurotic patients	2/10 r's $p < .05$
				Guilford-Martin Inventory		1/10 r's $p < .05$
				Therapists' judgments of patients, attitudes		58% agreement on attitudes towards father; 69% agreement on attitudes toward mother
Custom	Harlow (1951)	Scored for dominance-submission on a 4-point scale	40	Weightlifters versus nonweightlifters	Weightlifters & nonweightlifters	7/11 t tests $p < .05$

(Continued on next page)

TABLE 49-1 (continued)

TEST	E	N	Ss	METHOD OF ANALYSIS	CRITERION	RESULTS
Custom	Lazarus et al. (1951)	35 25	Psych. patients Repressors & Intellectualizers	Rated for expression of hostility and sexuality	Percept. acc. of hostile & sexual stimuli Repressors versus intellectualizers	$r = .45$, $p < .01$; $r = .55$, $p < .01$; t test $p < .05$
Custom	Cass (1952[b])	42	Well-adjusted & maladjusted children	Rated for parent-child conflict using a scoring manual of examples	Well-adjusted versus maladjusted children	t test $p < .001$
Custom	Kimball (1952)	117	Prep school	Rated for attitude toward father Rated for aggression	Academic underachievement versus normal achievement	Critical ratio $p < .05$ (father); Critical ratio $p < .01$ (aggression)
Custom	Dorris, Levinson & Hanfmann (1954)	21	College freshmen	Rated for ego-threat, passivity, and masculinity	High versus low authoritarians	12/16 hypotheses supported at $p < .05$ or better (t test)
Custom	Zimmer (1955)	73	AAF crew members	Prediction of criterion based on clinical impression	Sociometric rankings on 8 personality variables	$r = .10, .10, .21$ (all N.S.)
Custom	Burwen, Campbell, & Kidd (1956)	312	Air Force Cadets	Rated on 5-point scale of superior-subordinate orientation	Test of leadership knowledge Superior-subordinate cluster Scale of alienation O.T. ratings of behavior	$r = .27$, $p < .001$ $r = .32$, $p < .001$ $r = -.45$, $p < .001$ $r = .50$, $p < .01$
Custom	Walter & Jones (1956)	33	Psychiatric patients	Ratings on a 4-point scale of positive and negative attitudes	Social adjustment ratings based on interview data	6/10 r's $p < .05$ or better
Custom	Rychlak et al. (1957)	18	Japanese-born college students in USA	Ratings of inclusion with 10 personality categories based on scoring manual		
Custom	Willingham (1958)	164	Naval Aviation Cadets	Rated for acceptance of environment	4 morale tests	r with 4 tests = .27
Custom	Ebner & Shaw (1960)	48	Psychiatric patients & normal Ss	Rated for activity-passivity	Psychiatric patients versus normals	t test $p < .05$
Custom	Efron (1960)	92	Psychiatric patients	Rated for suicide potential	Expression versus nonexpression of suicidal thoughts	Correct identification = 43% & 30% (both N.S.)

[1] Preliminary form.
[2] High-school form.
[3] Where results are broken down by sex, N is reported by sex.

1945), and most of the others are also at least a decade old .It is not suggested here that new tests are best. Certainly, any test that could be of value ten years ago in the assessment of personality is very much up to date. It is interesting to note, however, what might be referred to as the sociology of test construction. Shortly after the war, a spate of sentence completion tests were made available, but more recently other tests appear to have caught the creative fancy of people in the field.

A notable exception to this trend is provided by a sentence completion form constructed by Stotsky and Weinberg (1956). In follow-up studies by Stotsky (1957), Connors, Wolkon, Haefner, and Stotsky (1960), and Wolkon and Haefner (1961), the Stotsky-Weinberg Sentence Completion Test has appeared to be a sensitive and useful instrument for assessing ego strength in psychiatric subjects.

SUBJECTS

Captive groups have traditionally been the major source of subjects for psychological experimentation. So, too, has it been the case with sentence completion research. Three groups have been most used; college students, psychiatric patients, and armed forces personnel. The last-named group may indeed, reflect the captivity of the psychologist as well as the subject. The danger in this restriction of subject populations is obvious. If we wish to know something about other people in the world, we are going to have to bring such specimens into our laboratories.

The problem of population restriction has been exacerbated in sentence completion research by the tendency for specific sentence completion forms to be used with specific populations. Of the 16 studies cited in the summary table that used college students as subjects, 11 of them involved the ISB, though the ISB was used in less than a thrrd of all the studies cited. (A chi square for independent samples, as outlined by Siegel, 1956, was computed, yielding a chi-quare value of 711, d.f. $=$1, p $<$.001.) This finding indicates that the ISB has been primarily a "college" test. Only in the Rotter and Willerman (1947) study was the ISB used with a psychiatric population. On the other hand, all three of the studies cited using the Forer, all three of the Stotsky-Weinberg studies, and two of the three studies cited using the SSCT employed psychiatric populations. Whatever the reason for such narrow usage, it is undeniably the case that cross-validation and generalizability have been thereby inhibited.

CRITERIA

Often in the history of psychological testing, tests have been devised to replace inadequate assessment techniques, only to be validated against these very same techniques. Though these bootstrap operations have, on occasion, appeared to work, they can hardly be regarded as the method of preference. The establishment of appropriate validating criteria has often been regarded as an especially difficult problem for projective tests:

Criteria can be obtained for overt, observable behavior. But that is not the forte of projective instruments. Their special attraction and most frequent use lies in the description of personality dynamics, which are mostly covert and inaccessible. How is one to establish criterion measures for such variables as confused sexual identification, inner emotional resources, or castration anxiety? At best, ways may be found by which these inner states can be inferred from observable or recordable behavior. The value of such behavior as criterion measures is qualified by the imperfect and sometimes undefinable relationship of the behavior to the inner states proper (Zimmer, 1956, p. 59).

This argument is both appealing and traditional and as such needs to be examined closely. All behavior presumably is tied to inner states, and in this regard the behavior of most interest to the projectivist is not special. What tends to distinguish the projective test user is his concern for inner states per se. The achievement test user, by contrast, though he may recognize the desirability of knowing the correlative intrapsychic forces, is primarily concerned with behavior and the implications of one set of behaviors for another set of behaviors.

Covert personality dynamics either relate in some predictable and orderly fashion to an observable, behavioral referent or they are indeed untestable. There is, fortunately, no good theoretical reason to suppose that personality dynamics are without behavioral referent. Certainly, a psychoanalytic position would suggest otherwise:

Mental phenomena are to be regarded as the result of the interplay of forces pressing respectively toward and away from motility. The organism is in contact with the outside world at the beginning and at the end of its reaction processes, which start with the perception of stimuli and end with motor or glandular discharge. Freud (1927) looks at the mental apparatus as modeled after an organism floating in water. Its surface takes up stimuli, conducts them to the interior, whence reactive impulses surge to the surface (Fenichel, 1945, p. 15).

The problem, then, for the projective test user becomes one of deducing a theoretically logical behavioral referent or outcome for the inner state under investigation. The measurement of this behavioral referent constitutes the criterion against which the projective test may be validated. Such procedures demand of the experimenter that his conceptual tools be valid if he is to assess the validity of his psychometric instruments. Given the complexity of personality and the primitiveness of personality theory, the task is formidable. There have, however, been researchers who were equal to the task.

Lazarus, Eriksen, and Fonda (1951) classified psychiatric patients according to their characteristic defense mechanisms. They isolated groups of intellectualizers and repressers, and they predicted that intellectualizers would express significantly more sex- and hostility-related responses on a specially devised sentence completion test than repressers. The data supported their predictions.

Harlow (1951) used a sentence completion test to test hypotheses derived from psychoanalytic theory concerning masculine inadequacy. Harlow speculated that weight lifting involves an excessive amount of narcissism and that weightlifters suffer from feelings of masculine inadequacy, have failed to identify with an adequate male object, and are attempting to obscure their underlying feelings of dependency and masculine inadequacy by the development of a strong masculine physique. Harlow gave groups of weightlifters and athletes who were not weightlifters sentence completion tests, which were scored for dominance and submissiveness. The two groups differed on 7 of 11 variables; all differences were statistically significant at the .05 level and were in the predicted direction.

In Harlow's study, two groups known to differ on X (weight lifting) were tested to see if they also differed on Y (feelings of masculine adequacy). The X variable was the criterion for the test, and the Y variable was the major focus of interest. This, basically, is the experimental form where the attempt is to go beyond simple empirical differences. Other research models are available. The experimenter might wish to determine whether his sentence completion test is useful in predicting academic success and failure. Two groups, a success group and a failure group (X variable), could be tested and the relationship between the test scores and the known group difference determined. Such a procedure need not involve the additional step of attributing a more "basic" determining difference distinguishing the two groups. This latter form is essentially the design used by Sechrest and Hemphill (1954), Hiler (1959), Hadley and Kennedy (1949), and many others. In the former case, the criterion is made to do double duty; it serves as a standard for test validation, and, additionally, it indicates another psychological event or process, which is typically of greater interest to the researcher.

Which research tactic is to be preferred must obviously be answered in the context of research goals. Clearly, the use of criteria as indicants is demanded when "inner states" are to be assessed; the use of single-purpose criteria is probably in order where "practical" psychometric goals are to be achieved. Both approaches have their uses, and both have inherent dangers: one, the danger of confusion and unjustified extrapolation, the other, the danger of sterility and triviality.

The choice of criteria is not only restricted by research purpose but is restricted as well by differences in sentence completion test structure and scoring procedure. Scoring procedures that yield a single variable summary score—as does the ISB, for example—have less plasticity and are likely to narrow relevant criteria more than a test like the Miale-Holsopple, which is analyzed impressionistically. Which test and what criteria to use, is again a problem to be resolved by individual research interests. Where the interest is in validating a specific test, the researcher will look for appropriate criteria; where the interest is in a given psychological process, the researcher will look for the appropriate test.

Matching test with criteria is, however, a task that requires greater sophistication than has often been given to this problem. As Zimmer points out: "When test and criterion are formulated and organized within different conceptual frameworks, the categories into which their materials have been arranged may not correspond to each other. If this is the case, it will be difficult to obtain a reliable estimate of the association between test and criterion. Any existing association may be obscured by the organization of the categories" (1956, p. 59).

THE UTILITY OF THE METHOD

Having noted repeatedly the dangers involved in making generalizations about a method as variable as the sentence completion, it is, nonetheless, in order that some general assessment of the method's validity be attempted.

Inspection of Figure 49–1 reveals that the power of the method is clearly related to the area of investigation. Sentence completion methods have been relatively unsuccessful in a number of research areas. So far,

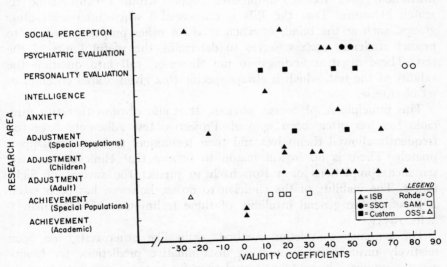

FIGURE 49–1. Distribution of validity coefficients abstracted from Table 49–1 and presented according to research area and S-C test used.

the method has been insensitive in the measurement of variables associated with social perception. The one reported correlation of a sentence completion test with a test of intelligence yielded a nonsignificant correlation of .11. The method has been used to predict the achievement of a variety of groups to a variety of criteria, and in general the results have not been encouraging.

Sentence completions have been only moderately successful in evaluating psychological adjustment in children. The use of the method to evaluate the adjustment of special, homogeneous groups, and for global personality assessment has yielded data of considerable variability. Rohde (1946) reports validities of .79 and .82, using the test for global personality evaluation. However, as noted previously, Rohde's methodology is open to criticism, and her findings are without corroboration.

Sentence completion tests—the ISB in particular—have, however, had consistent success in certain areas of psychological investigation. In the assessment of psychological adjustment in adults and in the evaluation of severity of psychiatric disturbance, sentence completion methods have proven to have considerable sensitivity and utility.

The differences between the areas in which the method has and has not been successful are not surprising. Sentence completion tests, like all other tests, are most successful when they are used to measure the variables they were constructed to measure. The ISB, for example, was designed to be a measure of pyschological adjustment, and its standardization groups were male and female college students. Used as such a measure with such groups, the reliability, validity, and usefulness of the instrument have received impressive support from a considerable research literature. That the ISB is unsuccessful when used with other groups, such as the blind, or when used for other purposes, such as to predict academic success, serves to determine the useful limits of the test. These negative findings do not, however, call into question the validity of the test, which is always specific to a given, stated criterion or set of criteria.

This principle is, of course, obvious. It is also obvious that this principle has too often been ignored. Projective test adherents have too frequently allowed themselves and their techniques to be used inappropriately. There is no logical reason to believe that clinicians can use sentence completions or a Rorschach to predict the success of flight cadets. The inability of the clinician to do so, however, has been taken as proof of the general invalidity of these techniques (cf. Holtzman & Sells, 1954).

The sentence completion method, again like other tests, has been relatively unsuccessful in making discriminative predictions for homogeneous groups. The sentence completion, for example, was not especially successful in predicting the success of graduate students in clinical psychology (Kelly & Fiske, 1951). It might be noted, however, that in the Kelly and Fiske study, the sentence completion, though not efficient by absolute standards, was relatively among the most successful predictors.

The sentence completion has not often been placed in direct competition with other projective devices, but when it has, it seems to have more than held its own. Murray et al. (1948) report that a sentence completion test was added to their evaluative techniques as an afterthought. After examining the performance of all tests, it was the only projective device they believed was worth retaining in their program. Certainly, if one compares the findings of standard reviews of the validity of other projective techniques, the support for the validity of the sentence completion method becomes even more impressive.[5]

Conclusions

Having reviewed much of what has been reported about the sentence completion method, several conclusions emerge.

1. The sentence completion is a valuable instrument in the assessment of personality that compares favorably to other standard instruments. A considerable, generally favorable, research literature tends to justify its wide clinical and research use.

2. Why the method works and how it works are not as clear. The relevance of the projection hypothesis to the sentence completion seems questionable, but alternate hypotheses of any conceptual power have yet to be advanced.

3. Most researchers, using the sentence completion, have seemed little bothered by the absence of a theoretical rationale underlying the use of the sentence completion method. A too general research practice involves the construction of custom tests with little more than face validity. These tests are then correlated with criteria, the validity of which are similarly suspect. Many of these studies, reported as though they were in final form, could more legitimately be regarded as pilot studies awaiting cross validation. The lack of cross validation, the absence of normative data, and the often gratuitous variations in procedure and structure have combined to retard standardization of the sentence completion and tended to make development diffuse and disorderly.

4. There have been sentence completion forms that have been developed more systematically, most notably, the Rotter ISB. Critics

---

[5] The reader is advised to consult Swensen (1957), Harris (1960), and Murstein (1963). These authors offer authoritative reviews of the DAP, Rorschach, and TAT, respectively. This author's view is that the sentence completion compares favorably to these other methods in reliability, validity, and utility.

of the ISB, while citing its psychometric advantages, have tended to regard it as undynamic and of relatively little use for general clinical purposes.

The objections to the ISB have tended to focus on two aspects of the test: (1) the quantification of its scoring system and (2) the use of a single-variable method of analysis. Proponents of the ISB have tended to endorse the test precisely because of these two features. There does appear to be essential soundness in both positions, and it is probably the case that the ISB sacrifices scope for efficiency.

5. The number of problems involved in the sentence completion method and the significant success it has achieved should both require and encourage additional research with the method. Much research has suggested that subjects can exercise considerable conscious control over their responses. One obvious research need, then, would be for the development of measures of dissimulation and defensiveness appropriate to the sentence completion. More systematic investigations of the inter-action effects of variations in instructions, set effects, stem structure, stem reference, and test length across populations should prove to be a valuable research contribution. Though the problem of context effects is obvious and would need to be explored, it might be possible to develop not only standard sets of stems but standard individual stems. Such standardization would provide normative data for the association value of individual stems.

6. But perhaps the greatest research need in regard to the sentence completion would be the refinement of extension of already available sentence completion forms. Specific tests have become almost traditionally associated with specific subject populations and validity criteria. Extending these tests to new subject populations and utilizing new classes of criteria would promote greater interresearch comparability, so that an already considerable research literature could be better integrated, better used, and better understood.

REFERENCES

ANASTASI, ANNE. *Psychological testing.* New York: Macmillan, 1954.

ARNOLD, F. C., & WALTER, V. A. The relationship between a self- and other-reference sentence completion test. *J. counsel Psychol.*, 1957, 4, 65–70.

BARRY, J. R. The relation of verbal reactions to adjustment levels. *J. abnorm. soc. Psychol.*, 1950, 46, 647–658.

BELLAK, L. On the problems of the concept of projection. In L. E. Abt & L. Bellak (Eds.), *Projective psychology.* New York: Knopf, 1950. Pp. 7–32.

BENTON, A. L., WINDLE, C. D., & ERDICE, E. *S U I sentence completions.* Unpublished monograph, State University of Iowa, 1952.

Benton, A. L., Windle, C. D., & Erdice, E. A review of sentence completion techniques. Project NR 151–075 Washington: Office of Naval Research, 1957.

Berger, I. L., & Sutker, A. R. The relationship of emotional adjustment and intellectual capacity to academic achievement of college students. Ment. Hyg., N.Y., 1956, 40, 65–77.

Bieri, J., Blacharsky, E., & Reid, J. W. Predictive behavior and personal adjustment. J. consult. Psychol., 1955, 19, 351–360.

Bijou, S. W. (Ed.) The psychological program in AAF convalescent hospitals. AAF aviation psychology research report No. 15. Washington: U.S. Government Printing Office, 1947.

Brown, Shirley W. The use of an incomplete sentences test for the study of attitudes towards Negroes. Unpublished doctoral dissertation, Ohio State Univer., 1950.

Burwen, L. S., Campbell, D. T., & Kidd, J. The use of a sentence completion test in measuring attitudes toward superiors and subordinates. J. appl. Psychol., 1956, 40, 248–250.

Cameron, N. A study of thinking in senile deterioration and schizophrenic disorganization. Amer. J. Psychol., 1938, 51, 650–664. (a)

Cameron, N. Reasoning, regression, and communication in schizophrenia. Psychol. Monog., 1938, 50, 1–34. (b)

Cameron, N., & Magaret, Ann. Experimental studies in thinking: I. Scattered speech in the responses of normal subjects to incomplete sentences. J. exp. Psychol., 1949, 39, 617–627.

Cameron, N., & Magaret, Ann. Correlates of scattered speech in the responses of normal subjects to incomplete sentences. J. gen. Psychol., 1950, 43, 77–84.

Campbell, D. T. A typology of tests, projective and otherwise. J. consult. Psychol., 1957, 21, 207–210.

Carr, A. C. Intra-individual consistency in response to tests of varying degrees of ambiguity. J. consult. Psychol., 1954, 18, 251–258.

Carr, A. C. The relation of certain Rorschach variables to expression of affect in the TAT and SCT. J. proj. Tech., 1956, 20, 137–142.

Carr, A. C. The psychodiagnostic test battery: rationale and methodology. In D. Brower & L. E. Abt (Eds.), Progress in clinical psychology. Vol. II. New York: Grune & Stratton, 1958. Pp. 28–39.

Carter, H. J. A combined projective and psychogalvanic response technique for investigating certain affective processes. J. consult. Psychol., 1947, 11, 270–275.

Cass, Loretta K. An investigation of parent–child relationships in terms of awareness, identification, projection and control. Amer. J. Orthopsychiat., 1952, 22, 305–313. (a)

Cass Loretta K. Parent-child relationships and delinquency. J. abnorm. soc. Psychol., 1952, 47, 101–104. (b)

Cattell, R. B. Principles of design in "projective" or misperception tests of personality. In H. H. & Gladys L. Anderson (Eds.), Projective techniques. New York: Prentice-Hall, 1951. Pp. 55–98.

Chance, June E. Adjustment and prediction of others' behavior. J. consult. Psychol., 1958, 22, 191–194.

Churchill, Ruth, & Crandall, V. J. The reliability and validity of the Rotter incomplete sentences test. J. consult. Psychol., 1955, 19, 345–350.

Conners, T., Wolkon, G. H., Haefner, D. P., & Stotsky, B. A. Outcome of post-hospital rehabilitative treatment of mental patients as a function of ego strength. J. counsel. Psychol., 1960, 7, 278–282.

Copple, G. E. Effective intelligence as measured by an unstructured sentence-completion technique. J. consult. Psychol., 1956, 20, 357–360.

Costin, F., & Eiserer, P. E. Students' attitudes toward school life as revealed by a sentence completion test. *Amer. Psychol.*, 1949, 4, 289.

CROMWELL, R. L., & LUNDY, R. M. Productivity of clinical hypotheses on a sentence completion test. *J. consult. Psychol.*, 1954, 18, 421–424.

CRONBACH, L. J. *Essentials of psychological testing.* New York: Harper, 1960.

DEAN, S. I. Adjustment testing and personality factors of the blind. *J. consult. Psychol.*, 1957, 21, 171–177.

DENENBERG, V. H. The relationship between a measure of kinesthesis and two indices of adjustment. *J. gen. Psychol.*, 1960, 62, 43–52.

DOLE, A. A. The vocational sentence completion blank in counseling. *J. counsel. Psychol.*, 1958, 5, 200–205.

DOLE, A. A., & FLETCHER, F. M., JR. Some principles in the construction of incomplete sentences. *Educ. psychol. Measmt*, 1955, 15, 101–110.

DORRIS, R. J., LEVINSON, D. J., & HANFMANN, EUGENIA. Authoritarian personality studied by a new variation of the sentence completion technique. *J. abnorm. soc. Psychol.*, 1954, 49, 99–108.

EBBINGHAUS, H. Ueber eine neue methode zur prüfung geistiger fähigkeiten und ihre awendung bei schulkindern. *Z. Psychol. Physiol. Sinnesorg.*, 1897, 13, 401–459.

EBNER, E., & SHAW, F. J. An investigation of modes and responses to contradictions. *Psychol. Rep.*, 1960, 6, 206.

EFRON, H. Y. An attempt to employ a sentence completion test for the detection of psychiatric patients with suicidal ideas. *J. consult. Psychol.*, 1960, 24, 156–160.

ELLSWORTH, R. B. The regression of schizophrenic language. *J. consult. Psychol.*, 1951, 15, 387–391.

FARBER, M. L. English and Americans: a study in national character. *J. Psychol.*, 1951, 13, 241–249.

FENICHEL, O. *Psychoanalytic theory of neurosis.* New York: Norton, 1945.

FISKE, D. W. An intensive study of variability scores. *Educ. psychol. Measmt*, 1957, 17, 453–465.

FISKE, D. W., & RICE, LAURA. Intra-individual response variability. *Psychol. Bull.*, 1955, 52, 217–250.

FISKE, D. W., & VAN BUSKIRK, C. The stability of interpretations of sentence completion tests. *J. consult. Psychol.*, 1959, 23, 177–180.

FITZGERALD, B. J. Some relationships among projective test, interview, and sociometric measures of dependent behavior. *J. abnorm. soc. Psychol.*, 1958, 56, 199–203.

FLANAGAN, J. C. (Ed.), *The aviation psychology program in the AAF. Aviation psychology research report No. 1.* Washington: U.S. Government Printing Office, 1947.

FORER, B. R. A structured sentence completion test. *J. proj. Tech.*, 1950, 14, 15–29.

FORER, B. R. Research with projective techniques: Some trends. *J. proj. Tech.*, 1957, 21, 358–361.

FORER, B. R. Sentence completion. In A. C. Carr (Ed.), *The prediction of overt behavior through the use of projective techniques.* Springfield, Ill.: Charles C Thomas, 1960. Pp. 6–17. (a)

FORER, B. R. Word association and sentence completion methods. In A. I. Rabin & Mary R. Haworth (Eds.), *Projective techniques with children.* New York: Grune & Stratton, 1960. Pp. 210–224. (b)

FORER, B. R., & TOLMAN, RUTH S. Some characteristics of clinical judgment. *J. consult. Psychol.*, 1952, 16, 347–352.

FRANK, L. K. Projective methods for the study of personality. *J. Psychol.*, 1939, 8, 389–413.

FRANK, L. K. *Projective methods.* Springfield, Ill.: Charles C Thomas, 1948.

FREUD, S. *The ego and the id.* London: Hogarth, 1927.

FRIESEN, E. P. The incomplete sentences technique as a measure of employee attitudes. *Personnel Psychol.*, 1952, 5, 329–345.

GETZELS, J. W., & JACKSON, P. W. Occupational choice and cognitive functioning. *J. abnorm. soc. Psychol.*, 1960, 61, 119–123.

GOLDE, PEGGY, & KOGAN, N. A sentence completion procedure for assessing attitudes toward old people. *J. Geront.*, 1959, 14, 355–360.

GRIGG, A. E., & KELLEY, H. P. A scale for self-description. *J. clin. Psychol.*, 1960, 16, 153–158.

GUERTIN, W. H. An analysis of gross errors on a sentence completion test. *J. clin. Psychol.*, 1959, 15, 414–416.

GUILFORD, J. P. *Psychometric methods.* New York: McGraw-Hill, 1954.

HADLEY, J. M., & KENNEDY, VERA E. A comparison between performance on a sentence completion test and academic success. *Educ. psychol. Measmt*, 1949, 9, 649–670.

HANFMANN, EUGENIA. Projective techniques in the assessment program of the Office of Strategic Services. In *Exploring individual differences.* Washington: Amer. Council on Educ., 1947. Pp. 19–29.

HANFMANN, EUGENIA, & GETZELS, J. W. Studies of the sentence completion test. *J. proj. Tech.*, 1953, 17, 280–294.

HARDY, VIRGINIA T. Relations of dominance to non-directiveness in counseling. *J. clin. Psychol.*, 1948, 4, 300–303.

HARLOW, R. G. Masculine inadequacy and compensatory development of physique. *J. Pers.*, 1951, 19, 312–323.

HARRIS, D. B., & TSENG, S. C. Children's attitudes toward peers and parents as revealed by sentence completions. *Child Developm.*, 1957, 28, 401–411.

HARRIS, J. G. Validity: the search for a constant in a universe of variables. In Maria A. Rickers-Ovsiankina (Ed.), *Rorschach psychology.* New York: Wiley, 1960.

HILER, E. W. The sentence completion test as a predictor of continuation in psychotherapy. *J. consult. Psychol.*, 1959, 23, 544–549.

HOLSOPPLE, J. Q., & MIALE, FLORENCE R. *Sentence completion: a projective method for the study of personality.* Springfield, Ill.: Charles C Thomas, 1954.

HOLT, R. R. Clinical and statistical prediction: a reformulation and some new data. *J. abnorm. soc. Psychol.*, 1958, 56, 1–12.

HOLTZMAN, W. H., & SELLS, S. B. Prediction of flying success by clinical analysis of test protocols. *J. abnorm. soc. Psychol.*, 1954, 49, 485–490.

HOLZBERG, J., TEICHER, A., & TAYLOR, J. L. Contributions of clinical psychology to military neuropsychiatry in an army psychiatric hospital. *J. clin. Psychol.*, 1947, 3, 84–95.

HOROWITZ, M. F. A study of clinicians' judgments from projective test protocols. *J. consult. Psychol.*, 1962, 26, 251–256.

HOWARD, K. L. The convergent and discriminant validation of ipsative ratings from 3 projective techniques. *J. clin. Psychol.*, 1962, 18, 183–188.

HUTT, M. L. The use of projective methods of personality measurements in army medical installations. *J. clin. Psychol.*, 1945, 1, 134–140.

IZARD, C. E., ROSENBERG, N., BAIR, J. T., & MAAG, C. Construction and validation of a multiple-choice sentence completion test; an interim report. *USN Sch. Aviat. Med. Res. Rep.*, 1953.

JENKINS, R. L. Quantitative aspects of sentence completion in the study of the improvement of schizophrenic patients. *J. proj. Tech.*, 1961, 25, 303–311.

JENKINS, R. L., & BLODGETT, EVA. Prediction of success or failure of delinquent boys from sentence completion. *Amer. J. Orthopsychiat.*, 1960, 30, 741–756.

JESSOR, R. N., & HESS, H. F. Levels of aspiration behavior and general adjustment:

An appraisal of some negative findings. *Psychol. Rep.*, 1958, 4, 335–339.

KAHN, M. W. Psychological test study of a mass murderer. *J. proj. Tech.*, 1960, 24, 148–160.

KAREN, R. L. A method for rating sentence completion test responses. *J. proj. Tech.*, 1961, 25, 312–314.

KELLEY, T. L. Individual testing with completion test exercises. *Teach. Coll. Rec.*, 1917, 18, 371–382.

KELLY, E. L., & FISKE, D. W. The prediction of success in the VA training program in clinical psychology. *Amer. Psychol.*, 1950, 5, 395–406.

KELLY, E. L., & FISKE, D. W. *The prediction of performance in clinical psychology.* Ann Arbor: Univer. of Michigan Press, 1951.

KIMBALL, BARBARA. The sentence-completion technique in a study of scholastic underachievement. *J. consult. Psychol.*, 1952, 16, 353–358.

KING, F. W. A normative note on sentence completion cross-sex identification responses. *J. consult. Psychol.*, 1958, 22, 63–64.

KIRK, B. A. Evaluation of in-service counselor training. *Educ. psychol. Measmt*, 1956, 16, 527–535.

LAZARUS, R. S., ERICKSON, C. W., & FONDA, C. P. Personality dynamics and auditory perceptual recognition. *J. Pers.*, 1951, 19, 471–482.

LINDGREN, H. C. The use of a sentence completion test in measuring attitudinal changes among college freshmen. *J. soc. Psychol.*, 1954, 40, 79–92.

LINDZEY, G. On the classification of projective techniques. *Psychol. Bull.*, 1959, 56, 158–168.

LOCKE, B. Comparison of naval offenders with nonoffenders on a projective sentence completion test. *U.S. Armed Forces Med. J.*, 1957, 8, 1825–1828.

LUFT, J. Implicit hypotheses and clinical predictions. *J. abnorm. soc. Psychol.*, 1950, 45, 756–759.

LUFT, J., WISHAM, W., & MOODY, H. A projective technique to measure adjustment to hospital environment. *J. gen. Psychol.*, 1953, 49, 209–219.

MACBRAYER, CAROLINE T. Differences in perception of the opposite sex by males and females. *J. soc. Psychol.*, 1960, 52, 309–314.

MACFARLANE, JEAN W., & TUDDENHAM, R. D. Problems in the validation of projective techniques. In H. H. & Gladys L. Anderson (Eds.), *An introduction to projective techniques.* Englewood Cliffs, N.J.: Prentice-Hall, 1951. Pp. 26–54.

McGREEVY, J. C. Interlevel disparity and predictive efficiency. *J. proj. Tech.*, 1962, 26, 80–87.

MASLING, J. M. The effects of warm and cold interaction on the interpretation of a projective protocol. *J. proj. Tech.*, 1957, 21, 377–383.

MEEHL, C. F. *Clinical versus statistical prediction.* Minneapolis: Univer. of Minnesota Press, 1954.

MEEHL, C. E. Wanted—a good cookbook. *Amer. Psychol.*, 1956, 11, 263–272.

MELTZOFF, J. The effect of mental set and item structure upon response to a projective test. *J. abnorm. soc. Psychol.*, 1951, 46, 177–189.

MEYER, M. M., & TOLMAN, RUTH S. Parental figures in sentence completion test, in TAT, and therapeutic interviews. *J. consult. Psychol.*, 1955, 19, 170.

MILLER, N., & GEKOSKI, N. Employee preference inventory: A forced-choice measure of employee attitude. *Engng. industr. Psychol.*, 1959, 1, 83–90.

MISHLER,, E. G. A scalogram analysis of the sentence completion test. *Educ. psychol. Measmt*, 1958, 18, 75–90.

MOONEY, R. L., & GORDON, L. V. *Manual: The Mooney problem check lists.* New York: Psychological Corp., 1950.

MORTON, R. B. An experiment in brief psychotherapy. *Psychol. Monogr.*, 1955, 89, 1–17.

MURRAY, H. A., & MACKINNON, D. W. Assessment of OSS personnel. *J. consult. Psychol.*, 1946, **10**, 76–80.

MURRAY, H. A., MACKINNON, D. W., MILLER, J. G., FISKE, D. W., & HANFMANN, EUGENIA. *Assessment of men.* New York: Holt, 1948.

MURSTEIN, B. I. *Theory and research in projective techniques.* New York: Wiley, 1963.

NASH, H. Incomplete sentences tests in personality research. *Educ. psychol. Measmt.*, 1958, **18**, 569–581.

NUNNALLY, J. C. *Tests and measurements.* New York: McGraw-Hill, 1959.

OSTERWEIL, J., & FISKE, D. W. Intra-individual variability in sentence completion responses. *J. abnorm. soc. Psychol.*, 1956, **52**, 195–199.

PAYNE, A. F. *Sentence completions.* New York: N.Y. Guidance Clinic, 1928.

PECK, R. F., & McGUIRE, C. Measuring changes in mental health with the sentence completion technique. *Psychol. Rep.*, 1959, **5**, 151–160.

PESKIN, H. Unity of science begins at home: A study of regional factionalism in clinical psychology. *Amer. Psychol.*, 1963, **18**, 96–100.

PILTZ, R. J. Problems in validity for the Copple sentence completion test as a measure of "effective intelligence" with Air Force personnel. *Dissert. Abstr.*, 1957, **17**, 1914–1915.

ROHDE, AMANDA R. Explorations in personality by the sentence completion method. *J. appl. Psychol.*, 1946, **30**, 169–181.

ROHDE, AMANDA R. A note regarding the use of the sentence completion test in military installations since the beginning of World War II. *J. consult. Psychol.*, 1948, **12**, 190–193.

ROHDE, AMANDA R. *The sentence completion method: Its diagnostic and clinical application to mental disorders.* New York: Ronald, 1957.

ROSENBERG, S. Some relationships between attitudes expressed toward the parent in a sentence completion test and case history data. *J. proj. Tech.*, 1950, **14**, 188–193.

ROTTER, J. B. The incomplete sentence test as a method of studying personality. *Amer. Psychol.*, 1946, **1**, 286.

ROTTER, J. B., RAFFERTY, JANET E., & SCHACHTITZ, EVA. Validation of the Rotter incomplete sentences blank for college screening. *J. consult. Psychol.*, 1949, **13**, 348–356.

ROTTER, J. B., & RAFFERTY, JANET E. *Manual: the Rotter incomplete sentences blank.* New York: Psychol. Corp., 1950.

ROTTER, J. B., & RAFFERTY, JANET E. Rotter incomplete sentences blank. In A. Weider (Ed.), *Contributions toward medical psychology: theory and psycho-diagnostic methods.* New York: Ronald, 1953. Pp. 590–598.

ROTTER, J. B., RAFFERTY, JANET E., & LOTSOF, A. B. The validity of the Rotter incomplete sentences blank: High school form. *J. consult. Psychol.*, 1954, **18**, 105–111.

ROTTER, J. B., & WILLERMAN, B. The incomplete sentence test. *J. consult. Psychol.*, 1947, **11**, 43–48.

ROTTER, J. B. Word association and sentence completion methods. In H. H. & Gladys L. Anderson (Eds.), *An introduction to projective techniques.* Englewood Cliffs, N.J.: Prentice-Hall, 1951.

ROZYNKO, V. V. Social desirability in the sentence completion test. *J. consult. Psychol.*, 1959, **23**, 280.

RYCHLAK, J. F., MUSSEN, P. H., & BENNETT, J. W. An example of the use of the incomplete sentence test in applied anthropological research. *Hum. Organ.*, 1957, **16**, (1):25–29.

SACKS, J. M. The relative effect upon projective responses of stimuli referring to the subject and of stimuli referring to other persons. *J. consult. Psychol.*, 1949, **13**, 12–20.

SACKS, J. M., & LEVY, S. The sentence completion test. In L. E. Abt & L. Bellak

(Eds.), *Projective psychology*. New York: Knopf, 1950. Pp. 357–402.

SAMUELS, H. The validity of personality-trait ratings based on projective techniques. *Psychol. Monogr.*, 1952, 60, No. 5.

SCHAFER, R. Psychological tests in clinical research. *J. consult. Psychol.*, 1949, 13, 328–334.

SECHREST, L. B., & HEMPHILL, J. K. Motivational variables in the assuming of combat obligation. *J. consult. Psychol.*, 1954, 18, 113–118.

SHAY, MARJORIE M. The construction of multiple-choice sentence completion test. Master's thesis, Univer. of Purdue, 1950.

SHOR, J. Report on a verbal projective technique. *J. clin. Psychol.*, 1946, 2, 279–282.

SIEGEL, S. *Nonparametric statistics for the behavioral sciences*. New York: McGraw-Hill, 1956.

SMITH, W. E. A comparison of the responses of stutterers and non-stutterers in a college population on the Rotter incomplete sentences blank. Unpublished master's thesis, Bowling Green State Univer., 1952.

SOUELEM, O. Mental patients' attitudes toward mental hospitals. *J. clin. Psychol.*, 1955, 11, 181–185.

STEIN, M. I. The use of a sentence completion test for the diagnosis of personality. *J. clin. Psychol.*, 1947, 3, 46–56.

STEIN, M. I. The record and a sentence completion test. *J. consult. Psychol.*, 1949, 13, 448–449.

STEPHENS, M. W. The incomplete sentences blank: Sources of variance in retest reliability. *J. clin. Psychol.*, 1960, 3, 331–333.

STONE, H. K., & DELLIS, N. P. An exploratory investigation into the levels hypothesis. *J. proj. Tech.*, 1960, 24, 333–340.

STOTSKY, B. A. Comparison of normals and schizophrenics on a work-oriented projective technique. *J. counsel. Psychol.*, 1957, 13, 406–408.

STOTSKY, B. A., & WEINBERG, H. The prediction of the psychiatric patient's work adjustment. *J. counsel. Psychol.*, 1956, 3, 3–7.

SUNDBERG, N. D. The practice of psychological testing in clinical services in the United States. *Amer. Psychologist*, 1961, 16, 79–83.

SWENSEN, C. H. Empirical evaluation of human figure drawings. *Psychol. Bull.*, 1957, 54, 431–466.

TALLAND, G. A. A review of J. Q. Holsopple & Florence R. Miale: *Sentence completion: a projective method for the study of personality*. In O. Buros (Ed.), *Fifth mental measurements yearbook*. Highland Park, N.J.: Gryphon, 1959. Pp. B213–B214.

TENDLER, A. D. A preliminary report on a test for emotional insight. *J. appl. Psychol.*, 1930, 14, 123–136.

TOUCHSTONE, F. V. A comparative study of Negro and white college students' aggressiveness by means of sentence completion. *Dissert. Abstr.*, 1957, 17, 1588–1589.

TRAUBE, M. R. *Completion-test language scales. Contributions to education*, No. 77. New York: Bureau of Publications. Teachers College, Columbia Univer., 1916.

TRITES, D. K. Psychiatric screening of flying personnel: Evaluation of assumptions underlying interpretation of sentence completion tests. *USAF Sch. Aviat. Med. Rep.*, 1955.

TRITES, D. K. Evaluation of assumptions underlying interpretation of sentence completion tests. *J. consult. Psychol.*, 1956, 20, 8.

TRITES, D. K., HOLTZMAN, W. H., TEMPLETON, R. C., & SELLS, S. B. *Research on the SAM sentence completion test*. San Antonio, Texas: USAF School of Aviation Medicine, Randolph Field, July, 1953.

WALTER, V. A., & JONES, A. W. An incomplete sentence test and the attitudes of manual arts therapy patients. *J. counsel Psychol.*, 1956, 3, 140–144.

West, J. T. An investigation of the constructs "effective intelligence" and "social competence" with the Copple sentence completion test utilizing a school of social work population. *Dissert. Abstr.*, 1958, **19**, 1121.

White, Mary A. A study of schizophrenic language. *J. abnorm. soc. Psychol.*, 1949, **44**, 61–74.

Willingham, W. W. The sentence-completion test as a measure of morale. *USN Sch. Aviat. Med. Res. Rep.*, 1958.

Wilson, Isabel. The use of a sentence completion test in differentiating between well-adjusted and maladjusted secondary school pupils. *J. consult. Psychol.*, 1949, **13**, 400–402.

Zimmer, H. Prediction by means of two projective tests of personality evaluations made by peers. *J. clin. Psychol.*, 1955, **11**, 352–356.

Zimmer, H. Validity of sentence completion tests and human figure drawings. In D. Brown & L. E. Abt (Eds.), *Progress in clinical psychology*. Vol. II. New York: Grune & Stratton, 1956. Pp. 58–75.

Wolkin, G. H., & Haefner, D. P. Change in ego strength of improved and unimproved psychiatric patients. *J. clin. Psychol.*, 1961, **17**, 352–355.

50

The Relative Effect on Projective Responses of Stimuli Referring to the Subject and of Stimuli Referring to Other Persons[1]

JOSEPH M. SACKS

The relative efficacy of first-person stems in comparison to third-person ones is the central focus of this study. The majority of psychologists comparing the two versions favored the first-person set, and the majority of VA psychiatric patients also said that this set more accurately portrayed their feelings. The first-person approach also resulted in significantly greater agreement with psychotherapists' ratings of their patients.

Despite this superiority, the author believes that little is known about the impact of the stems. There were, for example, more negative feelings expressed toward father and superiors in the third-person stems than in the first-person ones. Does this mean that the more impersonal stems are more suited for negative expressions than the more personal ones? Unfortunately, the study had too many uncontrolled factors to permit such a conclusion. To evaluate such a hypothesis seriously, it would be necessary to scale the items for distance from self and to quantify the degree of negativeness in the stems. Moreover, the effect of order of presentation should be more clearly studied. For example, the superiority of the first-

---

[1] Abstract of a thesis submitted to the Graduate School of New York University in partial fulfillment of the requirements for the degree of Doctor of Philosophy. Published with the permission of the Chief Medical Director, Department of Medicine and Surgery, Veterans Administration, who assumes no responsibility for the opinions expressed or conclusions drawn by the author.

823

person stems disappeared when they were presented after *the third-person stems. Last, an item analysis for accuracy of predicting such criteria as adjustment, psychotherapy outcome, and various personality ratings should clarify the dimensions involved in this version of the SCT and their stability across different criteria.*

The study is concerned with the problem of determining the relative effect on projective responses of (1) stimuli that refer directly to the subject and (2) stimuli that refer to persons other than the subject. The stimuli used in this study are sentence completion items.

The object of the study is to investigate the validity of the assumption, widely held by those who construct and employ projective techniques, that the subject reveals more about himself when he is talking about other people or about impersonal, unstructured objects than when he is talking about himself.

The problem is based on the hypothesis that the responses of individuals to the two types of stimuli described above (1 and 2) will differ significantly in terms of the amount of disturbance revealed in the areas of personality to be studied or the types of problems and attitudes revealed.

Background and Need for the Study

THE SENTENCE COMPLETION TEST

One of the pioneer workers with the sentence completion method in the field of personality was Tendler (1930), who distinguished between diagnosis of thought reactions and of emotional responsiveness. The items of his test were intended to stimulate admiration, anger, love, happiness, etc. Tendler believed that the presentation of stimuli in the form of incomplete sentences would arouse a particular emotional set and yet allow for free responses. In analyzing the responses of 250 college girls, Tendler noted that the same stimulus evokes different responses from different individuals; individuals differ in the associative flow of responses; responses indicate fears, aversions, likes, interests, and attachments; they may have positive or negative ego reference or social reference.

Rohde advocated use of the SCT as a tool for clinical psychologists and other professional people who deal with youth problems. Direct questioning tends, she maintained, to make the individual self-conscious and puts him on the defensive. Freedom of expression is limited in that the questions usually control the answers; but projective techniques avoid such resistance or control. They reveal latent needs, sentiments, attitudes, and aspirations which the subject would be unwilling or unable to recognize or to express in direct communication. "The sentence completion device in which the subject is asked to read to himself the forepart of a sentence is essentially a projection technique utilizing free association" (Rohde, 1946, p. 175).

In Shor's Self-Idea-Completion Test (SIC), the 50 items "are arranged in a definite sequence to permit a carry-over or generalization of attitude from immediate to basic human interest" (Shor, 1946, p. 280). The author emphasizes the importance of adapting stimuli to the current situation and cultural background of the groups tested. Shor suggests that administration be adapted to the dynamics of each case. An actively anxious patient, for example, might release rich material by the oral method, while another patient might be able to express himself better if left alone to write the responses. No formal scoring system is offered, but Shor recommends investigating areas of rejection, evidences of resistance, and other methods of evasion, noting recurrent themes and atypical associations and evaluating the level of personality projected.

Stein (1947) described a sentence completion test which was originally developed as an aid in the selection of OSS personnel during the war. Items were selected to contribute relevant information concerning at least one of ten areas considered important for personality evaluation: family, past, drives, inner states, goals, cathexes, energy, time perspective, reaction to others, and reaction of others to the subject. In this test, for the first time, two different types of items were used: the more "projective" questions, in which the proper name of some person or the third personal pronoun is employed, and personal questions, in which the first person is used. The two types were mixed in random order.

Symonds has reported on studies using this type of test in the OSS assessment program. Comparisons were made between the test responses of candidates and data from OSS records. It was tentatively concluded that "the sentence completion test cannot be used to differentiate good and bad adjustment by any direct comparison of items or by psychometric methods. The sentence completion test is descriptive and not evaluative" (Symonds, 1947, p. 321).

On the other hand, Rotter and Willerman (1947) claimed fairly high validity for the sentence completion method as an evaluative technique. The validity of their Incomplete Sentence Test, used in AAF hospitals, was determined by correlating the psychologist's initial evaluation of the severity of each patient's disturbance with the patient's total score on the test.

Carter (1947) combined a modification of Tendler's Emotional Insight Test with a psychogalvanometer to investigate certain affective processes. He found that changes in palmar skin conductivity and reaction time were significantly greater in individuals with problems and in psychoneurotics than in normals. However, the oral responses of the control and experimental groups varied little.

STUDIES CONCERNED WITH REFERENCE TO THE SELF AND TO OTHERS

If it can be demonstrated through the medium of the SCT that the individual reveals more about himself when he is talking about other people in his projective responses than when he is talking about himself, such a finding could be applied to the construction of this specific type of test. In a broader sense, it would suggest that a survey be made of other techniques of personality evaluation which depend largely on what the individual says about himself—i.e., case histories, autobiographies, and personality inventories—to see whether greater emphasis should be put on semistructured questions dealing with the subject's attitudes toward other people. On the other hand, if it can be clearly demonstrated that the individual reveals more when he is speaking about himself, follow-up studies in other projective techniques like the Rorschach, Thematic Apperception Test, and Picture-Frustration Study would be indicated.

Such an investigation has already been made with regard to direct and indirect forms of a personality questionnaire by Ellis (1947). Significant differences between the average scores of problem and nonproblem children were found only for one of the direct forms. Moreover, the direct forms contained more items discriminating between the two groups than did the indirect forms.

Spencer (1938) administered the Experience Appraisal Blank to a group of 192 high-school students who were instructed not to sign their names and were assured that their responses would be kept confidential because their identities would not be known. About 22 per cent of the subjects said they would have left some of the questions unanswered if their signatures had been requested, and about 9 per cent said they would have answered some of the questions untruthfully. The latter had the highest average conflict scores, while those who said they would have willingly answered all questions truthfully had the lowest average conflict scores in the entire group.

Combs (1947) made an analysis of material produced in autobiographies and in TAT stories of the same subject. He found that subjects tend to express more socially acceptable attitudes and feelings in the autobiographies and more aggressive, "prohibited" attitudes and feelings in the TAT stories.

Methodology

Four areas of personality were arbitrarily selected for study, based on the findings from various personality inventories, indexes, and projective methods. These areas were Family Attitudes, Sex Attitudes, Interpersonal Attitudes, and Self-Attitudes. The first area was divided into three categories: attitude toward mother, attitude toward father, and attitude toward family unit. The second area was divided into two categories: attitude toward women and attitude toward heterosexual relationships. The third area was divided into four categories: attitude toward friends and acquaintances, attitude toward superiors at work or school, attitude toward people supervised, and attitude toward colleagues at work or school. The fourth area was divided into six categories: fears, guilt feelings, attitude toward own abilities, attitude toward past, attitude toward future, and goals.

The SCT used in this experiment was constructed in the following manner: 20 staff psychologists of the Veterans Administration New York Regional Office Mental Hygiene Service were requested to submit three test items for each of the 15 categories above. These items were assembled, and to them were added other items obtained from previous SCT studies. This list of 280 items, ranging from 14 to 26 items per category, was submitted to the same group of 20 psychologists, who were then requested to select the four items in each category which they believed best suited to elicit the subject's attitudes in that category. In each category, the four items most frequently chosen became the test items. The 60 items were printed in such order that each category was represented once in the first 15 questions. The same order of categories was followed in each group. Two forms of the test were used: In Form A, all the items were worded in the first person. In Form B, a form of the third-personal pronoun or a proper name was substituted for the first-personal pronoun in each item. Sample items of the two forms show their similarities and differences. Form A: 4. If I were in charge. ... 9. When I was a child. ... 16. If my father would only. ... Form B: 4. If Bob were in charge. ... 9. When John was a child ... 16. If his father would only. ...

The SCT was administered to 100 subjects who were patients of Veterans Administration New York Regional Office Mental Hygiene Clinic. Ninety-six of the subjects were males, and 4 were females. They ranged in age from 19 to 51 years, with a median age of 27.5 years. They included 59 psychoneurotics, 24 psychotics, 13 character disorders, and 4 patients with organic and narcoleptic disorders.

The subjects were numbered consecutively in the order in which the test was administered to them. Odd-numbered subjects took Form A first, followed by Form B. Even-numbered subjects took Form B first, followed by Form A.

The subject's responses were typed on a rating sheet according to categories. Three psychologists independently rated the subject's degree of disturbance in each category on the basis of his four responses in that category. The two forms of the test were rated independently.[2]

Ratings of the subject's degree of disturbance in each category were also obtained from the psychiatrist by whom he was being treated. These ratings were based on the psychiatrist's clinical impressions.

Those ratings on which two of the three psychologists (judges) agreed were compared with the corresponding psychiatrists' (criterion) ratings. Chi squares were obtained, and corrected coefficients of contingency were calculated for the total test, for each area, and for each category on both forms of the test. In addition, the percentages of complete agreements, partial agreements, partial disagreements, and complete disagreements between judges' and criterion ratings were computed as a basis for comparing Form A with Form B.

A sample of 49 subjects were requested to compare their responses on Form A and on Form B, item by item, and to indicate which responses expressed their real feelings better. The means of these choices were compared.

The seven psychologists who participated most extensively in the experiment were asked to record their preference for one form of the test and to state their reasons for choosing it.

For a sample of 50 subjects, psychologists wrote interpretative summaries of the four responses in each category. The two forms were interpretated independently by two different psychologists. These interpretations were submitted to the psychiatrists who were treating the subjects with a request to rate the content of the statements in terms of their agreement with clinical findings. The two forms of the tests were compared with respect to the proportions of statements having various degrees of agreement with clinical findings.

For a sample of 50 subjects, two psychologists independently rated each response in terms of positive or negative feelings. The two forms of the test were compared with respect to the numbers of responses which, by agreement of the two psychologists, showed each of these types of feelings.

The number of agreements by two of the three psychologists making ratings of degree of disturbance was compared with the number of agreements expected by chance. The same procedure was followed for the number of unanimous agreements by the psychologists.

---

[2] The following three-point scale was used: 2—Severely disturbed. Appears to require therapeutic aid in handling emotional conflicts in this area. 1—Mildly disturbed. Has emotional conflicts in this area but appears able to handle them without therapeutic aid. 0—No significant disturbance noted in this area.

Results

The results which were obtained from a comparison of the distribution of ratings by psychologists based on the subjects' responses to the SCT and by psychiatrists based on their clinical impressions of the subject are summarized in Table 50–1.

TABLE 50–1   *Distributions of Ratings by Psychiatrists and Psychologists*

	CHI SQUARE	P	C	SE
Form A $(N = 100)$	113.80	.001	.38	.03
Form B $(N = 100)$	57.04	.001	.27	.04
Form A Taken First $(N = 50)$	96.83	.001	.48	.04
Form B Taken First $(N = 50)$	31.19	.001	.27	.05
Form A Taken after Form B $(N = 50)$	29.66	.001	.27	.05
Form B Taken after Form A $(N = 50)$	34.34	.001	.29	.05

TABLE 50–2   *Comparison of Agreement between Ratings by Psychiatrists and Psychologists*

	FORM A %	FORM B %	DIFF. %	SD DIFF.	t	P
Complete Agreements						
Both Forms, All Subjects	47.2	43.8	3.4	2.05	1.65	.10
Form A Taken First and Form B Taken First	51.6	42.3	9.3	2.90	3.21	.00
Form A Taken Second and Form B Taken Second	42.8	45.4	2.6	2.90	.89	.26
Complete Disagreements						
Both Forms, All Subjects	15.0	17.3	2.3	1.52	1.52	.12
Form A Taken First and Form B Taken First	12.2	16.2	4.0	2.03	1.97	.05
Form A Taken Second and Form B Taken Second	17.8	18.5	0.7	2.25	.29	.38

The judges' (psychologists') ratings tended to agree more closely with the criterion (psychiatrists') ratings on Form A for 100 subjects. This trend was even more marked on Form A for the 50 subjects who took Form A first.

A comparison of the two forms of the test in terms of the percentage of agreement between ratings by psychiatrists and psychologists shows the extent to which they agreed or disagreed on each form. Ratings were considered in complete agreement when both the psychiatrists and the psychologists rated the subject severely disturbed, mildly disturbed, or not showing significant disturbance. Complete disagreements were those in which the psychiatrists or the psychologist rated the subject severely disturbed, and the other judge rated him as not showing significant disturbance. These results are presented in Table 50–2.

As Table 50–2 shows, there were significant differences in favor of Form A taken first with respect to the percentages of complete agreements and complete disagreements between judges' and criterion ratings. However, there were no significant differences between the two forms of the test for all subjects and for those subjects who took each form second. In Form A taken first, there was a clearly closer relationship between ratings than in Form A taken after Form B, but there were no significant differences between Form B taken first and Form B taken after Form A.

In Form A, the distribution of the judges' and criterion ratings were found to differ significantly from chance in 8 of the 15 categories: attitudes toward mother, father, family unit, heterosexual relationships, superiors at work or school, colleagues at work or school, attitudes toward future, and goals. In Form B, the distributions deviated significantly from chance in only 3 categories: attitudes toward father, heterosexual relationships, and superiors at work or school.

Cases with 8 or more complete agreements had 13.5 mean hours of treatment (SD 8.6), while cases with 3 complete agreements or less had 6.4 mean treatment hours (SD 3.7). The difference between these figures would occur by chance less than one time in a thousand. There was a tendency for a larger number of indeterminate ratings and of no-responses to occur among the cases with low agreement.

None of the factors which differentiated the high-agreement and low-agreement groups were found to be significantly different when the subjects who took Form A first were compared with those who took Form B first. Their mean treatment hours, for example, were, respectively, 10.1 (SD 7.4) and 8.1 (SD 5.4). This difference is not significant at the 5 per cent level of confidence.

Under a combination of the most favorable conditions found in this experiment—i.e., Form A taken first, 9 or more treatment hours, considering only the 8 categories showing significant relationships—21 subjects were found. The ratings of the psychologists on these cases corresponded with those of the psychiatrists to a degree that compares favorably with results obtained from other projective studies (Garfield, 1947; Harrison, 1940). The coefficient of contingency was .57 (SE .08), and 76 per cent of the ratings were in close agreement or partial agreement with the criterion.

Of the 49 subjects who were asked to review their responses item by item and to indicate whether the responses to Form A or B represented their feelings better, 67 per cent chose more responses to Form A than to Form B, 2 per cent (one subject) chose more responses to Form B than to Form A, and 31 per cent indicated that in the largest number of items the responses to both forms represented their feelings equally well.

In the opinions of six of the seven psychologists who participated most extensively in rating and interpreting the responses, Form A is preferred for clinical use over Form B.

A significantly greater proportion of interpretations of the subjects' attitudes based on Form A (49.1 per cent) was in close agreement with clinical findings than that of interpretations based on Form B (39.4 per cent). This difference is significant at the 1 per cent level. Form A had a smaller number of complete disagreements (14.7 per cent) than Form B (18.6 per cent), the difference approaching the 5 per cent level of confidence.

On the whole, the two forms did not differ significantly in eliciting responses expressing positive feelings, negative feelings, indeterminate feelings, ambiguous feelings leading to conflicting ratings, and failures to respond. In the individual categories, a significantly larger number of negative responses was expressed in Form B with regard to attitudes toward father and superiors.

The extent to which the psychologists agreed in their ratings is indicated by their deviation from chance expectancy: less than one in a thousand for the numerical ratings. The results were similar for both forms, in which two out of three psychologists agreed on 92 per cent of all ratings and three psychologists agreed on 40 to 45 per cent of all ratings.

Discussion

The principal finding of this study is that significant differences occurred between responses to one form of a sentence completion test worded in the first person (Form A) and to another form consisting of the same items worded in the third person (Form B). The evidence for these differences is as follows:

1. There was a larger percentage of complete agreements and a smaller percentage of complete disagreements between judges' and criterion ratings of degree of disturbance in favor of Form A taken first over Form B taken first.

2. Significant relationships between judges' and criterion ratings were

found in eight categories on Form A but in only three categories on Form B.

3. There was a larger proportion of close agreements between content interpretations and clinical findings in favor of Form A.

4. There were larger proportions of responses expressing negative feelings in Form B in attitudes toward father and superiors.

5. A larger number of responses to Form A as more truly expressing their feelings was chosen by 67 percent of 49 subjects who were asked to indicate their preferences, item by item, while only 2 per cent chose more responses to Form B.

6. A preference for Form A as an instrument for clinical use was given by six of the seven psychologists who participated most extensively in rating and interpreting the SCT responses.

Thus, while comparison of ratings of the total number of subjects on Forms A and B showed no significant differences between the forms, these figures included subjects who took Form A after Form B as well as those who took Form A first. This creates an artificial situation with regard to comparing the forms, since if either test were given alone there would be no question of its being first or second in order.

It must be noted that these differences were found in subjects who are neuropsychiatric patients. Therefore, they can be applied to the general population only with reservations.

The differences in favor of Form A taken first are consistent with the results of Ellis, who found significant differences between the average scores of problem and nonproblem children only on the direct form of a personality inventory. The direct form also contained more items discriminating between the two groups than did the indirect forms of the questionnaire.

The larger proportion of responses expressing negative feelings in Form B is in accord with the findings of Combs (1947), in comparing autobiographies with TAT records. That these differences appeared in the SCT only with respect to attitudes toward father and superiors suggests that these two are the most important areas of hostility among the categories studied.

The validity figures obtained in this study under optimal conditions for Form A are in accord with those of Rotter and Willerman, who found a triserial coefficient of .61 between ratings on their version of the test and the criterion. Our results are also consistent with those of Harrison (1940), who obtained 75 per cent agreement between inferences made from TAT protocols and clinical records. On the other hand, we do not agree with Lorge and Thorndike, who concluded that "verbal replies in association and completion tests are largely unrelated to the real behavior of a person" (1941, p. 99), since we include in "real behavior" attitudes expressed in a clinical treatment situation.

Conclusions

1. The results of this study tend to support the hypothesis stated in the introduction of the problem: that the projective responses of individuals to stimuli referring to other people will be significantly different from their responses to stimuli referring to themselves in terms of the amount of disturbance revealed in the areas of personality studied and in the content of attitudes indicated.

2. Five of the six significant differences found between the two forms of a projective sentence completion test were in favor of the first-person form.

3. The first-person form of a sentence completion test (SCT) has been demonstrated to be an effective, though not exact, method of determining the degree of the subject's disturbance in several categories; namely, attitudes toward mother, father, family unit, heterosexual relationships, superiors, colleagues, future, and goals. Agreements among judges and between judges and criterion raters were beyond chance expectancy to the extent of less than one in a thousand. Under the optimal conditions found in the experiment, 76 per cent of judges' ratings based on SCT responses of subjects were in complete or partial agreement with criterion ratings based on clinical findings. Such results are comparable with validity data found in studies of other projective techniques.

4. The first-person form of the SCT was also found to be an effective technique for determining the content of a subject's attitude in the categories and areas studied. Seventy-seven per cent of the interpretations of the attitudes of 50 subjects were in close or partial agreement with clinical findings.

5. Further investigation is needed to demonstrate conclusively that the differences found between the two forms of the SCT were not due to extraneous factors. Suggestions for a more rigorous control of such factors include:

(1) Use of an impersonal form of the SCT in which only third-person pronouns are used, since names tended to arouse associations with specific people. (2) A minimum standard of ten treatment hours of subjects by the psychiatrists making criterion ratings. (3) Periodic reviews of ratings by judges and criterion raters to encourage a common frame of reference. (4) Correlation of SCT findings on both forms with findings from other projective techniques. (5) Determination of optimum intellectual level for obtaining valid SCT responses. (6) Item analyses to determine specific stimuli and responses, or groups of them, which may be associated with high and low agreement in ratings, diagnostic classifications, and dynamisms of adjustment.

REFERENCES

CARTER, H. J. A combined projective and psychogalvanic response technique for investigating certain affective processes. *J. consult. Psychol.*, 1947, 11, 270–275.

COMBS, A. W. A comparative study of motivations as revealed in thematic apperception stories and autobiographies. *J. clin. Psychol.*, 1947, 3, 65–74.

ELLIS, A. A comparison of the use of direct and indirect phrasing in personality questionnaires. *Psychol. Monogr.*, 1947, 61, No. 3.

GARFIELD, S. L. The Rorschach test in clinical diagnosis. *J. clin. Psychol.*, 1947, 3, 375–380.

HARRISON, R. Studies in the use and validity of the TAT with mentally disordered patients, II. A quantitative study. *Charact. & Pers.*, 1940, 9, 122–133.

LORGE, I., & THORNDIKE, E. L. The values of responses in a completion test as indications of personality traits. *J. appl. Psychol.*, 1941, 25, 191–199.

ROHDE, AMANDA R. Explorations in personality by the sentence completion method. *J. appl. Psychol.*, 1946, 31, 169–181.

ROTTER, J. B., & WILLERMAN, B. The incomplete sentences test as a method of studying personality. *J. consult. Psychol.*, 1947, 11, 43–48.

SHOR, J. Report on a verbal projective technique. *J. clin. Psychol.*, 1946, 2, 279–282.

SPENCER, D. The frankness of subjects on personality measures. *J. educ. Psychol.*, 1938, 29, 26–35.

STEIN, M. I. The use of a sentence completion test for the diagnosis of personality. *J. clin. Psychol.*, 1947, 3, 47–56.

SYMONDS, P. M. The sentence completion test as a projective technique. *J. abnorm. soc. Psychol.*, 1947, 42, 320–329.

TENDLER, A. D. A preliminary report on a test for emotional insight. *J. appl. Psychol.*, 1930, 14, 123–136.

51

The Effect of Mental Set and Item Structure on Response to a Projective Test [1,2]

JULIAN MELTZOFF

The projective hypothesis that the subject is unable to censor his responses to projective techniques so as to refrain from manifesting significant aspects of his personality is not supported in this study. The author is able to demonstrate convincingly that the "set" with which the subject takes the SCT is a key determinant of the nature of his response. Persons who were particularly ego-involved as a result of the structuring of the test situation tended to manifest more positive responses than any other kind. At the same time, approximately one-third of their responses were negative or neutral, being due for the most part to the stimulus structure of the stems. Approximately 70 per cent of the positive or negative responses of the college population studied followed the stimulus properties of the stems. Both the instructions and stimulus properties of the test, therefore, largely determine the content

[1] This paper is based on a dissertation submitted to the faculty of the University of Pennsylvania in partial fulfillment of the requirements for the degree of Doctor of Philosophy. The writer wishes to express his sincere appreciation to Professor Morris S. Viteles for his guidance throughout all phases of this research and to Professors Malcolm G. Preston, Harold A. Rashkis, and Mildred A. Gebhard. The author is indebted to the psychologists of the Philadelphia Veterans Administration Mental Hygiene Clinic and to the fraternities of the University of Pennsylvania for their excellent co-operation.

[2] Reviewed in the Veterans Administration and published with the approval of the Chief Medical Director. The statements and conclusions published by the author are the result of his own study and do not necessarily reflect the opinion or policy of the Veterans Administration.

835

of the completions. How, then, does one account for the relatively encouraging validity studies reported?

First, let it be noted that not all responses followed the negative or positive sentence stems. Probably the shifts have considerable diagnostic import. Second, neutral stems showed greater variability than did the positive or negative ones. Approximately 55 per cent of the neutral stems were given positive endings, 33 per cent negative endings, 5 per cent neutral endings, and approximately 7 per cent of the endings were ambiguous or omitted altogether. It seems possible, therefore, that the neutral stems had the greatest value in the assessment of personality in this study. Their efficacy in other kinds of studies may depend on the character of the criterion (see Cromwell & Lundy in this Volume, Chap. 54). Certainly a worth-while study would be to classify the stems according to stimulus structure and to determine the relationship of each of these categories to various behavioral criteria.

There has been a renaissance of the ego in contemporary psychology, as attested to by a growing body of literature and research.[3] Murphy defines the ego as a "group of activities concerned with the enhancement and defense of the self" (1947, p. 984). This investigation is concerned specifically with the defense of self-esteem rather than the more general "self."

Underlying this concept is the assumption that when a person's self-esteem is threatened, activities are aroused to defend it in some manner. If this assumption is true, defensive behavior in particular situations in which self-esteem is threatened should be deducible.

DEFENSE SETS AND DEFENSIVE BEHAVIOR

It can first be postulated that, in general, an individual becomes set to defend when faced with an esteem-threatening situation of any kind and specifically so in an esteem-threatening test situation. This is stated as a postulate because it is not intended here to attempt to demonstrate the existence of these not very tangible mental sets.[4] Specific hypotheses have been formulated and tested, however, in order to explain varied psychological phenomena such as selective recall[5] and level of aspira-

---

[3] Two of the most comprehensive discussions of this subject can be found in Allport (1943) and Sherif and Cantril (1947).

[4] For a review of the literature on mental set, see Gibson (1941).

[5] See Alper (1946) and Rosenzweig (1941).

tion[6] in terms of defensive behavior in the face of self-esteem threat. Experiments have also been carried out to demonstrate that when an individual is administered a personality inventory, he may attempt to defend his self-esteem by distorting his responses.

The possibility of such distortion has been noted by more than a score of authors cited by Meehl and Hathaway, who conclude from their own research with the Minnesota Multiphasic, "The conscious or unconscious *tendency* of subjects to present a certain picture of themselves in taking a personality inventory has a considerable influence upon their scores" (1946, p. 560). In fact, widely used personality inventories such as the one mentioned above have built-in lie scales and suppressor variables to detect and compensate for intentional and self-deceptive distortions.

The effect of signing one's name on inventories has been investigated in several studies. Research by Maller (1930), Olson (1936), and Spencer (1938) all show more frank and, by implication, more valid results when subjects performed anonymously than when names were signed. Although findings with personality inventories tend to support the defense hypothesis, it has not been tested experimentally for projective techniques. Indeed, it is contrary to some of their basic assumptions. The assumptions underlying the sentence completion technique, according to Stein are:

1. When an individual is put under pressure to respond with the first idea which occurs to him he usually offers significant material which he does not censor.

2. When faced with the problem of completing or structuring an unstructured situation, an individual's responses will be indicative of the true nature of his own reactions and sentiments.

3. In talking about others an individual is apt to reveal himself (1947, p. 52).

For the purpose of this study, it will be accepted that in completing, structuring, or giving meaning to a relatively unstructured stimulus situation, significant aspects of personality may be revealed. There is ample evidence to support the assumption that in talking about others an individual is apt to reveal himself.

Murray has stated that "almost everyone is put on the defensive by a direct attempt to penetrate below his peripheral personality" (1938, p. 529) but claims that by following the instructions of the TAT, S "is 'set' for the fullest expression, not for reticence" (p. 728). Rohde asserts that the sentence completion technique is not at all invalidated even if S suspects the purport of the test, because he is "projecting his personality regardless of his intentions" (1946, p 173). Fosberg (1938) found no significant differences in Rorschach responses given under instructions encouraging Ss to create both good and poor impressions.

---

[6] See Holt (1946).

Many others have cited resistance to censorship as a virtue of projective devices.

Some authors, however, have recognized that censorship can occur on projective tests. According to Cattell,

> It seems wrong to assume that the average person is completely taken off his guard by projective techniques so that he does not know what he is exposing. He may listen politely to the instructions that his "creative imagination" is being tested, but the psychologist is more naive than the subject if he believes that most subjects do not intuitively realize that they may be giving themselves away (1944, p. 187).

McClelland, Clark, Roby, and Atkinson, in a study of the projective expression of the need for achievement on the TAT, found that the stories of one of their groups performing under "ego-involving instructions . . . proved too inhibited to analyze" (1949, p. 254). Rotter and Willerman observed in research with a sentence completion test that some of their Ss "were saying in effect that their private feelings were 'none of your business'" (1947, p. 44).

Tompkins (1947) considering the problem of censorship on the TAT in relation to the concept of psychological distance, states: the strength of repressive factors is weakened by allowing the individual to achieve distance between himself and the character of his stories. If we would ask the individual to tell us what *he* would do if he were the person in the picture, the repressive forces would be alerted and the privacy of inner thoughts guarded (1947, p. 78).

Tomkins asserts that both the nature of the picture and the test itself contribute to the distance. The end product of an increase in psychological distance, as described above, can be formulated in terms of a decrease of self-esteem threat. Something remote from oneself in the sense of not being closely related to one's system of attitudes and activities revolving about oneself cannot be thought of as a threat to self-esteem. Under such circumstances, there is presumably no need for defense.

It seems empirically true that some process of censorship is present even on projective tests. If any marked alteration of responses can be shown to take place as a result of a change in S's conception of the purpose of the test, it would become necessary to ascertain which of his responses represented the "true nature" of his reactions.

THE ROLE OF THE STIMULUS

The importance of the stimulus itself is often overlooked in our interpretation of responses. Projective tests require of the stimulus that it be "relatively unstructured." An obvious difficulty arises in attempting to define the limits of an unstructured situation. A wide variety of stimuli are being used as unstructured material. Some are alleged to be more structured than others, but they are still deemed to be sufficiently unstructured to allow for valid interpretation of projections. Sentence completion tests, whose use in clinical practice has expanded considerably in recent years, employ such relatively unstructured stimuli.

Although it is not necessarily peculiar to this type of test, the partial sentences that are used as stimuli contain a characteristic which will be referred to as stimulus tone.[7] This term refers to the direction of the mood or feeling evoked by the stimulus, i.e., pleasant, hopeful, unpleasant, hopeless, etc. Little attention has been paid to this stimulus property, although Tendler, who constructed one of the first sentence completion tests for the evaluation of personality, included stimuli which were designed to "arouse a particular emotional set and yet allow for all that is implied in free response" (1930, p. 124). The actual freedom allowed is subject to serious question, as the stimulus tone appears to establish a set which has a distinct and systematic effect on response. If this is the case, then we could hardly expect to obtain the "true nature of his own reactions and sentiments" referred to in the discussion of assumptions. Survey of existing sentence completion tests reveals in many instances a heavy weighting of negatively toned stimulus words, and if our hypothesis is correct they tend to elicit mainly maladjusted responses.[8] The concept of what constitutes an unstructured stimulus situation is clearly in need of clarification if this is the case.

OBJECTIVES

In summary, there are several objectives to this investigation. The research is designed to examine some of the basic assumptions of projective techniques of the sentence completion type by testing a specific hypothesis deduced from the general assumption of defense in the face of self-esteem threat. Projective technique assumptions will be further examined by studying the effects of different types of item structure on response. Through the arousal of different mental sets and the production of different degrees of esteem threat, it is intended to study the characteristics of self-esteem defense in a projective test situation and to discover the specific methods[9] of alteration employed for each of the different item types when self-esteem is threatened in contrast to when it is not.

GENERAL PLAN OF THE EXPERIMENT

In order to study the effects of the stimulus tone, a test of the sentence completion type containing an equal proportion of three types of items

---

[7] For definition of stimulus tone, see "Method and Procedure."

[8] For definition of response tone, see "Treatment of the Data."

[9] An analysis of specific differences in the content of the responses under the various test conditions will appear in a future publication.

was administered under four different test conditions. Comparison of responses under the different conditions enable us to determine whether response distortion can and does occur. Two of these conditions provide extreme sets in order to determine whether Ss are capable of distorting responses. The S was to respond as if he were an extremely well-adjusted individual on one and an emotionally disturbed individual on the other. The two other conditions were one in which S was self-esteem threatened and one in which he was guaranteed anonymity and given no special instructions. The tone of the responses was judged, and the data were treated in a factorial design to determine the effects on response of the stimuli, test conditions, and their interaction.

HYPOTHESES AND EXPECTED RESULTS

There are two main experimental hypotheses, each of which subsumes several specific hypotheses. The hypotheses and results expected are as follows:

HYPOTHESIS I. *Other things being equal, the tone and neutrality of the responses to a sentence completion test are direct functions of the S's mental set, as determined essentially by test instructions.*

Specifically, in stating this hypothesis it was anticipated that the pattern of the differences in responses between the various test conditions would be as follows for the three types of responses.

Positive responses. It was hypothesized that there would be a hierarchial arrangement from greatest to least number of positive responses in the order: Condition A (simulated well-adjusted), Condition B (self-esteem threatened), Condition C (Anonymous), and Condition D (simulated emotionally disturbed).

It was expected that even naive Ss would be able to create successfully a facade on a projective test of this type and produce a large number of well-adjusted responses when instructed to simulate good adjustment under Condition A. Similarly it was anticipated that Ss whose self-esteem was threatened under Condition B would attempt to appear well adjusted by giving a large number of positive responses. With the need for self-defense reduced by anonymity under Condition C, the production of fewer positive responses than under either Condition A or B was predicted.

Negative responses. It was hypothesized that there would be a hierarchial arrangement from greatest to least number of negative responses in the order Conditions D, C, B, A. It was expected that the Ss who were asked to act the role of an emotionally disturbed individual under Condition D would be relieved of any responsibility for their productions by the instructions and would thereby express conflictual content freely. It was hypothesized that both the self-esteem threatened Ss of Condition B and those simulating good adjustment under Condition A would avoid giving responses suggestive of maladjustment and would produce fewer such responses than those performing anonymously under Condition C.

Neutral responses. It was hypothesized that the greatest number of neutral responses would be given by the self-esteem-threatened Ss, who, in addition to exhibiting a tendency to enhance their self-esteem by producing a preponderance of well-adjusted responses, would attempt to conceal personal inadequacies and difficulties by means of noncommittal or evasive responses. A minimum of neutral responses was expected when individuals were acting the role of another person, since it was thought that defensive behavior would no longer be necessary.

Ambiguous responses. The most ambiguous responses were anticipated under Condition C. It was expected that, when assured of anonymity, responses would become less stereotyped, less conforming to social patterns, more idiosyncratic, and consequently more difficult to evaluate.

HYPOTHESIS II. *Other things being equal, response tone is a direct function of the tone of the stimulus.*

Specifically, it was hypothesized that positive stimuli would tend to elicit more positive responses than any other type, that negative stimuli would tend to elicit more negative responses than any other type; and that in the absence of a stimulus tone, the tone of the responses to neutral stimuli would be primarily a function of factors other than that of the stimulus tone. It was expected that there would be more ambiguous and neutral responses to neutral stimuli than to any other type and more positive than negative responses with this population.

SUPPLEMENTARY HYPOTHESES

Response time. It was further hypothesized that time spent censoring, rejecting, and selecting responses when self-esteem was threatened would be reflected in decreased speed of performance under this condition.

Omissions. It was expected that omissions of responses would appear more frequently under the self-esteem-threatened condition, since rejection of items is usually considered to be an indication of emotional blocking.

Self-reference. Another index of the extent to which an individual is permitting self-expression is the use of self-reference. It was expected that a person who was trying to conceal rather than reveal would avoid any direct reference to himself. It was hypothesized that such responses would be most frequent when Ss were acting the role of another person.

Method and Procedure

SUBJECTS

The experimental population consisted of a total of 120 male undergraduate first-year fraternity members of the University of Pennsylvania, of whom approximately 90 per cent were freshmen. Ten subjects were selected at random from each of 12 fraternities, which in turn were selected at random from the total number of fraternities available for experimental purposes. The subjects were assigned rather than being volunteers. The requirement of being first-year members was established in order to maximize the chances of psychological naiveté, facilitate the drafting of subjects, and contribute to the realism and effectiveness of some of the test instructions.

CONSTRUCTION OF EXPERIMENTAL TASK

A group of 90 incomplete sentences was assembled. Both for purposes of internal consistency and adherence to the basic assumptions of this type of technique, all sentences were worded in the third person.[10] The items were considered by the experimenter to consist of 30 each of three types—positive, negative, and neutral. They were presented in random order for judging to five psychologists, who were furnished with the following operational definitions and examples of the three types of stimuli:

Positive stimulus. A positive stimulus, in general, is one which appears to be biased in the direction of psychological or social desirability. More specifically, this includes phrases which make reference to satisfying, nonconflictual, pleasant, complimentary, or happy thoughts, feelings, actions, reactions, or events. E.g., *He loves . . .; He feels wonderful when . . .; A person who helps others . . .*

Negative stimulus. A negative stimulus, in general, is one which appears to be biased in the direction of psychological or social undesirability. More specifically, this includes phrases which make reference to unsatisfying, conflictual, unhappy, unpleasant, or disparaging thoughts, feelings, actions, reactions, or events. E.g., *He hates . . .; It is terrible when . . .; Cruel people . . .*

Neutral stimulus. A neutral stimulus is one which contains no intrinsic suggestions in either of the above directions. E.g., *His sister . . .; He is usually . . . ; A person's life . . .*

---

[10] Sacks (1949) has compared the validity of items beginning in the first person, as opposed to the third person, and tentatively recommends the former. Since it is difficult to justify such a technique as projective regardless of its validity, and since the assumptions of projective techniques are being tested, it was necessary to word all items in the third person for the purposes of this experiment.

The judges were instructed to try to disregard their own personal associations to the phrases in rating and to place each of them in one of these three categories. Working independently, complete agreement of the five judges were obtained on 86.6 per cent, or 78 of 90 items. From among the 78 elegible items, 20 of each type were selected for the final test of 60 items. Selection was based on content distribution.

In order to eliminate a possible constant effect due to position of a stimulus in the series, the stimuli were assembled in small 60-page booklets, with a different random order for each subject. Blank face sheets were placed on all booklets except those randomly assigned to the self-esteem-threatened Condition B, for which spaces were provided on the face sheets for the entry of identifying information.

TEST CONDITIONS AND ADMINISTRATION

By means of randomization, each S was given an equal chance of taking the test under any one of the four test conditions. Instructions were given to each subject individually and privately. Precautions were taken to discourage intersubject communication and were successful as far as can be ascertained. The instructions under the four conditions were similar except for a few key variations:[11]

Condition A (Simulated well-adjusted). Working anonymously, Ss were instructed to try to create the impression by their responses of being emotionally stable and well-adjusted individuals.

Condition B (Self-esteem threatened). Each S's name was checked off against a list, and he was required to fill out the test face sheet with his name, age, fraternity, school and class, number of credits completed, and signature. He was told that his name had been given for this study involving the relationship between personality and grades and was informed that the president of his fraternity and university authorities were interested in the results.

Condition C (Anonymous). The Ss were given verbal assurances of anonymity and told that it was the test rather than themselves that was under investigation.

Condition D (Simulated emotionally disturbed). The Ss, working anonymously, were instructed to act the role of emotionally disturbed individuals and to create the impression by their responses of being maladjusted.

All the Ss were instructed in the usual manner to add words to the short phrases presented so as to make complete sentences and to work as quickly as they could. With the exception of the self-esteem-

---

[11] For full instructions to subjects and details of administration, order Document 3116 from American Documentation Institute, 1719 N Street, N.W., Washington 6, D.C., remitting $1.00 for microfilm (images 1 inch high on standard 35 mm. motion picture film) or $6.45 for photocopies (6×8 inches) readable without optical aid.

threatened Ss under Condition B, all were informed in advance that their tests would be completely unidentifiable since they themselves were to mix up their booklets with a large number of already completed ones (actually dummies) which were shown to them.

The two extreme and opposite test conditions, A and D, were designed to provide optimum conditions for S's trying intentionally to distort responses and thereby to enable us to ascertain whether or not purposeful alteration of responses is possible. Under Condition D, it was made clear to S that he was not responsible for the nature of his productions and that he could without fear of criticism respond with any associations that came to mind, since he was anonymously acting the role of another person.

Condition B was designed to create self-esteem threat in that S was fully identified and informed that the purpose of the test was to evaluate him personally. This approaches the normal condition of administration in which the S is identified and usually realizes the test is designed to uncover information about him. The instructions of Condition C were designed to lessen self-esteem threat through the task orientation and their assurances of anonymity, but they were otherwise identical. Comparison of the responses under these various conditions permits the determination of whether or not response alteration is possible. If so, the effect of self-esteem threat on response can then be compared with known, intentional distortions.

Treatment of the Data

RATING CRITERIA

In order to test the experimental hypotheses, it was necessary to devise an adequate method of arriving at unbiased classifications of responses into the three response categories.[12] Accordingly, criteria for positive, negative, and neutral responses were formulated and each response was submitted to five judges. Agreement of four of the five judges was decided in advance to be the minimum requirement necessary for acceptance of the categorization of any particular response. Agreement of this magnitude or higher for any particular classification can be expected by chance less than five times in one hundred.

Responses on which the judges' agreement failed to meet this standard were classified as *ambiguous* responses and treated as a separate category.

Stated in the most general terms, the criteria for the three response types are as follows.

---

[12] A similar scoring scheme was used by Rotter and Willerman (1947). Their scoring categories included from +3 to +1 for "conflict or unhealthy responses," o for neutral, and from −1 to −3 for "positive or healthy responses."

Positive response. A positive response is one that is suggestive of a happy or hopeful attitudinal state and is the type of response one would expect from a person who is well adjusted or subject to favorable external press in the area defined by the response.

Negative response. A negative response is one that is suggestive of an unhappy or maladjusted attitudinal state and is the type of response one would expect from a person who is poorly adjusted or subject to unfavorable external press in the area defined by the response.

Neutral response. A neutral response is one in which the subject has avoided personal identification or has responded by referring to an area not usually considered to have positive or negative significance.

Specific and detailed criteria, including illustrative samples that were not drawn from the experimental responses were evolved and submitted to a board of experts[13] for criticisms and suggestions.

RATING PROCEDURE

Twenty psychologists[14] who had previous experience with sentence completion tests served as judges. The group was randomly divided into four teams of five judges each in order to keep the total number of ratings per judge down to a feasible number. Judges were trained in the use of the criteria, given a preliminary rating test, and not allowed to proceed with the experimental ratings until they had met pre-established standards of efficiency.[15]

Responses were abstracted from the original records and transcribed with absolute fidelity onto rating sheets. The responses of all Ss to any particular item were presented in the already random order of administration, throughout which the four conditions of administration were randomly distributed. One-quarter of the items were assigned at random to each of the four teams for judging, and the items were presented to the judges in random order. No identifying marks were on the rating sheets, and a judge had absolutely no way of knowing under what condition of administration a particular response had been produced or which of the stimuli had previously been judged as positive, negative, or neutral.

The agreement of the judges on each team was highly satisfactory; the combined mean agreement was 91 per cent.

---

[13] The members of the board were: Professor Silvan S. Tomkins, Princeton University; Professor Morris I. Stein, University of Chicago; Dr. Harold A. Rashkis, formerly of the University of Pennsylvania; and Dr. John E. Davis, Jr., Eastern Pennsylvania Psychiatric Institute.

[14] All the judges in this experiment were psychologists at the Philadelphia VA Mental Hygiene Clinic.

[15] More detailed discussion of the rating procedure, training of judges, method of evaluating training, and full presentation of rating criteria are available in ADI Document 3116. See footnote 11, above.

STATISTICAL TREATMENT

The data were treated in a factorial design. The 30 Ss under each of the four test conditions, all of whom had taken the full test containing an equal number of positive, negative, and neutral items, were randomly divided into three subgroups of ten subjects each, making a total of 12 subgroups. Each analysis dealt with the responses of each subgroup of 20 items of a single type, while their remaining 40 responses to the other two groups of 20 items were treated in two separate analyses. By this means, a different group of Ss could be represented in each column of the statistical design and an independent estimate of error obtained. This permitted three separate analyses to be carried out for each type of response. The responses of a group of subjects of one type of item were not dependent on their responses to another type of item, and consequently an analysis based on one arrangement of subgroups was not dependent on an analysis based on a different arrangement of subgroups.

TABLE 51-1   *Totals and Percentages of Each Type of Response Obtained under the Four Test Conditions*

RESPONSE TYPE	A		B		C		D	
	NO.	PER CENT*	NO.	PER CENT	NO.	PER CENT	NO.	PER CENT
Positive	1,116	62	1,047	59	814	45	260	14
Negative	469	26	454	25	697	39	1,331	74
Neutral	48	3	176	10	107	6	56	3
Ambiguous	157	9	118	6	176	10	146	9
Omitted	10	0	5	0	6	0	7	0

* Percentages are rounded.

Despite the fact that the same Ss were employed in the separate analyses of positive, negative, and neutral responses, it was possible to make independent comparisons of these findings, just as were done for the three analyses of any *particular* type of response, so long as the results for each analysis were based on *different* arrangements of subgroups.[16]

Following the analyses of variance, t tests were carried out between each of the four test conditions and between each of the three item types.

---

[16] Fuller explanation of the statistical design is available in ADI Document 3116. See footnote 11, above.

Results[17]

For all three analyses of positive responses, the variance for test conditions, item types, and interaction of conditions × item types was greater than could be expected from fluctuations in random sampling alone ($p < .001$).

As illustrated in Table 51–1, positive responses appeared with decreasing frequency in the order A, B, C, D, with the greatest number being produced by the Ss acting well adjusted and the least by those acting emotionally disturbed. Subjects performing anonymously under Condition C gave fewer positive responses than those who were self-esteem-threatened under Condition B. The differences between all test conditions, except between Conditions A (simulated well adjusted) and B (self-esteem-threatened), were statistically reliable ($p < .001$) in all three analyses.

The greatest number of positive responses was given to positive stimuli, and the least to negative stimuli, as can be seen in Table 51–2. All differences between the mean number of positive responses elicited by each of the three stem types were significant ($p < .001$) in all three analyses.

NEGATIVE RESPONSES

Again in all three analyses, the variance for test conditions, item types, and interaction was greater than could be expected by chance ($p < .001$), and the differences between all test conditions except between A and B were significant ($p < .001$). However, essentially the reverse relationship to that obtained for positive responses was found, as shown in Table 51–1. The greatest number of negative responses was produced under Condition D, where the subjects were simulating emotional disturbance, and the next greatest frequency was obtained under the anonymous condition, C. The Ss who were simulating good adjustment under Condition A, as well as those who were self-esteem-threatened under Condition B, gave comparatively few responses suggestive of maladjustment.

All differences between item types in the mean number of negative responses evoked were statistically reliable for all three analyses ($p < .001$). The greatest number of negative responses was to negative stimuli and the least to positive stimuli, as illustrated in Table 51–2.

---

[17] The aforementioned ADI Document should be consulted for analysis of variance tables, interaction charts, and tables of means, differences between means, and t and P values of all differences. See footnote 11, above.

NEUTRAL RESPONSES

The variance for test conditions was significantly greater than could be expected by chance ($p < .001$) in all three analyses. Neutral responses were most frequent in the face of self-esteem threat and least frequent under the extreme but opposite conditions, A and D, as shown in Table 51–1. The only differences that were reliable in all three analyses were between Condition B (self-esteem-threatened) and the remaining three conditions.

The variance for item types was significant in two of the three analyses ($p < .001$, $< .05$). There was a significantly greater number ($p < .05$) of neutral responses to negative stimuli than to either positive or neutral stimuli for two of the three analyses, while the results of the third analysis were in the inconclusive range ($p < .10$–$.20$).

TABLE 51–2   *Totals of Each Type of Response to the Three Types of Item*

RESPONSE TYPE	ITEM TYPE			TOTAL
	+	−	N	
Positive	1683	249	1305	3237
Negative	431	1730	790	2951
Neutral	82	174	131	387
Ambiguous	200	236	161	597
Omitted	4	11	13	28

AMBIGUOUS AND OMITTED RESPONSES

Although the total number of ambiguous responses was greatest for the anonymous condition, C, and least for the self-esteem-threatened condition, B, the variance was significant in but one of the three analyses. Fewer than 1 per cent of the items were omitted under any condition, and no meaningful comparisons can be made.

INTERACTION

The interaction variance for both positive and negative responses was significant ($p < .001$) in all three analyses. Examination of all interactions leads to the same conclusions.

1. The effects of the test conditions varied from one type of item to another. The mental sets imposed by variations of instructions had most differential effect with neutral stimuli and least with negative stimuli. Negative stimuli tended to evoke negative responses, regardless

of the test condition, and in general exhibited the strongest effect among the three types of stimuli.

2. The effects of the item types varied from one test condition to another. The different types of stimuli had least differential effect against the strong tendency of the mental set under Condition D (simulated emotionally disturbed) to elicit negative responses. In general, when the stimulus tone was in the same direction as the mental set imposed by the test instructions (i.e., positive stimuli combined with Conditions A [simulated well adjusted] and B [self-esteem-threatened] or negative stimuli combined with Condition D), there was reinforcement. When the stimulus tone was in the direction opposite to that of the set imposed by the instructions (i.e., positive stimuli combined with Condition D or negative stimuli with Conditions A and B), there was an antagonistic effect.

TEST TIME

The time it took the subjects to complete the test ranged from 9 min. 49 sec. for one subject under Condition C (anonymous) to as high as 66 min. 16 sec. for another subject under Condition B (self-esteem-threatened). The average time for all subjects was 26 min. 18 sec. The mean time under Condition A (simulated well adjusted) and D (simulated emotionally disturbed) were essentially the same, with 27 min. 48 sec. for the former and 26 min. 42 sec. for the latter. The shortest average time was found under the anonymous condition, C, with a mean of 17 min. 30 sec.; the average time under the self-esteem-threatened condition, B, was almost twice as great, with a mean of 33 min. 12 sec.

The difference in time between Conditions A (simulated well adjusted) and D (simulated emotionally disturbed) was not significant.

TABLE 51–3   *Differences between Test Conditions in Response Time*

TEST CONDITIONS	DIFFERENCES BETWEEN MEANS, IN SECONDS	t	P
A–B	323.73	1.63	.10
A–C	617.20	4.24	.01
A–D	68.54	.44	.60–.70
B–C	940.93	5.78	.01
B–D	392.27	2.29	.02–.05
C–D	548.66	5.21	.01

Except for the inconclusive differences between Conditions A and B, the remainder of the differences were all statistically reliable, as shown in Table 51–3.

SELF-REFERENCE

The use of self-reference in the form of the words *I, me, my,* or *mine* was not common in completions of sentences beginning in the third person except under Condition D (simulated emotionally disturbed). Whereas 63 per cent of the Ss under Condition D referred to themselves directly in this fashion one or more times, such responses appeared in the records of only about one-fourth of the Ss under the remaining condtions.

Discussion of Results

In view of the consistently high degree of statistical reliability throughout the three analyses of each experimental variable, the main experimental hypotheses cannot be rejected. It has been demonstrated that both the nature of the stimulus and S's mental set in the test situation can directly affect the quality of his responses on a projective test of this type.

MENTAL SET

It was hypothesized that *other things being equal, the tone and neutrality of the responses to a sentence completion test are direct functions of S's mental set, as determined essentially by test instructions.*

Evidence of the capacity of Ss to alter their responses to a projective test as a result of mental set can be drawn particularly from a comparison of the opposite and extreme test conditions, A (simulated well adjusted) and D (simulated emotionally disturbed). In order to succeed in creating the impression of good adjustment, one would have to produce a predominance of positive responses; and in order to succeed in conveying the impression of maladjustment, the converse would hold. The Ss performed in precisely these respective manners, with those under Condition A giving predominantly responses suggestive of good adjustment and those under Condition D giving chiefly responses suggestive of poor adjustment. This strongly suggests that Ss are capable of censoring responses to a projective test of this type and of manipulating their responses to serve their purpose in taking the test. Prior research has already demonstrated the susceptibility of personality inventories to such manipulation. Now it can be seen that, contrary to common assumption, the S's persona is not invariably stripped off by the mechanism of projection to lay bare his defenseless inner self. It is not at all that simple.

Even if now satisfied that naive Ss can perform in this sophisticated manner, we are faced with the question of whether or not they actually do so, and, if so, under what circumstances. What would happen in a practical situation in which the Ss were not directly told to make their responses look well adjusted or maladjusted but were simply put into a self-esteem-threatening situation (as seems to be the case in general practice), allowed to mobilize their own modes of defense, and compared with a group in a nonself-esteem-threatening situation? The comparison of the responses under Condition B (self-esteem-threatened) and C (anonymous) contributes to the understanding of this question. Both groups of Ss were instructed to work quickly, and, in accordance with the assumptions underlying the technique, it would be expected that they would give uninhibited expression of their own attitudes and feelings. In keeping with the hypotheses and the rationale we have been following, however, it was expected that where self-esteem threat was minimized, there would be no need to conceal, evade, or enhance, except for purposes of self-deception, provided that the assurances of anonymity were fully accepted by the Ss. Significantly enough, comparison of these two test conditions reveals a greater number of well-adjusted responses, along with fewer maladjusted responses, and more evasive responses, under the self-esteem-threatened condition, B. In addition, the increase of mean performance time suggests that the Ss blocked much more frequently and spent considerably longer time in censorship activity. From this it can be inferred that the introduction of the variable of self-esteem threat results in a loss of immediate spontaneous responses and the substitution of a carefully studied facade. Thus the S presents the examiner with the very persona behind which he thought he had been peering. The evidence for this lies in the further comparison of Conditions A (simulated well adjusted) and B (self-esteem-threatened).

If the Ss under Condition B were actually attempting to enhance themselves, it would be expected that the results would approach those of Condition A, where the Ss were intentionally instructed to present the facade of a well-adjusted individual. Under both conditions, the Ss gave a preponderance of well-adjusted responses and relatively few maladjusted ones. Thus, Ss gave well-adjusted responses both when instructed to do so and without such instructions when self-esteem was threatened.

Evidence of the difference between these two conditions is to be found in the consideration of neutral responses. In the criteria statements, neutral responses are assumed to be evasions and, as such, are to be thought of as defensive behavior on a different level from the production of positive responses.[18] The evasive type of defense was most prominent under the self-esteem-threatened condition, B, the frequency being significantly higher than under Condition A (simulated well adjusted).

Certain essential differences should be noted between Conditions C (anonymous) and D (simulated emotionally disturbed). The instructions of Condition D were intended to enable the Ss to perform without threat to self-esteem and with least inhibition. In acting the role of another person, it was hoped that they would express material that they ordinarily would not allow themselves to admit to others and still deeper material that they themselves could not tolerate if recognized as applicable to themselves. Protected by the fact that they are acting a role, they should even be able to refer to themselves in the first person with impunity. Evidence for this was seen in the use of the words *I, me, my,* and *mine* in responses. Not only was the total number of such references overwhelmingly and significantly greater under Condition D than for any other condition, but the majority of the Ss employed such words here, whereas only a small minority did so under the other conditions.

There were many less neutral responses under Condition D (simulated emotionally disturbed) and C (anonymous), which suggests that the need for evasion or self-deception was no longer a factor. On the other hand, the fact that the Ss responded more slowly under Condition D is an apparent contradiction. Under Condition D, however, Ss were obliged to struggle against the effects of the positive stimuli, which comprised one-third of the total number of stimuli. It is possible that had only neutral stimuli been presented, the time relationships would have been altered. Before the real meaning of the effect of the instructions to simulate emotional disturbance can be ascertained, further research is necessary. In any event, it serves in this experiment as one of the bases against which to compare the anonymous condition, C. Responses under Condition C bore similarities to those under Condition D as well as to those under A (simulated well adjusted) and B (self-esteem-threatened), while responses under Conditions A and B were markedly different from those under Condition D.

STIMULUS TONE

It has been hypothesized that *other things being equal, response tone is a direct function of the tone of the stimulus.*

The Ss responded primarily with positive responses to positive stim-

---

[18] Preliminary research showed a group of psychologists to be exceptionally skilled in the technique of giving evasive responses. The psychologists in the preliminary study openly resented being tested, whereas the college students were compliant. It seemed as though the psychologists, in Rotter and Willerman's words (1947), were telling the examiner, "It's none of your business," whereas the college students were saying, "Although it is undoubtedly your business, I will tell you only nice things about myself."

uli, and with negative responses to negative stimuli. The effect of negative stimuli was even stronger than that of positive stimuli. With a
group of this type, it would be indeed surprising if they were to give
about seven times as many maladjusted as well-adjusted responses on
any test.[19] It would be still more surprising if they were to give four
times as many maladjusted responses, even when intentionally trying to
appear as well adjusted as possible, and twelve times as many when
performing anonymously. Yet this is exactly what happened when responses to negative stimuli alone are considered.The same Ss reversed
the picture by giving approximately four times as many well-adjusted
as maladjusted responses to positive stimuli for all conditions combined.
The effect of the stimulus is obviously of considerable import.

Neutral stimuli that were biased in neither direction and could easily
be organized in any fashion gave the S the greatest freedom of response.
With this type of stimulus, the group responded as might be expected
of a group of this sort, with the balance clearly in favor of well-adjusted
responses.

It was anticipated that more neutral responses would be given to
neutral stimuli than to any other kind because of the restrictions imposed
by negative and positive stimuli. Instead, in keeping with the assumption that neutral responses represent defensive behavior, the Ss evidently
called upon this kind of solution most frequently when faced with
negative stimuli. It is reasonable to believe that negative stimuli
represented more of a threat than neutral ones and consequently brought
out this kind of defense more often. Similarly, positive stimuli, being
least threatening, elicited the least number of neutral responses.

In order to demonstrate further how responses may be affected by
the stimulus tone, a comparison was made between the responses to all
stimuli (three stimuli of each type) dealing with the family, father, and
brother. These afford a clinically interesting comparison of the effect
of the stimulus tone on response. The three positive stimuli combined
yield a total of 74 per cent well-adjusted responses and but 15 per
cent responses suggestive of maladjustment in the area of family relations. Three negative stimuli dealing with the same area yielded 85 per
cent maladjusted responses and barely 1 per cent well-adjusted ones.
Three neutral stimuli in the same area elicited 58 per cent well-adjusted
and 36 per cent maladjusted responses.

These percentages are based on three responses of each of 120 Ss.
Thus the same S with one type of stimulus appeared maladjusted in
family relationships and with another type of stimulus appeared well

---

[19] In a previous study (Rotter & Willerman, 1947) with the Rotter Incomplete
Sentences Test, such a heavy weighting of maladjusted responses was not obtained
even from a group of "seriously disturbed" patients.

adjusted. When the stimuli were unbiased, more than twice as many responses were well adjusted as maladjusted, as would be expected for this group. Although it has not been demonstrated that the items under comparison are exactly equivalent, there is little doubt that a systematic effect is operating that is a direct result of these differences in tone.

Implications

The results of this investigation demonstrate that the responses to a projective test of this type vary systematically according to the conditions under which the test is administered. The total situation in which the stimuli are presented, including the S's conception of the purpose of the test and the extent to which it threatens his self-esteem, influences the results obtained. The methods of dealing with threat studied in this experiment were self-enhancement and evasiveness. It is likely that other, more subtle means of defense that were not uncovered by the scoring system used were present.

Since almost any test situation of any importance represents a potential threat to self-esteem, distortions should be expected and allowances made for them in interpretation. Either further effort should be made to decrease self-esteem threat, or the responses obtained in many cases must be considered as tantamount to the best efforts of the Ss to appear as well adjusted as possible. One method of decreasing self-esteem threat that is suggested by this study is to encourage S to act the role of another person. Further research is required to help determine what is actually being measured by the "emotionally disturbed" test condition.[20] It is possible that some of the productions under these instructions may reflect aspects of personality that are ordinarily inhibited.

Clearly, the findings of this research do not support the projective technique assumption that responses will be projected without censorship. Of course, the findings of this study cannot be generalized to include all projective techniques, but they should be of interest in considering other methods in which content is directly interpreted. By the same token, generalizations cannot be made beyond the experimental population of college students. A known neurotic group might very well be more threatened than these Ss and react still further in the direction of the findings. On the other hand, they might be unable to muster defenses as effectively. Intelligence may be a factor in the facility with which one can manipulate responses to serve definite ends. It would be

---

[20] Role playing has been used therapeutically, but its significance for testing has not been clearly demonstrated.

desirable to compare clinical groups on the extent and mode of defense employed.

The results of the experiment also emphasize the need in projective test construction for seriously considering the set aroused by the stimulus. Although the over-all picture was that of individuals not only responding to a stimulus but reacting purposefully in a total situation, the effect of the stimulus itself as a determiner of response should be recognized. It has been demonstrated in this experiment how opposite impressions about the same individuals can be gained by means of shifting the tone of the stimulus so that it is possible to find oneself unwittingly diagnosing the test as well as the Ss.

In this regard, it can be argued that it is not that the basic assumptions of the technique are at fault, but rather that there has been a failure to follow the rules of test construction required by these assumptions. This failure seems to be the result of an unclear conception of the limits of a "relatively unstructured" stimulus situation. On the basis of this research, these limits can be established in at least one dimension.

The results of this experiment suggest that an unstructured stimulus is one that is not biased in either a positive or negative direction. This finding should be applicable for types of stimuli other than incomplete sentences. If the stimuli are not neutral, their potential effects should at least be kept clearly in mind in interpretation and appropriate allowances made. Positive and negative stimuli could perhaps be profitably employed if accompanied by neutral stimuli related to the same topic. Thus, if S were to respond with similarly toned responses to three differently structured stimuli about the same topic, the examiner would be in a better position to make inferences than if he simply had a response to a positive or negative stimulus. Some indication of the intensity of S's feeling or attitude could be obtained from responses that reversed the tone of the stimulus, particularly where the response to the analogous neutral stimulus supported the finding. If S merely were to follow the respective sets of the positive and negative stimuli, the response to the neutral stimulus could help resolve the issue. If no such internal controls are attempted, it is probably safest to employ only neutral stimuli.

The findings of this investigation by no means invalidate the type of personality investigation represented by the sentence completion test. The multitude of different responses and the clusters of responses around particular areas of adjustment found in individual test records have not yet been analyzed. Distinct differences and consistencies in content characterize individual records, and it is felt that personality differences between Ss account for these characteristics. Rather than abandonment of the technique, which has proved most useful in clinical practice, refinements of construction, administration, and interpretation based on reformulation of and adherence to basic assumptions are required.

Summary and Conclusions

A projective test of the sentence completion type composed of three different types of stimuli was administered under four different conditions to 120 college students. The stimulus phrases were judged by clinical psychologists to be positively toned, negatively toned, or neutral. The test conditions were designed to provide two mental sets that favored response distortion by requesting Ss to act the role of well-adjusted and emotionally disturbed individuals, a condition in which self-esteem was threatened, and a condition under which self-esteem threat was reduced through verbal assurances of anonymity. The responses were judged by clinical psychologists to be positive (suggestive of good adjustment in the area defined by the response), negative (suggestive of poor adjustment in the area defined by the response), or neutral (evasive).

Results supported both the main experimental hypotheses and lead to the following conclusions.

1. *Other things being equal, the tone of the responses to a projective test of the sentence completion type is a direct function of the mental set of the subject as determined essentially by test instructions.*

(a) Subjects are able to manipulate responses on a projective test of this type so as to create the impression of either good or poor adjustment.

(b) When self-esteem is threatened by the test situation, the subjects respond in practically the same manner as those who are instructed to act well adjusted with the exception that they give more evasive responses and take a longer time to respond.

(c) Subjects working anonymously, and without having self-esteem threatened by the test situation, respond most rapidly and give significantly more maladjusted responses along with fewer well-adjusted and evasive responses than those who are self-esteem-threatened.

2. *Other things being equal, the tone of the responses to a projective test of the sentence completion type is a direct function of the tone of the stimuli.*

(a) Positive stimuli tend to elicit responses that are suggestive of good adjustment.

(b) Negative stimuli tend to elicit responses that are suggestive of poor adjustment, and they allow least freedom of response.

(c) Neutral stimuli do not directly affect the tone of the responses and allow most freedom of response.

REFERENCES

ALLPORT, G. W. The ego in contemporary psychology. *Psychol. Rev.*, 1943, 50, 451–478.

ALPER, T. G. Task-orientation vs. ego-orientation in learning and retention. *Amer. J. Psychol.*, 1946, 59, 236–248.

CATTELL, R. B. Projection and design of projective tests of personality. *Charact. & Pers.*, 1944, 12, 177–194.

FOSBERG, I. A. Rorschach reactions under varied instructions. *Rorschach Res. Exch.*, 1938, 3, 12–31.

GIBSON, J. J. A critical review of the concept of set in contemporary experimental psychology. *Psychol. Bull.*, 1941, 38, 781–817.

HOLT, R. R. Level of aspiration: Ambition or defense? *J. exp. Psychol.*, 1946, 36, 398–416.

MCCLELLAND, D. C., CLARK, R. A., ROBY, T. B., & ATKINSON, J. W. The projective expression of needs. IV. The effect of the need for achievement on thematic apperception, *J. exp. Psychol.*, 1949, 39, 242-255.

MALLER, J. B. The effect of signing one's name. *Sch. & Soc.*, 1930, 31, 882–884.

MEEHL, P. E., & HATHAWAY, S. R. The K factor as a suppressor variable in the Minnesota multiphasic personality inventory. *J. appl. Psychol.*, 1946, 30, 525–564.

MURPHY, G. *Personality—A biosocial approach to origins and structure.* New York: Harper, 1947.

MURRAY, H. A., et al. *Explorations in personality.* New York: Oxford Univer. Press, 1938.

OLSON, W. C. The waiver of signature in personal reports. *J. appl. Psychol.*, 1936, 20, 442–450.

ROHDE, AMANDA R. Exploration in personality by the sentence completion method. *J. appl. Psychol.*, 1946, 30, 169–181.

ROSENZWEIG, S. Need-persistive and ego-defensive reactions to frustration as demonstrated by an experiment on repression. *Psychol. Rev.*, 1941, 48, 347–349.

ROTTER, J. B., & WILLERMAN, B. The incomplete sentences test as a method of studying personality. *J. consult. Psychol.*, 1947, 11, 43–48.

SACKS, J. M. The relative effect upon projective responses of stimuli referring to the subject and of stimuli referring to other persons. *J. consult. Psychol.*, 1949, 13, 12–20.

SHERIF, M., & CANTRIL, H. *The psychology of ego-involvements.* New York: Wiley, 1947.

SPENCER, D. The frankness of subjects on personality measures. *J. educ. Psychol.*, 1938, 29, 26–35.

STEIN, M. I. The use of a sentence completion test for the diagnosis of personality. *J. clin. Psychol.*, 1947, 3, 47–56.

TENDLER, A. D. A preliminary report on a test for emotional insight. *J. appl. Psychol.*, 1930, 14, 123–136.

TOMKINS, S. S. *The thematic apperception test.* New York: Grune & Stratton, 1947.

52

Validation of the Rotter Incomplete Sentence Test for College Screening

JULIAN B. ROTTER, JANET E. RAFFERTY, AND EVA SCHACHTITZ

The Rotter Incomplete Sentences Blank has proved to be one of the most successful of the projective techniques in so far as validity studies are concerned. In this report, the primary validation study on the college form is described. The strength of the technique lies in the fact that, unlike many scoring systems, reliability is not so low as to preclude satisfactory validity figures. Split-half coefficients (not really applicable in an unhomogeneous test) are a respectable .83 and .84 for women and men, respectively, whereas interscorer reliability is a gratifying .96 and .91.

Using teacher and counselor judgments of adjustment, Rotter and colleagues obtained biserial correlations of .64 and .77 for women and men, respectively. This, needless to say, is very good for a 40-item test which takes no more than 20 minutes to complete for the average student. Further, the validity coefficients are not far from those reported in other studies.[a]

The high reliability figures are a function of the clearly written manual and unambiguous quantitative scoring system. The high validity coefficients would appear to be a function of the great flexibility of this

---

[a] J. B. Rotter and B. Willerman. "The Incomplete Sentences Test as a Method of Studying Personality," Journal of Consulting Psychology, 11 (1947), 43–48. Ruth Churchill and V. J. Crandall. "The Reliability and Validity of the Rotter Incomplete Sentence Test," Journal of Consulting Psychology, 19 (1955), 345–350; also Chap. 53, this book.

*test, with the possibility of shaping stems for any purpose. In my judg-
ment, for example, 26 of the 40 stems are neutral. Accordingly, this
makes the test maximally sensitive to projection by giving the subject
little leeway to follow the stimulus properties of the stems.*

*If there is a possible weakness, it lies in the question of whether the
test is sensitive only to those maladjusted persons who have already
decided to seek therapeutic help. In that case, why not simply ask the
entering student whether he'd like counseling and save the cost and
time of the psychologist's skills for more difficult diagnostic problems?
Rotter and colleagues indicate, however, that six specially selected
maladjusted cases in the female group were not known to have sought
help. Nevertheless, more work needs to be done on the sensitivity of
the test to persons not committed to psychotherapy.*

The use of the incomplete sentences technique for personality assessment was given decided impetus by its application in the armed services (Holzberg, Teicher, & Taylor, 1947; Hutt, 1945; Shor, 1946; Stein,
1947; Symonds, 1947).[1] The version used by Rotter and Willerman
(1947) indicated relatively high validity for determining the degree of
mental disturbance in patients in an AAF convalescent hospital, and
their study demonstrated that it was possible to have both objective
scoring and certain advantages of the projective techniques. The freedom
of response, enabling the subject to express his own conflicts rather than
conforming to a "yes", "no", "?" categorization, is retained, as well as a
certain amount of ambiguity or disguise of purpose. The latter is
perhaps better expressed by saying that the subject is less knowledgeable
as to what is a "good" as against a "bad" answer. It seemed probable
that the development of new scoring manuals could make this test useful
in a variety of other screening problems.

The present study is concerned only with the validation of the test
as used to obtain an over-all score for degree of conflict or maladjustment of college men and women. Employed in this way, the test might
be given to incoming freshmen or to special classes to determine which
students are in need of personal help. In addition to such screening,
the test results may provide significant material for individual clinical
evaluation of the subject of particular value in structuring the first interview or counseling session. It has been applied in general experimental
procedures, in which adjustment and the effects of treatment processes

---

[1] Reviews of previous work with incomplete sentences are given by Bell (1948),
Rohde (1946; 1948), and Symonds (1947).

were assessed, and in vocational and remedial counseling programs to determine the extent to which maladjustment is an important factor in the presenting problem.

The Test and Administration

The present test is a modification of the one used earlier by Rotter and Willerman (1947), which modified from forms used by Shor (1946), Hutt (1945), and Holzberg et al. (1947) at the Mason General Hospital.[2] The 40 items and instructions are presented in Figure 52–1.

No further instructions are given except to repeat the printed instructions and to urge subjects to complete all the items. Administration to a group of any number of subjects is possible. The approximate average time for administration is 20 minutes.

Complete These Sentences to Express Your Real Feeling. Try to Do Every One. Be Sure to Make a Complete Sentence.

1.	I like . . .	21.	I failed . . .
2.	The happiest time . . .	22.	Reading . . .
3.	I want to know . . .	23.	My mind . . .
4.	Back home . . .	24.	The future . . .
5.	I regret . . .	25.	I need . . .
6.	At bedtime . . .	26.	Marriage . . .
7.	Boys . . .	27.	I am best when . . .
8.	The best . . .	28.	Sometimes . . .
9.	What annoys me . . .	29.	What pains me . . .
10.	People . . .	30.	I hate . . .
11.	A mother . . .	31.	This school . . .
12.	I feel . . .	32.	I am very . . .
13.	My greatest fear . . .	33.	The only trouble . . .
14.	In high school . . .	34.	I wish . . .
15.	I can't . . .	35.	My father . . .
16.	Sports . . .	36.	I secretly . . .
17.	When I was a child . . .	37.	I . . .
18.	My nerves . . .	38.	Dancing . . .
19.	Other people . . .	39.	My greatest worry is . . .
20.	I suffer . . .	40.	Most girls . . .

Fig. 52–1. The Rotter Incomplete Sentences Blank

---

[2] Rohde (1948) has recently pointed out that some of the items of the incomplete sentence tests used in the Army are similar to items in a test copyrighted by her and Hildreth in 1941 and described in the psychological literature in 1946. The Rohde-Hildreth test was in turn modified from a test of Payne's which had not been described in the psychological literature prior to 1946.

Development of the Scoring Manuals

Previous experience has suggested that a criterion group containing fewer cases, each of whom has been carefully selected and intensively studied, is of more use than a large group poorly classified and studied only cursorily. In this research, subjects were obtained both from individual and group administrations, after which experienced psychologists were asked to classify each one as maladjusted, normal, or questionable.[3] The following general definition of maladjustment was used:

"Clearly maladjusted individuals are those students who are definitely in need of personal counseling and therapy because of personality problems. Normal students are defined as ones who would not usually be considered to be in need of treatment."

In addition to the general rating of adjustment, the psychologists rated each subject on a three-point scale in the following areas of adjustment: family, social, sexual, health, and vocational-educational. For this purpose, rating scales based on behavioral examples were used.

Subjects rated in this manner came from two sources, those who had come to the Ohio State Psychological Clinic and those in small remedial psychology courses. Combined, they formed the criterion groups. Information about them was varied, ranging from that gained through intensive clinical interviews to that obtained from test data, observations in the psychology courses, and brief interviews. In the female group there were 42 college women, 20 classified as "definitely of normal adjustment," 15 as "clearly maladjusted," and 7 as "questionably adjusted." Of the 33 male students, 13 were rated as normal, 15 as maladjusted, and 5 of questionable adjustment.

On the basis of the criterional cases, scoring booklets for both males and females were developed containing examples for each item. Using the Rotter-Willerman method of scoring, all responses were divided into three categories: conflict, or unhealthy; positive, or healthy; and neutral. Conflict responses were those associated with a maladjusted or unhealthy frame of mind, while positive answers were of a healthy, hopeful, or humorous nature. A continuum with three levels of conflict responses (C_3, C_2, C_1) and positive responses (P_3 P_2, P_1) was established. With neutral responses (N) at the center, a seven-point scale was obtained, ranging from 0 to 6. The extreme positive score (P_3) was scored as zero, the extreme conflict score (C_3) as six. Scoring examples were chosen on the basis of the frequency of occurrence of certain kinds of responses in criteria cases. In addition, the general clinical experience

[3] Grateful acknowledgment is made to Dr. John Kinzer, Dr. Emily Stogdill, Dr. Mary Alice Price, and Mr. Robert Morton for providing cases for this and the latter parts of the study.

of the authors and specific experience with the Army form of the test contributed to the evaluation of the degree of maladjustment indicated by a given response.

Replies for each category were varied. Conflict responses ran the gamut from hostility reactions, pessimism, symptom description, hopelessness, and suicidal wishes to statements of unhappy experiences, while positive answers might be humorous or flippant remarks, optimistic expressions, or acceptance statements. Generally speaking, the neutral responses were on a simple descriptive level. Some replies, such as "A mother . . . has children" are to be a large extent merely repetitious of the stimulus. Other common neutral answers are stereotypes, catch phrases, song titles and essentially meaningless and fragmentary completions. Examples are: "Back home . . . on the farm"; "I regret . . . that I have but one life to give for my country"; "Boys . . . will be boys"; "People . . . are funny"; "Sometimes . . . I feel like a motherless child"; "When I was a child . . . I spake as a child"; etc. Though it might be hypothesized that such responses, as well as humorous or flippant remarks, would be highly correlated with maladjustment, it was found that avoidance answers of this type correlated at least as well with good adjustment as with bad. This finding is in agreement with the earlier convalescent hospital study.

In an attempt to discover and eliminate common scoring problems, once the manual had been developed, the papers of 16 additional females and 20 males, whose adjustment was not as adequately deter-- mined as the criterion group, were examined and rated. Frequent responses not included previously in the scoring manual were used to expand it to its final form. In this step, the adjustment of the subjects was not as well established, and the basis for placing a response in a given category rested primarily on the judgment of the authors, based on a study of the whole record. Altogether, the protocols of 58 female and 53 male subjects were used in developing the scoring manuals.

The actual scoring examples for item 35 are given below for illustrative purposes.

MALES

My father . . .

C_3. promises many things and never keeps them; is the male responsible for my existence; wasn't very good; was a fool; and I have many arguments; is an alcoholic.

C_2. and I never were buddies; is in pretty bad shape; is hard to understand; is stern.

C_1. is in bad health; is good to me, but we have little spiritual communion; cannot supply me with everything; never had much of a chance; lives in . . . ; is proud; is sensitive.

N. is home; is a salesman; is dead; had all his teeth pulled; is a hard worker; is living.

P₁. is good to me; is very intelligent, though not highly educated; is an idol to me; is an excellent mechanic; is a good hard-working man; is the kindest, most honest man I have ever known.

P₂. is extremely caustic and reactionary, but I love him; is OK; is all right; is a good man.

P₃. is the greatest dad in the world; is a swell guy; is a good joe; is a good companion.

FEMALES

My father . . .

C₃. hasn't been home since I was twelve years old; still frightens me; is a stranger to me; is alcoholic.

C₂. isn't going to change and I wish he would; is not ambitious enough; is pretty strict; and I were never too close; has always made us work very hard at home; is (was) so good to me; antagonizes me; is angry with me; isn't sociable at home; is dead but I think of him a lot.

C₁. is really a good person but does not know how to warm up to people; seems more understanding than my mother; I wonder if I'll ever meet anyone as grand; worries about me too much; is a very quiet man; is the best man I know; is dead [with no feeling expressed about father's death].

N. is a successful businessman; is a . . . [occupation]; raised a large family; is hard-working; is in . . . [place].

P₁. is a character; cultivated my interest in sports; [activity with father, e.g., and I discuss current events daily]; is OK; is all right; has my respect and admiration; is a good man; is wonderful.

P₂. is a very handsome and intelligent metallurgist; has a complete head of hair — hurrah!; is very nice.

P₃. has a wonderful sense of humor; is very congenial; is a lot of fun; is a good guy.

Validation of the Scoring Manuals

Cases used for validation of the female manual were taken from three kinds of sources: A, classes in effective study; B, classes in mental hygiene; and, C, a limited number of cases individually declared, by competent clinicians, to be adjusted or maladjusted. In Groups A and B, the instructors were asked to rate every member of the class as either maladjusted or adjusted, i.e., as needing personal counseling or not. Thus forced to classify all subjects he possibly could in one or the other category, the instructor made judgments in many cases where he was relatively unsure of his rating. A number of errors of judgment would be expected in this group, which will, in this report, be referred to as "forced choice" cases.

Inadequate numbers of maladjusted females were available, so that most of the clear-cut cases were used in the development of the manual. In order to strengthen the criterion for the female group, a few advanced student clinicians were asked to secure tests from any college students whom they knew to be clearly maladjusted or well adjusted. In this fashion, six cases considered maladjusted and four well adjusted were obtained. These ten comprise Group C.

The male subjects included the following groups: A, forced-choice cases from effective study classes; B, forced-choice cases from mental hygiene classes; C, self-referrals to the psychological clinic for treatment; and D, cases from the Occupational Opportunities Service, referred for personal counseling by the vocational advisers.

Two females and one male, all forced-choice cases, were dropped from the initial group when further experience with the subjects convinced the instructors of the classes that they had been incorrectly classified. For the final study, 82 female and 123 male records were used. The distribution of male and female cases used is given in Table 52–1.

TABLE 52–1   *Sources of Subjects for Male and Female Cross-Validation Study*

| | FEMALES | | | MALES | | |
GROUP	AD-JUSTED	MALAD-JUSTED	TOTAL	AD-JUSTED	MALAD-JUSTED	TOTAL
A	24	17	41	48	13	61
B	26	5	31	9	8	17
C	4	6	10	0	15	15
D	0	0	0	0	30	30
Total	54	28	82	57	66	123

After all cases were collected, the following procedure was applied: the papers were numbered at top and bottom by one author and all identity removed, and they were then shuffled. In this manner bias was avoided, since the adjusted and maladjusted papers were interspersed, and the scorer, who had no previous familiarity with the papers, did not know whether they had been classified adjusted or maladjusted.

Test Reliability

Since it is hoped that the test is sensitive to changes in adjustment, test-retest reliability is not a good measure of reliability. Internal consistency, as measured by the split-half method, is of some interest in providing an estimate of reliability but is not strictly applicable since the items cannot be said to be measuring the same thing or be graded for difficulty. In a test of this kind, where scoring must be done from examples and it is possible for some subjectivity to appear in scoring (although each item is generally supposed to be scored independently of all others), interscorer reliability is perhaps of greatest interest. In light of this, consequently, two methods were used to estimate the reliability of the test. (1) For reliability of scoring, two judges, both advanced students in clinical psychology who were thoroughly familiar with the test and methods of scoring, independently scored the same 50 male records and 50 female records and their interscorer reliability was determined by the product-moment correlation. (2) The reliability of the instrument was estimated by the split-half method. The test was divided into equivalent items on an a priori basis and the correlation between halves computed by the product-moment method for both the males and females.

The correlations, standard errors, means, and standard deviations for interscorer reliability for 50 female and 50 male records are given in Table 52–2.

TABLE 52–2   *Interscorer Correlations on the Incomplete*
Sentences Blank

SCORER	r	SE	M	SD
		FEMALES ($N = 50$)		
X			126.7	19.82
	.96	.01		
Y			125.0	21.17
		MALES ($N = 50$)		
X			128.8	15.86
	.91	.02		
Y			125.1	16.90

When one judge scored 71 female records and the test was divided into halves on an a priori basis, the product-moment correlation between the equivalent halves was found to be .83, as corrected by the Spearman-Brown prophecy formula.

Similarly, one judge scored 124 male subjects and determined equivalent halves on an a priori basis. The correlation between the halves was found to be .84 corrected by the Spearman-Brown prophecy formula.

Test Validity

The main measure of test validity was obtained by determining the biserial coefficients between scores on the Incomplete Sentences Blank and the classification of adjusted or maladjusted. A secondary clue to validity could be obtained by comparing the maladjusted cases rated by the forced-choice technique with the obviously more serious cases who had found their way into clinics or sought help in some form.

Since the groups involved are not large enough to make a statistical comparison for females, this was done only for males.

The actual distribution of all cases is given in Tables 52–3 and 52–4. Group means and biserial validity coefficients are given in Tables 52–5 and 52–6.

The difference between the means of the forced-choice maladjusted males and the clinic cases was significant beyond the .01 level of confidence.

Although the forced-choice method in one of the classrooms (Group B) showed little differentiation, the success of the test with other groups produced relatively high validity coefficients. The relatively small number of selected female cases which showed no overlap in score suggests that the lower biserial was due to the smaller percentage of clearly maladjusted girls in the maladjusted group.

By using a cutting score of 135, it is seen (Table 52–3) that the test correctly identifies 68 per cent of the maladjusted females and 80 per cent of the adjusted females. With the same cutting score (Table

---

TABLE 52–3   *Distribution of Scores on the Incomplete Sentences Blank for Females**

SCORE	ADJUSTED (54)		MALADJUSTED (28)	
180–184			(1)	A
175–179				
170–174				
165–169				
160–164			(4)	ABCC
155–159			(4)	AAAC
150–154			(2)	CC
145–149	(2)	AB	(3)	AAC
140–144	(5)	AAAAB	(4)	AAAA
135–139	(4)	ABBB	(1)	B
130–134	(5)	AAABB	(1)	A
125–129	(6)	AAAABB	(1)	A
120–124	(6)	AABBBB	(1)	A
115–119	(8)	AAAABBCC	(1)	B
110–114	(5)	AABBC	(2)	AA
105–109	(6)	AABBBB	(2)	AB
100–104	(1)	B	(1)	B
95–99	(1)	B		
90–94	(3)	BBB		
85–90	(1)	C		
80–84	(1)	A		

* Letters refer to the source groups as described in the text.

52–1), 69 per cent of the maladjusted males and 89 per cent of the adjusted males are correctly placed.

Evaluation of Results

In order to obtain an adequate sample of cases for cross-validation purposes, it was necessary to draw on cases from a number of sources and by so doing to produce criteria of different strength. It was particularly difficult to obtain an adequate sample of maladjusted female cases, and this appears to be reflected in lower biserial coefficient of validity. In light of the weakness of the criteria, the results appear to indicate relatively high efficiency in screening and suggest that increase in score is in some way directly proportionate to increase in conflict or maladjustment. It might be thought that the higher score is a reflection of readiness to accept help. However, the six specially selected maladjusted cases in the female group were not individuals who were known to have sought help.

Interscorer reliability for experienced scorers is high enough to suggest that scoring was reasonably objective.

The similarity of results of the present study with the previous study of personality screening in an AAF convalescent hospital (Rotter &

TABLE 52–4		*Distribution of Scores on the Incomplete Sentences Blank for Males**		
SCORE	ADJUSTED (57)		MALADJUSTED (67)	
180–184			(1)	D
175–179			(5)	CCCCD
170–174			(2)	DD
165–169			(3)	CDD
160–164			(6)	ACCCDD
155–159			(8)	ACCDDDDD
150–154	(1)	A	(2)	AC
145–149	(1)	A	(1)	A
140–144			(6)	ABCDDD
135–139	(4)	AAAA	(12)	AAABBCDDDDDD
130–134	(5)	AAABB	(3)	BDD
125–129	(6)	AAABBB	(5)	AACDD
120–124	(10)	AAAAAAAAAA	(8)	AABBBCDD
115–119	(9)	AAAAAAAB	(4)	ACDD
110–114	(11)	AAAAAAABBB		
105–109	(5)	AAAAA	(1)	B
100–104	(2)	AA		
95–99	(3)	AAA		

* Letters refer to the source groups as described in the text.

Willerman, 1947) suggests that this method of scoring by example might be utilized for a number of screening problems. It appears that one of the greatest advantages of the incomplete sentence method is its flexibility. Experienced psychologists can devise special items and scoring examples for many specific problems. The method shows promise for a number of other screening problems, as in industry or the schools. It also has particular potentialities as an objective attitude scale, and as such it could be used to reveal attitudes toward race, politics, industrial relations, institutions, and so forth.

General Observations

Further analysis of the results of this study have produced some observations of interest to the general problem of measuring maladjustment. Many of these are suggestive of further research.

Generally speaking, it was found that there is a tendency for all individuals to twist responses. For example, it was noted that well-adjusted students twist answers, so that in reply to stimuli which presuppose a negative answer the subject responds in a positive or healthy manner. For example, in response to the stimulus, "What annoys me . . .", a well-adjusted individual might reply, "people who squeeze the tooth paste in the middle"; or to "What pains me . . ., a blow in the solar plexis." In reply to the same stimuli, however, the poorly adjusted individuals might respond; "What annoys me . . . are people"; "I can't . . . think straight"; "What pains me . . . is my home life."

It was found also that poorly adjusted students twist responses in reply to stimuli which suggest a positive answer. For example, instead of replying to "I like . . . a great many things," as would a well-adjusted

TABLE 52–5		Relationship between Psychologist's Rating of Adjustment and Scores on the Incomplete Sentences Blank for Females			
GROUP	N	M	SD	BISERIAL r	SE
Adjusted	54	120.15	15.64		
A	24	124.5			
B	26	117.96			
C	4	108.25			
Maladjusted	28	140.93	20.93		
B	17	140.53			
B	5	125.00			
C	6	155.33			
All students	82	127.24	19.98	.64	.10

TABLE 52–6   *Relationship between Psychologist's Rating of Adjustment and Scores on the Incomplete Sentences Blank for Males*

GROUP	N	M	SD	BISERIAL r	SE
Adjusted	57	119.37	11.70		
A	48	118.88			
B	9	122.00			
Maladjusted	67	144.31	18.97		
A	13	137.38			
B	8	125.57			
C	16	154.5			
D	30	146.33			
All students	124	132.85	20.30	.77	.06

person, he responds, "I like . . . to be alone." Where a healthy individual would reply, "The happiest time . . . is now," the maladjusted subject says, "The happiest time . . . ends badly." In opposition to a positive response such as "The best . . . is yet to come," a conflict response is "The best . . . friends are animals like dogs and cats."

As has been previously stated, it might be hypothesized that neutral as well as humorous or flippant remarks would be correlated to a high degree with maladjustment. However, in general, it seems that the maladjusted individuals take the test, as well as themselves, in all seriousness, so that the tests give them an opportunity to express their feelings of helplessness and desire for sympathy and help. In reading the papers, one often gets the impression that the plaintive cry of the poorly adjusted individual is that "no one understands me" and that these tests give some measure of outlet. On the other hand, the well-adjusted persons, with their abundance of flippant and neutral responses, seem to be saying in effect that their feelings are private property.

In analyzing the responses made by the maladjusted and adjusted individuals, an apparent correlation was found between the length of the response and the adjustment of the individual. The maladjusted individual often writes long, involved sentences as if compelled to express himself fully so as not to be misunderstood. On the other hand, the well-adjusted person frequently replies to the stimuli with short concise statements. On an inspection basis, with a cutting score of six or more statements that were more than one line in length, it was found that nine of fourteen such papers had been rated as maladjusted. For example, one poorly adjusted person wrote, "I feel . . . a deep sympathy for the needs and troubles of people and have a desire to help." An adjusted person wrote, "I feel . . . fine."

Another aspect of the completions appears to be related to length of response. This is a measure of the amount of emotional involvement as shown by the strength of language used: such devices as the exclamation mark and underlining. For example, "Most girls . . . around here are stuck on *themselves!!*" or "Most girls . . . are no damn good!" or "Boys . . . are mostly asses!" or "My nerves . . . are shot to hell" or "The only trouble . . . wish I had only ONE." All these examples illustrate a great degree of emotional involvement. Stein (1947) has also noted the relationship of lengthy and strongly termed responses to maladjustment.

Although perseveration or frequent repetition of the same responses was not particularly frequent in this college group, experience with the test has indicated that these manifestations tend to occur more frequently in more disturbed groups of maladjusted individuals. A rigidity or perseveration score might be of value for some experimental studies.

Summary

Manuals for scoring of an incomplete sentence test, adapted from an earlier one used by Rotter and Willerman, were developed for male and female college students in order to appraise degree of conflict or maladjustment. In developing the manuals, 58 female and 53 male subjects were used.

Validity and reliability of the test were determined on new groups of 82 female and 124 male subjects. To prevent bias, the source of the records was unknown to the scorers. Interscorer reliability of the test for two experienced scorers was .96 for the female manual and .91 for the male manual. Split-half reliability was .83 for the female manual and .84 for the male manual. However, split-half reliabilities are not strictly applicable to this type of test because of the nonequivalence of items.

The biserial validity coefficients obtained between ratings of adjusted or maladjusted and test score was .64 for females and .77 for males. It was considered that the lower coefficient for females was a function of the less adequate criterion used.

In general, the test appears to be promising for use with college students for a variety of screening and experimental problems when a measure of degree of conflict or maladjustment is required.

REFERENCES

BELL, J. E. *Projective techniques.* New York: Longmans, Green, 1948.
HOLZBERG, J., TEICHER, A., & TAYLOR, J. L. Contributions of clinical psychology to

military neuropsychiatry in an army psychiatric hospital. *J. clin. Psychol.*, 1947, 3, 84–95.

HUTT, M. L. The use of projective methods of personality measurement in army medical installations. *J. clin. Psychol.*, 1945, 1, 134–140.

ROHDE, AMANDA R. Explorations in personality by the sentence completion method. *J. appl. Psychol.*, 1946, 30, 169–181.

ROHDE, AMANDA R. A note regarding the use of the sentence completions test in military installations since the beginning of World War II. *J. consult. Psychol.*, 1948, 12, 190–193.

ROTTER, J. B., & WILLERMAN, B. The incomplete sentences test as a method of studying personality. *J. consult. Psychol.*, 1947, 11, 43–48.

SHOR, J. Report on a verbal projective technique. *J. clin. Psychol.*, 1946, 2, 279–282.

STEIN, M. I. The use of a sentence completion test for the diagnosis of personality. *J. clin. Psychol.*, 1947, 3, 46–56.

SYMONDS, P. M. The sentence completion test as a projective technique. *J. abnorm. soc. Psychol*, 1947, 42, 320–329.

53

The Reliability and Validity of the Rotter Incomplete Sentence Test

RUTH CHURCHILL AND VAUGHN J. CRANDALL

Substantial support for the Rotter Incomplete Sentences Blank (ISB) is evidenced in this report in which college students and mothers (aged 35 to 45) from the Fels Research Project served as subjects. Interscorer reliabilities in the upper .90's by untrained personnel attest to the ease of scoring. The reliabilities, ranging from .38 to .54 for retesting from six months to three years after the initial testing, though not high, indicate that the test measures more than immediate situational influences. Given to freshmen, the test was able to predict those subsequently entering counseling, with obtained biserial correlation values of .42 and .37 for women and men, respectively. When the adjustment ratings of mothers were correlated with their ISB scores, a product-moment correlation of .49 resulted. While these values are not earth-shattering, it should be noted that maladjustment is not the sole determinant of entering counseling. The ISB adjustment score does not, of course, take into account motivation for change.

In sum, the study serves to reinforce the earlier positive findings with the ISB as an indication of adjustment and to extend its applicability to other populations than the one in which the test was originally standardized.

The Rotter Incomplete Sentences Blank (ISB) has been suggested for several uses. The authors of the ISB have stated that "the test might be given to incoming college freshmen, or to special classes to determine which students are in need of personal help" (Rotter, Rafferty, & Schachtitz, 1949, p. 348), and "The test appears to be promising for use with college students for a variety of screening and experimental problems when a measure of degree of conflict or maladjustment is required" (p. 355).

To the best of the present writers' knowledge, there have been no published studies of the reliability and validity of the ISB at colleges other than Ohio State University, where the test was developed. In addition, as reviews of the ISB in the *Fourth Mental Measurements Yearbook* by Cofer (Buros, 1953, pp. 243-244) and by Schofield (Buros, 1953, pp. 244-245) have noted, the test-retest reliability of the ISB has yet to be evaluated. In the present study, ISB data were gathered to answer these and other questions.

1. What is the ISB interscorer reliability among scorers with limited psychological experience who are not trained by the authors of the test? The ISB manual reports interscorer reliabilities of .96 for female ISB records and .91 for male records (Rotter & Rafferty, 1950, p. 7). The scorers had considerable psychological training and were trained by the authors. Whether such high agreement would be found among scorers with less psychological experience and who had not been trained by the ISB authors remains an open question. Such a question is important, since institutions using the ISB must rely exclusively on the ISB manual for scorer training and may not have the services of an experienced clinical psychologist as a scorer.

2. How consistent is ISB behavior over varying periods of time? An evaluation of the test-retest reliability of the ISB is necessary. If the test is to be used as a screening instrument at college entrance to predict later difficulties, it must measure relatively stable personality characteristics rather than temporary moods or reactive states. If the test is to be used in research, the relationship of ISB performance to other variables may depend on the reliability of the ISB, particularly when the ISB has been administered at a time different from that when the other variables were measured.

3. What are the effects of previously having taken the ISB on retest performance? If ISB's are to be used as a measure of change in adjustment, the effect of the original test performance on retest performance should be known.

4. Are the normative data presented in the ISB manual applicable to students in colleges other than that from which the normative data were drawn? The manual presents normative distributions of ISB scores of male and female college freshmen at Ohio State Uni-

versity. The degree to which these norms are applicable to students in other colleges and universities is yet unknown.

5. How well does the ISB identify adjusted and maladjusted individuals? If colleges are to use the ISB to discover students likely to encounter difficulties in adjustment, it is well to discover whether or not students who earn high scores on the test at college entrance later manifest such difficulties.

Method

SUBJECTS

College students and adult women made up the two major samples of the present study. All the college students in the study were attending Antioch College, where ISB's have been regularly administered to all incoming students as part of their entering battery of placement tests. Antioch College is a small coeducational liberal arts college with a program which alternates periods of academic study with off-campus work. The student body comes from all parts of the United States, with the largest number, 36 per cent, coming from the Middle Atlantic states.

The adult women in the study were all members of a long-term longitudinal research project at the Fels Research Institute for the Study of Human Development. All these women were married and were mothers of one or more children. Most of them were between 35 and 45 years of age. Their educational backgrounds and intellectual levels were considerably higher than national averages. All these Ss were middle-class, with a preponderance of them belonging to the lower-middle socioeconomic class.

SCORING

Three individuals scored the college student ISB's. Two were senior students at Antioch College majoring in psychology. The third scorer had a B.A. degree in psychology. The ISB's of the mother sample were scored by two persons, both of whom had B.A. degrees in psychology.[1] Thus, none of the scorers had had graduate training in psychology or any extensive psychological experience. These scorers were trained by one of the authors (VJC), using the directions and scoring examples of the ISB manual (Rotter & Rafferty, 1950).

[1] The authors would like to express their gratitude to Misses Ruth Kamrass and Barbara Stunden and to Mrs. Piero Bellugi, who scored the college student ISB's, and to Mrs. Toby Helfand and Mrs. Piero Bellugi, who scored the mother ISB's.

The college student ISB's were scored in strict accordance with the ISB manual. Certain modifications were necessary, however, in the scoring of the ISB's of the mother sample. The adult form, rather than the college form, of the ISB was given to the mothers. Since no manual exists for the adult form of the ISB, the mothers' ISB's were scored with the college-form manual. Whenever possible, the examples of that manual were used. The scorers, however, were instructed to score in terms of the general instructions for each sentence whenever the specific examples for that sentence were judged to be inapplicable for adult females.

SAMPLING

For estimations of interscorer reliability, three scorers independently rated 40 ISB's selected randomly from Antioch College freshmen women students entering in 1953. Two scorers independently scored 45 ISB's of the mother sample.

College student samples were used to evaluate ISB test-retest reliability over varying intervals of time. All students originally had been tested at entrance to college. Six groups of students were retested. One group of men and one group of women were retested at six months. One group of men and one group of women were retested after a one-year interval. One group of men and one group of women students were retested three years after their original testing. Sixty Ss were randomly chosen for each of these six groups and were asked by mail to participate in a group retest session. Students who were unable to attend this session (approximately one-third) were tested individually. About 5 per cent of the students whose participation was requested could not be contacted, and another 8 per cent refused to participate. Forty-five retest ISB's for each of the six groups were selected at random from those obtained in the retesting sessions. Each of the three scorers scored 15 Ss' original test and retest ISB's in each of the six groups. Original test ISB's and retest ISB's were mixed together and all identifying data removed.

The procedure for evaluating ISB test-retest reliability in the mother sample was similar to that used in the college student sample except that, for the mothers, the retest interval varied somewhat from individual to individual. For the 39 mothers used in this reliability study, the retest interval ranged from 13 to 24 months, with a mean of 17 months and a median of 20 months. All original and retest ISB's were administered to the mothers in individual sessions.

To evaluate the screening validity of the ISB for college students, a list was compiled of all college students requesting psychological counseling in the last four years who had entered counseling within two years of the time of their original ISB. (It seemed unreasonable to expect

ISB scores to predict behavior more than two years in the future.) There were 65 women and 24 men in this counseling group. The ISB scores of this group were compared with the scores of a noncounseling group consisting of all students in the test-retest study who had not undergone psychological counseling (123 women and 132 men).

In the mother sample, the validity of the ISB was evaluated by comparing the ISB scores of 44 mothers with a clinical psychologist's ratings of the personal-social adjustment of these mothers.[2] The psychologist, a Fels Institute Home Visitor, had routinely visited these mothers in their homes at least twice a year as part of the Fels longitudinal study of maternal behavior to observe these mothers in interaction with their children. In addition, the mothers had, at various times, been interviewed by the Home Visitor concerning their relationships, not only with their children, but also with their husbands, with their friends, and with the community at large. On the basis of this information, the Home Visitor rated the personal-social adjustment of the mothers, using a graphic rating scale specifically constructed for the present study.

TABLE 53–1   *Means and Standard Deviations of Incomplete Sentences Blank Scores for College Group, by Scorers*

	WOMEN		MEN	
SCORER	MEAN	SD	MEAN	SD
First tests				
Scorer A	131.6	14.80	128.8	16.28
Scorer B	127.9	17.63	129.3	13.67
Scorer C	131.1	13.89	130.1	15.30
Retests				
Scorer A	133.2	20.95	132.4	17.12
Scorer B	128.8	24.08	133.5	15.03
Scorer C	133.0	17.97	126.8	16.67

Results

INTERSCORER RELIABILITY

In a student sample (original ISB's of 40 randomly selected freshmen women), the product-moment correlations between scorers were: Scorers A and B, .94; Scorers B and C, .94; Scorers A and C, .95. Interscorer agreement on 45 ISB's of the mother sample was .98. These reliabilities compare favorably with the correlation of .96 for college female ISB's

---

[2] Mrs. Anne Preston was the Fels Home Visitor who rated the adjustment of the mothers.

reported in the ISB manual. Table 53-1 summarizes the data on the means and standard deviations of the three scorers for the male and female college student ISB's. Analyses of variance were performed on the means, and Bartlett's test for homogeneity of variance (Anderson & Bancroft, 1952, pp. 141-144) was run on the variances. Analyses of variance resulted in the following F's: original test of female Ss, .75; retests of female Ss, .60; original tests of male Ss, .08; and retests of male Ss, 2.19. None of these F's was significant. Likewise, none of the tests for homogeneity of variance resulted in significant differences. The following $Q/1$ values were obtained: original test of female ISB's, 2.74; female retests, 3.70; original tests of male Ss, 1.35; and male retests, 0.80. Thus, in no group, male or female, original test or retest, was there a significant difference among the means or variances of the scores assigned by the three scorers. These results are promising. They suggest that high interscorer agreement can be found among ISB scorers with minimal psychological training who have been trained exclusively with the ISB manual.

TEST-RETEST EFFECTS ON MEANS AND VARIANCES

Table 53-2 gives the test-retest data. The mean test-retest differences did not differ significantly from zero. An F of 1.35 was obtained which was not significant for 6 and 264 degrees of freedom. The variances of

TABLE 53–2   *Test-Retest Reliability of the Incomplete Sentences Blank for College Students*

	ORIGINAL TESTS		RETESTS		
GROUP	MEAN	SD	MEAN	SD	r
Women: 6 months retest	129.9	15.88	131.9	15.81	.54
Women: 1 year retest	127.4	14.43	130.7	21.46	.50
Women: 3 years retest	133.3	15.36	132.3	24.82	.44
Men: 6 months retest	127.8	15.00	133.4	16.44	.43
Men: 1 year retest	128.5	13.53	125.7	16.62	.52
Men: 3 years retest	132.0	16.37	133.6	15.18	.38

these differences, however, were not equal from group to group. Bartlett's test for homogeneity of variance resulted in a $Q/1$ of 11.02, significant at the .05 level for five degrees of freedom. Inspection suggests that the greater variability of the variances of the retest scores for women after one and three years accounts for this finding. If a combined hypothesis that the mean test-retest differences equal zero and that the variances of these test-retest differences also equal zero is tested by Fisher's procedure for combining two independent probabilities (Fisher, 1936, p. 104), the results are not significant. In general, then, it would appear that retest performance showed no consistent pattern of difference from original test performance.

TEST-RETEST RELIABILITY

Table 53-2 also summarizes the test-retest reliability data. The reliability coefficients, ranging from .38 to .54, are not very satisfactory. These coefficients indicate that, if the ISB is to be used for experimental problems, as suggested by the test authors, there should be no great time lapse between ISB administration and the measurement of experimental variables to be correlated with ISB performance. However, all correlations were significantly different from zero beyond the .01 level of confidence, indicating that the ISB measures more than momentary moods or reactive states.

The test-retest reliability of ISB performance in the mother group was also evaluated. Their original test mean was 132.6, with a standard deviation of 18.01. Their retest mean and standard deviation were 135.5 and 20.48, respectively. The mothers had a median interval of twenty months between testing. The correlation of their test-retest scores was .70. This figure is considerably higher than any of the test-retest correlations of the college women. While no exact reason can be given for the greater test-retest reliability of the mothers' ISB's, there are at least two likely explanations. First, the test and retest situations for the mothers were exactly the same. On the other hand, the college students wrote their original ISB's as part of a required series of placement tests given when they arrived on campus, while their participation in the retest administration was voluntary. A second possibility may have been the difference in the environments of the two samples. While it can be assumed that most of the mothers' lives were relatively stable, the college students were moving from home environments to college and job environments entailing many new experiences and adjustments.

NORMATIVE DATA

The means and standard deviations of the original tests in Table 53-2 also serve to confirm the normative means and standard deviations reported by the test authors in their manual. They reported a mean of 127.4 and a standard deviation of 14.4 for 85 freshmen women and a mean of 127.5 and a standard deviation of 14.2 for 214 freshmen men at Ohio State University (Rotter & Rafferty, 1950, p. 11). In the present study, an analysis of variance was run on four samples of women (Rotter's sample and the three Antioch College original test samples). The analysis yielded an F value of 1.13, which was not significant. Bartlett's test for homogeneity of variance for the four samples yielded a nonsignificant $Q/1$ value of 3.32. When an analysis of variance was run on Rotter's male sample and the three Antioch College samples of men, a nonsignificant F of 0.55 was obtained. Bartlett's test for homogeneity of variance on these samples yielded a nonsignificant $Q/1$ of 2.00. The comparability of these ISB data from students of two different colleges (a large state university and a small liberal arts college with a work-study program) suggests that the norms presented in the ISB manual may be found to be applicable in a variety of college settings.

VALIDITY DATA

Table 53–3 indicates that ISB's given at college entrance did differentiate students who entered psychological counseling within two years from those who did not. The biserial correlations between ISB scores and presence in, or absence from, the counseling group were moderate for both men and women. They were lower than the biserial correlations of .50 for women and .62 for men reported by Rotter and Rafferty in the ISB manual (1950, pp. 8-9). However, different criteria were used in the two studies. Rotter and Rafferty used direct ratings of adjustment, while the present study used a criterion of entering or not entering psychological counseling. The mother sample data of the present study appear relevant here. The mothers' adjustment was rated by a clinical psychologist, a criterion more directly comparable to that used by Rotter and Rafferty. The product-moment correlation of .49 between the psychologist's ratings and the ISB scores of the 44 mothers compares favorably with Rotter's biserial correlation of .50 for female students.

| | WOMEN | | MEN | |
| | COUN-SELING | NONCOUN-SELING | COUN-SELING | NONCOUN-SELING |
STATISTIC				
N	65	123	24	132
Mean	141.8	129.6	140.1	129.3
SD	19.5	15.6	17.9	15.2
r_{bis}		.42		.37
t		4.61		3.03
p		<.01		<.01

TABLE 53–3   *Incomplete Sentences Blank Scores of Students Seeking and Not Seeking Psychological Counseling*

While the data in Table 53–3 indicate that college students who sought psychological counseling were differentiated from those who did not, they do not indicate how accurately a student would be assigned to the counseling or noncounseling groups on the basis of his ISB score. When the cutting score of 135 suggested in the ISB manual (Rotter & Rafferty, 1950, p. 9) was applied to the ISB's summarized in Table 53–3, that score correctly classified 64 per cent of the noncounseling women and 63 per cent of the noncounseling men and correctly identified 66 per cent of the women and 54 per cent of the men in psychological counseling.

Summary

In the present study, the reliability and validity of the Rotter Incomplete Sentences Blank were investigated in samples of college students from a small liberal arts college and in a sample of middle-class mothers. The following results were obtained: (1) High interscorer agreement was found among scorers who had relatively little psychological training (a B.A. in psychology or less) and who were trained exclusively on the ISB manual. In all cases, interscorer reliabilities were above .90. Scores assigned to the various samples of Ss had comparable means and variances from scorer to scorer. (2) Moderate test-retest reliability behavior was found for periods up to three years, suggesting that the ISB measures more than temporary moods. The test-retest reliability of the mothers' ISB's was somewhat higher than that found in the college students. This difference may have been due to the greater stability of the mothers' environment or to the fact that the test-retest situations were more similar for the mothers than for the students. (3) No consistent changes in means and variances were found upon retest. (4) The normative data obtained in the present study did not differ significantly from the normative data presented by the ISB authors. This finding suggests that the authors' ISB norms may be found to be applicable in a variety of college settings. (5) When entering psychological counseling versus not entering psychological counseling was used as a criterion of college student adjustment, the ISB was found to have moderate screening validity, somewhat lower than that reported by the authors of the test. That this lower validity may have been due to the criterion used in the present study is suggested by the fact that, for the mother sample, where the criterion of adjustment was similar to that employed by Rotter and Rafferty, their validity figures were duplicated.

REFERENCES

Anderson, R. L., & Bancroft, T. A. Statistical theory in research. New York: McGraw-Hill, 1952.

Buros, O. K. (Ed.) The fourth mental measurements yearbook. Highland Park, N.J.: Gryphon, 1953.

Fisher, R. A. Statistical methods for research workers. Edinburgh: Oliver & Boyde, 1936.

ROTTER, J. B., RAFFERTY, JANET, & SCHACHTITZ, EVA. Validation of the Rotter incomplete sentences blank for college screening. *J. consult. Psychol.*, 1949, 13, 348–356.

ROTTER, J. B., & RAFFERTY, JANET. *Manual for the Rotter incomplete sentences blank, college form.* New York: Psychological Corp., 1950.

54

Productivity of Clinical Hypotheses on a Sentence Completion Test[1]

RUE L. CROMWELL AND
RICHARD M. LUNDY

*The characteristics of a good sentence stem—a topic whose importance
is seemingly belied by the lack of research devoted to it—is the main
focus of this study. The authors demonstrated that some stems were
consistently judged to be superior as sources of interpretative hypotheses
for two independent samples of subjects and judges. They further stated
that many of the good items referred to the first person, whereas the
poorer items referred to the third person. The good items referred to
the present and were emotionally charged, whereas the poor items
referred to the past and contained little affect.*

*They offer no quantitative support for these conclusions, and it can
be readily demonstrated that, in fact, they are unwarranted. I have
classified the 65 stems with regard to affect as consisting of 4 positive,
14 negative, and 47 neutral stems. It is, therefore, noteworthy that the
four most productive stems were all negative. Further, the alleged
superiority of the first-person stems in comparison to the third-person
stems breaks down when one takes cognizance of the fact that all the
negative stems which refer to persons are in the first person. The simplest
and most justifiable conclusion is, therefore, that the negative stems
proved most effective in describing this neuropsychiatric population.*

[1] Acknowledgments are offered to the staff and trainees of Chillicothe VA Hospital
and to the VA psychologists throughout the country who assisted in this research.

This paper is published with the permission of the Chief Medical Director, Department of Medicine and Surgery, Veterans Administration, who assumes no responsibility
for the opinions expressed or conclusions drawn by the authors.

Clearly, further research is needed on other kinds of stems and their efficacy for other populations. (See, for example, in this volume, Sacks, Chap. 50).

Reviews of the literature on the sentence completion test (Rotter, 1951; Sacks & Levy, 1950) indicate that the SCT is frequently used in the diagnosis of adult personality problems. Rotter and Willerman (1947) used the test as a method of studying personality in the military setting; Machover (1949) discusses its function as a part of the total diagnostic program in a psychiatric hospital; Stein (1947) and Sacks (1949) suggest methods of interpreting material produced on the SCT. Also, Sacks and Levy (1950) have emphasized the use of the SCT as an instrument in forming clinical hypotheses about the emotional attitudes and mechanisms of the patient.

In these and other studies (e.g., Hadley & Kennedy, 1949; Lehner, 1947; Meltzoff, 1951; Rosenberg, 1950), sentence stems incorporated into tests have been selected on a priori basis or from clinical experience, depending on the purpose of the test. Though tests so designed may furnish hypotheses to the clinician about patients, the degree to which the various stems are used in making those hypotheses remains unknown. The impression of the authors is that some stems consistently produce many clinical hypotheses, while others consistently do not. This research has been designed to find those stems which are consistently most productive. It is assumed that, with a given test length, the more useful the material is in making and supporting hypotheses, the better position the clinician is in when evaluating the patient.

Types of SCT instructions have been discussed by Rotter (1951), Sacks and Levy (1950), and Meltzoff (1951). Instructions emphasizing (1) "real feelings" and (2) speed are commonly recognized. These two kinds are studied here in relation to their effect on productivity of hypotheses for the test as a whole.

Procedure

CONSTRUCTION OF TEST

Sixty-five stems were chosen for the test. This seemed to be the maximum number a hospital patient could complete in one session without undue effort and fatigue. Forty stems were taken from the Rotter Incomplete Sentences Blank, Adult Form, because a great deal of research has already been done on them in other situations. The remaining 25 stems were created to secure further information about ward adjustment of patients,[2] patient identification, and the utility of stems using the third-person pronoun.

Two different sets of instructions were used. They were alternated from patient to patient. One set emphasized speed, and the other emphasized "real feelings" as in the Rotter ISB, as follows:

"Set S. This is a test of your *speed* of thinking. Complete the following sentences as *quickly* as you can. Write down on each line the first idea that occurs to you. It makes no difference whether the statement you write is true or not. Do not start until the examiner tells you to begin."

"Set F. Compete these sentences to express your real feelings. Try to do every one. Be sure to make a complete sentence."

With the subjects who received the speed instructions, a stop watch was used as a prop.

The order of the sentence stems, as well as the instructions, was varied from subject to subject. The stems were reproduced on five pages, 13 stems to a page. The order of the pages was systematically alternated throughout both subject samples. By this means the subjects, and the clinical judges also, did not consistently respond to the same stem order on every test. For the second sample of 30 subjects, the stems were reshuffled and a new order was arranged on each page. This complete rearrangement of stem order was made to prevent context variables from affecting the results.

SUBJECTS

The SCT"s, thus constructed, were administered to 60 patients soon after their admission to Chillicothe VA Hospital. The subjects were divided into two samples of 30 each (Sample A and Sample B). No regard was given to the reason for admission or the diagnosis. If a patient was too disturbed or uncooperative to complete as many as 55 of the 65 stems, he was not used in the research.

JUDGES

After the protocols had been completed by the patients, they were sent in pairs, together with a standard set of instructions, to clinical psychologists who acted as judges. Thirty-five judges were selected by geographical stratified sampling of VA neuropsychiatric hospitals throughout the country. Four judges were selected locally. This method of

---

[2] Another study is being planned to investigate the use of the SCT in predicting ward adjustment.

selection afforded a wide sample of theoretical approaches currently used among VA psychologists.[3] Each of the 39 judges evaluated either one or two of the 60 protocols. No judge judged protocols from both Sample A and Sample B.

The judges were asked to make hypotheses about the subject from the completed protocol in the same way they would if they were writing a case report of the individual. They were then asked to list these formulated hypotheses and to put after each one the code numbers of the completed sentences used in deriving the hypothesis. Inferences about ward adjustment were also made and listed separately.

Results

From the lists of personality inferences returned by the judges, the number of times each judge used each stem was tabulated. No attention was given to the nature of the hypotheses or the number of stems used for a single hypothesis. The number of times any judge referred to any one stem ranged from zero to six times.

The number of times an individual judge referred to completed stems in a single protocol ranged from 15 to 112. If a simple frequency count were used in evaluating the productivity of individual stems, the judges making frequent references to stems would have a greater influence on the results than those judges who made infrequent references to them. To control this factor, the number of times each stem was used by each judge was divided by the total number of times he made references to *all* stems. The resulting weighted scores allowed each judge of each protocol to contribute equally to the results.

The weighted scores were summated for each of the 65 sentence stems for both Sample A and Sample B, giving each stem two productivity scores. These two sets of scores were correlated to see if the stem productivity was consistent from one sample to the other. The product-moment correlation was $+.745$.

The next step was to find a cutting point in the data in order to select the most productive stems for a final test form suitable for administration. By inspection, a cutting point was determined between the 45th and 46th stem, arranged in order of productivity. Of the 45 best stems in Sample A, 41 were also among the best 45 of Sample B. A rank-difference correlation of $+.401$ was obtained between the ranking of the best 45 in Sample A and their ranking in Sample B. This correlation is considerably below the correlation for all 65 stems, thus indicating

---

[3] Among these 39 judges, 7 called their approach psychoanalytic; 13, modified, broad, eclectic, or neopsychoanalytic; 8, eclectic; 4, learning or social learning; 3, Sullivanian; 1, Jungian; 1, client-centered; 1, neo-Adlerian; 1, perceptual-cultural.

that some stems which were consistently poor in productivity were eliminated. This final selection of 45 stems represents a compromise between
the goals of high productivity and optimal test length for behavior
sampling.

In order to obtain the most reliable ranking, the productivity scores
from Samples A and B were added together for each stem. With the
Spearman-Brown formula, we can estimate the correlation between these
final productivity scores (combined from A and B) and the productivity
scores from a proposed second set of judges and protocols similarly
obtained. This inferred correlation coefficient, computed as +.85, is the
estimated reliability of this final ranking of the stems:

1. People who push me around	34. The happiest time
2. My greatest worry	35. He wants
3. My greatest fear	36. I want to know
4. I like to break	37. I wish
5. Marriage	38. What pains me
6. The only trouble	39. I should obey
7. The future	40. The best
8. Sometimes	41. What worried us was
9. My mind	42. My nerves
10. I'll try to	43. Men
11. I suffer	44. My friends
12. I like	45. At bedtime
13. A mother	46. Back home
14. I need	47. Our
15. I am very	48. Telling the truth
16. I failed	49. It
17. I can't	50. This place
18. Other people	51. In the service
19. Most women	52. They will
20. I secretly	53. In school
21. My father	54. Dancing
22. I regret	55. She needs
23. I	56. In the past we
24. People	57. They
25. She	58. AWOL
26. He	59. My superior officer
27. I am best when	60. They had
28. I hate	61. Negroes
29. I feel	62. It seemed very
30. What annoys me	63. Reading
31. Fighting	64. Where I worked
32. When I was a child	65. Sports
33. I should	

The final step in the analysis was to compare the "real feeling"
instructions with the speed instructions in terms of total test produc-

tivity. The difference was not significant. However, the design did not permit comparison of instructions from ratings by the same judge. This finding, therefore, may have resulted from uncontrolled judge variability that masked real differences between instructions.

Discussion

In general, the results have supported the hypothesis that there are consistent individual differences in the productivity of sentence completion stems. The choice of stems for a test does make a difference as to how valuable the test is in sampling behavior. The correlation of +.745 between stem productivity scores of two subject samples attests to the consistency with which some stems are more productive than others.

By setting the cutting point at 45 and dropping the poorest 20 stems, we derived a test form that seems to be of appropriate size for personality evaluation in neuropsychiatric hospitals. It extracts a good deal of information from the average patient without becoming a burdensome task. Nevertheless, the test size could be shortened or lengthened to meet the needs of the individual clinician. For a short screening blank, the first 15 stems could be used. Ten of the first 15 stems in Sample A were among the most productive 15 in Sample B. The test could also be used flexibly as a time-limit rather than a work-limit test. The patient could start at the beginning and work until it was convenient for him to stop.

In this empirical investigation, there arises the question of what qualities make a stem productive or nonproductive. To pursue this question, the first ten stems may be compared with the last ten stems in the list above. It appears from examining these extremes of productive and nonproductive stems that no single factor differentiates the two groups. Many of the good stems refer to the first person (I, me, my), whereas many of the poor stems have third-person or impersonal references. Also, the poor stems often refer to activities with little "emotional" involvement. The good stems, on the other hand, are often built around hostilities, worries, troubles, and fears. Finally, the poor stems refer more often to past situations, whereas the productive stems deal more with the present and the future.

It is interesting to note that the SCT does not appear to be a fertile technique for investigating past and childhood experiences. Not only are past-tense references prevalent among the poor stems listed above, but stems such as "Back home" and "When I was a child" are low in the list. Whether it is because of the patients' ability to respond, the interests of the clinician in using the test, or the inherent nature of the stems, it seems that the SCT in the hospital situation is more fertile in sampling statements of present attitudes and future goals.

A next step in the development of this SCT would be a validation of clinical hypotheses derived from it. Such a study would yield a final SCT that is both productive and of known validity.

Summary and Conclusions

An incomplete sentences test of 65 stems was given to 60 newly admitted VA neuropsychiatric hospital patients. The order of the stems and two different sets of instructions were alternated from subject to subject. Thirty-nine clinical psychologists in various VA hospitals made personality inferences from the protocols and listed the completed sentences used in making the inferences.

The major findings were:

1. A correlation showed the individual differences in stem productivity to be significantly consistent from the first sample of 30 subjects to the second sample of 30 subjects.

2. A test of 45 highly productive stems was devised as appropriate for psychological evaluation in neuropsychiatric hospitals.

3. Results suggested that many of the more productive stems referred to the first person, the present and future, and "emotional" aspects of the subject.

4. No difference was found between speed and "real feeling" instructions with respect to test productivity.

REFERENCES

Hadley, J. M., & Kennedy, Vera E. A comparison between performance on a sentence completion test and academic success. *Educ. psychol. Measmt*, 1949, 9, 649–670.

Lehner, G. F. J. Projections of men and women to items referring to the same and the opposite sex on a sentence completion test. *Amer. Psychologist*, 1947, 2, 407. (Abstract)

Machover, S. (Ed.). Case reports in clinical psychology, Brooklyn, N.Y.: Kings County Hospital, Vol. 1, No. 1, August, 1949.

Meltzoff, J. The effect of mental set and item structure upon response to a projective test. *J. abnorm. soc. Psychol.*, 1951, 46, 177–189.

Rosenberg, S. Some relationships between attitudes expressed toward the parent in a sentence completion test case history data. *J. proj. Tech.*, 1950, 14, 188–193.

Rotter, J. B. Word association and sentence completion methods. In H. H. Anderson & Gladys L. Anderson (Eds.), *An introduction to projective techniques.* Englewood Cliffs, N.J.: Prentice-Hall, 1951. Pp. 279–311.

ROTTER, J. B., & WILLERMAN, B. The incomplete sentences test as a method of studying personality. *J. consult. Psychol.,* 1947, 11, 43–48.

SACKS, J. M. Effect upon projective responses of stimuli referring to the subject and to others. *J. consult. Psychol.,* 1949, 13, 12–21.

SACKS, J. M., & LEVY, S. The sentence completion test. In L. E. Abt & L. Bellak (Eds.), *Projective psychology.* New York: Knopf, 1950. Pp. 357–402.

STEIN, M. I. The use of a sentence completion test for the diagnosis of personality. *J. clin. Psychol.,* 1947, 3, 47–56.

55

The Stability of Interpretations of Sentence Completion Tests[1]

DONALD W. FISKE AND CHARLES VAN BUSKIRK

The crux of Fiske and Van Buskirk's study is that a judge's median Q-sort correlation of different subjects' relative need strengths gleaned from their SCT performance exceeded his median correlation for a single subject on different occasions about 25 per cent of the time. One limitation to the study was the sparse number of subjects (four college students and four patients). Another is the fact that taking a test repeatedly may alter the set of the subject. He may become bored with giving the same answer again and avoid monotony by creating a response of a different genre. This may give a false picture of the validity of the SCT, if one inaccurately reasons that response stability is necessary for validity. Perhaps the key point of this paper, then, is that undoubtedly some stems lead to more unstable responses than others. Since Stephens[a] has shown that unstable items are positively correlated with changing behavior, it is clear as to why retest reliability of the SCT may be low, whereas its validity is high. Validity in this case is measured on a given occasion. Some weeks or months later, the actual behavior may change, and the SCT will reflect this fact. Under these circumstances, test-retest reliability does not give a true picture of the

[1] We are greatly indebted to Ralph Heine, Joanne Powers, and Loren Chapman for serving as judges in this experiment. We also wish to thank Sol Garfield for making it possible to collect the Downey data. This study was supported in part by a grant from the Social Science Research Committee of the University of Chicago.

[a] M. W. Stephens. "The Incomplete Sentences Blank: Sources of Variance in Retest Reliability," *Journal of Clinical Psychology*, 16 (1960), 331–333.

test's reliability. Care should be taken, therefore, to separate intrinsically unstable items from those which reflect true changes in behavior.

In previous studies of repeated administrations of sentence completion tests, Osterweil and Fiske (1956; Fiske, 1957) have found that the great majority of responses are changed from one testing to the next. In terms of manifest content, only a few of a person's responses will be the same on two administrations.

This finding raises a question: if the manifest content changes so markedly, does the personality picture inherent in the protocol also change from one time to the next, or does the same picture emerge from two protocols even though their manifest content is different? Osterweil and Fiske (1956) decided that two different protocols from the same person would probably lead to slightly different interpretive pictures. But how should the extent and the significance of such differences be assessed? In view of the fact that projective techniques are commonly used to obtain an individualized picture of a person, the present authors formulated this specific and practical question: are the differences between the interpretations of protocols from the same person less than the differences between interpretations of protocols of different persons? Thus interindividual variation—variation between individuals —provides a frame of reference for evaluating the extent of intraindividual variability—variation or inconsistency within a person over time.

Method

Our judges interpreted each protocol in terms of an ordering of needs with respect to salience or strength in the hierarchical configuration of an individual's personality. More concretely, each judge did a Q sort of 30 need variables. We used a conceptual framework developed by Van Buskirk and Yufit (1956) to obtain personality profiles in connnection with a study of academic adjustment being conducted by the Examiner's Office at the University of Chicago. In this approach, a need is a valued goal with characteristic feelings and actions associated with it: examples are Harmavoidance, Emotionality, Affiliation, Sentience, and Disjunctivity. Each judge was given a list of the variables and their definitions.[2]

In their Q sorts, the judges used a fixed distribution with 10 steps. Q sorts were used because the correlation between sorts permits a rapid

---

[2] Copies of the variables and their definitions can be obtained from the authors.

and objective determination of the relative agreement or disagreement between two interpretations. Such a measure is appropriate because we were interested in the relative position of each need, not in its absolute strength.

SUBJECTS

We began by using available protocols. From a group of University of Chicago students tested nine times at weekly intervals (Fiske, 1957), we picked four Ss and took their first, fifth, and ninth protocols—these being obtained at one-month intervals. The four men formed a sample stratified on intraindividual variability: out of 30 men, we selected the 3rd, 11th, 19th, and 26th in terms of consistency of manifest content over the full nine trials.

At a later time, we decided that our first group of Ss might be too homogeneous and that our Sentence Completion Test might be too short. We then tested four patients at Downey VA Hospital, two men and two women. These were essentially a random sample, except that one was taken from each of four buildings and each had to be willing to take the test and sufficiently in contact to do so. Their ages were 32 to 56. As it happened, all four were diagnosed as paranoid schizophrenics. However, the four case histories were quite different. The intervals between the successive pairs of the three tests ranged from 20 to 38 days.

INSTRUMENTS

The Sentence Completion Test administered to the Chicago students was a 25-item form derived from one compiled and developed by Osterweil and Fiske (1956). The Sacks Sentence Completion Test (Sacks & Levy, 1950) was used with the Downey patients. It has 60 items.

JUDGES

Arrangements were made to permit each author to judge each protocol blindly. In addition, one experienced clinician judged the Chicago protocols, and the Downey protocols were judged by one experienced clinician and by a research psychologist with less clinical experience.

PROCEDURE

The protocols were presented to the judges in a random order with respect to subject and to the orders of each S's three protocols (first, second, or third testings), with the restriction that no pair of protocols from the same S were next to each other. Half the judges had the same order and the other half had this order reversed. The judges did their judging in several sessions.

The 12 sorts made by a judge on one of the S samples were intercorrelated. The intercorrelations for each judge were analyzed separately —the several judges providing replications of the basic design. This approach made it possible to eliminate interjudge differences from the comparisons of interpretations. Furthermore, the primary effect of any unreliability in the judge (variation in judgments over time) would be only to depress all the correlations between his interpretive sorts.

Results

The unit of analysis was the interpretation of a single protocol by a single judge. For a given judge, we compared this interpretation with

---

TABLE 55–1   *Median Intercorrelations with Protocols from the Same (Intra) and from Different (Inter) Persons**

STUDENT SUBJECTS

SUBJECT	TRIAL	JUDGE I INTRA	INTER	JUDGE II INTRA	INTER	JUDGE III INTRA	INTER
	1	.54	.04	.37	.15	.70	.51
A	2	.60	−.07	.43	−.05	.77	.45
	3	.40	−.10	.22	−.05	.68	.48
	1	.38	.11	.79	.00	.43	**.55**
B	2	.47	.04	.74	.02	.60	.32
	3	.34	−.23	.82	.17	.55	.03
	1	.05	−.07	−.06	−.32	.40	**.51**
C	2	.32	−.07	.20	**.28**	.48	**.53**
	3	−.05	**.19**	.14	.13	.55	.49
	1	.55	−.11	.12	−.04	.44	.40
D	2	.42	−.12	−.16	**.29**	.40	**.51**
	3	.51	.04	.06	.01	.48	.36

PATIENT SUBJECTS

SUBJECT	TRIAL	JUDGE I INTRA	INTER	JUDGE II INTRA	INTER	JUDGE IV INTRA	INTER	JUDGE V INTRA	INTER
	1	.62	.17	.21	**.37**	.78	.51	.21	**.32**
E	2	.60	.32	.28	.18	.76	.58	.35	.16
	3	.69	.38	−.07	**.02**	.79	.63	.21	**.32**
	1	.84	.16	.55	.15	−.09	−.22	−.04	**.12**
F	2	.80	.26	.58	.21	.30	**.40**	.04	**.29**
	3	.77	−.06	.48	.28	.21	**.58**	.22	**.32**
	1	.54	.42	.51	.21	.36	**.51**	.29	.29
G	2	.58	.32	.42	**.44**	.31	**.48**	.29	**.36**
	3	.47	.37	.39	.12	.18	−.21	−.04	**.25**
	1	.74	.17	.59	.21	.72	.51	.50	.31
H	2	.64	.21	.63	.33	.72	.51	.44	.25
	3	.73	.23	.63	.26	.77	.42	.62	.41

* Bold-faced values are interperson medians that exceed the corresponding intraperson medians.

the other two interpretations from the same S and with the nine interpretations from the other Ss. The Q sort form of the interpretations
permitted us to compute a correlation between any two of them. We
used the median correlation of each class of protocols; that is, we compared the median of the two within-person correlations with the median
of the between-person correlations. The results are presented in Table 55–1.

Among 84 comparisons of this sort, there were 21 protocols (25 per
cent) where the median interperson correlation exceeded the median
intraperson correlation. In other words, in one-quarter of the instances,
the interpretation of a protocol tended to agree better with interpretations for other cases than with those for the same case. Other analyses
of the total distributions of the correlations gave a similar picture to
this result found with the medians: about 25 per cent misclassification.

Note that the criterion was simply whether the within-person median
is above (or below) the between-person median, not whether it is
significantly different.

When we examined the stability of the Ss separately, we found there
was only one in each set of four Ss (A and H respectively) who was
consistently differentiated by all three or all four judges. For the remaining Ss, reversals in which the between-person median exceeded the
within-person median occurred in 11 to 44 per cent of the judge-protocol
combinations.

In terms of judges, there were reversals in six out of seven instances:
only one judge successfully differentiated all 12 protocols in one set
(Judge I for patient Ss).

Discussion

There was a possibility that each set of cases was perhaps so homogeneous that differentiation between them was very difficult. As a check
on this, we examined the overlap between protocols in terms of their
manifest content. We counted the number of items on which each pair
of protocols had the same or almost the same response, using a strict
criterion for sameness (cf. Fiske, 1957).

For each protocol, we found the protocol with which it overlapped
most. For 22 of the 24 protocols, the highest overlap was with another
protocol from the same person. For the other two, there was little
overlap and there were tied values; but on a chance basis they would
probably be misclassified. Thus, the manifest content differentiated the
individual cases better than the judges' interpretations. The same result
was obtained in a comparison of the median intraperson overlap with
the median interperson overlap in manifest content.

We may therefore conclude that the judges' results are not due to the homogeneity of manifest content among the Ss compared: the different Ss gave different and distinctive responses.

As another check, we compared the median correlations between cases in each group with the median of a sample of correlations between student cases and patient cases. Again, there was no evidence that the homogeneity of each group accounts for our results.

The limited numbers of Ss and judges restrict the confidence in any broad generalization from these findings. However, we feel that the data clearly indicate that one protocol differs in manifest content so much from other protocols of the same S that its interpretation will frequently resemble the interpretations of his other protocols *less* than it resembles interpretations for other Ss. This finding contradicts the assumption that the uniqueness of a single personality can be delineated in an interpretation of a sample of behavior obtained at one point in time.

The purpose of this paper is to point out the existence of this problem. The complexity of the problem is indicated by the considerable variation between Ss and also between judges in the extent of differentiation. The extent of overlap may also be different for other interpretive systems and for other techniques. It may be less (or more!) for the extensive sample of behavior provided by a full diagnostic battery. On the basis of our findings, however, it would seem necessary for clinicians performing individual diagnostic evaluations to establish that their formulations not only differentiate between cases but also are stable over time.

Summary

Sets of sentence completion protocols were judged in terms of a Q sort of need variables. Since each set contained three protocols from each of four subjects, it was possible to compare the agreement between interpretations of each subject's three protocols with the agreement between interpretations for different subjects. In 25 per cent of the comparisons, the agreement was higher with protocols for different subjects than with the other protocols from the same subject. Thus, a single protocol may be an insufficient basis for an interpretation that differentiates one person from other people.

REFERENCES

Fiske, D. W. An intensive study of variability scores. *Educ. psychol. Measmt*, 1957, 17, 453–465.

Osterweil, J., & Fiske, D. W. Intra-individual variability in sentence completion responses. *J. abnorm. soc. Psychol.*, 1956, 52, 195–199.

Sacks, J. M., & Levy, S. The sentence completion test. In L. E. Abt & L. Bellak (Eds.), *Projective psychology*. New York: Knopf, 1950. Pp. 357–402.

Van Buskirk, C., & Yufit, R. I. A quantitative, ideographic method for scoring projective data. *Amer. Psychologist*, 1956, 11, 364. (Abstract)

56

The Prediction of the Psychiatric Patient's Work Adjustment[1]

BERNARD A. STOTSKY AND HENRY WEINBERG

The ability of the SCT to predict adjustment of a psychiatric inpatient group to a therapeutic work situation is demonstrated in this study. Even further, the SCT was able to predict the extent of improvement six months later with equal facility. Why does the SCT fare so well? If research studies are an index of potential utility, then the SCT should be the "king" of projective techniques. In the Stotsky and Weinberg study, it may be noted that the nine variables studied focus strongly on positive reactions, persistence, and drive. These variables are the kinds that are most accessible to consciousness and within the control of the subject. These are also readily observable characteristics, thus presumably enabling the criterion judges to make reliable ratings. The word presumably is used because in actuality no reliability values for the ratings are provided in the study. In any event, the fact that both the prediction variable and the criterion involve behavior which is highly conscious and overt should make for reasonably high validity.

Does this mean that the information provided by the SCT could be obtained just as easily by asking the subject to rate himself on these behaviors? We can't say, because no such self-ratings were collected. It is possible, however, that culturally conditioned response habits of referring to the self may vitiate the meaningfulness of data collected through direct interviews, even though the subject does not necessarily

[1] From VA Hospital, Brockton, Massachusetts. Acknowledgment is made to V. Zilaitis and Evelyn Lafer for their assistance. The authors are preparing a more theoretical article on the topic of work and the ego.

899

wish to suppress this information. The SCT may, however, be a kind of preconscious test with just enough novelty to allow the subject to project many conscious overt aspects of himself without arousing the conditioned limiting reactions that occur when one is directly asked something about himself. It is, however, high time for the diagnostic efficiency of all our projective techniques to be ascertained by comparing the information they present with simple self-reports in response to direct questions.

Carefully controlled work assignments are being used increasingly as a way of rehabilitating chronic psychiatric patients who have lost their ability to work productively as a result of long hospitalizations. To utilize this mode of treatment effectively, psychologists must learn more about the role of work in the psychological economy of the individual so that ultimately they can use such knowledge in the rehabilitation process. As a first step in this direction, a means of assessing the strengths and weaknesses of the individual in the work area becomes necessary.

Method

The technique utilized in this study is a form of the sentence completion test. Although this is not the only technique possible, it has several features which especially recommend it. From the modest beginnings in the work of Tendler (1930), there has been an accelerated use of the sentence completion test in more refined, sophisticated ways for the exploration of specific areas of personality (Gilmore, 1951; Kimball, 1950; Lorge & Thorndike, 1941; Rohde, 1946; Rotter & Willerman, 1947; Sacks, 1949; Shor, 1946; Stein, 1947). Especially relevant have been the studies of Gilmore (1951) and of Kimball (1950) with underachievers in the school situation. Although all investigators have used incomplete sentences, the content of the sentence stems has varied with the purpose and theoretical orientation of the investigator.

The content of the stems used here was determined by nine ego-strength dimensions or variables which were presumed to be related to successful adjustment to work demands. They were not intended to cover all types of personality problems, nor is the test meant to be a general measure of personality in the same sense as the TAT or Rorschach. Altogether, there were 81 incomplete sentence stems, of which 69 were specifically related to the variables under investigation. The remaining 12 were inserted as relatively neutral items to offset the repetitive effect of such a large number of items centering around work, persistence, goals, and reactions to people in work situations. Although some of the incomplete sentence stems had been used in unpublished studies, a large proportion of the items were made up "fresh" by the authors for this experiment.

The selected dimensions of ego strength translated into work-relevant sentence stems were the following:

1. Reactions to situations of difficulty (16 items)
2. Need achievement (after Murray) (6 items)
3. Specificity of goals (5 items)
4. Reaction to failure (5 items)
5. Self-reliance (10 items)
6. Persistence on the job in the face of boredom, distractions, temptations, and the prospect of hard work (17 items)
7. Reactions to superiors (4 items)
8. Reactions to peers (4 items)
9. Reactions to subordinates (2 items)

The remaining 12 items were neutral with respect to this study.

The items were arranged in such a fashion as to ensure that stems relating to any one dimension were not clustered too closely together. The following are representative samples of the items and the test variables to which they refer.

Item No.		Variable No.
72	Once the going got rough on the new job he	1
31	The main driving force in my life is	2
70	Dick worked best at	3
8	Bob's defeat made him	4
12	Finding no one who could help him,	5
14	When he saw that he would have to learn a lot of new things in his work, he	6
3	When Frank saw his boss coming, he	7
43	The others who were working with him	8
50	The men under me	9

SUBJECTS

The sample consisted of 80 patients in the Manual Arts (MAT) and Educational Therapy (ET) subsections of the Physical Medicine Rehabilitation Service (PMRS) at a VA neuropsychiatric hospital. MAT and ET had been selected because patients regarded as having the best prognoses for rehabilitation were assigned to these activities. The assignments to these sections were not made on the basis of psychological test findings. Of the 80 patients, 78 carried diagnoses of schizophrenia; one patient was diagnosed sociopathic personality, and one depressive reaction.

PROCEDURE

The tests were administered to the patients in groups ranging from three to eight. The instructions given to the subjects were as follows:

"Please complete each of these sentences in whatever way you wish. Work fast and answer with the first thing that comes to mind. If you have any difficulty in completing a sentence, put a circle around the number and come back to it after you have finished the rest."

A scoring key for the nine test variables was developed from the data by one of the authors, who was entirely unfamiliar with any of the patients.[2] Coding categories were set up for the purpose of classifying responses to each of the 81 sentence stems. Each response was scored in terms of whether it represented a positive, negative, or neutral reaction to the particular situation to which the material related. Responses were scored +1 for positive, −1 for negative, and 0 for neutral reactions. The scores for the individual items were then summed to obtain the total scores for the test variables to which they referred. Interrater agreement for 125 samples each of +1 and 0 items was greater than 90 per cent, but for 125 samples of −1 items, it was only 72 per cent. Subsequent analysis was therefore limited to the distribution of +1 and 0 scores. The actual coding was done by three judges. Interjudge agreement, as determined by the scoring of sample items, was greater than 90 per cent for all three judges for the scoring of 400 individual responses. After scoring was completed, the scores for each variable were computed by combining the +1 scores for that variable. Every patient thus ended up with nine scores, one for each variable.

Criteria of performance were based on ratings by PMRS therapists on a 23-item work performance scale developed by one of the authors (Stotsky, 1956). Using this scale each therapist rated patients in his care on such aspects of work performance as work habits and skills, work attitudes, and interpersonal relations on the job. The ratings were then used to divide patients into a high or low group in each of the PMRS activities, the highs consisting of patients scoring above the median and the lows of patients scoring below the median for the work performance scale. Highs and lows from the six MAT and ET activities were combined into two groups, one consisting of 40 highs and the other of 40 lows. The groups were then compared for each of the variables of the sentence completion test.

A second set of comparisons was made in terms of the outcome of treatment as observed six months later. The outcome was considered positive if the patient had progressed to a regular work assignment at the hospital for either a half or a full day or if he had left the hospital

---

[2] The test and the scoring key are available for experimental purposes and may be obtained by writing either of the two authors.

on trial visit or complete discharge. It was considered negative when the patient had remained at the same assignment in MAT or ET or had been reassigned to activity assignments for the more regressed patients, such as Occupational Therapy or Corrective Therapy.

TABLE 56–1   *Comparison for Sentence Completion Test Variables of Patients Rated High with Patients Rated Low on Work Performance in Manual Arts or Educational Therapy Activties (N=80)*

	MEDIAN	SCORES BELOW MEDIAN*		SCORES ABOVE MEDIAN		χ^2	p
VARIABLE		HIGH	LOW	HIGH	LOW		
1. Positive reaction to difficulty	5	23	35	17	5	9.0	.01
2. Need achievement	1	22	32	18	8	5.7	.02
3. Goal specificity	1	22	34	18	6	7.2	.01
4. Positive reaction to failure	1	18	33	22	7	12.2	.001
5. Self-reliance	4	20	26	20	14	1.8	.18
6. Persistence	3	10	31	30	9	22.1	.001
7. Positive reaction to superiors	2	23	32	17	8	4.7	.05
8. Positive reaction to peers	2	20	31	20	9	6.5	.02
9. Positive reaction to subordinates	1	20	36	20	4	12.3	.001
Over-all score	21.5	12	28	28	12	12.8	.001

* Includes scores at the median.

On the assumption that differences in work performance and in the outcome of treatment are related to differences in personality functioning, it was predicted that there would be a positive relationship between scores on the nine variables of the sentence completion test and the two criteria: (1) current work performance as rated by PMRS therapists and (2) outcome of treatment as measured six months later.

Statistical comparisons were made by means of the median test in accordance with the recommendations of Keith Smith (1953). A fourfold categorization was made, the medians serving as cutting points.

Results

1. *Against work performance ratings.* All relationship between the test variables and work performance ratings were positive. Eight of the

nine chi squares were significant at the .05 level, five of the nine at the .01 level. Only variable 5, "self-reliance," was not related significantly to work performance ratings. Of all the variables, No. 6, "persistence on the job in the face of boredom, distractions, temptations, and the prospect of hard work," discriminated best between the two groups, categorizing 61 out of 80 (76 per cent) correctly. The best discriminations between highs and lows for combinations of two variables were obtained by combining variables 6 and 3, 6 and 7, 6 and 8, and 6 and 9. By classifying as highs, those patients obtaining scores above the median of *either* variable and as lows those patients scoring at or below the median, each of these combinations was able to categorize 80 per cent of the patients accurately.

Further analysis of the data showed all nine variables to be significantly interrelated, with probabilities ranging from .05 to .001. Due to the presence of highly skewed distributions with large numbers of 0 and 1 scores, it was not possible to use more refined correlational techniques for further analysis. However, for each patient, an over-all score was obtained from the sum of the individual variable scores. The mean over-all score for the 40 highs was 25.2 and for the 40 lows, 12.8. Comparison of the groups by the median test (median 21.5) showed 28 highs

---

TABLE 56–2   *Relation of Positive and Negative Outcome of*
Treatment to Sentence Completion
Test Variables (N=80)

VARIABLE	MEDIAN	SCORES BELOW MEDIAN*		SCORES ABOVE MEDIAN		χ^2	p
		POSI-TIVE	NEGA-TIVE	POSI-TIVE	NEGA-TIVE		
1. Positive reaction to difficulty	5	25	33	16	6	5.6	.02
2. Need achievement	1	23	31	18	8	5.0	.03
3. Goal specificity	1	21	35	20	4	14.1	.001
4. Positive reaction to failure	1	18	33	23	6	14.3	.001
5. Self-reliance	4	12	34	29	5	27.4	.001
6. Persistence	3	12	29	29	10	16.2	.001
7. Positive reaction to superiors	2	22	33	19	6	8.9	.01
8. Positive reaction to peers	2	18	33	23	6	14.3	.001
9. Positive reaction to subordinates	1	26	30	15	9	1.7	.19
Over-all score	21.5	12	28	29	11	14.5	.001

* Includes scores at the median.

above the median and 28 lows below, for a total accuracy of 56 out of 80 (70 per cent). Actually, the over-all score discriminated the groups less well than the scores for variable 6.

2. *Against criterion of adjustment six months later.* The next step was to determine the extent to which test scores could predict patient status after six months of rehabilitation treatment. The difficulties inherent in such a prediction quickly become evident when we consider the diverse, almost uncontrollable influences operating in the patient's life. For example, such factors as (1) unforeseen changes in the personality of the patient, (2) complications introduced by such other types of treatment as psychotherapy, shock, and drugs, (3) the effect of the attitudes and behavior of doctors, psychologists, nurses, aides, etc., (4) the attitudes and behavior of the family, (5) changes in the rehabilitation program resulting from psychiatric decisions, (6) budgetary considerations, (7) turnover of personnel, and (8) the kind of social and work environment to which the patient must return—might all affect the results. Nevertheless, despite these possibly complicating factors, the usefulness of a personality test still lies in its ability to predict with accuracy and efficiency at least as great as, if not greater than, other methods.

Of the 80 patients studied, 41 showed a favorable outcome of treatment in terms of either progressing to a higher level assignment or leaving the hospital.

For eight of the test variables and for over-all score on the test, high scores were significantly related to favorable outcome of treatment. Variable 5, "Self-reliance," was best able to differentiate those patients with positive outcomes from the ones with negative outcomes, correctly categorizing 63 out of 80 (79 per cent). The over-all score classified 57 out of 80 (71 per cent) accurately. For combinations of variables, 3 and 5 best differentiated the patients, classifying 66 out of 80 (83 per cent) correctly.

Discussion

Eight of the nine variables studied were significantly related to successful performance in MAT and ET. Likewise, eight of the variables were significantly related to ultimate outcome of treatment as measured six months later. The variable "Positive reactions to subordinates" did not correlate significantly with outcome. "Self-reliance," though not significantly related to performance in MAT and ET, was best able to predict outcome of treatment. This latter finding may be explained in the following terms: self-reliance items may be measuring the striving and determination of patients to assert their independence and break their identification with the hospital community. If this is so, self-reliance would be of much greater significance in determining outcome, which involves progress toward or actual separation from the hospital, than in assessing adjustment to work activities, since the latter places greater emphasis on interpersonal factors. In the latter case, independence and self-sufficiency, if too strongly asserted, could produce difficulties in working with therapists or patients.

The results may be interpreted as supporting the validity of the test as a measure of certain personality variables presumed to be related to successful work performance in rehabilitation activities and to outcome of rehabilitation treatment. The test, by successfully predicting to the two criteria at levels far enough beyond chance, can be regarded as useful to the practicing clinician who is called on to make judgments concerning the rehabilitation potential of patients. The results from this study are sufficiently encouraging to warrant further experimental use of the test as a measure of motivation for vocational objectives.

REFERENCES

GILMORE, J. V. A new venture in the testing of motivation. *Coll. Bd. Rev.*, 1951, 15, 221–226.

KIMBALL, BARBARA. The relationship between nonintellective factors and scholastic achievement. Unpublished doctoral dissertation, Harvard Univer., 1950.

LORGE, I., & THORNDIKE, E. L. The value of responses in a completion test as indicators of personality traits. *J. appl. Psychol.*, 1941, 25, 191–199.

ROHDE, AMANDA R. Explorations in personality by the sentence completion method. *J. appl. Psychol.*, 1946, 31, 169–181.

ROTTER, J. B., & WILLERMAN, B. The incomplete sentences test as a method of studying personality. *J. consult. Psychol.*, 1947, 11, 43–48.

SACKS, J. M. The relative effect upon projective responses of stimuli referring to the subject and of stimuli referring to other persons. *J. consult. Psychol.*, 1949, 13, 12–20.

SHOR, J. Report on a verbal projective technique. *J. clin. Psychol.*, 1946, 2, 279–282.

SMITH, K. Distribution—free statistical methods and the concept of power efficiency. In L. Festinger & D. Katz (Eds.), *Research methods in the behavioral sciences*. New York: Dryden, 1953. Pp. 536–577.

STEIN, M. I. The use of a sentence completion test for the diagnosis of personality. *J. clin. Psychol.*, 1947, 3, 47–56.

STOTSKY, B. Vocational tests as predictors of performance of schizophrenics in two rehabilitation activities. *J. clin. Psychol.*, 1956, 12, 236–242.

TENDLER, A. D. A preliminary report on a test for emotional insight. *J. appl. Psychol.*, 1930, 14, 123–136.

WEINBERG, H. Unconscious conflict in cases of peptic ulcer. Unpublished doctoral dissertation, Harvard Univer., 1951.

ACKNOWLEDGMENTS

For permission to reprint the material in this book, grateful acknowledgment is made to all the authors and their publishers with regard to the following chapters:

1: *The Journal of Psychology*, 1939, **8**, 389–413.
2: *The Journal of Abnormal and Social Psychology*, 1950, **45**, 619–627.
3: *The American Journal of Orthopsychiatry*, 1953, **23**, 107–119. Copyright, the American Orthopsychiatric Association, Inc.; reproduced by permission.
4: *Perceptual and Motor Skills*, 1961, **12**, 107–125.
5: *Journal of Projective Techniques*, 1959, **23**, 263–267.
6: *Ibid.*, pp. 287–290.
7: *Ibid.*, pp. 268–272.
8: *The Journal of Abnormal and Social Psychology*, 1953, **48**, 443–445.
9: *Journal of Projective Techniques*, 1958, **22**, 432–439.
10: *American Psychologist*, 1963, **18**, 96–100.
11: *Psychological Bulletin*, 1960, **57**, 65–85.
12: *Journal of Personality*, 1951, **19**, 245–264.
13: *Psychological Monographs*, 1952, **66**, No. 5.
14: John Wiley & Sons, Inc. (Bernard I. Murstein, *Theory and Research in Projective Techniques: Emphasizing the TAT*, 1963, pp. 125–139, 148–163).
15: *Psychological Bulletin*, 1958, **55**, 121–147.
16: *The Journal of Abnormal and Social Psychology*, 1953, **48**, 25–32.
17: *Journal of Projective Techniques*, 1954, **18**, 151–164.
18: *Ibid.*, 1956, **20**, 172–180.
19: *Journal of Consulting Psychology*, 1956, **20**, 99–104.
20: *Journal of Projective Techniques*, 1956, **20**, 418–428.
21: *Ibid.*, 1953, **17**, 34–50.
22: *Psychological Bulletin*, 1949, **46**, 393–429.
23: *Journal of Consulting Psychology*, 1960, **24**, 262–275.
24: D. Van Nostrand Co., Inc. (B. M. Bass and I. A. Berg, Eds., *Objective Approaches to Personality Assessment*, 1959, pp. 136–140).
25: *The American Journal of Psychiatry*, 1951, **107**, 577–581.
26: D. Van Nostrand Co., Inc. (J. W. Atkinson, Ed., *Motives in Fantasy, Action and Society*, 1958, pp. 596–616).
27: *Journal of Consulting Psychology*, 1957, **21**, 115–120.
28: *Psychological Monographs*, 1950, **64**, No. 9.
29: John Wiley & Sons, Inc. (Bernard I. Murstein, *Theory and Research in Projective Techniques: Emphasizing the TAT*, 1963, pp. 195–229).
30: *Journal of Consulting Psychology*, 1956, **20**, 449–456.

31: *The Journal of Experimental Psychology*, 1952, 44, 391–399.
32: *The American Journal of Orthopsychiatry*, 1956, 26, 567–576. Copyright, the American Orthopsychiatric Association, Inc.; reproduced by permission.
33: *Journal of Consulting Psychology*, 1954, 18, 389–395.
34: *The Journal of Abnormal and Social Psychology*, 1957, 55, 218–221.
35: *Psychological Bulletin*, 1957, 54, 431–466.
36: *Journal of Projective Techniques*, 1959, 23, 30–32.
37: *Journal of Consulting Psychology*, 1962, 26, 156–161.
38: *Ibid.*, 1959, 23, 129–133.
39: *Ibid.*, p. 560.
40: *Ibid.*, 1958, 22, 394.
41: *Journal of Clinical Psychology*, 1962, 18, 276–279.
42: *Journal of Projective Techniques*, 1953, 17, 210–216.
43: *Psychological Bulletin*, 1963, 60, 233–251.
44: *Journal of Consulting Psychology*, 1959, 23, 25–33.
45: *Ibid.*, 1957, 21, 355–357.
46: *Journal of Projective Techniques*, 1960, 24, 353–354.
47: *Ibid.*, 1956, 20, 127–136.
48: *Journal of Clinical Psychology*, 1960, 16, 432–435.
49: *Journal of Projective Techniques and Personality Assessment*, 1965, 29, 12–45.
50: *Journal of Consulting Psychology*, 1949, 13, 12–20.
51: *The Journal of Abnormal and Social Psychology*, 1951, 46, 177–189.
52: *Journal of Consulting Psychology*, 1949, 13, 348–356.
53: *Ibid.*, 1955, 19, 345–350.
54: *Ibid.*, 1954, 18, 421–424.
55: *Ibid.*, 1959, 23, 177–180.
56: *Journal of Counseling Psychology*, 1956, 3, 3–7.

NAME INDEX

Abel, Theodora M., 124, 370, 673–674
Abramson, H. A., 718
Abramson, L. S., 120
Abt, L., 50, 696 n
Ackner, B., 398, 411
Adair, John, 293 n, 294 n, 295
Adams, A. J., 124–125
Adcock, C. J., 397, 400, 406
Addington, M. C., 709, 744
Adkins, Margaret M., 458, 548, 600
Adorno, T. W., 101–102
Ainsworth, Mary D., 409
Albee, G. W., 308, 494, 648, 663, 674
Albizer-Miranda, C., 97
Alden, Priscilla, 129
Allen, R. M., 230–231, 233, 237, 240, 274
Allport, Gordon W., 2, 35-45, 56, 425, 478, 583
Alper, Thelma G., 91, 836 n
Alpert, R., 529
Amatruda, C. S., 478
Amen, E. W., 528
Ammons, R. B., 100
Anastasi, Anne, 79, 494, 497
Anderson, A. L., 715–716, 762
Anderson, R. L., 878
Angoulvent, N., 705
Apicella, F. S., 451
Arenberg, D., 90
Arluck, E. W., 126
Armstrong, Mary A., 527
Arnheim, R., 249
Arnold, F. C., 72, 792, 799
Arsfield, P., 399, 407
Arthur, Grace, 706
Atkinson, John W., 49, 63, 127–128, 147, 157, 197, 201, 203, 433–454, 520, 523, 525, 536, 652–663, 838
Auld, F., 53, 65, 96-98, 530

Bach, G. R., 458, 600
Bachrach, A. J., 428, 515–516
Bailey, M. A., 720
Bair, J. T., 794
Baldwin, Marcella V., 38, 145–161
Balinsky, B., 126, 363
Balken, Eva R., 483, 485, 590
Balloch, J. C., 226, 232, 237, 239 n
Bancroft, T. A., 878
Bandura, Albert, 250
Barker, A. J., 643
Barkley, B. J., 705
Barnett, I., 226, 239 n, 243
Barrera, S. E., 125, 387
Barron, F., 81, 740
Barry, J. R., 803
Bartlett, F. C., 209, 324, 878–879
Bateson, G., 3, 11 n
Baughman, E. Earl, xvii, 132, 136, 201, 221–251, 257–269, 273–291, 355, 395, 401–402, 404, 413, 417
Beall, G., 760
Beardslee, D., 451
Beck, S. J., 133, 239, 248, 257 n, 259, 277, 279, 338, 373–374, 401–402, 413, 417, 421, 470
Beier, E. G., 522
Belden, A. W., 226, 235, 239 n
Bell, J. E., 704, 860 n
Bellak, Leopold, 91, 124, 196, 318, 425-427, 431, 482, 525, 527, 579, 696 n, 781 n
Bellak, Sonya S., 525, 527
Bellugi, Mrs. Piero, 875 n
Belmont, L., 45
Bender, Lauretta, 704–705, 707–708, 742, 752–753, 762–763
Bendig, A. W., 409
Benedict, F. G., 159

SUBJECT INDEX

accomplishment, pride of, 435; scholastic, 442

achievement, 5; in TAT, 466; see also n Achievement

act, motivation and, 439–440

action, in DAP drawings, 637; see also animal movement

activity, goal-directed, 435

adaptation level, in projective techniques, 49–66

adaptive behavior, 91

adjustment level, in DAP, 647

administrative method, influence of, 118–122

adolescent, B-G scoring system for, 705–712; in reality situation, 96

A-E scale (authoritarianism-equalitarianism), 102

affective reactions, 436

age, body image and, 617; Z score and, in P&S test, 744

age regression, hypnosis and, 126

agression or aggressive behavior, 65, 123; ambiguity and, 91; case history of, 549–552; DAP and, 623; denial of, 58; fantasy, 81, 458, 549–550, 580; and fantasy punishment, 556; forceful language and, 580–582; "guess who" technique in, 603; guilt and, 555; in H-T-P drawings, 692–698; impulse-control balance and, 548–549; indexes of, 575–585; maternal response to, 599–605; misrecognition of, 579–580; as motive, 449; overt and covert behavior and, 575–585, 603; remoteness of, 550, 558; repressed, 580; Rorschach and, 411; self-ratings in, 578, 582–583; in TAT, 451, 486, 489, 500, 502; ten "signs" of, 576, 585; verbal and emotional, 54; see also hostility

aggressive anxiety, 81

aggressive fantasy, 458, 549–550, 580

airplane reaction, in Rorschach, 419

alcohol and alcoholism, 124–125; 472; B-G test and, 708; in DAP, 641, 644; sex and, 57, 561, 565, 572; in TAT, 524

Allport-Vernon-Lindzey Study of Values, 41

ambiguity, defined, 51; versus nonambiguity, 89–92; in TAT, 538–539

ambiguous stimuli, 25, 28, 49, 53, 63

American Psychiatric Association, 84, 426

American Psychoanalytic Association, 44

American Psychological Association, 307 n, 535

animal movement, FM response and, 98, 120, 273, 338, 406

animals, versus human beings, in TAT, 525–528

annihilation, feelings of, 478

Antioch College tests, 875–879

antisocial behavior, degree of, 553; discriminative power and, 557; impulse-control balance and, 548–549, 557; remoteness rating in, 550; TAT and, 547–549; see also behavior

anxiety, avoidance and, 450; criterion measure in, 592–594; diagnosis of, 40; of examiner, 336, 339–340, 344–351; rho correlation in, 595; in Rorschach, 99; "signs" of, 587–597; testing situation and, 123

apathy, 478

A response, Rorschach, 135

arms and hands, in DAP drawings, 627–630

aspiration, level of, 836–837; TAT score in, 466

921